THE PRINCIPLES OF EQUITY & TRUSTS

THE PRINCIPLES OF
EQUITY & TRUSTS

Third Edition

GRAHAM VIRGO QC (HON)

Professor of English Private Law, University of Cambridge;
Pro-Vice-Chancellor for Education, University of Cambridge;
Fellow of Downing College, Cambridge; Bencher of Lincoln's Inn

OXFORD
UNIVERSITY PRESS

OXFORD

UNIVERSITY PRESS

Great Clarendon Street, Oxford, OX2 6DP,
United Kingdom

Oxford University Press is a department of the University of Oxford.
It furthers the University's objective of excellence in research, scholarship,
and education by publishing worldwide. Oxford is a registered trade mark of
Oxford University Press in the UK and in certain other countries

Published in the United States of America by Oxford University Press
198 Madison Avenue, New York, NY 10016, United States of America

British Library Cataloguing in Publication Data

Data available

Library of Congress Control Number: 2017963191

ISBN 978-0-19-880471-0

Printed in Great Britain by Bell and Bain Ltd, Glasgow

PREFACE

PREFACE

Equity is an ancient country with rich resources. Its inhabitants are courteous, precise, and careful in their thinking and their speech; they place much weight on fundamental principles of justice and good faith. The territory of Equity is large. Some areas are well ordered, with elegant structures which continue to be of real practical benefit. Other areas have been left to grow wild. But, if the encroaching vegetation is stripped away, more structures can be identified which might be of real contemporary significance. The boundaries of this country are not particularly clear, but at the centre of it is a particular State, known as Trust. Some people, typically schooled in a particular way of thinking about the world, have said that Trust should devolve from Equity and become its own independent country, leaving the rest of the territory to be taken over by any other country which might be able to make use of its ancient resources. But the inhabitants of Equity are fiercely patriotic and wish to preserve their country for the benefit of all.

Over the years Equity's empire has been extensive. Equity has had much influence on other territories, especially commercially, although some might say that this influence is waning. They would be wrong. The territory of Equity is itself under threat. Some people wish to invade it and impose their will on its running, despite its many years of peaceful, benevolent existence. One group appear to have particular designs on Equity. This is a strange evangelical sect known as the 'unjust enrichmentarians'. The members of this sect are mainly benign, but they have their own strange dialect and wish to reform what they consider to be the unsophisticated attitudes of the ancient Equity people, not realizing that the new structures they wish to impose typically replicate what Equity already has and in a much less sophisticated way.

Despite the threats which Equity faces in the twenty-first century, it is a country which should be explored. Indeed all law students who wish to practise law are required to visit the country. Before doing so they may have heard a variety of rumours about what the country is actually like, including that it is old-fashioned and backward-looking; its inhabitants speak a strange language and are only concerned with making money. But these rumours should not put you off from visiting and properly exploring the country. To see how the country actually operates you need to go off the beaten track and explore for yourself. But you might get lost in the dense forests, particularly when the mist descends. What you need is a guidebook to show you the right path to take. This is your guidebook to the country of Equity and the state of Trust.

This book seeks to guide the law student through Equity and the law of trusts. Throughout this book my aim has been to ensure that different paths are identified clearly; that interesting features are identified and analysed; that the contemporary practical relevance of Equity and trusts is apparent; that wrong turnings and mistakes in the development of the law are examined and alternative solutions are suggested; that the views of different judges and commentators are considered and assessed. A good guidebook should not simply describe the legal landscape, but should comment on it as well. I have sought throughout to make it clear where description ends and commentary begins. I have also sought to avoid swamping the reader with excessive detail, particularly in the footnotes, but I have not wanted to dumb the subject down. Some of the concepts and issues are difficult, but I have aimed to take the reader through them carefully and to provide them with the terminological, analytical, and critical tools to cope with the demands of the subject.

I am indebted to many people for their help and support in writing this book. I am very grateful to those who have taught me Equity and trusts over the years, notably John Hopkins, Dr Charles Harpum QC, Professor Edward Burn, the late Professor Gareth Jones, and the late Tony Oakley. I am also grateful to those who have commented on the text or discussed areas of difficulty and controversy with me, in particular Dr Daniel Clarry, Professor Matthew Conaglen, Professor Paul Davies, Professor Norma Dawson, William Day, Justice Paul Finn, Professor David Fox, Amy Goymour, Dr Rachel Leow, Professor Richard Nolan, Ajay Ratan, Rajiv Shah, Shivani Sharma-Saul, Professor Lionel Smith, Dr Peter Turner, Dr Stephen Watterson, Professor Sarah Worthington, and Professor Tang Hang Wu. More generally I would like to thank all those I have taught Equity and trusts to over the years, who have helped me to formulate my ideas about the nature and structure of the subject. I would like to thank the Fellowship of Downing College, Cambridge and members of the Faculty of Law in Cambridge and of XXIV Old Buildings, Lincoln's Inn. Finally, I wish to thank my wife Cally and children, Elizabeth and Jonathan, for their constant support whilst I have been working on this edition of the book, which is dedicated to the three of them.

The Old Schools, Cambridge
6 November 2017

NEW TO THIS EDITION

Akers v Samba Financial Group [2017] UKSC 6, [2017] AC 424 on the nature of trust rights

Akita Holdings Ltd v The Honourable Attorney General of the Turks and Caicos Islands [2017] UKPC 7, [2017] AC 590 on unconscionable receipt

Angove's Pty Ltd v Bailey [2016] UKSC 47, [2016] 1 WLR 3179 on the constructive trust

Bainbridge v Bainbridge [2016] EWHC 898 (Ch), [2016] WTLR 943 on rescission for mistake

Barnett v Creggy [2016] EWCA Civ 1004, [2017] Ch 273 on limitation periods

Barnsley v Noble [2016] EWCA Civ 799, [2017] Ch 191 on exemption clauses

Burnden Holdings (UK) Ltd v Fielding [2016] EWCA Civ 557, [2017] 1 WLR 39 on limitation periods

Charity Commission for England and Wales v Mountstar [2016] EWHC 876 (Ch), [2016] Ch 612 on judicial directions to charities

The Commissioners for Her Majesty's Revenue and Customs v The Investment Trust Companies [2017] UKSC 29, [2017] 2 WLR 1200 on the interpretation of an unjust enrichment claim

Dowding v Matchmore Ltd [2016] EWCA Civ 1233, [2017] 1 WLR 749 on the joint venture constructive trust

Ivey v Genting Casinos (UK) Ltd [2017] UKSC 67, [2017] 3 WLR 1212 on dishonesty

Law Commission *Making a Will* (Law Com CP No. 231, 2017) consultation paper on possible reforms to the law of wills

Lowick Rose LLP v Swynson Ltd [2017] UKSC 32, [2017] 2 WLR 1161 on subrogation

Marr v Collie [2017] UKPC 17, [2017] 2 FLR 674 on the common intention constructive trust

Patel v Mirza [2016] UKSC 42, [2017] AC 467 on illegality

Preedy v Dunne [2015] EWHC 2713 (Ch), [2015] WTLR 1795 on proprietary estoppel of a trust

Salt v Stratstone Specialist Ltd [2015] EWCA Civ 745, [2015] 2 CLC 269 on rescission

OUTLINE CONTENTS

PART I EQUITY

PART II THE EXPRESS TRUST

PART III TRUSTS FOR PURPOSES

PART IV IMPLIED TRUSTS

PART V BENEFICIARIES

DETAILED CONTENTS

PART I EQUITY

PART II THE EXPRESS TRUST

123–132, 138–141

PART III TRUSTS FOR PURPOSES

PART IV IMPLIED TRUSTS

PART V BENEFICIARIES

PART VI TRUSTEES AND THEIR RESPONSIBILITIES

TABLE OF CASES

TABLE OF STATUTES

TABLE OF STATUTORY INSTRUMENTS

TABLE OF EUROPEAN LEGISLATION

PART I

EQUITY

PART I

EQUITY

1

AN INTRODUCTION TO EQUITY

1.1 THE RELEVANCE OF EQUITY

Alan was married to Belinda. They had three children: Colin, Deborah, and Elizabeth. Alan had been having an extramarital affair with Fiona, who fell pregnant and gave birth to Georgina. Alan kept his relationship and the birth of Georgina a secret from his wife and children, but he paid a regular monthly allowance to Fiona for the benefit of Georgina. A year ago, Alan drafted his will. He decided that he wanted to leave £50,000 to each of his children, but he did not want his wife or legitimate children to find out about Georgina. He decided that he would make a gift of £50,000 in his will to Huw, his best friend, but he wrote a letter to Huw stating that, on Alan's death, Huw should use this money for the benefit of Georgina. Alan also told Fiona what he had done. Soon afterwards, Alan was killed in a car crash. The executors of Alan's estate gave Huw the £50,000 bequest according to the terms of the will. Huw was short of money, having recently lost his job, and he did not like Fiona, so he decided to keep the £50,000 for himself. He used the money to buy a sports car and he invested the rest in shares, which have increased in value. Fiona was very upset that Alan's clear intent to benefit Georgina had been ignored. She approached Huw to get him to use the money for the benefit of her daughter. Huw waved a copy of the will in her face and told her that it clearly stated that he was to receive a gift of £50,000; it said nothing about using this money for the benefit of Georgina. Fiona reminded Huw of the letter that Alan had sent to him, requesting the money be used for the benefit of Georgina. Huw responded by saying that the letter did not form part of the will and so had no legal effect. Fiona has come to you for legal advice.

At the core of this problem there is a blatant unfairness. Alan, the testator, had intended some of his property to be used after his death for the benefit of Georgina, his illegitimate daughter. He trusted his best friend to abide by his wishes, but Huw has ignored them. But what Huw told Fiona is correct: Alan's letter did not form part of the will and it is a fundamental requirement of English law that a document cannot take effect as a will unless it is in writing and signed by the testator in the presence of at least two witnesses.[1] The formal will could not have been clearer: Huw was to get £50,000 and nothing was said about what Huw should do with the money. On the face of the will, it appears that the money belongs to Huw and he can do whatever he wants with it. But this does not seem fair: this is not what Alan wanted. His illegitimate daughter does not get anything under his will, whereas Alan wanted all four of his children to benefit equally. Should Huw be able to rely on the clear words of the statute so that the letter written by Alan has no legal effect after Alan's death, or should Georgina's intended benefit and Alan's expectation be protected? Should Huw be allowed to get away with this, when he knew exactly what Alan wanted?

Equity provides the answers to these questions. This simple problem encapsulates what that body of law which is called 'Equity' is actually about. When someone seeks to rely on their strict rights in circumstances under which they can be considered to be acting unfairly, Equity might be available to ensure a just result. In this case, Huw's blatant disregard of what Alan wanted, when Huw knew what Alan wanted, means that Equity will require Huw to hold the car and the shares for the benefit of Georgina.[2]

1.2 WHAT IS EQUITY?

At the beginning of their legal studies, law students soon realize that there is a fundamental division in the legal system between sources of law created by the legislature and by judges. This judge-made law is often called the 'common law'. But 'Common Law', with capital letters, is used in another, more specific sense, to indicate that body of law which was made and developed by the judges in the Common Law courts, as opposed to that body of law which was made and developed by the judges in the Chancery courts. It is this latter body of law which is called 'Equity'.[3]

Equity has certain characteristics that distinguish it from the Common Law. These characteristics derive from the historical origins of Equity.[4] From medieval times, the Common Law was a rule-based, formalistic body of law that dealt with contracts, torts, and property rights, amongst other things. Where there was no remedy provided in the Common Law courts, or where the result reached by the application of the Common Law might be considered to be harsh, it was possible to petition the king, and later the Lord Chancellor, to provide a remedy through the exercise of his discretion. It was this discretionary jurisdiction that eventually developed to become the distinct body of law called Equity. Crucially, this historical relationship between Common Law and Equity indicates the two fundamental features of Equity as a body of law. First, it exists to modify the harshness and rigidity of the Common Law; so Equity is characterized by flexibility. Secondly, Equity was founded on the exercise of the Lord Chancellor's discretion, by reference to his conscience, and so it is a jurisdiction that is grounded on fairness, justice, and morality. You might think that any body of law that is characterized as being flexible and discretionary is a recipe for disaster: where are the rules, the principles, and the

---

[1] Wills Act 1837, s. 9. See Section 5.2.2.(ii), p. 109.
[2] See Section 5.2.2.(ii), p. 110 for further analysis of this solution by reference to the doctrine of secret trusts.
[3] Worthington, *Equity*, 2nd edn (Oxford: Oxford University Press, 2006), pp. 3–21.
[4] This is considered in more detail in Section 1.3, p. 5.

predictability? The reality is that, over the years, Equity became much more rule-based and principled, with identifiable doctrines being recognized. This was largely because the Equity jurisdiction was transferred from the Chancellor to judges, whose decisions had value as precedent for future decisions so that, increasingly, like cases could be treated in the same way. But even today Equity is characterized by many judges and commentators as being flexible and seeking to secure the just result. But, rather than being characterized as securing justice, a better way of describing Equity is that it restrains injustice by stopping the unconscionable conduct of a particular person.[5] Whether this characterization remains valid in the twenty-first century will be one of the key issues that will be considered in this book.

1.3 A BRIEF HISTORY OF EQUITY

To understand why we have two different streams of judge-made law at Common Law and in Equity we need to go back in time to the Middle Ages.[6] This was the period during which judge-made law started to develop rapidly. Before this period, the law was local, being administered in local courts. The king developed a legal system that was common to all of England, known as 'common law'. It was during this period that legal principles, some of which are still relevant today, started to emerge. But the general attitude of the judges was strict and inflexible. Although there was room for judicial creativity, the judges tended to interpret the law rigidly and developed it through the elaboration of ever more complicated rules. In particular, claims brought by individual litigants had to fall within clearly established forms of action; if they did not, they would fail. Claims were initiated by writs, and cases were heard in front of a judge and jury. Claimants were bound by very strict rules of pleading and proof.

This common law system was restrictive. But if no remedy was awarded, or was even available, it was possible to petition the king to seek justice in a particular case. Eventually, this function was delegated by the king to his chief minister, the Lord Chancellor.

Originally, the Lord Chancellor was an ecclesiastical figure who presumably had regard to biblical notions of fairness and justice to determine whether a remedy should be awarded in an individual case, but he was clearly influenced by Greek and Roman authors too, notably the works of Aristotle and Homer. Ultimately, however, the Chancellor's decision was influenced by the exercise of his own conscience. It was through the exercise of conscience that the characteristic of Equity as a discretionary system emerged. This was famously described by John Selden, a legal author writing in the seventeenth century, as follows:

> Equity is a roguish thing: for law we have a measure, know what to trust to; equity is according to the conscience of him that is chancellor, and as that is larger or narrower, so is equity. [It is] as if they should make the standard for the measure we call a foot a chancellor's foot; what an uncertain measure would this be! One chancellor has a long foot, another a short foot, a third an indifferent foot. Tis the same in the chancellor's conscience.[7]

Eventually, so many petitions came to the Chancellor that it was necessary to establish a separate court, known as the Court of Chancery, to deal with them, and it was the law that was developed and applied in this court that became known as Equity. This law was very

---

[5] Evershed, 'Reflections on the fusion of Law and Equity after seventy-five years' (1954) 70 LQR 326, 329.
[6] Baker, *Introduction to Legal History*, 4th edn (Oxford: Oxford University Press, 2002), pp. 97–116.
[7] *Table Talk of John Selden*, ed. Pollock (London: Selden Society, 1927), p. 43.

different from that administered by the Common Law courts. It was much more discretionary, but, crucially, the judges in the court benefited from distinct powers and remedies that had been developed by the Chancellors. Two of these were especially significant. First, the court could subpoena the litigants to enable them to be interrogated in the court. That made it easier to determine what the fair result should be as between the particular parties. Secondly, whereas the remedy typically awarded in the Common Law courts was pecuniary to compensate for loss suffered, in Equity the Chancellors had fashioned the injunction, which enabled the court to compel a party to act or to desist from acting in a particular way.[8] Failure to comply with the terms of the injunction would constitute contempt of court, for which the sanction could be imprisonment.

Over the years, the distinction between the Common Law and Equity approaches to decision-making became so marked that there developed a struggle between the Common Law and Chancery courts, with each considering that its approach should prevail over the other. This struggle came to a head in the *Earl of Oxford's case*,[9] in which Equity prevailed. Lord Chancellor Ellesmere in that case recognized that Equity's function was 'to soften and mollify the extremity of the law'. Later, Lord Chancellor Cowper summarized the relationship between Common Law and Equity well when he said: 'Equity is no part of the law, but a moral virtue which qualifies, moderates and reforms the rigour, hardness and edge of the law'.[10]

From the seventeenth century onwards, Equity as a body of law became more systematic. Various Lord Chancellors made their mark in the Court of Chancery in rationalizing the law. For example, in the eighteenth century Lord Nottingham developed the law of perpetuities, which still applies today,[11] and early in the nineteenth century Lord Eldon consolidated many equitable rules to make Equity much more principled.[12]

Even though Equity's function in moderating the rigours of the Common Law remained clear, the legal system that emerged in the nineteenth century was far from ideal. The dual court structure, resulting from having distinct Common Law and Chancery courts in which different bodies of law were applied, caused great inconvenience and injustice: it meant that the claimant had to choose the right court in which to pursue the claim. If the wrong court were chosen, the claimant would then have to start all over again in the other court. This resulted in lengthy delays and inordinate costs in pursuing litigation. This was reflected by Charles Dickens in the mid-nineteenth century, in his novel *Bleak House*, which starts with the following description of Equity, as practised in the courts of the time:

> On such an afternoon, some score of members of the High Court of Chancery bar ought to be—as here they are—mistily engaged in one of the ten thousand stages of an endless cause, tripping one another up on slippery precedents, groping knee-deep in technicalities, running their goat-hair and horse-hair warded heads against walls of words, and making a pretence of equity with serious faces, as players might.

Everyone is yawning 'for no crumb of amusement ever falls from JARNDYCE AND JARNDYCE (the cause in hand), which was squeezed dry years upon years ago'. That case involved a disputed inheritance and, as Dickens writes, 'this scarecrow of a suit has, in course of time, become so complicated, that no man alive knows what it means'. By the end of the novel, judgment is given, but the legal costs that have been incurred are so great that they consume most of the estate that was disputed in the first place.

---

[8] See further Section 21.2, p. 628.

[9] (1615) 1 Ch Rep 1. See Ibbetson, 'The Earl of Oxford's Case', in *Landmark Cases in Equity*, ed. Mitchell and Mitchell (Oxford: Hart, 2012), ch. 1.

[10] *Lord Dudley v Lady Dudley* (1705) Prec Ch 241, 244.　　　[11] See Section 4.6, p. 102.

[12] *Gee v Pritchard* (1818) 2 Swans 402, 414.

The complexity of litigation in the nineteenth century was to some extent resolved by the enactment of the Judicature Acts of 1873 and 1875. The effect of these statutes was to abolish the Common Law and Chancery courts and replace them with a single High Court, which was divided into what is now known as the Chancery Division, the Queen's Bench Division, and the Family Division. Each Division is responsible for its own area of the law, with the Chancery Division tending to deal with the Equity business, the Queen's Bench Division dealing with contract and tort, and the Family Division dealing with matrimonial and other family disputes. But, because the Divisions together form a unified High Court, it should not matter to the resolution of the dispute in which Division the claimant chooses to sue. The Divisions are a matter of administrative convenience and do not have any jurisdictional significance. This was made absolutely clear by the Judicature Act 1873, which stated that Equity, as a body of law, could be applied in any Division of the High Court. The effect of this was that remedies that derived from Common Law or Equity could be awarded, regardless of the court in which the claim was heard.[13]

The Judicature Acts are highly significant in English legal history, but their significance must not be exaggerated. The effect of this legislation was to fuse the administration of Common Law and Equity, but the statutes did not fuse the two bodies of law.[14] Equity was not abolished by the Judicature Acts. Indeed, the Judicature Act 1873 recognized that Equity prevailed where there was a conflict or variance between the rules of Common Law and Equity.[15] One of the most important applications of this principle occurred almost a decade later in *Walsh v Lonsdale*.[16] In this case, a lease was purported to be made, but was unenforceable at Common Law because the formalities for its creation were never completed. But, because the parties had agreed to enter into a lease, Equity was able to enforce the agreement and treat the lease as having been validly made. In other words, the flexibility of Equity was able to make the agreement work despite the failure to comply with the requirements of the Common Law.

Equity is still sometimes described as operating to modify the rigidity of the Common Law. But, to the extent that this indicates that Equity is vague and unprincipled, it is untrue: much of Equity today is rule-based and certain; precedent is followed and there are identifiable principles. Further, the characterization of the Common Law as being rigid and unyielding in the face of injustice is unconvincing, since the rapid advances of the Common Law during the twentieth century and continuing into the twenty-first century in, for example, the laws of negligence and unjust enrichment, show that it is creative and nuanced. Today, rather than seeing the Common Law and Equity as being in conflict, the better characterization is that they are complementary, working together, although sometimes and unfortunately contradicting each other.

1.4 THE CONTEMPORARY CONTRIBUTION OF EQUITY TO ENGLISH LAW

It is all very well to identify a body of judge-made law, give it a name, identify certain vague characteristics, and then seek to justify this by reference to constitutional, political, and legal developments many hundreds of years ago. The crucial question is whether Equity remains relevant today. As will be illustrated throughout this book, it clearly is, both in

---

[13] See now the Senior Courts Act 1981, s. 49(2).   [14] Evershed (1954) LQR 326, 341.
[15] Supreme Court of Judicature Act 1873, s. 25(11). See now the Senior Courts Act 1981, s. 49(1).
[16] (1882) 21 Ch D 9.

terms of explaining long-established doctrines of private law and also as a mechanism for providing new solutions to contemporary problems: Equity is not, as it is sometimes quaintly put, 'past the age of child-bearing'. Equity can still be used to create new doctrines and to develop existing ones to provide solutions to contemporary problems that are ignored by the Common Law.

The best way of illustrating the continued relevance of Equity to English law is by reference to particular legal subjects. As you will see, the modern contribution of Equity relates both to the identification of significant rights, duties, powers, and liabilities, but also to important remedies.

1.4.1 THE LAW OF CONTRACT

Many aspects of the law of contract have been influenced by Equity. This influence has taken three main forms.

(i) Validity of consent

First, there are situations in which Equity operates to determine whether a party's promise is more apparent than real. There is a variety of situations in which a party to a contract has appeared to have made a real promise, but in circumstances under which it should not be considered to be valid. The Common Law has various doctrines to identify whether a party's consent is real, but Equity's approach is more nuanced and flexible. So, for example, the Common Law recognizes that, where a party's promise has been induced by fraudulent misrepresentation, this will be sufficient to enable the contract to be set aside. But Equity will recognize this even where the misrepresentation was negligent or innocent. Equity recognized a wider concept of mistake than at Common Law to vitiate a contract, although this has since been rejected.[17] Further, where the contractual document appears to be clear on its face but does not reflect the actual intention of the parties, Equity is willing to rectify the document,[18] whereas the Common Law takes the document at face value. Where a party's promise is valid, Equity will sometimes enforce it by means of the remedy of specific performance, at least where compensatory damages would be an inadequate remedy for a party's failure to perform.[19]

(ii) Fairness of the transaction

Equity is sometimes willing to examine the procedural fairness of a transaction, as regards the process by which the contract was made. If one party can be shown to have exploited its relationship with the other party, or if this exploitation can be presumed from the nature of the transaction, the contract may be set aside by virtue of the doctrine of undue influence.[20] Equity is even willing to assess the fairness of the substance of the contract. If this is considered to have involved one party taking unfair advantage of a weaker party, Equity may be willing to set the contract aside by virtue of the doctrine of unconscionable bargaining.[21]

(iii) Supplementing the law of contract

Finally, there are situations in which no contract has been formed but one party has made a promise on which the other party has relied. In such a case, the Common Law is unable

---

[17] *Great Peace Shipping Ltd v Tsavliris Salvage (International) Ltd* [2002] EWCA Civ 1407, [2003] QB 679.
[18] *Frederic E Rose (London) Ltd v William H Pim Junior and Co Ltd* [1953] 2 QB 450.
[19] See Section 21.4, p. 634.   [20] *Royal Bank of Scotland plc v Etridge (No 2)* [2002] 2 AC 773.
[21] *Hart v O'Connor* [1985] AC 1000.

to assist because the strict requirements for a contract have not been satisfied, usually through the absence of any consideration being provided by the relying party. But it is unconscionable for a party to say something and then deny it in cases in which the other party has relied upon the representation, and so Equity will prevent the representor from doing so by means of the doctrine of promissory estoppel.[22] So, for example, if the defendant owes the claimant £1,000 and offers to pay the claimant £800, which the claimant accepts, at Common Law the defendant remains liable to pay the outstanding £200.[23] However, the claimant's promise to accept £800 in satisfaction of the debt will mean that the claimant is estopped from relying on the strict terms of the contract and is bound by the promise in Equity, even though it is not supported by any consideration.

1.4.2 TORT

Equity recognizes a variety of civil wrongs, especially claims for breach of trust[24] or breach of fiduciary duty.[25] Although it is rare to describe them as torts, many of these wrongs have much in common with the torts that are recognized at Common Law. For example, whereas the Common Law recognizes a tort of inducing a breach of contract, Equity recognizes the equivalent wrong of inducing a breach of trust or breach of fiduciary duty, commonly called the 'action for dishonest assistance'.[26] Although there is an analogy with the Common Law tort, they are not identical, since the Common Law tort is one of strict liability, whereas the equitable wrong requires proof of fault.

Similarly, Equity recognizes an action for breach of confidence where the defendant is in a relationship with the claimant by virtue of which there is a duty to maintain confidences and the defendant breaches that duty, for example by disclosing the confidential information to another.[27] This action has been characterized as a tort,[28] although its equitable foundations[29] remain significant in determining the nature of the claim and the remedies which are awarded. The essence of the action was correctly identified by Deane J in *Moorgate Tobacco Co Ltd v Philip Morris Ltd (No 2)*:[30] 'its rational basis ... lies in the notion of an obligation of conscience arising from the circumstances in or through which the information was communicated or obtained'. A duty of confidence may relate to trade secrets,[31] national security,[32] and even personal confidences.[33] This action for breach of confidence is gradually being expanded from the protection of secret information to encompass liability for the protection of privacy.[34] Where privacy is protected, although this action remains formally one of breach of confidence, no relationship of confidence is required;[35] it is enough that the information is personal and private[36] and the defendant knows, or ought to know, that the claimant could reasonably expect their privacy to be

---

[22] See *Central London Property Trust Ltd v High Trees House Ltd* [1947] I KB 130.

[23] *Foakes v Beer* (1884) 9 App Cas 605.   [24] See Chapter 17.   [25] See Chapter 15.

[26] See Section 20.3.2, p. 613.   [27] *Coco v AN Clark (Engineers) Ltd* [1969] RPC 41.

[28] *Walsh v Shanahan* [2013] EWCA Civ 411, [55] (Rimer LJ).

[29] *Moorgate Tobacco Co Ltd v Philip Morris Ltd (No 2)* (1984) 156 CLR 414, 438 (Deane J); *Stephens v Avery* [1988] Ch 449, 455 (Sir Nicolas Browne-Wilkinson V-C).

[30] (1984) 156 CLR 414, 438. See also *Vestergaard Frandsen A/S v Bestnet Europe Ltd* [2013] UKSC 31, [2013] 1 WLR 1556, [22].

[31] *Saltman Engineering Co Ltd v Campbell Engineering Co Ltd* [1948] 65 RPC 203.

[32] *Attorney-General v Guardian Newspapers Ltd (No 2)* [1990] AC 109.

[33] *Argyll v Argyll* [1967] 1 Ch 302.

[34] *OBG Ltd v Allan* [2007] UKHL 21, [2008] AC 1, [255] (Lord Nicholls) and [272] (Lord Walker).

[35] *Attorney-General v Guardian Newspapers Ltd (No 2)* [1990] 1 AC 109, 281 (Lord Goff); *A v B plc* [2003] QB 195, 207 (Lord Woolf CJ).   [36] *Douglas v Hello! Ltd (No 3)* [2005] EWCA Civ 595, [2006] QB 125, [83].

protected.[37] The essence of this extension of the action for breach of confidence is that the abuse of personal information that was not intended to be made public will result in civil liability.

1.4.3 UNJUST ENRICHMENT

The law of unjust enrichment was recognized by the House of Lords in 1991,[38] but this was simply the formal recognition of a principle whose elements had been developing for many hundreds of years, which remain relevant to the contemporary understanding of this principle.[39] Much of this development had occurred in the Common Law, but Equity has had a significant influence on that development too. The essence of the law of unjust enrichment is that where the defendant has been enriched at the expense of the claimant in circumstances which fall within one of the recognized grounds of restitution, a restitutionary remedy will be awarded that is assessed by reference to the value of the enrichment received by the defendant.[40] The function of restitutionary remedies is to correct what has been described as 'normatively defective transfers of value' from one party to another by restoring the parties to their pre-transfer position.[41] A transfer of value will be 'normatively defective' if one of the recognized grounds of restitution can be identified, such as mistake, duress, and total failure of basis. These grounds were all developed by the Common Law. But Equity has influenced the interpretation and recognition of the grounds of restitution too. So, for example, the defendant will be liable to make restitution to the claimant of the value of any benefit received if the defendant unduly influenced the claimant to transfer the benefit or the defendant induced the claimant to transfer the enrichment as the result of a non-fraudulent misrepresentation.

This equitable jurisdiction within the law of unjust enrichment will be especially significant if the defendant has unconscionably induced the claimant to make a gift to the defendant. So, for example, in *Allcard v Skinner*,[42] the claimant was a nun who was persuaded by the defendant, her Mother Superior, to make gifts to her. Eventually, the claimant left the convent and, some years later, sought to recover the gifts. It was held that she would have been able to do so but for the delay in bringing the claim, on the ground that she had been unduly influenced by the defendant to make the gifts. Similarly, where the claimant has mistakenly made a gift to the defendant by deed, the defendant will be required to make restitution to the claimant if it would otherwise be unconscionable for the defendant to retain the gift.[43]

1.4.4 LAND LAW

Equity has had a profound influence on the development of land law, both as regards the recognition of different interests in land[44] and by protecting particular property interests. This is illustrated by three examples. The first concerns the law of mortgages. At Common

---

[37] *Primary Group (UK) Ltd v Royal Bank of Scotland plc* [2014] EWHC Ch 1082, [223] (Arnold J).
[38] *Lipkin Gorman (a firm) v Karpnale Ltd* [1991] 2 AC 548.
[39] *The Commissioners for Her Majesty's Revenue and Customs v The Investment Trust Companies* [2017] UKSC 29, [2017] 2 WLR 1200, [40] (Lord Reed).
[40] *Banque Financière de la Cité v Parc (Battersea) Ltd* [1999] 1 AC 221, 227 (Lord Steyn). The different questions which need to be considered to establish unjust enrichment have been described as 'signposts towards areas of inquiry' rather than being 'legal tests': *The Commissioners for Her Majesty's Revenue and Customs v The Investment Trust Companies* [2017] UKSC 29, [2017] 2 WLR 1200, [41] (Lord Reed).
[41] Ibid. [42].   [42] (1887) 36 Ch D 145.
[43] *Pitt v Holt* [2013] UKSC 26, [2013] 2 AC 108. See Section 9.3.3, p. 264.
[44] See Section 1.5.1, p. 15.

Law, a mortgagee would be able to retain the mortgaged property if there was the slightest delay in the mortgagor discharging the mortgage. This was considered to be unfair in Equity and so the equity of redemption was developed as a mechanism for avoiding the harshness of the Common Law, to enable the mortgagor to redeem the mortgaged property having repaid the loan to the mortgagee. Secondly, where the defendant represented to the claimant that the latter would obtain an interest in land and, in reliance on that representation, the claimant acted to their detriment, Equity would fashion a remedy to satisfy the expectations of the claimant by means of the doctrine of proprietary estoppel. Here, Equity could create an interest in property because of the defendant's unconscionable conduct in reneging on their representation.[45] Thirdly, where a couple have cohabited and the property is registered in the name of one of them, if the relationship ends, Equity will provide the party who does not have registered title with an interest in the family home by means of a common intention constructive trust.[46]

1.4.5 COMMERCIAL LAW

Equity has been especially influential in the development of modern commercial law.[47] For example, Equity recognizes that there are certain relationships that are characterized as relationships of trust and confidence, in which one party, known as the 'principal', is dependent on another, known as the 'fiduciary'.[48] The fiduciary is expected to be loyal to the principal and to maintain the highest standards of behaviour in looking after the principal's interests. Failure to maintain these standards will mean that the fiduciary is liable to the principal for breach of duty. A wide variety of relationships have been characterized as fiduciary, but many of them are relevant in the commercial world. So, for example, an agent owes fiduciary duties to their principal, a director owes fiduciary duties to their company, and solicitors are in a fiduciary relationship with their clients.

Equity has also proved to be significant in the recognition of a variety of security interests, such as the floating charge[49] and the lien[50] to secure a debt owed to the claimant.

1.4.6 EQUITABLE REMEDIES

Equity has had a profound influence on the development of English law by virtue of its remedial jurisdiction. Equity has created a wide variety of remedies that are available where Common Law compensatory damages are inadequate, including specific performance of contracts and account of profits to require the defendant to disgorge to the claimant any profits made as a result of a breach of an equitable duty.

One of the most significant contributions of Equity to the remedial arsenal is through the creation of the injunction to make the defendant act or refrain from acting in a particular way. The creative function of Equity is especially well illustrated by the freezing order, which was created in the 1970s to deal with the problem of a defendant who seeks to hide their assets or to take them out of the jurisdiction to prevent the claimant from enforcing a judgment for damages against the defendant.[51] To avoid this problem, Equity

---

[45] *Thorner v Major* [2009] UKHL 18, [2009] 1 WLR 776. See Section 10.4.3, p. 308.

[46] *Curran v Collins* [2015] EWCA Civ 404, [2015] Fam Law 780. See Section 10.2.4.(i), p. 293.

[47] See Yip, 'The commercial context in trust law' [2016] Conv 347 and Yip and Lee, 'The commercialisation of Equity' (2017) 37 LS 647 for analysis of the relevance of the commercial context to the development of trust law and Equity. [48] See further Section 15.2, p. 420.

[49] *Snell's Equity*, 33rd edn, ed. McGhee (London: Sweet and Maxwell, 2014), ch. 40.

[50] See further Section 19.4.2, p. 577. [51] See further Section 21.2.2.(v), p. 630.

created a new form of injunction to freeze some or all of the defendant's assets to ensure that any judgment could be enforced against the defendant. For example, the order might mean that the defendant is not able to gain access to money that has been credited to their bank account. The freezing order has proved to be of real significance to international commercial litigation in the English courts.

1.4.7 THE TRUST

The most important contribution of Equity to English law is undoubtedly the trust. The crucial feature of the trust is that property is held by one person for the benefit of another. This is recognized through the division of property rights. One person, known as the 'trustee', holds the legal title to the property. As far as the Common Law is concerned, that person is absolutely entitled to the property. But Equity can see that the legal owner holds the property for the benefit of somebody else, the 'beneficiary'. The beneficiary therefore has an equitable interest in the property. The trustee is obliged by Equity to look after the property for the benefit of the beneficiary, and indeed is in a fiduciary relationship with the beneficiary. If the trustee fails to manage the property properly, they will have breached the trust and will be liable to compensate the beneficiary for any loss suffered or to disgorge any benefits that they personally obtained from the property.

The trust remains of profound significance in English law today. For example, within the family, it can be used to enable parents to ensure that property is managed for the benefit of their children without the children being tempted to dissipate the property. So, for example, Alan, in the example that opened this chapter, may have wished to benefit his three legitimate children in his will, but he might have been concerned that, if £50,000 was paid to each of them, they would be tempted to spend it immediately and not to invest it wisely for their future. So Alan might have provided in his will that the money was to be paid to Huw to be held on trust for Alan's children until they reached the age of 25, by which time Alan might have considered that they would be mature enough to be able to invest the money wisely for themselves. As the trustee, Huw would be expected to manage the property for the benefit of the three children until they reached 25. They could be given the income before they attained that age, but the capital would remain under Huw's control.

This basic idea of letting somebody else manage property for the benefit of others explains why the trust has also proved to be so significant commercially. For example, investors may wish to rely on the expertise of fund-managers to manage their money and so will be willing to transfer their money into an investment trust. The fund managers will be trustees who will use their financial expertise to ensure that the money is invested wisely for the benefit of the investors. Similarly, the pension is founded on the trust idea too.[52] Employees will pay their money into a pension fund, in which it will be managed by trustees for the benefit of the pensioners, who will start to receive income and capital benefits when they retire.

1.4.8 THE POTENTIAL SIGNIFICANCE OF EQUITY

Throughout this book many cases will be considered which will show that there remains great scope for Equity to provide solutions to difficult problems. For now, this will be illustrated by reference to one case in which, although Equity was not able to assist on the

---

[52] See further Section 3.6.2.(ix), p. 56.

particular facts, had those facts been slightly different (or, more accurately, had it been possible to prove certain key facts), Equity could have assisted. The case is *Re Farepak Food and Gifts Ltd*,[53] which arose from the insolvency of a company. Farepak Food and Gifts Ltd operated a Christmas savings scheme to enable people to spread their Christmas savings over the year. People participating in the scheme, who typically came from low-income families, would make monthly contributions; in November, they would receive a voucher, Christmas hamper, or other goods as they wished, to the value of the total amount credited to them. The average contribution was between £250 and £300. In October 2006, the company went into insolvent administration. It was unable to fulfil the Christmas orders for that year, meaning that many of its customers would not be able to get the Christmas food or presents that they had expected to obtain. The company had about £1 million credited to its account and the administrators of the company sought directions as to how this should be distributed. This came to the court on 15 December. If any of the customers were to get any of their food or presents for Christmas, they needed to show that the money held by the administrators belonged to them. They could not show that this belonged to them at Law, because legal title to the money had passed to the company. So they needed to show that they had a proprietary interest in the money in Equity to enable them to claim the money back. They could establish this if they could show that the money was held by the company on trust for them.

Three different arguments were used in an attempt to show that the money was held on trust for the customers. The first argument was that there had been an express declaration that the property was held on trust for the customers. The trial judge found that the directors of the company had indeed purported to declare a trust of the money that had been received from the customers, but that the wrong bank account had been identified. He was willing to rectify the deed of declaration, by means of the equitable remedy of rectification,[54] so that it accorded with the directors' intention. However, the declaration of trust involved the directors preferring some of the company's creditors over others, which they are not allowed to do by operation of the law of insolvency.[55] Consequently, there had been no valid declaration of trust.

The second argument was that the money had been paid for a particular purpose, namely the purchase of Christmas hampers and presents, and since that purpose had failed, the money was held by the company on what is known as a 'resulting trust' for the customers.[56] This argument failed because it could not be shown that the money that was received by the company was to be used for that particular purpose.[57] When the company received the money, it could do what it wanted with it; the money was not credited to a particular account for the purchase of goods on behalf of the customers. Rather than the customers *owning* anything in the company's bank accounts, the company *owed* the value of what it had received. In other words, the relationship between the customers and the company was one of contract and not trust; it involved a debt and not property rights.

The third argument was that the company had acted unconscionably in receiving the money from the customers after the directors had decided that the company would cease trading, so that the money was held on constructive trust for the customers, a trust that arose by operation of law. The judge noted that a trust could be recognized where the money had been received in such circumstances. However, it could not be established on

---

[53] [2006] EWHC 3272 (Ch).   [54] See further Section 21.7, p. 654.

[55] See the Insolvency Act 1986, s. 239.

[56] This is called a *Quistclose* trust after the case in which it was first recognized: *Barclays Bank v Quistclose Ltd* [1970] AC 567. See Section 8.4, p. 239.

[57] For elaboration of this requirement, see Section 8.4.3.(i), p. 241.

the facts[58] that the money had been received after the decision to cease trading had been made. But, although it was of no help to the customers, there is at least the possibility of Equity securing a fair result in this type of case if it can be shown that a company has received money when it had already decided to cease trading.

All of the customers' arguments failed. It followed that, even though the judge expressed sympathy for the customers' predicament, Equity could not help them. As the judge said:

> It will doubtless seem to some that the points which currently seem to stand in the way of what they propose are technical and unmeritorious. Some of them are certainly technical. But they are real points, I fear, and they arise out of the way that this company conducted its business. They must be disposed of properly and on the basis of law, not purely on the basis of sympathy and Christmas.[59]

But, although the result seems unfair, the potential significance of Equity to reach a just result in this type of case is apparent. On different facts, perhaps only very slightly different, an express trust, resulting trust, and especially a constructive trust might have been recognized to give the customers an equitable proprietary interest in the money that they had paid. This would have meant that, since the money in the company's bank account belonged to them, they would rank above other creditors on the company's insolvency and so would be much more likely to recover what the company owed to them.

1.5 FUNDAMENTAL FEATURES OF EQUITY

At the heart of Equity is a fundamental division between the recognition and protection of property rights and personal rights. In a variety of situations, Equity will recognize that the claimant has an interest in property, or that the defendant is personally liable to pay the claimant a sum of money to compensate for loss suffered or to give up a gain made. Sometimes, the claimant may have both property and personal rights arising at the same time. It is then important to determine which right it is better for the claimant to assert.

Often, but not always, it will be preferable for the claimant to rely on a right to property that is in the defendant's hands. Generally, these property rights take one of two forms. First, the claimant may be able to assert a right to recover particular property from the defendant. Secondly, the claimant may have a right to a security interest in the property. This will be relevant where the defendant owes the claimant a sum of money. So, for example, if the defendant owes the claimant £1,000 and the claimant has a security interest over a particular piece of property owned by the defendant, it follows that, if the defendant has not paid the £1,000 to the claimant, that property can be sold and £1,000 of the purchase price will be paid to the claimant to discharge the debt.

Claiming property rights has three significant advantages for the claimant, depending on the nature of the property right that is claimed. First, the claimant's property right will give them priority over other creditors of the defendant. This will be significant where the defendant is insolvent. If the defendant does not have enough money to pay off all of their creditors, it will be necessary to distribute the defendant's money according to a prioritized list of creditors. If, however, the claimant can show that the defendant has property in which the claimant has a proprietary interest, then, at least as regards that property, the claimant will rank above all other creditors and will be able to make a claim against the

---

[58] This was partly due to the limited time available to prepare and present arguments in court, because of the need to reach a decision in time for Christmas.

[59] [2006] EWHC 3272 (Ch), [59] (Mann J).

property, either to recover the property itself or to force a sale and recover value where there is a security interest over the property.

Secondly, where the claimant has a property interest that is not a security interest, if the property in which the claimant has the interest has increased in value, the claimant will get the benefit of that increase. So, for example, if the claimant has a proprietary interest in shares that are held by the defendant, the claimant will be able to gain both the benefit of any dividends paid in respect of the shares and any increase in the value of the shares. Of course, if the claimant has a property interest in shares that have fallen in value, it may be preferable for the claimant to pursue a personal rather than a proprietary claim. So, for example, if the defendant trustee has misappropriated £200,000 from a trust fund that was held for the claimant beneficiary, the claimant will have a proprietary claim against the defendant to recover the £200,000 that was misappropriated and, alternatively, a personal claim for the amount misappropriated. If the defendant used the £200,000 to buy a house, the claimant will be able to claim the house instead of the money.[60] But if the value of the house has fallen to less than £200,000, it will be preferable for the claimant to rely on the personal claim to recover the amount of £200,000. In reality, in such a case it is unlikely that the defendant will have enough money to repay the claimant in full. The defendant may well be insolvent and so the claimant, who would be treated as an unsecured creditor as regards their personal claim, will have an equal claim with all the defendant's other creditors to the defendant's assets. It may, therefore, still be worth pursuing a proprietary claim to recover the value of the house, even though it is less than what the defendant actually owed to the claimant.

A third advantage of asserting a proprietary right, which applies where the claimant has a property interest which is not a security interest, is that they will be able to assert the proprietary right even where the property has been received and retained by a third party without proving that this recipient was aware that somebody else might have a right in the property, save where the recipient had provided some value for the property.[61]

This analysis indicates that whether the claimant pursues a proprietary or personal claim will often depend on the particular facts of the case, but a proprietary claim is generally more advantageous than a personal claim. It is then necessary to determine when the claimant will have a proprietary claim.

1.5.1 PROPRIETARY RIGHTS

(i) Different rights in property

Different people may have different rights or interests in a particular piece of property. This is true regardless of whether the rights are recognized at Common Law or in Equity. For example, Ivan owns a house with a garden. He is the registered owner of the land and so has legal title to it. But other people may have rights in the land as well. For example, his wife Jane occupies the house too. The purchase money from the house was borrowed from a bank, which will have a security interest over the house to the extent of the amount borrowed; this is a mortgage. Ivan rented part of the house to a friend, Kate, who has a leasehold interest. Another friend, Laura, is allowed to live in the house and she would be licensed to live there. Mike, Ivan's next-door neighbour, is allowed to park his car on Ivan's drive and Nadia has been given the right to cross Ivan's land to get to another property. So it can be seen from this example that rights in property are not confined to ownership; they also encompass possession and rights of varying kinds to use the property.

---

[60] See further Section 19.4, p. 574.　　　[61] See Section 19.5.1, p. 584.

The same is true of proprietary rights in Equity, but Equity is even more imaginative[62] in its recognition of property rights. Equity is able to recognize rights to assets and the use of property, but also to the value of property and rights that may arise in the future.

The significance of equitable property rights is illustrated by the different rights that may arise on the creation of a trust. Imagine a situation in which Oliver wishes to create a trust for the benefit of his three children. He transfers £100,000 to Pat to hold on trust for the children. Once the money has been transferred to Pat, she will have legal title to it. It follows that, as far as the Common Law is concerned, the money belongs to Pat and nobody else will have any interest in it. But if Pat has accepted the money as being held on trust for Oliver's children, Equity will not allow her to keep that money for herself absolutely so that she can benefit from it; it would be unconscionable if she were to do that. Consequently, Equity will recognize that the children have a proprietary interest in the money. But that interest will vary depending on the nature of the trust that has been created.

Three different scenarios illustrate the point:

(1) Pat is to hold the money on trust for the three children equally. If the children are over the age of eighteen and they all agree, they can claim the money whenever they want it.[63] This is a very strong equitable property right. Pat's function as a trustee in this case will be simply to administer the fund on behalf of the three children as they wish. This is called a bare trust.

(2) Pat is to hold the money on trust for the three children equally, but this time the children are under the age of eighteen. Consequently, Pat will be required to administer the property in the best interests of the children, but they will have no say in the administration of the property. Here, the property interests of the children are not as strong, in that they cannot call for the transfer of legal title whenever they like, although it is clear that they each have a one-third interest in the property. This is a fixed express trust.

(3) Oliver may have told Pat to hold the property on trust for his three children, but added that Pat was to distribute the property to them as she wished. Here, the children, even if they are over the age of eighteen, cannot identify a particular part of the trust fund that belongs to them in Equity. They have nothing more than an expectation that they might receive some property, but the amount that they receive and whether they receive anything at all will depend on the exercise of Pat's discretion. That is why this is called a discretionary trust.[64] The rights to the trust property in such a trust are clearly very different from the previous two examples. The children have no rights to any particular property. In fact, they only have a right to be considered by Pat in the exercise of her discretion to distribute the property between them.

(ii) Methods of creating proprietary rights

Equitable proprietary rights need to be created specifically. If somebody is the legal owner of property, it does not follow that that person also has an equitable interest in that property. So, if you have bought this book, you will have the legal ownership of it. But there is no equitable proprietary interest subsisting in this book until some event happens that creates that equitable interest. There are a variety of events that will operate to create equitable interests in property. By far the most significant is the express creation of that interest, as occurs where an express trust is created. Secondly, this may arise by virtue of a presumed intent that property should be held by the legal owner on behalf of the claimant.[65] Thirdly,

---

[62] See further Section 2.9, p. 34.   [63] See Section 11.4.1, p. 334.
[64] See Section 3.6.2.(iii), p. 54.   [65] See Section 8.2, p. 217.

the equitable proprietary interest may arise by operation of law, often because the defendant can be considered to have acted unconscionably.[66]

It follows from the principle that a particular event is required to create equitable property rights that all property does not have both a legal and an equitable owner. A related point is that one person alone cannot have both the legal and equitable ownership of property.[67] So, for example, when an event has occurred to create an equitable proprietary interest, that event must result in different interests being in two different people. Consequently, a trustee cannot hold property on trust just for themselves. This is because the trustee will have legal title to the property, but it is nonsense to say that they hold that property on trust for themselves. It does not follow, however, that a trustee cannot be both trustee and beneficiary. This is possible where the trustee holds property for themself and another, but it is only because of the interest of that other person that it is possible to conclude that a trustee also has an equitable interest themself.

A further consequence of the fundamental principle that there must always be at least one person other than the trustee who has an equitable interest in property is that if, subsequently, one person alone acquires both the legal and equitable interest, the equitable interest will be destroyed. So, for example, if you, as owner of this book, agree to hold the book on trust for your friend, you will continue to have the legal title to the book, but your friend will have an equitable proprietary interest in it. If your friend asks for the legal interest to be transferred to them,[68] then, once the legal title has been transferred, the equitable interest cannot continue to exist for the benefit of the legal owner alone and it will have been destroyed.

(iii) Different characteristics of legal and equitable proprietary rights

The distinction between legal and equitable proprietary rights is significant for a number of reasons, since each type of property right functions in a different way. If an equitable proprietary interest has not been created, the legal owner of property will be its beneficial owner in the sense that they can obtain the benefits of the property, including its use and its fruits, such as the dividends paid in respect of shares. Once an equitable interest has been created, however, the legal owner will no longer have the beneficial ownership of the property; it is the equitable owner who is the beneficial owner and who has the right to receive the benefits of the property. In this situation, the legal owner will be obliged to administer and manage the property on behalf of the equitable owner. The legal owner of the property will determine how that property is to be used and is obliged to bring legal proceedings if it is destroyed or damaged.[69]

Where the legal owner of property in which somebody has an equitable proprietary interest transfers that property to a third party who obtains legal title to it, normally the equitable owner retains title so that the third party will hold that property on trust for the equitable owner. The equitable proprietary right can, however, be defeated in two different ways:

(1) If the legal owner of the property is authorized to transfer the property to the defendant, the equitable interest in that property will be overreached and dissipated, but an equitable interest will be transferred to any substitute property.[70] This is called the overreaching doctrine. So, for example, if Quentin holds shares on trust for Rachel, Susan, and

---

[66] See Section 9.3.1, p. 258.

[67] *Westdeutsche Landesbank Girozentrale v Islington LBC* [1996] AC 669, 706 (Lord Browne-Wilkinson).

[68] See Section 11.4, p. 334, for discussion of when the beneficiary can demand transfer of the legal title to property.

[69] *Leigh and Sillivan Ltd v The Aliakmon Shipping Co Ltd* [1986] AC 785; *MCC Proceeds Inc v Lehman Brothers International (Europe)* [1998] 4 All ER 675.

[70] See further Section 11.2.1, p. 316.

Tariq, the terms of the trust document may state that the trustee is authorized to sell the shares. If Quentin sells the shares to Usman, then, because this is an authorized transaction, legal title to the shares will be transferred to Usman, and Rachel, Susan, and Tariq will no longer have an equitable interest in the shares. Quentin will, however, have legal title to the purchase money, which will come within the terms of the trust, so that Rachel, Susan, and Tariq will then have an equitable interest in that money.

(2) Where, however, property is held on trust and is transferred to a third party in breach of trust, the equitable proprietary interest will not be defeated by virtue of the over-reaching doctrine because the transaction was unauthorized. If, however, the property was transferred to a third party who was not aware that it had been transferred in breach of trust and the third party provided some value for the transfer, the equitable proprietary interest will be defeated and the third party will have absolute legal title to the property. It is a fundamental principle of Equity that the receipt of property by a bona fide purchaser for value will defeat any equitable interest in that property. Legal property rights will, however, not be defeated by receipt of the property by a bona fide purchaser for value, save where the property is money.[71]

(iv) Hierarchy of rights

A further key characteristic of equitable proprietary rights is that it is possible to plan for successive rights to property so that provision can be made for the present and future beneficial use of the property.

So, for example, Vernon may wish to determine what should happen to his property on his death and beyond. He may provide in his will that on his death his estate should be held on trust for the benefit of his wife, Wanda, for life, with remainder for Xerxes. This will mean that Wanda will get the benefit of the property whilst she is alive, but, on her death, the benefit will pass to Xerxes, even if Wanda would have preferred the benefit to pass to all of her three children equally. The ability to provide for consecutive interests in property is an important feature of Equity. It is possible to provide for such consecutive interests at Common Law too, but only as regards land; in Equity, this can occur as regards both land and personal property.

1.5.2 PERSONAL RIGHTS IN EQUITY

Although the major contribution of Equity to English law has been the recognition of equitable proprietary interests, the recognition of equitable personal rights has also been of real significance to the development of the law. Probably the most significant rights are those that arise from a fiduciary relationship, which is a particular relationship between the principal and the fiduciary which can be characterized as one of trust and confidence, such as the relationship of solicitor and client.[72] Fiduciaries owe their principals particular duties, which are distinct from, and additional to, the ordinary Common Law negligence standard of skill and care. In particular, fiduciaries owe their principals a duty of loyalty and self-denial. In addition to the proprietary connotations of the trust, where there is a division between legal and equitable proprietary rights, the fiduciary obligation is an essential characteristic of the express trust, for all express trustees owe fiduciary duties to their beneficiaries. So, for example, if a trustee misappropriates trust property for themself, the beneficiaries will be able to rely on their equitable proprietary rights and make a

---

[71] *Miller v Race* (1758) 1 Burr 452.   [72] See Section 15.2.1, p. 420.

claim to recover the property.[73] But they will also have personal rights against the trustee for breach of fiduciary duty and the trustee may be liable either to compensate the beneficiaries for the loss that they have suffered or account for the profit that the trustee has made as a result of the breach.[74]

The dividing line between proprietary and personal rights may sometimes be difficult to draw, and will depend on the particular circumstances of the case. This is particularly well illustrated by the law relating to rescission. If a claimant has transferred property to the defendant pursuant to a contract that is voidable in Equity, perhaps because of non-fraudulent misrepresentation or undue influence, the claimant will be able to rescind the contract in Equity and recover the property. The effect of rescission is that the defendant, who has legal title to the property, will hold that property for the claimant, who will have an equitable proprietary interest in it. In other words, the defendant will hold the property on trust for the claimant. Before the contract is rescinded, however, Equity recognizes that the claimant has a right to rescind the contract, and this right is called a 'mere equity'. This can be defined as a right that, if exercised, will enable the claimant to recover any property that has been transferred under the contract, and so operates like a proprietary right. Consequently, the mere equity to rescind can be defeated if the property has been obtained by a third party who provided some value for it and was acting in good faith, In other circumstances, however, this mere equity to rescind will not have any proprietary connotations where the voidable contract is executory, in the sense that the claimant has not yet transferred any property to the defendant. In such circumstances, the mere equity relates only to the personal right of the claimant to terminate their obligations under the contract.

1.6 SHOULD EQUITY BE ASSIMILATED INTO THE COMMON LAW?

This chapter has shown that there is a fundamental distinction in the law between the Common Law and Equity. Although the administration of Common Law and Equity have been assimilated so that Equity can be applied in any court, Common Law and Equity have not been substantively assimilated. In other words, they have not been fused. One of the great controversies concerning the function of Equity today is whether the separate existence of the Common Law and Equity can still be justified or whether the two should be fused.

1.6.1 ARE EQUITY AND COMMON LAW ALREADY ASSIMILATED?

Before considering whether the Common Law and Equity should be assimilated, the prior question must be whether they are already assimilated. The answer is clearly 'no'. This will be shown throughout this book, but for now two illustrations of the significant differences between Common Law and Equity will make the point:

(1) It remains a fundamental principle that equitable proprietary interests and legal proprietary interests are distinct. The notion of the trust depends on a separation of these interests. Since the Common Law does not recognize equitable interests in property, it follows that it does not recognize the trust.

---

[73] See further Chapter 19.   [74] See further Chapter 18.

(2) The characteristics of proprietary rights are dependent on whether they are classi-fied as legal or equitable. For example, if the defendant steals a car that belongs to me at Common Law, then the usual remedy that will be available to me is a pecuniary remedy to compensate me for the loss suffered: I will not usually be able to recover the car from the defendant. Where, however, I have an equitable interest in the car, for example because it is held on trust for me, and that car is stolen, I will be able to assert my equitable property rights to recover the car itself. Another difference between legal and equitable property interests relates to the ability to claim money that has been stolen from the claimant. If the claimant has a legal interest in money and that money is paid into an active bank account, the Common Law is unable to identify the money in the mixture and so any proprietary claim to that money will fail.[75] Where, however, the claimant has an equitable interest in the money, Equity is able to identify value in a mixture and the proprietary claim to the money will not be defeated by the mixing.

1.6.2 ARE COMMON LAW AND EQUITY BEING ASSIMILATED?

Although Common Law and Equity remain distinct, there is growing evidence that they are becoming assimilated. This is illustrated by three particular examples:

(1) When a defendant is liable to pay damages to the claimant, it has long been rec-ognized that the defendant will also have to pay interest to the claimant for the defend-ant's use of the money. Section 35A of the Senior Courts Act 1981 provides that simple interest should be available—that is, interest awarded on the sum due to the claimant. There is, however, an equitable jurisdiction to award compound interest, in which case interest is awarded on both the capital sum and on the interest that has already accrued. Traditionally, compound interest was only available for claims brought in Equity, such as claims for breach of trust.[76] However, the House of Lords in *Sempra Metals Ltd v IRC*[77] recognized that compound interest should be available for claims regardless of whether they arose at Common Law or in Equity.

(2) Traditionally, Common Law pecuniary remedies are compensatory, whereas those awarded in Equity are gain-based, in the sense that they are assessed by reference to the value of the gain made by the defendant rather than the loss suffered by the claimant. So, for example, where the defendant has breached a contract, the usual remedy will be compensatory damages, whereas where the defendant has breached a fiduciary duty, the typical remedy will be an account of profits, which is assessed by reference to the value of the gain made by the defendant as a result of the breach of duty. There is, however, grow-ing evidence of the assimilation of these remedies. So, for example, the House of Lords has recognized that the remedy of an account of profits may exceptionally be available where the defendant has breached a contract.[78] Equally, compensatory damages can be awarded for the commission of equitable wrongs.[79] Further, there appears to be a growing assimilation of the principles relating to the award of compensatory remedies for equitable wrongdoing with those concerning Common Law wrongdoing, at least where the equi-table wrong has occurred in a commercial context.[80]

---

[75] See Section 19.3.2.(iii), p. 557.
[76] *Westdeutsche Landesbank Girozentrale v Islington LBC* [1996] AC 669.
[77] [2007] UKHL 34, [2008] 1 AC 561.   [78] *Attorney-General v Blake* [2001] 1 AC 268.
[79] *Target Holdings Ltd v Redferns* [1996] AC 421; *AIB Group (UK) plc v Redler* [2014] UKSC 58, [2015] AC 1503.
[80] Ibid. See further Section 18.2.2.(ii), p.514.

(3) The orthodox analysis of the law of rescission of contracts is that the rules differ depending on whether the jurisdiction to rescind is asserted at Common Law or in Equity. The key difference in the application of these rules is that rescission at Common Law is effected by the election of the party seeking rescission of the contract,[81] whereas rescission in Equity is effected by a court order, with the court having a discretion to determine whether rescission is appropriate and, if it is, what the conditions for rescission should be.[82] A significant consequence of this has been that rescission at Common Law will be barred if the parties cannot be restored precisely to their pre-contractual position, whereas rescission can be effected in Equity by the court if the parties can be restored substantially to their pre-contractual positions. In fact, the Judicature Act 1873 itself might have operated to ensure that the equitable rules of rescission prevailed over those of the Common Law, so that all rescission should be effected by order of the court. This is because that Act provided that where there is a conflict or variance between the rules of Equity and the Common Law with reference to the same matter, the rules of Equity will prevail.[83] This might be interpreted to mean that, where there is a concurrent jurisdiction to rescind in Equity and the Common Law, the equitable rules should apply to the extent that they conflict. This interpretation of the legislation was acknowledged by Carnwath LJ in *Halpern v Halpern (No 2)*,[84] a case concerning rescission of a contract for duress, in which it was recognized that rescission for duress, which takes place at Common Law, should be subject to the more flexible, equitable interpretation of the bar that rescission will be denied if the claimant cannot restore the defendant to their pre-contractual position. This would appear to be a situation, therefore, in which the Common Law is being assimilated with Equity.

1.6.3 SHOULD EQUITY AND THE COMMON LAW BE ASSIMILATED?

For a number of commentators[85] and judges, having two separate systems of law is illogical and unprincipled. Some commentators have analysed private law generally by reference to a scheme that makes no reference to Equity at all. The main proponent of this scheme was Professor Peter Birks,[86] who distinguished between events and responses. He identified four types of event that trigger responses in private law. These events are consent, wrongs, unjust enrichment, and other events. Equity has no specific place in this scheme but operates within each event, and it is for this reason, among others, that this scheme should be rejected as not providing a useful map with which to analyse private law. In particular, much of Equity has to fit within the fourth category, especially because the principle of unconscionability is undoubtedly an event that triggers an equitable response, but is not founded on contract, wrongdoing or unjust enrichment.[87] Once this is recognized, it becomes clear that there must be a distinct place for the recognition of equitable events within private law.

---

[81] *Car and Universal Finance Co Ltd v Caldwell* [1965] 1 QB 525.

[82] *Lagunas Nitrate Co v Lagunas Syndicate* [1899] 2 Ch 392, 457 (Rigby LJ); *Spence v Crawford* [1939] 3 All ER 271, 280 (Lord Thankerton).

[83] Judicature Act 1873, s. 25(11). See now Senior Courts Act 1981, s. 49.

[84] [2007] EWCA Civ 291, [2008] QB 88, [70].

[85] See, especially, Burrows 'We do this at Common Law but that in Equity' (2002) 22 OJLS 1. See also Worthington, *Equity*, ch. 10.

[86] See e.g. Birks, 'Property, unjust enrichment and tracing' (2001) 54 CLP 231.

[87] See Section 9.3.8, p. 274.

For other judges and commentators, the very existence of two systems is not a matter of concern. For example, Lord Millett has said:[88]

> Those who favour the fusion of law and equity might perhaps reflect that the three greatest systems of jurisprudence in the Western world have all been dual systems. Jewish law had its written and oral law; Roman law its civil and praetorian or bonitary law; English law common law and equity. In each case the duality served a similar function. One system provided certainty; the other the necessary flexibility and adaptability to enable justice to be done. But the common law and equity are not two separate and parallel systems of law. The common law is a complete system of law which could stand alone, but which if not tempered by equity would often be productive of injustice; while equity is not a complete and independent system of law and could not stand alone.

This is the preferable view. There is evidence of assimilation of the systems in certain areas, or perhaps this might be preferably characterized as cross-fertilization, but the continued existence of a separate body of law known as Equity is essential. For example, complete assimilation of Common Law and Equity would not result in the abolition of the trust, but would render its analysis much more complex, and the subtleties and nuances of the law would be lost.[89] Kitto J[90] has described Equity extra-judicially as follows: '[I]t will be salutary for the lawyer to remind himself that equity is the appendix that the Chancery was composing for the saving of the common law, and is not an independent system of law.'

This remains true of Equity today. It is not an independent system of law, but it has a distinct identity and function to modify the rigours of the Common Law.

---

[88] 'Proprietary restitution', in *Equity in Commercial Law*, ed. Degeling and Edelman (Sydney: Law Book Co., 2005), p. 309.

[89] See Virgo, 'Restitution through the Looking Glass: restitution within Equity and Equity within restitution', in *Rationalizing Property, Equity and Trusts: Essays in Honour of Edward Burn*, ed. Getzler (Oxford: Oxford University Press, 2003), p. 106. See also Martin, 'Fusion, fallacy and confusion: a comparative study' [1994] Conv 13.

[90] 'Foreword', in *Equity: Doctrine and Remedies*, ed. Meagher, Gummow, and Lehane (London: Butterworths, 1975).

2

THE CHARACTERISTICS OF EQUITY

2.1 FUNDAMENTAL PRINCIPLES

Judges who apply the rules and principles of Equity often make decisions with reference to a number of recognized equitable maxims. Sometimes these maxims are cited by judges and used by commentators without any obvious understanding as to what they really mean or why they are being used;[1] this is not acceptable. The maxims are a useful method of paraphrasing a complex body of law: they are guidelines rather than rules. They are useful because, as Lord Upjohn recognized in *Boardman v Phipps*,[2] rules of Equity have to be applied to such a great diversity of circumstances that they can be stated only in the most general terms and applied with particular attention to the specific circumstances of each case.

But it is always important to unpack carefully what each maxim actually means. It is for this reason that it is essential to be aware of the existence of the maxims before you study the details of Equity. They are important because they can help you to get a better understanding of how the equitable jurisdiction operates, but they must be treated with caution, since they may require very careful interpretation and analysis. Also, some of the maxims are inconsistent with each other, or one may take precedence over the other, so it is important to determine when the application of one maxim will give way to another one.

---

[1] This has sometimes been described as a 'mantra': *Jones v Kernott* [2011] UKSC 53, [2012] 1 AC 776, at [19] (Lord Walker and Lady Hale).　　　　　　　　　　　　　　　　　　　　　[2] [1967] 2 AC 46, 123.

In this chapter, a number of new maxims are identified as a way of summarizing some complex principles or rules in a pithy statement. Some of the other maxims that will be examined in this chapter have been recognized for hundreds of years. Maybe that is the reason why some of them have become increasingly misleading, since the reality of the law that operates behind the maxims may have changed, but the maxim appears to remain the same. Consequently, the maxims are often subject to exceptions, and sometimes it may even be necessary to redefine them to ensure that they are fit for purpose today and, if it is found that they are not, reject them. Although there are traditionally twelve different maxims of Equity,[3] some of these should no longer be regarded as valid. For example, it is sometimes said that 'Equity will not suffer a wrong without a remedy.' If this is interpreted simply as meaning that where there is an identifiable equitable wrong, Equity will fashion a remedy, this is not saying anything peculiar about Equity; the same is true of the Common Law. It may, however, mean that where wrongdoing has occurred that could not be remedied at Law, it is possible to resort to Equity for a remedy. This was indeed how Equity originated.[4] But this is no longer the case. In *Holmes v Milage*,[5] it was recognized that 'it is an old mistake to suppose that because there is no effectual remedy at law, there must be one in equity'. This particular maxim should consequently be regarded as liable to deceive and useless, and so should be rejected.

There are fourteen maxims that are useful and relevant today as guidelines for the operation of the equitable jurisdiction. These maxims are as follows:

(1) Equity is discretionary.

(2) Equity is triggered by unconscionability.

(3) Those who seek Equity must do Equity.

(4) Those who come to Equity must come with clean hands.

(5) Equity treats as done what ought to be done.

(6) Equity protects the weak and vulnerable.

(7) Equity is cynical.

(8) Equity is imaginative.

(9) Equity follows the Law.

(10) Equity looks to substance rather than to form.

(11) Equity will not assist a volunteer.

(12) Equity assists the diligent.

(13) Equity is equality.

(14) Equity acts *in personam*.

2.2 EQUITY IS DISCRETIONARY

It was seen in Chapter 1 that there is a tendency to treat the application of Equity as being a discretionary regime that seeks to secure a just and fair result, without obvious regard to identifiable rules or principles that produce certainty and predictability.[6] The reality is

---

[3] Meagher, Gummow, and Lehane, *Equity: Doctrines and Remedies*, 5th edn, ed. Heydon, Leeming and Turner (London: Butterworths, 2014), ch. 3; *Snell's Equity*, 33rd edn, ed. McGhee (London: Sweet and Maxwell, 2016), ch. 5.

[4] See Section 1.3, p. 5.   [5] [1893] 1 QB 551.   [6] See Section 1.2, p. 4.

very different, in that much of Equity can be characterized as doctrinal, in the sense that it is made up of identifiable rules that are to be applied strictly, without any role for judicial discretion. In *Re Diplock*,[7] the Court of Appeal recognized that:

> if a claim in equity exists, it must be shown to have an ancestry founded in history and in the practice and precedents of courts administering equity jurisdiction. It is not sufficient that because we may think that the 'justice' of the present case requires it, we should invent such a jurisdiction for the first time.[8]

But doctrinal Equity is not fixed in stone. As Sir George Jessel MR recognized in *Re Hallett's Estate*,[9] 'doctrines are progressive, refined, and improved'. It follows that the Equity that was developed in the nineteenth century may be very different in the twenty-first century because it has been adapted to cope with the very different problems that arise today.

The recognition of specific doctrines within Equity does not mean that there is no role for the exercise of judicial discretion, but it is important to be clear as to what discretion means in this context. There is an assumption discernible in the cases and in the literature that judicial discretion is a bad thing because it is uncontrolled and unpredictable, and the judge simply cannot be trusted to exercise their discretion appropriately. This suspicion of the judiciary was recognized by Lord Camden in *Doe v Kersey*,[10] who said:

> The discretion of a Judge is the law of tyrants; it is always unknown; it is different in different men; it is casual, and depends upon constitution, in temper and passion. In the best it is often times caprice; in the worst it is every vice, folly and passion to which human nature is liable.

The assumption is that the exercise of judicial discretion is inevitably arbitrary, as recognized 500 years ago by Sir Thomas More who said in *Utopia*:

> The law and Judges should avoid arcane interpretations and debates about law but should instead judge the overall equity or justice of a situation and decide accordingly.[11]

But Hart[12] recognized that discretion is fundamentally different from arbitrary choice: discretion by its nature is guided by rational principles, so that a decision which is not susceptible to principled justification is not an exercise of discretion at all but involves the making of an arbitrary choice. Hart rejected arbitrary choice as a basis for judicial decision-making. He was right to do so; judicial decision-making must be founded on recognized principles. Whilst the role of judicial discretion is essential to ensure that justice is achieved, if the resort to justice is to be defensible and predictable, there needs to be identifiable principles to guide that discretion and to ensure that like cases are treated alike, for the benefit of the parties, their advisers and, if the case goes to trial, the judge.

A principle is appropriately defined as a reason of general application.[13] The difficulty relates to the identification of those principles, but they have emerged over time through the constant evolution of Equity. The principles are typically founded on what the judge considers to be just and fair; not determined through the exercise of arbitrary choice,

---

[7] [1948] Ch 465, 481–2.

[8] See also Denning, 'The need for a new Equity' (1952) 5 CLP 8: '[T]he Courts of Chancery are no longer courts of equity ... They are as fixed and immutable as the Courts of law ever were.'

[9] (1880) 13 Ch D 696, 710.   [10] (1795) (CP) quoted in Bower's Law Dictionary (1839).

[11] (1516) Book 1, 45.

[12] 'Discretion', written in 1956 and published in (2013) 127 Harvard Law Review 652.

[13] Gardner, 'Ashworth on principles' in *Principles and Values in Criminal Law and Criminal Justice: Essays in Honour of Andrew Ashworth*, ed. Zedner and Roberts (Oxford: Oxford University Press, 2012), p. 9.

but rather as an external normative standard against which the defendant can be judged. Some of these equitable principles can be identified at a high level of abstraction, such as fair dealing, trust, and conscience,[14] but then various sub-branches can be identified from these principles,[15] often influenced by the particular context. So, for example, Toulson LJ said of the equitable remedy of rectification[16] that:[17]

> its origins lie in conscience and fair dealing, but those origins cannot be invoked to justify
> an unprincipled approach: far from it. Particularly as rectification is normally invoked in
> a contractual context, it seems to me that its principles should reflect the approach of the
> law to contracts, in particular to the formation and interpretation of contracts. Similarly,
> as rectification most commonly arises in a commercial context, it is plainly right that the
> applicable principles should be as clear and predictable in their application as possible.

Whether the equitable approach should be considered to be primarily principled or discretionary has proved to be especially significant in respect of the constructive trust, which arises by operation of law rather than intention.[18] Traditionally, in England, the constructive trust arises by operation of law by virtue of clearly defined principles and is known as an institutional constructive trust. In other jurisdictions, notably Australia and Canada, the constructive trust arises through the exercise of judicial discretion, and is known as the remedial constructive trust. As a consequence of scepticism about judicial discretion, in England the remedial constructive trust is not recognized, as confirmed by the Supreme Court.[19] Lord Neuberger subsequently expressed his concerns about the recognition of the remedial constructive trust extra-judicially.[20] He noted that 'the notion of a remedial constructive trust displays equity at its flexible flabby worst' and he considered it to be 'unprincipled, incoherent and impractical'.[21]

But even in Australia the remedial constructive trust is founded on principle. It has been recognized that '[u]nstructured judicial discretion ... has no place in the law of constructive trusts in Australia.'[22] And Deane J in *Muschinski v Dodds* emphasized that:[23]

> The fact that the constructive trust remains predominantly remedial does not, however,
> mean that it represents a medium for the indulgence of idiosyncratic notions of fairness
> and justice. As an equitable remedy, it is available only when warranted by established
> equitable principles or by the legitimate processes of legal reasoning, by analogy, induc-
> tion and deduction, from the starting point of a proper understanding of the conceptual
> foundations of such principles ... proprietary rights fall to be governed by principles of law
> and not by some mix of judicial discretion, subjective views about which party 'ought to
> win' ... and 'the formless void' of individual moral opinion...

In England the characterization of the constructive trust as institutional, which cannot be modified by the exercise of judicial discretion, does not reflect the operation of the constructive trust in the real world.[24] The reality of the constructive trust is that it arises by

---

[14] See Section 2.3.1, p. 27.

[15] *Shearer v Spring Capital Ltd* [2013] EWHC 3148 (Ch), [250] (Daniel Alexander QC).

[16] Considered in Section 21.7, p. 654.

[17] *Daventry District Council v Daventry and District Housing Ltd* [2011] EWCA Civ 1153, [2012] 1 WLR 1333, [196].   [18] See Section 9.1.1, p. 254.

[19] *FHR European Ventures LLP v Cedar Capital Partners LLC* [2014] UKSC 45, [2015] AC 250, [47].

[20] 'The remedial constructive trust: fact or fiction', delivered in August 2014 to the Banking Services and Finance Law Association Conference, New Zealand.

[21] See also Birks, 'The remedies for abuse of confidential information' [1990] LMCLQ 460, 465.

[22] *State Trustees Ltd v Edwards* [2014] VSC 392, [143] (McMillan J).

[23] (1985) 160 CLR 583, 615.   [24] See further Section 9.4, p. 275.

operation of law at the point when the defendant's conduct can be characterized as uncon-scionable, as defined with reference to recognized principles, but this constructive trust (institutional if we have to call it that) can be modified in the exercise of judicial discretion, but itself in a principled and not an arbitrary way.[25]

It follows that, whilst it remains appropriate to recognize the maxim that Equity is dis-cretionary, it must not be forgotten that discretion does not mean arbitrary choice. The exercise of judicial discretion must constantly be grounded with reference to principle. This is then consistent with the rule of law.[26] The key consideration then relates to the identification of appropriate principles. That is what this book seeks to identify.

2.3 EQUITY IS TRIGGERED BY UNCONSCIONABILITY

Although doctrine and principle is vital to modern Equity, the very existence of the most important equitable principle might undermine the doctrinal coherence of the subject if it is not defined tightly and coherently. That principle is unconscionability. Today, one of the main justifications for the operation of the equitable jurisdiction is that the defendant has acted unconscionably. Indeed, in *Westdeutsche Landesbank Girozentrale v Islington LBC*,[27] the key justification for the recognition of a trust was the principle that 'Equity operates on the conscience of the owner of the legal interest.'[28] But what does conscience mean for these purposes?

2.3.1 THE MEANING OF CONSCIENCE AND UNCONSCIONABILITY

Gleeson CJ has said that the use of the word 'unconscionable' 'may be merely an emphatic method of expressing disapproval of someone's behavior, but its legal meaning is consider-ably more precise.'[29] But identifying that precise legal meaning is not easy. The preferable view is that unconscionability means 'contrary to good conscience.'[30] But is unconscio-nability a state of mind or does it relate to a normative standard for evaluating conduct, morality, or simply a sense of guilt?

2.3.2 THE HISTORY OF CONSCIENCE

Legal history can assist in determining how conscience and unconscionability should be interpreted today.[31] The words themselves have been used for hundreds of years, so it is vital to identify their origins to see if they can be of assistance in understanding their con-temporary application. The history of conscience in Equity is complex and uncertain.[32] Although what follows is a gross simplification of rigorous historical scholarship, it is

---

[25] See Section 9.4, pp. 277–9.

[26] See generally Harding, 'Equity and the rule of law' (2016) 132 LQR 278.

[27] [1996] AC 669.   [28] Ibid., 705 (Lord Browne-Wilkinson).

[29] *Australian Competition and Consumer Commission v CG Berbatis Holdings Pty Ltd* (2003) 214 CLR 51, [7].

[30] McConvill and Bagaric, 'The yoking of unconscionability and unjust enrichment in Australia' (2002) 7 Deakin LR 225, 249.

[31] See Havelock, 'The evolution of equitable conscience' (2014) 8 Journal of Equity 128.

[32] One of the best investigations is that of Klinck, 'The unexamined "conscience" of contemporary Canadian Equity' (2001) 46 McGill LJ 571.

possible to identify six different stages in the development of conscience as an equitable construct, in broadly chronological order.

(i) The Chancellor's conscience

Conscience originally referred to the conscience of the Chancellor as the measure of equity, with conscience being a reference to the individual moral judgment of the judge,[33] albeit one influenced by theological learning and canon law, since the Chancellor was typically a cleric.[34] Conscience in this moral sense was criticized for its inherent uncertainty being, as Selden famously acknowledged, like making the Chancellor's foot the measure of the standard foot.[35]

(ii) Personal knowledge

As Chancery procedure developed, references to conscience involved the ascertainment of legally relevant facts from the judge's personal knowledge or belief rather than by reference to what was alleged and proved.[36]

(iii) The defendant's conscience

The focus shifted to the assessment of the defendant's conscience, as determined by the court, but with reference to what the defendant knew or believed to be true, rather than what they believed to be morally right. This interpretation of conscience derived from the ability of Equity to compel the defendant's appearance at court and to examine the defendant on oath with a view to extracting a confession.[37] It also reveals a focus of the Chancery court on intervening to purge or purify what was considered to be the corrupt conscience of the defendant, and has been described as a 'cathartic jurisdiction'.[38] This was recognized by Lord Ellesmere in the *Earl of Oxford's Case*:[39]

> The office of the Chancellor is to correct men's conscience for frauds, breaches of trust, wrongs and oppressions of what nature soever they be…

(iv) The foundation of equitable doctrine

Under the influence of Lord Chancellors, notably Lord Eldon, who were lawyers rather than clerics, equitable principles were identified and were often justified with reference to conscience. Through the development of a doctrine of precedent, categories of like cases were identified which were informed by past decisions and past values, notably unconscionability. So, rather than seeking to identify unconscionability in each case, it was sufficient that a case fell within a particular category of liability, the existence of which could be justified by reference to the old language of conscience.[40] Here unconscionability operates as a matter of opinion, but one which has been 'formed and inferred by considered decisions in similar but not identical cases, by the values of the community, that is by the palimpsest of past legal and community traditions'.[41]

---

[33] Christopher St German's *Doctor and Student* (1523, 1531).
[34] Baker, *An Introduction to English Legal History*, 4th edn (Oxford: Oxford University Press, 2002), p. 99.
[35] Selden, *Table Talk of John Selden* (London: Selden Society, 1927), p. 43.
[36] McNair, 'Equity and conscience' [2007] OJLS 659.   [37] Ibid., p. 676.
[38] Ashburner's *Principles of Equity*, 2nd edn, ed. Browne (London: Butterworth and Co., 1933), p. 39.
[39] (1615) 1 Ch R 1, 6. See also *Allcard v Skinner* (1887) LR 36 Ch D 145, 189 (Bowen LJ).
[40] Rossiter and Stone, 'The Chancellor's new shoe' (1988) 11 UNSWLJ 11, 24.
[41] Ibid., p. 26. See also Finn, 'Unconscionable conduct' (1994) 8 JCL 37.

(v) Chancery is conscience

Conscience was also used simply to describe the Chancery jurisdiction, but without pro-viding any justification for the exercise of that jurisdiction.[42] Arguably, it is this sense of conscience which was recognized by Lord Nottingham in *Cooke v Fountain*:[43]

> With such a conscience as is only *naturali et interna* this Court has nothing to do; the con-science by which I am to proceed is merely *civilis et politica* and tied to certain measures; and it is infinitely better for the public that a trust, security, or agreement, which is wholly secret, should miscarry, than that men should lose their estates by the mere fancy and imagination of a chancellor.

(vi) Rhetorical conscience

Throughout the history of Equity the language of conscience and unconscionability has also been used simply as a rhetorical device which the judge could hide behind to exercise a choice without reference to principle.[44] The wheel may appear to have gone full circle, with the modern judge, who seeks to interpret conscience in this way,[45] appearing to act like the former Lord Chancellor and exercising judgment without reference to principle. But that is not the case. For the first interpretation of conscience was highly principled, with reference to theological interpretations of conscience, with very close attention to biblical text and commentary by scholars. Modern approaches to conscience, which actually hide behind the language of conscience, do not reflect the original, principled notion of conscience.

(vii) Summary

This review of the history of conscience reveals a variety of different interpretations over time, although a general trend can be identified away from conscience as a test of morality, to conscience underpinning equitable doctrine. At times conscience has referred explicitly to the conscience of the defendant, but typically it has been interpreted objectively, with reference to what the court considers the defendant's conscience should dictate.

2.3.3 A NEW TAXONOMY OF CONSCIENCE

In order to ensure precise analysis, consistent application and appropriate communication of meaning a new taxonomy of conscience needs to be adopted, involving a fundamental distinction between the defendant's conscience and the conscience of the court.[46]

(i) The defendant's conscience

The conscience of the defendant is often used as a component of particular causes of action.[47] This can be interpreted in two different ways:

(1) The subjective assessment of the defendant's mind, with regard to what the defend-ant knew, intended, or suspected. Inevitably, for reasons of proof, even this subjective

---

[42] Watt, *Equity Stirring* (Oxford: Hart, 2009), p. 106.   [43] (1676) 3 Swanst 585, 600.

[44] Kluck, *Conscience, Equity and the Court of Chancery in Early Modern England* (Farnham: Ashgate, 2010), p. 10.

[45] See e.g. *Pitt v Holt* [2013] UKSC 26, [2013] 2 AC 108, [126] (Lord Walker). See also *National Westminster Bank v Morgan* [1985] AC 686, 703 (Lord Scarman).

[46] Havelock, 'Conscience and unconscionability in modern equity' (2015) 9 Journal of Equity 1 argues that the use of the language of unconscionability is so confused that the word should be rejected.

[47] See Section 20.2.3.(i), p. 596.

test of conscience has objective connotations, because proof of a subjective state of mind is difficult, so the courts have regard to what the defendant would reasonably have known or suspected in order to determine what the defendant did think. As will be seen, this use of unconscionability will be rare and is primarily relevant to establish that the defendant holds property on constructive trust.[48]

(2) The objective assessment of the defendant's conduct, in the light of the facts as the defendant knew, believed, or suspected them to be. This is consistent with the historical development of conscience in Equity: the court determines what the defendant's conscience should reasonably require them to do in the light of the defendant's own awareness of the facts. Perhaps, in order to distinguish this from the next category of conscience, it would be appropriate to call this 'dishonesty'. This interpretation of conscience has proved to be significant to establish the defendant's personal liability for receipt of property transferred in breach of trust where the defendant no longer retains the property,[49] or where the defendant has assisted a breach of trust.[50]

(ii) The court's conscience

The alternative sense of conscience, which is much more prevalent, refers to the conscience of the court generally or the judge particularly. But, whilst this might appear to indicate that the judge can determine the result by reference to arbitrary choice, in fact this interpretation of conscience is properly analysed as involving principled discretion;[51] rather than treating the judge's conscience as a rhetorical device behind which they can hide by asserting that a particular result is justified by good conscience, the judge needs to go further and explain why good conscience demands such a result. As Lord Sumption has recognized: 'Good conscience … involves more than a judgment of the relative moral merits of the parties.'[52] The exercise of judicial discretion with reference to identified principles is similar to objective dishonesty, since the identification of such fault is determined by the judge on the evidence and so can be characterized as a principle which triggers equitable intervention. But the conscience of the court is much more extensive in its operation as regards the identification of many other principles, which will be identified throughout this book.

2.4 THOSE WHO SEEK EQUITY MUST DO EQUITY

The judicial discretion to determine whether an equitable remedy should be awarded is affected by the significant maxim that anybody who seeks an equitable award must themselves do equity. What this means is that, when granting an equitable remedy, the judge should ensure that the claimant is willing to act fairly towards the defendant in the future. So, for example, in *Chappell v Times Newspapers Ltd*,[53] an injunction was denied to employees who wished to restrain their employer from dismissing them, because the employees had refused to undertake that they would not strike in future.

To ensure that the claimant does indeed 'do' equity, the judge can attach conditions to the grant of an equitable remedy. So, for example, following *Ramsden v Dyson*,[54] when the claimant seeks to recover land from the defendant, but the claimant knows that the defendant has spent money on the land in the mistaken belief that the land belongs to

---

[48] See Section 9.3.1, p. 258.
[49] See Section 20.2, p. 592.   [50] See Section 20.3, p. 611.   [51] See Section 2.2, p. 24.
[52] *Angove's Pty Ltd v Bailey* [2016] UKSC 47, [2016] 1 WLR 3179, [28] (Lord Sumption).
[53] [1975] 1 WLR 482.   [54] (1866) LR 1 HL 129.

the defendant, it can be a condition of the claimant recovering the land that the defendant is reimbursed for this expenditure. Similarly, in *Re Berkeley Applegate (Investments Consultants) Ltd*,[55] it was recognized that a beneficiary cannot claim property from a trustee without reimbursing the trustee for costs that they have incurred as a trustee and for the trustee's labour in administering the property.

2.5 THOSE WHO COME TO EQUITY MUST COME WITH CLEAN HANDS

Whereas the last maxim was concerned with the claimant's conduct in the future, the maxim that those who come to Equity must have clean hands[56] relates to the claimant's past conduct. This maxim means that equitable relief will be denied to a claimant whose conduct can be considered to be improper in some way.[57] This maxim, like the previous one, is clearly based on the historical origins of Equity as being founded on conscience, judged objectively.

In *Dering v Earl of Winchelsea*,[58] it was held that improper conduct involves impropriety in a legal, and not a moral, sense. Also, the improper conduct must relate to the relief that is sought in some way. Consequently, just because the claimant's general conduct is unacceptable does not mean that Equity will deny relief to the claimant. So, for example, in *Argyll (Duchess) v Argyll (Duke)*,[59] the duchess was able to obtain an injunction to restrain her former husband from publishing confidential information, even though it was her adultery that had led to the breakdown of their marriage in the first place. In that case, Ungoed-Thomas J recognized that, although a person coming to Equity must come with clean hands, 'the cleanliness required is to be judged in relation to the relief sought'.[60]

A further restriction on the operation of the 'clean hands' maxim was once recognized, namely that it is possible to obtain an equitable remedy despite the claimant having unclean hands if it is not necessary for the claimant to rely on the improper conduct to obtain the remedy.[61] This was, however, rejected by the Supreme Court in *Patel v Mirza*[62] by virtue of its artificiality. Today, whether participation in a transaction tainted by illegality should bar an equitable claim will depend on the exercise of judicial discretion, guided by reference to a variety of recognized factors such as whether it would be proportional to deny relief.

2.6 EQUITY TREATS AS DONE THAT WHICH OUGHT TO BE DONE

This maxim[63] has been of particular significance in the development of Equity, but there is a tendency to rely on it too readily without regard to its rationale. The true function of the maxim is illustrated by the fact that, where the parties have entered into a contract that is specifically enforceable, Equity will treat the contract as having been performed.[64] The maxim is also relevant where the defendant has agreed to transfer property to another party,

---

[55] [1989] Ch 32.
[56] *Fitzroy v Twilim* (1786) 1 TR 153. See Chafee, 'Coming into equity with clean hands' (1949) 47 Mich L Rev 877 and 1065 and Pettit, 'He who comes to equity must come with clean hands' [1990] Conv 416.
[57] *Dunbar v Plant* [1998] Ch 412, 422 (Mummery LJ).
[58] (1787) 1 Cox Eq Cas 318.   [59] [1967] Ch 302.   [60] Ibid., 322.
[61] *Tinsley v Milligan* [1994] 1 AC 340.   [62] [2016] UKSC 42, [2017] AC 467. See Section 8.2.5, p. 224.
[63] *Banks v Sutton* (1732) 2 P Wms 700, 715 (Jekyll MR).
[64] *Re Anstis* (1886) 31 Ch D 596, 605 (Lindley LJ).

but has not done so. In such a scenario, the Common Law will look at the reality and will treat the defendant as still owning the property. But, if the contract is specifically enforceable, Equity will treat the defendant as having done what they had promised to do, namely transfer the property to the claimant, who will then be treated as owning the property in Equity. Since the defendant now has legal title and the claimant now has a title recognized in Equity, the defendant will hold the property on constructive trust for the claimant. This will still be the case even if the defendant has done nothing wrong in not transferring the property to the claimant. So, for example, if the defendant enters into a contract with the claimant for the sale of land, title to the land will not be transferred until completion. But, once the contract for sale is made, Equity will treat the transfer as having occurred, so the vendor will hold the land on constructive trust for the purchaser.[65] This trust is of a peculiar kind because the vendor also retains a beneficial interest in the property until the purchaser has paid the full purchase price, at which point the vendor is a bare trustee for the purchaser.[66] The maxim has also proved to be significant in respect of leases. It provides the basis for the important decision in *Walsh v Lonsdale*[67] that Equity will treat a person who has agreed for valuable consideration to take a lease as though that person is a lessee of property.

The maxim that Equity treats as done that which ought to be done has been applied in contexts other than contracts for the sale of land or chattels. This is illustrated most quaintly by *Frederick v Frederick*,[68] in which Thomas agreed with the Court of Aldermen in the City of London that he would take up his freedom of the City within one year in consideration of his marriage to Leonora. He married Leonora, but he failed to take up his freedom before he died. It was held that his estate could be distributed as though he were a freeman. As Lord Macclesfield recognized:

> Where one for valuable consideration agrees to do a thing, such executory contract is to be taken as done, and the man who made the agreement shall not be in better case than if he had fairly and honestly performed what he agreed to do.[69]

This principle has also been applied in the commercial context, and is especially significant as regards the law of assignment. So, for example, if Ann enters into a contract with Barry for valuable consideration to assign immediately property that does not yet exist (known as 'future property'), this is not an effective assignment, because there is not yet any property to assign. But immediately the property comes into existence, Equity will treat it as having been assigned to Barry, without Ann having to do anything more, so Barry will own the property in Equity. This also illustrates a restriction on the operation of the maxim. It is not a pure fiction, in that Equity will not pretend that the property is in existence when this is not the case. But it is only when that which ought to be done *can* be done that the maxim will operate.

2.7 EQUITY PROTECTS THE WEAK AND VULNERABLE

There are many examples of Equity intervening to protect the weak and the vulnerable, who are in a position in which they might easily be exploited. This is illustrated by the undue influence doctrine, which is a construct of Equity. This can be used to set aside a

---

[65] *Rayner v Preston* (1881) 18 Ch D 1. See Section 9.3.6, p. 272.
[66] *Lloyds Bank plc v Carrick* [1996] 4 All ER 630.   [67] (1882) 21 Ch D 9.
[68] (1721) 1 P Wms 710.   [69] Ibid., 713.

contract where one party actually unduly influenced[70] the other party, or is presumed to have done so.[71] Equity will also intervene where there is inequality of bargaining power between the parties and the defendant has unconscionably taken advantage of the claimant's special disability.[72] So, for example, in *Cresswell v Potter*,[73] the claimant, who was a telephonist, had released her interest in the matrimonial home to her husband as part of a divorce settlement. This release of the interest was set aside because the claimant was characterized as being poor and ignorant as to the operation of property transactions. Also, the transaction was unfair, since it had been at a significant undervalue and the claimant had not received any independent legal advice as to whether the release on those terms was appropriate.

Another situation in which Equity operates to protect the weak and the vulnerable is the law relating to fiduciaries.[74] A fiduciary relationship is a relationship of trust and confidence in which the principal trusts and has confidence in the fiduciary to manage the principal's property and affairs. The fiduciary is placed in a position of responsibility in which they might be tempted to exploit the principal. It is for this reason that the highest standards of behaviour are expected from the principal.

2.8 EQUITY IS CYNICAL

A number of the traits of Equity that have been identified so far might be considered to be laudable. That Equity is cynical is more negative, but in fact this maxim, although not formally recognized by the courts, underpins a number of equitable rules that exist typically to protect the vulnerable and to prevent exploitation.

There are a variety of situations in which Equity appears to be cynical about human nature. So, for example, where one party makes a gift to another, the Common Law will treat that as being valid, so that the gift belongs to the donee. But Equity is suspicious of a benevolent intent and, in a number of different scenarios, Equity will presume that the donor did not intend to make a gift, so that the recipient will hold the putative 'gift' on a trust for the claimant.[75]

Similarly, Equity assumes that certain types of relationship may be such that one party is likely to exploit the other, so there is a presumption that any transaction between them might be exploitative which means that it can be set aside. So, for example, Equity will presume that a parent has influence over their minor child,[76] that a doctor has influence over their patient,[77] that a solicitor has influence over their client,[78] and that a trustee has influence over their beneficiary.[79]

Much of the law on fiduciaries can be considered to be influenced by Equity's cynicism: Equity requires the highest standards of fiduciaries because of fears that people occupying such positions of trust and confidence may be tempted to prefer their own interests over those of their principals. It is for this reason that a fiduciary who makes any profit from their relationship will be liable to disgorge it to the principal, even if this was part of a transaction that was for the benefit of the principal.[80]

---

[70] *Bank of Credit and Commerce International SA v Aboody* [1990] 1 QB 923.
[71] *Royal Bank of Scotland v Etridge (No 2)* [2001] UKHL 44, [2002] 2 AC 773.
[72] *Hart v O'Connor* [1985] AC 1000.   [73] [1978] 1 WLR 255n.   [74] See Chapter 15.
[75] See Section 8.2.1, p. 218.   [76] *Lancashire Loans Ltd v Black* [1934] 1 KB 380.
[77] *Mitchell v Homfray* (1881) 8 QBD 587.   [78] *Wright v Carter* [1903] 1 Ch 27.
[79] *Ellis v Barker* (1870) LR 7 Ch App 104.   [80] See e.g. *Boardman v Phipps* [1967] 2 AC 46.

2.9 EQUITY IS IMAGINATIVE

Whereas the Common Law has a tendency to be rigid and unimaginative in its operation, Equity is much more imaginative in its application and development. This is illustrated by two significant equitable rules.

First, where a claimant's money is mixed with money belonging to the defendant or another party, the Common Law holds that the claimant's property is no longer identifiable in the mixture, so that the claimant will no longer have any property rights in the money.[81] Equity, however, treats the mixture as a fund and, as long as it is possible to know, or presume, what the claimant's proportionate contribution to the fund was, Equity will recognize that the claimant continues to have a proprietary interest in that proportion of the fund.[82] So, for example, if the defendant stole £100 from the claimant and credited this sum to a bank account that is already £100 in credit, the Common Law is unable to say which part of the credit belongs to the claimant and consequently legal title to the £100 will pass to the defendant. Equity is, however, able to identify the claimant's value in the fund. Since the claimant contributed 50 per cent of the value to the bank account, it follows that the claimant will have a 50 per cent share of the fund. Therefore, if the fund doubles in value, the claimant will be able to claim half of the overall value of the fund.

This imaginative approach to property and value is also illustrated by the role of Equity in the very different context of rescission of contracts. The remedy of rescission, either at Common Law or in Equity, is barred where the claimant has received benefits from the defendant under the contract and is unable to restore those benefits. This is known as the bar of *restitutio in integrum* being impossible. At Law, rescission is barred if the claimant has received a benefit in kind from the defendant, because the Common Law is unable to value such benefits. But Equity is not so inhibited. Where a claimant has received goods or services from the defendant under a contract that is voidable, Equity is willing to value the benefit in kind and make it a condition of rescission that the claimant repays this value to the defendant.[83]

2.10 EQUITY FOLLOWS THE LAW

The maxim that Equity follows the Law has long been recognized, although its interpretation and application is not straightforward. It is certainly the case that Equity recognizes legal rules. So, for example, Equity recognizes legal estates, rights, interests, and titles. But if Equity were to have followed the Law absolutely, there would have been no scope for the development of separate equitable doctrines and a separate identity for the equitable jurisdiction. It is for this reason that the American judge Cardozo J recognized that 'Equity follows the law, but not slavishly nor always.'[84] A more accurate statement of this maxim is simply to say that 'Equity recognizes the Common Law', or that 'Equity is a gloss on the Law.'

One particular example of Equity following the Law arises where two parties own a house which is registered in their joint names. If the parties' relationship fails, they will both claim a beneficial interest in the property. Equity will presume that the beneficial interest in the property corresponds to their legal interest, so that they will share

---

[81] *Taylor v Plumer* (1815) 3 M & S 562; *Agip (Africa) Ltd v Jackson* [1990] Ch 265, 285 (Millett J).

[82] *El Ajou v Dollar Land Holdings plc* [1993] 3 All ER 717, 735–6 (Millett J).

[83] *O'Sullivan v Management Agency and Music Ltd* [1985] AC 686; *Cheese v Thomas* [1994] 1 WLR 129; *Mahoney v Purnell* [1996] 3 All ER 61.

[84] *Graf v Hope Building Corp* (1920) 254 NY 1, 9.

the beneficial interest equally, save where this presumption can be rebutted by a contrary intention.[85]

2.11 EQUITY LOOKS TO SUBSTANCE RATHER THAN FORM

In *Parkin v Thorold*,[86] Lord Romilly MR recognized that:

Courts of Equity make a distinction in all cases between that which is matter of substance and that which is matter of form; and, if they do find that by insisting on the form, the substance will be defeated, they hold it to be inequitable to allow a person to insist on such form, and thereby defeat the substance.

There are numerous examples of this maxim being applied. For example, it provides the basis for the equitable remedy of rectification. Where the words of a contract do not reflect the common intentions of the parties, Equity is exceptionally willing to rewrite the document to reflect those intentions.[87]

Similarly, Equity will identify a trust, even though the settlor has not explicitly stated that they intended to create one, where it is possible to identify an obligation that the recipient of property holds that property for somebody else.[88] At the other extreme are circumstances in which the settlor has purported to create a trust, but Equity, having regard to the substance of the transaction, concludes that the trust is a sham.[89]

Despite this emphasis on the substance of the transaction, there are a number of cases in which Equity is concerned with the process of decision-making rather than the substance. So, for example, where trustees under a discretionary trust have a discretion to determine which objects to benefit and by how much, Equity is much more concerned with whether the discretion is exercised rather than with how it is exercised.[90]

2.12 EQUITY WILL NOT ASSIST A VOLUNTEER

A 'volunteer' is somebody who has not provided consideration for a particular transaction, such as a donor of a gift. The main application of this maxim is where a donor purports to make a gift to the donee, but the gift is not effective at Law, so that legal title is retained by the donor. It has been recognized that Equity will not perfect an imperfect gift,[91] and this rule is clearly founded on that of Equity not assisting a volunteer. In fact, there are numerous exceptions to this maxim, and Equity is perfectly content to intervene and provide assistance to a volunteer. So, for example, if the donor has done all that is necessary to transfer legal title to the donee, Equity will treat title as having been passed to the donee (by virtue of the maxim that Equity treats as done that which ought to be done),[92] even though the donee has not provided any consideration for the transaction.[93] Consequently, the donor will still have legal title, but, since Equity recognizes that the property belongs to the donee, they will have an equitable proprietary interest in it. Since

---

[85] *Jones v Kernott* [2011] UKSC 53, [2012] 1 AC 776, [51] (1) (Lady Hale and Lord Walker). See Section 10.2.2.(ii), p. 285. [86] (1852) 16 Beav 59, 66. [87] *The Olympic Pride* [1980] 2 Lloyd's Rep 67.
[88] See Section 4.2.2.(iii), p. 73. [89] See Section 4.2.3, p. 77.
[90] See Section 14.2.2.(i), p. 403.
[91] See especially *Milroy v Lord* (1862) 4 De GF & J 264, 45 ER 1185. See Section 5.3.3.(ii), p. 227.
[92] See Section 2.6, p. 31. [93] See Section 5.3.3.(iii), p. 128.

there is a split of legal and equitable title arising by operation of law, the property will be held on constructive trust for the donee by the donor. The maxim that Equity will not assist a volunteer will also be trumped by the principle of unconscionability,[94] so that a donor who has purported to make a gift, but who does so ineffectively, may be considered to hold the property on constructive trust for the donee if the donor's conduct can be characterized as being unconscionable.[95]

2.13 EQUITY ASSISTS THE DILIGENT

Even if a claim is not time-barred under statute, the claimant may be prevented from obtaining an equitable remedy if there has been delay in seeking the remedy. This provides the basis for the equitable doctrines of laches[96] and acquiescence.[97]

2.14 EQUITY IS EQUALITY

The maxim that Equity is equality means that, for example, where there are equitable interests in property, Equity presumes that they will be treated equally. So, for example, where the trustees have a power to appoint to a charitable purpose and a non-charitable purpose and that power is not exercised, the court will allocate half of the fund for charitable purposes and half for non-charitable purposes.[98] The general significance of the maxim has, however, been doubted in the law of trusts, because it would rarely accord with the intention of the person who created the trust,[99] although the maxim has proved to be significant in the context of determining the respective interests of a cohabiting couple in the family home.100

The maxim that Equity is equality was applied controversially in Re Bower's Settlement Trusts,101 in which the testator left the residue of his estate in his will to the beneficiaries in unequal shares. There was also a direction in the will that, if one of the beneficiaries were to die, his share should accrue to the other beneficiaries. Morton J applied the equitable maxim so that the deceased beneficiary's share was distributed equally between the other beneficiaries rather than proportionately in accordance with their existing share of the residue. Whether this literal application of the maxim was appropriate was considered in *Re Steel*.[102] In that case, legacies of different amounts were left in a will, which also contained a clause stating: 'Any residue remaining to be divided between those beneficiaries who have only received small amounts.' Megarry V-C considered whether the application of the equitable maxim required 'mathematical equality' and concluded that it might mean 'proportionate equality'[103]—that is, distribution in accordance with the existing proportions. He concluded that mathematical equality was appropriate on the facts of the case, although he considered that proportionate division would have been appropriate in *Re Bower's Settlement*.

---

[94] See Section 2.3, p. 27.
[95] *Pennington v Waine* [2002] EWCA Civ 227, [2002] 1 WLR 2075. See Section 5.3.3.(iii), p. 130.
[96] See Section 17.3.3.(ii), p. 489.   [97] See Section 17.3.4, p. 490.
[98] *Hoare v Osborne* [1866] LR 1 Eq 585.
[99] *McPhail v Doulton* [1971] AC 424, 451 (Lord Wilberforce).
[100] See Section 10.2.2.(ii), p. 285.   [101] [1942] Ch 197.   [102] [1979] Ch 218.
[103] Relying on *Steel v Dixon* (1881) 17 Ch D 825, 830 (Fry J).

2.15 EQUITY ACTS *IN PERSONAM*

This is a maxim that is often mentioned in cases, but its significance remains a matter of real controversy and a cause of confusion. The origins of the maxim can be identified in the fact that in its formative period Equity operated to create personal interests and not proprietary rights: when Equity intervened, it did not do so to deprive the legal owner of property, but ensured only that legal property rights were exercised conscionably. So, for example, whereas the Common Law would ensure that a claimant physically received property to which they were entitled, Equity would not order the transfer of property, but would impose a personal order against the defendant, breach of which would involve contempt of court, which was punishable by imprisonment.

But this is no longer true: Equity clearly operates to create property rights. Indeed, that is the essence of the trust, which recognizes that the beneficiaries have a proprietary interest recognized in Equity in the trust assets and is not confined to a personal remedy against the trustee for breach of trust. But the maxim that Equity operates *in personam* can be interpreted in another way, by distinguishing between *in rem* rights (which are good against the world) and *in personam* rights (which are good against a particular person). Equitable rights are not *in rem* in this sense, but are always *in personam*. This is because all equitable property rights are defeated if the property is obtained by a bona fide purchaser for value,[104] and so cannot be good against everybody in the world.

[104] See Section 1.5.1, p. 15.

3

AN INTRODUCTION
TO THE TRUST

3.1 GENERAL CONSIDERATIONS

The trust is at the heart of Equity, and it is not possible to understand the nature and function of equitable principles and policies without a clear understanding of the trust. Although the trust has been recognized for hundreds of years, its nature and function has not been constant. Grbich correctly recognized that 'the term "trust" is not clear and unchanging like a crystal, it is the skin round a living and growing concept'.[1] This chapter will identify the essence of that concept; subsequent chapters will examine the details of when a trust will be recognized and how it operates.

The origins of the trust can be traced back to the thirteenth century, when it was essentially a conveyancing device for the holding of land to avoid financial liabilities and restrictions on the inheritance of property.[2] This forerunner of the modern trust was called the use.[3] At its most basic, this device was used to transfer land to people who would hold it for the use of the transferor for life and then for selected family members. In that way, the transferor could ensure that the land was inherited by a member of their family rather than forfeited to a lord. The use was also deployed where a tenant of land was fighting abroad, for example in the Crusades, so that trustees could be appointed to manage the land on their behalf. The person who transferred the land would today be called the settlor, but they might alternatively be described as the trustor, since they trusted the transferee to hold the land for the benefit of themself or somebody else. The transferee of the land was called a trustee, because they were trusted by the transferor. The person for whom the land was held was called the beneficiary, because they benefited from the use of the land.

Although this tripartite structure can be identified in the modern trust device, the context in which the trust arises today is very different. It has developed from a trust of

---

[1] '*Baden*: awakening the conceptually moribund trust' (1974) 37 MLR 643, 648.

[2] Moffat, *Trusts Law*, 6th edn, ed. Garton (Cambridge: Cambridge University Press, 2015), ch. 2.

[3] See Milsom, *Historical Foundations of the Common Law*, 2nd edn (London: Butterworths, 1981), ch. 9; Baker, *An Introduction to English Legal History*, 4th edn (Oxford: Oxford University Press, 2002), ch. 14.

land, to a trust of all kinds of property within the family, including money and shares, to its significant use today as a commercial device for the management of a portfolio of financial assets.[4]

3.2 DEFINITION OF THE TRUST

The trust has been defined in many different ways,[5] but one of the most helpful definitions was suggested by Maitland:

> When a person has rights which he is bound to exercise upon behalf of another or for the accomplishment of some particular purpose he is said to have those rights in trust for that other or for that purpose and he is called a trustee.[6]

This definition identifies certain key features of the trust. It is concerned with one person, the trustee, acting on behalf of another or for an identified purpose. It is concerned with the exercise of rights. It is concerned with the imposition of obligations on the trustee. This definition does not, however, refer to property being held by the trustee. It is an essential requirement of any trust that identified property is held for the benefit of another, but property is difficult to define and great care must be taken when determining what the subject matter of the trust is.[7] In the easiest cases, the subject matter of the trust will be tangible assets such as land or a car. But the subject matter of the trust can include intangibles, even encompassing personal rights such as debts owed. It follows that it is preferable to describe the subject matter of the trust, as Maitland did, as being rights, such as the right to be paid money or the right to use land. Despite this, lawyers generally say that the subject matter of the trust is property. This is convenient shorthand and will be used in this book, but it must be remembered that any reference to 'property' is actually a reference to the rights relating to particular things, whether those things are tangible or intangible.

From this, it can be deduced that there are, in fact, two fundamental features of the trust:

(1) a person holds property rights for a person or purpose—the property component; and

(2) that person is obliged in Equity to exercise those rights for that person or purpose—the obligation component.

The significance of these two components has been identified particularly well in Parkinson's definition of the express trust, this being a trust that is expressly created by the settlor:[8]

> An express trust is an equitable obligation binding a person ('the trustee') to deal with identifiable property to which he or she has legal title for the benefit of others to whom he or she is in some way accountable. Such obligations may either be for the benefit of persons who have proprietary rights in equity, of whom they may be one, or for the furtherance of a sufficiently certain purpose which can be enforced by someone intended to have a right of enforcement under the terms of the trust or by operation of law.

---

[4] See Langbein, 'The secret life of the trust: the trust as an instrument of commerce' (1997) 107 Yale LJ 165.

[5] See Hart, 'What is a trust?' (1899) 15 LQR 294. See also the Convention on the Law Applicable to Trusts and on their Recognition, scheduled to the Recognition of Trusts Act 1987.

[6] Maitland, *Equity: A Course of Lectures*, 2nd edn, ed. Brunyate (Cambridge: Cambridge University Press, 1936), p. 44.   [7] See further Section 3.5.1, p. 44.

[8] 'Reconceptualising the express trust' (2002) 61 CLJ 657, 683 (footnotes omitted).

It is these two components of holding property rights for people or purposes and the personal obligations of the trustee that distinguish the trust from other legal concepts.[9] In the usual case, one person holds the legal title to property, but does not have absolute ownership of it. This is the trustee. As far as the Common Law is concerned, that person is the legal owner, but Equity can see that the legal owner holds the property for the benefit of somebody else, the beneficiary. The beneficiary under a trust has rights that are recognized only by Equity. The trustee's ownership is wholly burdensome. The trusteeship obliges the trustee to manage the property in the exclusive interest of the beneficiary, and imposes onerous duties and liabilities upon the trustee. All of the advantage of the trust is with the beneficiary.

Of the two core components of the trust, it is the property component rather than the obligation component that has traditionally been emphasized in the cases and by commentators. It is the fact that legal and equitable title to property are split that is the essence of the trust and which means that the law of trusts is traditionally considered to form a branch of property law. Whilst the property component is undoubtedly significant, more recent analysis of the trust has emphasized the importance of the obligation component.[10] Most significantly, Langbein has developed the 'contractarian account of the trust',[11] by virtue of which he concludes that the trust should be considered to be a bargain concerning how the trust assets should be managed and distributed. In particular, the 'trust deal', as he puts it, defines the powers and responsibilities of the trustee in managing the trust property. Langbein does not purport to argue that the trust should be defined only by reference to the obligation component, with that obligation deriving from a contract. He considers that the trust is a 'hybrid of contract and property', and that it 'straddles our categories of property and contract, because it embodies a contract about how property is to be deployed'.[12]

This contractarian account of the trust is undoubtedly useful, especially because it does not undermine the significance of the property component to the trust. It is clearly the case, as will be seen on a number of occasions throughout this book, that the nature of the duties and powers of trustees and the particular function of the trust are typically dependent on the terms of the document that governs the trust. In many cases, the 'law of trusts' is simply a body of default rules that can be rejected by the settlor in creating the trust and which apply where no alternative provision has been made in the trust instrument.

But the key problem with Langbein's thesis is his emphasis on a contract or bargain between the settlor and the trustee. In the commercial context of the trust, there will typically be negotiation and agreement between the settlor and the trustee as to the terms of the trust. But, despite the significance of the trust in modern commercial life, the trust is still relevant in other contexts, such as within the family, where such agreement and negotiation is less likely to take place. But even in commerce, to describe the trust as a bargain can be highly misleading as regards its components and characteristics, which cannot necessarily be regarded as contractual for the following reasons:

(1) The typical trust structure involves a settlor transferring property to the trustee to hold on trust for the beneficiary. Any bargain that establishes the trust will be between

---

[9] See Section 3.7, p. 58.   [10] See e.g. Parkinson (see n. 8).

[11] 'The contractarian basis of the law of trusts' (1995) 105 Yale LJ 625. See also Maitland (see n. 6), p. 28.

[12] (1995) 105 Yale LJ 625, 669 and 671.

the settlor and the trustee. But, once the trust has been created, the settlor has no rights to enforce the bargain and usually has no rights relating to the trust, except where they have reserved for themselves a power to revoke the trust,[13] to appoint trustees, to direct investment by the trustees,[14] or to amend the trust. Enforcement of the trust is left to the beneficiaries who were not parties to the bargain and who are volunteers, since they will not usually have provided any consideration in respect of the creation of the trust.[15] Although third parties to a contract can now enforce rights arising under the contract in certain circumstances by virtue of statute,[16] beneficiaries had been able to enforce their rights under the trust long before this statute was enacted.

(2) A testator may create a trust under their will that becomes effective only on their death. The person who is appointed as trustee of such a trust cannot usually be regarded as having entered into any contract with the testator. Whilst it is true that the trustee is not obliged to accept the office, so that anybody who becomes a trustee must consent to do so, it is not possible to deduce from this any contract between the testator and trustee.

(3) As we will see later,[17] it is possible for a settlor to declare themself as trustee. There clearly cannot be a contract between the settlor and trustee in such circumstances.[18]

It follows that the 'contractarian' analysis of the trust cannot be regarded as a universal explanation of the express trust, but it does not follow that Langbein's thesis should be rejected completely. He identifies an important truth relating to the law of trusts, namely that the obligations of the trustee can be modified by the terms of the trust instrument. It is not helpful to consider that instrument as being a bargain or a contract, but it clearly has a vital role in determining the nature of the trustee's obligations.

It follows from this analysis that the definition of the trust must consist of two components.[19] The property component emphasizes that it is only possible to have a trust of property, and that the rights relating to that property are split between the legal proprietary rights of the trustee[20] and the equitable proprietary rights of the beneficiary. This is significant because, as we will see later,[21] it follows that, if the trustee becomes insolvent, the trust property cannot be transferred to the trustee's creditors, since that property belongs to the beneficiaries in Equity. Also, if that property has been misappropriated and transferred to a third party who retains it, the beneficiaries have a claim based on their equitable property rights to recover that property.[22] The obligation component emphasizes that the trustee owes an obligation to the beneficiaries as regards the management and use of that property. This is significant because it means that a trustee is unable to benefit from that property for themself, save to the extent that they might also be a beneficiary of the trust.

---

[13] *Choithram International SA v Pagarani* [2002] 1 WLR 1, 11.

[14] *Vestey's Executors v IRC* [1949] 1 All ER 1108.   [15] See Section 5.3.2.(ii), p. 126.

[16] Contracts (Rights of Third Parties) Act 1999.   [17] See Section 4.2.2.(vi), p. 74.

[18] Langbein gets round this problem by unconvincingly concluding that there can be no trust in such circumstances.

[19] Or 'dimensions': Jaffey, 'Explaining the trust' (2015) 131 LQR 377, 393. Jaffey identifies these as the property and the contractual dimensions, although the latter aspect turns on a highly artificial characterization of contract and fails to consider the testamentary trust, where there is no agreement between the testator and the trustee.

[20] Although it is sometimes possible for a trustee to hold equitable property rights on trust for the beneficiary. See Section 3.5.2.(ii), p. 46.

[21] See Section 3.4.1, p. 43.   [22] See Section 19.4, p. 574.

3.3 FUNDAMENTAL PRINCIPLES RELATING TO THE TRUST

In *Westdeutsche Landesbank Girozentrale v Islington LBC*,[23] Lord Browne-Wilkinson identified four fundamental principles relating to all trusts that he considered to be uncontroversial. Although, as will be seen, the interpretation and operation of some of these principles are controversial in some contexts, they remain useful in determining how and when a trust will be recognized.

3.3.1 CONSCIENCE

Equity operates on the conscience of the owner of the legal interest. In the case of an express trust created by a settlor or testator, it would be unconscionable for the legal owner to fail to carry out the purposes for which the property was vested in them. In the case of a trust that arises by operation of law, the law imposes a trust by reason of the legal owner's unconscionable conduct.

3.3.2 AWARENESS OF FACTS THAT AFFECT CONSCIENCE

Since the equitable jurisdiction to enforce trusts depends upon the conscience of the holder of the legal interest being affected in some way, they cannot be a trustee of the property if they are ignorant of the facts that are alleged to affect their conscience. In other words, in the case of an express trust created by a settlor or testator, the holder of the legal interest must be aware that they are intended to hold the property for the benefit of others, or, in the case of a trust arising by operation of law, of the factors that are alleged to affect their conscience, at least as a general rule.[24]

3.3.3 IDENTIFIABLE PROPERTY

In order to establish a trust, there must be identifiable trust property that constitutes the subject matter of the trust. It is, at least as a general rule, a vital component of the trust that the trustee is obliged to keep the trust property segregated from their own property,[25] so that the property is not available to the trustee as part of their own assets.[26] If the trustee is allowed to mix the property that has been received with their own property, this will be a significant factor that suggests that the property is not held on trust.[27]

3.3.4 EQUITABLE PROPRIETARY INTEREST

From the date on which the trust is established, the beneficiary has, in Equity, a proprietary interest in the trust property. This proprietary interest will be enforceable in Equity against anybody who receives that property or its identifiable substitute, other than a purchaser for value of the legal interest without notice of the equitable proprietary interest.

---

[23] [1996] AC 669, 706.   [24] See Section 9.3.1.(ii), p. 261 and Section 12.2.4, p. 341.
[25] *Re Lehman Brothers International (Europe) (in administration)* [2012] UKSC 6, [2012] WTLR 1355, [2] (Lord Hope).
[26] *The Commissioners for Her Majesty's Revenue and Customs v The Investment Trust Companies* [2017] UKSC 29, [2017] 2 WLR 1200, [69] (Lord Reed).
[27] *Pearson v Lehman Brothers Finance SA* [2010] EWHC 2914 (Ch), [225] (Briggs J).

3.4 FUNCTIONS OF THE TRUST

There are a variety of reasons why someone would wish to create a trust with the consequent separation of legal and equitable title, whether in the context of the family or commerce.

3.4.1 SEGREGATION OF ASSETS

The trust enables assets to be segregated from those of the settlor, which protects them from the consequences of the settlor's insolvency. This is because, if the settlor becomes insolvent, they will no longer have any proprietary interest in the assets, so they will not be available to their creditors. Segregation of assets is also relevant as regards the trustee, since, if the trustee becomes insolvent, the trust assets will not be available for the trustee's creditors because the assets belong to the beneficiaries in Equity.[28]

3.4.2 ASSET PARTITIONING

Asset partitioning refers to the ability to take an asset and to create different rights in it. In the family context, asset partitioning can be significant because it enables the settlor or testator to provide for the successive enjoyment of property, such as when property is left to Adam for life with remainder to Brenda. This means that Adam will have the benefit of the property for his life, but, on his death, the property will then pass to Brenda.

3.4.3 MANAGEMENT OF PROPERTY

There may be a particular advantage in having trustees manage and administer the property on behalf of the beneficiaries. This may be because the trustees have particular financial and investment experience, or because the beneficiaries are too young to manage the property themselves or cannot be trusted with the property, so that it is preferable for somebody else to manage the property on their behalf.

3.4.4 CONVENIENT PROPERTY-HOLDING

The trust might be a convenient way of holding property for the mutual benefit of a group of people linked by a common interest. This is one of the main reasons why the trust is used in the commercial world. For example, it is used as a mechanism for managing pension funds,[29] under which the fund is held by trustees for the benefit of employees, or as a mechanism for a group of people investing their funds by means of a unit or investment trust, under which trustees hold investments in a range of securities in trust for investors who have purchased units or shares in the trust fund.

3.4.5 TAX AVOIDANCE

The trust can also provide a mechanism for mitigating or avoiding a tax liability, since if the settlor pays tax at a higher rate, the transfer of property to trustees may result in a lower rate of tax being charged. The trust cannot, however, be used as a mechanism to evade

---

[28] Convention on the Law Applicable to Trusts and on their Recognition, scheduled to the Recognition of Trusts Act 1987, Article 11 (a) and (b).   [29] See Section 3.6.2.(ix), p. 56.

the payment of tax that is already due, since that is a criminal offence.[30] A wide variety of tax-avoidance schemes have been developed using the trust as the means of implementing the scheme. The fundamental principle relating to the validity of such schemes is that it is legitimate to arrange one's affairs to reduce a tax liability,[31] but, if the main purpose or one of the main purposes of creating the trust is to avoid or reduce tax and this is considered to be abusive, in the sense that the creation of the trust is not a reasonable course of action, the General Anti-Avoidance Rule will apply so that the tax advantage obtained will be counteracted by making an adjustment to the tax liability.[32]

3.5 RIGHTS AND INTERESTS UNDER A TRUST

As we have seen, it is a fundamental requirement of a trust that property is held by a trustee on trust for another. But this apparently simple proposition raises some very difficult questions, such as: what is meant by 'property' for these purposes, and what is the nature of the rights and interests of the trustee and beneficiaries?

3.5.1 PROBLEMS OF TERMINOLOGY

When the different interests relating to trusts are examined, we immediately face a problem with the terminology used by courts and commentators. Various concepts are bandied about, such as 'ownership', 'title', 'estate', 'right', 'interest', 'benefit', and 'property'. Each concept can be defined in a number of different ways, so that two judges may use the phrase 'equitable interest' and yet each mean something different from the other. As Viscount Radcliffe[33] recognized, the problem is that 'our legal system has not produced a sufficient variety of words to represent the various meanings which can be conveyed by the words "interest" and "property"'.

There are certain terms that should be avoided or which should be used with caution. For example, 'ownership' of an asset suggests that the 'owner' has all rights relating to a particular asset. But this is alien to the very concept of a trust, because the rights relating to the trust asset are partitioned between the trustee and the beneficiaries, so that a trustee who 'owns' the property at Law does not have the benefit of all the rights relating to the asset. Even the word 'property' is ambiguous,[34] since it can be used to refer to a particular asset or to describe the rights relating to that asset. In this book, 'property' will be used to refer to assets, both tangible and intangible, and including debts and shares, since this accords with the terminology used by judges in the cases.

The focus should then be placed on the rights that particular groups of people have to particular assets. If the rights are recognized at Common Law, they can be described as 'legal proprietary rights'; if they are recognized in Equity, they are 'equitable proprietary rights'. Sometimes, judges use the word 'interest' rather than 'rights', as when a person is described as having 'an interest in' an asset. This usage is also recognized by statute, since, for example, the disposal of an equitable interest must be by writing.[35] An 'interest' can simply be described as a compendium of rights relating to a particular asset. Where these

---

[30] *IRC v Willoughby* [1997] 1 WLR 1071, 1079 (Lord Nolan).
[31] *IRC v Duke of Westminster* [1936] AC 1, 19 (Lord Tomlin).
[32] Finance Act 2013, Pt 5 and Sch. 43. See further on the doctrine of sham trusts, in Section 4.2.3, p. 77.
[33] *Commissioner of Stamp Duties v Livingston* [1965] AC 694, 712.
[34] See Gray, 'Property in thin air' (1991) 50 CLJ 252.
[35] Law of Property Act 1925, s. 53(1)(c). See Section 11.3, p. 324.

rights are recognized in Equity rather than at Common Law, they are properly characterized as an 'equitable interest'.

Judges and commentators have often used the word 'beneficial' followed by 'rights',
'interest', or 'ownership'. This is a particular source of confusion. Sometimes, a beneficial
interest is simply a different way of describing an equitable interest in property. But 'beneficial' does not always correspond with 'equitable', because the absolute legal owner of
property also has a beneficial interest in it without any equitable interest. 'Beneficial interest' is therefore best used descriptively to identify a person's right to receive some or all of
the benefit of property, such as the use of the property or its fruits. So, if the legal owner of
property has absolute title to the property, they will also have the beneficial interest in the
property. But if the legal owner holds that property on trust for another, that other person
will have the beneficial interest in the property as well as an equitable proprietary interest
in it. It is also possible for the legal owner of property to hold that property on trust for
themself and another person, in which case both the legal owner and the other beneficiary
will have beneficial interests in the property.

3.5.2 OPERATION OF RIGHTS RELATING TO TRUSTS

The law of trusts is primarily concerned with the variety of rights that different people
might have following the creation of a trust. There are a number of principles and concepts
that need to be analysed carefully to determine the variety of rights that can arise.

Imagine a simple case in which Adam seeks to declare a trust of land that he intends to
convey to Brenda and Claire, for them to hold on trust for David.

(i) Settlor's rights

Before the trust is created, it will be assumed that Adam has the legal right to the land,
which will be registered in his name so that he has legal title to it. He will also be considered to have the beneficial right, since he is entitled to the benefit of the property. So, he
will be entitled to receive the fruits of the land and to occupy it; there will not, however,
be any equitable interest in the land. It is a fundamental principle of the law of trusts that,
where a person has legal and beneficial title to property, they have an absolute or sole
right to the property and there is no equitable interest in it. A particular event needs to
be identified to create the equitable interest and to separate it from the legal interest. This
was recognized by Lord Browne-Wilkinson in *Westdeutsche Landesbank Girozentrale v
Islington LBC*:[36]

> A person solely entitled to the full beneficial ownership of money or property, both at law
> and in equity, does not enjoy an equitable interest in that property. The legal title carries
> with it all rights. Unless and until there is a separation of the legal and equitable estates,
> there is no separate equitable title.

Once the land has been validly conveyed to the trustees, Adam will lose both the legal
right to the land and the beneficial interest in it, so that he will drop out of the picture. If,
however, the trust has not been validly declared, legal title will still have been transferred
to Brenda and Claire, but an equitable proprietary interest will be created in Adam's favour
following the failure of the express trust, by means of what is known as a resulting trust.[37]

---

[36] [1996] AC 669, 706. See also *Commissioner of Stamp Duties (Queensland) v Livingston* [1965] AC 694,
712 (Viscount Radcliffe); *Vandervell v IRC* [1967] 2 AC 291, 311 (Lord Upjohn), 317 (Lord Donovan); *Re Bond
Worth Ltd* [1980] 1 Ch 228, 253 (Slade J).   [37] See Section 8.3.2, p. 231.

(ii) Trustees' rights

Once Adam has conveyed the land to Brenda and Claire, they will have joint legal title to it and will be treated at Law as the joint owners of the property. Since, however, they hold the property on trust, they will not have a beneficial interest in the property. The existence of the trust strips the trustees of the benefits of legal ownership.

Although many trusts involve the trustee having legal title to property, this is not always the case. It is possible to declare a trust of an equitable proprietary interest in property. So, for example, a beneficiary of a trust is able to declare that they hold their equitable proprietary interest on trust for another. It follows that there can be a chain of trusts. So, for example, money might be transferred to Emma to hold on trust for Frank. He might declare a trust of his equitable proprietary interest for Grace. So Emma has the legal title to the money that is held on trust for Frank, who holds his equitable interest on trust for Grace. This chain could continue indefinitely. It is only the trust of the money held by Emma for Frank that involves a trust of legal rights; all of the other trusts will involve a trust of the beneficiary's equitable interest in the money that is held on trust for them.[38] The possibility of creating such chains of trusts of the equitable proprietary interest is very significant commercially in respect of trusts of securities and of the rights to such securities.

(iii) Beneficiary's rights

Returning to the trust of land held by Brenda and Claire for David, once the trust has been validly created, David will have an equitable right in the land. He will also have the beneficial interest in the land, so that, depending on the nature of the trust, he may be entitled to take possession of the land and may be entitled to receive income obtained from it.

3.5.3 MERGER OF LEGAL AND EQUITABLE INTERESTS

In the same way that the person with sole legal and beneficial title to property does not also have an equitable proprietary interest, once an equitable interest has been created, it will be lost if the property is transferred to a person who has sole legal and beneficial title to it. Another way of expressing this principle is by recognizing that one person cannot hold property on trust for only themself.[39] This is illustrated by *Re Cook*,[40] in which land was held on trust by a husband and wife for themselves. Since there were two of them, each could hold the legal title to the land on trust for themself and the other. But, when the husband died, the entire interest in the property, both legal and equitable, vested in the wife. It was held that the legal interest had swallowed up the equitable, so that there was a merger of the two interests, and it followed that the trust was terminated. As Harman J recognized, 'you cannot have a trust existing when nobody is interested under it except the trustee, because nobody can enforce it and there is, in fact, no trust in existence'.[41]

3.5.4 OVERREACHING AND OVERRIDING OF EQUITABLE INTERESTS

Where property is held on trust for another, the trustee will usually have administrative powers and duties in respect of the management of the trust property.[42] These powers and duties can include the sale of trust property. The effect of such a sale on legal and equitable

---

[38] *Pearson v Lehman Brothers Finance SA* [2010] EWHC 2914 (Ch), [226] (Briggs J).
[39] *Re Selous* [1901] 1 Ch 921, 922 (Farwell J).   [40] [1948] Ch 212.   [41] Ibid., 215.
[42] See Chapter 13.

proprietary rights is a matter of real significance to the law of trusts. When determining what the effect of the transaction involving the trust property might be, it is vital to distinguish between authorized and unauthorized transactions.

(i) Authorized dealings

Where the trustee is authorized to sell the trust property, the effect of the transaction is to overreach the beneficiary's equitable proprietary interest. What this means is that, as the property is transferred to the purchaser, the beneficiary loses their equitable proprietary interest in the property and an equivalent proprietary interest is created in the asset that is obtained in exchange, which in a sale of trust property will be the purchase price.[43] The notional effect of the overreaching doctrine is that, as the property leaves the trust, the equitable proprietary interest is destroyed and an identical interest is created in the exchange product that comes into the trust. This doctrine of overreaching applies in all cases except where the trust instrument provides otherwise.[44] The effect of the overreaching doctrine is that the third party acquires the property absolutely and does not hold it on trust for the beneficiary, since the beneficiary no longer has an equitable interest in the property. The overreaching doctrine is not confined to sale of trust property; it will also apply where the trustee lawfully distributes trust property to beneficiaries of the trust. Those beneficiaries will receive the property absolutely and, since there is no exchange product, there will be no replacement property in which the remaining beneficiaries have an equitable proprietary interest.

(ii) Unauthorized dealings

Where a trustee transfers trust property to a third party by a transaction that is unauthorized, the overreaching doctrine will not apply, but legal title can still pass to the third party. It follows that the beneficiary will retain an equitable interest in the property, so that the third-party recipient will hold it on trust for the beneficiary, even though the third party might have been unaware of the beneficiary's equitable proprietary interest. This equitable proprietary interest will be destroyed, however, if the third party was a bona fide purchaser for value of the trust property.[45] This can appropriately be described as overriding,[46] as distinct from overreaching, of the equitable proprietary interest. So, if the trust property is sold by the trustee without authority under the trust instrument to do so, and if the purchaser has provided some value for the transfer and was unaware of the existence of the beneficiary's equitable proprietary interest and could not reasonably have been aware of it, the purchaser will take free of that equitable proprietary interest which will have been destroyed.[47] In such circumstances, the beneficiary's only claim is against the trustee for breach of trust.[48]

3.5.5 THE NATURE OF EQUITABLE RIGHTS

Although it is clear that, where a trustee holds property on trust, the beneficiaries have an equitable right to the trust property, we have not yet considered what the nature of this

---

[43] Harpum, 'Overreaching, trustees' powers and the reform of the 1925 legislation' (1990) 49 CLJ 277, 278; Fox, 'Overreaching', in *Breach of Trust*, ed. Birks and Pretto (Oxford: Hart, 2002), ch. 4.

[44] Nolan, 'Understanding the limits of equitable property' (2006) 1 Journal of Equity 18, 25.

[45] *Independent Trustee Services Ltd v GP Noble Trustees Ltd* [2012] EWCA Civ 195 [2013] Ch 91, [106] (Lloyd LJ).

[46] Briggs, '*Akers v Samba*: Equity's darling reigns supreme' (Chancery Bar Association Annual Lecture, 5th April 2017).   [47] *Akers v Samba Financial Group* [2017] UKSC 6, [2017] AC 424.

[48] Ibid., [83] (Lord Sumption). See Chapter 18.

right might be. This is a matter of particular controversy. There are four different ways of categorizing the beneficiary's equitable right.

(i) Right *in rem*

The equitable right can be characterized as a proprietary right against a particular asset. This is the most common way of analysing the right.[49] A key characteristic of such a property right is traditionally considered to be that the holder of the right is able to exclude anybody in the world from making use of the asset in which they have the right.[50] That is certainly the consequence of having a legal proprietary right. But an equitable proprietary right operates differently. First, as we have seen, it can be defeated if a third party obtains the property in good faith and for value. So equitable rights are not binding against everybody and consequently they are weaker than legal property rights, which are not defeated by receipt by a bona fide purchaser for value.

Secondly, if a third party steals the trust property, the beneficiary has no claim in the tort of conversion against the third party,[51] whereas the trustee would. The beneficiary would be able to sue in conversion if they had been in possession of the property, but then the beneficiary would be relying on their possessory right rather than their equitable proprietary right.[52] Similarly, where the property is negligently damaged, the beneficiary has no direct claim against the tortfeasor for property damage or economic loss, because such a claim can be brought only by a person who has a legal proprietary interest or possessory interest in the property.[53] A claim can be brought if the trustee is made a party to the proceedings,[54] but not if the trustee consented to the interference with the property, because then the third party will not have committed any wrong.

(ii) Rights *in personam*

Maitland[55] characterized the beneficiary's equitable rights as being personal rights against the trustee rather than property rights against a thing. Clearly, beneficiaries do have personal rights against the trustee, for example where there has been a breach of trust, but Maitland considered that beneficiaries have only personal rights and do not have any proprietary rights. This does not, however, explain how the beneficiary acquires rights that can bind third parties even if the third party is unaware of the right.[56] For example, if the trustee holds a car on trust for the beneficiary and the trustee gives the car to a third party, who is consequently not a bona fide purchaser for value, it is clear that the beneficiary can assert their equitable right against the third party, even though the third party was unaware of the beneficiary's right to claim the property. Similarly, if the trustee is declared bankrupt, the trustee in bankruptcy cannot claim the trust property in priority to the beneficiary's rights, which would be the case if the beneficiary's rights against the trustee were only personal. Further, where the subject matter of the trust is a personal right, such as where a trustee holds the value credited to a bank account on trust, if the trustee becomes insolvent the beneficiary's contractual claim to the value that is credited to the account will be an unsecured claim which ranks equally with all other such claims, since this is a personal claim at Common Law. The beneficiary, however, has an equitable right to the

---

[49] See Scott, 'The nature of the rights of the *cestuis que* trust' (1917) 17 Columbia L Rev 269.
[50] Nolan, 'Equitable property' (2006) 122 LQR 232, 234.
[51] *MCC Proceeds Inc v Lehman Bros International (Europe)* [1994] 4 All ER 675.
[52] *Healey v Healey* [1915] 1 KB 938.
[53] *Leigh and Sillivan Ltd v Aliakmon Shipping Co Ltd* [1986] AC 785, 809 (Lord Brandon).
[54] *Shell UK Ltd v Total UK Ltd* [2010] EWCA Civ 180, [2011] QB 86. See further Section 3.5.5.(iv), p. 50.
[55] Maitland (see n. 6), Lectures IX–XI.   [56] Jaffey, 'Explaining the trust' (2015) 131 LQR 377, 379.

amount credited which has priority over unsecured claims, so that it appears to operate as a proprietary right.

(iii) Right against rights

By virtue of the difficulties in analysing the beneficiary's equitable right as a right to a particular asset or as a personal right, McFarlane and Stevens[57] treat the beneficiary's[58] equitable right as being a right against rights, namely the beneficiary's right against the trustee's rights of ownership.[59] In other words, rather than saying that the trustee holds property on trust for the beneficiary, McFarlane and Stevens consider that we should say instead that the trustee holds their right of ownership of the property on trust for the beneficiary, who has an equitable right against that right of ownership.

This analysis is used to explain the characteristics of equitable rights, especially that they persist against third parties who acquire rights that derive from the trustee's rights, such as where the trustee transfers ownership to a third party. The third party is then bound by the beneficiary's right as against the third party's right to ownership, save where the third party is a bona fide purchaser for value. Where, however, the third party has stolen the trust property, the beneficiary cannot sue the third party in the tort of conversion because the third party's rights to the property do not then derive from the trustee's rights. So, if the third party stole a car that is held on trust, the third party's right to the car does not derive from the trustee's ownership of it, since the third party's right will be an original possessory right. This thesis is also used to explain how the beneficiary obtains equitable rights where the trustee has only a personal right. So, for example, where the beneficiary asserts an equitable right in respect of a bank account, they are not asserting a right to the bank account, but instead to the trustee's personal right to be paid by the bank; this is the beneficiary's right against a right. If this personal right is acquired by a third party, such as the trustee in bankruptcy of the trustee, it will be a right that can continue to be enforced by the beneficiary even though the trustee in bankruptcy was unaware of the beneficiary's existence, in the same way that a third party who acquires ownership of property from the trustee will be bound by the beneficiary's right against the third party's right of ownership.

McFarlane and Stevens' thesis is useful in explaining the characteristics of equitable rights by avoiding the need to characterize them as proprietary or personal. It also avoids the need to distinguish between legal and equitable ownership of property, since it rejects any notion of equitable ownership and replaces it with a notion of equitable rights. It further explains how there can be trusts of equitable rights. So, for example, Brenda's equitable right as a beneficiary can be held on trust for Clare, so that Clare has a right against Brenda's equitable right against the trustee's right of ownership to the property. The thesis also enables notions of equitable rights to be exported to jurisdictions with no tradition of Equity, because any legal system can recognize the concept of a right against a right.

Although McFarlane and Stevens' thesis does purport to explain the nature of a beneficiary's equitable right, it should be rejected primarily because it involves an artificial and unnecessarily complex analysis for the following specific reasons:

(1) The language of a right against a right is alien to Equity jurisprudence. This language is not used by the courts, in which the focus is instead on property rights, and

---

[57] 'The nature of equitable property' (2010) 4 J Eq 1. See also McFarlane, *The Structure of Property Law* (Oxford: Hart, 2008), pp. 25–32; Edelman, 'Two fundamental questions for the law of trusts' (2013) 129 LQR 66.

[58] Their analysis is not confined to the rights arising under a trust, but is also used to explain a wide variety of equitable rights, such as those relating to equitable leases, charges, and assignments.

[59] See also Smith, 'Trust and patrimony' (2008) 38 Revue générale de droit 379, who describes the beneficiary's interest as rights in rights.

the judges recognize that a beneficiary does have a proprietary interest in the trust property.[60] Similarly, there are statutes that refer to interests under a trust as being 'interests in property'.[61]

(2) The thesis fails to explain adequately the essentially proprietary nature of the beneficiary's interest under a trust. That interest is assignable, can be traded, can be held on trust for another, can sometimes enable the beneficiary to direct the transfer of trust property to themself,[62] and may result in a tax liability because the beneficiary has an immediate claim to the trust property. All of these consequences might be considered to be consistent with the right against a right analysis, but are much easier to understand by treating the beneficiary's interest as proprietary.

(3) It is a fundamental principle of Equity that a trust will not fail for want of a trustee.[63] If a trust is created by the settlor, but the trustee declines to act as trustee, the beneficiary can apply to the court to have a trustee appointed. The right of the beneficiary to have a trustee appointed cannot be considered to be a right against the trustee's right of ownership, because there will be no trustee at that particular moment. It is much more satisfactory to analyse this right as arising because Equity will ensure that the beneficiary's proprietary right to the trust property is respected.

(iv) Modified proprietary rights

Despite its flaws, the 'right against rights' thesis does at least purport to explain the key characteristics of equitable rights, which the *in rem* and *in personam* theories cannot satisfactorily do. The preferable view is that equitable rights should be regarded as proprietary, which is why they can persist against third parties.[64] But equitable proprietary rights are modified rights, in that they do not have the same characteristics as legal proprietary rights.[65] This is because equitable proprietary rights are properly treated as subsidiary property rights; they are subsidiary to legal proprietary rights. That is why legal proprietary rights are not defeated by the property being received by a bona fide purchaser for value and why the legal owner of property can bring the full range of claims for tortious interference with the property.

The modified nature of the equitable proprietary rights also explains how, although the trustee's claim against a bank for money credited to a bank account is a personal claim, it is transformed into a proprietary right of the beneficiary if the trustee became insolvent or if the money credited to the account was misappropriated by a third party. This arises because of the ability of Equity to identify property in a fund.[66] Equity is imaginative[67] and sees that, where trust money is credited to a bank account, the beneficiary of the trust has a right to the value in the fund. It is not the fund itself that is held on trust, but rather the value in the fund, the credit, even where the fund is made up of value from different sources, such as where money from the trustee is credited to the account as well. Once this

---

[60] See e.g. *Westdeutsche Landesbank Girozentrale v Islington LBC* [1996] AC 699, 705 (Lord Browne-Wilkinson); *Re Lehman Brothers International (Europe) (No 2)* [2009] EWCA Civ 1161, [2010] 1 BCLC 496; *Pearson v Lehman Brothers Finance SA* [2010] EWHC 2914 (Ch), [225] (Briggs J).

[61] See e.g. Trusts of Land and Appointment of Trustees Act 1996, s. 22(1).   [62] See Section 11.4, p. 334.
[63] See Section 12.4.5, p. 350.

[64] See *Akers v Samba Financial Group* [2017] UKSC 6, [2017] AC 424, [16] (Lord Mance), [82] (Lord Sumption).

[65] In *Akers v Samba Financial Group*, ibid., [51], Lord Mance described these equitable proprietary rights as 'protected rights that were always limited'. This is the same idea as 'modified rights'.

[66] Nolan, 'Property in a fund' (2004) 120 LQR 108.   [67] See Section 2.9, p. 34.

conceptual jump has been made, it is easy to treat the beneficiary's rights to the value in the fund as a proprietary right, which persists against third parties save if they are a bona fide purchaser for value, even though the trustee has only a personal right against the bank. This was recognized by Briggs J in *Pearson v Lehman Brothers Finance SA*:[68] '[N]o-one doubts the beneficial interest of clients in a solicitor's client account. Yet the subject matter of that fund consists entirely of the solicitor's purely personal rights as a customer of the client account bank or banks.' In fact, this notion of a modified property right in Equity is doing essentially the same thing as McFarlane and Stevens' 'right against rights' thesis, but simply uses the language and concepts used by the judges, which is, frankly, easier to understand and to articulate.

The modified nature of the beneficiary's proprietary rights against trust property is especially important when analysing the claims of beneficiaries to recover trust property that has been received by third parties, even where the original property has been substituted for new property.[69] So, for example, where shares are held on trust and have been misappropriated by the trustee and given to a third party, who then sells the shares and uses the proceeds to buy a car, the beneficiary of the trust can assert an equitable proprietary right against the car. This could be explained, using the language of McFarlane and Stevens, on the basis that the beneficiary has a right against the trustee's right to the ownership of the shares that persists against the third party, and which continues when the shares are sold and the car is purchased in its place. But it is so much easier, conceptually and analytically, to recognize that the beneficiary has an equitable proprietary right to the shares that can then be asserted against the car when it is substituted for the shares. But, being recognized in Equity, this proprietary right is modified and would be defeated if the shares had been purchased by the third party in good faith.

(v) Choosing between 'right against rights' and 'modified proprietary rights'

The potential significance of choosing between the 'right against rights' thesis and the 'modified proprietary rights' thesis is illustrated by the important and difficult decision of the Court of Appeal in *Shell UK Ltd v Total UK Ltd*.[70] In that case, the claimant stored oil at a terminal. The tanks and pipelines were held on trust for the claimant by two companies. The defendant negligently overfilled a fuel storage tank, which exploded and damaged the tanks and pipelines in which the claimant had a beneficial interest. The question for the court was whether the claimant could sue for damage to property in which it had a beneficial interest and whether it could also sue for consequential economic loss. The defendant accepted that it was liable for the destruction of the claimant's property,[71] having conceded that it did not matter that the claimant had only an equitable interest in the property. Although it was held that the claimant did not have a direct claim against the defendant for consequential economic loss, because it was neither the legal owner of the property nor in possession of it, it was recognized that such a claim could be brought if the trustees were joined as parties to the proceedings. The inclusion of the trustees meant that their legal title to the property could be used to establish the claim, even though the loss was suffered by the beneficiary. The fact that the beneficiary did not have a direct claim against the tortfeasor in its own right might be regarded as undermining the proprietary nature of the beneficiary's rights. But the court clearly considered the beneficiary to have an equitable proprietary interest and recognized that it would be a triumph of

---

[68] [2010] EWHC 2914 (Ch), [227].   [69] See Section 19.1.4, p. 539.
[70] [2010] EWCA Civ 180, [2011] QB 86. See further Section 11.2.1.(ii), p. 317.
[71] [2010] EWCA Civ 180, [2011] QB 86, [5].

form over substance to deny the beneficiary a remedy simply because legal title to the property was vested in bare trustees,[72] since the 'beneficial owner' of the property had a closer relationship to the tortfeasor than the bare trustees who only had legal title to the property.[73] Crucially, the beneficiary was able to recover compensation for the economic loss it had suffered as a result of the defendant's negligence, even though the beneficiary was not the legal owner and was not in possession of the property, because it was recognized that a duty of care in tort could be owed to the beneficiary of a trust as well as to the legal owner of the property.

But, although the beneficiary in *Shell UK* could recover damages for the defendant's negligent interference with trust property in which the beneficiary had an equitable proprietary interest, the beneficiary could not establish a direct claim against the tortfeasor, because the beneficiary did not have legal or possessory title to the property. It follows that, although the court did not use this language, the equitable proprietary right of the beneficiary could be considered to be a modified right. It is a proprietary right that, if tortiously interfered with by a third party, enables the beneficiary to assert the right and obtain a remedy, but only if the trustee is made a party to the proceedings. This is because property tort claims are Common Law claims based on interference with legal property and possessory rights. The beneficiary consequently has no direct claim against the tortfeasor, since their property interest is modified and is hidden behind that of the legal owner. The legal owner does have a direct claim against the tortfeasor, but the loss will be that of the beneficiary, so that any damages recovered by the trustee will be held on trust for the beneficiary. If the trustee refuses to sue the tortfeasor, the beneficiary could then either sue the trustee for breach of trust or could use an exceptional procedure, known as the *Vandepitte* procedure,[74] whereby the beneficiary can name the trustee as defendant and bring proceedings against the third party. This is what happened in *Shell UK*.

The result of *Shell UK* might alternatively be analysed with reference to the 'right against rights' thesis, but such an analysis is inelegant and unconvincing. The 'right against rights' explanation would focus on the fact that the beneficiary had a right to the damages that would be obtained by the trustee suing the tortfeasor for the interference with the trustee's legal proprietary right. But this is artificial simply because the trustee had no right to obtain damages, since the trustee will not have suffered any loss; the loss was suffered by the beneficiary and the right arising from this loss need to be attached to the trustee's right to sue for interference with the proprietary right. Rather than using the language of 'right against rights', the claim in *Shell UK* depended on the beneficiary's loss being attached to the trustee's tortious claim. That is why the case is more elegantly analysed as involving a modified proprietary right. In *Shell UK*, the implicit recognition that the beneficiary's right was a proprietary right was significant, since this enabled the court to compensate the beneficiary for provable economic loss arising from a breach of a duty of care owed directly by the tortfeasor to the beneficiary, albeit that, being a modified right, the beneficiary did not have a direct claim in tort and needed the voluntary or involuntary involvement of the trustee whose legal property right had been interfered with by the tortfeasor. Consequently, the effect of the decision of the Court of Appeal in *Shell UK* is preferably justified by reference to the beneficiary's right being a modified proprietary right rather than a right against the trustee's right.

---

[72] Ibid., [143].   [73] Ibid., [136].

[74] After *Vandepitte v Preferred Accident Insurance Corporation of New York* [1933] AC 70, 79 (PC) (Lord Wright). See further Section 11.2.1.(ii), p. 317.

3.6 CLASSIFICATIONS OF TRUSTS

As we examine the details of the law of trusts, we will see that trusts can arise in a wide variety of circumstances. It is helpful at the outset to identify a system of classifying trusts to assist in determining when trusts will be recognized and what their different attributes might be. There are a variety of ways in which trusts can be classified, but the most significant methods are by reference to the event that creates the trust and by the context in which the trust arises.

3.6.1 BY EVENT

Trusts can be classified by reference to particular events to determine when the trust arises. This event-based scheme was propounded by Birks,[75] who identified four events that trigger the recognition of trusts:[76] consent, wrongdoing, unjust enrichment, and other events. What this means is that the trust can be regarded as arising either where one party has consented to the creation of a trust, where the defendant has committed a wrong, where the defendant has been unjustly enriched at the expense of the claimant in circumstances that fall within one of the recognized grounds of restitution, or by other events yet to be identified.

Whilst this events-based classification has proved significant for a number of commentators, it has yet to be endorsed by the courts and should not be adopted. Particularly as regards trusts, it is a system of classification that does not reflect the state of the law and is too uncertain to be of any predictive value.

The following specific criticisms can be made of this classificatory scheme:

(1) The usefulness of such a scheme depends in part on how wide the final 'other events' category might be: if it is potentially very large, its uncertainty undermines the success of the whole scheme. In fact, this category is potentially very wide, for there are a variety of events that will trigger the recognition of trusts which cannot be considered to be founded on consent, wrongdoing, or unjust enrichment. For example, the trust may arise as a result of the defendant's unconscionable conduct not amounting to a recognized wrong.[77]

(2) There is no case in which it has explicitly been recognized that the defendant who has been unjustly enriched at the expense of the claimant holds the enrichment on trust for the claimant. The preferable view is that unjust enrichment creates only a personal liability to repay the value of the enrichment received, rather than triggers a trust so that the enrichment is held on trust for the claimant.[78] So, for example, a defendant who has received money paid by the claimant by mistake will be liable only to repay the value of the money received by virtue of the defendant's unjust enrichment, but will not hold the money on trust for the claimant.[79]

---

[75] Birks, 'Equity in the modern law: an exercise in taxonomy' (1996) Univ WALR 1, 9. See also Chambers, *Resulting Trusts* (Oxford: Clarendon Press, 1997), p. 5.

[76] Birks' classification system was intended to be of more general significance than to be used simply to determine when trusts are recognized.   [77] See Section 9.3.1, p. 258.

[78] See Section 19.1.4.(ii), p. 540.

[79] A trust may exceptionally arise in such circumstances, but only where the defendant can be considered to have acted unconscionably in not repaying the money and not because of the defendant's unjust enrichment. See Section 9.3.1, p. 258.

(3) As regards a trust arising from the commission of a wrong, it has never been suggested that a trust will arise from the commission of a tort or breach of contract, although it has been recognized that a constructive trust can arise where the defendant has profited from the equitable wrong of a breach of fiduciary duty.[80]

(4) So we are left with consensual trusts. But using the language of consent is odd when we are concerned with trusts, since the typical trust scenario is that in which the settlor expressly conveys property to be held on trust. There need not be an agreement or even an understanding between the settlor and trustee for the trust to be valid. Although a trustee must voluntarily accept the trusteeship and, in doing so, can be considered to have consented to the trust, the use of the language of consent is rather artificial. The key problem with using 'consent' as an event that justifies the recognition of trusts is that it implies a contract, but, as we have already seen,[81] the essence of a trust is not contractual. There is usually no contract between any of the settlor, trustee, or beneficiary, primarily because of the absence of consideration between the parties.

It follows that classification of trusts by event is, at best, unhelpful and, at worst, distorts our understanding of when trusts can and should arise.

3.6.2 BY CONTEXT

Alternatively, trusts can be characterized by reference to descriptive categories that are determined by reference to the context in which the trust arises.[82] These categories are not mutually exclusive, since a particular trust might fall within more than one category. Eleven contextual categories of trust can be identified, as follows.

(i) Express trusts

The main form of trust is the express trust, which is created intentionally by the settlor (if the trust is created by somebody whilst they are alive who 'settles' property on trust) or the testator (if the trust is created by somebody in a will). The settlor of a trust may either declare that they hold property on trust for somebody else or that they intend to transfer property to somebody else to hold on trust for another.

(ii) Fixed trust

A fixed trust arises where the interest of the beneficiary is identified in the trust instrument: for example, 'in trust for my children in equal shares'. The interests of the beneficiaries are established immediately the trust is validly created. These interests may be successive over time, such as 'for my wife for life; remainder to my children'.

(iii) Discretionary trusts

Another form of express trust is the discretionary trust under which the trustees have a discretion to distribute the property as they wish to people from a particular class of potential beneficiaries, known as the objects. For example, the trust may give the trustees a discretion to use the trust property to pay for the education of children of employees of

---

[80] *FHR European Ventures LLP v Cedar Capital Partners LLC* [2015] UKSC 45, [2015] AC 250. See Section 15.7.3, p. 454.   [81] See Section 3.2, p. 40.

[82] Or what has been called 'identity-based classification': McBride, 'On the classification of trusts', in *Restitution and Equity*, Vol. 1: *Resulting Trusts and Equitable Compensation*, ed. Birks and Rose (Oxford: Mansfield Press, 2000), p. 24. McBride also identifies an 'aim-based' classification of trusts.

a particular company. The trustees would be free to decide how they could allocate trust funds to such children and in such amounts as they considered to be appropriate. The objects of a discretionary trust do not have an equitable proprietary interest in the trust property, since the trustee's discretion may not be exercised in their favour. Instead, they have a chance, known as a mere equity, that the trustees might exercise the discretion in their favour. Lewison LJ has described the rights of an object of a discretionary trust as being

> a right to be considered as a potential recipient of benefit by the trustees. That is an interest which equity will protect. The trustees must apply some objective criterion in deciding whether or not to exercise their discretion in favour of a particular beneficiary; so that each beneficiary has more than a mere hope. But that right is not a proprietary interest in the assets held by the trustees, although it can be described as an interest of sorts . . .[83]

(iv) *Inter vivos* trusts

Trusts may be created *inter vivos*, which simply means that they are created whilst the settlor remains alive.

(v) Testamentary trusts

A testator can, in their will, leave their property to a beneficiary, known as a 'devisee' or 'legatee', absolutely, so that, once the testator's estate has been administered and all of their debts have been discharged, the estate will be transferred to the legatee. But the testator may wish to leave some or all of their property on trust. Once the estate has been administered, the trust property will then be transferred to a trustee to hold on the trusts identified in the will. This might be a discretionary trust or it could be a fixed trust in which the testator has created successive interests.

(vi) Bare trust

A bare trust arises where property is vested in the trustee for the sole benefit of the beneficiary, who is of full age. In a bare trust, the trustee has no discretion as to the management and disposal of the trust property, but is bound to follow the instructions of the beneficiary. A bare trustee is described as not having any active duties relating to the trust property.[84]

(vii) Public and private trusts

Trusts may be created for public purposes as well as for individuals or a class of people. Trusts for people are private trusts, since they are not created for the benefit of the public. Charitable trusts, which are the most common form of public trusts, must operate for the benefit of the public.[85] In addition, some public trusts arise in a commercial context by virtue of statute or regulation in the exercise of a public function and so, whilst operating as trusts, may not bear all the indicia of a trust as recognized in Chancery.[86] So, for example, money received by a financial firm from a client has been held on trust for the client even though the money had not been segregated into a client trust account as was required by the Financial Service Authority's regulations.[87]

---

[83] *JSC Mezhdunarodniy Promyshlenniy Bank v Pugachev* [2015] EWCA Civ 139, [2016] 1 WLR 160, [13].

[84] *Re Cunningham and Frayling* [1891] 2 Ch 567.   [85] See Section 6.2.2.(ii), p. 155.

[86] *Re Lehman Brothers International (Europe) (in administration)* [2012] UKSC 6, [2012] WTLR 1355, [189] (Lord Collins).   [87] Ibid.

(viii) Protective trusts

A protective trust is a method of protecting a beneficiary against the effects of bankruptcy or other misfortune.[88] The typical protective trust involves the beneficiary being given a life interest that is determinable on the occurrence of a designated event, such as the beneficiary's bankruptcy or on the assignment of the interest. If the event occurs, the life interest is forfeited, but the property will then be held on a discretionary trust, with the original beneficiary being a member of the class who might still be able to benefit from the exercise of the trustees' power to distribute the trust property.

These are called protective trusts because they provide a mechanism for protecting the beneficiary from adverse events. So, if the beneficiary becomes bankrupt, the termination of their life interest means that there is no property available to the beneficiary's creditors because they no longer have an equitable proprietary interest in that property. The use of this trust has proved to be especially important where a parent is concerned about a profligate child losing property on being declared bankrupt. Because the protective trust is a particularly significant mechanism for defeating the claims of creditors, it is subject to a number of restrictions. For example, the protective trust cannot be created by a settlor to protect their own property from creditors on being declared bankrupt.[89]

The nature of the protective trust and the consequences of forfeiture can be determined by the trust instrument, but, if that instrument simply says that the beneficiary has a life interest and the property is held on protective trust,[90] the statutory regime under section 33 of the Trustee Act 1925 applies, by virtue of which, if the life interest is forfeited on the beneficiary no longer having a right to receive income, the trust property will be held on discretionary trust for the original beneficiary, their spouse or civil partner, their children, or more remote issue.

The consequences of forfeiture may sometimes be beneficial to the beneficiary, especially where the effect is to protect trust property from creditors, but it may sometimes have adverse consequences for the beneficiary. So, for example, in *Re Baring's Settlement Trusts*,[91] a wife had a protected life interest with income payable to her until an event happened by virtue of which the income became payable to somebody else. She failed to obey a court order to return her infant children to the jurisdiction of the court and consequently her husband obtained a sequestration order against her property. This was sufficient to forfeit her life interest, because she no longer had a right to receive the income from the trust property and so a discretionary trust arose. In *Gibbon v Mitchell*,[92] the claimant voluntarily surrendered his protected life interest in favour of his children by a deed, with a view to minimize his inheritance tax liability, but he did not realize that this would result in the forfeiture of the life interest and bring a discretionary trust into effect. Consequently, the deed of surrender was set aside on the ground that he had made a serious mistake.[93]

(ix) Pension fund trusts

Pension schemes can be established without using the mechanism of a trust. So, for example, an employee's employment contract might provide that, in return for the employee's financial contributions, the employer will pay the employee a pension on retirement or a lump sum on death. The trust mechanism is, however, used for large pension schemes as a way of managing substantial sums of money for the benefit of the employees who contributed to the scheme. A typical contributory pension scheme provides defined benefits for

---

[88] See Sheridan, 'Protective trusts' (1957) 21 Conv 110.   [89] *Re Burroughs-Fowler* [1916] 2 Ch 251.
[90] *Re Wittke* [1944] Ch 166.   [91] [1940] Ch 737.   [92] [1990] 1 WLR 1304.
[93] On the role of mistake generally to set aside trusts and dispositions to trusts, see Section 9.3.3, p. 263.

the members of the scheme either as a proportion of their final salary or their average salary. Members of the scheme, who are typically employees of a company or group of companies, contribute a percentage of their salary to the scheme; their employer contributes as well. The fund is held on trust by trustees for the benefit of the employees, who receive payments following their retirement.

Hayton recognized that 'the species of pension trust should be regarded as having evolved from the trust genus as a drastically different species from the species of traditional family trust'.[94] This may well be true, but the pension trust is still a trust and is influenced by fundamental principles of trust law, although the employment context of the pension trust means that some of the principles are applied differently.[95] Some of the key differences between pension trusts and the traditional trust for the family are as follows:[96]

(1) The context of the pension fund trust is different from that of the family trust. The context of the pension trust is one of work and remuneration, whereas the context of the family trust is family and friendship.[97]

(2) The typical tripartite structure of the family trust does not operate in the same way for pension trusts. In the typical family trust, the settlor, acting voluntarily, transfers property to a trustee to hold on trust for the beneficiary. In the pension trust, each member is a settlor of a separate settlement within the head trust,[98] but is also the beneficiary. As beneficiaries, the members are not volunteers, since their contract of employment treats the provision of their pension rights as part of their pay and they are bound to contribute to the fund from their salary; the employer is contractually bound to make contributions as well. The receipt of benefits by the beneficiaries subsequently can be considered to be deferred remuneration for their services to their employer.[99]

(3) The pension trust lies at the interface of trust, employment, and contract law. The contractual nature of the pension scheme is vital to its operation. That scheme forms part of the wider contractual relationship between the employer and employee, and the terms and conditions of the scheme derive from the contract of employment. This contract may contain wide-ranging powers to amend the scheme.

(4) Whereas trustees of traditional trusts are required to promote the best interests of the beneficiaries exclusively, this is not true of pension trustees,[100] who must have regard to the interests of other participants in the scheme, including the employer[101] and the Pensions Protection Fund, an insurance scheme that underwrites pension schemes that are in deficit when they are wound up.[102] These other participants are affected by the exercise of the trustees' discretions if the employer becomes insolvent or if the fund falls into deficit.

(5) The significance of the pension trust, and the dangers of abuse of powers and misappropriation of trust assets by employers, has meant that these trusts are regulated by

---

[94] 'Pension trusts and traditional trusts: drastically different species of trusts' [2005] Conv 229, 245.

[95] But not always: see the law on distribution of surplus funds following the termination of a pension trust, in Section 8.3.2.(iii), p. 238. See also Lord Millett, 'Pension schemes and the law of trusts: the tail wagging the dog?' (2000) 14 TLI 66, 74.

[96] Milner, 'Pension trust: a new trust forum' [1997] Conv 89; Lord Millett (see n. 95); Hayton (see n. 94).

[97] Moffatt, 'Pension funds: a fragmentation of trust law?' (1993) 56 MLR 471, 488.

[98] *Air Jamaica v Charlton* [1999] 1 WLR 1399, 1408 (Lord Millett).

[99] *Imperial Group Pension Trust v Imperial Tobacco Ltd* [1991] 1 WLR 589, 597 (Browne-Wilkinson V-C).

[100] Fox, 'Discretion and moral hazard in pension trusts' (2010) 69 CLJ 240, 242.

[101] *Edge v Pensions Ombudsman* [2000] Ch 602, 627 (Chadwick LJ).

[102] *Independent Trustee Services Ltd v Hope* [2009] EWHC 2810 (Ch).

statute, notably the Pensions Act 1995, which provides safeguards for the protection of beneficiaries, including a requirement to appoint professional advisers and a minimum funding requirement to prevent a shortfall of funds.[103] The Pensions Act 2004 resulted in the creation of a Pensions Regulator to reduce the possibility of pension funds being misappropriated.

(x) Resulting trusts

In certain recognized situations a trustee will hold property on trust for the person who transferred property to the trustee. In these situations, the property will result back to the settlor or the estate of the testator, and so the trust is called a resulting trust.[104] So, for example, a trustee will hold property on trust for the settlor who sought to create an express trust that has failed. Similarly, where a transferor has transferred property to the transferee for no consideration, it will be presumed that the transferor intended the transferee to hold the property on trust for themself, by virtue of the principle that Equity is cynical about the making of gifts.[105] Whereas an express trust arises because it was expressly intended, the resulting trust arises because the transferor is presumed to have intended that it be held on trust for them.

(xi) Constructive trusts

The constructive trust[106] arises through the application of legal rules rather than being expressly created by the settlor or testator, or through the presumed intent of a transferor. These trusts arise in a number of different circumstances, but primarily where the recipient of property can be considered to have acted unconscionably, such as where the property was obtained fraudulently.

(xii) Common law trust

In *Akers v Samba Financial Group*[107] the Supreme Court recognized what was described as a 'common law trust', which referred to a trust recognized by English common law, but which could have as its subject matter property in another jurisdiction, even if that jurisdiction does not recognize the trust, such as, in that case, Saudi Arabian shares. This could still be a valid trust in England and could be enforced by the English courts as far as it is possible to do so. As Lord Mance said:

> in the eyes of English law, a trust may be created, exist and be enforceable in respect of any assets located in a jurisdiction, the law of which does not recognize trusts in any form.[108]

3.7 DISTINGUISHING TRUSTS FROM OTHER CONCEPTS

To get a better understanding of when a trust will be recognized and how it operates, it is useful to contrast the trust with other legal mechanisms, to determine where the boundaries between them lie. Sometimes, the boundaries are clear, but increasingly they are becoming more difficult to define.

---

[103] Nobles, 'Pensions Act 1995' (1996) 59 MLR 241.   [104] See Chapter 8 of this volume.
[105] See Section 2.8, p. 34.   [106] See Chapter 9 of this volume.   [107] [2017] UKSC 6, [2017] AC 424.
[108] Ibid., [34].

3.7.1 CONTRACT

Trust and contract are very different concepts. Contract is based upon agreement, requiring either a deed or consideration, and creates a personal right against the other party. The trust is an equitable concept, dependent typically upon the intention of the settlor or testator, and creates proprietary and personal rights in the beneficiary that the beneficiary is able to enforce despite being a volunteer and not being a party to any bargain. Whereas one contracting party can sue the other for breach of contract, once the trust has been created, the settlor cannot sue the trustee for breach of trust and cannot seek the termination of the trust.

Despite these fundamental differences between trusts and contracts, there are a growing number of situations in which the dividing line between them is blurred. For example, there are a number of situations in which a trust derives from a contract and it has been recognized that a single transaction can give rise to both a trust and a contract.[109] We have already seen this in respect of pension fund trusts, which derive from the employment contract. A trust will also arise where property is transferred pursuant to a contract for a particular purpose and that purpose subsequently fails.[110] Contracts can also have an important role in modifying the application of the rules in the law of trusts and even exclude them.[111] This is particularly so since, increasingly, trustees are professionals whose duties and responsibilities are determined by their contract of appointment, which will often exclude their liability for breach of trust.[112]

3.7.2 DEBT

The relationship of creditor and debtor is one of personal liability, since the debtor is personally liable to the creditor for the value of the debt. If, however, the debtor becomes insolvent, their assets will be available to all of their creditors, who will not have priority over each other unless one of them has a security interest over the debtor's property. The relationship of beneficiary and trustee is fundamentally different because the beneficiary does have an equitable proprietary interest in the trust assets, so that they will be able to claim those assets in priority to the trustee's creditors if the trustee becomes insolvent.

It does not follow that the creditor–debtor relationship is alien to the trust. The trustee may be personally liable to the beneficiary for breach of trust and this liability will create a debt owed to the beneficiary, so that, to this extent, the beneficiary is the creditor of the trustee.[113]

The significance of whether the beneficiary can be considered to be creditor of the trustee is particularly well illustrated by *Re Lehman Brothers International (Europe) (No 2)*,[114] which arose from the collapse of Lehman Brothers bank in 2008, leaving a lot of money owing to a number of creditors. In order to find a way of ensuring that the bank's creditors were repaid some of the money that was due to them, the administrators of the bank applied for a scheme of arrangement.[115] These schemes enable a company to rearrange its contractual or similar liabilities with creditors so that, for example, the creditors will receive part of the money due to them in return for their debts being discharged, this being preferable to the risk of them receiving nothing at all. Such a scheme will be valid only if 75 per cent of the creditors agree to it. Since this can have the effect of depriving

---

[109] *Charity Commission for England and Wales v Framjee* [2014] EWHC 2507 (Ch), [2015] 1 WLR 16, [42] (Henderson J).   [110] See Section 8.4, p. 239.
[111] See Section 3.2, p. 39.   [112] See Section 17.3, p. 473.
[113] *Sharp v Jackson* [1899] AC 441, 426 (Earl of Halsbury LC).
[114] [2009] EWCA Civ 1161, [2010] 1 BCLC 496.   [115] Under Companies Act 2006, Pt 26.

those who voted against the scheme of their rights, the scheme also needs the sanction of the courts. The question in this case concerned the identification of those creditors whose consent needed to be obtained. It was held that former clients of the company who had equitable rights in property that was held by the company on trust for them were not creditors, so that the court had no jurisdiction to sanction a scheme of arrangement relating to their interests. A creditor was defined as anybody with a monetary claim against the company that, when payable, would constitute a debt.[116] In other words, a creditor was somebody to whom money was owed. But a proprietary claim to trust property did not constitute a claim in respect of a debt owed by the company, since the beneficiaries of the trust would have a claim to the property that was held on trust rather than to the value of that property. It was recognized, however, that a person who had security rights in the company's property would be classed as a creditor of the company, since they would not have a claim to recover particular property, but a claim only to the value of what was due to them, albeit that, by virtue of their security over property, this claim would rank above those of other unsecured creditors of the bank. So the creditor with a security interest is still properly characterized as a creditor.

The boundary between trust and debt is also illustrated by *Duggan v Governor of Full Sutton Prison*,[117] in which the Court of Appeal held that a rule in the Prison Rules, that any prisoner who had cash in prison was required to pay it into an account under the governor's control, created a relationship of debtor and creditor, but did not impose a trust, since there was nothing in the Prison Rules to indicate that a trust was intended. It followed that the governor was not obliged to invest the money in an interest-bearing account for the benefit of the prisoners, since he had not received the money as trustee.

The boundary between trust and debt is sometimes blurred. It is, for example, possible for a debt itself to be the subject matter of a trust. It is also possible to ensure that what might otherwise be a debt is treated as a trust where money is lent for a particular purpose and, if that purpose fails, the borrower will hold the money on trust for the creditor.[118]

3.7.3 BAILMENT

The trust and bailment may appear to have much in common, since both involve obligations to look after property for the benefit of another,[119] with the trustee holding the property for the beneficiary and the bailee for the bailor. One key difference, however, depends on the location of the legal ownership,[120] since the trustee typically obtains legal ownership to property, whereas the bailor retains legal ownership. The significance of this is illustrated by the consequences of the trustee or the bailee selling the property to a third party without authority to do so. If the bailee sells the property in such circumstances, the bailor can sue the third party for the tort of conversion, even if the third party was a good faith purchaser of the property for value, since bona fide purchase does not defeat the bailor's legal title to the property. If, however, the trustee sells the property in breach of trust to a purchaser for value in good faith, the beneficiary will not have a claim in conversion because they do not have a legal proprietary interest in the property,[121] and the equitable proprietary interest will be defeated by virtue of the recipient being a bona fide purchaser for value.

---

[116] [2009] EWCA Civ 1161, [2010] 1 BCLC 496, [58] (Patten LJ).
[117] [2004] EWCA Civ 78, [2004] 1 WLR 1010.
[118] As recognized in *Barclays Bank plc v Quistclose Investments Ltd* [1970] AC 567. See Section 8.4, p. 239.
[119] Maitland (see n. 6), p. 45.
[120] *MCC Proceeds Inc v Lehman Bros International (Europe)* [1998] 4 All ER 675, 688 (Mummery LJ).
[121] Ibid.

The essence of the distinction between trust and bailment is therefore that the bailee does not have legal title to the property and is obliged to manage the property on behalf of the legal owner, whereas the trustee has legal title to the property and is obliged to manage the property on behalf of the beneficiary, who has an equitable interest in the property. The nature of the duties of management and the consequences of misapplication of the property will depend on whether a trust or a bailment can be identified, and this will turn on what the transferor of the property intended. But there will sometimes be circumstances under which a bailment will be converted into a trust, such as where the bailee has sold the property that they were looking after and the proceeds of sale are mixed with their own money. Legal title will then be transferred to the bailee, but they will hold the value of the property that was sold on trust for the bailor.[122]

3.7.4 AGENCY

Both trust and agency relationships are fiduciary, so that trustees and agents are both subject to fiduciary duties, such as that they must not make an unauthorized profit, and are liable to account for any such profit made.[123] But the essential difference between a trust relationship and an agency relationship again relates to proprietary rights. The agency relationship is a personal relationship. This means that any property that is transferred by the principal to the agent either still belongs to the principal at Law or, if legal title has passed to the agent, the principal will not have any equitable proprietary interest in the property; rather, the agent is simply liable to account to the principal for the value of the property received, so the relationship is one of creditor and debtor.

There will be circumstances, however, in which the line between agency and trust is very difficult to discern and in which an agency relationship can be converted into a trust relationship. This will occur where the agent has received property either from the principal or from a third party on behalf of the principal, so that the agent holds the property on trust for the principal. Whether a trust can be identified from an agency relationship will depend on the principal's intention. But a very significant factor in determining what the principal intended concerns whether the agent was under a duty to keep goods or money received separate from their own goods or money,[124] since this suggests that the agent has not received the property beneficially for their own purposes. If the agent is entitled to mix money received in their own bank account, there will only be a personal liability to account for the value received.[125] Sometimes, the trust will arise by regulation, such as by virtue of the rule that solicitors must keep the money of their clients in a separate account.[126] Alternatively, the trust may arise where the property has been transferred to an agent for a particular purpose that has failed.[127]

The decision whether a particular relationship should be characterized as an agency or a trust relationship will ultimately depend on the intention of the party creating the relationship. To assist with the identification of this intention, three principles were identified in *Pearson v Lehman Brothers Finance SA*:[128]

(1) If the agent is absolved by the principal from one or more of the basic duties of trusteeship, it does not necessarily follow that a trust cannot have been intended to be

---

[122] See e.g. *Re Hallett's Estate* (1879) 13 Ch D 696.   [123] See Section 15.6, p. 438.

[124] *Paragon Finance v DB Thakerar and Co* [1999] 1 All ER 400, 415 (Millett LJ); *Bailey v Angove's Pty Ltd* [2016] UKSC 47, [2016] 1 WLR 3179, [19] (Lord Sumption).   [125] *Re Stenning* [1895] 2 Ch 433.

[126] Solicitors Regulation Authority Accounts Rules 2011, r. 14.   [127] See Section 8.4, p. 239.

[128] [2010] EWHC 2914 (Ch). Briggs J's judgment was affirmed on appeal but these principles were not considered: [2011] EWCA Civ 1544, [2012] 2 BCLC 151.

created, but this does suggest that it may not have been. So, for example, if an agent is permitted to use the principal's money for their own purposes, this might indicate that there was no trust relationship, but it is not fatal to a finding of a trust if other aspects of the relationship point in favour of a trust being recognized.

(2) The law should not confine the recognition and operation of a trust to circumstances that resemble a traditional family trust, where the fulfilment of the parties' commercial objective calls for the recognition of a proprietary interest in the principal.[129] But, equally, the law should not unthinkingly impose a trust where purely personal rights between the principal and the agent sufficiently achieve their commercial objective. Ultimately, the finding of a trust should turn on the objective intention of the parties.

(3) There is, at least at the margins, an element of policy in recognizing a trust, especially as regards whether the property in the hands of the putative trustee should not be available for distribution to that person's creditors if they become insolvent. But, equally, the clients of putative trustees should be appropriately protected from that person's insolvency, which will be the case if a trust is recognized.

The identification of these three principles is important, but they have the potential to undermine the significance of certainty and clarity of the law, which is especially important in the commercial context. The emphasis in the third principle on the relevance of policy in determining whether there is a trust, something that is implicit in the recognition of the second principle, suggests that there is a critical role for judicial discretion in determining whether or not a trust should be recognized, with particular regard to the proprietary consequences of such a recognition. This is at odds with some other recent pronouncements that are critical of the role of judicial discretion in identifying proprietary interests.[130]

3.7.5 ASSIGNMENT

An assignment involves transferring rights from one person, the assignor, to another, the assignee. So, for example, if Brian owes money to Anne, she can assign the debt to Claudia so that Brian will then owe the money to Claudia. This does not involve the creation of any trust, since the essence of assignment is the transfer of existing rights rather than the creation of new rights.

The boundary between assignment and trust is not, however, as clear-cut as might first appear, especially because the creation of a trust can be used to avoid limitations on the assignment of rights. For example, in *Don King Productions Ltd v Warren*,[131] two boxing promoters entered into a partnership. They agreed that the benefit of all of their existing contracts with particular boxers should be brought into the partnership. They fell out and the partnership needed to be dissolved. One of the questions for the court concerned whether all of the boxing contracts had been transferred to the partnership. It certainly seems as though there had been an assignment of rights to the partnership, but this would not have been valid because many of the contracts contained anti-assignment clauses. The court got around this restriction by holding that the clauses did not prevent the person who was to receive the benefit of the contracts from holding those benefits on trust for somebody else. In other words, the prohibition on assignment was sidestepped by treating the agreement to transfer rights as an agreement to hold the rights on trust. This might

---

[129] *Target Holdings v Redferns* [1996] AC 421, 435 (Lord Browne-Wilkinson).
[130] See in particular the examination of the remedial constructive trust, in Section 9.4, p. 275.
[131] [2000] Ch 291. See also *Barbados Trust Co v Bank of Zambia* [2007] EWCA Civ 148, [2007] 1 Lloyd's Rep 495.

be considered to be incorrect, since the prohibition on assignment could be construed as intending to prohibit the creation of the trust as well, which would have had the practical effect of transferring the benefit of the rights to the partnership. But, since the contracts referred only to a prohibition on assignment and did not refer to a prohibition on creating a trust, the preferable construction is that they did not prohibit the transfer of rights by trust, because assignment and trust are functionally different. Since an assignment involves the transfer of an existing right and a trust involves the creation of a new right, it follows that, where a right to the benefit of a contract is transferred directly from Anne to Claudia, this involves an assignment. If, however, Anne declares that she holds those rights for the benefit of Claudia, this involves the creation of a new equitable proprietary right. This distinction, whilst recognized in *Don King Productions*, is not as clear as might first appear. If, for example, Anne declares a trust of the benefits of a contract for Claudia, this will involve the creation of a new equitable right to the benefits, but Claudia is able to call for the transfer of the benefits,[132] which will have the practical effect of the benefits being assigned to Claudia. Since, however, this will have occurred through the use of the trust mechanism, any anti-assignment limitation can be avoided.

3.7.6 GIFTS

Although the traditional trust involves the gratuitous transfer of property to the trustee for the benefit of the beneficiary, neither of whom have provided any consideration for the transfer, there is a significant difference between trusts and gifts. This can be illustrated by distinguishing between three scenarios:

(1) The typical gift involves two parties, where the donor transfers all rights to property to the donee without any obligation attached.[133] The donee consequently receives the property that has been donated absolutely and beneficially.

(2) The typical trust involves the settlor transferring property to the trustee, who is subject to an obligation to hold that property on trust for the benefit of the beneficiary. Since the trustee has not received the property beneficially, it cannot be considered to have been given to them. Since the beneficiary has not received the property absolutely, there has been no gift to them either, although once the trust has been terminated and the beneficiary receives the property absolutely, it can be seen that there has been an effective gift of the property to the beneficiary via the mechanism of a trust.

(3) In between these two scenarios is a third one, in which property is transferred subject to a condition. Whether these transfers constitute gifts or trusts will depend on the intention of the transferor, objectively determined by the courts.[134] This is practically significant because, whether the transaction is characterized as a gift or a trust, will determine the nature of the condition.

The distinction between gifts subject to a condition and trusts is illustrated by *Attorney-General v The Cordwainers' Co*,[135] in which the testator had left an inn to the Cordwainers' Company on condition that it paid annuities to certain relatives of the testator and made some payments for charitable purposes. Over the years, the rents obtained from the inn increased, so that there was a substantial surplus and the question for the court concerned who was entitled to it. It was held that the original devise of the inn constituted a gift to the Cordwainers' Company subject to a condition rather than a trust and, subject to

---

[132] See Section 11.4, p. 334.   [133] *Re Endacott* [1960] Ch 232, 242 (Lord Evershed MR).
[134] See Thomas, 'Conditions in favour of third parties' (1952) 11 CLJ 240.   [135] (1833) 3 My & K 534.

satisfactory performance of the duties arising from the condition, the Company was entitled to keep the surplus rents from the property beneficially. In other words, the testator intended that the Company should receive the inn absolutely as a gift subject to the continued performance of the condition. This can be compared with *Re Frame*,[136] in which property was bequeathed to a housekeeper on condition that she adopted one of the testator's daughters and made payments to the testator's other children. The daughter opposed the adoption order, which was refused by the court. The housekeeper argued that this was a gift subject to a condition and that, since the condition had become impossible to perform, she was entitled to receive the property absolutely. It was held that, although the testator had used the word 'condition', he had actually intended to create a trust for his children, as was made clear from the imposition of the obligation to pay money to his other children.

There is one other construction of a gift subject to a condition, which is that the condition creates a charge on the property that has been transferred. This means that the third party who is to benefit from the condition has a right to receive payment, but, once the condition has been satisfied, the donee of the property receives the property absolutely. So, for example, in *Re Oliver*,[137] the testator left land to his nephew, who was required to pay out certain legacies. The nephew took possession of the land, which was then sold in order to pay the legacies. The question was whether the nephew held the land as a trustee, for, if he did so, he would be liable to pay rent for his period of occupation. It was held that he did not hold the land as trustee. The third parties who were entitled to receive legacies had only charges on the land for the value of the legacies that were due to them. It followed that the nephew was not subject to fiduciary duties and, once the obligation to pay the legacies had been discharged, he could retain the land or the proceeds of sale beneficially. Until the obligation is discharged, the third parties will have an equitable security interest in the property by virtue of the charge, but that interest will be destroyed if the property is purchased by a bona fide purchaser for value.

3.7.7 INTERESTS UNDER A WILL OR INTESTACY

Where a testator dies, their property will pass to executors, who will receive the property absolutely, but subject to a fiduciary duty to ensure that it is transferred to those entitled under the will. Where the deceased has not left a will, they will have died intestate. There will be no executors of the estate, but the courts will appoint administrators to ensure that the deceased's property is transferred to those who are entitled to it under the law of intestacy. Executors and administrators are collectively described as the 'personal representatives' of the deceased.

A beneficiary under a will has neither a legal nor an equitable interest in any of the deceased's property until the executors have discharged all of the deceased's debts or have taken the risk of conveying the property prematurely to the relevant beneficiary.[138] Until this has occurred, the beneficiary cannot claim any property from the estate for themself and has only an expectation of the property being distributed to them, which is characterized as a mere equity. The same is true of those who are entitled on intestacy.[139] This is because, until the estate has been completely administered with all debts paid, it is impossible to say of what the estate consists.[140] This illustrates the key difference between a beneficiary's interest under a will or on an intestacy and an interest under a fixed trust. The former

---

[136] [1939] Ch 700.   [137] (1890) 62 LT 533.
[138] *Commissioner of Stamp Duties (Queensland) v Livingston* [1965] AC 694.
[139] *Eastbourne Mutual Building Society v Hastings Corporation* [1965] 1 WLR 861.
[140] *Commissioner of Stamp Duties (Queensland) v Livingston* [1965] AC 694, 708 (Viscount Radcliffe).

interests are not proprietary; they consist only of a personal right to ensure that the estate is administered, rather than a right that attaches to a specific piece of property. Interests under a trust are properly characterized as proprietary, since they relate to identifiable trust assets.[141] Despite this, if property from an unadministered estate has been misappropriated, any person who is entitled to the estate can bring a proprietary claim to recover the property from the third-party recipient.[142] This might suggest that the beneficiary does have a proprietary interest in the estate before it is administered. In fact, the beneficiary is acting only on behalf of the estate and in lieu of the personal representatives, who might themselves be implicated in the misappropriation of the property.[143] Consequently, if the misappropriated property is recovered, it will be restored to the estate rather than to the beneficiary, this simply being a consequence of the beneficiary's right to ensure that the estate is properly administered.[144]

The significance of this analysis of interests under a will is illustrated by *Commissioner of Stamp Duties (Queensland) v Livingston*.[145] A testator had left his estate to his wife. Following his death, and whilst the estate was still being administered, the widow died intestate. Her estate was liable to pay tax if she held a beneficial interest in the property left to her by her husband. It was held that she did not have such an interest because administration of the estate was not complete; rather, on the husband's death, full ownership of the estate had passed to the executors and the wife had not acquired any proprietary interest in it.

The nature of a beneficiary's interest in an unadministered estate is also illustrated by *Re Leigh's Will Trusts*,[146] in which the testatrix was the sole administratrix and beneficiary of her husband's unadministered estate. In her will, she bequeathed all of the shares that she owned in a particular company. She did not own any shares in the company, but her husband did. The court confirmed that she had no proprietary interest in any particular asset in the estate whilst it remained unadministered, but that she had a right to ensure that the estate was properly administered. This was a chose in action, which could be transmitted in her will. It followed that the legatee under her own will was entitled to receive the shares.

The fact that the right to have the estate properly administered is a mere equity that is transmissible means that a legatee who is entitled to land under the testator's estate can enter into a valid contract to sell the land even before the estate has been administered.[147] Although the land cannot be conveyed until administration of the estate has been completed and the property has been vested in the legatee, this will not prevent the legatee from entering into a contract to sell the property once it has been conveyed.

The nature of the proprietary interest of the executor or administrator is significant. Legal title to the property in the deceased's estate will be automatically vested in the personal representatives on the deceased's death. There will be no equitable proprietary interest in that property, since there will have been no event to create such an interest and nobody other than the personal representative who could have it; as we have already seen,[148] one

---

[141] See Section 3.5.5.(i), p. 48. Interests of objects under a discretionary trust have more in common with a beneficiary's interest under a will or on an intestacy, because there is only an expectation of property being received rather than a right to it. See Section 11.2.2.(i), p. 320.

[142] *Re Diplock's Estate* [1948] Ch 465. See Section 19.3.3.(i), p. 559.

[143] *Commissioner of Stamp Duties (Queensland) v Livingston* [1965] AC 694, 714 (Viscount Radcliffe).

[144] Bailey, 'Equitable interests: position of beneficiaries under will or intestacy—whether administration complete: tracing' (1965) 23 CLJ 44, 46. [145] [1965] AC 694.

[146] [1970] Ch 277. [147] *Wu Koon Tai v Wu Yau Loi* [1997] AC 179, 188 (Lord Browne-Wilkinson).

[148] See Section 3.5.3, p. 47.

person alone cannot have both the legal and equitable proprietary interest. But the personal representatives cannot be considered to have the beneficial interest in the property either,[149] since, as fiduciaries, they are not in a position to benefit from the property. So, where is the beneficial interest? It might be considered to be located in those people who are entitled to the estate, but since they have only a mere equity, they have only an expectation of benefit and they cannot enforce their beneficial interest by, for example, requiring the personal representative to transfer possession of property to them or the income derived from the property forming the deceased's estate. The better view, therefore, is that the beneficial interest in the property should be considered to be in suspense pending the administration of the estate.[150]

3.7.8 POWERS

A fundamental distinction exists between trusts and powers, since trusts impose obligations that *must* be performed, whilst powers are discretionary, so they *may* be performed. But the distinction between trusts and powers can be difficult to draw because a particular trust instrument may impose both trust obligations on the trustees *and* create discretionary powers that may be exercised by the trustees. It is important to distinguish between trusts and powers, both because it is necessary to determine whether the trustee must or may act, and because trusts can be executed by the court, whereas powers cannot. So, for example, if a trustee dies without making an appointment of trust property to the beneficiaries, if there is a trust obligation to make an appointment, the court will do so, but if there is a power, it will lapse on the trustee's death.[151]

The significance of the distinction between trusts and powers is illustrated by reference to the distribution of trust property to objects of the trust. A hierarchy of trusts and powers can be identified.

(i) Fixed trust

Under a fixed trust, the duty to distribute trust property to the beneficiaries must be discharged. If not, the court will ensure that the duty is performed by appointing the trust property according to the terms of the trust.

(ii) Discretionary trust

The discretion of a discretionary trustee can be characterized as a power, in the sense that the trustee can choose who is to benefit. But this power must be exercised and so it appears to be a trust. Because it has these dual components of trust and power, it is sometimes called a 'trust power'. It is a trust because there is an obligation to appoint, but it is a power because the trustee has a discretion regarding who is to benefit from the appointment of trust property and by how much.[152] The trustee of a discretionary trust is subject to a duty to survey the class of beneficiaries and to exercise their discretion in favour of one or more members of that class. If the trustee fails to do so, the trust power will not lapse, but will be executed by the court, either by making an order for equal division among the beneficiaries or in such proportions as appear to be appropriate in the circumstances.[153]

---

[149] *Commissioner of Stamp Duties (Queensland) v Livingston* [1965] AC 694, 707 (Viscount Radcliffe).
[150] By analogy with the trust created by a testator, but which arises on the death of a legatee: see *Ottaway v Norman* [1972] Ch 698, discussed in Section 5.2.2.(ii), p. 113.   [151] *Brown v Higgs* (1803) 8 Ves 561.
[152] Ibid., 570 (Lord Eldon).   [153] See Section 14.2.3.(i), p. 404.

(iii) Fiduciary power

This power is a power of appointment that is given to a trustee in their capacity as a trustee. It is a true power because the trustee is not obliged to exercise it at all.[154] But its fiduciary nature means that the trustee must consider whether or not the power should be exercised.[155] If the power is not exercised, it will lapse and the property that is subject to the power will devolve on default of appointment according to the terms of the trust. So, for example, if there is a fixed trust and the trustee has a fiduciary power to distribute a proportion of the property as they might wish, if that power lapses, the property that could have been appointed by the exercise of the power will be appointed according to the terms of the fixed trust.

Fiduciary powers can be divided into three categories:

(1) *general power*—a power to appoint property to anyone the trustee chooses;

(2) *special power*—a power to appoint to a person from a selected group; and

(3) *intermediate power*—a power to appoint property to anybody except certain people or a certain group of people.

(iv) Power coupled with a trust

Another category of powers involves a power to make an appointment, but a trust arises if the appointment is not made. This gives the trustee a discretion to determine whether or not to make an appointment, but if the power is not exercised before the trustee dies, the power will lapse and will be replaced with a trust obligation in favour of the objects of the power. So, for example, in *Burrough v Philcox*,[156] the testator gave life interests in his property to his two children with remainder to their issue. His will provided that if his children should die without issue, the survivor had a power to dispose of the property in his will amongst the testator's nephews and nieces in such proportions as the surviving child thought proper. It was held that the testator had created a trust in favour of his nephews and nieces, but this was subject to a power of selection in the surviving child. If the surviving child had made a selection in their own will, this would have been effective, but if, as occurred, no such selection had been made, the property was held on trust for the nephews and nieces who took in equal shares. This construction is justifiable because the testator was considered to have a general intention to benefit the class of nephews and nieces as a whole, but this was subject to a particular intention for his surviving child to have a discretion to select from that class.[157] If that power were not exercised, the general intention to benefit the whole class would apply through the imposition of a trust, which did not lapse following the death of the testator.

(v) Mere powers

Powers may also be given to people who are not trustees or otherwise in a fiduciary relationship. These are called 'mere powers' and the donee of the power is not even required to consider the exercise of it.[158] A trustee may be given a mere power if the power is given to them in a personal capacity, rather than as a trustee.

---

[154] *Breadner v Granville-Grossman* [2001] Ch 523, 540 (Park J).

[155] *Re Gulbenkian* [1970] AC 508, 525 (Lord Upjohn); *McPhail v Doulton* [1971] AC 424.

[156] (1840) 5 My & Cr 72.

[157] Ibid., 91 (Lord Cottenham). This can be contrasted with *Re Weeke's Settlement* [1897] 1 Ch 289, in which it was not possible to find a general intention on the part of the testatrix to benefit the class.

[158] *Re Gulbenkian's Settlements* [1970] AC 508, 518 (Lord Reid).

(vi) Determining whether a trust or power has been created

Whether the settlor or testator has created a trust obligation or a discretionary power depends on their intent, as deduced from careful construction of the trust instrument. If mandatory language is used, this suggests that there is a trust obligation that must be exercised, such as by use of the phrase 'to be distributed'. Discretionary language, on the other hand, suggests a fiduciary power, such as the trustee 'may appoint'. If there is an express gift over in default of appointment, this suggests that a fiduciary power will have been created,[159] because the provision of such a gift over negatives the possibility of a duty on the trustee to distribute, since the settlor or testator had made contingency plans that would take effect if the property were not distributed.

In *McPhail v Doulton*,[160] a clause in the trust instrument stated that the trustees should apply the income from a fund for employees and their relatives and dependants in such amounts, at such times, and subject to such conditions as the trustees thought fit. The trustees were not obliged to exhaust the income of the fund each year and could realize capital if the income was not sufficient. It was held by the House of Lords that this had created a trust power rather than a fiduciary power because of the use of the words 'shall distribute'—that is, mandatory language. Lord Wilberforce[161] recognized that the distinction between trust and power was narrow and artificial, and depended on 'delicate shading'.

Similarly, in *Breadner v Granville-Grossman*,[162] Park J illustrated the distinction between trusts and powers by reference to a trust for the distribution of income. If the power were a trust power, the trustees would be bound to distribute the income, but would have a discretion as to how it should be divided between the objects. If, however, it were a fiduciary power, the trustees would have two discretions: first, as to whether or not to distribute the income and, secondly, if they decided to exercise that discretion, as to how the income should be divided between the beneficiaries. Typically, in such a case, there would be a default trust that applies if the trustees were not to exercise their discretion to distribute the income, for example by requiring the undistributed income to be accumulated or by requiring it to be distributed to a named beneficiary, whose right to distribution would have been defeated had the trustees exercised their discretion to distribute.

[159] Hopkins, 'Certain uncertainties of trusts and powers' (1971) 29 CLJ 68, 72.
[160] [1971] AC 424. See further Section 4.4.3.(i), p. 90.   [161] [1971] AC 424, 448.
[162] [2001] Ch 523, 540. Approved in *Schmidt v Rosewood Trust Ltd* [2003] UKPC 26, [2003] 2 AC 709, [40].

PART II

THE EXPRESS TRUST

4

THE REQUIREMENTS OF AN EXPRESS TRUST

4.1 FUNDAMENTAL PRINCIPLES

In order to create a private trust expressly, whether immediately by a settlor or by a will following the death of a testator, there are a number of requirements that need to be satisfied. Each of these requirements will be examined in this chapter, but before doing so it is important to emphasize that express trusts arise from the express intention of the party who creates the trust. This is an obvious point, but its significance is often ignored. The creator of the trust is given a great deal of flexibility as to the terms and operation of the trust. Consequently, many of the requirements for the creation of the trust will be easily met by careful drafting of the trust instrument or will, or by providing mechanisms to resolve problems, such as giving the trustees the power to resolve any uncertainty in the terms of the trust.[1] Most of the problems that arise as regards whether a trust has been validly created do so from a failure to obtain legal advice or from a failure to follow it. But this does not mean that the requirements for the creation of a trust are insignificant: if any of them are not satisfied, the trust will be void.

The fundamental principle that is of relevance to this chapter is that judges will try to uphold a trust if they can; the settlor's or testator's intention to create a trust should be respected. This was recognized in *McPhail v Doulton*[2] by Lord Wilberforce, who said that 'a trust should be upheld if there is sufficient practical certainty in its definition for it to be carried out, if necessary with the administrative assistance of the court, according to the expressed intention of the settlor'. As one commentator has recognized: '[T]he court will bend over backwards to construe sense into instruments.'[3] But there comes a point at which this desire to uphold the trust cannot be fulfilled because of insufficient practical certainty, either because it is not clear what the settlor or testator wanted to achieve, or because it is not clear what the trustees are to do in carrying out the trust and the court is unable to execute the trust.[4] In older cases, the courts tended to adopt a much stricter approach to the construction of trusts, so that virtually any uncertainty relating to

---

[1] See Section 4.4.6.(i), p. 97.   [2] [1971] AC 424, 450.

[3] Grbich, '*Baden*: awakening the conceptually moribund trust' (1974) 37 MLR 643, 650.

[4] *IRC v Broadway Cottages* [1955] Ch 20, 30 (Jenkins LJ).

a trust's administration would result in its invalidity. More recently, the courts have tended to strive to uphold a trust if they possibly can.[5]

The first three requirements to establish an express trust revolve around the need to establish certainty, whether of intent to create a trust, subject matter, or beneficiaries.[6] Although these three certainties are distinct, they often overlap. So, for example, it has been recognized that uncertainty in the subject matter of a trust has a 'reflex action' that creates doubt as to whether the settlor or testator did actually intend to create a trust.[7]

4.2 INTENTION TO CREATE A TRUST

The creator of an express trust, whether a settlor or a testator, must intend to create the trust.

4.2.1 CAPACITY TO CREATE A TRUST

An intention will be valid only if the settlor or testator had the capacity to create a trust. So, for example, a settlement made by a child is voidable by the child before or reasonably soon after their eighteenth birthday,[8] on the basis that it might not be in the best interests of a child to make a trust where the child lacks the ability to determine whether a trust should be created, because of immaturity.[9] Further, a settlement made by a mentally incapacitated person is void,[10] although the court may make a settlement of property or execute a will on behalf of a person who lacks the mental capacity to do so.[11]

4.2.2 CERTAINTY OF INTENT

Various principles can be identified to determine whether the settlor or testator did have the necessary intent to create the trust rather than simply to make a gift,[12] but ultimately this is a question of fact that depends upon careful construction of the trust document or will.

(i) Essential test

The key test to establish whether there was an intention to create a trust is to consider whether the creator of the trust wanted somebody to hold property for the benefit of another person, so that they are under a duty to do so. This will be sufficient to create a trust, even though the creator of the trust did not understand that this was the effect of what they were doing.[13]

(ii) Use of the word 'trust'

The word 'trust' need not be used to create a trust.[14] Even if the word 'trust' is used, it does not follow that a trust has been created. For example, depending on the context, the use of

---

[5] *Pearson v Lehman Brothers Finance SA* [2010] EWHC 2914 (Ch), [245] (Briggs J).

[6] These 'three certainties' were recognized by Lord Langdale in *Knight v Knight* (1840) 3 Beav 148, 173.

[7] *Mussoorie Bank v Raynor* (1882) 7 App Cas 321, 331 (Sir Arthur Hobhouse).

[8] *Edwards v Carter* [1893] AC 360.

[9] The Law Commission has provisionally recommended that the age of capacity to make a will should be reduced from 18 to 16: *Making a Will* (Law Com CP No. 231, 2017), p. 168.

[10] *Re Beaney* [1978] 1 WLR 770.   [11] Mental Capacity Act 2005, s. 18(1)(h), (i).

[12] See also *Pearson v Lehman Brothers Finance SA* [2010] EWHC 2914 (Ch), discussed in Section 3.7.4, p. 61, for identification of principles to assist in determining whether a trust or an agency relationship was intended.   [13] See *Paul v Constance* [1977] 1 WLR 527, discussed in Section 4.2.2.(vi), p. 75.

[14] *Charity Commission for England and Wales v Framjees* [2014] EWHC 2507 (Ch), [2015] 1 WLR 16, [28(a)] (Henderson J).

the word 'trust' might not be intended to refer to the private law institution of a trust, but might instead be used in a 'higher' public law sense to refer to the trust that is bestowed on public officials as regards how they deal with particular property for the benefit of citizens.[15]

(iii) Substance of intention

The court needs to look at the substance of the creator's intent to determine whether they wished to impose an obligation on the other party to hold property for somebody else, or were simply requesting that they do so. Words that involve a request are described as 'precatory' words. So, if the creator says that they 'desire',[16] or 'wish',[17] or 'request', or are 'confident'[18] that the party receiving property will hold it for somebody else, this lacks the necessary element of *requiring* the other party to do so and will not be evidence of a sufficiently certain intent to create a trust. Even if the creator uses the word 'trust' in the sense of trusting that the other party will hold the property for someone else, this is not a sufficiently certain intent to create a trust.[19]

(iv) Objective assessment

As in the law of contract, whether a trust was intended is to be assessed objectively rather than subjectively, by reference to the terms of any agreement or the relationship between the parties.[20] What this means is that, rather than being concerned with what the creator of the trust actually intended, we are concerned with what the reasonable person would conclude that the creator of the trust intended.[21] Consequently, the court can infer an intent to create a trust from the circumstances of the case, the conduct of the parties, and careful construction of any relevant document. So, for example, in *Re Adams and the Kensington Vestry*[22] the testator provided in his will:

> I give, devise, and bequeath all my real and personal estate and effects . . . unto and to the absolute use of my dear wife . . . in full confidence that she will do what is right as to the disposal thereof between my children, either in her lifetime or by will after her decease.

It was held that this created an absolute gift to the wife and did not impose any legal obligation on her to hold the property on trust for the children. Rather, the testator was considered to have intended to impose merely a moral obligation on her to provide for the children, but that was not legally enforceable. The court emphasized that in some of the earlier cases too much weight had been placed upon the use of particular words that had previously been recognized as being sufficient to create a trust, whereas the court should be concerned with construing the whole of the document to determine whether a trust could be considered to have been intended. Later, in *Comiskey v Bowring-Hanbury*,[23] a similar bequest was made that was construed as creating a trust. In that case the testator had left his estate to his wife:

> in full confidence that she will make such use of it as I should have made myself and that at her death she will devise it to such one or more of my nieces as she may think fit and in default of any disposition by her thereof by her will . . . I hereby direct that all my estate and

[15] *Kinloch v Secretary of State for India* (1882) 7 App Cas 619, 625 (Lord Selborne LC); *Town Investments Ltd v Department of the Environment* [1978] AC 359, 382 (Lord Diplock).

[16] *Re Diggles* (1888) 39 Ch D 253. [17] *Re Hamilton* [1895] 2 Ch 370.

[18] *Mussorie Bank Ltd v Raynor* (1882) 7 App Cas 321. [19] *Re Williams* [1897] 2 Ch 12.

[20] *Pearson v Lehman Brothers Finance SA* [2010] EWHC 2914 (Ch), [225] and [249] (Briggs J).

[21] *Twinsectra Ltd v Yardley* [2002] UKHL 12, [2002] 2 AC 164, [71] (Lord Millett). The court will, however, have regard to the actual intention of the settlor when determining whether the trust is a sham. See Section 4.2.3, p. 77. [22] (1884) 27 Ch D 394. See also *Lamb v Eames* (1871) LR 6 Ch 597.

[23] [1905] AC 84.

property acquired by her under this my will shall at her death be equally divided among the surviving said nieces.

The House of Lords held that the testator intended to make a bequest to his wife with an 'executory gift over' of the property at her death to such of her nieces as should survive her, which was to be shared according to the wife's will but otherwise equally. In other words, the bequest to the wife was subject to a trust for the nieces on the wife's death. Although the wife was given a discretion as to how the gift would be shared between the nieces, if she did not state in her will what the shares were, the gift would be shared equally.

In some cases, however, the fact that particular words are used in a settlement or a will that have previously been recognized as being sufficient to create a trust is strong evidence that a trust was intended, especially where the document is drafted by a lawyer.[24]

(v) Interpretation of intent

In cases of ambiguity, the court will need to make sense of the expressed intent. In *Re Gulbenkian*,[25] Lord Upjohn said:

> It is then the duty of the court by the exercise of its judicial knowledge and experience in the relevant matter, innate common sense and desire to make sense of the settlor's . . . expressed intentions, however obscure and ambiguous the language that may have been used, to give a reasonable meaning to that language if it can do so without doing violence to it.

So, for example, in *Gold v Hill*,[26] the deceased had told his solicitor to make arrangements if anything happened to him, and 'to look after' his mistress and their children. Carnwath J considered the words used to be ambiguous. The deceased might have intended there to be an absolute gift to his mistress, expecting that she would use it for herself and their children, but this expectation would not have been enforceable. Alternatively, the deceased might have intended property to be held on trust for the mistress and their children. The judge concluded that the most likely interpretation of the deceased's intent was that he wanted the solicitor to hold money as trustee for the mistress.

(vi) Self-declaration of trust

The problem of whether there was an intention to declare a trust is especially acute where a person purports to hold their own property for the benefit of another—the so-called 'self-declaration of trust'.[27] This is illustrated by *Jones v Lock*,[28] in which a father, having returned from a business trip without a gift for his infant son, produced a cheque for £900 payable to himself and said it was a gift to the baby. He placed it in the baby's hand and then said, 'I am going to put it away for him'. He took the cheque and locked it in a safe. He died six days later. The key question was whether he had given the cheque to his son, or held it on trust for him, or whether it remained part of his estate. It was held that he had not made an effective gift of the cheque, because, being payable to himself, it needed to be endorsed to the baby by adding his own signature, but neither had he intended to declare a trust of the cheque. In particular, Lord Cranworth stated that it would be dangerous if 'loose conversations of this sort' were sufficient to declare a trust and all that the father had meant was that he intended to provide for his son, rather than to create a proprietary interest in the cheque for the child. So the cheque remained part of the father's estate.

---

[24] *Re Steele's Will Trust* [1948] Ch 603, following *Shelley v Shelley* (1868) LR 6 Eq 540.
[25] [1970] AC 508, 522.   [26] [1999] 1 FLR 54.   [27] See further Section 5.3.2.(i), p. 125.
[28] (1865) 1 Ch App 25. See also *Richards v Delbridge* (1874) LR 18 Eq 11.

The decision that somebody has declared that they hold their property on trust for somebody else is particularly sensitive in the context of family property disputes. So, for example, in *Paul v Constance*,[29] the deceased was married to the defendant, but he had left her and had gone to live with the claimant. The deceased was injured at work and received damages. To avoid the embarrassment of having a joint bank account with the claimant, he had an account in his own name to which the damages were credited. Money that he and the claimant had both won from playing bingo was credited to this account, and money was drawn from it to pay for both of them to go on holiday. On his death, the claimant sought a declaration that the money credited to this account was held on trust for her, so that it would not pass to the defendant. It was held that the evidence supported the conclusion that the money was intended to be held on trust, particularly because, on a number of occasions, the deceased had confirmed that the money was the claimant's as much as it was his own. These verbal statements proved decisive. Similarly, in *Rowe v Prance*,[30] the defendant had been having an extramarital affair with the claimant for fourteen years. The defendant told her that he would divorce his wife, sell the matrimonial home, and use the proceeds to buy a yacht, which would be their home whilst they sailed around the world. The defendant did not divorce his wife and neither did he sell the matrimonial home, but he did buy a yacht. This was registered in his sole name because, he had said, the claimant did not have an Ocean Master's Certificate, although neither did he. The relationship between them ended and the claimant successfully sought a declaration that the yacht was held on trust for them both, there being a crucial finding of fact that the defendant had often described the boat as 'ours'. Consequently, he held the yacht on trust for them both in equal shares.

(vii) Commercial context

Identifying whether there was an intention to create a trust has also proved significant in commercial disputes, especially those in which a party is bankrupt or insolvent. There is a general reluctance to find a trust arising from a commercial relationship,[31] but where there is clear evidence of the necessary intent, a trust will be found. One factor pointing to the finding of a trust is whether there is an obligation to segregate property, although this is not conclusive. So, for example, in *R v Clowes (No 2)*,[32] investors were induced to invest in the defendant's investment scheme by a misrepresentation in brochures that the money would be securely invested. The brochures also stated that all money received from investors would be held in designated client accounts and that the clients would be beneficial owners of all of the securities purchased on their behalf. In fact, most of the money was mixed in one bank account and the money was used by the defendant for his personal use. The issue for the Court of Appeal was whether the defendant was guilty of theft, which turned on whether the money paid by the clients was held on trust for them. If it were, the defendant would have appropriated property belonging to another person, since the clients had a proprietary interest in it.[33] It was held that the money was intended to be held on trust rather than simply creating a relationship of debtor and creditor, as indicated by the terms of the brochure. Watkins LJ[34] recognized that a requirement to keep money separate is normally an indicator that a trust was intended. If mingling of money is contemplated, then that normally negatives the intent to create a trust, unless other factors support a

[29] [1977] 1 WLR 527.   [30] [1999] 2 FLR 787.

[31] *Henry v Hammond* [1913] 2 KB 515, 521 (Channell J); *Neste Oy v Lloyd's Bank plc* [1983] 2 Lloyd's Rep 658; *Re Multi Guarantee Co Ltd* [1987] BCLC 257.

[32] [1994] 2 All ER 316. See also *Re Kayford* [1975] 1 WLR 279 and *Re Farepak Food and Gifts Ltd* [2006] EWHC 3272 (Ch), discussed in Section 1.4.8, p. 13.   [33] Theft Act 1968, s. 5(1).

[34] *R v Clowes (No 2)* [1994] 2 All ER 316, 325.

finding of a trust. Similarly, in *Re Lewis's of Leicester Ltd*,[35] a company, which traded as a department store, licensed other traders to trade within the shop. Some of these traders, known as 'concessionaires', paid takings into tills controlled by the company, which takings were then paid into a separate bank account; at the end of the month, the company paid this money to the concessionaires minus a commission. The company entered into administration and the question for the court was whether the money paid into the bank account was intended to be held on trust for the concessionaires. It was held that it was, because the payment was made into a separate bank account, although the company was also a beneficiary of this trust to the extent of its right to receive a commission.

(viii) Intention to make a gift

If there is an intention to make a gift, but legal title to the property is not successfully transferred, this transaction cannot be saved by treating it as a trust.[36] This is because an intention to make a gift involves an intention to transfer property absolutely without intending to impose any obligations on the donor to hold the property for someone else. Consequently, an intention to make a gift contradicts any intention to declare a trust.

(ix) Testamentary trusts

Generally a will should be interpreted in the same way as a contract,[37] even though a will is a unilateral rather than bilateral document. It follows that, when determining whether a testamentary trust has been created, the focus should be on the identification of the meaning of particular words with reference to their natural and ordinary meaning, save, if they are used in a technical sense, the overall purpose and other provisions of the will should be considered; the facts known or assumed by the testator when the will was executed should be taken into account; and the judge should exercise common sense.[38] But the judge should ignore evidence of the testator's intention and other extrinsic evidence. The only exception to this is where section 21 of the Administration of Justice Act 1982 applies. This enables extrinsic evidence to be taken into account to assist in the interpretation of the will, and this can include evidence of the testator's actual intention, but only where part of the will is meaningless; the language used is ambiguous; or evidence other than that of the testator's intention shows that the language used in the will is ambiguous in the light of the surrounding circumstances. It follows that, when determining whether a will has created a trust, an objective test is adopted save where any of the triggers for section 21 apply.[39]

The application of these principles of construction is illustrated by *Re Freud (deceased)*,[40] where the court had to construe the will of the painter Lucien Freud to determine whether his residuary estate was held on trust for any of his children. One clause of the will stated that the residuary estate was to be given to Freud's solicitor and one of his children. There was no mention of this being held on trust. Since the clause was not meaningless or ambiguous, section 21 of the Administration of Justice Act 1982 was inapplicable and so no extrinsic evidence of the testator's intent could be admitted. The judge considered other clauses of the will which referred to the solicitor and daughter as trustees, but this word was not used in the clause which referred to the residuary estate. Further, the relevant will

---

[35] [1995] 1 BCLC 428.

[36] *Jones v Lock* (1865) 1 Ch App 25; *Richards v Delbridge* (1874) LR 18 Eq 11. See also Section 5.3.3.(ii), p. 127.   [37] *Marley v Rawlings* [2014] UKSC 2, [2015] AC 129, [19] (Lord Neuberger).

[38] Ibid. See also *Loring v Woodland Trust* [2014] EWCA Civ 1314, [2015] 1 WLR 3238.

[39] See *Re Freud (deceased)* [2014] EWHC 2577 (Ch), [2014] WTLR 1453, [15] (Richard Spearman QC).

[40] Ibid.

had revoked an earlier will in which the clause relating to the residue had stated that it was to be held on trust. The different language of the subsequent will suggested that a trust was not intended. It was consequently concluded that the testator objectively intended the solicitor and daughter to take the property personally and absolutely rather than as trustees. In fact, evidence was submitted by the solicitor and daughter that the testator had communicated to them before his death that his intention was that they should hold the property for others, on what is called a fully secret trust,[41] but, since this was extrinsic evidence, it could not be relied on to identify a testamentary trust, although such evidence might be used to identify an express trust which operates outside of the will.[42]

The significance of taking into account the facts known or assumed by the testator when the will was executed is illustrated by *Loring v Woodland Trust*.[43] The testatrix had made her will in 2001 and had left to her children and grandchildren such sum as would be exempt from Inheritance Tax. At the time she made the will this was £325,000. Subsequently, the rules relating to Inheritance Tax liability changed so that it was also possible to rely on a deceased spouse's exemption from Inheritance Tax if that exemption had not yet been used. The testatrix's husband had died in 1984 and his exemption had not been used. Following the testatrix's death some of the beneficiaries of her estate claimed the benefit of the testatrix's husband's tax exemption, amounting to another £325,000. The issue for the Court of Appeal was whether the testatrix had intended to bequeath this additional amount to her family. It was held, following consideration of the circumstances at the time the will was executed, that the testatrix should be treated as intending to leave as much money to her family as possible without incurring liability to Inheritance Tax. Consequently, her family received £650,000 under the will.

The interpretation of the terms of a will may also be determined by subsequent legislative developments. So, for example, in *Re Hand's Will Trust*[44] 'children' of the testator were held to include 'adopted children', for otherwise the will would be discriminatory contrary to the European Convention on Human Rights.

4.2.3 SHAM TRUSTS

There are cases in which the settlor appears objectively to have intended to create a trust but in which, on closer inspection, this intention is not genuine since the settlor has an ulterior motive to create a different set of rights and obligations. This is a 'sham trust', and it will be void and unenforceable.[45] The essence of a sham was identified by Diplock LJ in *Snook v London and West Riding Investments Ltd*:[46]

> it means acts done or documents executed by the parties to the 'sham' which are intended by them to give to third parties or to the court the appearance of creating between the parties legal rights and obligations different from the actual legal rights and obligations (if any) which the parties intend to create.

Whether the trust is a sham will depend upon careful consideration of the evidence, but a number of principles can be identified to assist in this analysis:[47]

(1) There must be an intention to create a false or misleading appearance that a trust has been created.[48]

---

[41] See Section 5.2.2.(ii), p. 117.   [42] See further Section 5.2.2.(ii), p. 109.
[43] [2014] EWCA Civ 1314, [2015] 1 WLR 3238.   [44] [2017] EWHC 533 (Ch), [2017] 3 WLR 559.
[45] See *Midland Bank plc v Wyatt* [1995] 1 FLR 696, 707 (Young QC).   [46] [1967] 2 QB 786, 802.
[47] See Conaglen, 'Sham trusts' (2008) 67 CLJ 176.
[48] *Shalson v Russo* [2005] EWHC 1637 (Ch), [2005] Ch 281.

(2) A trust may be a sham even if it is not declared with any dishonest or fraudulent motive. In *Midland Bank plc v Wyatt*,[49] the claimant bank obtained a charging order over the Wyatts' interest in the matrimonial home. Before this, Mr Wyatt had purported to declare a trust of his interest in the home for the benefit of his wife and children. This was held not to be a valid declaration of trust because he lacked any real intent to hold the interest on trust for the benefit of his family. Rather, the trust was purportedly declared to act as a safeguard if his company were to face financial difficulties. Consequently, it was a sham. It was recognized that this conclusion would be reached even though there was no evidence that it had been created fraudulently or dishonestly, but as the result of, for example, mistaken legal advice. The crucial test was whether the trust was entered into for some ulterior motive other than to create a genuine trust. It has subsequently been suggested that a 'finding of sham carries with it a finding of dishonesty'.[50] Whether that is correct depends on what is meant by 'dishonesty'. This is a word the definition of which has caused a great deal of controversy in Equity,[51] although it appears essentially to be determined objectively by reference to what the reasonable person would consider to be dishonest. Whatever the meaning of 'dishonesty', the better view is that it is not a separate requirement which needs to be proved to establish a sham, although usually the finding of a sham will mean that the parties purporting to create a trust acted dishonestly.

(3) Where the settlor purports to declare a trust with somebody else as trustee, the trust will be treated as a sham only if both the settlor and the trustee intend[52] it to be so.[53] So, in *A v A*,[54] a trust was held not to be a sham because the trustees did intend to hold property on the stated trusts. The reason for requiring both parties to share the intention to mislead is unclear. Conaglen suggests that it is because a high threshold must be met to ensure that apparent trusts are not upset too readily, so as to maintain the security of transactions.[55] To reach this threshold, what must be established is effectively a conspiracy between the parties to the transaction, namely the settlor and trustee, to mislead. Of course, where the settlor purports to declare themself as trustee, only the settlor's intent to mislead can be relevant.

(4) A trust that was not a sham when created cannot be made a sham subsequently,[56] but a trustee who purports to treat a valid trust as a sham may be liable for breach of trust instead. A trust that was a sham when it was created can, however, be converted into a genuine trust if, for example, new trustees are appointed who are unaware of the sham intent, and who exercise their powers and duties in accordance with the terms of the trust.[57]

(5) Various factors are relevant to the determination of whether there was an intention to mislead, such as the artificiality of the transaction,[58] and the extent to which the settlor

---

[49] [1997] 1 BCLC 242.

[50] *National Westminster Bank plc v Jones* [2001] BCLC 98, [59] (Neuberger J); *ND v SD* [2017] EWHC 1507 (Fam), [184] (Roberts J). See also Conaglen (see n. 47), p. 187.

[51] See further Section 20.3.2.(iii), p. 614.

[52] Although it may be sufficient for one party, who was reckless as to the transaction in the sense that they did not know or care that it was misleading, to be deemed to have intended it to mislead: *Midland Bank plc v Wyatt* [1995] 1 FLR 696, 699–700 (Young QC); *A v A* [2007] EWHC 99 (Fam), [2007] 2 FLR 467, [52] (Munby J). But if this is the test, the courts should acknowledge that an intention to mislead is not required and mere recklessness is sufficient.

[53] *Shalson v Russo* [2005] EWHC 1637 (Ch), [2005] Ch 281, [188] and [190] (Rimer J).

[54] [2007] EWHC 99 (Fam).   [55] See n. 47, pp. 188–90.

[56] *A v A* [2007] EWHC 99 (Fam), [2007] 2 FLR 467, [43] (Munby J).   [57] Ibid., [45].

[58] *National Westminster Bank plc v Jones* [2001] 1 BLCL 98, [39] (Neuberger J).

can control the trustee's decision-making powers or treat the trust fund as their own to do with as they wish.[59]

(6) A declaration of trust can also be set aside by statute[60] where it is made to defraud creditors,[61] such as where the settlor's purpose is to put assets beyond the reach of creditors[62] or to prejudice creditors' interests in a claim against the settlor.[63]

Conaglen has argued[64] that the doctrine of sham trusts is a distinct doctrine from that involving certainty of intent, since the focus is on establishing the true subjective intent of the person declaring the trust. This has been challenged by Douglas and McFarlane,[65] who argue that there is no distinct doctrine of sham trusts since the focus is simply on establishing the objective intent of the settlor to determine whether the settlor did not intend the trust to take effect on the terms which were set out in the trust deed. Whilst establishing a sham can have regard to the oral communication between the parties, this still involves an objective interpretation to determine what these communications would have reasonably conveyed to the recipient. This is an attractive analysis, since it will mean that there is no distinct doctrine of sham which needs to be considered. But there is really no significant disagreement between Conaglen and Douglas and McFarlane since the key issue relating to sham involves identifying what the parties intended behind the face of the trust document and this will inevitably involve objective assessment of the evidence to determine how it should be interpreted.

4.2.4 ABSENCE OF CERTAINTY OF INTENT

Where there is uncertainty as to whether there was an intent to create a trust, no valid trust will have been declared. If the creator of the putative trust purported to declare themself as trustee, the purported declaration will be of no legal effect at all. But, where the creator of the putative trust transferred property to somebody else, that person may take the property beneficially[66] and they can then use that property how they wish.

4.3 IDENTIFIABLE SUBJECT MATTER

4.3.1 NATURE OF SUBJECT MATTER

Trusts can be declared over all kinds of property, including land, money, shares, and chattels, and even intangible property, such as a covenant[67] or a debt.[68] So, for example, in *Swift v Dairywise Farms Ltd*,[69] it was recognized that milk quotas, which exempt the holder from a financial levy, can be held on trust.

---

[59] See *Shalson v Russo* [2005] EWHC 1637 (Ch), [2005] Ch 281, [195] (Munby J), although this was not made out on the facts. See also *JSC Mezhdunarodniy Promyshlenniy Bank v Pugachev* [2017] EWHC 2426 (Ch), [441] (Birss J). [60] Insolvency Act 1986, s. 423.

[61] See also Insolvency Act, s. 339, where the transferor is declared bankrupt within five years of a transaction at undervalue, without needing to prove an intent to defraud creditors. See e.g. *Hill v Haines* [2007] EWCA Civ 1284, [2007] 50 EG 109 (CS). [62] *IRC v Hashmi* [2002] EWCA Civ 981, [2002] WTLR 1027.

[63] *Hill v Spread Trustee Co Ltd* [2006] EWCA Civ 542, [2007] 1 WLR 2404, where the purpose in making a settlement was to induce HM Customs & Revenue to make an incorrect assessment of capital gains tax; this was caught by s. 423 of the Insolvency Act 1986. [64] (2008) 67 CLJ 176.

[65] 'Sham trusts' in *Modern Studies in Property Law*, vol. 9 (eds Conway and Hickey) (2017, Hart Publishing), Ch. 13.

[66] *Lassence v Tierney* (1849) 1 Mac & G 551, 561 (Lord Cottenham LC); *Hancock v Watson* [1902] AC 14; *Watson v Holland* [1985] 1 All ER 290. [67] See Section 5.3.3.(iii), p. 132.

[68] *Lord Strathcona Steamship Co Ltd v Dominion Coal Co Ltd* [1926] AC 108, 124 (Lord Shaw).

[69] [2000] 1 WLR 1177. See also *Armstrong DLW GmbH v Winnington Networks Ltd* [2012] EWHC 10 (Ch), [2013] Ch 156 (EU carbon emission allowances were held on trust).

4.3.2 DESCRIPTION OF SUBJECT MATTER

A declaration of trust can be valid only if the subject matter of the trust has been described with sufficient clarity. As with the law on certainty of intention to create a trust, this will ultimately be a question of fact as to whether the description of the subject matter enables the property to be identified clearly. So, for example, in *Palmer v Simmonds*,[70] a testators' declaration that the 'bulk' of her estate should be held for certain people was not sufficiently certain. Other examples of testamentary gifts that have failed for uncertainty of subject matter include 'the remaining part of what is left',[71] 'such parts of my … estate as she shall not have sold',[72] 'all my other houses',[73] and 'such minimal part of my estate [to which my wife is] entitled for maintenance purposes'.[74]

On the other hand, in *Re Last*,[75] it was held that the reference to 'anything that is left' of the testator's estate was sufficiently clear. Consequently, when the testator had bequeathed her estate to her brother apparently absolutely, but then added in the will that anything left was to be transferred to other people, this was interpreted as giving the brother a life interest in the estate, with the residue of the estate passing to the other people on his death. Further, in *Re Golay's Will Trusts*,[76] a 'reasonable income' was held to be sufficiently certain, because it was considered to be possible to determine what is objectively considered to be 'reasonable'. This decision might appear to undermine the rationale behind the need for certainty of subject matter, namely that the court is able to administer the trust if the trustee fails to do so. But, in this case, the court was able to identify criteria to determine what is a reasonable income, namely by reference to the beneficiary's previous standard of living.

4.3.3 IDENTITY OF SUBJECT MATTER

Even if the subject matter of the trust is clearly defined, the property must be identifiable;[77] if it is not, the trust will be void for uncertainty.[78] The question of identity of property is especially significant where a defined part of a particular type of property is to be held on trust, but it is not clear which part of the whole is subject to the trust. So, for example, if Angela declares that she holds twenty of the one hundred sheep that she owns on trust for Brian, it is not clear which twenty sheep in the flock are held on trust for Brian, so the trust will fail.

The leading case on identifying trust property is *Hunter v Moss*.[79] The defendant in that case owned 950 out of 1,000 issued shares in a company and declared that he held 5 per cent of the company's issued shares, namely 50 shares, on trust for the claimant. This appears to be a trust that would be void for uncertainty of subject matter, since it was not clear which 50 shares were held on trust. But, despite this, it was held that there was a valid declaration of trust over 50 shares. In making this decision, a number of significant principles were identified.

(i) Clarifying identity on death

It was recognized that if there had been a declaration of trust of 5 per cent of the shares in a will, this would clearly have been valid, because the executors of the will would have been

---

[70] (1854) 2 Drew 221.   [71] *Sprange v Barnard* (1789) 2 Bro CC 585.   [72] *Re Jones* [1898] 1 Ch 438.
[73] *Boyce v Boyce* (1849) 16 Sim 476.   [74] *Anthony v Donges* [1998] 2 FLR 775.
[75] [1958] P 137.   [76] [1965] 1 WLR 969.
[77] *Westdeutsche Landesbank Girozentrale v Islington London Borough Council* [1996] AC 669, 705 (Lord Browne-Wilkinson).
[78] *Re Stapylton Fletcher Ltd* [1994] 1 WLR 1181; *Re Goldcorp Exchange Ltd* [1995] 1 AC 74 (PC).
[79] [1994] 1 WLR 452.

able to resolve any uncertainty as to the identity of the subject matter.[80] This is because, on the testator's death, title to the shares will pass to the executors, who will distribute the estate according to the terms of the will.[81] It would then be for the executors to choose any 50 of the shares and transfer them to the person designated in the will as the trustee.

(ii) Types of share

It was recognized that if there had been a lifetime declaration of trust by a settlor of 50 shares and the settlor held shares in two companies, A and B, this would have been void for uncertainty of subject matter because it would not be clear whether the settlor intended the shares in company A or company B to be held on trust. Similarly, if the settlor held shares of different classes in one company and it was not clear which shares of which class were to be held on trust, the trust would be void for uncertainty in the identity of the subject matter.

(iii) Chattels in a bulk

The issue in *Hunter v Moss* was different because the shares were of a single class and in a single company. The problem was that the settlor had not identified which 50 shares were to be held on trust. In earlier cases, this uncertainty of identity of property had proved decisive, albeit in the context of sale of goods. So, for example, in *Re London Wine Co (Shippers) Ltd*,[82] a company acquired a stock of wine that was deposited in various warehouses. Quantities of wine were sold to customers, but the wine remained in the warehouses as part of the general stock, without being allocated to particular sales contracts. The company went into receivership and the question for the court was whether the wine was held on trust for the customers. It was held that there was no trust because particular bottles had not been segregated from the bulk.[83] Similarly, in *Re Goldcorp Exchange Ltd*,[84] customers had paid a company for gold bullion. Before it was delivered to them, the company became insolvent. The question for the Privy Council was whether the customers had proprietary rights in the bullion which would mean that their claims ranked above those of other creditors of the company. The claims of a few customers succeeded because their bullion had been segregated from the bulk, but most claims failed because there had been no segregation, so that legal title did not pass to the customers, and the bullion was not held on trust because the customers could not identify their property in the bulk. The particular result in these sale-of-goods cases would now be different in England following the enactment of the Sale of Goods (Amendment) Act 1995, which provides that a purchaser of an unascertained part of a bulk of goods acquires property rights in that bulk.

Re *London Wine* was distinguished in *Hunter v Moss* on the ground that it concerned the appropriation of chattels and the passage of legal title, whereas *Hunter v Moss* concerned shares and the declaration of trust, in respect of which there was no suggestion that legal title had passed.

(iv) Tangible and intangible property

It appears from the previous principle that there is a crucial distinction between trusts of tangible property and trusts of intangibles, such as shares, with a more benevolent approach to identification applying to intangibles.[85] It follows that if I purport to hold 10 of

---

[80] See *Re Clifford* [1912] 1 Ch 29; *Re Cheadle* [1900] 2 Ch 620.
[81] See Section 3.7.7, p. 64.   [82] [1986] PCC 121. See also *Re Wait* [1927] 1 Ch 60.
[83] Compare *Re Stapylton Fletcher Ltd* [1994] 1 WLR 1181, in which some wine had been segregated and so was held on trust.   [84] [1995] 1 AC 74.
[85] See *Re Harvard Securities Ltd* [1997] 2 BCLC 369, 383 (Neuberger J).

my 20 bottles of wine of the same label and vintage on trust for you, there will not have been a valid declaration of trust, even if all of the bottles look the same, because it is not clear which bottles from the bulk are to be held on trust for you. I must specifically identify which bottles are to be held for you. If, however, I am purporting to hold 50 of my 100 shares on trust for you, the subject matter will be identifiable as half of my shareholding. But can this distinction between chattels and intangibles be defended? If all of the bottles look the same, surely it should be sufficient that any 10 of them are held on trust for you? But, although the bottles of wine may appear to be the same, this might not be the case: for example some might be corked.[86] Similarly, if I declare that I hold 20 of my 100 sheep of the same breed on trust for you without identifying which sheep will form the 20, they cannot all be treated as identical because, for example, some may have a disease and others not. But intangibles of the same type will always be exactly the same. So, for example, shares of the same class and in the same company are exactly the same, in the sense that it does not matter which shares from the fund are allocated to the trust. It is true that shares are numbered, but this should not be sufficient to make them different, since the numbering is used simply to account for the shares rather than to affect the quality of the property.[87] The same is true of money in a fund: it does not matter which money credited to the fund is held on trust. The key principle that can be derived from *Hunter v Moss* is that a trust of part of a mass will not fail for uncertainty where there has not been an appropriation of any specific part of the mass for the beneficiary, as long as the mass itself is sufficiently identified and as long as the beneficiary's proportionate share of the mass is not uncertain.[88]

(v) Intention to create a trust from a particular fund

It is not sufficient to conclude that the rules on identification turn simply on whether the subject matter is tangible or intangible. Even where the subject matter of the trust is intangible, a trust will not be created from a fund if the settlor did not intend part of that fund to be held on trust. This principle is illustrated by *MacJordan Construction Ltd v Brookmount Erostin Ltd*,[89] as regards a claim that money was held on trust. In that case, a building contract provided that the client would retain 3 per cent of the contract price as trustee for the builder, pending confirmation that the building work was satisfactory. A separate retention fund was intended to be set up, but this never occurred. The client became insolvent and the builder claimed that money in the client's bank account was held on trust. But, since the client had never assumed an obligation to establish the retention fund from that account, the claim failed. *Hunter v Moss* was different, since the settlor had intended that some of the shares that he owned should be held on trust for the claimant. In other words, the shareholding was the equivalent of a fund that was sufficiently identified[90] and part of which was held on trust for the claimant because this is what the settlor had intended.

(vi) Practical implications

The decision in *Hunter v Moss* does cause some practical difficulties, primarily because it is not possible to identify any clear rationale as to how the trust works in practice.[91]

Although it may not matter at the time the trust is declared which shares are held on trust, it may matter subsequently. So, for example, if 50 of 950 shares are held on trust by

---

[86] See Hayton, 'Uncertainty of subject-matter of trusts' (1994) 110 LQR 335, 337.
[87] See Goode, 'Are intangible assets fungible?' [2003] LMCLQ 379, 384.
[88] *Pearson v Lehman Brothers Finance SA* [2010] EWHC 2914 (Ch), [225] (Briggs J).
[89] (1991) 56 BLR 1. Approved in *Re Goldcorp Exchange Ltd* [1995] 1 AC 74.
[90] *Pearson v Lehman Brothers Finance SA* [2010] EWHC 2914 (Ch), [230] (Briggs J).
[91] Ibid., [232] (Briggs J).

the settlor, who then sells 500 shares, whose shares have been sold? This type of problem is dealt with in the context of claims to recover property by means of the tracing rules.[92] For present purposes, the details and function of these rules do not matter. What is significant is that they incorporate a principle that everything is to be presumed against the trustee.[93] The same principle could be used in the present context, so that the trustee who has sold 500 shares should be presumed to have sold the shares that they beneficially own rather than the shares that are held on trust: the trustee is under a duty to segregate the shares, and, if they have failed to do so and the shares that were not sold fall in value, they should be presumed to belong to the trustee absolutely. But, if the shares have increased in value, they should be presumed to belong to the beneficiary. Since the presumption works against the trustee, it should follow that, if the trustee had sold 50 shares and used the proceeds to buy a lottery ticket, one of which won the jackpot of £1 million, the beneficiary should be able to assert that the shares that were sold belonged to him and so can claim the jackpot that had been obtained using his money. Whether such a result can be considered to be fair will be examined when the tracing rules are analysed.[94]

Of course, if the trustee were to sell 930 of the 950 shares, it must follow that 30 of the shares that were held on trust would have been sold. The beneficiary of the trust would then have a claim against the trustee for breach of trust in respect of the sale of those shares, or, if the proceeds of sale were used to buy an asset, a claim to part of that asset.

(vii) Alternative constructions of the transaction

The problem of how some shares from a shareholding can be held on trust can be dealt with in a variety of ways, depending on how the transaction is construed, of which the following are examples:

(1) If Angela transfers 950 shares to Brian, to hold 50 of them on trust for Claire and 900 for David, this will be a valid trust because it will be for Brian to determine which shares should be held on which trust. This follows the same pattern as a testator leaving 50 shares to Edward in his will, where it is for the executor to resolve the uncertainty as to identity.[95]

(2) If Angela declares herself trustee of 50 of the 950 shares, she may intend that the beneficiary should have a beneficial interest in any 50 shares or that the beneficiary is to get a one-nineteenth interest in the shares, so that they will be tenants in common of the whole. The latter analysis was adopted by the New South Wales Court of Appeal in *White v Shortall*.[96] In that case, it was held that there had been a valid self-declaration of trust over 222,000 shares out of a holding of 1.5 million shares. This was not analysed as a trust of specific assets held for one person, but rather as a trust of a fund consisting of all of the shares, which were held for two beneficiaries, namely the settlor and the other party. Consequently, it was not necessary for each beneficiary to be able to point to particular shares to say that they had a proprietary interest in them; rather, each had an interest in all of the shares. This is an attractive analysis because it resolves the need to identify particular assets which are held on trust. Campbell J recognized that an implication of this construction is that the settlor would be free to deal with the shareholding as he wished, including the disposal of shares, as long as at least 222,000 shares remained and the beneficiary could call for the transfer of any of the 222,000 shares whenever he wished. In the meantime, the beneficiary could claim an appropriate proportion of the dividends declared in respect of the whole shareholding or of any capital returned by the company to the shareholders.

---

[92] See Section 19.3, p. 559. [93] See Section 19.3.3.(iii), p. 562. [94] See Section 19.3.3.(iii), p. 561.
[95] See Section 4.3.3.(i), p. 80. [96] [2006] NSWSC 1379.

Goode[97] has defended this co-ownership analysis of the trust in cases such as *Hunter v Moss* by reference to the proprietary nature of shares, which he analyses as being no more than fractions of a single asset, namely the issuing company's share capital. Consequently, when some of the shares are declared to be held on trust, the beneficiary simply becomes a co-owner of a single legally indivisible asset. This is why shares are distinguishable from tangible property—because of the nature of the asset of which they form part. This co-ownership analysis is attractive. What is surprising is that it was not adopted in *Hunter v Moss* itself, because the structure of the trust seems to be consistent with it: the settlor in that case did not actually declare a trust of 50 shares, but instead a trust of 5 per cent of the company's issued shares. This was treated by the court as meaning a trust of 50 shares owned by the settlor, since he owned 950 of the company's 1,000 issues shares, but it could just as easily, and more satisfactorily, have been treated as a trust of 5 per cent of the shareholding as a single asset, in other words one-nineteenth of all the shares he owned. This would be consistent with the approach adopted in *White v Shortall*. This co-ownership analysis of the trust has been expressly affirmed in *Pearson v Lehman Brothers Finance SA*,[98] by Briggs J, who said that 'such a trust works by creating a beneficial co-ownership share in the identified fund, rather than in the conceptually much more difficult notion of seeking to identify a particular part of that fund which the beneficiary owns outright'. A consequence of this beneficial co-ownership analysis will be that any loss arising from a shortfall in the value of the fund would be shared between the beneficiaries in proportion to their respective interests in the fund.[99]

4.3.4 CERTAINTY OF DIVISION OF BENEFICIAL SHARE

Certainty of subject matter requires certainty both of the identity of the property that is to be held on trust and of the proportionate amount of each beneficiary's share.[100] If an express trust is purportedly declared, but it is unclear what proportion of the whole each of the beneficiaries has, the trust will be void for uncertainty. So, in *Boyce v Boyce*,[101] a beneficiary was to determine which of the testator's houses she would have, but she died before doing so. The trust failed for uncertainty. It might, however, sometimes be possible to resolve the uncertainty. The trustees may have been given a discretion to divide the beneficial shares as they consider appropriate, or it might be possible for the court to apply the maxim that 'Equity is equality' and so divide the property equally between the beneficiaries.[102]

4.3.5 FUTURE CERTAINTY

A trust will not fail for uncertainty as to subject matter merely because the subject matter is, at present, uncertain, if the terms of the trust are sufficient to identify the subject matter in the future.[103] In those cases in which the subject matter of the trust relates to what is left of the property after the trustee's death,[104] there can be no immediate trust of the property because it will not be certain at the time of creation what, if anything, can be held on trust. This could, however, be interpreted instead as a floating trust that crystallizes only on the trustee's death. So, if Angela leaves Brian £1,000 in her will, with an obligation on Brian to

---

[97] [2003] LMCLQ 379, 384.

[98] [2010] EWHC 2914 (Ch), [232] (Briggs J). This analysis was affirmed by the Court of Appeal: [2011] EWCA Civ 1544. See also *LBIE v Rab Market Cycles* [2009] EWHC 2545 (Ch), [56] (Briggs J).

[99] *Pearson v Lehman Brothers Finance SA* [2010] EWHC 2914 (Ch), [244] (Briggs J).   [100] Ibid., [243].

[101] (1849) 6 Sim 476.   [102] *Burrough v Philcox* (1840) 5 Myl & Cr 72. See Section 2.14, p. 36.

[103] *Pearson v Lehman Brothers Finance SA* [2010] EWHC 2914 (Ch), [225] (Briggs J). See *Tailby v Official Receiver* (1888) 13 App Cas 523.   [104] As in *Sprange v Barnard* (1789) 2 Bro CC 585.

leave what is left of this money to Claire, Brian will be free to use the £1,000 as he wishes, but will be obliged to leave anything that is not spent on trust for Claire. This floating trust has been recognized in English law, but only in the specific context of secret trusts.[105] There is no reason why this concept cannot be applied more generally.

4.3.6 ABSENCE OF CERTAINTY OF SUBJECT MATTER

Where a trust is void for uncertainty as to subject matter, there are various consequences depending on the nature of the uncertainty. Where the identity of the subject matter is unclear, there is nothing to which any trust can attach. So, if property has been transferred by Angela to Brian with the intention that part of it be held on trust, but the identity of that part is uncertain, Brian will take the property absolutely. Part of it cannot be held on resulting trust for Angela because it is unclear which part was intended to be held on trust. If, however, the trust fails because of uncertainty in the division of beneficial shares, then all the property will be held by Brian on resulting trust for Angela,[106] because it is clear that Brian was not intended to have any of that property beneficially.

4.4 CERTAINTY OF OBJECTS

The identity of the objects of a trust will depend on the type of express trust that is being considered. Usually, the objects will refer to the beneficiaries, but for purpose trusts, such as charitable trusts, the relevant object will be the designated purpose.[107]

Where the trust is an express trust for persons, the key principle relating to certainty of objects is that the objects of the trust must be defined with sufficient certainty to enable the trustees, or, if they default, the court, to execute the trust according to the settlor's or testator's intention.[108] If it is unclear who the objects are, the trust will be void. Different tests of certainty of objects have been developed for different types of trust and power. In each case, six different matters need to be considered:

(1) the essential test of certainty;

(2) whether it is possible to define with sufficient certainty the description of the class, known as conceptual certainty;

(3) the ease of proving that somebody is an object, known as evidential certainty;

(4) ascertaining where an object of the class is located;

(5) the size of the class; and

(6) how sensible the settlor's or testator's intent was, known as the test of capriciousness.

4.4.1 FIXED TRUSTS

(i) The essential test of certainty

A fixed trust is a trust under which the trustees are required to distribute the trust property to the beneficiaries in the proportions identified by the trust document. The trustees have no discretion as to which people are to benefit from the trust and in what proportions; the

---

[105] See *Ottaway v Norman* [1972] Ch 698, discussed in Section 5.2.2.(ii), p. 118.
[106] See *Boyce v Boyce* (1849) 6 Sim 476.   [107] See Section 6.1.2.(iii), p. 146.
[108] Emery, 'The most hallowed principle: certainty of beneficiaries of trusts and powers of appointment' (1982) 98 LQR 551, 552.

objects of the trust are fixed from the start. Consequently, it must be possible to identify who all the beneficiaries are.[109] This is known as the 'complete list test' and it requires that a list can be compiled of all beneficiaries at the time when the trust property is to be distributed. It does not matter that a complete list cannot be drawn up when the trust is created. So, for example, a trust for Angela's grandchildren, including those born subsequently, will be valid even though the names of all of the grandchildren cannot be listed when the trust is created. If it is not possible to draw up a complete list of objects at the time of distribution, the trust will be void from the start.

(ii) Conceptual certainty

The need to satisfy the complete list test means that, if the definition of the objects is unclear, it will not be possible to compile a complete list, so that the trust will be void. So, for example, a fixed trust for the settlor's friends will be void for conceptual uncertainty, because it is not possible to define clearly who is 'a friend'.[110]

(iii) Evidential certainty

Even if the definition of the objects is certain, if it is not possible to prove who the objects are, the complete list test will not be satisfied. So, for example, if Angela creates a trust of £1,000 to be divided equally amongst the people who were in the school football team with her, this will be conceptually certain. But the school may no longer have any records of who played in the school team, so the trust will fail for evidential uncertainty, because it is not possible to complete the list of objects, unless some other evidence of membership of the team emerges.

(iv) Ascertainability

It does not matter that the location or continued existence of particular beneficiaries cannot be established.[111] The property will be distributed amongst those who can be ascertained and the share of anybody who cannot be ascertained can be paid into court.

(v) Size of the class

The question of the size of the class of objects has proved to be significant when considering the validity of discretionary trusts,[112] but there is no evidence that this is a relevant consideration when determining the validity of a fixed trust. This is presumably because all of the necessary work is being done by the complete list test. If it is possible to list all of the objects, there should be no concerns about the size of the class being such that the trust cannot be administered. Further, the size of the class is relevant to discretionary trusts because the trustees have to select from within the class, and if the class is too large, the act of selection will not be administratively workable. There is no such concern for fixed trusts because trustees do not select from within the class; instead they distribute amongst the whole class, which makes the administration of the trust a great deal easier despite the size of the class. But, by its very nature, the class in fixed trusts tends to be small.

(vi) Capriciousness

The question of whether the settlor's or testator's intent is capricious has proved to be significant when considering the validity of fiduciary powers of appointment,[113] but there

---

[109] *IRC v Broadway Cottages Trust* [1955] Ch 20, which actually involved a discretionary trust for which a different test of certainty is now used. See Section 4.4.3.(i), p. 89.   [110] But see Section 4.4.2.(i), p. 88.
[111] *Re Gulbenkian* [1970] AC 508, 524 (Lord Upjohn).   [112] See Section 4.4.3.(v), p. 93.
[113] See Section 4.4.4.(vi), p. 94.

is no evidence to suggest that this is of any relevance to the validity of a fixed trust. It follows that if the settlor or testator has chosen the objects by reference to a description that
cannot be described as sensible, this will not invalidate the trust. So, for example, there is
nothing inherently wrong with a settlor creating a trust of £1,000 to be divided equally
amongst those members of his cricket club who have ginger hair.

4.4.2 FIXED TRUSTS SUBJECT TO A CONDITION

(i) The essential test of certainty

A fixed trust can also arise where the trustees are obliged to distribute trust property to
beneficiaries subject to whether or not a particular condition has been satisfied. This condition must be certain as well. The test of certainty varies depending on whether the condition is a condition precedent, which needs to be satisfied before the property can be
distributed, or a condition subsequent, in which case, if the condition is satisfied, a beneficiary will no longer be entitled to the trust property. Whether a condition is characterized as being precedent or subsequent may sometimes be difficult to determine and raises
subtle issues of construction of the language used.

Condition subsequent

A stricter test of certainty is applied to conditions subsequent, whereby a vested interest
in trust property is defeated by a subsequent event, than to conditions precedent.[114] A
condition subsequent will be valid only if it can be known with certainty from the start the
exact event that will result in the defeat of the beneficiary's interest.[115] If this cannot be established, the condition will be void.[116] For example, in *Clayton v Ramsden*,[117] a condition
subsequent that would have the effect of forfeiting property held on trust if the beneficiary
were to marry a 'person not of the Jewish faith' was void for uncertainty as to the meaning
of being a member of that faith. A similarly strict approach was adopted in *Re Jones*,[118] in
which half the money held on trust for the testator's daughter was to be forfeited if she had
a social or other relationship with a named person. This was held to be void for uncertainty, because a relationship could encompass 'the existence of a relative state of facts between two people', which was considered might extend to two people standing next to each
other in a bus queue.[119] The condition was void even though the trustees were expressly
identified as being the arbiters of whether the daughter had entered into such a relationship,[120] and even though the court had suggested a definition of what might constitute a
relationship, albeit a very wide definition.

Although the accepted approach to conditions subsequent is that they should be construed strictly, more recent cases have tended to adopt a more benevolent approach to
construction. So, in *Re Tepper's Will Trusts*,[121] beneficiaries were entitled to income from
the testator's estate when they reached the age of 25, provided that they 'did not marry
outside of the Jewish faith'. This was characterized as being a condition subsequent and it
was to be valid only if it could be determined with certainty what was meant by the 'Jewish
faith'. Scott J recognized that this could be considered to be conceptually uncertain, as had
been concluded in *Clayton v Ramsden*, but he was willing to have regard to extrinsic evidence to resolve the uncertainty, which involved him asking what the 'testator sitting in his

---

[114] *Blathwayt v Lord Cawley* [1976] AC 397, 429 (Lord Cross).
[115] *Clavering v Ellison* (1859) 7 HLC 707, 725 (Lord Cranworth).
[116] *Clayton v Ramsden* [1943] AC 320; *Re Jones* [1953] Ch 125.
[117] [1943] AC 320.   [118] [1953] 1 Ch 125 .   [119] Ibid., 126.
[120] See further Section 4.4.6.(i), p. 97.   [121] [1987] Ch 358.

armchair' might have meant by 'the Jewish faith'. In *Blathwayt v Lord Cawley*,[122] a condition subsequent that would result in the forfeiture of a beneficial interest if the beneficiary were to become a Roman Catholic was held to be sufficiently certain. These cases indicate that the courts appear now to be more concerned with respecting the wishes of the settlor or testator by upholding the condition subsequent if they can.

It is only necessary to consider whether the condition subsequent is conceptually certain; it is not necessary to consider matters such as evidential certainty or the size of the class, because these are negating, rather than entitling, conditions. In other words, the beneficiary already has an interest under a trust that is subsequently forfeited if the condition is satisfied. The condition is either certain and valid, or uncertain and invalid.

Condition precedent

A condition precedent, which must be satisfied before property can be distributed, will be valid if it can be said of just one person that they satisfy the condition. This was recognized in *Re Barlow's Will Trusts*,[123] in which the testatrix had left some pictures in her will on trust for sale, but had directed that her executor should allow any members of her family or her friends to buy them at a lower value. The key question was whether it was clear who her 'friends' were or whether this direction was void for uncertainty. It was held that this was sufficiently clear. Although it was accepted that 'friends' was not conceptually certain for discretionary trusts or fiduciary powers,[124] because there are many degrees of friendship ranging from an intimate relationship to a mere acquaintance, and it was not clear what the testatrix had in mind in this case, it was held that this was not the relevant test to be applied when determining whether a condition precedent was valid. Rather, in this context, it was sufficient that one person undoubtedly fulfilled the condition and it did not matter that it was difficult to say whether or not anybody else did.[125] Consequently, 'friends' was sufficiently certain as a description for a condition precedent because there would be some people with whom the testatrix was so close that anybody would characterize them as friends. Similarly, a gift to anybody who is 'tall' would be difficult to define comprehensively, but some people would easily be able to show that they satisfy the condition, which would therefore be valid.

This approach to the validity of conditions precedent must be right. There is no obligation on the trustee to survey the class,[126] but rather the onus is placed on the object to show that they satisfy the condition. If the object is able to show this, the trustee will be obliged to transfer the property to that object. So, in *Re Barlow's Will Trust*, the direction in the will created an option for friends of the testatrix to purchase pictures from her collection; it did not create a class of objects. The trustee was not required to bring this option to the attention of all of the testator's friends, and anybody wishing to exercise the option bore the burden of proving that they were a friend and so satisfied the condition. Only if the trustees considered that the burden had been reasonably satisfied would they be required to sell a picture at the reduced price. If the trustees were unsure whether an applicant was a friend according to this test, they could apply to the court for directions, although it is unclear how the court could resolve this problem if the trustees could not.

This laxer test of certainty for transfers subject to a condition precedent is justified simply because the test is being used as a threshold requirement for a particular object to establish an entitlement to the property. The fact that the concept might be uncertain so that others could not meet the threshold should not prevent those who can show that they do from obtaining the property and so giving effect to the settlor's intent.

---

[122] [1976] AC 397.   [123] [1979] 1 WLR 278.
[124] See Section 4.4.3.(ii), p. 91 and Section 4.4.4.(ii), p. 96.   [125] See *Re Allen* [1953] Ch 810.
[126] As there is for discretionary trusts, see Section 14.2.2.(i), p. 403.

(ii) Conceptual certainty

Lord Denning, in *Re Tuck's Settlement Trust*,[127] recognized that conceptual uncertainty would not render a condition precedent void, whereas it would invalidate a condition subsequent. But it is unclear why this should be so. If the concept underlying the condition is uncertain so that it can never be established whether anybody satisfies it, it is effectively void. The better view therefore is that conceptual uncertainty will render any condition ineffective, either as a matter of law or simply in practice.[128]

(iii) Evidential certainty

Since the burden of proving that the condition has been satisfied is borne by the object, evidential uncertainty will not invalidate the condition, but will simply mean that the condition cannot be shown to have been satisfied by that particular object.

(iv) Ascertainability

The fact that an object cannot be ascertained will not invalidate the condition, since the object needs to establish that the condition has been satisfied. If, however, no object can be ascertained, the condition will lapse and the property will pass to those entitled to the residue.

(v) Size of the class

Since the burden is placed on the object to establish that the condition is satisfied, it is difficult to conceive that a fixed trust subject to such a condition will be administratively unworkable from the perspective of the trustee, by virtue of the size of the class.

(vi) Capriciousness

Although there is no authority on the point, presumably if the condition can be characterized as capricious, in the sense that the settlor or testator had no sensible intent for imposing it, the condition should be disregarded.

4.4.3 DISCRETIONARY TRUSTS

(i) The essential test of certainty

In a discretionary trust, the trustees are given a discretion as to which objects are to be benefited by distribution of trust property and in what proportion.[129] Confusingly, this type of trust is sometimes described as a 'trust power',[130] since there is an obligation to make an appointment, but the trustee has a discretion as to who will benefit. This power must be exercised by the trustees, failing which it will need to be exercised by the court. In order for the power to be exercised, it is essential that the trustees know from the outset who the potential beneficiaries might be. If this is unclear, the trust will be void for uncertainty.[131]

It is consequently important to have a clear test of certainty of objects for discretionary trusts. Initially, no distinction was drawn by the courts between fixed trusts and

---

[127] [1978] Ch 49, 60.

[128] Although the conceptual uncertainty may be resolved, for example by referring the matter to a third party to define the concept. See Section 4.4.6.(ii), p. 99.

[129] See Section 3.7.8.(ii), p. 66. For analysis of the obligation to exercise this discretion, see Section 14.2.2.(i), p. 403.

[130] For criticism of the use of this term in this context, see Bartlett and Stebbing, 'Trust powers: a reappraisal' [1984] Conv 227.   [131] *Sprange v Barnard* (1789) 2 Bro CC 585.

discretionary trusts, so that the same complete list test of beneficiaries was used for both types of trust.[132] This rule was thought to be necessary in order to make a distribution possible by the court if the trustees failed to make a selection in breach of trust. In such circumstances, it was assumed that the court would apply the equitable maxim that 'Equity is equality'[133] and would authorize distribution of the trust property amongst all of the objects equally;[134] such distribution would only be possible if a complete list of the beneficiaries could be drawn up.

But satisfying the complete list test causes many more difficulties for discretionary trusts than for fixed trusts. This is because fixed trusts tend to involve only a small number of objects. Discretionary trusts, however, could involve many more objects. So, for example, a trust to distribute amongst such of the inhabitants of a town as the trustees wish, would be void for uncertainty according to the fixed list test because of the difficulties in listing such a substantial number of objects, but also because the nature of the class is likely to fluctuate as people move into and out of the town, are born or die. Consequently, the House of Lords in *McPhail v Doulton*[135] rejected the fixed list test of certainty of objects for discretionary trusts. This is because, if the trustees fail to exercise their discretion, the court will be willing to find a solution to the problem without resorting to the maxim that 'Equity is equality'. The general significance of this maxim was doubted by Lord Wilberforce in *McPhail v Doulton*,[136] especially because it would rarely accord with the intention of the settlor. Indeed, as he recognized, in some trusts equal division among many will be beneficial to nobody, since the trust assets would be disbursed so thinly as to be essentially worthless. In fact, as Lord Wilberforce identified, there are many cases in which equal division of trust assets has not taken place.[137]

The complete list test is not totally irrelevant to discretionary trusts, but will be applicable only where it appears that the settlor's intent is that, if the trustee does not make a selection from the objects, there will be division among them all, whether equally or in different proportions.[138] Such a construction of the settlor's intent would be available only where the list of potential objects is small. Although it has been suggested[139] that, if it were not possible to satisfy the complete list test from the start, this type of trust would immediately be void, the better view is that it should be void only if the trustee fails to make a selection within a reasonable time and if, at that point, it is not possible to compile a complete list of objects. This would at least mean that the settlor's intent is more likely to be fulfilled.

To determine what the general test of certainty of objects is for discretionary trusts, it is necessary to consider with some care the decision of the House of Lords in *McPhail v Doulton*.[140] In that case the settlor established a fund for the benefit of the employees and ex-employees of a company, and their relatives and dependants. It was recognized that the settlor had purported to create a discretionary trust, but the validity of this trust turned on whether 'relatives' and 'dependants' were sufficiently certain objects. Lord Wilberforce, giving the leading judgment, held that it was sufficient that it could be said with certainty that any given individual was or was not a member of the relevant class, and it was not necessary to ascertain everybody who was in the class.[141] This is sometimes known as the 'given postulant test'.[142] It is important to stress that 'any' in 'any given person' does not

---

[132] *IRC v Broadway Cottages Trust* [1955] Ch 20.   [133] See Section 2.14, p. 36.
[134] *Burrough v Philcox* (1840) 5 My & Cr 72.   [135] [1971] AC 424.   [136] Ibid., 451.
[137] See e.g. *Moseley v Moseley* (1673) Cas temp Finch 53; *Warburton v Warburton* (1702) 4 Bro Parl Cas 1.
[138] *Burrough v Philcox* (1840) 5 Myl & Cr 72.   [139] See Emery (see n. 108), 571.
[140] [1971] AC 424.
[141] Ibid., 454. Note Matthews, 'The comparative importance of the rule in *Saunders v Vautier*' (2006) 122 LQR 266, 276, who suggests that this test should also apply to fixed trusts.
[142] The language of Harman J in *Re Gestetner Settlement* [1953] Ch 672, 688.

mean that it is enough that one person satisfies the test, but instead refers to anybody at all who might be considered to be a potential object.[143]

Following the decision of the House of Lords, the case was remitted to the Chancery Division to determine whether the trust was valid in the light of Lord Wilberforce's test. Although this case is known as *Re Baden's Deed Trusts (No 2)*,[144] it is the same case as *McPhail v Doulton*. Both the trial judge and the Court of Appeal concluded that the discretionary trust was valid, by applying Lord Wilberforce's test, but that test was interpreted in different ways by the three judges, both as regards the determination of conceptual certainty and especially as regards evidential certainty.

(ii) Conceptual certainty

The test of certainty of objects will not be satisfied if it is not possible to define the description of the class with sufficient clarity.[145]

In *Re Baden (No 2)*, the Court of Appeal recognized that both 'relatives' and 'dependants' were conceptually certain. 'Dependants' were defined as those who are wholly or partly financially dependent on somebody else.[146] 'Relatives' were defined by Sachs and Megaw LJJ as descendants from a common ancestor,[147] whereas Stamp LJ defined them as the next of kin or nearest blood relations.[148] Subsequently, in *Re Barlow's Will Trusts*,[149] the normal meaning of 'family' was considered to be those related by blood. Which definition is adopted could be significant, since defining 'relatives' as blood relations creates a much smaller potential class than defining them by reference to a common ancestor.

Sachs LJ usefully considered whether other concepts might meet the test of conceptual certainty and concluded that the description of an object as 'someone under a moral obligation' was not conceptually certain, whereas 'first cousins' would be.[150] Many other descriptions of a class could be used and it will be necessary to determine in each case whether the concept is sufficiently certain. So, for example, 'an inhabitant of West Yorkshire' has been considered to be conceptually certain,[151] as has 'being of Jewish blood', which has been defined as being of 'some Jewish blood'.[152] A trust for 'my friends' would presumably be considered to be conceptually uncertain because there are so many different degrees of friendship, ranging from intimacy to mere acquaintance; without more, it will be unclear what degree of relationship was intended by the creator of the trust.[153] Nevertheless, in *Re Barlow's Will Trusts*,[154] Browne-Wilkinson J did provide some guidance as to the definition of 'a friend', albeit in the different context of determining whether a condition precedent is certain.[155] He considered that the reasonable characteristics of friendship include a long-standing relationship, which was social rather than business or professional, and in which the parties met frequently when they had an opportunity to do so. In the light of this attempt at a definition of the concept of friendship, there is a strong argument that the concept of 'a friend' is sufficiently certain even for a discretionary trust, although this point has not yet been resolved by the courts and Browne-Wilkinson J did assume that 'friends' was not sufficiently certain for the purposes of establishing a discretionary trust.

---

[143] *McPhail v Doulton* [1971] AC 424, 453 (Lord Wilberforce).   [144] [1973] Ch 9.
[145] Ibid., 19 (Sachs LJ). See also *McPhail v Doulton* [1971] AC 427, 457 (Lord Wilberforce).
[146] [1973] Ch 9, 21 (Sachs LJ) and 30 (Stamp LJ).   [147] Ibid., 22 (Sachs LJ) and 22 (Megaw LJ).
[148] Ibid., 29, following *Harding v Glynn* (1739) 1 Atk 469.   [149] [1979] 1 WLR 278.
[150] [1973] Ch 9, 20 (Sachs LJ).
[151] *R v District Auditor, ex p West Yorkshire Metropolitan County Council* [1986] RVR 24.
[152] *Re Tuck's Settlement Trust* [1978] Ch 49, 64 (Lord Russell of Killowen). See also Section 4.4.6.(ii), p.99.
[153] *Re Barlow's Will Trusts* [1979] 1 WLR 278, 281 (Browne-Wilkinson J).   [154] Ibid.
[155] See Section 4.4.2.(i), p. 88.

(iii) Evidential certainty

In *Re Baden (No 2)*, the three judges all agreed that the discretionary trust was evidentially certain, but used very different tests to reach this conclusion.

Sachs LJ concluded that the courts would never be defeated by evidential uncertainty.[156] He recognized that the given postulant test was concerned only with conceptual certainty and that, once the meaning of the class was clear, it was simply a question of fact on the evidence whether a person fell within that class. If a particular person were not proved to be within the class, then they should be considered to be outside it. But this would not render the trust void; it would simply mean that the particular person was not an object under the trust.

Megaw LJ adopted a very different approach to evidential certainty.[157] He concluded that it was not necessary to show that a particular person either was or was not a member of the class, because it was not necessary to ascertain every member of the class for a discretionary trust to be valid. Rather, he suggested that it was enough that it could be shown of a substantial number of objects that they were within the class. Consequently, the trust would be valid even though, as regards a significant number of potential objects, it could be proved neither that they were nor that they were not within the class. He considered that what is meant by 'a substantial number' is a matter of common sense and degree in respect of the particular trust.

Stamp LJ concluded that it was not enough to be able to show that one person fell within or outside the class; rather, the test of evidential certainty required it to be shown of any given person that they either were or were not within the class.[158] This does not, however, require a complete list of objects to be drawn up. Instead, it would be enough to show of anybody who might potentially be an object that they were or were not an object, but if there were uncertainty about any one person as to whether or not they were within the class, the trust would fail. According to this test, if 'relatives' were defined as descendants of a common ancestor, Stamp LJ would have held the trust to be void, because this relationship would be very difficult to prove. However, since he defined the concept as meaning the next of kin, he concluded that it was evidentially certain.

In determining which of these three approaches to evidential certainty is preferable, it is important to go back to the essential test identified by Lord Wilberforce in *McPhail v Doulton*, namely whether 'it could be said with certainty whether any given individual was or was not a member of the class, and [the trust] did not fail simply because it was impossible to ascertain every member of the class'.[159] This suggests that it is not enough that the given object cannot be proved to be a member of the particular class, as Sachs LJ suggested; neither does Megaw LJ's substantial numbers test accord with the test of Lord Wilberforce. Stamp LJ's approach is most consistent with the test propounded by Lord Wilberforce. Megaw LJ had suggested that this was not an appropriate test to adopt because it would involve a return to the fixed list test. But that is not correct: the second part of Lord Wiberforce's crucial dictum makes it clear that it is not necessary to ascertain the whole of the class. But the first part of the dictum makes clear that it must be possible to say of any given person that they were or were not within the class. If this cannot be shown, it follows that the trustees could not be sure whether they should distribute to that person or not, and also what the range of the class might be. The trust should consequently be held to be void for uncertainty of objects, unless it is possible to resolve this evidential uncertainty in some other way.[160]

---

[156] [1973] Ch 9, 20.   [157] Ibid., 24.
[158] Ibid., 28.   [159] [1971] AC 424, 454.
[160] As to which, see Section 4.4.6, p. 97.

But even though Stamp LJ's approach is the most consistent with the given postulant test propounded by Lord Wilberforce, it does mean that discretionary trusts are more likely to be found to be void, and this would not be consistent with the fundamental principle that the settlor's or testator's intent will be respected if at all possible by upholding the trust. In the light of that policy, the approach of Sachs LJ is to be preferred, because this removes evidential certainty as a means of invalidating trusts. His approach places the evidential burden on the potential object, who is in the best position to bear it. If that object cannot discharge the burden, they should not be considered to be an object and should not benefit under the trust—but this will not prevent anybody else from proving that they do fall within the class of objects.

(iv) Ascertainability of objects

The fact that it cannot be established where a particular object is, or even whether they are still alive,[161] does not invalidate the trust. Rather, the inability to ascertain the location of an object simply means that that person cannot receive a distribution from the trust.

(v) Size of the class

A further consideration when assessing certainty of objects relates to whether the class of objects is so wide that it cannot be considered to be anything like a class.[162] In such circumstances, the trust will be considered to be administratively unworkable and will be void. Lord Wilberforce in *McPhail v Doulton*[163] tentatively suggested that a discretionary trust for the benefit of 'all the residents of Greater London' would be administratively unworkable and so void.

In *R v District Auditor, ex p West Yorkshire Metropolitan County Council*,[164] this principle was used for the first time to invalidate a trust. In that case, a local authority purported to create a discretionary trust for the benefit of any, some, or all of the inhabitants of the county of West Yorkshire, which amounted to 2.5 million objects. The judge was willing to assume that the definition of the class was conceptually certain, although he did acknowledge that there might be some argument about what 'inhabitant' meant. He considered, however, the size of the class to be so wide that it was incapable of forming anything like a class and so was administratively unworkable.

If the size of the class is what makes a trust administratively unworkable,[165] it is then necessary to determine how big the class must be before it is unworkable. It has been recognized that a class of hundreds of thousands is not inherently defective,[166] but a class of 2.5 million is clearly too big. In *Re Harding*,[167] it was recognized that a trust for the black community of four London boroughs would have been treated as void for being administratively unworkable had it not been a charitable trust.[168] Further, in *Re Hay's Settlement Trust*,[169] Sir Robert Megarry V-C recognized that a discretionary trust for anyone other than a few specified people would be administratively unworkable.

But the key issue here concerns why a trust should be void because the class is too wide. A variety of suggestions have been made by judges and commentators, as follows:

(1) The trustees will not be able to perform their duty to ascertain the range of objects[170] if the size of the class is so large that it cannot be treated as anything like a class.

---

[161] *McPhail v Doulton* [1971] AC 424, 457 (Lord Wilberforce).
[162] *Re Gulbenkian's Settlements* [1970] AC 508, 518 (Lord Reid) and 524 (Lord Upjohn); *McPhail v Doulton* [1971] AC 424, 457 (Lord Wilberforce). [163] [1971] AC 424, 457.
[164] [1986] RVR 24. [165] See *Re Hay's Settlement Trusts* [1982] 1 WLR 202, 213–14 (Megarry V-C).
[166] *Re Baden (No 2)* [1973] Ch 9, 20 (Sachs LJ). [167] [2007] EWHC 3(Ch), [2008] Ch 235.
[168] See further Section 6.1.2.(iii), p. 147. [169] [1982] 1 WLR 202, 213.
[170] A duty recognized by Lord Wilberforce in *McPhail v Doulton* [1971] AC 424, 449.

But it was recognized by Sachs LJ in *Re Baden (No 2)*[171] that the size of the class can be infinitely variable and that the trustees need only to be aware of the width of the field so that they can adapt their method of selecting objects. This suggests that trustees are able to exercise their discretion even if the class is very large.

(2) If the trustees fail to exercise their discretion, the court would not be able to execute a trust with a very large class of objects.[172] But it is unclear why this is necessarily the case. Indeed, there are alternative mechanisms available to the court other than judicial execution of the trust, such as appointing replacement trustees or determining a scheme of arrangement.[173]

(3) There is no criterion for the exercise of the discretion where the class is large, so it is not possible to ascertain what the settlor's intention is.[174] But many discretionary trusts lack such a reference point, regardless of the size of the class. For example, a trust for the settlor's children, to be distributed in accordance with the trustee's absolute discretion, will be valid even though no guidance is given as to how the discretion is to be exercised. But, at least in such a case, the small size of the class does make it easier for the trustee to weigh up the claims of all of the objects.

(4) The principle of administrative workability might reflect a policy against excessive delegation[175] to the trustees by the settlor or testator who are expected to describe the objects with sufficient clarity.

Since no consistent rationale for the size of the class rule can be identified and because it is inconsistent with the fundamental principle of respecting the settlor's or testator's intention in creating the trust, this rule should be rejected[176] and the issues instead should be examined when considering the test of evidential certainty.[177] It was concluded earlier[178] that the preferable interpretation of evidential certainty is that, if an object cannot be proved to be within a class, they should be considered to be outside it. This should be a sufficient filter to deal with the administrative workability problem. This can be illustrated by a discretionary trust for relatives, as in *McPhail v Doulton*. This is conceptually certain since 'relatives' can be defined as all descendants from a common ancestor. This could constitute millions of people and even billions, but most people will not be able to prove that they are related to the settlor, and this should be sufficient to make the exercise of the trustees' discretion workable. Admittedly, with better research tools available for tracing a family tree, especially using the Internet, the class of provable objects will be larger, but this should not render such a trust void. And it must not be forgotten that a discretionary trust for relatives was held to be valid in *Re Baden (No 2)*.

(vi) Capriciousness

A discretionary trust may also be treated as void on the ground of capriciousness, in that the settlor had no sensible intent in establishing the trust. In *R v District Auditor, ex p West Yorkshire Metropolitan County Council*,[179] it was recognized that the Council did have a sensible reason for wishing to benefit the inhabitants of West Yorkshire, so that the discretionary trust was not capricious. But there will be circumstances under which the

---

[171] [1973] Ch 9, 20.
[172] *Morice v Bishop of Durham* (1805) 10 Ves 522, 527 (Lord Eldon); *Re Manisty's Settlement* [1974] Ch 17, 29 (Templeman J); *R v District Auditor, ex p West Yorkshire Metropolitan County Council* [1986] RVR 24.
[173] See further Section 14.2.3.(i), p. 404.   [174] Grbich (see n. 3), p. 652; Emery (see n. 108), p. 558.
[175] Harpum, 'Administrative unworkability and purpose trusts' (1986) 45 CLJ 391.
[176] See also McKay, '*Re Baden* and the third class of uncertainty' [1974] Conv 269.
[177] Hardcastle, 'Administrative unworkability: a reassessment of an abiding problem' [1990] Conv 24.
[178] See Section 4.4.3.(iii), p. 92.   [179] [1986] RVR 24.

creation of a discretionary trust can be considered to be capricious. Consideration should be given to the nature of the class to determine whether the settlor had a good reason to benefit that particular class; if it is arbitrary, the trust is likely to be void. So, for example, in *Re Manisty's Settlement*,[180] Templeman J—albeit in the context of a case concerning fiduciary powers rather than discretionary trusts—suggested that a power given to trustees to benefit the 'residents of Greater London' would be capricious because the terms of the power negatives any sensible intention on the part of the settlor. But, why should benefiting the residents of Greater London be capricious when benefiting the inhabitants of West Yorkshire is not? Numbers may be one reason, but the connection between the settlor and the chosen objects must be significant as well. In *West Yorkshire*, the settlor was the county council for that area, which was consequently especially interested in the needs of those living there. If a settlor chooses to establish a trust for the residents of an area with which they had no connection and who they had no reason to benefit, this could be considered to be a capricious motive, as was indeed recognized by Templeman J in *Re Manisty* itself:

> The terms of the power negative any sensible intention on the part of the settlor … If the settlor had any … sensible intention or expectation, he would not have required the trustees to consider only an accidental conglomeration of persons who have no discernible link with the settlor … The settlor gives the trustees an unlimited power which they can exercise sensibly, not a power limited to what may be described as a 'sensible' class, but a power limited to a class, membership of which is accidental and irrelevant to any settled purpose or to any method of limiting or selecting beneficiaries.[181]

No discretionary trust has, however, been invalidated for capriciousness.

4.4.4 FIDUCIARY POWERS

(i) Essential test of certainty

Fiduciary powers are held by trustees and other fiduciaries. They are different from discretionary trusts, or trust powers, because there is no obligation on the trustee to distribute among the objects, although, because the trustee is a fiduciary, they must consider the exercise of the power.[182] The essential test of certainty of objects for fiduciary powers was settled in *Re Gulbenkian's Settlements*,[183] which recognized that the test was met if it could be determined that any individual was or was not a member of the class. In that case, a settlement contained a power to appoint in favour of Gulbenkian, his wife, children, remoter issue, or anybody who employed him or with whom he resided. This was held by the House of Lords not to be void for uncertainty because it could be said of any given person that they were or were not a member of the class. In reaching this conclusion, the House of Lords rejected the approach of the Court of Appeal[184] that it was sufficient that it could be shown that just one person fell within the class.[185] The need for a clear test of certainty was recognized by the House of Lords because, although it could not compel trustees to exercise a fiduciary power, people who are entitled to the fund in default of its exercise are entitled to restrain the trustees from exercising the power in favour of objects who are not within the class. Consequently, it is vital that both trustees and the court are able to determine who are and who are not objects of the power.

---

[180] [1974] Ch 17, 27.   [181] Ibid.
[182] See Section 3.7.8.(iii), p. 67. For analysis of the exercise of the power, see Section 14.2.3.(ii), p. 404.
[183] [1970] AC 508.   [184] [1968] Ch 126, 134 (Lord Denning MR) and 138 (Winn LJ).
[185] This test is still used to determine the validity of conditions precedent. See Section 4.4.2.(i), p. 88.

(ii) Conceptual certainty

In *Re Gulbenkian's Settlements*,[186] the objects of the power included those with whom a particular person had been 'residing'. It was held that this was not conceptually uncertain because the court could determine whether a particular person matched the description. But this does appear to be at odds with the stricter approach to conceptual certainty adopted in *Re Baden (No 2)*, in which particular concepts needed a clear definition to be valid. That may be because *Re Baden (No 2)* involved a discretionary trust and Gulbenkian a fiduciary power or, more likely, that *Re Baden (No 2)* was decided slightly later, by which time the courts had adopted a more sophisticated approach to the problem of certainty of objects.

(iii) Evidential certainty

Presumably, the same test of evidential certainty applies to fiduciary powers as that which applies to discretionary trusts.[187]

(iv) Ascertainability

As with discretionary trusts, the fact that a particular person is an object, but their whereabouts or existence cannot be ascertained, cannot defeat the validity of the power. This is even clearer for a fiduciary power, since there is not even an obligation to exercise the power. If the trustees were to want to exercise the power in favour of somebody who could not be located, the power simply could not be exercised.

(v) Size of the class

Whether a fiduciary power can be void for administrative unworkability has been a controversial matter.[188] Fiduciary powers have been recognized as valid where the trustees are able to exercise the power in favour of the whole world, other than members of a limited class,[189] or even to such people as the trustees think fit without any limit at all.[190] It follows that a fiduciary power cannot be struck down for being administratively unworkable simply because of the breadth of the class.[191] This is surely right. Bearing in mind that the essence of a fiduciary power is that the fiduciary only needs to consider its exercise, the fact that a class is very broad does not prevent the trustee from fulfilling their duty. A discretionary trust can be considered to be different, because the power of distribution must be exercised.

(vi) Capriciousness

A fiduciary power may be invalidated by virtue of being capricious in the sense that there was no sensible intention of the settlor to benefit the objects. A power will be characterized as capricious if there is no discernible link with the settlor,[192] but it will not be capricious simply because of the size of the class. So a power to benefit anybody in the world will not be treated as capricious because no class that could be considered to be capricious has

---

[186] [1970] AC 508.   [187] See Section 4.4.3.(iii), p. 92.

[188] *Blausten v IRC* [1972] Ch 256, 272, in which Buckley LJ suggested, obiter, that a power might be invalid for administrative unworkability.

[189] *Re Manisty's Settlement* [1974] Ch 17; *Re Hay's Settlement Trust* [1982] 1 WLR 202.

[190] *Re Beatty* [1990] 1 WLR 1503.

[191] *Re Hay's Settlement Trust* [1982] 1 WLR 202, 212, in which Megarry V-C appeared to confine the administrative workability principle to discretionary trusts. But note Gardner, 'Fiduciary powers in Toytown' (1991) 107 LQR 214, who suggests that the decision in *Mettoy Pension Trustees Ltd v Evans* [1990] 1 WLR 1587, which appears to allow discretionary trust remedies for fiduciary powers of appointment (see Section 11.2.3.(ii), p. 323), might mean that the administrative workability test should also apply to fiduciary powers.

[192] *Re Manisty's Settlement* [1974] Ch 17, 29.

been identified.[193] But a power to distribute to anybody who has read this book might be capricious, depending on context, because membership of the class appears to be accidental and irrelevant to any purpose or method of limiting or selecting objects.[194] But, if it is legitimate to have a power for anybody in the world or almost anybody in the world, where there is no discernible link between the objects and the settlor, why should a power for any smaller class be regarded as capricious? If the settlor wants to benefit only those who have read this book what is wrong with that? Why should a settlor's purpose in giving the power be limited by the need to be sensible? The test of capriciousness is unacceptably vague, is inconsistent with the policy of respecting the settlor's intent, and should be rejected.

4.4.5 SUMMARY OF THE LAW

The various tests relating to certainty of objects apply as shown in Table 4.1, in which a tick (✓) indicates that it is relevant and a cross (×) indicates that it is not relevant.

Table 4.1 Tests relating to certainty of objects

	Essential test	Conceptual certainty	Evidential certainty	Ascertainability	Size of the class	Capriciousness
Fixed trust	Complete list	✓	✓	×	×	×
Fixed trust: subject to condition precedent	One person satisfies condition	×	×	×	×	?
Discretionary trust	Any given individual	✓	× (?)	×	✓	✓ (?)
Fiduciary Power	Any given individual	✓	× (?)	×	×	✓

4.4.6 RESOLVING UNCERTAINTY

There are a variety of methods by virtue of which uncertainty as to objects might be resolved.

(i) Trustees as arbiter

The creator of the trust might give to the trustees an express power to resolve uncertainty relating to the identity of objects. There is, however, a need to balance two conflicting principles where the validity of such a power is considered. First, there is the principle against excessive delegation to the trustee by the settlor and especially the testator, who cannot rely on the trustee to make the will for them, for example by saying that all of the testator's property is to be distributed by the trustee as they wish.[195] Further, it is not acceptable to exclude the jurisdiction of the court to determine whether the objects are certain. Against this is the principle that the settlor's or testator's intention should be respected, so that if the creator of the trust wishes the trustees to be the arbiters who will resolve uncertainty, then so be it.

---

[193] *Re Hay's Settlement Trust* [1982] 1 WLR 202, 212 (Megarry V-C).

[194] *Re Manisty's Settlement* [1974] Ch 17, 26 (Templeman J).

[195] *In Bonis Smith* (1869) LR 1 P & D 717 (Lord Penzance); Gordon, 'Delegation of will-making powers' (1953) 69 LQR 334.

This conflict of principles has tended to be resolved by recognizing that trustees are able to be arbiters about questions of evidential certainty, but not conceptual certainty. So, for example, in *Re Coxen*,[196] it was held to be legitimate for the testator to allow the trustees to determine whether a condition for revoking a gift had been satisfied, as long the terms of the condition were defined with sufficient certainty. So, in that case, the trustees held a house on trust to permit the testator's wife to live in it, but the house was to be transferred to those entitled to the residuary estate if the trustees considered that she had ceased to live there permanently. It was held that this condition was not void for uncertainty, because the decision as to whether she had ceased to live there permanently was legitimately for the trustees to determine and because the meaning of 'ceasing to live somewhere permanently' was considered to be conceptually certain. The opinion of the trustees was simply relevant to determine evidential certainty, namely whether the condition was satisfied on the facts. Similarly, in *Dundee General Hospitals Board of Management v Walker*,[197] the House of Lords, in an appeal from Scotland, recognized that it was valid for a trust to state that whether or not a hospital had been taken over by the State could be determined by the trustees in their sole and absolute discretion. But it was noted that the trustees would need to act reasonably in determining this: an important check on the otherwise unfettered discretion of the trustees.

But, if the defining concept is unclear, leaving it to the trustees to define the concept will not be sufficient to save the trust. So, for example, in *Re Wright's Will Trusts*,[198] it was held that a residuary gift to trustees to use it in 'their absolute discretion for such people and institutions as they think may have helped me or my late husband' was void for being conceptually uncertain. Similarly, in *Re Jones*,[199] a fund was held on trust for the testator's daughter, but she would forfeit half of her rights to the fund if, in the opinion of the trustees, she had a 'social or other relationship' with a named person. The notion of 'social or other relationship' was considered to be conceptually uncertain and this could not be resolved by reliance on the trustee's opinion as to what this meant. Consequently, this condition subsequent was held to be void. In *Re Wynn*,[200] the trustees were empowered by a clause in a will to resolve all questions of doubt arising from the execution of the trust. This was held to be void because the right of a beneficiary to have uncertainty resolved by the court could not be removed by the creator of the trust.

In *Re Leek*,[201] Sachs LJ recognized that a power in a discretionary trust to appoint to anybody whom the trustee considered to have a 'moral claim' on the settlor meant that the trustees were the arbiters and could determine who had a moral claim. This might be considered to be incorrect because this appears to make the trustees the arbiters of conceptual certainty. But, in fact, subtle construction of the power suggests that the right result was achieved. A distinction needs to be drawn between a trust for those who have a moral claim on the settlor, with those having a 'moral claim' being determined by the trustees, and a trust for those whom the trustees think have a moral claim on the settlor. The first construction involves the trustees defining 'moral claim' and this is not acceptable. The second construction involves the objects being those whom the trustees think have a moral claim on the settlor, in which case the trustees are not the arbiters of whether the power applies, but rather form an essential part of the definition of the power.[202] This construction was adopted in *Re Coates*,[203] in which it was recognized that a power given by the testator to his wife in his will to pay a small sum of money if she 'feels that I have

---

196 [1948] Ch 747.   197 [1952] 1 All ER 896.   198 [1981] LS Gaz 841.
199 [1953] Ch 125.   200 [1952] Ch 271.   201 [1969] 1 Ch 563.
202 Which suggests that *Re Wright's Will Trust* [1981] LS Gaz 841, discussed in Section 4.4.6.(i), p. 98, was decided incorrectly.   203 [1955] Ch 495.

forgotten any friends' was not void for uncertainty. It was recognized that the wife could determine whether the testator had forgotten to include any friends in his will. In other words, the relevant concept was not 'friends I have forgotten', but 'those people whom my wife considers are friends I have forgotten'.

(ii) Third party as arbiter

It has been recognized that it is acceptable to resolve questions of evidential uncertainty relating to the identification of objects by referring the matter to a third party whom the settlor has made an arbiter of the matter. So, for example, in *Re Tuck's Settlement Trusts*,[204] any uncertainty about whether a person was married to an 'approved wife of Jewish blood' who worshipped according to the Jewish faith could legitimately be resolved by referring the matter to a chief rabbi, as the settlement had authorized. Lord Denning drew an analogy with the law of contract, under which parties who agree to refer a matter of doubt or difficulty to a third party for decision are bound by that decision. Similarly, he considered that a settlor or testator could leave a decision to a third party and that this would not oust the jurisdiction of the court, to which the trustee could always apply for directions.

The analogy with the law of contract is not exact, however, since, under the law of trusts, the court does have a supervisory jurisdiction for the benefit of the beneficiaries. But, as has already been seen, it is legitimate for the creator of the trust to leave the trustee to resolve questions of evidential certainty, so it should also be legitimate for such matters to be resolved by third parties. But Lord Denning went further and recognized that conceptual uncertainty could also be resolved by a third party.[205] He did not consider that this would oust the jurisdiction of the court, since trustees can still apply to the court for directions as to whether the third party has misconducted themself or has come to an unreasonable decision. The key reason for Lord Denning's decision was that the intent of the settlor or testator should be respected: if the creator of the trust wanted the objects to be defined by reference to the views of a third party, then so be it.

There is a difficult balancing act between respecting the intention of the creator of the trust and ensuring that the supervisory jurisdiction of the court is not ousted. Older decisions were more likely to reject references to trustees or third parties as arbiters of the definition of concepts;[206] the pendulum has certainly swung the other way now.[207] But there is an alternative way of analysing the use of third parties as arbiters of whether the definition of objects is uncertain: an approach adopted by Eveleigh LJ in *Re Tuck's Settlement Trusts*,[208] namely that the third party is not being used to resolve uncertainty in the definition of the class, but forms part of the definition of the class. So, for example, rather than saying that the objects are those of the Jewish faith and that, if it is uncertain who satisfies this definition, this can be resolved by the chief rabbi, instead the definition of the class is those people whom the chief rabbi considers to be of the Jewish faith. In other words, the relevant concept is not objectively those people of Jewish faith, but those people whom the chief rabbi considers to be of Jewish faith.

Whichever construction of the role of third parties is adopted, it does not follow that the supervisory jurisdiction of the court is ousted completely, because the third party can be required to give explanation to the court as to the basis for reaching their decision. If

---

[204] [1978] Ch 49.   [205] Ibid., 61.

[206] See e.g. *Re Rook* [1915] Ch 673, in which the identity of an institution was to be resolved by trustees, which was considered to be repugnant and contrary to public policy because it ousted the jurisdiction of the court.

[207] Largely prompted by the decision of the House of Lords in *Dundee General Hospitals Board of Management v Walker* [1952] 1 All ER 896. See Section 4.4.6.(i), p. 98.   [208] [1978] Ch 49.

this is found to be an unreasonable decision, the court will be able to intervene and set the interpretation of the concept aside.[209]

(iii) Severance

Where a discretionary trust is established for two classes, one of which satisfies the test of certainty and the other does not, one obvious solution is to enable the uncertain class to be severed, otherwise the whole trust will fail for uncertainty. So, for example, this might be a solution where a trust is declared for the settlor's relatives and those for whom the settlor has a moral obligation. In *Re Leek*,[210] however, Sachs LJ held that severance was not available in such circumstances, although he considered this to be unacceptable because severance is available in the law of contract. Similarly, in *Re Wright's Will Trusts*,[211] the class consisted of identifiable named charities and other bodies that could not be identified, but the Court of Appeal refused to give effect to the gift in favour of the named charities only, since no severance of the named and unidentified charities was allowed. But severance has been recognized as regards charitable trusts, where gifts have been made to charities and non-charities and is valid as regards the former only.[212]

There is no reason of logic or principle why the uncertain objects should not be severed from the certain. This would reflect the intention of the creator of the trust at least in part, rather than frustrate that intention completely.

(iv) Wide definition of beneficiaries

In *Schmidt v Rosewood Trust Ltd*,[213] the Privy Council recognized the legitimacy of the modern practice of those drafting trusts to include very widely defined classes of object, which give the trustees the widest possible discretion in determining who should benefit. The main obstacle to this would be one of administrative unworkability in exercising the discretion to appoint to objects within the class,[214] but this could be avoided if the power were fiduciary rather than a trust power, since administrative unworkability does not invalidate fiduciary powers.[215] This has been recognized through the mechanism of an intermediate power,[216] whereby the trustees have power to appoint property to anybody in the world other than a small class of excluded people. Such a power was recognized as valid in *Blausten v IRC*,[217] but only because it was possible for the trustees to specify particular objects within this class with the settlor's written consent. If this qualification had not been added, the intermediate power would have been held to be void, for two reasons: first, because the class would have been so wide as not to form a true class, and secondly, because the width of the class would prevent the trustees from considering whether to exercise the power. Both of these arguments were rejected by Megarry V-C in *Re Hay's Settlement Trust*.[218] In recognizing the validity of intermediate powers, he did not consider that the size of the class would prevent the trustees from exercising their duty, which, as regards fiduciary rather than trust powers, was simply to consider whether or not to exercise the power rather than being required to exercise it. Further, he considered that a requirement of needing the settlor's consent to specify members of the class would make no difference to the number of people who were potentially included within the class.

---

[209] *Re Coates* [1955] 1 Ch 495, 500 (Roxburgh J); *Re Tuck's Settlement Trust* [1978] Ch 49, 62 (Lord Denning).
[210] [1969] 1 Ch 563, 586.   [211] (1999) 13 TLI 48 (decided 1982).
[212] *Re Clarke* [1923] 2 Ch 407. See Section 6.4.2.(iii), p. 173.
[213] [2003] UKPC 26, [2003] 2 AC 709, [35].   [214] See Section 4.4.3.(v), p. 93.
[215] See Section 4.4.4.(v), p. 96.   [216] This is also sometimes called a 'hybrid' power.
[217] [1972] Ch 256.
[218] [1982] 1 WLR 202, 208. See also *Re Manisty's Settlement* [1974] Ch 17 and *Breakspear v Ackland* [2008] EWHC 220 (Ch), [2009] Ch 32 (Briggs J).

(v) Letter of wishes

A letter of wishes[219] is a means of communication, by a settlor to the trustees, of non-binding requests to take certain matters into account when exercising their discretionary powers.[220] Although these letters may relate to a number of different powers of trustees, they are often concerned with the power of appointment to objects of the trust. These letters can be used to avoid the dangers of having uncertain objects in trusts by referring to descriptions in a letter that are conceptually uncertain but which may assist the trustees in exercising their discretion. So, for example, the trust may be for the inhabitants of a particular neighbourhood, but the letter of wishes might state that the settlor would prefer the trustees to distribute to her friends among those living in that area. This does not bind the trustees, in that they are not required to distribute to such objects, but it can certainly be of assistance to them when determining how they should exercise their discretion.

4.4.7 ABSENCE OF CERTAINTY OF OBJECTS

If a settlor purports to declare a trust, and there is clear intention to do so and certainty of subject matter, but the objects of the trust are unclear, the express trust will be void—but what should happen to the property that will have been transferred to the trustee? It would not be appropriate for the trustee to receive this property absolutely, since we know that the settlor did not intend them to obtain the benefit of the property; the settlor intended that it be held on trust for the benefit of somebody else. It cannot be held on an express trust, simply because it is unclear who the objects of the trust are. Consequently, the logical solution is to conclude that the trustee should hold the property on trust for the settlor; this is known as a 'resulting trust'.[221] It follows that the settlor can demand the transfer of the legal title from the trustee[222] and, if the settlor so wishes, declare another trust, but this time ensuring that the objects are certain. If the trust were a testamentary trust, the trustee would hold the property for the benefit of those entitled to the deceased's residuary estate.

4.5 THE BENEFICIARY PRINCIPLE

Once it has been established that the three certainties have been established, it is then necessary to determine whether the beneficiary principle is satisfied. This requires property to be held on trust for identified beneficiaries or objects. This requirement clearly overlaps with that of certainty of objects, for if there are certain objects there must be identifiable beneficiaries. But, in fact, the beneficiary principle has a distinct function. Where, for example, a trust for the settlor's relatives is both conceptually and evidentially certain, it may still be the case that the settlor no longer has any relatives alive. Consequently, the class of beneficiaries will be empty. It follows that there will be nobody available to enforce the trust. This results in the trust being invalid, because an express trust for persons must have identifiable people in whose favour the court can decree performance.[223] This is the prime reason why beneficiaries need to be identified.

---

[219] See Section 11.2.2.(ii), p. 322.
[220] *Breakspear v Ackland* [2008] EWHC 220 (Ch), [2009] Ch 32, [5] (Briggs J).
[221] *Briggs v Penny* (1851) 3 Mac & G 546, 557 (Lord Truro LC). On the resulting trust, see Section 8.3.2.(i), p. 232.   [222] See Section 11.4, p. 334.
[223] See *Morice v Bishop of Durham* (1805) 10 Ves 522.

A logical consequence of recognizing the beneficiary principle is that an express trust must be a trust for persons. A trust for purposes will not be valid. So, in *Morice v Bishop of Durham*,[224] a trust for 'such objects of benevolence and liberality as the Bishop of Durham in his own discretion shall most approve of' was held to be void, because there were no identifiable beneficiaries.[225] Consequently, it is generally the case that a trust for purposes will not be recognized, but there are some significant exceptions to this:[226]

(1) Charitable trusts are express trusts for purposes that are valid. This is a long-standing exception to the beneficiary principle,[227] but it does not undermine the rationale of the principle, because the Attorney-General and the Charity Commission are charged with the duty of enforcing charitable trusts.

(2) Sometimes, an express trust appears to be a trust for purposes on its face, but it is possible to identify persons who will indirectly benefit from the trust and so the beneficiary principle will be satisfied.[228]

(3) Non-charitable purpose trusts have been recognized as effective in certain, very exceptional, cases. These are old cases and, although they are likely to be followed as regards their particular facts, they are unlikely to be extended, because they contravene the beneficiary principle. They have been described as 'troublesome, anomalous and aberrant'.[229] They include trusts for animals, memorials, and masses. Where such purpose trusts are valid, the purpose must be described with sufficient certainty.[230]

4.6 THE PERPETUITY RULE

4.6.1 THE RULE AGAINST REMOTENESS OF VESTING

Property must be vested in individuals within a recognized period of time, and, if it might not vest within that time, any interest in that property might be void.[231] The purpose of this rule is to prevent wealth being locked away indefinitely, otherwise the rich would be in a position to control their assets for many generations. So, for example, if Alan's will creates successive interests, with a life interest for his daughter Brenda, then for her son Clive for life, and remainder to Clive's first-born child, each interest will be valid only if it is vested in each person within the perpetuity period.[232] An interest will be vested when it does not depend on a prior condition being fulfilled, such as the beneficiary attaining a specified age, or where the benefit of the interest depends on the exercise of the trustee's discretion.

This rule about vesting of interests also applies to an equitable interest under a trust that is subject to a condition precedent before it becomes vested, so that the condition precedent must be satisfied within the perpetuity period, and if it is not, the interest will lapse.[233] The rule about remoteness of vesting also applies where an interest under a trust can be lost on the occurrence of a condition subsequent,[234] so that the condition subsequent must

---

[224] (1805) 10 Ves 522.
[225] This was also held not to be a charitable trust: see Section 7.1.1.(ii), p. 189.
[226] This is considered in more detail in Chapter 7.   [227] See Section 6.1.2.(i), p. 146.
[228] *Re Denley's Trust Deed* [1969] 1 Ch 373. See Section 7.2.1, p. 190.
[229] *Re Endacott* [1960] Ch 232, 251 (Harman LJ); *Re Wood* [1949] Ch 498.
[230] *Re Astor's Settlement Trust* [1952] Ch 534.
[231] In the United States, there is a growing tendency to allow a settlor to create family trusts that are perpetual. See Waggoner, 'US perpetual trusts' (2011) 127 LQR 423.
[232] Perpetuities and Accumulations Act 2009, s. 1(2).   [233] Ibid., s. 1(3).   [234] Ibid., s. 1(4).

occur within the perpetuity period, and if it will not, the condition will not be effective. The rule also applies to wills under which property is left to a legatee with an obligation to leave it to somebody else, known as the 'doctrine of executory bequests'.[235] The rule also applies to the exercise of powers of appointment,[236] so that the power must also be exercised within the perpetuity period.

4.6.2 THE PERPETUITY PERIOD

The perpetuity period was determined at common law by reference to a relevant life in being plus twenty-one years. This would mean that, in the example, above, if Brenda's life were the relevant life in being, her life interest would clearly vest within the perpetuity period, as would Clive's, but, assuming that he has no children when Brenda dies, his children's interest would be void, since it might not vest until more than twenty-one years after Brenda's death.

The common law perpetuity period was reformed by statute, so that it was possible to specify a perpetuity period of no more than eighty years.[237] The law on perpetuities has been reformed again by the Perpetuities and Accumulations Act 2009, which has introduced a single perpetuity period of 125 years,[238] even if the trust instrument specifies a different period.[239] The perpetuity period generally starts when the trust instrument or will takes effect,[240] although where the trust instrument is made in the exercise of a special power of appointment, the perpetuity period will start when the instrument that created that power takes effect.[241]

4.6.3 THE 'WAIT AND SEE' RULE

Whether the perpetuity period was satisfied was originally determined at common law at the time when the trust was created, so if it were possible that the property might vest outside the perpetuity period, the interest in that property would be void. Under the Perpetuities and Accumulations Act 2009 there is a 'wait and see' rule[242] that applies where an interest would be void on the ground that property might not vest until after the perpetuity period has passed. In such circumstances, the interest in the trust property is not to be treated as void until it is clear that the property must vest, if at all, after the end of the perpetuity period. Everything done before this point remains valid. Similarly, a power of appointment will not be treated as void until it is established that the power will not be exercised within the perpetuity period. If a gift is made in favour of a class of people, it might not be possible to ascertain all members of the class within the perpetuity period because, for example, some of the members of the class are unborn, such as where there is a trust for 'my children, grandchildren and great-grandchildren'. In such a case, rather than treating the whole trust as void because part of it might vest outside the perpetuity period, it is possible to close the class artificially so that those who are ascertainable within the perpetuity period will benefit from the trust. This is done by excluding from the class those whose interests might vest outside the perpetuity period, as long as their exclusion does not mean that there are no members of the class.[243]

---

[235] Ibid., s. 1(5).   [236] Ibid., s. 1(6).   [237] Perpetuities and Accumulations Act 1964, s. 1.
[238] Perpetuities and Accumulations Act 2009, s. 5(1).
[239] Although trusts made before the Act came into force in 2010, which have a perpetuity period determined by reference to lives in being and where it is difficult to ascertain whether the lives have ended, may be subject to a perpetuity period of one hundred years: ibid., s. 12.   [240] Ibid., s. 6(1).
[241] Ibid., s. 6(2).   [242] Ibid., s. 7.   [243] Ibid., s. 8.

4.6.4 DURATION OF PURPOSE TRUSTS

The statutory perpetuity rule relates to the vesting of property in people and ensures that the property is vested within 125 years, and so this determines the duration of the trust. The statutory perpetuity period does not, however, apply to purpose trusts. No perpetuity rule applies to charitable purpose trusts, since such trusts are, by definition, for the benefit of the public and so there is a public interest in such trusts potentially lasting forever.[244] There is no such public interest as regards non-charitable purpose trusts, so that, even though the statutory perpetuity rule does not apply to such trusts,[245] they are still caught by the common law perpetuity rule.[246]

---

[244] See Section 6.1.2.(ii), p. 146.
[245] Perpetuities and Accumulation Act 2009, s. 18.   [246] See Section 7.2.2, p. 191.

5

FORMALITIES

5.1 GENERAL CONSIDERATIONS

In the last chapter, we examined the requirements for the creation of an express trust. This chapter is concerned with the process of creating an express trust and related matters. There are essentially two processes that need to be considered, both of which might involve formality requirements. The first process involves possible formality requirements relating to the creation of the trust itself, such as the need to evidence the transaction in writing. The second involves identifying possible formalities for the transfer of property to the trustees, which might, for example, require the completion and submission of particular documents to a third party. This process of transferring property to the trustees is described as 'constituting' the trust. A trust can be effective only once property has been validly transferred to the trustees.

In the course of examining these processes, it will be seen that the principles involved have application outside of the particular context of trust creation. This application of the principles provides further evidence of the significant role of Equity in English law, especially as regards commercial transactions.

5.2 FORMALITIES FOR TRUST CREATION

5.2.1 DECLARATION OF TRUST

(i) By a settlor

In most cases, a trust can be declared by a settlor without any formality requirements. So, for trusts of personalty, such as money, shares, and chattels, writing is not required; an oral declaration of the trust is sufficient.[1] Declarations of trusts of land or of interests in land must, however, be proved by writing that is signed by the person declaring the trust.[2] Such signed writing is not, however, required for resulting, implied, or constructive trusts of land.[3] If express trusts of land are not proved by signed writing, the trust is unenforceable

---

[1] *Paul v Constance* [1977] 1 WLR 527.   [2] Law of Property Act 1925, s. 53(1)(b).
[3] Ibid., s. 53(2). See further Section 5.2.2.(i), p. 108.

rather than void.[4] In other words, the trust is valid, but it cannot be enforced by the beneficiary. So, if the trustees wish to be bound by the trust, they can be, but they cannot be compelled to fulfil their trust obligations if they do not wish to do so.[5] The function of the requirement of writing is merely to evidence the settlor's intention to declare the trust rather than being needed to create it, so the declaration of trust itself need not be in writing and the written evidence need not be contemporaneous with the declaration of trust.[6] Although the signature will normally be that of the settlor, it can be that of the trustee.[7] These formalities are required as a safeguard against fraud and abuse, to ensure that the settlor is aware that they want a trust to be declared, and as a means of standardizing transactions.[8]

(ii) By a testator

Trusts of land declared by will must be evidenced by signed writing.[9] Trusts of other property declared by a will do not have any specific formality requirements, but any testamentary trust must comply with the formality requirements under the Wills Act 1837 regardless of the nature of the property: if the will is not valid, then, generally,[10] the trust will not be valid either. Testamentary formalities include that the will must be in writing and be signed either by the testator or by somebody else at the direction of the testator and in the testator's presence.[11] There also need to be two witnesses present at the time to attest and sign the will. These formalities are imposed to reduce the chances of mistake, fraud, undue influence and ill-considered and hasty dispositions of property by a will.[12] The Law Commission has reviewed the law relating to the making of wills and has made various tentative recommendations for reform, including the creation of a power to dispense with formalities in certain circumstances.[13]

5.2.2 FAILURE TO COMPLY WITH FORMALITIES

(i) By settlors

Where a trust of land is declared orally, the statutory formalities will not have been satisfied and so the trust will not be enforceable by the intended beneficiary. But this rule can cause real injustice. For example, if Alan transfers land to Brian to hold on trust for Clare, but Alan does this orally, Clare will not be able to enforce the trust as the purported beneficiary because of Alan's failure to comply with the formality requirements. But Brian will now have legal title to the land, assuming that Alan fulfilled the formalities to convey legal title to Brian.[14] Alan will not have intended Brian to have the benefit of the land, but, since

---

[4] *Gardner v Rowe* (1828) 5 Russ 258. Compare with the Law of Property Act 1925, s. 53(1)(c), discussed in Section 11.3, p. 324. Swadling, 'The nature of the trust in *Rochefoucauld v Boustead*', in *Resulting and Constructive Trusts*, ed. Mitchell (Oxford: Hart, 2010), ch. 3, considers s. 53(1)(b) to be concerned with the method of proving the trust rather than whether it is enforceable. But, if the trust cannot be proved by the admission of oral evidence, it will inevitably be unenforceable.

[5] But in some circumstances it may be possible to treat the land as being held on constructive trust, which does not require writing to be enforceable. See Section 5.2.2.(i), p. 108.

[6] *Rochefoucauld v Boustead* [1897] 1 Ch 196.   [7] *Gardner v Rowe* (1828) 5 Russ 258.

[8] Fuller, 'Consideration and form' (1941) 41 Columbia L Rev 799; Youdan, 'Formalities for trusts of land, and the doctrine in *Rochefoucauld v Boustead*' (1984) 43 CLJ 306, 314; Feltham, 'Informal trusts and third parties' [1987] Conv 246, 248.   [9] Law of Property Act 1925, s. 53(1)(b).

[10] Subject to what is discussed in Section 5.2.2.(ii), p. 109.

[11] Wills Act 1837, s. 9, as amended by the Administration of Justice Act 1982, s. 17. See *Barrett v Bem* [2011] EWHC 1247 (Ch), [2011] WTLR 1117.   [12] See *Making a Will* (Law Com, CP, No. 231, 2017), p. 56.

[13] Ibid., p. 102.   [14] As to the nature of these formalities, see Section 5.3.2.(ii), p. 125.

Clare cannot enforce the trust, this will be the effect of Alan's failure to comply with the statutory formalities. Such a result is manifestly unfair.

Equity has intervened in cases such as this through the application of the principle that 'Equity will not permit a statute to be used as an instrument of fraud'. In other words, Equity will not allow a party to rely on statutory requirements to perpetrate a fraud on the settlor or beneficiary. This maxim can be relevant in two different ways.

Two-party scenarios

Alan may orally declare that he holds land on trust for Brian. Since the trust was not evidenced by signed writing, it is not enforceable. If Alan wishes to renege on the declaration, then, since it remains his own property at Law and he did not acquire the property subject to a trust, it is unlikely that Equity will consider his reliance on the formality requirements of the Law of Property Act 1925 to constitute a fraud on Brian.[15] But it will be different where, for example, Alan orally transfers land to Brian to be held on trust for Alan. It will be considered fraudulent for Brian to deny the trust if he knew that Alan intended him to hold the property on trust for Alan.[16] Brian might argue that the trust has not been validly declared because it was not evidenced in writing contrary to the requirements of the Law of Property Act 1925, but this would be to use the statute as an instrument with which to perpetrate a fraud. Equity will not countenance this and so will recognize that Brian holds the land on trust for Alan. Fraud for the purposes of the operation of the equitable maxim is not restricted to fraud on the part of Brian in procuring the transfer of property, but includes Brian's reliance on the transfer of legal title to the property to defeat Alan's beneficial interest in it. This is illustrated in an extreme way by *Bannister v Bannister*,[17] in which A, who was widowed, owned a cottage and entered into an oral agreement with B, her brother-in-law, whereby she would convey the cottage to him on the understanding that she would be allowed to live in it rent-free for as long as she wished. B allowed her to occupy only one room and then sought possession of that on the basis that A had no right of occupation. It was held that B was acting fraudulently by setting up the absolute character of the conveyance to defeat A's life interest and so the property was held on trust by B for A to occupy for as long as she wished.

The leading case on the operation of the equitable maxim in a two-party scenario is *Rochefoucauld v Boustead*.[18] In that case, the Comtesse de la Rochefoucauld owned coffee plantations in what was then known as Ceylon. She mortgaged the land and the mortgagee sold the land to the defendant. The defendant had previously orally agreed to hold the land on trust for the Comtesse, subject to repayment by her to the defendant of the purchase price and expenses. The defendant sold the land at a profit, but was then declared bankrupt. The question for the Court of Appeal was whether the Comtesse could claim this profit. This turned on whether there had been a valid declaration of trust in her favour. Since there was no writing, the trust of the land appeared not to be enforceable under the Statute of Frauds 1677, the precursor of the Law of Property Act 1925. It was held, however, that the statute could not be used to prevent proof of fraud and, since the defendant knew that the property had been sold to him to be held on trust for the Comtesse, it would be fraudulent for him to deny the trust, and so the Comtesse was allowed to prove by oral evidence that a trust had been intended.

---

[15] Youdan (see n. 8), p. 325. But there might be circumstances under which Brian might have a claim based on proprietary estoppel if he had relied on a representation by Alan that the property will be held on trust for Brian. See Section 10.4, p. 305.   [16] Youdan (see n. 8), p. 327.

[17] [1948] 2 All ER 133. See also *Neale v Willis* (1968) 19 P & CR 839.   [18] [1897] 1 Ch 196.

The trust in *Rochefoucauld v Boustead* was specifically recognized as being an express trust,[19] which was significant since it meant that the Comtesse's claim was not time-barred.[20] Subsequent cases have characterized the trust as either being constructive,[21] because it operates to prevent the transferee of the property from benefiting from fraud,[22] or resulting, because it arises from the failure of an express trust.[23] Characterizing the trust as express is, however, consistent with the language of the Law of Property Act 1925, since there is a valid trust, but it is simply unenforceable because of the absence of writing.

Three-party scenarios

Where Alan conveys land to Brian and Alan has orally communicated to Brian that he should hold the property on trust for Clare, although the express trust for Clare is unenforceable by her, it will be fraudulent for Brian to deny the trust and to rely on his legal rights to the property. But what is the appropriate solution in this scenario? There are three solutions that are potentially available, depending on how the facts are analysed.

(1) Brian should hold the land on resulting trust for Alan.[24] This trust does not need to be evidenced in writing.[25] A resulting trust will be recognized, amongst other reasons, where Alan does not intend Brian to receive the property that has been transferred beneficially.[26] This is precisely the situation in which Alan transfers land to Brian to hold on trust for Clare, where the trust is declared orally. Brian is intended to hold the property for Clare rather than to benefit himself from its receipt. Where a resulting trust is recognized, Brian will hold the property on trust for Alan, who will then be able to terminate the trust and recover the property. Alan can then declare the trust for Clare as was originally intended, this time satisfying the formality requirements in doing so and, in the light of Brian's conduct, possibly choosing a different person to act as trustee.

(2) Brian should hold the land on constructive trust for Clare.[27] Such a trust does not need to be evidenced in writing,[28] but whether such a trust can be recognized will depend on whether Brian's conduct can be characterized as unconscionable.[29] The fact that Brian seeks to deny the trust when he is aware that Alan intended the property to be held on trust for Clare might be sufficient to trigger the constructive trust. Recognizing that Brian holds the property on trust for Clare does at least have the advantage of respecting Alan's initial intention as to what should happen to the property. But, against this conclusion is the fact that, by treating Brian as a trustee for Clare, albeit by virtue of a constructive trust that arises by operation of law, the evidential requirements of section 53(1)(b) of the Law of Property Act 1925 are avoided.

(3) Brian should hold the land on express trust for Clare for the same reasons as an express trust was recognized in *Rochefoucauld v Boustead*. Where Alan has orally declared a trust of land whereby Brian is to hold the land for Clare, this is a valid trust, but one that is not enforceable. But if Brian seeks to rely on his legal rights, Equity will not permit him to use the statute as an instrument of fraud and the trust will become enforceable.

---

[19] Ibid., 208 (Lindley LJ).   [20] Swadling (see n. 4), p. 98.

[21] See e.g. *Bannister v Bannister* [1948] 2 All ER 133, discussed under two-party scenarios.

[22] See McFarlane, 'Constructive trusts arising on a receipt of property *sub conditione*' (2004) 120 LQR 667, 675 who considers that the constructive trust arises to prevent the recipient of the property from reneging on the understanding subject to which the property was received. This would be consistent with some other situations in which a constructive trust is recognized. See Section 9.3.5, p. 268.

[23] *Hodgson v Marks* [1971] Ch 892.   [24] Youdan (see n. 8), p. 326.

[25] Law of Property Act 1925, s. 53(2).   [26] See Section 8.3, p. 29.

[27] This is the preferred analysis of Youdan (see n. 8), p. 335.   [28] Law of Property Act 1925, s. 53(2).

[29] See Section 9.3.5, p. 268.

Of these three options, the first is the most inconvenient. The second and third are no different in terms of result, but only in terms of analysis. Even so, the third option is the preferable way of analysing these cases. Equity will not permit Brian to act fraudulently and so, as long as Brian was aware of Alan's intention that he should hold the property for Clare, Equity will enforce the trust despite the failure to comply with the statutory formalities. It would be different if Brian had discovered Alan's intention that the property was to be held on trust for Clare only after he had received the property from Alan, since it is not fraudulent to receive property as a gift and then to rely on the formality requirements of the statute to show that Brian should retain the property free of the trust.[30]

(ii) By testators

The need for formalities

Where a testator intends to create a trust in a will, the formality requirements might not be satisfied for a variety of reasons, such as where there is only one witness or the witnesses attested the will in the absence of the testator. Since the will is not valid by virtue of the failure to comply with formalities, any testamentary trust will be void too. Alternatively, the testator may have been fraudulently induced to leave property to somebody in their will, but on the understanding that that person would hold the property on trust for another. If this understanding has not been expressed in writing, the person receiving the property will not be bound to hold the property on trust, because the strict requirements of the Wills Act 1837 have not been satisfied.

It is important that the formalities of the Wills Act are respected to ensure that the testator's intentions are expressed clearly and accurately, and that the testator has not been defrauded or unduly influenced, but also to ensure that the testator does not reserve for themselves a power to dispose of property by a future unattested document that fails to comply with the statutory formality safeguards. It was for the last reason that a gift in a will in *Re Jones*,[31] which purported to reserve to the testator the power to alter the settlement in the future, was held not to be valid.

Modification of formality requirements

Various mechanisms have, however, been developed by Equity to ensure that the strict formality rules for wills do not necessarily frustrate the testator's intent. So, for example, informal documents can be incorporated into a will if they are expressly identified by the will and if they existed when the will was executed.[32] This is called the 'doctrine of incorporation by reference'. Alternatively, informal documents can be incorporated into the will after it has been executed if the incorporation is confirmed by another formal document, known as a 'codicil', which refers to those documents. Another device with which to fulfil the testator's intent arises if property is left in a will to such people as will be identified subsequently, in which case the bequest is valid if the identification of these legatees is made by reference to facts of independent legal significance rather than dependent on the testator's subsequent decision. It does not matter that the determination of the legatees is made subsequently and outside of the will. So, for example, if a father states in his will that he will leave his property to whichever of his two sons does not obtain property from a third party, the decision of the third party will determine who will benefit under the father's will,

---

[30] Youdan (see n. 8), p. 327.
[31] [1942] Ch 328. Compare *Re Schintz's Will Trusts* [1951] Ch 870, in which the power to amend or revoke the settlement, whilst invalid, was considered to be otiose and did not invalidate the will as a whole.
[32] *Re Edward's Will Trusts* [1948] Ch 440.

and this is valid because it is determined by reference to a decision that is verifiable and is independent of the testator.

Failure to comply with the testamentary formalities may, however, be intended by the testator, and this raises distinct and complex problems for Equity. There might be particular reasons why a testator does not want it to be generally known who is to benefit under their will, typically because the testator wishes to benefit a lover or an illegitimate child, but without making any reference to this on the face of the will, because a will is admitted to probate and is open for public inspection.[33] In such a situation, the testator might decide to leave property to a named person in a will, but in the expectation that the property will be used for the benefit of these unnamed people. This may occur in two different ways. First, the testator may make it clear in the will that the property is to be held by a named person on trust for an unnamed person and that the name of this person is to be communicated separately to the trustee. This is known as a 'half-secret trust'. In this case, it is clear from the will that the trustee is receiving property as a trustee and not beneficially, so the opportunity to act contrary to the testator's intent is reduced. But is such a trust valid, when the name of the beneficiary is not disclosed on the face of the will? This certainly appears to be contrary to the Wills Act 1837, since this involves a disposition of property to take effect after the testator's death where significant terms of the trust have not been incorporated in the will.[34]

The other scenario is known as a 'fully secret trust'. Here, the will purports to leave property to a named person beneficially, but the testator intends the legatee to hold the property on trust for the benefit of another and this intention will have been communicated to the legatee separately. In this situation, there is much greater scope for the testator's intention to be defeated because, according to the clear words of the will, the legatee is to have the property absolutely. There is nothing on the face of the will to indicate that there is any trust. But if the legatee, being aware of the testator's intention, seeks to rely on their legal rights to the property under the will, they will be seeking to use the formality requirements of the Wills Act as an instrument with which to perpetrate fraud. There would appear, therefore, to be a strong case for equitable intervention in such circumstances, but, again, it is necessary to consider whether, as a matter of policy, it is appropriate to give effect to the testator's intent to declare a trust after their death when this has not been expressed in the will.

The significance of the secret trust where a testator wishes to provide for illegitimate children is illustrated by *Re Freud (deceased)*.[35] The case concerned the appropriate construction of the will of Lucian Freud, the artist, who allegedly had at least fourteen children. On the face of the will, Freud's residuary estate was left to his solicitor and one of his children, who were the claimants, absolutely. The defendant, one of Freud's other children, argued that the estate was not given to the claimants for their absolute benefit, but was held on trust, the terms of which were not set out in the will, so that it was a half-secret trust.[36] The case actually turned on the appropriate construction of the will to determine whether Freud had intended to declare a trust, albeit that the terms of the trust were not disclosed.[37] It was held, following objective construction of the will, that there was no intention to declare a trust, so that the residuary estate was indeed given to the claimants absolutely. They had, however, acknowledged that they had received communications

---

[33] Senior Courts Act 1981, s. 124.

[34] Kincaid, 'Secret and semi-secret trusts: justifying distinctions between the two' [1995] Conv 366, 367.

[35] [2014] EWHC 2577 (Ch), [2014] WTLR 1453.

[36] He also argued that this was not a valid trust so that there would be an intestacy of the residue, part of which he would be entitled to receive.   [37] See further Section 4.2.2.(ix), p. 76.

from Freud before his death as to how the residuary estate should be used. So it appears, therefore, that this was in fact a fully secret trust, even though there was nothing on the face of the will to indicate this. Crucially, the claimants stated that the defendant was not one of the beneficiaries of this trust.

If Equity is to intervene in these cases, what would be the most appropriate solution? Where the statutory formalities have not been satisfied and a trust of land to be held for a third party is declared whilst the settlor is alive, one possible solution is to hold that the land transferred to the intended trustee should be held on resulting trust for the settlor, who then has the opportunity to declare the trust again, this time complying with the formalities.[38] But this resulting trust solution could not work in the same way for secret trusts, since the testator will be dead. Consequently, the property could be held on resulting trust for those entitled to the testator's residuary estate, but there is no guarantee that they will respect the testator's intent and declare a trust for the intended beneficiaries. Where the intended beneficiaries are the testator's mistress and illegitimate children, such a declaration of trust may well be the last thing that those members of the family who inherit the testator's residuary estate will want. So Equity needs to find some other solution—one that carries the property forward rather than returns it back to the testator's estate.

Since half-secret and fully secret trusts raise distinct issues, it is appropriate to consider them separately. But there are certain general principles relating to all secret trusts that need to be considered first.

General principles relating to secret trusts

The key controversy involving secret trusts concerns whether their recognition is compatible with the Wills Act 1837: if the secret trust is valid, property that is transferred to a legatee will be held on trust for another in circumstances in which either there is no indication of a trust on the face of the will (the fully secret trust), or the will identifies the trust, but not the terms and the objects (the half-secret trust). In both cases, property is to be disposed after the testator's death according to terms that are not declared in the will, contrary to the strict formality requirements of that Act.

The recognition of secret trusts has sometimes been justified on the basis that the legatee, who receives property under the will knowing that the testator intended them to hold it on trust for somebody else, cannot then rely on the formality requirements of the Wills Act to invalidate the trust, since this would involve the use of that statute as an instrument of fraud. Such trusts are therefore treated as testamentary trusts, which are recognized despite the failure to comply with the formalities of the Wills Act. The preferable view, however, is that both fully secret and half-secret trusts are valid not as exceptions to the formality requirements under the Wills Act, but because they operate outside the will and are therefore not caught by those requirements. This is known as the 'dehors- (or outside) -the- will' theory. Secret trusts are properly analysed as express trusts that are validly declared during the testator's lifetime,[39] following communication by the testator and acceptance by the trustee. These trusts arise independently of the will by reason of the personal obligation accepted by the legatee. Although these trusts are not constituted until the subject matter of the trust is vested in the trustee by the executor following the testator's death,[40] it does not follow that they are testamentary trusts, because they have already been created *inter vivos*; it is only the constitution that occurs on death and automatically once property has been transferred by the executors to the trustee.

---

[38] See Section 5.2.2.(i), p. 108.

[39] Oakley, *Constructive Trusts*, 3rd edn (London: Sweet and Maxwell, 1996), p. 262.

[40] See Rickett, 'Thoughts on secret trusts from New Zealand' [1996] Conv 302, 306.

The dehors-the-will theory of secret trusts was recognized by Sir Robert Megarry V-C in *Re Snowden*:[41]

> the whole basis of secret trusts … is that they operate outside the will, changing nothing that is written in it, and allowing it to operate according to its tenor, but then fastening a trust on to the property in the hands of the recipient.

The dehors-the-will theory is not, however, a perfect explanation of the secret trust. The fact that the trust is declared whilst the testator is still alive, but is constituted only following the testator's death, means that Equity allows the trust to bind property in the testator's estate that may have been acquired after the trust had been declared. This contravenes the usual rule that it is not possible to declare an immediate trust of future property,[42] although this might instead be treated as a trust of the testator's promise to leave future-acquired property to the trustee rather than a trust of the property itself.[43]

Analysing both fully secret and half-secret trusts as express trusts that are created *inter vivos* and not by the will is important when considering how both types of trust are created and operate. Certain principles relating to their creation and operation can be identified:

(1) The formality requirements of the Wills Act 1837 are not relevant to the recognition of secret trusts. For example, in *Re Young*,[44] a testator made a bequest to his wife and imposed a condition that she should make certain bequests that he had previously communicated to her, including a gift of £2,000 to his chauffeur. The chauffeur had witnessed the will, which meant that he could not receive a legacy under it.[45] It was held, however, that the chauffeur was still entitled to the gift, because it arose from an oral trust declared by the testator and was not a bequest under the will, so that the testamentary formalities were irrelevant.

(2) Since secret trusts are not constituted until after the testator's death, the terms of the trust can be changed by the testator after it has been declared, for example by the will being revoked or altered, or by the property being disposed of in some other way.[46] It might, however, be possible to invoke the doctrine of proprietary estoppel to invalidate any attempt to revoke the trust or to change its terms.[47] This will apply where the testator has made a clear representation about the validity of the trust, followed by detrimental reliance on the part of the beneficiary.[48]

(3) If the trustee were to die before the testator, then this would presumably invalidate the trust. This appears to be the case as regards fully secret trusts.[49] As regards half-secret trusts, it might be argued that the death of the trustee should not invalidate the trust because of the maxim that a trust will not be allowed to fail for want of a trustee,[50] unless the identity of the trustee is especially significant. This maxim would clearly be relevant to half-secret trusts, because the existence of the trustee is obvious on the face of the will, but there is no reason why the maxim should not also be extended to fully secret trusts, since the testator will have relied on the legatee to hold the property on trust after the testator's death.[51] Of course, where the trustee has died before the testator, the testator will usually have the opportunity to appoint another trustee.

---

[41] [1979] Ch 528, 535.   [42] *Re Ellenborough* [1903] 1 Ch 697.

[43] See further Section 5.3.3.(iii), p. 137.   [44] [1951] Ch 344.

[45] Wills Act 1837, s. 15. Now see the Wills Act 1968, which allows a witness to a will to take under it if the will would have been valid without the particular witness's attestation.

[46] Kincaid, 'The tangled web: the relationship between a secret trust and the will' [2000] Conv 420, 426.

[47] Pawlowski and Brown, 'Constituting a secret trust by estoppel' [2004] Conv 388.

[48] See further Section 10.4, p. 305.   [49] *Re Maddock* [1902] 2 Ch 220, 231 (Cozens-Hardy LJ).

[50] For the view that a half-secret trust would also fail, see Wilde, 'Secret and semi-secret trusts: justifying distinctions between the two' [1995] Conv 366, 373.   [51] Kincaid (see n. 46), p. 440.

(4) The trustee will be free to revoke their acceptance of the trust before the testator's death, so that the trustee will no longer be bound by their undertaking to hold the property on trust. Again, the testator will have the opportunity to appoint a new trustee, but if there were not sufficient time to do so before the testator's death, it would be appropriate for the court to appoint a new trustee.[52] If a trustee seeks to renounce the trust after the testator's death, this will be too late and the trustee will be bound by the trust until a replacement trustee can be appointed.[53]

(5) What should happen where the beneficiary of the trust dies before the testator? In *Re Gardner (No 2)*,[54] it was held that the personal representatives of the deceased beneficiary could claim their share of the estate. Usually, where a legatee dies before the testator, the gift lapses, unless the legatee has acquired a prior interest in the property. But the putative beneficiary does not have any such interest under a secret trust because the trust will not be constituted until after the testator's death, when legal title is vested in the trustee. *Re Gardner (No 2)* should consequently be regarded as wrongly decided. The lapsed gift should instead have been held by the trustee on resulting trust for those entitled to the residuary estate of the testator.

(6) If secret trusts are characterized as express trusts, then, where the subject matter of the trust is land, the declaration of the trust must be evidenced by signed writing.[55] This was recognized in *Re Baillie*,[56] as regards a half-secret trust of land. In *Ottaway v Norman*,[57] however, a fully secret trust of land was held to be enforceable even though it was not evidenced in writing. This might mean that fully secret trusts of land operate as constructive trusts, since such trusts of land are valid despite the absence of writing,[58] or—as is perhaps more likely—that the court failed to appreciate the significance of the oral declaration of the trust in that case. The preferable view is that, regardless of whether the trust is a fully secret or half-secret trust of land, the trust can be validly declared even though it is not evidenced by signed writing because the trustee's conduct, in consciously allowing the testator to leave them the land in the expectation that the trustee will hold it on trust for another, means that the trustee should not be allowed to use the formality requirements of the Law of Property Act 1925 as an instrument of fraud. The use of this doctrine does not mean that the trust itself is not an express trust.[59]

Half-secret trusts

The typical half-secret trust arises where a testator leaves property to a named person in a will to hold on the trusts that have been, or will be, declared.[60] It is clear from the will that the legatee takes as a trustee rather than beneficially. But, since the intended beneficiary has not been identified in the will, the strict formalities of the Wills Act 1837 have not been satisfied. Despite this, the courts have been willing to enforce such trusts, albeit subject to stringent conditions.

Time of communication

The terms of the trust must be communicated to the trustee before, or contemporaneously with, the execution of the will.[61] Communication of the terms after the will has been

---

[52] Ibid., p. 441.   [53] See further Section 12.2.4, p. 340.   [54] [1923] 2 Ch 230.

[55] Law of Property Act 1925, s. 53(1)(b).   [56] (1886) 2 TLT 660, 661 (North J).

[57] [1972] Ch 698. See Section 5.2.2.(ii), p. 118.   [58] Law of Property Act 1925, s. 53(2).

[59] As in *Rochefoucauld v Bousted* [1897] 1 Ch 196. See Section 5.2.1.(i), p. 107.

[60] If the trusts are declared in writing subsequently, it may be possible to incorporate them into the will if the conditions for incorporation are satisfied. See Section 5.2.2.(ii), p. 109.

[61] *Johnson v Ball* (1851) 5 De G & Sm 85.

executed will mean that the half-secret trust fails and the property will then be held on resulting trust for residuary beneficiaries of the testator's estate; similarly where the terms are not communicated to the trustee at all.[62] In *Re Keen*,[63] it was recognized that giving a sealed envelope to one trustee was sufficient communication of the identity of the beneficiary, even though it was not read until after the testator's death, because the trustee had the means of knowing who the beneficiary was before the testator's death. Further, it did not matter that the envelope was given to only one of the two trustees named in the will.

It was recognized in *Re Keen* that the reason why communication of the terms of the trust after the will has been executed cannot be effective to declare a half-secret trust is because this involves the testator reserving a power to change a will informally, contrary to the Wills Act 1837.[64] But this is not convincing. No such rule of communication applies to fully secret trusts[65] and it is not consistent with the dehors-the-will theory of secret trusts, since such trusts are not declared by the will, but are declared independently by the testator and are constituted only following the testator's death. It follows that it should be sufficient that the terms of the half-secret trust are communicated before the testator's death.[66]

Consistency with terms of the will

Despite the terms of the half-secret trust being communicated before the will was executed in *Re Keen*, the trust was still held to be invalid because it was inconsistent with the terms of the will. In that case, the testator had left £10,000 in his will to his trustees, to be disposed of by them to such people or charities as he would notify to them during his lifetime. It was held that the trust was not valid because the communication of the name of the beneficiary had occurred before the will was executed, contrary to the terms of the will, which was interpreted by the court as requiring the name to be communicated after the will was made, because of the use of the phrase 'as he would notify' rather than 'as he had notified'. It follows that it is a vital feature of the law relating to half-secret trusts that the evidence that is adduced to prove the terms of the trust must be consistent with the terms of the will. So, for example, in *Re Huxtable*,[67] the will stated that £4,000 was to be held on trust for charitable purposes to be agreed between the testator and trustee. It was held that oral evidence could be admitted to establish what the charitable purposes were, but not to establish that the testator had intended only the income to be used for such purposes, because this was not consistent with the will, which stated that the whole sum was to be held on trust.

Changes to the terms of the trust

Changes to the terms of a half-secret trust after the will has been executed will not be effective, at least if the changes to the terms have not been communicated to the trustees. This was recognized in *Re Cooper*,[68] in which the testator declared a half-secret trust of £5,000 in his will and communicated the terms of the trust to his trustees before the will was executed. A month later, the testator made a new will that purported to cancel the previous one. This new will stated that the £5,000 bequeathed to his trustees was to be increased to £10,000 and that the trustees knew the testator's wishes as regards the use of

---

[62] *Re Pugh* [1967] 1 WLR 1262.   [63] [1937] Ch 236.

[64] See also *Re Bateman's Will Trusts* [1970] 1 WLR 1463.

[65] Holdsworth, 'Secret trusts' (1937) 53 LQR 501. See Section 5.2.2.(ii), p. 119. This is also the rule for half-secret trusts in Ireland (*Re Browne* [1944] IR 90) and New South Wales (*Ledgerwood v Perpetual Trustee* [1997] 41 NSWLR 532).

[66] Communication of the terms after the testator's death will not suffice for a fully secret trust (*Re Boyes* (1884) 26 Ch D 531) and should not do so either for a half-secret trust.   [67] [1902] 2 Ch 793.

[68] [1939] Ch 811.

this sum. The fact that the amount had been increased was not, however, communicated to the trustees. It was held that the first £5,000 was held on the terms of the secret trust, as had previously been communicated, but the additional £5,000 was held on resulting trust for those entitled to the testator's residuary estate, because this additional amount had not been communicated to the trustees. It was, however, recognized that if the amount of the subsequent bequest had been lower than the amount that had been communicated to the trustees, there would have been a valid trust, because the greater included the lesser.[69] It was also accepted that, if the later bequest had been only slightly more than the sum communicated, this would have been caught by the half-secret trust by virtue of the *de minimis* principle, namely that small differences in amounts are not significant.

Trustees as beneficiaries

In *Re Rees*,[70] the testator declared a half-secret trust. When the will was executed, he told the trustees that any surplus after making certain payments could be retained by them beneficially. It was held that the surplus could not belong to the trustees, but rather was held on resulting trust for those entitled to the testator's residuary estate. This was because the testator's oral communication to the trustees about the surplus conflicted with the terms of the will, which stated that the trustees were to receive the property as trustees rather than beneficially.

In *Re Tyler*,[71] Pennycuick J said that he did not find the reasoning in *Re Rees* to be easy. On the face of it, the reasoning is unconvincing: if the will says that the property is held on trust for certain people, why cannot some of those people be the trustees who could benefit from the surplus? But, although this was not acknowledged in *Re Rees*, it is surely because the trustees' assertions that they were entitled to the surplus raised a real danger of fraud on their part, since they were seeking to obtain a personal benefit that was not identified on the face of the will. Where the trustees are intended to benefit from the testator's estate, but this is not expressed in the will, the high standards of behaviour expected from the trustees as fiduciaries should be such that they should not receive the property beneficially. If this is the correct analysis, it means that, even if the trustees in *Re Rees* were intended to benefit under the half-secret trust itself rather than to obtain any surplus, they would not have been able to do so.

Theoretical basis for recognizing half-secret trusts

If evidence of the terms of the half-secret trust were not admitted, the trustee would hold the property on resulting trust for those entitled to the testator's residuary estate,[72] because it is clear that the trustee cannot receive the property beneficially. So, why is it possible to allow evidence of the terms to be admitted so that the trustee holds the property on the secret trust for the beneficiaries chosen by the testator? Two different explanations have been suggested.

The first is the doctrine of incorporation by reference,[73] which enables informal documents to be incorporated into a will if they are expressly identified by the will and existed when the will was executed.[74] The requirements for this doctrine do appear to be consistent with the requirements for the half-secret trust, since the testator must have communicated the terms of the trust, including the identity of the beneficiaries, to the intended trustee before or at the time the will was made and reference to the trust must be made in

---

[69] Ibid., 818 (Sir Wilfrid Greene MR).   [70] [1950] Ch 204.   [71] [1967] 1 WLR 1269, 1278.
[72] *Re Pugh's Will Trusts* [1967] 1 WLR 1262.
[73] Matthews, 'The true basis of the half-secret trust?' [1979] Conv 360.
[74] See Section 5.2.2.(ii), p. 109.

the will. Once these conditions are satisfied, it would then be possible to incorporate the terms of the secret trust into the will, so that the formality requirements of the Wills Act 1837 could then be considered to be satisfied. This theory also explains why communication of the terms of the trust after the will has been executed will not be effective, unless the will is confirmed by a codicil that refers to the communication.[75]

Although the use of the doctrine of incorporation by reference to explain the law on half-secret trusts appears to explain the requirements of that trust, this is not a sufficient explanation for a number of reasons. First, the doctrine of incorporation by reference relates only to the incorporation of documents in a will and does not extend to the incorporation of oral communications, because such communications clearly do not comply with the formality requirements of the Wills Act 1837 that all parts of the will need to be in writing.[76] But it has been recognized that oral communication of the terms of the trust are sufficient for a half-secret trust to be valid.[77] Secondly, a document can be incorporated into a will even though it has not been communicated to the trustee, whereas communication of the terms of the trust to the trustee is a vital requirement for a half-secret trust to be valid. Thirdly, the main advantage of the use of the doctrine of incorporation by reference to explain the half-secret trust is to justify the requirement of communication of terms before execution of the will. But that requirement has already been criticized as being inconsistent with the requirements for fully secret trusts and also the dehors-the-will theory. It follows that the incorporation by reference doctrine cannot adequately explain why half-secret trusts are recognized.

An alternative explanation of the half-secret trust is that such trusts should be recognized to prevent a fraud from being perpetrated on the intended beneficiaries if a legatee, having agreed to hold property on trust, fails to do so.[78] Although fraud has proved significant to the recognition of the fully secret trust,[79] it appears not to be relevant to the half-secret trust, since, as the trust is apparent on the face of the will, there is little scope for the trustee to defraud the beneficiaries, save where the trustee might assert that the communication of the terms of the trust occurred after the will had been executed. Even then, there is no scope for the trustee benefiting from the half-secret trust failing, unless they were otherwise entitled to the testator's residuary estate.

Fraud cannot, therefore, explain why half-secret trusts are recognized if it is interpreted restrictively so that it only arises where the trustee wishes to benefit from the invalidity of the trust. But, if fraud were instead interpreted as encompassing unconscionable conduct objectively determined, it could be used to justify the recognition of these trusts. Trustees can be considered to act unconscionably where they seek not to be bound by their undertaking to the testator to hold property on trust for another. The trust could then be recognized to prevent such unconscionable behaviour from occurring. Such a principle was effectively recognized by the House of Lords in *Blackwell v Blackwell*,[80] in which the testator had left money in his will to five legatees to be applied for the benefit of people whose names he had previously communicated to them. Before the will was executed, the testator had informed the trustees orally that the money was to be used for the benefit of his mistress and his illegitimate son. It was held that this was a valid trust. It was specifically recognized that the Wills Act 1837 did not purport to interfere with the equitable jurisdiction, which ensures that, where a bequest is made in a will without revealing who the beneficiary is, evidence outside of the will can be adduced to establish the identity of

---

[75] See Section 5.2.2.(ii), p. 109.

[76] Critchley, 'Instruments of fraud, testamentary dispositions and the doctrine of secret trusts' (1999) 115 LQR 631, 644.   [77] *Blackwell v Blackwell* [1929] AC 318.

[78] Ibid.   [79] See Section 5.2.2.(ii), p. 117.   [80] [1929] AC 318.

that beneficiary. But the crucial trigger for the exercise of this equitable jurisdiction was considered to be communication and acceptance of the trust by the legatee.

It follows that the essential condition for recognizing a half-secret trust is that the testator has communicated the purpose of the trust to the legatee, who then either acquiesces or promises to comply with this purpose, and the testator then relies on this by executing the will so as to leave property to the trustee.[81] In other words, this operates as a form of estoppel, because of the key requirements of communication, acceptance, and reliance. It will then be unconscionable for the legatee not to fulfil the undertaking that they have given to carry out the purposes for which the bequest was made.[82] This satisfactorily explains why the half-secret trust is recognized and why there are particular requirements for the recognition of such a trust.

Summary of the law on half-secret trusts

The requirements for the recognition of half-secret trusts, the nature of such trusts, and the justification for their recognition is fraught with difficulty, largely because of confused analyses of these trusts by judges and commentators. But half-secret trusts can be analysed simply and the decision of the House of Lords in *Blackwell v Blackwell* provides the key to this. A half-secret trust is an express trust that is declared by the testator in their will. The trust should be valid only where the terms of the trust have been communicated to the trustee, either before or after the will was executed,[83] in circumstances under which the trustee has accepted the trusteeship or, by acquiescing, can be assumed to have accepted the trusteeship. It will then be unconscionable for the trustee to break this undertaking once the trust has been constituted by transfer of property to the trustee after the testator's death.

Fully secret trusts

Whereas the half-secret trust is apparent on the face of a will, a fully secret trust is completely hidden from the will. The will instead indicates that a gift is made to a particular person absolutely, but the testator intends the legatee to hold the gift on trust for somebody else. This may be because the testator wants to benefit somebody without anybody knowing or suspecting that there is a different beneficiary, such as a mistress or illegitimate child. Alternatively, the testator might be uncertain as to who should be benefited at the time that the will is executed and leaves property to some trusted person, such as a solicitor, to dispose of it according to instructions that are to be communicated subsequently.[84]

According to the terms of the will in such cases, the legatee is to receive the property absolutely. But, assuming that the terms of the trust were communicated to the legatee, their reliance on the strict terms of the will to ignore the testator's intention to hold property on trust for another would be unconscionable. The legatee should consequently not be allowed to receive the property beneficially and so the fully secret trust has been recognized as valid, but subject to stringent conditions.

That the recognition of a fully secret trust is prompted by a desire to prevent fraud is illustrated most clearly by the old case of *Thynn v Thynn*,[85] where a father in his will had made his wife his executrix. Their son persuaded his mother that it would be better for him to be the executor and that he would hold the estate on trust for her. The son arranged for the father's will to be cancelled and a new will was prepared that made the son the

---

[81] *Re Cooper* [1939] Ch 811, 816 (Sir Wilfrid Greene MR).
[82] *Re Keen* [1937] Ch 236, 245 (Lord Wright MR).
[83] Although this probably does not reflect the state of English law. See Section 5.2.2.(ii), p. 114.
[84] See e.g. *Re Snowden* [1979] Ch 528.   [85] (1684) 1 Vern 296.

executor. When it came to the father signing the new will, which was read out to him by the will-writer, the father said that he could not hear what was being said. He did sign the will, but clearly in very suspicious circumstances. On the father's death, the son obtained the estate and denied that he held this on trust for his mother. It was held that the trust was valid, even though it had not been declared in writing as required by statute, because of the son's fraud.

A fully secret trust will be recognized if the following conditions are satisfied.[86]

Testator's intention

The testator must have intended to create an express trust that satisfies the three certainties of intention, subject matter, and objects,[87] so that the legatee will be subject to an obligation to hold the identified property on trust for identified beneficiaries.[88]

The fully secret trust may not, however, be intended to arise immediately on the testator's death. So, for example, the testator might intend to create an obligation on the legatee to dispose of the property in a particular way by their own will. This type of trust is illustrated by *Ottaway v Norman*,[89] in which the testator in his will left his bungalow, its contents, and some money to his housekeeper. The testator made an agreement with the housekeeper that she would leave the bungalow in her will to the testator's son. She made a will in accordance with this arrangement. But, four years later, she made a new will that left the bungalow to the defendant. The testator and the housekeeper having died, the testator's son successfully sought a declaration that the defendant held the bungalow on a fully secret trust for him. The son also argued that his father intended that the housekeeper could spend the money as she wished, but that anything that was left was to pass to the son. It was recognized that, had this been intended, it would have created a valid trust. The housekeeper would then have been free to spend all of the money as she wished, but anything that was left on her death would have to be left to the son in her will. It was recognized that this trust obligation would be in suspense[90] during the housekeeper's life, but would have attached to her estate immediately on her death. Consequently, if she had not left the residue of the money to the son in her will, it would still be held on trust for the son by the executor of her estate. It was not, however, possible to establish that the father had intended the housekeeper to be obliged to leave the residue to the son, because there was no evidence that she was intended to keep the money left to her by the testator separate from her own money. Since no such requirement was intended, it followed that there was no ascertainable fund to which the trust could attach.

Although the analysis of the suspensory trust obligation in *Ottaway v Norman* was *obiter*, it is nonetheless significant. It follows that, if the testator in that case had intended the housekeeper to leave any residue to the testator's son, the son would have had an equitable proprietary interest in that residue. But what sort of trust would this be? The normal secret trust that arises immediately on the testator's death has been analysed as an express trust that is made *inter vivos*, but which is constituted on death.[91] But that cannot be true of the suspensory trust, since, on the testator's death, the trust property is still uncertain and might never exist if the legatee dissipates all of it. Any trust of the residue could be constituted only on the death of the legatee. Consequently, this is better analysed as a constructive trust that attaches to any residue of the testator's estate at the time

---

[86] *Ottaway v Norman* [1972] Ch 698, 711 (Brightman J). See also *Brown v Pourau* [1995] 1 NZLR 352, 367 (Hammond J).   [87] See Section 4.1, p. 72.

[88] *Ottaway v Norman* [1972] Ch 698, 711 (Brightman J).   [89] Ibid.

[90] A concept recognized by the High Court of Australia in *Birmingham v Renfrew* (1937) 57 CLR 666. See also *Re Cleaver* [1981] 1 WLR 939. See Section 9.3.5.(iii), p. 271.   [91] See Section 5.2.2.(ii), p. 111.

of the legatee's death.[92] It is only at that point that the subject matter of the trust will be certain. During the period from the testator's death until the legatee has died, the legatee is best regarded as the absolute owner of the property subject to fiduciary responsibilities arising out of the arrangements with the testator to prevent them from making gifts and settlements *inter vivos* with the intention of defeating the undertaking. The potential interest of the person whom the testator intended to receive the residue enables them to obtain an injunction to prevent such a disposition and to recover any property that has been so disposed. On the death of the legatee, if no provision has been made in their will for the residue to be given to the other person, the executor of the legatee's estate will hold the residue on constructive trust for that person. But, crucially, if the legatee legitimately dissipates the legacy received from the testator, there will be no property to be held on constructive trust for the other person.

Communication to legatee

The testator must have communicated the trust, its terms, and the identity of the trust property and the beneficiaries to the legatee before the testator's death.[93] So, for example, in *Re Boyes*,[94] the testator left a legacy to his solicitor, who was told that it was to be held on trust, but who was not told for whom. After the testator's death, a letter was found amongst the testator's papers stating that the residuary estate was to be held for the testator's mistress. It was held that this was not sufficient to create a valid secret trust and so the estate was held on resulting trust for the testator's next of kin. The secret trust was invalid because the legatee had to know who the beneficiary was before the testator died: it would be only once all of the key terms had been communicated that the trustee could have accepted the trust so that its performance was binding on him.

As with half-secret trusts, the delivery of a sealed letter during the testator's lifetime will be sufficient communication, provided that the legatee knows that the letter contain the terms of the trust and accepts it as such.[95]

Acceptance by legatee

The trust must be accepted by the legatee expressly or by acquiescence.[96] Alternatively, the legatee may expressly or impliedly agree that property should be disposed of in the legatee's will in a particular way.[97] Unlike the requirements for a half-secret trust,[98] it does not matter whether these conditions of communication and acceptance are satisfied before or after the will is made,[99] but they must be satisfied before the testator's death. Once the legatee has accepted the trust it cannot be disclaimed.[100]

Where testamentary gifts are made to two or more people as tenants in common and secret trusts are communicated to some of them, only those people are bound by the trusts and the others take beneficially.[101] Where, however, the gift is made to two or more people as joint tenants and the secret trusts are communicated only to some of them, they are all bound if the trust was communicated before the will was executed;[102] if the communication occurred after execution, it is only those who accepted the trusts who will be bound.[103] The reason for this distinction appears to be that, where the communication occurred before the will was executed, the will was made on the faith of the promise that all parties would be bound by the trust and it would be unconscionable for any of the

---

[92] Hayton, 'Ottaway v Norman' [1972] Conv 129, 132.   [93] *Wallgrave v Tebbs* (1855) 2 K & J 313.
[94] (1884) 26 Ch D 531.   [95] *Re Keen* [1937] Ch 236, 242 (Lord Wright MR).
[96] *Moss v Cooper* (1861) 1 J & H 352, 366 (Wood VC).   [97] *Ottaway v Norman* [1972] Ch 698.
[98] See Section 5.2.2.(ii), p. 114.   [99] *Moss v Cooper* (1861) 1 J & H 352, 367 (Wood VC).
[100] See Glister, 'Disclaimer and secret trusts' [2014] Conv 11.   [101] *Tee v Ferri* (1856) 2 K & J 357.
[102] *Re Young* [1951] Ch 344.   [103] *Moss v Cooper* (1861) 1 J & H 352.

parties to break that undertaking. If, however, the communication occurred after the will was executed, only the promisor will be bound by their undertaking, because the gift will not have been tainted with fraud in procuring the execution of the will.[104] But this is an unconvincing distinction since, even where the acceptance occurred after the will was executed, the testator had an opportunity to change the will and failed to do so. The better view is that, if the testator has been induced by the promise of one of the parties to leave property on secret trust, such that the gift would not have been made without the promise, the trust should bind all parties regardless of whether they are joint tenants or tenants in common, and regardless of whether or not the promise was made before or after the will was executed.[105]

Burden and standard of proof

The person seeking to establish the secret trust bears the burden of proving that the trust has been created.[106] As regards the standard of proof, it was recognized in *Ottaway v Norman*[107] that clear evidence was required before the court would be willing to conclude that the testator had intended something different from what appeared on the face of the will. An analogy was drawn with the equitable doctrine of rectification of documents,[108] under which a high standard of proof is required to show that the document does not reflect the actual intention of the parties so that it should be altered through the exercise of the equitable jurisdiction.

In *Re Snowden*,[109] however, Megarry V-C accepted that the ordinary civil standard of proof on a balance of probabilities applied to establish a fully secret trust,[110] save where fraud was asserted against the alleged trustee. In that case, the testatrix made her will six days before she died. She left her residuary estate to her brother absolutely. Six days after her death, the brother died. He left his property to his son. The testatrix's solicitors, who had prepared and witnessed the will, gave evidence that the testatrix wanted her brother to divide her estate for her so that she could be fair to everyone. The question for the court concerned the standard for proving this trust. Megarry V-C doubted the relevance of the analogy with the equitable doctrine of rectification when determining the standard of proof for recognizing secret trusts, because such trusts operate outside the will and do not require the formal terms of the will to be altered.[111] Rather, the will identifies who should receive property and then a trust external to the will is imposed on the legatee to reflect the testator's intent. Crucially, although Megarry V-C accepted that fraud is sufficient to establish a secret trust, he did not consider that it was required. It followed that there was no single standard of proof for all secret trusts; the standard depended on whether or not fraud was being proved. If fraud were alleged, then it would have to be established by the clearest evidence. But if fraud were not alleged, the lower civil standard of proof on the balance of probabilities would apply. On the facts of the case, Megarry V-C considered that fraud did not need to be proved, but even the lower civil standard of proof had not been satisfied. The testatrix was not considered to have intended to impose any legally enforceable obligation on her brother, but had simply left property to him for him to determine what he thought she would have done had she made up her mind as to what should happen to her property. This was a moral, rather than a legal, obligation and so there was no

---

[104] *Re Stead* [1900] 1 Ch 237, 241 (Farwell J).
[105] Perrins, 'Can you keep half a secret?' (1972) 88 LQR 225, 226.
[106] *Jones v Badley* (1868) LR 3 Ch App 362.   [107] [1972] Ch 698.   [108] See Section 21.7, p. 654.
[109] [1979] Ch 528.
[110] This is the standard of proof to establish mutual wills: *Re Cleaver* [1981] 1 WLR 939, 948 (Nourse J). See Section 9.3.5.(iii), p. 271.   [111] See Section 5.2.2.(ii), p. 111.

intention that he should hold the property on a fully secret trust. Consequently, the first requirement of a fully secret trust had not been proved to have been satisfied.[112]

The difficulty with *Re Snowden* relates to when fraud must be proved to establish a fully secret trust. Since, as will be seen, the recognition of all fully secret trusts can be justified by the need to prevent fraud, in the sense of unconscionable conduct, in defeating the testator's expectation that property will be held on trust,[113] it would appear that, when determining the standard of proof, fraud is to be interpreted in a narrow sense to mean deliberate and conscious wrongdoing amounting to deceit. Consequently, where the alleged secret trustee denies the existence of the trust and claims to take the property beneficially, a higher standard of proof must be satisfied, as in *Ottaway v Norman*. Where, however, the issue is simply whether the conditions for establishing a fully secret trust have been satisfied, such as whether the testator intended such a trust to be declared, as in *Re Snowden*, there is no allegation of fraud and the balance-of-probabilities standard applies. Similarly, for half-secret trusts, there will usually be no fraud in this narrow sense because the trust is clear on the face of the will. But, even with half-secret trusts, fraud in the narrow sense might be relevant if, for example, the trustee denies that the communication of the terms of the trust occurred before the will was executed and the trustee is entitled to the residuary estate, and so would take the property beneficially if the trust fails.

But this analysis of *Re Snowden* creates a paradox: it means that the worse the trustee's conduct is alleged to be, the higher the standard of proof that needs to be satisfied before the trust is recognized. It follows that, since fraud in this narrow sense of deceit need not be proved to establish a fully secret trust, it would be preferable not to plead it and for the beneficiary of the trust simply to satisfy the standard of proof on the balance of probabilities.

In *Re Snowden*, an alternative solution could have been adopted that would have enabled a secret trust to be identified. The court might have found that the testatrix intended to benefit a particular class, namely her nearest relatives, but had left it to her brother to decide how this could be best achieved. This should have created a secret trust in favour of her relatives, but subject to a power of selection in her brother.[114] The brother could not have been compelled to exercise this power during his lifetime, but, if the power had not been exercised, on his death the property could have been distributed equally amongst the testatrix's nearest relatives.

Failure to establish all requirements of a fully secret trust

If it is possible to prove that the testator intended a trust, and that this was communicated to and accepted by the legatee, but it is not possible to prove, for example, who the intended beneficiaries were, or if the terms of the trust are unlawful or uncertain,[115] the property will be held on resulting trust for those entitled to the testator's residuary estate.[116] Where it is not possible to prove even that the testator intended the legatee to take the property as a trustee, they will take the property beneficially.

Non-testamentary applications

Although a fully secret trust can arise only in the testamentary context, the principles recognized in the secret trust cases have been applied to transactions outside of wills. So, for example, in *Gold v Hill*,[117] the testator nominated his solicitor as the beneficiary of a

---

[112] See Section 5.2.2.(ii), p. 118.
[113] See Section 5.2.2.(ii), p. 122. The same is true of half-secret trusts. See Section 5.2.2.(ii), p. 122.
[114] Hodge, 'Secret trusts: the fraud theory revisited' [1980] Conv 341, 342.
[115] *Re Pugh's Will Trust* [1967] 1 WLR 1262. [116] *Re Boyes* (1884) 26 Ch D 531.
[117] [1999] 1 FLR 54.

life insurance policy. He then told the solicitor that he wanted him to use the proceeds of the policy to look after his partner and children. Following the testator's death, the solicitor received the proceeds of the policy. It was held that the solicitor held this money on trust for the partner and children, by analogy with a secret trust. This was not precisely the same mechanism as a secret trust because the solicitor was nominated as beneficiary of the policy rather than in a will, but the effect was the same since the solicitor was intended to hold the money on trust for others and this became effective only on the death of the testator. At that point, the solicitor received the proceeds of the policy, but he was then obliged to apply the money for the benefit of the testator's partner and children. The nomination was effective only on the date of death, so it was sufficient that the nature of the trust had been communicated by then.

The principles arising from the fully secret trust doctrine have also been applied where the testator failed to revoke an existing gift in reliance on the donee's assurances as to what he would do with the gift,[118] and also where a person failed to make a will in reliance on the assurances of the next of kin, who would be entitled to the estate on an intestacy, as to what they would do with the property.[119]

Theoretical basis for recognizing fully secret trusts

In the same way as the half-secret trust is recognized to prevent the trustee from acting unconscionably in avoiding their undertaking to the testator to hold property on trust for another, the fully secret trust can be justified in the same way, namely to prevent fraud.[120] This involves fraud as interpreted in its wider objective sense, since it does not require positive proof of the trustee's intention to deceive the testator. Although sometimes judges have suggested that fraud in its narrower sense of 'deception'[121] constitutes the basis for the recognition of fully secret trusts, the better view now is that this needs to be proved only sometimes and is not a requirement for the recognition of all fully secret trusts.[122]

A unified theory of secret trusts?

Although half-secret and fully secret trusts appear to be juridically different,[123] since one appears on the face of the will and the other does not, the better view is that they are not different. They are both express trusts that arise dehors the will, even though they are constituted only once the testator has died. Both types of trust should be recognized in order to prevent fraud in the wider sense of unconscionable conduct in betraying the undertaking made to the testator.[124] It follows that the requirements for both types of trust should be the same, namely an intention to create a trust, communication of the terms to the trustee before the testator's death, and acknowledgement or acquiescence of the trust by the trustee. Analysed like this, half-secret and fully secret trusts are defensible and workable.

Should secret trusts be recognized today?

The reasons for recognizing secret trusts might be considered to be much weaker today than they were in the nineteenth and early twentieth centuries. The desire to keep certain beneficiaries off the face of the will, namely mistresses and illegitimate children, might not

---

[118] *Moss v Cooper* (1861) 1 J & H 352.

[119] *Stickland v Aldridge* (1804) 9 Ves 516; *Re Gardner (No 2)* [1923] 2 Ch 230, 233 (Romer J).

[120] *McCormick v Grogan* (1869) LR 4 HL 82; *Re Snowden* [1979] Ch 528, 536 (Sir Robert Megarry V-C). See Hodge (see n. 114) and McFarlane (see n. 22), p. 677, who conclude that the secret trust is consequently a constructive trust. [121] *McCormick v Grogan* (1869) LR 4 HL 82, 97 (Lord Westbury).

[122] *Re Snowden* [1979] Ch 528. [123] Sheridan, 'English and Irish secret trusts' (1951) 67 LQR 314.

[124] Hodge (see n. 114); cf. Critchley (see n. 76), p. 652.

be considered to be a sufficient reason to allow a secret trust to be valid, especially because illegitimate children can now claim from the testator's estate.[125] Another reason for wishing to use secret trusts is because the testator might be indecisive as to who should benefit from their estate and may wish somebody else to make the decision on their behalf, as in *Re Snowden*.[126] This is not an acceptable reason for avoiding the operation of the Wills Act 1837, which exists to prevent such informal arrangements in the distribution of an estate. A possible solution[127] is to require the communication of the key terms of both half-secret and fully secret trusts before the will is executed, since this would ensure that the policy of maintaining secrecy would be preserved, but would prevent the secret trust from being used where the testator is indecisive as to who should be benefited.

5.3 FORMALITIES FOR THE CONSTITUTION OF TRUSTS

5.3.1 GENERAL PRINCIPLES

(i) The nature of constituting a trust

In addition to possible formality requirements relating to the creation of trusts, the question of formalities may also be relevant to determine when a trust is constituted. For a trust to be effective, it is not enough simply to declare the trust; it is also necessary to ensure that title to property has been vested in the trustee or trustees. This process of vesting of title is known as 'constituting' the trust. What is required to constitute a trust depend on the circumstances in which the trust is declared and the nature of the property that is intended to be held on trust. Where a trust is not effectively constituted, a complex body of law has developed whereby Equity may be able to intervene and validate the trust. This body of law may also be of relevance where a gift has not been effectively transferred at Law.

(ii) Timing

The question of timing is also significant. The declaration of trust and its constitution need not be contemporaneous.[128] So the settlor can declare the trust one day and legal title to property can be transferred to the trustee much later. It follows that, once the trust has been declared, the settlor can change their mind about creating the trust before it has been constituted. Once the trust is constituted, however, the settlor cannot recover the property that has been transferred, even though the trustee and beneficiary will not have provided any consideration for it. The question of timing is significant for another reason: if Ann wishes to declare a trust but does so only after title to property has been transferred to Bill, there can be no trust, for Bill will already have received the property absolutely.

(iii) Modes of disposing property

There are three modes of disposing property. As we will see, identifying which mode is intended by the transferor is vital to understanding the operation of the law in this area, since if the transferor intended one mode of disposal that is ineffective, Equity will not, at least as a general rule, give effect to their intention by applying a different mode.[129]

---

[125] Inheritance (Provision for Family and Dependants) Act 1975.
[126] [1979] Ch 528. See Section 5.2.2.(ii), p. 120.
[127] Watkin, 'Cloaking a contravention' [1981] Conv 335, 340.
[128] As with the secret trust. Section 5.2.2.(ii), p. 111.
[129] *Milroy v Lord* (1862) 4 De G F and J 264.

Transfer of legal ownership beneficially

Where the transferor has legal title to property, they may intend to transfer that property to the transferee absolutely so that the transferor divests themself of legal ownership and the other party takes the property beneficially. This transfer of legal ownership may involve, for example, the conveyance of land, the sale or gift of chattels, the assignment of debts, or the transfer of shares. Where there is an intention to transfer property absolutely to the transferee, there will be no intention on the part of the transferor that the property should be held on trust.

If the transferor agreed to give property to the transferee, but failed to do so, for example because an attempted transfer failed or the transferor changed their mind, Equity will not, at least as a general rule,[130] be in a position to help the transferee. This is because 'Equity will not assist a volunteer',[131] meaning somebody who has not provided consideration for the transfer, such as a donee. The principle that Equity will not assist a volunteer is closely related to another principle that 'Equity will not perfect an imperfect gift'. This is consistent with Equity's general suspicion of gifts.[132] If a donor has acted unwisely in agreeing to make a gift and regrets doing so, then it is not for Equity to intervene and to compel the gift to be made;[133] rather, the donor should be allowed to change their mind about the gift. Of course, if the intended transferee has provided valuable consideration for the property, such as the purchase price, then there is likely to be a contract, and, if the transferor then fails to transfer the property, the transferee can sue for breach of contract and Equity might even exceptionally assist by specifically enforcing the transferor's promise to transfer the property.[134] But this does not involve the perfection of a gift, because the transferee provided consideration. It is this that marks the significant difference between 'gift' and 'contract'.

Transfer on trust

The transferor may instead intend to transfer the legal or equitable title to property to the transferee to be held on trust either for the transferor or a third party. In such circumstances, the trustee is not intended to receive the property absolutely and, usually, neither is the trustee intended to receive the property beneficially.

Declaration of self as trustee

Finally, rather than transferring legal title to the transferee, the person who has legal and beneficial title to the property might instead declare that they hold that property on trust for another person. In such a situation, the owner of the property will become the trustee of it. They will retain legal title to the property, but will no longer have a beneficial interest in it;[135] this will then be with the beneficiary. Alternatively, the person with legal title to the property might declare that they hold the property on trust for themself and another.[136] They would then retain a beneficial interest in the property, but it would not be an absolute beneficial interest, because the other beneficiary would have a beneficial interest as well.

5.3.2 CONSTITUTION OF EXPRESS TRUST

There are two methods for constituting an express trust, depending on who the intended trustees are.

---

[130] See Section 5.3.3.(iii), p. 127.   [131] See Section 2.12, p. 35.
[132] See Section 2.8, p. 33.
[133] *Pennington v Waine* [2002] EWCA Civ 227, [2002] 1 WLR 2075, [62] (Arden LJ).
[134] See Section 21.4, p. 634.   [135] *Richards v Delbridge* (1874) LR 18 Eq 11, 14 (Jessel MR).
[136] *Paul v Constance* [1977] 1 WLR 527. See Section 4.2.2.(vi), p. 75.

(i) Declaration of self as trustee

The first method of constituting a trust is straightforward. Where a settlor declares themself as trustee of property in which the settlor either has a legal or an equitable interest,[137] the trust will be constituted automatically because title to the trust property will already be vested in the settlor.

Intention to declare self as trustee

The key difficulty as regards this method of constitution turns on whether the settlor intended to declare themself as a trustee.[138] But once this intent has been established, then, as long as the settlor does have title to the property, the trust will be automatically constituted[139] and the court will enforce it on behalf of the beneficiaries, even though they are volunteers.

More than one trustee

One particular problem involving the constitution of a trust where the settlor declares themself as trustee relates to where the settlor intends others to be trustees as well. Must title to the property be transferred to these other trustees for the trust to be constituted? This issue was considered in the important decision of the Privy Council in *T Choithram International SA v Pagarani*.[140] In that case, the settlor, a rich businessman who was seriously ill, executed a deed to establish a charitable foundation by means of a trust. He appointed himself as one of the trustees and verbally declared that he gave all of his estate to the foundation, which was interpreted as meaning to the charitable trust, since this was the mechanism by which the foundation operated.[141] He died before legal title to his shares had been transferred to the trustees. It was held, however, that a trust of his estate had been validly constituted because title to the estate was already vested in him and it did not matter that title had not yet been vested in the other trustees. It followed that the trust was constituted immediately the settlor had declared that he gave his estate to the foundation. This was effective even though the trust property was not vested in all of the trustees, because the settlor's conscience was considered to have been affected by the trust immediately it had been declared, such that it would then have been unconscionable for him to deny the trust. Consequently, had the settlor survived, he would have been obliged to ensure that legal title to the trust property was vested in all of the trustees. It follows that, as long as one trustee has title to the property, the trust can be considered to have been constituted, even though the settlor and that one trustee were the same person so that there was no transfer of title to anybody.

(ii) Vesting of title in trustees

The other method of constituting a trust is for the settlor to vest title to the property in trustees. Whether any formalities are required for such vesting of title will depend on the nature of the trust property. So, for example, title to registered land is transferred by registration,[142] whereas title to unregistered land is transferred by a deed.[143] Title to shares is transferred by completion and delivery of a form of transfer followed by registration of title in the share register;[144] copyright is transferred by writing;[145] and chattels are

---

[137] *Timpson's Executors v Yerbury* [1936] 1 KB 645, 664 (Romer LJ).   [138] See Section 4.2.2.(vi), p. 75.
[139] *Middleton v Pollock* (1876) 2 Ch D 104.   [140] [2001] 1 WLR 1.
[141] See Rickett, 'Completely constituting an *inter vivos* trust: property rules?' [2001] Conv 515, 516.
[142] Land Registration Act 2002.   [143] Law of Property Act 1925, s. 52 (1).
[144] Companies Act 2006, ss. 544, 770–4; Stock Transfer Act 1963, s. 1.
[145] Copyright, Designs and Patents Act 1988, s. 90(3).

transferred either by a deed of gift[146] or by an intention to give coupled with a delivery of possession.[147]

If the settlor is already the beneficiary of a trust, they can declare a trust of their equitable interest and have this interest held on trust by trustees for other beneficiaries. But this will require the assignment of an existing equitable interest to the trustees, which will require writing.[148] This is illustrated by *Kekewich v Manning*,[149] in which shares were held on trust for A for life with remainder to B absolutely. B assigned his equitable interest in the remainder to C to hold on trust for D. This created a valid trust of the equitable interest in the remainder for D.

Once title has been vested in the trustees, the trust will be completely constituted and effective from that point, and cannot then be revoked.[150] It is irrelevant that the trustees and beneficiaries have not provided any consideration for the constitution of the trust.[151]

The precise moment at which a trust is validly constituted might be a matter of some significance, as illustrated by *Re Ralli's Will Trusts*.[152] In that case, a testator had left his estate on trust for his wife for life and then for his two daughters, Helen and Irene, absolutely. Helen made a marriage settlement whereby she covenanted to settle any property acquired subsequently for Irene's children. The testator's widow and Helen having died, the claimant, who was Irene's husband, was the sole trustee of the testator's will and also of Helen's marriage settlement. The question in issue in the case was whether the claimant held Helen's half of the testator's residuary estate on trust for Helen's estate or on the trusts of her marriage settlement, the beneficiaries of which were the claimant's three children. It was held that he held Helen's share of the residuary estate on the trusts of the marriage settlement. This was because the property was vested in him as trustee of the marriage settlement and it did not matter that it had come to him as a trustee of the trusts under the testator's will. In other words, the trust of the marriage settlement was constituted once the property had come to him, albeit in a different capacity from his position as trustee of the trust in question. It follows that it is the fact of legal title vesting in the trustee that constitutes the trust, regardless of the reason why the legal title was vested in the trustee.[153]

5.3.3 INCOMPLETELY CONSTITUTED TRUSTS

When a trust is not completely constituted, it cannot take effect as an express trust. Equity might still be able to rescue something from the apparently failed transaction, but, for Equity to intervene, a major doctrinal obstacle needs to be surmounted. This is the principle that 'Equity will not assist a volunteer'. The volunteer, for these purposes, is the intended beneficiary, who will not have provided any consideration for the transfer of trust property to the trustee. This causes no problems where the trust has been constituted, for the effect of the constitution is that the beneficiary can obtain the benefit of the trust property regardless of the fact that they are a volunteer. But, where the trust has not been constituted, the lack of consideration provided by the intended beneficiary means that they have no rights to enforce. It is this characteristic of being a volunteer that has enabled Equity to draw an analogy with another form of failed transaction, the failed gift, under which a donor purports to make an outright gift to the donee, but fails to transfer the

---

[146] *Jaffa v Taylor Gallery Ltd* (1990) The Times, 21 March.
[147] *Re Cole (a Bankrupt)* [1964] Ch 175; *Thomas v Times Book Co Ltd* [1966] 1 WLR 911.
[148] Law of Property Act 1925, s. 53(1)(c). See Section 11.3.1, p. 325.   [149] (1851) 1 De GM & G 176.
[150] *Re Bowden* [1936] Ch 71.   [151] See *Paul v Paul* (1882) 20 Ch D 742.   [152] [1964] Ch 288.
[153] See also the rule in *Strong v Bird* (1874) LR 18 Eq 315, discussed in Section 5.3.3.(iii), p. 140.

property effectively or at all. The fundamental principle here is that there is no Equity to perfect an imperfect gift,[154] because, again, Equity will not assist the donee volunteer.

(i) Failed trusts

The leading case that recognizes the general principle that Equity will not assist a volunteer beneficiary to save an incompletely constituted trust is *Milroy v Lord*.[155] In that case the settlor purported to transfer shares to Lord by deed to be held on trust for the claimant. The settlor handed Lord the share certificates, but this was not sufficient to vest the legal title in him, since further formalities still had to be completed. Although Lord had a power of attorney as the settlor's agent, which would have enabled him to transfer the shares into his name, this power was not exercised and the shares remained registered in the name of the settlor. It was held that, since legal title to the shares had not been vested in Lord, the trust had not been constituted and so was not valid. It was recognized that the settlor needed to have done everything required by the nature of the trust property to ensure that the property was transferred to the trustee, but that, since he had not done this, title to the shares remained in him. The court did consider whether the fact that Lord had the power of attorney, which would have enabled him to have the shares transferred into his name, would be sufficient to treat the trust as perfected. But this was rejected on the ground that Lord held this power as the settlor's agent and the court was not willing to compel the agent to transfer the shares if it would not have been able to make the settlor do so. An alternative result might have been to treat the settlor as holding the shares on an express trust for the claimant, but this was clearly not what the settlor had intended and so would not have been an appropriate solution.

(ii) Failed gifts

Where a gift has been made imperfectly, Equity will not, as a general rule,[156] perfect it. So, for example, if a donor purports to make a gift before their death and fails to do everything at Law to transfer title to the donee, the court will not compel the personal representatives of the donor to complete the act that the donor failed to do.[157] Also, where a gift is imperfect, the court will not give a benevolent construction to the donor's words so that an intention to make a gift is treated as though the donor had declared themself to be a trustee of the property for the donee.[158] This is because an intention to make a gift is fundamentally different from an intention to declare oneself a trustee: a donor intends to divest themself of all responsibility for the property, whereas a trustee assumes onerous obligations in respect of the property, so that the imposition of trusteeship on a donor would impose a responsibility that they would not have anticipated.

(iii) Saving failed trusts and gifts

Although the principles that Equity will not assist a volunteer and will not perfect an imperfect gift are fundamental, Equity recognizes a further qualifying principle, namely that 'Equity will not strive officiously to defeat a gift',[159] whether this is an outright gift to the donee or a gift held on trust for the beneficiaries. Although a failed gift or an incompletely constituted trust cannot be saved by treating the donor or settlor as an express trustee of the property for the donee or the beneficiaries, simply because this will not have been intended, Equity has found other ways of fulfilling the settlor's or donor's intention.

---

[154] *Milroy v Lord* (1862) 4 De GF & J 264.   [155] Ibid.   [156] See Section 5.3.3., (iii), p. 127.
[157] *Re Rose* [1949] Ch 78.   [158] *Milroy v Lord* (1862) 4 De GF & J 264.
[159] *T Choithram International SA v Pagarani* [2001] 1 WLR 1, 11 (Lord Browne-Wilkinson).

Settlor or donor has done everything necessary to transfer title

Where the settlor or donor has done all that is necessary to transfer title to the trustee or donee, but this has not happened for reasons outside the control of the settlor or donor, then, although at Law the settlor or donor has retained legal title, Equity will assume that title has passed to the trustee or donee. But this passing of title is recognized only in Equity. It follows that legal title remains in the settlor or donor, and equitable title will be in the intended trustee or donee. This division of legal and equitable title means that there is a trust and, since this arises by operation of law, it is properly analysed as a constructive trust.[160] The beneficiary of this trust, namely the intended trustee or donee, can then seek the transfer of the property to them.[161] Once legal title has been transferred, the trustee will hold it on trust for the intended beneficiary and the donee will receive it absolutely.

The application of this principle is particularly well illustrated by *Re Rose*.[162] The transferor in that case purported to transfer shares to the transferees in March 1943, with one transfer intended to be a gift to his wife and the other for the transferee to hold on trust. The transferor completed the relevant documentation and delivered it to the company to which the shares related. The transfer was eventually registered by the directors of the company in June of that year. The transferor then died. If the transfer had been effective in March, estate duty would not have been payable on the transfers by the transferor's estate, but duty would have been payable by the estate if the transfer were effective only in June. The Court of Appeal held that, although the transfer was not legally effective until June, when the shares were registered in the name of the transferees, it was effective in Equity in March, because the transferor had done everything in his power to effect the transfer by that date. Whilst it was acknowledged that an intention to make a gift could not be interpreted as an intention to declare a trust, this referred to an express trust and did not prevent the court from recognizing that the shares were held on a constructive trust by the transferor for the transferees. Crucially, if the transferor has done everything that they can do to effect the transfer, then they will hold the property on constructive trust for the transferee.

Earlier, in a case coincidentally also called *Re Rose*,[163] the testator had bequeathed in his will shares in a company to Hook, but only if the shares had not already been transferred to him before the testator's death. The testator had executed the transfer documents in accordance with the company's regulations, which he then transferred to Hook with the share certificate, but the shares had not been registered in Hook's name by the time of the testator's death. The question for the court was whether the shares had been transferred whilst the testator was alive or whether there was a transfer under the will, which might have been inoperative at Law. It was held that, because the testator had done all that he needed to do to vest legal title to the shares in Hook, Equity should treat this as having occurred, so that the gift of shares had been effective whilst the testator was alive.

In both cases, the settlor or donor was considered to have done everything that they needed to do to ensure that title to the shares was transferred to the trustee or donee, respectively. But the facts of such cases need to be analysed carefully to ensure that the settlor or donor has, indeed, done everything necessary to ensure that the property is transferred. In *Re Paradise Motor Co Ltd*,[164] for example, the transferor of shares was considered to have done all that was necessary to effect the transfer even though he had not

---

[160] See further Section 5.3.3.(iii), p. 131.   [161] See Section 11.4, p. 334.

[162] *Rose v Inland Revenue Commissioners* [1952] Ch 499. See also *Zeital v Kaye* [2010] EWCA Civ 159, [2010] WTLR 913, [40] (Rimer LJ).

[163] *Midland Bank Executor and Trustee Co Ltd v Rose* [1949] Ch 78. Approved by Lord Wilberforce in *Vandervell v IRC* [1967] 2 AC 291, 330.   [164] [1968] 1 WLR 1125.

signed the transfer document, since this was considered to be a mere irregularity and not essential. This can be contrasted with *Re Fry*,[165] in which the donor, who lived abroad, needed to obtain HM Treasury consent to transfer shares. Although he had applied for this consent, it had not been obtained. It was held that it was not possible to say that the donor had done everything necessary to effect the transfer of the shares, because HM Treasury might have required more information to be provided. In fact, in both of the *Re Rose* cases, it might have been held that the settlor and donor had not done everything necessary to effect the transfer of legal title to the shares, since consent of the directors of the company was required before the transfer of shares could be registered and the directors might have requested more information before giving their consent.[166] The preferable view, therefore, is that the possibility that a third party might require the settlor or donor to do something else before legal title can be transferred should not mean that the settlor or donor has not done everything necessary to effect the transfer. It will always be the case that the settlor or donor could have done more to effect the transfer of legal title to the shares, such as simply requesting the company to register the trustee or donee as shareholder,[167] but it should be sufficient that the donor has done everything that it is essential for them to do to effect the transfer and without which the transfer could not take place.

It follows that where a donor intends to give shares to a donee but, even though the donor had done all that they needed to do to ensure that they were transferred, legal title remains in the donor, Equity will regard the shares as being held on constructive trust for the donee, who can then demand transfer of the legal title. Even then, legal title to the shares will be transferred only where the formalities for transfer are satisfied. Similarly, where a settlor intends to transfer shares to the trustee to hold for the beneficiary, but, despite the settlor having done everything necessary to transfer legal title, they retain legal title, the settlor will hold the shares on constructive trust for the intended trustee. The settlor can still arrange for legal title to be transferred to the intended trustee, who will then hold the shares on the anticipated express trust for the beneficiary. In both cases, the settlor or donor will not be able to withdraw from the transaction, since a constructive trust will have been automatically constituted.

If the property that is intended to be transferred to the trustee or the donee comprises shares, the fact that the shares are held on constructive trust by the settlor or donor has significant practical implications. For example, any distribution of dividends will be paid to the settlor or donor, but, since they derive from the shares that are held on trust, the dividends will also be held on trust. Also, the settlor or donor will be required to exercise the voting rights attached to the shares for the benefit of the beneficiaries.

The *Re Rose* principle has been applied to transfers involving property other than shares. So, for example, in *Mascall v Mascall*,[168] a father had intended to make a gift of his house to his son. He handed the land certificate to the son and executed the transfer document. The son then needed to submit the transfer for stamping and to ask the Land Registry to register his title, but, before this could be done, the father and son fell out and the father sought a declaration that the gift was void. It was held that the gift had been effective in Equity, because the father had done all that he needed to do to effect the transfer of the house to the son. Although it was possible for the father to have sought registration of the change in title himself, this was not considered to be relevant because the test was whether

---

[165] [1946] Ch 312.

[166] McKay, 'Share transfers and the complete and perfect rule' (1976) 40 Conv 139, 146; Lowrie and Todd, 'Re Rose revisited' (1998) 57 CLJ 46, 49.

[167] *Pennington v Waine* [2002] EWCA Civ 227, [2002] 1 WLR 2075, [116] (Clarke LJ).

[168] (1984) 50 P & CR 119. See Dowling, 'Can Roses survive on registered land?' (1999) 50 NILQ 90.

the father had done everything in his power in the ordinary way to transfer title, and it was usual for the donee to seek registration.

Unconscionability

The *Re Rose* principle has been extended to apply even where the settlor or donor had not done everything necessary to effect a transfer of title, but where the settlor or donor had done enough to effect the transfer such that any attempt to deny the validity of the transfer by the settlor or donor would be considered to be unconscionable. This was recognized by the Court of Appeal in *Pennington v Waine*.[169] In that case, the donor told her nephew that she wanted to give him 400 shares in a company and wanted him to become a director of the company, for which he needed to own at least one share. They both signed the share transfer form, which was delivered to the company's auditor. The donor died before the auditor had delivered the form to the company. The issue for the court was whether the donor had done enough to transfer the shares so that they did not form part of her residuary estate. The problem was that this was not a case in which, technically, the donor had done all that she needed to do to transfer the title to the shares. This was because, although she had completed the transfer form and had delivered it to the auditor of the company, the auditor was considered to be acting as her agent. Since he had not done everything in his power to transfer title to the shares, it followed that the donor had not done so either, since the omissions of the agent were considered to be the omissions of the principal. Further, the donor could have demanded the return of the share transfer form at any point before the agent had delivered it, which meant that the simple transfer of the form to the agent did not establish that the donor had done all within her power to effect the transfer.

Despite this, it was still held that the nephew had an equitable interest in the shares, so that they did not form part of the donor's residuary estate. The reason for this was recognized most clearly by Arden LJ, who held that, since the nephew had been told of the gift of the shares and he had been made a director of the company, it would have been unconscionable for the donor to revoke the gift before her death. Two policy objectives were considered to be significant in reaching this decision: first, to uphold the donor's intent to transfer the shares, and secondly, to prevent the donor, or her personal representatives, from acting unconscionably by revoking the gift.

Whenever the word 'unconscionable' is used as the basis for a test in Equity, there are genuine concerns about lack of certainty and principle.[170] In *Pennington v Waine*, Arden LJ recognized[171] that there was no comprehensive list of what factors would make it unconscionable for the donor to recall the gift and that the court should evaluate all relevant considerations. On the facts of the case, these considerations included that the donor intended to make an immediate gift and did so of her own free will; she had informed her nephew of the gift; her agent had told the nephew that he did not need to take any action to register the shares; and the nephew had agreed to become director of the company, which required the shares to be transferred to him. This was sufficient to make any attempt of the personal representatives of the donor to revoke the gift to be unconscionable.

But why were these particular factors considered to be relevant? The better view is that they indicate that the donor had made a representation to the nephew on which he had relied, albeit not to his detriment. It follows that the key test of unconscionability is a form of estoppel, but without needing to prove detriment.[172] That unconscionability in *Pennington*

---

[169] [2002] EWCA Civ 227, [2002] 1 WLR 2075.   [170] See Section 2.3, p. 27.
[171] [2002] EWCA Civ 227, [2002] 1 WLR 2075, [64].
[172] As in *Banner Homes Group plc v Luff Developments Ltd* [2000] Ch 372. See Section 10.3.2, p. 303.

v Waine can be established by virtue of the intended donee's reliance on the intended gift was subsequently recognized by Briggs J in *Curtis v Pulbrook*.[173] But Briggs J also considered that the reliance had to be detrimental, which it was not in that case so the failed gift could not be saved by a constructive trust, and that the nephew in *Pennington* had detrimentally relied on the intended gift by agreeing to become a director of the company on the assumption that he had received an effective gift of qualifying shares.[174] But, since legal title to the shares had not been transferred to the nephew, it is difficult to see how his reliance on the gift was detrimental. Rather, by agreeing to become a director, he had simply relied on the gift being made and there was nothing in the decision of the Court of Appeal to suggest that he had acted to his detriment in reliance on the gift being made.

In fact, rather than using the language of unconscionability, it would have been preferable for the Court of Appeal in *Pennington v Waine* to conclude that the donor, or her personal representatives, could not revoke a gift where she was estopped from doing so. The use of unconscionability as the key test with its connotations of fault was inappropriate, especially since it was specifically derived from the decision of the Privy Council in *T Choithram International SA v Pagarani*.[175] But that was in the very different context of a settlor's self-declaration of himself as an express trustee, where it would be unconscionable for him not to transfer title to his co-trustees. But the settlor in that case had already declared himself to be a trustee, whereas unconscionability in *Pennington* was used to convert a donor into a trustee. Rather than treating unconscionability as the test determining whether Equity will intervene, it is better to regard that as the conclusion that will be reached once it can be shown that the donor is estopped from denying the gift. In other words, proof of estoppel establishes that it is unconscionable for the donor to seek to revoke the gift. On the facts of *Pennington v Waine* itself, it might have been concluded that there was insufficient evidence of the nephew's reliance on the donor's representation, save for his agreement that he would become a director of the company, which required him to own at least one share. Consequently, the finding of unconscionability in that case is difficult to defend.

A further issue arising from *Pennington v Waine* concerned the nature of the trust by virtue of which the donor held the shares for the donee. According to Clarke LJ, it was an express trust, since he considered the aunt to have assigned an equitable interest in the shares to the nephew, so that she held the shares on trust for him. But this cannot be correct because the donor intended to make an immediate gift of the shares without intending to hold them on trust for the nephew, and it is a fundamental principle that Equity will not save a gift by treating it as a declaration of trust.[176] Further, if the aunt had indeed assigned an existing equitable interest to the nephew, there needed to have been a prior event to create such an interest, and there was no such event. She was the absolute owner of the shares and nothing had occurred before the attempted transfer of the shares to create an equitable interest in them.

The preferable analysis of the trust in *Pennington* is that of Arden LJ, who treated the trust as constructive. This is consistent with the recognition of the principle of unconscionability, which is regarded as one of the events that triggers the recognition of constructive trusts.[177] This also does not undermine the principle that Equity will not save a gift by finding a declaration of trust, because constructive trusts arise by operation of law and do not depend on intent, so that they do not require there to be any declaration of trust. Further,

---

[173] [2011] EWHC 167 (Ch), [2011] 1 BCLC 638, [43].

[174] The significance of detrimental reliance was also raised but not examined in *Zeital v Kaye* [2010] EWCA Civ 159, [2010] WTLR 913, [45] (Rimer LJ).   [175] [2001] 1 WLR 1. See Section 5.3.2.(i), p. 125.

[176] *Milroy v Lord* (1862) 4 De GF & J 264. See Section 5.3.3.(i), p. 127.   [177] See Section 9.3.8, p. 274.

the key reason why an intention to make a gift will not be treated as an intention to hold on trust arises from the fundamental difference between donors and trustees:[178] a donor intends to divest themself of all responsibility for the property, whereas the trustee assumes onerous obligations in respect of the property. But that is not the case as regards a constructive trustee, who will not be subject to such onerous duties, this being a bare trust.[179]

Covenants to settle

Where title to property has not been transferred to the trustee, but the settlor has covenanted or promised to settle property either on a new or an existing trust, the beneficiaries of that trust might wish to enforce the covenant either by compelling the settlor to transfer the property or by seeking damages for breach of the covenant. But the beneficiaries will not usually be in a position to enforce such a covenant, because they are not party to any contract made with the settlor, such a contract typically being between settlor and trustee, and they will not have provided any consideration for the covenant to enable them to enforce it, so that they are volunteers and Equity will not assist a volunteer.[180] Nevertheless, there will be circumstances under which the beneficiaries can enforce the covenant, either because they have a statutory right to do so or because consideration is interpreted more widely in Equity than at Common Law, so that the beneficiaries may not actually be volunteers.

Contracts (Rights of Third Parties) Act 1999

Today, the significance of the principle that Equity will not assist a volunteer is significantly reduced because of the Contracts (Rights of Third Parties) Act 1999, the effect of which is that somebody who is not a party to a contract will be able to enforce a term in it either if the contract expressly states that the third party can enforce it,[181] or if a term in the contract purports to confer a benefit on the third party,[182] although this latter provision will not apply if the parties to the contract did not intend the term to be enforceable by the third party.[183] The third party will be able to enforce a term only if they are identified in the contract by name, or as a member of a class, or as answering a particular description, although they need not be in existence when the contract was made,[184] so that a child or grandchild of a settlor born after the contract was made can still rely on the Act to enforce a term. If the third party is able to rely on the Act, they can obtain any remedy that would have been available had they been a party to the contract, and it is irrelevant that the third party had not provided any consideration. Where a third party has a right to enforce a term of the contract under the Act, the contract cannot be rescinded or varied so as to extinguish or alter the third party's right without that party's agreement, in three situations:[185]

(1) if the third party communicated to the promisor their assent to the term;

(2) if the promisor is aware that the third party has relied on the term; and

(3) if the promisor can reasonably be expected to have foreseen that the third party would rely on the term and the third party did rely on it.

The relevance of this Act as regards covenants to settle property on trust is that a beneficiary of that trust could enforce a covenant to convey property to the trustees for the

---

[178] Maitland, Equity: A Course of Lectures, 2nd edn, ed. Brunyate (Cambridge: Cambridge University Press, 1936), p. 74. See Doggett, 'Explaining Re Rose: the search goes on?' (2003) 62 CLJ 263, 264.

[179] See Section 9.5, p. 279.   [180] Jefferys v Jefferys (1841) 1 Cr & Phill 138, 141 (Lord Cottenham).

[181] Contracts (Rights of Third Parties) Act 1999, s. 1(1)(a).   [182] Ibid., s. 1(1)(b).

[183] Ibid., s. 1(2).   [184] Ibid., s. 1(3).   [185] Ibid., s. 2.

benefit of the beneficiary even though they are a volunteer. So, for example, if Ann covenants with Belinda to transfer property to Belinda to be held on trust for Clive, but Ann fails to transfer the property to Belinda, Clive will have a direct cause of action against Ann for breach of the covenant, because the term purports to confer a benefit on Clive, who is identified by name. Clive could then sue for damages to compensate him for the loss arising from the breach. But it may alternatively be possible for Clive to enforce the covenant by requiring Ann to transfer the property to Belinda, since the remedy of specific performance is specifically recognized as being available under the Act if it would have been available had Clive been a party to the contract.[186] The availability of specific performance under the Act does, however, cause some difficulty, since it is not available to a volunteer.[187] Since most parties in the position of Clive will be volunteers, it has been suggested that the rule relating to the availability of specific performance should not apply under the Act[188] and the covenant would then be specifically enforceable as long as compensatory damages are not an adequate remedy, this being an essential requirement for specific performance.[189] This would, however, be inconsistent with fundamental equitable principles, notably that Equity will not assist a volunteer, so the preferable view is that the remedy of specific performance will not be available to a third party to the contract unless they had provided consideration for the promise.

Although the enactment of the 1999 Act reduces the significance of the principle that volunteers cannot enforce a covenant to settle property on trust, it does not render that principle irrelevant. This is because the 1999 Act applies only to those covenants that were entered into after 11 May 2000[190] and in which the beneficiary is identified by name or by description. It follows that it remains necessary to consider the old cases that recognize that volunteers cannot enforce a covenant and those that identify methods for avoiding this principle. These methods continue to be relevant, because the 1999 Act does not affect any right or remedy of a third party that exists apart from the Act.[191]

Definition of a volunteer

Where Ann covenants with Belinda to transfer property to Belinda to hold on trust for Clive and Ann fails to transfer the property to Belinda, Clive will have an equitable claim against Ann outside of the 1999 Act if Clive had provided consideration for the transfer so that he is not a volunteer. As we have seen, the beneficiary will rarely have provided any valuable consideration, such as money or services, for the covenantor's promise. At Common Law, a party to a covenant will be able to enforce it even though they are a volunteer if the covenant is contained in a deed. Equity does not, however, treat a covenant in a deed as any different from a covenant in any other form. Equity does, however, define consideration more widely than at Common Law, since it includes the so-called 'marriage consideration'. This means that where a covenant to transfer property to be held on trust is made in consideration of a marriage, the husband, wife, and any issue of the marriage are able to enforce the covenant,[192] although it cannot be enforced by any other relative.[193] Illegitimate children and children from a former marriage do not fall within the marriage consideration. If the beneficiary falls within the marriage consideration and the covenant is made in consideration of a marriage, they can sue for breach of the covenant and obtain damages or, if damages is not an adequate remedy, specific performance of the covenant.

---

[186] Ibid., s. 1(5).   [187] See Section 21.4, p. 635.

[188] See Andrews, 'Strangers to justice no longer: the reversal of the privity rule under the Contracts (Rights of Third Parties) Act 1999' (2001) 60 CLJ 353, 361.   [189] See Section 21.4, p. 634.

[190] Contracts (Rights of Third Parties) Act 1999, s. 10(2). The Act applies to covenants entered into after 11 November 1999 if the contract expressly provides that the Act shall apply: ibid., s. 10(3).

[191] Ibid., s. 7.   [192] *Pullan v Koe* [1913] 1 Ch 9.   [193] *Re D'Angibou* (1880) 15 Ch D 228.

The significance of whether a person falls within the marriage consideration is illustrated by *Re Plumptre's Marriage Settlement*,[194] in which a marriage settlement was made whereby money from the wife's father was covenanted to be settled upon trust for the wife with remainder to her next of kin. Her next of kin sought to enforce the covenant, but, because they were not within the marriage consideration, they were considered to be volunteers and were not able to do so.

Even where valuable consideration for the covenant is provided by a third party, it will not enable the beneficiaries to enforce the covenant. So, in *Re Cook's Settlement Trusts*,[195] a son covenanted to pay the proceeds of sale of any pictures sold during his father's lifetime to be held on trust for his children, who were volunteers because the settlement was not made in consideration of the settlor's marriage. The father had, however, provided valuable consideration for this covenant. The son gave one of the pictures by Rembrandt to his wife, who sold it. The issue for the court was whether the trustees were required to enforce the son's covenant to require the proceeds of sale to be transferred to the children's trust. It was held that, because the son's own children were volunteers, they could not require the trustees to enforce the covenant on their behalf. It was irrelevant that their grandfather had provided consideration for the covenant.

Covenant relating to property acquired in the future

Whether consideration has been provided for the covenant to settle property on trust has proved to be of especial significance where a settlor purports to declare a trust of property that the settlor has not yet acquired, but which they expect to receive in the future. This cannot be a valid trust at the time of declaration because there is no property that can be held on trust. But, once the settlor acquires the property and transfers it to the trustee, the trust will be constituted and effective. But what will happen if the settlor obtains the property and does not transfer it to the trustee? Can the trustee or beneficiary compel the settlor to convey the property to the trustee by treating the declaration of trust as an enforceable covenant to transfer the property?

A covenant to transfer future property to a trust is not enforceable at Common Law, even if consideration has been provided, simply because the property is not in existence when the contract is made. But, if consideration has been provided, the covenant is enforceable in Equity,[196] because of the principle that 'Equity treats as done what ought to be done'.[197] The covenant will be treated as a promise to transfer the property once it is acquired. Once the covenantor has acquired the property, Equity will assume that it has already been transferred to the trust, so that the covenantee obtains an equitable interest in it.[198] The application of this principle means that, although legal title remains in the covenantor, equitable title is in the covenantee, so that the property, once acquired, is held on constructive trust for the covenantee. The application of this principle is illustrated by *Pullan v Koe*,[199] in which the effect of a marriage settlement was that property was settled on the husband, wife, and any children of the marriage. The wife covenanted to settle on the same trusts any property worth £100 or more that she acquired after the marriage. She received a present of £285 from her mother, which was credited to her husband's bank account. Some of this money was used to buy bonds and the interest on these bonds was also credited to the account. Her husband died and the trustees of the marriage settlement claimed the bonds from her husband's executors. It was held that the gift from her mother

---

[194] [1910] 1 Ch 609. See also *Re Pryce* [1917] Ch 234.   [195] [1965] Ch 902.
[196] *Holroyd v Marshall* (1862) 10 HL Cas 191, 220 (Lord Chelmsford).   [197] See Section 2.6, p. 31.
[198] *Norman v Federal Commissioner of Taxation* (1963) 109 CLR 9, 24 (Windeyer J) (High Court of Australia).   [199] [1913] 1 Ch 9.

was held on trust and, since the bonds had been bought with this money, they became trust property as well. Crucially, the court was willing to enforce the covenant in the marriage settlement in favour of those within the marriage consideration, namely the wife and her children, because they were not volunteers. It followed that, when the wife received the gift from her mother, Equity assumed that it had already been transferred to the trust by virtue of the wife's covenant.[200]

The principle that Equity treats as done what ought to be done is applicable only in favour of a person who is entitled to enforce the covenant, so it cannot be relied on by a volunteer.[201] So, for example, in *Re Kay's Settlement*,[202] the settlor, who was unmarried, executed a settlement of property to herself for life and then to her as-yet-unborn children. The settlement contained a covenant to settle after-acquired property. She later married and had three children. She acquired property, but refused a request by the trustees of the settlement to transfer this property to the trust. It was held that she was not liable to do so because this was not a settlement made in consideration of marriage, so that her children were volunteers and not in a position to enforce the covenant against her. Similarly, in *Re Brooks' Settlement Trusts*,[203] property was held under a marriage settlement on trust for the wife for life and after her death on trust for her children. One of her children, Arthur, purported to assign to trustees what he might become entitled to in the future. The mother then appointed a sum of money to Arthur. It was held that the assignment had not been effective and so the trustees were required to pay the money to Arthur. Since the trustees had not provided consideration for Arthur's promise, it was not enforceable by them.

Mechanisms for assisting volunteers

Although volunteers are not able to enforce covenants to settle or transfer property as a general rule, there are certain exceptional circumstances under which remedies might be available to them, either directly or indirectly.

Constitution of trust despite unenforceable covenant

Where a settlor covenants to transfer property to a trust and the covenant is unenforceable for want of consideration, the trust will be completely constituted if the settlor nonetheless transfers property to the trustees. The settlor will then not be able to recover the property and the beneficiaries will be able to enforce the trust.[204] Similarly, where the settlor covenants that they will hold property to be acquired in the future on trust, this trust will be automatically constituted on receipt of the property by the settlor by virtue of the principles relating to declaration of oneself as trustee.[205]

Beneficiary party to the covenant under a deed

In *Cannon v Hartley*,[206] it was recognized that, even though the beneficiary is a volunteer, if the covenant is made with them by deed, it is possible for the beneficiary to sue at Common Law for breach of the covenant and obtain damages. But, being a volunteer, it will not be possible for them to obtain the equitable remedy of specific performance.[207] The payment of damages to the beneficiary will not constitute the trust, since the damages will be paid to the beneficiary personally to compensate them for the loss suffered from breach of the covenant.

---

[200] See *Smith v Lucas* (1881) 18 Ch D 531, 543 (Jessel MR).
[201] *Re Plumptre's Marriage Settlement* [1910] Ch 609, 619 (Eve J).
[202] [1939] Ch 329. See also *Re Ellenborough* [1903] 1 Ch 697.   [203] [1939] Ch 993.
[204] *Paul v Paul* (1882) 20 Ch D 742.   [205] See Section 5.3.2.(i), p. 125.   [206] [1949] Ch 213.
[207] See Section 21.4, p. 635.

Action for damages brought by trustees at Law

Since the settlor has made the covenant with the trustees rather than the beneficiaries, the fact that the covenant has been breached by the settlor not transferring property to the trust will enable the trustees to sue for breach of the covenant at Common Law, at least where the covenant is contained in a deed, since they are unlikely to have provided valuable consideration. But what remedy would be available for the trustees? Specific performance would be available only if the trustees had provided valuable consideration. Damages would be available only to compensate the trustees for their loss, rather than that of the beneficiary,[208] and since the trustees were not intended to benefit from the receipt of the property, it might be concluded that they would not have suffered any loss themselves in not receiving the property. Where, however, the settlor has promised to pay an agreed sum, the trustees will be able to sue for this amount without needing to prove loss. When they receive this money, they will hold it on trust for the beneficiaries, since the trustees were never intended to receive this amount beneficially[209] and receipt of this sum would constitute the trust.

It has been recognized that the decision whether to sue the settlor for breach of the covenant is a decision to be made by the trustees. The beneficiaries cannot make the trustees enforce the covenant, because they are volunteers and Equity will not enable them to obtain indirectly what they cannot obtain directly.[210] It has sometimes been recognized that the trustees should be directed by the court not to sue on the covenant,[211] although the better view is that, although they can do so if they wish,[212] they are not bound to do so.[213] Although, in *Beswick v Beswick*,[214] Lord Reid did recognize, *obiter*, that a trustee would be bound to recover the money and account for it to the beneficiary, the preferable view is that the trustee should be under a duty to do so only where the trust has been constituted, for then the trustee's fundamental duty is to get in the trust property for the benefit of the trust.[215]

Specific performance sought by trustees

There may be circumstances under which the trustees are able to seek specific performance of the covenant that will result in the settlor being required to transfer the property so that the trust will become constituted. This may be the result even if the trustees are able to obtain specific performance in a different capacity from that of being trustees. This is illustrated by *Beswick v Beswick*,[216] although in a different context from that of covenants to transfer property to a trustee. In that case, Peter, a coal merchant, made an arrangement with his nephew to transfer his business to the nephew, who in turn promised to employ Peter as a consultant and, on Peter's death, to pay his widow £5 a week for life. After Peter's death, the nephew stopped paying the money to Peter's widow. She was unable to sue on the contract because she was not a party to it. She was, however, appointed administratrix of Peter's estate and, in that capacity, she was able to seek specific performance of the covenant in her favour as Peter's widow. Although such a result could also apply in respect of

---

[208] Compare where there is a trust of the promise. See Section 5.3.3.(iii), p. 137.

[209] Rickett, 'Two propositions in the constitution of trusts' [1981] CLP 189, 196.

[210] *Re Pryce* [1917] 1 Ch 234.

[211] Ibid.; *Re Kay's Settlement* [1939] Ch 329; *Re Cook's Settlement Trusts* [1965] Ch 902.

[212] *Davenport v Bishopp* (1843) 2 Y & C Ch Cas 451, 460 (Knight-Bruce V-C); Elliott, 'The power of trustees to enforce covenants in favour of volunteers' (1960) 76 LQR 100, 114; Rickett, 'The constitution of trusts: contracts to create trusts' [1979] CLP 1, 13.   [213] *Re Ralli's Will Trust* [1964] Ch 288, 301 (Buckley J).

[214] [1968] AC 58, 71.   [215] Meagher and Lehane, 'Trusts of voluntary covenants' (1976) 92 LQR 427.

[216] [1968] AC 58.

covenants to settle property on trust, there was one significant feature in *Beswick v Beswick* that enabled the widow as administratrix to seek specific performance of the nephew's covenant, namely that her husband had provided valuable consideration for it. In the normal situation of a settlor covenanting to transfer property to the trustees to hold on trust, neither the trustee nor the beneficiary will have provided consideration, so specific performance will not be available.

Trust of the promise

It has sometimes been recognized that, since the settlor's promise to transfer property to the trust is a chose in action and so property in its own right, it is capable of being held on trust by the trustees for the benefit of the beneficiary. A trust of the promise will be constituted immediately the promise is made, since the rights arising from this promise are held on trust and it is irrelevant that the beneficiary of the trust is a volunteer. The trustee would consequently be required to enforce the trust for the benefit of the beneficiaries. This can be compared with the general rule on covenants to transfer property to the trustees, under which trustees are not bound to enforce the covenant because there is no trust obligation.[217] Finding a trust of the promise is consequently significant because, since there is a completely constituted trust, the trustees are subject to an obligation to enforce the promise for the benefit of the beneficiaries. Consequently, if Alan covenants to transfer property to Barbara to hold on trust for Clare, if Alan's promise can be considered to be held on trust by Barbara for Clare, once Alan receives the property and does not transfer it to Barbara, she could sue for damages,[218] which would be held on trust for the volunteer beneficiaries, or for specific performance of the covenant if consideration has been provided. If Barbara refuses to act, Clare can seek the relief against Alan, joining Barbara as a co-defendant.[219] Whether a covenant to settle future property can be the subject matter of a trust in its own right has sometimes been doubted,[220] largely on the ground that it relates to future property and so does not create an enforceable debt. But this view is misconceived, because it is the covenant that is the subject matter of the trust and not the property that will be acquired in the future. This is illustrated by *Fletcher v Fletcher*,[221] in which the settlor had covenanted to pay trustees £60,000, which was to be held on trust for the settlor's illegitimate son, Jacob. The question for the court was whether Jacob could enforce the covenant, even though he was a volunteer. It was recognized that there could be a trust of a covenant for the benefit of a third party and that Jacob could either sue in the name of the trustees at Common Law or in his own name in Equity.

But although a trust of the promise is perfectly acceptable in principle, it will be established only where the promise is intended to be held on trust for another.[222] Proof of such an intention will be difficult to establish and cannot be assumed.[223]

Where a trust of the promise has been created, if the promisor fails to transfer the promised property to the trustee once it has been acquired, the trustee will be able to seek damages for breach of the covenant to compensate for the loss suffered, but, being a volunteer, will not be able to enforce the covenant specifically.[224] It might be thought that the trustees

---

[217] See Section 5.3.3.(iii), p. 132.

[218] *Lloyd's v Harper* (1880) 16 Ch D 290, 321 (Lush J); *Coulls v Bagot's Executor and Trustee Co Ltd* (1967) 40 ALJR 471, 486 (Windeyer J).

[219] *Les Affréteurs Réunis SA v Leopold Walford (London) Ltd* [1919] AC 801.

[220] *Re Cook's Settlement Trusts* [1965] Ch 902.   [221] (1844) 4 Hare 67.

[222] *Re Schebsman* [1944] Ch 83, 89 (Lord Greene MR).

[223] Cf. Feltham, 'Intention to create a trust of a promise to settle property' (1982) 98 LQR 17, 18.

[224] *Cannon v Hartley* [1949] Ch 213.

will have suffered no personal loss as a result of the failure to transfer property to be held on trust. The loss will have been suffered by the beneficiary, but this loss cannot be attributed to the trustees.[225] But, if the covenant was to pay a sum of money or transfer property to the trust, the trustee's loss will simply be the amount of money or the value of the property that was not received. It follows that the trustees should be able to recover substantial damages for the settlor's breach of covenant. That this is how damages will be assessed is illustrated by *Re Cavendish Browne's Settlement Trusts*,[226] in which it was recognized that the trustees were entitled to recover damages from the administrators of the deceased settlor for breach of the covenant to transfer property to the trust. The damages were assessed with reference to the value of the land that would have been transferred to the trustees had the covenant been performed.

A distinction was recognized in *Re Cook's Settlement Trusts*[227] between a debt that can be the subject of an immediate trust even though it will arise only in the future, by virtue of the doctrine of trust of the promise, and a covenant to settle after-acquired property that might never be acquired, which cannot be held on trust. This distinction between debt and covenant is, however, very fine. Certainly, a covenant to settle after-acquired property can be converted into a trust of the promise if such a trust is intended.[228] It seems that the distinction recognized in *Re Cook* turns on the likelihood of the property being acquired by the covenantor, with the greater the likelihood of acquisition the more likely that the case will be treated as a trust of the promise rather than a simple covenant.

Even if the necessary intent to create a trust of the promise can be identified on the facts, there is an important issue of policy to be considered, namely whether it is appropriate that the covenantor should be able to create such a trust. Whilst it is acceptable to say that the promise is property that can be held on trust, surely this promise belongs to the covenantee and it is the covenantee who should be able to declare a trust of it, as a form of equitable assignment of the promise to the beneficiary, for otherwise the promisor will be imposing a trust on the promisee's property behind their back and so depriving the promisee of the benefit of the promise without their consent or even knowledge? If this is correct, a trust of the promise should not have been recognized in *Fletcher*, because the trustees of the settlement did not know about the promise until the settlor's death and wanted to decline the trust once they had heard of it. The focus on the covenantor's intent has, however, been justified on the ground that, if the declaration of such a trust were to depend on the intention of the promisee, there is a genuine risk that such a trust would not be declared, since the effect of such a trust would be to deprive the promisee of any benefit of the promise.[229] Of course, in many cases in which there is an issue as to whether a trust of a promise has been declared, the effect of the promise will be to confer a benefit on the beneficiary, who will be able to enforce it under the Contracts (Rights of Third Parties) Act 1999, at least where the beneficiary has been identified by name or by description.[230]

Donatio mortis causa

Where a donor purports to make a gift at a time when they expect to die, but title to the property has not passed whilst the donor is alive, title might pass following the donor's death. In some cases this may apply automatically on the death of the donor, without the need for equitable intervention, such as where a chattel has been delivered during the

---

[225] See also *Shell UK Ltd v Total UK Ltd* [2010] EWCA Civ 180, [2011] QB 86, discussed in Section 3.5.5.(v), p. 51, as regards the attribution of loss arising from damage to trust property.

[226] [1916] WN 341. See Goddard, 'Equity, volunteers and ducks' [1988] Conv 19.   [227] [1965] Ch 902.

[228] Barton, 'Trusts and covenants' (1975) 91 LQR 236; Meagher and Lehane (see n. 215).

[229] Rickett (see n. 209), p. 7.   [230] See Section 5.3.3.(iii), p. 132.

donor's lifetime to which title is perfected on the donor's death. Where, however, the property is a chose in action or land, the effect of the donor's death will be to vest title in the donor's personal representatives rather than the donee. The equitable doctrine of *donatio mortis causa* can be relied on by the donee in such circumstances to compel the personal representatives to perfect the donee's title, even though the donee is a volunteer.

Donatio mortis causa means a gift made in prospect of the donor's death. This is the essential rationale of the equitable doctrine: if the donor anticipated their imminent death and made the gift to the donee in these circumstances, it is just for Equity to perfect the gift even though the donor had not made a will.

Three conditions must be satisfied for this doctrine to apply.[231] First, the gift must have been made in contemplation of the donor's impending death in the near future for a specific reason,[232] such as because of a terminal illness or because the donor was about to embark on a hazardous journey. Secondly, the gift must be conditional on death and the donor should intend the property to revert to them should the donor recover. Thirdly, the property must have been delivered to the donee or essential indicia of title passed to the donee with a view to the donor parting with the dominion over the property rather than merely parting with its physical possession. 'Parting with dominion' means parting with the ability to control the property. What is required to be delivered will depend on the nature of the property. So, for example, with chattels, it may be sufficient to hand over a key to the place where the property is located;[233] with choses in action, it is sufficient to hand over documents that constitute evidence of title.[234] As regards land, it was recognized in *Sen v Headley*[235] that giving the donee the keys to a box containing the title deeds to a house constituted constructive delivery of the title deeds and was sufficient to deliver dominion over the unregistered land.[236]

The doctrine of *donatio mortis causa* functions by means of a constructive trust: once the donor has died, title to the relevant property will have passed to the donor's personal representative. Where the conditions for the doctrine are satisfied, Equity will require the personal representative to hold the property on trust for the donee. This is a trust that arises by operation of law and so it is constructive in effect.[237]

Although there are no reported cases in which the doctrine of *donatio mortis causa* has been used to constitute an express trust, there is no reason to conclude that the doctrine could not be applicable in such circumstances. So, if Alan, contemplating death, wishes Barbara to hold property on trust for Clare, and Alan delivers the indicia of title to the property to Barbara, then, once Alan has died, the trust should be considered to have been constituted. Alan's executors will hold the property for Barbara, who will hold it for Clare.

If the donor, in anticipation of their death, purports to make a transfer to the donee and the donor then makes a recovery, the donor can revoke the transfer and recover the property.[238]

The doctrine of *donatio mortis causa* is open to criticism on the ground that it is open to abuse by those who might wish to take advantage of the donor, especially because the

---

[231] *Sen v Headley* [1991] Ch 425.

[232] See *King v Dubrey* [2015] EWCA Civ 581, [2016] Ch 221. Jackson LJ, at [53]–[54], considered that the doctrine serves little useful purpose today and should not be expanded.

[233] *Re Cole* [1964] Ch 175; *Woodard v Woodard* [1995] 3 All ER 980 (delivery of car keys). But delivering a key and then taking it back will not constitute parting with the dominion: *Re Johnson* (1905) 92 LT 357.

[234] *Birch v Treasury Solicitor* [1951] Ch 298.   [235] [1991] Ch 425.

[236] For registered land, it may be sufficient to deliver the land certificate, although it is not strictly an indicia of title to the land.

[237] *Duffield v Elwes* (1827) 1 Bli (NS) 497, 530 (Lord Eldon). On constructive trusts generally, see further Section 9.1.3, p. 255.   [238] *King v Dubrey* [2015] EWCA Civ 581, [2016] Ch 221, [57] (Jackson LJ).

donor's intention to make a gift need not be evidenced in writing. In reviewing the doctrine, the Law Commission has acknowledged the possibility of abuse, but its tentative conclusion is that the doctrine might continue to serve a useful purpose by softening the hard edges of the formalities rules relating to wills.[239] Consequently, the Law Commission's tentative conclusion is that the doctrine should not be abolished. As Cumber[240] has recognized, '[i]t is hard to think of a better example of equity assisting a volunteer and perfecting an imperfect gift.'

The rule in Strong v Bird

Where a donor has promised to make a gift to a donee, but legal title to the property has not been transferred, another method of perfecting title is by means of the rule in *Strong v Bird*.[241] The essence of this rule is that, where the donee of a promised gift obtains title to the gift in another capacity, this will be sufficient to perfect the gift. The rule usually applies where the donee receives the gift as executor.[242] So, for example, if Alan promises to give money to Barbara, but the money is not transferred before Alan's death, if Barbara receives the money in her capacity as executor of Alan's estate, the fact that Barbara now has legal title to the money as executor will be sufficient to perfect her title to the money in a personal capacity. The underlying principle is that the gift will be treated as perfected if the donee no longer needs the assistance of the court to perfect it, as long as the intention to give continues.[243]

The rule has been applied beyond the particular context of perfecting gifts to executors. For example, in *Strong v Bird* itself, the rule was applied to effect the release of a debt. In that case, A was B's mother-in-law, who lived with B. A paid a sum of money to B each month. B borrowed money from A and it was agreed that B would repay the debt over time by A deducting a sum each month from what she paid to B. A did this for two months and then continued to pay the full amount to B. On A's death, B was appointed A's executor. The question for the court was whether the debt that B continued to owe A could be considered to have been released through B's appointment as executor. It was held that the debt was released when B obtained probate of A's will.

The rule has also been applied where B is appointed administrator of A's estate.[244] This extension of the rule has been criticized[245] because the appointment of an administrator, unlike that of an executor, is not an act of the deceased, but is a matter of chance by operation of law. But the better view is that the rule should apply to administrators too,[246] because the key rationale of the rule is that legal title has been obtained by B in one capacity that is sufficient to perfect B's title to the property in a personal capacity, and it is immaterial whether this occurred through the act of the testator or by operation of law.

The application of the rule in *Strong v Bird* depends on the donor purporting to make an immediate gift of property or to release immediately a debt that fails for want of formalities, and the intention to make the gift or release the debt must have continued until the donor's death. So, for example, in *Re Gonin*,[247] a mother wanted to leave her house to her daughter, who had looked after the mother and her husband for many years, but the mother incorrectly thought that she could not do so because the daughter had been born illegitimately. So the mother wrote a cheque for her daughter for £33,000 instead. This was

---

[239] *Making a Will* (Law Com CP N0. 231, 2017), p. 236.
[240] 'Donatio mortis causa: a doctrine on its deathbed?' [2016] Conv 56.   [241] (1874) LR 18 Eq 315.
[242] [1908] 2 Ch 251.
[243] *Rowlandson v National Westminster Bank Ltd* [1978] 1 WLR 798, 802 (John Mills QC).
[244] *Re James* [1935] Ch 449.   [245] *Re Gonin* [1979] Ch 16, 34 (Walton J).
[246] Kodilinye, 'A fresh look at the rule in *Strong v Bird*' [1982] Conv 14, 17.   [247] [1979] Ch 16.

found after the mother's death, but it could not be cashed because the authority to pay on a cheque is terminated when the bank is informed of the drawer's death. The daughter was appointed administratrix of the mother's estate and sought to rely on the rule in *Strong v Bird* to claim the house. Her claim failed because there was no evidence of a continuing intent on the part of the mother to make an immediate gift of the house to the daughter, especially because she had written a cheque for her instead. Similarly, the rule did not apply in *Re Wale*,[248] in which the testatrix had purported to settle certain investments, and then forgot about the settlement and treated the investments as her own. The rule in *Strong v Bird* was not applicable because there was no continuing intent to settle the investments.

The rule in *Strong v Bird* will not apply where the donor intends to make a gift subsequently by will,[249] since this would be a way of avoiding the formalities of the Wills Act 1837. Although the rule does have an effect after the donor's death, it does not infringe the requirements of the Wills Act because the donor needs to have intended to make an immediate lifetime gift.

Although the rule in *Strong v Bird* has been applied to perfect gifts and to release debts, there is no reason to think that it cannot be applied in the specific context of covenants to settle property on trust.[250] So, if Alan covenants to transfer property to Barbara to be held on trust for Clare and Alan fails to convey legal title to Barbara, the trust will not have been constituted. If, however, Barbara is appointed executor of Alan's estate, there is no reason why the rule in *Strong v Bird* cannot be applied to perfect her title as trustee so that the trust will be completely constituted. This scenario of a trust being constituted by the trustee obtaining the property in a different capacity has previously been recognized in *Re Ralli's Will Trust*.[251] That case did not involve the application of the rule in *Strong v Bird* because the settlor had not intended to make an immediate gift, but an analogy at least can be drawn between the two cases such that it should not matter in what capacity a trustee receives title to property; it is the conveyance of legal title to the trustee that will constitute the trust.

---

[248] [1956] 3 All ER 280.   [249] *Re Innes* [1910] 1 Ch 188.
[250] Kodilinye (see n. 246), p. 21; Jaconelli, 'Problems in the rule in *Strong v Bird*' [2006] Conv 432, 444.
[251] [1964] Ch 288, see Section 5.3.2.(ii), p. 126.

PART III
TRUSTS FOR PURPOSES

6

CHARITABLE TRUSTS

6.1 GENERAL CONSIDERATIONS

In Part II, we examined private trusts for individual beneficiaries. In Part III, we are concerned with trusts for purposes. The beneficiary principle requires there to be identifiable people who are able to enforce the trust.[1] It follows that a trust for purposes will generally not be valid. One significant exception to this principle, however, is that charitable trusts have long been recognized as valid, even though they are trusts for purposes rather than for particular people. These express trusts are treated favourably by the law because they provide a benefit to the public or a section of the public. Charitable trusts can usefully be characterized as public trusts since they promote purposes beneficial to the community,[2] as distinct from trusts for people, which are private trusts because they provide benefits to private individuals.

Charities play a significant role in the community and they are increasingly important to the delivery of public services. There are over 167,000 charities registered with the Charity Commission[3] with a total annual income of over £74 billion.[4] They are consequently numerically, financially, and politically significant. Equity has had a very important role in creating and developing the law relating to the creation, definition, and operation of charities.

6.1.1 THE ESSENCE OF CHARITABLE TRUSTS

A charity is an institution that is established exclusively for charitable purposes and is subject to the jurisdiction of the High Court,[5] which means that the charity must be established under English law even though the charitable purpose is to be fulfilled abroad. A trust can be used as the mechanism for implementing a charitable purpose,[6] but other legal mechanisms can also be used. So, for example, it is possible to incorporate a charitable company[7] or to use an unincorporated association to effect a charitable purpose.

---

[1] See Section 4.5, p. 101.   [2] *Gaudiya Mission v Brahmachary* [1998] Ch 341, 430.
[3] Charity Commission, *Recent Charity Register Statistics*, October 2017: www.gov.uk/government/publications/charity-register-statistics/recent-charity-register-statistics-charity-commission
[4] Ibid.   [5] Charities Act 2011, s. 1(1).   [6] Ibid., s. 9(3).
[7] The Charities Act 2011, Pt 11, creates a new form of incorporation specifically for charities, called a 'charitable incorporated organization'. This is not a company, but has some of the hallmarks of a company, such as limited liability.

Regardless of the type of legal mechanism that is used to implement a charitable purpose, the people who have the general control and management of the administration of a charity are called the 'charity trustees'.[8] Charity trustees are distinct from trustees of a charity. The latter are the trustees of a charitable trust, who will also be called charity trustees. But, where the mechanism for implementing a charitable purpose is not a trust, those people who control and manage the charity will still be called charity trustees and not trustees of a charity. So, for example, the directors of an incorporated charity are charity trustees for the purposes of the Charities Act 2011, but are not trustees of the charity. This is generally a distinction of only technical, rather than practical, significance, since charity trustees are still subject to fiduciary duties and have administrative responsibilities in just the same way as they would if they were trustees of a trust.

Whatever mechanism is used to effect a charitable purpose, an institution can be considered to be charitable only if three conditions are satisfied:

(1) it must be established for a purpose that the law regards as charitable;[9]

(2) its purposes must benefit the public or a sufficient section of the public;[10] and

(3) it must be wholly and exclusively charitable.[11]

6.1.2 ADVANTAGES OF BEING A CHARITABLE TRUST

There are a number of significant advantages in creating a charitable, rather than a private, trust.

(i) No need for ascertainable beneficiaries

Where the charity is established as a trust, it will be valid even though there are no ascertainable beneficiaries who are in a position to enforce the trust, so that the beneficiary principle is not satisfied. This is not a problem because responsibility for enforcing charitable trusts formally lies with the Attorney-General, acting on behalf of the Crown, and practically lies with the Charity Commission.

(ii) Duration

Whereas private trusts are subject to the perpetuity rule,[12] meaning that they can last for only a limited time, charitable trusts can exist perpetually. The oldest registered charity is the King's School, Canterbury, which was founded 1,400 years ago. The rules on the vesting of property in charitable trusts do operate in the same way as for private trusts,[13] and so the property must vest in the charity within 125 years.[14]

(iii) Certainty of purpose

Whereas, for private trusts, there are strict rules as to certainty of intent to create a trust and certainty in defining the objects,[15] the rules on certainty for charitable trusts are much more flexible. The courts are more likely to find that a trust was intended in a charitable rather than a commercial context.[16] It is sufficient that there is an intention to apply property for a charitable purpose and it does not matter that the trust fails to provide

---

[8] Charities Act 2011, s. 177.   [9] See Section 6.3, p. 158.   [10] See Section 6.2.2, p. 152.
[11] See Section 6.4, p. 174.   [12] See Section 4.6, p. 102.
[13] *Re Lord Stratheden and Campbell* [1894] 3 Ch 265. Also, a charity's power to accumulate income is restricted to twenty-one years: Perpetuities and Accumulations Act 2009, s. 14(4).
[14] Perpetuities and Accumulations Act 2009, s. 5. See Section 4.6.2, p. 103.   [15] See Section 4.1, p. 72.
[16] *Charity Commission for England and Wales v Framjee* [2014] EWHC 2507 (Ch), [2015] 1 WLR 16, [28(d)] (Henderson J).

with reasonable certainty what that purpose is.[17] If there is doubt about this, the Charity Commission or the courts can prepare a scheme for the use of the property for particular charitable purposes. It is even possible for the trustees of a charitable trust to execute a deed which limits[18] or widens[19] the terms of the trust in circumstances where the trust has been created in general or vague terms, rather than treating the trust as void, provided this limitation of the terms does not conflict with the terms on which any donors to the trust made their donations.[20] This has been justified on the basis that the trustees have implied authority to include terms in the trust deed on behalf of the donors.

The purposes of a charitable trust must be wholly and exclusively charitable; if they are not, the whole trust will be void.[21] The courts will, however, seek to adopt a benign construction of trust instruments to uphold the charitable trust if it is possible to do so, to avoid rendering the trust void.[22] For example, if a potential charitable trust can be construed in two ways, with one way making it charitable and effectual, and the other non-charitable and void, the courts will adopt the former construction, if at all possible.[23]

(iv) Tax advantages

One of the main reasons why creators of trusts will want the trust to be characterized as charitable is because there are significant tax advantages that result from this, both for the charity and the donors to it. For the charity, these advantages include relief from income and capital gains tax. A number of the key charity cases that have reached the courts have involved disputes with HM Revenue and Customs as to whether or not a trust is charitable, with a decision that the institution is not charitable resulting in a significant tax liability.

(v) Cy-près

Where a private trust fails and there are still trust funds available, those funds will usually be returned to the settlor by means of a resulting trust.[24] Where a charitable trust fails, however, the surplus funds may be applied for another similar charitable purpose, by virtue of the cy-près doctrine.[25] This can be regarded as advantageous in that the creator of the trust and donors to it will know that, once property has been received by that trust, it will be used for charitable purposes, even if the particular trust fails.

(vi) Reputational benefits

There are also certain benefits of good reputation arising from being a registered charity that enhance the charity's ability to raise funds.[26]

(vii) Equality

Although the Equality Act 2010 operates to remove discrimination and encourage equality, a limited exemption exists for charities which can adopt discriminatory charitable objects if they can be objectively justified as a proportionate means of achieving a legitimate

---

[17] *Moggridge v Thackwell* (1802) 7 Ves Jun 36.   [18] See *Attorney-General v Mathieson* [1907] 2 Ch 383.
[19] In *Re Orphan Working School and Alexandra Orphanage's Contract* [1912] 2 Ch 167 the trustees were allowed to widen the terms of the trust.
[20] *Khaira v Shergill* [2014] UKSC 33, [2015] AC 359, where the trustees had included a term delegating the authority to remove trustees and appoint new ones.   [21] See Section 6.4.2.(ii), p. 176.
[22] *IRC v McMullen* [1981] AC 1, 14 (Lord Hailsham).
[23] *Re Koeppler's Will Trusts* [1986] Ch 423; *Guild v IRC* [1992] 2 AC 310.
[24] See Section 8.3.2.(iii), p. 236.   [25] See Section 6.5, p. 177.
[26] *The Independent Schools Council v The Charity Commission for England and Wales* [2011] UKUT 421 (TCC), [2012] Ch 214, [14].

aim or are a means of preventing or compensating for a particular disadvantage.[27] It follows that it might be possible for a charity to provide benefits solely for women or people with disability if this can be objectively justified as a legitimate aim.[28] The extent to which charities might discriminate was considered in *Catholic Care (Diocese of Leeds) v Charity Commission for England Wales (No 2)*,[29] which concerned a Roman Catholic charity which provided adoption services and had the practice of not making those services available to same-sex couples. Whilst it was accepted that it was relevant when examining objective justifications to consider that donors might withhold their donations if the charity did not adopt a discriminatory policy, it had not been established that the policy in favour of heterosexual couples was objectively justified.

6.1.3 DISADVANTAGES OF BEING A CHARITY

There are certain disadvantages of a trust being charitable in that, because of the public nature of the trust, there are significant administrative and bureaucratic obligations. All charities need to be registered by the Charity Commission, which can involve an administrative burden in establishing that the hallmarks of a charity are satisfied. Once registered, Part 8 of the Charities Act 2011 imposes strict duties on charity trustees to prepare annual accounts, to arrange for their audit, and to send annual reports to the Charity Commission on their activities. There are criminal penalties for failure to submit reports and returns.

6.1.4 REGULATION AND SUPERVISION OF CHARITIES

There are a variety of mechanisms for regulating and supervising charities.

(i) The Attorney-General

The Attorney-General is responsible for enforcing the charitable trust in the name of the Crown.[30] The Attorney-General acts as the protector of the charity and has been described as the 'representative of the beneficial interest'.[31] There is a need for the Attorney-General to protect the property of the charitable trust because no private person has a beneficial interest in the trust's property.

(ii) Charity Commission

The general administration of charities is carried out by the Charity Commission,[32] but the Commission also has a quasi-judicial function. The Charities Act 2011[33] identifies various objectives of the Commission, including increasing public trust and confidence in charities, promoting compliance by charity trustees with their legal obligations, and promoting the effective use of charitable resources. The Charity Commission has a number of key general functions, which include:[34]

(1) determining whether or not institutions are charities;

(2) identifying and investigating misconduct or mismanagement of charities; and

(3) maintaining an up-to-date register of charities.

---

[27] Equality Act 2010, s. 193(2)(a).
[28] This does not allow discrimination by reference to skin colour: s. 194(2).
[29] [2012] UKUT 395 (TCC), [2013] 1 WLR 2105.
[30] *Gaudiya Mission v Brahmachary* [1998] Ch 341, 350 (Mummery LJ).
[31] *Weth v Attorney-General* [1999] 1 WLR 686, 691 (Nourse LJ).
[32] Charities Act 2011, s. 13.   [33] Ibid., s. 14.   [34] Ibid., s. 15.

The register of charities contains the name of every charity registered by the Charity Commission,[35] other than charities that are exempted by statute, charities with a gross income of less than £5,000, and certain charities with a gross income of less than £100,000 that are excepted from registration by the Commission or under regulations made by the Secretary of State.[36] The Charity Commission is required to remove from the register any institution that it no longer considers is a charity, and any charity that has ceased to exist or no longer operates.[37] A charity that is included on the register is conclusively presumed to be a charity, save where rectification of the register is sought.[38] Anybody who might be affected by the registration of an institution as a charity, such as a testator's next of kin, can object to its inclusion on the register or apply for it to be removed.[39] Where a charity is required to be registered, it is the duty of the charity trustees to apply for registration.[40] Charity trustees are also under a duty to inform the Commission if the charity ceases to exist or if there is a change in the charity's trusts.[41]

The Charity Commission has various regulatory powers. For example, it can institute an inquiry with regard to a charity or a class of charities,[42] and it can then give directions to the charity trustees to take particular actions in the interests of the charity.[43] The Charity Commission can also give advice to charity trustees relating to the administration of the charity or the performance of the trustees' duties.[44] It can also sanction actions that are expedient in the administration of the charity, such as a particular application of charity property, even if the charity trustees do not have the power to take such action.[45]

The Charity Commission has a concurrent jurisdiction with the High Court as regards various matters,[46] such as establishing a scheme for the administration of the charity, appointing, discharging, or removing a charity trustee, and transferring property. But the Charity Commission does not have jurisdiction to determine title to property, or to determine the existence or extent of any trust,[47] and it should not exercise its concurrent jurisdiction if the matter is more appropriately adjudicated by the court because of its contentious nature, or because it raises special questions of law or fact.[48]

There has been concern that the Charity Commission has not exercised its powers appropriately in determining whether an institution is or is not a charity.[49] The function of the Charity Commission is to apply the law as it has been developed by the courts and by Parliament. But the Charity Commission has at times developed its own interpretation of those principles and made decisions that lack 'legal rigour'.[50]

(iii) The Tribunals

The First-tier and Upper Tribunal[51] have jurisdiction to hear appeals and applications in respect of decisions, orders, and directions of the Charity Commission, such as a decision to register or not to register a charity, or to remove an institution from the register of charities. The Charity Commission or the Attorney-General may also refer matters to the Tribunals, including matters relating to the powers of the Commission itself and to the operation of the law of charity. It is possible to appeal from the First-tier Tribunal to the Upper Tribunal on a point of law.[52] The Tribunals have a potentially very important role

---

[35] Ibid., s. 29.   [36] Ibid., s. 30(2).   [37] Ibid., s. 34.   [38] Ibid., s. 37(1).   [39] Ibid., s. 36.

[40] Ibid., s. 35(1).   [41] Ibid., s. 35(3).   [42] Ibid., s. 46.   [43] Ibid., s. 84.

[44] Ibid., s. 110.   [45] Ibid, s. 86.   [46] Ibid., s. 69(1).   [47] Ibid., s. 70(1).   [48] Ibid., s. 70(8).

[49] See generally Synge, *The 'New' Public Benefit Requirement: Making Sense of Charity Law?* (2015) (Oxford, Hart Publishing).

[50] See Luxton and Evans, 'Cogent and cohesive? Two recent Charity Commission decisions on the advancement of religion' [2011] Conv 144, 151.

[51] Charities Act 2011, Pt 17.   [52] Tribunals, Courts and Enforcement Act 2007, s. 11.

in developing charity law, as illustrated by the Upper Tribunal's decision relating to the charitable status of independent schools.[53]

The Tribunals have jurisdiction with respect to disputes relating to the internal or functional administration of a charitable trust, but only if the charity is established under English law.[54] Proceedings involving such matters, which are known as 'charity proceedings',[55] may be brought only by the charity, by any of the charity trustees, by anybody interested in the charity, or, where the charity is a local charity, by two or more inhabitants of the area of the charity.[56] A person is 'interested in the charity' if they have an interest in securing the due administration of the charity that is greater than or different from that possessed by ordinary members of the public.[57] Generally, such proceedings must be authorized by the Charity Commission but they will not be if they can be dealt with under the Commission's own regulatory powers. This requirement of authorizing proceedings ensures that charities do not waste money in pursuing litigation relating to internal disputes[58] and that charities are not harassed by hopeless challenges.[59]

Decisions of the Charity Commission and of certain charities may be examined by the Tribunals through judicial review proceedings. This will be available only as regards decisions of charities where the charity has the characteristics of a public body. So, for example, in *Scott v National Trust*,[60] it was recognized that, in principle, decisions of the National Trust were subject to judicial review, since that charity is of importance to the nation and is regulated by a specific Act of Parliament. In that case, members of hunts and various farmers had sought a judicial review of the National Trust's decision not to renew licences to hunt deer on its land. It was held that the claimants could not seek judicial review of this decision because judicial review is available only where the claimant has no alternative remedy, and charity proceedings were an alternative remedy because this was a special statutory procedure to monitor the decisions of charities. A further restriction on the availability of judicial review proceedings was recognized in *RSPCA v Attorney-General*,[61] which concerned the legitimacy of the charity's policy of excluding existing members and preventing new members from joining if their reason for wishing to be members was to challenge the charity's policy against hunting with dogs. It was held that an existing member of the charity who was then excluded would have *locus standi* to bring charity proceedings, but an unsuccessful applicant for membership was not sufficiently interested in the charity. Neither would an unsuccessful applicant be able to bring judicial review proceedings, because this procedure could not be used to circumvent the statutory requirement of charity proceedings that the claimant was interested in the charity. The only route available for unsuccessful applicants was to make a complaint to the Charity Commission or to the Attorney-General.

(iv) The High Court

Provision is also made for the Charity Commission to apply to the High Court for directions relating to the administration of charities in certain circumstances, such as where an interim manager has been appointed by the Charity Commission to manage a charity.[62] In *Charity Commission for England and Wales v Mountstar*,[63] Snowden J considered when

---

[53] *The Independent Schools Council v The Charity Commission for England and Wales* [2011] UKUT 421 (TCC), [2012] Ch 412. See Section 6.3.2.(ii), p. 163.

[54] *Gaudiya Mission v Brahmachary* [1998] Ch 341.   [55] Charities Act 2011, s. 115(8).

[56] Ibid., s. 115(1).   [57] *Re Hampton Fuel Allotment Charity* [1989] Ch 484, 494 (Nicholls LJ).

[58] *Muman v Nagasena* [2000] 1 WLR 299, 305 (Mummery LJ).

[59] *Scott v National Trust* [1998] 2 All ER 705.   [60] Ibid.   [61] [2002] 1 WLR 448.

[62] Charities Act 2011, s. 78(5)(b).   [63] [2016] EWHC 876 (Ch), [2016] Ch 612.

it would be appropriate for the court to give such directions. The case concerned whether it was appropriate for the interim managers to decide to discontinue an appeal against the decision of HM Revenue and Customs to reject the charity's claims for gift aid. Snowden J recognized that it would not be appropriate for the court to be asked to sanction what is essentially a business decision, save where the consequences of that decision could be characterized as 'momentous'. That was the appropriate characterization of the decision in this case because the appeal related to a very large sum of money which the charity had sought to be treated as gift aid. In the light of this, the decision of the interim managers to discontinue the appeal was considered and was upheld, because the prospects of success on the appeal were negligible since the interim manager's decision was such as a reasonable trustee, properly instructed and ignoring irrelevant considerations, would have reached. It was also recognized that the court would be wary of allowing a charity trustee to surrender the exercise of their discretion to the court.[64]

6.1.5 A BRIEF HISTORY OF THE LEGAL DEFINITION OF CHARITY

There was no formal definition of 'charity' in English law until the enactment of the Charities Act 2006, now consolidated in the Charities Act 2011. Before then, a definition of charity emerged through limited statutory provision, decisions of the courts, and, more recently, decisions of the Charity Commission as to whether or not to register a charity. The history of the definition of charity remains significant today because the new statutory definition builds on these earlier developments.

(i) The Preamble to the Charitable Uses Act 1601

The Charitable Uses Act 1601 featured a Preamble that identified a number of charitable purposes. These proved to be highly significant for the subsequent development of the law of charity. These purposes included: the relief of aged, impotent, and poor people; the maintenance of sick and maimed soldiers and mariners; schools and universities; repairs of bridges, churches, and highways; houses of correction; marriages of poor maids; and the relief or redemption of prisoners. The purpose of this statute was to correct abuses in the administration of charitable trusts but the courts used the Preamble to assist in the determination of whether a particular purpose was charitable. The list was not considered to be exhaustive, but provided a foundation for the development of the law of charity by analogy with the identified purposes and with regard to the 'spirit or intendment' of the Preamble.[65] If a particular purpose did not fall within the Preamble expressly or by analogy, it could not be regarded as charitable, even though it was beneficial to the public.

(ii) The four heads of charity

Over the next 300 years, the law of charity developed with reference to the Preamble. At the end of the nineteenth century, in *Commissioners for Special Purposes of Income Tax v Pemsel*,[66] Lord Macnaghten extracted a number of key principles from the cases to assist in the definition of charity. He identified four heads of charity, namely for the relief of poverty, the advancement of education, the advancement of religion, and other purposes that are beneficial to the community. In *Scottish Burial Reform and Cremation Society v Glasgow Corporation*,[67] Lord Wilberforce clarified the law further. He considered

---

[64] Ibid., [64].   [65] *Morice v Bishop of Durham* (1804) 9 Ves 399, 405 (Sir William Grant MR).
[66] [1891] AC 531, 583.   [67] [1968] AC 138, 154.

the identification of the four heads of charity by Lord Macnaghten to be valuable, but to be only a classification of convenience, so that certain purposes might not fit neatly into any of the headings. Crucially, he recognized that any charity must be for the benefit of the public 'within the intendment of the Preamble', as interpreted by the courts.

The effect of these decisions is that a trust would be considered to be charitable if it were to fall within the spirit and intendment of the Preamble, but the four heads of charity identified by Lord Macnaghten provided a useful checklist with which to test whether the purpose was charitable. But it was also necessary to establish that the purpose was for the public benefit. Benefit was, however, presumed[68] for trusts for the relief of poverty and for the advancement of education and religion, although this presumption could be rebutted by showing that the particular purpose was not beneficial.[69] Benefit needed to be proved for a trust to fall within the fourth head of being another purpose that was beneficial to the community. Different tests of what constituted the public were developed for each of the four heads of charity.

(iii) Charities Acts 2006 and 2011

The Charities Act 2006, which came into force in 2008, provided for the first time a statutory definition of 'charity', albeit one that built on the previous law. A charitable purpose was defined as being a recognized purpose of charity and one that is for the public benefit.[70] The Charities Act 2011 came into force in 2012 and consolidated the various statutory provisions relating to charities into one statute, but without significantly adding to or altering the law deriving from the 2006 Act.

6.2 CHARITIES ACT 2011

6.2.1 HEADS OF CHARITY

The Charities Act 2011 identifies thirteen descriptions of recognized charitable purposes.[71] The object of a charity must satisfy at least one of these purposes. Some of them replicate previously recognized heads of charity, such as the advancement of education and religion. Others simply codify subsequent developments in the definition of charity, either through decisions of the courts or the Charity Commission, such as the advancement of culture or environmental protection. The final head of charity is 'other purposes' which recognizes that the heads of charity are not static and can be developed by analogy with the Preamble to the 1601 Act, as subsequently interpreted by the courts and the new heads of charity under the 2006 Act.[72] This development of the definition of 'charitable purposes' can be undertaken through decisions of the Charity Commission, the First-tier and Upper Tribunals, or the courts.

6.2.2 PUBLIC BENEFIT

Every charity must fulfil the public benefit requirement. The rebuttable presumption of benefit for trusts involving the relief of poverty or the advancement of education and

---

[68] *National Anti-Vivisection Society v IRC* [1948] AC 31, 56 (Viscount Simonds). The presumption only ever related to the establishment of the benefit rather than to whether it was for the benefit of a sufficient section of the community: *The Independent Schools Council v The Charity Commission for England and Wales* [2011] UKUT 421 (TCC), [2012] Ch 412, [63] and [67].

[69] See e.g. *Gilmour v Coats* [1949] AC 426, discussed in Section 6.3.3.(ii), p. 167.

[70] Charities Act 2011, s. 2(1).   [71] Ibid., s. 3(1).   [72] See Section 6.3.13, p. 174.

religion has been abolished,[73] so in every case public benefit needs to be established on the facts. All charities, whether new or existing, must demonstrably satisfy this public benefit requirement. If a charity fails to do so, it will not be registered or it will cease to be registered as a charity.

The Charities Act 2011 does not provide any definition of 'public benefit', so its meaning must be deduced from previous cases and decisions of the Charity Commission. The Charity Commission is, however, required to produce guidance as to the interpretation of public benefit,[74] and did so in 2008.[75] That guidance purported to build on the common law without creating any new law or definitions, but sought to clarify the law in a number of significant respects by identifying principles and factors to assist in the assessment of public benefit.

The validity of this guidance was considered by the Upper Tribunal in *The Independent Schools Council v The Charity Commission for England and Wales*,[76] in which various aspects of it were found wanting, either as being incorrect as a matter of law or as being ambiguous and obscure. So, for example, the statement in the guidance that an organization that excluded people from the opportunity to benefit because of their inability to pay fees would not satisfy the public benefit requirement was found to be wrong, since it is sufficient that the organization provides a more-than-token benefit to the poor.[77] Further, the suggestion in the guidance that the organization must make 'reasonable' provision for the poor, with reasonableness determined by the Charity Commission or the courts, was rejected as being inconsistent with the state of the law, which only requires trustees to provide a more-than-token benefit, above which level they can determine themselves what provision should be made. It followed that the Charity Commission was required to correct the guidance, which it did in new guidance which was published in 2013.[78]

When establishing whether the public benefit requirement is satisfied, there are two distinct aspects which must both be established, as recognized in the Charity Commission's guidance, relating to the identification of a benefit and the determination of what constitutes the public or a section of the public.

(i) Identifiable benefit or benefits

The charity must provide a benefit that is capable of being recognized or described, but it need not be measured. The use of the word 'benefit' in the context of the public benefit test has sometimes caused confusion to the courts, since 'benefit' has also been used to describe the charitable purpose. A key distinction therefore needs to be drawn between two uses of the word 'benefit'. A charitable purpose does need to be beneficial, and this is determined as a matter of law with reference to the heads of recognized charitable purposes and the spirit of the Preamble. Benefit for purposes of the public benefit test needs to be identified as a question of fact, although it is not necessary to establish any consensus of opinion as to whether the purpose is beneficial.[79] So, for example, in *Re Shaw*,[80] George Bernard Shaw's request in his will that his residuary estate should be used to create a forty-letter alphabet to replace the existing twenty-six-letter one was not considered to be of any general utility to the public. The opinion of the testator or the donor of a gift that the

---

[73] Charities Act 2011, s. 4(2).   [74] Ibid., s. 17(1).
[75] Charity Commission, *Charities and Public Benefit* (January 2008).
[76] [2011] UKUT 421 (TCC), [2012] Ch 412.   [77] See Section 6.2.2.(ii), p. 155.
[78] Charity Commission, *Public Benefit: The Public Benefit Requirement* (September 2013).
[79] *Re Grove-Grady* [1929] 1 Ch 557, 572 (Lord Hanworth MR).   [80] [1957] 1 WLR 729.

purpose is beneficial is not relevant; the decision is a matter for the judge, having regard to all of the evidence. So, for example, in *Re Hummeltenberg*,[81] benefit to the public could not be identified from a training college for mediums, despite the testator's belief that it was beneficial.

The benefit must relate to the charity's aims; incidental benefits that are not related to those aims will be disregarded. Further, the benefit must not give rise to more than an incidental personal benefit.[82] Any identifiable benefit will be balanced against any detriment or harm arising from that charitable purpose, so that, if the detriment exceeds the benefit, the public benefit requirement will not be satisfied.[83] So, for example, in *National Anti-Vivisection Society v IRC*,[84] it was held that the public benefit test was not satisfied where an organization sought to ban experimentation on animals, because the detriment to the public through adverse effects on medical research arising from such a ban outweighed the putative benefit arising from the welfare of the animals. This decision also illustrates how the interpretation of public benefit can change over time. A decision fifty years earlier[85] had held that a society, the purpose of which was to stop experiments on animals, was charitable as being for a purpose that was beneficial to the community. By the time of *National Anti-Vivisection Society*, an awareness of the benefits to medical research arising from experiments on animals meant that such a charitable purpose was no longer considered to be beneficial to the public.

In assessing the balance of benefits, it is also necessary to consider any private benefits that are received by people or organizations that are not beneficiaries of the charity. Such private benefits will not necessarily defeat the public benefit test, but they must be incidental to the fulfilment of the charity's aims, such as where they are a necessary by-product of the fulfilment of those aims.

It has sometimes been recognized that indirect benefits to the general public arising from the fulfilment of the charitable purpose will be relevant to the public benefit inquiry. So, for example, a trust for a private hospital will benefit the State by relieving the demand for beds in public hospitals,[86] or the provision of private accommodation for the elderly might delay the need for such people to rely on public services for their care.[87] But this recognition of indirect benefits to the public has not been applied universally.[88] In particular, it does not appear to be relevant to the advancement of education, for otherwise it would be possible to establish the public benefit from independent schools indirectly by showing that the existence of such schools reduces the demand for places at State schools and so is an indirect benefit to the public. Such an argument was not countenanced by the Charity Commission in its original guidance on *Charities and Public Benefit*, which demanded that independent schools identify public benefit by showing how the education at a particular independent school can be made available to the wider community, for example through the provision of scholarships and bursaries or making facilities available for use by the State sector. The validity of this approach was considered by the Upper Tribunal in *The Independent Schools Council v The Charity Commission for England and Wales*,[89] which identified various direct and indirect benefits that might be provided by independent schools, such as allowing local State school students to use school facilities,

---

[81] [1923] 1 Ch 237.   [82] Charity Commission (see n. 78) , Pt 6.   [83] Ibid., Pt 4.
[84] [1948] AC 31, 57 (Lord Wright).   [85] *Re Fouveaux* [1895] 2 Ch 501.
[86] *Re Resch's Will Trusts* [1969] 1 AC 514.
[87] *Joseph Rowntree Memorial Trust Housing Association Ltd v Attorney-General* [1983] Ch 159.
[88] See also *Helena Housing Ltd v The Commissioners for Her Majesty's Revenue and Customs* [2012] EWCA Civ 569, [2012] WTLR 1519, concerning the provision of housing regardless of whether the beneficiary was in need. See further Section 6.3.10, p. 173.
[89] [2011] UKUT 421 (TCC), [2012] Ch 412. See Section 6.3.2.(ii), p. 163.

including swimming pools and sport halls, the sharing of teachers with local State schools, the dissemination of teaching materials, and allowing other members of the community to use the school's facilities. Some of these might be characterized as direct benefits that relate to the charitable purpose of advancing education. Allowing members of the public to use the school's facilities was, however, held not to be a relevant benefit to the public, since it would not advance education. But other indirect benefits would be relevant to establishing the public benefit requirement, such as where students from the school involve themselves in community projects as part of the school's citizenship education programme. Crucially, whilst the Upper Tribunal acknowledged the argument that education in independent schools might be a relevant benefit to the public because it takes students out of the State sector who would otherwise have to be educated at the expense of the State, the Tribunal concluded that this would make little, if any, difference to the determination of an independent school's charitable status, because the benefit is speculative and an independent school could probably establish the relevant benefit without resorting to this argument.

(ii) To the public

The benefit must be available to the public in general or to a section of the public. Defining what is meant by 'the public', or a section of it, is crucial to the law of charity to distinguish between public and private trusts. The policy of the law is clear, namely that it is not appropriate for a settlor to obtain the benefits of charitable status through the mechanism of a trust where the beneficiaries are, in fact, a private group of people, such as the settlor's close family or friends. Consequently, the class of actual and potential beneficiaries must be a public class. It may be quite a small class, but it must not be numerically negligible[90] and the members of that class must not be linked by a contract or by a quality that depends on their relationship to a particular individual.[91]

The key concern relates to the availability of the opportunity to benefit from the fulfilment of the charity's purpose, even though relatively small numbers are likely to benefit from that purpose. The opportunity to benefit must not be unreasonably restricted, for example by reference to geographical location. It does not follow that the benefit cannot be restricted to a particular area, but such a restriction must not be unreasonable. Restricting the benefit to people living in a particular town is likely to be acceptable as constituting an appropriate section of the public, whereas limiting it to people living in a particular street will not, although this will depend on the particular aims of the charity. The public benefit test can still be satisfied even though the beneficiaries are abroad,[92] but the charity must be registered in England and Wales.[93]

The opportunity to benefit must also not be unreasonably restricted by the ability of potential beneficiaries to pay fees. It does not follow that charities cannot charge for the services or facilities that they provide, such as charging school fees[94] or fees for a private hospital,[95] and they can even make a profit as long as this is reasonable and necessary to carry out the charity's aims, such as by enhancing the facilities that are provided. In other words, the profit must be ploughed back into the charitable work.[96] If, however, the charges restrict the benefits only to those who can afford the fees, it may follow that the benefits are not available to a

---

[90] A gift to a care home of thirty-three residents failed this test in *Re Duffy* [2013] EWHC 2395 (Ch). For criticism of this test see Synge, 'Charitable status: not a negligible matter' (2016) 132 LQR 303.

[91] *Re Compton* [1945] Ch 123; *Oppenheim v Tobacco Securities Trust Co Ltd* [1951] AC 297.

[92] *Re Niyazi's Will Trusts* [1978] 1 WLR 910.   [93] *Gaudiya Mission v Brahmachary* [1998] Ch 341.

[94] *The Abbey, Malvern Wells Ltd v Ministry of Housing and Local Government* [1951] 1 Ch 728; *The Independent Schools Council v The Charity Commission for England and Wales* [2011] UKUT 421 (TCC), [2012] Ch 412.

[95] *Re Resch's Will Trusts* [1969] 1 AC 514.   [96] *IRC v Falkirk Temperance Café Trust* 1927 SC 261.

sufficiently large section of the public. This is all a matter of degree, however, and the Charity Commission will consider all of the benefits that are provided by a charity that charges fees, since there may be sufficient benefits available to people who cannot afford fees to satisfy the public benefit requirement. Satisfying the public benefit test where a charity charges fees has proved particularly significant as regards independent schools.[97] The fact that fees are charged by such schools does not automatically render the school non-charitable, but it will be necessary for the school to show that sufficient benefit is provided to members of the public who are unable to afford fees, such as through the provision of scholarships and bursaries, for otherwise the poor will be excluded from the charity's work.[98]

(iii) Political objectives

Charities cannot pursue political objectives.[99] This might be regarded as being relevant to the definition of appropriate charitable purposes as a matter of law, but the courts have tended to analyse the pursuit of political objectives in the context of the public benefit test.

When analysing whether a charity is pursuing a political objective, an important distinction needs to be drawn between those cases in which an organization's main purpose is political and those in which the political objective is merely incidental to the charity's main non-political purpose. An organization will be considered to be pursuing a political purpose where its main purpose is of a party-political nature, or where it advocates or opposes a change in the law or policy, or decisions of central or local government authorities, either in England or abroad.[100] Courts are unwilling to consider whether the pursuit of party-political purposes is for the benefit of the public because the law wishes to remain politically neutral.[101] A number of reasons can be identified as to why the courts are not willing to consider whether purposes seeking a change in law or policy are for the benefit of the public:

(1) The court usually has no means of judging whether the proposed change will be for the public benefit.[102]

(2) Even if there were evidence of the public being benefited by the change in law or policy, the court should abide by the principle that the law is right as it stands, for otherwise it would trespass on the functions of the legislature.[103]

(3) The Attorney-General has a duty to formulate a scheme for the execution of a charitable trust if required, and it would not be appropriate for such a law officer to intervene and seek a change in the law.[104]

Thus, in *National Anti-Vivisection Society v IRC*, another reason why the society was not considered to be charitable was that its main purpose was to campaign for a change in the law to abolish vivisection, which was held to be a political purpose.[105]

---

[97] See Section 6.3.2.(ii), p. 163.

[98] *The Independent Schools Council v The Charity Commission for England and Wales* [2011] UKUT 421 (TCC), [2012] Ch 412, [178]. See further Section 6.3.2.(ii), p. 163.

[99] *Bowman v Secular Society Ltd* [1917] AC 406; *McGovern v Attorney-General* [1982] Ch 321.

[100] *McGovern v Attorney-General* [1982] Ch 321, 339 (Slade J); Charity Commission, *Speaking Out: Guidance on Campaigning and Political Activities by Charities*, CC9 (2008).

[101] See the Charity Commission's report on *Campaigning and Political Issues Arising in the Run-Up to the 2017 General Election* (2017).

[102] *Bowman v Secular Society Ltd* [1917] AC 406, 442 (Lord Parker).

[103] *McGovern v Attorney-General* [1982] Ch 321, 337 (Slade J); *Hanchett-Stamford v Attorney-General* [2008] EWHC 330 (Ch), [2009] Ch 173, [16] (Lewison J).

[104] *National Anti-Vivisection Society v IRC* [1948] AC 31, 62 (Lord Simonds).

[105] See also *Hanchett-Stamford v Attorney-General* [2008] EWHC 330 (Ch), [2009] Ch 173.

A charity will legitimately be using political means to further a non-political purpose where it is campaigning for a change in the law for the benefit of those who are objects of the charity's purpose, raising awareness of a particular issue, influencing and changing public attitudes, or influencing government policy or legislation. The key characteristic of such activities that makes them non-political is that the campaigning is a means of furthering the organization's charitable purposes, but without becoming the dominant means by which it carries out those purposes.[106] So, for example, it would be legitimate for a student union, which is a charity, to organize a demonstration against an increase in tuition fees. This would be for the benefit of the students, but would be incidental to the charity's main purposes relating to the advancement of education.

The rule preventing charities from pursuing political purposes has been criticized as being outdated.[107] The reasons given for the illegitimacy of pursuing such objectives are unconvincing,[108] especially the reason that the law is incapable of judging whether a change in the law or government policy is good or bad. Indeed, in *National Anti-Vivisection Society v IRC*,[109] the House of Lords judged that a proposed change in the law, in the form of the abolition of vivisection, was not in the public interest because benefits to the public in terms of scientific and medical research outweighed the harm to animals arising from vivisection. Also, the crucial distinction between political purposes that are a main objective or only incidental is a distinction that can be very difficult to draw in practice. Consequently, there should be no objection to a charity pursuing political objectives in the sense that the charity is seeking a change in law or policy, whether at home or abroad.[110] This should only be qualified in two respects. First, a charity should not be allowed to pursue a political objective if the detriment to the public outweighs the benefit, as determined either by the courts or the Charity Commission. So, for example, a charity that seeks a change in the law in favour of racial or sexual discrimination should not be regarded as pursuing an objective that is beneficial to the public. Secondly, a charity should not pursue party-political objectives, since the benefits of charity law, particularly the fiscal advantages, should not be available in support of such purposes. But, otherwise, there is no need for a special rule relating to political objectives; this should be assessed in the normal way by reference to the public benefit criteria.[111]

But, as English law stands, it is clear that, where a main purpose of an organization is political, the trust will be invalid as a charitable trust. This is the case even if there are other charitable purposes, because a charity's purposes must be wholly and exclusively charitable.[112] Where, however, the organization's purposes might be carried out either in a way that is non-political or a way that is political, the courts will adopt a benign approach to the construction of the purpose, and will assume that the trustees will act in a lawful and proper manner and not in a way that can be considered to be political.[113]

---

[106] Charity Commission (see n. 101), CC9.

[107] Stevens and Feldman, 'Broadcasting advertisements by bodies with political objects, judicial review, and the influence of charities law' [1997] PL 615, 622; Santow, 'Charity in its political voice: a tinkling cymbal or a sounding brass?' [1999] CLP 255. But note the more liberal approach to the recognition of the advancement of human rights as a specific charitable purpose following the enactment of the Charities Act 2011. See Section 6.3.8, p. 171.

[108] See Garton, '*National Anti-Vivisection Society v Inland Revenue Commissioners*' in *Landmark Cases in Equity*, ed. Mitchell and Mitchell (Oxford: Hart, 2012), p. 555.   [109] [1948] AC 31.

[110] As has been recognized by the High Court of Australia in *Aid/Watch Incorporated v Commissioner of Taxation* [2010] HCA 42, which concerned an organization that campaigned for effective Australian and multinational foreign aid policies. This was considered to be for the public benefit.

[111] See Walton, '*McGovern v Attorney-General*: constraints on judicial assessment of charitable benefit' [2014] Conv 317.

[112] See Section 6.4, p. 174.   [113] *Re Koeppler's Will Trusts* [1986] Ch 423, 437 (Slade LJ).

(iv) Duties of charity trustees

Charity trustees are required to have regard to the Charity Commission's guidance on public benefit when exercising their powers or duties.[114] It does not follow that the trustees are required to follow the guidance, but it must be considered. Charity trustees are also required to report annually on how they have carried out the aims of the charity for the benefit of the public.

6.3 CHARITABLE PURPOSES

6.3.1 THE PREVENTION OR RELIEF OF POVERTY

(i) Charitable purpose

Under the common law of charity, the first of the four heads of charitable purpose recognized in *Pemsel's case*[115] was the relief of aged, impotent, and poor people. This head has now been divided into the relief of the poor in paragraph (a) of the Charities Act 2006, with 'relief of those in need' now covered by paragraph (j).[116] Paragraph (a) covers both the relief of poverty and also the prevention of poverty.[117]

'Poverty' is a relative term.[118] It encompasses, but is not confined to, complete destitution.[119] It also includes those people who do not have access to the normal things of life that most people would take for granted. It can extend to people of moderate means and may even include people who suffer only temporary financial hardship arising from a sudden change in their circumstances.[120] In *Re Coulthurst*,[121] a fund for the widows and orphans of officers of a bank whose financial circumstances were such that they were most deserving of assistance, was held to be charitable. A trust to set up the unemployed in trade or business was held to be charitable as being for the relief of poverty.[122] The imposition of a minimum income qualification did not prevent a particular trust from being for the relief of poverty, at least where preference was given to widows with young dependent children.[123]

A trust to provide 'dwellings' for the 'working classes' has been held not to be charitable because there was no requirement of being poor to benefit from it,[124] whereas a testamentary gift to construct a working men's hostel in Cyprus was held to be charitable, because 'hostel' suggested modest accommodation for working men of relatively low income who were in temporary need.[125] This charity was valid even though it was for the relief of poverty abroad. Clearly, the decision whether a gift is for the poor requires some very subtle distinctions to be drawn.

Sometimes, the creators of trusts have tried hard to squeeze their gifts within the charitable definition of poverty, none more so than the testator in *Re Gwyon*,[126] who left a fund to provide underpants for boys in Farnham, subject to various conditions, such as each boy not being supported by another charity and his parents not receiving poor relief. Boys could obtain new pants each year, but only by showing the old ones with the writing

---

[114] Charities Act 2011, s. 17(5).

[115] Charities Act 2011, s. 3(1). For the rationale behind the recognition of this head of charity, see Dunn, 'As "cold as charity"? Property, Equity and the charitable trust' (2000) 20 LS 222.

[116] [1891] AC 531. See Section 6.1.5.(ii), p. 151.   [117] See Section 6.3.10, p. 172.

[118] *Re Clarke* [1923] 2 Ch 407.   [119] *Re Coulthurst* [1961] 661, 665 (Sir Raymond Evershed).

[120] See e.g. *AITC Foundation's Application for Registration as a Charity* [2005] WTLR 1265, in which a charity was registered for the relief of poverty suffered by those who had invested in companies that had collapsed.

[121] [1951] Ch 661.   [122] *IRC v Oldham Training and Enterprise Council* [1996] STC 1218.

[123] *Re De Carteret* [1933] Ch 103.   [124] *Re Sanders' Will Trusts* [1954] Ch 265.

[125] *Re Niyazi's Will Trusts* [1978] 1 WLR 910.   [126] [1930] 1 Ch 255.

'Gwyon's Present' still decipherable on the waistband. The motive for this gift is unclear, but it was held not to be for the relief of poverty because the conditions did not sufficiently identify that the eligible boys had to be poor.

(ii) Public benefit

The presumption that trusts for the relief of the poor satisfied the benefit element of the public benefit test was removed by the Charities Act 2006,[127] so that it is now necessary to establish in each case that such trusts satisfy both elements of the public benefit test. Benefit from the prevention or relief of poverty is easily proved. As regards the definition of 'public', it has long been recognized that this test is interpreted more liberally where the charitable purpose is for the relief of the poor than for other charitable purposes, primarily because of the benefit to the State from poverty being relieved, so that it is easier to justify allowing fiscal privileges to such charities. The 'public' can encompass a very small class of potential beneficiaries, such as poor relatives of the testator,[128] or poor people from a small geographical area, such as a parish or town.[129] Consequently, there can be a family connection between the creator of the charitable trust and the pool from which the beneficiaries is drawn where the charitable purpose is for the relief of poverty, when this would not be allowed for other charitable purposes. But the line must not be crossed so that the benefits of a charity are available where the trust is a private trust for the benefit of poor people. It follows that the class must consist of a particular description of poor people, rather than a gift to particular poor people with the relief of poverty simply being the motive for the gift.[130] There is, therefore, a distinction between a trust 'for the relief of my poor relatives' and a trust 'for the relief of poverty suffered by my son and daughter'.

The proper interpretation of the public benefit test in respect of a trust for the relief of poverty was considered in the important case of *Dingle v Turner*.[131] The question for the House of Lords was whether a trust for the relief of poor employees should be treated as charitable in the same way as could a trust for the relief of poor relatives, even though the class was defined by reference to common employment with a particular company. The case concerned a trust to pay pensions to poor employees of a particular company who were aged or incapacitated. The company had over 600 employees and a substantial number of ex-employees. The House of Lords held that the public benefit test was satisfied.

In reaching this decision, the Lords distinguished their earlier decision in *Oppenheim v Tobacco Securities Trust Co Ltd*,[132] which had held, in the context of the charitable purpose of advancing education, that a trust that provided for the education of children of a particular company did not satisfy the public benefit test. In *Dingle* it was held that, if trusts for poor relations satisfied the public benefit test (and since they had been recognized for such a long time their validity could not be impeached), then the same should be true of a trust for poor employees; it would be illogical to distinguish between different sorts of poverty trust. Also, a number of poor employee charities had been recognized as valid for a number of years. Finally, there are fewer concerns about trusts for the relief of poverty obtaining fiscal advantages as a result of being characterized as charitable, as compared to trusts for the advancement of education, simply because company benevolent schemes that are free of tax do not constitute an attractive fringe benefit, since employees tend to be optimistic enough to think that they will not need to apply to such schemes.

---

[127] See now Charities Act 2011, s. 4(2). See Section 6.2.2, p. 153. [128] *Re Segelman* [1996] Ch 171.
[129] *Re Lucas* [1922] 2 Ch 52; *Re Monk* [1927] 2 Ch 197.
[130] *Re Scarisbrick's Will Trusts* [1951] Ch 622. See also *Re Segelman* [1996] Ch 171.
[131] [1972] AC 601.   [132] [1951] AC 297. See Section 6.3.2.(ii), p. 161.

It follows that the public benefit test for trusts for the relief of poverty can encompass a potentially narrow class of beneficiaries and the fact that the class is defined by reference to a personal nexus, such as having a common relative or employer or being a member of the same club, will not prevent the test from being satisfied. This was confirmed by the Upper Tribunal in *Attorney-General v Charity Commission for England and Wales*.[133]

6.3.2 THE ADVANCEMENT OF EDUCATION

(i) Charitable purpose

In the Preamble to the Charitable Uses Act 1601 the only references to educational matters are to schools of learning, free schools, and scholars in universities. 'Education' is now widely defined to encompass improving and disseminating human knowledge.[134] Before 2006, the definition was even wider, to include promoting arts and culture, but this is now a distinct charitable purpose,[135] so the definition of education is likely to narrow.

Various principles can be identified relating to the determination of educational charitable purposes. At its core, 'education' relates to teaching, including paying teachers,[136] whether at home or abroad.[137] But it is not confined to formal instruction in the classroom, and encompasses instruction, training, and practice containing spiritual, moral, mental, and physical elements.[138]

'Education' also encompasses research. In assessing whether the research is educational, the court will have regard to its aims and utility. In *Re Hopkins' Will Trust*,[139] the key issue was whether a gift to the Francis Bacon Society, to identify evidence in support of his authorship of the plays attributed to Shakespeare, was charitable. In holding that it was, the court observed that it was not required to determine whether Bacon did write the plays attributed to Shakespeare, but only whether this was a legitimate subject of research. It was held that it was not so manifestly futile and improbable as to be an object that was devoid of the possibility of any result. In *Re Shaw*,[140] on the other hand, a gift in the will of George Bernard Shaw for the development of a phonetic alphabet was held not to be educational because its object merely tended to the increase of knowledge without being combined with teaching or education.[141] This was, however, qualified in *Re Hopkins* as regards academic research, which will still be regarded as educational even though the researcher is not required to engage in teaching or education in the conventional sense. Such research will be considered to be educational if it is of educational value to the researcher, or might lead to something that would pass into the store of educational material, or might improve the sum of communicable knowledge, including the formation of literary taste and appreciation. Conducting research into the authorship of the plays attributed to Shakespeare was considered to be educational in the third sense, since it related to the formation of literary taste and appreciation. The first attribute of research, namely that it is of educational value to the researcher, is doubtful, especially because this would not appear to meet the public benefit requirement. Consequently, the preferable view is that research should be considered to be educational only where it involves some element of dissemination of the results. This had been recognized in *Re British School of Egyptian Archaeology*,[142] in

---

[133] (2012) UKUT 420 (TCC), [2012] WTLR 521. See also Charity Commission (see n. 78), Annex A.

[134] *Incorporated Council of Law Reporting for England and Wales v Attorney-General* [1973] Ch 73, 102 (Buckley LJ).

[135] See Section 6.3.6, p. 169.   [136] *Case of Christ's College, Cambridge* (1757) 1 Wm Bl 90.

[137] *Manoogian v Sonsino* [2002] EWHC 1304, [2002] WTLR 989.

[138] *IRC v McMullen* [1981] AC 1, 15 (Lord Hailsham).   [139] [1965] Ch 669.   [140] [1957] 1 WLR 729.

[141] It also did not satisfy the public benefit test. See Section 6.2.2.(i), p. 153.   [142] [1954] 1 WLR 546.

which a trust to excavate and discover Egyptian antiquities, to hold exhibitions, to publish works, and to train students was held to be for educational purposes, both as regards the dissemination of knowledge and the teaching of students. Indeed, in *Re Hopkins* itself, Wilberforce J accepted[143] that research that is of a private character, such as being for the benefit only of members of a particular society, would not normally be educational. In *Incorporated Council of Law Reporting for England and Wales v Attorney-General*,[144] a trust for the publication of law reports was considered to advance education because it assisted research into the law and disseminated knowledge of the law.

The advancement of education has also been held to include the study and dissemination of ethical principles,[145] the organization of conferences to discuss issues of public and international interest at which the participants learned from and instructed each other,[146] and even a trust to organize and encourage football and other games and sports at schools and universities.[147]

(ii) Public benefit

The requirement of public benefit has proved especially significant when determining whether trusts for the advancement of education are charitable, and will be even more so now that benefit can no longer be presumed.[148]

Definition of the public

It has been in the context of this charitable purpose that the tax advantages of being a charity have proved to be important, especially as regards whether independent schools should be treated as charitable. Also, employers might seek to provide tax-free benefits to employees by providing for the education of their children, but this will be effective only if a benefit to the public can be identified. The definition of 'public' for these purposes was the key issue in the leading case of *Oppenheim v Tobacco Securities Trust Co Ltd*,[149] in which income of a trust fund was to be used to provide for the education of children of employees or former employees of British-American Tobacco Co Ltd and its subsidiary or allied companies. Even though these companies together employed over 110,000 people, it was held that the public benefit test was not satisfied. Lord Simonds emphasized that the key test to identify whether the public element of the public benefit test was satisfied was whether the potential beneficiaries formed a section of the community. This meant that they were not numerically negligible and the quality that distinguished them from other members of the community did not depend on their relationship to a particular individual or individuals, such as a member of their family. This relationship was called the 'personal nexus'. In this case, the group of beneficiaries was identified by reference to employment with a particular employer and such common employment did not make the employees a section of the community. It would, however, have been different if the trust had provided for the education of children of those engaged in the tobacco industry in a named town, because then the personal nexus would have been absent. Since there was, however, a personal nexus in this case, the trust was a private trust that was void for perpetuity.

The decision of the House of Lords in *Oppenheim* does not sit easily with the later decision of the same court in *Dingle v Turner*.[150] That case also concerned the provision of benefits by an employer for employees, but the charitable purpose there related to the relief

---

[143] [1965] Ch 669, 681.   [144] [1972] Ch 73.

[145] *Re South Place Educational Society* [1980] 1 WLR 1565.   [146] *Re Koeppler's Will Trusts* [1986] Ch 423.

[147] *IRC v McMullen* [1981] AC 1. This would also now be charitable under head (g) involving the advancement of amateur sport. See Section 6.3.7, p. 170.   [148] Charities Act 2011, s. 4(2).

[149] [1951] AC 297.   [150] [1972] AC 601. See Section 6.3.1.(ii), p. 159.

of poverty and, despite the personal nexus between the employees and their employer, the public benefit test was satisfied. The two cases can be reconciled on the basis that they were concerned with different charitable purposes; in *Oppenheim*, the House of Lords did acknowledge that the common nexus test did not apply to trusts for the relief of poverty, at least where the personal nexus involved a common relative. *Dingle v Turner* simply extended this to where the nexus related to a common employer. But is it satisfactory to reconcile these cases simply on the ground that they were concerned with different charitable purposes? Why should this make such a difference? In *Oppenheim*, Lord MacDermott dissented. He considered that the identification of a class of beneficiaries with reference to a personal nexus was an important factor in suggesting that the class was not a section of the public, but he did not consider it to be a decisive factor. Other relevant factors included the size of the class, the needs of the members of that class and the advantage to the public in having those needs met, the interests of the settlor in the fortunes of the members of the class, the purpose of the trust, and its scope and value. He applied these factors to the facts of *Oppenheim* and concluded that the public benefit test was satisfied because of the large size of the class, which included children of former employees and employees of subsidiary companies.

Lord MacDermott's approach to the identification of a section of the community commended itself to the judges in *Dingle v Turner*. Lord Cross said that he did not consider the distinction between personal and impersonal relationships, when identifying a section of the public, to be satisfactory. He emphasized that, ultimately, whether the class of potential beneficiaries did represent a section of the public was a matter of degree, having regard both to the numbers in the class and to the purposes of the trust. The other four judges agreed with the judgment of Lord Cross.

But Lord Cross in *Dingle v Turner* went one stage further in his analysis, a step that was not supported by three of the other judges, one of whom was Lord MacDermott. Lord Cross suggested that, in determining whether the public benefit test is satisfied, the availability of fiscal privileges should be taken into account. In particular, if the purpose of the creator of the trust is to obtain fiscal privileges, the trust should not be charitable. The automatic availability of fiscal privileges to charities has been a cause of concern for many years. In 1955, the Radcliffe Commission recommended that fiscal privileges should be allowed only to certain charities.[151] This is not the law. There is one solution to the problem identified by Lord Cross, however, which depends on whether it is the purpose or the motive of the creator of the trust to attract fiscal privileges. If the purpose is to advance education, but the motive is to attract fiscal privileges, the trust should be regarded as charitable. If, however, the purpose, or one of the purposes, is to attract fiscal privileges, this is not a charitable purpose. Consequently, the purposes of the trust will not be exclusively charitable and so the trust will not be a charity.[152]

So where is the law left concerning the identification of public benefit for the advancement of education following *Oppenheim* and *Dingle*? Although it has been suggested that the consequence of the comments in the later case of *Dingle* is that *Oppenheim* must be treated as wrongly decided,[153] those comments were *obiter* and nothing was said in *Dingle v Turner* to suggest that *Oppenheim* should have been decided differently. It was simply the approach of Lord MacDermott in *Oppenheim* that commended itself to Lord Cross in *Dingle*. *Oppenheim* was followed in *IRC v Educational Grants Association Ltd*,[154] although this was decided before *Dingle v Turner*. The *Educational Grants Association* case

---

[151] *Report of the Radcliffe Commission*, Cmd 9474 (London: HMSO, 1955), paras. 54–60.
[152] Watkin, 'Charity: the purport of '"purpose"' [1978] Conv 277, 282.
[153] Hayton, '*Dingle v Turner*' [1972] Conv 209, 212.   [154] [1967] Ch 123.

concerned a company that was established for the advancement of education. The company had a close relationship with Metal Box Co Ltd and most of its income was applied for the education of children connected with that company. It was held that Educational Grants Association Ltd was not charitable because the income was not being applied for the benefit of a sufficient section of the public.

If the facts of *Oppenheim* and *Educational Grants Association* were to arise today, it is clear that the Tribunals, or more likely the Charity Commission, would apply the personal nexus test to determine whether the beneficiaries constituted a sufficient section of the public. But, in assessing this, it would be appropriate to have regard to the factors identified by Lord MacDermott and affirmed by Lord Cross. The fact that the creator of the trust is seeking to obtain fiscal immunity should also be regarded as a relevant factor; this is a legitimate motive for seeking charitable status, but it cannot be regarded as a charitable purpose in its own right. It is not appropriate for companies to use the law of charity to provide tax-free benefits to employees. This unacceptably confuses the public law of charity with the private endeavours of companies.

Although much of the discussion about public benefit in respect of the advancement of education has focused on the personal nexus test, it must not be forgotten that, for all trusts involving the advancement of education, it must be shown that there is a factual benefit and that this benefit is available to the public or a section of the public, so even if there is no personal nexus, it does not automatically follow that the public benefit test has been satisfied.[155] So, for example, if the charitable purpose relates to research, this needs to be disseminated and not restricted to the use of the researcher or to the members of a particular society.[156] Where eligibility to obtain the benefits of the charity is restricted, this does not mean that the benefit is no longer available to a section of the public, as long as the restriction is reasonable and is not based on a personal nexus. So, for example, a scholarship to study at a particular school or university may legitimately be restricted to people from a particular town or to people who attain a certain level of academic achievement, but it cannot be restricted to relatives of the donor.

Independent schools

A matter of long-standing controversy has related to the satisfaction of the public benefit requirement by independent schools, so that they can be registered as charities and obtain fiscal advantages. About 7 per cent of the school population in England and Wales attend a private school, and pay an average fee of over £12,000 per year. Whether such schools do satisfy the public benefit requirement was considered by the Upper Tribunal in *The Independent Schools Council v The Charity Commission for England and Wales*.[157]

As regards the benefit component, it was accepted that independent schools which provide mainstream education do advance education and so do provide a benefit. Whilst the dis-benefit to society of paying fees, with consequent effects on social mobility, was balanced against the benefit arising from the advancement of education, it was recognized that great weight is to be attached to a purpose that would ordinarily be charitable, and value judgements influenced by a social and political agenda are unlikely to be sufficient to establish detriment. Consequently, the benefit element was established.

The key question concerned whether an independent school provided a benefit for a sufficient section of the community, bearing in mind that fees were charged. It was

---

[155] *The Independent Schools Council v The Charity Commission for England and Wales* [2011] UKUT 421 (TCC), [2012] Ch 214, [141].

[156] *Re Hopkins' Will Trust* [1965] Ch 669, 681 (Wilberforce J). See Section 6.3.2.(i), p. 160.

[157] [2011] UKUT 421 (TCC), [2012] Ch 214.

recognized that a hypothetical independent school, the sole object of which was to advance the education of children whose families could afford to pay for their education, would not satisfy the public benefit test, because a trust that excludes the poor from the benefit cannot be a charity. But it was also recognized that such a hypothetical school is unlikely to exist. The key test of public benefit was to consider what a reasonable trustee, acting in the interests of the community as whole, would do in all of the circumstances of the particular school and to consider what provision such a reasonable trustee would make for poor students above the token level, including provision of partial scholarships and bursaries, and remission of fees for those who become unable to pay their school fees.

Once the level of benefit is above the minimum below which no reasonable trustee would go, the level and method of provision is for the trustees and not for the Charity Commission or the courts.[158] Where this line is to be drawn depends on each individual case and does not depend on a general test of reasonableness. In assessing whether minimum provision for poor students had been made, it was appropriate to consider both whether students had access to funds from third parties, such as grant-making educational charities, and from the school itself, in the form of scholarships and bursaries. It is also appropriate to consider indirect benefits that advance the school's educational purpose, such as giving access to facilities to local State school students. However, the ancillary benefit to the wider community of reducing the financial burden on local authorities by having students educated outside the State sector was considered to be too speculative and of too little weight to be taken into account. Ultimately, whether a particular school had provided more than a mere token public benefit is a matter for the trustees to determine and will depend on the school's particular circumstances.

Political purposes

An otherwise valid purpose for the advancement of education will not be charitable if it involves political propaganda masquerading as education, since the trust will not then be exclusively charitable. We have already seen that a political purpose is one that relates to a political party, or to changes in law or policy.[159] A trust for education about party-political principles or dogma will not be charitable. So, for example, in *Re Hopkinson*,[160] a trust for the advancement of adult education with reference to the principles of the Labour Party was held not to be charitable. In *Southwood v Attorney-General*,[161] a trust to advance the education of the public about disarmament was held not to be charitable because the main purpose was political, in the sense of seeking a change in government policy, and the court was not in a position to determine whether unilateral disarmament was for the public benefit. It would have been different if the trust's purpose had been more balanced and less partisan, as in *Re Koeppler's Will Trust*,[162] in which the trust sought to educate the public in the differing ways of securing peace and avoiding war, but no particular political stance was adopted, and the trust was intended to facilitate genuine discussion and the trading of ideas. This was held to be a legitimate charitable purpose as involving the advancement of education.

The identification of political purposes has been of particular significance as regards the operation of students' unions of colleges and universities. Such unions are charities since they have a charitable purpose connected with the advancement of education, by fostering and representing the interests of students to further the educational purposes of the college or university, and must operate for the public benefit. Consequently, such organizations must not use their funds for political purposes. There is a fine line between

---

[158] Ibid., [220].   [159] See Section 6.2.2.(iii), p. 156.   [160] [1949] 1 All ER 346.
[161] (2000) 80 P & CR D 34.   [162] [1986] Ch 423.

what is and is not acceptable political campaigning by students' unions. As a basic rule, if the campaigning relates to an issue that furthers the interests of the students of that union in a way that assists in the educational aims of the university or college, then it will not be a political purpose.[163] But funds of the union cannot be spent on political purposes. Consequently, a students' union was restrained from making payment to a publicity campaign against the abolition of free milk for school children,[164] and another was restrained from making payments to the National Student Committee to Stop War in the Gulf,[165] since, in both cases, the campaign was not related to the interests of the students of those particular unions. Funds, could however, be spent on campaigns to improve street lighting near the campus or to demonstrate against tuition fees. Students are not prevented from demonstrating about political matters, but they cannot use funds from their students' union to enable them to do so, because such funds must be used for the public benefit, as defined by the law.

6.3.3 THE ADVANCEMENT OF RELIGION

(i) Charitable purpose

Religion

Although advancement of religion has long been recognized as a charitable purpose, the only reference to religion in the Preamble to the Charitable Uses Act 1601 is to 'the repair of churches'. The notion of advancing religion has been expanded dramatically since then. Over the years, various charities relating to Christian denominations have been recognized as advancing religion, whether involving the Church of England, non-denominational churches, or the Catholic[166] religion. In *Thornton v Howe*,[167] a trust for the publication of the works of Joanna Southcote was considered to be for the advancement of religion, Joanna Southcote having claimed that she was with child by the Holy Ghost and would give birth to a second Messiah. A faith-healing movement has also been held to involve the advancement of religion.[168] Other religions have been recognized as well, including charities relating to the advancement of Judaism,[169] Islam, and the Unification Church.[170]

The interpretation of 'religion' was widened significantly by the Charities Act 2006,[171] which defines religion as including a belief in more than one god and even a religion that does not involve a belief in a god. It follows that trusts for the advancement of Buddhism, Hinduism, and Sikhism will undoubtedly be religious. In addition, the Charity Commission[172] has provided guidance on the interpretation of religion, which identifies four characteristics:

(i) a belief in a supreme being or entity, which includes a 'spiritual principle', which is the object or focus of the religion;

(ii) a relationship between the believer and supreme being or entity by showing worship, reverence, or veneration;

(iii) a belief system which has a certain level of cogency, coherence, seriousness, and importance; and

(iv) the promotion of an identifiable, positive, beneficial, moral, or ethical framework.

---

[163] *Charity Commission, Students' Unions: A Guide*, OG48.C3 (2001).
[164] *Baldry v Feintuck* [1972] 1 WLR 552. [165] *Webb v O'Doherty* (1991) The Times, 11 February.
[166] See e.g. *Gilmour v Coats* [1949] AC 426. [167] (1862) 31 Beav 14.
[168] *Funnell v Stewart* [1996] 1 WLR 288. [169] Since the Religious Disabilities Act 1846.
[170] Popularly known as the 'Moonies'. [171] See now Charities Act 2011, s. 3(2)(a).
[172] Charity Commission, *Guidance on Charitable Purposes* (2013).

Whilst this purports to be a statement of the statutory definition of religion in the light of the interpretation of religion by the courts, it goes beyond the statutory definition, especially by including the reference to the relationship between believer and supreme being.[173]

The courts have, however, held that certain belief systems cannot be characterized as religious. So, for example, in *Re South Place Ethical Society*,[174] the Society's objects of studying and disseminating ethical principles and cultivating rational religious sentiment was held not to involve the advancement of religion, since religion was concerned with man's relationship with God, and ethics with man's relations with man. In that case, Dillon J also indicated that religion required faith in a god and worship of that god. This is now inconsistent with the statutory definition of religion, which does not require a belief in a god. In the end, the Society was held to be charitable as being for the advancement of education and for other purposes beneficial to the community. But, even with the new statutory definition of religion, a trust for the advancement of ethical principles or humanism would not be a trust for the advancement of religion, since there still needs to be a belief in some form of supreme being or entity that is worshipped, venerated, or revered.

Similarly, is Scientology a religion? In 1999, the Charity Commission[175] decided that the Church of Scientology should not be registered as a charity because, although followers of Scientology believe in a supreme being, they do not worship, but engage in one-to-one counselling, called 'auditing', and study the works of L. Ron Hubbard, a science-fiction writer.[176] In Australia, however, Scientology has been held to be a religion for tax purposes.[177] It is likely that the effect of the wider definition of religion under the Charities Act 2006 will mean that Scientology can now be classed as a religion,[178] but it will still be necessary to establish public benefit, which was a further reason why the Charity Commission refused to register it as a charity in 1999. It still has not been registered, presumably for that reason.[179]

The Charity Commission has decided that the Gnostic Centre for the advancement of Gnosticism, under which the followers believe that the world was created by a lesser god and the true God is a higher being, was not charitable because there was no evidence of the teaching of a clear and identifiable moral framework.[180] This is a new requirement that has not previously been recognized in the case law. The Druid Centre, which promotes paganism, however, has been considered to be charitable as advancing religion, because of a belief in a supreme entity and the promotion of ethical codes,[181] relating primarily to the preservation of ancient monuments.

Advancement

The advancement of religion has been defined as taking positive steps to promote or spread religious belief.[182] This may occur, for example, through religious instruction, persuading unbelievers, religious services, and pastoral or missionary work. It was because

---

[173] See Iwobi, '"Out with the old, in with the new": religion, charitable status and the Charities Act 2006' (2009) 29 LS 619, 649.   [174] [1980] 1 WLR 1565.

[175] *Church of Scientology (England and Wales)*, Charity Commission decision, 17 November 1999.

[176] Edge and Loughrey, 'Religious charities and the juridification of the Charity Commission' (2001) 21 LS 36.

[177] *Church of the New Faith v Commissioner of Pay-Roll Tax (Victoria)* (1982) 154 CLR 120.

[178] And was so characterized by the Supreme Court in *R (on the application of Hodkin) v Registrar of Births, Deaths and Marriages* [2013] UKSC 77, [2014] AC 610, for purposes of determining that a Scientology chapel was a place of worship and so could be registered for weddings. Lord Toulson, at [57], defined a religion as 'any spiritual or non-secular belief system'.   [179] See Section 6.3.3.(ii), p. 168.

[180] *The Gnostic Centre*, Charity Commission decision, 16 December 2009. See Luxton and Evans (n. 50).

[181] *The Druid Foundation*, Charity Commission decision, 21 September 2010.

[182] *United Grand Lodge of Ancient Free and Accepted Masons of England v Holborn Borough Council* [1957] 1 WLR 1080, 1090 (Donovan J).

freemasonry does not involve promoting or spreading religious belief that it was held, in *United Grand Lodge*,[183] not to involve the advancement of religion, even though the object of freemasonry was identified as belief in a supreme creator and leading a moral life.

(ii) Public benefit

Before the enactment of the Charities Act 2006, all charitable trusts for the advancement of religion were presumed to be beneficial to the public. Benefit has now to be proven by evidence that is acceptable to the court;[184] the faith of a particular religion that prayer and intercession will confer a benefit on the public is not sufficient.[185]

The leading case on the interpretation of the 'public' in respect of advancing religion is *Gilmour v Coats*,[186] in which a gift was made in trust for a Carmelite Priory. Carmelite nuns are Catholics who devote their lives to prayer, contemplation, penance, and self-sanctification and do not engage in work outside of the convent. The question for the House of Lords was whether this was a charitable trust. It was accepted that the trust was for the advancement of religion, but its validity as a charity turned on whether there was a sufficient public benefit. It had been argued that the nuns' prayers benefited the public and the religious life practised by the nuns, involving self-sacrifice of worldly things, was a source of edification to Catholics and others. This was held not to be sufficient to establish a benefit for the public, because a belief in the efficacy of prayer could not be proved to be a benefit, and edification by example was too vague and intangible to constitute a relevant benefit, so the presumption of benefit was rebutted. It would have been different had the nuns not been cloistered and if they had gone out to benefit the community. It had also been argued that a benefit to a sufficient section of the public could be established, because any female Roman Catholic could be accepted to be a nun if she had a vocation, in the same way as a scholarship that was awarded on the basis of open competition satisfied the public benefit test. This argument was rejected on two grounds: that it is dangerous to reason by analogy from one head of charity to another, and because even a gift for education on condition that the person who is educated remains cloistered for life would not be charitable. This assumes that, even for purposes of education, it is the fact that the person who is educated will go out to benefit society that establishes the benefit to the public. It is the fact that the nuns were cloistered that was the key reason why the House of Lords held that the public benefit test was not satisfied, so that the trust was not charitable.

Gilmour v Coats can usefully be contrasted with *Re Hetherington*,[187] in which the testatrix had left her residuary estate to a Roman Catholic church for masses to be held for her soul. This was held to be charitable because, although there was no express requirement that the masses were to be celebrated in public, the gift was to be construed as one that would be carried out by the methods that were charitable, so that the public could attend.[188] This was considered to be beneficial because those who attend a religious rite are edified and improved by their attendance. Benefit was also identified in that the priests who celebrated the mass were to be paid a stipend that would relieve the Roman Catholic Church of part of its liability to pay priests, so there was a clear financial benefit to the Church that would enable its resources to be allocated elsewhere.

The interpretation of public benefit in *Gilmour v Coats* involving engagement of the religious with the surrounding community was also recognized in *Neville Estates Ltd v*

---

[183] Ibid.
[184] See generally Harding, 'Trusts for religious purposes and the question of public benefit' (2008) 71 MLR 159.
[185] *Gilmour v Coats* [1949] AC 426. [186] Ibid. [187] [1990] Ch 1.
[188] An example of benign construction of charitable trusts. See Section 6.1.2.(iii), p. 147.

Madden,[189] in which it was decided that land held by the Catford Synagogue was held for charitable purposes for the advancement of the Jewish religion. The members of the synagogue were considered to be a sufficient section of the public because they spent time in the community, whereas the Carmelite nuns were excluded from the community.

The significance of the public benefit to trusts for the advancement of religion is especially well illustrated by the decision of the Charity Commission[190] in refusing to register the Church of Scientology as a charity because the public benefit requirement was not satisfied, since practice of the religion was essentially private, being limited to a private class of individuals and involving private activities of auditing and training.

It is clear from these cases that both elements of public benefit need to be considered carefully, but they can often be established in the same way. Some benefit must be identified from the advancement of religion that cannot be too vague or intangible. The benefit from prayer or from edification by example will not suffice; there needs to be some direct engagement with the community. This will also satisfy the public requirement. So, for example, in *Funnell v Stewart*,[191] it was held that a trust for faith-healing was a valid charitable trust for the advancement of religion. Public benefit was established because, although faith-healing sessions were not advertised, they were open to the public. Consequently, potential attendance by members of the public was sufficient. It was assumed that such attendance would be beneficial without the need to assess whether faith healing was effective. Since, today, benefit can no longer be presumed, it might now be necessary to assess the efficacy of faith healing to determine whether there is a benefit to the public, by considering both the numbers who attended and how many had benefited from their attendance.

6.3.4 THE ADVANCEMENT OF HEALTH OR THE SAVING OF LIVES

The advancement of health includes the prevention or relief of sickness, disease, or human suffering.[192] Although advancing health and saving lives is a new head of charitable purpose, it has long been recognized as charitable. In particular, trusts for hospitals have been charitable for hundreds of years, including trusts for private hospitals, even though the patients had to pay fees for admission and treatment, as long as the hospital was not a commercial profit-making concern. In *Re Resch's Will Trusts*,[193] such a trust was held to satisfy the public benefit test, even though the payment of fees would exclude the poor, because the fees were approximately at cost price and, although some poor people would be excluded from the services of the hospital, others would not if the hospital had a medical benefit scheme or patients could negotiate a reduction of, or exemption from, the charges. It was further recognized that there would also be an indirect benefit to the State from the creation of private hospitals, because the existence of such hospitals reduces the demand for beds in public hospitals. This indirect benefit analysis of benefit to the public is, however, difficult to justify. If it is of general application, it would mean that independent schools could easily be established as charitable, because the existence of such schools reduces the demand for places at State schools. But such arguments have not been countenanced by the Charity Commission, which demands that public schools identify public benefit by showing how the education at the school can be made available to the wider community. Consequently, even as regards trusts for private hospitals, it is preferable that the benefit to the public is established directly without reference to vague and indirect benefits obtained by the State.

---

[189] [1962] Ch 832.

[190] *Application for Registration as a Charity by the Church of Scientology* (England and Wales) (1999).

[191] [1996] 1 WLR 288.   [192] Charities Act 2011, s. 3(2)(b).   [193] [1969] 1 AC 514.

6.3.5 THE ADVANCEMENT OF CITIZENSHIP OR COMMUNITY DEVELOPMENT

This head of charitable purpose includes rural or urban regeneration, and the promotion of civic responsibility, volunteering, the voluntary sector, or the effectiveness or efficiency of charities.[194]

Aspects of this new head of charitable purpose were previously recognized at common law in respect of purposes that are beneficial to the community. But, as always, it is important to satisfy the public benefit requirement and to ensure that the purposes of the trust are exclusively charitable. The significance of these requirements is illustrated by *IRC v Oldham Training and Enterprise Council*,[195] in which the objects of the Council included the promotion of vocational education and training, and the retraining of the public, which could also be characterized as advancing education, and the promotion of industry, commerce, and enterprise for the benefit of the public in Oldham. It was held that it was sufficient that the organization benefited a section of the public, namely the inhabitants of Oldham, and that providing assistance in finding work for the unemployed was a matter of general public utility, since the State would be relieved of the burden of providing unemployment benefit.[196] But, since the Council also had the object of promoting trade, commerce, and enterprise and of providing support services and advice to new businesses, which could involve promoting the interests of individuals, it followed that the Council also provided private benefits. Although the promotion of such objects might confer some benefits on the community, this was considered to be too remote. Since the objects as a whole were not exclusively charitable,[197] it followed that the Council was not a charity.

6.3.6 ADVANCEMENT OF THE ARTS, CULTURE, HERITAGE, OR SCIENCE

Before the Charities Act 2006 recognized a distinct head of charitable purpose involving the advancement of arts, culture, heritage, or science, trusts for such purposes would be upheld as charitable only if they were considered to be for the advancement of education or for other purposes beneficial to the community. Today, such purposes do not need to be squeezed within the definition of education and are explicitly recognized as charitable purposes in their own right, but they must still satisfy the public benefit test.

When assessing the public benefit of trusts for such purposes, there must be some utility for the public in carrying out the particular purpose. So, where the trust purports to advance the arts or culture, it is necessary to consider whether there is any artistic merit in the specific purpose. So, for example, a trust for the promotion of the work of the composer Delius[198] was considered to be educational. Roxburgh J, in that case, suggested that the music of the composer must be worth appreciating, which suggests that if the trust relates to the work of an inadequate composer, the necessary benefit to the public might not be identified. That there may be cases in which the advancement of culture or heritage is not beneficial is illustrated by *Re Pinion*,[199] in which the testator left his studio and contents, which included furniture and china of generally poor quality, to be displayed to the public as a museum. It was held that this was not charitable, because it was not educational, but presumably it would not be charitable today because the quality of the contents were such that it could not be considered to advance culture or heritage, either because it

---

[194] Charities Act 2011, s. 3(2)(c).   [195] [1996] STC 1218.
[196] Another example of an indirect public benefit. See also Section 6.2.2.(i), p. 154, and Section 6.3.4, p. 168.
[197] See further Section 6.4, p. 174.   [198] *Re Delius* [1957] Ch 299.   [199] [1965] Ch 85.

would not meet the definition of the charitable purpose as a matter of law or, more likely, because it would not satisfy the public benefit test as a matter of fact. In *Re Pinion*, the quality of the proposed exhibits was examined and found wanting. They were described as 'worthless' and a 'haphazard assembly of items'. One expert witness expressed surprise that 'so voracious a collector should not by hazard have picked up even one meritorious object' and the Court of Appeal concluded that no useful object could be served by foisting on the public 'this mass of junk'.

Even if the trust does promote culture or heritage and is regarded as beneficial, it must still be shown that the benefit is available for a sufficient section of the public and that the purposes are exclusively charitable. So, for example, in *Williams' Trustees v IRC*,[200] a trust to maintain an institute and meeting place for the benefit of Welsh people in London, with a view to creating a centre to promote the moral, social, spiritual, and educational welfare of Welsh people, was held not to be charitable. This was because the trust was not considered to fall within the spirit and intendment of the Preamble, and so could not be regarded as some other reason that was beneficial to the community. This appears to have been because the institute was characterized as an ordinary social club,[201] but it was also suggested that a sufficient section of the public could not be identified.[202] If the validity of this trust as a charity were to be considered today, the public benefit might be identified because the class would not, presumably, be numerically small and would not be defined with reference to a personal nexus.[203] Some of the purposes of the charity would also fall within the new head of advancing culture or heritage, especially since the trust sought to foster the study of the Welsh language, history, music, literature, and art. The problem, however, would still be that there were other purposes that were non-charitable, including providing a meeting place for 'social intercourse study reading rest recreation and refreshment'. Since these purposes are not exclusively charitable,[204] the trust still could not be treated as charitable.

6.3.7 ADVANCEMENT OF AMATEUR SPORT

Before the enactment of the Charities Act 2006, trusts for the provision of sporting facilities or the encouragement of sport were not charitable, as such. But if the facilities or sporting activities were for pupils of schools or universities,[205] or if the game was itself of an educational nature, the trusts would be for the advancement of education. Alternatively, if the sports facilities were for the armed forces, they might be regarded as being beneficial to the community by contributing to the safety and protection of the country.[206] With the recognition of the advancement of amateur sport as a charitable purpose in its own right, such artificial interpretation of other charitable purposes is not required.

'Sport' is defined to mean sport or games that promote health by involving physical or mental skill or exertion.[207] Clearly, this encompasses team sports, such as football, and solo sports, such as athletics, but it would also encompass chess[208] and bridge[209] because of the mental skill involved. Other games will be more borderline, such as darts, and these will require careful assessment of the skill and exertion involved.

The public benefit requirement will apply in the normal way. So, in *IRC v Baddeley*,[210] in which playing fields were provided for members of a particular Methodist church, it

---

[200] [1947] AC 447.   [201] Ibid., 460 (Lord Normand).   [202] Ibid., 458 (Lord Simonds).
[203] See Section 6.2.2.(ii), p. 155.   [204] See Section 6.4, p. 174.   [205] *IRC v McMullen* [1981] AC 1.
[206] *Re Gray* [1925] Ch 362.   [207] Charities Act 2011, s. 3(2)(d).
[208] See *Re Dupree's Deed Trusts* [1945] Ch 16, which held that arranging a chess tournament was educational.
[209] *Hitchin Bridge Club*, decision of the Charity Commission, 2011.   [210] [1955] AC 572.

was held that the trust failed to meet the public benefit requirement, because the class consisted of members of a particular church within a limited geographical area and so constituted a class within a class, meaning that it was not of general public benefit.

Specific provision was made by the Recreational Charities Act 1958 to treat the provision of recreation or leisure facilities as charitable if the facilities are provided in the interests of social welfare and for the public benefit. This statute was consolidated in section 5 of the Charities Act 2011, and it has proved significant in treating community centres and church halls as charitable. Some of these will now be charitable by virtue of the formal recognition of the promotion of amateur sport as a charitable purpose, but, to the extent that these facilities are intended to be used for non-sporting activities, they might still be charitable by virtue of section 5 of the Charities Act 2011. Such facilities will be provided in the interests of social welfare only if they are provided with the object of improving the conditions of life of the people who are primarily intended to use the facilities, and either if such people need the facilities by reason of their youth, age, infirmity, disability, poverty, or social and economic circumstances, or if the facilities are available to members of the public at large, or to female members of the public at large. The operation of the Act is illustrated by *Guild v IRC*,[211] which held that a town's sports centre was charitable. The centre provided facilities for recreation and leisure occupation that were available to the public at large. It was recognized that the statutory requirement that the facilities are provided with the object of improving the conditions of life for the persons for whom the facilities are primarily intended did not require the beneficiaries to be suffering from some form of social disadvantage or deprivation; it was sufficient that the facilities were provided with the object of improving the conditions of life for members of the community generally.

6.3.8 ADVANCEMENT OF HUMAN RIGHTS

In addition to the advancement of human rights, this new charitable purpose includes providing for conflict resolution or reconciliation or for the promotion of religious harmony, equality, or diversity. Some of these purposes have previously been recognized as charitable, either by virtue of being for the advancement of education or for other purposes beneficial to the community. In *Re Strakosch*,[212] however, a trust to appease racial feelings between the Dutch-speaking and English-speaking sections of the South African community was held not to be charitable because the scope of the gift was too wide and vague. If it had been defined more clearly, particularly with reference to education, it might have been held valid. Similar problems as to the vagueness of the gift would arise in respect of the new charitable purpose under the Charities Act 2011.

One of the key difficulties relating to a trust for the advancement of human rights is that charities with such a purpose must not pursue political objectives, especially those that relate to seeking a change in law or policy either of England and Wales or of a country abroad.[213] There is a fine line between pursuing political activities as a means to a charitable end and pursuing purposes that are political in their own right. This is illustrated by *McGovern v Attorney-General*,[214] which concerned whether a trust created by Amnesty International was charitable. That trust contained various objectives, which included attempting to secure the release of prisoners of conscience, and procuring the abolition of torture and inhuman or degrading treatment or punishment. It was held that this was not a charitable trust, because seeking the release of prisoners of conscience was considered to be a political purpose through seeking the reversal of administrative decisions

---

[211] [1992] 2 AC 310.   [212] [1949] Ch 529.
[213] See Section 6.2.2.(iii), p. 156.   [214] [1982] Ch 321.

of governmental authorities, albeit abroad. This was not considered to be a legitimate charitable objective, since the English court has no adequate means of judging whether a proposed change in the law of a foreign country would be for the benefit of the public in England, and there would also be a public-policy dimension to the recognition of such a trust, since it might prejudice the relations of the United Kingdom with that foreign country. Other purposes, such as relieving the suffering of needy prisoners of conscience, were charitable, but since this was one purpose amongst others that were not charitable, the trust was not wholly and exclusively charitable. Similarly, in *R v Radio Authority, ex p Bull*,[215] a charity to promote awareness of human rights, but with the object of bringing pressure to bear on a government to change its policies, was considered to have a political purpose and so not to be charitable.

Both of these cases were decided before the Charities Act 2006 recognized the new charitable purpose of promoting human rights, but they would be likely to be decided the same way today because the law on the definition of political purposes has not changed. The significance of the recognition of the new charitable purpose is that it is now a legitimate charitable purpose to monitor human rights abuses, to seek redress for victims of such abuse, and to raise awareness of human rights issues, but a charity still must not cross the line and actively seek to procure changes in law or governmental policy as regards human rights issues. A consequence of the state of the law is that Amnesty International has been divided into Amnesty International, which is a registered charity with non-political purposes, and Amnesty International Ltd, which is not registered as a charity and which pursues political objectives.

6.3.9 ADVANCEMENT OF ENVIRONMENTAL PROTECTION

This charitable purpose includes acting both for the protection and improvement of the environment.[216]

6.3.10 RELIEF OF THOSE IN NEED

The first of the old charitable purposes under *Pemsel's case*,[217] namely for the relief of poverty, also included the relief of the aged and impotent. These last two purposes have now been separated and form a new charitable purpose, albeit one that is defined more expansively. This charitable purpose is for the relief of those in need either by reason of youth, age, ill-health, disability, financial hardship, or other disadvantage.[218] Since the relief of the needy no longer falls within the same head as the relief of poverty, it is clear that somebody can be in need even if they are not poor, which was acknowledged even under the old law, but that the beneficiary of the charitable purpose must still be in need in some way. The relief may be provided in a wide variety of ways, but the statute makes clear that it can include the provision of accommodation or care.[219]

The courts have considered the meaning of being in need 'by virtue of age'. In *Joseph Rowntree Memorial Trust Housing Association Ltd v Attorney-General*,[220] a scheme to build self-contained dwellings to be let on long leases to elderly people at 70 per cent of the cost of the premises, with the remaining expense being met by a State housing grant, was held to be a charitable scheme for the relief of aged people, even though beneficiaries had to make a substantial financial contribution and, if they were to sell their lease, they could

---

[215] [1998] QB 294.   [216] Charities Act 2011, s. 3(1)(i).
[217] *Commissioners for Special Purposes of Income Tax v Pemsel* [1891] AC 531. See Section 6.1.5.(ii), p. 151.
[218] Charities Act 2011, s. 3(1)(j).   [219] Ibid., s. 3(2)(e).   [220] [1983] Ch 159.

make a profit. It was confirmed that the relief of aged people did not require them to be poor, but that there had to be a need that was attributable to their age and that the charity sought to relieve this need, here through the provision of suitable accommodation for old people, with communal services and a warden. It did not matter that, for old people to benefit from the charity, they had to enter into a contract with it in order to lease a property, but it was crucial that the charity did not profit from the transaction. Although the beneficiaries might profit through the sale of their lease, this was considered to be incidental to the charitable purpose. If, however, housing stock is provided both to those in need and others who are not in need, this will not be for an exclusively charitable purpose.[221]

The old word 'impotence' that appeared in the Preamble has been replaced by 'disability' and need arising by reason of some disadvantage. This would include trusts for the benefit of the blind[222] and the prevention of cruelty to children.[223]

6.3.11 ADVANCEMENT OF ANIMAL WELFARE

Before the enactment of the Charities Act 2006, trusts for the advancement of animal welfare could be charitable only within the fourth head of *Pemsel's case*, being another purpose beneficial to the community. Now, animal welfare is identified as a specific charitable head, although this has not significantly altered the law as regards the definition of the charitable purpose.[224] Animal welfare has been held to include providing for the welfare of particular types of animal, such as cats,[225] or providing for the welfare of all animals, such as the Royal Society for the Prevention of Cruelty to Animals (RSPCA).[226] It has even included improving methods of slaughtering animals.[227] It does not include providing for the welfare of a particular animal, which might exceptionally be valid as a non-charitable purpose trust.[228]

It will also be necessary to show that there is a public benefit in advancing animal welfare. The benefit to the public from the advancement of animal welfare has been described as indirect,[229] and arises from the promotion of humanity and morality by repressing brutality and elevating the human race.[230] Even this indirect benefit to the public might be difficult to establish. So, for example, in *Re Grove-Grady*,[231] a trust to buy land to provide a sanctuary for all creatures so that they would be safe from molestation or destruction by man was held not to be charitable because there was no public benefit. This was because the effect of the trust was that no animal within the designated area could be destroyed, even if this were in the interests of people or other creatures living there, or even those of the animal itself. It was considered that no benefit to the community would arise from such a purpose. A trust for the prevention of cruelty to animals would have been different, because there is public benefit arising from the promotion of humane sentiments in man and the elevation of the human race.[232] In *National Anti-Vivisection Society v IRC*,[233] a society, the purpose of which was to suppress experiments on animals, was held not to be charitable because any public benefit arising from the advancement of animal welfare was outweighed by detriment to medical science and research, and consequently to public health. So, rather than being for the public benefit, this purpose was considered to be for the public disadvantage.

---

[221] *Helena Housing Ltd v The Commissioners for Her Majesty's Revenue and Customs* [2012] EWCA Civ 569, [2012] WTLR 1519.   [222] *Re Fraser* (1883) 22 Ch D 827.

[223] *Commissioners for the Special Purposes of Income Tax v Pemsel* [1891] AC 531, 572 (Lord Herschell).

[224] *Hanchett-Stamford v Attorney-General* [2008] EWHC 330 (Ch), [2009] Ch 173.

[225] *Re Moss* [1949] 1 All ER 495.   [226] *Tatham v Drummond* (1864) 4 De GJ & Sm 484.

[227] *Re Wedgwood* [1915] 1 Ch 113.   [228] See Section 7.2.2.(i), p. 192.

[229] *Hanchett-Stamford v Attorney General* [2008] EWHC 330 (Ch), [2009] Ch 173, [13] (Lewison J).

[230] *Re Wedgwood* [1915] 1 Ch 113, 122 (Kennedy LJ).   [231] [1929] 1 Ch 557.

[232] See *Re Wedgwood* [1915] 1 Ch 113.   [233] [1948] AC 31. See Section 6.2.2.(iii), p. 156.

6.3.12 PROMOTION OF EFFICIENCY OF PUBLIC SERVICES

'Public services', for the purposes of this charitable head, includes the armed forces, the police, fire, and rescue services, and the ambulance services.[234] Efficiency has been held at common law to include physical efficiency, so a trust to promote outdoor sport for members of an army regiment was a charitable purpose,[235] as was a trust to buy and maintain a library for an officers' mess, since it tended to improve the efficiency of the army.[236]

6.3.13 OTHER BENEFICIAL PURPOSES

Other purposes will be considered to be charitable if they:[237]

(1) have been recognized as charitable purposes under existing charity law or under section 5 of the Charities Act 2011 concerning recreational and similar trusts;[238] or

(2) can reasonably be regarded as analogous to, or within the spirit of, the twelve purposes identified by the Charities Act 2011, or with the purposes recognized under existing charity law or section 5 of the Charities Act 2011 concerning recreational and similar trusts;[239] or

(3) can reasonably be regarded as analogous to, or within the spirit of, the purposes that have been recognized under charity law as falling within paragraph (2) or which have previously been recognized as falling within this third paragraph.[240]

Although this is a somewhat opaque head of charity, it operates as a safety net to ensure that charitable purposes can continue to be developed by analogy with the existing law of charity or with the heads recognized under the Charities Act itself. But the effect of the third paragraph is that a purpose can be considered to be charitable by analogy to a purpose that is already recognized under the law of charity. The recognition of charitable purposes by analogy is a long-standing feature of charity law. A good example of such analogous reasoning is *Incorporated Council of Law Reporting for England and Wales v Attorney-General*,[241] in which the Council of Law Reporting was registered as a charity either because it advanced education[242] or fulfilled a purpose that was otherwise beneficial to the community. That the Council fulfilled such a purpose was justified by analogy with the charitable purposes that were recognized in the Preamble, some of which involved charities taking on functions, such as providing sea walls, that would otherwise have to be undertaken by the State. So, too, if the law reports were not published by the Incorporated Council, the State would have had to make provision for their publication to ensure the due administration of the law.

6.4 EXCLUSIVELY CHARITABLE

6.4.1 INCLUSION OF NON-CHARITABLE PURPOSES

A trust can be regarded as charitable only if all of its purposes are charitable.[243] This means that the trust cannot have a mixture of charitable and non-charitable purposes.

---

[234] Charities Act 2011, s. 3(1)(l).
[235] *Re Gray* [1925] Ch 362. See also now the purpose of advancing amateur sport. See Section 6.3.7, p. 170.
[236] *Re Good* [1905] 2 Ch 60.   [237] Charities Act 2011, s. 3(1)(m).   [238] Ibid., s. 3(1)(m)(i).
[239] Ibid., s. 3(1)(m)(ii).   [240] Ibid., s. 3(1)(m)(iii).   [241] [1972] Ch 73.
[242] See Section 6.3.2.(i), p. 161.
[243] Charities Act 2011, s. 1(1)(a). See *Latimer v CIR* [2004] UKPC 13, [2004] 1 WLR 1466, [32].

So, for example, if the purposes of a trust are described as being 'charitable *or* benevolent', this will not be exclusively charitable, because a benevolent purpose can be wider than the legal definition of 'charitable purposes', which would mean that the trustees would be able to apply trust funds for purposes that are not necessarily charitable. If, however, the trust provides for funds to be applied for 'charitable *and* benevolent purposes', this will be charitable, because any purpose must be charitable even if it is benevolent as well. Consequently, the validity of such trusts as charities will often turn on whether the words 'or' or 'and' are used. It follows that great care must be taken when seeking to draft a charitable trust.

The leading case to consider whether a trust's purposes were exclusively charitable is *Chichester Diocesan Fund and Board of Finance Incorporated v Simpson*,[244] in which Caleb Diplock, in his will, directed his executors to apply the residue of his estate for such charitable institutions 'or benevolent object or objects' as the executors in their absolute discretion should select. It was held that the gift was void because the executors could choose benevolent objects that extended beyond what the law recognized as charitable, and it was not possible to interpret the clause so that 'or' meant 'and' through the identification of an overriding charitable intention. Similarly, a trust for charitable or philanthropic purposes has been held not to be exclusively charitable,[245] neither was a trust for a charitable institution 'or one operating for the public good',[246] nor a trust for worthy purposes.[247] A trust for charitable and deserving objects was, however, held to be exclusively charitable.[248] But it does not necessarily follow that the identification of two purposes that are connected by 'and' will be valid.[249] For example, in *Attorney-General of the Bahamas v Royal Trust Co*,[250] a gift 'for any purposes for and/or connected with the education and welfare of Bahamian children and young people' was held to be void. 'Welfare' was considered too wide to necessarily be confined to a charitable purpose and the use of 'or', albeit as well as 'and', meant that the gift could be used for non-charitable purposes.

Although a trust for the benefit of a particular locality, including a trust for the benefit of Great Britain, would not appear to be exclusively charitable, such trusts have been held to be valid charitable trusts,[251] because they are benevolently interpreted as being confined to charitable purposes within the identified locality.[252] These are highly anomalous cases, but they do exemplify the principle of benign construction of charitable gifts.[253] It is unfortunate that this same benign construction is not adopted where the gift includes non-charitable purposes so that it could be assumed that the gift would be applied only for the charitable purpose.

6.4.2 CONSEQUENCE OF INCLUDING NON-CHARITABLE PURPOSES

Where the purposes of a trust are not exclusively charitable, there are various alternative consequences. Which one applies will depend on how the language of the trust is construed.

---

[244] [1944] AC 341.   [245] *Re Macduff* [1896] 2 Ch 451.

[246] *Attorney-General of Cayman Islands v Wahr-Hansen* [2001] 1 AC 75 (PC).

[247] *Re Atkinson's Will Trusts* [1978] 1 WLR 586.   [248] *Re Sutton* (1885) 28 Ch D 464.

[249] See e.g. *Re Eades* [1920] 2 Ch 353 ('religious, charitable and philanthropic objects' was not exclusively charitable).   [250] [1986] 1 WLR 1001.

[251] *Nightingale v Goulbourn* (1847) 5 Hare 484.

[252] *Attorney-General of the Cayman Islands v Wahr-Hansen* [2001] 1 AC 75, 81 (Lord Browne-Wilkinson).

[253] See Section 6.1.2.(iii), p. 147.

(i) Incidental purposes

If the non-charitable purpose is incidental or subsidiary to the main charitable purpose, it will not prevent the trust from being charitable.[254] In *Latimer v The Commissioner for Inland Revenue*,[255] it was recognized by Lord Millett that a distinction should be drawn between ends, means, and consequences relating to charitable purposes. The ends must be exclusively charitable, but if non-charitable benefits are merely means to that end or the incidental consequences of carrying out the charitable purposes, and are not ends in their own right, the charitable status will not be lost. So, for example, if the trust deed authorizes charity trustees to charge their fees and expenses to the trust, this will not cause the trust to lose its charitable status, because charging such fees is not a purpose of the trust; rather, it helps to further the trust's charitable purposes and so can be regarded as ancillary to that purpose—that is, it is a means to that end. So, in *Re Coxen*,[256] a fund was held on trust for medical charities, but provision was made for the payment of £100 for a dinner for those aldermen who attended a meeting to discuss the business of the trust, who would also receive a guinea each if they were to attend the whole of the meeting. This was held to be a valid charitable trust since the dinner and the payments were incidental to the main medical purpose of the trust, and might even be regarded as resulting in the better administration of the trust. In *Attorney-General v Ross*,[257] a students' union was held to be a charitable trust even though one of its objects related to affiliation to the National Union of Students (NUS), which was a non-charitable organization, since this was an ancillary purpose that helped the charitable purpose of furthering the educational function of the institution. In *Funnell v Stewart*,[258] private worship was held to be ancillary to the charitable purpose of faith healing because it assisted in the advancement of that purpose.

(ii) Void trust

If the non-charitable purpose is not ancillary to the main charitable purpose, the trust will be declared void, unless it can exceptionally be regarded as a valid non-charitable purpose trust.[259] If the trust is declared void, the funds will be held on resulting trust for the settlor or testator's estate.[260] A consequence of the decision in *Chichester Diocesan Fund and Board of Finance Incorporated v Simpson*,[261] that a testamentary gift to charitable institutions or benevolent objects was void, was that the testator's next of kin could claim the gifts that been made to various charities by the executor. The nature of these claims was complex and controversial.[262]

(iii) Severance

Exceptionally, where a trust's purposes are not exclusively charitable, it may be possible to divide the fund into parts, so that some are applied to charitable purposes and the rest will either be held on a valid non-charitable purpose trust or on a resulting trust for the settlor or those entitled to a testator's residuary estate. This solution will only be possible where the language of the trust instrument can be construed as directing such a division. For example, in *Salusbury v Denton*,[263] a fund was to be used to found a school or to provide for the poor, and the remainder was to be used for the benefit of the testator's relatives. It was held that the fund was divisible, with the first part being used for the charitable purposes and the rest for the next of kin. Severance was possible because the will contemplated division of the estate.[264] In *Re Coxen*,[265] Jenkins J recognized that severance will be appropriate

---

[254] See generally Gravells, 'Charitable trusts and ancillary purposes' [1978] Conv 92.
[255] [2004] UKPC 13, [2004] 1 WLR 1466, [36].   [256] [1948] Ch 747.   [257] [1986] 1 WLR 252.
[258] [1996] 1 WLR 288.   [259] See Section 7.2, p. 190.   [260] See Section 8.3, p. 229.
[261] [1944] AC 341.   [262] See Section 19.3.3.(i), p. 560.   [263] (1857) 3 K & J 529.
[264] See also *Re Clarke* [1923] 2 Ch 407.   [265] [1948] Ch 747, 753.

where the amount applicable to the non-charitable purpose can be quantified, but where such quantification is not possible, the trust will fail completely.

(iv) Retrospective validation

In 1954 the Charitable Trusts (Validation) Act was enacted to provide that any charitable trust created before 16 December 1952 that was invalid because the fund could be used for non-charitable purposes should be treated as though all of the objects were charitable. Since this Act had only retrospective effect, it does not affect the general principle relating to modern trusts needing to have exclusively charitable purposes. But if the Act was able to validate old trusts despite the inclusion of non-charitable purposes, why could it not be applied prospectively? This has been described as 'logically indefensible':[266] if the law is unjust, then it should have been changed for all trusts.

6.5 CY-PRÈS

Where a charitable trust fails because, for example, it is impossible or impracticable to apply funds for the identified charitable purpose or because that purpose ceases to be charitable, it is necessary to consider whether the funds should either be returned to the creator of the trust by means of a resulting trust, or whether they might be applied for a slightly different charitable purpose by virtue of the cy-près doctrine. Cy-près means as 'near as possible'. This doctrine applies differently depending on whether the failure of the charitable purpose occurs before the trust commences or subsequently. Essentially, where there is an initial failure of the charitable purpose, the property will be applied cy-près only if the donor can be considered to have an intention that the property should be used for the benefit of charity generally rather than be confined to the particular charitable purpose. Once, however, property has been used for a charitable purpose and there is a subsequent failure of that purpose, the property will be applied cy-près whether or not the donor had an intention to benefit charity generally. It follows that it is important to work out whether there has been a failure of charitable purpose and, if there has, whether it is an initial or a subsequent failure.

Where property is to be applied cy-près, the courts and the Charity Commission have the power to make schemes so that the property is applied for a similar charitable purpose.[267] In making a scheme, the court or the Charity Commission should have regard to the spirit of the original gift, the desirability of ensuring that the property is applied for charitable purposes that are close to the original purposes, and the need for the charity that might receive the property to have purposes that are suitable and effective in the light of current social and economic circumstances.

6.5.1 INITIAL FAILURE

To establish an initial failure of charitable purpose, it is necessary to consider whether, at the time the trust is to take effect, the identified purpose is impossible or impracticable to fulfil. Even though a charity no longer exists in its original form, the court may find that the charitable purpose continues elsewhere, so that it has not failed and so that the cy-près doctrine is not engaged. So, for example, in *Re Faraker*,[268] the testatrix left £200 to 'Mrs Bailey's [*sic*] Charity, Rotherhithe'. Hannah Bayly's Charity had been founded in

---

[266] Cross, 'Some recent developments in the law of charity' (1956) 72 LQR 187, 203.
[267] Charities Act 2011, s. 67.   [268] [1912] 2 Ch 488. See also *Re Lucas* [1948] Ch 424.

1756 for the benefit of poor widows in Rotherhithe. In 1905 the Charity Commissioners had consolidated various local charities with the funds being held on trust for the benefit of the poor of Rotherhithe, but no specific mention was made of widows. It was held that the consolidated charities were entitled to the legacy. Although Hannah Bayly's charity no longer existed, its purpose continued in the consolidated charities, so the purpose had not failed. As Cozens-Hardy MR recognized: 'Hannah Bayly's Charity is not extinct, it is not dead . . . it cannot die.'[269] A charity will, however, be considered to have ceased to exist if its funds no longer remain in existence. So, where a testatrix had left money for the work of a hospital in Australia treating tuberculosis, but the hospital had closed down before the testatrix's death because tuberculosis had been controlled in the locality, then, since the hospital had not left any funds to continue this purpose, it followed that there was an initial failure of the gift.[270] Martin[271] has criticized this decision on the ground that the key question should not have been whether the funds continued to exist, but whether the charitable purpose continued to exist, and, presumably, the purpose of eliminating tuberculosis continued elsewhere. It may have been significant, however, that the testatrix had left her estate to the particular hospital in Australia where her daughter had been treated for some years and had died. Whilst the judge found that her intention had not been to make the gift to the Red Cross Society, which ran the hospital, she may have intended her estate to be used only for the work of the particular hospital at which her daughter had been treated rather than for the purpose of treating tuberculosis generally. As always in cases of this kind, the intention of the donor is vital and must be construed very carefully.

Further, where a bequest is intended to be for a particular charitable institution, rather than for the institution's charitable purpose, and the institution has ceased to exist before the testator's death, there will be an initial failure of the gift.[272] This distinction between a gift to a charitable purpose and a gift to an institution is influenced by whether the intended recipient of the gift is an unincorporated or an incorporated charity. The significance of this distinction was recognized in *Re Finger's Will Trusts*,[273] in which a testatrix left her estate to eleven charities. One of these was the National Radium Commission, which was an unincorporated charity, and another was the National Council for Maternity and Child Welfare, which was an incorporated charity. Before the testatrix's death, both of these charities ceased to exist. It was held that the gift to the unincorporated association was valid as a charitable purpose trust, whereas the gift to the incorporated charity failed.[274] The reason for this distinction is that an unincorporated charity does not have a separate legal identity,[275] so a gift to such a charity must be a gift for a charitable purpose rather than to the institution.[276] If that purpose can still be fulfilled, then there has been no initial failure, unless the continued existence of the institution was essential to the gift. So, the gift to the National Radium Commission was for the work of the Commission and would be applied for a similar purpose, on condition that the charitable purpose continued and that the testatrix's intention to make the gift was not conditional on the Commission continuing in existence at the time the gift was to take effect, continued. Since the purpose did continue and the gift was found not to be conditional on the continued existence of the Commission, it was applied for that purpose. There had been no failure of purpose and so the cy-près doctrine was not engaged.

---

[269] [1912] 2 Ch 488, 493.   [270] *Re Slatter's Will Trusts* [1964] Ch 512.

[271] 'The construction of charitable gifts' (1974) 38 Conv (NS) 187, 191.

[272] *Re Rymer* [1895] 1 Ch 19; *Re Stemson's Will Trust* [1970] Ch 16.   [273] [1972] Ch 286.

[274] Although it was applied for similar purposes by virtue of the cy-près doctrine. See Section 6.5.1.(ii), p. 180.

[275] See further Section 7.4, p. 195.   [276] *Re Vernon's Will Trusts* [1972] Ch 300n.

Where, however, a gift is to an incorporated charity, then, since such a charity has an independent legal existence, the gift will be to that body beneficially,[277] save where it was intended to take as a trustee.[278] In *Re Finger's Will Trusts*, the gift to the National Council for Maternity and Child Welfare consequently failed even though its work continued, unless the gift was intended to be held on trust for that organization's purpose rather than being an absolute gift to the corporation. No such purpose trust could be identified and so this gift failed.

Where a testamentary gift was made to a charitable company that had entered into insolvent liquidation before the death of the testator, but, by the time the testator had died, the company had not been formally dissolved, there was no initial failure and the testamentary gift belonged to the company beneficially and so could be distributed among its creditors.[279]

(i) General charitable intent

Where the charitable purpose fails before the commencement of the trust, the funds can be applied cy-près for a similar charitable purpose only if the settlor or testator had a general charitable intent. What this means is that the creator of the trust was more concerned that the funds should be used for charitable purposes generally rather than concerned to benefit only the specific charity that they had identified. If there is a charitable intent to benefit charity generally, the fund will be applied cy-près. Where there is no general charitable intent, the fund will be held on resulting trust for the settlor or for those entitled to the testator's residuary estate.

Identifying whether there was a general charitable intent requires careful construction of the trust documents and surrounding circumstances. For example, in *Re Rymer*,[280] the testator left a sum of money in his will to the rector of St Thomas's Seminary for the education of priests in the diocese of Westminster in London. When his will was made, there was such a seminary that did educate priests in that diocese, but, by the time of the testator's death, the seminary had closed and its students had been transferred to a different seminary near Birmingham. It was held that the testator did not have a general charitable intent, and so the bequest lapsed and went to the residuary legatees. This was because the gift was interpreted as being for a particular seminary rather than for any seminary. A key distinction was drawn between whether the mode of attaining the charitable object was simply machinery or whether it related to the substance of the gift. Here, the identification of the particular seminary related to the substance of the gift, rather than simply being a mechanism to enable an appropriate seminary to be identified. Similarly, in *Re Good's Will Trusts*,[281] the testator left funds to buy land and to build six rest homes of a particular type. The money was insufficient for the purpose and it was held that it could not be applied cy-près to a similar charitable purpose, because the purpose was so specific that a general charitable intention could not be identified.

An example of a case in which a general charitable intention was identified is *Biscoe v Jackson*,[282] in which £10,000 was left for charitable purposes, of which £4,000 was to be applied to establish a soup kitchen for the parish of Shoreditch and a cottage hospital adjoining it. After the testator's death, it was not possible to acquire the land to carry out the provisions in the will. The will was, however, held to show a general charitable intent to benefit the poor of Shoreditch and so the money was applied cy-près for that purpose.

---

[277] Ibid.
[278] See *Liverpool and District Hospital for Diseases of the Heart v Attorney-General* [1981] Ch 193.
[279] *Re ARMS (Multiple Sclerosis Research) Ltd* [1997] 1 WLR 877.   [280] [1895] 1 Ch 19.
[281] [1950] 2 All ER 653.   [282] (1873) 35 Ch D 460.

(ii) Defunct or non-existent charity

Whether property can be applied cy-près following an initial failure of purpose may turn on whether the particular charity that has been identified by the donor is defunct or never existed, since this may affect whether a general charitable intent can be identified on the facts. The significance of this distinction is illustrated by *Re Harwood*,[283] in which the testatrix left bequests to the Wisbech Peace Society and the Peace Society of Belfast. The Wisbech Peace Society had existed when the will was made, but it had ceased to exist by the time of her death. The Peace Society of Belfast had never existed. It was held that the gift to the Wisbech Peace Society could not be applied cy-près, but the other gift could. This was because a general charitable intent could not be identified where the money was intended to be given to a particular society that had ceased to exist, because the naming of the society suggested an intention to benefit only that society. Where, however, the society had never existed, it was possible to identify a general charitable intent, because it was assumed that the testatrix had intended to benefit any society that was formed with the intention of promoting peace and which was connected with Belfast. Consequently, that gift could be applied cy-près. This decision has been described as remarkable.[284] It is certainly difficult to see how the testatrix's intention can be differentiated depending on whether or not the charity that she wished to benefit had or had not existed, since in both cases she had intended to benefit a particular institution.

The significance of this distinction between defunct and non-existent charities was considered further in *Re Spence*,[285] in which a testatrix had left the residue of her estate for the benefit of the patients of the 'Old Folks Home at Hillworth Lodge Keighley'. By the time of her death, the home had closed. It was held that the gift could not be applied cy-près. Although it was noted that this case was different from *Re Harwood*, since that had concerned a gift to an institution whereas this was a gift for a purpose, namely for the benefit of the patients of the home, this was not considered to be a relevant distinction to draw. The relevant distinction was instead one of particularity and generality. Where a particular institution or purpose was specified, it is that institution or purpose but no other that is to be the object of the benefaction; the specific displaces the general. Where the testator has not specified any particular charitable institution or purpose, a general charitable intention could be identified. Although Megarry V-C in *Re Spence* appeared to confirm the distinction recognized in *Re Harwood* between defunct and non-existent charities, his emphasis on the identification of particular and general purposes or institutions would suggest that, where an institution is specifically identified to receive a bequest, there cannot be a general charitable intent even though the institution never existed. Certainly, in *Re Spence* itself, the identification of a specific charitable purpose meant that, since that purpose had failed, the bequest could not be applied cy-près.

There will, however, sometimes be circumstances under which, despite the identification of a particular charitable purpose or institution that has become defunct, the court will still be able to find a general charitable intent. This is illustrated by *Re Finger's Will Trust*,[286] in which the gift to the National Council for Maternity and Child Welfare, an incorporated charity, had failed because the charity had ceased to exist by the time of the testatrix's death and it was found that the gift was intended to be for the institution rather than for its charitable purpose. The question then was whether this gift could be applied cy-près by virtue of the identification of a general charitable intent. In *Re Harwood*,[287] it had been held that it would be difficult, but not impossible, to find such an intention

---

[283] [1936] Ch 285.   [284] *Re Finger's Will Trusts* [1972] Ch 286, 299 (Goff J).   [285] [1979] Ch 483.
[286] [1972] Ch 286. See Section 6.5.1, p. 178.   [287] [1936] Ch 285.

where there was a gift to an identifiable body that had ceased to exist. In the special circumstances of *Re Finger's Will Trust*, such an intention was found. These circumstances included that the testatrix did not think that she had any relatives, she left almost all of her estate to charity,[288] and the Council was only a coordinating body, so it was unlikely that she intended to benefit that body alone. Consequently, the gift could be applied cy-près for similar purposes.

(iii) Charity by association

Where a testator, for example, makes a number of gifts to charities with similar purposes, but one of those charities does not in fact exist, the court will be willing to find a general charitable intention and so the gift to the non-existent charity will be applied cy-près by virtue of the principle that it was intended to be used for general charitable purposes because of its association with gifts to existing charities. So, for example, in *Re Satterthwaite's Will Trusts*,[289] the testatrix left her estate to seven animal charities, an anti-vivisectionist society, and the London Animal Hospital. No such hospital existed when the will was made. It was held that the gift that was purportedly made to the hospital could be applied cy-près because the testatrix had a general charitable intent in favour of kindness to animals, as evidenced by the other dispositions that she had made, and even though she had made one gift to an anti-vivisection society, which was not charitable.[290] In *Re Jenkins's Will Trusts*,[291] however, the testatrix bequeathed her residuary estate to seven institutions, one of which was the British Union for the Abolition of Vivisection, which was not a charity because of its political purpose.[292] The other six institutions were charities with purposes relating to animal welfare. It was held that the gift to the anti-vivisection institution failed because it was not possible to identify an intention that the gift for the non-charitable purpose should take effect as a gift for other charitable purposes simply because there were other charitable gifts, and even though the non-charitable gift had a close relation to those other purposes. The difference between the two cases is that, in *Re Satterthwaite*, the testatrix intended to benefit an institution that did not exist, but would probably have been charitable had it existed; in *Re Jenkins*, the institution did exist, but it was not pursuing a charitable purpose. The general charitable intent was identified in *Re Satterthwaite* because of the close connection between the different charitable purposes. In *Re Jenkins*, a non-charitable purpose could not have been rendered charitable simply by virtue of its association with other charitable purposes.

The doctrine of charity by association was analysed further in *Re Spence*,[293] in which Megarry V-C described the doctrine as arising where there were bequests to various charities with kindred objects. The doctrine of charity by association was not applied in that case, however, where the testatrix had made a bequest for the benefit of old people in a particular home that no longer existed and for blind patients in another home that did exist. It was held that a general charitable intent could not be identified through association with a valid charitable gift to blind patients, because there was only one other gift and the objects were not considered to be kindred. Megarry V-C also recognized that the doctrine would be much less likely to apply where the chosen charity existed when the will was made, but had ceased to exist by the time of the testator's death, or where the charitable purpose had ceased to be possible and practicable, rather than where the institution had never existed or the purpose could never be fulfilled.

---

[288] The finding of a general charitable intent in *Re Finger's Will Trust* was distinguished in *Re Spence* partly because, in the latter case, over one-third of the testatrix's estate was not applied for charitable purposes.
[289] [1966] 1 WLR 277.   [290] See Section 6.3.11, p. 173.   [291] [1966] Ch 249.
[292] See Section 6.2.2.(iii), p. 156.   [293] [1979] Ch 483.

6.5.2 SUBSEQUENT FAILURE

Once a trust fund has been dedicated to a charitable purpose, the fact that the purpose then fails cannot destroy the charitable nature of the fund. Consequently, when there is subsequent failure of the purpose, the fund will not be held on resulting trust for the settlor or those entitled to the testator's residuary estate. Rather, the courts will find a similar charitable purpose and the fund will be transferred to it, regardless of whether the settlor or testator had a general or particular charitable intent,[294] except where the creator of the trust has expressly provided that the fund should be returned to the settlor, or to those entitled to the testator's residuary estate, or passed to a third party, if the purpose subsequently fails.[295]

Where a testator has sought to create a charitable trust, the failure of the charitable purpose will be subsequent where it occurs after the testator's death even though it occurred before the gift was vested in the charity, as will be the case if the property is given to an individual for life with remainder to the charity.[296] So, for example, in *Re Slevin*,[297] the testator made a gift to an orphanage that was in existence at his death, but which ceased to exist soon afterwards and before the legacy was paid. It was held that the gift could be applied cy-près. This is in accordance with the normal rules relating to legacies to individuals or companies. If a testator has made a bequest to a legatee who was alive when the testator died, but the legatee has died before the legacy is paid, the legatee's estate will still be entitled to receive the gift because it has become the property of the legatee on the death of the testator. If a company is dissolved between the death of the testator and the date of payment, the legacy will still be available to the company's creditors because it belonged to the company on the testator's death. Similarly, if a bequest has been made to an established charitable trust and it becomes impossible or impracticable to apply the gift to that purpose between the date of the testator's death and the date on which the bequest is due to be paid, the gift will have already become the property of the trustees of the charity and, if the particular purpose can no longer be satisfied, the property will be applied for an analogous charitable purpose. In other words, at the death of the testator, the gift will have been impressed with charity and therefore must be used for a charitable purpose even if the original charitable purpose is subsequently no longer possible. This is particularly well illustrated by *Re Wright*,[298] where the testatrix had left her residuary estate subject to a life interest to be held on trust for a convalescent home. When she died in 1933, the provision of such a home was capable of being carried out, but, when the life tenant died in 1942, it was no longer practicable. The Court of Appeal held that the test of practicability should be applied at the date of the testatrix's death rather than when the funds became available on the death of the life tenant. This was because the former date was that on which the rights of the charity and the next of kin, who would take the residuary estate if the gift to the charity failed, were ascertained. This was consequently a case of subsequent failure of the charitable purpose because that purpose had been practicable when the testatrix died and so the funds could be applied cy-près.

In *Re Tacon*,[299] the time for determining the practicability of fulfilling the charitable purpose was clarified. It was held that, where the gift is vested but liable to be defeated on the occurrence of a particular event, it is not sufficient merely to consider whether the purpose was practicable at the date of the testator's death; it is also necessary to consider whether it would be practicable at some future date. In that case, the testator had left his

---

[294] *Re Wright* [1954] Ch 347, 362 (Romer LJ).   [295] *Re Peel's Release* [1921] 2 Ch 218.
[296] *Re Woodhams* [1981] 1 WLR 493.   [297] [1891] 2 Ch 236.
[298] [1954] Ch 347.   [299] [1958] Ch 447.

residuary estate to his daughter for life with remainder to her children, but if she did not have any, part of the residuary estate was to be used to found a convalescent hospital. At the date of the testator's death, the value of the residuary estate was sufficient to establish such a hospital. His daughter died childless thirty years later, by which time the value of the residuary estate had fallen significantly, so that the charitable purpose was no longer practicable. It was held that, in a case such as this in which the gift for the charitable purpose was vested but defeasible, it should be assumed that the gift would take effect at some time in the future. In the light of that, it was considered that, had the question of practicability in the future been assessed at the time of the testator's death, the purpose would have been considered to be practicable because it would not have been anticipated that the value of money would have fallen in the meantime or that estate duty would have increased substantially to reduce the amount available.

A charitable purpose will also be considered to have failed subsequently where the purpose has been fulfilled and there is a surplus of trust funds. So, for example, in *Re King*,[300] the testatrix left the residue of her estate for a stained-glass window to be installed in a church. The residue was over £1,000 and the cost of the window was about £700. It was held that the surplus of the estate could be applied cy-près towards the installation of another window in the church.

6.5.3 ALTERATION OF THE ORIGINAL CHARITABLE PURPOSES

At common law, the cy-près doctrine is applicable only where the objects of the trust became impossible or impracticable in whole or in part. Where the purpose is subject to a condition that makes it impossible or impracticable to achieve the main purpose, the court can, as part of its cy-près jurisdiction, sever the condition so that the main purpose could be achieved. So, for example, in *Re Dominion Students' Hall Trusts*,[301] a condition of a trust for the maintenance of a hostel for male students of 'the overseas dominions of the British Empire' restricted the benefits to dominion students of European origin, which made it impossible to fulfil the purpose at all. The offending condition was excised because it defeated the charity's principal object of promoting community of citizenship among all members of the British Commonwealth. In *Re Robinson*,[302] a condition of a gift for an evangelical church that the preacher should wear a black gown was removed because it was impracticable, since preachers in the evangelical tradition did not wear gowns. In *Re Lysaght*,[303] the Royal College of Surgeons refused to accept a generous benefaction towards medical studentships because it was subject to a condition that meant that Jewish or Roman Catholic students were not eligible to receive studentships, a condition that the Royal College considered to be alien to the spirit of its work. This rendered the fulfilment of the charitable purpose impossible because the testatrix wanted only the Royal College of Surgeons to be the trustee of the fund. It was held that, since the conditions relating to religious disqualification concerned the machinery of the trust and did not form an essential part of her intention to found medical studentships, a scheme was ordered whereby the Royal College held the bequest on trust, but without the offending condition. In all of these cases, the condition that was excised was not considered to be essential to the fulfilment of the donor's dominant charitable intent. In other words, the relevant condition was subsidiary only to that purpose.

---

[300] [1923] 1 Ch 243. See also *Re North Devon and West Somerset Relief Fund* [1953] 1 WLR 1260.
[301] [1947] Ch 183.   [302] [1923] 2 Ch 332.
[303] [1966] Ch 191. See also *Re Woodhams* [1981] 1 WLR 493.

Altering the original charitable purpose is not, however, available at common law where the fulfilment of the purpose remains possible, but it is not useful or convenient, such as where property had been left for use as a hospital but for which purpose the site was simply not suitable,[304] or where the purpose was outmoded or was provided for from other sources. The cy-près doctrine can now be applied in such situations by virtue of section 62 of the Charities Act 2011, which relaxes the requirement of impossibility and impracticability.

Section 62 enables the original purposes of a charitable gift to be altered by the Charity Commission in certain circumstances to allow some, or all, of the donated property to be applied cy-près. These circumstances include:

(a) where the original purposes of the gift have been wholly or partly fulfilled or cannot be carried out or cannot be carried out according to the directions given and the spirit of the gift;

(b) where the original purposes provided a use for only part of the property given;

(c) where the property given and other property applicable for similar purposes can be used more effectively together for common purposes having regard to 'the appropriate considerations';

(d) where the original purposes referred to an area that has ceased to be a unit, such as a parish, or by reference to a class of persons or to an area that have ceased to be suitable, having regard to 'the appropriate considerations'; or

(e) where the original purposes have wholly or partly:

(i)   been adequately provided for by other means;

(ii) ceased to be charitable in law, because for example they are useless or harmful to the community, such as anti-vivisection; or

(iii) ceased to provide a suitable and effective method of using the property having regard to 'the appropriate considerations'.

The references to 'the appropriate considerations' in paragraphs (c), (d), and (e)(iii) refer to the spirit of the relevant gift and the social and economic circumstances that prevail at the time of the proposed alteration of the original purposes.

The effect of section 62 is not to alter the conditions for property to be applied cy-près, other than as regards the identification of when there has been a failure of the original purpose of the charitable gift.[305] But the jurisdiction is a significant one, since it involves altering the original purposes of the charity to enable property to be applied in a different way from that intended by the donor.

The significance of section 62 is especially well illustrated by *Varsani v Jesani*,[306] which concerned a Hindu religious sect that had split into two factions, one of which recognized the divine status of the successor to the sect's founder and the other of which did not. Consequently, neither group could worship together in the charity's temple. Both factions sought a scheme to divide the charity's funds under what is now section 62 on the ground that the original purpose of the charity had ceased to provide a suitable and effective method of using the property, having regard to the spirit of the gift. It was held that what is now section 62 applied, so a scheme as to the division of the charity's property between the two groups would be directed, even though the original purposes of the charity were neither impossible nor impracticable. Section 62 was engaged because the property of the charity was no longer being used in a suitable and effective manner for the

---

[304] *Re Weir Hospital* [1910] 2 Ch 124.   [305] Charities Act 2011, s. 62(3).   [306] [1999] Ch 219.

original purpose of the charity, namely to promote the faith of the sect, since the minority faction had been excluded from the temple. The alternative was to conduct an inquiry to determine which faction followed the true faith; that faction could then have exclusive use of the temple. This was not considered to be a suitable and effective method of using the property, having regard to the spirit in which the donors had given property on trust for the purpose of promoting the faith of the sect by the community worshipping together.

Another example of the significant jurisdiction created by what is now section 62 includes *Re Lepton's Charity*,[307] in which, in 1715, the testator had left land on trust with £3 of the income each year to be paid to a Protestant dissenting minister in Pudsey, and the surplus to be distributed to the poor and aged of the town. The land was eventually sold for nearly £800. The question for the court was whether what is now section 62 could be used to vary the will and raise the annual payment to the minister to £100. A scheme was ordered to vary the will on the ground that regard should be had to the charitable purposes in the trust as a whole, in particular the relative value of the payment to the minister and the residue. The spirit of the gift was intended to provide the minister with a modest, but not negligible, income, which originally amounted to three-fifths of the income. By 1970, this had become derisory, and so it was appropriate to alter the charitable purposes to pay the minister proportionately more. The application of what is now section 62 in this case suggests an expansion of the statutory jurisdiction, since there was no alteration of the original charitable purpose, but only of the amount that could be paid to the minister. However, the amount that would otherwise be due was so inadequate that this could be regarded as defeating the original charitable purpose.

Section 62 will be engaged only if the case falls within one of the recognized conditions for that provision to apply. If it does not, the court can still rely on its inherent common law jurisdiction to amend the terms of the charitable trust. So, for example, in *Re JW Laing Trust*,[308] in 1922 the settlor had transferred £15,000 worth of shares to be held on charitable trust, with the capital and income to be wholly distributed within ten years of his death. The settlor died in 1978. By 1982, the capital had not been distributed and was worth £24 million, with an annual income of £1.2 million. The trustee applied for a scheme to discharge it from the obligation of distributing within ten years of the settlor's death. The application was refused under what is now section 62, because the obligation to distribute was an administrative provision and was not an original purpose of the charitable gift that related to the charitable objects for which the gift was to be applied. The scheme was, however, approved in the exercise of the court's inherent jurisdiction at common law, because the requirement as to distribution was inexpedient in the altered circumstances of the charity since 1922 and it appeared that the settlor had not attached much significance to the condition when the trust was created. This reliance on the court's inherent jurisdiction can be justified on the basis that the condition did not affect the spirit of the gift and so can be distinguished from *Re Lepton's Charity*, in which the statutory jurisdiction was engaged because the amount to be paid to the minister did affect the spirit of the gift.

Another example of the continuing significance of the court's inherent jurisdiction is *Oldham Borough Council v Attorney-General*.[309] In that case, land had been conveyed in 1962 to the Council on trust for use as playing fields. The Council wished to sell the land to developers for a substantial sum of money and to use the proceeds to buy other playing fields with much better facilities. It was held that the court could not authorize the sale under what is now section 62, because, even though the retention of the site was part of the original purposes of the charity, none of the identified circumstances under the

---

[307] [1972] Ch 276.   [308] [1984] Ch 143.   [309] [1993] Ch 210.

statute applied. It was recognized, however, that the court had an inherent jurisdiction to authorize a scheme to sell charitable property and to reinvest the proceeds on the same charitable trusts. This jurisdiction was not available where the identity of the property was essential to the charitable purpose, such as where the purpose of the trust related to the maintenance of a house of architectural merit, or an area of land of outstanding natural beauty. In such a case, the property could only be sold by virtue of the statutory jurisdiction under what is now section 62 because the sale of the property would involve the alteration of the charitable purpose. In this case, however, the property could be sold because the retention of the specific land was not essential to carrying out the purposes of the charitable trust, namely to provide facilities for inhabitants.

6.5.4 CHARITY COLLECTIONS

Where property has been given by a donor for a specific charitable purpose that fails initially, that property will be held on resulting trust for the donor.[310] It could not be applied cy-près because, being for a specific charitable purpose, no general charitable intent would be identifiable. Where, however, the donor cannot be identified or found or has formally disclaimed their right to have the property returned, the property is treated as if it were given for charitable purposes generally and can be applied cy-près.[311] This will be possible only where the donor cannot be identified or found after prescribed adverts have been published, inquiries have been made, and a prescribed period of time has elapsed. Property will be conclusively presumed to belong to donors who cannot be identified if it consists of the proceeds of cash collections by means that cannot distinguish one gift from another, such as by a collecting box, or is the proceeds of a lottery or raffle. The court or the Charity Commission can direct that property should be treated as belonging to donors who cannot be identified where the amounts involved make it unreasonable to incur expense with a view to returning the property or the amount involved and the lapse of time make it unreasonable for the donors to expect the property to be returned. Where the property is applied cy-près, the donor of the property is deemed to have parted with the proprietary interest when the gift was made, although provision is made for a donor who had not been identified or found to make a claim to the property within six months of the scheme to apply the property cy-près having been made.

6.5.5 CHARITY SOLICITATIONS

Where property has been given in response to a solicitation for a particular charitable purpose and that solicitation is accompanied by a statement that, if the purpose fails, the property will be applied cy-près as though the property had been given for a general charitable purpose, the property will be so applied if the purpose fails, except where the donor, at the time of making the gift, wanted to be given the opportunity for the property or its value to be returned if the purpose failed.[312]

6.5.6 SMALL CHARITIES

Where a charity has a gross income of less than £10,000, does not hold land on trust for charitable purposes, and is not exempt or a charitable company, the charity trustees can determine their own cy-près application of property with the concurrence of the Charity Commission, for example by transferring all of the charity's property to another charity,

---

[310] See Section 8.3.2, p. 231.   [311] Charities Act 2011, s. 63(1).   [312] Ibid., s. 65.

or by replacing some or all of the charity's purposes, where the original charity's purposes are no longer conducive to a suitable and effective application of the charity's resources.[313]

6.5.7 APPRAISAL

At the heart of the cy-près doctrine is the distinction between initial and subsequent failure of purpose. On which side of the line a particular case falls will affect whether a general charitable intent needs to be identified. The recognition that no such intent is required where there is subsequent failure involves the elevation of a rule of evidence into a rule of law.[314] This is because, in cases of subsequent failure, the old rule was that there was a presumption of general charitable intent, but this was a presumption that could be rebutted. Luxton[315] has advocated a more rational approach to the cy-près doctrine as follows.

(1) Where there is an initial failure of charitable purpose, there should be a presumption that the property will be held on resulting trust, save where that presumption can be rebutted by evidence of a general charitable intent.

(2) Where there is a subsequent failure, there should be a presumption that the property has been dedicated to charitable purposes, although this can be rebutted by evidence of an absence of a general charitable intent on the part of the donor, but the presumption should become irrebutable after the perpetuity period to prevent the dead hand of the donor removing property from charitable purposes many years after their death.

---

[313] Ibid., s. 268.
[314] Luxton, 'Cy-près and the ghost of things that might have been' [1983] Conv 107.   [315] Ibid.

7

NON-CHARITABLE PURPOSE TRUSTS

7.1 GENERAL CONSIDERATIONS

7.1.1 GENERAL INVALIDITY OF NON-CHARITABLE PURPOSE TRUSTS

Non-charitable purpose trusts are generally void for two reasons.

(i) Need for identifiable beneficiaries

It is a fundamental principle of the law of trusts that the objects of the trust are people rather than purposes, because there need to be ascertained or ascertainable beneficiaries who are in a position to enforce the trust.[1] The recognition of charitable trusts, as we saw in the last chapter, is a significant qualification to this principle, since these are purpose trusts that are valid, but only because they are for the benefit of the public or a section of the public. Responsibility for enforcing such trusts formally lies with the Attorney-General and practically lies with the Charity Commission. But, where the purpose is not charitable, there is nobody who can request such a trust to be enforced. This is significant because a trustee will not be subject to equitable obligations unless there is somebody who can enforce the correlative equitable right. In other words, there is no duty without a corresponding right, and if there is no equitable duty, there can be no valid trust.

The leading case in which a non-charitable purpose trust was held to be void is *Re Astor's Settlement Trusts*.[2] This involved a settlement to hold the shares of a company on trust for various purposes, including the maintenance of good understanding, sympathy, and cooperation between nations, and the preservation of the independence and integrity of newspapers. The trusts were not charitable, either because they did not fall within any of the relevant heads of charity or because the purposes were political and so not for

---

[1] *Morice v Bishop of Durham* (1804) 9 Ves 399, 405 (Sir William Grant MR); *Re Astor's Settlement Trusts* [1952] Ch 534; *Leahy v Attorney-General for New South Wales* [1959] AC 457; *Re Endacott* [1960] Ch 232, 246 (Lord Evershed MR).

[2] [1952] Ch 534. See also *Bowman v Secular Society Ltd* [1917] AC 406, 441 (Lord Parker).

the public benefit. Consequently, being for non-charitable purposes, the trusts were void, since there were no identifiable beneficiaries.

(ii) Certainty of purpose

In *Re Astor's Settlement Trusts*, the non-charitable purpose trust was also held to be void because the identified purposes were considered to be too uncertain. Similarly, in *Morice v Bishop of Durham*,[3] a trust for 'such objects of benevolence and liberality as the Bishop of Durham' should approve was held to be void because the objects were uncertain. Whereas, for charitable trusts, the courts will strive to resolve any uncertainty to hold the trust valid once it is clear that the settlor or testator had a charitable intent,[4] such benevolent construction will not be adopted for non-charitable purpose trusts. Consequently, even if the absence of beneficiaries to enforce the trust did not result in invalidity, and as will be seen this is sometimes the case,[5] the purpose must be defined with reference to clear concepts, and the means by which the trustees are to attain the purpose must also be prescribed with a sufficient degree of certainty. This is important because, if the trustees were to surrender their discretion to the court or were unable or unwilling to perform their obligations under the trust, the court would need to be able to administer the trust. This is much less of a problem for charitable trusts, because the Attorney-General and the Charity Commission can formulate schemes for the administration of the trust, can enforce the trust, and can prevent maladministration of it.

7.1.2 CHARITABLE PURPOSES

When considering whether a purpose trust is valid, it is always important to consider first whether the purpose is charitable, since the two factors that render the trust obligation imperfect do not apply to charitable trusts. The beneficiary principle does not apply to such trusts and uncertainty in the definition of the purposes is much more likely to be resolved to ensure that the trust is upheld. If it is concluded that the purpose is not charitable, its non-charitable status will generally render the trust void. So, for example, in *Re Shaw's Will Trust*,[6] George Bernard Shaw's residuary estate was left to be applied to the creation of a forty-letter alphabet. This was held not to be a charitable purpose[7] and so the trust was void as a non-charitable purpose trust. Similarly, in *Re Endacott*,[8] a gift of the testator's residuary estate to a parish council to provide some useful memorial to him was not charitable, even though it purported to be a 'public trust', and so was void as being for a non-charitable purpose.

Although these cases would probably be decided in the same way today, it is important to realize that the gradual expansion and clarification of recognized charitable purposes, as confirmed by the Charities Act 2011, will mean that some purposes that were once regarded as non-charitable and void will now be valid under the law of charity, as long as the public benefit test is satisfied. So, for example, trusts for amateur sport were once regarded as non-charitable and void, but today this is a recognized charitable purpose.[9]

7.1.3 CRITIQUE OF THE GENERAL INVALIDITY PRINCIPLE

Although non-charitable purpose trusts have long been regarded as generally void, it is difficult to identify any clear rationale as to why this should be the case. If the purpose is defined clearly, the only obstacle to validity is the absence of ascertainable beneficiaries to

---

[3] (1804) 9 Ves 399; affirmed (1805) 10 Ves 522.   [4] See Section 6.1.2.(iii), p. 146.
[5] See Section 7.2.2, p. 191.   [6] [1957] 1 WLR 729.   [7] See Section 6.2.2.(i), p. 153.
[8] [1960] Ch 232.   [9] See Section 6.3.7, p. 170.

enforce the trust. But, if the trustees are willing to perform the trust, there is no problem of enforceability. The trustees might still fail to comply with the terms of the trust and misapply the trust property, but those who are entitled to the trust property if the trust were to fail would be in a position to enforce the trust if they wished to do so,[10] or the settlor or testator could provide for the appointment of a third party to enforce the trust if necessary.[11] In other words, the problems of enforcement could be resolved.[12]

Matthews[13] has, however, argued that the beneficiary principle is not simply dependent on the beneficiaries being in a position to enforce the trust. Rather, it is the fact that the beneficiary has a proprietary right and the trustee owes them duties that is significant. If this is correct, it follows that a third-party enforcer of the trust who does not have a proprietary interest in trust property would not be sufficient to satisfy the beneficiary principle. This approach is not, however, consistent with a number of key cases that have recognized that non-charitable purpose trusts are valid, because beneficiaries can be identified even though they do not have any equitable proprietary interests in trust property.[14] Also, a third-party enforcer of a non-charitable purpose trust who is not beneficially entitled to the trust property can still be regarded as having a sufficient proprietary interest in the trust property, since they would be able to claim the property in the hands of a third party if it had been misappropriated,[15] albeit not for their own benefit, but instead to return the property to the trust for use for the identified purpose.

7.2 EXCEPTIONAL CIRCUMSTANCES UNDER WHICH NON-CHARITABLE PURPOSE TRUSTS ARE VALID

Despite the general principle of invalidity, there are two exceptional categories of case in which non-charitable purpose trusts have been recognized as valid.

7.2.1 DIRECT OR INDIRECT BENEFIT TO INDIVIDUALS

A trust that appears to be for a non-charitable purpose might be valid if the purpose can be regarded as directly or indirectly benefiting ascertained individuals. Although these individuals will not have a proprietary interest in the trust property, the benefit that they obtain from the purpose gives them a factual interest, so that they have *locus standi* to enforce the trust if necessary. This was recognized in *Re Denley's Trust Deed*.[16] In that case, trustees held land as a sports ground for the use and enjoyment of employees of a particular company for twenty-one years from the death of the last survivor of a group of named individuals. The trustees also had the power to allow the facilities to be used by other people. It was held that, although the trust was expressed as a purpose, namely use and enjoyment, it directly or indirectly benefited individuals and so was valid, since such a trust did not fall within the mischief of the beneficiary principle. Goff J did, however, recognize that the trust would not have been valid had the purpose been abstract or impersonal. This would be the case, for example, had the purpose been to seek a change in the law, such as the abolition of vivisection, which had no direct or indirect benefit for particular people.

---

[10] See *Re Shaw's Will Trust* [1957] 1 WLR 729.   [11] See further Section 7.3.4, p. 194.

[12] See Pawlowski and Summers, 'Private purpose trusts: a reform proposal' [2007] Conv 440.

[13] 'The new trust: obligations without rights?', in *Trends in Contemporary Trust Law*, ed. Oakley (Oxford: Clarendon Press, 1996), p. 3.

[14] See especially *Re Denley's Trust Deed* [1969] 1 Ch 373. See Section 7.2.1, p. 190.

[15] Hayton, 'Developing the obligation characteristic of the trust' (2001) 117 LQR 96, 102.

[16] [1969] 1 Ch 373.

If the facts of *Re Denley* were to arise today, the trust might potentially be regarded as valid as a charitable trust, since the purpose was for the advancement of sport.[17] But the validity of this trust in the law of charity would turn on whether the public benefit test were satisfied, and this might be difficult to establish because most of those who benefited from the purpose were the employees of the same company, so that there was a personal nexus.[18] The fact, however, that the trustees had a discretion to allow people other than employees to use the facilities might have been sufficient to satisfy the public benefit test and render the trust charitable.

The principle that a non-charitable purpose trust can be valid as long as identifiable individuals are benefited can also be used to explain the validity of trusts in the earlier decisions in *Re the Trusts of the Abbott Fund*[19] and *Re Gillingham Bus Disaster Fund*,[20] in which money was collected from the public for people in distress: in the former case, for two deaf and blind sisters; in the latter, for the victims and families of a bus crash. In both cases, the trusts could have been construed as express private trusts, with the beneficiaries being the people in distress. But, in both cases, the trustees had a great deal of discretion as to the use of the money collected, and in *Gillingham Bus* they even had a power to apply the surplus for other worthy causes which they could select. Consequently, these cases are preferably analysed as being trusts for the purposes of benefiting the people in distress rather than for the particular people themselves. Since the class of people who could be benefited was limited, it followed that neither trust could be charitable, because the public benefit requirement was not satisfied. Also, in *Gillingham Bus* the inclusion of 'other worthy causes' would mean that the trust was not exclusively charitable.[21] Since, however, there were ascertainable beneficiaries who directly benefited from the carrying out of the purposes, they were in a position to enforce the trusts and so there was no objection to the trusts being recognized as valid, consistent with the approach adopted in *Re Denley*.

7.2.2 TESTAMENTARY TRUSTS OF IMPERFECT OBLIGATION

There are some exceptional cases in which non-charitable purpose trusts created by wills have been recognized as valid.[22] These are difficult to justify, save as being concessions to human weakness or sentiment.[23] Such trusts are sometimes described as being 'trusts of imperfect obligation',[24] to acknowledge that the so-called 'obligation' of the trustee to perform the trust is imperfect in that the trustee is allowed to carry out the purpose of the trust if they wish to do so, but is not obliged to do so. Consequently, such trusts are preferably analysed as powers to act rather than obligations to do so.[25]

A testamentary trust of imperfect obligation must fall within one of the recognized categories of case in which such trusts have previously been treated as valid. The trust cannot be of indefinite duration and so must comply with that part of the perpetuity rule, known as the 'rule against inalienability',[26] which operates in this context to ensure that property

---

[17] See Section 6.3.7, p. 170.

[18] See *Oppenheim v Tobacco Securities Trust Co Ltd* [1951] AC 297, discussed in Section 6.3.2.(ii), p. 161, as regards a trust for the advancement of education of children of employees that did not satisfy the public benefit test because of the personal nexus. But compare this with *Dingle v Turner* [1972] AC 601, discussed in Section 6.3.1.(ii), p. 159, in which a trust for the relief of poverty of employees of a company did satisfy the public benefit test, despite the personal nexus. Clearly, much will turn on the nature of the charitable purpose as to whether the public benefit test is considered to have been satisfied. [19] [1900] 2 Ch 326.

[20] [1959] Ch 62. [21] See *Re Atkinson's Will Trusts* [1978] 1 WLR 586, discussed in Section 6.4.1, p. 175.

[22] See Brown, 'What are we to do with testamentary trusts of imperfect obligation?' [2007] Conv 148.

[23] *Re Shaw's Will Trust* [1957] 1 WLR 729. [24] Hart, 'What is a trust?' (1899) 15 LQR 294, 302.

[25] For the distinction between trusts and powers, see Section 3.7.8, p. 66.

[26] Dawson, 'The rule against inalienability: a rule without a purpose' (2006) 26 LS 414.

is not bound up for non-charitable purposes indefinitely. Although the Perpetuities and Accumulations Act 2009 has reformed the law on perpetuity,[27] that Act is concerned with the remoteness of vesting of equitable interests in people. Since non-charitable purpose trusts are concerned with the use of property for purposes rather than the vesting of interests in people, the 2009 Act expressly does not apply to non-charitable purpose trusts,[28] but the common law rule on the duration of such trusts still applies, namely that a trust cannot continue for longer than the life of an identified person or persons in being plus twenty-one years. If no person is identified, the trust should last for only twenty-one years.[29] If the trust might last for a longer period, it will be void from the outset,[30] save where the court is willing to construe it as lasting for no longer than the perpetuity period.

(i) Trusts for a particular animal

A trust for the welfare of animals will be a valid charitable trust,[31] but a trust for the care of a single animal will not be charitable, presumably because the public benefit requirement will not have been satisfied, since the only benefit is to the animal's owner. But such a trust will be valid as a trust of an imperfect obligation even though it is for a non-charitable purpose, as long as it complies with the perpetuity rule. So, for example, in *Re Dean*,[32] a trust for the maintenance of the testator's horses and hounds for fifty years, as long as they lived that long, was held to be valid even though it was not charitable and nobody could enforce it. Being for fifty years and without reference to the life of a specified person, this does appear to have infringed the perpetuity rule, although the court may have assumed that the horses and hounds would not have lived for longer than twenty-one years.

(ii) Trusts to erect and maintain monuments and graves

Trusts for the erection or maintenance of tombs or monuments have long been regarded as valid, even though they are not charitable because of the absence of any public benefit,[33] but they must still satisfy the perpetuity rule. So, for example, in *Pirbright v Salwey*,[34] a trust to maintain a grave and to decorate it with flowers was held to be valid, and in *Re Hooper*,[35] a trust for the care and upkeep of family graves and monuments was held to be valid for twenty-one years only. It was held that, after the end of the perpetuity period, any surplus money should be given to whoever was entitled to the residue of the estate.

(iii) Trusts for the saying of private masses

Trusts for the saying of masses that the public are entitled to attend will be charitable.[36] A trust for the saying of masses in private will not satisfy the public benefit requirement to be a charity, but will be valid as a non-charitable purpose trust if the perpetuity rule is not infringed.[37]

(iv) Trusts for other purposes

In *Re Endacott*,[38] it was recognized by the Court of Appeal that these anomalous cases in which testamentary purpose trusts have been recognized should not be extended. In that

---

[27] See Section 4.6, p. 102.   [28] Perpetuities and Accumulations Act 2009, s. 18.
[29] *Re Hooper* [1932] 1 Ch 38.
[30] The wait-and-see rule under the Perpetuities and Accumulations Act 2009, s. 7, will not apply. See Section 4.6.3, p. 103.   [31] See Section 6.3.11, p. 173.
[32] (1889) 41 Ch D 552. See also *Pettingall v Pettingall* (1842) 11 LJ Ch 176; *Mitford v Reynolds* (1848) 16 Sim 105.
[33] *Trimmer v Danby* (1856) 25 LJ Ch 424; *Mussett v Bingle* [1876] WN 170.   [34] [1896] WN 86.
[35] [1932] 1 Ch 38.   [36] See Section 6.3.3.(ii), p. 167.
[37] *Re Endacott* [1960] Ch 232, 246 (Lord Evershed MR).   [38] Ibid.

case the testator had left his estate to a parish council to provide 'some useful memorial' to himself. This was construed to be a trust for a non-charitable purpose that was not valid, even though it might be regarded as analogous to trusts to erect and maintain monuments and graves. Reasoning by analogy, which has proved to be so significant to the development of the law of charity,[39] appears not to be available for non-charitable purpose trusts.

There have, however, been other testamentary dispositions that have been held to be valid even though they involve non-charitable purposes. So, for example, in *Re Thompson*,[40] a legacy to promote and further fox hunting was upheld as valid on the basis that the legacy could be paid to the legatee on him giving an undertaking that it would be applied as the testator wished. Although this was a gift rather than a trust, the requirement of the legatee giving an undertaking as to the use of the money is significant. Such an undertaking could be required in the other anomalous cases, and was in fact required of the trustee in *Pettingall v Pettingall*,[41] in respect of a trust for the upkeep of the testator's horse. Such an undertaking could be enforced by the residuary legatees applying to the court if the undertaking were breached or the fund were misapplied.[42] Such undertakings by trustees could also be given in situations outside the recognized cases of testamentary trusts of imperfect obligation, such as in the circumstances of *Re Endacott*. There is consequently no reason why the recognition of such trusts should be limited to these exceptional cases so that any non-charitable purpose in a testamentary trust should be valid if the appropriate undertaking is given, and as long as the trust satisfies the perpetuity rule and the purpose is sufficiently certain. If the trustee does not give an undertaking to apply the fund for the non-charitable purpose, the fund should be held on resulting trust for those entitled to the testator's residuary estate.

7.3 OTHER MECHANISMS FOR IMPLEMENTING NON-CHARITABLE PURPOSES

In addition to the clearly recognized situations in which a non-charitable purpose trust has been held to be valid, there are other mechanisms available to enable property to be transferred to another for use for non-charitable purposes, not all of which involve the law of trusts.

7.3.1 FIDUCIARY POWER FOR NON-CHARITABLE PURPOSES

Although it is a fundamental principle of the law of trusts that a valid power cannot be spelt out of an invalid trust,[43] so that what purports to be a non-charitable purpose trust cannot be treated as a power that the trustee may, rather than must, exercise for the non-charitable purpose,[44] it does not follow that a trust cannot be created where the trustee is expressly given the power to use the trust property for the identified purpose.[45] The trustee would not be required to exercise the power and, if they did so, this would not be a breach of trust. Since such a power need not be exercised, it might be considered not to

---

[39] See Section 6.3.13, p. 174.   [40] [1934] Ch 342.   [41] (1842) 11 LJ Ch 176.

[42] Marshall, 'The failure of the *Astor* trust' (1953) 6 CLP 151, 153.

[43] *IRC v Broadway Cottages Trust* [1955] Ch 20, 36 (Jenkins LJ).

[44] *Re Shaw* [1957] 1 WLR 729, 746 (Harman J); *Re Endacott* [1960] Ch 232, 246 (Lord Evershed MR). Of course, the recognition of testamentary trusts of an imperfect obligation is a clear exception to this principle. See Section 7.2.2, p. 191.

[45] Morris and Leach, *Rule against Perpetuities*, 2nd edn (London: Stevens, 1962), p. 320.

be necessary to identify beneficiaries who could enforce it. But trustees are still required to consider the exercise of the power[46] and might exercise the power improperly, so the preferable view is that a fiduciary power to allow the property to be applied by a trustee for a non-charitable purpose would still be caught by the beneficiary principle and could be valid only if it were to fall within one of the recognized exceptions to that principle.

7.3.2 POWER ATTACHED TO GIFT

A non-charitable purpose might also be achieved by giving property to a person subject to a power that it should be used for a non-charitable purpose, failing which a gift over would take effect. The donee would not be obliged to use the property for that purpose, but if they were to fail to do so, the gift would lapse and the gift over would apply. This has been recognized as effective as regards charities, so that where a gift is made to a charity subject to a condition to perform a non-charitable purpose, failing which the gift will vest in another charity, this is not caught by the perpetuity rule.[47] So, for example, in *Re Tyler*,[48] the testator left money to a charity, the London Missionary Society. He also committed to the care of the trustees of the charity the keys of his family vault to keep it in good repair; if the Society were to fail to so keep the vault, the money was to be transferred to another charity. Even though the gift had been made to a charity, this particular purpose was not charitable. It was held that both the gift and the gift over were valid and were not caught by the perpetuity rule. This might be justified because the condition attached to the gift was not considered to have created an obligation on the part of the trustees to maintain the vault, but only a power. This power was not caught by the perpetuity rule because, as Fry LJ recognized, that rule applies to property and not to motives. Where, however, a gift was made to a charity subject to a duty to apply the property for a non-charitable purpose, this was held to be void. In *Re Dalziel*,[49] the testatrix had left a substantial sum of money to a hospital on condition that the income should be used for the repair of her family mausoleum, with a gift over to another charity if the hospital were to fail to so repair it, but that gift over was subject to the same conditions. It was held that the testatrix had purported to impose a duty on the hospital to maintain the mausoleum, and that this and the gift over were void as being contrary to the perpetuity rule.

7.3.3 MANDATE OR AGENCY

It has been recognized that a gift can be transferred to a donee who is appointed as agent for the donor and with authority to apply the gift for a non-charitable purpose.[50] If the agent were to misapply the gift, they would be liable for breach of fiduciary duty.[51] If they were to fail to apply the gift as they were mandated to do, it would be returned to the donor except where it was agreed that the money was no longer recoverable.

7.3.4 APPOINTMENT OF AN ENFORCER

A number of foreign jurisdictions allow non-charitable purpose trusts to be created.[52] They do this as a means of attracting tax business to their countries, and such trusts are

---

[46] See Section 3.7.8.(iii), p. 67.   [47] Perpetuities and Accumulations Act 2009, s. 2(3).
[48] [1891] 3 Ch 252.   [49] [1943] Ch 277.
[50] *Conservative and Unionist Central Office v Burrell* [1982] 1 WLR 522.
[51] See Chapter 15 in this volume.
[52] For example, Bermuda, British Virgin Islands, Cayman Islands, Cyprus, Isle of Man, and Jersey.

significant as part of international tax planning and international commerce.[53] The use of non-charitable purpose trusts is important because, as they lack beneficiaries with equitable proprietary interests, it is possible to structure transactions and companies without beneficial ownership, which has the advantage of avoiding tax liability and protecting assets from creditors. For such purpose trusts to be valid, they require an enforcement mechanism, which usually involves the appointment of a person, typically known as the 'enforcer' or 'protector', to enforce the trust by application to the court if the purpose is not being carried out.[54] If this enforcer mechanism were recognized in England and Wales, it would enable non-charitable purpose trusts to be treated as generally valid, since the existence of the enforcer would ensure that the trust is performed properly.[55] Such a development would probably require legislation to ensure that the ambit of the trust is clearly defined, and the powers and responsibilities of the protector clearly identified, although Hayton[56] has argued that the law already allows any settlor to identify expressly a person with *locus standi* to enforce the trustee's duties, which has the practical effect of allowing non-charitable purpose trusts to be treated as valid by ensuring that the beneficiary principle is satisfied. But this goes too far. The traditional attitude of the English authorities, at the very least, requires the beneficiary to be in a position to enforce the trust, save for those exceptional circumstances under which a non-charitable purpose trust is recognized.

7.4 UNINCORPORATED ASSOCIATIONS

7.4.1 THE NATURE OF THE PROBLEM

The fact that trusts for non-charitable purposes are generally not valid creates particular problems when property is transferred to an unincorporated association. On the face of it, property-holding by an unincorporated association does not raise any issues relating to the law of trusts. An unincorporated association is essentially a non-commercial club or society, like a sports club or a drama group. If property is given to such an association, it might be assumed that the association will own the property like anybody else. But there is a tricky legal problem here, simply because the association is not like anybody else: legally, it is not a person. If you give me money, that money will belong to me; if you pay a company money, that money will belong to the company, because the law recognizes that the company has a separate legal personality[57] and so can own property. But unincorporated associations have no legal personality and so cannot own property. So what happens to the property that is transferred to an unincorporated association, such as subscriptions and donations of money or gifts of land? How is it held? Equity might be able to provide a solution to this problem by enabling the property to be held on trust. But, since unincorporated associations exist for purposes and because non-charitable purpose trusts are generally not valid, the trust solution may not be available.[58] In fact, Equity can explain to some extent how property can be held for the purposes of unincorporated associations, although the analysis is somewhat complex and contract has a significant role to play as well.

[53] See Matthews, 'The new trust: obligations without rights', in *Trends in Contemporary Trust Law*, ed. Oakley (Oxford: Clarendon Press, 1996), pp. 18–22.

[54] See Waters, 'The protector: new wine in old bottles', in *Trends in Contemporary Trust Law*, ed. Oakley (Oxford: Clarendon Press, 1996), ch. 4, p. 63.   [55] Pawlowski and Summers (see n. 12).

[56] 'Developing the obligation characteristic of the trust' (2001) 117 LQR 96, 98.

[57] *Salomon v Salomon & Co Ltd* [1897] AC 22.

[58] See generally *Leahy v Attorney-General for New South Wales* [1959] AC 457, 479.

This question of property-holding is not only of theoretical significance. It can also be of real practical importance, especially when the unincorporated association is dissolved, for how the property has been held will affect who is entitled to receive the property on dissolution.

7.4.2 THE DEFINITION OF UNINCORPORATED ASSOCIATIONS

An unincorporated association was defined by Lawton LJ in *Conservative and Unionist Central Office v Burrell*,[59] as:

> two or more persons bound together for one or more common purposes, not being business purposes, by mutual undertakings each having mutual duties and obligations, in an organisation which has rules which identify in whom control of it and its funds rests and on what terms and which can be joined or left at will. The bond of union between the members of an unincorporated association has to be contractual.

The key elements of this definition are that the association must be non-profit-making and its members must be bound together by identifiable rules,[60] such as a constitution of the association. Such associations may exist for a variety of purposes, such as social or recreational purposes, or to secure personal advantages for the members, or even in pursuit of an altruistic purpose, such as seeking a change in the law. A good example of an unincorporated association is an amateur football club,[61] which is not a business and which will typically have its own constitution. In *Burrell* itself, it was held that the Conservative Party was not an unincorporated association because it consisted of a number of different components, namely local constituency parties, parliamentary parties, and Central Office, which were not contractually bound together as one association by a single constitution.

7.4.3 PROPERTY-HOLDING FOR UNINCORPORATED ASSOCIATIONS

Since the unincorporated association does not have a legal personality, the association as an entity cannot own property. So a football ground and a club house that are colloquially described as 'belonging' to an amateur football club cannot be owned by the club, neither can the subscriptions paid by members or property donated to the club. The crucial questions then concern who might own such property, since clearly the property must be owned by somebody, and, once the various options have been identified, how can the unincorporated association be set up to ensure that property is owned and managed appropriately?[62] A variety of mechanisms for property ownership can be identified, of varying degrees of efficacy. A particular mechanism might be expressly chosen by the transferor of property, but usually no mechanism has been chosen and it is necessary to construe carefully the nature and circumstances of the transaction to determine which mechanism is applicable on the facts. In practice, in cases of doubt, judges have a tendency to adopt the mechanism that is most likely to validate the transfer of property, although this is not always the case.

In most cases in which property is transferred to an unincorporated association, it will be vested in the treasurer or other officers of the association. Typically, the transferor will not intend the officers to receive the property beneficially, but will intend the property to

---

[59] [1982] 1 WLR 522, 525.　　　[60] *Re Koeppler's Will Trust* [1986] Ch 423, 431 (Slade LJ).

[61] A professional football club will be incorporated rather than organized as an unincorporated association.

[62] See generally Waters (see n. 54).

be used for the benefit of the association. The key question is whether this is for the benefit of the association's purposes or members and, if for the members, whether it is for the benefit of present or future members.

(i) Charitable trust

It is possible that property that is to be used for the benefit of the unincorporated association could be held on a charitable purpose trust, but only if there is a recognized charitable purpose and if the trust is for the public benefit.[63] With the recognition of the advancement of amateur sport as a distinct charitable purpose, it will be easier to treat the property transferred to sports clubs as being held on trust for the charitable purposes of that club. It will be important to consider the circumstances carefully to determine whether a valid charitable trust has been created. If property appears to be held for charitable purposes, but the association has a rule that, on dissolution, the property will be divided between the members themselves, this will negate the charitable purpose,[64] because the purpose is not exclusively charitable.

(ii) Non-charitable purpose trust

Unincorporated associations were once considered to be an exception to the general principle that non-charitable purpose trusts are void, but this exception was rejected by the Privy Council in *Leahy v Attorney-General for New South Wales*.[65] In that case, the testator left his property to be held on trust for an order of nuns, which was an unincorporated association. It was held that this was not charitable and was not intended to be a private trust for the members of the order, since there were many members of the order who were spread all over the world and the property was only a house with twenty rooms that could not have been intended to belong to each nun beneficially. Consequently, this was a trust for the non-charitable purposes of the order, which was held to be void.

There will, however, be circumstances under which a property might legitimately be held on trust for the purposes of the unincorporated association, even though those purposes are not charitable, if the trust can be considered to be for the direct or indirect benefit of the members of that association within the *Denley* principle.[66] In such circumstances, the members of the association will be in a position to enforce the trust since they factually benefit from the purpose. Although *Re Denley* itself did not involve an unincorporated association, it did involve the employees benefiting from the use of a sports ground. This construction might be applicable therefore where members of an amateur football club benefit from the provision of a football ground. The land can be held on trust for the purposes of the club and its members will be in a position to enforce the trust, even though they do not have a proprietary interest in the land. Such a trust, being a non-charitable purpose trust, must comply with the common law perpetuity rule and last for no more than a life in being of an identified person or persons plus twenty-one years. This mechanism for property-holding by the club must be intended by the settlor, in that the settlor must intend the property to be held for the purposes of the club rather than for the members themselves.[67]

The application of the *Denley* principle to unincorporated associations was, however, doubted by Vinelott J in *Re Grant's Will Trusts*,[68] since he considered that it applied only to discretionary trusts where the use of the property was at the discretion of the trustees,

---

[63] See Section 6.2.2, p. 152.   [64] *Neville Estates Ltd v Madden* [1962] Ch 832, 850 (Cross J).

[65] [1959] AC 457.   [66] [1969] 1 Ch 373. See Section 7.2.1, p. 190.

[67] See Section 7.4.3.(iii), p. 198, for consideration of cases in which the property is intended to be held for the members.   [68] [1980] 1 WLR 360, 368.

as was the case in *Re Denley*. But there is no reason to confine the *Denley* principle in this way. In *Re Denley* itself, the discretion of the trustees was not considered to be significant and *Re Denley* was applied, amongst other mechanisms, in *Re Lipinski's Will Trust*[69] to explain how property could be used for the purposes of an unincorporated association.

(iii) For members at the time

Rather than intending to benefit the purposes of the association, the transferor of property may wish to benefit the members of the association at the time the property is transferred. The property may either be treated as belonging to the members absolutely, or it will be held on trust for them, with legal title in an officer such as the treasurer, so that the members have equitable interests in the property.

Regardless of whether the members own the property absolutely or beneficially under a trust, their interest would be as joint tenants.[70] Their interest in the property would arise because they were members at the time of the transfer of the property, but this interest does not depend on them continuing to be members. Consequently, they would retain their interest in the property even once they had ceased to be members. They would be able to sever their share whenever they liked, even after they had ceased to be a member. Also, new members who join the association after the property was acquired would not have any interest in the property.

There are advantages of analysing property-holding by unincorporated associations in this way, including that, where the property is held on trust for the members, the beneficiary principle is satisfied, since the members at the time of the acquisition are the beneficiaries and the perpetuity rule will not be infringed because the members are free to dispose of the income and capital.[71] But this type of mechanism is unlikely to be what the donor of the property wanted, because it does not operate for the benefit of the association's purposes, but only for the benefit of the members at the time of the transfer, each of whom can sever their own interest for their own benefit at any time. Consequently, this is unlikely to be a mechanism that will be adopted by transferors. It is, anyway, a mechanism that can be excluded by the rules of the association if those rules prevent members from severing their shares in the property held for the benefit of the association.[72]

(iv) On trust for present and future members

To avoid the unfortunate consequences of the property being transferred for the benefit of the members at the time of the transfer, the transferor might instead wish the property to be held on trust for 'present and future members'. This would clearly satisfy the beneficiary principle, but such a trust has traditionally been regarded as void for infringing the perpetuity rule, since the property would be available indefinitely for future members, whose interests would vest outside the perpetuity period. But a trust for present and future members would presumably not now be caught by the perpetuity rule as it has been amended by statute. Under the Perpetuities and Accumulations Act 2009, the perpetuity period is 125 years, but the trust will remain valid throughout that period to see if it terminates in time.[73] If it does not, the trust will terminate automatically at the end of the period and the property will be distributed to the members at that time.

---

[69] [1976] Ch 235, 247 (Oliver J).
[70] *Neville Estates Ltd v Madden* [1962] Ch 832, 849 (Cross J). See also *Leahy v Attorney-General for New South Wales* [1959] AC 457, 479.
[71] Warburton, 'The holding of property by unincorporated associations' [1985] Conv 318, 221.
[72] Matthews, 'A problem in the construction of gifts to unincorporated associations' [1995] Conv 302.
[73] Perpetuities and Accumulations Act 2009, s. 7(2).

But a trust for present and future members would still be subject to the same significant limitation as a trust just for members at the time when the property is transferred, namely that each member would retain an interest in the trust property even if they had ceased to be a member. What is needed is a mechanism whereby the property can benefit both present and future members of the association, but a member would cease to enjoy the benefit if they were to cease to be a member of the association.

(v) For members subject to their existing contractual rights

The preferable construction to adopt is to treat the property as either being given absolutely or held on trust for the members at the time of the transfer, but subject to their contractual rights and liabilities towards one another as members of the association.[74] These contractual rights will be derived from the association's rules or constitution, since all unincorporated associations must, by definition, have rules that bind the members[75] and which form the basis of an express or implied contract between them.[76]

This mechanism, known as the contract-holding theory, ensures that the property is available for all members, including those members who join the association in the future. The essence of property-holding according to this theory was identified by Lewison J:[77]

> It is true that this is not a joint tenancy according to the classical model; but since any collective ownership of property must be a species of joint tenancy or tenancy in common, this kind of collective ownership must, in my judgment, be a subspecies of joint tenancy, albeit taking effect subject to any contractual restrictions applicable as between members.

The significance of this contractual modification of the classical model of joint tenancy is that the members cannot sever the joint tenancy at will. Further, members at the time of the transfer who subsequently resign from the association will no longer have contractual rights relating to the property; the property will belong beneficially to the remaining members. Later members who join the association will be able to benefit from the property because they will have beneficial rights in the property arising from the rules of the association that they have joined.

The contract-holding theory is the mechanism of property-holding that is now usually recognized by the courts, but it will not be available if the transferor of the property clearly intended the property to be held for the purposes of the association, or for the members at the time the property was transferred, or for present and future members. But those constructions are not satisfactory, because usually a trust for the purposes of the association will be void, and trusts for the members, either at the time of the transfer or present and future members, will have the unfortunate consequence that a person who ceases to be a member will still have a beneficial interest in the property. Consequently, the contract-holding theory is by far the most satisfactory and workable explanation of property-holding in respect of unincorporated associations.

Whilst the members of the unincorporated association may own property without the intervention of a trust, in practice, where there are a significant number of members, property will most conveniently be held on trust for the members by the treasurer or other officers of the association,[78] and land can only be held on trust for the members regardless

---

[74] *Neville Estates Ltd v Madden* [1962] Ch 832, 849 (Cross J).   [75] See Section 7.4.2, p. 196.

[76] *Re Bucks Constabulary Widows' and Orphans' Fund Friendly Society (No 2)* [1979] 1 WLR 936, 943 (Walton J); *Artistic Upholstery Ltd v Art Forma (Furniture) Ltd* [1999] 4 All ER 277.

[77] *Hanchett-Stamford v Attorney-General* [2008] EWHC 330 (Ch), [2009] Ch 173, [47].

[78] *Re Bucks Constabulary Widows' and Orphans' Fund Friendly Society (No 2)* [1979] 1 WLR 936, 939 (Walton J).

of whether they are characterized as joint tenants or tenants in common.[79] Typically, the treasurer will hold the property on a bare trust in accordance with the rules of the association.[80] Each member will then have a beneficial interest in the property and so the beneficiary principle will be satisfied, since each member can ensure that the property is applied in accordance with the rules of the association. Being a bare trust for persons, namely the members at that time, the statutory perpetuity rule will apply and, since the trust might be terminated within 125 years of its creation, it will be valid until that time,[81] with the wait-and-see rule applying.[82] Further, the class-closing rule will apply, so that the fact that future members might benefit after the 125-year period will not invalidate the trust, since it is possible to exclude those potential members whose interests might vest outside the perpetuity period.[83]

That the contract-holding theory can operate within the law of trusts was recognized in *Re Lipinski's Will Trusts*,[84] in which the testator had left part of his residuary estate on trust for the Hull Judeans (Maccabi) Association, an unincorporated association, to build and improve new buildings. The Association existed to promote the participation of Anglo-Jewish youth in sport, cultural, and communal activities, as well as to inculcate good citizenship and self-discipline, and to cultivate an interest in Jewish history, the Hebrew language, and national traditions. This was held to be a valid trust for the members of the Association, so that the gift accrued to the funds of the Association according to the terms of the contract between the members.

Even where the transfer of the property cannot be construed as being intended to be held on trust, it will typically be held by the treasurer, but in accordance with the contractual rules of the association that bind all members.[85] This is illustrated by *Re Recher's Trusts*,[86] in which a testamentary gift was made to an anti-vivisection society, which was an unincorporated association. Since the society had political objectives, the gift could not be held for charitable purposes.[87] The gift was not construed as being a gift to the members at the time of the testator's death, nor to present and future members beneficially, nor as a gift in trust for the purposes of the society. Rather it was a gift to the members at the time of the testator's death, but subject to the contract between them, which took effect in favour of the existing members as an accretion to the funds that were the subject matter of the contract between all of the members, including those who joined in the future.

Unincorporated associations are of very different sizes. In smaller ones there is likely to be only one class of member, so all members will be treated alike. Consequently, if the property that has been received for the purposes of the association is disposed of, the value of that property will be distributed equally between the members. But larger unincorporated associations are likely to have different classes of member, so, if property is sold, it will be necessary to determine whether all the members should share in the proceeds of sale regardless of their class of membership.[88] This was the key issue in *Re Horley Town*

[79] Law of Property Act 1925, ss. 34 and 36.

[80] *Re Horley Town Football Club* [2006] EWHC 2386 (Ch), [2006] WTLR 1817, [118] (Lawrence Collins J).

[81] See further Section 4.6.3, p. 103.   [82] Perpetuities and Accumulations Act 2009, s. 7.

[83] Ibid., s. 8.

[84] [1976] Ch 235. See also *Re Bucks Constabulary Widows' and Orphans' Fund Friendly Society (No 2)* [1979] 1 WLR 936; *Re Horley Town Football Club* [2006] EWHC 2386 (Ch), [2006] WTLR 1817.

[85] Warburton (see n. 71), p. 324.

[86] [1972] Ch 526. See also *Re Grant's Will Trusts* [1980] 1 WLR 360; *Universe Tankships Inc of Monrovia v International Transport Workers Federation* [1983] 1 AC 366 (gift to members of trade union); *Artistic Upholstery Ltd v Art Forma (Furniture) Ltd* [1999] 4 All ER 277.   [87] See Section 6.2.2.(iii), p. 156.

[88] This will also be relevant where the unincorporated association is dissolved. See Section 7.4.4, p. 203.

Football Club,[89] which concerned the sale of a football ground by an amateur football club. The ground was held on trust for the members of the club, whose rights were determined by the club's constitution. There were, however, a number of different classes of member, including full, associate, and temporary members, with the last of these being people such as members of visiting teams who were granted membership simply to use the club's facilities on a one-off basis. It was held that, for the purposes of the contract-holding theory, a member was somebody who could vote to have the assets sold. According to the club's constitution, this could either be by majority at an annual general meeting or otherwise by unanimous resolution. Consequently, it was only the current full members, and not the associate or temporary members, who had a beneficial interest in the property. There were other members, such as youth and junior members, who paid subscriptions, but, because they were not entitled to vote, they did not have a beneficial interest in the property. As regards those members who did have a beneficial interest, it was held that the proceeds of sale should be distributed amongst them equally.

The application of the contract-holding theory is not restricted to explain property-holding and how the value of assets are distributed to the members. The theory can also impact on the personal liabilities of the members. For example, in *Howells v Dominion Insurance Co Ltd*,[90] thirty-two members of a football club were held liable for repayment of an insurance payment that had been mistakenly paid to the club, amounting to £76,000. This is a logical consequence of the application of the contract-holding theory. The original payment would have accrued to the fund that was the subject matter of the contract between the members, so that the money belonged to the members equally. Since the money had been paid by mistake, there was a liability to repay it, so it followed that the liability to repay should be borne by the members equally as well.

It is an important feature of the contract-holding theory that the members of the association must be able to alter their rules by an appropriate majority provided by the rules, or unanimously if no provision is made, so as to provide that the funds or part of them can be applied for a new purpose or distributed amongst the members for their own benefit, for otherwise the gift or the trust for the benefit of the members could continue indefinitely, which would undermine the policy that underpins the perpetuity rule. If, however, the rules of the association prevent the members themselves from determining that the assets will be distributed amongst themselves, then, if there is no mechanism for the members to change the rules to provide for such distribution, the transfer of property to the members cannot be validated by the contract-holding theory and, if some other mechanism of property-holding cannot be identified, the gift will be void. This was recognized in *Re Grant's Will Trusts*,[91] in which the testator left his estate for the benefit of a Labour Party constituency association. It was held that this was not a valid gift because the rules of the association provided that the rules could only be changed by the National Executive Committee of the Labour Party. It was held that, for a gift to the members beneficially subject to their contractual rights to be valid, it was essential that the members were free to dispose of the property as they wished or to divide it amongst themselves beneficially, and they could not do this because they were controlled by an outside body. Since the gift could not alternatively be construed as one to existing members as joint tenants, it followed that the gift was void.

The contract-holding theory can, therefore, be used to explain how a gift can be made for the purposes of an unincorporated association, and can be held on trust for present

---

[89] [2006] EWHC 2386 (Ch), [2006] WTLR 1817. [90] [2005] EWHC 552 (QB).
[91] [1980] 1 WLR 360.

and future members. But the use of this theory within the law of trusts might not sit easily with fundamental principles of the law of express trusts. It is an essential feature of the contract-holding theory that, when a member retires from the association, they will lose their equitable proprietary interest in the assets that are available for carrying out the association's purposes. This interest would then accrue to the remaining members of the association.[92] If this involves a disposition of an existing equitable interest, it will require writing to be effective.[93] The preferable view, however, is that the departing member's interest is not transferred to the other members. Rather, it is destroyed, and the destruction of such interests does not require writing to be effective.[94]

(vi) Agent for the transferor

Rather than treating a gift of property as being a gift to the present members or as being held on trust for the members or the purposes of the association, an alternative mechanism of property-holding is for the property to be transferred to an officer of the association, but as agent for the transferor and with authority to apply the property for the transferor's intended purposes. This agency solution has proved significant where an organization does not satisfy the definition for being an unincorporated association, so that the contract-holding theory is unavailable. So, for example, in *Conservative and Unionist Central Office v Burrell*,[95] the Conservative Party was held not to be an unincorporated association because of the absence of a contractual link between the different components of the party. The Conservative Party did, however, receive substantial funds. It was held that these funds were paid to the treasurer of the Party, who had title to the money but as agent for the donors, so that the treasurer was authorized to use the money only for the purposes of the Party.

Where the recipient of the money is an agent for the donor, there will typically be no trust relationship, so that title to the money passes to the agent beneficially, subject to a personal obligation to use the money for the designated purpose. If the agent then fails to apply the money within the scope of the authority given by the donor, this will constitute a breach of fiduciary duty and the agent will be personally liable to the donor.[96] But there will be circumstances under which an agent who has received the money from the donor will hold it on trust[97] for the donor, subject to a power to apply it for the designated purpose. Where that purpose fails, the donor will then be able to recover the money.[98]

The treatment of the officer of an association as agent for the transferor of property provides a workable solution for property-holding for the benefit of organizations that are not unincorporated associations in most cases, but it is subject to certain disadvantages. One is that the authority of the agent will be personal and will be revoked where the agent has died or has been declared bankrupt. This might be dealt with by treating the agent as being the person who occupies a particular office, such as the treasurer of the organization, so that the death of the person who has been acting as treasurer will not revoke the authority; the person appointed to that position should have the same authority to use the property, even though they have not been expressly appointed as such. Another disadvantage of the agency approach is that the agency will lapse where the transferor of the property has died, because agency cannot survive the death of the principal. A final disadvantage is that the

---

[92] Baughen, 'Performing animals and the dissolution of unincorporated associations: the "contract-holding theory" vindicated' [2010] Conv 216, 225.

[93] By virtue of Law of Property Act 1925, s. 53(1)(c). See Section 11.3, p. 324.

[94] See Section 11.3.3, p. 327.   [95] [1982] 1 WLR 522.   [96] See Chapter 18 of this volume.

[97] For analysis of the distinction between the agency and trust relationships, see Section 3.7.4, p. 61.

[98] See further Section 8.3.2.(iii), p. 236.

agency theory cannot apply to legacies left to organizations, because an agency cannot be established at the time of death between the testator and the chosen agent. To avoid these limitations of the agency theory, the transfer to the officer of the association might instead be analysed as a gift with a power that the gift be used for a particular purpose. Such a power cannot bind the recipient as to how the gift should be used, but, if the recipient accepted the gift on the basis that it would be used for the particular purpose, they might be estopped from using it for a different purpose.[99]

7.4.4 DISSOLUTION OF UNINCORPORATED ASSOCIATIONS

Where an unincorporated association is dissolved, the disposal of any surplus assets will depend on which construction of property holding has been recognized. The cases reveal a complicated approach to the consequences of dissolution. In some of the earlier cases, the nature of the unincorporated association proved significant, but this is of little, if any, relevance today.

(i) Determining when the association is dissolved

The dissolution of an unincorporated association may occur by court order or by resolution of the members according to the rules of the constitution, or, if there is no such provision, by unanimous agreement of the members. Since the definition of an unincorporated association is that it consists of at least two members, it follows that, if the number of members falls below two, either because of death or resignation, the association will automatically be dissolved.[100] The association will also be regarded as dissolved if it can be considered to have become moribund. This was recognized in *Re GKN Bolts & Nuts Ltd etc Work Sports and Social Club*,[101] which concerned a social club for employees that was held to have gradually ceased to operate. It was recognized that an unincorporated association could be dissolved without a court order or members' resolution when it had been inactive for a prolonged period of time. But it was still necessary to establish some element of deliberation on the part of the members to confirm that the association was being treated as dissolved. This was established on the facts because the members had resolved to abandon issuing membership cards and had resolved to sell the sports ground that was the final asset available for the benefit of the association.

(ii) Distribution of surplus assets

When an unincorporated association is terminated, it may have surplus assets that derive from the members through the payment of subscriptions, or from gifts from members or third parties. The key question is to determine what should happen to these assets. There are three possible consequences:

(1) The assets may be returned to the people who provided them in the first place.

(2) The assets may be transferred to the Crown on the ground that nobody owns them—that is, they become bona vacantia.

(3) The assets may be transferred to the members at the time of the dissolution.

Which consequence applies will depend on how the assets were held in the first place.

---

[99] Smart, 'Holding property for non-charitable purposes: mandates, conditions and estoppels' [1987] Conv 415, 418. [100] *Hanchett-Stamford v Attorney-General* [2008] EWHC 330 (Ch), [2009] Ch 173.
[101] [1982] 1 WLR 774.

Resulting trust for transferors of property

A resulting trust can arise when property is held on an express trust that fails.[102] In such circumstances, the property that was held on the express trust will be held on a resulting trust for the settlor. Consequently, if property has been held on trust for the purposes of the unincorporated association and the association is dissolved, the property will be held on resulting trust for the people who originally transferred the property to the trust. If property has been held on trust for the members at the time the property was transferred, the dissolution of the unincorporated association will have no effect on the trust, since the validity of the trust does not depend on the unincorporated association continuing. In other words, the express trust will not have failed. The property will continue to be held for the members who contributed to the funds, whether they are past or present members, and who will be able to claim their proprietary interest whenever they wish.[103]

Where the effect of the dissolution of the association is to terminate the express trust, the property transferred will not be held on resulting trust for the transferors of the property if they can be considered to have divested themselves of all of their rights to the property. This will be the case if, for example, money has been paid to the association by a member in return for contractual benefits. If the society is then dissolved, the member cannot then claim recovery of the money. This is illustrated by *Cunnack v Edwards*,[104] in which a friendly society had been formed to raise funds to provide annuities for widows of members of the society who had died. The last member died in 1879 and the last widow died in 1892, at which point there was a surplus of £1,250 that was claimed by the personal representatives of the last members. The society was held to be moribund and so had been terminated. It was held that the next of kin of the members could not claim the surplus assets by means of a resulting trust because they had parted outright with their subscriptions when they had paid them in return for contractual benefits, namely that their widows would be provided for once the members had died.

This principle was applied in *Re West Sussex Constabulary's Widows, Children and Benevolent (1930) Fund Trusts*.[105] This case concerned a fund that had been established to provide for the widows and children of deceased members of the West Sussex police force. The funds were derived from subscriptions from members, the proceeds of entertainments, raffles, collecting boxes, and donations and legacies. The police force was amalgamated with other forces and the fund was dissolved, with a surplus. It was held that the members could not recover their subscriptions, since they were considered to have divested themselves of any interest in the money in return for contractual benefits in favour of their widows and children. The proceeds of raffles and entertainments were not held on resulting trust either, because the relationship between the payers and the association was considered to be one of contract rather than trust, in that money was paid to participate in the competition or to enjoy the entertainment, so that the payers had divested themselves of any interest in the money paid. Similarly, the money raised from street collections was not held on resulting trust, because the donors had parted with it completely with no intention that the money should be returned. But money paid by identified donors or testators for the specific purposes of the fund was held on resulting trust for them or their estates once the fund was dissolved.

---

[102] See further Section 8.3.2, p. 231.

[103] *Re Hobourn Aero Components Air Raid Distress Fund* [1946] Ch 86; affirmed [1946] Ch 194. Cf. *Re Printers and Transferrers Amalgamated Trades Protection Society* [1899] 2 Ch 184, in which the distribution was confined to the members at the time of the dissolution in proportion to the amount that they had contributed. This is, in fact, consistent with the approach adopted through the application of the contract holding theory, although the court had held that the applicable mechanism was a resulting trust. See Section 7.4.4.(ii), p. 205.

[104] [1896] 2 Ch 679.   [105] [1971] Ch 1.

The essential feature of these two decisions is that, where the payer of money receives, or expects to receive, some contractual benefit in return for their payment, they will be considered to have given up any rights to the return of their money. The reasoning employed in *Cunnack v Edwards* has been doubted on the ground that property can be held on resulting trust even though the contributor had received all of the expected contractual benefits.[106] In fact, the result in *Cunnack* can be justified for the exceptional reason that a relevant statute at the time required the rules of the association to state all of the possible uses of the society's assets and no use was identified in favour of the members. In other words, the resulting trust was excluded by a statutory provision. In *Air Jamaica v Charlton*,[107] it was held that surplus funds arising from the discontinuance of a pension scheme should be held on resulting trust for the employer and the employees who had contributed to the fund, in proportion to their contributions and regardless of any benefit that they had received from the fund. This is the better view: the fact that a member had received contractual benefits from the association should not prevent a resulting trust from arising.

Bona vacantia *to the Crown*

Where property is ownerless, it will be considered to be *bona vacantia* and will be transferred to the Crown. This consequence would arise where property has been held on trust for the purposes of an unincorporated association or its present members and, once the association has been dissolved, it is not possible to identify who transferred the property to the association, such as where a member who had paid subscriptions can no longer be identified. This solution was adopted in both *Cunnack v Edwards* and *Re West Sussex Constabulary's Widows, Children and Benevolent (1930) Fund Trusts*[108] once it had been recognized that property could not be held on resulting trust because the members had parted with their proprietary rights to the money paid. Similarly, in the latter case, the proceeds of raffles, sweepstakes, and entertainments, and money received from donors through collecting boxes, went to the Crown.[109]

Contractual entitlement

It is readily apparent that explaining what is to happen to the property given to an unincorporated association on its dissolution by reference to the resulting trust or *bona vacantia* is artificial and unsatisfactory. One of the key advantages of the contract-holding theory is that the consequences of dissolution are much easier to explain and understand. The consequence of that theory is that the assets belong to the members at the time of the dissolution according to their contractual rights under the rules of the association. Those rules may provide for a particular method of distribution of the assets on dissolution, which would be binding on the members. But, if no such provision is made, a term will be implied into the rules to the effect that the surplus should be distributed equally between the members at the time of the dissolution.[110] This is an application of the principle that 'Equity is equality'.[111]

[106] *Davis v Richards and Wallington Industries Ltd* [1990] 1 WLR 1511, 1542 (Scott J); *Air Jamaica Ltd v Charlton* [1999] 1 WLR 1399, 1412 (Lord Millett). [107] [1999] 1 WLR 1399.

[108] [1971] Ch 1.

[109] If this had been a charitable trust, such donations could have been applied cy-près. See Section 6.5.2, p. 182.

[110] *Re Bucks Constabulary Widows' and Orphans' Fund Friendly Society (No 2)* [1979] 1 WLR 936. The same approach will be adopted as regards distribution of the proceeds of sale amongst members even though the association has not been dissolved: *Re Horley Town Football Club* [2006] EWHC 2386 (Ch), [2006] WTLR 1817. See Section 7.4.3.(v), p. 199. [111] See Section 2.14, p. 36.

This operation of the contract-holding theory on the dissolution of an unincorporated association was considered in *Re Bucks Constabulary Widows' and Orphans' Fund Friendly Society (No 2)*,[112] which held that, where property is held by the members with reference to the contract governing the association, the property will belong to those who are members at the time of the dissolution and nobody else will have acquired any other rights in the property, except if other trusts have been validly declared of the property for the benefit of other people, or contractual arrangements have been entered into with others in respect of the property.[113] That case concerned an unincorporated association that provided for the relief of widows and orphans of deceased members of the Bucks Constabulary. Its funds were derived from voluntary contributions from its members. The Constabulary amalgamated with others and the Society was dissolved. The Society's rules did not provide for distribution of the assets on dissolution, so a term was implied into the rules that the assets should be distributed to those people who were members at the time of the dissolution. Previous members were not able to participate since, on ceasing to be members, they ceased to have any interest in the fund, because they were no longer party to the contract governing the members of the association.

The significance of the contract-holding theory to the distribution of surplus assets on the dissolution of the unincorporated association is particularly well illustrated by *Hanchett-Stamford v Attorney-General*,[114] which concerned the Performing and Captive Animals Defence League, an unincorporated association that was formed in 1914 to procure a ban on the use of performing animals. Eventually, the membership of the association dwindled to two. When the penultimate member died, there were substantial assets, including a property worth £675,000 and stocks and shares worth over £1.7 million. The question for the court was what should happen to this property. It was held that, since one of the association's purposes was to seek a change in the law, its purposes were not exclusively charitable and so the surplus funds could not be applied cy-près.[115] The association was held to have automatically dissolved on the death of the penultimate member, since the requirement that an association had two members was no longer met. It was further recognized that the assets available for the association's purposes belonged to the members beneficially subject to their contractual rights, which included the right to the assets on dissolution. Whilst the association was functioning, the members were precluded from severing their interests, but, on dissolution, the contractual restrictions fell away and those who were members at the time of the dissolution were entitled to the assets free from the contractual restrictions. It followed logically that the last surviving member was entitled to all of the assets rather than that those assets should be treated as ownerless.[116]

Where distribution of assets occurs by reference to the contract-holding theory, usually the assets will be distributed equally between the members at the time of the dissolution,[117] regardless of how long they have been members or the amount of subscriptions that they have paid.[118] But sometimes the terms of the contract between the members will result in a different form of distribution. For example, in *Re Sick and Funeral Society of St John's Sunday School, Golcar*,[119] a society had been formed at a Sunday school to provide for sickness and death benefits for its members, who could be teachers and children. Junior members under the age of 13 paid half the weekly subscription and received sickness benefits at half the rate. Following dissolution of the society, it was held that the effect of the rule of

---

[112] [1979] 1 WLR 936.   [113] Ibid., 940 (Walton J).   [114] [2008] EWHC 330 (Ch), [2009] Ch 173.

[115] See Section 6.4.2.(ii), p. 176.

[116] As Walton J had suggested, *obiter*, in *Re Bucks Constabulary Widows' and Orphans' Fund Friendly Society (No 2)* [1979] 1 WLR 936, 943.   [117] Ibid., 952.

[118] *Re GKN Bolts & Nuts Ltd etc Work Sports and Social Club* [1982] 1 WLR 774.   [119] [1973] Ch 51.

the association was that junior members were entitled to only a half-share of the assets as compared with the ordinary members. In addition, it was confirmed that members who had been excluded from the association by virtue of failing to pay their subscriptions were not entitled to share in the distribution of assets, even if they had paid the arrears of their subscriptions after the association had been dissolved. They would, however, have been able to share in the distribution had they paid the arrears before dissolution, because they would then have been members at the time of the dissolution.

(iii) Choosing between the different mechanisms

With the general recognition of the contract-holding theory of property-holding by unincorporated associations, it follows that there is very little scope for property to be held on resulting trust for those who transferred property to the association or to treat property as *bona vacantia* following the dissolution of an unincorporated association.

As regards the claims of the members to assets that they contributed in the form of subscriptions, for example, those assets will not be held on resulting trust for the present and past members where the contract-holding theory applies. This is because, when the members transfer property, such as by paying subscriptions, it becomes the property of all of the members of the association by virtue of the contract that binds them all. The effect of that contract is that only the members at the time of the dissolution will be entitled to share in the assets, unless the terms of the contract exclude the possibility of any such claim.[120] But, otherwise, the fact that the members at the time of the dissolution may have obtained benefits by virtue of their membership of the association will not prevent them from sharing in the distribution of the assets on dissolution. Where property has been transferred by third parties for the benefit of the association, that too will be distributed to the members at the time of the dissolution. The only situation in which such property would be held on resulting trust is where the property is transferred on trust for the purposes of the association and this is, exceptionally, a valid non-charitable purpose trust. The only situation in which the property could be treated as *bona vacantia* is where the last member of the association and their family cannot be identified.

---

[120] As in *Cunnack v Edwards* [1896] 2 Ch 769. See Section 7.4.4.(ii), p. 204.

PART IV

IMPLIED TRUSTS

8

RESULTING TRUSTS

8.1 GENERAL CONSIDERATIONS

8.1.1 THE NATURE OF THE RESULTING TRUST

A resulting trust arises where property has been transferred to the defendant and a recognized trigger for the trust occurs, which might arise at the time of transfer or subsequently, so that the property is then held by the defendant on trust for the claimant. The trust is called 'resulting' since the beneficial interest in the property returns, or 'results', back in Equity to the person who transferred the property in the first place.

It is an essential feature of a resulting trust that an interest in property has either been transferred to the defendant or created for the defendant.[1] Consequently, if the claimant purports to transfer property to the defendant but the disposition is unsuccessful, so that title and possession remains in the claimant and the defendant acquires no interest in the property, there is no interest that can be held on trust for the claimant.

The resulting trust is a real trust with property being held by a trustee for a beneficiary. The recognition of such a trust can be significant for the beneficiary because it means that the trustee will be personally liable to the beneficiary for breach of trust, such as where trust property is transferred to a third party, even though the trustee was not aware of the existence of the trust.[2] The beneficiary will also have an equitable proprietary interest in the trust property that may enable them to claim the property from the trustee or a third party who has received it. This will be significant where the trustee is insolvent, since the beneficiary of the trust will have a claim that ranks above those of other creditors of the trustee.[3]

---

[1] *Re Vandervell (No 2)* [1974] Ch 269, 289 (Megarry J).

[2] For analysis of personal liability for breach of trust, see Chapter 18 of this volume.

[3] See Section 19.1.3.(i), p. 538.

8.1.2 THE CATEGORIES OF RESULTING TRUST

The orthodox view of resulting trusts is that they are of limited significance[4] and operate only within two recognized categories.[5]

(i) Presumed resulting trusts

Where the claimant transfers property to the defendant or purchases property that is vested in the defendant's name alone or in joint names, and the claimant does not receive any consideration for this transaction from the defendant, who is consequently a volunteer, it will be presumed that the defendant holds the property on resulting trust for the claimant.[6]

(ii) Automatic resulting trusts

Where property has been transferred to the defendant to be held on an express trust that fails, either initially or subsequently, that property will be held on resulting trust for the settlor or those entitled to the testator's residuary estate. Since the property was transferred on trust, the resulting trust does not operate to establish that the transferee holds the property as trustee, but operates instead simply to establish that the trustee now holds the property on trust for the settlor or those entitled to the testator's residuary estate.[7]

(iii) Other categories of resulting trust?

The resulting trust has been recognized in other situations as well, such as where property has been transferred pursuant to a contract that has been rescinded[8] and where property has been transferred for a specific purpose that has failed.[9] The analysis of these situations is more controversial, since the trust that arises might not be a resulting trust, but might be some other form of trust, although the preferable view is that only the latter scenario involves a resulting trust. It has also been argued that, in most cases in which a defendant has been unjustly enriched at the expense of the claimant, any property received by the defendant should be held on resulting trust for the claimant. If this were correct, it would dramatically expand the operation of the resulting trust, and the preferable view is that, for this and other reasons, the resulting trust should not be triggered by the defendant's unjust enrichment.[10]

8.1.3 THEORETICAL FOUNDATION OF THE RESULTING TRUST

Although resulting trusts have long been recognized, the theoretical foundation for their recognition remains highly controversial.

(i) The significance of intention

Although the courts have distinguished between automatic and presumed resulting trusts, in *Westdeutsche Landesbank Girozentrale v Islington LBC*,[11] Lord Browne-Wilkinson

---

[4] See Rickett and Grantham, 'Resulting trusts: a rather limited doctrine', in *Restitution and Equity*, Vol. 1: *Resulting Trusts and Equitable Compensation*, ed. Birks and Rose (Oxford: Mansfield Press, 2000), p. 59; Tettenborn, 'Resulting trusts and insolvency', in *Restitution and Insolvency*, ed. Rose (London: Mansfield Press, 2000), p. 167.

[5] See *Re Vandervell (No 2)* [1974] Ch 269, 289 (Megarry J); *Westdeutsche Landesbank Girozentrale v Islington LBC* [1996] AC 669, 689 (Lord Goff) and 708 (Lord Browne-Wilkinson).

[6] *Tinsley v Milligan* [1994] 1 AC 340, 371 (Lord Browne-Wilkinson); *Chen v Ng* [2017] UKPC 27, [27]: an agreed statement of the parties that consideration had been paid was held to be non-binding, because it was untrue, had not been relied on, and was intended only to benefit one party.

[7] *Tinsley v Milligan* [1994] 1 AC 340, 371 (Lord Browne-Wilkinson).   [8] See Section 8.5.2, p. 252.

[9] See Section 8.4, p. 239.   [10] See Section 8.5.1, p. 249.   [11] [1996] AC 669, 708.

suggested, *obiter*, that all resulting trusts should be considered to be presumed trusts. He said that:

> Both types of resulting trust are traditionally regarded as examples of trusts giving effect to the common intention of the parties. A resulting trust is not imposed by law against the intentions of the trustee (as is a constructive trust) but gives effect to his presumed intention.

This has proved to be a significant dictum that might provide a coherent explanation of all resulting trusts.[12] The dictum itself is, however, rather confused. First, the reference to the common intention of the parties cannot be correct. Such a common intention has proved significant to the common intention constructive trust, which is largely concerned with determining the beneficial interests of cohabiting couples in the family home,[13] but not to the resulting trust. Secondly, if intention is relevant to explain when a resulting trust is recognized, it cannot be the intention of the trustee that applies; the only relevant intention should be that of the transferor, who is effectively in the position of the settlor of the trust. Thirdly, if an intention is presumed, it is not clear what the transferor is being presumed to have intended.

In fact, the intention of the transferor is significant for the proper analysis of all resulting trusts.[14] For a resulting trust to be recognized, the transferor should intend that the property be held on trust for them in certain circumstances. There are five different ways of establishing such an intention, some of which might be relevant to the resulting trust.

Express intention

If the transferor of property expressly intends the transferee to hold the property on trust for them, this trust will not be resulting, but will be a straightforward express trust.

Inferred intention

There will be circumstances under which it is not possible to prove an express intention on the part of the transferor that property should be held on trust for them, but it might be possible to infer such an intent having regard to all of the circumstances of the case. Again, the trust that arises is properly analysed as an express trust, because an inferred intent is an actual intent.[15] But an inferred intention must still be proved. As Megarry J said in *Re Vandervell's Trusts (No 2)*:[16] '[T]he mere existence of some unexpressed intention in the breast of the owner of the property does nothing: there must at least be some expression of that intention before it can effect any result.' But this intention need not be expressed formally; it can be deduced from the evidence. As Lord Neuberger has said: 'An inferred intention is one which is objectively deduced to be the subjective actual intention of a party in the light of their actions and statements; it involves concluding what a party intended.'[17]

---

[12] See further Section 8.1.3.(ii), p. 215.

[13] See Chapter 10 of this volume. It appears that the resulting trust has no role to play in respect of the family home, see Section 8.2.2, p. 221.

[14] *Westdeutsche Landesbank Girozentrale v Islington LBC* [1996] AC 669, 708 (Lord Browne-Wilkinson). Compare constructive trusts that are imposed by law regardless of the claimant's intention. See Chapter 9 of this volume.

[15] *Jones v Kernott* [2011] UKSC 53, [2012] 1 AC 776, [51](3) (Lady Hale and Lord Walker).

[16] [1974] Ch 269, 294.

[17] *Stack v Dowden* [2007] UKHL 17, [2007] 2 AC 432, [126]. See also *Jones v Kernott* [2011] UKSC 53, [2012] 1 AC 776, [51](3) (Lady Hale and Lord Walker). See further Section 10.2.2.(iv), p. 287.

Imputed intention

Whereas an inferred intention involves determining what a party did actually intend, an imputed intention involves concluding what a party would have intended had they considered the matter.[18] An intention that property should be held on resulting trust may be imputed to the transferor where it is possible to conclude that this is what the transferor would have intended had they thought about the consequences of the transfer, such as that the transaction might fail in whole or in part. This imputed intention arises by operation of law rather than proven fact. An imputed intention is attributable to a party even though they had no such actual intention, and even though it cannot be deduced from their actions and statements.[19] Whilst a majority of the Justices in the Supreme Court in *Jones v Kernott* recognized that there was a conceptual difference between the inference and imputation of intention, they considered that the difference in practice might not be great.[20]

Presumed intention

A legal presumption arises where proving one fact enables another fact to be found without needing to adduce any evidence to prove that other fact.[21] This presumed fact can then be rebutted by the other party adducing evidence that contradicts it. A fact is presumed because it reflects common experience and is a consensus of judicial opinion as to the most likely inference to be drawn in the absence of any evidence to the contrary.[22] So, proof of one fact may be sufficient to trigger a presumption that the transferor intended property to be held on trust for them. An imputed intent and a presumed intent are similar, since both are recognized by operation of law and reflect common experience. But, whereas an imputed intent is irrebuttable, a presumed intent might be rebutted by contrary evidence.

In the context of resulting trusts, the proof of a particular type of transaction, such as a voluntary transfer of property, will trigger a legal presumption that the transferor intended the property to be held on trust for them;[23] this intention would be the fact that is presumed following proof of the fact that the transaction had occurred. The legal presumption of an intention to declare a trust would not need to be invoked, however, where the transferor was able to adduce evidence to establish an express or implied intention that a trust should be declared. In other words, intention will be presumed only where there is a gap in the evidence, but common experience suggests that it would have been likely that the transferor would have had such an intention.

Absence of intention

Finally, rather than a positive intent that property should be held on trust for the transferor being proved, implied, imputed, or presumed, it may simply be sufficient to show that the transferor did not intend the recipient to benefit from the receipt of the property, either because the necessary intention was absent or had been vitiated. This analysis of intention has been developed by commentators[24] and was specifically recognized by Lord Millett in *Air Jamaica v Charlton*,[25] albeit in giving the advice of the Privy Council. He also

---

[18] *Jones v Kernott* [2011] UKSC 53, [2012] 1 AC 776, [47] (Lady Hale and Lord Walker). See also Lord Kerr, [73], who described this as an attribution of intention.

[19] *Stack v Dowden* [2007] UKHL 17, [2007] 2 AC 432, [126] (Lord Neuberger).

[20] [2011] UKSC 53, [2012] 1 AC 776, [34] (Lady Hale and Lord Walker), [58] (Lord Collins). This was not the view of the dissenting Justices, Lords Kerr and Wilson. See further Section 10.2.2.(iv), p. 290.

[21] Swadling, 'Explaining resulting trusts' (2008) 124 LQR 72, 74.   [22] *Pettit v Pettit* [1970] AC 777, 823.

[23] Swadling, 'A new role for resulting trusts?' (1996) 16 LS 110, 116.

[24] Notably, Birks, 'Trusts raised to reverse unjust enrichment: the *Westdeutsche* case' [1996] 4 RLR 3 and Chambers, *Resulting Trusts* (Oxford: Clarendon Press, 1997), p. 8.   [25] [1999] 1 WLR 1399, 1412.

recognized this theory in *Twinsectra Ltd v Yardley*,[26] but none of the other judges considered it. In *Air Jamaica*, he said:[27]

> Like a constructive trust, a resulting trust arises by operation of law, though unlike a constructive trust it gives effect to intention. But it arises whether or not the transferor intended to retain a beneficial interest—he almost always does not—since it responds to the absence of any intention on his part to pass a beneficial interest to the recipient.

Such an absence of intention to benefit could itself be express, inferred, imputed, or presumed, so this is not necessarily a distinct method of establishing intention; rather, it is a different type of intention that can be established by reference to any of these four methods.

(ii) Intention and the categories of resulting trust

It is clear that an express or implied intention that property should be held on trust for the transferor cannot be used to explain the operation of the resulting trust, simply because proof of such an intent establishes an express trust. But the other three forms of intent can be of use to explain the operation of these trusts.

Presumed resulting trust

Although presumed resulting trusts are clearly established in the law, it is important to be clear about what it is that is being presumed. The presumption might simply be of a resulting trust, but that would be incorrect because legal presumptions involve presumptions of fact and a presumption that a resulting trust exists would be a presumption of a legal response rather than fact.[28] It has, anyway, been recognized that the presumption of resulting trust is not a rule of law, but a presumption of intention.[29] So, what is the transferor presumed to intend? The presumption is preferably analysed as being that, where the claimant has voluntarily transferred property to the defendant or paid the purchase price for property held by the defendant, the claimant intended the property to be held on trust for themself. This is what Mee has described as being a presumed intention to make the transferee trustee for the transferor.[30] This is a presumption that can be rebutted by the transferee of the property adducing evidence that the transferor did not intend the property to be held on trust, for example by showing that the transferor intended to make a gift.

Chambers fits the presumed resulting trust into his theory that all resulting trusts respond to the absence of an intention to benefit the defendant by treating the presumption as being that the claimant did not intend the transfer of a property to be an absolute gift to the defendant, rather than a presumption that the claimant intended the property to be held on trust.[31] Whether the presumption is analysed as an absence of intent to benefit or a positive intent that the property will be held on trust will make no difference to the result in most cases: these are simply different sides of the same coin. If the claimant is presumed to have intended property to be held on trust for themself so that the claimant

---

[26] [2002] UKHL 12, [2002] 2 AC 164, 190. See also *Prest v Petrodel Resources Ltd* [2013] UKSC 34, [2013] 2 AC 415, [49].

[27] [1999] 1 WLR 1399, 1412. This analysis was endorsed by the Singapore Court of Appeal in *Chan Yuen Lan v See Fong Mun* [2014] SGCA 36, [44]. [28] Swadling (see n. 21), p. 79.

[29] *Stack v Dowden* [2007] UKHL 17, [2007] 2 AC 432, [60] (Baroness Hale); *Jones v Kernott* [2011] UKSC 53, [2012] 1 AC 776 (Lord Walker and Lady Hale).

[30] 'Presumed resulting trusts, intention and declaration' (2014) 73 CLJ 86. Swadling (see n. 21) considers instead that the presumption is of an express declaration of trust, which Mee convincingly argues is not consistent with the state of the authorities. [31] Chambers (see n. 24), p. 21.

has a beneficial interest in it, the claimant could also be presumed not to intend the defendant to benefit from the property. Consequently, in this context at least, the debate about whether resulting trusts should be analysed by presuming a positive intention to declare a trust or an absence of intention to benefit is largely sterile since it generally makes no difference to the result. But there is a very significant doctrinal problem with explaining the presumed resulting trust with reference to the absence-of-intent theory, namely whether a presumption of an absence to benefit should be sufficient to create a resulting trust in all cases. Where, for example, the claimant has transferred property to the defendant by mistake, the fact that might be presumed from the circumstances of the transfer is the absence of an intention to benefit the defendant. But it does not follow from this presumption of fact that the property should be held on resulting trust for the mistaken transferor, rather than there simply being a personal liability to return the value of the property transferred. Another presumption would be needed that the property is held on resulting trust, but that would be a presumption of law and so an invalid presumption. These difficulties can be avoided by analysing the presumption as being a positive fact, namely an intention that the property should be held on trust for the transferor.

Automatic resulting trust

Swadling has been unable to identify a rationale for the recognition of automatic resulting trusts where an express trust has failed, and he has concluded that such trusts defy legal analysis.[32] He considered that this category of resulting trust cannot be explained by relying on a presumption of an intention to declare a trust, because this category of resulting trust simply arises by operation of law where an express trust has failed, and no additional facts are required to be proved.[33]

Those commentators who have propounded the 'absence of intent to benefit' explanation of the resulting trust explain the automatic resulting trust simply on the basis that the claimant will not have intended the defendant to benefit from the receipt of the trust property where the trust has failed. Swadling[34] has rightly criticized this, since the theory does not explain why property should be held on a resulting trust rather than there simply being a personal liability to restore the value of property to the claimant.

It is possible, however, to explain the recognition of automatic resulting trusts without referring either to presumed intent or absence of intent.[35] Rather, the automatic resulting trust should be considered to arise by operation of the law imputing an intention that, in the circumstances that have happened, a trust would be declared for the claimant. This imputed intention does not purport to reflect what the claimant did intend, but rather what the claimant can objectively be considered to have intended if they had considered the possibility of the express trust failing. This might be described as being the same as a presumed intent, but an imputed intention is irrebuttable and responds to the legal consequence of an express trust having failed. That the automatic resulting trust responds to an imputed intention was effectively recognized by Harman J in *Re Gillingham Bus Disaster Fund*,[36] in which the surplus of a fund was held on resulting trust for those who had made donations to it. It was held that the recognition of an automatic resulting trust does not rest on the state of mind of the transferor, since, in most cases, the transferor does not expect the money to be returned, but the trust arises where the expectation of the transferor that the trust will absorb the fund completely is 'for some unforeseen reason cheated of fruition, and is an inference of law based on after-knowledge of the event'.

---

[32] Swadling (see n. 21), p. 102.   [33] Ibid., 95.   [34] Ibid., 99.
[35] See further Section 8.3.1.(iii), p. 230.   [36] [1958] Ch 300, 310. See Section 8.3.2.(iii), p. 237.

Other categories of resulting trust

If lack of intention that the defendant should benefit from the receipt of the property does form the theoretical foundation for the recognition of the resulting trust, it would follow logically that such a trust might be recognized in any case in which the claimant's intention to benefit the defendant can be regarded as vitiated, such as where the claimant has transferred property to the defendant by mistake, or as the result of duress, or on a basis that has subsequently failed totally. This would dramatically expand the operation of the resulting trust and would have unsettling effects on the rights of third parties and the security of commercial transactions.[37] Whether such an expansion of the role of the resulting trust is defensible will be considered at the end of this chapter, but for now it is sufficient to conclude that the absence-of-intention analysis has received the judicial support only of Lord Millett and is plainly inconsistent with the classical[38] analysis of such trusts adopted by Lord Browne-Wilkinson in *Westdeutsche Landesbank*,[39] in which the focus was on a positive intent that such a trust be declared, albeit one that is presumed.

(iii) Summary

The presumptions and rules relating to the recognition of resulting trusts are preferably analysed as being a 'default mechanism to fill in evidential lacunae as to the location of the beneficial interest'[40] either where the claimant has voluntarily transferred property or provided money to buy property, or where an express trust can be considered to have failed. Resulting trusts should be regarded as responding to a positive intention on the part of the transferor of property, albeit an intention that is either presumed or imputed depending on the context in which the resulting trust arises.

8.2 PRESUMED RESULTING TRUSTS

Where the claimant has transferred property to the defendant or paid the purchase price for property that has been acquired by the defendant, it will be presumed that the claimant intended the defendant to hold that property on trust for them. The justification for this presumption is that Equity assumes that people do not act altruistically, but rather with some degree of self-interest and an expectation of some return,[41] so that they would wish to obtain a beneficial interest in the property received by the defendant.[42] But this presumption of an intention to declare a trust can be easily rebutted by the transferee showing that the transferor did intend the transferee to take the property beneficially, for example by proving that the transferee was intended to receive the property absolutely as a gift.[43] Such a donative intention will itself be presumed, in the form of the presumption of advancement, where the relationship between the transferor and the transferee is such that the transferor bears some responsibility for the transferee, so that a gift is likely to have been intended. But this presumption of advancement can also be rebutted by the transferor proving that no gift was intended.

---

[37] Consequences acknowledged by the Singapore Court of Appeal in *Chan Yuen Lan v See Fong Man* [2014] SGCA 36, [48], even though that court adopted the absence-of-intention analysis of the resulting trust.

[38] The word used by Raja JA, ibid., [40].   [39] [1996] AC 669, 708. See also Lord Goff, 689.

[40] Rickett and Grantham, 'Resulting trusts: the true nature of the failing trust cases' (2000) 116 LQR 15, 20.

[41] Note the principle that 'Equity is cynical'. See Section 2.8, p. 33.

[42] See *Stack v Dowden* [2007] UKHL 17, [2007] 2 AC 432, [60] (Baroness Hale).

[43] *Westdeutsche Landesbank Girozentrale v Islington LBC* [1996] AC 669, 708 (Lord Browne-Wilkinson).

The practical effect of these different presumptions relates to the allocation of the onus of proof.[44] Where the transferor has invoked the presumption of resulting trust by establishing a transfer of property or contribution to the purchase price for which the transferee had provided no consideration,[45] the burden will then be placed on the transferee to show that a gift was intended. Where the presumption of advancement applies, the burden will be on the transferor to show that they intended to have a beneficial interest in the property.

8.2.1 VOLUNTARY TRANSFER OF PROPERTY

Where the claimant transfers property to the defendant or directs a trustee for the claimant to transfer property to the defendant, and the transfer is for no consideration, whether the property is presumed to be held on resulting trust for the claimant might depend on the nature of the property that has been transferred.

(i) Land

Where the claimant voluntarily transfers land to the defendant, it has sometimes been assumed that there is no presumption of resulting trust, by virtue of section 60(3) of the Law of Property Act 1925, which states: 'In a voluntary conveyance a resulting trust for the grantor shall not be implied merely by reason that the property is not expressed to be conveyed for the use or benefit of the grantee.' Although somewhat opaque in meaning, the effect of this provision might be to disapply a presumption of resulting trust where land is conveyed to the defendant (the grantee) for no consideration, simply because the conveyance did not state that the property was conveyed for the defendant's use or benefit. The better view, however,[46] is that this provision is simply a statutory reminder to conveyancers that a resulting trust will not be implied simply because a conveyance of property does not expressly state that the property is for the use or benefit of the grantee. The provision has no effect on whether or not a resulting trust of land will be presumed where the transferor voluntarily conveys it to the transferee.

(ii) Personalty

A resulting trust can certainly be presumed where personalty, such as shares and money, is voluntarily transferred to the defendant. In such circumstances, there are three separate principles that need to be considered:

(1) If the claimant asserts that they intended the defendant to take the property beneficially, that is the end of the matter; there can be no trust and the presumption of resulting trust will not be engaged. If the claimant intended the property to be held by the defendant on trust for the claimant or for a third party, the property will be held on an express trust

---

[44] *Russell v Scott* (1936) 55 CLR 440, 451 (Dixon and Evatt JJ).

[45] *Sayre v Hughes* (1868) LR 5 Eq 376, 380 (Stuart VC); *Re Vandervell's Trusts (No 2)* [1974] Ch 269, 294 (Megarry J). But Penner, 'Resulting trusts and unjust enrichment: three controversies', in *Constructive and Resulting Trusts*, ed. Mitchell (Oxford: Hart, 2010), p. 240, suggests that the transferor does not need to prove that the transaction was for no consideration; any transfer will suffice to invoke the presumption, even if the transferor was contractually obliged to make it or to contribute to the purchase price. But, where the transferor was liable to transfer the property or to contribute to the purchase price, the presumption will be easily rebutted by the transferee. The better view, however, is that the transferor does need to prove that the transferee did not provide consideration, for it is the fact that the transaction is a gift that triggers Equity's cynical suspicions about the possible exploitation of the donor by the donee.

[46] Swadling, 'A hard look at *Hodgson v Marks*', in *Restitution and Equity*, Vol. 1: *Resulting Trusts and Equitable Compensation*, ed Birks and Rose (London: Mansfield Press, 2000), p. 74.

and the presumption of a resulting trust is irrelevant. Being an express trust of personalty, writing is not required.[47]

(2) If the claimant does not assert that they intended the defendant to receive the property beneficially, there will be a presumed resulting trust in favour of the claimant, unless the relationship between the claimant and defendant is such that the presumption of advancement is engaged.[48]

(3) Where the presumption of an intention that the property is held on trust is engaged, the defendant can seek to rebut it by adducing evidence of relevant facts and circumstances to conclude that the claimant did not intend the property to be held on trust for them, such as that it was intended to be an outright transfer by way of gift.

These three principles were recognized in *Aroso v Coutts and Co*,[49] in which it was also acknowledged that the presumption of resulting trust is easily rebutted. The application of the principles is illustrated by the facts of that case. A father had allowed his children to draw money from his bank account. After a family row, he revoked this power, and transferred his money to a new bank account for himself and his nephew. The father died and his children claimed that the money credited to the bank account was held on resulting trust by the nephew for their father's estate, to which they were entitled as his next of kin. It was recognized that the money was held on a presumed resulting trust because the nephew had given no consideration for the transfer of assets into the joint names of himself and his uncle. The nephew was, however, able to rebut this presumption by relying on the mandate form, which clearly expressed an intention that the money should be held by them both jointly and that the survivor was to take beneficially.

In *Re Vinogradoff*,[50] a grandmother transferred £800 stock into her own name and that of her granddaughter, who was 4 years old. It was held that the presumption of resulting trust applied and had not been rebutted, so that they both held the stock on trust for the grandmother and it was irrelevant that the granddaughter was a child, who could not have held the property as an express trustee.[51] This result is difficult to defend, since, even if the presumption of resulting trust was applicable in such a case, the granddaughter should have been able to rebut it on the ground that, by virtue of her youth, her grandmother could not have intended her to hold the property on trust for them both.

The presumption of resulting trust should also be relevant where the claimant has transferred property to the defendant for no consideration, but the transfer is involuntary, such as where the defendant has stolen money from the claimant. Although normally in such a case the defendant will hold the property on constructive trust, because of their unconscionable conduct in obtaining the property,[52] there is no reason why the presumption of resulting trust cannot be engaged because the property has been transferred for no consideration in return.[53] The defendant might, however, seek to rebut the presumption by pleading that the claimant was unaware of the transfer and so could not have intended the property to be held on trust, but the success of this plea will turn on whether it is considered to be appropriate for the defendant to rely on the illegality of the transfer to rebut the presumption, which will turn on the court's analysis of the facts.[54]

---

[47] See Section 5.2.1.(i), p. 105.   [48] See Section 8.2.4, p. 222.
[49] [2001] 1 WTLR 797, 806 (Lawrence Collins J).   [50] [1935] WN 68.
[51] Law of Property Act 1925, s. 20. See Section 12.4.1, p. 347.   [52] See Section 9.3.1, p. 258.
[53] Tettenborn (see n. 4), p. 165.   [54] See Section 8.2.5, p. 224.

8.2.2 PURCHASE IN THE NAME OF ANOTHER

Where the claimant buys property in the name of the defendant, it is presumed that the property will be held on resulting trust for the claimant. Similarly, where the claimant has contributed to the purchase price of property that is in the name of the defendant, that property will be presumed to be held on resulting trust for the claimant in shares proportionate to their contribution.[55] This presumption applies regardless of the nature of the property.[56] The presumption will be rebutted either by establishing that the presumption of advancement applies by virtue of the relationship between the claimant and defendant, or by the defendant adducing evidence that the claimant intended the defendant to receive the property outright, such as where it was intended to be a gift. The evidence that will be required to rebut the presumption will depend on the circumstances of the case.[57] In some cases, the presumption of resulting trust will be strong and difficult to rebut, such as where the claimant has invested their money in shares that are registered in the name of their solicitor; it will be difficult to establish that the claimant intended the solicitor to receive the shares as a gift. But, in other circumstances, the relationship between the parties, whilst not sufficient to establish a presumption of advancement, will suggest that a gift is more likely to have been intended. In *Fowkes v Pascoe*,[58] for example, a woman had purchased annuities in the joint names of herself and her daughter-in-law's son. Although it was presumed that he held the annuities on resulting trust, this presumption was easily rebutted in the light of the circumstances of the case, which included that the woman was wealthy, he was living in her house, and she was already providing for him financially. All of this suggested that she had intended him to have a beneficial interest in the annuity.

The practical importance of the presumption of resulting trust is particularly well illustrated by *Abrahams v Trustee in Bankruptcy of Abrahams*,[59] in which a wife had paid her own share and that of her estranged husband in purchasing a winning National Lottery ticket. It was held that there was nothing to rebut the presumption of resulting trust, so that all of the winnings were held on trust for her.[60]

In the cases that we have considered so far, the claimant paid money directly for the purchase of property, whether an annuity or a share of a ticket. Will the presumption of resulting trust apply where the claimant has provided value, but it contributes only indirectly to the purchase of property? The presumed resulting trust arises at the date on which the property is acquired, so it is at that point that it is necessary to consider whether the claimant has provided or contributed to the purchase price.[61] It has been recognized that, where a party obtains a discount on the purchase price by exercising a statutory right to buy property, this can be treated as a financial contribution by that party to the purchase price.[62] Similarly, it has been recognized that, where the claimant is the mortgagor who has borrowed money that is to be used in the purchase of the property, they are to be treated as having contributed the proportion of the purchase price that is attributable to the amount borrowed.[63] If, however, the claimant is not the mortgagor, but they make subsequent

---

[55] *Westdeutsche Landesbank Girozentrale v Islington LBC* [1996] AC 669, 708 (Lord Browne-Wilkinson).

[56] Section 60(3) of the Law of Property Act 1925 will not apply.

[57] *Fowkes v Pascoe* (1875) 10 Ch App 343.   [58] Ibid.   [59] [2000] WTLR 593.

[60] If the parties were reversed so that the husband had paid for his wife's share, the presumption of advancement would have been applicable. See Section 8.2.4, p. 222.

[61] *Curley v Parkes* [2004] EWCA Civ 1515, [14] (Gibson LJ).

[62] *Laskar v Laskar* [2008] EWCA Civ 347, [2008] 1 WLR 2695.

[63] *Curley v Parkes* [2004] EWCA Civ 1515, [14] (Gibson LJ). See also *Carlton v Goodman* [2002] EWCA Civ 545, [2002] 2 FLR 259; *McKenzie v McKenzie* [2003] 2 P & CR DG6.

contributions to discharge the mortgage loan, this will not be regarded as a relevant contribution to the purchase price to enable a resulting trust to be presumed, since it is the obtaining of the mortgage loan that is considered to be the contribution to the purchase price and not the repayment of that loan.[64] The significance of this distinction was considered in *Laskar v Laskar*.[65] In that case the defendant had bought her council house with her daughter. They were jointly and separately liable on the mortgage, the daughter being included because the mother could not otherwise have obtained the mortgage. The property was purchased as an investment, and rent from tenants who leased the property was used to pay the mortgage instalments. It was recognized that the presumption of resulting trust applied[66] and, since both mother and daughter were jointly liable on the mortgage, it followed that they were deemed to have contributed the loan money equally, even though there was no expectation that the daughter would actually have to pay anything. This was justified because there was no agreement or understanding between them that one of them would be responsible for repayment and because the use of the rent obtained from the property to repay the mortgage affected both of them equally, so their beneficial interest should be apportioned accordingly. In fact, the daughter obtained a one-third beneficial interest and the mother two-thirds, because the mother had also contributed a statutory discount on the purchase price for the property by virtue of her being a tenant of a council house.

More remote contributions to the purchase price will not, however, be sufficient to give rise to the presumption of a resulting trust. So, for example, payment of household bills by one party to enable the other to pay the mortgage will not suffice,[67] neither will non-financial contributions to the running and maintenance of the family home.[68] It is for this reason that the resulting trust has proved to be of very limited significance in determining the allocation of property rights in the family home following the breakdown of a relationship between cohabiting parties, where one party has paid the purchase price and the other has made other contributions, often non-financial. Different doctrines have been developed to deal with that problem.[69] It has now been recognized that, where a couple are joint legal owners of the family home, the presumptions of resulting trust and advancement should not be used to determine their beneficial interests in the property.[70] This has subsequently been extended to where the property has been registered in the name of one party only,[71] and even where the property has been purchased as an investment rather than a family home.[72]

8.2.3 TRANSFER TO A COMPANY

The presumption of resulting trust has also been invoked where property is held by a company which is controlled by one person who had either transferred the property to the company or provided the consideration for its purchase. This was recognized in *Prest v Petrodel Resources Ltd*,[73] which arose from a claim for ancillary relief on divorce. The wife claimed that her husband had used various offshore companies, which he controlled

---

[64] Piska, 'Distinctions without a difference? Explaining *Stack v Dowden*' [2008] Conv 451, 459.

[65] [2008] EWCA Civ 347, [2008] 1 WLR 2695.

[66] Although this is now more likely to be treated as a common intention constructive trust. See *Marr v Collie* [2017] UKPC 17, [2017] 3 WLR 1507. Section 10.2.4(iv), p. 295.　　　　[67] *Gissing v Gissing* [1971] AC 886.

[68] *Burns v Burns* [1984] Ch 317. See further Chapter 10.　　　[69] See Chapter 10.

[70] *Stack v Dowden* [2007] UKHL 17, [2007] 2 AC 432. See Section 10.2.4.(ii), p. 294.

[71] *Abbott v Abbott* [2007] UKPC 53. See Section 10.2.4.(i), p. 293.

[72] *Marr v Collie* [2017] UKPC 17, [2017] 3 WLR 1507. See Section 10.2.4(iv), p. 295..

[73] [2013] UKSC 34, [2013] 2 AC 415.

and in which he owned all the shares, to hold the legal title to seven residential properties. The Supreme Court recognized that it was not possible to pierce the corporate veil, but the properties were held by the companies on trust for the husband, who consequently had a beneficial interest in them which enabled them to be transferred to the wife as ancillary relief. Lord Sumption, with whom the other Justices concurred, recognized that this was an ordinary presumed resulting trust, the presumption being that the companies were not intended to acquire a beneficial interest in the properties. Both forms of the presumption of resulting trust were applicable. Some of the properties were transferred by the husband for nominal consideration, which triggered the voluntary transfer presumption. Other properties were purchased by the companies, with consideration provided by the husband, which triggered the purchase money resulting trust. Neither presumption had been rebutted.[74]

But the operation of the presumptions of resulting trust where property has been obtained by a company, such that the company holds the property on trust for its controller, is not without difficulty. The application of the presumptions in *Prest* required careful consideration of what was being presumed and, crucially, why; but such analysis was lacking in the case. It has already been seen that what is being presumed is that the transferor or payer does not intend to benefit the recipient, because they should be assumed to be acting for reasons of self-interest rather than altruisitically in transferring the property or paying the money, but is presumed to have intended the recipient to hold the property on trust for the transferor or payer. But where the property is transferred or the money is paid for the benefit of a company which the transferor or payer controls, then, even though the company has a separate legal personality, the transferor or payer benefits from the property being received by the company, since the value of the controller's shares will have increased. Crucially, the controller will be no worse off after transferring the property or paying the purchase price. Consequently, it does not follow that the controller did not intend to benefit the company and it might even be a more appropriate presumption that they did so intend. The only justification for the deployment of the presumptions in *Prest* was because of the peculiar fact pattern, involving a husband whose conduct throughout the litigation had been silent and obstructive, since he was clearly seeking to hide assets from his wife, such that it was appropriate to infer that he did not intend his companies to benefit from the properties. Indeed, Lord Sumption recognized that these types of case were highly fact sensitive.[75] But such policy-motivated decision-making is more consistent with the family law context of the litigation, rather than the doctrinal elegance and principle of the law of trusts within the equitable jurisdiction.

8.2.4 PRESUMPTION OF ADVANCEMENT

Where the transferor of property or the contributor of the purchase price is the husband,[76] fiancé,[77] father,[78] or a person who stands *in loco parentis*[79] of the recipient of the property, it is presumed that a gift was intended. This is known as the 'presumption of advancement'.[80] The presumption has not been applied where property has been transferred to or purchased for a mistress,[81] or where a wife purchases property for her husband,[82] or a

---

[74] Ibid., [49].   [75] Ibid., [52].   [76] *Tinker v Tinker* [1970] P 136.
[77] Law Reform (Miscellaneous Provisions) Act 1970, s. 2 (1).   [78] *Grey v Grey* (1677) 2 Swans 594.
[79] *Bennet v Bennet* (1879) 10 Ch D 474.
[80] Glister, 'The presumption of advancement', in *Constructive and Resulting Trusts*, ed. Mitchell (Oxford: Hart, 2010), ch. 10.   [81] *Lowson v Coombes* [1999] Ch 373.
[82] *Heseltine v Heseltine* [1971] 1 WLR 342.

mother for her child.[83] The presumption does not apply where property has been trans-ferred into the joint names of a husband and wife, since the common intention construc-tive trust will apply instead.[84]

Although the presumption of advancement may once have been justified as reflecting common experience because of the moral obligation of one person to make provision to advance another and set them up in life,[85] it is increasingly difficult to defend both in its general application and its discriminatory effect as between men and women. The pre-sumption of advancement was abolished by section 199 of the Equality Act 2010, although the relevant provision is not yet in force, and there is no sign that the Government intends to bring it into force; so it remains important to be aware of the nature and operation of the presumption.

Although it has been recognized that the presumption of advancement can be rebutted by comparatively slight evidence of a contrary intention not to make a gift,[86] it can only be re-butted by acts and declarations of the parties, but, as regards declarations, only if it was made before, during, or immediately after the time the property was purchased or transferred, and only then if it constituted part of the transaction of purchase or transfer.[87] A declaration made by a party after the transaction and which did not form part of that transaction can still be admitted to rebut the presumption of advancement, but only if it operates against the interests of the person making the declaration and not in their favour. If such subsequent declarations were admitted in favour of the person declaring them, it would be easy for a party to manufacture evidence to further their own interests. The operation of these prin-ciples relating to the rebuttal of the presumption is illustrated by *Shephard v Cartwright*,[88] in which a father had purchased shares that were registered in the names of his children. The shares were sold and the proceeds deposited for the benefit of the children. The presumption of advancement was consequently engaged. Five years later, the father procured the written consent of the children to enable him to withdraw money from their deposit account. The children were not aware of what they had signed. The question for the court was whether this document was sufficient to rebut the presumption of advancement. Since this was evi-dence that did not form part of the original transaction, it could be admitted only if it was evidence of the children admitting that their father had not intended a gift. But, since the children were not aware of what they had signed, it could not be used in this way. This can be contrasted with *Warren v Gurney*,[89] in which a father had purchased a house and conveyed it to one of his daughters. The presumption of advancement was rebutted by contemporane-ous declarations of the father to the effect that a gift was not intended and by the fact that he had retained the title deeds to the property. Similarly, in *McGrath v Wallis*,[90] a family home was acquired and was conveyed into the name of the son since, because the father was unemployed, only the son was acceptable as the mortgagor. At the time of the transfer, a declaration of trust had been drafted indicating that the father was to have an 80 per cent beneficial interest and the son 20 per cent. This had not been signed and so it was not a valid declaration of trust, but it was sufficient to rebut the presumption of advancement.

---

[83] Although the presumption has been applied in such circumstances in Australia (*Nelson v Nelson* (1995) 132 ALR 133) and, in England, Neuberger LJ, in *Laskar v Laskar* [2008] EWCA Civ 347, [2008] 1 WLR 2695, [20], acknowledged that the presumption might apply as between mother and child, but it would be a weak presumption, especially where the child was over the age of 18 and managed their own affairs.

[84] *Gibson v Revenue and Customs Prosecution Office* [2008] EWCA Civ 645, [2008] 2 FLR 1672, [27] (Arden LJ). See Section 10.2, p. 284.   [85] *Bennet v Bennet* (1879) 10 Ch D 474, 476 (Sir George Jessel MR).

[86] *Pettit v Pettit* [1970] AC 777, 814 (Lord Upjohn); *McGrath v Wallis* [1995] 2 FLR 114.

[87] *Shephard v Cartwright* [1955] AC 431. Criticized by Fung, 'The scope of the rule in *Shephard v Cartwright*' (2006) 122 LQR 651 as anachronistic.   [88] *Shephard v Cartwright* [1955] AC 431.

[89] [1944] 2 All ER 472.   [90] [1995] 2 FLR 114. See also *Lavelle v Lavelle* [2004] EWCA Civ 223.

8.2.5 THE PRESUMPTIONS AND ILLEGAL TRANSACTIONS

The distinction between presumptions of resulting trust and advancement has proved to be especially significant where property was transferred pursuant to an illegal transaction. Illegality encompasses a wide variety of conduct encompassing criminal activity and conduct that is otherwise considered to be unlawful or immoral. As regards the operation of the presumptions of resulting trust and advancement, the most relevant form of illegality concerns the transfer of property to the defendant in order to hide it from creditors or other people, such as an ex-spouse. But the illegality may also involve tax evasion and benefit fraud. The effect of illegality on private law claims generally has been altered by the very important decision of the Supreme Court in *Patel v Mirza*.[91]

Before *Patel v Mirza*, for reasons of public policy, it was not possible to plead an illegal purpose.[92] This did not prevent the presumption of resulting trust or advancement from being engaged, but it did mean that the party against whom the presumption applied would not be able to assert their illegal purpose to rebut the presumption. So, for example, where a husband transferred property to his wife to hide it from his creditors, it was presumed that he had intended to make a gift of the property to her, by virtue of the presumption of advancement. The husband would not be able to rebut this presumption by adducing evidence that his purpose was to hide his assets from his creditors rather than to benefit his wife, because that would involve pleading an illegal purpose.[93]

That the presumption of resulting trust applied despite the claimant's involvement in an illegal transaction if it was not necessary to rely on the illegality was recognized by the House of Lords in *Tinsley v Milligan*.[94] Tinsley and Milligan had been in a lesbian relationship. They had both contributed to the purchase of a house, but it was registered in the sole name of Tinsley on the understanding that they would have joint beneficial interests in it. This arrangement was to make it appear that Milligan was a lodger, so that she could make fraudulent claims for housing benefit to which she was not entitled. Both parties had participated in the fraud and benefited from it. Subsequently, their relationship ended and Tinsley brought an action for possession of the house, asserting that she had sole ownership of it. Milligan counterclaimed that she had a beneficial interest in the property, because the nature of their relationship was such that a resulting trust could be presumed. Tinsley argued that Milligan could not ask the court to enforce the trust in her favour because of her illegal conduct in perpetrating benefit fraud. By a majority, it was held that Milligan's counterclaim should succeed: to trigger the presumption of resulting trust, she simply needed to show that she had contributed to the purchase price and she did not need to refer to the illegal purpose to show this.[95] The only way in which Tinsley could have sought to rebut this presumption was by showing that Milligan had intended Tinsley to have sole title to the property to enable her to perpetrate the fraud. But Tinsley could not establish this because it would have involved her pleading that the transaction

---

[91] [2016] UKSC 42, [2017] AC 467.

[92] *Tinsley v Milligan* [1994] 1 AC 340. This principle of public policy derived from *Holman v Johnson* (1775) 1 Cowp 341, 343 (Lord Mansfield). The principle was extended to common intention constructive trusts (*Davies v O'Kelly* [2014] EWCA Civ 1606, [2015] 1 WLR 2725) and to express trusts (*Collier v Collier* [2002] EWCA Civ 1095, [2002] BPIR 1057).   [93] *Tinker v Tinker* [1970] P 136.

[94] [1994] 1 AC 340.

[95] Lord Goff dissented on the ground that to obtain relief in Equity the applicant must come with clean hands. See Section 2.5, p. 31. In fact, the clean hands maxim is a principle of justice which is designed to prevent those guilty of serious misconduct from securing a discretionary equitable remedy, such as an injunction or specific performance: *Dunbar v Plant* [1998] Ch 412, 422 (Mummery LJ). It follows that the maxim should not be relevant where a party seeks to vindicate an equitable proprietary right.

was intended to effect an illegal purpose. It did not follow, however, that a party was always prevented from relying on an illegal purpose. In *Silverwood v Silverwood*,[96] money was given by a grandmother to two of her grandchildren. It was presumed that this was held on resulting trust for the grandmother. The grandchildren sought to rebut this presumption by pleading that the grandmother had intended the transfer of the money to be a gift. It was held that the executor of the grandmother's will could plead that the purpose behind the transfer of the money was actually to perpetrate a fraud on the Department of Social Security, since it had enabled the grandmother to obtain income support. Here, the illegal purpose was being pleaded to defeat an attempt to rebut a presumption rather than to rebut a presumption of resulting trust. This involves a very fine distinction being drawn and one that is difficult to defend. If it is legitimate to rely on the illegal purpose to prevent a presumption being rebutted, as in *Silverwood v Silverwood*, why in cases such as *Tinsley v Milligan* cannot the illegal purpose be used to rebut the presumption of resulting trust?

As regards the presumption of advancement, although it had been recognized that it was not possible to rely on an illegal purpose to rebut the presumption of an intention to make a gift,[97] this was not an absolute bar. In *Tribe v Tribe*,[98] it was held that the claimant was entitled to plead an illegal purpose to rebut the presumption of advancement where they had withdrawn from the illegal transaction before any part of the illegal purpose had been fulfilled: the so-called 'withdrawal principle'. In that case a father had illegally transferred shares to his son to conceal them from his creditors. Once the threat from his creditors had passed, the father asked his son to return the shares to him. The son refused to do so. The son argued that the presumption of advancement applied and the father was unable to rebut this by pleading his illegal purpose to establish that a gift had not been intended. It was held that, since none of the creditors had been aware of the transfer of shares, it followed that they had not been deceived and so no part of the illegal purpose had been carried into effect.[99] Consequently, the father could be considered to have withdrawn from the illegal transaction and could rely on his actual purpose to rebut the presumption of advancement. It was irrelevant that the father had sought to recover the shares only once the threat from the creditors had passed. The principle recognized in *Tribe v Tribe* was developed from the principle known as *locus poenitentiae*, which required the claimant to repent of the illegality before relying on their illegal purpose to rebut a presumption. Millett LJ in *Tribe v Tribe* confirmed that repentance was no longer required, it being sufficient that the claimant had voluntarily withdrawn from the transaction before any part of the illegal purpose had been satisfied.[100]

The law on the effect of illegality on the operation of the presumptions of resulting trust and advancement was much criticized. The result depended on which presumption applied, which was arbitrary and simply turned on where the burden of proof lay. Where a resulting trust was presumed, the claimant would be able to establish a beneficial interest that the defendant would not be able to rebut, despite the claimant's illegal purpose. When the presumption of advancement applied, the property would be presumed to have been an outright gift to the defendant and the claimant would not be able to rebut this presumption by pleading their true intent. The Law Commission reviewed the law of illegality

---

[96] (1997) 74 P & CR 453.   [97] *Tinker v Tinker* [1970] P 136.   [98] [1996] Ch 107.

[99] See *Collier v Collier* [2002] EWCA Civ 1095, [2002] BPIR 1057, in which the purpose of deceiving creditors by transferring property to the claimant's daughter had been fulfilled and so the transferor of the property could not be considered to have withdrawn from the illegal transaction.

[100] See Samet, '*Locus poenitentiae*: repentance, withdrawal and luck', in *Constructive and Resulting Trusts*, ed. Mitchell (Oxford: Hart, 2010), ch. 12, for a critique of the move from repentance to withdrawal.

generally and in particular as regards the law of trusts.[101] It concluded that the principle that a party cannot plead an illegal purpose 'was deeply embedded' and 'produces complex and arbitrary results, depending on the detailed intricacies of trust law'.[102] Consequently, the Law Commission recommended statutory reform of the law to introduce a statutory discretion as to the appropriate result where a trust was created to conceal the beneficiary's interest in connection with a criminal purpose. This discretion would be exercised only exceptionally. The Law Commission identified various factors to assist the court in the exercise of this discretion, such as the conduct and intention of the parties, the value of the beneficial interest, whether enforcing the beneficial interest would further the criminal purpose, and whether refusing to enforce the interest would have any deterrent value. Where the intended beneficiary is not allowed to enforce the beneficial interest, the court should have a power to determine who should be entitled to it, whether it be the settlor, trustee, or another beneficiary, but the property should not be declared to be ownerless and transferred to the State.

Although there was no legislative response to the Law Commission's proposals, the broad thrust of those proposals was adopted by the Supreme Court in *Patel v Mirza*. In that case the claimant had transferred £620,000 to the defendant, a City trader who had suggested the scheme, so that the defendant could use the money to bet on share price movements based on inside information. Such insider dealing is a crime.[103] The inside information was not forthcoming and so the agreement was not carried out. The claimant sought restitution of the money paid on the ground that the defendant had been unjustly enriched at his expense, since the basis for the transfer had failed totally. Because the parties had committed a conspiracy to commit insider dealing, and so were tainted by illegality, the defendant refused to make restitution. In the Supreme Court the nine Justices unanimously held that the defendant should recover the money he had paid to the claimant. The logic of restitution prevailed, despite the taint of illegality arising from the conspiracy to commit insider dealing, such that all the Justices recognized that it was appropriate to restore the status quo rather than to allow the defendant to profit from his participation in the illegal transaction. As Lord Sumption recognized,[104] 'an order for restitution would not give effect to the illegal act or to any right derived from it'.

The wider significance of *Patel v Mirza* relates to the operation of illegality in private law. There was consensus that the rationale behind the illegality defence is that it would be contrary to the public interest to enforce a claim if to do so would be harmful to the integrity of the legal system.[105] But there was disagreement amongst the Justices as to whether the defence should be discretionary and context-dependent in its operation or certain and principled. By a majority of six to three the discretionary approach was adopted.

This approach to illegality was identified by Lord Toulson and was approved by the other Justices in the majority. It involves a trio of considerations, as follows:[106]

> . . . one cannot judge whether allowing a claim which is in some way tainted by illegality would be contrary to the public interest, because it would be harmful to the integrity of the legal system without (a) considering the underlying purpose of the prohibition which has been transgressed, (b) considering conversely any other relevant public policies which may be rendered ineffective or less effective by denial of the claim, and (c) keeping in mind the possibility of overkill unless the law is applied with a due sense of proportionality. We are, after all, in the area of public policy.

---

[101] *The Illegality Defence*, Law Com No. 320 (London: HMSO, 2010).   [102] Ibid., p. 2.
[103] Criminal Justice Act 1993, Part V.   [104] [2016] UKSC 42, [2017] AC 467, [268].
[105] Ibid., [120] (Lord Toulson).   [106] Ibid., [101].

These three considerations will operate in the following way.

(1) It is necessary to consider the reasons why the conduct was made illegal, although no guidance was given as to how this should be achieved and why it is relevant to the operation of the illegality defence.

(2) It is then necessary to consider the policies which would be affected by denying the claim, but again it is unclear what these policies might be and how they might be identified.

(3) Various factors were identified to assess the question of proportionality of denying relief, although Lord Toulson emphasized that this was not a closed list because of the infinite possible variety of cases involving illegality. The identified factors included the seriousness of the conduct and whether there was a marked disparity in the parties' respective culpability. But the question of proportionality requires a quantitative assessment against some objective guide, and no such guide was identified.

Lord Sumption[107] rejected the approach of the majority considering it to be 'far too vague and potentially far too wide to serve as the basis on which a person may be denied their legal rights. It converts a legal principle into an exercise of judicial discretion, in the process exhibiting all the vices of "complexity, uncertainty, arbitrariness and lack of transparency" which Lord Toulson attributes to the present law.' Lord Toulson's response to this was to acknowledge that the trio of considerations might result in uncertainty, but he considered that the existing law was already riven with uncertainties and, anyway, certainty was not a relevant consideration when dealing with people who were contemplating unlawful activity. But surely Lord Sumption's analysis is correct. Whilst the trio of considerations purport to be principled, there is a significant danger that, when applied by a judge, they will not provide the guidance to judicial decision-making that is required of a legal principle. It is, for example, unclear how the considerations were applied on the facts of *Patel v Mirza* itself, although it is clear that they did not operate to defeat the unjust enrichment claim.

Whilst most of the analysis of the law by the Supreme Court focused on illegality as it relates to the law of unjust enrichment, the decision is of profound importance to the law of trusts and to Equity more generally. Any allegation of illegality in an equitable claim will now have to be examined with reference to the trio of considerations to determine what the effect of the illegality should be. But there are two particular implications of the decision which have specific relevance to resulting trusts, namely the continued validity of *Tinsley v Milligan*,[108] and its recognition of the 'no-reliance' principle, and of the withdrawal principle.

The majority recognized that the 'no-reliance' principle should be rejected, primarily because of its perceived procedural nature and its arbitrary consequences. It follows now that an equitable claim will not be defeated simply because the claimant needs to establish the illegality of the transaction to make the claim. Even so, the majority considered that *Tinsley v Milligan* would have been decided the same way today, but without the artifice of considering whether or not it was necessary to rely on the illegality to establish the presumption of resulting trust or to rebut that presumption. Rather, the majority would have required the nature of the illegality to be considered explicitly, but would have concluded that it would have been disproportionate to have prevented Milligan from enforcing her equitable proprietary interest which had arisen under the presumption of a resulting trust, because this would have resulted in Tinsley being unjustly enriched.[109]

---

[107] Ibid., [265].   [108] [1994] 1 AC 340.
[109] [2016] UKSC 42, [2017] AC 467, [110] (Lord Toulson) and [136] (Lord Clarke).

The continued operation of the withdrawal principle, allowing a claim to succeed if the claimant has voluntarily withdrawn from the illegal transaction, is doubtful following *Patel v Mirza*. Lord Toulson did not consider that this principle was relevant on the facts of the case, so he did not examine it. But the principle appears to be inconsistent with the trio of considerations which he identified, or, if it remains relevant, it will be subsumed into one of the relevant factors to assess the disproportionality of denying relief. It follows that *Tribe v Tribe* would presumably be decided in the same way, with the presumption of advancement being rebutted because no part of the illegal purpose had been satisfied, save if the application of the trio of considerations would defeat the claim. And there we have the problem with the new law of illegality. Everything will turn on the interpretation of the trio of considerations, which is a matter of significant uncertainty.

8.2.6 THE FUTURE OF THE PRESUMPTIONS

Chambers has suggested that the presumptions of resulting trust and advancement are not needed because they do not fill a necessary function.[110] He considers that the courts should instead assess in each case what the claimant actually intended in transferring property or paying money. If the abolition of the presumption of advancement is brought into force, it might be concluded that there is no longer any need for the presumption of resulting trust either. But whether this is right simply turns on whether the presumption can still be considered to reflect common experience. If, for example, the claimant transfers property to the defendant for no consideration, is it still appropriate to assume that the claimant did not intend a gift? If we adopt a cynical view of human relations, and it is perhaps right to do so, the presumption of resulting trust is still of legitimate evidential significance and the defendant does have the opportunity to rebut it. It must not be forgotten that the real significance of the presumption of resulting trust relates to the allocation of the burden of proof between the parties. The most significant criticism of the presumptions is how they have operated in respect of illegal transactions, but following the decision of the Supreme Court in *Patel v Mirza*[111] the effect of illegality on a transaction will depend on the operation of the trio of considerations which will not obviously be influenced by the operation of the presumptions. Lord Sumption was the only Justice in *Patel v Mirza* to defend the no-reliance principle, although he considered that its application was inappropriate in *Tinsley v Milligan* only because the case turned on the procedural implications of the presumption of resulting trust. He said that the focus should instead have simply been on whether there was an intention to make a gift.[112] This is potentially a radical reappraisal of the law of resulting trusts, which would imply that there is no role for presumptions at all. But surely the point of the presumptions is that they assist in determining whether there was an intention to make a gift or to declare a trust. Whilst the distinction between presumptions of resulting trust and advancement is open to objection in their operation, the existence of the presumptions is surely defensible in assisting in the determination of the appropriate intention.

Mee[113] has argued that there is no longer any need for the presumed resulting trust but instead the common intention constructive trust should do the work.[114] But, whilst the latter trust is undoubtedly of growing importance and has expanded at the expense of the presumed resulting trust, it is too early to say that the latter has been defeated by the

---

[110] 'Is there a presumption of resulting trust?', in *Constructive and Resulting Trusts*, ed. Mitchell (Oxford: Hart, 2010), ch. 9, p. 270.   [111] [2016] UKSC 42, [2017] AC 467.

[112] Ibid., [238]. See also Lord Mance, [200].

[113] 'The past, present, and future of resulting trusts' (2017) CLP 1.   [114] Section 10.2, p. 284.

former. There is still a need for the presumption of a resulting trust outside the personal relationship context, as long as the presumed intent that property be held on trust for the transferor can be considered to be of evidential usefulness.

8.3 TOTAL OR PARTIAL FAILURE OF EXPRESS TRUST

8.3.1 JUSTIFICATIONS FOR THE RESULTING TRUST

The second category of resulting trust has been called the 'automatic' resulting trust.[115] It is said to arise where:[116]

> a transfer to B is made on trusts which leave some or all of the beneficial interest undisposed of. B automatically holds on a resulting trust for A to the extent that the beneficial interest has not been carried to him or others.

The automatic resulting trust will arise only where property has been transferred to a trustee on an express trust so that the trustee has legal title to the property that can then be held on trust for the settlor. But the language of 'failing to dispose of all of the beneficial interest' has caused difficulties for judges and commentators, since it assumes that a beneficial interest is carved out of the property transferred to the trustee which is retained by the settlor or testator. This is artificial. It is preferable instead to focus on the express trust failing. This may be an initial failure, where all of the requirements for an express trust have not been satisfied, or a subsequent failure, where an express trust has been created effectively and then terminates for some reason, leaving surplus assets. But where an express trust has failed, why should a resulting trust arise? It might be considered to be sufficient, for example, to enable the settlor to have a personal claim to recover the value of the property transferred, by an action founded on the unjust enrichment of the trustee.[117] But this will be disadvantageous to the settlor if the trustee has become insolvent, since the settlor will rank with the other unsecured creditors of the trustee; the recognition that the property is held on resulting trust will mean that the settlor's claim has priority over other creditors. But is it possible to justify the claimant having a proprietary interest by means of a resulting trust? Various justifications have been suggested for the resulting trust arising where an express trust has failed.

(i) Retention of beneficial interest

Where the settlor purports to create an express trust, but fails to do so effectively, legal title will typically pass to the trustee, but the settlor will retain the beneficial interest in the property, so that the trustee holds the property on trust for the settlor. This notion of retaining the beneficial interest is consistent with both older[118] and more recent authorities.[119] In *Westdeutsche Landesbank Girozentrale v Islington LBC*,[120] Lord Browne-Wilkinson explained this resulting trust as arising because of the failure to exhaust the

---

[115] *Re Vandervell's Trusts (No 2)* [1974] Ch 269, 294 (Megarry J). Although Lord Browne-Wilkinson, in *Westdeutsche Landesbank Girozentrale v Islington LBC* [1996] AC 669, 708, preferred to treat even this trust as a presumed resulting trust. See Section 8.3.1.(iii), p. 231.

[116] *Re Vandervell's Trusts (No 2)* [1974] Ch 269, 294 (Megarry J).

[117] See further Section 8.5.1, p. 249.

[118] See Mee, '"Automatic" resulting trusts: retention, restitution or reposing trust?', in *Constructive and Resulting Trusts*, ed. Mitchell (Oxford: Hart, 2010), ch. 7.

[119] See *Vandervell v IRC* [1967] 2 AC 291, 313 (Lord Upjohn) and 329 (Lord Wilberforce).

[120] [1996] AC 669, 708.

claimant's beneficial interest in the express trust. But this is the assertion of a conclusion rather than an explanation as to why the beneficial interest is retained or not exhausted. Some event needs to be identified that explains how and why such an interest can be retained. Further, the assertion that an automatic resulting trust arises on the subsequent failure of an express trust cannot be explained by stating that the settlor has retained the beneficial interest, because the settlor will not have retained any beneficial interest once the trust has been operating effectively.

(ii) Hybrid trust

Mee has suggested a more convincing explanation of the automatic resulting trust.[121] He has argued that, where a settlor has purported to create an express trust that is ineffective, for example because of a failure to identify any beneficiaries, the trust will not have completely failed because the settlor will have successfully created a trust by transferring property to the trustee, so that the settlor reposes trust in the trustee; the settlor will simply not have successfully declared the particular trust that was intended because of the failure to identify the beneficiaries. In such circumstances, Mee argues, Equity allocates the beneficial interest to the settlor by operation of a rule of law that has been devised to fill any gaps in the beneficial interest under the trust. This is a hybrid trust, because it depends on the decision of the settlor to create an express trust. This decision means that the beneficial interest under the trust must be in somebody other than the trustee, for otherwise there would be no trust. If it is not clear who should have that beneficial interest, the equitable default rules are brought into effect by means of the resulting trust, and the trustee then holds the property on trust for the settlor. Mee suggests that the equitable default rules resemble implied terms in a contract and cover matters that the settlor may not have consciously considered.

This is certainly a better explanation of the automatic resulting trust than simply asserting that the beneficial interest is retained. But the hybrid justification is unnecessarily complicated and artificial. Mee effectively distinguishes between two types of trust: a non-technical express trust, which arises whenever property is transferred to a person to be held on an unspecified trust; and a technical express trust, which fails because the requirements of such a trust have not been specified. Where the latter trust fails, the former will not, and Equity simply allocates the beneficial interest under the former trust that the settlor has established. But these different notions of what constitutes a trust are artificial and contradict fundamental principles of the law of trusts. If, for example, no beneficiary has been identified, there is simply no express trust, and such a trust cannot be constructed simply from the fact that the trustee has transferred property to a person trusting that they will hold the property for somebody else.

(iii) Imputed or presumed intention

But Mee's thesis needs to be modified only slightly to provide a perfectly acceptable justification for the recognition of automatic resulting trusts. Rather than relying on a notion that the non-technical express trust has not failed, it is actually vital that there has been a failure of the express trust, either initially or subsequently. When there is such a failure, Equity intervenes to impute an intention that the property that has been transferred to the trustee should be held on resulting trust for the settlor.[122] This intention is imputed because, as Mee recognizes, it is 'plausible to suggest that such a rule would reflect the legal response which settlors as an abstract class would be likely to prefer'.[123] In other words,

---

[121] Mee (see n. 118).   [122] See Section 8.1.3.(i), p. 214.   [123] Mee (see n. 118), p. 211.

where there is an initial or subsequent failure of an express trust, it is appropriate for Equity to recognize that the recipient of the property was intended to be a trustee rather than to receive the property beneficially; had the settlor considered the possibility of the trust failing, they would have intended to have a beneficial interest in the property.[124] At the very least, this enables the settlor to demand the transfer of the legal title and then to declare new trusts if they wish.[125]

Although the intention that the property should be held on trust for the settlor where the express trust has failed might be interpreted as an imputed intent so that it is irrebuttable, the intention might instead be analysed as a presumed intention, which could be rebutted exceptionally by contrary evidence.[126] For example, if the settlor had given some thought to the possibility of the trust failing and intended, if this happened, that the trustee should receive the property beneficially or intended simply to give up all rights to the asset, so that the trustee should obtain it absolutely,[127] this could be used to displace the presumed intention of a resulting trust. If this presumed-intent analysis were adopted, the presumption would be a strong one that would require very clear evidence to rebut it, simply because it is highly unlikely that the settlor would have even considered the possibility of the express trust failing, let alone that they would wish the trustee to receive the property absolutely if the express trust had failed. But analysing this intention as a presumed one is at least consistent with the approach to resulting trusts adopted in *Westdeutsche Landesbank* by Lord Browne-Wilkinson,[128] who concluded that these resulting trusts do not arise automatically, but are presumed trusts because of the possibility that the settlor might have intended to abandon the property that had been transferred if the express trust had failed.[129] Such an intention to transfer the property absolutely would rebut the presumption and so would negate the resulting trust. As Scott J recognized in *Davis v Richards and Wallington*,[130] where 'the intention of a contributor that a resulting trust should not apply is the proper conclusion, it would not be right . . . for the law to contradict that intention'.

As between treating the intention that the property be held on resulting trust where an express trust has failed as either an imputed or a presumed intention, the preferable explanation is that the so-called automatic resulting trust responds to the settlor's presumed intention that the property will be held on resulting trust, albeit that the intention can only exceptionally be rebutted by clear evidence to the contrary.

8.3.2 FAILURE OF AN EXPRESS TRUST

An automatic resulting trust will arise only where property has been transferred on an express trust that has failed. A failure of trust may arise from the outset or subsequently, but a trust will not fail simply because the settlor's purpose in creating the trust has been frustrated, for example by a change of circumstances; the trust must be illegal or impossible to perform.[131]

A trust may fail for a variety of reasons.

---

[124] *Re Gillingham Bus Disaster Fund* [1958] Ch 300, 310 (Harman J). See Section 8.1.3.(ii), p. 216.

[125] Alternatively, the settlor could transfer the beneficial interest to a third party. Such a transaction would require signed writing. See Section 11.3, p. 324. [126] Rickett and Grantham (see n. 40), p. 17.

[127] See Section 8.3.2.(iii), p. 236. [128] [1996] AC 669, 708.

[129] See *Re West Sussex Constabulary's Widows, Children and Benevolent (1930) Fund Trusts* [1971] Ch 1, discussed in Section 8.3.2.(iii), p. 237. [130] [1991] 1 WLR 1510, 1541.

[131] *Twinsectra Ltd v Yardley* [2002] UKHL 12, [2002] 2 AC 164, [98] (Lord Millett).

(i) Initial failure of express trust

Where an express trust is intended, but fails to be established, property that has been transferred to the putative trustee will be held on resulting trust for the settlor. The trust that fails must have been an *inter vivos* trust. If it is a testamentary trust that fails, the property will not be held on resulting trust, but will simply fall into residue and be distributed to those who are entitled to the testator's residuary estate.

An example of an automatic resulting trust arising from the initial failure of an express trust is *Essery v Cowlard*,[132] in which a marriage settlement declared that property of the intended wife was to be transferred to trustees to be held on trust for her, her husband, and their children. The marriage did not take place, although the parties lived together. It was held that the contract for marriage had been rescinded and the trust failed. Consequently, the property was held on resulting trust for the settlor. Similarly, in *Re Ames' Settlement*,[133] following a marriage the husband's father transferred £10,000 to trustees to be held on trust for the couple and their children. Eighteen years later, the marriage was declared void *ab initio* for non-consummation. It was held that the money was held on resulting trust for the father's estate, because the money had been transferred on the basis that there was a valid marriage. Since the marriage was treated as void from the start, the money had been transferred to the trustees on a basis that never existed, so it was to be returned to the settlor's estate.

Where, however, property is transferred to trustees for a charitable purpose that fails from the outset, that property may be applied cy-près for other charitable purposes if a general charitable intention can be identified.[134] If such an intention cannot be identified, the property will be held on resulting trust for the settlor.

(ii) Invalidity of express trust

A trust might alternatively fail from the outset because the trust is legally invalid, for a variety of reasons. For example, a charitable trust might fail because the purpose is not wholly or exclusively charitable. If so, the property transferred to the trustees will be held on resulting trust for the settlor or the estate of the testator.[135] The cy-près doctrine will not apply because the property has never been subject to a valid charitable purpose. Further, in *Air Jamaica v Charlton*,[136] an express trust of surplus funds that should have arisen following the discontinuance of a pension scheme was void for infringing the perpetuity rule. It was held that the surplus of the fund should be held on resulting trust for the employer and the employees who had contributed to the fund in proportion to their contributions and regardless of any benefit that they had received from the fund.

A resulting trust has also been recognized as arising where an express trust fails through failure to comply with the relevant formalities for establishing such a trust, even where the settlor purports to declare a trust in favour of themselves. This is illustrated by *Hodgson v Marks*.[137] Mrs Hodgson was an 83-year-old widow who owned a house. Her lodger, Evans, had supervised the investment of her money. She transferred the house to Evans under an unenforceable[138] oral agreement that she would retain a beneficial interest in the property. She received no consideration in return for this transaction. Evans was registered as the owner of the house, which he then sold to Marks. It was held that Mrs Hodgson had not

---

[132] (1884) 26 Ch D 191.   [133] [1947] Ch 217.   [134] See Section 6.5.1, p. 177.
[135] *Morice v Bishop of Durham* (1804) 9 Ves 399; on appeal (1805) 10 Ves 522; *Chichester Diocesan Fund and Board of Finance Inc v Simpson* [1944] AC 341. See Section 6.4.1, p. 175.   [136] [1999] 1 WLR 1399.
[137] [1971] Ch 892.
[138] By virtue of the Law of Property Act 1925, s. 53(1)(b). See Section 5.2.1.(i), p. 105.

intended to transfer the property to Evans as a gift and so he held the house on resulting trust for her.

Hodgson v Marks is a difficult case. Since Mrs Hodgson had transferred the property to Evans for no consideration, this could be analysed as a case in which a presumed resulting trust had been triggered. But the presumption of a resulting trust of land might have been removed by statute and it was assumed in argument that a presumed resulting trust would not have arisen.[139] This does not prevent land from being held on resulting trust, but with no presumption of an intention that a trust be declared, it would be necessary to show that Mrs Hodgson actually intended the land to be held on trust for her. She did have such an express intention, but this would mean that the trust was express, and being a trust of land, it could only be enforced if evidenced by signed writing, which takes us back to where we started. This vicious circle can be avoided, however, if we focus instead on the resulting trust being automatic rather than presumed. Since Mrs Hodgson had intended to create an express trust, and had failed to do so effectively because of the absence of writing, Equity could intervene and find a resulting trust in her favour. Indeed, Russell LJ expressly recognized[140] that, where an express trust fails, a resulting trust can be implied regardless of whether the failure of trust is due to uncertainty, perpetuity, or failure to comply with the formalities. The resulting trust therefore arose automatically. But this is difficult to justify as well, since the initial express trust had not failed. An oral trust of land is a valid trust; it is simply a trust that cannot be enforced because of the absence of writing.[141] So, to explain the result in this case, either it is necessary artificially to define a failure of an express trust as including a valid trust that is unenforceable, or some other trust needs to be identified. In fact, the result of the case is preferably achieved by concluding that Evans, and those who claimed through him, could not be allowed to use a statute as an instrument of fraud to deny that Evans held the property as trustee rather than absolutely, so that the express trust was enforceable.[142] In other words, there was no need to rely on the resulting trust, presumed or automatic, in this case.[143]

One particular example of an express trust failing for legal invalidity is where title to property has been transferred to the trustee, but no beneficiaries have been identified. Whether a resulting trust can be recognized in such a situation was considered by the House of Lords in *Vandervell v IRC*.[144] Vandervell had decided to make a gift to the Royal College of Surgeons to found a chair of pharmacology, but he wanted to do this in a tax-efficient way both for the College and for himself. Consequently, he planned to transfer a block of shares in his own private company, Vandervell Products Ltd, to the Royal College. He would then arrange for dividends to be declared on these shares, which would provide the money to found the chair. Vandervell Trustees Ltd, a trust company that acted as trustee for Vandervell's philanthropic schemes, would be given an option to buy these shares for £5,000. The option was included in case it might be desirable in the future to convert the company into a public company, since it would then be preferable for the shares to be under the control of Vandervell or those who would act as he directed.

Although complicated, the transaction was structured in this way to ensure that the College could recover tax that had been deducted from the dividends before they were

---

[139] Law of Property Act 1925, s. 60(3). See Section 8.2.1.(i), p. 218.   [140] [1971] Ch 892, 933.

[141] See Section 5.2.1.(i), p. 105.

[142] See *Rochefoucauld v Boustead* [1897] 1 Ch 196. See Section 5.2.2.(i), p. 107.

[143] Swadling (see n. 21), p. 74. See also Mee, 'Resulting trusts and voluntary conveyances of land' [2012] Conv 307.

[144] [1967] 2 AC 291. See Simpson, 'On the nature of resulting trusts: the *Vandervell* legislation revisited', in *Restitution and Equity*, Vol. 1: *Resulting Trusts and Equitable Compensation*, ed. Birks and Rose (Oxford: Mansfield Press, 2000), ch. 1.

paid and that Vandervell would not be personally liable to pay any tax on the dividends because he would have no interest in the shares. Vandervell directed his bank, which held the shares on trust for him, to transfer the shares to the Royal College,[145] and the company declared £157,000 dividends, which was paid to the College. No express provision had been made for the declaration of trusts of the shares that were to be purchased by the trustee company on exercising the option. The issue was therefore whether the option to purchase the shares, as a property right, was held on resulting trust for Vandervell. If it were, he would be liable to pay tax on the dividends received by the Royal College, because he had a beneficial interest in the shares after all. The House of Lords held that Vandervell did indeed have a beneficial interest in the option and so was liable to pay tax on the dividends. This was because it was found that Vandervell had granted the option to the trust company to be held on trust. However, the objects of that trust had not been identified, and so the express trust was void for want of objects and so failed. Lord Wilberforce specifically recognized that the beneficial interest in the option could not remain in the air and had to be vested in somebody, and so concluded that it remained in Vandervell until an express trust of the option had been validly declared.[146] But a simpler explanation of the result is that, since the intended express trust had failed, an equitable interest in the option arose automatically by virtue of either an imputed or presumed intention that the property should be held on trust.

The imputed or presumed intention explanation of automatic resulting trusts has already been justified[147] on the ground that if the settlor had contemplated the express trust failing, they would have intended the property to be held on resulting trust. But a resulting trust was the very last thing that Vandervell wanted because his beneficial interest in the option meant that he was liable to pay tax. There are two responses to this difficulty.

(1) The intention is imputed and arises by operation of law without regard to the particular facts, it being a rule of law that, where an express trust fails, a resulting trust will be recognized, even if this is detrimental to the claimant's interests. This appears to have been the preferred approach of Lord Wilberforce, who concluded that there was no room for a presumption to operate in this case,[148] suggesting that there was an irrebuttable imputed intent that the option be held on trust for Vandervell.

(2) There is a presumed, rather than imputed, intention that the property held by the trustee on a failed express trust is held for the settlor on a resulting trust. This presumption can be rebutted by the settlor proving that such a trust was never intended. On the facts of the case, Vandervell might have been able to establish that he did intend the option to be held by the trust company for his children, although this would have meant that the settlement for the children would have borne the tax liability. Since he clearly did not intend the option to belong to the trust company beneficially, the choice would simply be between him or his children having the beneficial interest. Faced with such a choice, he might simply not have been able to adduce sufficient evidence to rebut the presumption of resulting trust.

As between these two analyses, the approach of the judges in *Vandervell v IRC* clearly reflects the first involving an imputed intention, so that there is no role for a presumed intention. But that is inconsistent with the later *obiter dictum* of Lord Browne-Wilkinson in *Westdeutsche Landesbank Girozentrale v Islington LBC*[149] that even the resulting trust

---

[145] This was a valid transaction. See Section 11.3.3, p. 327.   [146] [1967] 2 AC 291, 329.

[147] See Section 8.3.1.(iii), p. 230.

[148] [1967] 2 AC 291, 329. See also *Re Vandervell's Trusts (No 2)* [1974] 1 Ch 269, 294 (Megarry J).

[149] [1996] AC 669, 708.

arising from a failed express trust operates by virtue of a presumed intention that can be rebutted if the settlor intended to transfer the property absolutely. That is the preferable method of analysing the automatic resulting trust, which would mean that, had Vandervell been able to rebut the presumption of resulting trust, he would not have been liable to pay tax on the dividends, but instead the tax liability would have been borne by the children's settlement.

But this was not the end of the *Vandervell* litigation. Vandervell subsequently arranged for the trustee company to exercise the option to buy the shares. The trust company used money from the children's settlement to do so. It then treated the shares as being held on trust for the children and paid the dividends to their settlement. Vandervell eventually executed a deed transferring any interest that he might have had in the shares to the trusts of his children's settlement. Vandervell then died and a further dispute related to whether the dividends should be paid to Vandervell's estate or to the children's settlement. This was considered in *Re Vandervell's Trusts (No 2)* and turned on whether the shares were held on resulting trust for him.[150] The trial judge, Megarry J,[151] held that, once the option, which was held on resulting trust for Vandervell, had been exercised by the trustee company, the shares were also held on resulting trust for Vandervell, even though the company had used money from the children's settlement to buy the shares. This was because, as the House of Lords had previously held, the option belonged to Vandervell beneficially and the money simply enabled him to exercise his right to buy the shares, which also belonged to him beneficially. The source of the money was considered to be irrelevant to the beneficial ownership of the shares, although, since it derived from the children's settlement, his estate was liable to repay the money to the settlement.

This decision was overturned by the Court of Appeal,[152] which held that, although the option had been held on resulting trust for Vandervell, the shares were not held on resulting trust for him. Lord Denning MR decided that the shares were instead held on an express trust for the children's settlement, so that the dividends were properly paid to the children's settlement. He identified an intention that the trust company should hold the shares on express trust for the children's settlement from the following facts: the money to exercise the option had come from that settlement, and this would have constituted a breach of trust had the trustees not intended the shares to be added to the settlement; the trust company had written to the Inland Revenue declaring that the shares were held for the children; and the dividends had been paid to the settlement. All of this was done with Vandervell's assent. The problem with this analysis is that, since the House of Lords had previously recognized that Vandervell had an equitable interest in the option and the children had ended up with an equitable interest in the shares, there appears to have been a transfer of one equitable interest from Vandervell to the children, but such a disposition can be valid only if it is effected by writing.[153] Lord Denning MR dealt with this objection by concluding that Vandervell's equitable interest in the option had been destroyed when the option had been exercised by the trust company; the children's equitable interest in the shares was then created, and the creation of a new interest in personalty does not require writing.[154] The conclusion that the equitable interest in the option had been destroyed was considered to follow logically from the circumstances in which an automatic resulting trust will be triggered, namely where there is a gap in the beneficial ownership of property. But, where that gap is plugged by the creation of an express trust, the equitable interest under the resulting trust will be automatically destroyed.[155]

---

[150] If they were, then Vandervell's estate would have been liable to pay tax on the dividends.
[151] [1974] Ch 269. [152] Ibid. [153] Law of Property Act 1925, s. 53(1)(c). See Section 11.3, p. 324.
[154] [1974] Ch 269, 320. See also Lawton LJ, 325. [155] See further Section 11.3.4, p. 329.

The conclusion of the Court of Appeal is open to criticism for two reasons.

(1) The express trust of the shares was apparently declared by the trust company, although there had been no resolution of the board of directors to declare such a trust.

(2) The option and the shares should not be considered to be two distinct pieces of property. The option was a limited right that was carved out of the bundle of rights inherent in the shares.[156] The trust company, as the legal owner of the option, had the right to exercise it and so become owner of the shares at Law, but it never had the right to exercise the option for its own benefit. Consequently, both the option and the shares were held on resulting trust for the grantor of the option, namely Vandervell, until his beneficial interest was displaced by the valid creation of a new trust. The decision of the Court of Appeal is actually inconsistent with the earlier decision of the House of Lords: the House of Lords had held that Vandervell had failed to divest himself absolutely of the shares by virtue of his beneficial interest in the option, so he was liable to pay tax on the dividends paid in respect of the shares. Once the option was exercised, Vandervell retained a beneficial interest in the shares until he had instructed his trustees that they should be held on the trusts of his children's settlement, but this could be effected only by writing since it would have involved the disposition of an existing equitable interest, namely the interest arising under the resulting trust.

It follows that Vandervell should be considered to have retained a beneficial interest in the shares, so that his estate remained liable to pay tax on any dividends paid in respect of the shares.

(iii) Subsequent failure of trust

Where property has been validly held on trust which subsequently fails because it becomes impossible to continue to perform, if the trust makes no provision for what is to happen to the surplus trust property in such circumstances, it will usually be held on resulting trust for the settlor or the testator's residuary estate.

This subsequent failure of trust is likely to arise only where there is a valid trust for purposes that has become impossible to perform. Where property is held on trust for an individual who dies, the consequence of the death will depend on the nature of the beneficiary's interest. If it is a life interest, the property will be held on trust for the person entitled to the remainder. If the deceased had an interest in remainder, the property will form part of their estate. Consequently, once a trust for persons has become effective, there can be no failure of trust to justify the imposition of a resulting trust.

Where the trust is a charitable purpose trust that subsequently fails, the surplus fund will automatically be applied cy-près.[157] Where the trust is a non-charitable purpose trust that is exceptionally valid initially[158] and subsequently fails, the property may, however, be held on resulting trust for the settlor. So, for example, in *Re the Trusts of the Abbott Fund*,[159] money was collected for the support of two sisters, who were deaf and dumb, and who had been defrauded of their inheritance. The money that had been collected for them was held on trust for their benefit, but no provision was made in the trust instrument for the disposal of the fund on the death of the survivor. At her death, there was a surplus of over £366. It was held that this should be held on resulting trust for the contributors to the fund.

---

[156] Battersby, 'Some thoughts on the Statute of Frauds in relation to trusts' (1975) 7 Ottawa LR 483, 500.
[157] See Section 6.5, p. 177.
[158] See Section 7.2, p. 190. Where the trust is void at the outset, this will be an initial failure of trust and the property will be held on resulting trust for the settlor. See Section 8.3.2.(i), p. 232.
[159] [1900] 2 Ch 326.

This was a valid purpose trust for the sisters because they had been in a position to enforce it,[160] rather than a trust for the sisters beneficially which would have enabled them to call for the transfer of the trust funds to themselves. On their deaths, the purpose had failed and a resulting trust arose automatically. Similarly, in *Re Gillingham Bus Disaster Fund*,[161] a fund was established for the care of those injured following a bus crash and then to other worthy causes. The public contributed £9,000 to the fund, partly by identified subscribers, but largely from street collections. There was a surplus, which was held on resulting trust for the donors because, as Harman J recognized, there was an inference of law, based on after-knowledge of the circumstances, that the donors parted with their money only for the purposes of the trust and, if those purposes were fulfilled, the money should be held on resulting trust for them. This applied both as regards the identified and anonymous donors of money. The latter were still considered to be beneficiaries of the resulting trust even though they were unascertained, and the Crown could not claim their money as *bona vacantia*. This money was paid into court, where it was never claimed. Nearly twenty years later, it was eventually used to pay for a memorial to the victims of the crash.[162]

There are circumstances, however, in which the surplus will not be held on resulting trust for those who had given money for the particular purpose in the first place.

Absolute gifts

Where a gift has been expressed as being applicable for a particular purpose, it might also be possible to identify an intention on the part of the settlor that an individual should take the property beneficially. For example, in *Re Osoba*,[163] the testator left property to his widow on trust for her maintenance and for the training of his daughter. Following the death of the widow and the completion of the daughter's education, there was a surplus. It was held that the testator had intended to make absolute gifts to the beneficiaries, because he had given the whole of the residuary estate for their benefit, with the identified purposes simply being expression of motives for the use of the money rather than requirements that it be used for that purpose. Consequently, there had actually been no subsequent failure of the trust.

Bona vacantia

Where the surplus is considered to be ownerless, it will be transferred to the Crown on the basis of its being *bona vacantia*. This is illustrated by *Re West Sussex Constabulary's Widows, Children and Benevolent (1930) Fund Trusts*,[164] in which a fund that had been established to provide for widows and children of deceased members was wound up with a surplus. It was held that money subscribed by the members passed to the Crown as *bona vacantia* because they had divested themselves of any interest in the money in return for contractual benefits in favour of their widows and children. Similarly, money that had been raised from street collections passed to the Crown as *bona vacantia* because the donors had divested themselves of any interest in the money paid. This was because the relationship between the donor and the donee was one of contract rather than trust,[165] and, if property has not

---

[160] By virtue of what is now recognized as the *Denley* principle: *Re Denley's Trust Deed* [1969] 1 Ch 373. See Section 7.2.1, p. 190.

[161] [1958] Ch 300, affirmed [1959] Ch 62. See also *Re Hobourn Aero Components Air Raid Distress Fund* [1946] Ch 86.

[162] This can be compared with a trust for charitable purposes where surplus money provided by unknown donors can be applied cy-près: Charities Act 2011, s. 65. See Section 6.5.5., p. 186.

[163] [1979] 1 WLR 247.

[164] [1971] Ch 1. See also *Cunnack v Edwards* [1896] 2 Ch 679. See Section 7.4.4.(ii), p. 204.

[165] [1971] Ch 1, 10 (Goff J).

been held on an express trust, there is no scope for an automatic resulting trust to arise. Money paid by identified donors was, however, held on resulting trust for each donor.

Contract holding

Where money has been added to a fund that is held by reference to the terms of a contract, that contract will provide either expressly or impliedly what is to happen to any surplus funds. This is particularly well illustrated by money transferred for the purposes of an unincorporated association.[166] According to the contract-holding theory, the money will be held on the terms of the contract binding the members. On the dissolution of the association, any surplus funds will be distributed amongst the members at the time of the dissolution and will not be held on resulting trust for the contributors or transferred to the Crown as *bona vacantia*.[167] This contract-holding solution would now be available in many of the cases in which property has previously been held on resulting trust or has been applied *bona vacantia*.[168]

Pension fund trusts

Finally, and much more controversially, the surplus will not be held on resulting trust where it is not possible to impute an intention that it should be so held. This has been recognized in the context of pension fund trusts. In *Davis v Richards and Wallington Industries Ltd*,[169] a pension fund was wound up with a surplus of £3 million. The fund had been derived from contributions from employers and employees, and from funds transferred from other pension schemes. It was recognized that usually, in such circumstances, the surplus would be held on resulting trust for the employers and employees who had contributed to the fund, even though the employees would have received all that they had bargained for under their employment contract.[170] On the facts, however, it was held that the employer alone was entitled to the surplus, since express provision had been made for this in the trust deed. It was recognized that a resulting trust could be excluded by an express or an implied term in a contract. In other words, the express or implied intent of a contributor will rebut the resulting trust.[171] But Scott J went on to consider what would have been the result had the trust deed been invalid. Although normally the surplus would then have been held on resulting trust for the contributors, he concluded that it would have been paid to the Crown as *bona vacantia*, since it would not have been possible to impute an intention to the employees that any surplus should be held on resulting trust for them. This was because it would not have been practicable to apportion the surplus with reference to the value of the benefit that each member had received, and the judge refused to impute an intention that would lead to an unworkable result. He also considered that such an intention could not be imputed because the employees could not receive sums by way of resulting trust in excess of the maximum permitted by statute.

This analysis is difficult to defend. Whilst it was acceptable for the judge to analyse the automatic resulting trust with reference to an imputed intent,[172] although it would have

---

[166] See Section 7.4.4.(ii), p. 203.

[167] *Re Bucks Constabulary Widows' and Orphans' Fund Friendly Society (No 2)* [1979] 1 WLR 936. See Section 7.4.4.(ii), p. 206.

[168] *Hanchett-Stamford v Attorney-General* [2008] EWHC 330 (Ch), [2009] Ch 173.

[169] [1990] 1 WLR 1511.   [170] Contradicting the reasoning in *Cunnack v Edwards* [1896] 2 Ch 679.

[171] [1990] 1 WLR 1511, 1541 (Scott J).

[172] This was, however, rejected by Lord Millett, in *Air Jamaica Ltd v Charlton* [1999] 1 WLR 1399, 1412, who preferred to analyse the trust as arising in favour of the contributors to a pension scheme because they did not intend to pass a beneficial interest to the trustee of the pension fund. In other words, he focused on the absence of intent to benefit analysis of the resulting trust. Section 8.1.3, p. 214.

been preferable to treat this as a presumed intent which was rebuttable,[173] this is an intention that is imposed by Equity to reflect what the contributors would have intended had they considered the matter. Such an intention should not be defeated by impracticability in implementing the trust. Rather, the surplus should be apportioned in proportion to the contributors' contributions to the fund and without regard to any benefits that they had received. This was the solution that was adopted in apportioning the surplus of a dissolved pension fund in *Air Jamaica Ltd v Charlton*,[174] and is consistent with the essence of the resulting trust. To the extent that the claimant has contributed to an express trust that has failed, the amount of that contribution should be held on resulting trust for the claimant. If the value of the fund has fallen, the amount held on trust for the claimant should be reduced proportionately. But where, as in these pension funds cases involving distribution of surpluses, the value of the fund has increased, this increase should be shared amongst the contributors in proportion to the amount that they had contributed. Further, since the resulting trust arises outside of the pension scheme, there is no reason why it should be affected by statutory entitlements to pension payments.[175]

There is, however, a significant restriction on using the resulting trust to deal with the distribution of surplus funds on the termination of a pension fund trust, namely that the employees would get back only a proportionate share of what they had contributed to the fund. An alternative, and preferable, solution would be to extend the contract-holding theory to pension trusts.[176] This is because pension funds are held on trust for the members of the scheme according to the contractual terms that govern that scheme. Consequently, on dissolution of the trust, the surplus funds should be distributed to the members at that time in accordance with the terms of the contract, which would normally mean an equal division between the members of the scheme unless provision had been made for an alternative distribution. The existence of this contractual provision for the distribution of the surplus would then exclude the resulting trust. In other words, the presumption that a resulting trust of the surplus was intended should be rebutted by the employees' contractual rights.

8.4 THE *QUISTCLOSE* TRUST

8.4.1 GENERAL PRINCIPLES

Where property has been transferred for a specific purpose, such as where money has been lent to a borrower to be used in a particular way, the recipient of that property must use it for that purpose and may hold it on trust for the transferor if the purpose fails. This trust is of real commercial significance, since where, for example, money has been lent, the recognition of the trust will mean that the debt owed by the borrower will be converted into a trust that will give the lender a proprietary interest in the money and so priority over the borrower's creditors if the borrower becomes insolvent. This trust has become known as the *Quistclose* trust, after the name of the case in which the House of Lords first recognized it.[177] The nature of this trust has proved to be a controversial matter and has been analysed either as an express trust for people, an express trust for purposes, or as a resulting trust. But, if it is properly analysed as a resulting trust, what

---

[173] See Section 8.3.1.(iii), p. 230.   [174] [1999] 1 WLR 1399, 1413. See Section 8.3.2.(ii), p. 232.
[175] [1999] 1 WLR 1399, 1413.
[176] Vinelott, 'Equity and its relevance to superannuation schemes today' (1992) 62 TLI 119, 124.
[177] *Barclays Bank Ltd v Quistclose Investments Ltd* [1970] AC 567.

sort of resulting trust is it? Does it fall within the traditional categories of a presumed or automatic resulting trust, or is it a distinct type of resulting trust? Before these difficult questions are answered, it is useful to identify how the *Quistclose* trust operates in practice.

8.4.2 THE OPERATION OF THE *QUISTCLOSE* TRUST

The operation of the *Quistclose* trust is illustrated by the two leading cases that have recognized this trust.

(i) *Barclays Bank Ltd v Quistclose Investments Ltd*

In *Barclays Bank Ltd v Quistclose Investments Ltd*,[178] Quistclose had lent money to Rolls Razor Ltd specifically to enable it to pay a dividend that it had previously declared, but which it could not afford to pay. The money that was borrowed was paid into a bank account that was specially opened for the purpose. Rolls Razor went into liquidation, so the dividend could not be paid. The bank wished to use the money in the account to discharge Rolls Razor's overdraft. The House of Lords held that the bank could not use the money in this way because it was held on trust for Quistclose, even though the money had been lent to Rolls Razor.

Lord Wilberforce gave the only reasoned speech. He considered that the loan had created a primary trust in favour of the creditors who were owed dividends, with an equitable right for Quistclose to ensure that the money was applied for the purpose of paying those creditors. If the primary purpose were carried out, then Quistclose would have a simple claim for repayment of the debt. If, however, the primary purpose failed, it was then necessary to consider whether a secondary trust of the money arose. It was recognized that the money would be held on trust for Quistclose if this had been agreed expressly or impliedly.[179] If there were no trust for Quistclose, it would be confined to its personal remedy for recovery of the loan from the borrower. On the facts, it was held that the parties had intended to create a trust for the benefit of Quistclose if the primary trust to pay the dividend had failed. It was found that the mutual intention of the parties and the essence of the bargain between them was that the money lent should not become part of Rolls Razor's assets, but was to be used exclusively to pay those creditors who were entitled to the dividend. If the dividend could not be paid, the money was then to be returned to Quistclose. It was further held that the bank was bound by this secondary trust if it had notice either of the primary trust or the circumstances that gave rise to it when the money was credited to the borrower's bank account. Barclays Bank did have such notice, because it was aware that the money had been paid for a specific purpose to benefit third parties rather than the borrower.[180]

Lord Wilberforce acknowledged that the recognition of a trust in favour of the creditor in such circumstances had been recognized in a number of earlier cases,[181] but he also defended the recognition of the trust on policy grounds, namely that money that had been paid for a particular purpose should not be available for the borrower's general creditors whom the lender had not intended to benefit.

---

[178] Ibid.   [179] Ibid., 581–2 (Lord Wilberforce).

[180] It is unclear why such notice was required, since Quistclose had an equitable proprietary interest in the money credited to the bank account regardless of the bank's knowledge or notice. The bank's notice did, however, mean that it could not defeat the lender's claim by virtue of being a bona fide purchaser for value. See Section 19.5.1, p. 584.   [181] Including *Toovey v Milne* (1819) 2 B & Ald 683.

(ii) *Twinsectra Ltd v Yardley*

In *Twinsectra Ltd v Yardley*,[182] a solicitor, Sims, received money from a lender, Twinsectra, on behalf of Yardley, who had made arrangements to borrow the money. Sims undertook to Twinsectra to retain the money until it was used to acquire property. In breach of this undertaking, the money was paid to another solicitor, Leach, who paid some of it out on Yardley's instructions for other purposes. Sims became bankrupt and Twinsectra sued Leach for dishonestly assisting a breach of trust committed by Sims,[183] but this liability depended on whether Sims had held the money on trust. All of the judges in the House of Lords recognized that the money had been held on trust for Twinsectra. Lord Hoffmann, with whom Lords Slynn, Steyn, and Hutton agreed, recognized that the money was held on an express trust. Lord Millett, with whom Lords Hutton and Steyn also agreed, held that the money was held on a *Quistclose* trust, which he characterized as being a resulting trust. He recognized that such a trust did not arise simply because money is paid for a particular purpose, since many loans are made for particular purposes. What is required is that the money was not intended to be at the free disposal of the borrower, but was to be used exclusively for the specific purpose and for no other. Since the money had been lent for the exclusive purpose of buying property and had been applied for a different purpose, it followed that the money was held by Sims on resulting trust for Twinsectra, but subject to a power for the money to be used by Yardley in accordance with the undertaking.

8.4.3 THE REQUIREMENTS OF A *QUISTCLOSE* TRUST

Where the claimant wishes to establish that the defendant holds property on a *Quistclose* trust, the following matters must be considered.

(i) Particular purpose

The property that is transferred must be intended to be used for a particular purpose. In many of the cases, the relevant transaction has been a loan that is to be used to enable the borrower to pay their creditors.[184] But the property may be transferred for many other purposes, including to be used to purchase property,[185] or to be invested.[186] This transfer for a purpose has meant that the *Quistclose* trust has been described as a type of purpose trust.[187]

(ii) Exclusive use for stated purpose

It is an essential feature of the *Quistclose* trust that the property that has been transferred is not at the free disposal of the recipient.[188] This can be established by showing that the property is to be used exclusively for the stated purpose, since this establishes that the recipient was not free to use the transferred property simply as they wished. In *Bellis v Challinor*,[189] a *Quistclose* trust was not recognized because the terms of the transfer left the money transferred at the free disposal of the recipient with no restriction on its use for a particular purpose; consequently the payment was considered to be an immediate

---

[182] [2002] UKHL 12, [2002] 2 AC 164.   [183] See Section 20.3.2.(iii), p. 616.

[184] As in *Quistclose* itself. See also *Carreras Rothmans Ltd v Freeman Mathews Treasure Ltd* [1985] Ch 207.

[185] As in *Twinsectra v Yardley* [2002] UKHL 12, [2002] 2 AC 164. See also *Re EVTR* [1987] BCLC 646.

[186] *Box v Barclays Bank* [1998] Lloyd's Rep Bank 185.

[187] *Cobbold v Bakewell Management Ltd* [2003] EWHC 2289 (Ch), [16] (Rimer J).

[188] *Twinsectra v Yardley* [2002] UKHL 12, [2002] 2 AC 164, [74] (Lord Millett); *Charity Commission for England and Wales v Framjee* [2014] EWHC 2507 (Ch), [2015] 1 WLR 16, [28(b)] (Henderson J).

[189] [2015] EWCA Civ 59, [2016] WTLR 43.

loan which was not held on trust but became the property of the transferee who was free to dispose of the money as they wished, subject to a personal liability to repay the amount borrowed. Crucially, in such a case, since there is no trust, the lender would bear the risk of the borrower's insolvency.[190]

(iii) Separate fund

It has been recognized that, where the recipient of the money is obliged to keep it separate, this will be objective evidence that the payer and the recipient did not intend the money to be at the free disposal of the recipient,[191] but it is not a requirement for the recognition of a *Quistclose* trust.[192] So, for example, in *Quistclose*, the borrower was required to pay the loan money into a special bank account. There was no such requirement in *Twinsectra Ltd v Yardley*, although it would have been assumed that the money would have been paid into the solicitor's client account. This is consequently simply a factor of strong evidential significance. The true role of an obligation to keep the money separate was recognized in *R v Clowes (No 2)* by Watkins LJ,[193] who said that 'a requirement to keep moneys separate is normally an indicator that they are impressed with a trust, and that the absence of such requirement, *if there are no other indicators of a trust*, normally negatives it'.

(iv) Failure of purpose

In many cases, it will be clear that the identified purpose has failed, but this may some-times require more careful analysis. For example, in *Re EVTR*,[194] the claimant deposited £60,000 for the sole purpose of enabling the company to buy equipment. The money was used to buy equipment, but, before that equipment was delivered, the company went into receivership and the purchase was terminated. A large part of the purchase price was re-paid to the company. It was held that, although the equipment had been purchased, the purpose had ultimately failed because the equipment had not been delivered, and so the money that had been repaid was held on trust for the claimant.

(v) Intention

In *Challinor v Bellis*[195] Briggs LJ identified an additional requirement before a *Quistclose* trust could be recognized, namely that there should be an intention on the part of the transferor to create a trust, albeit that this should be determined objectively. In fact, as Briggs LJ went on to recognize, the relevant intention to create the trust can be deduced from the fact that the transferor intended to enter into the arrangement involving the transfer of money for a particular purpose, even if the invitation to do so came from the transferee or a third party.

8.4.4 THE NATURE OF THE *QUISTCLOSE* TRUST

The nature of the *Quistclose* trust is controversial.[196] Various explanations of it have been suggested.

---

[190] Ibid., [64].

[191] *Twinsectra v Yardley* [2002] UKHL 12, [2002] 2 AC 164, [95] (Lord Millett). See *Henry v Hammond* [1913] 2 KB 515, 521 (Channell J); *Biber v Teathers Ltd (in liquidation)* [2012] EWCA Civ 1466, [2013] WTLR 1, [14] (Patten LJ).

[192] *Charity Commission for England and Wales v Framjee* [2014] EWHC 2507 (Ch), [2015] 1 WLR 16, [28(c)] (Henderson J).   [193] [1994] 2 All ER 316, 325 (emphasis added).

[194] [1987] BCLC 646.   [195] [2015] EWCA Civ 59, [2016] WTLR 43, [55].

[196] See Swadling (ed.), *The Quistclose Trust: Critical Essays* (Oxford: Hart, 2004). See also Millett, 'The *Quistclose* trust: who can enforce it?' (1985) 101 LQR 269.

(i) Express trust for the third party

The initial analysis of the *Quistclose* trust was that it involves a primary express trust for the benefit of third parties. This analysis was adopted by Lord Wilberforce in *Quistclose* itself,[197] in which he recognized that the money lent was held on trust for the creditors of the borrower. Once this primary trust fails, it will be replaced by a secondary resulting trust for the lender. This analysis is consistent with the core principles relating to automatic resulting trusts: where an express trust has failed, the property will be held on resulting trust for the settlor. This secondary trust might even be analysed as an express trust itself, contingent on the failure of the primary trust, since it was intended that, if the primary trust failed, the money lent would be held on trust for the lender.[198]

But this analysis of the *Quistclose* trust is not satisfactory. It cannot explain all of the cases in which the *Quistclose* trust has arisen, since in some of them the primary trust cannot be for identifiable beneficiaries, but is for abstract purposes. Indeed, as Lord Millett recognized in *Twinsectra v Yardley*,[199] the loan in that case was paid for a purpose and not for a beneficiary, and non-charitable purpose trusts are generally void.[200] Also, where the trust is for identified beneficiaries, if they are all adults, they could unanimously terminate the trust and require the transfer of the property to themselves[201] regardless of whether the purpose had been satisfied or not. Indeed, if the primary trust in *Quistclose* itself had been an express trust for the creditors of Rolls Razor, the insolvency of the company would not have rendered the performance of the trust impossible; the creditors could still have been paid their dividends from the money that had been lent to the borrower.

(ii) Express trust for the lender

Lord Hoffmann in *Twinsectra v Yardley* recognized that the money in that case was held by Sims on an express trust for Twinsectra, subject to the power of Sims to apply the money for the agreed purpose. This express trust arose from the fact that the money was paid to a solicitor's client account and so was held on trust. The terms of that trust were identified from the undertaking made by Sims, which made it clear that the money was not held on trust for Yardley, who did not have the free use of the money, but was held for Twinsectra until the money was applied for the acquisition of property.[202] Sims simply had a power to apply the money in accordance with the undertaking that he had made.

But, if this is an express trust for the lender, it does not fit with the orthodox analysis of the rights of beneficiaries in respect of express trusts, since it would follow that the lender would be able to compel use of the money for the promised purpose, or revoke the loan and require payment immediately even though the purpose was still capable of being fulfilled, or require the borrower to use the money for another purpose. But any such rights of the lender would be inconsistent with the requirements of the *Quistclose* trust.[203]

(iii) Beneficial interest in suspense

The Court of Appeal in *Twinsectra v Yardley* had held that the money in that case was held on an express non-charitable purpose trust.[204] The effect of this would be that the

---

[197] [1970] AC 567, 580. See Section 8.4.2.(i), p. 240.

[198] See *Re Australian Elizabeth Theatre Trust* (1991) 102 ALR 681, 691 (Gummow J).

[199] [2002] UKHL 12, [2002] 2 AC 164, [79]. [200] See Section 7.1.1, p. 188.

[201] By virtue of the rule in *Saunders v Vautier* (1841) 4 Beav 115. See Section 11.4, p. 334.

[202] [2002] UKHL 12, [2002] 2 AC 164, [12]–[13] (Lord Hoffmann).

[203] Payne, '*Quistclose* and resulting trusts', in *Restitution and Equity*, Vol. 1: *Resulting Trusts and Equitable Compensation*, ed. Birks and Rose (Oxford: Mansfield Press, 2000), ch. 5.

[204] [1999] Lloyd's Rep Bank 438.

beneficial interest in the money would be in suspense until the identified purpose had been carried out or had failed.[205] This was rejected by Lord Millett in *Twinsectra Ltd v Yardley*,[206] both on the ground that it was unorthodox and because it is the function of the resulting trust to fill the gap where a transfer has not exhausted the entire beneficial interest, so that there is no possibility of that interest being in suspense.[207]

(iv) Express trust for the borrower

An alternative construction is that the money in a *Quistclose* trust is held on an express trust for the borrower. But this is inconsistent with an essential feature of the *Quistclose* trust, namely that the property is not available at the borrower's free disposal. So, in *Twinsectra Ltd v Yardley*, Sims could not have held the money on trust for Yardley, so that Yardley could have sought the transfer of the money to him. The money was available only for the use of Yardley for the particular purpose. The 'trust for the borrower' analysis could not have operated in *Quistclose* either, since the borrower was the trustee and it is not possible to be trustee for oneself. Consequently, if the beneficial interest had been in the borrower, it would follow that there was no trust and the borrower would be free to do what it wished with the money; this would undermine the whole point of the *Quistclose* trust.

(v) Loan subject to contractual undertaking

Chambers[208] analysed the *Quistclose* trust as involving a transfer of property to the borrower, but with the lender merely having a contractual right that is specifically enforceable in Equity to prevent the property from being applied for any other purpose. This would mean that there was no initial trust at all. According to Chambers's theory, a resulting trust would arise if the purpose for which the money was lent had failed, because then the claimant would not have intended the recipient of the property to have the benefit of the property. This theory was adopted by the Court of Appeal in *Twinsectra*,[209] but was rejected by Lord Millett[210] on the following grounds:

(1) It does not provide a solution where there is a non-contractual payment.

(2) It is inconsistent with Lord Wilberforce's recognition in *Quistclose* that the borrower is subject to a fiduciary obligation.

(3) It does not explain the evidential significance of the requirement that the transferred money should be kept separate from the borrower's money.

(4) It does not explain how proprietary rights can be conjured out of a contractual relationship so that the claimant has a proprietary, rather than only a personal, claim and so obtains priority over the borrower's creditors.

(vi) Resulting trust from the outset

In *Twinsectra Ltd v Yardley*, Lord Millett recognized that the *Quistclose* trust is an orthodox example of a resulting trust that arises at the outset: the lender has not disposed of the

---

[205] *Carreras Rothman v Freeman Matthews Treasure* [1985] Ch 207, 223.

[206] [2002] UKHL 12, [2002] 2 AC 164, [90] and [92].

[207] As had been recognized by the House of Lords in *Vandervell v IRC* [1967] 2 AC 291, discussed in Section 8.3.2.(ii), p. 233.   [208] Chambers (see n. 24), ch. 3.

[209] [1999] Lloyd's Rep Bank 438, 456 (Potter LJ).

[210] Relying in particular on the criticisms of Ho and Smart, 'Re-interpreting the *Quistclose* trust: a critique of Chambers' analysis' (2001) 21 OJLS 267.

whole of the beneficial interest in the property transferred[211] since the money is transferred on terms which do not leave it at the free disposal of the recipient but is to be used for an exclusive purpose. In *Challinor v Bellis*,[212] however, Briggs LJ emphasized that this resulting trust is not orthodox since it is not presumed to exist save if there is a contrary intention on the part of the transferor. Rather, the transferor must objectively intend to have created a trust, which will be established if the transferor intended to enter into particular arrangements which have the effect in law of creating a trust.[213] But this looks very much like an intention to create an express trust which is resulting in effect, which intention will be imputed if the conditions for establishing the trust have been established.[214] Certainly, as Briggs LJ recognized, the *Quistclose* trust does not operate like a presumed resulting trust.

In *Twinsectra*, Lord Millett considered that the money that had been lent was held on resulting trust for Twinsectra, subject to Sims's power[215] to apply the money for the specified purpose. This resulting trust could be enforced by the lender to ensure that the money lent is not misapplied. When the lender's purpose becomes frustrated, they can then revoke the borrower's power to apply the money for that purpose and demand repayment. Since the beneficial interest in the money remains in the lender throughout, it follows that the money is held on resulting trust immediately it is paid to the borrower. Although Lord Millett gave a dissenting speech, it was approved by Lords Hutton and Steyn, and has subsequently been described as 'authoritative' and 'compelling'.[216]

Lord Millett's analysis of the *Quistclose* trust is consistent with his general approach to resulting trusts, namely that they respond to the transferor's absence of intention to pass the entire beneficial interest in property to the transferee. But, can Lord Millett's analysis be reconciled with the principled analysis of the resulting trust that has been adopted in this chapter? Lord Millett's emphasis on the lender retaining a beneficial interest in the money lent[217] suggests that he was treating the *Quistclose* trust as being an automatic resulting trust. Such a trust will arise only where property has been transferred on an express trust and that trust has failed. But Lord Millett's analysis in *Twinsectra* is not consistent with these requirements for two reasons. First, he did not seek to establish any express trust, being content to assert that Twinsectra had not intended to transfer a beneficial interest to Sims so that a resulting trust arose immediately. According to Lord Millett, there is only ever one trust, and that is a resulting trust. Secondly, as he acknowledged, in many of the *Quistclose* cases the purpose of the transfer had not failed, so that there was no failure of trust. In *Quistclose* itself, since the money did not belong to the borrower, the borrower's insolvency did not prevent the money from being paid to the creditors. The fact, however, that the borrower was insolvent meant that the lender's reason for lending the money, namely to save the borrower from insolvency, had failed and that enabled the lender to revoke the mandate of the borrower to pay the money to its creditors. It appears, therefore, that this resulting trust is different from those that have been considered earlier in this chapter. It follows that either the *Quistclose* resulting trust constitutes a distinct third category of resulting trust or Lord Millett's analysis is incorrect.

---

[211] [2002] UKHL 12, [2002] 2 AC 164, [100]. *Twinsectra Ltd v Yardley* [2002] UKHL 12, [2002] 2 AC 164, [100] (Lord Millett) (see also [7] (Lord Steyn), [13] (Lord Hoffmann) and [25] (Lord Hutton)); *Latimer v IRC* [2004] UKPC 14, [2004] 1 WLR 1466, 1478 (Lord Millett); Lord Millett, '*Quistclose* trusts: *Twinsectra v Yardley* explained' (2011) 1 T&T 7.   [212] [2015] EWCA Civ 59, [2016] WTLR 43, [57].

[213] Ibid., [56].

[214] See Section 8.4.4.(vi), p. 245 for an explanation of the *Quistclose* trust as a form of automatic resulting trust.

[215] Lord Millett recognized that, in some cases, the borrower may be under a duty to apply the money for a particular purpose.   [216] *Challinor v Bellis* [2015] EWCA Civ 59, [2016] WTLR 43, [54] (Briggs LJ).

[217] Also recognized ibid., [62] (Briggs LJ).

(vii) The preferable analysis

Although there are various theories to explain the *Quistclose* trust, that trust can in fact be explained very simply and consistently with fundamental principles of the law of resulting trusts. Before that explanation is given, there are two fundamental points that need to be emphasized. First, the confusion in this area of the law derives from seeking to treat the so-called *Quistclose* trust as a unique form of trust. It is not.[218] Great confusion has arisen from the identification of a particular context in which trusts might arise, and from giving it a name by reference to a case that apparently identified new trust principles and a new type of trust. Secondly, there is no single trust template that applies where property has been transferred for a particular purpose.[219] There will be different responses depending on the particular circumstances of the case.[220]

Where property is transferred exclusively for a particular purpose, such as to enable the borrower to pay creditors, this will normally purport to be an express non-charitable purpose trust. An express trust will be intended because the payer will not intend the money to be at the free disposal of the recipient.[221] The consequences of this will depend on the particular circumstances of the transfer.

(1) In *Twinsectra Ltd v Yardley*, property was transferred to Sims to be held on an express trust. This may have arisen simply because the money was paid into a solicitors' client account,[222] or because the money was not at Sims's free disposal because it was to be applied for a particular purpose. This was a non-charitable purpose trust. Since the trust was for an abstract purpose of purchasing property, it followed that the trust was void because of the absence of any beneficiaries.[223] Consequently, the express trust failed initially and so the money paid to Sims was held on resulting trust for Twinsectra. Sims did indeed have a power to apply the money for the agreed purpose, and, had he done so, this would not have been a breach of trust, since it was authorized, and it would have exhausted the resulting trust such that the transferor's beneficial interest would have been extinguished.[224] But, until that power was exercised, it could be revoked by Twinsectra, and it was so revoked once the money had been misapplied. The power would also be revoked if there was a lack of clarity as to the identification of the purpose.[225] This analysis is consistent with that adopted by Lord Millett, but is more principled by identifying an express trust and showing that it had failed, so justifying the recognition of the resulting trust. There is no need to rely on the vague notion that Twinsectra had retained a beneficial interest in the money; a beneficial interest was created following the initial invalidity of the express trust.

(2) In *Quistclose*, the money lent to the borrower was intended to be held on an express trust because, again, it was clear the money was not at the free disposal of the borrower.[226] This too could be regarded as a non-charitable purpose trust.[227] This purpose may have

---

[218] Millett (see n. 196), 290.

[219] Glister, 'The nature of *Quistclose* trusts: classification and reconciliation' (2004) 63 CLJ 632, 633.

[220] Lord Millett, 'Foreword', in *The Quistclose Trust*, ed. Swadling (Oxford: Hart, 2004).

[221] *Challinor v Bellis* [2015] EWCA Civ 59, [2016] WTLR 43, [56] (Briggs LJ).

[222] As recognized by Lord Hoffmann: [2002] UKHL 12, [2002] 2 AC 164, [12].   [223] See Section 7.1.1, p. 188.

[224] *Challinor v Bellis* [2015] EWCA Civ 59, [2016] WTLR 43, [62] (Briggs LJ).

[225] Ibid., [63] (Briggs LJ).

[226] This has been doubted by Swadling, 'Orthodoxy', in *The Quistclose Trust: Critical Essays*, ed. Swadling (Oxford: Hart, 2004), p. 19. But, if there was no valid express trust, there was at least an attempt to create one that failed, so there would be a resulting trust. In other words, the case would then be treated in precisely the same way as *Twinsectra v Yardley*.

[227] Rickett, 'Different views on the scope of the *Quistclose* analysis: English and Antipodean insights' (1991) 107 LQR 608, 648. It was recognized as a purpose trust by Briggs LJ in *Challinor v Bellis* [2015] EWCA Civ 59, [2016] WTLR 43, [53]. See also *Twinsectra v Yardley* [2000] Lloyd's Rep PN 239, [75] (Potter LJ); *Cooper v PRG Powerhouse Ltd* [2008] EWHC 498 (Ch).

been specifically to pay dividends or to ensure that the company did not collapse. If the latter, this would be an invalid purpose trust, since the purpose was abstract; consequently, the trust failed initially, so that there would be an immediate automatic resulting trust with a power for the borrower to use the money to pay the dividend. This would reflect precisely the result in *Twinsectra*. Alternatively, if the purpose was to pay dividends to creditors, which was the purpose identified by Lord Wilberforce, this was not an abstract purpose, but one that benefited particular individuals. This express purpose trust would therefore be valid by virtue of the principle recognized in *Re Denley's Trust Deed*,[228] namely that the indirect benefit to individuals meant that the beneficiary principle would be satisfied, so that the creditors could enforce the trust. Subsequently, once the borrower had become insolvent, the purpose trust could not be performed, because a company cannot pay dividends once it has gone into liquidation. At this point, the express trust would have failed and the money would be held on resulting trust for the lender. Clearly, the lender could not have any beneficial interest in the money once the express trust was up and running, but that would not prevent a beneficial interest springing back to the lender once the trust had failed subsequently. This analysis is consistent with the structure of Lord Wilberforce's analysis in *Quistclose* (although he regarded the express trust as being one for persons rather than purposes, but this would have meant that the express trust would not have failed[229]), is not contradicted by anything said by Lord Millett in *Twinsectra*, and, most importantly, is consistent with the basic principles of resulting trusts.

(3) Other fact patterns can be suggested. For example, a lender might lend money to the borrower to pay creditors. This might be construed as a trust for persons rather than for purposes, but, if no particular beneficiaries could be identified, the express trust would fail initially for lack of beneficiaries[230] and a resulting trust would arise immediately.

(4) There could also be an express rather than a resulting trust, such as an express trust for the lender,[231] either declared by the lender or the borrower, or an express trust for the third-party creditors. But an express trust would be recognized only where this was consistent with the express or inferred intention of the relevant settlor. In *Charity Commission for England Wales v Framjee*[232] a charitable trust, known as the Dove Trust, was established to enable members of the public to raise money for the benefit of charities of their choice. So, for example, an individual might decide to run a marathon for a charity and would request donors to pay money to the Dove Trust which would then be distributed to the chosen charity. This had administrative and tax advantages. Unfortunately the Dove Trust owed significantly more to charities than it had received. It was consequently necessary to determine how the money it had received but which had not yet been paid out was held. Henderson J decided that the money was held by the Dove Trust on a single express sub-trust for the other charities, this trust having been declared by the trustees of the Dove Trust. This construction did at least avoid the problems of having numerous resulting trusts for each donor.

Where the borrower holds the money on trust for the lender, in many cases it will not make any difference whether the trust is express or resulting. It has, however, been suggested that, where the trust is resulting, the lender would not be able to terminate it and

---

[228] [1969] 1 Ch 373. Applied in the *Quistclose* trust context in *Carreras Rothman Ltd v Freeman Matthews Treasure Ltd* [1985] Ch 207, although Gibson J said that the effect of the case was that the beneficial interest was in suspense. [229] See Section 8.4.4.(i), p. 243.

[230] See *Vandervell v IRC* [1967] 2 AC 291, discussed in Section 8.3.2.(ii), p. 233.

[231] *Latimer v IRC* [2004] UKPC 13, [2004] 1 WLR 1466, [41] (Lord Millett). Such an express trust was recognized by the majority in *Twinsectra Ltd v Yardley* [2002] UKHL 12, [2002] 2 AC 164.

[232] [2014] EWHC 2507 (Ch), [2015] 1 WLR 16.

demand repayment of the money whilst the purpose was still capable of being fulfilled, whereas an express trust could be terminated by the lender at any point,[233] unless a term could be implied into the contract of loan that the lender would not seek repayment as long as the purpose was capable of being fulfilled.[234]

The real significance of this analysis of the *Quistclose* trust is that, where money is paid for a particular purpose that fails, that money can be held on an automatic resulting trust for the lender. Crucially, the money can be held on resulting trust only where the lender intended it to be held on an express trust, but that trust failed either initially or subsequently. This express trust will be found where the lender intended the money lent to be used for an exclusive purpose and the borrower was obliged to keep the money separate from their own assets.[235] If either or both of these factors are not established it will be difficult to show an intention that the money was to be held on an express trust. Because it is difficult to identify these factors in the *Quistclose* case itself, the money lent might not have been held on an express trust, and so, whichever mode of analysis is adopted, the lender should have had only a personal claim for repayment of the debt and not an equitable proprietary claim to the money.

Although the use of trusts to enable lenders to obtain priority over the borrower's creditors has proved to be controversial, this is much more defensible when it can be shown to involve the logical application of basic equitable principles through the mechanism of express and resulting trusts. It follows that the so-called *Quistclose* trust is not a peculiar trust, but simply involves the application of the law relating to automatic resulting trusts. Where A has requested B to transfer money to C on the basis that the money will be used for a specific purpose, if C fails to use it for that purpose there will be a failure of the express trust so that the money is held by C on an automatic resulting trust for B. If the money has been dissipated by C, so that B has no proprietary claim to it, B may be able to sue C for breach of trust, but only if C knew of the terms of A's request to B before disposing of the money.[236] The need for awareness of the terms of the transfer before C can be liable for breach can be justified by the principle that a trustee needs to be aware of the terms of the trust before they can be liable for breach of trust.[237]

(viii) Should the *Quistclose* trust be recognized?

The previous analysis has focused on explaining how the *Quistclose* trust can be recognized, but there is a more fundamental question: should it be? Bearing in mind that the effect of recognizing the trust is to give, for example, the lender of money priority over the borrower's unsecured creditors in circumstances where the lender had not sought to ensure that the loan is secured, is this defensible, or should the lender be confined to a personal claim? This has been considered by Hudson,[238] who concludes that the trust cannot be justified by a policy of incentivizing desirable transactions, nor by reference to unconscionability, nor by reference to fairness. She considers that the strongest justification is by reference to the need to respect party intention, which means that the *Quistclose* trust should primarily be interpreted as express. At the very least, such an approach to the analysis of the trust indicates that it should be confined to the clearest of cases where the conditions for recognizing the trust have been satisfied, for only then is it possible to justify the proprietary advantages of recognizing the trust.

---

[233] Glister (see n. 219), p. 649.

[234] Birks, 'Retrieving tied money', in *The Quistclose Trust*, ed. Swadling (Oxford: Hart, 2004), p. 126.

[235] See *Challinor v Bellis* [2015] EWCA Civ 59, [2016] WTLR 43, [56] (Briggs LJ).

[236] Ibid., [61] (Briggs LJ).   [237] See Section 3.3.2, p. 42.

[238] 'A normative approach to the *Quistclose* trust' (2017) 80 MLR 775.

8.5 EXPANSION OF THE RESULTING TRUST

Although the resulting trust has an important role to play commercially, that role is restricted to carefully defined circumstances. But Birks[239] and Chambers,[240] in particular, have sought to expand the role of the resulting trust dramatically by reference to their thesis that this trust responds to the claimant's absence of intention that the defendant should receive property beneficially. Their thesis is of potential significance where the defendant is unjustly enriched at the claimant's expense and where a transaction is rescinded.

8.5.1 UNJUST ENRICHMENT

The law of unjust enrichment is engaged where the defendant is unjustly enriched at the expense of the claimant.[241] Where the claimant establishes an unjust enrichment claim, the defendant will be liable to pay the value of the enrichment that has been received to the claimant. To establish such a claim, the claimant will need to show that the defendant has been enriched (which for present purposes means that the defendant has received money or other property); that this enrichment was obtained from the claimant; and that the circumstances of the defendant's enrichment are unjust in that the case falls within one of the recognized grounds of restitution. The function of these grounds is to establish that the claimant's intention to transfer the enrichment to the defendant can be regarded as absent or defective in some way. This may be because the claimant made a mistake, or was compelled to transfer the enrichment, or was unduly influenced by the defendant, or transferred the enrichment expecting to receive something in return and nothing was forthcoming, known as 'total failure of basis or consideration'. Once the elements of the claim have been established, the defendant will be liable to restore the value of the enrichment to the claimant, subject to any defences, such as that the defendant has changed their position in good faith. A typical example of an unjust enrichment claim will be where Ann has paid £1,000 to Bill thinking that she was liable to pay him the money, when in fact she was liable to pay somebody else. Bill will be required to repay £1,000 to Ann, save to the extent that he has changed his position, for example by spending the money without realizing that it had been paid by mistake. If Bill has not changed his position, he will be liable to make restitution of the value received, because Ann's intention to benefit Bill can be considered to be vitiated by the mistake.

Birks and Chambers reasoned from this vitiation of intention in the law of unjust enrichment to conclude that, in many cases of unjust enrichment, the enrichment received by the defendant should be held on resulting trust for the claimant.[242] This is because they consider the resulting trust to arise whenever the claimant lacked the intent to benefit the defendant.[243] Where an intention to transfer an enrichment has been vitiated, it follows, they conclude, that the enrichment received must be held on resulting trust for the claimant because the claimant would not have intended to benefit the defendant. This has significant implications, primarily by converting a well-established personal claim to restore

---

[239] See e.g. 'Trusts raised to reverse unjust enrichment: the *Westdeutsche* case' (1996) 4 RLR 3.

[240] See n. 24, Pt II; Chambers, 'Resulting trusts', in *Mapping the Law*, ed. Burrows and Lord Rodger (Oxford: Oxford University Press, 2006), ch. 13.

[241] As recognized by the House of Lords in *Lipkin Gorman (a firm) v Karpnale Ltd* [1991] 2 AC 548.

[242] Alternatively, note Häcker, 'Proprietary restitution after impaired consent transfers: a generalized power model' (2009) 68 CLJ 324, who argues that the transferor of property whose consent to the transfer of property has been impaired, such as where the transfer was induced by fraud or by duress, has a power *in rem* to bring a trust into existence by election, although the power cannot be exercised once the property had been obtained by a bona fide purchaser for value. [243] See Chambers (see n. 24), ch. 5.

value to the claimant into a proprietary claim, since the property that has been transferred to the defendant will be held on trust. This will be of great practical significance where the defendant is insolvent, for then the claimant's claim will rank above the defendant's unsecured creditors.

But why should the claimant be given such priority? The biggest drawback with the absence-of-intent theory of the resulting trust concerns whether the recognition of such a potentially wide doctrine of resulting trust will give claimants excessive proprietary protection.[244] If the defendant is to be considered to hold property on resulting trust whenever the claimant's intention to benefit the defendant is vitiated, it follows that the defendant will hold property on resulting trust in most cases in which the defendant will have been unjustly enriched, since much of the law of unjust enrichment turns on the claimant's intention to benefit the defendant being vitiated, for example by mistake or duress. This will enable the claimant to bring a proprietary claim rather than simply to recover the value of the property transferred, which will be advantageous where the defendant is insolvent. This is a serious concern and it follows that, if the absence-of-intent theory is to be recognized, it is vital to define restrictively the circumstances in which the claimant's intention to benefit the defendant should be regarded as vitiated.

Consequently, Chambers adapted his absence-of-intent thesis to ensure that the resulting trust would arise only where the defendant were not free to use the property that had been transferred for their own benefit.[245] It follows that, in most cases in which the basis for a transfer has failed, a resulting trust will not be recognized because the defendant will have been free to use the property for their own benefit when it was transferred, with the vitiation of the claimant's intention to benefit the defendant arising only subsequently when the benefit that the claimant expected to receive was not forthcoming. So, for example, if Carol were to deliver apples to David for him to make cider, with Carol expecting payment in return, David would be free to use the apples for his own benefit and would not hold them on resulting trust for Carol, even once David had told Carol that he would not pay for them, so that the basis for Carol's delivery will have failed. Carol would, therefore, not have an equitable proprietary interest in the apples, but would have a personal claim either to sue for breach of contract or, since the contract would have been discharged for breach, for the value of the apples in unjust enrichment.

If a resulting trust will not be triggered by the 'absence of intent to benefit' theory where the defendant was free to use the property transferred for their own purposes, the application of this principle becomes more complicated where the property has been transferred pursuant to a contract that was void *ab initio*. Since such a transaction was never legally valid, it might be concluded that the defendant never received the property beneficially, and so such benefits should be held on resulting trust for the claimant. The decision of the House of Lords in *Sinclair v Brougham*[246] is consistent with this argument, since it was recognized that property which was transferred pursuant to a void transaction would be held on resulting trust for the transferor. In that case the claimants had deposited money with a building society which did not have capacity to borrow the money. It was held that, because this transaction was ultra vires, and so null and void, the building society held the money on trust for the depositors. This case was, however, overruled by the House of Lords in *Westdeutsche Landesbank Girozentrale v Islington LBC*,[247] which held that no resulting trust arises when property is transferred to the defendant under a void contract.

---

[244] *Westdeutsche Landesbank Girozentrale v Islington LBC* [1996] AC 669, 716 (Lord Browne-Wilkinson).
[245] See n. 24, p. 145.   [246] [1914] AC 398.
[247] [1996] AC 669, 713 (Lord Browne-Wilkinson, with whom Lords Slynn, 718, and Lloyd, 738, concurred). Lord Goff was simply prepared to distinguish the case: ibid., 688.

The claimant in that case was a bank that had paid the defendant local authority a sum of money in respect of a transaction that was held to be null and void because the defendant lacked capacity to enter into it. The defendant conceded that it was liable to repay this money to the claimant, so the only question before the House of Lords was whether the claimant could claim compound interest from the defendant in respect of the amount that was due to it. Compound interest was at that time only available in respect of equitable claims, so the claimant needed to establish that it had an equitable proprietary interest in the money that the defendant had received. The claimant sought to show this by arguing that, since the transaction was void, the purpose of the transaction had failed and so the money was held on resulting trust for the claimant. This was rejected by the House of Lords for a number of reasons:

(1) because if a resulting trust were recognized, it would give unacceptable priority to the claimant if the defendant were to become insolvent—priority that would not be available if the transaction were merely voidable;

(2) because of a reluctance to import equitable principles into commercial dealings;[248] and

(3) because the claimant, having entered into a commercial transaction, took the risk of the defendant's insolvency.[249]

This must be correct. Where the claimant intends to transfer a benefit to the defendant for a particular purpose and that purpose can never be satisfied, there is no obvious reason why the property should be held on resulting trust for the claimant.

This is a significant decision in undermining the absence-of-intent analysis of the resulting trust. Chambers reconciled the decision with his absence-of-intent thesis by concluding that the defendant was free to use the money transferred for its own benefit.[250] But that was incorrect as a matter of law since, because the transaction was null and void from the start, the defendant could not have used the money for their own purposes. Further, the reasons suggested by the House of Lords for refusing to recognize a resulting trust in that case are of wider significance in supporting a restrictive role for the resulting trust.

Another problem with the attempt by Birks and Chambers to expand the role of the resulting trust by reference to proof of an absence of intent to benefit the defendant is that they assume that an intention to transfer property is either vitiated or it is not. In fact, vitiation of intention is a matter of degree. This is especially well illustrated by claims for recovery of mistaken payments. In the law of unjust enrichment, it is sufficient to show that the claimant's mistake caused them to pay money to the defendant.[251] But different, and more stringent, tests of mistake are required to set aside a contract,[252] or to show that legal title to property has not been transferred to the defendant.[253] In each case, it can be concluded that the claimant's intention to contract with or transfer property to the defendant has been vitiated, but different tests of mistake are required. Similarly, even if the resulting trust can be justified by reference to the absence of intent to benefit the defendant, it does not follow from the fact that the claimant transferred property to the defendant by mistake that the property will be held on resulting trust. That vitiation of intention must be a matter of degree is, in fact, a crucial part of Birks's and Chambers's theory of the resulting trust. For there to be a resulting trust where property is transferred to the defendant by

---

[248] Ibid., 704 (Lord Browne-Wilkinson).   [249] Ibid., 684 (Lord Goff).
[250] See n. 24, p. 162.   [251] *Kleinwort Benson Ltd v Lincoln City Council* [1999] 2 AC 349.
[252] *Great Peace Shipping Ltd v Tsavliris Salvage (International) Ltd* [2002] EWCA Civ 1407, [2003] QB 679.
[253] Virgo, *The Principles of the Law of Restitution*, 3rd edn (Oxford: Oxford University Press, 2015), p. 574.

mistake, for example, legal title to that property must be vested in the defendant. So, the absence-of-intent theory assumes that the claimant's intention to transfer legal title has not been vitiated,[254] but, rather, it is the claimant's intention to benefit the defendant that has been vitiated, whatever that means. Anyway, this chapter has shown that the resulting trust does not respond to an absence of intent, but to an imputed or presumed[255] intention that the property should be held on resulting trust for the claimant, and there is no reason why such an intention should be imputed or presumed simply because the defendant has been unjustly enriched at the expense of the claimant.

It does not follow, however, that there can be no circumstances where property has been transferred to the defendant in which the claimant has a claim in unjust enrichment where that property might also be held on resulting trust. This might arise, for example, where property has been held on an express trust that has failed, such as in the context of *Barclays Bank Ltd v Quistclose Investments Ltd*,[256] or where the claimant has voluntarily transferred property to the defendant in circumstances under which a resulting trust will be presumed. But, in the common cases in which the claimant has a claim in unjust enrichment, the recognized categories of resulting trust will not be engaged. So, for example, where property has been transferred to the defendant in circumstances under which there has been a total failure of basis in that the claimant has received nothing in return, there will be no presumption of resulting trust because the claimant's expectation that they would receive something in return for the transfer will not make it a voluntary transfer and the relevant presumption will not be engaged. Where the claimant has transferred property to the defendant by mistake, such as where the claimant believes that they are discharging a liability owed to the defendant that does not exist, the transfer will not be voluntary and so the presumption of resulting trust will not be engaged. If, however, the transfer was intended to be a gift, but the claimant was mistaken, for example, as to the identity of the donee, the presumption of resulting trust would appear to be engaged because the transfer was intended to be voluntary,[257] but the fact that the donor intended to make a gift, albeit that it was to the wrong person, can be relied on by the donee to rebut the presumption, simply because an intention to make a gift is inconsistent with the presumed intent that the property should be held on trust for the donor.[258] Consequently, the donor would only have a claim in unjust enrichment against the donee for the value of the gift; there would be no proprietary claim.

Outside of these established categories of the resulting trust, where the overlap with a claim in unjust enrichment is a matter of coincidence rather than design, the resulting trust is not a mechanism for effecting a proprietary restitutionary response to the defendant's unjust enrichment at the claimant's expense.[259]

8.5.2 RESCISSION

Where property has been transferred to the defendant pursuant to a contract that is voidable, because, for example, the claimant was induced to enter into it as a result of

[254] Mee (see n. 118), p. 227.

[255] This being consistent with the analysis of Lord Browne-Wilkinson in *Westdeutsche Landesbank Girozentrale v Islington LBC* [1996] AC 669, 708. See Section 8.3.1.(iii), p. 231.

[256] [1970] AC 567. See Section 8.4.4.(vii), p. 246.

[257] Worthington, 'Proprietary restitution: void, voidable and uncompleted contracts' (1995) 9 TLI 113, 114.

[258] See Swadling (see n. 23), p. 116, who considers that the fact that the intention of the donor to make a gift is known to the court will mean that the presumption of resulting trust will not even be engaged.

[259] O'Dell, 'The resulting trust', in *Structure and Justification in Private Law*, ed. Rickett and Grantham (Oxford: Hart, 2008), ch. 19, although the constructive trust may have a role in effecting a proprietary restitutionary response. See Section 9.3.1, p. 258.

misrepresentation or undue influence, the claimant can apply to the court to seek an order to rescind the contract in Equity. The effect of rescission will be that the property which has been transferred will be held on trust by the defendant for the claimant. This has sometimes been analysed as a resulting trust. For example, *El Ajou v Dollar Land Holdings plc*[260] recognized this as an 'old-fashioned institutional resulting trust'. But what sort of resulting trust would it be? It could not be an automatic resulting trust, because property had not previously been transferred to the defendant on an express trust. But neither could it be a presumed resulting trust, because the transfer had not been voluntary; the property was transferred pursuant to a contractual obligation rather than purportedly as a gift. This could, instead, be regarded as a resulting trust triggered either by the defendant's unjust enrichment, since the defendant will be unjustly enriched once the contract has been rescinded, or simply a resulting trust established by showing that the claimant did not intend the defendant to enjoy the benefit of the property once the contract had been rescinded. But neither explanation is consistent with the fundamental principles relating to resulting trusts as they have been identified in this chapter. The preferable explanation of the trust that arises on rescission of a contract is that it is a constructive trust that follows from the defendant's unconscionable conduct in inducing the contract.[261] Indeed, Millett J recognized in *Lonrho plc v Fayed (No 2)*[262] that where a contract has been rescinded for fraudulent misrepresentation, any property transferred would be held on constructive trust.

8.5.3 CONCLUSIONS

It follows that there is no need to expand the resulting trust to encompass claims in unjust enrichment and following rescission of a contract. In addition, the absence-of-intent theory as an explanation of the resulting trust should be rejected as being unprincipled, inconsistent with much authority, and unacceptable for policy reasons in expanding potential proprietary claims. Instead, the resulting trust can arise only where the circumstances of the transfer of property falls within one of the recognized cases in which a resulting trust is presumed or where an express trust has failed. In both situations, the underlying trigger for the resulting trust is most appropriately considered to be the transferor's imputed or presumed intention that the property should be held on trust for them.

---

[260] [1993] 3 All ER 717, 734.
[261] This has been recognized by Etherton C in *National Crime Agency v Robb* [2014] EWHC 4384 (Ch), [2015] Ch 520, [49]. See Section 9.3.2, p. 263.   [262] [1992] 1 WLR 1, 12.

9

CONSTRUCTIVE TRUSTS

9.1 FUNDAMENTAL PRINCIPLES

9.1.1 THE ESSENCE OF CONSTRUCTIVE TRUSTS

A constructive trust is a true trust like any other, where the constructive trustee has legal title to identifiable property that is held for the benefit of the beneficiaries. But the distinctive feature of a constructive trust is that it arises by operation of law, without regard to the intentions of the parties.[1] The constructive trust clearly differs, therefore, from an express trust, which is created by the settlor's intent,[2] and the resulting trust, which is triggered by the imputed or presumed intention of the transferor that property is to be held on trust for them.[3]

9.1.2 THE THEORETICAL FOUNDATION OF CONSTRUCTIVE TRUSTS

If the constructive trust is not created by intention (whether actual, imputed, or presumed), what is it that triggers the trust? This is a matter of particular controversy. It has sometimes been suggested that the constructive trust is a response to the defendant's unjust enrichment,[4] but the better view is that the doctrine of unjust enrichment should trigger only personal remedies and not the creation of equitable proprietary interests.[5] In the 1970s, some judges, led by Lord Denning MR, used the constructive trust as a mechanism with which to create equitable property rights where justice and good conscience demanded it.[6] But this is unprincipled and uncertain. More recently, Lord Browne-Wilkinson recognized that unconscionability on the part of the defendant was the general principle that underpins the recognition of the constructive trust in all cases.[7] Careful analysis of the different circumstances under which the constructive trust has been recognized reveals that

---

[1] *Air Jamaica v Charlton* [1999] 1 WLR 1399, 1412 (Lord Millett).   [2] See Section 4.2, p. 72.

[3] See Section 8.1.3.(iii), p. 217.

[4] See Birks, *Unjust Enrichment*, 2nd edn (Oxford: Oxford University Press, 2005), p. 302.

[5] See Section 19.1.4.(ii), p. 540.   [6] *Eves v Eves* [1975] 1 WLR 1338.

[7] *Westdeutsche Landesbank Girozentrale v Islington London Borough Council* [1996] AC 669, 705. See also *Paragon Finance Ltd v D B Thakerar* [1999] 1 All ER 400, 409 (Millett LJ).

unconscionability is indeed a significant trigger for this trust, but it does not necessarily explain all of the recognized categories. As Sir Terence Etherton noted:[8]

> The search for an acceptable, universally acknowledged, principle for the establishment of a constructive trust, which gives coherence to past decisions and provides a clear guide for the future, will certainly prove elusive in relation to the many different areas of law and fact in which constructive trusts arise.

Similarly, Lord Scott[9] has recognized that it is not possible to prescribe exhaustively the circumstances under which a constructive trust will be created, so the focus should instead be placed on recognizing particular factual circumstances under which the constructive trust will and will not be relevant. Consequently, rather than seeking a simple unifying theory of the constructive trust from the outset and then attempting to squeeze the recognized cases into this theory, it is more useful to identify the particular categories of case in which the constructive trust has previously been recognized and then to consider whether there is one single principle that can be identified to explain all constructive trusts.[10]

9.1.3 THE NATURE OF CONSTRUCTIVE TRUSTS

Why are these trusts called 'constructive trusts'? The use of the word 'constructive' suggests that there is something artificial about them, in that they are construed by the courts, but it does not follow that the trust itself is artificial in any way. These are genuine trusts, under which property is held by a trustee on trust for somebody else. The artificiality relates to the way in which they are created. Because these trusts arise by operation of law, there is no requirement that they need to be formally declared. It is for this reason that constructive trusts of land do not need to be evidenced in writing.[11] Once created, the trust functions in the same way as an express trust, save that the constructive trustee is not subject to the same obligations as an express trustee.[12] In particular, the fact that the beneficiary of such a trust has an equitable proprietary interest in the trust property means that, if the trustee becomes insolvent, the beneficiary's claim to the trust property will rank above the claims of other unsecured creditors of the trustee.

9.2 TYPES OF CONSTRUCTIVE TRUST

Much of the complexity of the law in this area arises because the judges use the language of the constructive trust in five distinct ways.

9.2.1 INSTITUTIONAL CONSTRUCTIVE TRUST

The institutional constructive trust is the orthodox mode of analysing these trusts, which are treated as arising by operation of law on the occurrence of a certain event where a constructive trust has previously been recognized.[13] Under this category of the constructive trust, the court simply recognizes that the trust has already arisen, without having any discretion as to whether or not to do so.

---

[8] 'Constructive trusts: a new model for Equity and unjust enrichment' (2008) 67 CLJ 265.
[9] In *Cobbe v Yeoman's Row Management Ltd* [2008] UKHL 55, [2008] 1 WLR 1752, [30].
[10] See Section 9.3.8, p. 274.   [11] Law of Property Act 1925, s. 53(2).
[12] See Section 9.5, p. 279.
[13] See e.g. *Halifax Building Society v Thomas* [1996] Ch 217, 229 (Peter Gibson LJ).

9.2.2 REMEDIAL CONSTRUCTIVE TRUST

This is simply a remedy that can be awarded where a judge, in the exercise of their discretion, considers that it is appropriate that the defendant should hold property on trust for the claimant. A consequence is that the creation of the equitable proprietary interest in the property that is held on trust occurs by virtue of the exercise of judicial discretion and it is this that distinguishes the remedial from the institutional constructive trust, as was recognized by Lord Browne-Wilkinson in *Westdeutsche Landesbank Girozentrale v Islington LBC*:[14]

> Under an institutional constructive trust the trust arises by operation of law as from the date of the circumstances which give rise to it: the function of the court is merely to declare that such trust has arisen in the past. The consequences that flow from such a trust having arisen (including the potentially unfair consequences to third parties who in the interim have received the trust property) are also determined by rules of law, not under a discretion. A remedial constructive trust, as I understand it, is different. It is a judicial remedy giving rise to an enforceable obligation: the extent to which it operates retrospectively to the prejudice of third parties lies in the discretion of the court.

The remedial constructive trust is recognized in Australia, Canada, and New Zealand, but it has been rejected in England.[15] Whether it should be recognized in this jurisdiction will be considered later in this chapter.[16]

9.2.3 CONSTRUCTIVE TRUST AS REMEDY

Where the claimant has an existing equitable interest in property that has been misappropriated and that property, or substitute property that can be regarded as representing the original property,[17] has been received by a third-party defendant, the claimant will wish to recover the property from the defendant.[18] A mechanism for doing so is the constructive trust. The court can order that the defendant holds the property on constructive trust for the claimant who can then call for the property to be transferred to them. Here, the constructive trust operates simply as a remedial mechanism to enable the transfer of the property to the claimant in Equity. It is different from the remedial constructive trust, because that involves the creation of an equitable proprietary interest that had not previously existed. Where the constructive trust as remedy is used, there is already an equitable proprietary interest in existence, which will typically have been created by an express trust; the constructive trust simply operates as a conduit for the transfer of property from the defendant to the claimant. Whether it is appropriate to use the language of the constructive trust as remedy in this context is, however, a matter of some controversy. It has been suggested that, if the claimant's original equitable interest arose under an express trust, the defendant who has received the property or its substitute should hold that property on the same trust.[19] But this argument is unconvincing. The defendant who has received the property will not be under the same trust obligations as the original express trustee, such as being subject to an obligation to invest the trust property. The better view, therefore, is that the recipient does indeed hold the property on a distinct trust, which, because it arises by operation of law, should be characterized as a constructive trust.

---

[14] [1996] AC 669, 714.

[15] *FHR European Ventures LLP v Cedar Capital Partners LLC* [2014] UKSC 45, [2015] AC 250, [47].

[16] See Section 9.4, p. 275.   [17] By virtue of the tracing rules, see Section 19.3, p. 551.

[18] As occurred in *Foskett v McKeown* [2001] 1 AC 102. See Section 19.1.6.(vi), p. 546.

[19] Lord Millett, 'Proprietary restitution', in *Equity in Commercial Law*, ed. Degeling and Edelman (Sydney: Law Book Co., 2005), pp. 315–16. See also *Foskett v McKeown* [2001] 1 AC 102, 108 (Lord Browne-Wilkinson).

9.2.4 LIABILITY TO ACCOUNT AS A CONSTRUCTIVE TRUSTEE

English law recognizes two specific equitable causes of action involving liability of third parties arising from breach of a trustee's or fiduciary's duty, known as the actions for unconscionable receipt of property in breach of trust or fiduciary duty,[20] and dishonestly assisting a breach of trust or fiduciary duty.[21] The liability of the defendant in these claims is traditionally described as a liability to account as a constructive trustee.[22] But such language is misleading, since it might be interpreted as requiring the defendant to hold property on a constructive trust.[23] That is not the case. The defendant's liability for both causes of action is a personal liability, either to restore the value of any property received in breach of trust or fiduciary duty, or to compensate the claimant for loss suffered as a result of the defendant's assistance with a breach of trust or fiduciary duty. The defendant holds nothing on trust for anybody. This was recognized in *Dubai Aluminium Co Ltd v Salaam* by Lord Millett,[24] who concluded that the defendant's liability is better described as an equitable liability to account to the claimant.

9.2.5 COMMON INTENTION CONSTRUCTIVE TRUST

Although the constructive trust traditionally arises without regard to the intention of the parties, there is a distinct form of constructive trust that is triggered with reference to the express, implied, or imputed intention of the parties, and which is known as the common intention constructive trust. This is a trust that arises from an agreement or understanding of the parties as to whether they have a beneficial interest in property and, if so, what the extent of that interest might be.

This is especially significant where a couple have cohabited and their home is registered either in the name of them both[25] or in the name of one of them only.[26] Although the language of the constructive trust is used in these cases,[27] this is very different from the ordinary constructive trust, because it responds to the intention of the parties; for that reason, it will be treated separately in this book.[28]

9.3 CIRCUMSTANCES IN WHICH AN INSTITUTIONAL CONSTRUCTIVE TRUST WILL BE RECOGNIZED

Of the five types of constructive trust, it is the institutional constructive trust that is most significant in English law. The remedial constructive trust is not recognized in England and Wales. The constructive trust as remedy is relevant to equitable proprietary claims,

---

[20] See Section 20.2.3.(i), p. 596.   [21] See Section 20.3.2, p. 613.

[22] It was rather confusingly described as 'a remedial constructive trust in cases of ancillary liability' by Henderson J in *The High Commissioner for Pakistan in the United Kingdom v Prince Mukkuram Jah* [2016] EWHC 1465 (Ch), [2016] WTLR 1763, [125].

[23] This appears to have been Lord Sumption's, incorrect, assumption in *Angove's Pty Ltd v Bailey* [2016] UKSC 47, [2016] 1 WLR 3179, [29].

[24] [2002] UKHL 48, [2003] 2 AC 366, 404. See also *Paragon Finance plc v DB Thakerar and Co* [1999] 1 All ER 400, 408 (Millett LJ) and *Williams v Central Bank of Nigeria* [2014] UKSC 10, [2014] AC 1189, [9] (Lord Sumption) and [64] (Lord Neuberger).

[25] *Stack v Dowden* [2007] UKHL 17, [2007] 2 AC 432, discussed in Section 10.2.4.(ii), p. 294 and *Jones v Kernott* [2011] UKSC 53, [2012] 1 AC 776, discussed in Section 10.2.4.(iii), p. 294.

[26] *Curran v Collins* [2015] EWCA Civ 404, [2015] Fam Law 780, discussed in Section 10.2.4.(i), p. 293.

[27] Which have been extended to commercial arrangements: *Yaxley v Gotts* [2000] Ch 162; *Banner Homes Group Plc v Luff Developments Ltd* [2000] Ch 372; *Crossco No 4 Unlimited v Jolan Ltd* [2011] EWCA Civ 1619. See also *Yeoman's Row Management Ltd v Cobbe* [2008] UKHL 55, [2008] 1 WLR 1752. See Section 10.3.3, p. 304.

[28] See Chapter 10 of this volume.

and so is considered in Chapter 19. Liability as a constructive trustee does not involve the recognition of a constructive trust of property, and the common intention constructive trust, being triggered by the intention of the parties, is clearly distinct from the core categories of the constructive trust and so will be considered in Chapter 10. Consequently, we need to focus on the institutional constructive trust and the identification of the categories of case in which such a trust has been recognized.

The orthodox view in English law is that the constructive trust is a substantive institution which will be recognized in certain circumstances;[29] this is a real trust. But Birks[30] suggested that all constructive trusts are fictions, because the declaration of trust only exists in the eye of the law. This argument was developed by Swadling[31] who considers that the label 'constructive trust' simply masks a liability on the part of the defendant either to pay money to the claimant or to transfer a right to the claimant. In other words, the label simply describes different remedies for particular grievances. But is this trust really fictional? Surely it simply involves a different method of declaring a trust, but it does involve a real trust with real proprietary interests. The deemed declaration of a constructive trust is a deliberate attempt by Equity to recognize a real trust in certain well-defined circumstances. There is no fiction. If the trust were not real then it would indeed be fictional, which is why the so-called constructive trust which is recognized where the defendant is held liable for unconscionable receipt or dishonest assistance should not be called a trust at all, since it is only a cipher for a personal remedy. Since the constructive trust is a real trust it follows that, from the date of creation of the trust, the beneficiary has an equitable proprietary interest in the trust property which can be vindicated as appropriate.

9.3.1 UNCONSCIONABLE RETENTION

A significant category of the institutional constructive trust arises where it is unconscionable for the defendant to retain property received from the claimant. Although unconscionability is at the heart of this category, as it is with all categories of constructive trust, it is distinct because unconscionability is determined with specific regard to the fault of the defendant in receiving and retaining property from the claimant. This category of constructive trust was recognized by Lord Browne-Wilkinson in *Westdeutsche Landesbank Girozentrale v Islington LBC*,[32] when he was considering the difficult decision of *Chase-Manhattan Bank NA v Israel-British Bank (London) Ltd.*[33] In *Chase Manhattan Bank*, the claimant had mistakenly paid the defendant the same amount of money twice. It was held that, although legal title in the money that had been mistakenly paid had passed to the defendant, it was still possible for the court to recognize that the claimant had an equitable proprietary interest in the money. As Goulding J said,[34] 'a person who pays money to another under a factual mistake retains an equitable property in it and the conscience of the other is subjected to a fiduciary duty to respect his proprietary rights'. But Goulding J did not explain how this equitable proprietary interest could have arisen.

In *Westdeutsche Landesbank*,[35] Lord Browne-Wilkinson suggested that Goulding J was wrong to conclude that the claimant had an equitable proprietary interest in the money

---

[29] See e.g. *Metall und Rohstoff AG v Donaldson, Lufkin and Jenrette Inc* [1990] 1 QB 391, 478–80 (Slade LJ) and *Halifax Building Society v Thomas* [1996] Ch 217, 229 (Peter Gibson LJ).

[30] 'Property, unjust enrichment and tracing' [2001] CLP 231, 242.

[31] 'The fiction of the constructive trust' (2011) 64 CLP 1.

[32] [1996] AC 669, 714–15. See Section 8.5.1, p. 249. See also *Hussey v Palmer* [1972] 1 WLR 1286, 1290 (Lord Denning MR) and *The Commissioners for Her Majesty's Revenue and Customs v The Investment Trust Companies* [2017] UKSC 29, [2017] 2 WLR 1200, [70] (Lord Reed).   [33] [1981] Ch 105.

[34] Ibid., 119.   [35] [1996] AC 669, 715.

from the moment at which it had been received by the defendant simply because it had been paid by mistake, since there needed to be an identifiable event to create the equitable interest, and the fact that the claimant has paid money to the defendant by mistake is not a sufficient event to create such an interest. Although Lord Browne-Wilkinson did not express his conclusion in these terms, the effect of his analysis of *Chase Manhattan Bank* is that the fact that the defendant has been unjustly enriched at the expense of the claimant by virtue of the receipt of a mistaken payment is not a sufficient reason to trigger a constructive trust.[36] But Lord Browne-Wilkinson did suggest that the money paid by mistake was subsequently held on constructive trust for the claimant, so that the claimant did indeed have an equitable proprietary interest in the money. This constructive trust arose because the defendant became aware that the claimant had paid the money to it by mistake within two days of its receipt of the money. As Lord Browne-Wilkinson said: 'Although the mere receipt of the moneys, in ignorance of the mistake, gives rise to no trust, the retention of the moneys after the recipient bank learned of the mistake may well have given rise to a constructive trust . . . '.[37] In other words, the justification for the recognition of the claimant's equitable proprietary interest in the money paid by mistake was that the defendant's conscience had been affected by its knowledge of the mistake whilst it was in possession of the money. Once the defendant was aware of the mistake, it should have repaid the money to the claimant, and its failure to do so constituted the unconscionable conduct that justified the recognition of the constructive trust.

Lord Browne-Wilkinson went on to recognize that a thief who stole a bag of coins would similarly hold that property on a constructive trust, because of the thief's unconscionable conduct in committing theft and retaining the stolen property.[38] Constructive trusts will be triggered by this principle of unconscionable retention in other circumstances as well, such as where the defendant has obtained property by fraud.[39]

The significance of the constructive trust was confirmed in *Re Farepak Food and Gifts Ltd*,[40] which recognized that claimants, who had paid in advance for goods or services, could claim that the money was held on constructive trust for them where the defendant, at the time of receiving payment, had already decided that the goods and services would not be provided because it would cease trading, although this could not be established on the facts of the case. However, in *Bailey v Angove's Pty Ltd*[41] the Supreme Court did not accept that a constructive trust would be recognized where money had been paid to the defendant pursuant to a contract and, at the time of payment, the defendant knew that imminent insolvency would prevent it from performing any of its obligations under the contract. In reaching this conclusion the reasoning in *Nesté Oy v Lloyd's Bank Plc*[42] was

---

[36] Neither would it be a sufficient reason to trigger a resulting trust. See Section 8.5.1, p. 249.

[37] [1996] AC 669, 715. See also *Bank of America v Arnell* [1999] Lloyd's Rep 399; *Papamichael v National Westminster Bank plc* [2003] 1 Lloyd's Rep 341, 372 (Judge Chambers QC); *Commerzbank AG v IMB Morgan plc* [2004] EWHC 2771 (Ch), [2005] 1 Lloyd's Rep 298, [36] (Lawrence Collins J); *Re Farepak Food and Gifts Ltd* [2006] EWHC 3272 (Ch), [40] (Mann J); *Armstrong DLW GmbH v Winnington Networks Ltd* [2012] EWHC 10 (Ch), [2013] Ch 156. In Australia see *Wambo Coal Co Pty Ltd v Ariff* [2007] NSWC 589.

[38] [1996] AC 669, 716. See also *Bankers Trust Co v Shapira* [1980] 1 WLR 1274 and *Armstrong DLW GmbH v Winnington Networks Ltd* [2012] EWHC 10 (Ch), [2013] Ch 156, [276] (Stephen Morris QC).

[39] *Stocks v Wilson* [1913] 2 KB 235, 244 (Lush J); *Halley v The Law Society* [2003] EWCA Civ 97, [48] (Carnwath LJ); *Papamichael v National Westminster Bank plc* [2003] 1 Lloyd's Rep 341, 374 (Judge Chambers QC); *Commerzbank AG v IMB Morgan plc* [2004] EWHC 2771 (Ch), [2004] All ER (D) 450 (Nov), [36] (Lawrence Collins J); *Sinclair Investment Holdings SA v Versailles Trade Finance Ltd* [2005] EWCA Civ 722; *Campden Hill Ltd v Chakrani* [2005] EWHC 911 (Ch).

[40] [2006] EWHC 3272 (Ch). See Section 1.4.8, p. 13. See also *Armstrong DLW GmbH v Winnington Networks Ltd* [2012] EWHC 10 (Ch), [2013] (Ch) 156, [129] (Stephen Morris QC).

[41] [2016] UKSC 47, [2016] 1 WLR 3179. See Watts (2017) 133 LQR 11.   [42] [1983] 2 Lloyd's Rep 658.

rejected, namely that a constructive trust would be triggered because a reasonable and honest person would have repaid the money which had been received after the directors of the recipient company had concluded that the company was insolvent. The justification for the Supreme Court's decision turns on what good conscience is considered to require and that, just because a reasonable person would have returned a payment, it does not follow that it should have been returned. But this misses the point about the basis for recognizing the constructive trust on the ground of unconscionable retention. The prior question is whether the defendant is liable to make restitution to the claimant, which will be the case if money has been paid on a basis which is not fulfilled in any way. If there is such a restitutionary liability and the defendant is aware of the circumstances which establish the claim then the retention of the money should be considered to be unconscionable, so triggering a constructive trust. That is why money paid by mistake may be held on constructive trust, as was acknowledged by Lord Sumption, although he considered that this will only occur where the mistake was 'fundamental', without explaining what this means. Lord Sumption suggested that only where the claimant had made such a mistake would their intention to benefit the defendant have been vitiated completely. That is why he concluded that, in a case where the claimant had paid money to the defendant expecting something in return which was not forthcoming, a constructive trust would not be recognized because this would not have 'vitiated the intention of the [claimant] to part with its entire interest in the money'.[43] But this is confusing rules about intention to pass title at Law with the very different question as to whether the defendant's retention of the money was unconscionable in the light of the defendant's knowledge of the circumstances of the transfer. If the defendant was aware that the claimant had transferred money expecting to receive something in return which was not forthcoming, and the defendant failed to pay the money back, the defendant's retention of the money should be treated as unconscionable; although this should only be the case where the basis for the payment has actually failed and not where it might potentially fail in the future. This is not, however, what the Supreme Court held in *Bailey*, although that decision is demonstrably confused and creates significant inconsistency in the law.

But if *Bailey* is regarded as correctly reflecting the state of the law where the defendant has failed to perform any part of the contract, what should happen where the contract was void and the defendant was aware of this? There will be a personal liability to make restitution where the contract is void and, if the defendant is aware of the invalidity but does not repay the money, they could be considered to have acted unconscionably so that the money paid pursuant to the void contract will be held on constructive trust. If this is correct, it would follow that, on the facts of *Westdeutsche Landesbank* itself, in which money had been paid by a bank in respect of a contract with a public authority that was void, the defendant public authority would have held the money on constructive trust for the claimant bank had the money not ceased to be identifiable before the defendant discovered that the transaction was void. It would follow that, once a defendant has discovered that a contract in respect of which money has been paid is void, the defendant's continued retention of that money will be unconscionable. This does, however, appear to be inconsistent with *Bailey v Angove's Pty Ltd* simply because the fact that the contract was void will not be sufficient to vitiate the claimant's intention to transfer the benefit to the defendant.

There are three other particular problems relating to the unconscionable retention head of constructive trusts.

---

[43] [2016] UKSC 47, [2016] 1 WLR 3179, [30].

(i) What has happened to the legal title?

It is a fundamental principle of the law of trusts, including the law of constructive trusts, that the trustee has legal title and the beneficiary has an equitable interest in the trust property. So, in all cases in which a constructive trust has been recognized, the trustee must have legal title[44] to the property. But this causes serious problems where, for example, property has been stolen, since, in such circumstances, the claimant's legal title to the property will not have passed to the defendant until it ceases to be identifiable at Law, because, for example, it has become mixed with the defendant's own property.[45] But, if the legal title has not passed, how can the defendant thief hold the stolen property on constructive trust for the victim? Since the property will still belong to the victim, it would appear that the thief cannot hold the property on constructive trust for them.[46] This was specifically recognized as a problem in *Shalson v Russo*.[47] Despite this, Lord Browne-Wilkinson, in *Westdeutsche Landesbank*,[48] and the High Court of Australia[49] have recognized that a thief will indeed hold property on constructive trust for the victim. An explanation for this result has been suggested by Tarrant, who has argued that the thief holds their rights to possess the stolen property on trust for the victim.[50] It has been recognized that a thief does indeed have a possessory title to the stolen property, so, for example, if that property is unlawfully taken from a thief by a third party, the thief can assert their possessory rights against that third party.[51] It has further been recognized that the thief, or the person who obtains the stolen property from the thief, has a good title to the stolen property against anybody in the world except for the victim of the theft.[52] It follows that the victim of theft has both a residuary legal title in the stolen property and also an equitable proprietary interest in the thief's possessory title by virtue of the thief's unconscionable retention.[53] The victim then has a choice as to whether to rely on their legal property right to assert a claim against the thief or the subsequent possessor of the stolen property, or instead to assert a claim founded on their equitable rights to the property against the thief or subsequent possessor of it. The advantage of relying on the equitable property right is that the remedies in Equity to vindicate property rights are much more extensive than at Law,[54] and that the claimant is able to make a claim to recover the stolen property or its proceeds even though it has become mixed with other property.[55]

(ii) The degree of fault

What degree of fault is required on the part of the defendant before their conduct in retaining the property can be considered to be unconscionable? If the claimant paid money by mistake or if the transaction was invalid, it is clear that the defendant's knowledge of the mistake or the invalidity of the transaction will be sufficient to characterize them as

---

[44] Although it is possible to have a trust of an equitable interest.   [45] See Section 19.3.2, p. 556.

[46] Barkehall Thomas, 'Thieves as trustees: the enduring legacy of *Black v S Freedman and Co*' (2009) 3 J Eq 52; Chambers, 'Trust and theft', in *Exploring Private Law*, ed. Bant and Harding (Cambridge: Cambridge University Press, 2010), ch. 10.   [47] [2003] EWHC 1637 (Ch), [2005] Ch 281, [110] (Rimer J).

[48] [1996] AC 696, 716.   [49] *Black v F S Freedman and Co* (1910) 12 CLR 105.

[50] Tarrant, 'Property rights to stolen money' (2005) 32 UWALR 234, 245; Tarrant, 'Thieves as trustees: in defence of the theft principle' (2009) 3 J Eq 170, 172. See also Fox, *Property Rights in Money* (2008, OUP), p. 140. This analysis was approved by the New South Wales Court of Appeal in *Fistar v Riverwood Legion and Community Club Ltd* [2016] NWSCA 81, [37] (Leeming JA).

[51] *Costello v Chief Constable of Derbyshire* [2001] 3 All ER 150.

[52] *Islamic Republic of Iran v Barakat Galleries Ltd* [2009] QB 22, [15] (Lord Phillips).

[53] See *Armstrong DLW Gmbh v Winnington Networks Ltd* [2012] EWHC 10 (Ch), [2013] Ch 156, [276] (Stephen Morris QC).   [54] See further Section 19.4, p. 574.

[55] See Section 19.3.3.(iii), p. 561.

acting unconscionably in not repaying the money to the claimant. Presumably, it will also be sufficient that the defendant believes or suspects that the claimant was mistaken or that the transaction was invalid.[56] But, should it be sufficient that the defendant ought to have known of the mistake or the invalidity of the transaction? If unconscionability were to encompass an objective test of what the defendant ought to have known, it would significantly widen the circumstances in which a constructive trust will be recognized. But, due to the policy of the law to restrict claims to recover property, particularly because of the adverse effect that they have on the defendant's creditors where the defendant is insolvent, the better view is that the rules for the imposition of constructive trusts should be interpreted very restrictively. Consequently, the defendant's conscience should be considered to be affected only where they were actually aware of the claimant's mistake or the invalidity of the transaction[57] and, in the light of that knowledge or suspicion, they should have returned the benefit received.[58]

(iii) Timing

At what point must the defendant's conscience be affected? Clearly, if the defendant knew of the mistake or the invalidity of the transaction at the time the property was received, it would be appropriate to recognize that the property was held on constructive trust for the claimant from that moment. Lord Browne-Wilkinson's interpretation of *Chase-Manhattan Bank* suggests that acquiring knowledge of the mistake two days after receipt of the money would have been sufficient to characterize the defendant's conduct as unconscionable. But, what if the defendant discovers the mistake months or even years later? The natural limit to the period during which we should consider whether the defendant's conscience has been affected is once the defendant has lost the property that they had received from the claimant, or the proceeds of, or substitute for, that property.[59] In other words, the question of recognizing a constructive trust is bound up with the question of following and tracing of property:[60] if the claimant's property ceases to be identifiable according to the following and tracing rules, a constructive trust cannot be imposed, simply because there will be no identifiable fund to which the trust can attach.[61] This is the reason why a constructive trust was not recognized on the facts of *Westdeutsche Landesbank*, because, when the defendant learned that the transaction was void, the claimant's money had ceased to be identifiable.[62]

9.3.2 RESCISSION OF CONTRACT

Another situation in which the courts have recognized that property is held on constructive trust for the claimant is where the court has rescinded in Equity a contract which the claimant had made with the defendant.[63] In *El Ajou v Dollar Land Holdings plc*,[64] however, although Millett J affirmed that when a transaction is rescinded an equitable title can vest

---

[56] Although in *Papamichael v National Westminster Bank plc* [2003] 1 Lloyd's Rep 341, 373, Judge Chambers QC said that actual knowledge is required.

[57] In *Westdeutsche Landesbank Girozentrale v Islington LBC* [1996] AC 669, 705 Lord Browne-Wilkinson emphasized that the defendant's conscience will only be affected where they knew 'of the factors which are alleged to affect' their conscience.

[58] *Fitzalan-Howard (Norfolk) v Hibbert* [2009] EWHC 2855 (QB), [49] (Tomlinson J).

[59] *Westdeutsche Landesbank Girozentrale v Islington LBC* [1996] AC 669, 707 (Lord Browne-Wilkinson); *Re Goldcorp Exchange Ltd* [1995] 1 AC 74.   [60] See Section 19.3, p. 551.

[61] *Papamichael v National Westminster Bank plc* [2003] 1 Lloyd's Rep 341, 372 (Judge Chambers QC).

[62] [1996] AC 669, 689 (Lord Goff) and 707 (Lord Browne-Wilkinson).

[63] *Lonrho plc v Fayed (No 2)* [1992] 1 WLR 1, 12 (Millett J). See also *Daly v Sydney Stock Exchange* (1986) 65 ALR 193, 204 (Brennan J).   [64] [1993] 3 All ER 717, 734.

in the claimant retrospectively, he characterized the trust that arises as a result of the rescission as a resulting rather than a constructive trust.[65] Characterization of the trust as
resulting is not, however, consistent with the key principles relating to the law of resulting
trusts, namely that such a trust arises either where there has been a failure of an express
trust or where there is a voluntary transfer to the defendant.[66] Consequently, the preferable
analysis of the trust that arises on rescission of a contract is that it is a constructive trust
that is triggered by the defendant's unconscionable conduct that makes the transaction
voidable in the first place, whether this is because of misrepresentation or undue influence.
This analysis was adopted by Etherton C in *The National Crime Agency v Robb*.[67] He recognized that, when a transaction induced by fraudulent misrepresentation is rescinded, the
property which was transferred pursuant to the transaction will be held on constructive
trust for the transferor, assuming that it is possible to identify the transferred property or
its traceable proceeds in the hands of the defendant.[68]

Regardless of whether the defendant is characterized as a resulting or constructive
trustee, it is clear that until the transaction is rescinded, which requires an order of the
court,[69] the claimant only has a mere equity to seek rescission of the transaction,[70] which
is not sufficient for the claimant to establish a claim to vindicate their equitable proprietary
rights.[71] It is for this reason that the claimant will be barred from rescinding the transaction if a third party acquires an equitable interest in the property for value and without
notice of the claimant's right to rescind.[72] Although it has been recognized that, where the
contract was induced by fraud, the claimant will have obtained an equitable proprietary
interest in the property which was transferred from the moment they elected to rescind,[73]
and that this operates retrospectively from the date when the equity to rescind arose,[74] the
better view is that rescission in Equity is a remedy which is effected by the court rather
than by the exercise of a power of election by the claimant. Whether the equitable proprietary right arises on making the election to rescind or when the court makes its order
matters, since the equity to rescind will be defeated where the property has been obtained
by a *bona fide* purchaser for value.

9.3.3. VOLUNTARY TRANSACTIONS MADE BY MISTAKE

There is an equitable jurisdiction to set aside gifts and dispositions to trusts made by deed
where the transferor had made a mistake.[75] This was recognized in *Lady Hood of Avalon v
Mackinnon*.[76] In that case, Lady Hood made an appointment to one of her two daughters
in 1888. She made appointments to her other daughter in 1902 and 1904. Forgetting that
she had made the appointment to her first daughter many years earlier, she made another

---

[65] See Section 8.5.2, p. 253.   [66] See Section 8.1.2, p. 212.
[67] [2014] EWHC 4384 (Ch), [2015] Ch 520 [49].   [68] Ibid., [51].
[69] See Section 21.6.2.(ii), p. 639.
[70] *Phillips v Phillips* (1862) 4 De GF & J 208; *Shalson v Russo* [2003] EWHC 1637 (Ch), [2005] Ch 281, [111] (Rimer J).
[71] *Phillips v Phillips* (1862) 4 De GF and J 208; *Shalson v Russo* [2003] EWHC 1637 (Ch), [2005] Ch 281, [111] (Rimer J); *The National Crime Agency v Robb* [2014] EWHC 4384 (Ch), [2015] Ch 520, [80] (Etherton C).
[72] *Westminster Bank Ltd v Lee* [1956] Ch 7.
[73] *Banque Belge pour l'Etranger v Hambrouck* [1921] 1 KB 321, 332 (Atkin LJ); *Lonrho plc v Fayed (No 2)* [1992] 1 WLR 1, 12 (Millett J); *El Ajou v Dollar Land Holdings plc* [1993] 3 All ER 717, 734 (Millett J); *Shalson v Russo* [2003] EWHC 1637 (Ch), [2005] Ch 281, 316, [122] (Rimer J).
[74] *The National Crime Agency v Robb* [2014] EWHC 4384 (Ch), [2015] Ch 520, [80] (Etherton C).
[75] There is no equitable jurisdiction to set aside contracts on the ground of mistake: *Great Peace Shipping Ltd v Tsavliris Salvage (International) Ltd* [2002] EWCA Civ 1407, [2003] QB 679; *Van der Merwe v Goldman* [2016] EWHC 790 (Ch), [2016] 4 WLR 71.   [76] [1909] 1 Ch 476.

appointment to her to ensure that both daughters were treated equally. This was regarded as a sufficiently serious mistake to enable the court to rescind the deed, since the claimant had never intended to make double provision for the daughter. Where this jurisdiction to rescind is exercised, the property that has been transferred will be held on trust for the transferor. Since this jurisdiction is triggered by unconscionability, the trust is properly characterized as constructive.

The operation of this equitable jurisdiction to rescind voluntary dispositions[77] was examined and authoritatively clarified by the Supreme Court in *Pitt v Holt; Futter v Futter*.[78] Lord Walker identified three interlinked elements before the equitable jurisdiction is engaged.

(i) The donor must have been mistaken

Lord Walker[79] defined mistake by distinguishing between three different states of mind: an incorrect conscious belief, an incorrect tacit assumption, and mere causative ignorance but for which the claimant would not have acted as they did. He decided that only the first two can be characterized as mistake. Although he accepted that it might be difficult to distinguish between beliefs, assumptions, and ignorance, he emphasized that the court should not shrink from drawing an 'inference of conscious belief or tacit assumption when there is evidence to support such an inference'.[80] Consequently, if it can be shown that the claimant had an incorrect belief or acted on an incorrect assumption as to fact or law, the claimant can be considered to be mistaken. If, however, the claimant had no idea about the possible existence of a fact, this suggests ignorance rather than mistake, unless a tacit assumption about the fact can be inferred. This notion of an incorrect tacit assumption proved to be significant on the facts of *Pitt v Holt*. The case concerned a claim to set aside a voluntary disposition made to a trust on the ground that the disposition had been made by mistake. Following a road accident in which he was seriously injured, Mr Pitt received significant compensation. His wife was appointed his receiver and she sought professional advice concerning the investment of this money. As a result of this advice she placed the money in a discretionary trust for the benefit of her husband, herself, and their children. Mr Pitt later died, and his estate was found to be liable to pay inheritance tax on the sum held on trust. This liability could have been easily avoided had the trust contained a provision that at least half of the settled property applied during Mr Pitt's lifetime would be used for his benefit, but both the professional advisers and the Court of Protection, which had approved the trust, apparently overlooked the relevant tax liability. Lord Walker considered that Mrs Pitt had made a mistake relating to the inheritance tax liability: she either had an incorrect conscious belief as regards the tax consequences of the settlement, or a tacit assumption that it would not result in adverse tax consequences. In fact, the trial judge had held[81] that Mrs Pitt had not made any mistake because she had not considered the question of inheritance tax liability at all, relying completely on her advisers. The Supreme Court disagreed and found that she was mistaken. But the trial judge's finding of

---

[77] The equitable jurisdiction has been recognized as extending to gifts and other voluntary transfers of property: *Pagel v Farman* [2013] EWHC 2210 (Comm), [2013] WTLR 1575; *Spaul v Spaul* [2014] EWCA Civ 679, [52] (Rimer LJ); *Re Pallen Trust* 2015 BCCA 222 (Court of Appeal for British Columbia). The equitable jurisdiction is not, however, engaged where the transaction was neither a gift nor a voluntary disposition: *The Co-Operative Bank Plc v Hayes Freehold Ltd* [2017] EWHC 1820 (Ch), [130] (Carr J).

[78] [2013] UKSC 26, [2013] 2 AC 108. See Davies and Virgo, 'Relieving trustees' mistakes' [2013] RLR 73. The decision has been followed by the Royal Court of Guernsey (*Nourse v Heritage Corporate Trustees Ltd*, 01/2015) and the Grand Court of the Cayman Islands (*Schroder Cayman Bank and Trust Co Ltd v Schroder Trust AG* (2015) FSD 122/2014).   [79] [2013] UKSC 26, [2013] 2 AC 108, [108].

[80] Ibid.   [81] *Pitt v Holt* [2010] EWHC 45 (Ch), [2010] 1 WLR 1199, [50] (Robert Engelhart QC).

fact suggests that, because Mrs Pitt had no belief as to the tax liability, she must have made an incorrect tacit assumption that there would be no such liability.

This recognition that an incorrect tacit assumption constitutes a mistake, potentially expands the notion of mistake significantly. It means that if, for example, the claimant has forgotten certain facts, such that they have already transferred a benefit to the defendant,[82] the claimant can be considered to have acted on an assumption which was incorrect. But such circumstances of forgetfulness about particular facts could be characterized as involving mere causative ignorance. The line between assumption and ignorance is consequently unclear. It would certainly have been more straightforward for the Supreme Court to have confined mistake to an incorrect conscious belief, which is how it was previously defined. In *Great Peace Shipping Ltd v Tsavliris Salvage (International) Ltd*[83] Lord Phillips MR described a mistake as an 'erroneous belief'. It would follow that forgetfulness or ignorance about particular facts would not constitute a mistake, because they do not involve belief. After the decision of the Supreme Court in *Pitt v Holt*, this does not represent the law.

(ii) The mistake was sufficiently serious

Prior to the decision of the Supreme Court, a controversial issue concerned whether a mistake as to the consequences of a voluntary transfer could constitute a relevant mistake, or whether the mistake had to relate to the legal effect of the transaction.[84] This was a significant issue since a common reason for a donor wishing to set aside a voluntary transfer was because of its adverse tax consequences, rather than the legal effect of the transfer. In *Pitt v Holt* Lord Walker rejected the need to distinguish between consequences and legal effect and focused instead on the seriousness of the mistake.[85] Crucially, he recognized that:[86]

> the true requirement is simply for there to be a causative mistake of sufficient gravity; and, as additional guidance to judges in finding and evaluating the facts of any particular case, that the test will normally be satisfied only where there is some mistake either as to the legal character or nature of a transaction, or as to some matter of fact or law which is basic to the transaction.

This expands the types of mistake which might be sufficient to engage the equitable jurisdiction to rescind a deed, since a mistake as to the tax consequences of the disposition might be relevant if sufficiently serious. The distinction between effect and consequence has not disappeared completely, however, but may remain of evidential significance since, as Lord Walker recognized,[87] a mistake as to the essential nature of a transaction is likely to be more serious than a mistake as to its consequences.

(iii) The mistake is sufficiently grave

Finally, the assertion of the donee's rights would be objectively unjust or unconscionable which would render the mistake of sufficient gravity to rescind the disposition. The determination of unconscionability requires close examination of the facts, including 'the circumstances of the mistake and its consequences for the person who made the vitiated disposition', whether the defendant had changed their position, and 'other matters relevant to the exercise of the court's discretion'.[88] Lord Walker used the language of

---

[82] As in *Lady Hood of Avalon v Mackinnon* [1909] 1 Ch 476. See Section 9.3.3, p. 263.

[83] [2002] EWCA Civ 1407, [2003] QB 679, [28].

[84] As Millett J had recognized in *Gibbon v Mitchell* [1990] 1 WLR 1304.

[85] Relying on *Ogilvie v Littleboy* (1897) 13 TLR 399, 400 (Lindley LJ). Affirmed by the House of Lords: *Ogilvie v Allen* (1899) 15 TLR 294.   [86] *Pitt v Holt* [2013] UKSC 26, [2013] 2 AC 108, [122].

[87] Ibid., [123].   [88] Ibid., [126].

'unconscionableness', as he called it, interchangeably with that of 'justice' and 'unfairness',[89] so that the test of gravity appears to turn simply on an assessment of fairness determined through the exercise of judicial discretion. In *Gresh v RBC Trust Co (Guernsey) Ltd*,[90] the Royal Court of Guernsey held that a request by a member of a pension fund to be paid a lump sum distribution in the mistaken belief that it was not subject to tax, did not engage the equitable jurisdiction to rescind the transaction because there was nothing which rendered the retention of the distribution unfair or unjust as between the member and the pension fund.

On the facts of *Pitt v Holt* it was held that Mrs Pitt's mistake as to the tax consequences of the disposition to the trust was sufficiently serious and grave to trigger the equitable jurisdiction to rescind the disposition for mistake. In reaching the decision that this disposition could be rescinded, a matter of particular significance was the fact that the disposition did not form part of an artificial or abusive tax avoidance scheme[91] and also that it had been authorized by the Court of Protection. Similarly, in *Wright v National Westminster Bank plc*,[92] a trust was set aside by virtue of the settlor's mistaken belief that income from the asset which was settled on trust would continue to be available to him and his wife to maintain their existing standard of living.[93]

In addition to considering the appeal in *Pitt v Holt*, the Supreme Court also considered an appeal in *Futter v Futter*. This appeal focused on the validity of a trustee's exercise of discretion.[94] In the Supreme Court the appellants sought for the first time to rely on the equitable jurisdiction to set aside a disposition for mistake. Although the Supreme Court declined to permit the appellants to raise this on appeal, even had it been properly raised earlier, Lord Walker considered that it would have been difficult to establish that the mistake was sufficiently serious and grave to justify rescission. In *Futter v Futter* the trustees of a discretionary trust had exercised powers of advancement[95] on the understanding that, although this would result in a tax liability, that liability could be set off against allowable losses. The decision to exercise the power was made after the trustees had obtained advice from solicitors, but the advice ignored the effect of a statute which provided that the tax liability could not be set off. The settlor and the beneficiaries incurred a significant tax liability as a result of the trustees' mistake. Unlike the disposition made by Mrs Pitt, this case involved an artificial tax avoidance scheme which had gone wrong.[96] Lord Walker described such schemes as constituting 'a social evil',[97] and emphasized that the court might refuse to award equitable relief to rescind a voluntary disposition on the ground of public policy, suggesting that there are moral questions which need to be examined by the court in determining whether it is appropriate to exercise the jurisdiction to rescind the disposition. It does not appear to be unconscionable for the Revenue to keep tax paid as part of an artificial avoidance scheme entered into by mistake. It follows that many claims based upon a mistake as to the fiscal implications of a disposition seem destined to fail.

The determination of whether a voluntary disposition should be rescinded in Equity appears to involve the exercise of arbitrary judicial choice rather than the exercise of a

---

[89] Ibid.   [90] (2016)18 ITELR 753.

[91] See also *Kennedy v Kennedy* [2014] EWHC 4129 (Ch), [2015] WTLR 837, [39] (Etherton C); *Re Pallen Trust*, 2015 BCCA 222 (Court of Appeal for British Columbia).

[92] [2014] EWHC 3158 (Ch), [2015] WTLR 547. See also *Freedman v Freedman* [2015] EWHC 1457 Ch, [2015] WTLR 1187.

[93] In *Re Pallen Trust* 2015 BCCA 222 the Court of Appeal for British Columbia applied the principles recognized in *Pitt v Holt* to rescind a dividend paid to a discretionary trust on the ground that the dividend had been paid on the mistaken assumption that it would reduce a tax liability.

[94] See Section 12.8.7, p. 369. This issue was also considered in *Pitt v Holt*. See Section 12.8.7, p. 370.

[95] See Section 14.5, p. 414.   [96] *Pitt v Holt* [2013] UKSC 26, [2013] 2 AC, [135].   [97] Ibid.

principled discretion.[98] Confusingly, the distinction between seriousness of the mistake and its gravity assessed by reference to unconscionability is likely to merge to form a single test turning on the justice of the case. The real problem with the approach of Lord Walker in *Pitt v Holt* is the inclusion of the third test involving the 'unconscionableness' of the defendant's receipt. There is no need for such a test. It should be enough that the mistake is sufficiently serious before a voluntary disposition can be rescinded.

Where, however, the voluntary disposition is set aside, the property transferred to the donee or trustee will be held on trust for the donor or settlor.[99] The fact that the gravity of the mistake must be so serious that it is unconscionable for the recipient to retain the property that has been transferred suggests that the trust that will be imposed is properly analysed as a constructive trust. This is because it can be considered to respond to the donee's unconscionable conduct in retaining the property, albeit that this is to be determined objectively rather than with reference to the donee's knowledge or suspicion about the mistake: if the donee knows or suspects the mistake, then the constructive trust will arise under the separate head of unconscionable retention of property,[100] which can apply where property has been transferred by mistake,[101] albeit usually not pursuant to a voluntary transaction. Consequently, there might be circumstances under which the mistaken voluntary transaction head of constructive trusts overlaps with that of unconscionable retention. But the mistaken voluntary transaction might also potentially overlap with the presumed resulting trust, since the voluntary transfer might be considered to trigger the presumed intent that the property transferred is held on resulting trust for the transferor.[102] But the transferor's intention to make a gift will either rebut the presumption or might even prevent it from being engaged in the first place.

9.3.4 FIDUCIARIES *DE SON TORT*

One of the best examples of the significance of the constructive trust to resolve problems arising from unconscionable conduct is where a person who has not been properly appointed either as a trustee,[103] or an executor,[104] or any other type of fiduciary, such as an agent,[105] intermeddles with trust or estate matters, or does acts that are characteristic of the fiduciary office. Such 'fiduciaries *de son tort*'[106] will be treated as though they have been properly appointed to the respective office and so will be subject to fiduciary duties in the ordinary way. The preferable view is that a person who meddles with a trust is considered to be an express trustee,[107] whereas a person who acts as a fiduciary, although not properly appointed as such, will hold any property obtained by intermeddling on constructive trust for the principal. This is especially well illustrated by *James v Williams*.[108] A mother of three children had died intestate. The family home was to be held on a statutory trust for the children equally. Although the son, William, was meant to be the administrator of

---

[98] See Section 2.2, p. 24.

[99] Etherton justified the stricter test for this reason: 'The role of equity in mistaken transactions' (2013) 27 TLI 159.   [100] See Section 9.3.1, p. 258.

[101] As in *Chase-Manhattan Bank NA v Israel-British Bank (London) Ltd* [1981] Ch 105.

[102] See Section 8.2, p. 217.

[103] *Blyth v Fladgate* [1891] 1 Ch 337; *Mara v Browne* [1896] 1 Ch 199; *Taylor v Davies* [1920] AC 636, 651 (Viscount Cave); *Dubai Aluminium Co Ltd v Salaam* [2002] UKHL 48, [2003] 2 AC 366. See further Section 12.3.9, p. 345.   [104] *James v Williams* [2000] Ch 1.

[105] *Lyell v Kennedy* (1889) 14 App Cas 437.

[106] Perhaps better described simply as *de facto* trustees or executors. See *Dubai Aluminium Co Ltd v Salaam* [2002] UKHL 48, [2003] 2 AC 366, 403 (Lord Millett).   [107] See Section 12.3.9, p. 346.

[108] [2000] Ch 1.

the estate, he took possession of the property as if it were his own, even though it was established that he was aware that he was not solely entitled to the property. It was held that, by virtue of his knowledge, he was an executor *de son tort*, and so he held the property on constructive trust for himself and his two siblings. Here, the constructive trust was clearly triggered by William's unconscionable conduct in treating the property as his own.

9.3.5 BREACH OF UNDERTAKING

Where the claimant has transferred property to the defendant in circumstances in which the defendant has undertaken to deal with the property for the benefit of a particular person and the defendant breaches that undertaking, Equity may intervene and require the defendant to hold the property on constructive trust for the person whom the defendant had agreed to benefit.[109] This will arise only where the defendant was under a legally binding obligation to deal with the property in a particular way. Here, too, the constructive trust can be considered to be triggered by the defendant's unconscionable conduct in reneging on the undertaking with the claimant, on the basis of which the claimant had relied by transferring the property to the defendant.[110] This category of constructive trust will be triggered in four different circumstances.

(i) Undertaking by purchasers

Where a purchaser has bought land and has made an undertaking[111] that they would respect the rights of a third party, that party's rights can be protected by means of a constructive trust.[112] This has proved to be especially important in respect of licences over land. In *Ashburn Anstalt v Arnold*,[113] the Court of Appeal recognized that a purchaser would not normally be bound by the rights of a contractual licensee save where the land could be held on constructive trust for the benefit of the licensee. Such a constructive trust would be recognized where the purchaser had undertaken to respect the rights of the licensee. Similarly, in *Binions v Evans*,[114] the defendant and her husband lived rent-free in a cottage on an estate. On the husband's death, the trustees of the estate agreed that the defendant could continue to live in the cottage for the rest of her life, without needing to pay rent. The estate sold the cottage to the claimant and the contract of sale stated that the sale was subject to the defendant's right. The claimant sought to eject the defendant, but failed. Lord Denning MR said that the claimant had taken the property subject to a constructive trust for the defendant. This analysis was affirmed in *Ashburn Anstalt*,[115] in which the court emphasized the significance of the purchaser's express undertaking to respect the rights of the third party, for only then will the conscience of the purchaser be affected if they seek to ignore the third party's rights. The simple fact that property is sold 'subject to' the rights of the third party will not be sufficient to trigger the constructive trust.

There are other circumstances where a purchaser of property has given an oral undertaking to respect the rights of another where the purchaser's attempt to renege on the undertaking is founded on the informality of the undertaking that does not comply with

---

[109] *Ottaway v Norman* [1972] Ch 698; *Re Cleaver* [1981] Ch.

[110] See Allan, 'Once a fraud, forever a fraud: the time-honoured doctrine of parol agreement trusts' (2014) 34 LS 419.

[111] McFarlane, 'Constructive trusts arising on a receipt of property *sub conditione*' (2004) 120 LQR 667; Hopkins, 'Conscience, discretion and the creation of property rights' (2006) 26 LS 475.

[112] Alternatively, the third party may have a cause of action against the purchaser by virtue of the Contracts (Rights of Third Parties) Act 1999. See Section 5.3.3.(iii), p. 132.   [113] [1989] Ch 1.

[114] [1972] Ch 359.   [115] See also *DHN Food Distributors Ltd v Tower Hamlets BC* [1976] 1 WLR 852.

statutory formalities. In such a situation the purchaser may be prevented from reneging on the undertaking by virtue of the principle that 'Equity will not permit a statute to be used as an instrument of fraud.' So, for example, in *Lyus v Prowsa Developments Ltd*,[116] land was bought expressly subject to the claimant's contractual rights, but the defendants sought to defeat those rights by relying on the provisions of the Land Registration Act 1925, by virtue of which the rights were not enforceable at Law because they had not been registered. The court decided that the defendant held the land on constructive trust for the claimant because the defendant was acting fraudulently in relying on its statutory rights rather than complying with the undertaking. It was, however, recognized in *Chaudhury v Yavuz*[117] that *Lyus* was an exceptional case and that a constructive trust will not be recognized if the contractual rights of the claimant have not been specifically identified in the contract by virtue of which the defendant agreed to buy the property or if the claimant's rights are capable of protection on the land register, since the defendant's denial of the claimant's rights in such circumstances will not be sufficiently unconscionable. This is because the defendant will not be considered to have undertaken a new obligation to give effect to the claimant's rights if they had not been specifically identified and it is appropriate for the defendant to assume that the claimant will protect their rights by registering them. The implications of these qualifications is illustrated by *Chaudhury v Yavuz* itself, where the defendant had purchased a property which included a metal staircase that was used by the claimant to access the upper floor of his own property Even though the claimant had a right of way over the staircase and it was obvious that he needed to use it to gain access to the upper floor of his property, it was held not to be unconscionable for the defendant to obstruct the claimant's use of the staircase, because the claimant had not registered his right of way and no express reference was made to that right in the contract of sale.

The constructive trust has also been recognized where the purchaser's undertaking relates to the declaration of a trust of land in favour of the vendor or a third party, where the trust is unenforceable because it has not been evidenced in writing.[118] In such cases, it is, however, preferable to analyse the trust as being express rather than as arising by operation of law,[119] since a valid trust has been declared, but it is simply unenforceable because of the absence of writing.

(ii) Secret trusts

It was seen earlier[120] that a testator might wish to leave property to friends or next of kin without making this explicit on the face of their will. One way in which to achieve this is to set up a secret trust under which the trustee is informed outside of the will how the property should be distributed. Once the testator has died and the trustee has received the property, the latter might decide to use the money for themselves. According to the strict terms of the will, this might appear to be perfectly legitimate. Equity is not, however, concerned only with the words in the will; Equity is also concerned with the nature of the dealings between the parties. Consequently, Equity will hold the trustee to the terms of the

---

[116] [1982] 1 WLR 1044. See also *Lloyd v Dugdale* [2001] EWCA Civ 1754.

[117] [2011] EWCA Civ 1314, [2013] Ch 249, [62] (Lloyd LJ). See also *Groveholt Ltd v Hughes* [2012] EWHC 3351 (Ch), [2013] 1 P and CR 20.

[118] As required by the Law of Property Act 1925, s. 53(1)(b); see Section 5.2.1.(i), p. 105. See *Bannister v Bannister* [1948] 2 All ER 133, McFarlane (see n. 111), p. 675 and Liew, 'Reanalysing institutional and remedial constructive trusts' (2016) 74 CLJ 528, who argues that the constructive trust here is a remedy which replicates the rights arising under the express trust.

[119] *Rochefoucauld v Boustead* [1897] 1 Ch 196, 208 (Lindley LJ), discussed in Section 5.2.2.(i), p. 107. See Swadling, 'The nature of the trust in *Rochefoucauld v Boustead*', in *Resulting and Constructive Trusts*, ed. Mitchell (Oxford: Hart, 2010), ch. 3.   [120] See Section 5.2.2.(ii), p. 110.

understanding and the property will be held on trust for those whom the testator intended to benefit.

Whether this trust is analysed as a constructive or express trust may depend on the type of secret trust that is involved. A fully secret trust is one that is not apparent from the will in any way. The recipient of the property will hold the property on trust to prevent them from profiting from fraud.[121] Clearly, this is consistent with the constructive trust being triggered by unconscionable conduct. The other type of secret trust is the half-secret trust, under which reference to the trust is made in the will, but the details of the trust are transmitted separately. Here, the trust appears to be express. The classification of the trust as constructive or express really matters only when the subject matter of the trust is land, for then, if it is an express trust, it must be evidenced in writing.[122] In *Ottaway v Norman*,[123] a fully secret trust of land was upheld even though it was not evidenced in writing, which suggests that this was a constructive trust. In *Re Baillie*,[124] a half-secret trust of land was required to be evidenced in writing, which suggests that it is an express trust. Despite this apparent distinction, both fully secret and half-secret trusts are preferably analysed as being express trusts, since they are made when the testator communicates the terms of the trust to the trustee, albeit that they are constituted only on the testator's death.[125]

(iii) Mutual wills

Sometimes, two people, such as a husband and wife, might agree to make wills that give the property of the first of them to die to the survivor and, after the survivor's death, to agreed legatees. This is called a mutual wills contract or simply mutual wills.[126] The key problem with mutual wills arises when the survivor has received property from the first to die and then leaves it in their will inconsistently with what they had previously agreed. In such circumstances, what can those who should have benefited according to the original agreement do to enforce their rights? One solution is contractual in that, following the enactment of the Contracts (Rights of Third Parties) Act 1999,[127] a person who is not party to a contract is able to enforce the terms of that contract in their own right, either if the contract expressly provides that the party can enforce it or if the contract confers a benefit on them, save, in the latter case, where the parties did not intend the party to be able to enforce the terms of the contract. But this will give the third party to the agreement only a personal right to sue the survivor's estate for breach of contract. Since the third party will not have provided consideration for the contractual right, they will not be able to obtain the equitable remedy of specific performance.[128] A better solution is to recognize that the property is held on trust for those who should have received the property under the survivor's will.[129] This could be an express trust, depending on the parties' intent, but often it is best analysed as a constructive trust arising by operation of law that responds to the survivor's unconscionable conduct in not leaving the property as the parties had agreed,[130] this being unconscionable because the other party had relied on the survivor's promise. The beneficiary of this trust can consequently enforce it even though they were not a party to the mutual wills contract.

---

[121] *McCormick v Grogan* (1869) LR 4 HL 82.
[122] Law of Property Act 1925, s. 53(1)(b). See Section 5.2.1.(i), p. 105.   [123] [1972] Ch 698.
[124] (1886) 2 TLR 660.   [125] See Section 5.2.2.(ii), p. 122.
[126] See *Marley v Rawlings* [2014] UKSC 2, [2015] AC 129, [34] (Lord Neuberger). See generally Hudson and Sloan, 'Testamentary freedom: mutual wills might let you down', in *Modern Studies in Property Law*, ed. Barr (Oxford: Hart, 2015), vol. 8, p. 157; Liew 'The ambit of the mutal wills doctrine' (2016) 132 LQR 664.
[127] See further Section 5.3.3.(iii), p. 132.   [128] See Section 5.3.3.(iii), p. 133.
[129] *Dufour v Pereira* (1769) 1 Dick 419; *Re Hagger* [1930] 2 Ch 190.
[130] *Ollins v Walters* [2008] EWCA Civ 782, [2009] Ch 212, [37] (Mummery LJ).

The doctrine of mutual wills depends on there being a legally binding contract between the two testators not to revoke their wills.[131] It does not matter that the survivor does not receive any property under the first testator's will,[132] since it is the existence of the agreement that is vital to the doctrine: if the defendant fails to comply with the original undertaking, albeit an undertaking owed to the other testator rather than the ultimate beneficiaries, the defendant's conscience will be affected and this is sufficient to trigger the constructive trust.

The operation of the doctrine of mutual wills is especially well illustrated by *Re Cleaver*.[133] A husband and wife made wills in each other's favour, with gifts to the husband's children. On his death, the widow changed her will to leave the property to only one child. It was held that the wife held this property on constructive trust for all of the three children. The widow was allowed to enjoy the property acquired from her husband during her lifetime, but this was subject to a fiduciary duty that crystallized on her death. The fiduciary nature of this duty meant that she was only prevented from dispositions of property that were calculated to defeat the agreement, but she was not prevented from disposing of small amounts of the property.

The doctrine of mutual wills causes a number of conceptual and doctrinal problems. For example, when does the constructive trust arise, what property is caught by the trust, and what can the survivor do with that property? The nature and function of this trust was analysed in *Ottaway v Norman* by Brightman J,[134] who said, *obiter*, that if property is left to one person on the understanding that it would be disposed of in their will in favour of another person, a trust is created in favour of that other person which is in suspense until the death of the testator, at which point the trust crystallizes on the survivor's estate, which must be dealt with as the two testators had agreed. This analysis followed that of the High Court of Australia in *Birmingham v Renfrew*,[135] in which it was held that the husband, who had revoked his will in breach of an undertaking to his wife, who had died before him, held the residue of his property at his death on constructive trust. The husband could use the property that he had received from his wife as he wished during his lifetime, but on his death the trust crystallized on his estate.

The function of the constructive trust arising from the making of a mutual wills contract was reconsidered in *Ollins v Walters*[136] with potentially significant implications. In that case, a husband and wife had made wills in almost identical terms in which they each left to the other their entire residuary estate. Ten years later, codicils were drafted to each of the wills, in which each agreed not to change their will without the other's consent. The wife died and the husband disputed the existence of a mutual wills contract. It was held on the facts that mutual wills had been created and that, on the death of the wife, a constructive trust had arisen by operation of law that bound the conscience of the husband immediately in respect of the wife's property that had been left to him, rather than being a trust that was postponed until his death and only taking effect when the property or what was left of it came into the hands of the husband's personal representatives.[137] But the Court of Appeal did not consider the implications of this observation, which would appear to be that the property that was received by the survivor from the estate of the first person to die could not be disposed of by the survivor and must be left in their will as the parties had originally agreed. Provision could, however, be made in the mutual wills contract for the survivor to have a fiduciary power to use this property as they wished. As Mummery

---

[131] *Dufour v Pereira* (1769) 1 Dick 419; *Re Goodchild* [1997] 1 WLR 1216; *Ollins v Walters* [2008] EWCA Civ 782, [2009] Ch 212.   [132] *Re Dale* [1994] Ch 31.

[133] [1981] 1 WLR 939.   [134] [1972] Ch 698.   [135] (1937) 57 CLR 666.

[136] [2008] EWCA Civ 782, [2009] Ch 212.   [137] Ibid., [42] (Mummery LJ).

LJ recognized, disputes 'about the actual operation of the trust in practice usually turn on construction of the contract in all the relevant circumstances'.[138]

As between these two modes of analysing the constructive trust, as either being in suspense or arising immediately, the former analysis is not free from difficulty. In particular, if the constructive trust is suspended until the survivor's death, what happens if the intended third-party beneficiary dies before the survivor? Since the trust will crystallize only on the survivor's death, the logical solution would be for the property that derived from the first testator's estate to be held on resulting trust for those who are entitled to the residuary estate, which would be the surviving party, by analogy with the resulting trust that arises when an express trust initially fails for want of beneficiaries.[139] But this doctrinal difficulty will be avoided if the analysis of the constructive trust recognized by the Court of Appeal in *Ollins v Walters* is adopted, for then the constructive trust would arise immediately the deceased party's property had been received by the surviving party, and the death of the beneficiary of this trust will not defeat their beneficial interest, which would pass to those entitled to the beneficiary's residuary estate, unless this beneficiary was intended only to have a life interest that would be terminated on death. It follows that, as between the suspensory constructive trust and the immediate constructive trust coupled with a power to benefit from the property, the latter is the preferable way of analysing the trust that arises from mutual wills.

(iv) Perfecting an imperfect gift

The constructive trust has also been used to perfect an imperfect gift, where the donor has sought to make a gift of property to the donee, but has failed to transfer legal title. It has been recognized that the donor might hold the property on constructive trust for the donee where it would be unconscionable for the donor to revoke the gift.[140] This is properly treated as falling within the category of breach of an undertaking, since it appears that the donor would be considered to have acted unconscionably in seeking to revoke a gift where the donor had represented to the donee that the gift would be made and the donee had relied on this representation in some way.

9.3.6 CONTRACT FOR THE SALE OF LAND

All of the heads of constructive trust that have been examined so far can be justified by reference to the principle that the defendant has acted unconscionably in some way. One other category of institutional constructive trust is recognized in the context of contracts for the sale of land.[141] Where the purchaser has entered into a contract for the sale of land, the vendor will hold that land on constructive trust for the purchaser; this cannot be explained by reference to any principle of unconscionability, unless the defendant seeks to renege on the contract, but the constructive trust arises even if the defendant wishes to carry out the agreement. The constructive trust in this context can be justified by the separate principle that 'Equity treats as done what ought to be done'.[142] Contracts for the sale of land are specifically enforceable in Equity, so Equity is willing to treat the contract as having been performed immediately it is made, so that the vendor holds the property on trust for the purchaser by operation of law.[143]

---

[138] Ibid., [43] (Mummery LJ).   [139] See Section 8.3.2.(i), p. 232.
[140] *Pennington v Waine* [2002] EWCA Civ 227, [2002] 1 WLR 2075, discussed in Section 5.3.3.(iii), p. 130.
[141] *Lysaght v Edwards* (1876) 2 Ch D 499, 506 (Jessel MR).   [142] See Section 2.6, p. 32.
[143] Turner, 'Understanding the constructive trust between vendor and purchaser' (2012) 128 LQR 582, justifies the trust as a means of supporting the contractual bargain between vendor and purchaser.

The constructive trust in this context is simply an equitable mechanism to protect the interests of the purchaser, but it operates in a very limited way. This is illustrated by *Rayner v Preston*,[144] in which the vendor agreed to sell a house that he had insured. After the contract was made, but before the sale was completed, the house was damaged by fire. The insurers paid insurance money to the vendor, which the purchaser sought to recover. The purchaser's claim failed,[145] because, as Cotton LJ said, the vendor is a trustee of the property only in a 'qualified sense', because Equity will give effect to the contract of sale by transferring the property to the purchaser. But it was only the property that was held on constructive trust and not the insurance policy. That the constructive trust of the property that has been contracted to be sold is a qualified trust is supported by *Shaw v Foster*,[146] in which Lord Cairns recognized that, although the vendor is the trustee and the purchaser has a beneficial interest in the property, the trustee also has a personal and substantial interest in the property, and a right to protect it. This is different from other trustees, who do not automatically have such an interest in the trust property. The unusual position of the vendor trustee was further emphasized by Sir George Jessel MR in *Lysaght v Edwards*:[147]

> the position of the vendor is something between what has been called a naked or bare trustee, or a mere trustee (that is, a person without beneficial interest), and a mortgagee who is not, in equity (any more than the vendor), the owner of the estate, but is, in certain events, entitled to what the unpaid vendor is, [namely] possession of the estate and a charge upon the estate for his purchase-money.

The peculiar nature of the constructive trust relating to sale of land was further emphasized by the Supreme Court in *Southern Pacific Mortgages Ltd v Scott*,[148] where it was held that, after the exchange of contracts, the purchaser of property could not grant an equitable proprietary interest in the property in favour of the vendor before the legal title had been transferred to the purchaser. Consequently, where the vendor had agreed to sell her house to the purchaser following the purchaser's promise that the vendor could remain in occupation at a low rent, the vendor had no equitable proprietary right in the house until legal title had passed to the purchaser, by which time a mortgage had been obtained, which took priority over the vendor's rights. Whilst the Supreme Court did not analyse the nature of the purchaser's equitable interest under the constructive trust, the effect of the decision is that the purchaser was unable to declare a sub-trust of the property, implying that the purchaser's equitable interest is of a more fragile kind than that of a beneficiary under a typical constructive trust.

9.3.7 BREACH OF FIDUCIARY DUTY

Where a fiduciary, such as an agent or director of a company, has profited from their fiduciary position,[149] they will hold this profit on constructive trust for their principal.[150] Where this profit has been derived directly from interference with the principal's property,

---

[144] (1881)18 Ch D 1. See also *Lake v Bayliss* [1974] 1 WLR 1073; *Freevale Ltd v Metrostore (Holdings) Ltd* [1984] Ch 199; *Englewood Properties Ltd v Patel* [2005] EWHC 188 (Ch), [2005] 3 All ER 307.

[145] It would now succeed under the Law of Property Act 1925, s. 47, which enables the purchaser to recover such sums once the conveyance has been completed.   [146] (1872) LR 5 HL 321, 338.

[147] (1876) 2 Ch D 499, 506 (Jessel MR). See also *Royal Bristol Permanent Building Society v Bomash* (1887) 35 Ch D 390, 397 (Kekewich J); *Cumberland Consolidated Holdings Ltd v Ireland* [1946] KB 264, 269 (Lord Greene MR).   [148] [2014] UKSC 52, [2015] AC 385.

[149] See Section 15.6, p. 438.

[150] Where an express trustee has made such a profit it will be held on the express trust for the beneficiaries.

such as misappropriation of the principal's money,[151] or by exploiting an opportunity which should have been available to the principal, the constructive trust is justifiable on the ground that the profits properly belong to the principal. Where, however, the profits derive from a third party, whether they should be held on constructive trust for the principal has proved to be more controversial. This has particularly been the case where the fiduciary has been bribed to breach their fiduciary duty. In such circumstances the profit cannot be considered to have derived from the principal. Consequently, the orthodox view was that only the personal remedy to account for the value of the bribe was available.[152] This was, however, rejected by the Supreme Court in *FHR European Ventures LLP v Cedar Partners LLC*.[153] It was held that, wherever a fiduciary is liable to account for profits made as a result of a breach of fiduciary duty, they will be held on constructive trust for the principal, even though those profits did not derive from interference with the principal's property or from the exploitation of an opportunity which should have been exploited for the principal. Consequently, wherever a fiduciary receives a bribe in breach of fiduciary duty, that bribe will be held on constructive trust. The constructive trust was explicitly characterized as institutional and is justified because the fiduciary is treated as though they had acquired the bribe on behalf of the principal, who therefore has an equitable proprietary interest in it. This assumption that the bribe has been acquired for the principal has been defended by virtue of the need to ensure fiduciary fidelity,[154] and what Hayton has called the 'good person' philosophy, namely that fiduciaries are expected to act as good people for the benefit of their principals.[155]

9.3.8 THEORETICAL FOUNDATIONS OF THE INSTITUTIONAL CONSTRUCTIVE TRUST

It was noted at the start of this chapter that judges and commentators have observed that it is not possible to identify one single unifying principle to explain all of the situations in which an institutional constructive trust is recognized. But, having reviewed the different circumstances under which such trusts are recognized, it is clear that there is a common theme that runs through almost all of them, namely that the constructive trust is a response to the defendant's actual or potential unconscionable conduct.[156] 'Unconscionability' can be interpreted in both a narrow and a wide sense.[157] The narrow sense of unconscionability is used in the category of unconscionable retention of property. Unconscionability here focuses on the conscience of the defendant and involves a subjective test relating to the defendant's knowledge or suspicion of the circumstances of receipt. But unconscionability can be used in a wider, more objective, sense, in which Equity intervenes by recognizing a constructive trust to ensure that the defendant does not profit from what is considered to amount to unconscionable conduct. This explains why the constructive trust is recognized where the defendant might renege on an undertaking to the claimant, or where the defendant fiduciary has profited from breach of their fiduciary duty, or where the defendant retains a profit following rescission of the underlying transaction. This wider sense of unconscionability has now been explicitly recognized in the context of mistaken voluntary transfers. Unconscionability cannot, however, explain the so-called constructive trust

---

[151] *Keown v Nahoor* [2015] EWHC 3418 (Ch), [41] (D Halpern QC).
[152] *Lister and Co v Stubbs* (1890) 45 Ch D 1.   [153] [2014] UKSC 45, [2015] AC 250.
[154] 'Bribes and secret commissions again' (2012) 71 CLJ 583. See also Smith, 'Constructive trusts and the no-profit rule' (2013) 72 CLJ 260.
[155] 'The development of equity and the "good person" philosophy in common law systems' [2012] Conv 263, 272.
[156] See *De Bruyne v De Bruyne* [2010] EWCA Civ 519, [2010] 2 FLR 1240, [49] (Patten LJ).
[157] See further Section 2.3.1, p. 27.

that arises when a contract is made for the sale of land. As will be seen,[158] it is also not a satisfactory explanation of the requirements of the common intention constructive trust, because of the emphasis on the parties' intention. For that reason, the trusts that arise in these two circumstances are better characterized as implied or imputed trusts, rather than constructive trusts, because they do not respond to the defendant's unconscionable conduct. It follows that the designation of a trust as being constructive is properly confined to those trusts that respond to the defendant's actual or potential unconscionable behaviour. This was recognized by Millett LJ in *Paragon Finance plc v DB Thakerar and Co*:[159]

> A constructive trust arises by operation of law whenever the circumstances are such that it would be unconscionable for the owner of property . . . to assert his own beneficial interest in the property and deny the beneficial interest of another . . . In these cases the plaintiff does not impugn the transaction by which the defendant obtained control of the property. He alleges that the circumstances in which the defendant obtained control make it unconscionable for him thereafter to assert a beneficial interest in the property

9.4 THE REMEDIAL CONSTRUCTIVE TRUST

Whereas an institutional constructive trust arises by operation of law from the date of the event that gives rise to it, the remedial constructive trust arises through the exercise of the judge's discretion whenever it is considered to be just to recognize that the claimant has an equitable proprietary interest.[160] The recognition of such a remedy would have a profound effect on the law, since it would apparently enable judges to create equitable proprietary interests where it was felt that the justice of the case demanded it. As a consequence the court could transfer an asset which belongs to the defendant, and in which the claimant did not have a pre-existing legal or equitable interest, to the claimant. The key difference between the institutional and the remedial constructive trust is that, to recognize a remedial constructive trust, it is not necessary to establish that the claimant has a pre-existing proprietary right; the purpose of the remedial constructive trust is to create such a proprietary right.[161]

In some jurisdictions such as Australia,[162] Canada,[163] and New Zealand,[164] the remedial constructive trust is recognized. It is not recognized in England and Wales, as confirmed by the Supreme Court in *FHR European Ventures LLP v Cedar Partners LLC*.[165] The Supreme Court cited the judgment of Lord Browne-Wilkinson in *Westdeutsche Landesbank Girozentrale v Islington LBC*[166] in support of this conclusion, but, whilst he did not formally recognize the remedial constructive trust, he was clearly not adverse to its recognition, because it would enable the consequences of proprietary relief to be tailored to the particular circumstances of the case.

---

[158] See Chapter 10 of this volume.

[159] [1999] 1 All ER 400, 408. See also *Stack v Dowden* [2007] UKHL 17, [2007] 2 AC 432, [128] (Lord Neuberger).

[160] *Westdeutsche Landesbank Girozentrale v Islington LBC* [1996] AC 669, 714 (Lord Browne-Wilkinson). See also *Re Sharpe* [1980] 1 WLR 219; *Metall und Rohstoff AG v Donaldson Lufkin & Jenrette Inc* [1990] 1 QB 391, 479 (Slade LJ); *Re Goldcorp Exchange Ltd* [1995] 1 AC 74, 104 (Lord Mustill); *London Allied Holdings v Lee* [2007] EWHC 2061 (Ch).

[161] *Re Polly Peck International plc (No 2)* [1998] 3 All ER 812, 830 (Nourse LJ).

[162] *Muschinski v Dodds* (1985) 160 CLR 583; *Grimaldi v Chameleon Mining NL (No 2)* (2012) 200 FCR 296, [569] (Justice Finn). [163] *Pettkus v Becker* (1980) 117 DLR (3d) 257.

[164] *Powell v Thompson* [1991] 1 NZLR 597.

[165] [2014] UKSC 45, [2015] AC 250, [47] (Lord Neuberger). See also *Angove's Pty Ltd v Bailey* [2016] UKSC 47, [2016] 1 WLR 3179, [27] (Lord Sumption). [166] [1996] AC 669, 716.

Lord Neuberger, who delivered the speech of the Supreme Court rejecting the remedial constructive trust, subsequently expressed his concerns about the remedial constructive trust extra-judicially.[167] He was opposed to its recognition in England and Wales for the following reasons:

(i) It would render the law unpredictable.

(ii) It would be an affront to the common law view of property rights and interests.

(iii) It would involve the courts usurping the role of the legislature: the creation of new property rights should be left to Parliament.[168] This reflects a concern about use of the remedial constructive trust to undermine priorities on insolvency as identified by statute. The Court of Appeal in *Re Polly Peck International plc (No 2)* had explicitly refused to recognize the remedial constructive trust for this reason. It was considered that the variation of property rights should be a matter for Parliament rather than for the discretion of the judiciary, especially where the creation of an equitable proprietary right by a judge would exclude assets from distribution to the unsecured creditors of the defendant.[169] In *Polly Peck*, the claimant sought to recover money from an insolvent company and argued that this money was held on a remedial constructive trust to enable it to gain priority over the defendant's other creditors. The Court of Appeal refused to recognize such a trust, especially because the distribution of assets on insolvency was governed by the Insolvency Act 1986 and it was not for the courts to interfere with this statutory regime. As Mummery LJ recognized:[170] 'The insolvency road is blocked off to remedial constructive trusts, at least when judge-driven in a vehicle of discretion.' Nourse LJ went further and said that, even had the defendant been solvent, he would not have recognized a remedial constructive trust because proprietary rights should be varied only by statute.

But the real concern about the recognition of the remedial constructive trust is simply that we need clear rules as to whether or not equitable proprietary rights have been created, and the remedial constructive trust is antithetical to such clarity and predictability.[171] Birks consequently described the remedial constructive trust as a remedy that is 'ugly, repugnant alike to legal certainty, the sanctity of property and the rule of law'.[172] Despite this, there have still been calls for the recognition of the remedial constructive trust in English law. In *London Allied Holdings v Lee*,[173] Etherton J suggested that *Polly Peck* was concerned only with the recognition of the remedial constructive trust where the defendant was insolvent, and indeed Mummery and Potter LJJ in *Polly Peck* did focus on that context. Etherton J considered that the way was therefore clear for the recognition of such a trust where the defendant was solvent and advocated the judiciary having a discretion to fashion such a remedy by analogy with the discretion to fashion the remedy in respect of proprietary estoppel.[174] He concluded that:

---

[167] 'The remedial constructive trust: fact or fiction', delivered on 10 August 2014 to the Banking Services and Finance Law Association Conference, New Zealand.

[168] But the Supreme Court in *FHR European Ventures LLP v Cedar Capital Partners LLC* [2014] UKSC 45, [2015] AC 250 surely did create a new property right in bribe money which had not existed previously. See Section 9.3.7, p. 274 and Section 15.7.3, p. 454.

[169] [1998] 3 All ER 812. See also *Cobbold v Bakewell Management Ltd* [2003] EWHC 2289 (Ch), [17] (Rimer J); *Re Farepak Food and Gifts Ltd* [2006] EWHC 3272 (Ch), [38] (Mann J); *Sinclair Investments (UK) Ltd v Versailles Trade Finance Ltd* [2011] EWCA Civ 347, [2012] Ch 453, [37] (Lord Neuberger MR).

[170] [1998] 3 All ER 812, 827.

[171] Millett, 'Equity: the road ahead' (1995) 9 TLI 35, 42; Birks, 'Property and unjust enrichment: categorical truths' [1997] NZ Law Rev 623, 641; Birks, 'The remedies for abuse of confidential information' [1990] LMCLQ 460, 465.

[172] 'Property and unjust enrichment: categorical truths' [1997] NZ Law Rev 623, 641. See also Millett, 'Equity's place in the law of commerce' (1998) 114 LQR 399.

[173] [2007] EWHC 2061 (Ch), [247].   [174] See Section 10.4.3, p. 308.

there still seems scope for real debate about a model more suited to English jurisprudence, borrowing from proprietary estoppel; namely a constructive trust by way of discretionary restitutionary relief, the right to which is a mere equity prior to judgment, but which will have priority over the intervening rights of third parties on established principles . . . [175]

But the problem with the recognition of the remedial constructive trust is that the remedy must be triggered by a cause of action. What should that cause of action be? It could be equitable wrongdoing, but as has already been seen, the constructive trust that is recognized where there is a breach of fiduciary duty is institutional in form, arising by operation of law rather than judicial discretion.[176] Similarly, unconscionable retention of property triggers an institutional, rather than a remedial, constructive trust. The remedial constructive trust might be considered to be an appropriate response to the defendant's unjust enrichment—indeed Etherton LJ's reference to 'discretionary restitutionary relief' might suggest that this is what he was contemplating—but as we saw in respect of resulting trusts,[177] the fact that the defendant has been unjustly enriched at the claimant's expense is not a sufficient reason to recognize an equitable proprietary interest; the claimant should instead be confined to a personal claim against the defendant. A remedy without a cause of action is meaningless, so the remedial constructive trust should not be recognized in English law.

It does not follow, however, that only the rigid institutional constructive trust should be recognized. There does not need to be a fundamental dichotomy between recognizing either the institutional or the remedial constructive trust; with one apparently grounded on principle and the other on perceived judicial discretion. It was observed in Chapter 2[178] that the exercise of judicial discretion must be grounded on recognized principle or else it becomes the exercise of an arbitrary choice. It is possible to identify a model of the constructive trust which is principled but also flexible, without recourse to arbitrary choice.[179] This model builds on the orthodox institutional constructive trust, as has already been examined in this chapter, by virtue of which the trust arises automatically by operation of law if the case falls within one of the recognized categories of constructive trust. This trust should, however, be capable of modification by the judge to qualify some of the proprietary implications of a constructive trust being recognized. Whilst this modified constructive trust model has not yet been recognized in English law, its recognition is not necessarily inconsistent with authority, including the decision of the Supreme Court in *FHR* itself. Crucially, the recognition of a modified constructive trust would assuage some of Lord Neuberger's concerns. Significantly, it would not be remedial in the sense that a judge creates equitable proprietary rights through the exercise of their discretion. Consequently, it should not be considered to subvert the statutory insolvency regime, for what Equity has created Equity can take away, as long as it is done on a principled basis. Indeed, the very creation of equitable proprietary rights by operation of judge-made law might be regarded as upsetting the statutory insolvency regime, but there are numerous examples of Equity doing that. Modification of the institutional constructive trust is much less controversial than, for example, the *Quistclose* trust,[180] which clearly has the potential to subvert the statutory insolvency regime.

---

[175] See also *Thorner v Major* [2009] UKHL 18, [2009] 1 WLR 776, [20], in which Lord Scott indicated that the remedial constructive trust should be used where the defendant has represented that the claimant would receive property in the future, for example in the defendant's will, in reliance on which the claimant acted to their detriment. This is presently dealt with through the doctrine of proprietary estoppel. See further Section 10.4.3, p. 308.

[176] See Section 9.3.7, p. 274.   [177] See Section 8.5.1, p. 249.   [178] See Section 2.2, p. 25.

[179] See further Virgo, 'The genetically modified constructive trust' (2016) 2(2) Canadian Journal of Comparative and Contemporary Law 579. Liew, 'Reanalysing institutional and remedial constructive trusts' (2016) 74 CLJ 528, develops a similar approach and calls this the 'transformative constructive trust'.

[180] See Section 8.4, p. 239.

A key benefit of recognizing the modified constructive trust is that the old debate about institutional versus remedial constructive trust can be regarded as sterile. Rather, the modified constructive trust can be classified as institutional but with scope for the judge to modify it on a principled basis. Once it is accepted that the constructive trust can be modified, it is important to consider when such modification might be justified. In assessing this the three key implications of recognizing proprietary interests in Equity need to be borne in mind,[181] namely: (i) priority over unsecured creditors when the defendant is insolvent; (ii) obtaining the benefit of any increase in the value of the property held on constructive trust; and (iii) where the property, or its identifiable substitute, has been received by a third party, recovering the property from that party even if they were unaware of the circumstances which triggered the constructive trust in the first place. But there may be other considerations to take into account, such as there being other remedies which can do the same work more effectively or that third parties, such as creditors of the defendant, should not be considered to be tainted by the defendant's unconscionable conduct and so should not be disadvantaged by the constructive trust. The relevance of these factors to the modification of the constructive trust can be illustrated by considering the operation of the trust in two particular scenarios.[182]

9.4.1 STOLEN PROPERTY

Where a thief holds stolen property on constructive trust for the victim,[183] should this trust ever be modified to deprive the victim of any of these proprietary benefits of the constructive trust? First, if the thief has become insolvent, should the thief's creditors be able to assert a claim against the stolen assets? Since the stolen property never legitimately formed part of the thief's pool of assets, there is no reason why the thief's creditors should gain priority over the victim. Secondly, if the stolen asset has increased in value, there is no reason why the claimant should be deprived of the benefit of this increase, since the thief should not profit from their crime in any way. Thirdly, should innocent third parties who have obtained possession of the asset or its identifiable substitute have any better claim than the thief?[184] If the third party neither knew nor suspected that the property had been stolen, surely their claim should be at least as good and possibly even better than that of the victim of the theft. It follows that the constructive trust of stolen property should not be modified to benefit creditors of the thief or the thief themself, but there might be a case to treat the constructive trust as revoked once the asset has been received by an innocent third party who has not provided value for the receipt.[185]

9.4.2 MISTAKEN PAYMENT

Where money paid by mistake is held on constructive trust because of the defendant's unconscionable retention,[186] should this trust ever be modified? First, if the defendant has become insolvent, there is no reason why the defendant's creditors should have a better claim to the trust property than the claimant. Since the asset has been received from the claimant it should be restored to the claimant. If the defendant's receipt is unconscionable

---

[181] See Section 19.1.3, p. 538.

[182] See also the analysis of bribed fiduciaries in Section 15.7.3, p. 452.   [183] See Section 9.3.1, p. 259.

[184] If the third-party recipient of the stolen property or its traceable substitute had provided value and acted in good faith, the victim's equitable proprietary claim would be defeated. See Section 19.5.1, p. 584.

[185] In *Relfo Ltd v Varsani* [2014] EWCA Civ 360, [2015] 1 BCLC 14, Arden LJ, [1], stated that money or its substitute can be recovered from a third party where the money was stolen by the fiduciary, if the money or its substitute was *knowingly* received by the third party. See also *FHR European Ventures LLP v Cedar Capital Partners LLC* [2014] UKSC 45, [2015] AC 250, [44] where Lord Neuberger indicated that bribe money held on constructive trust by a fiduciary could be claimed from a *knowing* recipient.   [186] See Section 9.3.1, p. 258.

then an equitable proprietary interest should be recognized. By virtue of the analogy with theft, there is no reason why the creditors of the defendant should obtain any advantage over the claimant. Secondly, the defendant should not be allowed to gain from the retention of the asset, save where that gain cannot be causatively linked to the receipt. So, if the asset is invested and increases in value, the defendant should hold that increase on constructive trust. But, suppose the defendant used money paid by mistake to buy a lottery ticket which wins the jackpot. Determining whether that jackpot is held on constructive trust should depend on whether it can be shown that, but for the receipt of the money paid by mistake, the defendant would not have bought the ticket. If the defendant would have bought the ticket anyway, and used the money paid by mistake by chance, this would be an appropriate reason to modify the constructive trust so that the jackpot is not held on trust. If the defendant did not rely on the receipt to buy the ticket, there is no reason why the claimant should have a proprietary claim to the jackpot. Thirdly, should the equitable proprietary right of the claimant be defeated by innocent receipt by a third party who has not provided value for the property? Whilst the law assumes that the claimant should have a proprietary restitutionary claim against such a third-party recipient,[187] this is difficult to defend. The claimant should be confined to a personal claim in unjust enrichment against the direct recipient of the mistaken payment and not have a proprietary claim against an innocent third-party recipient, at least where the only reason why the equitable proprietary right was created was because of the defendant's unconscionable retention. If the third party's receipt cannot similarly be characterized as unconscionable, there is no reason why the claimant should have a proprietary claim against that recipient.

It is important to emphasize that this modified constructive trust is speculative, especially because the institutional constructive trust appears so entrenched in England. But it is the failure to consider carefully what is meant by institutional versus remedial constructive trusts that has resulted in an unsophisticated analysis of the constructive trust. If it was accepted instead that the constructive trust arises by virtue of recognized principles but can be modified in a principled way, the constructive trust would cease to be the blunderbuss that it is today.

9.5 THE NATURE OF CONSTRUCTIVE TRUSTEESHIP

Although a constructive trust is a real trust, it does not follow that a constructive trustee is under the same obligations as any other type of trustee. A constructive trustee will have legal title to property that is held on trust for the benefit of others and will be obliged to convey the trust property to the beneficiary, but the duties of that trustee will be less onerous than those of an express trustee.[188] For example, constructive trustees are under no obligation to invest[189] and neither are they required to observe the usual duty of care.[190] Since a constructive trustee may not know that they are a trustee,[191] it would be unreasonable to impose such obligations, including the fiduciary duty of loyalty to the beneficiaries.[192]

---

[187] *Re Diplock's Estate* [1948] Ch 465, 539. See Section 19.3.3.(i), p. 560.
[188] Smith, 'Constructive fiduciaries', in *Privacy and Loyalty*, ed. Birks (Oxford: Clarendon Press, 1997), ch. 9.
[189] *Lonrho plc v Fayed (No 2)* [1992] 1 WLR 1, 12 (Millett J).   [190] See Section 13.2, p. 374.
[191] Cf. Lord Browne-Wilkinson's assertion in *Westdeutsche Landesbank Girozentrale v Islington London Borough Council* [1996] AC 669, 705, that it is a fundamental principle of the law of trusts that a trustee must know that they are a trustee. Such a principle can apply only to express trusts.
[192] See Section 15.1.2, p. 418.

10

INFORMAL ARRANGEMENTS RELATING TO PROPERTY

10.1 GENERAL CONSIDERATIONS

10.1.1 FORMALITIES

We have already come across a variety of formality requirements relating to property. For example, wills must be written and witnessed,[1] and the creation of trusts of land must be evidenced by signed writing.[2] There are other significant formality requirements that relate to property, such as contracts for the sale or other disposition of interests in land needing to be in writing, so that oral contracts for the sale of land are void.[3]

In many cases, the formality requirements will be satisfied and the transaction relating to property will be valid. But there are situations in which the parties have not complied with the formality requirements and instead enter into informal, typically oral, arrangements relating to property. The question then is whether the transaction can be rendered effective despite the informality of the arrangement. Equity has an important role to play in rendering such informal arrangements effective. This has sometimes been recognized explicitly by the relevant statute. In particular, the formality requirements for trusts of land[4] and contracts for the sale of land[5] do not apply to the creation or operation of resulting, constructive, or implied trusts. Consequently, these trusts have a significant role to play in validating informal arrangements relating to property, as does the doctrine of equitable or proprietary estoppel.

The use of these trusts and the doctrine of estoppel to render informal transactions valid is controversial. As Dixon[6] said of the doctrine of proprietary estoppel (although the point applies to trusts as well):

> If statute requires the claimant's alleged property right to have been created with a certain type of formality, why, in the absence of such formality, can the claimant run to the back door, break in using estoppel as a jemmy, and run off with some or all of the landowner's proprietary valuables?

---

[1] Wills Act 1837. See Section 5.2.1.(ii), p. 106.
[2] Law of Property Act 1925, s. 53(1)(b). See Section 5.2.1.(i) p. 105.
[3] Law of Property (Miscellaneous Provisions) Act 1989, s. 2(1).   [4] Law of Property Act 1925, s. 53(2).
[5] Law of Property (Miscellaneous Provisions) Act 1989, s. 2(5).
[6] 'Confining and defining proprietary estoppels: the role of unconscionability' (2010) 30 LS 408, 409.

Whether such equitable intervention should be considered to be appropriate, even though it has been provided for to some extent by statute, needs to be borne in mind throughout this chapter.

10.1.2 THE ROLE OF EQUITY

The informal arrangements relating to property that will be examined in this chapter are primarily significant as regards land and typically arise in one particular scenario. Imagine a case in which Alan and Belinda agree that a property will be purchased. That property is registered in Alan's name only, but he and Belinda both contribute to the purchase price, either directly by paying money to the vendor, or indirectly by contributing mortgage payments. Belinda might make other contributions, such as paying for gas and electricity, which enables Alan to take sole responsibility for the mortgage payments. The question for Equity is whether Belinda, in these circumstances, can be considered to have a beneficial interest in the property.

This scenario will typically arise because Alan and Belinda are in a relationship that breaks down. If they are married, the question of their rights in the property will largely be determined by the court's wide discretionary powers to grant ancillary relief.[7] But, if they cohabited, there is no statutory jurisdiction to determine their property rights. This is where the law of trusts has a significant role to play. But the scenario involving Alan and Belinda may arise for other reasons. They may be related, but not cohabiting, such as where they are father and daughter. Or they may be unrelated and involved in a purely commercial transaction, whereby the property is purchased as an investment or for development. But, despite the different contexts, the key questions are the same, namely whether Belinda has a beneficial interest in the property and how Equity might assist her.

Another scenario can be imagined involving Alan and Belinda. They are cohabiting and buy a house in which to live. This house is registered in both of their names, but Belinda paid most of the purchase price, or they may have contributed equally to the purchase price, but Belinda has spent more on paying for services and in repairing and improving the property. What is the extent of Belinda's beneficial interest in the property in these circumstances? What difference, if any, does it make that the property was registered in their joint names rather than only in the name of Alan?

Regardless of whether the property has been conveyed into the names of one or both of the parties, Equity may have a significant role to play in determining their respective interests in the property. A number of different types of trust and other equitable mechanisms may be relevant.

(i) Express trust

Where the property has been registered at Law in the name of one or both of the parties, the beneficial interests in that property may have been determined by an express declaration of trust.[8] Since the subject matter of the trust that we are considering is land, such a trust will need to be evidenced in signed writing to be enforceable.[9] Where the relationship between the parties is domestic rather than commercial, it is much less likely that

---

[7] By virtue of the Matrimonial Causes Act 1973. See *Miller v Miller; McFarlane v McFarlane* [2006] UKHL 24, [2006] 2 AC 618. A similar scheme applies for civil partners under the Civil Partnership Act 2004, Sch. 5, and marriage of same-sex couples: Marriage (Same Sex Couples) Act 2013, s. 11. But note the role of the resulting trust in *Prest v Petrodel Resources Ltd* [2013] UKSC 34, [2013] 2 AC 415. See Section 10.1.2.(ii), p. 282.

[8] *Stack v Dowden* [2007] UKHL 17, [2007] 2 AC 432, [49] (Lady Hale).

[9] Law of Property Act 1925, s. 53(1)(b).

they will even have considered what their respective beneficial interests in the property might be, let alone prepared any written document to identify these interests. It is for this reason that resulting, constructive, and implied trusts will be significant in determining what their beneficial interests are, because such trusts do not need to be evidenced in writing.[10] But, it is important to be aware that many of the problems that are examined in this chapter could be easily avoided if the parties were to consider their beneficial interests when acquiring the property and prepare a document confirming what these interests were.

(ii) The resulting trust

We saw in Chapter 8 that one of the typical situations in which a resulting trust will arise is where one party has contributed to the purchase price of property that is registered in the name of another. In such circumstances, it will be presumed that the contributor of the purchase price intended the property to be held by the other party on trust for them.[11] Such a resulting trust may not be the best solution for the contributor, since their beneficial interest in the property will be limited to the value of their financial contribution. The resulting trust cannot reflect other contributions, whether they are indirect financial contributions or non-financial contributions relating to the running of the family home. It is for this reason that other solutions have been sought. It has been recognized in the context of a cohabiting couple who purchase a property in their joint names for their joint occupation, that the resulting trust will usually have no role to play in determining their beneficial interests in the family home, regardless of whether they have made a financial contribution to the acquisition of the property.[12] This has now been extended to where the property was purchased as an investment by parties who are in a personal relationship.[13] This is partly justified for policy reasons, since the dramatic inflation in property prices has made the division of property with reference to initial financial contributions artificial and also produces a result which is unjust.[14] It was, however, recognized by Lord Sumption in *Prest v Petrodel Resources Ltd*[15] that, where the home of a married couple was transferred to a company, it was appropriate to infer that the property was held by the company on resulting trust for the spouse who owned and controlled the company. Since the occupation of the company's property as the controller's matrimonial home will not be readily justified as being in the company's interests, and is not consistent with the company having a beneficial interest in the property, it was considered to be unlikely that the presumption of resulting trust would be rebutted. Presumably the same result would have been reached had the couple been unmarried.

(iii) The remedial constructive trust

At one time, a constructive trust of the home was recognized simply on the grounds of justice and good conscience.[16] This was subsequently rejected[17] on the ground that the recognition of interests in property needed to be principled and not simply determined

---

[10] Ibid., s. 53(2).   [11] See Section 8.2.2, p. 220.

[12] *Jones v Kernott* [2011] UKSC 53, [2012] 1 AC 76, [53] (Lady Hale and Lord Walker). See further Section 10.2.2, p. 286 and Section 10.2.3, p. 292. This approach has been rejected by the Singapore Court of Appeal: *Chan Yuen Lan v See Fong Mun* [2014] SGCA 36.

[13] *Marr v Collie* [2017] UKPC 674, [2017] 3 WLR 1507. See further Section 10.2.4.(iv), p. 295, below.

[14] *Jones v Kernott* [2011] UKSC 53, [2012] 1 AC 76, [56] (Lord Collins).

[15] [2013] UKSC 34, [2013] 2 AC 415, [51]. See further Section 8.2.3, p. 221.

[16] *Heseltine v Heseltine* [1971] 1 WLR 342; *Hussey v Palmer* [1972] 1 WLR 1286; *Eves v Eves* [1975] 1 WLR 1338.

[17] See *Burns v Burns* [1984] Ch 317, 342 (May LJ); *Stack v Dowden* [2007] UKHL 17, [2007] 2 AC 432.

by reference to the exercise of judicial discretion. The remedial constructive trust has, anyway, been rejected in English law.[18]

(iv) The institutional constructive trust

In Chapter 9, the institutional constructive trust was analysed, this being a trust that arises by operation of law where the defendant can be considered to have acted unconscionably.[19] This type of constructive trust can also be relevant where property has been acquired by one party and another party seeks to assert a beneficial interest in it. This is particularly significant in the commercial context where the property has been acquired to be developed by both parties as a joint venture and the defendant who has legal title to it wishes to exclude the other from the arrangement.[20]

(v) The common intention constructive trust

The trust which has been of particular significance in determining the beneficial interests in the family home has been the common intention constructive trust. This is a trust which arises from an agreement or understanding of the parties as to whether they have a beneficial interest in the property and, if so, what the extent of that interest might be. Although this trust can be established by reference to the intentions of the parties, and so looks like an express trust, it is not, simply because any agreement or understanding between the parties will have been expressed orally rather than in writing. Consequently, as an express trust of land, it will be unenforceable, but as a constructive trust, it will be valid and enforceable despite the absence of writing.[21] But the fact that this trust is construed by reference to the parties' common intentions rather than unconscionable conduct, which is the key hallmark of an institutional constructive trust,[22] shows that the 'common intention constructive trust' is a distinct form of trust. It is preferably analysed as being an implied trust,[23] although, as will be seen, even this categorization is far from satisfactory because of the uncertainty as to what, if anything, is being implied. But, at least categorizing it as an implied trust forces us to see that these trusts are different from all of the other trusts that have been considered so far in this book.

(vi) Proprietary estoppel

Proprietary estoppel is another equitable doctrine that may be relevant to identify a beneficial interest in property owned at Law by another party. The essence of this doctrine is that, where the claimant has relied to their detriment on an assurance that they will acquire an interest in property belonging to the defendant, the court may recognize that the claimant has a beneficial interest in that property. The role of proprietary estoppel has proved controversial, both as to when it applies and also as to how it relates to other doctrines, especially the common intention constructive trust.[24] But it is clear that, in some cases at least, proving proprietary estoppel may enable the court to recognize that the defendant holds property on trust for the claimant and that this trust could be characterized as either being constructive, or preferably, an implied trust.

---

[18] *FHR European Ventures LLP v Cedar Capital Partners LLC* [2014] UKSC 45, [2015] AC 250. See Section 9.4, p. 275. [19] *Stack v Dowden* [2007] UKHL 17, [2007] 2 AC 432, [128] (Lord Neuberger).
[20] See Section 9.3.5.(i), p. 268. [21] Law of Property Act 1925, s. 53(2). [22] See Section 9.3.8, p. 274.
[23] *Jones v Kernott* [2011] UKSC 53, [2012] 1 AC 776, [16] (Lady Hale and Lord Walker).
[24] In *Southern Pacific Mortgages Ltd v Scott* [2014] UKSC 52, [2015] AC 385, [28], Lord Collins recognized that the distinction between the constructive trust and proprietary estoppel is only likely to matter as regards the identification of the appropriate remedy.

10.2 COMMON INTENTION CONSTRUCTIVE TRUST

10.2.1 BACKGROUND

The common intention constructive trust has proved to be most significant in determining the beneficial interests in a house bought by a cohabiting couple as the family home. If their relationship breaks down, it will be necessary to consider the extent of their respective interests in the property. If there has been an express declaration of trust in writing, this will be straightforward, but in most cases this will not have occurred and so the common intention constructive trust will be deployed. The common intention constructive trust has replaced the resulting trust as the means of dealing with the proprietary consequences of a relationship breakdown. It has been recognized that it was developed 'to mitigate the arithmetic rigour of the resulting trust when ascertaining property rights upon the breakdown of a relationship in the domestic context'.[25]

The requirements for establishing a common intention constructive trust have developed over the years since its effective origins in the decisions of the House of Lords in *Pettit v Pettit*[26] and *Gissing v Gissing*.[27] One of the most significant reformulations of the common intention constructive trust was undertaken by Lord Bridge in *Lloyds Bank plc v Rosset*.[28] He recognized that, where the property has been registered in the name of one of the parties, the common intention constructive trust could arise in two different ways:

(1) Where the parties had expressed a common intention to share the beneficial interest, followed by detrimental reliance by the claimant that is referable to that common intention. This detrimental reliance would make it unconscionable for the defendant to deny the claimant's beneficial interest in the property and give rise either to a constructive trust or proprietary estoppel. This detrimental reliance might take the form of non-financial contributions to the home, such as renovating the property.

(2) Where a common intention to share the beneficial interest can be inferred because the claimant has made a financial contribution to the purchase price of the property or to the payment of mortgage instalments. In such circumstances, the beneficial interest of the claimant would not necessarily reflect precisely the value of their financial contribution.

This structured approach to the common intention constructive trust was subject to much criticism, especially as regards the exclusion of non-financial contributions when inferring a common intention.[29] In the absence of any express evidence of intention, there was a tendency for the courts to determine the extent of the claimant's beneficial interest by reference to what the court considered to be fair in the light of the whole course of dealing between the parties in relation to the property.[30] This came very close to resurrecting the discredited remedial constructive trust solution.[31]

The House of Lords reconsidered the requirements for the common intention constructive trust in *Stack v Dowden*.[32] Whilst purporting to build on the old authorities, which have not been overruled,[33] this decision has put the common intention constructive trust

---

[25] *Chan Yuen Lan v See Fong Mun* [2014] SGCA 36, [95] (Rajah JA).   [26] [1970] AC 777.
[27] [1971] AC 886.   [28] [1991] 1 AC 107.
[29] See e.g. *Stack v Dowden* [2007] UKHL 17, [2007] 2 AC 432, [63] (Lady Hale).
[30] *Oxley v Hiscock* [2004] EWCA Civ 546, [2005] Fam 211, [69] (Chadwick LJ).
[31] See Section 10.1.2.(iii), p. 282.   [32] [2007] UKHL 17, [2007] 2 AC 432.
[33] Sloan, 'Keeping up with the *Jones* case: establishing constructive trusts in the sole legal owner scenarios' (2015) 35 LS 226, 251 suggests that there is still a need for a Supreme Court decision to determine whether the law of common intention constructive trusts is finally liberated from the *Rossett* criteria. Whilst technically correct, the subsequent pronouncements of judges at all levels assumes that those criteria no longer apply. The law on the common intention constructive trust practically starts with *Stack v Dowden*.

on a new footing, such that the key principles now derive from that decision and later authorities that have interpreted it, those principles being difficult to reconcile with the old cases. Although all five judges in *Stack v Dowden* gave reasoned judgments, the leading judgment was that of Lady Hale, with which three of the other judges agreed. Although Lord Neuberger agreed with the result, he adopted very different reasoning.[34] The decision of the majority in *Stack v Dowden* was subsequently clarified by the Supreme Court in *Jones v Kernott*.[35]

10.2.2 UNDERLYING PRINCIPLES

When determining the nature and extent of the beneficial interests of a cohabiting couple in the family home, the relevant principles are as follows.

(i) Express declaration of trust

Regardless of whether the property has been conveyed into the names of one party or both of them, the beneficial interest may have been allocated by the parties expressly in writing, so that it will be held on an express trust.[36] If so, that is the end of the matter.[37]

(ii) The presumptions

By virtue of the principle that 'Equity follows the Law', it is to be presumed that the beneficial interest in the property mirrors the legal interest. This means that it is very important to distinguish between cases of sole and joint legal ownership:[38]

(1) Where the property is registered in the name of one party only, it is to be presumed that that party has the sole beneficial interest in the property and the other party has none; there is no presumption of equality of interest.[39] The presumption of sole beneficial interest applies even where the parties wanted to register the property in their joint names but were dissuaded from doing so because it was impractical or undesirable, such as that they would have been unable to obtain a mortgage if it was registered in their joint names.[40] It follows that the presumption is triggered solely by the state of the register.

(2) Where the property is registered in the names of both parties, they clearly both have a beneficial interest in it and it is presumed that this is an equal beneficial interest; they are presumed to have a beneficial joint tenancy. This has been described as the 'default option'.[41] There is no need to prove any financial contribution to the acquisition of the property for a beneficial interest to be presumed, since this simply follows from the property being registered in the names of both parties. It follows that this has nothing to do with the presumption of a resulting trust, since that presumption depends on a party contributing to the purchase price of the property.[42]

---

[34] See Section 10.2.3, p. 292.   [35] [2011] UKSC 53, [2012] 1 AC 76.

[36] *Goodman v Gallant* [1986] Fam 106; *Pankhania v Chandegra* [2012] EWCA Civ 1438, [2013] WTLR 101, [28] (Mummery LJ).

[37] Although Gardner has tentatively suggested that, even where there has been an express declaration of trust, events after the declaration might vary the allocation of the beneficial interests: 'Family property today' (2008) 124 LQR 422.

[38] *Jones v Kernott* [2011] UKSC 53, [2012] 1 AC 776, [16] (Lady Hale and Lord Walker), [68] (Lord Kerr).

[39] *Graham-York v York* [2015] EWCA Civ 72, [2015] HLR 26, [25] (Tomlinson LJ).

[40] *Thompson v Hurst* [2012] EWCA Civ 1752, [2014] 1 FLR 238, [20] (Etherton LJ).

[41] *Jones v Kernott* [2011] UKSC 53, [2012] 1 AC 776, [15] (Lady Hale and Lord Walker).

[42] Ibid., [53], (Lady Hale and Lord Walker).

Although there might have been a continuing role for a resulting trust to be presumed where the property has been registered in the name of one party only and the other has contributed to the purchase price,[43] the Privy Council in *Abbott v Abbott*[44] subsequently rejected the resulting trust even in that context.[45] The presumption of resulting trust is inapplicable, at least in the context of determining beneficial interests in the home of a cohabiting couple, because the law has moved on in response to changing social and economic conditions.[46] Similarly, where the matrimonial home is transferred into the joint names of husband and wife, the presumption of advancement will give way to the presumption of equal beneficial ownership.[47]

(iii) Rebuttable presumption

The presumptions relating to the location and extent of the beneficial interests can be rebutted by the party who wishes to show that their location and extent are different from the location and extent of the legal interests. The process for rebutting the presumptions will differ depending again on whether the case involves sole or joint legal ownership:

(1) Where the property is registered in the name of one party only, the other will first need to establish that there was a common intention,[48] objectively determined[49] and which may be express or inferred from conduct,[50] that they would have a beneficial interest in the property. Having done so, that party will then need to establish what proportion of the beneficial interest would be fair, having regard to the whole course of dealing between the parties such that it is possible to impute an intention as to the appropriate share of the beneficial interest.[51] The burden of proving that the other party should have a beneficial interest at all is a heavy one[52] and does not involve the imputation of intent with reference to what the court considers to be fair, but just what the parties expressly agreed or can be inferred to have agreed, with regard to direct and, it appears, indirect financial contributions.[53] Imputation of intent and the question of fairness is relevant to the quantification of the beneficial interest stage. The other party will need to establish that they acted to their detriment in reliance on the common intention that they would have an interest in the property.[54] This brings the doctrine of the common intention constructive trust closer to that of proprietary estoppel,[55] and provides a justification for the recognition of an equitable proprietary interest the legal title to which is in the other party, since denying

---

[43] *Stack v Dowden* [2007] UKHL 17, [2007] 2 AC 432, [114] (Lord Neuberger).

[44] [2007] UKPC 53, [2008] 1 FLR 1451.

[45] See also *Negus v Bahouse* [2007] EWHC 2628 (Ch), [2008] FLR 381; *Tackaberry v Hollis* [2007] EWHC 2633 (Ch), [2008] WTLR 279; *Frost v Clarke* [2008] EWHC 742 (Ch); *Williamson v Sheikh* [2008] EWCA Civ 990.

[46] *Stack v Dowden* [2007] UKHL 17, [2007] 2 AC 432, [60] (Lady Hale). For the rejection of the presumption of resulting trust where a couple in a personal relationship buy property as investment rather than as a home for them, see *Marr v Collie* [2017] UKPC 17, [2017] 3 WLR 1507, Section 10.2.4.(iv), p. 295.

[47] *Gibson v Revenue and Customs Prosecution Office* [2008] EWCA Civ 645, [2008] 2 FLR 1672, [27] (Arden LJ).

[48] In *Capehorn v Harris* [2015] EWCA Civ 955, [2015] Fam Law 1347, [17], Sales LJ called this an 'actual agreement'.

[49] *Jones v Kernott* [2011] UKSC 53, [2012] 1 AC 776, [46] and [51] (Lady Hale and Lord Walker); *Curran v Colins* [2015] EWCA Civ 404, [2015] Fam Law 780, [34] (Arden LJ).

[50] *Capehorn v Harris* [2015] EWCA Civ 955, [2015] Fam Law 1347, [17] (Sales LJ).   [51] Ibid.

[52] More so where the property is purchased as an investment rather than a home: *Geary v Rankine* [2012] EWCA Civ 555, [2012] 2 FLR 1409, [18] (Lewison LJ).

[53] *Bhushan v Chand* [2015] EWHC 1298 (Ch), [6] (Davies HHJ).

[54] *Curran v Collins* [2015] EWCA Civ 40, [2015] Fam Law 780 [20] (Arden LJ) and [77] (Lewison LJ), relying on *Grant v Edwards* [1986] Ch 638, 654 (Browne-Wilkinson V-C). See also *Smith v Bottomley* [2013] EWCA Civ 953, [2014] 1 FLR 626, [31] (Sales J).

[55] See further Section 10.4, p. 305.

an interest to the party who has relied on the common intention can be characterized as unconscionable.[56]

(2) Where the property is registered in the name of both parties, the party who claims that the beneficial interest is apportioned otherwise than equally bears the burden of proving that a different apportionment was intended by the parties. So, for example, the claimant might wish to argue that the beneficial interest should be apportioned 75:25 rather than the presumed 50:50 division. The burden of proving such different apportionment is a heavy one and Lady Hale indicated in *Stack v Dowden*[57] that it would be a very unusual case in which the beneficial interest is not shared equally—although, as we will see,[58] *Stack v Dowden* was, in fact, one of the unusual cases in which a different apportionment of the beneficial interest was recognized, as was the decision of the Supreme Court in *Jones v Kernott*.[59] The reason why the presumption will be difficult to rebut is that, where a couple in an intimate relationship buy a property in which to live together, often with the assistance of a mortgage for which they are jointly and severally liable, this is strong evidence of an emotional and economic commitment to a joint enterprise.[60] The existence of this joint enterprise strongly supports the presumption of equal beneficial interests in the property.

(iv) Rebutting the presumption

The essential test for rebutting the relevant presumption relates to the common intentions of the parties as to whether a party has a beneficial interest and, if they do, what the proportion of that interest is. This common intention was described by Lady Hale in *Stack v Dowden*[61] as being the parties' shared intention, which is actual, inferred, or imputed in the light of their whole course of conduct in relation to the property. Crucially, the focus is on what the parties did intend, or must be taken to have intended, rather than the court simply identifying a result that it considers to be fair.[62]

Relevant factors

Before *Stack v Dowden*, the common intention could be established only with reference to financial contributions to the acquisition of property.[63] Now, a much wider variety of factors can be considered to identify the parties' intentions. This has been described as a holistic approach that requires the court to survey the whole course of dealing between the parties in so far as it relates to the acquisition of the property rather than to the success of their relationship or the normal demands of everyday life.[64] Although each case will turn on its particular facts, the following factors were identified by Lady Hale in *Stack v Dowden* as being significant:

(1) advice or discussions at the time of the purchase that cast light on the parties' intentions;

(2) consideration of the reasons why the house was acquired in their joint names or in the name of one of them;

---

[56] See Sloan (see n. 33), p. 228.
[57] [2007] UKHL 17, [2007] AC 432, [69] and see [33] (Lord Walker); *Fowler v Barron* [2008] EWCA Civ 377, [2008] 2 FLR 831, [51] (Toulson LJ).   [58] See Section 10.2.4.(ii), p. 294.
[59] [2011] UKSC 53, [2012] 1 AC 776. See Section 10.2.4.(iii), p. 294.
[60] *Jones v Kernott* [2011] UKSC 53, [2012] 1 AC 776, [19] (Lady Hale and Lord Walker).
[61] [2007] UKHL 17, [2007] AC 432, [59].
[62] See also *Holman v Howes* [2007] EWCA Civ 877. But note the effect of the decision of the Supreme Court in *Jones v Kernott* [2011] UKSC 53, [2012] 1 AC 776. See Section 10.2.2.(iv), p. 289.
[63] See especially *Lloyd's Bank plc v Rosset* [1991] 1 AC 107, 133 (Lord Bridge).
[64] *Stack v Dowden* [2007] UKHL 17, [2007] AC 432, [61] (Lady Hale) and see also [34] (Lord Walker).

(3) the purpose for which the house was acquired;

(4) the nature of their relationship;

(5) whether they had children for whom they shared a responsibility to provide a home;

(6) how the purchase was financed, initially and subsequently;

(7) how they arranged their finances;

(8) how they discharged their outgoings on the property and other household expenses; and

(9) their characters and personalities.

This is not an exclusive list of factors; there could be other factors that are relevant in particular cases. Lady Hale emphasized that, where the couple own the home jointly and are jointly liable for the mortgage, the arithmetical calculation of how much each paid may not be that significant when determining the proportions of their beneficial interests, since it may be more important that they intended each to contribute as much to the household as they could and that they would share the eventual benefit or burden equally. The parties' intentions may also change over time, such as where one party has financed or built an extension to the property, but only where the improvements are significant.[65]

The function of these factors is important. They are not being considered to show that the claimant had detrimentally relied on any understanding that they would acquire a beneficial interest; such detrimental reliance needs to be shown in sole ownership cases, but only once the common intention has been established.[66] The factors are relevant only as evidence to determine what the parties intended. But it is unclear why some of these factors are relevant in deducing a common intention relating to beneficial interests,[67] such as the fact that they have had children. Although they purport to be of evidential significance, they could simply be a smokescreen behind which the court can exercise its discretion to determine an allocation of the beneficial interest that is fair and just, even though the court is not meant to reason in this way.[68]

Express common intention

If it can be shown that the parties had an express understanding or agreement as to the apportionment of the beneficial interest in the property, it is entirely appropriate that this apportionment is recognized by the courts, even though this does not correspond with the allocation of the legal title to the property and does not comply with the relevant formalities to create an enforceable express trust. This actual common intention will be established on the facts, without the need to consider the factors identified by Lady Hale.

Inferred common intention

If an express common intention cannot be established, it is necessary to consider whether such an intention can be objectively inferred from the evidence. The factors identified by Lady Hale will be of particular significance when inferring a common intention as to the allocation of the beneficial interests. But it is important to be clear about what the nature of this inference entails. The court is simply trying to establish from all of the available evidence that there was a genuine agreement or understanding between the parties as to the

---

[65] Ibid., [34] (Lord Walker). See further Section 10.2.4.(iii), p. 294.

[66] *Curran v Collins* [2015] EWCA Civ 404, [2015] Fam Law 780, [77] (Lewison LJ). See Section 10.2.4.(i), p. 293.

[67] *Stack v Dowden* [2007] UKHL 17, [2007] AC 432, [106] (Lord Neuberger).

[68] See further Section 10.2.2.(iv), p. 290.

allocation of the beneficial interest. An inferred intent is an actual intent, albeit one which can be deduced objectively from the parties' conduct.[69]

Imputed common intention

The most controversial aspect of Lady Hale's analysis of common intention in *Stack v Dowden* is her acceptance that this intention might be imputed. This does not involve proving an actual intent shared by the parties, but rather involves the attribution of an intention that they might not have shared, but which the court considers they would have agreed had they thought about the allocation of the beneficial interest. It is at this point that the proof of a common intention could disintegrate into a determination of an allocation of the beneficial interest that the court considers to be fair. Indeed, Etherton has said that 'there is now a hair's breadth between the [common intention constructive trust] . . . and a remedial constructive trust'.[70]

The relevance of an imputed intention was criticized by Lord Neuberger in *Stack v Dowden*,[71] as being wrong in principle and as requiring the judge to engage in a difficult, uncertain, and subjective exercise in construing an intention that does not exist. It is unclear whether the court should consider a hypothetical negotiation between the parties, which would favour an unreasonable party, or what reasonable people would have agreed in the circumstances, which would give greater scope for the court to impose its own view of a fair result. The imputation of intention is also inconsistent with earlier decisions of the House of Lords that held that the court should only be concerned with the identification of the parties' real intention rather than an imputed intention with reference to what the parties would have decided had they thought about the matter.[72] It has even been suggested[73] that the House of Lords in *Stack v Dowden* did not intend courts to find a common intention by imputation, but Lady Hale expressly referred to the imputation of intention being sufficient to establish common intent.

It was because of the continued uncertainty about the significance of inferred and imputed intention to the identification of a common intention that the judges in the Supreme Court reconsidered the principles underlying the common intention constructive trust in *Jones v Kernott*.[74] The majority in that case, consisting of Lady Hale, Lord Walker, and Lord Collins, concluded that the court should primarily be concerned with searching for the parties' actual shared intentions, subject to two exceptions where an intention would be imputed: first, as the result of a presumption of resulting trust, although that was not considered to be generally applicable in a domestic context;[75] secondly, and more significantly, where it was clear that the parties intended to share the beneficial interest but it was not possible to determine a common intention as to the proportions in which the interest was to be shared.[76] Where imputation of an intention is required, the court must consider what is fair having regard to the whole course of dealing in respect

---

[69] *Jones v Kernott* [2011] UKSC 53, [2012] 1 AC 776, [51](3) (Lady Hale and Lord Walker). Cf. Lord Wilson, [88].

[70] 'Constructive trusts and proprietary estoppel: the search for clarity and principle' [2009] Conv 104, 125.

[71] [2007] UKHL 17, [2007] AC 432, [144].

[72] *Pettitt v Pettitt* [1970] AC 777; *Gissing v Gissing* [1971] AC 886, 898 (Lord Morris), 900 (Viscount Dilhorne), and 904 (Lord Diplock). Cf. the judgments of Lord Reid, who advocated the imputation of intention: *Pettitt v Pettitt* [1970] AC 777, 795; *Gissing v Gissing* [1971] AC 886, 897.

[73] *Tackaberry v Hollis* [2007] EWHC 2633 (Ch), [2008] WTLR 279.

[74] [2011] UKSC 53, [2012] 1 AC 776.

[75] Confirmed in *Marr v Collie* [2017] UKPC 17, [2017] 3 WLR 1507, Section 10.2.4.(iv), p. 295.

[76] [2011] UKSC 53, [2012] 1 AC 776, [31] (Lady Hale and Lord Walker).

of the property,[77] which will include the financial contributions made by the parties, but other factors as well, including those identified by Lady Hale in *Stack v Dowden*.[78] It was recognized in *Graham-York v York*,[79] that, in determining what is fair, the court is not seeking to effect redistributive justice, so, in that case, the fact that the defendant had abused the claimant did not justify the court in redistributing property interests to effect compensation. Fairness relates instead to the course of dealing between the parties in respect of the property, with reference to the claimant's financial and non-financial contribution to the property.

The majority in *Jones v Kernott* accepted that, although there was a conceptual difference between the inference and imputation of a common intention, the difference in practice might not be great.[80] Crucially, as Lady Hale and Lord Walker recognized:

> the court will try to deduce what [the parties'] actual intentions were at the relevant time. It cannot impose a solution upon them which is contrary to what the evidence shows that they actually intended. But if it cannot deduce exactly what shares were intended, it may have no alternative but to ask what their intentions as reasonable and just people would have been had they thought about it at the time. This is a fallback position which some courts may not welcome, but the court has a duty to come to a conclusion on the dispute put before it.[81]

But this removes any rational difference between inference and imputation. That is why Lords Wilson and Kerr, whilst agreeing with the result in the case, disagreed with the approach of the other three judges.[82] Lords Wilson and Kerr recognized that the inference of an intention involves deducing the parties' actual intention objectively from their conduct[83] to determine what the parties must be taken to have intended in fact. If it is not possible to discover this actual intention then the common intention could only be imputed, or attributed, and they emphasized that the concept of inference should not be strained in order to avoid imputing an intention.[84] But, in determining whether such an intention can be imputed, Lords Wilson and Kerr emphasized that the parties' share of the value of the property should only reflect what the court considers to be fair having regard to the whole course of dealing between the parties.[85] Unlike the majority, the minority considered that the imputation of an intention had nothing to do with what the parties did intend or could be considered to have intended had they thought about it.

The preferable view is that there should be a clear conceptual division maintained between inferring and imputing a common intention. An inferred common intention is an actual intention which can only be established on the evidence. If such an intention cannot be established, the court should seek to impute the intention.[86] This is an objective test which should be assessed by reference to what reasonable people would have intended had they been in the position of the parties. A wide variety of factors should be considered in establishing this, but it is dangerous to resort to uncertain notions of fairness. If a common intention cannot be imputed then, where the property is registered in joint names, the presumption of a joint tenancy will not have been rebutted so the parties will share the value of the property equally.

---

[77] Ibid., [51](4) (Lady Hale and Lord Walker), [64] (Lord Collins).
[78] See Section 10.2.2.(iv), p. 287.   [79] [2015] EWCA Civ 72, [2015] HLR 26, [22] (Tomlinson LJ).
[80] [2011] UKSC 53, [2012] 1 AC 776, [34] (Lady Hale and Lord Walker), [58] (Lord Collins).
[81] Ibid., [47] (Lady Hale and Lord Walker).   [82] Ibid., [67] (Lord Kerr).
[83] Ibid., [68](iii) (Lord Kerr),   [84] Ibid., [72] (Lord Kerr), [89] (Lord Wilson).
[85] Ibid., [68](iv) (Lord Kerr), [88] (Lord Wilson).
[86] See Pawlowski, 'Imputing a common intention in single ownership cases' (2015) 29 TLI 3.

Ambulatory intention

The common intention of the parties as to the allocation of the beneficial interests might change over time, a so-called 'ambulatory intention',[87] but compelling evidence will be required to establish a subsequent change in the beneficial ownership,[88] such as significant capital expenditure to the property to extend or improve it or the separation of the parties over a substantial period.[89] But, at any point in time, the common intention of the parties must be the same for all purposes and cannot vary depending on the particular circumstances which might exist in the future. For example, the parties cannot intend to have a joint tenancy with survivorship should one of them die, a tenancy in common in equal shares if they separate amicably, and a tenancy in common in unequal shares should they separate acrimoniously.

Summary

The practical effect of the new approach to the common intention constructive trust introduced by *Stack v Dowden* is that it is no longer necessary to find either an express agreement plus detrimental reliance or financial contributions to the acquisition of the property. Rather, the courts start with the allocation of legal title to the property and will only conclude that the allocation of the beneficial interest is different if this is what the parties can be considered to have intended, whether expressly, impliedly, or by virtue of an imputed intention.

10.2.3 LORD NEUBERGER'S APPROACH

In *Stack v Dowden* Lord Neuberger adopted a more principled approach to the common intention constructive trust. Although his approach reached the same result as that adopted by the other judges in the case, none of them approved of his analysis, even though it is much more consistent with the established authorities and fundamental principles of the law of trusts.

The significant difference between the approach adopted by Lord Neuberger and that of the other judges is that he considered the resulting trust to have a significant role to play in the analysis. He recognized that the starting point is that the beneficial interest should follow the legal interest so that, where the property is registered in the names of both parties, they should have equal beneficial interests in it; where it is registered in the name of one party only, the other should be presumed to have no beneficial interest. Where, however, the parties have made financial contributions to the purchase price, their beneficial interests should be presumed to be held in the same proportions as their financial contributions through the application of the presumed resulting trust.[90] He considered this to be preferable to simply presuming that the beneficial interest follows the legal interest, because the property may have been placed in the joint names of the parties for reasons that cast no light on their intentions as regards the beneficial interests, such as resulting from a decision made by their solicitor or because the mortgage lender preferred to have the security of two borrowers. This is, however, a presumption of resulting trust that can be rebutted by a common intention that the beneficial interests were different, in which case the property would be held on a constructive trust according to that common intention. But he emphasized that this common intention could be established only expressly or impliedly, and could not be imputed.[91]

---

[87] *Stack v Dowden* [2007] UKHL 17, [2007] AC 432, [62] (Lady Hale).

[88] [2007] UKHL 17, [2007] AC 432, [138] (Lord Neuberger); *Jones v Kernott* [2011] UKSC 53, [2012] 1 AC 776, discussed in Section 10.2.4.(iii), p. 294.   [89] Ibid. See Section 10.2.4.(iii), p. 294.

[90] [2007] UKHL 17, [2007] AC 432, [110] (Lord Neuberger).   [91] Ibid., [125].

When considering whether any of the presumptions had been rebutted, Lord Neuberger would have adopted a more restrictive approach to the use of the circumstances of the parties' relationship to establish the common intention. In particular, how the parties conducted their day-to-day living and finances could not be considered to be a reliable guide to their intentions in relation to the beneficial ownership of the property.[92] For example, he considered that the fact that the parties had a joint bank account and used money from that account to pay the mortgage would not suggest an intention to have joint beneficial interests in the property. Further, the fact that the parties had a close and loving relationship might rebut the presumption of resulting trust, since it would indicate that a contribution to the purchase price might have been a gift. Lord Neuberger also placed much less emphasis on the significance of factors arising after the property had been acquired, except where there were discussions, statements, or actions that implied a positive intention that the beneficial interest should be apportioned differently.[93] Lord Neuberger's approach was, however, clearly rejected by all of the judges in the Supreme Court in *Jones v Kernott*, both because none of them recognized the significance of the resulting trust in cohabitation cases and because they all recognized that a common intention could be imputed, although they differed as to when and how this might be established.[94] Lord Neuberger's approach has also been rejected by the Privy Council,[95] by a Board of which Lord Neuberger was a member. It is, however, an approach which has been endorsed by the Singapore Court of Appeal.[96]

10.2.4 APPLICATION OF THE PRINCIPLES

The legitimacy of the approach to the common intention constructive trust following the analysis of the House of Lords in *Stack v Dowden* and the Supreme Court in *Jones v Kernott* is best assessed by seeing how these principles have been applied in particular cases.

(i) Single-ownership cases

Although *Stack v Dowden* and *Jones v Kernott* were cases where the property was registered in the names of both parties, it is clear that the principles which derive from those cases are applicable where the property has been registered in the name of one party only.[97]

Although *Oxley v Hiscock*[98] was decided before *Stack v Dowden*, and the explicit focus on achieving a fair result was rejected by the House of Lords, nothing was said in *Stack* to suggest that the result in *Oxley v Hiscock* was incorrect. In that case, the claimant and the defendant had bought a house in which they cohabited. The property was registered in the sole name of the defendant because of a concern that it would otherwise be vulnerable to a claim from the claimant's former husband. The purchase price of £127,000 was funded by: £36,300, being the net proceeds of the sale of the claimant's previous property; £60,700 contributed by the defendant; and a mortgage loan of £30,000 that was paid off through roughly equal financial contributions by the claimant and the defendant. The parties

[92] Ibid., [143].   [93] Ibid., [146].   [94] See Section 10.2.2.(iv), p. 289.
[95] *Marr v Collie* [2017] UKPC 17, [2017] 3 WLR 1507, Section 10.2.4.(iv), p. 295.
[96] *Chan Yuen Lan v See Fong Mun* [2014] SGCA 36.
[97] See *Crown Prosecution Service v Piper* [2011] EWHC 3570 (Admin); *Geary v Rankine* [2012] EWCA Civ 555, [2012] 2 FLR 1409; *Aspden v Elvy* [2012] EWHC 1387 (Ch), [2012] 2 FLR 807; *Thompson v Hurst* [2012] EWCA Civ 1752, [2014] 1 FLR 238; *Gallarotti v Sebastianelli* [2012] EWCA Civ 865, [2012] WTLR 1509; *Graham-York v York* [2015] EWCA Civ 72, [2015] HLR 26; *Curran v Collins* [2015] EWCA Civ 404, [2015] Fam Law 780, *Capehorn v Harris* [2015] EWCA Civ 955, [2015] Fam Law 1347. See generally Sloan (see n. 33).
[98] [2004] EWCA Civ 546, [2005] Fam 211.

separated and the property was sold for £232,000. The claimant sought a declaration that the proceeds were held by the defendant on trust for both of them in equal shares. It was held that a common intention to share equally could not be inferred; instead, the claimant obtained 40 per cent of the proceeds, which reflected the relative scale of her contributions to the acquisition of the house fixed by reference to her direct contributions. A similar result would have been achieved had the presumption of resulting trust been applied.[99]

Abbott v Abbott[100] is a case involving sole legal ownership in which *Stack v Dowden* was applied. Although this was a decision of the Privy Council, the panel included three of the judges who had sat in *Stack v Dowden*, including Lady Hale and Lord Neuberger. The case concerned a house that had been registered in the name of the husband only. Following the divorce of the couple, the wife sought to establish a beneficial interest in the property. The dispute arose in Antigua and Barbuda, which does not have property adjustment legislation for divorcing couples, so the common intention constructive trust was applicable. Being a sole-ownership case, it was recognized that the wife needed to show a common intention that she was to acquire a beneficial interest in the property and, having done that, what the beneficial interest was intended to be. A common intention that the wife was to have a beneficial interest was inferred because she was jointly liable for mortgage repayments, to which her salary contributed, although her husband contributed more than she did. In quantifying the extent of her beneficial interest, the court had regard to the whole course of the parties' conduct in relation to the property. Since they had organized their finances jointly, with a joint bank account and joint liability for mortgage repayments, and the land on which the property was built had been a gift from the husband's mother to the couple, it was held that the beneficial ownership should be split equally between them.

Abbott v Abbott is potentially significant because Lady Hale applied the holistic approach to both the identification of the beneficial interest stage of the inquiry and to the quantification stage. In fact, she did not distinguish clearly between the two stages.[101] Subsequently, however, in *Capehorn v Harris*[102] the Court of Appeal emphasized that the two stages of the inquiry are distinct. The first stage requires an actual agreement to have been made between the parties as to the sharing of the beneficial interest, although this may be inferred but not imputed from conduct. At the second quantification stage the court can impute an intention that each party is entitled to the share of the beneficial interest which the court considers to be fair having regard to the whole course of dealing between them in relation to the property.[103]

Whilst the results of *Oxley v Hiscock* and *Abbott v Abbott* suggest that the presumption that the party with the legal title had the whole of the beneficial interest can be rebutted relatively easily, since the circumstances for rebuttal were not particularly unusual, more recent cases, notably *Capehorn v Harris*, indicate that the presumption will not be easily rebutted. In particular, it was recognized in *Curran v Collins*,[104] that, in these sole-ownership cases, it is not enough to establish the common intention; the party who is asserting a share in the beneficial interest must also have relied to their detriment on this common intention. This is a requirement which does not apply in the joint-ownership context, and may prove to be a significant restriction on the identification of a share of the beneficial interest in sole-ownership cases. It was certainly a test that was not satisfied in that case, where the defendant had made it clear that the properties which had been purchased were

---

[99] Gardner, 'Quantum in *Gissing v Gissing* constructive trusts' (2004) 120 LQR 541, 544.
[100] [2007] UKPC 53, [2008] 1 FLR 1451.   [101] Lee, '*Stack v Dowden*: a sequel' (2008) 124 LQR 209, 210.
[102] [2015] EWCA Civ 955, [2015] Fam Law 1347. See also *Geary v Rankine* [2012] EWCA Civ 555, [2012] 2 FLR 1409, [20] (Lewison LJ).   [103] [2015] EWCA Civ 955, [2015] Fam Law 1347, [17] (Sales LJ).
[104] [2015] EWCA Civ 404, [2015] Fam Law 780.

his alone, so that the claimant could not have reasonably believed that there was a common intention to share the beneficial interest. Although the reason given by the defendant for this, namely that it would be too expensive to put the claimant on the title deeds, was considered to be specious, this was not regarded as being sufficient to draw the inference that the claimant could reasonably consider herself to have a share in the beneficial interest in the property. Further, the claimant had not relied to her detriment in any way on the defendant's representation, since she had made no direct or indirect financial contributions to the purchase of the properties. Consequently, she did not have a beneficial interest in any of the properties. This is surely correct. It is not appropriate for an equitable proprietary interest to be created where the claimant, who does not have legal title to the property, has not contributed to the purchase of that property in any way.

(ii) Joint-ownership cases

Stack v Dowden[105] was a case in which the family home had been conveyed into the names of both parties. Two-thirds of the purchase price was contributed by the claimant, and one-third from a mortgage loan in their joint names, to which they had both contributed. On the breakdown of their relationship, the issue for the court concerned the quantification of the claimant's beneficial interest. Since the property was registered in their joint names, the starting point was to presume that they shared the beneficial interest. The question then was whether this presumption could be rebutted by the identification of a common intent that the beneficial interest should be apportioned differently. It was held that this was an exceptional case in which the proportion of the beneficial interest was different from the legal interest, so that the claimant had a 65 per cent interest and the defendant 35 per cent. Lady Hale concluded that the parties had not intended their share of the beneficial interest to be equal, because the claimant had contributed substantially more of the purchase price than the defendant and the parties had not pooled their resources for the common good.[106] But it is not clear whether the House of Lords considered that the common intention could be inferred or imputed, although the nature of the factors identified suggest an imputed intent. Subsequently, however, in *Jones v Kernott*[107] Lady Hale and Lord Walker emphasized that the relevant intention in *Stack v Dowden* had been inferred.

In fact, the same result could have been achieved by the straightforward application of the presumption of resulting trust, which was how Lord Neuberger affirmed the result, but by a different route. The claimant had contributed 65 per cent of the purchase price and on that basis, he said, she was entitled to a 65 per cent share of the beneficial interest.

(iii) Ambulatory intent

Whether an initial common intention as regards the allocation of the beneficial interest can be considered to have changed over time was considered in *Jones v Kernott*.[108] In that case, the couple had purchased a house in 1985 which was conveyed into their joint names. They separated in 1993. It was accepted that, at that time, they held the property beneficially in equal shares. The claimant continued to live in the house with their children, whilst the defendant had acquired alternative accommodation and made no further contribution towards the acquisition of the property. The claimant assumed sole responsibility for paying the mortgage, and for repairs and improvements to the property. The defendant

---

[105] [2007] UKHL 17, [2007] 2 AC 432.

[106] Ibid., [92].

[107] [2011] UKSC 53, [2012] 1 AC 776, [30].

[108] Ibid. See also *Geary v Rankine* [2012] EWCA Civ 555, [2012] 2 FLR 1409, where it was held that the defendant's intention had not changed.

severed the joint tenancy in 2008, at which point the claimant asserted that their beneficial interests were no longer equal. The Supreme Court held that the initial presumption
of equality of beneficial interests continued until the parties separated, but thereafter the
common intention of the parties had changed. The property was purchased for £30,000
and by the time of the trial it was worth £245,000. The couple had jointly contributed to
the mortgage for eight years and five months and the claimant had contributed to it by
herself for fourteen and a half years. It was held that the value of the property should be
divided between them as to 88 per cent for the claimant and 12 per cent for the defendant.

Whilst the judges in the Supreme Court unanimously recognized that the parties' initial
common intention as to the allocation of the beneficial interest had changed over time,
there was a clear division of opinion as to how this ambulatory intention was to be ascertained. Three of the judges accepted that the intention could be inferred, because the
trial judge had found that the common intention of the parties as to the extent of their
beneficial interest had changed on their separation. This was supported by the fact that
the defendant no longer contributed to the purchase of the property but had acquired a
new property for himself. Lady Hale and Lord Walker concluded that a changed common
intention as to the allocation of the beneficial interest could be inferred, because this is
what reasonable people would have intended had they thought about it at the time. Lords
Kerr and Wilson, on the other hand, considered that a changed common intention could
not be inferred on the facts, but could only be imputed. They agreed with the other judges
as to the appropriate division of the value of the property, but only because this was the
fair solution.

(iv) Application beyond cohabitants

It is clear from the leading cases that the common intention constructive trust can be used
to determine the beneficial interests in the family home of a cohabiting couple.[109] The trust
has been extended beyond cohabiting couples to other personal relationships in which
the property that is purchased is the parties' home, described as the 'domestic consumer
context'.[110] So, for example, it has been applied where a house was purchased by a mother
and son in joint names as a home for them both,[111] and where two close male friends had
bought a flat together in the name of one of them,[112] and it seems that the presumption of
joint beneficial ownership will be more easily rebutted where the parties are not a couple
or are not living together.

Limits to the operation of the common intention constructive trust were recognized
after *Stack v Dowden* where property was purchased as an investment rather than as a
family home, which would trigger the presumption of resulting trust rather than the *Stack
v Dowden* presumption.[113] But this has now been rejected by the Privy Council in *Marr v
Collie*,[114] with both Lord Neuberger and Lady Hale on the Board. The case concerned two
men who were in a personal relationship for a number of years, during which they purchased various properties as investments. These properties were registered in their joint
names but one of the men was primarily responsible for making payments associated with
the purchases. After their relationship had ended, the issue arose as to what beneficial
interest they each had in the properties. The Privy Council rejected the proposition that

---

[109] Even if the property is not their primary residence: *Kali & Burlay v Chawla* [2007] EWHC 2357, [17]
(Judge Hodge QC).   [110] *Stack v Dowden* [2007] UKHL 17, [2007] AC 432, [58] (Lady Hale).
[111] *Adekunle v Ritchie* [2007] WTLR 1505.
[112] *Gallarotti v Sebastianelli* [2012] EWCA Civ 865, [2012] WTLR 1509.
[113] *Laskar v Laskar* [2008] EWCA Civ 347, [2008] 1 WLR 2695.
[114] [2017] UKPC 17, [2017] 3 WLR 1507.

the common intention constructive trust should be confined to 'the domestic setting' and it was extended to where the property had been purchased as a commercial investment if there was a personal relationship between the parties. It follows that the resulting trust model will generally not apply where a personal relationship has broken down, regardless of the reason why the property was purchased.

The Privy Council justified its decision in this way:[115]

> It is entirely conceivable that partners in a relationship would buy, as an investment, property which is conveyed into their joint names with the intention that the beneficial ownership should be shared equally between them, even though they contributed in different shares to the purchase. Where there is evidence to support such a conclusion, it would be both illogical and wrong to impose the resulting trust solution on the subsequent distribution of the property.

But this misses the point that the 'resulting trust solution' is itself a presumption to assist the court in determining the right result, and this presumption can be rebutted by contrary evidence. The real issue should be whether this is an appropriate presumption on which to rely: where there is a differential financial contribution to the purchase of the property should this be presumed to affect the quantification of the beneficial interests?

The Privy Council also considered the effect of a 'clash of presumptions' between the presumption relating to the resulting trust and that relating to the common intention constructive trust. It was recognized that:[116]

> ...save perhaps where there is no evidence from which the parties' intentions can be identified, the answer is not to be provided by the triumph of one presumption over another. In this, as in so many areas of law, context counts for, if not everything, a lot. Context here is set by the parties' common intention—or by the lack of it. If it is the unambiguous mutual wish of the parties, contributing in unequal shares to the purchase of property, that the joint beneficial ownership should reflect their joint legal ownership, then effect should be given to that wish. If, on the other hand, that is not their wish, or if they have not formed any intention as to beneficial ownership but had, for instance, accepted advice that the property be acquired in joint names, without considering or being aware of the possible consequences of that, the resulting trust solution may provide the answer.

But this is very confused, because the Privy Council failed to use the language of presumption and sought to identify a common intention as triggering a particular result, whereas the proper approach is to start with a presumption as to what the common intention should be and then consider whether that presumption has been rebutted. The reasoning of the Privy Council should actually have been as follows:

(i) If the property is registered in joint names there is a presumption that the parties have an equal beneficial interest in it.

(ii) If the parties have made different financial contributions then they should be presumed to have intended to have different beneficial interests.

(iii) These presumptions can be rebutted if it can be established that the parties' common intention was contrary to what they were presumed to have intended. This stage must logically come at the end in order to rebut any presumption. If the presumption cannot be rebutted then it continues to apply. The real issue is whether the only presumption should be the first one, which is the *Stack v Dowden* approach, or whether the second

---

[115] Ibid., [49].   [116] Ibid., [54].

presumption has a legitimate role to play, which would bring in the presumption of a resulting trust. The preferable view is that the second presumption does indeed have a vital role, at least where the property is purchased as an investment and regardless of the relationship between the parties. But crucially this three-stage analysis shows that it is unhelpful to talk about a 'clash' of presumptions; rather there is a hierarchy of presumptions relating to beneficial interest and quantification of that interest which are not inconsistent, and which can be rebutted by evidence of the parties' intention.[117]

It is, however, clear that, following *Marr v Collie*, the *Stack v Dowden* presumption will apply in the domestic context even though the property is not bought as a family home but as an investment. Presumably, the *Stack v Dowden* presumption does not apply in a purely commercial context in which the purchase of property is at arm's length, meaning that the presumption of resulting trust would be applicable. Consequently, where the property is not purchased as a home and the claimant has contributed to the purchase price, the presumption of resulting trust should continue to apply. Where there is a joint venture between the claimant and the defendant as regards the development of the property, which is registered in the name of the defendant, the defendant might hold the property on constructive trust for the claimant.[118]

10.2.5 DOCTRINAL FOUNDATIONS OF THE COMMON INTENTION CONSTRUCTIVE TRUST

In assessing the legitimacy of the common intention constructive trust as interpreted by the House of Lords in *Stack v Dowden* and in subsequent cases, it is important to be able to identify a sound doctrinal basis for the trust.

That the beneficial interest should be presumed to follow the legal interest can be considered to be consistent with fundamental principles of Equity, particularly the maxims that 'Equity should follow the Law' and that 'Equity is Equality',[119] and, much more significantly, as reflecting common experience as to what the intention of the parties is likely to be and the consensus of judicial opinion as to the most likely inference to be drawn in the absence of any evidence to the contrary.[120] That this presumption should be rebutted in accordance with the common intention of the parties is also perfectly acceptable, since it is appropriate that the identification and quantification of beneficial interests should be determined with reference to the consent of the parties, as long as the intention of the parties is properly established.[121] The real problem with the law following *Stack v Dowden* and *Jones v Kernott* concerns the recognition that it is possible to impute a common intention to the parties concerning the quantification of their beneficial interest. This does not purport to be a real intention on their part, but one that is imposed on the basis that, had the parties considered the matter, this is what the court considers they would have intended, and with reference to a variety of factors the significance of which is difficult to assess. Can this resort to imputed intention be justified?

---

[117] See further George and Sloan, 'Presuming too little about resulting and constructive trusts?' [2017] Conv 303.   [118] See Section 10.3, p. 302.

[119] See Section 2.14, p. 36.   [120] See Section 8.1.3.(i), p. 214.

[121] Although note Gardner (see n. 37), p. 435 who criticizes this approach on the ground that statute requires such intention to be expressed in writing (Law of Property Act 1925, s. 53(1)(b)) and the principle that enables this requirement to be avoided, namely that a statute cannot be used as an instrument of fraud, is available only where the claimant has relied on the common intention (*Rochefoucauld v Boustead* [1897] 1 Ch 196, discussed in Section 5.2.2.(i), p. 107) and he considers that such reliance is no longer required to establish the common intention constructive trust. But see now *Curran v Collins* [2015] EWCA Civ 404, [2015] Fam Law 780, Section 10.2.4.(i), p. 293.

If the imputed common intention is simply a smokescreen to enable the court to achieve what it considers to be a fair result, it would be preferable to state this explicitly as Lords Kerr and Wilson did in *Jones v Kernott*,[122] and it would not then be necessary to search for any doctrinal foundation for the trust, since it would be blatantly remedial and unprincipled. But this approach to the imputation of intention was explicitly rejected in *Stack v Dowden* and is inconsistent with the approach of the majority in *Jones v Kernott*. The imputation of intention might instead respond to unconscionable conduct of the defendant, which would mean that the constructive trust is properly characterized as an institutional constructive trust.[123] But it has never been a requirement of the common intention constructive trust that the defendant's conduct can be characterized as unconscionable.

An alternative way in which to justify the imputed intention is by analysing it with reference to the law of unjust enrichment. Indeed, all aspects of the common intention constructive trust might be analysed in this way. If it can be shown that the defendant has been unjustly enriched at the expense of the claimant, the defendant will be liable to make restitution to the claimant to the extent of that enrichment. It has been suggested that the defendant's unjust enrichment would justify the recognition of a beneficial interest in the family home.[124] So, for example, if the family home of a cohabiting couple is registered only in the name of the defendant and the claimant has contributed to the purchase price, paid for utilities, and has decorated the property, she would have a beneficial interest in the house to the extent that the defendant has been enriched by her contributions, including the services that she has provided. Sir Terence Etherton has argued that the appropriate remedy would be the remedial constructive trust to reverse the defendant's unjust enrichment[125] and that this would give the court the discretion to recognize a beneficial interest in the property if it were considered appropriate to do so.[126]

The use of the law of unjust enrichment to explain all or part of the common intention constructive trust is, however, inappropriate for a number of reasons:

(1) Unjust enrichment liability arises only if there is no agreement or understanding between the parties.[127] Consequently, to the extent that there is an express or implied common intention, it will not be possible to have resort to the law of unjust enrichment. So unjust enrichment could only ever apply where there is an imputed intention.

(2) To establish unjust enrichment, it must be shown that the defendant has been enriched at the expense of the claimant in circumstances which fall within one of the recognized grounds of restitution, such as mistake or total failure of basis for a transfer.[128] But, where a cohabiting party has contributed to the purchase price, for example, it will be difficult to establish that they had been mistaken or expected to receive something in return that is not forthcoming. Etherton suggests that a new ground of restitution should be recognized for policy reasons, namely unconscionability, which would arise from the intimacy of the personal relationship between the parties.[129] But there is no authority for

---

[122] See Section 10.2.2.(iv), p. 289.   [123] See Section 9.3.8, p. 274.

[124] See Etherton, 'Constructive trusts: a new model for Equity and unjust enrichment' (2008) 67 CLJ 265; Gardner (see n. 37), p. 433.

[125] As occurs in Canada: *Kerr v Baranow* 2011 SCC 10, (2011) 328 DLR (4th) 577. See McInnes, 'Cohabitation, trusts and unjust enrichment in the Supreme Court of Canada' (2011) 127 LQR 339. Also in Scotland: see *Satchwell v McIntosh* 2006 SLT 117; *McKensie v Nutter* 2007 SLT 17; and in Jersey: *Flynn v Reid* [2012] JRC 100.   [126] Etherton (see n. 124), p. 283.

[127] Virgo, *The Principles of the Law of Restitution*, 3rd edn (Oxford: Oxford University Press, 2015), ch. 7.

[128] See Section 8.5.1, p. 249.

[129] See n. 124, p. 283. This would reflect the approach adopted in Australia, albeit without reference to unjust enrichment, where the constructive trust is imposed to prevent the unconscionable retention of disproportionate contributions to the shared home: *Baumgartner v Baumgartner* (1987) 164 CLR 137.

the recognition of such a ground and it would be one that would be difficult to define. Gardner has argued that it is sufficient that there was an absence of basis for the enrichment.[130] But this too is not supported by authority. Further, it has been recognized that, where property is registered in joint names and has increased in value—although that increased value can be characterized as an enrichment—it is not unjust because the joint owner of the property is entitled to it,[131] neither can the increase in value be considered to be at the expense of the other party.[132]

(3) The law of unjust enrichment cannot be used to create proprietary interests.[133] Consequently, unjust enrichment cannot be used to explain the common intention constructive trust.

The preferable view is that an imputed common intention cannot be justified doctrinally and should be rejected. If it is appropriate to recognize the common intention constructive trust, that common intention should be established only by reference to an express or inferred agreement or understanding as to the existence and quantification of beneficial interests; there should be no role for an imputed intent to rebut the presumption that the beneficial interest should follow the legal interest.

10.2.6 CRITICISM OF THE LAW

The law on the common intention constructive trust can be criticized in a number of respects.[134] First, following the reformulation of the trust in *Stack v Dowden* and its further analysis in *Jones v Kernott*, although the presumption that the beneficial interest should follow the legal interest is helpful, there is continuing uncertainty as to when and how this presumption will be rebutted. The presumption is meant to be rebutted only in exceptional circumstances, but it has been rebutted in a significant number of the reported cases, including *Stack v Dowden* and *Jones v Kernott*, which suggests that it is easily rebutted, although some recent cases suggest a more restrictive approach is being adopted. But it is unclear what makes a case exceptional and so permits the holistic inquiry by reference to a myriad of factors, the significance of which is unclear. Gardner has suggested that rebuttal of the presumption should turn on whether or not the parties have a 'materially communal relationship' in the sense that they pooled all of their material resources, including money, assets, and labour, such as where they have a joint bank account.[135] Where there is such a relationship, this will strongly suggest that they have joint beneficial interests; where they do not have such a relationship, this will strongly suggest that their beneficial interests are determined with reference to their contributions, both financial and non-financial. This analysis is consistent with *Abbott v Abbott*,[136] in which joint beneficial interests were recognized where the parties shared a bank account, and *Stack v Dowden*,[137] in which differential beneficial interests were recognized where the couple's financial affairs were

---

[130] See n. 37, p. 438.

[131] *Davis v Jackson* [2017] EWHC 698 (Ch), [2017] WTLR 465, [85] (Snowden J).

[132] If the other party had made mortgage payments, the value of these payments could constitute an enrichment at that party's expense, but it would still be necessary to show that the enrichment was unjust by reference to one of the recognized unjust factors. This point was ignored in *Davis v Jackson* [2017] EWHC 698 (Ch), [2017] WTLR 465, [88]. [133] *Foskett v McKeown* [2001] 1 AC 102.

[134] Although Gardner, 'Problems in family property' (2013) 72 CLJ 301 has defended the law on the ground that it can be stated easily.

[135] See n. 37, p. 431. See also Gardner, 'Rethinking family property' (1993) 109 LQR 263.

[136] [2007] UKPC 53, [2008] 1 FLR 1451. See Section 10.2.4.(i), p. 293.

[137] [2007] UKHL 17, [2007] 2 AC 432. See Section 10.2.4.(ii), p. 294.

kept separate. It is also consistent with *Jones v Kernott* where the earlier separation of the parties meant that it was appropriate for differential beneficial interest to be recognized. But Gardner's analysis cannot be used to explain the relevance of the holistic approach by virtue of which all factors are to be taken into account when assessing the common intention, such as whether the couple had children, and it is not supported by all subsequent decisions.[138] The absence of certainty as to the application of the law is a matter of real concern, especially as regards the conduct of negotiations between the parties following the breakdown of their relationship.[139] In this context, in particular, there is a need for certainty of principle and law to enable legal advisers to advise their clients clearly and to prevent the dispute from being litigated.

Secondly, despite the apparent move in *Stack v Dowden* and *Jones v Kernott* to consider a wide range of factors to displace the presumption of equality in those cases where the property is jointly registered, in practice[140] the focus of the courts has largely been on the respective financial contributions of the parties, which brings the common intention constructive trust much closer to the resulting trust, at least as regards the result rather than the nature of the analysis.

Thirdly, the continued relevance of imputed intention makes a mockery of the purported aim of seeking out the common intention of the parties. The quest to identify a common intention has previously been described as a myth,[141] and it continues to be so after the decisions in *Stack v Dowden* and *Jones v Kernott*. The real danger of the willingness to impute a common intention is that the courts are actually seeking to redistribute the beneficial interests in property to achieve a just result, but without the benefit of any clear principles.

The problem with the use of the common intention constructive trust to determine beneficial interests in the family home is that the courts have been seeking to redistribute the beneficial interest in property, but are restricted by the use of the trust device within the law of property, with the consequent need for certainty of principle and logical conclusions. The use of the trust device does not commend itself to the manipulation of the law and evidence to obtain what is considered to be a fair result which involves redistribution of the beneficial interest in the property. The common intention constructive trust, as it has been developed by the courts, is not fit for purpose. The law is at a junction and a decision has to be made as to whether a property-based solution or a redistributive solution should be adopted. The Supreme Court had the opportunity in *Jones v Kernott* to adopt a property-based solution to determine the beneficial interest in the family home, but instead opted for the redistributive solution and rejected the role of the resulting trust in this context, at least where the property is purchased in the joint names of the couple for their joint occupation and where they both have responsibility for the mortgage.[142] This is unfortunate. The court should instead have brought the presumption of resulting trust back into the picture, as advocated by Lord Neuberger and adopted by the Singapore Court of Appeal.[143] Beneficial interests in the family home should, first, be presumed to

---

[138]   E.g. *James v Thomas* [2007] EWCA Civ 877, [2007] 3 FCR 696.

[139]   Cloherty and Fox, 'Proving a trust of a shared home' (2007) 66 CLJ 517, 518.

[140]   Not in all cases: see *Crown Prosecution Service v Piper* [2011] EWHC 3570 (Admin) where an equal share of the beneficial interest was recognized, despite a much smaller financial contribution, because this reflected the common intention of the parties.

[141]   Glover and Todd, 'The myth of common intention' (1996) 16 LS 325.

[142]   *Jones v Kernott* [2011] UKSC 53, [2012] 1 AC 776, [35] (Lady Hale and Lord Walker). But it does not necessarily follow that a resulting trust can be presumed where title to the property is registered in the name of one party only.

[143]   *Chan Yuen Lan v See Fong Mun* [2014] SGCA 36, [153]. See also Dixon, 'The never-ending story: co-ownership after *Stack v Dowden*' [2007] Conv 456.

follow the legal interest; should, secondly, be presumed to be determined by the financial contribution to the acquisition of the property; and, in both cases, the presumption should be rebutted by the parties' express or inferred common intention, but only where such an intention can be clearly proved. Beyond this, the law of trusts should not go. As Deane J recognized in the Australian case of *Muschinksi v Dodds*,[144] 'proprietary rights fall to be governed by principles of law and not by some mix of judicial discretion, subjective views about which party "ought to win" and the "formless void" of individual moral opinion'. This trusts approach would have the added advantage of removing the artificial distinction that has emerged between allocation of the beneficial interest in domestic and commercial contexts.[145] It would be appropriate even in the commercial context for the presumption of resulting trust to be rebutted by the common intention of the parties that the beneficial interest should be apportioned differently, although it would be more likely that the presumption would be rebutted in the domestic context.

If it is felt that this trust law solution is too restrictive by not giving sufficient weight to the claimant's non-financial contributions to the acquisition and maintenance of the property, and to the relationship as a whole, the only alternative solution is a statutory one, to give the courts discretion to redistribute the beneficial interest in the family home to achieve fairer results. Such statutory intervention has occurred in other jurisdictions[146] and it has been recommended by the English Law Commission.[147] After conducting a comprehensive review of the law and its application in practice, the Law Commission recommended that, although cohabitants should not have the same rights and remedies as married couples or civil partners as regards the identification of beneficial interests in the family home, a new statutory scheme should be created, which would apply specifically to cohabiting couples who separate. The scheme would apply, save where it was specifically disapplied by the couple, where two key conditions were satisfied:

(1) The couple had a child together or had lived together as a couple in a joint household for a specified minimum period (possibly between two and five years).

(2) The party who was seeking relief had made 'qualifying contributions to the relationship giving rise to certain enduring consequences at the point of separation'.[148]

If these conditions were satisfied, the court would be given a structured discretion to order adjustment of the beneficial interests in the property. This discretion would be exercised in such a way as to ensure that the 'pluses and minuses of the relationship were shared between the couple',[149] so that benefits retained by the defendant and economic disadvantage suffered by the claimant would need to be reflected in the relief that was awarded. The court would be given wide powers to ensure that the relief was appropriate, such as by making a financial award, transferring property, or creating a settlement of the property. If this scheme were to apply, the law on implied trusts and estoppel would be excluded.

There is much to commend this recommended scheme, especially that it is not seeking to force a solution using the trust device with its consequent limitations. Such a scheme would be explicitly redistributive in approach, and would enable the judge to obtain what is considered to be the just and fair result. But the scheme would not be comprehensive: it could be excluded by the parties; it would not cover cohabitants whose relationship was

---

[144] (1985) 160 CLR 583, 616.

[145] Albeit a distinction which is proving to be of increasing significance in contemporary Equity. See Section 18.2.2, p. 512.   [146] See e.g. the New South Wales De Facto Relationships Act 1984.

[147] *Cohabitation: The Financial Consequences of Relationship Breakdown*, Law Com No. 307 (London: HMSO, 2007).   [148] Ibid., 3.

[149] Ibid., para. 1.19.

not intimate, such as parent and child; and it would not deal with disputes involving a third party, such as a bank claiming an interest in the family home. It follows that, even if this statutory scheme were adopted, there would be a continuing role for the common intention constructive trust. The Government responded cautiously to the Law Commission's recommendations and stated that it had no immediate plans to implement the recommendations. Attempts in 2013, 2014, and 2016, to implement some of the recommendations, by means of a private member's bill,[150] failed. Consequently, the trust will continue to have a vital role in determining beneficial interests in the family home.

10.3 JOINT VENTURE CONSTRUCTIVE TRUST

Where the claimant and the defendant have entered into an arrangement involving the acquisition of property by one of them, that party may be required to hold the property on constructive trust for both of them if it can be considered to be unconscionable for the party acquiring the property to deny subsequently that the other has any beneficial interest in the property. Since this is a trust that responds to the defendant's unconscionability, it follows that the trust is properly characterized as an institutional constructive trust rather than a common intention constructive trust.[151] The crucial feature of this category of institutional constructive trust is that there is a joint venture between the claimant and the defendant.

This is sometimes described as the '*Pallant v Morgan* equity' after a case of that name that recognized this form of trust.[152] In *Pallant v Morgan*,[153] the agents of two neighbouring landowners agreed in an auction room just before an auction of land that the claimant's agent would refrain from bidding and that, if the defendant's agent were successful in his bid, the land would be divided between them. The defendant's bid was successful, but he denied that the claimant had any interest in the property. It was held that the defendant held the property on trust for both of them in equal shares, because the claimant had been kept out of the bidding process by a promise that, if the claimant did not bid, an agreement as to the division of the property would be reached.

10.3.1 REQUIREMENTS FOR THE JOINT VENTURE CONSTRUCTIVE TRUST

The following requirements need to be satisfied for the property to be held on constructive trust.[154]

---

[150] Cohabitation Rights Bill.

[151] Although in *Crossco No 4 Unltd v Jolan Ltd* [2011] EWCA Civ 1619, [2012] 1 P and CR 16 a majority of the Court of Appeal considered this to be a common intention constructive trust, whereas Etherton LJ, at [85], analysed it with reference to breach of fiduciary duty. See also *Dowding v Matchmore Ltd* [2016] EWCA Civ 1233, [2017] 1 WLR 749, [28]. Grower, 'Explaining the "*Pallant v Morgan* equity"', [2016] Conv 434 considers that the trust is simply a constructive trust which arises in response to an agent's breach of fiduciary duty.

[152] But note Hopkins, 'The *Pallant v Morgan* equity' [2002] Conv 35, who considers this doctrine to have been created by the Court of Appeal in *Banner Homes Group plc v Luff Developments Ltd* [2000] Ch 371, discussed in Section 10.3.2, p. 303, because *Pallant v Morgan* turned on the application of the law of agency. See also *Crossco No 4 Unltd v Jolan Ltd* [2011] EWCA Civ 1619, [2012] 1 P and CR 16, [88] (Etherton J), [128] (Arden LJ). Man Yip, 'The *Pallant v Morgan* equity reconsidered' (2013) 33 LS 549 does not consider *Pallant v Morgan* to have created a new doctrine of constructive trust but, rather, an orthodox constructive trust which derives from the agency relationship.   [153] [1953] Ch 43.

[154] *Banner Homes Group plc v Luff Developments Ltd* [2000] Ch 371, 397–9 (Chadwick LJ). See also *Kearns Bros Ltd v Hova Developments Ltd* [2012] EWHC 2968 (Ch).

(i) Arrangement or understanding

Before the property is acquired by the defendant, there needs to have been an express arrangement or understanding between the parties that, following the acquisition of the property, the claimant will acquire some interest in it. This arrangement or understanding need not be an enforceable contract, so it does not matter that it is too uncertain to constitute a valid contract.

(ii) Reliance

The claimant must have relied on the arrangement or understanding by doing something or omitting to do something that either confers an advantage on the defendant in respect of the acquisition of the property or is detrimental to the ability of the claimant to acquire the property on equal terms. For example, where the claimant's reliance on the arrangement means that they stay out of the market, although this will be a loss of opportunity to the claimant rather than a detriment, it will have conferred an advantage on the defendant.[155]

(iii) Inconsistent act

The defendant must have acted inconsistently with the arrangement or understanding, typically by denying that the claimant has any interest in the property. It is acting inconsistently with the arrangement or understanding once the claimant has relied on it that renders the defendant's conduct unconscionable and which triggers the constructive trust.[156] The defendant will not have acted inconsistently if they informed the other party before the property was acquired that they no longer intended to honour the arrangement or understanding.

10.3.2 APPLICATION OF THE JOINT VENTURE CONSTRUCTIVE TRUST

The significance of the joint venture constructive trust is particularly well illustrated by *Banner Homes Group plc v Luff Developments Ltd*,[157] in which the claimant and the defendant had formed a joint venture to purchase a site for development. They reached an agreement in principle to acquire a site through a company that they would incorporate and would own equally. The defendant incorporated the company and owned all of its shares. The company then acquired the site. The defendant had second thoughts about pursuing the joint venture with the claimant and, without informing the claimant, started to look for another partner. The defendant did not inform the claimant about what it was doing from fear that it would acquire the site for itself. The defendant then told the claimant that it was withdrawing from the joint venture. It was held that the defendant held the shares in the company on constructive trust for the claimant and the defendant equally. The requirements for recognizing the trust were all satisfied: there was an arrangement, reliance through the claimant not acquiring the property for itself, and an act of the defendant that was inconsistent with the agreement, which rendered it unconscionable for the defendant to retain the property for itself.

---

[155] The fact that the reliance need not be detrimental is one factor that distinguishes the joint venture constructive trust from proprietary estoppel. See further Section 10.4.1.(iv), p. 307.

[156] *Lonrho plc v Fayed (No 2)* [1992] 1 WLR 1, 10 (Millett J); *Paragon Finance plc v D B Thakerar & Co* [1999] 1 All ER 400, 409 (Millett LJ).

[157] [2000] Ch 371. See also *Holiday Inns Inc v Broadhead* (1974) 232 EG 951, recognized as involving an institutional constructive trust in *Cobbe v Yeoman's Row Management Ltd* [2008] UKHL 55, [2008] 1 WLR 1752.

Similarly, in *Yaxley v Gotts*,[158] the claimant and Gotts had informally agreed that Gotts would buy a house that the claimant would convert into flats. The claimant would own the ground-floor flat and would act as the managing agent for Gotts in respect of the other flats in the house. The property was, in fact, purchased by Gotts's son, the defendant, but the claimant assumed that Gotts had purchased it. The claimant converted the property and acted as managing agent. The claimant and Gotts fell out, and the defendant refused to allow the claimant to continue to manage the flats and denied that he had any interest in the ground-floor flat. It was held that the son held the leasehold interest of the flat on constructive trust for the claimant. Although this was characterized as a common intention constructive trust, it is better analysed as being an institutional trust that responded to the defendant's unconscionable conduct in reneging on the understanding between them.

On the facts, it was held that there had been no oral contract between the claimant and the defendant, so there was no question as to whether the effect of the decision was to enforce an invalid contract. But the Court of Appeal recognized that, had there been such an oral contract, it would still be possible to recognize that the property was held on constructive trust by virtue of the statutory exemption in section 2(5) of the Law of Property (Miscellaneous) Provisions Act 1989.

10.3.3 LIMITS ON THE OPERATION OF THE JOINT VENTURE CONSTRUCTIVE TRUST

In *Cobbe v Yeoman's Row Management Ltd*,[159] the claimant had entered into an oral agreement to purchase flats belonging to the defendant, a company controlled by Zipporah Lisle-Mainwaring,[160] with a view to redeveloping them and sharing the profits between the claimant and the defendant, the claimant having obtained planning permission at his own expense. No written contract was made. Believing that there was an understanding that the property would be sold to him, the claimant spent the next eighteen months obtaining planning permission. Before planning permission had been obtained, the defendant withdrew from the agreement. The claimant was not able to sue on the contract, since contracts relating to the sale of land must be in writing.[161] Writing is not, however, required where the claimant asserts a proprietary interest under a resulting, implied, or constructive trust. So the claimant argued that the property was held on a joint venture constructive trust. This argument failed, although the reasons for this are somewhat unclear. In *Herbert v Doyle*[162] Arden LJ explained the result on the basis that a constructive trust would not be recognized if the parties intended to make a formal agreement, or if further terms remained to be agreed or if the parties did not expect the agreement to be immediately binding. Subsequently, in *Dowding v Matchmore Ltd*,[163] the Court of Appeal considered that Arden LJ was not describing three different situations where a constructive trust would not be recognized, but rather was explaining the result in *Cobbe* in three different ways. In other words, the constructive trust was not recognized in *Cobbe* because the claimant expected to acquire an interest in the property under a legally enforceable contract.[164] Instead, a personal claim founded on unjust enrichment succeeded as regards

---

[158] [2000] Ch 162.   [159] [2008] UKHL 55, [2008] 1 WLR 1752.

[160] Who made the news in 2015 when she painted her London townhouse in red and white stripes as a result of a planning row: http://www.bbc.co.uk/news/uk-england-london-33645003

[161] Law of Property (Miscellaneous Provisions) Act 1989, s. 2(1).

[162] [2010] EWCA Civ 1095, [2015] WTLR 1573, [57].   [163] [2016] EWCA Civ 1233, [2017] 1 WLR 749.

[164] As was recognized by Lord Scott, at [37], and Lord Walker, at [87], in *Cobbe*: [2008] UKHL 55, [2008] 1 WLR 1752.

the value of the claimant's services in obtaining planning permission for the benefit of the defendant. It follows from this analysis of *Cobbe* that the joint venture constructive trust will only be recognized where the parties assumed that the oral agreement or understanding between them was sufficient and they were not anticipating that a contract would be made in the future. Presumably this is because the claimant in such circumstances will not have been relying on the oral agreement or understanding but will be relying on the contract which was anticipated.

10.3.4 JUSTIFYING THE JOINT VENTURE CONSTRUCTIVE TRUST

The joint venture constructive trust applies where property has been obtained by the defendant under an arrangement with the claimant that it is unconscionable for the defendant to ignore following the claimant's reliance on the arrangement. The consequence is that Equity gives effect to the underlying arrangement.[165] This arrangement relates to the sale of land and so should be in writing,[166] but it is appropriate to give effect to the arrangement in Equity because of the defendant's unconscionable conduct and the claimant's reliance on the understanding or arrangement, even though that reliance is not necessarily detrimental.

10.4 PROPRIETARY ESTOPPEL

The essence of proprietary estoppel is that, where the defendant has made a promise or given an assurance that the claimant will acquire an interest in specified property and the claimant has relied on this promise or assurance to their detriment, the claimant has a mere equity entitling them to equitable relief, which might involve the claimant acquiring an interest in the property. This will therefore be another route by which the claimant can obtain a proprietary interest, despite the informal nature of the arrangement.

Before the decision of the House of Lords in *Stack v Dowden*,[167] the generally accepted view was that proprietary estoppel and the common intention constructive trust were similar, if not identical,[168] because both depended on the claimant's detrimental reliance. But one consequence of the decision in *Stack v Dowden* is that the common intention constructive trust no longer depends on detrimental reliance and so, as Lord Walker recognized, proprietary estoppel and the common intention constructive trust have not been assimilated.[169]

Even though subsequent decisions have recognized that there is sometimes a role for detrimental reliance in the common intention constructive trust,[170] this trust cannot be assimilated with proprietary estoppel because they have different functions and requirements. These differences also mean that the joint venture constructive trust and proprietary estoppel are distinct doctrines. In particular, whereas the common intention and joint venture constructive trusts are used to identify the true beneficial owners of property and the size of their beneficial interests, a claim in proprietary estoppel creates a mere equity, which is satisfied by the court determining the minimum necessary to do justice, which may be

---

[165] Lord Neuberger, 'The stuffing of Minerva's owl? Taxonomy and taxidermy in Equity' (2009) 68 CLJ 537, 549.

[166] Law of Property (Miscellaneous Provisions) Act 1989, s. 2(1).

[167] [2007] UKHL 17, [2007] AC 432.

[168] *Yaxley v Gotts* [2000] Ch 162, 177 (Robert Walker LJ); *Oxley v Hiscock* [2004] EWCA Civ 546, [2005] Fam 211, [66] (Chadwick LJ).   [169] [2007] UKHL 17, [2007] AC 432, [37].

[170] See Section 10.2.2.(iii), p. 286.

no more than a monetary award.[171] Where proprietary estoppel is established, the court, in the exercise of its discretion, may decide that the defendant holds property on trust for the claimant. This trust could be characterized as constructive, because of the significance of unconscionability to estoppel, but this trust is truly remedial and exists only from the date of the court order, whereas the common intention and joint enterprise constructive trusts will exist from the date on which the property is acquired. This difference can be particularly significant as regards the effect of recognizing the trust on third-party property rights.

10.4.1 REQUIREMENTS FOR PROPRIETARY ESTOPPEL

Four requirements need to be satisfied to establish proprietary estoppel.[172]

(i) Representation

There must be a representation or assurance[173] made to the claimant by the owner of property that the claimant has, or will have, an interest in identified property.[174] This representation can be made by silence or inaction.[175] The representation must be sufficiently clear and unequivocal. This means that, where the representation relates to the acquisition of a proprietary interest in the future, it can be reasonably understood by the claimant to constitute a commitment or assurance by the defendant as to the defendant's future conduct.[176] This will need to be assessed in the context of the particular case. So, for example, in *Thorner v Major*,[177] the claimant had worked on a relative's farm for twenty-nine years without payment with the expectation that he would inherit the farm on the farmer's death. The farmer died intestate. Although the farmer had not made any express representation that the claimant would inherit the farm, this could be inferred from indirect statements and his conduct over the years. The House of Lords held that it was sufficient that the claimant reasonably understood that he had received assurances from the farmer that he intended the claimant to inherit the farm. It was irrelevant that what constituted the farm varied over time, as the farmer had bought and sold land, since the assurance clearly related to the farm as it existed at the farmer's death.

Where it is alleged that a trust is bound by a proprietary estoppel it will be necessary to show that the relevant representation has been made by all the trustees unanimously or by one of them with the authority of the others to do so.[178]

(ii) Reliance

The claimant must have relied on the representation or assurance and this reliance must have been reasonable in all of the circumstances. The reliance will only be relevant if it is considered to be reasonable for the claimant to have concluded that the defendant

---

[171] *Crabb v Arun District Council* [1976] Ch 179, 198 (Scarman LJ).

[172] *Thorner v Major* [2009] UKHL 18, [2009] 1 WLR 776, [29] (Lord Walker). See *Taylors Fashions Ltd v Liverpool Victoria Trustees Co Ltd* [1982] QB 133, 144 (Oliver J). See generally McFarlane, *The Law of Proprietary Estoppel* (Oxford: Oxford University Press, 2013), ch. 5.

[173] McFarlane and Sales, 'Promises, detriment, and liability: lessons from proprietary estoppel' (2015) 131 LQR 610, 612 describe this as an express or implied promise.

[174] *Jennings v Rice* [2002] EWCA Civ 159, [2003] 1 P & CR 100.

[175] This is defended by Samet: 'Proprietary estoppel and responsibility for omissions' (2015) 78 MLR 85.

[176] *Thorner v Major* [2009] UKHL 18, [2009] 1 WLR 776. See McFarlane and Robertson, 'Apocalypse averted: proprietary estoppel in the House of Lords' (2009) 125 LQR 535, 540.

[177] [2009] UKHL 18, [2009] 1 WLR 776.

[178] *Fielden v Christine-Miller* [2015] EWHC 867 (Ch), [2015] WTLR 1165; *Preedy v Dunne* [2015] EWHC 2713 (Ch), [2015] WTLR 1795,

intended the representation or assurance to be taken seriously.[179] This is an objective test, so it is not necessary to prove that the defendant knew of or foresaw the claimant's particular acts of reliance.

(iii) Detriment

The claimant must have suffered detriment as a result of the reliance on the defendant's representation or assurance. The detriment needs to have been sufficiently substantial to justify the intervention of Equity,[180] but need not involve expenditure.[181]

(iv) Unconscionability

Whilst not a distinct requirement as such, unconscionability constitutes a unifying factor that confirms the other elements of proprietary estoppel.[182] Unconscionability involves an objective value judgement of the nature of the defendant's conduct in the light of their representation and the claimant's detrimental reliance. The real function of unconscionability is that, once the first three requirements have been established, the court should step back and consider whether the conscience of the court has been shocked.[183] It follows that proprietary estoppel will not be established just because the defendant's conduct is unattractive;[184] something more will be required. So, for example, in *Cobbe v Yeoman's Row Management Ltd*,[185] the claimant and the defendant had entered into an oral, and so unenforceable, agreement for the sale of land. Despite the claimant's detrimental reliance on the defendant's assurance that the property would be sold to the claimant,[186] it was held that the defendant's conduct in reneging on the agreement, whilst dishonourable, was not unconscionable, because the claimant had taken the risk that a formal agreement would not be made.

10.4.2 EFFECT OF ESTOPPEL

Proprietary estoppel is an independent cause of action that enables the court to create property rights in land.[187] It follows that proprietary estoppel can properly be characterized as a 'sword', in that it enables new rights in property to be created, as opposed to promissory estoppel, which operates only as a defensive 'shield' where the claimant sues the defendant on a contractual right, having represented to the defendant that they would not enforce it and the defendant having then relied on that representation.[188]

Despite this clear differentiation between proprietary estoppel as a source of new rights and promissory estoppel as a defence, in *Cobbe v Yeoman's Row Management Ltd*, Lord Scott asserted that proprietary estoppel was a subspecies of promissory estoppel so that its function was to bar the defendant from asserting facts that stood in the way of the proprietary right claimed by the claimant.[189] But this treats proprietary estoppel as simply an evidential device to prevent the defendant from denying a particular state of affairs, such

---

[179] McFarlane and Robertson (see n. 176), p. 541.
[180] *Thorner v Major* [2009] UKHL 18, [2009] 1 WLR 776, [15] (Lord Scott).
[181] *Greasley v Cooke* [1980] 1 WLR 1306; *Campbell v Griffin* [2001] EWCA Civ 990, [2001] WTLR 981.
[182] *Cobbe v Yeoman's Row Management Ltd* [2008] UKHL 55, [2008] 1 WLR 1752, [92] (Lord Walker).
[183] Ibid.   [184] Lord Neuberger (see n. 165), p. 541.   [185] [2008] UKHL 55, [2008] 1 WLR 1752.
[186] As to the proper interpretation of the assurance, see Section 10.4.5.(i), p. 310.
[187] Lord Scott has recognized that proprietary estoppel can also be used to create rights over chattels or choses in action: *Cobbe v Yeoman's Row Management Ltd* [2008] UKHL 55, [2008] 1 WLR 1752, [14].
[188] *Central London Property Trust Ltd v High Trees House Ltd* [1947] KB 130.
[189] [2008] UKHL 55, [2008] 1 WLR 1752, [14] (Lord Scott).

as that there was no enforceable contract, whereas the reality is that proprietary estoppel enables the claimant to acquire rights in property that they did not previously have, as was recognized subsequently by the House of Lords in *Thorner v Major*.[190]

10.4.3 THE NATURE OF RELIEF

Once the requirements of proprietary estoppel have been satisfied, the court has a discretion to award the claimant the appropriate relief in the light of all relevant circumstances. This may mean that the court decides that the claimant should not obtain any relief, or that the benefits that they had already received are sufficient to satisfy the estoppel,[191] or that the claimant should receive only some of the assets promised by the defendant,[192] or, most relevant to this chapter, that the claimant should acquire a beneficial interest in the property, which will be held on constructive trust for the claimant.[193]

In exercising its discretion, the court must ensure that there is proportionality between the claimant's expectation and the detriment suffered, so that if the expectation is extravagant and out of proportion to the detriment suffered, this should be reflected in the relief awarded.[194] In *Davies v Davies*[195] Lewison LJ acknowledged that the clearer the expectation of the claimant, the greater the detriment suffered, and the longer the passage of time during which the expectation was reasonably held, the greater the weight which should be given to the expectation.

If the defendant has made a representation that the claimant relies on to their detriment and the defendant then changes their mind, the effect of this should be taken into account by the court when determining the appropriate relief. But there will be circumstances under which the nature of the claimant's detrimental reliance is such that the defendant should not be able to revoke the representation or assurance.[196] So, for example, in *Thorner v Major*, where the farmer had assured the claimant that he would leave his farm to him in his will, if he had subsequently changed his mind and left his farm to somebody else, the court would have needed to assess the appropriate relief, but it might be appropriate to say that the effect of the claimant's detrimental reliance on the assurance was that the farm could not be left to anybody else, unless this change of will was justified by a change in circumstances.[197] So, for example, if the farmer had sold the farm after making the representation to the claimant, but only because he needed to do so to pay for expensive medical treatment, the farmer's circumstances should be considered to have changed so significantly as to defeat the proprietary estoppel completely.

Lord Scott would have dealt with this problem of the defendant acting contrary to his representation by restricting proprietary estoppel to representations about present property interests and leaving representations about future property interests to be dealt with by means of a remedial constructive trust.[198] But, bearing in mind the discretion judges have in determining the appropriate proprietary relief, nothing is to be gained by distinguishing between proprietary estoppel and the remedial constructive trust in this way. In either case, the court will have a discretion to determine the appropriate relief and it is far

---

[190] [2009] UKHL 18, [2009] 1 WLR 776. See especially [67] (Lord Walker).
[191] *Sledmore v Dalby* (1996) 72 P & CR 196.
[192] *Jennings v Rice* [2002] EWCA Civ 159, [2003] 1 P & CR 100.
[193] *Re Basham* [1986] 1 WLR 1498; *Thorner v Major* [2009] UKHL 18, [2009] 1 WLR 776.
[194] *Jennings v Rice* [2002] EWCA Civ 159, [2003] 1 P & CR 100; *Joyce v Epsom and Ewell BC* [2012] EWCA Civ 1398, [51] (Davis LJ).   [195] [2016] EWCA Civ 463, [2017] 1 FLR 463, [41].
[196] Similar to the restrictions arising from the doctrine of mutual wills. See Section 9.3.5.(iii), p. 270.
[197] [2009] UKHL 18, [2009] 1 WLR 776, [89] (Lord Neuberger).   [198] Ibid., [20].

better to do this having satisfied the requirements of proprietary estoppel, than to leave the claim and remedy to be determined by the exercise of judicial discretion. The remedial constructive trust has, anyway, been rejected in English law.[199]

Even though the claim for proprietary estoppel is structured, the discretion to determine the appropriate relief can be criticized as lacking sufficient transparency in providing reasons for the chosen outcome and failing to take into account the aim of proprietary estoppel, which is to redress the unconscionability that arises where the claimant detrimentally relies on an expectation induced by the defendant.[200]

10.4.4 USES OF PROPRIETARY ESTOPPEL

Proprietary estoppel has been applied in a variety of different contexts. For example, it has been used to perfect an imperfect gift,[201] or where the claimant mistakenly believed that they had already obtained a proprietary interest, which belief was encouraged by the defendant.[202] Most of the cases relate to situations in which the claimant is led to expect an interest in property arising in the future,[203] such as where the claimant is led to believe that they will be left property in the representor's will.[204] Proprietary estoppel can also be of use to a cohabiting party to obtain a proprietary interest in the family home where the common intention necessary for a common intention constructive trust cannot be established.[205]

10.4.5 LIMITATIONS ON PROPRIETARY ESTOPPEL

There are three potentially significant restrictions on the application of the doctrine of proprietary estoppel.

(i) Commercial context

In *Cobbe v Yeoman's Row Management Ltd*,[206] the doctrine of proprietary estoppel was not established, although the reasons for this are somewhat confused. In that case, the claimant and the defendant had entered into an oral agreement for the sale of land. This was considered to constitute a 'gentleman's agreement' to sell the property. Although the claimant was well aware that the actual sale of the property depended on a formal agreement being made and the negotiations relating to that agreement were still continuing, he was encouraged by the defendant to believe that a formal contract would be forthcoming and, in reliance on that representation, he spent time and money obtaining planning permission. The defendant then withdrew from the negotiations. The claimant was unable to sue the defendant for breach of contract because the oral contract was unenforceable. He

---

[199] See Section 9.4, p. 275.

[200] See generally Gardner, 'The remedial discretion in proprietary estoppel' (1999) 115 LQR 438; Gardner, 'The remedial discretion in proprietary estoppel: again' (2006) 112 LQR 492; Mee, 'Proprietary estoppel and inheritance: enough is enough?' [2013] Conv 280.

[201] *Dillwyn v Llewlyn* (1862) 4 De GF & J 517. See also *Pascoe v Turner* [1979] 1 WLR 431.

[202] *Crabb v Arun District Council* [1976] Ch 179.

[203] *Ramsden v Dyson* (1866) LR 1 HL 129, 170 (Lord Kingsdown).

[204] *Re Basham* [1986] 1 WLR 1498; *Gillett v Holt* [2001] Ch 210; *Ottey v Grundy* [2003] EWCA Civ 1176, [2003] WTLR 1253; *Jennings v Rice* [2002] EWCA Civ 159, [2003] 1 P & CR 100.

[205] *Pascoe v Turner* [1979] 1 WLR 431; *Holman v Howes* [2007] EWCA Civ 877.

[206] [2008] UKHL 55, [2008] 1 WLR 1752.

sought to assert a right in the property by virtue of proprietary estoppel, but was unable to do so. In the end, he was confined to a personal claim in unjust enrichment, for the value of his services in obtaining planning permission.

Two different reasons were suggested in the House of Lords as to why proprietary estoppel could not be established:

(1) Lord Scott held that, for purposes of proprietary estoppel, the key test is to determine what fact the defendant was estopped from asserting. The defendant could not be estopped from asserting that the oral contract was unenforceable for want of writing, because the claimant had not claimed that the contract was enforceable. Neither could the defendant be estopped from asserting that the claimant had already acquired a proprietary interest, because the defendant was not asserting this. But this reasoning suffers from the fatal flaw identified earlier, namely that Lord Scott did not realize that proprietary estoppel was a cause of action in its own right that could generate property rights; it is not simply about preventing the defendant from pleading a fact, which is what promissory estoppel is about. Lord Scott assumed that the claimant needed to rely on a proprietary claim that the defendant was seeking to answer by asserting a fact that he could be estopped from asserting. But that is not what proprietary estoppel is about.

(2) Lord Walker held that proprietary estoppel could be established only where the claimant believed that the defendant was legally bound to transfer the proprietary interest to the claimant. In that case, both parties were business people who knew that there was no legally binding contract and that either of them was free to withdraw from the negotiations if they were to wish to do so. The claimant was therefore running a commercial risk as to whether a written contract would be made.[207] On the face of it, this is a more convincing explanation as to why proprietary estoppel failed on the facts of *Cobbe*. But it is a reason that does not explain many of the earlier cases in which the claimant was not led to believe that the defendant was legally bound to transfer property to the claimant, such as where the defendant represented that he would leave property to the claimant in his will. There is no expectation in such a case that the claimant has a legally enforceable claim against the defendant.

The reasoning in *Cobbe*, of both Lord Scott and Lord Walker, would appear to restrict the role of proprietary estoppel dramatically. Indeed, proprietary estoppel was even described as being 'dead' as a result of the decision.[208] The later decision of the House of Lords in *Thorner v Major*[209] showed, however, that there was still some life in proprietary estoppel, since the claimant's claim succeeded in that case as regards his detrimental reliance on the farmer's assurance that the claimant would be left the farm in the farmer's will, even though the claimant was not led to believe that he had a legally enforceable claim for the farm.

So how can the results in *Cobbe* and *Thorner* be reconciled? The context of the claims appears to be decisive, with the doctrine of proprietary estoppel being applied differently depending on whether the context is commercial or domestic.[210] In the commercial context, if the claimant takes the risk that a contract to sell land will be forthcoming, this should be sufficient to defeat proprietary estoppel. In that context, the claimant must act

---

[207] Ibid., [91].
[208] McFarlane and Robertson, 'The death of proprietary estoppel' [2008] LMCLQ 449.
[209] [2009] UKHL 18, [2009] 1 WLR 776.
[210] *Cobbe v Yeoman's Row Management Ltd* [2008] UKHL 55, [2008] 1 WLR 1752, [66]–[68] (Lord Walker); *Thorner v Major* [2009] UKHL 18, [2009] 1 WLR 776, [96]–[97] (Lord Neuberger).

in the belief that they had already obtained a legally enforceable right to property.[211] If the claimant takes the risk of such a right arising subsequently, then it should not be for Equity to assist them, because the claimant should have ensured that there was an enforceable contract with the defendant. So, if the claimant and the defendant had entered into an agreement that was 'subject to contract', there is no role for proprietary estoppel, because the risk of no contract being made has been placed on the claimant.[212] If the claimant acts to their detriment in the belief that a contract will be made, it is not appropriate for them to obtain a proprietary interest with the assistance of Equity.[213] Further, the introduction of equitable concepts into this commercial context would introduce unacceptable uncertainty.[214] In the domestic context, however, where, for example, a relative is led to believe that they will inherit land, there is a relationship of trust and confidence between the representor and the representee such that, even though the representee takes a risk in relying on the representation to their detriment, this should not defeat proprietary estoppel. In this domestic context, the parties would not normally enter into a contract, so there is a role for Equity to assist the claimant. This distinction was recognized extra-judicially by Lord Neuberger, who said:[215]

> Where parties can reasonably be expected to regulate their relationship by a binding contract if they want to do so, equity should fear to tread. Not so where the relationship between the parties is such that they cannot be expected to have recourse to contracts.

(ii) Enforcing an unenforceable contract

Another potential limitation on the application of proprietary estoppel is that it can enable a proprietary right to be acquired by means of an informal arrangement. This is a potentially significant problem where the claimant relies on proprietary estoppel to obtain an interest in property that they are seeking to purchase by means of an oral contract, as occurred in *Cobbe v Yeoman's Row Management Ltd*. In that case, the oral contract of sale was void because it did not comply with the requisite formalities.[216] An interest in the property could be obtained if it were held on trust for the claimant, where the trust is implied, resulting, or constructive.[217] The exception does not mention proprietary estoppel, so Lord Scott in *Cobbe* held that proprietary estoppel cannot render enforceable an agreement that the statute has already declared to be void.[218] This was another reason why he considered that proprietary estoppel would not succeed in that case.

If Lord Scott's conclusion is correct, this would be a significant limitation on the operation of proprietary estoppel, since it would mean that there is no scope for the doctrine to create beneficial interests in property by means of informal arrangements. The better view is that Lord Scott's conclusion can be avoided by two different arguments. First, where the relief awarded by the court is to recognize that the claimant has a beneficial interest in the relevant property, that property will be held on constructive trust for the claimant and this

---

[211] Lord Neuberger (see n. 165), p. 542.

[212] See also *Attorney-General of Hong Kong v Humphreys Estate (Queen's Gardens) Ltd* [1987] AC 114.

[213] McFarlane and Sales (see n. 173), p. 613, consider that proprietary estoppel could not have been made out because there was no promise made that could seriously be relied on that the property would be sold and which invited reliance by the claimant.

[214] *Thorner v Major* [2009] UKHL 18, [2009] 1 WLR 776, [81] (Lord Walker).

[215] See n. 165, p. 544.   [216] Law of Property (Miscellaneous Provisions) Act 1989, s. 2(1).

[217] Ibid., s. 2(5).

[218] [2008] UKHL 55, [2008] 1 WLR 1752, [29]. In *Pearson v Lehman Brothers Finance SA* [2010] EWHC 2914 (Ch), Briggs J left open whether the dictum of Lord Scott extended to the need to use writing to dispose of an equitable beneficial interest under s. 53(1)(c) of the Law of Property Act 1925. See Section 11.3, p. 324.

constructive trust will fall within the statutory exception. Secondly, proprietary estoppel does not enforce the unenforceable contract between the claimant and the defendant, so the policy behind the relevant statutory formality is not engaged.[219] This is because proprietary estoppel may operate even though the parties have not intended to conclude, or come close to concluding, a contract. Even if the parties had concluded an unenforceable contract, proprietary estoppel would be triggered by the defendant's unconscionable conduct rather than the contract. It is a distinct cause of action in its own right, so that any proprietary rights that arise derive from the estoppel rather than the contract.[220]

(iii) Proprietary estoppel of a trust

Where trustees have made a representation to a party on which that party has detrimentally relied, for example by occupying trust property, this will not be sufficient to bind the beneficiaries and defeat their equitable proprietary interests.[221] It will be possible for proprietary estoppel to result in a third party being granted a licence to occupy trust property, although such a licence could be defeated by the beneficiaries applying to the court for sale of the trust property.[222]

---

[219] Lord Neuberger (see n. 165), p. 546. This was the view of the Court of Appeal in *Yaxley v Gotts* [2000] Ch 162; *Jennings v Rice* [2002] EWCA Civ 159, [2003] 1 P & CR 8, [45] (Robert Walker LJ); *Kinane v Mackie-Conteh* [2005] EWCA Civ 45, [2005] WTLR 345.

[220] McFarlane, 'Proprietary estoppel and failed contractual negotiations' [2005] Conv 501.

[221] *Preedy v Dunne* [2015] EWHC 2713 (Ch), [2015] WTLR 1795.   [222] Ibid.

PART V

BENEFICIARIES

11

BENEFICIARIES

11.1 GENERAL CONSIDERATIONS

The beneficiary of a trust has a variety of equitable rights, and sometimes powers, arising under the trust. The nature of these rights and powers will depend on the nature of the trust which has been created. Once these rights have been created there are various rules relating both to their disposal and termination. Similarly, there are various rules relating to the exercise of any powers.

11.2 NATURE OF A BENEFICIARY'S RIGHTS

Once a private trust has been validly created and constituted, the beneficiary acquires equitable rights, which may be both proprietary and personal. All beneficiaries can enforce these rights against the trustee. It is a fundamental principle of Equity that, if the beneficiaries have no enforceable rights against the trustees, there cannot be a trust.[1]

The beneficiaries can disclaim their beneficial interest by declining their interest.[2] This right to decline, also known as the right to disclaim, exists because nobody is required to accept a gift if they do not wish to do so. But it is presumed that, once a beneficiary is aware of their interest, they will not wish to disclaim it; silence is treated as tacit acceptance.[3] If a beneficiary does wish to disclaim their interest, they must do so actively, within a reasonable time, and show unequivocally that they reject it.[4] A disclaimer operates retrospectively and the interest disclaimed passes to the other beneficiaries.[5]

The nature of the right that is enforceable by the beneficiary will depend on the nature of the trust that has been established, although some rights are common to all beneficiaries, namely the right to have trustees perform the trusts honestly and in good faith for the benefit of the beneficiaries.[6] In particular, the rights of beneficiaries under resulting and constructive trusts are limited, by virtue of the limited responsibilities of the trustees

---

[1] *Armitage v Nurse* [1998] Ch 241, 253 (Millett LJ).

[2] A disclaimer can be made verbally rather than by writing: *Re Paradise Motor Co Ltd* [1968] 1 WLR 1125. See Section 11.3.8, p. 333.   [3] *Standing v Bowring* (1885) 31 Ch D 282.

[4] *Re Paradise Motor Co* [1968] 1 WLR 1125, 1141 (Danckwerts LJ).

[5] *JW Broomhead (Vic) Pty Ltd v JW Broomhead Pty Ltd* [1985] VR 891, 934 (McGarvie J).

[6] *Armitage v Nurse* [1998] Ch 241, 253 (Millett LJ).

of such trusts. Consequently, the focus in this chapter will be on the beneficiaries' rights arising under express trusts.

11.2.1 FIXED TRUSTS

(i) Proprietary rights

Under a fixed trust, the beneficiaries have an equitable proprietary interest[7] in the assets that comprise the trust fund.[8] These interests can be vested or remote, being contingent on the occurrence of particular events. Where there is an interest in remainder following the death of a person with a life interest, the remainder interest is treated as vested even whilst the life tenant is alive, because the person with the remainder interest does not need to do anything to vest the property in themself. The proprietary right can be enforced in Equity against anybody who comes into possession of the original property or property that can be considered to represent the original property,[9] even if they are unaware of the equitable proprietary right, unless such a person has purchased the legal title for value and without actual or constructive notice of the equitable proprietary interest, the so-called bona fide purchaser for value. It follows that the beneficiary of a trust does not have the same rights against the recipient of trust property as the beneficiary has against the trustee.[10] A purchaser will have actual notice of the equitable proprietary interest if they were aware of it, and constructive notice if they ought to have been aware of it. So, if shares are held on trust by Arun for Bella and Arun sells those shares to Carol in breach of trust, Carol will obtain absolute title to the shares if she provided value for them and was not aware that Arun had breached the trust in selling the shares. If Carol had not provided value, or should have been aware of the breach of trust, Bella's equitable proprietary interest will continue to be vested in the shares, so that she will be able to assert this interest against the shares held by Carol or any substitute asset, by seeking the restoration of the shares or their substitute to the trust.[11] Alternatively, Bella could adopt Arun's transaction, which would mean that the shares would belong to Carol and the proceeds of sale would form part of the trust assets for Bella. If, however, Carol had provided value and acted in good faith, Bella will only be able to assert her equitable proprietary interest in the money received by Arun or any asset that has been purchased by Arun using that money.

Alternatively, the beneficiary's equitable proprietary interest might be overreached,[12] and so extinguished, if the property is transferred from the trust pursuant to an authorized transaction.[13] The effect of overreaching is that property legitimately leaves the trust so that the beneficiary no longer has a proprietary interest in it. If, however, property is substituted for the original trust asset, this substitute property will be subject to the trust and the beneficiary will have a proprietary interest in that asset. So, for example, if shares are held on trust by Arun for Bella and Arun sells those shares for £1,000 to Carol, as Arun is authorized to do, Bella's equitable proprietary interest will be transferred from the shares to the purchase price, and if the purchase price is used to buy new shares, it will be transferred to the new shares, which will be held by Arun on trust for Bella.

---

[7] Nolan, 'Equitable property' (2006) 122 LQR 232. See also Nolan, 'Understanding the limits of equitable property' (2006) 1 J Eq 18 and Waters, 'The nature of the trust beneficiary's interest' (1967) 45 Canadian Bar Review 219.

[8] *Westdeutsche Landesbank Girozentrale v Islington LBC* [1996] AC 669, 705 (Lord Browne-Wilkinson).

[9] See further Section 19.3.3, p. 559.

[10] *Akers v Samba Financial Group* [2017] UKSC 6, [2017] AC 424, [46] (Lord Mance).

[11] See Section 19.4.1, p. 574.

[12] Fox, 'Overreaching', in *Breach of Trust*, ed. Birks and Pretto (Oxford: Hart, 2002), ch. 4.

[13] See Section 3.5.4, p. 46.

The difference between Bella's equitable property right being overreached and that interest being defeated by Carol being a bona fide purchaser for value depends essentially on whether the transaction between Arun and Carol is authorized or unauthorized. If it is authorized, the proprietary interest will be overreached; if unauthorized, it will not be overreached, but, if Bella adopts the transaction subsequently, it will then be treated as though it were authorized. If it is unauthorized and not adopted by Bella, she will be able to assert her equitable proprietary interest against Carol in the normal way, unless Carol is a bona fide purchaser for value.

If the recipient of the trust property is not a bona fide purchaser or the trust has not been overreached, the beneficiary only has the right to have the trust property restored to the original trustee, or, if the trust was a bare trust which the beneficiary wishes to terminate,[14] to themselves.[15]

One consequence of the beneficiary having a proprietary interest in the trust property is that, if the trustee becomes insolvent, the property will not be available to the trustee's creditors, but will continue to be held on trust for the beneficiaries, whose proprietary rights will consequently prevail over those of the trustee's creditors even though the trustee owns the fund at Law.

The nature of the beneficiary's equitable proprietary interest might be affected by the terms of the trust. So, for example, a fixed trust might be subject to a power of selection vested in the trustee. In such a case, the beneficiaries will have a vested interest in the trust property, but this can be divested by the exercise of the power of appointment.[16]

The peculiar situation of testamentary trusts needs to be emphasized as regards when equitable proprietary rights arise. On the death of the testator, their estate passes to the executor, who has full ownership of it. The executor owes fiduciary duties to the beneficiaries to administer the estate and to implement any trusts created by the will, which can be enforced by the beneficiaries. But, until the estate has been administered by the executor, the intended beneficiaries do not have a proprietary interest in the property.[17]

(ii) Personal rights

Although beneficiaries of fixed trusts have proprietary rights in the trust assets that can be asserted against the trustee and third parties, they also have a variety of personal rights.

Rights to ensure proper administration of the trust

The beneficiaries have a right to compel the trustees to administer the trust properly. Beneficiaries can apply to the court if the trustees fail to take the necessary action to preserve trust property.[18] The court can direct the trustees to enforce a claim against third parties or allow the beneficiary to sue a third party for the benefit of the trust.[19] Beneficiaries cannot, however, order a trustee to depart from the terms of the trust.[20]

Right to be informed

The beneficiaries have a right to be informed that they have a right to the trust property once they have become entitled to it, such as on attaining a specified age.[21]

---

[14] Section 11.4.1, p. 334.
[15] *Akers v Samba Financial Group* [2017] UKSC 6, [2017] AC 424, [46] (Lord Mance).
[16] Bartlett and Stebbing, 'Trust powers: a reappraisal' [1984] Conv 227.
[17] *Commissioner for Stamp Duties v Livingston* [1965] AC 694. See Section 3.7.7, p. 65.
[18] *Fletcher v Fletcher* (1844) 4 Hare 67.   [19] See *Foley v Burnell* (1783) 1 Bro CC 274.
[20] *Re Brockbank* [1948] Ch 206.   [21] *Hawkesley v May* [1956] 1 QB 304, 322 (Havers J).

Rights following breach of trust

If the trustees have breached the trust, the beneficiaries can sue them for that breach.[22] The remedy will, however, involve a transfer of value to the trust rather than payment to the beneficiaries directly, save where the trust has come to an end.[23]

Rights against third parties

If a third party has received property in which the beneficiaries have a proprietary interest, but the third party no longer has that property, the beneficiaries may have a personal claim against the third party in the action known as 'unconscionable (or knowing) receipt'.[24] Beneficiaries also have rights against third parties who dishonestly encourage or assist a breach of trust.[25]

Tortious rights

Where the trust property has been stolen, the beneficiary has no direct personal claim in conversion against the thief because conversion cannot be used to protect the beneficiary's equitable property rights.[26] If, however, the beneficiary was in possession of the trust property at the time of the theft, they would have a claim in conversion, but based on their possessory right rather than an equitable property right.[27] Similarly, where a third party has negligently damaged the trust property, the beneficiary has no direct claim against the tortfeasor for economic loss since the beneficiary has no legal or possessory title to the property,[28] although it has been recognized that a claim can be made by the beneficiary if the trustee is made a party to the proceedings.[29] The significance of the trustee being made a party to the proceedings is that their legal title to the property can be used to establish the property tort claim, since this is a Common Law claim which is based on interference with legal property rights. The trustee has a direct claim against the tortfeasor, although any damages recovered will be held on trust for the beneficiary.[30] If the trustee refuses to sue the tortfeasor, the beneficiary could sue the trustee for breach of trust, or sue the tortfeasor themself, but only by making the trustee a party to the proceedings to establish the interference with a legal proprietary right as part of the cause of action. This ability to name the trustee as a defendant to enable the beneficiary to bring proceedings against a third party is known as the 'Vandepitte procedure'[31] and its application is not confined to tort claims, but has been recognized as regards claims for losses sustained by the beneficiaries consequent upon a third party breaching a contract with the trustee.[32] This is a shortcut procedure to avoid two claims, one involving the beneficiary applying to the court to require the trustee to sue and the other involving the trustee suing the third party,[33] but the beneficiary is actually suing on behalf of the trustee,[34] although any damages will be held by the trustee on trust for the beneficiary.

---

[22] See Chapter 18 in this volume.

[23] *Target Holdings Ltd v Redferns* [1996] AC 421, 435 (Lord Browne-Wilkinson). See further Section 18.2, p. 515.   [24] See Section 20.2.3.(i), p. 596.

[25] See Section 20.3.2, p. 613.

[26] *MCC Proceeds Inc v Lehman Bros International (Europe)* [1994] 4 All ER 675.

[27] *Healey v Healey* [1915] 1 KB 938.

[28] *Leigh and Sillivan Ltd v Aliakmon Shipping Co Ltd* [1986] AC 785, 812 (Lord Brandon).

[29] *Shell UK Ltd v Total UK Ltd* [2010] EWCA Civ 180, [2011] QB 86. See Section 3.5.5.(v), p. 51.

[30] Similarly where the trustee has a direct claim against a third party for breach of contract that caused loss to the beneficiary: *Pan Atlantic Insurance Co Ltd v Pine Top Insurance Co Ltd* [1989] 2 Lloyd's Rep 568.

[31] After *Vandepitte v Preferred Accident Insurance Corporation of New York* [1933] AC 70, 79 (PC) (Lord Wright).   [32] Ibid.; *The Alabzero* [1977] AC 744.

[33] *Barbados Trust Co Ltd v Bank of Zambia* [2007] EWCA Civ 148, [2007] 2 All ER (Comm) 445, [45] (Waller LJ).   [34] *Roberts v Gill and Co* [2010] UKSC 22, [2011] 1 AC 240, [62] (Lord Collins).

Right to trust documents

If the beneficiaries are to monitor the trustees' performance of their duties, it is important that they have access to documents relating to the management and administration of the trust and the powers of the trustee to distribute trust assets. Whether the beneficiaries have rights to such documents has proved controversial. It was at one time thought that the beneficiaries had a proprietary right to trust documents, because they belonged to the trust and so belonged in Equity to the beneficiaries, who consequently had a right to see all such documents.[35] Now, the better view is that the ability to obtain trust documents forms one part of the court's inherent jurisdiction to supervise the administration of trusts and depends on the exercise of the court's discretion.[36] Consequently, there is no right to inspect trust documents, although beneficiaries are entitled to see trust accounts.

The difficulties arising from the proprietary analysis of the perceived right to trust documents is illustrated by *Re Londonderry's Settlement*.[37] In that case, the daughter of the settlor was dissatisfied with the provision that the trustees had made for her and her children. She asked to see various documents relating to the administration of the trust, including minutes of meetings of the trustees. It was recognized that not all documents relating to a trust could be classified as trust documents and that beneficiaries only had a proprietary interest in trust documents. It was then necessary to determine which documents could be characterized as trust documents. In *Re Londonderry's Settlement* this was defined as those documents that contained information that the beneficiaries were entitled to know, but the court did not give any indication as to what beneficiaries are entitled to know, making it very difficult to be certain which documents the beneficiaries had a right to see.

But it is no longer necessary to determine whether a document is or is not a trust document: the Privy Council, in *Schmidt v Rosewood Trust Ltd*,[38] recognized that it is neither necessary nor sufficient that a beneficiary can assert a proprietary interest in a trust document for the beneficiary to be entitled to see that document. Rather, as Lord Walker, speaking for the Board, recognized,[39] the right to seek disclosure of trust documents is 'one aspect of the court's inherent jurisdiction to supervise, and if necessary to intervene in, the administration of trusts. The right to seek the court's intervention does not depend on entitlement to a fixed and transmissible beneficial interest.' The court has a discretion to determine whether documents relating to the trust should be released to beneficiaries, who consequently have no absolute right to the disclosure of such documents.

In exercising this discretion, there are a number of key considerations for the court to consider, including the following:

(1) The first is whether documents should be released completely or in a redacted form where certain parts of the document are hidden.[40]

(2) Another consideration is whether safeguards should be imposed to limit the use that might be made of the documents or the information that is disclosed to the beneficiaries.[41] These safeguards might include undertakings being made to the court by the beneficiaries or particular arrangements for the inspection of the document by a beneficiary.

---

[35] *O'Rourke v Darbishire* [1920] AC 581, 626 (Lord Wrenbury).
[36] *Schmidt v Rosewood Trust Ltd* [2003] UKPC 26, [2003] 2 AC 709; *Breakspear v Ackland* [2008] EWHC 220 (Ch), [2009] Ch 32; *Dawson Damer v Taylor Wessing* [2017] EWCA Civ 74, [2017] 1 WLR 3255, [47] (Arden LJ). [37] [1965] Ch 918.
[38] [2003] UKPC, [2003] 2 AC 709. Although a decision of the Privy Council and so only of persuasive authority, it has since been followed in England: *Breakspear v Ackland* [2008] EWHC 220 (Ch), [2009] Ch 32. See also *Murphy v Murphy* [1999] 1 WLR 282. [39] [2003] UKPC, [2003] 2 AC 709, [51].
[40] Ibid., [54]. [41] Ibid.

(3) When there are issues of personal or commercial confidentiality, the court may have to balance the competing interests of different beneficiaries, the trustees, and third parties when determining whether to disclose documents.[42] So, for example, correspondence between trustees and individual beneficiaries about their personal circumstances might not be disclosed for reasons of confidentiality. Similarly, it might not be appropriate to disclose correspondence between the trustees and a third party, such as enquiries made by a trustee to a doctor whether the beneficiary has a life-threatening illness.[43]

(4) A beneficiary with only a remote or wholly defeasible equitable interest will find it more difficult for the court to exercise its discretion to release trust documents than will a beneficiary with a present interest.[44] It follows that the exercise of the court's discretion will depend on the strength of each applicant's case for disclosure.

Whilst replacing the old test of a proprietary right to disclosure of trust documents with a judicial discretion to disclose might be considered to introduce too much uncertainty, in fact the modern approach to disclosure is clearer and more principled, because the court is no longer required to speculate as to whether a particular document is or is not a trust document. Rather, the judge has a structured discretion to determine, in the light of all relevant circumstances, whether it is appropriate to authorize disclosure.

11.2.2 DISCRETIONARY TRUSTS

(i) Proprietary rights

A discretionary trust is a trust for distribution subject to a power of selection which is exercisable by the trustees amongst the objects of the trust. It follows that the objects have no proprietary interest in the trust fund itself,[45] because nobody knows whether they will benefit under the trust until the trustees have exercised their discretion to distribute the trust property to members of the class. This is why we talk about the 'objects' of a discretionary trust rather than the 'beneficiaries': an object is simply a potential beneficiary. Although objects of a discretionary trust do have rights, these are generally not considered to be proprietary because they are not transmissible interests,[46] although the objects of a discretionary trust can claim against third parties who have misappropriated trust assets, which is one of the characteristics of a proprietary right.[47] They can, however, seek only the return of the misappropriated property to the trust and cannot obtain the misappropriated property for themselves, since the distribution of the property will still be determined by the exercise of the trustee's discretion. The objects may also seek the termination of the trust, but only if all the objects agree.[48]

(ii) Personal rights

Objects under a discretionary trust have a fundamental right to ensure that the trust is administered properly, in the sense that the trustees consider the exercise of their power of appointment and exercise that power in a reasonable time. Beneficiaries have a number of specific personal rights relating to this fundamental right to ensure proper administration of the trust.

---

[42] Ibid.   [43] *Breakspear v Ackland* [2008] EWHC 220 (Ch), [2009] Ch 32, [54] (Briggs J).
[44] *Schmidt v Rosewood Trust Ltd* [2003] UKPC, [2003] 2 AC 709, [54].
[45] *Gartside v IRC* [1968] AC 553, 617 (Lord Wilberforce); *Sainsbury v IRC* [1970] Ch 712, 725 (Ungoed-Thomas J).   [46] *Schmidt v Rosewood Trust Ltd* [2003] UKPC 26, [2003] 2 AC 709, [51] and [54].
[47] See Nolan, 'Equitable property' (n. 7), p. 257.   [48] See Section 11.4.2, p. 335.

Application to court

If the trustees fail to exercise their discretion, the objects can apply to the court, which has a variety of options open to it,[49] including directing the trustees to exercise their discretion, appointing new trustees, authorizing a scheme of distribution, or directing the trustees to distribute the trust assets.

Rights arising from breach of trust

If the trustees' power of appointment is exercised in breach of trust, the beneficiaries can apply to court to have the appointment set aside and even to have the trustees removed.

Right to be informed

Since the objects have a right to put their case to the trustees for the exercise of their discretion,[50] it follows that the objects should have a right to be informed that they are objects.[51]

Rights to trust documents

In the same way as beneficiaries of a fixed trust can request to see trust documents,[52] so too can the objects of a discretionary trust. Under the old theory of proprietary rights in trust documents, the objects would not have been able to see the documents, since they were not considered to have any proprietary rights in trust property, but, with the recognition by the Privy Council in *Schmidt v Rosewood Trust Ltd*[53] that the court has a discretion to disclose documents to beneficiaries which does not depend on the assertion of any proprietary rights, it follows that objects of a discretionary trust can request disclosure of trust documents. Indeed, this was specifically recognized in *Schmidt* itself.

The exercise of the court's discretion to order the release of trust documents will be affected by a variety of considerations, including those that have been identified as being relevant to the requests of beneficiaries under a fixed trust.[54] There are some further considerations that are specific to the claims of objects under a discretionary trust:

(1) The court will be less likely to exercise its discretion to disclose trust documents in favour of an object under a discretionary trust,[55] since the objects have only a theoretical possibility of benefiting under the trust.

(2) It is a fundamental principle that trustees are not required to give reasons for the exercise of their discretion,[56] because nobody would agree to be a trustee of a discretionary trust if their reasons for exercising the discretion were liable to be questioned in court,[57] and because it reduces the possibility of litigation about the rationality of the trustees' exercise of their discretion.[58] Since reasons need not be disclosed, it follows that the court should not compel disclosure of trust documents that reveal why the trustees exercised their discretion as they did.[59] There is consequently a fundamental, but not absolute, principle of confidentiality that needs to be respected when determining whether documents

---

[49] *McPhail v Doulton* [1971] AC 424, 456–7 (Lord Wilberforce).

[50] *Murphy v Murphy* [1999] 1 WLR 282.

[51] Hayton, 'The irreducible core content of trusteeship', in *Trends in Contemporary Trust Law*, ed. Oakley (Oxford: Clarendon Press, 1996), ch. 3. [52] See Section 11.2.1.(ii), p. 319.

[53] [2003] UKPC 26, [2003] 2 AC 709. See Ho, 'Trustees' duties to provide information', in *Exploring Private Law*, ed. Bant and Harding (Cambridge: Cambridge University Press, 2010), ch. 15.

[54] See Section 11.2.1.(ii), p. 319.

[55] *Schmidt v Rosewood Trust Ltd* [2003] UKPC 26, [2003] 2 AC 709, [54].

[56] *Re Beloved Wilkes's Charity* (1851) 3 Mac & G 400. [57] *Re Londonderry's Settlement* [1965] Ch 918.

[58] *Breakspear v Ackland* [2008] EWHC 220 (Ch), [2009] Ch 32, [55] (Briggs J).

[59] *Re Londonderry's Settlement* [1965] Ch 918.

should be disclosed. The principle that trustees are not required to give reasons for the exercise of their discretion has been criticized on the grounds that it is not especially onerous for them to give reasons, especially where they are professional trustees, and that providing reasons for a decision may avoid problems from arising in the future.[60]

(3) The documents that an object would be interested in seeing might include a so-called 'letter of wishes'. This is a letter written by a settlor to the trustees that contains non-binding requests for the trustees to take certain matters into account when exercising their discretionary powers.[61] This letter of wishes enables the settlor to express views about the objects of the trust that might be prejudicial and hurtful if they were to be revealed in the trust document. Consequently, it would seem that, since confidentiality is an important characteristic of these letters, they should not be disclosed to the objects. An alternative view has been expressed,[62] namely that such a letter supplements the trust deed and should be treated like any other trust document, although this ignores the fact that these letters do not bind the trustees, but they are certainly highly persuasive as regards the exercise of their discretion.

That letters of wishes may be released to the objects has now been recognized in *Breakspear v Ackland*.[63] In that case, the settlor had settled property on a discretionary trust for himself and his family. At the same time, he wrote a non-binding 'wish letter' that requested the trustees to take certain matters into account when exercising their discretionary powers to appoint trust property. Three of the objects of the trust sought disclosure of this letter so that they could evaluate their expectations under the trust. The trustees did not want to disclose the letter, because it was confidential and they considered that disclosure would cause discord in the family. The judge, following *Schmidt v Rosewood Trust Ltd*, recognized that disclosure depended on the exercise of his discretion rather than whether the objects had any proprietary rights to the letter. In determining whether the letter should be disclosed, he recognized that trustees were not required to disclose their reasons for exercising a power that was confidential and, since the wish letter existed to further that confidential process, the letter should be treated as confidential as well. The trustees or the court could, however, disclose the letter if it were considered to be in the best interests of the beneficiaries and the administration of the trust to do so. The key question in exercising this discretion was what the objective consequences of disclosure might be, rather than the subjective purpose for which disclosure was sought. In this case, the judge decided that the wish letter should be disclosed. This was because the risk of family division following disclosure was outweighed by the fact that the trustees would be seeking the approval of the court to a scheme of distribution of the trust fund. This was relevant because, in seeking this approval, the trustees would have surrendered the protection of confidentiality since, in order to sanction the scheme, it would be necessary for the court to consider the reasons for the exercise of the trustees' discretion, which would, in turn, require the court to see the wish letter. Had the trustees not been seeking court sanction of the scheme, the letter would not have been disclosed.

The decision whether to release the letter of wishes to the objects involves a finely balanced exercise of judicial discretion. On the one hand, disclosure of the letter might be considered to infringe the trustees' right to confidentiality in decision-making, which is reflected in the principle that they are not required to disclose reasons for their decisions.

---

[60] *Hartigan Nominees v Rydge* (1992) 29 NSWLR 405, 420 (Kirby P).
[61] *Breakspear v Ackland* [2008] EWHC 220 (Ch), [2009] Ch 32, [5] (Briggs J).
[62] *Hartigan Nominees Pty Ltd v Rydge* (1992) 29 NSWLR 405, 419 (Kirby P).
[63] [2008] EWHC 220 (Ch), [2009] Ch 32.

On the other hand, disclosure might be considered to be crucial to enable the objects to monitor the administration of the trust by the trustees. Bearing in mind the recognition in *Breakspear v Ackland* that these letters might be disclosed to the objects, so undermining their confidentiality, it is likely that they will become less popular following this decision.

Right to information

It was recognized in *Murphy v Murphy*[64] that the objects of a discretionary trust are entitled to ask the trustees for information as to the nature and value of the trust property, the amount of trust income, and how the trustees had been investing and distributing it. It was also recognized that the court has a discretion to require a third party to disclose to the objects of a discretionary trust the names and addresses of the trustees, where this would enable the objects to enforce their rights against the trustees. This discretion is more likely to be exercised in respect of discretionary trusts where there are a smaller number of objects, since the claims of an object of such a trust will be statistically stronger. In *Murphy v Murphy*, the court exercised its discretion to disclose the identity of the trustees in favour of the beneficiary, who was one of the settlor's children and so not a remote object, and who was not well-off, suggesting that the beneficiary would be more likely to receive a distribution from the trust fund.

11.2.3 FIDUCIARY POWER

(i) Proprietary rights

Where a trustee has a fiduciary power to distribute trust property to the objects, they are not obliged to exercise that power, but need only consider its exercise.[65] It follows that the objects who might benefit from the exercise of the power cannot be considered to have any proprietary interest in the trust fund, because they do not know whether they will receive any part of that fund. They have only a hope that the power will be exercised in their favour; they do not even have a right to be considered. Until the power is exercised, those who take the property in default of its exercise have an equitable proprietary interest in the property. If the power is exercised in favour of certain objects, this will defeat the equitable interest of those who take in default.

(ii) Personal rights

Release of the power

The object of a power can 'release the power', which means that they can no longer receive property in the exercise of the trustee's power of appointment.

Application to court

In *Re Manisty's Settlement*,[66] Templeman J considered that the only rights of an object of a power who was aggrieved by the trustee's conduct would be to apply to the court to remove the trustee and have them replaced. In *Mettoy Pension Trustees Ltd v Evans*,[67] however, it was recognized that the court has similar powers of intervention in respect of fiduciary powers as those that exist for discretionary trusts.[68] But, since the donee of a fiduciary power is required only to consider the exercise of the power and is not required to exercise the power, it is difficult to see why it is appropriate that all of the weapons in the judicial armoury should be available where a trustee has not considered the exercise of the

---

[64] [1999] 1 WLR 282, 290 (Neuberger J).   [65] See Section 3.7.8.(iii), p. 67.   [66] [1974] Ch 17, 25.
[67] [1990] 1 WLR 1587.   [68] See Section 11.2.2.(ii), p. 321.

power within a reasonable time. For example, failure to exercise a fiduciary power should not result in the creation of a scheme of arrangement or an order directing the trustees to distribute trust assets. It should be sufficient either for the court to direct the trustees to consider whether the power should be exercised or to replace the trustees if they refuse to consider the exercise of the power.

Right to be informed

The objects of the power have no right to be informed that they are objects.[69]

Trust documents

The court has a discretion to order the release of trust documents to the object of a fiduciary power, as was specifically recognized by the Privy Council in *Schmidt v Rosewood Trust Ltd*,[70] which concerned in part a claim by the object of a fiduciary power to see a trust document.

Right to information

Could the discretion in *Murphy v Murphy*[71] be exercised in favour of the object of a power of appointment, who could apply to the court for information about the identity of trustees and the investment of trust assets? There is no reason why the discretion of the court to release such information cannot be exercised in favour of such objects, especially since trust documents might be released to them.

11.3 DISPOSITION OF EQUITABLE INTEREST

If the beneficiary has an equitable interest in trust property, they may wish to transfer this interest to another person. Such a disposition of an equitable interest must satisfy statutory formality requirements. Section 53(1)(c) of the Law of Property Act 1925 states that the disposal of equitable interests or trusts must be in writing and signed by the person who is disposing of them, or their agent, who is authorized in writing or by a will to do so. Equitable interests include limited interests, such as life interests, and absolute interests, such as interests in the remainder, whether in land or personalty.

The rationale of section 53(1)(c) is to prevent fraud. Indeed, the provision originated in the Statute of Frauds 1677. Its function is to prevent hidden oral transactions in equitable interests to the detriment of those who are truly entitled to those interests.[72] Also, the requirement of writing enables the trustees to determine more easily who the beneficiaries are.

Writing is needed to effect the disposition of the equitable interest, rather than merely as evidence of an intention to do so. Consequently, unlike declaration of trusts of land where the absence of writing merely makes the trust unenforceable,[73] the absence of writing under section 53(1)(c) renders the disposition of the equitable interest void. The writing can consist of a number of connected documents.[74] It has been recognized in the context of formalities for guarantees, which must be in signed writing,[75] that offering the

---

[69] *Re Manisty's Settlement* [1974] Ch 17, 25 (Templeman J). See Hayton (n. 51), p. 50.

[70] [2003] UKPC 26, [2003] 2 AC 709.

[71] [1999] 1 WLR 282, 290 (Neuberger J). See Section 11.2.2.(ii), p. 323.

[72] *Vandervell v IRC* [1967] 2 AC 291, 311 (Lord Upjohn).   [73] See Section 5.2.1.(i), p. 105.

[74] *Re Danish Bacon Co Staff Pension Fund Trusts* [1971] 1 WLR 248, 255 (Megarry J).

[75] Statute of Frauds 1677, s. 4. The consequence of failure to comply with this provision is that the agreement is unenforceable rather than void.

guarantee by email does constitute writing, although the insertion of an email address by an internet service provider was not a sufficient signature for these purposes.[76] There is no reason to think that electronic mail will not suffice to dispose of an equitable interest, but the person's name must be appended to the email. Section 8 of the Electronic Communications Act 2000 creates a power to issue a statutory instrument to modify a statute to facilitate electronic communication. No such statutory instrument has been issued in respect of the disposition of equitable interests, but, although the matter is not free from doubt, there is no reason why electronic mail should not be sufficient to dispose of an equitable interest. Indeed, in *Pearson v Lehman Brothers Finance SA*,[77] Briggs J recognized that electronic documentation was sufficient to satisfy the writing requirement of section 53(1)(c).

This simple provision has generated a great deal of litigation. This is largely because, for many years, the existence of writing to effect a transfer of personalty such as shares, including the transfer of an equitable interest in personalty, triggered liability to pay stamp duty on the document. If writing was not required, the duty was not payable, which might involve a substantial saving of money. Consequently, it was often very important to determine whether writing was required to effect the transaction. Today, stamp duty, or an equivalent duty, is charged on particular types of transaction, such as the purchase of shares or the purchase of an interest in shares, regardless of whether the transaction is effected by writing or not. But, it is still of practical significance to determine whether a transfer of an equitable interest can be effected without the need for writing, since, if writing were required where, for example, the beneficiary has purported to transfer an equitable interest by making a phone call, the transfer would not be effective.

The key to understanding the numerous cases that have interpreted section 53(1)(c) is to bear in mind two key principles. The first is that the interest or trust must be subsisting at the time of the transaction. Consequently, the provision will not apply to a declaration of trust that creates an equitable interest; the equitable interest must already be in existence.[78] The second principle relates to the nature of the underlying transaction. If the effect of the transaction is to extinguish the equitable interest or trust, writing is not required, because the transaction would not involve the disposal of the interest but involves its destruction. If the effect of the transaction is to transfer an existing equitable interest from one party to another,[79] this does constitute a disposition of that interest, and so writing will be required for the transaction to be effective.

The best way in which to understand the operation of section 53(1)(c) is to consider particular types of transaction, and to determine whether, in each case, there is a subsisting equitable interest and whether that interest is being disposed of or destroyed.

11.3.1 ASSIGNMENT OF EQUITABLE INTEREST

As illustrated in Figure 11.1, if property is held on trust by Arun for Bella, she may wish to transfer the benefit of the trust property to Carol. This could be achieved by Bella assigning her interest directly to Carol. Since the equitable interest is already subsisting and the purpose of the assignment is that Carol will now have the equitable interest in the property, which will be held by Arun for Carol, there is a disposition rather than a destruction

---

[76] *J Pereira Fernandes SA v Mehta* [2006] EWHC 813 (Ch), [2006] 1 WLR 1543.
[77] [2010] EWHC 2914 (Ch), [414].
[78] *Kinane v Mackie-Conteh* [2005] EWCA Civ 45, [2005] WTLR 345.
[79] See *Akers v Samba Financial Group* [2017] UKSC 6, [2016] AC 424.

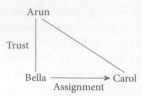

Figure 11.1 Assignment of equitable interest

of an existing equitable interest and section 53(1)(c) will be triggered: writing is required for the assignment to be valid.[80]

11.3.2 DIRECTION TO TRUSTEES TO HOLD ON TRUST FOR ANOTHER

If property is held on trust by Arun for Bella and she asks Arun to hold the property on trust for Carol, as illustrated in Figure 11.2, this also involves the disposition of an existing equitable interest and so writing is required. The effect of the direction to Arun is that Bella's equitable interest is intended to become Carol's and so this looks like an assignment of that interest. But, whereas an assignment involves a transaction directly between Bella and Carol, where there is a direction by the beneficiary to the trustee that the trustee should hold the trust property for the benefit of another, the transaction is actually between Arun and Bella. Since, however, the aim is still to ensure the disposition of an existing equitable interest to Carol, writing is required to effect the disposition.

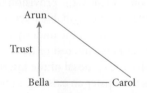

Figure 11.2 Direction to trustee to hold for another

That this type of transaction does fall within section 53(1)(c) was recognized in *Grey v IRC*.[81] In that case, the settlor had made a number of settlements in favour of his grandchildren. He transferred shares to the trustees to be held on trust for himself. He then orally instructed the trustees to hold the shares on the trusts of the settlements for his grandchildren. Documents were subsequently executed to confirm that the shares were held on trust for the grandchildren. The key issue for the House of Lords was whether the trusts of the shares were created by the settlor's oral direction or by the execution of the documents, and this turned on whether there had been a disposition of a subsisting equitable interest within section 53(1)(c). This mattered because, if writing had been required, the disposition would have been effected by the execution of the document, and so, as the law stood at the time, stamp duty would have been due. It was held that the effect of the direction to the trustees to hold the shares on trust for the grandchildren was to dispose of the settlor's existing equitable interest in the shares, and this could be effected only by writing and not

---

[80] See *Re Danish Bacon Co Ltd Staff Pension Fund Trusts* [1971] 1 WLR 248.   [81] [1960] AC 1.

orally. Consequently, the dispositions were effected when the documents were executed and so stamp duty was payable.

11.3.3 DIRECTION TO TRUSTEE TO CONVEY LEGAL ESTATE

Where Arun holds property on trust for Bella, she might direct him to transfer both the legal and equitable proprietary interests to Carol. As illustrated in Figure 11.3, the effect of this transfer will be that Carol holds the property absolutely. Since one person cannot hold both the legal and the entire equitable interest in one piece of property, it follows that the equitable interest must be extinguished by the disposition. Since this transaction involves the destruction rather than the disposition of the equitable interest, writing is not required. This is of practical significance, especially as regards shareholdings, where often legal title to shares will be held by a nominee on behalf of beneficiaries, who will usually wish to request their sale informally, by phone or email.

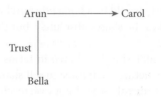

Figure 11.3 Transfer of property absolutely

That such a transaction does not require writing was recognized by the House of Lords in *Vandervell v IRC*.[82] Vandervell wanted to endow a chair of pharmacology for the Royal College of Surgeons, but to do so in a tax-efficient way. He was the beneficial owner of shares in Vandervell Products Ltd, which were held on trust for him by the National Provincial Bank. Vandervell requested the bank to transfer these shares to the Royal College of Surgeons. A substantial dividend was then declared, which was to be used by the Royal College to endow the chair; this would be tax-free because the Royal College was a charity. An option to purchase the shares for £5,000 was given to Vandervell Trustees Ltd. The Inland Revenue argued that Vandervell was liable to pay surtax[83] on the dividend that had been declared because he retained an equitable interest in the shares. The House of Lords held that this was correct, because Vandervell Trustees Ltd held the option on resulting trust for Vandervell,[84] so that he retained an equitable interest in the shares. The significance of the case for present purposes, however, is that the Inland Revenue had also argued that the National Provincial Bank had only conveyed the legal interest in the shares to the Royal College of Surgeons, so that Vandervell had retained the equitable interest because he had not disposed of his interest in writing within section 53(1)(c), as required by *Grey*. This argument was rejected and *Grey* was distinguished because, in that case, the legal title had remained with the trustee and the beneficiary was only dealing with the equitable interest. In *Vandervell*, however, the beneficiary had directed the trustee bank to dispose of both the legal and the equitable interest, resulting in the destruction of the latter interest.

Nolan[85] has suggested an alternative way of explaining why section 53(1)(c) is not engaged when the beneficiary directs the trustee to transfer the legal title to a third party absolutely, by reference to the doctrine of overreaching.[86] He has argued that, when a

---

[82] [1967] 2 AC 291. See Section 8.3.2.(ii), p. 233.
[83] This was the equivalent of a higher rate of income tax.   [84] See Section 8.3.2.(ii), p. 234.
[85] Nolan, '*Vandervell v IRC*: a case of overreaching' (2002) 61 CLJ 169.   [86] See Section 3.5.4, p. 46.

trustee acts on the beneficiary's instructions to transfer the property, the equitable interest in the trust is overreached as an authorized transaction, so that the third party acquires legal title to the property free of the equitable interest. Although there is no reference to such overreaching reasoning in the House of Lords' decision, this does provide a rational explanation of the result. Since the effect of the doctrine is that the equitable title is destroyed, it follows that there is no disposition and writing is not required. This is of practical significance since it means that where, for example, shares are held by a nominee for the beneficiary, they can orally request their transfer to a third party. The application of the overreaching doctrine has other implications. For example, if the beneficiary instructs the trustee to sell shares, but changes their mind before the shares are sold and notifies the trustee of this change of mind, if the trustee subsequently sells the shares, this will not overreach the equitable interest because the sale will be unauthorized.[87] Legal title would pass to the purchaser of the shares, but the equitable interest will not have been overreached. If, however, the third-party purchaser of the shares were to be acting in good faith, in the sense that there were unaware of the beneficiary's revocation of authorization to sell the shares, the third party would be a bona fide purchaser for value[88] and this would mean that the third party takes the shares absolutely, but the purchase price will be held on trust for the beneficiary.

A further consequence of analysing *Vandervell* in terms of overreaching is that, if the beneficiary has died after instructing the trustee to sell shares, the effect of the death is to revoke the instruction so that the sale would not overreach the equitable interest.[89] Lord Wilberforce in *Vandervell*[90] did, however, suggest that Vandervell's death would not have made any difference because Vandervell had done all that was necessary to transfer title by virtue of the *Re Rose*[91] principle, namely that title will be considered to have passed in Equity if the transferor has done everything to effect the transfer of title at Law. This principle could have had no effect on the legal title, so it could have affected only Vandervell's equitable interest, which would have been transferred from him to the Royal College of Surgeons. This would, therefore, involve the disposition of an existing equitable interest from one party to another, which would require writing, except if the *Re Rose* principle provides an exception to this statutory requirement, although no reason was suggested as to why that might be the case. Alternatively, the effect of the *Re Rose* principle might be that Vandervell held his equitable interest on trust for the Royal College, so that a new equitable interest will have been created and held on a sub-trust. But Vandervell would still have retained the original equitable interest and so would still be liable to pay surtax. Consequently, the better view is that the *Re Rose* principle would not be of assistance in such circumstances, and, had Vandervell died before legal title was transferred to the Royal College, his estate would have retained the equitable interest in the shares.

Vandervell was concerned with a scenario identical to that in which Bella directs Arun to transfer the property to Carol, as illustrated in Figure 11.3, above. If, however, Bella directs Arun to transfer property to Carol to hold on trust for David, as illustrated in Figure 11.4, below, should this be considered to be a disposition of an equitable interest, for which writing will be required, or the destruction of one equitable interest and the creation of a new interest, for which writing will not be required?

The effect of this transaction is that legal title will be transferred to Carol. Since, however, Bella's equitable interest will not have been destroyed, but will simply have been assigned to David, the transaction falls within section 53(1)(c).[92] This is because the effect

[87] Nolan (see n. 85) p. 183.   [88] See Section 11.2.1.(i), p. 316.   [89] Nolan (see n. 85), p. 184.

[90] [1967] 2 AC 291, 330.   [91] [1949] Ch 78, discussed in Section 5.3.3.(iii), p. 128.

[92] Battersby, 'Formalities for the disposition of equitable interests under a trust' [1979] Conv 17, 37.

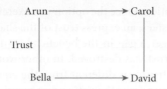

Figure 11.4 Transfer of property to be held on trust

of this transaction is that Bella's equitable interest is effectively being transferred to David. The result would presumably be different if Bella were to direct Arun to transfer property to Carol absolutely and then requested Carol to declare a trust of the property for David. In this scenario, there would be two separate transactions.[93] The first would involve the destruction of Bella's equitable interest, which would not require writing. Carol would then be able to declare a valid trust of the property for David without the need for writing, save as evidence of the trust if the subject matter is land.[94] But Carol cannot be compelled to declare such a trust. The only hope for David in such a case is if Carol has made an undertaking to Arun or Bella to declare the trust for David, so that her failure to do so can be considered to be unconscionable, so that she will then hold the property on constructive trust for David.[95]

11.3.4 DESTRUCTION OF AN EQUITABLE INTEREST ARISING UNDER A RESULTING TRUST

The dispute involving Vandervell's tax liability was not confined to whether he retained an equitable interest in the shares either by failure to dispose of an existing equitable interest or by the equitable interest in the option to purchase the shares being held on resulting trust for him. Subsequently, the option was exercised by Vandervell Trustees Ltd, which paid £5,000 to the Royal College of Surgeons for the shares, with the intention that the shares were to be held on trust for Vandervell's grandchildren. The Inland Revenue claimed that the company held these shares on trust for Vandervell, so that there was a continuing tax liability in respect of the dividends declared on the shares. Four years later, Vandervell executed a deed to release any right or interest that he held in the shares to the trustees. Vandervell died and his estate sued the company for the payment of any dividends paid on the shares after the option had been exercised. The claim failed in the Court of Appeal on the ground that Vandervell no longer had an interest in the shares.[96] Instead, the shares were held on the trusts of the grandchildren's settlements.

One of the questions for the court related to how Vandervell could have lost his equitable interest in the option that had arisen under a resulting trust. Lord Denning held that the resulting trust is born and dies without writing. It is certainly the case that a resulting trust arises without the need for writing,[97] but, once the equitable interest has been created, it is a real equitable interest, the disposition of which must involve writing by virtue of section 53(1)(c). The only way in which the need for writing can be avoided is if there is a destruction, rather than a disposition, of the interest. Lord Denning concluded that the equitable interest arising from a resulting trust would be destroyed once a gap in the beneficial ownership of property was filled by the creation of an express trust. On the facts, a resulting trust of the option had arisen because there was considered to be a gap in the

---

[93] Nolan (see n. 85), pp. 185–6.   [94] See Section 5.2.1.(i), p. 105.
[95] See Section 9.3.5, p. 268.   [96] [1974] Ch 269. See Section 8.3.2.(ii), p. 235.
[97] Law of Property Act 1925, s. 53(2).

beneficial ownership of the option. Once the option was exercised and the shares were reg-istered in the name of the trustees, an express trust of the shares had been created, which meant that there was no longer a gap in the beneficial ownership and so the equitable interest under the resulting trust was destroyed. In other words, the equitable interest in the shares under the express trust was different from the equitable interest in the option under the resulting trust because, once the option was exercised, it was destroyed and the subject matter of the express trust was the different property of the shares under a different trust.[98] So, although the effect of the transaction appeared to be a transfer of Vandervell's equitable interest to his children, the transaction instead involved the extinction of the re-sulting trust and the creation of a new equitable interest under an express trust; since this did not involve the disposition of a subsisting equitable interest, writing was not required.

11.3.5 DECLARATION BY BENEFICIARY AS TRUSTEE

Where Arun holds property on trust for Bella and she declares a sub-trust of that equitable interest for Carol, as illustrated in Figure 11.5, this should not require writing, since a new equitable interest is created for the benefit of Carol, which is different from the original equitable interest, and Arun retains his existing equitable interest.[99]

Some cases have, however, suggested that the proper interpretation of such a sub-trust may depend on the nature of the sub-trust. If Bella has active duties under the sub-trust, she will continue to hold the equitable interest on trust for Carol, who acquires a distinct equitable interest.[100] This will be the case if, for example, Bella declares a trust of her equi-table interest for Carol, David, and Elizabeth as she shall, in her discretion, select. But, if Bella has no such obligations, as will be the case if the sub-trust is a bare trust, the better view is that Bella will drop out of the picture and Arun will hold the property directly on trust for Carol;[101] to put it in the memorable words of Lindley LJ, the court will 'look through [the trustee] as nobody'.[102] Since Arun now holds for Carol rather than Bella, this appears to be a disposition of the equitable interest and so needs to be effected by signed writing.

The nature of this sub-trust was considered by the Court of Appeal in *Nelson v Greening and Sykes (Builders) Ltd*,[103] in which the vendor (A) was constructive trustee[104] of land for the purchaser (B), who held his interest on resulting trust for (C) who had provided the money for the purchase of the land.[105] The issue for the court did not concern formalities, but related instead to whether a charging order made against B's interest in the land as a trustee was valid. This turned on whether B had an interest in the land when the charging

Arun

Bella

Carol

Figure 11.5 Declaration of sub-trust

---

[98] See Section 8.3.2.(ii), p. 236, for criticism of this conclusion.

[99] See *DHN Food Distributors Ltd v Tower Hamlets LBC* [1976] 1 WLR 852.

[100] *Re Lashmar* [1891] 1 Ch 258, 269 (Fry LJ).

[101] See *Grainge v Wilberforce* (1889) 5 TLR 436; *Grey v IRC* [1958] Ch 375, 382 (Upjohn J).

[102] *Re Lashmar* [1891] 1 Ch 258, 268.   [103] [2007] EWCA Civ 1358, [2008] 8 EG 158.

[104] See Section 9.3.6, p. 272.   [105] See Section 8.2.2, p. 220.

order was made. If B had dropped out of the picture, so that A actually held the land directly for C, the charging order would not have been valid because B would not have had an interest that could have been charged. It was held that the order was valid since B had not dropped out of the arrangement. The cases which held that a party such as B could drop out were interpreted as simply giving the trustee A the option to deal directly with the beneficiary of the sub-trust, C, rather than with B, if it were more convenient to do so, but it did not follow that B ceased to be a trustee as a matter of law. If this decision is correct, it follows that, in all cases in which a beneficiary declares a trust of their equitable interest, this will involve the creation of a new equitable interest rather than the disposition of an existing interest, and so writing will not be required, regardless of whether B can be considered to have active duties under the sub-trust.[106]

11.3.6 SPECIFICALLY ENFORCEABLE CONTRACTS

In *Oughtred v IRC*,[107] shares were held on trust for Mrs Oughtred for life and, on her death, for her son Peter absolutely. To avoid tax liability on her estate when she died, Mrs Oughtred entered into a tax-avoidance scheme. This involved her orally agreeing with Peter that she would transfer to him other shares that she owned absolutely in return for Peter releasing to her his remainder interest in the shares, which were held on trust. Subsequently, a deed was executed that confirmed that the shares were held on trust for Mrs Oughtred absolutely. The Inland Revenue claimed that the deed had been effective to transfer Peter's equitable interest in the shares to his mother and so stamp duty was payable. Whether this was correct depended on whether the transfer of the equitable interest had been effected by writing or had already been effected orally. The majority of the House of Lords concluded that there had been a disposition of an existing equitable interest and this could be effected only by writing.

This appears to be consistent with the analysis in *IRC v Grey*, but what makes this case potentially different is Mrs Oughtred's argument that section 53(1)(c) did not apply because the earlier oral agreement with Peter had created a constructive trust of his equitable interest in the shares, which did not require writing.[108] This was because the agreement was specifically enforceable in Equity[109] and, by virtue of the maxim that 'Equity treats as done that which ought to be done',[110] she argued that Equity would treat the agreement as having been performed, so that the disposition of his equitable interest would already have occurred, so that Peter held his remainder interest on constructive trust for his mother by operation of law. A variety of different views on this argument were expressed by the judges. Lords Denning and Cohen did not consider that the oral contract excluded the application of section 53(1)(c), but did not provide reasons for this conclusion. Lords Jenkins and Keith did not consider the point, since they concluded that, because a document had been used to complete the transaction, stamp duty was payable even if there had been a constructive trust. But Viscount Radcliffe, dissenting, accepted Mrs Oughtred's argument, and concluded that she had acquired the equitable interest without the need for writing.

---

[106] For a historical defence of this position see Tham, 'Exploding the myth that bare sub-trustees "drop out"' (2017) TLI 76.   [107] [1960] AC 206.

[108] Law of Property Act 1925, s. 53(2).

[109] See further Section 21.4, p. 634. Contracts for the sale of shares are specifically enforceable only if damages are not an adequate remedy for breach of the contract. Since the shares in *Oughtred* were in a private company, there was no market for the shares, and so damages would not be have been an adequate remedy, since Mrs Oughtred would not have been able to buy equivalent shares from anybody else.

[110] See Section 2.6, p. 32.

It is Viscount Radcliffe's judgment that is of special interest when considering the nature of a specifically enforceable oral agreement. If he were correct and the agreement did create a constructive trust, on the facts of *Oughtred* this would have involved the creation of a sub-trust of Peter's reversionary interest. This has been described as a logical and practical solution.[111] Although Peter would not have had any active duties under this sub-trust, the modern view appears to be that the person in Peter's position would not drop out of the picture,[112] so that the mother would acquire a new equitable interest, which does not require writing to be valid. If this analysis is correct, the law relating to the operation of sections 53(1)(c) and 53(2) becomes even more artificial: if Bella purports to assign her equitable interest to Carol, this requires writing as being a disposition of an existing equitable interest, but if Bella agrees to assign the interest and this agreement is specifically enforceable, there is no need for writing by virtue of the creation of a new equitable interest by means of a constructive trust. This raises important questions of policy as to whether it is appropriate to identify a constructive sub-trust where an agreement is specifically enforceable by virtue of the principle that 'Equity treats as done that which ought to be done.'

However the judgments in *Oughtred* are analysed, that case does not provide a definitive answer to the problem of whether an oral agreement can be effective to transfer an equitable interest. Although it is a decision of the House of Lords, it raises many more questions than it answers. It is for this reason that the Court of Appeal was able to consider the matter afresh in *Neville v Wilson*.[113] In that case, the shareholders of a company had entered into an oral agreement for the informal liquidation of the company. Part of the agreement was that the company's equitable interest in the shares of another company should be divided amongst the shareholders. The question for the Court of Appeal was whether this oral agreement to assign the equitable interest in the shares was sufficient to dispose of the equitable interest or whether writing was required. It was held that, since the agreement was specifically enforceable, a constructive trust of the shares was created and so writing was not required. The nature of the agreement was analysed as rendering each shareholder a constructive trustee for the other shareholders and that nothing was decided in *Oughtred* that prevented such a decision. This decision was, however, doubted by Chadwick J in *United Bank of Kuwait plc v Sahib*[114] on the ground that it cannot be right that an oral contract can transfer an equitable right, whereas an oral disposition cannot. But, earlier in *Chinn v Collins*,[115] Lord Wilberforce had recognized, in the context of a tax-avoidance scheme, that, where legal title to shares was held by a nominee, an agreement to sell the shares would be effective to pass the equitable interest in them once the purchase price had been paid, without the need to satisfy any formalities regardless of whether the agreement was specifically enforceable.

If *Neville v Wilson* is right, it means that the requirement of writing under section 53(1)(c) can be easily avoided for many transactions. Rather than instructing a trustee to hold trust property for somebody else, the beneficiary should contract for value to dispose of the beneficial interest. If this agreement is specifically enforceable and, according to Lord Wilberforce, even if it is not, where the purchase price has been paid, a constructive trust will arise and an equitable interest will be created without the need to comply with formalities. But this shows how technical the law has become and, with a bit of legal creativity,

---

[111] Thornley, 'Trusts of personality: dispositions of interests—formality' (1960) 20 CLJ 31, 34.
[112] See Section 11.3.5, p. 330.
[113] [1997] Ch 144. Followed in *Slater v Simm* [2007] EWHC 951 (Ch), [2007] WTLR 1043, [24] (Peter Smith J). See also *Halloran v Minister Administering National Parks and Wildlife Act 1974* [2006] HCA 3 (High Court of Australia); Turner, 'The High Court of Australia on contracts to assign equitable rights' [2006] Conv 390.
[114] [1997] Ch 107, 129.   [115] [1981] AC 533, 548.

oral transactions can be effective to dispose of equitable interests by means of the constructive trust.

Thompson[116] has suggested a way of reconciling the different approaches adopted in the cases by distinguishing between executory and executed contracts. Where there is an agreement to sell shares, the contract will be executory until the purchase price has been paid and the vendor will retain an equitable interest in the property. It should follow that writing would be necessary to dispose of the vendor's equitable interest to the purchaser. Once the contract has been executed through the payment of the purchase price, the entire equitable interest would pass without writing by means of a constructive trust, presumably by virtue of the principle that 'Equity will treat as done that which ought to be done', namely that the shares had been transferred to the purchaser. It follows that writing was necessary in *Oughtred* because the contract remained executory, but was not needed in *Neville v Wilson* because the contract had been executed. This also explains the analysis of Lord Wilberforce in *Chinn v Collins*, in which he emphasized the significance of the price being paid before the equitable interest could be transferred without formality. But there is another view, namely that it is not appropriate to create an equitable proprietary interest by use of the principle that 'Equity treats as done that which ought to be done'. Consequently, the maxim should not be relied on in respect of oral agreements to transfer shares so as to create an equitable proprietary interest by means of a constructive trust, regardless of whether the agreement is executory or executed. The only appropriate method for creating an equitable proprietary interest by means of a constructive trust in these circumstances is where the vendor of the equitable interest can be considered to have acted unconscionably in some way, such as by reneging on the undertaking to transfer the equitable interest to the purchaser where it can be considered to be unconscionable to renege on that undertaking.[117] Such unconscionable conduct might be difficult to establish on the facts, save where there had been some reliance on the undertaking by the purchaser.

11.3.7 NOMINATION OF FUTURE BENEFITS

Where a person is entitled to receive a benefit in the future and nominates that this benefit should be received by somebody else, this does not involve the disposition of an equitable interest within section 53(1)(c) since the interest is not subsisting at the time of the disposition. So, for example, if a contributor to a pension scheme nominates that any benefits payable to their estate under the scheme on their death should be received by somebody else, this nomination does not need to be in writing.[118] Similarly, in *Gold v Hill*,[119] the deceased had nominated his solicitor as the beneficiary of a life insurance policy, with the intent that the solicitor should use the proceeds of the policy for the benefit of the deceased's partner. This nomination was held to be valid even though it was not in writing, because there would be no subsisting equitable interest until the proceeds of the policy had become due on the death of the deceased.

11.3.8 DISCLAIMER OF BENEFICIAL INTEREST

If a trustee holds property on trust for a beneficiary who disclaims the interest, this does not need to be in writing because the effect of the disclaimer is that the equitable interest is destroyed rather than transferred.[120]

---

[116] [1996] Conv 366, 370.   [117] See Section 9.3.5, p. 268.
[118] *Re Danish Bacon Co Ltd Staff Pension Fund Trusts* [1971] 1 WLR 248, 255 (Megarry J); *Baird v Baird* [1990] 2 AC 548 (PC).   [119] [1999] 1 FLR 54.
[120] *Re Paradise Motor Co Ltd* [1968] 1 WLR 1125.

11.4 TERMINATION OF THE TRUST

11.4.1 THE RULE IN *SAUNDERS V VAUTIER*

The rule in *Saunders v Vautier*[121] states that an adult beneficiary of a trust, who is of sound mind and is entitled to the whole beneficial interest, can direct the trustees to transfer the trust property to them. The consequence of this transfer will be the termination of the trust. In *Saunders v Vautier*, following the death of the testator, shares were held on trust for Vautier until he attained the age of 25. All of the dividends declared on the shares were to be accumulated in the trust and were then to be transferred to him on attaining that age. When Vautier attained the age of majority, which then was 21 but is now 18,[122] he claimed that he was entitled to have the shares and accumulated income transferred to him. It was held that, because he was now an adult and had an absolute indefeasible interest in the trust, he could claim the transfer of the trust property to him even though he had not attained the age of 25. It was then argued on appeal that Vautier's interest was actually contingent on him attaining the age of 25, which meant that the rule did not apply.[123] On the facts of the case, this argument was rejected and it was held that the interest was vested in him, although the enjoyment of it was postponed until he turned 25. It follows that the trust must be carefully construed to determine whether the beneficiary's interest is vested, as in *Saunders v Vautier* itself, or is contingent upon a particular condition. If it is contingent, then the rule will not be applicable,[124] because, if the contingency is not subsequently satisfied, somebody else would be entitled to the property, and it would not be appropriate for the person with the contingent interest to terminate the trust and obtain the benefit of the trust property absolutely. *Saunders v Vautier* was different because there was no gift-over and, if Vautier had not attained the age of 25, the gift would simply have fallen into residue and been distributed to those entitled to the testator's estate. Consequently, the bequest to Vautier was considered to be an immediate gift which vested on the death of the testator.

The rule was extended during the nineteenth century to include cases in which there are two or more beneficiaries.[125] In such cases, if it is possible to sever the interest of one party without harming the remainder, the rule can apply as regards that individual's interest only, because one beneficiary has an absolute right to that part. In other cases, such as where beneficiaries are entitled in succession,[126] with one being a life tenant and the other the person entitled to the remainder, the rule can apply, but only if, both of them being of full capacity, they both agree in the direction to the trustees that the trust fund be transferred to them. This is because each one by themselves does not have an absolute right to any part of the trust fund; they have only an absolute right if their interest is treated together with that of the other. The rule applies even if the settlor purports to exclude it.[127]

The essence of the rule is therefore that all those who are entitled to the whole of the beneficial interest can direct the trustees how the trust fund should be dealt with, as long as they are all of full capacity so that they can give a valid receipt for the trust property and as long as they all agree.[128] The effect of the rule is to terminate the trust and to ensure the

---

[121] (1841) 4 Beav 115. See Matthews, 'The comparative importance of the rule in *Saunders v Vautier*' (2006) 122 LQR 266.   [122] Family Law Reform Act 1969, s. 1.

[123] (1841) Cr & Ph 240.   [124] *Re Couturier* [1907] 1 Ch 470, 473 (Joyce J).

[125] *Re Sandeman's Will Trusts* [1937] 1 All ER 368; *Lloyds Bank plc v Duker* [1987] 1 WLR 1324.

[126] *Anson v Potter* (1879) 13 Ch D 141; *Re White* [1901] 1 Ch 570.

[127] *Stokes v Cheek* (1860) 28 Beav 620.

[128] See *Stephenson v Barclays Bank Trust Co Ltd* [1975] 1 WLR 882, 889 (Walton J).

transfer of the trust fund either to the beneficiaries, or to a third party if the beneficiaries so direct. It is not possible to apply the rule in *Saunders v Vautier* to override the existing trust but to keep the trust in operation.[129] So, for example, it is not possible to direct an existing trustee to appoint a nominee of the beneficiaries as trustee of the existing trust[130] or to direct how the trustees should invest the trust fund.

The fact that the rule in *Saunders v Vautier* results in termination of the trust means that, if the beneficiaries wish the trust fund to be transferred to a third party, this will not require writing because it will not involve the disposition of an equitable interest, since the equitable interest will be destroyed on the termination of the trust.[131]

The nature of the rule in *Saunders v Vautier* was considered by the High Court of Australia in *CPT Custodian Pty Ltd v Commissioner of State Revenue of the State of Victoria*[132] where it was recognized that the rule gives the beneficiaries a power rather than a right to terminate the trust, which corresponds with a liability on the part of the trustees rather than a duty to act. This is because, as recognized by Harris,[133] '[b]y breaking the trust, the beneficiaries do not compel the trustees to carry out any part of their office as active trustees; on the contrary, they bring that office to an end'.

The rule in *Saunders v Vautier* is of vital significance to the law of trusts, since the rule effectively acknowledges that the property that is held on trust for the beneficiaries is their property in Equity, so that they should be able to decide what they do with it. The strongest argument against the rule in *Saunders v Vautier* is that the operation of the rule means that the settlor's or testator's intention can be defeated, as occurred in *Saunders v Vautier* itself since the beneficiary obtained the benefit of the trust property before he attained the age of 25. But, why should the will of the creator of the trust prevail once the trust has been validly created, bearing in mind that the property is vested and belongs to the beneficiary in Equity and the rule requires that the beneficiary must be of full capacity, so that they do not need to be protected by Equity by virtue of age or mental incapacity?

11.4.2 DISCRETIONARY TRUSTS

Where property is held on discretionary trusts, it has already been seen that the objects do not have a proprietary interest in the trust fund.[134] Despite this, the rule in *Saunders v Vautier* is also applicable to such trusts.[135] Where the trustees are required to distribute the whole of the fund, but they have a discretion as to which object will benefit and by how much, it is possible to treat all of the objects as though they were one person,[136] who are then able to request the trustees to transfer the property to them. This will work, however, only if all of the trustees have capacity to do so, namely if they are adults and of sound mind, and if they all agree. So, for example, in *Re Nelson*,[137] trustees held the fund on trust for the testator's son, with a discretionary trust for the income to be applied for the benefit of the son, his wife, and only child. These three people requested the income to be transferred to them and, because between them they were absolutely entitled to the income, the trustees were obliged to do as the objects had requested.

---

[129] Ibid.   [130] *Re Brockbank* [1948] Ch 206.   [131] See Section 11.3, p. 325.
[132] [2005] HCA 3, [119] (Gleeson CJ, Mchugh, Gummow, Callinan, and Heydon JJ).
[133] 'Trust, power and duty' (1971) 87 LQR 31, 63.   [134] See Section 11.2.2.(i), p. 320.
[135] *Re Smith* [1928] Ch 915. See also *Schmidt v Rosewood Trust Ltd* [2003] UKPC 26, [2003] 2 AC 709, [40].
[136] *Re Nelson* [1928] Ch 920n.   [137] Ibid.

11.4.3 FIDUCIARY POWERS

The rule in *Saunders v Vautier* will even extend to where the trustees have a power of appointment where there is a gift over in default of appointment.[138] So, if Arun holds the property on trust with a power to appoint to Bella, Carol, and David, as Arun may select, and to David in default of appointment, then, if they all agree and are of full capacity, they can request the transfer of the property to themselves.

---

[138] Matthews (see n. 121), p. 269.

PART VI

TRUSTEES AND THEIR RESPONSIBILITIES

12
TRUSTEES

12.1 GENERAL CONSIDERATIONS

All trusts need trustees, but the nature of trusteeship varies according to the nature of the trust. There is a wide variety of different types of trustee and complex rules relating to their appointment, removal, and replacement. Once appointed, trustees have a wide variety of powers. Misuse of these powers will constitute breach of trust, but the determination of when the exercise of powers can be characterized as invalid and the consequences of such an exercise of a power raise issues of some complexity and controversy.

12.2 THE ESSENCE OF TRUSTEESHIP

A trustee holds an office that involves significant responsibility and onerous duties. This was recognized by Lord Hardwicke LC:[1]

> a trust is an office necessary in the concerns between man and man and . . . if faithfully discharged, attended with no small degree of trouble and anxiety . . . it is an act of great kindness in any one to accept it.

This office has a number of common characteristics and significant features.

12.2.1 HOLDING PROPERTY FOR ANOTHER

Trustees have the primary rights of ownership in trust property, but are not able to exploit the beneficial incidents of this ownership for themselves in their capacity as trustees, since they hold the property for other people or sometimes for particular purposes. Usually, the trustees will have legal title to the property vested in them, meaning that they own that property at Law. It is, however, possible to declare a trust over an equitable interest, which means that the trustees will have equitable title to the property, but still hold it for others. In fact, having title to property vested is not a prerequisite for somebody to be a trustee; it is sufficient that the trustee has such control of the property that they have nothing to do

---

[1] *Knight v Earl of Plymouth* (1747) Dick 120, 126.

but require that the property should be vested in them.[2] If a person could be recognized as a trustee only if title to the property were vested in them, it would mean that, from the period of appointment as a trustee to when title is vested, that person could not exercise the powers of a trustee. But, regardless of whether title to property is vested in a trustee or whether they have sufficient control of the property, the essential feature of a trustee is that they cannot obtain any benefit from that property.

12.2.2 JOINT TENANCY

Where there is more than one trustee, the trustees hold the property as joint tenants. It follows that none of them has a distinct interest or share in the property. Consequently, when one of the trustees dies, no part of the trust property will pass to the deceased trustee's estate. Rather, the property continues to remain vested in the surviving trustees.[3] Where a sole trustee dies, the trust property will pass to their personal representative, but subject to the trust, so the personal representative will be responsible as trustee for the property[4] until new trustees can be appointed.

12.2.3 IRREDUCIBLE CORE OF TRUST DUTIES

It is fundamental to the concept of a trust and to the identification of somebody as a trustee that the trustee owes an irreducible core of duties to the beneficiaries that are enforceable by the beneficiaries against the trustee.[5] If the beneficiaries have no rights that are enforceable against trustees, then there cannot be a trust. The fundamental duty of all trustees is to perform the trust honestly and in good faith for the benefit of the beneficiaries.

12.2.4 VOLUNTARY ASSUMPTION OF RESPONSIBILITY

Since the duties imposed on trustees are onerous, as a general principle nobody is required to accept the office of trustee if they do not feel that they can comply with the demands of trusteeship. Consequently, it is generally not possible to impose trusteeship on a person without their consent; the trustee must accept the demands of the office voluntarily. This was recognized by Lord Browne-Wilkinson in *Westdeutsche Landesbank Girozentrale v Islington LBC:*[6]

> The equitable jurisdiction to enforce trusts depends upon the conscience of the holder of the legal interest being affected. He cannot be a trustee . . . until he is aware that he is intended to hold the property for the benefit of others in the case of an express or implied trust or, in the case of a constructive trust, of the factors which are alleged to affect his conscience.

This is correct and uncontroversial as regards the express trustee. We have already examined the circumstances under which a constructive trust will be recognized.[7] Lord Browne-Wilkinson implicitly acknowledged that a constructive trustee need not know

---

[2] *Re Barney* [1892] 2 Ch 265, 273 (Kekewich J).   [3] Trustee Act 1925, s. 18(1).
[4] Ibid., s. 18(2). If the trustee dies intestate, the trust property will vest in the Public Trustee until the grant of administration: Administration of Estates Act 1925, s. 9. See Section 12.3.7, p. 344.
[5] *Armitage v Nurse* [1998] Ch 241, 253 (Millett LJ).   [6] [1996] AC 669, 705.
[7] See Section 9.3, p. 257.

that they are holding property on behalf of another, but must be aware of the circumstances that affect their conscience by virtue of which a constructive trust is triggered. So, for example, if money is paid by the claimant to the defendant by mistake, the defendant will hold that money on constructive trust for the claimant once the defendant becomes aware of the mistake,[8] but the defendant need not know that the money is now being held on trust for the claimant. But the constructive trust will be recognized in a wide variety of other circumstances under which it is not necessary to prove that the defendant was aware of the factors that are alleged to have affected their conscience.[9] But it is as regards the resulting trust, which Lord Browne-Wilkinson called an 'implied trust', that his statement is most controversial: he suggested that a resulting trustee must be aware that they are intended to hold the property for the benefit of somebody else. But this is not consistent with the preferable analysis of the resulting trust, namely that such a trust arises by operation of law where the claimant can be presumed to have intended that the property was held on trust for them, or such an intention can imputed,[10] and this does not require the defendant's conscience to be affected in any way or the defendant to have any awareness that a resulting trust has been presumed.[11]

If a person has not voluntarily accepted appointment as an express trustee, they cannot be liable for neglect of duty.[12] If no trustee accepts appointment, the trust will not fail for want of a trustee and the court will make an appropriate appointment, unless the settlor or testator made the validity of the trust dependent on the acceptance of appointment by a particular trustee.[13] In *Re Lysaght*,[14] for example, the testatrix had left money to the Royal College of Surgeons to establish a charitable trust for the provision of studentships for trainee surgeons, except for those of the 'Jewish or Roman Catholic' faiths. The Royal College said that it was unable to accept such a gift, since the religious discrimination was invidious and alien to its work. It was held that, normally, if a trustee were to feel unable to accept the trust, they should simply make way for one who would accept it. Where, however, as here, the identity of the trustee was clearly essential to the testator, the trust would fail for want of a trustee. But, on the facts, the trust was saved by deleting the offending term because this was considered to be an inessential part of the testatrix's paramount charitable intent to establish the studentships.

12.2.5 INABILITY TO CHALLENGE TRUST DEED

In *Khaira v Shergill*,[15] the Supreme Court recognized that trustees who have been appointed under the terms of a trust are not able to challenge the validity of the trust deed.[16] This is because the people who are appointed as trustees only have authority to involve themselves in the affairs of the trust as trustees and so are not able to impugn the document which gives them such status, for otherwise they would be denying their title to act as trustees and, without such title, they cannot challenge the trust. Whilst a superficially attractive argument, this does assume that nobody other than a trustee can have standing

---

[8] See Section 9.3.1, p. 258.   [9] See Chapter 9 of this volume.

[10] See Section 8.1.3.(iii), p. 217.

[11] Although where the automatic resulting trust arises following the initial or subsequent failure of an express trust, the trustee will have been aware that they were expected to hold the property for the benefit of others, albeit not necessarily for the settlor of the trust. See Section 8.3.2.(i), p. 232.

[12] *Ward v Ward* (1843) 2 HL Cas 777n.   [13] *Re Lysaght* [1966] Ch 191.

[14] Ibid.   [15] [2014]UKSC 33, [2015] AC 359.

[16] See *Attorney-General v Mathieson* [1907] 2 Ch 383.

to challenge the validity of a trust deed, which cannot be correct. It would be a much more appropriate argument to assume that the trust deed is valid, then allow the trustees to challenge the deed as putatively validly appointed trustees and, if successful, the court should then conclude that the trust is not valid.

12.3 TYPES OF TRUSTEE

We have already seen three different types of trustee, namely the express trustee appointed by a settlor or a testator,[17] the resulting trustee,[18] and the constructive trustee.[19] There are a number of other categories and types of trustee, some of which overlap.

12.3.1 AMATEUR TRUSTEE

Although this is not a specific legal category of trustee,[20] it is always significant to consider whether the trustee is being paid for their services. If the trustee is not being paid, less will be expected of them in fulfilling their duties, but these still remain onerous. In small family trusts, the trustee will usually be a member of the family or a friend who does not expect to be paid for their work, but assumes the responsibility of being a trustee from a sense of duty to the family.[21] Less skill and diligence will be expected of such trustees when compared with professional trustees.

12.3.2 PROFESSIONAL TRUSTEE

In the eighteenth and nineteenth centuries, trustees tended to be amateurs, who were often friends of the testator or settlor, or members of their family. But, with the growing recognition of the usefulness of the trust in commerce, trusts increasingly involved large funds and much greater administrative demands being placed on the trustee. A consequence of this was increased use of the professional trustee, who advertises their services as a trustee and who is remunerated for them.[22] The professional trustee might be a solicitor or a bank. A 'professional trustee' has been defined for the purposes of the Trustee Act 2000 as somebody who acts in the course of a profession or a business that involves providing services in connection with the management or administration of trusts.[23] Professional trustees have their own professional organizations, notably the Society of Trust and Estate Practitioners (STEP), which is the largest trust industry body in the UK.

The significance of this shift from the amateur to the professional trustee has been summarized by Lord Millett as follows:[24] 'Trusteeship too has become more professional. Clients no longer look to their trustees to be philosophers, guides and friends. They expect them to be professional fund-managers and even, sometimes, businessmen.'

---

[17] See Section 3.6.2.(i), p. 54.   [18] See Section 8.1.1, p. 211.   [19] See Section 9.5, p. 279.

[20] Although the 'lay trustee' is recognized in the context of remuneration for services and is defined as somebody who does not act in a professional capacity in providing services for the trust: Trustee Act 2000, s. 28(2). See Section 12.7.3.(ii), p. 358. The fact that a trustee is a professional rather than an amateur is also relevant when determining the duty of care to be expected of trustees: Trustee Act 2000, s. 1. See Section 13.2.2, p. 376.

[21] *Bartlett v Barclays Trust Co Ltd (No 1)* [1980] Ch 515, 534 (Brightman J).

[22] See Section 12.7.3, p. 357.   [23] Trustee Act 2000, s. 28(5).

[24] *Dubai Aluminium Co Ltd v Salaam* [2002] UKHL 48, [2003] 2 AC 366, [134].

The distinction between amateur and professional trustees is significant in a variety of ways, including that higher standards of care are expected from professional trustees[25] and amateur trustees are more likely to be relieved of liability for breach of trust.[26]

12.3.3 PENSION TRUSTEE

Trustees of pension funds are subject to the usual responsibilities of trustees of private trusts, although particular provision is made for alternative responsibilities by the statutory scheme in the Pensions Act 1995 as regards, for example, powers of investment and delegation,[27] and the duties of such trustees may sometimes differ from those of a trustee of a private trust. So, for example, trustees of a pension trust cannot delegate any of their investment functions.[28]

12.3.4 CHARITY TRUSTEE

A crucial distinction needs to be drawn between a trustee of a charity and a 'charity trustee'. 'Charity trustees' are defined as those people who have the general control and management of the administration of a charity.[29] It does not follow that such people are necessarily 'trustees of a charity', because the vehicle for the creation of a charity need not be a trust; it could be a company. In such a case, the directors of the company are charity trustees for purposes of the Charities Act 2011, but are not trustees of the charity.[30] This is generally a distinction of only technical, rather than practical, significance, since charity trustees are still subject to fiduciary duties and have administrative responsibilities in just the same way as they would if they were trustees of a trust.

12.3.5 JUDICIAL TRUSTEES

Where the administration of a trust by the trustees has broken down, the court may take on the full administration of the trust—but this is time-consuming and expensive.[31] A more convenient solution is for the settlor, trustees, or beneficiaries to apply to the court to have a judicial trustee appointed,[32] either to help the existing trustees to administer the trust, or to replace the trustees and take sole responsibility for the administration of the trust. The person appointed as a judicial trustee will either have been nominated and found by the court to be a fit and proper person to be a trustee, or, if such a person cannot be identified, will be a court official.[33] A judicial trustee is subject to the control of the court, which may give directions concerning the administration of the trust[34] and will supervise that administration. The judicial trustee is able to exercise the discretionary powers of a trustee, such as the power to compromise disputes, without obtaining directions from the court.[35]

---

[25] *Re Waterman's Will Trusts* [1952] 2 All ER 1054, 1055 (Harman J). See also the Trustee Act 2000, s. 1(1), discussed in Section 13.2.2, p. 376.

[26] See Section 17.3.2.(i), p. 482.   [27] Pensions Act 1995, s. 34.

[28] Trustee Act 2000, s. 36(5).   [29] Charities Act 2011, s. 177.

[30] *Re French Protestant Hospital* [1951] Ch 567.

[31] *Re Ridsel* [1947] Ch 597, 605 (Jenkins J).

[32] Under the Judicial Trustees Act 1896. See e.g. *Thomas and Agnes Carvel Foundation v Carvel* [2007] EWHC 1314 (Ch), [2008] Ch 395.

[33] Judicial Trustees Act 1896, s. 1(3).   [34] Ibid., s. 1(4).   [35] *Re Ridsel* [1947] Ch 597.

12.3.6 CUSTODIAN TRUSTEE

A custodian trustee is a corporate trustee which is authorized by statute to be appointed to have custody of trust property and related documents.[36] Such a trustee does not have general responsibility for the administration of the trust, since it has no discretion as to what to do with the trust property and must give effect to the decisions of the other trustees (known as 'managing trustees') relating, for example, to the investment of trust property. But custodian trustees are properly regarded as trustees,[37] rather than simply as bailees of the property in the sense that they only look after the property. What makes them real trustees is that they hold the trust property and income derived from it on trust for the beneficiaries according to the terms of the trust instrument; they cannot benefit from the property themselves; and they owe duties to the beneficiaries not to misapply the trust property and to avoid a conflict between personal interest and duty,[38] so they are subject to the irreducible core of trust duties that are a prerequisite for a trustee.[39]

There are a number of advantages in appointing a custodian trustee, which are more significant where the trust fund is large and the trust is expected to last for some time.[40] First, where the trust property is vested in a custodian trustee, it is not necessary to vest the property in the managing trustees each time a new one is appointed. If there are a number of trustees who are likely to change over time, this is a very significant advantage. Secondly, having the property vested in a custodian trustee also makes the selection and review of investments easier to implement. Finally, having a professional trustee to manage the trust property may reduce the possibility of a breach of trust.

12.3.7 PUBLIC TRUSTEE

The Public Trustee is an officer appointed by the Lord Chancellor under the Public Trustee Act 1906. The Public Trustee may act as an executor when asked to do so, as an administrator of small estates or, exceptionally, as a judicial trustee, custodian trustee, or even an ordinary trustee, but only as a last resort.[41] The functions of the Public Trustee are much more limited today than they used to be and essentially the office has a residuary function to act as a trustee where nobody else is suitable, able, and willing to act.

12.3.8 TRUST CORPORATION

Although a company can be a trustee, not all companies are trust corporations. A trust corporation is a special kind of trustee that is specifically appointed by the court to be a trustee or is entitled to be a custodian trustee.[42] Having a trust corporation is significant to the administration of the trust, since it can often act alone when two trustees would otherwise be required. So, for example, a trust corporation alone can give a valid receipt for the proceeds of sale under a trust for land, whereas two individual trustees would be required to give a valid receipt.[43]

---

[36] Public Trustee Act 1906, s. 4.
[37] Even though they do not count when determining the maximum number of trustees for the purposes of the Trustee Act 1925: Public Trustee Act 1906, s. 4(2)(g).
[38] *Re Brooke Bond and Co Ltd's Trust Deed* [1963] Ch 357.   [39] See Section 12.2.3, p. 340.
[40] Maurice, 'The office of custodian trustee' (1960) 24 Conv 196.
[41] https://www.gov.uk/government/organisations/official-solicitor-and-public-trustee.
[42] Trustee Act 1925, s. 68(18).   [43] Ibid., s. 14(2).

12.3.9 TRUSTEE *DE SON TORT*

In some circumstances, a person who has not been appointed as a trustee will be treated as though they were an actual trustee[44] where that person took it upon himself to do some acts that are characteristic of a trustee and discharged the duties of trustees on behalf of others.[45] This is called a trustee *de son tort*, meaning a 'trustee of their own wrong'. The key feature of a trustee *de son tort* is that they have intermeddled with the trust in some way[46] and becomes responsible as a trustee for that intermeddling.

Somebody will be treated as a trustee *de son tort* in two situations:

(1) The first is where a person has assumed the position of a trustee in fact even though they had not been properly appointed, but only where the person who has assumed the position of trustee intends to act as a trustee. This was recognized in *Mara v Browne*,[47] in which the defendant, who was a solicitor, advised the trustees of a marriage settlement to make certain investments that were inappropriate since they were speculative and caused loss to the trust. The trustees argued that the defendant had intermeddled with the trust and was liable as a trustee *de son tort*. This was rejected because he neither intended nor purported to act as a trustee in providing the advice; rather he was simply acting as a solicitor. A person will not be regarded as a trustee *de son tort* simply because they have a role in the administration of the trust,[48] such as being a professional adviser or agent,[49] and acts within the scope of their authority.[50] They need to go beyond any such role and actually do acts that are characteristic of a trustee, knowing that they are dealing with trust property and doing so on behalf of the beneficiaries of the trust.[51]

(2) The second is where a person has obtained such command or control of trust property that they can call for title to the property to be vested in them.[52] The degree of control required before somebody can be characterized as a trustee *de son tort* is illustrated by *Re Barney*,[53] in which two friends of the deceased had been asked to look after the financial interests of his widow, by looking over the accounts, checking her expenditure, and initialling any cheques that she drew on her bank account so that she could not draw any cheques without their concurrence. This was held not to be sufficient control of the widow's money to render the friends trustees *de son tort*, because, for example, they could not call for the money to be paid to them and could not determine how it should be invested.

Although the term 'trustee *de son tort*' suggests that a person will be treated as a trustee only if they have acted tortiously or wrongfully in some way, this doctrine does not require there to be proof of dishonesty, fraud, or any wrongdoing. Lord Millett has consequently suggested that such trustees are better described as '*de facto* trustees',[54] since, as regards their relations with the beneficiaries, they are treated on the facts just as though they had been properly appointed.

---

[44] *Taylor v Davies* [1920] AC 636, 651 (Viscount Cave).
[45] *Dubai Aluminium Co Ltd v Salaam* [2002] UKHL 48, [2003] 2 AC 366, [138] (Lord Millett).
[46] *Mara v Browne* [1896] 1 Ch 199, 209 (AL Smith LJ).
[47] Ibid.   [48] *Mara v Browne* [1896] 1 Ch 199.
[49] *Williams-Ashman v Price and Williams* [1942] Ch 219.
[50] *Barnes v Addy* (1874) LR 9 Ch App 244, 252 (Lord Selborne LC); *Williams-Ashman v Price and Williams* [1942] Ch 219, 228 (Bennett J).
[51] *Re Barney* [1892] 2 Ch 265; *Goddard v DFC New Zealand Ltd* [1991] 3 NZLR 580, 591 (Gallen J).
[52] *Re Barney* [1892] 2 Ch 265, 273 (Kekewich J); *Soar v Ashwell* [1893] 2 QB 390, 394 (Lord Esher MR).
[53] [1892] 2 Ch 265.
[54] *Dubai Aluminium Co Ltd v Salaam* [2002] UKHL 48, [2003] 2 AC 366, [138].

The nature of the trusteeship of the 'trustee *de son tort*' is of some practical significance since whether the trust is considered to be express or constructive will affect the nature of the trustee's duties. Trustees *de son tort* have sometimes been described as constructive trustees because they are regarded as having become so by construction.[55] But this description of constructive trusteeship has actually been employed in two distinct contexts, as was recognized by Lord Selborne LC in *Barnes v Addy*:[56]

> Those who create a trust clothe the trustee with a legal power and control over the trust property, imposing on him a corresponding responsibility. That responsibility may no doubt be extended in equity to others who are not properly trustees, if they are found either making themselves trustees *de son tort*, or actually participating in any fraudulent conduct of the trustee to the injury of the [beneficiaries].

Distinguishing clearly between these two contexts helps to bring into focus the nature of the trusteeship of a trustee *de son tort*:[57]

(1) The first context is the person who intermeddles with the trust. This is the trustee *de son tort* properly so-called. Here, the defendant is treated as being a trustee of an existing trust and is potentially strictly liable for breach of trust in intermeddling with the trust. The trustee is properly characterized as an express trustee,[58] because they have intermeddled with an existing trust and is simply deemed to have been appointed as a trustee to that trust.

(2) The second category is the person who receives property, knowing of a prior breach of trust. Here, the recipient of the property is liable because the receipt of trust property was unconscionable.[59] The recipient is a stranger to the trust and becomes liable only after the breach of trust has occurred.[60] Here, the defendant's liability is characterized as being accountable as though they were a constructive trustee. However, as we will see,[61] even here the language of constructive trusteeship is misplaced, because the defendant's liability is personal and is based on the value of the property received. No property is held by the defendant on trust for anybody else and, crucially, the defendant as a stranger to the trust is not regarded as a trustee of it.

Consequently, the language of constructive trusteeship is inappropriate, both as regards the recipient of trust property by a stranger and the intermeddler. The latter is properly regarded as an express trustee, albeit that they have not formally been appointed by the settlor or testator. It follows that a trustee *de son tort* shares the responsibilities of a properly appointed trustee. They are, for example, subject to the same fiduciary duties[62] and the same duties relating to the administration of the trust. They must account to the beneficiaries for the trust property.[63] They will be liable for breach of these duties in the same way as a properly appointed trustee.

---

[55] *Soar v Ashwell* [1893] 2 QB 390, 393 (Lord Esher MR); *Mara v Browne* [1896] 1 Ch 199, 209 (A L Smith LJ).

[56] (1874) LR 9 Ch App 244, 251.

[57] *Dubai Aluminium Co Ltd v Salaam* [2002] UKHL 48, [2003] 2 AC 366, [134]. See also *Paragon Finance plc v DB Thakerar and Co* [1999] 1 All ER 400, 408 (Millett LJ).

[58] *Soar v Ashwell* [1893] 2 QB 390, 394 (Lord Esher MR). Cf. Kay LJ, 405, who described the trustee *de son tort* as a constructive trustee.

[59] See Section 20.2.3.(i), p. 596.   [60] *Clarkson v Davies* [1923] AC 100, 110 (PC).

[61] See Section 20.1.2, p. 592.

[62] *Dubai Aluminium Co Ltd v Salaam* [2002] UKHL 48, [2003] 2 AC 366, [138] (Lord Millett).

[63] *Soar v Ashwell* [1893] 2 QB 390, 394 (Lord Esher MR).

12.4 APPOINTMENT OF TRUSTEES

12.4.1 BY THE SETTLOR

The settlor can choose anybody whom they like to be a trustee, except that a child cannot act as trustee of any trust.[64] It is even possible for a settlor to appoint themself as a trustee. Where the settlor does appoint themself as a trustee of property that they already own, the trust will be immediately constituted, since the settlor will already have the legal title vested.[65] So, for example, if Alan declares that he holds shares that he already owns on trust for Brenda, the trust will be immediately constituted because he already has legal title to the shares. If Alan wishes to appoint somebody else as a trustee of the shares, the trust will be properly constituted only once legal title to the shares has been effectively transferred to that person.[66]

Generally, a settlor can appoint as many or as few trustees as they wish, but, bearing in mind that trustees are usually required to act unanimously,[67] it is important not to appoint too many trustees because of the difficulties in arranging for all of the trustees to meet. For all trusts, it is sufficient to have only one trustee. The one significant restriction on the number of trustees appointed arises where the subject matter of the trust is land and the trust is not charitable,[68] since, for such a trust, the maximum number of trustees is limited to four.[69] If the settlor purports to appoint more than four trustees in a non-charitable trust of land, the first four who are named, and who are willing and able to act, will be the trustees.[70]

Once the settlor has appointed trustees on creating the trust, they cannot determine subsequent appointments of trustees, save where the settlor has reserved the power in the trust instrument to make such appointments.[71]

12.4.2 BY THE TESTATOR

Similar rules about the appointment of trustees apply where a trust is declared in a will. The testator can choose whomever they wish to be the trustee, other than a child, and can have as many trustees as they like, save for non-charitable trusts of land, in which, again, the number of trustees is limited to a maximum of four.[72] It is possible for the testator to choose the same person to be both executor and trustee. If different people are chosen as trustees and executors, the executors will hold the property in the testator's estate immediately on the testator's death until the property is vested in the trustees appointed by the will. If all of the trustees chosen by the testator have predeceased the testator, the testator's personal representatives will hold the property on trust until trustees are appointed.[73]

12.4.3 BY PEOPLE WITH THE POWER TO APPOINT

The trust instrument may give an express power to a particular person or people to appoint new trustees. Additionally, there are three specific statutory powers to appoint new trustees, although these powers may be excluded by the expression of contrary intention in the trust instrument.[74]

---

[64] Law of Property Act 1925, s. 20. Although it has been recognized that a child did hold personalty on a resulting trust: *Re Vinogradoff* [1935] WN 68. See Section 8.2.1.(ii), p. 219.

[65] See Section 5.3.2.(i), p. 125.   [66] See Section 5.3.2.(ii), p. 125.

[67] See Section 12.8.1, p. 362.   [68] Trustee Act 1925, s. 34(3)(a).

[69] Ibid., s. 34(2). See also the limitations on the number of trustees where additional trustees are appointed under statutory powers: see Section 12.4.3.(iii), p. 348.

[70] Trustee Act 1925, s. 34(2)(a).   [71] See Section 12.4.3, p. 347.

[72] Trustee Act 1925, s. 34(2).   [73] *Re Smirthwaite's Trust* (1871) LR 11 Eq 251.

[74] Trustee Act 1925, s. 69(2).

(i) General statutory power

The general statutory power applies where the trust instrument nominates particular people to appoint trustees; if no such people have been identified, or if they have been identified, but are not able and willing to act, the surviving or continuing trustees may appoint a new trustee.[75] The nominated people or trustees can appoint a new trustee by writing, but only in particular circumstances, which include where a trustee is dead, has been abroad for over a year, is a child, wishes to retire, refuses to act, or is unfit or incapable of acting. If all of the trustees are dead, the personal representative of the last trustee can appoint a successor.[76] It is possible for the person exercising this general power of appointment to appoint themselves as trustee.

The question whether a person has been nominated to make an appointment may raise some subtle issues of interpretation. For example, in *Re Wheeler and De Rochow*,[77] the trust instrument gave the power of appointment to nominated people if one of the trustees were to be 'incapable' of acting. One of the trustees became bankrupt and absconded. It was held that this rendered the trustee 'unfit' to act, but not 'incapable'. It followed that the power of appointment by nominated people was not engaged and so the remaining trustees were able to rely on the general statutory power to make an appointment on the ground that one of the existing trustees was unfit.

(ii) Replacement of trustees

Where a trustee has been removed under a power in the trust instrument,[78] that trustee will be treated either as if they were dead or, if a corporation, as though it wished to be discharged from the trust, and so the nominated people with the power to appoint or the trustees will be able to exercise their general statutory power of appointment.[79] If, once a trustee has been removed, there is a single trustee left who is not a trust corporation, the trustee who had been removed must be replaced, save where only one trustee was originally appointed.[80]

(iii) Additional trustees

In any trust in which there are no more than three trustees, the person with the general power to appoint trustees who is willing to act or, if there is no such person, the other trustees can appoint additional trustees, but the total number of trustees must not exceed four and the person with the power of appointment cannot appoint themself.[81]

(iv) Selecting trustees

The people exercising the statutory power of appointment have a free choice as to whom they can appoint. They can usually even appoint themselves.[82] They can also choose to appoint foreign trustees to administer the trust.[83] The courts have sometimes been reluctant to allow an appointment of foreign trustees save in the most exceptional circumstances.[84] Today, a more international attitude is adopted. The courts accept that, where trustees wish to exercise their power by appointing trustees who are based abroad, the court will simply assess whether this is a decision that a reasonable trustee would make in the best

---

[75] Ibid., s. 36(1).   [76] Ibid.   [77] [1896] 1 Ch 315.   [78] See Section 12.6.1, p. 352.

[79] Trustee Act 1925, s. 36(2).   [80] Ibid., s. 37(1)(c).

[81] Ibid., s. 36(6). Cf. the general power of appointment where the person making the appointment can appoint themself. There is no obvious justification for this difference.

[82] Trustee Act 1925, s. 36(1).

[83] *Re Smith's Trusts* (1872) 26 LT 820; *Richard v The Hon AB Mackay* (14 March 1987) (1997) 11 TLI 23.

[84] See e.g. *Re Whitehead's Will Trusts* [1971] 1 WLR 833, 837 (Sir John Vinelott).

interests of the beneficiaries.[85] There may be a variety of reasons why trustees would wish to appoint foreign trustees, including that the beneficiaries live abroad permanently or the trust property is located abroad.[86] Relocation of the trust by appointing foreign trustees may also avoid a tax liability, which is considered to be a legitimate reason to appoint foreign trustees.[87] So, in *Re Beatty's Will Trusts (No 2)*,[88] it was held to be reasonable to appoint trustees resident in Jersey to avoid capital gains tax on a trust estate that had included Van Gogh's *Sunflowers*, which had just been sold at auction for the then record price of £22.5 million. When determining whether the appointment of foreign trustees is reasonable, the court will also consider the professional experience of the proposed trustee and whether they are in a jurisdiction with trust law similar to that of England.

(v) Continuing trustees

The general statutory power of appointment of trustees may be exercised by a 'continuing trustee'. This is defined to include 'a refusing or retiring trustee, if willing to act in the execution of the provisions of' section 36 of the Trustee Act 1925.[89] It follows that a retiring trustee or group of trustees is able to appoint successors. But it has been held that a retiring or refusing trustee can participate in the exercise of the power of appointment only if they are competent, and ready and willing to act.[90] Further, when replacing a trustee who has been abroad for over a year, it is not necessary for that trustee to participate in the exercise of the power of appointment, because that trustee is being removed rather than retiring or refusing to act.[91]

Where two trustees wish to retire, it is not possible for them to appoint one trustee to replace them unless it is a trust corporation, because, where there were originally two trustees, it is not possible to reduce the overall number of trustees.[92]

12.4.4 AT THE DIRECTION OF THE BENEFICIARIES

The rule in *Saunders v Vautier*[93] gives a power to the adult beneficiaries of a trust who are between them absolutely entitled to the beneficial interest in the trust property to terminate the trust, and to direct the trustees to transfer the property to them if they are of full capacity and agree to the termination of the trust. It has been held, however, that this is an all-or-nothing power: it does not enable the beneficiaries to interfere with the administration of the trust, whilst keeping the trust on foot.[94] Specifically, it does not enable the beneficiaries either to control the exercise of the trustees' power to appoint trustees or enable the beneficiaries to replace a trustee with their own appointee.[95] If the beneficiaries wish to appoint new trustees, they need to exercise the power under *Saunders v Vautier* to terminate the trust and settle the property on new trusts for themselves with their nominated trustees. Apart from being a somewhat convoluted process to terminate and resettle the trust property, this may also have adverse tax consequences.

There is, however, now a statutory mechanism that enables the beneficiaries to secure the appointment of their nominated trustees. Where the rule in *Saunders v Vautier* is engaged (in that the beneficiaries are of full age, have capacity, and between them are

---

[85] *Richard v The Hon AB Mackay* (14 March 1987) (1997) 11 TLI 23, 25 (Millett J).

[86] Similar considerations will be relevant if the trustees wish to transfer all or part of the trust funds abroad.

[87] *Re Beatty's WT (No 2)* (4 March 1987) (1997) 11 TLI 77.

[88] Ibid.   [89] Trustee Act 1925, s. 36(8).   [90] *Re Coates to Parsons* (1886) 34 Ch D 370.

[91] *Re Stoneham's Settlement Trust* [1953] Ch 59.

[92] Trustee Act 1925, s. 37(1)(c). See *Adam and Co International Trustees Ltd v Theodore Goddard* [2000] WTLR 349; criticized by Barlow, 'The appointment of trustees: a disappointing decision' [2003] Conv 15.

[93] (1841) 4 Beav 115. See Section 11.4.1, p. 334.   [94] *Re Brockbank* [1948] Ch 206.   [95] Ibid.

absolutely entitled to the trust property), they may direct the trustees to appoint a particular person to act as a trustee, but they must all agree to the direction being made and must do so in writing.[96] This power will not be available where the trust instrument has nominated somebody to appoint trustees. The question of when somebody has been nominated is a matter of some uncertainty, although it appears that, if a person has been nominated and then dies, the nomination will cease, whereas if the person becomes incapacitated or is unwilling to act, they will remain nominated and so the beneficiaries' power to force an appointment will continue to be excluded.[97] In such a situation, if the beneficiaries wish to appoint trustees, they will need to terminate the trust and resettle. The beneficiaries' power of appointment cannot be used to appoint more than four trustees.[98]

This is a significant power that gives the beneficiaries a great deal of indirect influence over the management of the trust property, since the beneficiaries are not restricted in the choice of people whom they can direct the trustees to appoint and can therefore choose people whom they might consider will look after their own interests more appropriately.

12.4.5 BY THE COURT

It is a fundamental principle of the law of trusts that a trust will not fail for want of a trustee. Consequently, if the trustees, or other people with the power to appoint a trustee, fail to do so, the court will intervene and appoint a trustee. The court has a statutory power to appoint new trustees whenever it is expedient to do so and it is inexpedient, difficult, or impracticable otherwise to make an appointment.[99] It follows that this power will be relevant only where there is no other authorized person who is willing and able to make an appointment.[100] So, for example, in *Re May's Will Trusts*,[101] although one of the trustees was in Belgium at the time of the German invasion of that country during the Second World War, there was no evidence that she was incapable of exercising the power of appointment, and so the court was unable to exercise its statutory power of appointment.

Where the court does exercise its statutory power of appointment, it can appoint an additional trustee or replace an existing trustee who lacks capacity to act as a trustee, or is bankrupt, or is a corporation that is insolvent.[102] This power of the court to make an appointment may be relevant in a wide variety of circumstances, including where a sole trustee has died intestate or where the donee of a power to appoint cannot exercise it because they are underage.[103]

When the court is selecting an appropriate trustee, it should have regard to a number of principles that were identified in the important case of *Re Tempest*,[104] which concerned a trust that had been created by a will. One of the trustees appointed by the will had died before the testator. The will gave the power of appointing a new trustee to a group of people, but they were unable to agree who should be appointed. A petition was presented to the court requesting the appointment of Petre. A beneficiary opposed this on the ground that Petre was connected with a branch of the family with whom the testator had not been on friendly terms and which had been excluded from participating in the management of the testator's

---

[96] Trusts of Land and Appointment of Trustees Act 1996, s. 19(1). A similar power of direction is available to the beneficiaries where the trustee is incapable of acting because they lack capacity to act: ibid., s. 20.

[97] Hopkins, 'The Trusts of Land and Appointment of Trustees Act 1996' [1996] Conv 411, 430.

[98] Trusts of Land and Appointment of Trustees Act 1996, s. 19(5).

[99] Trustee Act 1925, s. 41(1). This power extends to the Charity Commission to appoint charity trustees: Charities Act 2011, s. 69(1)(b).

[100] *Re Gibbon's Trusts* (1882) 30 WR 287.   [101] [1941] Ch 109.

[102] Trustee Act 1925, s. 41(1).   [103] *Re Parsons* [1940] Ch 973.   [104] (1866) 1 Ch App 485.

property. It was held that the court could not appoint Petre as the replacement trustee. In reaching this decision, the court identified three key principles that were to be borne in mind when determining how it should exercise its discretion in selecting a new trustee:

(1) The court should have regard to the wishes of the settlor or testator, either as expressed in the trust instrument or evidenced by it. So, if the testator had said that a particular person or type of person should not be appointed as trustee, the court should not appoint such a person.

(2) If some of the beneficiaries want a particular person to be appointed as trustee, that person should not be appointed if it is contrary to the wishes of other beneficiaries, because trustees are bound to look after the interests of all of the beneficiaries rather than a particular class of beneficiaries.[105]

(3) A key consideration is whether the appointment of a particular person as trustee will promote or impede the administration of the trust. It is a relevant factor that the continuing trustees are opposed to the proposed appointment, but they should not be given a veto as to who should be appointed. The court should instead consider whether the objection of the continuing trustees is well founded; if it is not, it should be ignored. If a continuing trustee has refused improperly to work with the proposed trustee, that may in fact be a reason for the court to remove the continuing trustee.

Positive reasons must be identified for the court to appoint foreign trustees. A common reason for wishing to appoint such trustees is to avoid tax, but this is unlikely to be regarded as a legitimate reason for the court to make such an appointment.[106]

12.4.6　BY THE CHARITY COMMISSION

In charitable trusts, the Charity Commission can appoint a person to act as a trustee for a variety of reasons, including the need to replace a trustee removed by the Commission or because one or more existing trustees is unfit, incapable, or absent.[107]

12.4.7　VESTING OF TRUST PROPERTY

If a trustee has been appointed by deed, the vesting of most forms of trust property in the new trustee will be effected automatically.[108] This avoids the needs for a formal transfer of property from the old trustees to the new. But there will not be automatic vesting of stocks and shares because this depends on the registration of the new trustees in the share register. As regards registered land, title to the land will not pass until a proper entry of the vesting order is included on the register.

12.5　RETIREMENT

12.5.1　VOLUNTARY RETIREMENT

A trustee can voluntarily retire from the trust by deed if, after the retirement, there are still two people or one trust corporation to act as trustees, and the co-trustees and any person who has the power to appoint trustees consent to the discharge of the trustee and the

---

[105] See further Section 13.5, p. 391.
[106] *Re Beatty's WT (No 2)* (4 March 1987) (1997) 11 TLI 77. Cf. where the trustees wish the court to approve the exercise of their discretion in favour of such an appointment: see Section 12.4.3.(iv), p. 348.
[107] Charities Act 2011, s. 80(2).　　　　[108] Trustee Act 1925, s. 40.

vesting of trust property in the co-trustees.[109] A trustee who purports to retire, but fails to comply with the statutory requirements, will remain in office.[110]

A trustee who retires from the trust should obtain a formal discharge of liability from the beneficiaries. But, even if such a discharge is not obtained, the retired trustee will not be liable for breaches of trust that occur after their retirement, except where the trustee resigned in order to facilitate a breach of trust.[111] A trustee who has resigned will, however, remain liable for breaches of trust that occurred before the resignation.

12.5.2 BY DIRECTION OF THE BENEFICIARIES

Where the beneficiaries are, between them, absolutely entitled to the trust property, are all of full age and sound mind, and act unanimously, they can compel a trustee to retire from the trust by giving written directions to the trustee to do so, but only if, after the retirement, there will still be two people or one trust corporation to act as trustees, and either a new trustee is to be appointed or the continuing trustees consent to the retirement.[112] This power will not be available if the instrument nominates somebody to make trustee appointments.

This power of the beneficiaries to compel retirement is a significant one, especially when coupled with the power to force an appointment of a new or replacement trustee.[113] It has been criticized by Keppel-Palmer:[114] 'To allow beneficiaries the whip hand over trustees, by threatening to and replacing them on a whim, surely undermines the basis of trusteeship, especially in its stakeholding between the interests of beneficiaries.' But the statutory power to force a retirement can be regarded as a logical extension of the beneficiaries' power to terminate a trust under the rule in *Saunders v Vautier* and it is a power that has a number of safeguards against abuse. But it certainly has the potential to change the dynamics between the trustees and beneficiaries in a small trust where the beneficiaries are absolutely entitled to the trust property.

12.6 REMOVAL

12.6.1 BY THE TRUST INSTRUMENT

The trust instrument may provide for the removal of a trustee. Where such a power to remove has been exercised, the trustee will be treated as having died, so that either a person with the power to appoint trustees or the remaining trustees may appoint a new trustee.[115]

12.6.2 GENERAL STATUTORY POWER

The donee of a power to appoint trustees or the trustees themselves may remove one trustee and replace them with a new trustee on the specific grounds recognized by the Trustee Act 1925,[116] such as where the trustee has been abroad for over a year, is a child, or is incapable or unwilling to act as a trustee.

---

[109] Ibid., s. 39(1).
[110] *Jasmine Trustees Ltd v Wells and Hind (a firm)* [2008] Ch 194.
[111] *Head v Gould* [1898] 2 Ch 250, 272 (Kekewich J). See further Section 15.6.7.(iv), p. 447.
[112] Trusts of Land and Appointment of Trustees Act 1996, s. 19(2) and (3).
[113] See Section 12.4.4, p. 349.   [114] 'Discretion no more?' (1996) 146 NLJ 1779, 1786.
[115] Trustee Act 1925, s. 36(2). See further Section 12.4.3.(ii), p. 348.
[116] Trustee Act 1925, s. 36(1). See Section 12.4.3.(i), p. 348.

12.6.3 BY THE CHARITY COMMISSION

Where the Charity Commission has conducted an inquiry with regard to a charity[117] and concludes that there has been misconduct or mismanagement in the administration of the charity, the Commission can remove any charity trustee who has been involved in the misconduct or mismanagement.[118] The Commission also has the power to remove a charity trustee who has been declared bankrupt in the last five years, is incapable of acting because of a mental disorder, or is absent or refuses to act and this is impeding the proper administration of the charity.[119]

12.6.4 BY THE COURT

The court has a statutory power to remove a trustee and appoint a new trustee in their place.[120] In particular, the court can appoint a new trustee in substitution for an existing one on the grounds of incapacity to exercise the functions of a trustee, bankruptcy, or insolvency.[121]

The court also has an inherent jurisdiction to remove a trustee from the trust, but only where cogent grounds are established.[122] In *Letterstedt v Broers*,[123] Lord Blackburn identified certain key principles that were to be borne in mind by the court when exercising its direction to remove a trustee, which he described as a 'delicate jurisdiction'[124] that was ancillary to the court's principal duty to ensure that trusts are properly executed. The fundamental principle concerns the welfare of the beneficiaries and the preservation of the trust property. Consequently, a trustee might be removed where they have abused the trust by acts or omissions that endangered the trust property, or where they have exhibited dishonesty, incapacity, or want of reasonable fidelity. Also, a trustee might be removed where their continuing as a trustee prevents the trust from being properly executed, such as where the trustee is infirm or there is hostility between the trustee and the beneficiaries as regards the administration of the trust.

These principles were applied in *Re Wrightson*,[125] in which some of the trustees had committed a breach of trust and consequently a majority of the beneficiaries wanted the trustees removed. But this was not considered to be a sufficient reason for the court to remove them, because the court could still ensure that the trust was properly executed, a significant proportion of the beneficiaries did not want the trustees to be removed, and (a factor that was considered to be particularly significant) a change of trustees would have resulted in extra expense and loss to the trust estate.

Trustees have been removed by the court by virtue of a conflict between their personal interest and duty to the trust.[126] So, in *Moore v M'Glynn*,[127] the trustee of a will took on the testator's business and then established a similar line of business for himself in the neighbourhood. Rather than preventing him from carrying on his own business, he was removed from the trust. One of the most extreme examples of the application of these principles is in *Thomas and Agnes Carvel Foundation v Carvel*,[128] which, although it concerned the removal of an executor, involved exactly the same principles as for removal of a trustee. An American businessman, who made his money as one of the biggest sellers of

---

[117] By virtue of Charities Act 2011, s. 46. See Section 6.1.4.(ii), p. 149.

[118] Charities Act 2011, s. 79(2).   [119] Ibid., s. 80(1).

[120] Trustee Act 1925, s. 41. This power extends to the Charity Commission to remove charity trustees: Charities Act 2011, s. 69(1)(b).

[121] Ibid.   [122] *Re Edwards' Will Trusts* [1982] Ch 30, 42 (Buckley J).

[123] (1884) 9 App Cas 371 (PC).   [124] Ibid., 387.   [125] [1908] 1 Ch 789.

[126] Such a conflict involves a breach of fiduciary duty. See Section 15.5, p. 431.

[127] [1894] 1 IR 74.   [128] [2007] EWHC 1314 (Ch), [2008] Ch 395.

ice cream in the United States, and his wife made mutual wills[129] whereby they mutually agreed that the first to die would leave their money to the other and, on the death of that person, to a named foundation. The husband died first. A few years later, the wife changed her will to leave her estate to a corporation that was incorporated in her own name and that of her niece, who was also the executor. On the death of the wife, the niece sought to transfer the estate to the corporation. It was held that, since the niece had a clear conflict of interest and was dishonest, or at the very least did not understand her responsibilities as an executor, she should be removed.

12.7 PAYMENT TO TRUSTEES

The office of trustee is voluntary and generally gratuitous,[130] meaning that a trustee should not be paid for administering the trust.[131] This is consistent with one of the core duties of trustees, which is that they should not profit from their position as trustees.[132] There are, however, certain situations in which trustees have either a right or a legitimate expectation to receive payment in respect of their administration of the trust.

12.7.1 REIMBURSEMENT OF EXPENSES

Where trustees have incurred reasonable expenditure in administering the trust, they have a right to be reimbursed either from the trust fund or, sometimes, from the beneficiaries themselves.

(i) From the trust

If a trustee has properly incurred expenses when acting on behalf of the trust, they are either entitled to be reimbursed from the trust fund or can pay the expenses directly from that fund.[133] The trustees are not bound to make any payment to the beneficiaries until their expenses have been reimbursed,[134] and they have a lien on the trust property to secure their right to be reimbursed.[135]

The Trustee Act 2000 states that the expenses must be 'properly incurred'. Under the old common law rule, the expenses had to be reasonably incurred. Nothing should turn on the different word used, so the old cases on what is 'reasonable' remain relevant in determining what is 'proper'. This is particularly well illustrated by *Re Chapman*,[136] in which a barrister trustee had been paying income from the trust to a life tenant. He began to think that the life tenant was dead and he had been paying the income to an imposter. He incurred expense in investigating whether this was the case. The court held that there was no foundation for his suspicions and nobody else would have displayed such 'phenomenal scepticism'. Consequently, the expenses were considered to be so unreasonable as to be vexatious, oppressive, and wholly unjustifiable. His claim for reimbursement failed. In *Foster v Spencer*,[137] however, it was recognized that first-class air travel from Malaysia to attend to trust matters in England was a reasonable expense.

---

[129] See Section 9.3.5.(iii), p. 270.   [130] *Re Duke of Norfolk's Settlement Trust* [1982] Ch 61, 79 (Fox LJ).
[131] *Robinson v Pett* (1724) 3 P Wms 249, 250 (Lord Talbot LC).
[132] See Section 15.6, p. 438, for discussion of the no-profit principle.   [133] Trustee Act 2000, s. 31(1).
[134] *Stott v Milne* (1884) 25 Ch D 710.
[135] *Alsop Wilkinson v Neary* [1996] 1 WLR 1220, 1224 (Lightman J).
[136] (1894) 72 LT 66.   [137] [1996] 2 All ER 672.

If trustees are uncertain whether they have a right to be reimbursed from the trust, they should apply to the court for directions. It has been held that the right to be reimbursed from the trust fund enables the trustee simply to retain part of that fund so that they do not have a cause of action in debt or for damages against the fund. This is significant because it means that the trustees are unable to claim interest on the reimbursement that they retain.[138]

(ii) From the beneficiaries

If the trust fund is not sufficient to reimburse the trustee, they may look to the beneficiaries for reimbursement of expenses. It has been recognized that, where a trustee has incurred expenses by virtue of holding the trust property, they can be indemnified by the beneficiaries, who are between them absolutely entitled to the property, even if the expenses exceed the value of the trust property.[139] This is consistent with the rationale behind the rule in *Saunders v Vautier*[140] that adult beneficiaries of full capacity who are absolutely entitled to the trust property can terminate the trust and get the trust property vested in themselves. It was held in *Hardoon v Belilios* that '[t]he plainest principles of justice require that the [beneficiary] who gets all the benefit of the property should bear its burden unless he can show some good reason why his trustee should bear them himself'.[141]

It has been recognized in the Supreme Court of Victoria that the liability of the beneficiaries to indemnify the trustee is proportionate to their interest in the trust fund.[142] So, if there are four beneficiaries with equal interests in the fund, they would each be liable to indemnify the trustee 25 per cent of their expenses. It was also recognized in that case that, if one of the beneficiaries is insolvent or has disclaimed[143] their beneficial interest, they are not liable to indemnify the trustee, but the other beneficiaries do not have a corresponding increase in their own liability to indemnify. This is a suspect conclusion where a beneficiary has disclaimed their beneficial interest. Such a person no longer has a beneficial interest and clearly should not be liable to indemnify the trustee. But, when a beneficiary disclaims a beneficial interest, this is regarded as operating retrospectively, so that the beneficiary has never had a beneficial interest in the trust property. The other beneficiaries will therefore have an increased share in the trust property and this should be reflected in the extent of their liability to indemnify the trustee. Whether beneficiaries should have an increased liability to indemnify the trustee if one of their number is insolvent raises a difficult policy question as to who should bear the risk of such insolvency: should it be the trustee, as the Supreme Court of Victoria decided, or the other beneficiaries? Bearing in mind that trustees could obtain insurance against their own personal liability,[144] it would be preferable to place the risk of a beneficiary's insolvency on the trustee.

Since the liability of beneficiaries to indemnify the trustee is related to the rule in *Saunders v Vautier*, it appears that there will be no such liability if the conditions for that rule to be applicable are not satisfied.[145] This will be the case if one of the beneficiaries is a child, since they are not then all of full capacity.

If a trustee has incurred liability when not acting on behalf of the trust, the beneficiaries may still be liable to indemnify the trustee, but only if they requested this liability to be

---

[138] Ibid.   [139] *Hardoon v Belilios* [1901] AC 118 (PC).
[140] (1841) Cr & Ph 240. See Section 11.4.1, p. 334.   [141] [1901] AC 118, 123 (Lord Lindley).
[142] *JW Broomhead (Vic) Pty Ltd v JW Broomhead Pty Ltd* [1985] VR 891.
[143] See Section 11.2, p. 315.   [144] See Section 17.3.1.(ii), p. 479.
[145] See Hughes, 'The right of a trustee to a personal indemnity from beneficiaries' (1990) 64 ALJ 567.

incurred. So, in *Bush v Higham*,[146] a trustee was entitled to be indemnified by the beneficiary for interest payments when he had borrowed money at the beneficiary's request.

12.7.2 REIMBURSEMENT OF THE COSTS OF LITIGATION

Where trustees have incurred a liability to pay for the costs of litigation relating to the trust, this will constitute an expense that they might be reimbursed from the trust fund under the Trustee Act 2000.[147] Trustees may incur litigation costs either in suing somebody or in defending proceedings. In either case, it is necessary to consider whether the costs were properly incurred for the benefit of the trust.[148] In determining whether it was necessary for the trust to be involved in litigation, either in suing or defending proceedings, a fundamental principle is that trustees, especially of small trust funds, should avoid involving the trust in litigation unless the chance of success is such that it is desirable in the interests of the trust for the risk to be incurred. If it is found that the benefits were not properly incurred, the trustees will have to bear the cost personally and it is no defence that they were advised by a solicitor to commence proceedings.[149] In such a situation, the trustees must then seek to recover their costs from the solicitor rather than from the trust fund.

In assessing whether the costs of litigation were properly incurred, it is useful to distinguish between three types of dispute involving the trust.[150]

(i) Trust dispute

This is a dispute that concerns the nature and terms of the trust on which the property is held. Such a dispute might be characterized as 'friendly' if it involves matters such as the proper construction of the trust instrument or the proper administration of the trust.[151] Costs incurred in such friendly litigation will generally be considered to be reasonable and so recoverable from the trust fund,[152] except that the trustees will not recover costs if they acted in a partisan manner in seeking the guidance of the court, such as where they argue positively for a particular outcome of the question on which they seek the court's guidance.[153] If the trustees are in substance acting in the best interests of the trust rather than for their own benefit the litigation will be characterized as friendly, even if the trustees may obtain an incidental personal benefit.[154] Alternatively, a trust dispute might involve hostile litigation, such as where the settlor challenges the validity of the trust on the ground that they were unduly influenced to create it, or the trustees sue the settlor for the transfer of property to the trust.[155] There is no duty on the trustees to defend the trust where its validity is challenged,[156] but if the trustees do so and succeed, they may be entitled to their costs from the trust fund, for they have preserved the interests of the beneficiaries under the trust,[157] although usually some or all of the costs in such a case will be borne by the losing party rather than the trustees. Similarly, if the trustees successfully commence a

---

[146] (1728) 2 P Wms 453.   [147] Section 31(1). See Civil Procedure Rules, Pt 46.3.

[148] Section 31(1). See also *Holding and Management Ltd v Property Holding and Investment Trust plc* [1989] 1 WLR 1313, 1324 (Nicholls LJ).

[149] *Re Beddoe* [1893] 1 Ch 547.

[150] *Re Buckton* [1907] 2 Ch 406, 414–15 (Kekewich J); *Alsop Wilkinson v Neary* [1996] 1 WLR 1220, 1123–4 (Lightman J).

[151] *Spencer v Fielder* [2014] EWHC 2768 (Ch), [2015] 1 WLR 2786, [26] (Etherton C).

[152] *Re Buckton* [1907] 2 Ch 406.   [153] *Breadner v Granville-Grossman (costs)* [2006] WTLR 411.

[154] *Spencer v Fielder* [2014] EWHC 2768 (Ch), [2015] 1 WLR 2786, [27] (Etherton C).

[155] *Bonham v Blake Lapthorn Linnell* [2007] WTLR 189.

[156] *Alsop Wilkinson v Neary* [1996] 1 WLR 1220.

[157] *Re Holden, ex p Official Receiver* (1887) 20 QBD 43.

trust dispute against the settlor, they will be able to recover their costs if, having considered all of the circumstances of the case, it was reasonable to commence the litigation.[158] If the trustees take part in hostile litigation, either by bringing or defending a claim, and lose, they will generally not be entitled to be reimbursed their costs from the trust fund.[159]

(ii) Beneficiary dispute

This involves one or more of the beneficiaries challenging the propriety of an action that the trustees have taken or have failed to take, such as a claim for breach of trust under which the beneficiaries seek the removal of a trustee or seek a remedy for loss suffered. This is considered to be hostile litigation, so that the costs will be borne by the losing party.[160] If this is the trustees, they will have to bear the loss personally rather than seek reimbursement from the trust fund.[161] But, if the trustees do successfully defend themselves against an action for breach of trust, they will be entitled to recover their costs from the trust fund.[162]

(iii) Third-party dispute

This is a dispute between the trust and people other than the beneficiaries concerning rights and liabilities, such as a dispute in respect of a contract entered into by the trustees when administering the trust. Trustees are under a duty to protect and preserve the trust estate for the benefit of the beneficiaries, and so should represent the trust in a third-party dispute, save where they consider that pursuing an action against a third party would be fruitless.[163] Where it is reasonable to pursue or defend a third-party dispute, the trustee will be reimbursed for costs properly incurred even if the trustees lose the case.[164]

Since it may not be clear whether the proceedings are proper in a particular case, it is preferable for trustees to seek court authorization before they sue or defend proceedings, especially in respect of third-party disputes, and the trustee will be indemnified the cost of this application.[165] The directions given by the court are called a 'Beddoe order'.[166] If the court directs the action to be taken, the trustees will be reimbursed their costs even if they lose, unless the trustees failed to make full and proper disclosure to the court when seeking directions.[167] There is no breach of trust simply in commencing litigation without first obtaining a Beddoe order,[168] but the failure to obtain such an order means that the trustees will take the risk of having to pay the costs of the litigation personally if they lose and it cannot be shown that bringing or defending the proceedings was reasonable.

12.7.3 REMUNERATION FOR SERVICES PROVIDED

Although, generally, trustees will not be paid for services provided to the trust, there are some particular situations in which a trustee can be remunerated for what they have done for the trust.

---

[158] *Bonham v Blake Lapthorn Linnell* [2006] EWHC 2513 (Ch), [2007] WTLR 189.
[159] *Alsop Wilkinson v Neary* [1996] 1 WLR 1220, 1225 (Lightman J).
[160] *Armitage v Nurse* [1998] Ch 241, 262 (Millett LJ).
[161] *McDonald v Horn* [1995] 1 All ER 961, 971 (Hoffmann LJ).
[162] *Re Spurling's Will Trusts* [1966] 1 WLR 920, 935 (Ungoed-Thomas J).
[163] *Re Brogden* (1888) 38 Ch D 546. See Section 13.3, p. 378.
[164] *Alsop Wilkinson v Neary* [1996] 1 WLR 1220.
[165] *Re Beddoe* [1893] 1 Ch 547.   [166] After *Re Beddoe*, ibid.
[167] *McDonald v Horn* [1995] 1 All ER 961.
[168] *Bonham v Blake Lapthorn Linnell* [2006] EWHC 2513 (Ch), [2007] WTLR 189.

(i) Authorized by trust instrument

It is legitimate for the trust instrument to make express provision for payment out of the trust fund for the services of a trustee that is either a trust corporation or who is acting in a professional capacity,[169] which means that the trustee acts in the course of a profession or business that involves providing services in connection with the management or administration of a trust.[170] The trustee will be entitled to payment even if the services could have been provided by a lay trustee.[171]

(ii) Authorized by statute

Where no provision is made by the trust instrument or any other statute[172] for remuneration, the Trustee Act 2000 authorizes reasonable remuneration to be made from the trust fund in respect of any services provided to the trust by a trust corporation or by a trustee who acts in a professional capacity where, in the latter case, all of the other trustees have agreed in writing that the professional trustee may be paid for the services.[173] This provision does not apply to charitable trustees, since separate provision is made for them, or where a professional trustee is acting by themselves, since the safeguard of another trustee scrutinizing the remuneration will be absent.

Specific provision is made for the remuneration of charity trustees from charity funds where services are provided to the charity.[174] Such remuneration is tightly controlled and subject to a number of conditions, including that the maximum amount of remuneration is set out in a written agreement and is no more than is reasonable for the provision of the service by the trustee. Also, the other charity trustees must be satisfied that the provision of the service by that person is in the best interests of the charity.

(iii) Authorized by the court

The court has a residual jurisdiction to authorize payment to be retained by a trustee for services provided to the trust. There are two particular situations in which this jurisdiction might be exercised. First, where a trustee has been found liable for breach of fiduciary duty, it is possible for the court to award what is known as the 'equitable allowance' to reflect the value of the work done by the trustee despite the breach of duty.[175]

Secondly, the court has a residual jurisdiction to authorize remuneration, which will be relevant where no provision has been made in the trust instrument for payment and the statutory power is not engaged, such as where the trustee is not a professional. This jurisdiction of the court is of significance in four particular situations.

Past services

The court may authorize payment to be made to a trustee who has provided exceptional service for the benefit of the trust, as recognized by the Court of Appeal in *Re Duke of Norfolk's Settlement Trusts*.[176] The significance of this jurisdiction is particularly well illustrated by *Foster v Spencer*,[177] in which the trustees of a cricket club were awarded remuneration for their past services that were regarded as exceptional and unforeseen at the time of their appointment. In that case, the trust consisted of a cricket ground and

---

[169] Trustee Act 2000, s. 28(1).   [170] Ibid., s. 28(5).   [171] Ibid., s. 28(2).

[172] Specific statutory provision is made for remuneration of judicial trustees, the Public Trustee, and custodian trustees.   [173] Trustee Act 2000, s. 29(1).

[174] Charities Act 2011, s. 185. See Charity Commission, *Trustee Expenses and Payments*, CC11 (2011), for published guidance on best practice as regards paying charity trustees.

[175] See Section 18.5.3.(ii), p. 530.   [176] [1982] Ch 61.   [177] [1996] 2 All ER 672.

pavilion, which were in a state of disrepair. The trustees decided that the ground should be sold for redevelopment and a new site be obtained. This required a great deal of work on the part of two trustees in particular, since the sale and purchase was more difficult than could have been anticipated as a result of lack of clarity about the power to sell and difficulties in securing the site from squatters, who needed to be evicted. One of these trustees was a chartered surveyor and the other, who lived nearby, was a building contractor. Neither trustee had been appointed because of his professional experience, but each used his experience for the benefit of the trust. It was held that the work that had been involved was completely outside the scope of what could have been contemplated when they were appointed and so the court authorized reasonable payment to them from the trust fund for the work that they had done.

The legal basis for the court exercising its jurisdiction to authorize remuneration for services provided has proved controversial. It has been suggested that it is founded on an express or even an implied contract,[178] but that would be highly artificial; or simply that it is part of the court's inherent jurisdiction to secure the competent administration of the trust property,[179] although this is vague both as regards the rationale for authorizing the payment and the appropriate method for assessing it. But there is a preferable explanation for the award that is founded on the law of unjust enrichment. This was specifically recognized in *Foster v Spencer* itself by Judge Paul Baker QC, who held that, if the trustees were not remunerated for the work that they had done, the beneficiaries would have been unjustly enriched by the receipt of the services without having to pay for them.

There are three main components of a cause of action in unjust enrichment.[180] First, the defendant must have been enriched by the receipt of a valuable benefit.[181] In *Foster v Spencer*, the beneficiaries of the trust had obtained the valuable benefit of the trustees' professional and other services, for which they would have to have paid had they employed somebody to do this work for the trust. Secondly, this enrichment must have been obtained at the expense of the claimant, which was clearly satisfied because the trustees had provided the services. Thirdly, the claim must fall within one of the recognized grounds of restitution, such as mistake. It would be difficult to show that the trustees had actually been mistaken when they provided the services, since they knew what they were doing and there was no evidence that they had expected to be paid at that time. There is, however, another relevant ground of restitution, which is necessity. If it can be shown that the services were necessary to the defendant, in the sense that, if the claimant had not provided them, the defendant would have had to arrange for somebody else to do so, then this will be a reason why the defendant should be required to pay for the services.[182] Necessity was specifically recognized by Walton J as being relevant to the exercise of the court's jurisdiction to authorize remuneration in *Re Duke of Norfolk's Settlement Trusts*,[183] although without specific reference to the law of unjust enrichment. But the emphasis on necessity explains the requirement that the trustee's services must be essential to the trust, since, if they had not provided the services, somebody else would have had to be employed to do the work, so the beneficiaries had been saved an inevitable expense by virtue of what the trustee had done. The claim in unjust enrichment might, however, be defeated if the beneficiaries have a defence, such as that they changed their position in reliance on the

---

[178] *Re Salmon* (1912) 107 LT 108.

[179] *Re Worthington* [1954] 1 WLR 526; *Re Duke of Norfolk's Settlement Trusts* [1982] Ch 61, 77 (Fox LJ).

[180] *Banque Financière de la Cité v Parc (Battersea) Ltd* [1999] 1 AC 221, 227 (Lord Steyn).

[181] See *Benedetti v Sawiris* [2013] UKSC 50, [2014] AC 938.

[182] See Virgo, *The Principles of the Law of Restitution*, 3rd edn (Oxford: Oxford University Press, 2015), ch. 12.

[183] [1979] Ch 37, 58.

receipt of the enrichment,[184] although it is difficult to see how this would be relevant in a case involving remunerating trustees for services provided to the trust.

Once the elements of a claim in unjust enrichment have been established, the trustee will then be entitled to be reimbursed for the reasonable value of the services provided. This remedy is called a *quantum meruit*. It will be assessed by reference to what the beneficiaries would have paid in the market to obtain the service that was in fact provided by the trustees.[185] Since the remedy for a claim in unjust enrichment is restitutionary, we are concerned with the value of the gain obtained by the beneficiaries rather than the loss suffered by the truste. The assessment of the value of a service is fraught with difficulty. In *Foster v Spencer*, the trial judge held that the assessment of the value of the service lay in the discretion of the court, with regard to factors such as the size of the trust fund, the cost of engaging outside professional help, and the amount of time spent by the trustees. He concluded that one trustee, who provided the services of a chartered surveyor, should receive a commission of 5 per cent of the proceeds of sale from the land that was sold. The other, who was a building contractor, was paid an annual fee for his work of £5,000.

The analysis of the court's jurisdiction to award remuneration with reference to unjust enrichment is significant for two reasons:

(1) The assessment of the value of the services should not lie in the discretion of the court, as the judge had suggested. The focus should simply be on what the beneficiaries saved by not having to employ somebody to provide the service. The additional factors to which he referred, such as the size of the trust fund and the amount of time the trustees actually spent on the work, are simply not relevant, since the focus should be placed on the value of the benefit to the defendant (although the amount of time spent by the trustees may be of evidential significance in determining how much the beneficiaries had saved by not employing a third party to do the work).

(2) A claim in unjust enrichment creates a right to be paid if the elements of the claim are satisfied, whereas the traditional approach to the court's jurisdiction is that the amount of remuneration lies completely within the court's discretion. *Foster v Spencer* illustrates starkly the consequences of shifting legal analysis from a judicial discretion to a legal right to payment. In many cases, the same result will be achieved regardless of whether the focus is on judicial discretion or a right to unjust enrichment. Traditional Equity lawyers might prefer the former analysis as being consistent with the distinct and ancient equitable jurisdiction that is founded on the court's responsibility for ensuring the good administration of trusts.[186] But, as we have seen previously,[187] the divide between Common Law and Equity is narrowing. The law of unjust enrichment explains numerous long-standing Common Law claims, so there is no reason why it should not be used to explain claims in Equity too. And surely the unjust enrichment analysis is preferable. It means that a claim to remuneration is much clearer and predictable and that, where unjust enrichment can be established, trustees will be able to obtain remuneration for services provided to the trust without the need to seek authorization from the court. But, if in doubt, trustees should still apply to the court to seek authorization for the money to be paid.

Future services

The court also has an anticipatory jurisdiction to authorize remuneration of trustees in respect of future services for the trust, but this will be exercised only exceptionally and where the services are required to be provided by the trustee. The court refused to award

---

[184] See further Section 19.5.2, p. 585.   [185] *Benedetti v Sawiris* [2013] UKSC 50, [2014] AC 938.
[186] *Re Duke of Norfolk's Settlement Trusts* [1982] Ch 61, 79 (Fox LJ).   [187] See Chapter 1 of this volume.

remuneration for future services to the trustees in *Foster v Spencer*,[188] because the only work that they still needed to provide for the trust related to the distribution of the trust assets. This was not regarded as particularly onerous and did not require the trustees to possess any special expertise. Where the court does authorize remuneration for exceptional services to be provided in the future by a trustee, this can be justified on the grounds that the payment will prevent the beneficiaries from becoming unjustly enriched at the trustee's expense.[189]

Retention of remuneration obtained in a different capacity

Similar principles have been applied where a trustee has received remuneration for work done as a director of a company, where the trustee took on the appointment at the request of the other trustees and because the trust had a controlling interest in the company.[190] The trustee is able to retain the remuneration received as director if the work that they had done involved exceptional skill or effort, which has been defined as going beyond what would ordinarily be expected of a director who represents the interests of a substantial shareholder.[191] The court can also authorize the trustee to retain future remuneration that will be obtained as a director, but again only if the work done is exceptional and if it is expedient in the interest of the trust for the work to be done by the trustee director.[192]

Increasing remuneration under the trust instrument

The court's residual jurisdiction to authorize remuneration to be paid even extends to varying the authorized level of remuneration in the trust instrument for work already done and which will be done in the future. This was recognized in *Re Duke of Norfolk's Settlement Trusts*,[193] in which a trustee company was entitled under a settlement to remuneration in accordance with its usual scale of fees. Subsequently, additional property was added to the trust, which involved the trustee in exceptionally burdensome work beyond what could have been reasonably foreseen when it was appointed. The effect of this was that the level of remuneration, according to the charges in the trust instrument, was low. The trustee successfully applied to the court for the amount of remuneration authorized under the trust instrument to be increased.

Two arguments were made against the assertion of the court's jurisdiction in this case. The first was that, where remuneration has been authorized by the trust instrument, this is a beneficial interest that the court has no inherent jurisdiction to vary.[194] This argument was rejected simply because the trustee cannot be regarded as a beneficiary of the trust as regards the right to receive remuneration for work done.

Secondly, it was argued that the trust instrument constituted a contract that the court could not vary. Brightman LJ held that, even if the trust instrument did have contractual effect, this would not prevent the court from varying a clause that authorized remuneration. Fox LJ went further and rejected as artificial the contractual analysis of the power in the trust instrument to authorize payment.[195] He considered that the power to authorize payment derives instead from the power of the settlor to direct how their property should be dealt with. This is surely right. In most cases, the relationship between trustee and settlor is not contractual, since it is voluntary and does not involve a bargain.[196]

But, if the variation of beneficial interests and contractual explanations are rejected, how can the court's jurisdiction to increase the level of remuneration be rationalized? This

[188] [1996] 2 All ER 672.   [189] See Section 12.7.3.(iii), p. 359.
[190] *Re Keeler's Settlement Trust* [1981] Ch 156.   [191] Ibid., 163 (Goulding J).
[192] Ibid., 162.   [193] [1982] Ch 61.   [194] See further Section 16.1.2, p. 459.
[195] [1982] Ch 61, 76.   [196] See Section 3.2, p. 41.

might be justified, again, in terms of unjust enrichment, in that if the trustees are paid at a level far below the market value of their services, the beneficiaries will be unjustly enriched at their expense. This explanation is, however, flawed because a claim in unjust enrichment will fail where there was a legal basis for the transfer of an enrichment to the defendant, such as where it was transferred pursuant to a contract or a statutory obligation.[197] Consequently, where a trustee has provided services for the benefit of the beneficiaries in circumstances where express provision is made in the trust instrument for remuneration, that must provide a legitimate basis for payment and it is not possible to bring a claim in unjust enrichment to alter this provision. It would follow that the court should not have a jurisdiction to increase the level of remuneration in the trust instrument.

But, if the court did not increase the level of remuneration in those cases in which the level authorized by the trust instrument is well below the market rate, there may well be unfortunate consequences: the trustee might resign and a new trustee would need to be appointed, who would presumably be willing to do so only if paid the market rate for the work. The court's jurisdiction to increase the rate of remuneration in the trust instrument can therefore be regarded simply as a pragmatic response to ensure the proper administration of the trust by an existing trustee. It might still be analysed under the law of unjust enrichment in that the court's equitable jurisdiction to amend the rate of remuneration in the trust instrument might simply be regarded as a mechanism to remove the legal basis for the remuneration of the service under that instrument, so that the trustee could then be paid at the market rate, and this could legitimately be justified with reference to the law of unjust enrichment. Although none of the cases have analysed this jurisdiction in this way, unjust enrichment would provide a rational way of justifying the jurisdiction and for determining its ambit.

12.8 EXERCISE OF POWERS

Trustees typically have a number of powers that they may exercise relating to the administration of the trust[198] or the disposition of the trust estate to beneficiaries.[199] A number of rules and principles of general application have been developed relating to the exercise of these powers.

12.8.1 UNANIMITY OF DECISION-MAKING

As a general rule, trustees must be unanimous in exercising any powers vested in them[200] and a decision of a majority binds neither the minority nor the trust estate.[201] Trustees of charities[202] and pension trusts[203] can, however, act by a majority. For all other trusts, a majority decision will be effective only if it is authorized by the trust instrument.[204] Sometimes, statutory provision is made for majority decision-making. So, for example, where some trustees wish to pay money or securities into court, but the concurrence of some of them cannot be obtained, the court may order payment if a majority of the trustees agree.[205]

---

[197] *Kleinwort Benson Ltd v Lincoln CC* [1999] 2 AC 349, 407 (Lord Hope).
[198] See further Chapter 13 of this volume.   [199] See further Chapter 14 of this volume.
[200] *Re Allen-Meyrick's Will Trusts* [1966] 1 WLR 499, 505 (Buckley J).
[201] *Luke v South Kensington Hotel Co* (1879) 11 Ch D 121.
[202] *Re Whiteley* [1910] 1 Ch 600, 608 (Eve J).   [203] Pension Act 1995, s. 32(1).
[204] *Re Butlin's WT* [1976] Ch 251, in which the trust instrument was rectified to allow for majority decision-making as regards all decisions of the trustees. See further Section 21.7.2, p. 655.
[205] Trustee Act 1925, s. 63(3).

The significance of the general rule requiring unanimity of decision-making is illustrated by *Re Mayo*,[206] in which the trustees were under a duty to sell the trust property, but had a power to postpone sale if they so wished. One of the three trustees wished to sell, but the other two wished to postpone. Since there was no unanimity of decision, it was held that the duty trumped the power and they were obliged to sell. They could have postponed the sale only if they had all agreed to do so.

The fact that trustees of most private trusts must make their decisions unanimously, whereas trustees of charitable trusts are bound by a majority decision, is inconsistent and difficult to justify.[207] Some explanations for this difference of treatment have been suggested,[208] for example that the need for unanimity reduces the possibility of loss being caused to the trust. But this is an unconvincing explanation, since the same possibility of loss exists in charitable trusts and, in private trusts, the need for unanimity limits the possibility of trustees responding flexibly and quickly to particular problems concerning the administration of the trust. So, for example, if the trustees have appointed an agent to assist in the administration of the trust[209] and it is discovered that the agent is unreliable or untrustworthy, it will be possible to remove the agent only if all of the trustees agree. One trustee might not do so and the trust might then suffer loss. That trustee could be liable for breach of trust in such circumstances, but surely it would be preferable to prevent the loss from arising in the first place by allowing for a majority decision to remove the agent to be effective? A similar problem would arise if there were three trustees, two of whom agree to remove the agent immediately and the other of whom is simply not available to make a decision. Another suggested explanation for the difference of approach between private and charitable trusts is that charitable trusts are more likely to have a larger number of trustees, making a unanimity requirement much more difficult to implement. But the fact that charity trustees do have a larger number of trustees may, in fact, be a consequence of the rule that majority decision-making is sufficient in charities. If the unanimity rule were abolished for private trusts, there might be a greater incentive to increase the number of trustees appointed.

The better view therefore is that the majority rule that applies to charitable and pension trusts should be extended to all trusts. The strongest argument against this is that it would mean that a minority trustee would be bound by the decision of the majority. Since the liability of trustees is joint and several,[210] it would follow that, if the decision of the majority involves the trustees in committing a breach of trust, any trustee could be liable for this, even the minority trustee who did not vote in favour. But this could be dealt with sensibly by the exercise of the court's statutory discretion to relieve a trustee of liability where they had acted honestly and reasonably.[211]

12.8.2 PROVISION OF REASONS

Trustees are not required to give reasons to the beneficiaries for their decisions as to whether or not to exercise a power.[212] So, for example, in *Re Beloved Wilkes' Charity*,[213] the trustees had a power under a charitable trust to select a boy to be educated in preparation for him to become an Anglican priest, with preference for a boy living in certain

---

[206] [1943] Ch 302.
[207] See Jaconelli, 'Decision-taking by private and charitable trustees' [1991] Conv 30.
[208] Ibid., pp. 32–3.   [209] See further Section 13.7.1, p. 397.   [210] See Section 17.4.2, p. 494.
[211] Trustee Act 1925, s. 61. See Section 17.3.2, p. 481.
[212] *Re Londonderry's Settlement* [1965] Ch 918. The same rule applies to trustees of a pension trust: *Wilson v Law Debenture Trust Court plc* [1995] 2 All ER 337.
[213] (1851) 3 Mac & G 440.

designated parishes if, in the view of the trustees, a fit and proper candidate could be found from one of those parishes. The trustees chose a boy living outside the parishes and gave no reasons for doing so. It was held that the trustees were not required to explain why they had reached their decision and the selection was not set aside, there being no evidence that the trustees had exercised their discretion unfairly or dishonestly. If, however, the trustees do give reasons for their decisions, the court will look at the adequacy of the reasons; if they are found wanting, this may result in the decision being set aside.[214] Consequently, it is preferable for the trustees simply to state that they have met and reached a decision, without providing any further details, since it is not then possible to challenge their decision[215] unless there is additional evidence of bad faith or error in making the decision.

The justification for the general rule that there is no duty to provide reasons is that the effective administration of the trust would be undermined if the trustees were subject to investigation as to whether they had exercised their powers or fulfilled their duties in the best possible manner. Further, the rule is meant to avoid litigation and disputes within the family,[216] although it is just as likely that it creates an atmosphere of suspicion that could be resolved simply by the trustees providing some explanation for their decisions.[217]

12.8.3 SURRENDER OF POWERS TO THE COURT

The court will be willing to give directions on specific matters relating to the exercise of a power, but it is not possible for trustees to surrender their powers to the court completely in the expectation that the court will make all subsequent decisions on behalf of the trustees. This principle is illustrated by *Re Allen-Meyrick's Will Trusts*,[218] in which trustees held property on trust, with a power to apply the income for the maintenance of the testator's husband as they, in their absolute discretion, thought fit. The trustees had made some payments to the husband, but had not been able to agree on making any more once he had become bankrupt. Once it had become clear that they were not able to reach agreement as to whether any further payments should be made to the husband, they sought to surrender their discretion completely to the court. It was held that the court would not accept the surrender of such a discretionary power prospectively and absolutely where that power was to be exercised over a period of time, since this would relieve the trustees of their obligation to consider whether the power should be exercised and would require the court to gather all of the evidence of changes in circumstances to enable it to make appropriate decisions.[219] Consequently, the court refused to accept the proffered general surrender of discretion. Instead, where the trustees are unable to reach a decision, they should apply to the court for directions as to how the discretion should be exercised at that time. Where the trustees surrender their decision-making to the court in this way, the court has an unfettered discretion to determine what should be done in the best interests of the trust and of the beneficiaries. To enable the court to assess this, the parties are obliged to put before the court all of the available material to enable the discretion to be exercised.[220]

Rather than seeking directions from the court as to how the discretion should be exercised, the trustees may instead simply seek the approval of the court as to the proposed exercise of their powers or ask the court to construe the ambit of the powers.[221] Where the

---

[214] *Klug v Klug* [1918] 2 Ch 67.   [215] See *Re Londonderry's Settlement* [1965] Ch 918.
[216] *Hartigan Nominees Pty Ltd v Ridge* (1992) 29 NSWLR 405.   [217] Ibid., 420 (Kirby P).
[218] [1966] 1 WLR 499.   [219] Ibid., 503 (Buckley J).
[220] *Marley v Mutual Security Merchant Bank and Trust Co Ltd* [1991] 3 All ER 198; *RSPCA v Attorney-General* [2002] 1 WLR 448.
[221] See *Public Trustee v Cooper* [2001] WTLR 901, 924 (Hart J).

trustees seek court approval of a proposed exercise of a power, the court is concerned only to determine whether the proposed exercise is lawful, is within the scope of the power, and is a decision that would be made by a reasonable trustee.[222] A consequence of the court authorizing the exercise of a power is that the beneficiaries cannot then allege a breach of trust and seek a remedy for loss suffered as a result of the power being exercised. As a result, the court acts with caution and if there is doubt as to the propriety of what the trustees propose the court will withhold its approval.[223] To assist the court in determining whether the proposal is reasonable the trustees should disclose the reasons for what they are proposing.[224]

As a last resort, trustees or beneficiaries can apply for the court to administer the trust, but the court will make an administration order only if the issues cannot be resolved in any other way,[225] such as by surrendering a discretion on a one-off basis, seeking directions, or replacing the trustees.[226]

12.8.4 SURRENDER OF POWERS TO A THIRD PARTY

Although it might be considered to be fundamental to the exercise of a trustee's discretion that they exercise the discretion for themself, it was recognized in *Citibank v MBIA Assurance*[227] that a third party can legitimately instruct the trustees as to the exercise of their discretion and that the trustees will not be liable for breach of trust if they follow those instructions. This was regarded as legitimate because the trustees remained subject to a duty of good faith and continued to have a real discretion to exercise. The better view, however, is that such a surrender of a discretion to a third party contravenes fundamental principles of the law of trusts, especially the obligation of the trustees to exercise their powers for the benefit of the beneficiaries rather than for the benefit of the trustees or the third party.[228]

12.8.5 RELEASE OF POWERS

Where trustees are obliged to exercise the power, such as a power of appointment under a discretionary trust, it cannot be released, because otherwise the trustee would commit a breach of trust.[229] Even where the trustee has a fiduciary power, which they need not exercise, but the exercise of which they must consider,[230] that power cannot be released either.[231]

12.8.6 INVALID EXERCISE OF POWERS

Where the trustees have agreed to the exercise of a discretionary power, the courts will not interfere as long as the power is exercised in good faith and within the limits with which it has been given to them.[232] The court will also not consider the accuracy of the

---

[222] *Richard v The Hon AB Mackay* (14 March 1987) (1997) 11 TLI 23; *RSPCA v Attorney-General* [2002] 1 WLR 448.

[223] *Re MF Global UK Ltd* [2014] EWHC 2222 (Ch), [2014] Bus LR 1156, [32] (David Richards J).

[224] Ibid. [225] Civil Procedure Rules, Practice Direction, 64B.

[226] See Section 12.6.4, p. 353. [227] [2007] EWCA Civ 11, [2007] 1 All ER (Comm) 475.

[228] See further Chapter 15 of this volume. Failure to exercise a power for the benefit of the beneficiaries could also constitute fraud on the power. See Section 12.8.6.(vii), p. 368.

[229] *Re Mills* [1930] 1 Ch 654, 661 (Lord Hanworth MR). [230] See Section 3.7.8.(iii), p. 67.

[231] *Mettoy Pension Trustees Ltd v Evans* [1990] 1 WLR 1587.

[232] *Gisborne v Gisborne* (1877) 2 App Cas 300. See generally Nolan, 'Controlling fiduciary power' (2009) 68 CLJ 293.

trustees' conclusions.[233] So, for example, in *Tempest v Lord Camoys*,[234] the court refused to override the refusal of one of two trustees to agree with a course of action proposed by the other trustee involving the purchase of particular land and the raising of some of the purchase money on a mortgage. Jessel MR affirmed that, where trustees are given a pure discretion as to the exercise of a power, such as the power to buy land, the court will not compel them to exercise the power against their wishes, but will simply prevent them from exercising the power improperly.[235] So, in this case, the court refused to interfere with the trustees' discretion as to when they would purchase property and what property they would purchase.

There will, however, be certain circumstances under which the exercise of a discretionary power by trustees will be held to be invalid and void. Essentially, where the act done by the trustees in the exercise of their discretion is not within the scope of the power, the power will not be considered to have been exercised at all and the transaction will be void. Acting outside the scope of the power may occur for a number of different reasons.

(i) Formal defects

If there are formal or procedural defects, the exercise of the power will be ineffective, for example if the trustees fail to use a required formality, such as a deed, or to obtain a required consent for a transaction. Sometimes, in such circumstances, Equity might relieve against the defect, depending on its nature and effect, so that the exercise would be effective.

(ii) Unauthorized exercise

Where the trustees purport to exercise the power in a way that is not authorized,[236] such as where they seek to delegate to an agent where the power of delegation has been excluded by the trust instrument[237] or seek to make an appointment to somebody who does not fall within the class of objects in a discretionary trust,[238] the exercise of the power will be invalid.

(iii) Unlawful exercise of the power

The exercise of the power may be invalid because it infringes the law, such as the rule against perpetuities.[239] This is illustrated by *Re Hastings-Bass*,[240] in which funds from a trust in which Captain Hastings-Bass had a protected life interest were advanced[241] to his son to be held on other trusts in an attempt to save estate duty. But these trusts were void for perpetuity. The question for the Court of Appeal was whether the trustees had validly exercised their discretion to exercise the power of advancement. It was held that the advancement was effective to create a life interest in favour of the son, since that was not caught by the perpetuity rule, but the beneficial interests in the capital were void because of the perpetuity rule. Therefore, as regards the capital, the exercise of the power of advancement was unlawful.

---

[233] *Re Beloved Wilkes' Charity* (1851) 3 Mac & G 440, 448 (Lord Truro LC). See also *Dundee General Hospital v Walker* [1952] 1 All ER 896, 905 (Lord Reid).

[234] (1882) 21 Ch D 571.   [235] Ibid., 578.

[236] *Re Hastings-Bass* [1975] Ch 25, 41 (Buckley LJ).   [237] See further Section 13.7.1, p. 397.

[238] See e.g. *Schroder Cayman Bank and Trust Co Ltd v Schroder Trust AG* (2015) FSD 122/214 (Grand Court of the Cayman Islands).   [239] See Section 4.6, p. 102.

[240] [1975] Ch 25.   [241] See Section 14.5, p. 414, for consideration of the power of advancement.

(iv) Excessive exercise

Where an appointment is partly good and partly bad, the court will seek to sever the good from the bad so that the good exercise remains valid.[242] So, for example, if the trustee were to exercise a power of appointment in favour of two people, one of whom was an object within the power and the other not, the appointment to the former could be severed[243] and will be valid. Similarly, in *Re Hastings-Bass*,[244] the exercise of the power of advancement was valid to the extent that it did not infringe the perpetuity rule. It will not be possible, however, to sever the valid from the invalid exercise of the power where the valid part that would remain is not reasonably capable of being considered to be for the benefit of the person in whose favour the power was exercised.[245]

(v) Failure to exercise discretion

The trustees may have been unaware that they had any discretion to exercise before acting and so will not be considered to have made a decision at all. This is illustrated by the exceptional case of *Turner v Turner*,[246] in which appointments made under fiduciary powers were held to be void because the trustees had failed to apply their minds to the exercise of the discretion that had been entrusted to them. They were described as 'ciphers', who simply signed the deeds of appointment as they were requested to do by the settlor, who was not a trustee, without realizing that they had any discretion to exercise and without reading or understanding the documents. This vitiated the exercise of the power of appointment and so the purported appointment was a nullity. This is effectively an equitable form of the contractual *non est factum* doctrine, under which a signature on a contract will be invalid if the signer did not know what they were signing.

(vi) Bad faith

Where a power is exercised in bad faith, the exercise will be void. Bad faith appears to be determined by reference to the subjective state of mind of the trustee,[247] at least as regards their awareness of the consequences for the beneficiary of exercising the power. Bad faith has been equated with equitable fraud and dishonesty.[248] Whether a particular trustee has acted dishonestly has been interpreted as where a trustee intended to pursue a course of action knowing that it was contrary to the best interests of the beneficiaries or being recklessly indifferent to their interests, regardless of whether the trustee intended to benefit from the conduct.[249] A trustee would not be acting in bad faith if they were to believe themself to be acting in the best interests of the beneficiaries, even if the exercise of the power had adverse consequences for the beneficiaries. If, however, the trustee is a professional trustee, they would be considered to have acted dishonestly, and so presumably in bad faith, even if they were to have considered that the exercise of the power was in the best interests of the beneficiaries, if the belief was so unreasonable that no reasonable trustee in that profession would have shared that belief.[250] Although this was decided in the context of the operation of exemption clauses to exclude trustees' liability for breach of duty, there is no reason why this test should not be applied to determine whether the actual exercise

---

[242] *Re Oliphant* (1917) 86 LJ Ch 452.
[243] *Price v Williams-Wynn* [2006] EWHC 788 (Ch), [2006] WTLR 1633.
[244] [1975] Ch 25.   [245] *Pitt v Holt* [2011] EWCA Civ 197, [2012] Ch 132, [96] (Lloyd LJ).
[246] [1984] Ch 100.   [247] Nolan (see n. 232), p. 296.
[248] *Armitage v Nurse* [1998] Ch 241, 254 (Millett LJ).   [249] Ibid., 251.
[250] *Walker v Stones* [2001] QB 902, discussed in Section 17.3.1.(i), p. 477. See also *Barnes v Tomlinson* [2006] EWHC 3115 (Ch), [2007] WTLR 377, [79] (Kitchin J); *Fattal v Walbrook Trustees (Jersey) Ltd* [2010] EWHC 2767 (Ch), [81] (Lewison J).

of the power was valid. It follows that bad faith may be determined objectively, without regard to the defendant's knowledge or suspicion, where the trustee is a professional.

(vii) Fraud on the power

If the power is exercised for an improper purpose, it will be invalid by virtue of the doctrine of fraud on the power.[251] An improper purpose encompasses an exercise of the power for a collateral purpose,[252] or wantonly, or capriciously.[253] A 'capricious decision' has been described as one that is 'irrational, perverse or irrelevant to any sensible expectations of the settlor'.[254] Of course, since trustees are not required to give reasons for the exercise of their discretion,[255] it will be difficult to show that the exercise was capricious.

The notion of fraud for these purposes does not necessarily require conduct that amounts to fraud at Common Law or conduct that could be termed dishonest or immoral, but simply involves the power being exercised for a purpose that is either beyond the scope of the trust instrument or is not justified by that instrument.[256] So there will be fraud on the power if the trustee's purpose in exercising the power is to secure a benefit for themselves, or for a third party who is not an object of the power. For example, there was fraud in the exercise of a power in *Cloutte v Storey*,[257] in which a power of appointment was exercised by the trustees in favour of the child of one of them, who was a legitimate object of the power, but pursuant to a private arrangement in which the benefit was passed back to the trustees, who had made the appointment in the first place. In *Klug v Klug*,[258] one of two trustees, who was the mother of the beneficiary, refused to agree to the exercise of a power of advancement to provide funds to her beneficiary daughter to enable her to pay a legacy duty. The other trustee, who was the Public Trustee, considered this to be a proper exercise of the power. It appeared that the mother's refusal to exercise the power was motivated by anger that her daughter had married without her consent. This was considered to be an inappropriate reason for the trustee's decision to refuse to exercise the power. The court effectively discounted the mother's vote and ordered the power to be exercised. Further, in *Hillsdown Holdings plc v Pensions Ombudsman*,[259] a pension fund had a surplus, but its rules prevented the trustees from paying this to the employer. The trustees transferred the fund to another pension scheme, which was able to pay the surplus to the employer. Even though the employer had agreed to increase the members' benefits under the new pension scheme in return for receiving the surplus, it was held that the transfer of the funds to this other pension scheme constituted fraud on the power, because the transfer was motivated by the collateral purpose of benefiting the employer and so was void.

It is not, however, necessarily fraud on the power that the trustee or a third party benefits indirectly from the exercise of the power.[260] So, for example, if a father exercises a power of appointment in favour of his infant child and that child dies before attaining the age of majority, the father will receive the property as next of kin, but this will not invalidate the exercise of the power, except if the trustee intended when exercising the power to benefit from the appointment.

Where the doctrine of fraud on the power applies, the exercise of the power will be void, since the effect of the doctrine is simply that the power will not have been exercised,[261]

---

[251] *Balls v Strutt* (1841) 1 Hare 146, 149 (Sir James Wigram V-C).
[252] *Hillsdown Holdings plc v Pensions Ombudsman* [1997] 1 All ER 862, 883 (Knox J).
[253] *Pilkington v IRC* [1964] AC 612, 641 (Viscount Radcliffe).
[254] *Re Manisty* [1974] 1 Ch 17, 23 (Templeman J).   [255] See Section 12.8.2, p. 363.
[256] *Vatcher v Paull* [1915] AC 372, 378 (Lord Parker of Waddington).
[257] [1911] 1 Ch 18.   [258] [1918] 2 Ch 67.   [259] [1997] 1 All ER 862.
[260] *Vatcher v Paull* [1915] AC 372, 379 (Lord Parker of Waddington).
[261] *Clouette v Storey* [1911] 1 Ch 18.

although the court might be able to distinguish between the quantum of benefit that was properly appointed to one object, which will be valid, and the quantum of benefit that was improperly appointed, which will be invalid.

An unfortunate consequence of the doctrine rendering the exercise of the power void is that a third party may suffer, because they, being unaware of the hidden purpose of the trustee, would conclude that everything that was done was entirely in order. Consequently, it might be preferable to treat the doctrine as rendering the transaction voidable rather than void, such that it would be valid until it had been rescinded. This would prevent the disposition from being set aside if the third party had acquired rights under it for value and was acting in good faith, since this is a recognized bar to rescission.[262] This is not the law, although in *Pitt v Holt*[263] Lord Walker said that the decision in *Clouette v Storey*, which had recognized that the effect of the doctrine is to render the transaction void, might have to be 'revisited one day'. It is unfortunate that the Supreme Court in *Pitt v Holt* failed to recognize that fraud on the power should render the disposition voidable rather than void.

12.8.7 VOIDABLE EXERCISE OF POWER

Where trustees make a decision that has an adverse effect on the trust or the beneficiaries, the trustees may apply to the court to have the decision set aside on the ground that they had taken into account an irrelevant consideration or ignored a relevant consideration. This became known as the 'rule in *Hastings-Bass*'.[264] But the rule was reconsidered by the Supreme Court in conjoined appeals in *Pitt v Holt* and *Futter v Futter*.[265] As we have already seen,[266] *Re Hastings-Bass* itself actually involved the exercise of a power that was partially void because it infringed the perpetuity rule. In that case, Buckley LJ stated that the court would not interfere with a trustee's discretion unless the trustee would not have acted as they did had they not taken into account considerations that should not have been taken into account or had ignored considerations that ought to have been taken into account. This dictum was then taken out of context in *Mettoy Pension Trustees Ltd v Evans*,[267] in which it was formulated in positive terms as the 'Rule in *Hastings-Bass*'. It was subsequently invoked in a series of first-instance cases, including *Sieff v Fox*, in which it was formulated as follows:[268]

> Where trustees act under a discretion given to them by the terms of the trust, in circumstances in which they are free to decide whether or not to exercise that discretion, but the effect of the exercise is different from that which they intended, the court will interfere with their action if it is clear that they would not have acted as they did had they not failed to take into account considerations which they ought to have taken into account, or taken into account considerations which they ought not have taken into account.

Such a rule meant that, if the trustees failed to take into account the tax consequences of a disposition which ought properly to have been considered, the disposition might be unwound.[269] For example, in *Sieff v Fox* itself, trustees of a settlement, having received professional advice concerning potential tax liability, exercised their power of appointment in favour of a beneficiary. The tax advice was incorrect and the beneficiary was liable to pay

---

[262] See Section 21.6.4.(iv), p. 649.   [263] [2013] UKSC 26, [2013] 2 AC 108, [62].

[264] [1975] Ch 25.   [265] [2013] UKSC 26, [2013] 2 AC 108.

[266] See Section 12.8.6.(iv), p. 367.   [267] [1990] 1 WLR 1587.

[268] [2005] EWHC 1312(Ch), [2005] 1 WLR 3811, [119] (Lloyd LJ).

[269] *Abacus Trust Co (Isle of Man) v Barr* [2003] EWHC 114 (Ch), [2003] Ch 409; *Smithson v Hamilton* [2007] EWHC 2900 (Ch), [2008] 1 WLR 1453.

over £1 million of capital gains tax. The trustees successfully applied to have the appointment set aside on the ground that, had they known of the true tax position, they would not have made the appointment.

This formulation of the rule was reconsidered by the Supreme Court in *Pitt v Holt*, which affirmed the decision of the Court of Appeal, where Longmore LJ had described the rule in *Hastings-Bass* as an example of:[270]

> that comparatively rare instance of the law taking a seriously wrong turn, of that wrong turn being not infrequently acted on over a twenty year period but this court being able to reverse that error and put the law back on the right course.

Lord Walker in the Supreme Court recognized that:

> the label 'the rule in *Hastings-Bass*' is a misnomer . . . The rule would be more aptly called 'the rule in *Mettoy*' . . . But the misnomer is by now so familiar that it is best to continue to use it, inapposite though it is.[271]

The Supreme Court drew a fundamental distinction between an exercise of a discretionary power that is void for invalid exercise, known as 'excessive execution', and the exercise of a discretionary power that is voidable because, although acting within the scope of their power, the trustees breached their duty in exercising it, known as 'inadequate deliberation'.[272] Trustees never had the authority to do what they did in cases of excessive execution, so it is appropriate that Equity considers their actions to be void. But, in cases of inadequate deliberation, the disposition made was an authorized act of the trustees, so it should be treated as voidable at the instance of a beneficiary. Whether the exercise of the power will be avoided will be subject both to the discretion of the court and to the equitable bars for rescission, such as delay in seeking to avoid the transaction or that property which has been transferred has been received by a bona fide purchaser for value.[273]

This re-interpreted 'rule in *Hastings-Bass*' applies to cases of inadequate deliberation, but only where the trustee had breached their fiduciary duty.[274] A trustee will have breached their fiduciary duty if they failed to take into account a relevant matter or took into account an irrelevant matter when deciding to exercise the discretion. But the Supreme Court recognized that trustees who act upon professional advice in making authorized dispositions will not generally commit any breach of duty; this was the case in both *Pitt* and *Futter*.

In *Pitt v Holt*, Mrs Pitt had been appointed the receiver for her husband by the Court of Protection after he had been seriously injured in a road accident. Following the accident, he received a lump sum and an annuity, which was settled on trust for his benefit. Mr Pitt then died and a substantial inheritance tax liability was incurred. This could have been avoided by a very simple restructuring of the settlement, so that half of the fund was to be applied for his benefit during his lifetime, which was how the fund was actually applied anyway. The Supreme Court held that the settlement could not be avoided, at least by virtue of the rule in *Hastings-Bass*, because, although Mrs Pitt as receiver was in a fiduciary position, albeit not a trustee, she had not breached her duty in creating the trust, since she had reasonably relied on the advice of her advisers. It was, however, recognized that the settlement could be set aside on the separate ground of mistake.[275]

---

[270] [2011] EWCA Civ 197, [2012] Ch 132 at [227], cited with approval by Lord Walker at [2013] UKSC 26, [2013] 2 AC 108, [9].

[271] [2013] UKSC 26, [2013] 2 AC 108, [1].   [272] Ibid., [60].

[273] Such a bar would not be available to HM Revenue & Customs as regards a liability to pay tax, since this is a claim in debt for tax due. See Nolan and Cloherty, 'The rule in *Pitt v Holt*?' (2011) 127 LQR 499, 502.

[274] [2013] UKSC 26, [2013] 2 AC 108, [73].   [275] See Section 9.3.3, p. 264.

In the other case considered by the Supreme Court, *Futter v Futter*, trustees had exercised powers of advancement under a discretionary trust to enable assets to be transferred out of a settlement to avoid capital gains tax. This was not effective because the solicitors who were advising the trustees had misinterpreted the relevant statute. Although the trial judge had held that this rendered the exercise of the powers void, the Supreme Court held that the transactions were valid and not even voidable, because, although the trustees had ignored a relevant consideration as regards the fiscal consequences of the transaction, since they had been given the wrong advice by the solicitors, the trustees had not breached their duty in following that advice.

In both cases there was no basis for the beneficiaries to complain about the actions of their trustees because they had complied with their duty to act with reasonable skill and care.[276] Yet, in some circumstances, the trustees will commit a breach of trust in failing to appreciate the tax consequences of a disposition; where, for example, they fail to take, or properly consider, appropriate advice,[277] or where the trustee's instructions to the adviser were flawed because the trustee had failed to take reasonable care in obtaining information which was relevant to the instructions which were given.[278] In determining whether the trustee has taken sufficient care to ensure that their reliance on the advisor can be considered to be reasonable, it is relevant to consider the commercial experience and sophistication of the trustees,[279] since, the more experienced and sophisticated they are, the less likely it will be that the simple reliance on professional advice will be considered to be reasonable. But, where there has been no breach of fiduciary duty, there is no reason for the court to interfere with the trustees' exercise of their discretionary powers. The balance is now struck at a more appropriate level: beneficiaries are protected where the trustees breach their duties. An inevitable consequence of the decision in *Pitt v Holt* requiring proof of breach of duty is that, if the trustees did act reasonably in obtaining and relying on professional advice, it is much less likely that the transaction will be set aside where it has adverse fiscal consequences, whereas, if the trustees acted unreasonably in not obtaining or relying on professional advice, the transaction might be set aside because the trustees will have breached their duty. Although the beneficiary might have an alternative claim against the trustee for breach of trust, such a claim might be defeated by the operation of a clause excluding the trustee's liability.[280] Where the trustee has not breached their duty in making a disposition because they had acted reasonably in relying on professional advice, if that advice was negligent, the beneficiary will not necessarily be without a remedy because the trustee may have a claim in tort against the advisers. This will usually be the most satisfactory route to redress: the error was made by the advisers, so those advisers should bear the loss.

The rationalization of the rule in *Re Hastings-Bass* is to be welcomed. Whether the exercise of a discretionary power by a trustee or another fiduciary is void, voidable, or valid will depend on the circumstances in which the power is exercised. If the trustee acts outside the scope of the power, it is void, as will be the case if the trustee acts fraudulently in exercising the power. If the trustee acts within the scope of the power, it is valid, unless the trustee can be considered to have acted in breach of duty in doing so. The fact that the transaction has adverse fiscal consequences will not automatically result in an invalid exercise of the power. The essence of the rule in *Hastings-Bass* is to ensure that beneficiaries

---

[276] See further Section 13.2, p. 374.   [277] Trustee Act 2000, s. 5. See Section 13.4.2.(iii), p. 382.

[278] *Top Brands Ltd v Sharma* [2014] EWHC 2753 (Ch); [2015] 1 BCLC 516, [33] (HHJ Simon Barker QC).

[279] *Power Adhesives Ltd v Sweeney* [2017] EWHC 676 Ch, [27] (Chief Master Marsh).

[280] And such clauses are not readily challengeable: see *Armitage v Nurse* [1998] Ch. 241. See Section 17.3.1.(i), p. 474.

do not suffer from the inappropriate, but authorized, exercise of a power by the trustees. But the exercise of a discretionary power can only be considered to be inappropriate where it involves a breach of duty.

There remain, however, some outstanding concerns about the interpretation of the re-invented rule in *Hastings-Bass*. First, Lord Walker referred to the requisite breach of duty as a breach of 'fiduciary duty' rather than a breach of trust. Such use of language may lead to confusion. A failure to seek advice where appropriate,[281] or the exercise of a power without taking reasonable care,[282] may both be breaches of duty sufficient to trigger the rule in *Hastings-Bass*, but such breaches of trust are not also breaches of fiduciary duty which protect the fiduciary's core obligation of loyalty, and are breached when the fiduciary places themself in a position where their personal interest conflicts with the interest of their principal, for example.[283] But a breach of a trust duty through failing to take advice or acting negligently does not constitute disloyalty. The language of 'fiduciary duties' may have been introduced by Lord Walker because the rule in *Re Hastings-Bass* can be applied to non-trustees who are acting in a fiduciary capacity,[284] such as Mrs Pitt herself, but the more general language of breach of duty is preferable, regardless of whether it constitutes a breach of trust or breach of fiduciary duty.

Secondly, Lord Walker provided little guidance as to when the court would grant relief where there had been a breach of duty. It has been a matter of some controversy for some time whether the rule in *Hastings-Bass* is engaged only where the trustees can show that they *would* have acted differently had they taken into account a relevant consideration or ignored an irrelevant one, or only that they *might* have acted differently.[285] In *Pitt v Holt* Lord Walker refused to rule on whether it was necessary to show that the defendant would or might have acted differently, because he did not wish to 'inhibit the court in seeking the best practical application of the *Hastings-Bass* rule in a variety of different factual situations'.[286] He did, however, recognize that the court might, in practice, think that 'would not' is the appropriate test for family trusts, and 'might not' would be preferable for pensions trusts, but he refused to go any further.[287] This does at least reflect the growing dichotomy between family and commercial trusts,[288] but it is unclear why the different type of trust should affect the test which is applied here. The preferable view is that the 'might not' test should be applicable regardless of the type of trust. If a beneficiary has established that the trustees breached their duty, it would be a very difficult hurdle also to have to prove that the trustees *would* have acted differently had they not breached their duty. This would unduly limit the beneficiaries' right to expect that the trust should be properly administered. If the beneficiaries can establish that the trustees *might* have acted differently had there not been a breach of duty, the court should be able to set aside the disposition.

---

[281] See Section 13.4.2.(ii), p. 382.   [282] See Section 13.2, p. 374.
[283] See Section 15.5, p. 431.   [284] [2013] UKSC 26, [2013] 2 AC 108, [10].
[285] See e.g. *Abacus Trust Co (Isle of Man) v Barr* [2003] EWHC 114 (Ch), [2003] Ch 409, [21] (Lightman J); *Sieff v Fox* [2005] EWHC 1312 (Ch), 1 WLR 3811, [77] (Lloyd LJ).
[286] [2013] UKSC 26, [2013] 2 AC 108, [92].   [287] Ibid., [92].
[288] See also Section 18.2.2, p. 514.

13

THE ADMINISTRATION OF TRUSTS

13.1 GENERAL CONSIDERATIONS

Trustees are responsible for the administration of the trust. They are subject to certain key duties, which must be performed, and have a number of key powers, which may be performed, relating to trust administration. The nature of these duties and powers are examined in this chapter.

Before the key administrative duties and powers are considered, it is important to identify a number of general considerations which relate to them.

13.1.1 SOURCES OF DUTIES AND POWERS

Many of these duties and powers have been created by the judges or by statute, which has resulted in a complex and dense body of law. The statutory provisions in particular often prescribe administrative processes in mind-numbing detail. In this book, we are less concerned with the precise details of the procedures with which trustees must comply to fulfil their administrative responsibilities; instead the focus is on the rationale behind the duty or the power and its effect on the role of the trustee, the protection of the trust property, and the interests of the beneficiaries. But, sometimes, it will be necessary to examine key statutory provisions in some detail to determine what the law is trying to achieve, why it is trying to achieve it, and whether it is successful.

13.1.2 THE FUNCTION OF THE TRUST INSTRUMENT

Most of the duties or powers can be expanded, modified, or even excluded by the trust instrument.[1] It follows that the creator of a trust, whether settlor or testator, has a great deal of discretion as to the nature and extent of the trustee's administrative duties and powers.

---

[1] See e.g. Trustee Act 1925, s. 69(2), as regards the powers identified by that statute.

The judge-made rules of Equity and the various statutes provide a menu as to what duties and powers might be available. If they are not mentioned in the trust instrument, they will apply, but, if the creator of the trust does not want the trustee to have one or more of them, they can be excluded or modified; alternatively, the creator of the trust may wish to expand them, save exceptionally if the statute says that the duty or power applies regardless of what the trust instrument states.[2]

13.1.3 APPLICATION TO DIFFERENT TYPES OF TRUSTEE

In what follows, it will be assumed that the trustee whose administrative duties and powers we are considering is an express trustee. The Trustee Act 1925 does, however, define a trustee to include 'implied and constructive trustees',[3] and so the statutory powers and duties are considered to be of general application to all trustees.

13.1.4 BREACH OF TRUST

Breach of any of the administrative duties of a trustee or improper exercise of the administrative powers may involve liability for breach of trust. The nature of this liability is considered in Part VIII of this book. At this stage, it is sufficient to be aware that Equity requires strict compliance with administrative responsibilities. Normally, this means that liability for breach of trust is strict, so that no fault needs to be established and the trustee will be liable even though they considered that what they were doing was correct or was in the best interests of the beneficiaries.[4] But, as will be seen, some duties will be breached only if the trustee has acted unreasonably, so that it becomes necessary to consider issues of fault and the particular responsibility of the individual trustee.

13.1.5 RANGE OF DUTIES

Trustees are subject to a number of specific duties which will be examined in this and subsequent chapters. These duties can be considered to fall within three broad categories, as recognized by Lord Toulson in *AIB Group (UK) plc v Redler and Co*:[5]

(1) a custodial stewardship duty to preserve the trust assets, save to the extent that the trust instrument permits the trustee to do otherwise;

(2) a management stewardship duty to manage the trust assets with proper care; and

(3) a duty of undivided loyalty, which prohibits the trustee from taking advantage of their position without the fully informed consent of the beneficiaries.[6]

All the duties of a trustee can be considered to fall within one of these three categories.

13.2 THE DUTY OF CARE

Trustees are required to perform their administrative responsibilities diligently, and are subject to a duty to comply with the standard of skill and care expected of all trustees. There are two distinct tests of the duty of care: one at common law and the other statutory.

---

[2] See e.g. the power to raise money by selling or mortgaging trust property: Trustee Act 1925, s. 16(2). See Section 13.6.4, p. 396.   [3] Trustee Act 1925, s. 68(17).

[4] Although the trustee may be excused from liability in such circumstances. See Section 17.3.2, p. 481.

[5] [2014] UKSC 58, [2015] AC 1503, [51].

[6] This underpins the fiduciary duty of the trustee, which is considered in Chapter 15 of this volume.

Before the law is analysed, it is important to understand the possible different standards of care to which a trustee might be subject. There are essentially three choices:[7]

(1) A subjective test by virtue of which the trustee is judged by reference to what they are capable of achieving, having regard to their own skills, experience, and knowledge. A trustee will not be liable for breach of duty according to this standard even if they might be considered to have acted incompetently, if the trustee did the best that they could do in the circumstances.

(2) A pure objective test by virtue of which the trustee's conduct is judged against the standard of the reasonable or prudent trustee. According to this test, all trustees are expected to comply with the same standard of skill and care regardless of their skills, experience, and knowledge, or lack of them.

(3) A qualified objective test by virtue of which the trustee is judged against the standard of the reasonable person, but a reasonable person who is deemed to possess those skills, experience, and knowledge of the particular trustee. According to this test, the standard of skill and care expected of the trustee may be higher or lower than that of the reasonable person, depending on what skills, experience, and knowledge the trustee actually has.

13.2.1 COMMON LAW DUTY OF CARE

At common law, trustees are expected to exercise the same standard of diligence and care as an ordinary prudent person of business would exercise in the management of their own affairs.[8] What constitutes the 'affairs' of a business person has sometimes been interpreted to mean their private affairs,[9] or their own business.[10] In many cases, there will be no difference between the standard adopted for one's private affairs and one's business affairs, although a higher standard of care might sometimes be expected when acting in business than in private matters. Sometimes, an alternative test has been adopted, namely the standard that an ordinary prudent person would adopt when acting for the benefit of other people for whom they 'felt morally bound to provide',[11] which might be interpreted to mean that even greater care might be expected of the trustee than in managing one's own private or business affairs.

The common law duty of care has been applied in respect of a variety of administrative actions taken by trustees. So, for example, if a trustee were to wish to delegate administrative functions to an agent, this duty of care would apply as regards the need to delegate, the selection of the agent, and the supervision of the agent.[12] The duty of care could be satisfied if it were reasonably necessary to delegate certain functions or if it were consistent with business practice; similarly, as regards the duty of the trustee to select and review trust investments.[13] The application of the test is particularly well illustrated by *Speight v Gaunt* itself.[14] A trustee was instructed by the beneficiaries of the trust to invest the bulk of the trust assets in securities. On the advice of the beneficiaries, the trustee selected a

---

[7] See generally Getzler, 'Duty of care', in *Breach of Trust*, ed. Birks and Pretto (Oxford: Hart, 2002), pp. 42–3.

[8] *Speight v Gaunt* (1883) 9 App Cas 1, 19 (Lord Blackburn).

[9] *Learoyd v Whiteley* (1887) 12 App Cas 727, 733 (Lord Watson). See also *Mendes v Gruedalla* (1862) 2 J & H 259, 277 (Page Wood V-C).   [10] *Speight v Gaunt* (1883) 22 Ch D 727, 730 (Jessel MR).

[11] *Re Whiteley* (1886) 33 Ch D 347, 355 (Lindley LJ).

[12] See now the statutory duty of care, discussed in Section 13.2.2, p. 376.

[13] *Re Whiteley* (1886) 33 Ch D 347, 355 (Lindley LJ). See now Section 13.4.3, p. 384.

[14] (1883) 22 Ch D 727.

stockbroker, not realizing that the person selected was nearly insolvent. The stockbroker showed the trustee a forged note as evidence that the securities had been purchased. The trustee transferred the trust funds to him and the stockbroker then absconded with the money. The beneficiaries sued the trustee for imprudently choosing and relying on a dishonest agent. It was held that the trustee had not breached his duty of care because he had complied with the standards of business practice at the time, namely to transfer the payment before the securities were executed.

This standard of the ordinary prudent business person is the standard of care that applies to the amateur or gratuitous trustee.[15] It is a purely objective test[16] that pays no regard to the particular skills or experience of the trustee either to reduce or increase the standard of care. This is illustrated by *Re Vickery*,[17] in which the defendant trustee, who had been a missionary in London and who was utterly ignorant of business affairs, was judged against the standard of the reasonable trustee, rather than the reasonable missionary, but was still found not to have breached his duty of care when he chose a local solicitor to administer the trust, who had in fact been suspended from practice and who absconded with the trust property.

If, however, the trustee is a paid professional, a higher standard of care will be required, namely the standard that such a professional would be expected to exhibit[18] because the professional administrator holds themself out as having specialized skills and experience, for which they will be remunerated.[19]

The 'prudent business person' test involves an idealized figure against which the standard of the trustee's performance can be measured. This is an equivalent standard to that which is adopted for the tort of negligence; in fact, the equitable duty of care can be regarded as having now been assimilated into the Common Law tort of negligence and outside the exclusive jurisdiction of Equity.[20] It follows that liability for breach of this duty of care is subject to the same rules and remedies as the tort of negligence, including, for example, that the trustee's liability will be subject to the defence of contributory negligence.

Even if the trustees have apparently not satisfied the standard of skill and care, it does not follow that they will be liable to the beneficiaries, since the beneficiaries also need to show that, had the trustees complied with the relevant standard of skill and care, this would have affected the trust.[21] This is a difficult burden to satisfy. So, for example, in *Nestlé v National Westminster Bank plc*,[22] the trustee bank breached its duty of care in its management of the trust's investments, but it was not liable to the beneficiaries because it could not be shown that the trust would have benefited financially had there been better management of the investments.

13.2.2 THE STATUTORY DUTY OF CARE

The Trustee Act 2000 creates a statutory duty of care that now applies when trustees carry out most administrative powers and perform most duties. As regards all other powers and duties, the common law duty of care still applies, most notably to the dispositive powers of appointment of trust property to beneficiaries,[23] of maintenance,[24] and of advancement.[25]

---

[15] *Speight v Gaunt* (1883) 22 Ch D 727, 740 (Jessel MR).   [16] See Section 13.2, p. 375.

[17] [1931] 1 Ch 572, 573 (Maugham J).

[18] *Re Waterman's Will Trusts* [1952] 2 All ER 1054, 1055 (Harman J); *Bartlett v Barclays Bank Trust Co Ltd* [1980] Ch 515, 534 (Brightman J).   [19] *Re Waterman's Will Trusts* [1952] 2 All ER 1054, 1055 (Harman J).

[20] *Henderson v Merrett Syndicates Ltd* [1995] 2 AC 145; *Bristol and West Building Society v Mothew* [1998] Ch 1; *Swindle v Harrison* [1997] 4 All ER 705. See Getzler (n. 7), p. 71.

[21] It must also be shown that the loss arose from the breach of duty. See Section 18.3.2, p. 522.

[22] [1993] 1 WLR 1260. See further Section 13.4.3.(i), p. 385.

[23] See Section 14.2, p. 402.   [24] See Section 14.4, p. 412.   [25] See Section 14.5, p. 414.

One of the most controversial issues in this area concerns the extent, if any, to which the common law duty of care and the statutory duty of care are different.[26]

The statutory duty of care requires a trustee to exercise such care and skill as is reasonable in the circumstances, having regard in particular to any special knowledge or experience that they have or hold themselves out as having and, where the trustee is acting as a trustee in the course of a business or profession, to any knowledge or experience that it is reasonable to expect of a person acting in that kind of business or profession.[27] So, for example, a solicitor who acts as a professional trustee will be expected to comply with a higher standard of care than an amateur trustee, because of the knowledge and experience that it is reasonable to assume that the solicitor will have acquired.

This statutory duty of care applies to particular identified powers of trustees, whether they arise under the Trustee Act 2000 itself or other statutes or under the trust instrument.[28] The relevant powers include: any power of investment; the power to acquire land; the power to appoint agents, nominees, and custodians; and the power to insure trust property. The statutory duty of care can be excluded by the trust instrument.[29]

The standard of the statutory duty of care is essentially a purely objective test,[30] since it is the standard of reasonableness. All trustees have to comply with the standard of the reasonable trustee, even those trustees who are plainly incompetent and unsuited to the task. This is the threshold standard of care. The statute does, however, state that the test of reasonableness is assessed with regard to what is reasonable 'in the circumstances'. Could this be interpreted to mean that, if the defendant is unskilled, inexperienced, or incompetent, the standard of care would be reduced, so that the standard becomes subjective and it is sufficient that the defendant acted honestly? The better view is that the defendant's circumstances should not be taken into account to reduce the standard of care below that of the reasonable trustee. The incompetent trustee should not be absolved from responsibility simply because they are plainly unsuited to the task; every trustee should be expected to comply at least with the threshold standard of objective reasonableness. But what is reasonable in the circumstances should be influenced by factors such as the size of the trust fund and the complexity of the trust.

What is made explicitly clear by the statute, however, is that the standard of care expected of trustees can be raised if the trustee possesses particular knowledge or experience. This will occur in two situations. First, if the trustee is acting in the course of a business or profession, the standard of care is what it is reasonable to expect of a person in that business or profession.[31] This can be regarded as a purely objective test, which applies to all professional trustees, such as banks, solicitors, and trust corporations. So, for example, a solicitor who is a trustee will be expected to comply with a higher standard of care in administering the trust than will an amateur trustee.

Secondly, the pure objective test of reasonableness will be qualified if the trustee has particular knowledge or experience or holds themself out as having such knowledge and experience.[32] This will apply both where the trustee is not acting professionally but has built up experience having acted as a trustee previously, and where the trustee is a professional but has advanced knowledge or experience beyond that of a reasonable professional. So, for example, more will be expected of a solicitor trustee who has professional experience of trust work than of a solicitor trustee who only had experience of a criminal practice.

---

[26] See Section 13.2.3, p. 378.   [27] Trustee Act 2000, s. 1(1).   [28] Ibid., Sch. 1.
[29] Ibid., para. 7. But note the Pension Act 1995, s. 33, which prevents the exclusion or restriction of the duty of care as regards the exercise of investment powers in pension trusts.
[30] See Section 13.2, p. 375.   [31] Trustee Act 2000, s. 1(1)(b).   [32] Ibid., s. 1(1)(a).

13.2.3 THE RELATIONSHIP BETWEEN THE TWO TESTS

The creation of a statutory duty of care based on reasonableness in the circumstances was proposed by the Law Commission,[33] which rejected the common law language of the prudent person of business. A number of reasons were identified for this decision, including that adopting a 'prudent business person' test would simply involve a restatement of the common law test; that the statutory standard has explicit regard to the particular skills of the trustee; that the standard of care must be robust and demanding; and that there may, in fact, be little difference between the two alternatives. Indeed, the Law Commission stated that the 'statutory duty of care probably represents no more than a codification of the existing common law duty'.[34]

In light of this, are there any significant differences between the two tests, or should they be regarded as essentially the same test, but formulated in different language? The preferable view is that the statutory test does indeed constitute a codification of the common law test.[35] Both tests involve a purely objective core, whereby all trustees must comply with an objective standard, whether that is described with reference to the prudent business person or the reasonable person. The standard of care for both tests is higher where the particular trustee is a professional. Admittedly, the statutory test qualifies the objective test where the trustee has particular skills or experience, but this would presumably be true of the common law test too, since the justification for raising the standard expected from professional trustees is that they hold themselves out as having specific skills or experience. Presumably any trustee with particular skills or experience would also have to comply with a higher standard of care at common law, even if they were not a professional.

Consequently, it should not matter whether the common law or statutory test applies; the same rules on determining the standard of care will operate. But we have not yet had a case that explicitly confirms this conclusion. So it is still necessary to exercise some caution in assessing the relationship between the two tests, particularly because the statutory test is formulated more expansively than that at common law. But it could be of real practical significance that the tests are effectively identical. In particular, if the trust instrument purports to exclude the statutory duty of care, this should be interpreted as impliedly excluding the common law test as well.

13.3 DUTY TO SAFEGUARD TRUST ASSETS

The trustees are responsible for safeguarding the trust assets for the benefit of the beneficiaries. This means, for example, that, on appointment, a trustee must ensure that the trust funds are properly invested and that trust assets, such as securities and chattels, are kept securely.[36] This duty also means that, if money is owed to the trust, the trustees must take all reasonable steps to ensure that the debt is discharged. This is illustrated by *Re Brogden*,[37] in which a testator had covenanted to pay £10,000 to the trustees of his daughter's marriage settlement within five years of his death. This money was due from a family partnership run by the testator's sons. The trustees of the marriage settlement sought payment of the £10,000 from the sons on a number of occasions, but did not start doing

---

[33] Law Commission, *Trustees' Powers and Duties*, Law Com No. 260 (London: HMSO, 1999).
[34] Ibid., p. 25.
[35] See *Pitt v Holt* [2011] EWCA Civ 197, [2012] Ch 132, [107] (Lloyd LJ). This issue was not considered on appeal to the Supreme Court.   [36] *Re Miller's Deed Trust* (1978) 75 LS Gaz 454.
[37] (1888) 38 Ch D 546 See also *Re Greenwood* (1911) 105 LT 509.

so until four months after the end of the five-year period. The partnership was becoming less prosperous and the trustees did not wish to precipitate a crisis by suing for the money, which would jeopardize the solvency of the firm, but they did obtain security for the money that was due. Eventually, the partnership became insolvent and the security proved worthless. The trustees of the marriage settlement were held to be liable for breach of trust in not taking all reasonable steps to obtain payment of the £10,000, which was recognized as involving a duty to sue for payment if the money was not forthcoming.

It does not follow, however, that trustees must sue for money that is owed to the trust in every case. In the particular circumstances of the case, other courses of action might be more appropriate, but the trustees bear the burden of proving that it was not reasonable to sue for payment.[38] So, for example, in *Re Ezekiel's Settlement Trust*,[39] it was held to be appropriate for a trustee to enter into a compromise[40] as regards money that was owed to the trust, even though the beneficiary wanted the full amount due to be recovered through litigation. Resorting to litigation was not considered to be a reasonable course of action since there was an unacceptable risk that the trust might suffer a loss as the result of bearing the costs of the litigation. Similarly, in *Ward v Ward*,[41] a trustee was held not to have committed a breach of trust by failing to call for money owed to the trust by a beneficiary, since this would have resulted in the bankruptcy of the beneficiary.

13.4 DUTY TO INVEST

13.4.1 GENERAL PRINCIPLES

Trustees are subject to statutory duties under the Trustee Act 2000 to invest the trust fund, to review the trust investments from time to time, and to consider whether they should be varied.[42] Trustees also have a range of discretionary powers relating to the selection and sale of investments.

In the nineteenth century, the duties of trustees to invest and to review trust investments was not particularly significant, since the subject matter of many trusts was usually a landed estate, which simply had to be managed for the benefit of the beneficiaries. But, with the expansion of the trust into the commercial sphere, the subject matter of the trust is increasingly money and securities, such as shares. For some trusts, especially pension and unit trusts, the trust property may be worth many millions of pounds. Consequently, the duty to invest has become much more significant. Even for smaller family trusts, the obligation to invest trust property is much more important than it used to be.

(i) Duty of impartiality between beneficiaries

The paramount duty of trustees is to exercise their investment powers in the best interests of both present and future beneficiaries.[43] There are two significant, and possibly contradictory, principles that arise from this duty.[44]

Safeguarding the fund

Trustees must safeguard the trust fund for the benefit of the beneficiaries, present and future. The consequence of this principle is usually that trustees must at least preserve

---

[38] Ibid.   [39] [1942] Ch 230.
[40] By virtue of the power to compound liabilities under the Trustee Act 1925, s. 15. See Section 13.9, p. 400.
[41] (1843) 2 HL Cas 777n.   [42] Trustee Act 2000, s. 4(2).
[43] *Cowan v Scargill* [1985] Ch 270, 286–7 (Sir Robert Megarry V-C).
[44] See Law Commission, Law Com No. 260 (see n. 33), p. 18.

the capital value of the trust fund. This principle encourages trustees to adopt a conservative investment policy, which seeks to avoid taking significant risks with the investment by speculating with the trust fund.[45] This was the approach to investment in Victorian times, when trusts were intended to preserve capital and ensure that the beneficiaries had a steady, albeit conservative, stream of income.[46] As Legatt LJ has acknowledged, 'the importance of preservation of a trust fund will always outweigh success in its advancement . . . the virtue of safety will in practice put a premium on inactivity'.[47]

Maximizing the fund

A more modern approach to investment policy is to recognize that trustees must maximize returns for the benefit of the beneficiaries.[48] This principle encourages trustees to speculate with the trust fund, so as to obtain a good income from investments and to ensure that the capital value of the fund increases. This principle requires trustees to have the widest possible investment powers, so that they can invest the trust assets in the most appropriate way for the benefit of the trust.

(ii) Definition of investment

Although there is no statutory definition of 'investment', it was defined by P O Lawrence J in *Re Wragg*[49] as involving the application of 'money in the purchase of some property from which interest or profit is expected and which property is purchased in order to be held for the sake of the income which it will yield'. So, for example, if trustees purchase shares with money from the trust fund, the aim will be to ensure both that the capital value of the shares increases, so that, when they are eventually sold, they can be sold at a profit, and that the trust will obtain a regular income in the form of dividend payments, which can be distributed to the beneficiaries or used to purchase more shares. The definition of investment in *Re Wragg* suggests that the trustees cannot invest in items that will not provide an income stream, such as antiques or gold. The notes to the Trustee Act 2000, which are not binding, indicate, however, that trustees are permitted to invest in assets that are expected to produce either an income return or a capital return, so investment in assets that will not yield an income can still count as legitimate investments. To avoid the possibility of any doubt about this, it would be appropriate for the creator of the trust to include a specific power in the trust instrument to enable trustees to invest in such non-income-producing assets.

(iii) Portfolio theory

The old approach to selecting trust investments was to look at each investment independently, and to determine whether its acquisition and retention could be justified with regard to the dual principles of safeguarding the fund and maximizing growth. This approach to investment selection tended to be risk-adverse, so that trustees would not take significant risks with their investments.[50] The modern approach to investment practice is called 'portfolio theory'.[51] According to this theory, investors should have regard to

---

[45] *Learoyd v Whiteley* (1887) 12 App Cas 727, 733 (Lord Watson).
[46] *Nestlé v National Westminster Bank plc* [1993] 1 WLR 1260, 1281(Legatt LJ).
[47] Ibid., at 1284.   [48] *Re Wragg* [1919] 2 Ch 58, 65 (P O Lawrence J).
[49] Ibid.   [50] Ford, 'Trustee investment and modern portfolio theory' (1996) 10 TLI 102.
[51] Lord Nicholls of Birkenhead, 'Trustees and their broader community: where duty, morality and ethics converge' (1995) 9 TLI 71, 75; Ford (see n. 50); Thornton, 'Ethical investments: a case of disjointed thinking' (2008) 67 CLJ 396, 399–401. For a more mathematical analysis of modern portfolio theory, see Legair, 'Modern portfolio theory: a primer' (2000) 14 TLI 75.

the composition of their investments as a whole, known as the 'portfolio', to determine whether they are balanced and suit the needs of the particular trust. A balanced portfolio of investments will have a mixture of different types of investment and in different sectors, including sectors that are in competition with each other. In this way, if one sector does not perform well, the chances are that the other competing sector will perform better. This is called 'diversification' of the investment. So, for example, trustees might wish to invest in the shares of an umbrella manufacturer and also the shares of a suntan lotion manufacturer.[52] If there is a wet summer, the sale of umbrellas will increase, with a consequent good return on that investment; if there is a hot, dry summer, the better return will be on the shares in the suntan lotion manufacturer.

Another factor in ensuring that there is a balanced portfolio of investments is through careful management of the risk of loss. If the trust fund is large, it will be possible to include some investments in high-risk securities, which can then be balanced by investments in low-risk securities. In this way, if the high-risk securities do not perform well and a loss is suffered, the trust fund still has the low-risk securities to provide some stability in the value of the fund. Where the trust fund is small, it will not be prudent to invest in high-risk securities, because there will not then be sufficient funds to invest in low-risk securities to ensure a balance of risk. The significance of portfolio theory to the management of risk is that the emphasis is placed on the risk level of the entire portfolio rather than the risk being attached to each investment in isolation.[53] Consequently, an investment that, when examined in isolation, might be considered to be too risky for the trust such that the purchase of that investment would constitute a breach of trust, might be justified when considered in conjunction with the other less risky investments of the trust.

13.4.2 INVESTMENT POWERS

Trustees have extensive statutory powers relating to their duty to invest. These investment powers are provided by Part II of the Trustee Act 2000. They also apply to charity trustees.[54] A key function of the Trustee Act 2000 was to create statutory powers of investment that are consistent with modern investment practice.

(i) General power of investment

Part II of the Trustee Act 2000 makes provision for a general power of investment by trustees. This is a power to make any kind of investment that the trustee could make if they were absolutely entitled to the trust property,[55] save for investments in land other than loans that are secured on land, such as by a mortgage.[56] The general power of investment applies to most trusts, even those that were settled before 2001 when the Trustee Act came into force,[57] save that the general power can be expanded, restricted, or excluded by the trust instrument.[58] The general power of investment does not apply to trustees of pension schemes,[59] or authorized unit trusts,[60] or to charitable trustees who are managing

---

[52] See Ford (n. 50).

[53] *Nestlé v National Westminster Bank plc* (1996) 10 TLI 113, 115 (Hoffmann J).

[54] For additional rules on investment by charitable trustees, see Section 13.4.2.(vii), p. 383. See generally the Charity Commission's guidance, *Charities and Investment Matters: A Guide for Trustees*, CC14 (2016).

[55] Trustee Act 2000, s. 3(1).

[56] Ibid., s. 3(3). Investments in land are permitted, but these are covered by special powers under s. 8. See Section 13.4.2.(vi), p. 383.   [57] Trustee Act 2000, s. 7.

[58] Ibid., s. 6(1).   [59] Ibid., s. 36(3). Their investment powers are governed by the Pensions Act 1995.

[60] Trustee Act 2000, s. 37(1).

common investment or common deposit schemes,[61] since alternative statutory provision is made for these trustees.

(ii) Standard investment criteria

In exercising the general power of investment or any power of investment, such as one created by the trust instrument, the trustee is under a duty to have regard to the so-called 'standard investment criteria'.[62] These criteria also apply where trustees are reviewing the investments.[63] There are two criteria,[64] which reflect the key principles of portfolio theory.

Suitability

Trustees must consider the suitability to the trust of the particular investment. Whether an investment is suitable, or continues to be suitable, will require the trustees to consider various factors. Two of the most significant relate to the size of the trust fund and the anticipated length of the trust: the smaller the fund and the shorter the anticipated life of the trust, the more appropriate it will be to make a short-term investment, such as depositing the fund in an interest-bearing bank account; if the fund is large and the trust is anticipated to continue for a substantial period of time, it will be more appropriate to consider making a long-term investment. Another factor that will need to be considered concerns the degree of risk attaching to the investment. It is usually not appropriate for the trustees to take unacceptable risks with investments, for example by speculating in a start-up business. Such risks may, however, be more defensible if the risk can be spread by making some safer investments. This spreading of the risk will be easier to do if the fund is large.

Diversification

Trustees must also consider the need to diversify the investments, but only so far as this is appropriate to the circumstances of the trust. This also requires the trustees to consider the relative risk of loss and gain, but they must also ensure that they invest in competing sectors, so that if one sector is doing less well, another sector might do much better and give a better return.[65] In *Cowan v Scargill*,[66] Megarry V-C recognized that the 'circumstances of the trust' for these purposes include the size of the trust fund, since the degree of diversification that is practicable and desirable for a large fund may be impracticable and undesirable for a small fund.

(iii) Duty to obtain advice

Before exercising any power of investment, whether under the statute or by virtue of a power included in the trust instrument,[67] or when reviewing the trust investments,[68] a trustee is under a duty to obtain and consider proper advice about how the power should be exercised in the light of the standard investment criteria. The advice of a person will be considered to be 'proper' where the trustee reasonably believes that the person is qualified to give the advice by virtue of their ability in, and practical experience of, financial and other matters relating to the proposed investment.[69] The duty to obtain advice does not apply, however, where the trustee reasonably concludes that it is not necessary or appropriate to obtain such advice,[70] perhaps because the fund is relatively small so that the cost of obtaining the advice might be more than the value of the investment, or where the

---

[61] Ibid., s. 38. See Section 13.4.2.(vi), p. 383.   [62] Ibid., s. 4(1).   [63] Ibid., s. 4(2).
[64] Ibid., s. 4(3).   [65] See further Section 13.4.1.(iii), p. 380.   [66] [1985] Ch 270, 289.
[67] Trustee Act 2000, s. 5(1).   [68] Ibid., s. 5(2).   [69] Ibid., s. 5(4).   [70] Ibid., s. 5(3).

trustee is a professional investment adviser. The trustee is not required to follow the advice obtained, but it must be reasonable to decide not to do so.[71]

(iv) Duty of care

When exercising any power of investment, including the general power of investment, when considering the standard investment criteria, and when obtaining investment advice, the statutory duty of care applies,[72] so that the trustee must exercise such care and skill as is reasonable in the circumstances.[73]

(v) Delegation of investment powers

Investment powers can be delegated to an agent,[74] who will be bound by any restrictions on the exercise of those powers in the same way as would be the trustee.[75] So, for example, an agent who is authorized to exercise the general power of investment must also have regard to the standard investment criteria. An agent is not, however, required to obtain investment advice if they are the kind of person from whom it would have been proper for the trustees to obtain such advice,[76] such as a financial adviser.

(vi) Purchase of land

Trustees have a statutory power to acquire freehold or leasehold land in the UK, whether as an investment, or for occupation by the beneficiary, or for any other reason.[77] Trustees do not, therefore, have a statutory power to acquire land abroad, although this power can be provided by the trust instrument. The key reason why a default power to buy land abroad was not included in the Trustee Act 2000 is that trusts are not universally recognized abroad and the purchase of land for a trust in a country that does not recognize the trust might cause difficulties.

This statutory power is in addition to powers otherwise conferred on the trustee, such as by the trust instrument, and may be restricted or excluded by the trust instrument.[78] The statutory duty of care applies to the exercise of any power to acquire land.[79] The trustees who exercise the power to acquire land have all of the powers of an absolute owner in relation to that land for the purpose of exercising their functions as trustees.[80]

(vii) Common investment funds for charities

The court and the Charity Commission have the power to create a common investment scheme under which property transferred to the scheme by two or more participating charities is invested by trustees who are appointed to manage the fund.[81] This provides a useful mechanism for participating charitable trusts collectively to get the benefit of expert investment experience. The participating charities are entitled to the capital and income of the fund in proportion to the value that they contributed to the fund in the first place.

(viii) Duty to obtain the best price

When trustees are buying and selling trust property, they are under a duty to obtain the best price and must not be influenced by ethical or moral considerations. When selling trust property, the best way of satisfying this duty is by stirring up competition. This could be done by auctioning the property. But, in a private sale, if one purchaser is played off against

---

[71] See *Cowan v Scargill* [1985] Ch 270, 289 (Megarry V-C).   [72] Trustee Act 2000, Sch. 1, para. 1.
[73] See Section 13.2.2, p. 376.   [74] Trustee Act 2000, Pt IV. See Section 13.7, p. 397.
[75] Ibid., s. 13(1).   [76] Ibid., s. 13(2).   [77] Ibid., s. 8(1).   [78] Ibid., s. 9.
[79] Ibid., Sch. 1, para. 2.   [80] Ibid., s. 8(1).   [81] Charities Act 2011, s. 96.

another, there is a danger that both will be lost, and, if the trust suffers a loss as a result, the trustees could be liable for breach of trust. So, there must be a point at which the reasonable trustee would accept an offer to purchase property, even though there is a possibility that somebody else might make a higher offer. When it is reasonable to do this will depend on market conditions and how easy it is to sell the property.[82] If the market is strong, the reasonable trustee will be more likely to hold out for a better offer, but, if the market is weak, it will be more reasonable to accept an offer that might be considered to be relatively low.

There will be circumstances under which trustees may even have to act dishonourably for the benefit of the trust.[83] So, even where trustees have accepted an offer to sell property, if they subsequently receive a better offer, they should typically renege on the first and accept the second. In other words, there is a duty to 'gazump'.

The application of these principles is especially well illustrated by *Buttle v Saunders*.[84] In that case, the trustees had orally agreed to sell land to Mrs Simpson for £6,142. One of the beneficiaries of the trust, Buttle, wished to buy the land for a charity and offered £6,500 for it. The trustees felt that they had reached a stage in the negotiations with Mrs Simpson from which they could not honourably withdraw as a matter of commercial morality. Buttle sought an injunction to restrain the trustees from selling at a price lower than that which he had offered. In granting the injunction, Wynn-Parry J accepted that, whereas vendors who are not trustees can accept a lower offer for their property if they so wish, trustees are not vested with such complete freedom; rather they have an overriding duty to obtain the best price that they can for their beneficiaries. It does not follow, however, that the trustees must automatically accept an increased offer, however late it is made in the course of negotiations with another purchaser. Rather, the trustees have a discretion to act with proper prudence, bearing in mind that 'a bird in the hand is worth two in the bush'. In other words, there may be circumstances under which it is prudent to reject the higher offer, for example because of a real risk that the offeror will renege on it. But each case turns on its facts. In *Buttle*, the trustees were willing to take into account an irrelevant consideration, namely that it was commercially immoral to renege on the prior negotiations. They should instead have spent time probing Buttle's offer, since there was little risk that Mrs Simpson would have withdrawn her offer, because she had a leasehold interest in the property that was drawing to an end and she may well have paid more to stay in the property. In fact, in the end, Mrs Simpson increased her offer to that made by Buttle and this offer was accepted by the trust.

13.4.3 SELECTING INVESTMENTS

(i) General principles

When trustees select investments, they must have regard to the principles of portfolio theory, as embodied in the standard investment criteria.[85] A number of distinct principles can be identified to assist in the selection of investments:

(1) Trustees must ensure that the investments chosen are permitted by the terms of the trust.[86]

(2) The investments should be diversified, so that the trustees do not, for example, invest all of the funds in one account or the shares of one particular company.

---

[82] Samuels, 'The duty of trustees to obtain the best price' [1975] Conv 177, 181.
[83] *Cowan v Scargill* [1985] Ch 270, 288 (Megarry V-C).
[84] [1950] 2 All ER 193.   [85] See Section 13.4.2.(ii), p. 382.
[86] *Speight v Gaunt* (1883) 9 App Cas 1, 19 (Lord Blackburn).

(3) Trustees should avoid investments that are particularly risky.[87] The key aim is to obtain the best return for the beneficiaries having regard to the risks of the investments, and the prospects of income yield and capital appreciation.[88]

(4) Trustees are not generally required to consult the beneficiaries on the selection of investments, unless this is required by the trust instrument, and are not bound to act on the wishes of beneficiaries when selecting investments, but they should consider the comments of beneficiaries and take them into account as appropriate.[89]

(5) Different types of beneficiary will have different interests in the types of investment made and the trustees must ensure that they have regard not only to the interests of those who are entitled to the income, such as the life tenant, but also to the interests of those who will take in the future, such as those who are entitled to the remainder.[90] Consequently, the trustees have a duty to exercise their investment powers in the best interests of present and future beneficiaries, and should hold the scales impartially between different classes of beneficiary.[91]

The significance of this duty to balance fairly the interests of beneficiaries is illustrated by *Nestlé v National Westminster Bank plc*,[92] in which the bank was trustee of the testator's estate in which his sons had life interests and to which, on their deaths, his granddaughter would become absolutely entitled. She sued the bank for breach of trust, claiming that the fund, which was worth just over £250,000, should have been worth £1.8 million. She claimed that the investment policy adopted by the bank had focused on investments that favoured the life tenants, by providing good income, but little capital growth, to the detriment of her own interest in the remainder, which meant that the trust fund was worth less than it should have been. This occurred, she alleged, because the trustee bank had adopted a policy of reducing the life tenants' tax liability by investing in tax-exempt products that did not increase the capital value of the fund. Her claim failed because she had failed to discharge the burden of proving loss to the trust fund by showing that, had the trustees adopted a different investment policy, this would have increased the capital value of the trust fund. But the Court of Appeal did acknowledge the duty of trustees to balance or ensure fairness as between the interests of present and future beneficiaries impartially. Further, if it could have been shown that, had the trustees adopted a different investment policy, the value of the fund would have increased, the trustee bank might have been liable to compensate the fund with its liability founded on breach of trust. Even if loss were not established as a result of the investment decisions, if it could have been shown that the trustees had breached the duty of maintaining a fair balance, other remedies might have been available, such as injunctive relief or an application being made by the beneficiaries to have the trustees replaced.[93]

(ii) Ethical considerations

General principles

To what extent is it appropriate for trustees to take into account ethical considerations when selecting investments?[94] This was considered by Sir Robert Megarry V-C in the important case of *Cowan v Scargill*,[95] which concerned a pension fund for employees and former employees of the National Coal Board (NCB). The fund was managed by ten trustees,

[87] *Learoyd v Whiteley* (1887) 12 App Cas 727, 733 (Lord Watson).
[88] *Cowan v Scargill* [1985] Ch 270, 287 (Megarry V-C).
[89] *X v A* [2000] 1 All ER 490, 496 (Arden LJ).   [90] *Re Whiteley* (1886) 33 Ch D 347, 350 (Cotton LJ).
[91] *Cowan v Scargill* [1985] Ch 270, 287 (Mergarry V-C). For the general duty to balance the interests of beneficiaries, see Section 13.5, p. 391.
[92] [1993] 1 WLR 1260.   [93] See Section 12.6.4, p. 353.   [94] Thornton (see n. 51).
[95] [1985] Ch 270.

five of whom were appointed by the NCB and five by the National Union of Mineworkers (NUM). One of the latter trustees was Arthur Scargill, the NUM president. The pension fund had previously made overseas investments in oil and gas, industries that competed with the English coal-mining industry. When a revised investment plan was being considered by the trustees, the five NUM trustees refused to accept it unless there was no increase in overseas investment; existing overseas investment would be withdrawn at an appropriate time; and there would be no investment in energies that directly competed with coal. The NCB trustees applied to the court for directions as to whether it was appropriate to take such ethical considerations into account when making investment decisions. It was held that the NUM trustees had committed a breach of trust by taking into account ethical consideration when considering the investment plan. Further, where the purpose of the trust is the provision of financial benefits for the beneficiaries, the key duty of the trustees is to ensure that the investments provided the greatest financial benefits for present and future beneficiaries. Consequently, when the trust is a pension fund, the power of investment must be exercised to yield the best return for the beneficiaries, having regard to the risk of the investment, but without regard to ethical considerations. So, for example, a decision not to purchase South African investments could have been justified with reference to political instability in South Africa and concerns about the financial soundness of its economy, but not with reference to social and political factors such as working conditions in South Africa.

The court also held that it made no difference to the rules on the selection of investments that the trust was a pension fund, save that the large size of the fund meant that diversification of the fund was more significant, and because most of the funds had been contributed by the members of the scheme, so that it was important that the trustees exercised their investment powers in the best interests of the beneficiaries so that they might receive the benefits for which they had paid. In other words, if anything, ethical considerations were of even less significance to such trusts.

The importance of the decision in *Cowan v Scargill* is the recognition of the principle that trustees should put aside their personal interests and views when selecting investments. So, for example, if a trustee is personally opposed to the tobacco industry or the trade in armaments, the trust should still invest in such industries if they give a better financial return. This approach to ethical considerations when selecting investments is consistent with the general duty to safeguard assets, under which trustees must put aside moral considerations and, if it is appropriate to do so, gazump for the benefit of the trust.[96]

The operation of this principle when selecting investments is particularly well illustrated by a decision of the Scottish courts in *Martin v City of Edinburgh DC*,[97] in which the District Council was a trustee which had withdrawn trust investments in South Africa as a protest against that country's apartheid policy. It was held that this constituted a breach of trust, since the councillors had not considered the effect of the investment policy on the interests of the trust. Lord Murray said:[98]

> A trustee cannot be expected to divest himself of political beliefs or all moral, religious or other conscientiously held principles. He should recognise that he has preferences and do his best to exercise fair and impartial judgment on the issues before him. If he cannot then he should abstain from participating in deciding the issue or, in an extreme case, resign as trustee.

---

[96] *Buttle v Saunders* [1950] 2 All ER 193, 195 (Wynn-Parry J). See Section 13.4.2.(viii), p. 384.
[97] [1988] SLT 329.   [98] Ibid., 334.

Qualifications of the general principles

The general principle in favour of ignoring ethical and non-financial considerations when selecting investments is qualified in certain circumstances. But these qualifications will apply only exceptionally and there will be a heavy burden of proof placed on the person who asserts that such considerations should be taken into account.

(1) Where there is a choice of two investments that are equally economically beneficial to the beneficiaries, it is legitimate for the trustees to have regard to ethical considerations to choose between them.[99]

(2) If the beneficiaries are all adults with full legal capacity and who are absolutely entitled to the trust property, it is legitimate for the trustees to have regard to ethical considerations when selecting investments if all of the beneficiaries have strict views on such matters.[100] This effectively involves an application of the principle in *Saunders v Vautier*,[101] not to terminate the trust, but to qualify the normal rules on selecting investments. So, for example, if all of the beneficiaries are adults, absolutely entitled to the trust property, and have very strict moral views, such as being opposed to alcohol, tobacco, and sale of armaments, it might not be for their benefit to know that they are obtaining larger financial returns from investments in such activities, and they might prefer to receive less rather than more from tainted sources. Consequently, there might be situations in which investments that work to the beneficiaries' financial disadvantage may still be regarded as beneficial to them.

(3) The settlor or testator can exclude certain investments from the power of investment on ethical grounds or may explicitly require the trustees to have regard to ethical considerations when selecting investments.[102] This will involve a reduction of the general investment powers of trustees, but it is possible to do this by the trust instrument.[103]

(4) If a pension trust has an ethical investment policy, this must be explicit.[104]

Charities

The general principles relating to the selection of investments apply to charity trustees as well, but, crucially, there is greater scope for such trustees to have regard to ethical considerations. The extent to which charity trustees can have regard to ethical considerations was examined in *Harries v Church Commissioners for England*,[105] in which the Bishop of Oxford and the Christian Ethical Investment Group claimed that the Church Commissioners, whose charitable purpose was to promote the Christian faith through the Church of England, should not select investments that were incompatible with that purpose, even if it involved significant financial detriment to the charity.

Nicholls V-C identified the following general principles relating to investment by charitable trustees.

(1) When selecting investments, the trustees have a duty to further the purpose of the trust and should seek to obtain the maximum return by income or capital growth that is consistent with commercial prudence.

---

[99] This is criticized by Thornton as being unrealistic, since it is inconceivable that there would be no legitimate financial ground on which to distinguish between two investments: Thornton (see n. 51), p. 405.

[100] *Cowan v Scargill* [1985] Ch 270, 288 (Megarry V-C).

[101] (1841) Cr & Ph 240. See Section 11.4.1, p. 334.

[102] *Harries v Church Commissioners for England* [1992] 1 WLR 1241, 1247 (Nicholls V-C).

[103] Trustee Act 2000, s. 6(1). See Section 13.4.2.(i), p. 381.

[104] Pension Act 1995, s. 35.   [105] [1992] 1 WLR 1241.

(2) Usually, the best interests of the charity will require that the investments be chosen solely with reference to well-established investment criteria.

(3) Exceptionally, choosing certain types of investment will conflict with the aims of the charity and the trustees should then not invest in such investments even if this would result in significant financial detriment to the charity. So, for example, trustees of a charity the purpose of which is to conduct research into cancer would not be required to invest in tobacco companies, and trustees of a temperance charity would not be expected to invest in breweries and distilleries. Usually, the exclusion of such investments from the portfolio would not result in financial detriment to the charity, since the trustees should be able to make investments that produce an equivalent financial return.

(4) Exceptionally, purchasing certain investments might actually hamper the charity's work and so the trustees would not be expected to do so. For example, if the charity invested in an industry or a country that potential recipients of the charity's aid might consider to be ethically or morally suspect, the result of such investment might be that the potential recipients would not seek aid from the charity. Similarly, such investments might alienate potential donors from supporting the charity. In such a situation, the trustees would need to balance the difficulties of fulfilling its charitable purpose and the risk of financial loss from donors against the risk of financial detriment from not selecting the particular investments. The greater the risk of financial detriment, the more certain the trustees should be of countervailing disadvantages to the charity as a result of the reaction of those who might otherwise seek aid from, or donate money to, the charity.

In applying these principles, it was recognized that the Charity Commissioners had adopted an ethical investment policy and that it was legitimate for them to do so. The Commissioners had a policy of not investing in companies the main business of which involved armaments, gambling, alcohol, or tobacco. These had been excluded from the portfolio, because there was a significant body of opinion within the members of the Church of England that was opposed to such businesses on religious or moral grounds, and, crucially, there were alternative investments that the Commissioners could make to obtain an equivalent financial return. This was held to be legitimate. The Commissioners also had a policy of not investing in newspapers, because many newspapers were associated with particular political parties or political views, investment in which might compromise the neutrality of the Commissioners. This was also held to be a legitimate policy to adopt. The recognition of the relevance of the members' beliefs is particularly significant. It is unclear to what extent this is an application of principle (4) above, concerning the effects of a particular investment policy on recipients of aid or donors, or whether it is an extension of that principle, or even the recognition of a new principle.

The decision in *Bishop of Oxford* has been criticized for being unnecessarily restrictive on charity investment.[106] When trustees of charities are making decisions about giving away money to those who are to benefit from the charitable purpose, they are free to make controversial moral judgements, so, it has been suggested, they should be allowed to make similar moral judgements when determining their investment policies. But a distinction needs to be drawn between direct and indirect fulfilment of the charity's purposes. When making distributions, trustees are directly benefiting the objects and have a free discretion as to whom or what they will benefit subject to the restrictions of the trust instrument. But, when making investment decisions that have indirect effects on the fulfilment of the charity's objectives, the ultimate aim is to maximize the financial return for the furtherance

---

[106] See particularly Nobles, 'Charities and ethical investment' [1992] Conv 115.

of those purposes, and so restrictions are properly imposed on what the trustees can and cannot take into account when determining their investment policies. In other words, the distinction is between administrative and dispositive decisions, a distinction that is just as relevant to charitable trusts as it is to private trusts. Determining investment policy is an administrative matter and raises different considerations from making appointments of trust property.

The *Bishop of Oxford* case identifies some significant and useful principles to assist charity trustees in developing an investment policy. But how will these principles actually be applied in practice? For example, what about a charitable higher education institution that invests in the oil industry? If the students who study at that institution demand that the charity should sell those investments on ethical grounds, by virtue of concern about climate change, should the trustees do so? The starting point must be that the charity trustees need to secure the best financial return for the charity. It would be very difficult to argue that they should sell the investments if the trustees cannot obtain an equivalent financial return from other investments. But, assuming that there are satisfactory alternative investments available, should the trustees sell the oil investments? Although the use of such a charity's funds to buy investments in the oil industry is unlikely to be incompatible with the aims of a higher education institution, the views of a substantial majority of the student body should also be taken into account, since they indirectly benefit from the charity's investments, in the same way that the views of a significant proportion of the membership of the Church of England were relevant in justifying the Church Commissioners' ethical investment policy. Adopting a policy of investing in oil might affect relations between the charity and the student body, and may even influence application decisions by potential new students and donations from former students. The trustees have to balance the likelihood of these effects of maintaining investments in the oil industry against the financial returns that they can expect from such investments. The result of this balancing exercise could well be that the trustees could sell the investments in oil without committing a breach of trust, rather than that they would be required to do so.

13.4.4 TRUSTEES HOLDING A MAJORITY SHAREHOLDING IN A COMPANY

Where the trustees own sufficient shares in a company to give them a controlling interest in that company, they will be subject to additional obligations to safeguard the trust's investment in the company because, through their majority control, they are able to become actively involved in the management of the company. The significance of this duty is illustrated by *Bartlett v Barclays Bank Trust Co Ltd*,[107] in which a bank was a trustee of a fund that consisted of almost all of the shares in a private property company. No beneficiaries of the trust were on the board of the company and no directors were nominees of the trustee. The trust required money to pay estate duty, and the trustee and the board of directors considered that a public flotation of the company's shares would be the best way in which to raise this money. The board of directors was advised that this was more likely to be successful if the company invested in property development and it agreed to do so. The company invested in two projects without consulting the trustee. One project at Guildford was successful and the other, opposite the Old Bailey in London, was not, because planning permission could not be obtained. The profit from the former was used to finance the latter, but the company still suffered a substantial loss. The trustee did not

---

[107] [1980] Ch 515. See also *Re Lucking's Will Trusts* [1967] 3 All ER 726.

participate in the management of the development projects and was content to receive the same information at the annual general meeting as any ordinary shareholder would have received. Consequently, the trustee had not realized that the projects were risky and it had not intervened to stop them.

The beneficiaries successfully sued the trustee for breach of trust on the ground that the trustee should have acted to safeguard its investment. It was held that the trustee, as controlling shareholder, should have made sure that it received sufficient information to place itself in a position to make an informed decision as to whether any action was necessary for the protection of the trust's investment. Further, if the trustee were to become aware or was put on inquiry that the company's affairs were not being conducted as they should have been, the trustee should take appropriate action. This might involve consulting with the directors and, if necessary, convening a general meeting to remove and replace one or more of the directors,[108] either with a nominee or with the trustee. In *Bartlett*, the bank had not received sufficient and frequent information about the company's activities. Had it done so, it would have been able to intervene and stop the Old Bailey project, which was imprudent, hazardous, and wholly unsuitable as an investment vehicle for a trust. Consequently, the bank was liable for breach of trust.[109]

13.4.5 ENLARGEMENT OF INVESTMENT POWERS BY THE COURT

Although the statutory powers of investment are wide, there may be exceptional circumstances under which trustees might wish to have the powers widened by the courts either under the Trustee Act 1925[110] or the Variation of Trusts Act 1958.[111] Similarly, the powers of investment under the trust instrument may be restrictive and the trustees might wish to have the restriction removed. The courts are prepared to expand the investment powers of trustees although the extent to which they will do so has proved to be controversial.

The courts were, at one stage, willing to extend investment powers only in special circumstances,[112] but in *Trustees of the British Museum v Attorney-General*,[113] the court was willing to expand the circumstances under which it would widen investment powers, primarily because investment powers at the time were considered to be too restrictive and outdated. In that case, the court approved a scheme to give the trustees of the British Museum wide powers of investment of charitable funds to enable investment abroad. The court was influenced by a number of factors in reaching this decision, including the common practice at the time for trust instruments to give wider investment powers than the statutory powers of investment, that the trustees were eminent and responsible and were willing to obtain independent financial advice, and that the fund was large, being worth over £5 million, and so was more like a pension trust, which does have wide powers of investment.

Since that decision, statutory powers of investment have been dramatically modernized and expanded through the enactment of the Trustee Act 2000. Consequently, there will be much less need for applications to be made to court to widen investment powers, although there will still be situations in which trustees might wish to have their investment powers expanded, such as where the trustees wish to invest in land abroad, which is not permitted by the general statutory powers of investment, or to remove restrictions on investment

---

[108] Companies Act 2006, s. 168. [109] As to the nature of this liability, see Section 18.3.3, p. 522.
[110] s. 57. See Section 16.2.1, p. 460. [111] See Section 16.2.2, p. 460.
[112] *Re Kolb's Will Trusts* [1962] Ch 531; *Mason v Farbrother* [1983] 2 All ER 1078.
[113] [1984] 1 WLR 418. See also *Steel v Wellcome Custodian Trustees Ltd* [1988] 1 WLR 167.

powers in the trust instrument that are now out of line with the wide investment powers under the Trustee Act 2000. This will involve overturning the wishes of the settlor or testator and therefore raises sensitive issues that will be examined in Chapter 16.[114]

13.5 DUTY TO MAINTAIN A FAIR BALANCE BETWEEN BENEFICIARIES

Trustees are subject to a duty to act in the interests of all beneficiaries, and, where those interests conflict, the trustees are under a duty to maintain a fair balance between them and not to favour one beneficiary or class of beneficiary over another.[115] We have already examined this general duty in respect of its particular application to powers of investment,[116] but the duty is of wider significance. So, for example, in *Lloyds Bank plc v Duker*,[117] the testator's estate included 999 shares in a company that owned a hotel in Torquay. He left $^{46}/_{80}$ of the shares to his wife and the rest to five other beneficiaries. Although the wife appeared to be entitled to 574 shares, this being the relevant proportion, it was held that she could not claim all of these shares since, being a majority holding, it would be worth more than $^{46}/_{80}$ of the shares and this would contravene the general principle that trustees must not favour one beneficiary over another, but must hold an even hand between them. Consequently, the only fair solution was for the trustees to sell all of the shares and then divide the proceeds according to the proportions identified in the will.

The duty to maintain a fair balance can be expressly or implicitly excluded by the trust instrument, as will be the case where the trustees are given a power to choose between different beneficiaries or classes of beneficiary when exercising a power of appointment.[118]

The duty to maintain a fair balance between different classes of beneficiary is particularly important where there are beneficiaries with a life interest and others with an interest in remainder, since those interests will potentially conflict. The life tenant is entitled to receive income receipts and the people entitled to the remainder will eventually get the benefit of capital receipts, so it is necessary to be able to classify the receipts carefully.[119] This will also affect the value of the interest in remainder, which will be significant if the person entitled to it wishes to sell it. The significance of this conflict of interest between life tenants and those entitled to the remainder is illustrated by the following scenario:

> Property has been settled on Alan for life and thereafter to Brenda absolutely. Until Alan's death, he will be entitled to the net income derived from the property. If this income is abnormally high, it will still be payable to him and Brenda will receive nothing until Alan has died. If, for some reason, the income is abnormally low, or even non-existent, Alan cannot seek any compensation from the capital value of the property. So Alan will want the best possible income return and Brenda will be concerned that the capital value of the property increases.

---

[114] See Section 16.2.2.(iv), p. 463.
[115] *Nestlé v National Westminster Bank plc* [1993] 1 WLR 1261. See Section 13.4.3.(i), p. 385.
[116] See Section 13.4.1.(i), p. 379.   [117] [1987] 1 WLR 1324.
[118] *Edge v Pensions Ombudsman* [2000] Ch 602.   [119] See Section 13.5.1, p. 392.

This conflict between the interests of the income and capital beneficiaries is particularly marked when selecting investments. The income beneficiary will prefer investments that will produce the highest possible income, but will not be especially concerned by poor capital growth, so will be happy with a wasting asset, such as a short lease, which will produce income in the form of rent, but, after the expiry of the lease, will be worthless and so of no value to the capital beneficiary. The capital beneficiary will prefer investments that will preserve the capital value of the trust property and will have a good prospect of substantial future growth. They will not be concerned that there is no income stream in the short term. Consequently, the capital beneficiary will be content, for example, with investment in gold or antiques, which should increase in capital value over time.

13.5.1 CLASSIFICATION OF INCOME AND CAPITAL

(i) Receipts

Before the duty to maintain a fair balance is examined, it is important to analyse the basis by reference to which receipts to the trust are classified, and then allocated as income and capital. This is significant in determining which receipts benefit the income beneficiary and which benefit the capital beneficiary, but it is of wider significance, for example as regards taxation. A useful metaphor to apply is that of trees and fruit, with the growth of a tree representing capital growth and the fruit representing income. In many cases, the fruits of property will be treated as income, whereas other gains will be capital. So, for example, if a trust has a leasehold interest in a property, the rent that the trustees receive will be income and money received on selling the lease to a third party will be capital. In other cases, a receipt will simply be apportioned fairly between the income and capital beneficiaries. So, for example, where compensation is due to the trust fund and interest is payable on the sum due, this interest will be apportioned between the income and capital beneficiaries.[120]

Classification of income and capital has not been intuitive as regards distributions from companies. The general approach to classification has been that most distributions from companies have been treated as income, even if the distribution involves the transfer of shares, save for bonus shares.[121] Whilst it is appropriate to treat the payment of dividends as income, the distribution of shares would more naturally be classified as capital. This has now been recognized by section 2 of the Trusts (Capital and Income) Act 2013, the effect of which is essentially that distributions of corporate assets to a trust will be treated as a receipt of capital, subject to any contrary intention in the trust instrument. So, for example, the distribution of shares in a new company under a demerger will be treated as capital. This reform makes the classification of income and capital more intuitive and less artificial.

(ii) Expenses

Classification is also significant as regards trust expenses, since it is necessary to ascertain whether these are to be charged to income or to capital. A trust expense may relate to administrative matters, such as paying for professional fees or remunerating the trustees,[122] or may relate to the maintenance of the trust property, such as the cost of repairing a house.

Express provision may be made for the classification of trust expenses in the trust instrument, or the trustees may be given an express power to allocate expenses to income or

---

[120] *Jaffray v Marshall* [1993] 1 WLR 1285, 1294 (Nicholas Stewart QC).
[121] *Bouch v Sproule* (1887) LR 12 App Cas 385.   [122] See Section 12.7, p. 354.

capital. But, if no such provision is made, the law of trusts provides a default rule, which is that ordinary outgoings of a recurrent nature, such as rates and taxes, are charged to income, whereas expenses that are charged for the benefit of the whole of the trust estate, such as the cost of repairing trust property, insurance premiums, and payments to professional advisers, are classified as capital.[123] An expense will be incurred for the benefit of the whole estate where the purpose or object of the expense is to confer a benefit on both the income and capital beneficiaries.[124] It is, however, possible to apportion an expense between income and capital if part of the expense can be shown to relate to work carried out for the benefit of the income beneficiary alone. Whilst this apportionment must be based on evidence rather than on the trustees' view of what is a fair balance as between income and capital beneficiaries, it can still be regarded as founded on the principle of ensuring a fair balance between beneficiaries, since it is fair that the burden of the expense should be borne by the beneficiary who benefits from it.[125] Even the default rule that a trust expense will be classified as capital if it was incurred for the benefit of the trust can be considered to be founded on the principle of maintaining a fair balance, since the result of such a classification is that there will be less capital in the trust fund that can generate income for the income beneficiary. The only situation in which this would be unfair is where the income beneficiary gets substantially more benefit from the expense. But, in that case, as long as it can be shown that the expense was incurred for the income beneficiary, it will be possible to classify it as income completely or to apportion it between income and capital.

13.5.2 THE MEANING OF 'BALANCE'

In *Nestlé v National Westminster Bank plc*,[126] Staughton LJ recognized that trustees are obliged to administer the trust impartially or fairly without preferring one class of beneficiary over another. What this means is that, when the trustees are administering the trust, they should have regard to the effects of their decisions on both income and capital beneficiaries, and ensure that they are treated even-handedly. So, for example, in *Nestlé*, a relevant consideration when selecting investments was the adverse tax consequences of focusing on capital or income returns, which would justify the trustees in shifting the balance towards whichever of income or capital would result in a lower tax liability.[127]

The duty to ensure balance has been described as preserving 'an equitable balance'[128] between the different classes of beneficiary. But Hofmann J[129] preferred the language of fairness rather than 'balance in the scales', since the latter phrase suggests a more mechanistic approach to the exercise of the trustee's discretion to ensure impartiality between beneficiaries, whereas Hoffmann J wanted the particular circumstances of the beneficiaries to be taken into account when assessing what is a fair equitable balance. So, for example, if the income beneficiary is poor and the capital beneficiary relatively well off, it might be appropriate for the trustees to seek a higher income at the expense of capital, having verified the facts relating to their relative circumstances. But this emphasis on personal circumstances confuses trustees' administrative and dispositive responsibilities. The personal circumstances of the income or capital beneficiary are relevant considerations when trustees

---

[123] *Carver v Duncan* [1985] AC 1082, 1120 (Lord Templeman).
[124] *Revenue and Customs Commissioners v Trustees of the Peter Clay Discretionary Trust* [2008] EWCA Civ 1441, [2009] STC 469, [8] (Sir John Chadwick).
[125] Law Com No. 315, *Capital and Income in Trusts: Classification and Apportionment* (2009), para. 7.53.
[126] [1993] 1 WLR 1260, 1279.   [127] See Section 13.4.3.(i), p. 385.
[128] *Re Pauling's Settlement Trusts (No 2)* [1963] Ch 576, 586 (Wilberforce J). See also *Cowan v Scargill* [1985] Ch 270, 286 (Megarry V-C).   [129] *Nestlé v National Westminster Bank plc* (1996) TLI 112.

are deciding whether to exercise powers of appointment and in whose favour.[130] But the duty to maintain a fair balance is preferably characterized as an administrative duty, and consequently it should be assessed simply with reference to what is objectively fair and reasonable without regard to personal circumstances. In *Edge v Pensions Ombudsman*,[131] Chadwick LJ described the duty to act impartially as simply embodying the ordinary duty imposed on a trustee who is entrusted with the exercise of a discretionary power to exercise it for the proper purpose, taking into account relevant considerations and ignoring irrelevant ones, and it did not matter when exercising a power of appointment that the trustees preferred one group of beneficiaries over another. But that case concerned a dispositive, and not an administrative, power. The duty to maintain a fair balance relates to the latter and not the former type of power.

13.5.3 ALLOCATION OF RECEIPTS

One method of implementing this duty of ensuring a balance as regards the selection of investments would be to adopt what is known as a 'total return' investment policy. Adopting such a policy enables trustees to select investments on the basis of expected returns from the investment regardless of whether the return is classified as income or capital. Trustees would then have a discretion to allocate the investment returns to the income and capital beneficiary according to what they might expect to enjoy in the light of their respective interests in the fund, and in that way the trustees might maintain a balance between the two interests. The essence of a total return investment policy is that the trustees can select their investments without regard to the duty to balance the interests of the income and capital beneficiaries; the duty to balance arises only subsequently, when receipts are received that can then be allocated to income or capital. The aim of such an investment policy is simply to increase the investment return across the whole of the investment portfolio.

Although a total return investment policy would benefit trusts and beneficiaries, generally it cannot be adopted because it is inconsistent with the duty to maintain balance between the interests of beneficiaries when selecting investments. In other words, the effect of the present law is to concentrate the trustees' minds on the form of the return, whether it is income or capital, rather than the substance of maximizing the return of the whole portfolio regardless of the how the fruits of the investments are classified. The Charity Commission is, however, able to sanction charities to adopt a total return investment policy where it is expedient in the best interests of the charity.[132] In private trusts, trustees are able to adopt such an investment policy only if the terms of the trust enable them to select investments without regard to the form of likely receipts, and then to allocate receipts to income and capital subsequently.

The Law Commission considered whether trustees should be given a general statutory power to allocate receipts, and also expenses, to capital or income as the trustees consider appropriate, but was unable to recommend such a reform because of the significant tax implications of giving trustees a discretion to classify receipts.[133] Instead it recommended that, since charities do not usually pay tax,[134] a general statutory power should be created for charities with an endowment fund, by virtue of which not all of its property is available to be expended for charitable purposes, to adopt a total return investment policy, without requiring the prior sanction of the Charity Commission. This was enacted by section 104A of the Charities Act 2011.[135]

---

[130] See Section 14.2.2, p. 403.   [131] [2000] Ch 602, 627.
[132] Under the power in Charities Act 2011, s. 105.   [133] Law Com No. 315 (see n. 125), para. 4.25.
[134] See Section 6.1.2.(iv), p. 147.   [135] Inserted by the Trusts (Capital and Income) Act 2013, s. 4.

13.5.4 RULES TO RESTORE BALANCE

Various rules were developed in Equity to maintain or restore balance between income and capital beneficiaries, involving a duty either to sell and reinvest unauthorized trust property, called conversion, or to apportion capital or income between beneficiaries. Most of these rules were based on the presumed intention of the settlor or the testator that the income and capital beneficiaries should enjoy the benefits of the trust equally.[136] For example, if personal property was left by will to one person for life, with remainder to another person, and there was a significant risk that the property would fall in value, this would affect the interest of the person entitled to the remainder, since the capital value of the property would have fallen by the time they were entitled to the property. Consequently, the trustees would be under a duty to convert such property into authorized investments,[137] which would give the income beneficiary an income, for example in the form of dividends, and the beneficiary entitled to the remainder would obtain the benefit of the capital value of the investment. These complex rules to restore balance became increasingly insignificant in practice because they were usually excluded by the trust instrument. Further, with the recognition of portfolio theory, wasting or hazardous investments are more likely to be appropriate because they can be balanced by purchasing less risky investments, and also because the obligation to select and review investments according to the standard investment criteria[138] will provide sufficient protection to all classes of beneficiary against the effect of such investments. Consequently, the rules to restore balance were abolished for new trusts by section 1(2) of the Trusts (Capital and Income) Act 2013, save if the trust instrument makes specific provision for the operation of the rules.

13.5.5 ACCUMULATION OF INCOME

Where the trustees have a power or duty to accumulate income by adding it to capital rather than distributing it to the beneficiaries, there used to be statutory restrictions on the length of time of such accumulation.[139] The Perpetuities and Accumulations Act 2009 removed the restrictions on the accumulation of income,[140] other than for charitable trusts, under which income can be accumulated for no more than twenty-one years.[141] The exception for charities is sensible, since money held by a charitable trust should regularly be spent in order to further the trust's charitable purposes.

13.6 POWERS AND DUTIES RELATING TO PROPERTY

Trustees have a variety of powers and duties relating to trust property.

13.6.1 TRUSTS FOR SALE

A trust for sale is a trust under which there is a duty on the trustees to sell the trust property and either reinvest the proceeds or distribute them to the beneficiaries. The duty of sale is subject to a power to postpone the sale and trustees are not liable for postponing the sale of land for a limited period in the exercise of their discretion.[142] This power can be exercised only if all of the trustees agree to postpone the sale.[143]

---

[136] Law Com No. 315 (see n. 125), para. 6.10.

[137] Under the rule known as the first rule in *Howe v Lord Dartmouth* (1802) 7 Ves 137.

[138] Trustee Act 2000, s. 3(1). See Section 13.4.2.(ii), p. 382.

[139] Law of Property Act 1925, s. 164.   [140] Perpetuities and Accumulations Act 2009, s. 13.

[141] Ibid., s. 14.   [142] Trusts of Land and Appointment of Trustees Act 1996, s. 4.

[143] See Section 12.8.1, p. 362.

13.6.2 POWERS OVER LAND

Trustees of land have all of the powers of an absolute owner in respect of the land,[144] but they must have regard to the rights of the beneficiaries,[145] they have a duty to consult any adult beneficiary who has an interest in possession,[146] and they are subject to the statutory duty of care.[147] Trustees can convey land to the beneficiaries who are of full age and capacity, and who are absolutely entitled to the property, even if the beneficiaries have not requested the conveyance.[148]

The most significant power arising from trustees being in the position of absolute owners of the land is that they have a power to sell the land. Where trustees sell land that has been held on trust, they are able to give a valid written receipt only if the purchase money is received by two trustees or a trust corporation;[149] if it is not, the purchaser might be liable for loss or misapplication of the purchase money.

13.6.3 POWERS RELATING TO PERSONAL PROPERTY

Where property other than land, such as chattels or shares, is held on trust, there may be an express or an implied power to sell the property. Written receipt of payment by one trustee is sufficient to discharge the purchaser, so that they will not be liable for loss or misapplication of the purchase money.[150]

13.6.4 RAISING CAPITAL MONEY

Where trustees, other than charitable trustees, are authorized to pay or apply capital money for any purpose, they have the power to raise the money by, amongst other things, selling or mortgaging property.[151] But this does not authorize trustees to raise money by charging existing investments in order to purchase others.[152]

13.6.5 INSURANCE

Trustees may insure any trust property against the risk of loss or damage caused by any event and may pay the premiums from income or capital from the trust funds.[153] If, however, the property is held on bare trust for adult beneficiaries of full capacity who are absolutely entitled to the property, they can all direct that any trust property should not be insured.[154] Any insurance money that is paid in respect of loss or damage to the property should be treated as capital money under the trust rather than income,[155] and it may be used to reinstate the property.[156]

13.6.6 COURT POWER TO AUTHORIZE DEALINGS WITH TRUST PROPERTY

Where the trust instrument or any statute does not create a power for the trustees to deal with trust property, for example by sale, lease, mortgage, purchase, or investment, it is possible for the trustees or beneficiaries to apply to the court for the power to be conferred on the trustees, either for a specific transaction or generally.[157]

---

[144] Trusts of Land and Appointment of Trustees Act 1996, s. 6.   [145] Ibid., s. 6(5).

[146] Ibid., s. 11(1).   [147] Ibid., s. 6(9).   [148] Ibid., s. 6(2).

[149] Trustee Act 1925, s. 14(2).   [150] Ibid., s. 14(1).   [151] Ibid., s. 16.

[152] *Re Suenson-Taylor's Settlement Trusts* [1974] 1 WLR 1280.

[153] Trustee Act 1925, s. 19.   [154] Ibid., s. 19(2).

[155] Ibid., s. 20(1). For the relevance of this classification, see Section 13.5.1.(i), p. 392.

[156] Trustee Act 1925, s. 20(4).   [157] Ibid., s. 57(1) and (3). See further Section 16.2.1, p. 460.

13.7 THE POWER OF DELEGATION

Originally, a trustee was expected to perform all of their duties personally. In reality, this has proved to be impracticable, especially as the size of trust funds have increased, and over the years it has become possible for trustees collectively to delegate certain functions to other people, either through judicial development or subsequently by statute. The relevant statutory regime is now governed by the Trustee Act 2000.

A trustee may wish to delegate their powers for two reasons. The first is that the trustee may be incapable of discharging their duties for a limited period of time, for example because of an operation in hospital or a foreign business trip. If the trustee is incapable of discharging their duties for a substantial period of time, it would be preferable for the trustee to resign from the trust.[158] A second reason why a trustee might wish to delegate responsibilities is because they lack the expertise to discharge the particular responsibility and prefers an expert to do so instead.

13.7.1 DELEGATION TO AGENTS

Trustees have a statutory power collectively to appoint an agent with the authority to exercise any or all of the trustees' delegable functions.[159] For trusts other than charities, all functions are delegable except[160] those that relate to the distribution of trust assets,[161] the power to decide whether payments from trust funds should be made from income or capital,[162] the power to appoint a trustee,[163] and the power conferred by statute or the trust instrument to appoint a nominee or custodian.[164] For charitable trusts, the only functions that can be delegated are those that relate to carrying out the decisions of trustees, to the investment of trust assets, or to the raising of funds for the trust other than by means of a trade, which is an integral part of carrying out the trust's charitable purposes.[165]

Trustees may authorize one or more of their number to exercise delegable functions as an agent on behalf of all of the trustees,[166] but they cannot appoint a beneficiary as an agent even if the beneficiary is also a trustee.[167] The powers to appoint agents can be restricted or excluded by the trust instrument.[168]

The appointment of an agent can be on such terms as the trustees determine, including the remuneration of the agent.[169] But the agent cannot be authorized to exercise functions on the following terms, except where those terms are reasonably necessary:[170] permitting the agent to appoint a substitute; restricting the agent's liability owed to the trustees or beneficiaries; and permitting the agent to act in circumstances that give rise to a conflict of interest.

The person who is appointed as an agent to exercise a particular function is subject to the specific duties or restrictions that attach to that function.[171] So, for example, an agent who is authorized to exercise the general power of investment is bound to consider the standard investment criteria.[172]

There are particular restrictions on the delegation of trustees' asset management functions, which include investing trust assets, and acquiring and managing trust property.[173] Such functions must be delegated by an agreement that is in writing or is evidenced in

---

[158] See Section 12.5, p. 351. [159] Trustee Act 2000, s. 11(1). [160] Ibid., s. 11(2).
[161] See Section 14.1.3, p. 402. [162] See Section 14.4, p. 412. [163] See Section 12.4.3, p. 347.
[164] See Section 13.7.2, p. 398.
[165] Trustee Act 2000, s. 11(3). The Secretary of State has the power to prescribe more delegable functions, but has not done so and there are no plans to do so.
[166] Ibid., s. 12(1). [167] Ibid., s. 11(3). [168] Ibid., s. 26. [169] Ibid., s. 14(1).
[170] Ibid., s. 14(2) and (3). [171] Ibid., s. 13(1). [172] See Section 13.4.2.(ii), p. 382.
[173] Trustee Act 2000, s. 15(5).

writing;[174] a written policy statement must be prepared that gives guidance as to how the delegated functions should be exercised in the best interests of the trust, such as any ethical considerations that should be borne in mind; and the agreement must include a term that the agent will comply with the policy statement.[175] Trustees have a duty to assess whether the policy statement is being complied with and a duty to consider whether it needs to be revised or replaced, and, if they decide that it does, they are under a duty to so revise or replace it.[176]

If an agent incurs expenses when acting on behalf of the trust[177] or exercising the functions of an agent,[178] they can be reimbursed from the trust fund. There is also a statutory power to remunerate agents for services provided to the trust if the agent was engaged on terms that entitled them to be remunerated and the amount paid does not exceed what it is reasonable to be paid in the circumstances for the provision of that particular service.[179]

13.7.2 APPOINTMENT OF NOMINEES AND CUSTODIANS

Trustees also have the power to appoint a nominee in respect of particular trust assets, such as shares, which are then vested in the nominated person,[180] or to appoint a custodian of particular trust assets.[181] A custodian undertakes the safe custody of trust assets, or documents, or records relating to those assets. A person can be appointed as a nominee or custodian only if they are a professional nominee or custodian, or is a company controlled by the trustees.[182] The powers to appoint nominees or custodians can be restricted or excluded by the trust instrument.[183] The nominee or custodian can be reimbursed expenses[184] and can be remunerated for reasonable services provided.[185]

The power to appoint a nominee is significant, since it might be considered to contradict one of the key characteristics of a trustee, namely that trust property is vested in the trustee, who has control of the property.[186] Where a nominee is appointed, the trust property will be vested in the nominee, who then acquires legal title to it. But this is for the better administration of the trust and is therefore an appropriate power, especially because the trustee remains responsible for reviewing the arrangements and can therefore be regarded as retaining some control over the property.

The Official Custodian for Charities[187] holds investments and property on behalf of many charities, and can buy or sell investments or property if the charity trustees so instruct. The Official Custodian has no power to manage investments.[188] The Official Custodian has legal title to charity property and this is done to avoid having to transfer charity property on the successive appointment of new trustees.[189]

13.7.3 REVIEWING DELEGATION ARRANGEMENTS

Where trustees have appointed an agent, custodian, or nominee, the trustees are under a duty to keep the arrangements under review. The trustees must also consider whether it is necessary to exercise a power of intervention and, if it is, they must exercise the power.[190] A power of intervention includes the power to give directions and to revoke the authorization or appointment.

---

[174] Ibid., s. 15(1).   [175] Ibid., s. 15(2).   [176] Ibid., s. 22(2).   [177] Ibid., s. 31(2).
[178] Ibid., s. 32(3).   [179] Ibid., s. 32(1).   [180] Ibid., s. 16(1).   [181] Ibid., s. 17(1).
[182] Ibid., s. 19(2).   [183] Ibid., s. 26.   [184] Ibid., s. 32(3).   [185] Ibid., s. 32(1).
[186] *Webb v Jonas* (1888) 39 Ch D 660. See Section 12.2.1, p. 339.   [187] Charities Act 2011, s. 21.
[188] Ibid., s. 91(1)(a).   [189] *Muman v Nagasena* [2000] 1 WLR 299, 304 (Mummery LJ).
[190] Trustee Act 2000, s. 22(1).

13.7.4 LIABILITY OF TRUSTEES

Trustees are not liable for any acts or omissions of agents, nominees, or custodians, except if the trustee has failed to comply with the statutory duty of care[191] when entering into the arrangements or reviewing the arrangements.[192] The effect of this is that, if the trustees have exercised such skill and care as is reasonable in the circumstances, they will not be vicariously liable if the agent has caused loss by acting negligently.

If a trustee exceeds the statutory powers in authorizing a person to exercise functions as an agent or in appointing a nominee or custodian, the authorization or appointment is not invalidated.[193] Consequently, any action of the agent, nominee, or custodian that is within the scope of their own authority will be effective and binding on the trust.

13.7.5 SPECIFIC POWERS OF DELEGATION

Various statutes make provision for specific powers of delegation. So, for example, it is possible for an individual trustee to delegate by deed the execution or exercise of any of the trusts, powers, or discretions that are vested in them as a trustee[194] for up to a year by power of attorney.[195] The trustee must give written notice of the delegation within a week to all of the other trustees and to anybody who has the power to appoint new trustees under the trust. The exercise of this power of appointment is different from that under the Trustee Act 2000 in a number of respects. First, delegation under the Trustee Act 2000 involves delegation of functions by the trustees collectively, whereas the power under the 1925 Act enables an individual trustee to delegate for a limited period of time. Secondly, under the 1925 Act, it is possible to delegate to a trustee or a beneficiary, whereas delegation to a beneficiary is not permitted under the 2000 Act. Finally, the trustee who appoints an agent under the 1925 Act remains liable for the acts and omissions of the agent as if they were the acts and omissions of the trustee,[196] whereas trustees who have delegated under the 2000 Act are not vicariously liable, but are personally liable only for failing to comply with the statutory duty of skill and care.

Another specific power of delegation relates to trustees of land who can collectively delegate to a beneficiary of full age, who is beneficially entitled to an interest in possession in land that is subject to the trust, any of the trustees' functions relating to that land for any period or indefinitely.[197]

13.8 DUTY TO KEEP ACCOUNTS

Trustees must keep accounts of the trust and are required to disclose them to beneficiaries if they so request.[198] Trustees have the power, rather than a duty, to have the trust accounts audited, but not more than once every three years unless the nature of the trust or the dealings with the property make more regular audits reasonable.[199] The costs of the audit are to be paid from capital or income as the trustees direct.

---

[191] Ibid., s. 1(1).   [192] Ibid., s. 23(1).   [193] Ibid., s. 24.   [194] Trustee Act 1925, s. 25(1).

[195] Ibid., s. 25(2).   [196] Ibid., s. 25(7).

[197] Trusts of Land and Appointment of Trustees Act 1996, s. 9(1) and (5). Note also the Trustee Delegation Act 1999, s. 1, by virtue of which trustees of land who are also beneficiaries can delegate all trustee functions relating to the land.

[198] *Pearse v Green* (1819) 1 Jac & W 135, 140 (Plumer MR).   [199] Trustee Act 1925, s. 22.

13.9 POWERS TO COMPOUND LIABILITIES AND TO SETTLE CLAIMS

Trustees have various powers to settle any claims relating to the trust or to enter into a compromise,[200] or they can extend the time of payment of money owed to the trust.[201] The trustees are not liable for any losses that arise from the exercise of these powers if they have complied with the statutory duty of care.[202]

In *Alsop Wilkinson v Neary*,[203] it was held that a trustee against whom hostile litigation had been brought, which involved a challenge to the validity of a settlement, was not under a duty to defend the trust, but should remain neutral, leaving it to the rival claimants to the beneficial interest to fight their own battles.

---

[200] See *Re Earl of Strafford* [1980] Ch 28.   [201] Trustee Act 1925, s. 15.
[202] See Section 13.2.2, p. 376.   [203] [1996] 1 WLR 220. See Section 12.7.2.(i), p. 356.

14

DISPOSITIVE POWERS
AND DUTIES

14.1 GENERAL CONSIDERATIONS

14.1.1 NATURE OF DISPOSITIVE POWERS AND DUTIES

In Chapter 13, the powers and duties of trustees relating to the administration of the trust were examined. In this chapter, we are concerned with the powers and duties of trustees relating to the distribution of trust property to beneficiaries or objects. These powers are usually known as 'dispositive powers', or sometimes 'beneficial powers'. Although the line between administrative and dispositive powers is sometimes difficult to draw, it is a distinction that is recognized in the law,[1] and one that is of legal and practical significance, since different principles apply to dispositive, as opposed to administrative, powers and duties.

The essence of a dispositive power is that it enables the trustees to exercise a discretion relating to the distribution of trust assets to some or all of the beneficiaries or objects, having considered their respective claims. So, for example, with a discretionary trust, the trustees will have a power to choose which objects will receive trust property and the amount of property that they can receive.[2] The essence of a dispositive duty is that it requires the trustees to act in a particular way or to make a particular decision. So, for example, with a discretionary trust, there is a duty to distribute the trust property within a reasonable time.[3]

14.1.2 STANDARD OF SKILL AND CARE

The decision whether to exercise a dispositive power is a matter for the trustees to determine and is not subject to the duty of care[4] either at common law or under the Trustee Act 2000. But, once trustees have decided to exercise a dispositive power, the manner in which they exercise it or exercise any dispositive duty will be assessed against the reasonable

---

[1] *Re Butlin's Will Trust* [1976] Ch 251, 263 (Brightman J).

[2] See Section 14.2.2.(i), p. 403.   [3] See Section 14.2.2.(i), p. 403.

[4] See Section 13.2, p. 374.

standard of care. The statutory duty of care under the Trustee Act 2000 applies only to administrative functions, so the common law duty of care will apply to the exercise of dispositive functions, although, as was seen in Chapter 13,[5] the preferable view is that there is no relevant difference between statutory and common law duties of care.

14.1.3 NO DELEGATION

Whereas many administrative functions can be delegated to an agent, it is not possible for a trustee to delegate any dispositive function that relates to whether and in what way any of the trust assets should be distributed.[6] In other words, all decisions about the exercise of dispositive functions must be made by the trustees rather than delegated to an agent.

14.1.4 EXERCISE OF POWERS

Trustees are not permitted to release their dispositive powers[7] and must exercise their powers validly, so, for example, the powers must be exercised for a proper purpose and not capriciously. Consequently, the doctrine of fraud on the power applies.[8] If the trustees breach their duty in the exercise of the power by acting unreasonably, the exercise of the power may be voidable by virtue of the 'rule in *Hastings-Bass*'[9]

14.2 POWER OF APPOINTMENT

A significant power of trustees relates to the appointment of trust property. The power of appointment can be divided into a power to decide whether to appoint the trust fund to objects of the trust at all, and a power to decide which objects should receive trust property and in what proportion.

14.2.1 NATURE OF THE POWER OF APPOINTMENT

The nature of a power of appointment will depend on whether it is characterized as being a trust power or a fiduciary power.[10] If it is a trust power, the trustees are required to make the appointment, but have a discretion as to who should receive the trust property and how much. If it is a fiduciary power, the trustees may make the appointment if they wish to do so, but are obliged to consider whether the power should be exercised.[11] Consequently, all powers of appointment involve some choice for the trustee, whether it relates to the decision to exercise the power at all or simply who will benefit and by how much.

To determine whether a power of appointment is a trust power or a fiduciary power requires careful construction of the trust instrument to determine what the creator of the trust intended,[12] but, as a rule of thumb, if the trustees *must* exercise the power, it is a trust power, and if they *may* exercise it, it is a fiduciary power.

---

[5] See Section 13.2.3, p. 378.
[6] Trustee Act 2000, s. 11(2). A general non-fiduciary power of appointment can be delegated, but such a power is, by definition, not held by a trustee: *Re Triffitt's Settlement* [1958] Ch 852, 861 (Upjohn J); *Tasarruf Mevduati Sigorta Fonu v Merrill Lynch Bank and Trust Co (Cayman) Ltd* [2011] UKPC 17, [2012] 1 WLR 1721.
[7] See Section 12.8.5, p. 365.   [8] See Section 12.8.6.(vii), p. 368.
[9] *Pitt v Holt; Futter v Futter* [2013] UKSC 26, [2013] 2 AC 108. See Section 12.8.7, p. 370.
[10] See Section 3.7.8, p. 66.   [11] See Section 3.7.8.(iii), p. 66.   [12] See Section 3.7.8.(vi), p. 68.

14.2.2 EXERCISING THE POWER

(i) Trust power

A trust power must be exercised by the trustee in a proper manner and within a reasonable time.[13] What this means is that, for example, where the trust is an exhaustive discretionary trust, the trustees must distribute all of the income, and sometimes the capital too, within a reasonable time. If the trust is a non-exhaustive discretionary trust, they will have a power to accumulate, which means that they have a discretion to build up the income before deciding to distribute it.

Where the trustees are required to exercise their power of appointment, they must make such a survey of the range of objects as will enable them to carry out their duty to distribute the trust property.[14] The trustees should:

> examine the field, by class and category; might indeed make diligent and careful inquiries, depending on how much money he had to give away and the means at his disposal, as to the composition and needs of particular categories and of individuals within them; decide upon certain priorities or proportions, and then select individuals according to their needs or qualifications.[15]

It has been recognized that, in very large discretionary trusts, the trustee must assess the size of the class in a businesslike way,[16] this being the language of the common law duty of care, which still applies to the exercise of powers of appointment.[17] If the trustees make a distribution to the objects without conducting a reasonable survey of the class, and of the needs of particular categories and individuals, the trustees will be liable for breach of trust.

If a trustee exercises the trust power improperly, for example by distributing outside the range of objects as defined by the trust instrument, or by exercising the power capriciously,[18] for example by taking into account irrelevant considerations, the exercise of the power will be void.[19]

(ii) Fiduciary power

Where the trustees have a fiduciary power of appointment, they are subject to a duty to consider the exercise of the power periodically, but they are not required to exercise it.[20] Megarry V-C, in *Re Hay's Settlement Trusts*,[21] recognized a number of principles relating to the exercise of a fiduciary power of appointment, as follows:

(1) The power should not simply be exercised in favour of such objects as are at hand or who have made a claim.

(2) The trustees must consider who the potential objects are, as identified by the trust instrument. It is not necessary to make a complete list of objects or even to seek an accurate assessment of their number; it is sufficient that the trustee has appreciated the width of the field of objects.

(3) Once the trustees are aware of 'the size of the problem', they should consider in individual cases whether, in comparison with the other objects, an appointment is appropriate.

---

[13] *Tempest v Lord Camoys* (1882) 21 Ch D 571, 578 (Jessel MR).
[14] *McPhail v Doulton* [1971] AC 424, 457 (Lord Wilberforce).   [15] Ibid., 449.
[16] *Re Baden's Deed Trusts (No 2)* [1973] Ch 9, 20 (Sachs LJ).   [17] See Section 13.2.1, p. 375.
[18] *Re Manisty's Settlement* [1974] Ch 17.   [19] See Section 12.8.6, p. 385.
[20] *Re Hay's Settlement Trust* [1982] 1 WLR 202, 209 (Megarry V-C). See also *McPhail v Doulton* [1971] AC 424, 457 (Lord Wilberforce).   [21] [1982] 1 WLR 202, 209.

(4) In making an appointment, the trustees should not prefer the undeserving to the deserving, but it is not necessary to make an exact calculation between deserving claimants as to who is the most deserving.

If the trustees do decide to exercise the power, it must be exercised only within the scope of what the trustees are authorized to do, and they must exercise the power responsibly according to its purpose and not capriciously.[22] If the trustees do exceed their powers, the exercise will be void.

14.2.3 CONSEQUENCES OF FAILURE TO EXERCISE THE POWER

Where a trustee fails to exercise a trust power within a reasonable time, they will be liable for breach of trust by virtue of failing to make an appointment. Similarly, the trustees will be liable for breach of trust if they fail to consider whether or not to exercise a fiduciary power in a reasonable time. But, where trustees fail to make an appointment under a fiduciary power, they will not be liable, since they are not under any duty to do so.[23]

In addition to potential liability for breach of trust, there may be other consequences should trustees fail to exercise a power of appointment.

(i) Trust power

If a trustee fails to exercise a trust power, the court will endeavour to fulfil the settlor's or testator's intent by securing execution of the power.[24] There are a variety of ways in which the court might do this:

(1) The court may direct the trustees to exercise their discretion, albeit late, provided that there is no evidence of bias or obstinacy on the part of the trustees. So, in *Re Locker's Settlement*,[25] although the trustees held property on an exhaustive discretionary trust with a duty to apply all of the income to the objects of the trust, they accumulated the income for a number of years. It was held that, since they had failed to distribute the income within a reasonable time, the trustees had breached their trust. The court authorized the trustees to exercise their discretion, even though it was out of time, but they could make appointments only to those objects who would have benefited from the exercise of the power of appointment had it been exercised within a reasonable time. This late exercise of the power of appointment by the trustees is justified, rather than the discretion being exercised by somebody else, because the settlor had intended the trustees to exercise the discretion[26] and it is better that the discretion is exercised late rather than never.

(2) The court may replace the trustees under its inherent jurisdiction.[27]

(3) The court may authorize or direct representatives of the objects to prepare a scheme of distribution.

(4) If a proper basis for distribution can be identified, the court may be willing to exercise the discretionary power and will order the trustees to make the distribution.

(ii) Fiduciary power

It has been assumed that, if a trustee fails to exercise a fiduciary power of appointment within a reasonable time, the power will simply lapse and the court will not compel

---

[22] Ibid.   [23] *Brophy v Bellamy* (1873) 8 Ch App 798.
[24] *McPhail v Doulton* [1971] AC 424, 457 (Lord Wilberforce).   [25] [1977] 1 WLR 1323.
[26] Ibid., 1325 (Goulding J).   [27] See Section 12.4.5, p. 350.

performance,[28] unless there was an improper purpose behind the failure to exercise the power,[29] although the court might still be willing to compel the trustee to consider whether or not the power should be exercised.[30] In *Mettoy Pension Trustees Ltd v Evans*,[31] however, it was recognized that the court has similar powers of intervention for failure to exercise a fiduciary power as apply to the failure to exercise a trust power of appointment, including appointing replacement trustees,[32] ordering a scheme of distribution to be prepared by the objects of the power, or even directing the exercise of the power itself.

Mettoy Pension Trustees concerned a company that had gone into liquidation with a surplus in its pension fund. The company had a power of appointment in favour of the pensioners, with any surplus not appointed to them going to the company. The liquidator wished to release the company's power of appointment and pay the surplus from the pension fund to the creditors of the company. The company's power of appointment was characterized as a fiduciary power because the pensioners, as the objects of the power, were not volunteers, but had earned the right at least to have the exercise of the power considered, because their rights derived from their contract of employment and were earned by their service to the company. Being a fiduciary power, it was held that the power could not simply be released; the donor of that power had a duty to consider its exercise. But this was where the real difficulty in the case arose. The original donor of the power, the company, could not exercise it because it had gone into liquidation. The liquidator could not properly exercise the power, because he had a conflict of interest between his duty to the creditors of the company and his duty to the pensioners to consider whether it was appropriate to exercise the power. Since there was nobody else who could exercise the power,[33] it was held that the court would be willing to exercise the power according to a scheme of distribution that would need to be approved subsequently.

The decision in *Mettoy Pension Trustees* is significant in its apparent assimilation of the judicial responses where there is a failure to exercise a trust power and a fiduciary power. But this surely goes too far, since the effect of this assimilation of responses is to turn a fiduciary power, which *may* be exercised, into a trust power, which *must* be exercised. The assimilation of response is not, however, complete; it remains necessary to distinguish between trust powers and fiduciary powers where the power of appointment is not exercised. For example, presumably the court will not intervene where the trustees have decided, in good faith and after careful consideration of the circumstances, that they will not exercise a fiduciary power of appointment. Also, if a fiduciary power is not exercised within a reasonable time, that power will lapse if the trust instrument provides for a gift over to another person to take effect in such circumstances. So, for example, in *Re Allen-Meyrick's Will Trust*,[34] the trustees had a power to distribute income for the maintenance of A in their absolute discretion, and, subject to that power, to hold the trust property on trust for B and C in equal shares absolutely. The trustees failed to reach a decision as to whether to exercise the power for the benefit of A. It was held that, after a reasonable time had elapsed from the receipt of the income, their discretion to apply it for the benefit of A terminated, and the income was held for B and C.[35]

---

[28] *McPhail v Doulton* [1971] AC 424, 456 (Lord Wilberforce).   [29] *Klug v Klug* [1908] 2 Ch 67.

[30] *Re Hay's ST* [1982] 1 WLR 202, 209 (Sir Robert Megarry V-C).   [31] [1990] 1 WLR 1587.

[32] *Re Manisty's Settlement* [1974] Ch 17, 25.

[33] It was not considered whether the trustee of the pension fund was an appropriate person to exercise the power or whether any other person might be appointed to exercise the power: Gardner, 'Fiduciary powers in Toytown' (1991) 107 LQR 214, 217.   [34] [1966] 1 WLR 499.

[35] Ibid., 504 (Buckley J).

Another key difference between trust powers and fiduciary powers that have not been exercised is that, as regards trust powers, the court may be willing to allow trustees to exercise the power late,[36] but it has been held that a fiduciary power cannot be exercised late, although it is unclear to what extent this turned on the facts of the case rather than was the recognition of a general principle. In *Breadner v Granville-Grossman*,[37] a fixed trust had been established for four people, subject to the trustees exercising a fiduciary power of appointment before a particular date. The trustees exercised the power of appointment a day late and sought the confirmation of the court that the exercise of the power was valid. The court drew a distinction between acts and omissions. The court would have been willing to declare the act of exercising a power to be ineffective by virtue of the trustees having taken into account irrelevant considerations or ignoring relevant ones,[38] but it would not intervene where a trustee had omitted to exercise a power. In this case, the power had lapsed before it was exercised and the court was not willing to treat it as though it had been validly exercised in time. The general tenor of *Breadner v Granville-Grossman* is inconsistent with the approach of the court in *Re Locker's Settlement*,[39] in which the court authorized a tardy exercise of a trust power, and with *Mettoy Pension Fund*, in which judicial responses to failure to exercise a trust power and a fiduciary power were assimilated. Perhaps the explanation for the approach in *Breadner* was that the power was specifically time-limited, so that the power had lapsed by the passage of time according to the clear words of the trust instrument, whereas in *Re Locker's Settlement* the terms of the trust instrument did not expressly limit the time for performance. Or, perhaps, the distinction simply reflects the essential nature of trust powers and fiduciary powers: a trust power does not lapse even if it has not been exercised within a reasonable time, whereas fiduciary powers do. It is also significant that, in *Breadner*, the default trust came into effect and it would not have been appropriate to deprive the trust beneficiaries of their rights by resurrecting the lapsed fiduciary power.

14.3 DUTY TO DISTRIBUTE

Where beneficiaries have a right to receive payment of income or capital, or both, the trustees are under a duty to find the beneficiaries and to make distributions to them as the money becomes due, without any demand for payment first being required from the beneficiaries.[40] So, for example, if property is held on trust for Christine until she attains the age of 18, on attaining that age she has a right to receive the trust property. Failure to distribute to the beneficiaries with an entitlement to the property will constitute a breach of trust, although a trustee may be relieved from liability if they acted honestly and reasonably, and ought fairly to be excused.[41]

The trustees may have a power to accumulate income, which means that they can decide to build up the income before distributing it. If there is no power of accumulation in the trust instrument, the trustees are under a duty to distribute the income within a reasonable time of receiving it.

---

[36] See Section 14.2.3.(i), p. 404.   [37] [2001] Ch 523.

[38] This being an application of the rule in *Hastings-Bass*, save that now the exercise of the power will be voidable only where it amounted to a breach of duty by the trustees. See Section 12.8.7, p. 369.

[39] [1977] 1 WLR 1323.   [40] *Hawkesley v May* [1956] 1 QB 305, 324 (Havers J).

[41] Trustee Act 1925, s. 61. See Section 17.3.2, p. 481.

14.3.1 DUTY TO INFORM BENEFICIARIES AND OBJECTS OF THEIR STATUS

The trustees are under a duty to inform the beneficiaries under a fixed trust of their right to the trust property once they have become entitled to it, such as on attaining a specified age.[42] No such duty is placed on an executor to inform legatees that they are entitled to a legacy from the testator's estate, since a will is a public document, so it is appropriate to assume that the legatees are aware of their rights.[43] An express trust is a private document, so the beneficiaries will not necessarily know of their rights until the trustees inform them. The obligation of trustees to inform beneficiaries of their rights is a product of the fundamental principle of trustee accountability: trustees cannot be held accountable if beneficiaries are unaware of their rights.[44]

Although it has been suggested[45] that the trustees are not required to give the beneficiaries legal advice or to inform them of their right to terminate the trust under the rule in *Saunders v Vautier*,[46] the better view is that the trustees are indeed under a duty to inform them of this right, since it relates directly to the nature and extent of their interests under the trust, although it would not be appropriate for trustees to provide legal advice as to whether termination of the trust is an appropriate course of action to take.[47]

As regards the objects of a discretionary trust, since they have a right to put their case to the trustees for the exercise of their discretion,[48] it follows that the trustees should be under a duty to take reasonable steps to draw this right to the objects' attention.[49] What constitutes reasonable steps will depend on the size of the class: trustees will not be expected to search for all possible objects where the class is very large.[50] As regards fiduciary powers of appointment, it seems that the objects of the power have no right to be informed that they are objects.[51]

14.3.2 TRUSTEE PROTECTION AGAINST LIABILITY FOR OVERPAYMENT

Where there is doubt as to the beneficiary's entitlement or known beneficiaries cannot be found, there are various steps that the trustees can take to ensure that the duty to distribute is fulfilled without breach of trust. This is particularly significant where the trustees wish to distribute all of the trust assets so that there is no trust property left to meet the claims of beneficiaries who subsequently come forward. There are also sometimes concerns that, if the trustees make a distribution and creditors subsequently come forward (typically creditors of the deceased testator), the trustees will be personally liable to those creditors because there will no longer be an estate to meet the liabilities. The various mechanisms discussed below may also be of relevance in this scenario too.

---

[42] *Hawkesley v May* [1956] 1 QB 304, 322 (Havers J).   [43] *Re Lewis* [1904] 2 Ch 656.

[44] Fox, 'The irreducible core for a valid trust' (2011) 17 T&T 16, 20.

[45] *Hawkesley v May* [1956] 1 QB 304, 323 (Havers J).

[46] (1841) Cr & Ph 240. See Section 11.4.1, p. 334.

[47] Samuels, 'Must the trustees tell the beneficiary about *Saunders v Vautier*?' (1970) 34 Conv 29.

[48] *Murphy v Murphy* [1999] 1 WLR 282.

[49] Hayton, 'The irreducible core content of trusteeship', in *Trends in Contemporary Trust Law*, ed. Oakley (Oxford: Clarendon Press, 1996), p. 49.

[50] *Hartigan Nominees Pty Ltd v Rydge* (1992) 29 NSWLR 405, 432 (Mahoney JA).

[51] *Re Manisty's Settlement* [1974] Ch 17, 25 (Templeman J). Hayton (see n. 49), p. 50.

(i) Directions from the court

The trustees can apply to the court for directions[52] as to the claims of the beneficiaries and what they should do if an identified beneficiary cannot be found. If the trustees comply with the directions of the court, they cannot be liable to the beneficiary who did not receive any distribution or to creditors who come forward subsequently.[53]

(ii) Advertisement for claimants

In order to identify unknown beneficiaries, trustees[54] may give notice by advertising in the *Gazette*,[55] or a newspaper, of their intention to make a distribution, giving potential beneficiaries at least two months in which to provide the trustees with particulars of their claim to the trust assets.[56] After the expiration of the time fixed by the advertisement, the trustees can make the distribution to those people who have claims of which the trustees had notice and the trustees will not be liable to anybody of whose claim they did not have notice.[57] This limitation of liability cannot be excluded by the trust instrument.[58] But this provision does not prevent those who were entitled, but who did not come forward, from bringing a proprietary claim against the person who has received the property to which they were entitled, save where that property was received by a bona fide purchaser for value.[59]

The advertisement will protect the trustees from liability only if they have no notice of the beneficiaries' claims. Notice does not mean knowledge, as was held in *MCP Pension Trustees Ltd v Aon Pension Trustees Ltd*.[60] In that case, a pension scheme was administered by the defendant on behalf of the claimant trustee. The claimant knew that some new members had been transferred into the scheme from a different scheme. The defendant failed to maintain the scheme records properly, so that the names of the new members were removed from the relevant documents. The claimant sought to wind up the scheme and placed an advert requesting anybody with claims against the assets to make contact. Nobody came forward. The claimant distributed the assets, and then became aware of the claims of the new members and settled a number of them. The claimant sued the defendant for damages for negligently maintaining the records. The defendant's liability turned on whether the claimant was protected from liability by placing the advert: if it were protected, the claimant would not have suffered any loss for which the defendant would be liable.[61] In other words, the claimant was arguing that it was not protected from liability by placing the advert because it did have notice of the claims of the new members. It was held that 'notice' meant actual or constructive notice and included deemed knowledge of facts that were not actually known to the trustee at the time of the distribution. In this case, since the trustee had known that the members had been transferred to the new scheme, but had then forgotten this, it was held that the trustee still had actual notice of their claims and so was not protected by the advertisement. In other words, notice did not lapse with memory.

---

[52] Under the Civil Procedure Rules, Pt 64 and Practice Direction 64A.

[53] *Re Yorke* [1997] 4 All ER 907, 921 (Lindsay J).

[54] Including trustees of pension trusts: *MCP Pension Trustees Ltd v Aon Trustees Ltd* [2010] EWCA Civ 377, [2012] Ch 1.

[55] 'The Official Newspaper of Record', known as the *London Gazette*. It was first published in 1665 and claims to be the first newspaper in English.   [56] Trustee Act 1925, s. 27(1).

[57] Ibid., s. 27(2).   [58] Ibid., s. 27(3).   [59] Ibid., s. 27(2)(a).

[60] [2010] EWCA Civ 377, [2012] Ch 1.

[61] The claim was actually pursued by the claimant's insurance company through the claimant.

(iii) *Benjamin* order

A *Benjamin* order is made by a court to authorize the trustees to distribute all of the trust property or all of the assets of a deceased's estate even though, after all practical inquiries have taken place, the whereabouts, or even the continued existence, of all of the beneficiaries is not known. The purpose of the *Benjamin* order is to protect the trustees from liability if those beneficiaries who did not receive anything under the distribution subsequently come forward. The order is named after *Re Benjamin*,[62] in which case the testator had left a share of his estate to his son, should that son survive his father. The testator died in June 1893. His son had disappeared in September 1892 and could not be traced. An application was made to the court for directions as to what the trustees should do. Having considered the evidence, the judge concluded that it was highly probable that the son had died in September 1892 and that the trustees were free to distribute the estate on that assumption. A special order was made by the court to the effect that the trustees were at liberty to distribute the estate on the footing that the son had not survived his father.

The potential reach of a *Benjamin* order was expanded in *Re Green's Will Trusts*.[63] In that case, the testatrix had made her will in 1972, in which she left all her property to her son, Barry, with it going to charity if he did not claim it by 2020. He had not been heard of since 1943, when he was in a plane that disappeared over Berlin on a wartime bombing raid. Neither the plane nor the crew were ever found. The Air Ministry certified that all members of the crew were presumed dead. Barry's mother was convinced that her son had survived. It was held that, since it was virtually certain that Barry was dead (and the evidence of death in this case was considered to be much stronger than in *Re Benjamin*), a *Benjamin* order was made so that the executors of the will could distribute the estate on that assumption and even though this order conflicted with the testatrix's clear intention, as expressed in the will. Nourse J justified this decision as follows:

> The true view is that a *Re Benjamin* order does not vary or destroy beneficial interests. It merely enables trust property to be distributed in accordance with the practical probabilities, and it must be open to the court to take a view of those probabilities entirely different from that entertained by the testator.[64]

The result has been described as indefensible in its patronizing disregard of the testatrix's intent.[65]

Whilst it is true that the effect of making a *Benjamin* order is simply to protect the trustee and to enable trust property to be distributed without having to wait until what might be unprovable can be proved, the order may sometimes have substantive effects on the beneficial interest: if a trustee does distribute trust property on the assumption that a beneficiary is dead and that beneficiary then comes forward, the beneficiary will not be able to recover the property if it has been dissipated or has been sold to a bona fide purchaser for value.[66] In such circumstances, the beneficiary cannot sue the trustee for breach of trust, because the trustee will be protected by the *Benjamin* order. The only hope will be to bring a proprietary claim in respect of the property that was transferred or a personal claim against the recipient of the trust property.[67] But the real advantage of the *Benjamin* order is that it allows trust property to be distributed whilst leaving open the possibility of

---

[62] [1902] 1 Ch 723.   [63] [1985] 3 All ER 455.   [64] Ibid., 462.
[65] Luxton, 'Eluding the dead hand: a live issue?' [1986] Conv 138, 142.
[66] See further Chapter 19 in this volume.
[67] Under the rule in *Ministry of Health v Simpson* [1951] AC 251. See Section 20.2.3.(ii), p. 607.

the lost beneficiary coming forward and claiming what is rightfully theirs if any property remains undistributed.

(iv) Insurance

Another solution to the problem of a beneficiary appearing after the trust fund has been distributed is to take out a missing-beneficiary insurance policy, which provides a fund to meet the claim of a missing beneficiary without imposing liability on the trustee or depriving the overpaid beneficiary of what they have received. The use of such an insurance policy was endorsed in *Re Evans*,[68] in which the defendant was the administratrix of her father's estate, which was held on trust for her and her brother. She had not heard from her brother for thirty years and assumed that he was dead. She took out a missing-beneficiary insurance policy and then distributed the estate to herself. Her brother reappeared and issued proceedings against her concerning the purchase of the insurance policy. It was held that personal representatives of small estates should seek practical solutions to difficult administration problems, such as insurance, without the expense of resorting to the courts. Also, for small intestate administrations in which the representative will typically have an interest in the estate, it is not appropriate for sizeable sums to be tied up indefinitely for fear of the re-emergence of a long-lost beneficiary. Consequently, taking out a missing-beneficiary policy was entirely appropriate, even though the administratrix was personally interested in the estate, and was at a relatively small cost compared with the expense of applying to the court for a *Benjamin* order.

(v) Retention of a fund

The trustees may decide to make a distribution to the beneficiaries, but set aside a sum of money in a fund to be used to discharge any subsequent liabilities arising from overpaying beneficiaries, either to unpaid beneficiaries or to creditors who subsequently come forward.[69] This requires a careful balance of the risks of the beneficiaries being overpaid if new beneficiaries or creditors emerge subsequently. Specific provision is made by statute for the creation of such a fund to meet liabilities arising under a lease and then for the trustees to distribute the rest of the trust assets to those who are entitled to them.[70]

(vi) Payment into court

Trustees may pay the trust money into court[71] if they can establish genuine doubt, for example, as to the identity and location of the beneficiaries, or because of their inability to give receipts.[72] The effect of such payment into court is that the trustees retire from the trust.[73] The trustees will be discharged from their obligations to administer the funds[74] and their discretionary powers will be terminated.[75] They will, however, remain liable for past breaches[76] and responsible for any money that comes into their hands subsequently, but they will not be liable otherwise for anything that happens after they have paid money into the court.

(vii) Barrister's opinion

Where a barrister of at least ten years' standing gives an opinion about the construction of a trust or a will, the High Court may authorize distribution in reliance on that opinion

---

[68] [1999] 2 All ER 777. See also *MCP Pension Trustees Ltd v Aon Pension Trustees Ltd* [2010] EWCA Civ 377, [2012] Ch 1.   [69] See *Re Yorke* [1997] 4 All ER 907, 921 (Lindsay J).

[70] Trustee Act 1925, s. 26(1).   [71] Ibid., s. 63.   [72] *Re Knight's Trusts* (1859) 27 Beav 45.

[73] *Re Williams' Settlement* (1858) 4 K & J 87.   [74] *Re Lloyd's Trust* (1854) 2 WR 371.

[75] *Re Nettlefold's Trusts* (1888) 59 LT 315.   [76] *Barker v Peile* (1865) 2 Drew & Sm 340.

without hearing any further evidence.[77] The trustees will then be absolved from any liability in respect of the distribution.

14.3.3 WRONGFUL DISTRIBUTION

Where trustees have transferred trust property to the wrong beneficiary or have transferred too much property to one beneficiary, the trustees could bring a claim against the recipient for restitution. There are two potential claims that are open to the trustees in such circumstances.

(i) Proprietary claim

The trustee may seek to recover the property that has been transferred to the beneficiary, or the identifiable substitute for that property, on the ground that the trustee has a proprietary interest in that property.[78] Where property, such as money, is transferred to somebody by mistake, legal title to that property will typically pass. So, if the trustee has distributed money from the trust estate to a beneficiary who was not entitled to receive it, the trustee will have been mistaken in making the transfer, but this will not usually prevent legal title to that money from passing. But the trustee may be able to establish an equitable proprietary interest in the property. If the transfer of the property is outside the scope of the exercise of the power, that exercise of the power will be void and ineffective in Equity, so that the trustee will be able to recover the property in Equity.[79] If the transfer of the property is within the scope of the power, but involved a breach of duty because the exercise of the power in that way was not reasonable, the transfer of property will be voidable and, once avoided, can be recovered.[80] If the trustee had not breached their duty in exercising the power, a proprietary claim to the property transferred by mistake might be established instead, by resorting to the equitable jurisdiction to set aside voluntary dispositions for mistake.[81] This requires the claimant to establish that the mistake was serious and was of such gravity that it would be unjust for the donee to retain the property that was given to them. Where the mistaken transfer can be set aside, whether for involving the invalid exercise of a power or for mistake, the property will be held on constructive trust for the trustee, which will enable them to assert a proprietary claim against the overpaid beneficiary.[82]

(ii) Personal claim

Alternatively, the trustee may have a personal claim to recover the value of the property that has been transferred to the wrong person. Such a claim would arise within the law of unjust enrichment. The trustee will need to establish that the defendant recipient has received an enrichment directly[83] at the trustee's expense. This will be easily established. The trustee will then need to show that the claim falls within one of the recognized grounds of restitution, the most relevant here being that founded on mistake. It has been recognized that where a claimant transfers an enrichment as the result of a mistake either of fact or law but for which the transfer would not have been made,[84] the claimant

---

[77] Administration of Justice Act 1985, s. 48.   [78] See further Section 19.2, p. 548.

[79] See Section 12.8.6, p. 365.

[80] *Pitt v Holt* [2013] UKSC 26, [2013] 2 AC 108. See Section 12.8.7, p. 370.

[81] *Pitt v Holt* [2013] UKSC 26, [2013] 2 AC 108. See Section 9.3.3, p. 264.

[82] See Section 19.2.1, p. 549.

[83] *Commissioners for Her Majesty's Revenue and Customs v The Investment Trust Companies* [2017] UKSC 29, [2017] 2 WLR 1200.   [84] *Kleinwort Benson Ltd v Lincoln City Council* [1999] 2 AC 349.

will be able to recover the value of the enrichment subject to the defendant having a defence, such as that they changed their position in good faith in reliance on the receipt of the enrichment.[85] So, for example, if Alan, a trustee of a discretionary trust, has distributed money to Brenda, thinking that she falls within the class of objects when this is not the case, Alan will be able to sue Brenda for the amount of the money paid, which will then be repaid to the trust. It will not matter that Alan's mistake related to the fact that he thought that Brenda met the requirements to fall within the class of objects, or was a mistake of law relating to the construction of the trust instrument. If Brenda has spent the money that she received in good faith, then she will be able to rely on the defence of change of position.

There is, however, a matter of some uncertainty about the nature of this unjust enrichment claim in mistake following the decision of the Supreme Court in *Pitt v Holt*.[86] Since the exercise of a trustee's dispositive powers involves a voluntary disposition of property, the equitable jurisdiction for setting aside mistaken voluntary dispositions made by deed might be engaged instead. This would mean that it will not be sufficient that the mistake was a 'but for' cause of the transfer to be made, since it must be shown that the mistake was serious and of such gravity that it would be unjust for the recipient to retain the property. Cases decided after *Pitt v Holt* have assumed without analysis that this test applies to recover gifts even if the subject matter of the gift was not transferred by deed, albeit not in the context of dispositions made by trustees.[87]

14.4 POWER OF MAINTENANCE

Where a beneficiary is a minor, they will typically not be entitled to receive any income from the trust until the age of 18, which is the age of majority. But there may be circumstances under which the minor could benefit from the receipt of income now rather than have to wait until they are old enough to have a right to receive it. Similarly, an adult beneficiary may not yet be entitled to income under the trust, since he or she has a contingent interest in the property, but might benefit from receiving some income now. In such circumstances, the trustees may wish to exercise their statutory power of maintenance.[88] The effect of this power is that, as regards minors, the trustees can apply income from the trust for their maintenance, education, and benefit. As regards adult beneficiaries who are contingently entitled to the capital on the happening of a future event, the trustees have the power to apply income for their benefit now before the occurrence of the event on which the interest is contingent.

The language of the statutory power of maintenance has been described as not being easy to follow and drafted in such a way as to make the apprehension of its effect difficult to discern.[89] But, if the aims of the provision are clearly identified, it does become easier to understand. The statutory power of maintenance is to be read into every trust instrument in the absence of contrary intent.

---

[85] See Section 19.5.2, p. 585.   [86] [2013] UKSC 26, [2013] 2 AC 108.

[87] *Pagel v Farman* [2013] EWHC 2210 (Comm), [2013] WTLR 1575; *Spaul v Spaul* [2014] EWCA Civ 679, [52] (Rimer LJ); *Freedman v Freedman* [2015] EWHC 1457 (Ch); *Van der Merwe v Goldman* [2016] EWHC 790 (Ch), [2016] 4 WLR 71; *Bainbridge v Bainbridge* [2016] EWHC 898 (Ch), [2016] WTLR 943. See further Virgo, *The Principles of the Law of Restitution*, 3rd edn (Oxford: Oxford University Press, 2015), p. 182.

[88] Trustee Act 1925, s. 31(1).

[89] *Re Vestey's Settlement* [1951] Ch 209, 216 (Sir Raymond Evershed MR).

14.4.1 MINORS

As regards minors who have either a vested or a contingent interest in property, the trustees have the power to pay such income from the property as the trustees may think fit[90] either by paying it to the child's parent or guardian, or by applying it for the child's maintenance, education, or benefit.[91] This power can be exercised even though there is another fund available for the same purpose and even though somebody else is bound by law to provide for the maintenance or education of the child. Under the statute as originally enacted, the exercise of the trustees' discretion was subject to a proviso, as a result of which they had to consider various matters, such as the age of the child and their requirements; it also imposed a restriction on the amount of income which can be paid out. This proviso was removed by section 8(b) of the Inheritance and Trustees' Powers Act 2014, meaning that the trustees can consider all relevant matters in exercising their discretion and pay out as much income as they consider appropriate. The trustees can legitimately exercise the power even though this indirectly benefits one of the parents of the child, but they cannot set out to benefit the parent.[92]

14.4.2 TRUSTS THAT CARRY THE INTERMEDIATE INCOME

The power of maintenance applies to all minors with a vested interest, namely an interest that does not depend on a prior condition being satisfied, such as reaching a specified age. If the minor has a contingent interest, the power will apply only if the trust 'carries the intermediate income'.[93] The power of maintenance can also be exercised for the benefit of adult beneficiaries who have a contingent interest in trust property, but again only if the trust carries the intermediate income.[94] Where an adult beneficiary has a vested interest in trust property, there is no need for the power of maintenance to be exercised, since they are already entitled to the income.

The precise meaning of 'trusts that carry the intermediate income' is obscure, but essentially it arises where the beneficiary is entitled to the income from the date of the gift, such as on the death of the testator, until the property vests. This generally applies to all testamentary gifts except for contingent pecuniary legacies or where this is excluded by the will.[95] The power cannot be exercised in favour of an object of a discretionary trust because they have no right to the income.[96]

14.4.3 DUTY TO ACCUMULATE INCOME

During the infancy of the child, any surplus of the income that has not been applied for the maintenance of a child must be accumulated by investing it, and the accumulated income is treated as an accretion to the capital of the trust property to which the child is entitled when they reach the age of 18.[97] The income from these investments can be used for the maintenance of the child and the investments themselves can be applied for the maintenance of the child.

---

[90] Under s. 31 of the Trustee Act 1925 as originally enacted, the trustee's discretion was restricted by an objective standard of reasonableness. The provision was amended by s. 8(a) of the Inheritance and Trustees' Powers Act 2014 to give the trustees an unfettered discretion. As the Explanatory Note to the Act states, however, the 'general law on trustees' decision-making applies; the decision must be taken in good faith after due consideration of the circumstances'.   [91] Trustee Act 1925, s. 31(1).

[92] *Fuller v Evans* [2000] 1 All ER 636.   [93] Trustee Act 1925, s. 31(3).   [94] Ibid.

[95] Ker, 'Trustees' power of maintenance' (1953) 17 Conv 273, 275–9.

[96] *Re Vestey's Settlement* [1951] Ch 209.   [97] Trustee Act 1925, s. 31(2).

Once the beneficiary attains the age of 18, or has married or entered into a civil partnership at a younger age, and the trust property is vested in the beneficiary so that they are absolutely entitled to it, they have a right to those accumulations.[98] If a beneficiary becomes entitled to personalty on attaining a certain age, but that entitlement is subject to an overriding power of appointment, the beneficiary has no right to receive the accumulations because they are not absolutely entitled to the property since the power of appointment might be exercised and so defeat their interest.[99] If the property never vests in the beneficiary or the beneficiary is a minor with a vested interest who dies before attaining the age of 18, the accumulations will be added to capital.[100] This means, for example, that the interest of the child who died would devolve with the capital.

14.4.4 EXCLUSION OF THE STATUTORY POWER

The power of maintenance will be excluded if a contrary intention is expressed in the trust instrument.[101] The significance of this is illustrated by *Re Turner's Will Trust*,[102] in which the testator had created a trust for those of his grandchildren who attained the age of 28. An express power to apply the income for the maintenance, education, and benefit of the grandchildren was included, and the surplus income was to be accumulated. It was held that the direction to accumulate excluded the statutory power of maintenance.

The duty to accumulate income can also be excluded by a contrary intention in the trust instrument.[103] So, in *Re Delamere's Settlement Trust*,[104] the trustees had appointed income to the beneficiaries 'absolutely'. This was held to exclude the duty to accumulate.

14.5 POWER OF ADVANCEMENT

14.5.1 NATURE OF THE POWER

Whereas the power of maintenance relates to income, the statutory power of advancement relates to the payment of money or transfer or application of property[105] from the capital of the trust for the advancement or benefit of a beneficiary before that beneficiary has a right to receive the capital because their interest is contingent on the occurrence of a particular event.[106] The use of the word 'advancement' has a particular meaning, namely concerning the improvement of the beneficiary's condition, and does not relate to the act of advancing money from the trust.

The statutory power of advancement is to be read into every trust instrument in the absence of a contrary intention. It gives the trustees an absolute discretion to pay or transfer capital to the beneficiary directly, or to apply capital for the advancement or benefit of the beneficiary. The beneficiary who is entitled to the capital may be entitled absolutely or contingently, such as contingent on attaining a particular age, and whether in possession, in remainder, or in reversion, and even though the interest may be defeated by the exercise of a power of appointment or diminished by an increase in the class to which they belong.

---

[98] Ibid., s. 31(2)(i).

[99] *Re Sharp's Settlement Trusts* [1973] Ch 331. This does not apply where the trust property is land, since it is sufficient that the beneficiary has a determinable interest in the property.

[100] Trustee Act 1925, s. 31(2)(ii).   [101] Ibid., s. 69(2).   [102] [1937] Ch 15.

[103] Trustee Act 1925, s. 69(2).   [104] [1984] 1 WLR 813.

[105] The power to transfer or apply property was added by the Inheritance and Trustees' Powers Act 2014, s. 9(2). The extension to the application of property means, for example, that the power of advancement can be exercised to create another trust in favour of the beneficiary, with capital being transferred to new trustees to be held on trust for the beneficiary.   [106] Trustee Act 1925, s. 32(1).

14.5.2 EXERCISE OF THE POWER

The exercise of the power of advancement is, however, subject to certain requirements and restrictions.[107]

(i) Extent of advancement

In section 32 of the Trustee Act 1925 as originally enacted a significant restriction was that the capital paid to the beneficiary should not exceed one half of their presumptive or vested share. This restriction was removed by section 9(3)(a) of the Inheritance and Trustees' Powers Act 2014. It follows that the power of advancement has been extended to enable the whole of the beneficiary's prospective share to be paid, transferred, or applied for their advancement or benefit, but cannot exceed the beneficiary's prospective share.[108]

(ii) Subsequent absolute entitlement

If the person to or for whom capital has been paid, transferred, or applied becomes absolutely and indefeasibly entitled to a share in the property, the capital that has been paid, transferred, or applied must be taken into account as part of their share.[109] It is, however, possible for the trustees, when bringing the capital advanced into account, to choose, expressly or by implication, to treat the capital advanced to a beneficiary as a proportion of the overall value of the trust rather than according to its strict monetary value.[110] So, for example, if £10,000 is advanced to one of three beneficiaries at a time when the trust fund as a whole is worth £30,000, the trustees may choose to treat this as the distribution of the beneficiary's proportionate share, so that, even if the trust fund subsequently increases in value, that beneficiary is not entitled to receive any further distribution.

(iii) Avoiding prejudice to others

The payment, transfer, or application should not be made if it prejudices any person who is entitled to another interest in the capital, such as a life interest, unless that person is of full age and consents in writing to the advancement.[111]

(iv) Exclusion of the power

The power of advancement may be excluded by express or implied contrary intent in the trust instrument that it is not applicable.[112] The existence of an express power of advancement in the trust instrument does not necessarily exclude the statutory power, save where the powers are incompatible, such as where the trust instrument limits the amount of money that can be paid.[113]

(v) Proper exercise

The power of advancement, like any power of trustees, must be exercised for the proper purpose and not capriciously. So, for example, in *Klug v Klug*,[114] one of the trustees was willing to exercise the power of advancement in favour of the beneficiary, but the other trustee, who was the beneficiary's mother, refused to exercise the power because the claimant had married without her approval. It was held that the mother had failed to exercise her discretion at all and the court directed that the power of advancement out of capital should be made. It would have been different had the mother determined that the power

---

[107] Ibid.   [108] Ibid., s. 32(1)(a).   [109] Ibid., s. 32(1)(b).
[110] Ibid., s. 32(1A) as inserted by the Inheritance and Trustees' Powers Act 2014, s. 9(6).
[111] Ibid., s. 32(1)(c).   [112] Ibid., s. 69(2).   [113] *Re Evans' Settlement* [1967] 1 WLR 1294.
[114] [1918] 2 Ch 67.

should not be exercised because it would not have been in the claimant's best interest for the advancement to be made out of capital.

14.5.3 ADVANCEMENT OR BENEFIT

The key consideration when deciding whether the power of advancement should be exercised is whether it is for the advancement or benefit of the beneficiary. This phrase has traditionally encompassed the making of payments that contribute to the establishment in life of the beneficiary, such as by assisting them in training, obtaining a professional qualification[115] or an interest in a business, and even, for girls, the advancement in life on getting married.[116]

The use of the power has since been expanded to encompass a more immediate financial benefit. In *Pilkington v Inland Revenue Commissioners*,[117] the House of Lords recognized that the power could be used to pay capital to the beneficiary entitled to the capital to avoid inheritance tax liability on the death of the beneficiary entitled to income. In this case, the testator had left the income of his residuary estate on trust for his nieces and nephews, with the capital being held on trust for their children. One of the beneficiaries had a two-year-old daughter. The trustees decided to pay one half of the daughter's expectant share to the trustees of a new trust that was being created for her benefit. The main purpose of this payment was to avoid the tax liability that would arise on her father's death. It was held that, although this was an appropriate exercise of the power of advancement, because it was for the daughter's benefit, it was actually void for perpetuity, since the transfer of property to the new trust was an exercise of a power under the original trust, so the period of vesting started with the creation of the first trust. Since the daughter was not able to take under the new trust until she attained the age of 30, this was held to be too remote as a period of vesting.[118]

As regards the operation of the power of advancement, Viscount Radcliffe defined 'advancement or benefit' as encompassing 'any use of the money which will improve the material situation of the beneficiary',[119] and concluded that there was nothing in the words of section 32 of the Trustee Act 1925 that restricted the manner or purpose of the advancement. In particular, there was no objection that the property would be transferred to another trust by means of an effective resettlement of trust property.

Subsequently, the courts have held that the exercise of the power of advancement to enable transfers to be made to a specific charity could be considered to be for the material benefit of a rich minor who felt that he had a moral obligation to make appropriate donations to charity.[120] This is an even more extreme interpretation of 'benefit', since it actually involves a financial loss being caused to the beneficiary, albeit with the advantage of an improved moral well-being. A more restrictive interpretation of benefit was adopted in *X v A*,[121] in which it was held that a purported exercise of the power to pay capital to the beneficiary for charitable purposes did not improve her material situation. In that case the trust had been settled by a vicar, who had inherited his wealth from his family company. His strongly held view, shared by his wife, was that inherited wealth brought with it many disadvantages. His wife had a life interest in the property and she asked her trustees to

---

[115] *Re Pauling's Settlement Trusts* [1964] Ch 303.   [116] *Lloyd v Cocker* (1860) 27 Beav 645.

[117] [1964] AC 612.

[118] See now the Perpetuities and Accumulations Act 2009, discussed in Section 4.6.1, p. 102.

[119] *Pilkington v Inland Revenue Commissioners* [1964] AC 612, 635.

[120] *Re Clore's Settlement Trusts* [1966] 1 WLR 955.   [121] [2006] 1 WLR 741.

transfer capital from the trust fund for her to use it for charitable purposes. It was accepted that using capital from the fund to discharge a moral obligation would constitute benefit for purposes of the power, such as where, if the capital were not paid, the beneficiary would have paid the same amount from her own resources. But, in this case, the payment of the capital would not have improved her material situation, particularly because the amount she was seeking far exceeded the amount of her free assets. Crucially, the court emphasized that, although the beneficiary must feel that they have a moral obligation to make charitable donations, the moral obligation also needed to be recognized by the court objectively.

14.5.4 APPLICATION OF THE MONEY

In *Re Pauling's Settlement Trusts*,[122] it was recognized that, once the power of advancement had been exercised, the trustees were obliged to check that the money had been applied for the purpose for which it was advanced and could not leave the beneficiary free to spend the money how they wished. If the trustees were to become aware of such misapplication of the money paid, they should not pay any more to the beneficiary, but should pay it to a third party to spend it for the particular purpose.

---

[122] [1964] Ch 303, 334 (Willmer LJ). See further Section 17.3.5, p. 492.

15

FIDUCIARY DUTIES

15.1 GENERAL CONSIDERATIONS

Fiduciary law is one of the most significant contributions of Equity to the modern law, particularly in respect of commercial transactions. But it remains an area of the law that is fraught with controversy and uncertainty, as regards both the identification of fiduciary relationships and the determination of fiduciary duties. The fiduciary relationship has even been described as a 'concept in search of a principle'.[1]

15.1.1 ESSENCE OF FIDUCIARY RELATIONSHIPS

The essence of a fiduciary relationship is that the fiduciary has undertaken to act for or on behalf of somebody else in circumstances that give rise to a relationship of trust and confidence.[2] A fiduciary has been described by Birks as 'one who has discretion, and therefore, power, in the management of another's affairs, in circumstances in which that one cannot reasonably be expected to monitor him or take other precautions to protect his own interests'.[3] But these are simply hallmarks of a fiduciary relationship rather than a legal definition. Traditionally, a person is treated as a fiduciary because they are subject to fiduciary duties,[4] and so it is vital to determine what those duties are and when they might be recognized as arising.

15.1.2 ESSENCE OF FIDUCIARY DUTIES

The key obligation of a fiduciary is one of loyalty, in that the principal is entitled to the single-minded loyalty of the fiduciary.[5] Beneath the umbrella of this loyalty obligation are two fundamental duties, as recognized by Lord Herschell in *Bray v Ford*:[6]

---

[1] Mason, 'Themes and prospects', in *Essays in Equity*, ed. Finn (Sydney: Law Book Co., 1985), p. 246.

[2] *Bristol and West Building Society v Mothew* [1998] Ch 1, 18 (Millett LJ).

[3] 'Equity in the modern law: an exercise in taxonomy' (1996) 26 Univ WALR 1, 18. See also Shepherd, 'Towards a unified concept of fiduciary relationships' (1981) 97 LQR 51, 75.

[4] *Bristol and West Building Society v Mothew* [1998] Ch 1, 18 (Millett LJ). See Finn, *Fiduciary Obligations* (Sydney: Law Book Co., 1977), p. 2.

[5] *Bristol and West Building Society v Mothew* [1998] Ch 1, 18 (Millett LJ). See Worthington, 'Fiduciaries: when is self-denial obligatory?' (1999) 58 CLJ 500; Conaglen, 'The nature and function of fiduciary loyalty' (2005) 121 LQR 452.

[6] [1896] AC 44, 50.

it is an inflexible rule of a court of equity that a person in a fiduciary position . . . is not, unless otherwise expressly provided, entitled to make a profit; he is not allowed to put himself in a position where his interest and duty conflict.

These are the so-called 'no conflict' and 'no profit' duties, which are peculiar to fiduciaries.[7]

15.1.3 RELEVANCE OF FIDUCIARY DUTIES TO TRUSTEES

We have already seen that trustees are subject to a number of duties relating to the administration of the trust and the disposition of trust property. These are not fiduciary duties. But express trustees are considered to be in a fiduciary relationship of trust and confidence with their beneficiaries, and consequently they owe additional distinct fiduciary duties to the beneficiaries. Consequently, fiduciary law has a significant impact on the law of trusts.

15.1.4 WIDER SIGNIFICANCE OF THE LAW OF FIDUCIARIES

But the significance of the law of fiduciaries is not confined to imposing additional duties on trustees. The categories of fiduciary relationship are much wider and encompass a wide variety of commercial relationships, all of which can be characterized as relationships of trust and confidence. It follows that the law of fiduciaries is particularly relevant in the commercial world in imposing onerous duties on fiduciaries and significant remedies if the duties are breached.

Where the fiduciary is not a trustee, the person to whom the duties are owed is described as a 'principal'. So, for example, an agent will be in a fiduciary relationship and will owe fiduciary duties to their principal. In this chapter, the person to whom fiduciary duties are owed will be described as the principal, even though, in the trust context, the duties are actually owed to the beneficiaries.

15.1.5 REMEDIES FOR BREACH OF FIDUCIARY DUTY

The usual remedy where the fiduciary has breached a fiduciary duty is rescission of any transaction entered into by the fiduciary with or on behalf of the principal and the fiduciary will be liable to disgorge to the principal any profit made from the breach of duty.[8] But Equity can also require the fiduciary to compensate the principal for any loss suffered as a result of the breach of fiduciary duty.[9] It follows that the principal may have to elect between disgorgement and compensatory remedies. The choice of remedy will be determined by whether the loss suffered by the principal is greater than the profit obtained by the fiduciary. The principal will not be able to recover both compensatory and disgorgement remedies, since this would result in double recovery.[10] The fiduciary may also hold profit obtained from breaching the fiduciary duty on constructive trust for the principal, so that the principal has an equitable proprietary interest in the property held on trust, which will provide a basis for a proprietary claim.[11]

---

[7] *Bristol and West Building Society v Mothew* [1998] Ch 1, 16 (Millett LJ).   [8] See Section 18.5, p. 525.

[9] *Swindle v Harrison* [1997] 4 All ER 705; Conaglen, 'Equitable compensation for breach of fiduciary duty rules' (2003) 119 LQR 246. See further Section 18.4, p. 523.

[10] *Tang Man Sit v Capacious Investments Ltd* [1996] AC 514. See Watterson, 'An account of profits or damages? The history of orthodoxy' (2004) 24 OJLS 471. See Section 18.7, p. 535.

[11] See Section 15.7.3, p. 451.

15.2 DEFINITION OF A FIDUCIARY

Although a person is traditionally treated as a fiduciary because they are subject to fiduciary duties,[12] it is possible to identify certain principles that assist in the determination of whether a particular person is a fiduciary and who is therefore subject to fiduciary duties.

There is no legal definition of when somebody can be considered to be a fiduciary.[13] A 'fiduciary' is essentially somebody, person A, who is in a relationship with another person, B, in which B is entitled to expect that A will act either in B's best interests or in their joint interests, to the exclusion of A's own interest.[14] In determining whether a person is a fiduciary, it is first necessary to consider whether that person is in a relationship with another that falls within one of the recognized categories of fiduciary relationships. If it does not, it is then necessary to examine the factual circumstances of the relationship to determine whether there are sufficient hallmarks of a fiduciary relationship to enable the court to conclude that the relationship is indeed fiduciary.

15.2.1 RECOGNIZED CATEGORIES OF FIDUCIARY RELATIONSHIP

The recognized categories of fiduciary relationship include those involving agents,[15] solicitors,[16] company directors[17] including de facto directors,[18] and partners.[19]

The relationship of trustee and beneficiary is also a recognized category of fiduciary relationship. It is a matter of some uncertainty, however, whether all trustees can be considered to be in a fiduciary relationship. This will turn on what the hallmarks of such a relationship are considered to be. If, as Birks identified,[20] the exercise of a discretionary power in managing another's affairs is an essential feature of a fiduciary relationship, it would follow that a bare trustee could not be considered to be a fiduciary because such a trustee does not have such a discretionary power.[21] Similarly, a custodian trustee[22] will not be a fiduciary because their duties are simply to look after trust property, with no discretion as to its management. Although it has been recognized that a custodian trustee is indeed subject to fiduciary duties,[23] the better view is that this is incorrect because they have no discretion to exercise.

Whether resulting and constructive trustees are subject to fiduciary duties is a matter of some controversy. The preferable view is that a trustee should be considered to be subject to these distinct fiduciary duties only if they voluntarily assumed the position of

---

[12] *Bristol and West Building Society v Mothew* [1998] Ch 1, 18 (Millett LJ).

[13] *Grimaldi v Chameleon Mining NL (No 2)* [2012] FCAFC 6, [177] (Finn J). But see Glover, 'The identification of fiduciaries', in *Privacy and Loyalty*, ed. Birks (Oxford: Clarendon Press, 1997), ch. 10, who attempts to identify the hallmarks of a fiduciary relationship as involving an undertaking by the fiduciary, property, reliance, and power.

[14] Finn, 'Fiduciary law and the modern commercial world', in *Commercial Aspects of Trusts and Fiduciary Obligations*, ed. McKendrick (Oxford: Clarendon Press, 1992), p. 9.

[15] *De Bussche v Alt* (1878) 8 Ch D 286.   [16] *Brown v IRC* [1965] AC 244.

[17] *Aberdeen Rail Co v Blaikie Brothers* (1854) 23 LT 315. The duty is owed to the company and not to the shareholders: Companies Act 2006, s. 170(1). Shadow company directors also owe fiduciary duties: Companies Act 2006, s. 170(5).

[18] *Revenue and Customs Commissioners v Holland* [2010] UKSC 51, [2010] 1 WLR 2793; *Vivendi v Richards* [2013] EWHC 3006 (Ch), [2013] BCC 771, [142] (Newey J).

[19] *Featherstonhaugh v Fenwick* (1810) 17 Ves 298.

[20] See Section 15.1.1, p. 418. This hallmark was also recognized by the High Court of Australia in *Hospital Products Ltd v United States Surgical Corp* (1984) 156 CLR 41, 97 (Mason J), and by the Supreme Court of Canada in *Galambos v Perez* 2009 SCR 48, [2009] 3 SCR 247.   [21] See Section 3.6.2.(vi), p. 55.

[22] See Section 12.3.6, p. 344.   [23] *Re Brooke Bond and Co Ltd's Trust Deed* [1963] Ch 357.

trustee.[24] It follows that a constructive trustee should not be considered to be a fiduciary, because there is no voluntary assumption of the position of trustee, so that the trustee has not knowingly subjected themself to fiduciary obligations.[25] This should be true of all constructive trustees, regardless of whether the constructive trust arises by virtue of unconscionable conduct[26] or common intention.[27] Whether a resulting trustee is a fiduciary would depend on the category of resulting trust that is involved. If the resulting trust arises automatically from the failure of an express trust,[28] it would be appropriate to treat the resulting trustee as a fiduciary,[29] since the trustee would already owe fiduciary duties under the express trust that would have been voluntarily assumed. Where, however, the resulting trust is presumed,[30] there is no reason to impose fiduciary duties on the trustee because the trustee has not voluntarily assumed the position of trustee.

15.2.2 AD HOC FIDUCIARY RELATIONSHIPS

It has been recognized that the classes of fiduciary relationship are not closed,[31] so new categories of fiduciary relationship may be recognized, but if a particular relationship does not fall within one of the recognized categories, it might still be characterized as fiduciary if it is sufficiently similar to one of the recognized classes, with the hallmark of trust and confidence. So, for example, it has been recognized that members of a joint venture can be in a fiduciary relationship,[32] as can certain bailees,[33] certain public officials,[34] and employees in a relationship of confidentiality.[35]

The possibility of identifying fiduciary relationships outside the established categories is potentially very important as regards commercial transactions. The courts have generally refused to recognize that a commercial relationship that has been entered into at arm's length and on an equal footing is a fiduciary relationship,[36] because it lacks the hallmarks of trust and confidence. This was confirmed by the Privy Council in *Re Goldcorp Exchange plc*,[37] in which a restrictive interpretation of fiduciary duties was adopted.[38] In that case the claimants had bought bullion from the defendant company. The bullion had not been allocated to the claimants, who consequently argued that the defendant had breached its fiduciary duty to them. This argument was easily rejected because the court was unable to identify duties that could be characterized as fiduciary rather than merely contractual.

The identification of fiduciary duties, especially in a commercial context, can have profound consequences on the risks inherent in such relationships, since the characterization of the defendant as a fiduciary will often mean that they bear the risk of things going wrong. It is to be hoped that the recognition in *Re Goldcorp* that fiduciary duties

---

[24] See Edelman, 'When do fiduciary duties arise?' (2010) 126 LQR 302. See further Section 15.3.6, p. 427.

[25] Millett, 'Restitution and constructive trusts' (1998) 114 LQR 399, 405. See also Smith, 'Constructive fiduciaries', in *Privacy and Loyalty*, ed. Birks (Oxford: Clarendon Press, 1997), p. 263.

[26] See Chapter 9 of this volume.   [27] See Chapter 10 of this volume.   [28] See Section 8.3.2, p. 231.

[29] See Chambers, *Resulting Trusts* (Oxford: Clarendon Press, 1997), pp. 196–200.

[30] See Chapter 8.2, p. 217.   [31] *English v Dedham Vale Properties Ltd* [1978] 1 WLR 93.

[32] *Murad v Al-Saraj* [2005] EWCA Civ 969, [2005] WTLR 1573.

[33] *Aluminium Industrie Vaassen BV v Romalpa Aluminium Ltd* [1976] 1 WLR 676.

[34] *Reading v Attorney-General* [1951] AC 507 (police sergeant); *Attorney-General for Hong Kong v Reid* [1994] 1 AC 324 (acting director of public prosecutions).

[35] *Attorney-General v Guardian Newspapers Ltd (No 2)* [1990] 1 AC 109.

[36] *Polly Peck International v Nadir (No 2)* [1992] 4 All ER 769; *Re Goldcorp Exchange Ltd* [1995] 1 AC 74, 98 (Lord Mustill).   [37] [1995] 1 AC 74.

[38] See also *Hospital Products International v United States Surgical Corporation* (1984) 156 CLR 41 (High Court of Australia).

are fundamentally different from merely contractual obligations will prevent the concept from being abused purely from a desire to secure a just result. As Lord Mustill memorably said, 'high expectations do not necessarily lead to equitable remedies'.[39] Millett LJ has emphasized extrajudicially that: 'It is of the first importance not to impose fiduciary obligations on parties to a purely commercial relationship who deal with each other at arms' length and can be expected to look after their own interests.'[40]

It does not follow that fiduciary law has no role to play in commercial transactions. Many of the recognized categories of fiduciary relationship operate in the commercial context, such as partnerships, company directors, and solicitors. But the concern is with fiduciary duties being attached to ad hoc commercial relationships in which they have no legitimate role to play. A commercial relationship should be converted into a fiduciary one only in limited circumstances and the key test should be whether the defendant has voluntarily undertaken to act for another.[41] This was acknowledged by the Supreme Court of Canada in *Galambos v Perez*,[42] which held that an ad hoc fiduciary relationship should be recognized only if two conditions are satisfied:

(1) there is an express or implied undertaking by one party that they will act in the best interests of the other; and

(2) the party making the undertaking has a discretionary power to affect the other's legal or practical interests.

Consequently, in that case, where an office manager of a law firm had lent money to the firm to stave off its insolvency, it was held that a lawyer in the firm was not in a fiduciary relationship with the office manager because he was unaware that the loans had been made, so there was no undertaking that he would act in her best interests and he had no discretionary power that would affect her interests.

It has also been suggested that another hallmark of a fiduciary relationship is that it is reasonable or legitimate for the principal to expect that fiduciary duties will be complied with.[43] This is probably, however, not an additional requirement to those identified in *Galambos*, because, where there is an express or implied undertaking to act in the principal's best interests, the principal will have a legitimate expectation that the fiduciary will comply with their fiduciary duties.

These hallmarks of an undertaking or legitimate expectation and discretionary power are consistent with a number of cases that have recognized ad hoc fiduciary relationships. So, for example, in the employment context, although the relationship of employer and employee is not normally a fiduciary one,[44] it is possible for fiduciary duties to be recognized by virtue of specific contractual obligations imposed on the employee to act solely in the interests of the employer.[45] So, for example, in *Tesco Stores v Pook*,[46] a senior employee

---

[39] *Re Goldcorp Exchange plc* [1995] 1 AC 74, 98.

[40] 'Equity's place in the law of commerce' (1998) 114 LQR 214, 217–18. Cf. Mason, 'The place of Equity and equitable remedies in the contemporary common law world' (1994) 110 LQR 238, 245–6.

[41] Edelman (see n. 24).

[42] 2009 SCC 48, [2009] 3 SCR 247. See also *Alberta v Elder Advocates of Alberta Society* 2011 SCC 23, in which the Supreme Court of Canada recognized that fiduciary liability could extend to public authorities, albeit exceptionally. See Flannigan, 'A revised Canadian test for fact-based fiduciary accountability' (2011) 127 LQR 505. This has been recognized in England: *Bromley LBC v Greater London Council* [1983] 1 AC 768; *Charles Terence Estates Ltd v Cornwall Council* [2011] EWHC 2542 (QB).

[43] Conaglen, *Fiduciary Loyalty: Protecting the Due Performance of Non-Fiduciary Duties* (Oxford: Hart, 2010), ch. 9.   [44] *Customer Services plc v Ranson* [2012] EWCA Civ 841.

[45] *Nottingham University v Fischel* [2000] ICR 1461; *Customer Services plc v Ranson* [2012] EWCA Civ 841, [54] (Lewison LJ).   [46] [2003] EWHC 823 (Ch).

was found to be subject to fiduciary duties even though he was not a director, and so did not fall within a recognized category of fiduciary relationship, because he was a senior manager of the company whose contractual obligations rendered him a fiduciary.[47]

This restrictive approach to the recognition of ad hoc fiduciary relationships is not always reflected in the cases. This is illustrated by *English v Dedham Vale Properties Ltd*,[48] in which the defendant was considered to be a self-appointed agent and so a fiduciary. The defendant was a property development company that wanted to purchase the claimant's house, known as 'Rusty Tiles'. The purchase price that was agreed reflected the fact that planning permission for the development of Rusty Tiles was unlikely. But, before the contracts were exchanged, the defendant applied for planning permission in the name of the claimant and obtained it, although the defendant had failed to inform the claimant of this. Once the claimant had discovered that the defendant had obtained planning permission, it successfully claimed the profit that the defendant had made as a result of the development, on the ground that the defendant owed the claimant fiduciary duties. It was held that the defendant was a fiduciary because it had purported to act as an agent of the claimant when it obtained planning permission. But this is a highly artificial finding of such a relationship, since there was nothing on the facts to suggest that either party had ever contemplated that the defendant was acting as the claimant's agent. There was no evidence of any express or implied undertaking that the defendant would act in the claimant's best interests nor (which is probably the other side of the same coin) that the claimant had a legitimate expectation that the defendant would comply with its duties. The identification of a fiduciary relationship appears to have been motivated by a sense that the defendant had behaved in an underhand way and should not be allowed to profit from its conduct. But that is no basis for making somebody a fiduciary. Principles can be identified and should be respected. Crucially, ad hoc fiduciary relationships should be recognized only in exceptional circumstances.

15.3 NATURE OF FIDUCIARY DUTIES

Once it has been recognized that the defendant is a fiduciary in a fiduciary relationship, it is necessary to consider the nature and ambit of the fiduciary duties to which they are subject. The details of the law relating to these duties will be examined later. At this stage, it is useful to identify a number of principles to assist in their interpretation and application.

15.3.1 BREACH OF DUTY

For a fiduciary to be liable for breach of fiduciary duty, they must have breached the duty by an intentional act; unconscious omission is not sufficient.[49] But, crucially, a fiduciary will be held liable even if they did not act fraudulently or in bad faith and even if the fiduciary honestly thought that they were acting in good faith.[50] It follows that liability for breach of fiduciary duty is strict, since the fiduciary need not be aware of the disloyalty; they only need intentionally to do the act that constitutes disloyalty.

---

[47] Cf. Flannigan, 'The [fiduciary] duty of fidelity' (2008) 124 LQR 274, 288, who considers that all employees should be treated as fiduciaries by virtue of their status rather than by virtue of the facts.

[48] [1978] 1 WLR 93.   [49] *Bristol and West Building Society v Mothew* [1998] Ch 1, 19 (Millett LJ).

[50] *Murad v Al-Saraj* [2005] EWCA Civ 969, [2005] WTLR 1573, [67] (Arden LJ).

15.3.2 DISTINCTION BETWEEN FIDUCIARY AND NON-FIDUCIARY DUTIES

Not every breach of duty by a fiduciary is a breach of a fiduciary duty.[51] We have already seen that the core fiduciary duties are the no-conflict and the no-profit duties,[52] but fiduciaries will be subject to many other duties, such as the obligation to use proper skill and care in the discharge of their duties.[53] The breach of this obligation is not, however, a breach of a fiduciary duty, simply because the obligation arises from the fact that the defendant has assumed responsibility to another person and not from the fact that the defendant is a fiduciary.[54] Similarly, the duties to act in good faith, for proper purposes, and without exceeding the fiduciary's powers should not be characterized as fiduciary duties because they are also recognized in non-fiduciary relationships.[55]

This distinction between fiduciary and non-fiduciary duties might simply be treated as a matter of correct use of terminology without any substantive consequences. But whether the duty that has been breached is fiduciary or non-fiduciary will sometimes have substantive consequences,[56] both as regards the rules of causation and also as regards the determination of the appropriate remedy, with full disgorgement of profits being the typical remedy for breaches of fiduciary duty and equitable compensation for breach of non-fiduciary duties.[57]

15.3.3 PROSCRIPTIVE DUTIES

Fiduciary duties are generally considered to be proscriptive in effect. This means that the duties do not identify what fiduciaries must do, but rather identify what they should not do on the basis that, if a fiduciary were to act in a prohibited way, this would be disloyal to the principal. In other words, they operate negatively by preventing the fiduciary from acting in a particular way that could be considered to be disloyal to the principal, such as competing with the principal's business where the fiduciary has obtained a competitive advantage through the use of knowledge acquired whilst acting as a fiduciary. Crucially, fiduciary duties do not operate positively, or prescriptively, by requiring the fiduciary to do particular things.

But the principle that fiduciary duties are only proscriptive needs to be treated with some caution: even though the fiduciary duties are formulated in such a way as to identify what the fiduciary must not do, it may still follow that the fiduciary must act in a particular way in order to avoid liability. For example, if the fiduciary is acting for two principals whose interests conflict and the fiduciary obtains information from one principal that would be of benefit to the other, the fiduciary must disclose the information to the other.[58]

---

[51] *Bristol and West Building Society v Mothew* [1998] Ch 1, 16 (Millett LJ). See also *Hilton v Barker, Booth and Eastwood* [2005] UKHL 8, [2005] 1 WLR 567, [29] (Lord Walker).

[52] See Section 15.1.2, p. 418.   [53] See Section 13.2, p. 374, for analysis of the trustee's duty of care.

[54] *Henderson v Merrett Syndicates Ltd* [1995] 2 AC 145, 180 (Lord Goff) and 205 (Lord Browne-Wilkinson); *White v Jones* [1995] 2 AC 207, 274 (Lord Browne-Wilkinson).

[55] Conaglen (see n. 5), p. 457. Cf. *Bristol and West Building Society v Mothew* [1998] Ch 1, 18, in which Millett LJ described the duty to act in good faith as being a fiduciary duty; *Pitt v Holt* [2013] UKSC 26, [2013] 2 AC 108, [73] where Lord Walker described the trustee's duty to comply with the reasonable standard of skill and care as breach of fiduciary duty. But these duties are not peculiar to fiduciaries. See Section 12.8.7, p. 370. See generally Nolan and Conaglen, 'Good faith: what does it mean for fiduciaries and what does it tell us about them?', in *Exploring Private Law*, ed. Bant and Harding (Cambridge: Cambridge University Press, 2010), ch. 14, on the characterization of duties.   [56] *Bristol and West Building Society v Mothew* [1998] Ch 1, 16 (Millett LJ).

[57] See Chapter 18 of this volume.

[58] *Hilton v Barker Booth and Eastwood* [2005] UKHL 8, [2005] 1 WLR 567. See Section 15.5.3.(iii), p. 437.

Similarly, if the fiduciary acquires a business opportunity whilst acting as a fiduciary, they are not able to exploit it without disclosing the opportunity to the principal.[59] In both of these situations, the underlying fiduciary duty can still be characterized as proscriptive, since the duty actually requires the fiduciary not to place themselves in a position in which their work for two principals might conflict and not to exploit a business opportunity that they acquired as fiduciary; but, in order to avoid liability for breach of duty from arising, in both cases the fiduciary will need to act by disclosing information to the principal. In other words, whilst the duty is formulated proscriptively, in that the fiduciary should not allow themself to be in a position of disloyalty, if the fiduciary does find themself in such a position, certain action on the part of the fiduciary can function as a defence to avoid liability.

It has been argued that there is no reason why fiduciary duties cannot be formulated to encompass prescriptive duties that require the fiduciary to act in a particular way, and that this would still be consistent with the underlying fundamental obligation of loyalty.[60] In fact, fiduciary duties have sometimes been formulated as involving positive duties to act. So, for example, in *Item Software UK Ltd v Fassihi*,[61] it was held that a director, who had tried unsuccessfully to exploit a corporate opportunity for himself, was under a positive fiduciary duty to disclose to the company his intention to compete with it and was liable for the failure to disclose the attempted exploitation. This was different from disclosure that is needed to prevent a liability from arising, where the disclosure operates as a defence,[62] since in *Item Software* it was the failure to disclose the wrongdoing that constituted the breach of duty. In other words, it was the non-disclosure of misconduct by the fiduciary that constituted a distinct breach of fiduciary duty and this was a prescriptive, rather than a proscriptive, duty, because the director was required to act in a particular way. This fiduciary duty was considered to derive from the fundamental duty of a director to act in what they considered in good faith to be in the best interests of the company.[63] Breach of this positive duty involves proof of awareness of disloyalty on the part of the fiduciary, since they would only be liable if they were to consider that disclosure would, in fact, be in the principal's best interests, but had failed to disclose the misconduct.

This so-called 'duty to disclose misconduct' might be treated as an aspect of the usual proscriptive duty of a fiduciary to avoid a conflict between their personal interest and their duty to the principal. This would mean that the fiduciary was not allowed even to try to exploit an opportunity that would otherwise be available for the principal without first disclosing their intent to do so to the principal.[64] But this is not how the Court of Appeal analysed the duty in *Item Software* and, if the duty were to form part of the no-conflict rule, the fiduciary's liability would not depend on whether they considered that disclosure would be in the best interests of the principal. Although the Court of Appeal described failure to disclose misconduct as a breach of fiduciary duty, the preferable view is that this is actually a distinct non-fiduciary duty, since the duty to disclose misconduct was related

---

[59] See Section 15.6.7, p. 442.

[60] Ho and Lee, 'A director's duty to confess: a matter of good faith?' (2007) 66 CLJ 348, 357. See also Lee, 'In search of the nature and function of fiduciary loyalty: some observations on Conaglen's analysis' (2007) 27 OJLS 327.

[61] [2004] EWCA (Civ) 1244, [2005] 2 BCLC 91.   [62] See Section 15.5.3.(iii), p. 437.

[63] [2004] EWCA (Civ) 1244, [2005] 2 BCLC 91, [41] (Arden LJ); *Shepherds Investments Ltd v Walters* [2006] EWHC 836 (Ch), [2007] 2 BCLC 202, [132] (Etherton J); *Sinclair Investments (UK) Ltd v Versailles Trade Finance Ltd* [2011] EWCA Civ 347, [2012] Ch 453, [36] (Lord Neuberger MR).

[64] This is how the duty was interpreted by Etherton J in *Shepherds Investments Ltd v Walters* [2006] EWHC 836 (Ch), [2007] 2 BCLC 202.

to the director's duty to act in the best interests of the principal. Since this is a duty that is not peculiar to fiduciaries, it is preferably not characterized as a fiduciary duty, and so the decision does not undermine the fundamental principle that fiduciary duties are proscriptive[65] and that they involve strict liability.

It follows that fiduciary duties are properly characterized as proscriptive only. This emphasis on their proscriptive nature is of practical significance for the future development of fiduciary law, since it means that, once a defendant has been characterized as a fiduciary in a fiduciary relationship, it is not possible to impose positive duties on the fiduciary to act in a particular way simply because they are a fiduciary. So, for example, in *Breen v Williams*,[66] the High Court of Australia refused to compel a doctor to disclose medical records to his patient because the doctor was not necessarily in a fiduciary relationship with the patient, but, even if he were, no positive obligation of disclosure should have been recognized.

15.3.4 TERMINATION OF THE RELATIONSHIP

As a general rule, a fiduciary obligation does not continue after the termination of the relationship that gave rise to the duty.[67] Where the fiduciary is employed, the relationship will be terminated when the employment ends. The relationship may even finish earlier where the fiduciary continues to be formally appointed, but has no discretion to exercise.[68] There are, however, exceptional circumstances in which fiduciary obligations continue after the relationship has been terminated. For example, where the fiduciary resigns in order to exploit an opportunity that they discovered whilst acting as a fiduciary, the exploitation of the opportunity will constitute a breach of fiduciary duty.[69] Whilst this might be analysed as continuation of fiduciary duties after resignation, and so an exception to the general rule that fiduciary duties terminate on resignation, it is better analysed as a breach of duty whilst still in a fiduciary relationship, by virtue of the disloyalty in resigning in order to exploit the opportunity.[70] Indeed, if the fiduciary resigns for legitimate reasons and then exploits the opportunity, this will not constitute a breach of fiduciary duty.[71]

There are other potential qualifications to the rule that fiduciary duties end on the termination of the relationship. The first is where information is imparted to the fiduciary in confidence whilst the fiduciary relationship subsists. The obligation to maintain confidence is unrelated to the fiduciary continuing to be employed and so the obligation continues even after the relationship has been terminated,[72] although strictly the liability is for breach of confidence rather than for breach of fiduciary duty.[73] The second exception is where the principal remains dependent on the fiduciary despite the formal termination of the relationship, so that the fiduciary continues to be able to exert influence on the principal. So, for example, in *Demerara Bauxite Co Ltd v Hubbard*,[74] a

---

[65] *Item Software* was not followed by the Supreme Court of Victoria for this reason: *P and V Industries Pty Ltd v Porto* (2006) 14 VR 1. See also Harding, 'Two fiduciary fallacies' (2007) 2 J Eq 1.

[66] (1996) 186 CLR 71.

[67] *CMS Dolphin Ltd v Simonet* [2001] EWHC 415 (Ch), [2001] 2 BCLC 704, [95] (Collins J); *In Plus Group Ltd v Pyke* [2002] EWCA Civ 370, [2002] 2 BCLC 201, [71] (Brooke LJ).

[68] *In Plus Group Ltd v Pyke* [2002] EWCA Civ 370, [2002] 2 BCLC 201.

[69] *Foster Bryant Surveying Ltd v Bryant* [2007] EWCA Civ 200, [2007] 2 BCLC 239.

[70] Ibid., [69] (Rix LJ).   [71] See Section 15.6.7.(iv), p. 447.

[72] *Attorney-General v Blake* [1998] Ch 439 (CA); *Attorney-General v Guardian Newspapers Ltd (No 3)* [1990] 1 AC 109.

[73] *Bolkiah v KPMG* [1999] 2 AC 222, 235 (Lord Millett).   [74] [1923] AC 673.

solicitor purchased property from his former client, in circumstances under which the antecedent relationship of influence between the parties continued, so that the solicitor continued to be subject to fiduciary duties. The fiduciary relationship in such a case can be considered to have changed from a relationship falling within one of the recognized fiduciary relationships to one that is ad hoc and that arises on the particular facts of the case.

15.3.5 VARIABLE DUTIES

The ambit and interpretation of fiduciary duties may vary depending on the nature of the underlying fiduciary relationship. This may occur for two reasons. First, different categories of fiduciary may have different levels of duty. So, for example, the duties will be interpreted more strictly as regards trustees than for partners in a partnership. Secondly, a fiduciary may owe fiduciary duties in respect of some of their activities, but not all of them,[75] depending on whether the particular activity requires the fiduciary to be loyal to the principal.

15.3.6 ROLE OF CONTRACT

In many cases, the fiduciary relationship derives from a contractual relationship between the parties, such as agency or a joint venture. The contract between the parties can define, modify, and even exclude the fiduciary obligations.[76] As Langbein has recognized, 'the duty of loyalty is default law that yields to contrary terms'.[77] So, for example, particular fiduciary duties can be determined by the trust instrument, or a company's memorandum and articles of association, or the contract between agent and principal. The operation of the underlying contract can consequently be highly significant to the identification and interpretation of the relevant fiduciary duties.

Edelman[78] has argued that fiduciary obligations are express or implied duties that arise where one party voluntarily undertakes to act in the interests of the other. He considers that the test for implying such duties is the same as that for the implication of terms in a contract, namely whether a party, by their words or conduct, gave rise to an understanding or expectation in a reasonable person that they would behave in a particular way.[79] Whilst it is certainly the case that fiduciary duties can be expressly agreed or implied as a matter of fact, it is also the case that such duties will be imposed by law without regard to express or implied manifestations of consent,[80] so that it will not always be necessary to construe the nature of the undertaking to determine the duties that have been undertaken by the parties. Rather, where the hallmarks of a fiduciary relationship have been identified, either because the relationship falls within one of the recognized categories or is a de facto fiduciary relationship, fiduciary duties will be imposed by operation of law, but these duties may be modified or excluded by the parties.[81]

---

[75] *New Zealand Netherlands Society 'Oranje' Inc v Kuys* [1973] 1 WLR 1126, 1130 (Lord Wilberforce).

[76] *Kelly v Cooper* [1993] AC 205, 215 (Lord Browne-Wilkinson) (PC). See *Sargeant v National Westminster Bank plc* (1990) 61 P & CR 518.

[77] 'The contractarian basis of the law of trusts' (1995) 105 Yale LJ 625, 659. See also Duggan, 'Is Equity efficient?' (1997) 113 LQR 601, 624; Easterbrook and Fischel, 'Contract and fiduciary duty' (1993) 36 J L & Econ 425, 426; Duggan, 'Contracts, fiduciaries and the primacy of the deal', in *Exploring Private Law*, ed. Bant and Harding (Cambridge: Cambridge University Press, 2010), ch. 12.   [78] Edelman (see n. 24).

[79] Ibid., p. 317.   [80] Something contemplated ibid., p. 327.

[81] Conaglen, 'Fiduciary duties and voluntary undertakings' (2013) 7 J Eq 105.

15.3.7 THE PECULIAR POSITION OF COMPANY DIRECTORS

We have already seen that company directors are fiduciaries and owe fiduciary duty to their companies.[82] Although these duties have been developed primarily in respect of trustees, the corporate context has had a significant impact in defining the no-conflict and no-profit duties, since many of the key decisions on fiduciary law have involved directors. The Companies Act 2006, however, purported to codify the common law and fiduciary duties of company directors. It follows that, today, the fiduciary duties of directors are determined with reference to this statute rather than to the equitable rules. The statutory fiduciary duties of directors are based on equitable principles and replace those principles as regards the duties owed by directors.[83] But the equitable principles remain relevant when interpreting and applying the statutory duties,[84] and the remedies for breach of the statutory duties are the same as those that apply to the breach of the equivalent equitable duties.[85] The core no-conflict[86] and no-profit[87] duties are included in the statute as well. But, as will be seen,[88] this is not a simple codification. The statute has clarified the law as regards certain aspects of fiduciary duties, so it will be important to check whether the fiduciary is a director or not: if a fiduciary is a director, the relevant duty will need to be identified from the statute rather than from equitable principles, even though the statutory and equitable duties are broadly the same.

15.4 FUNCTION OF FIDUCIARY DUTIES

15.4.1 IMPOSITION OF STRICT STANDARDS

The two key fiduciary duties require the fiduciary to avoid conflict between personal interest and duty, and to avoid making an unauthorized profit from their position as a fiduciary. Both of these duties are interpreted very strictly, so that the fiduciary is liable even though they were acting honestly and to the best of their ability, without fraud or bad faith.[89] For example, a fiduciary will be liable to account to the principal for profits they had made in a personal capacity whilst acting for the principal, even though the fiduciary acted in good faith, made the profits from a transaction that was beneficial to the principal, and the profits could not have been obtained by the principal.[90] It follows that the highest standards of behaviour are expected from fiduciaries to avoid the imposition of liability. The imposition of such high standards has been subject to much criticism, but to understand the function of fiduciary duties, it is vital to be aware of the reasons why such high standards are imposed. A number of reasons have been suggested by judges and commentators, some of which are more persuasive than others.

(i) Morality

It has sometimes been suggested that the high standards expected of fiduciaries are imposed for reasons of morality.[91] This has been described as the 'altruistic theory' of fiduciary law.[92] According to this theory, fiduciary duties are imposed to protect vulnerable principals by requiring the fiduciary to act in the best interests of the principal. But such

---

[82] See Section 15.2.1, p. 420.   [83] Companies Act 2006, s. 170(3).
[84] Ibid., s. 170(4).   [85] Ibid., s. 178.   [86] Ibid., s. 175.
[87] Ibid., s. 176 (as regards accepting benefits from third parties).   [88] See Section 15.5.2, p. 432.
[89] *Regal (Hastings) Ltd v Gulliver* [1967] AC 134n, 386 (Lord Russell).   [90] See Section 15.6.7.(iii), p. 444.
[91] Alternatively for reasons of public policy: Simpson, 'Conflicts', in *Breach of Trust*, ed. Birks and Pretto (Oxford: Hart, 2002), p. 77.   [92] Duggan (1997) (see n. 77), p. 619.

a theory is at odds with the essential features of fiduciary law, primarily that it determines what the fiduciary cannot do rather than determining what the fiduciary must do. That the fiduciary duties are not founded on principles of morality was recognized by Lord Herschell in *Bray v Ford*.[93]

(ii) Evidential complexity

The strict approach to the application of fiduciary duties means that it is not necessary for the principal to prove that they have suffered harm as a result of the breach of duty or that any profit obtained by the fiduciary can be attributed to the breach. This makes it evidentially more straightforward to establish liability for breach of duty. In the nineteenth century, Equity's rules of evidence were too cumbersome to cope with proof of loss and gain and this may, therefore, provide a historical justification for the equitable approach to liability for breach of fiduciary duties. But the evidential rules are now more sophisticated. The laws of tort, contract, and unjust enrichment can cope with such evidential questions, and there is no reason why Equity cannot do so today.[94]

(iii) Control of discretion

Since it is a hallmark of a fiduciary relationship that the fiduciary has discretionary powers that are to be exercised for the benefit of the principal, the strict nature of fiduciary duties might be justified as a means of controlling the exercise of this discretion and protecting the principal against the abuse of this discretion.[95]

(iv) Resisting temptation

In *Bray v Ford*,[96] Lord Hershell, in recognizing the no-conflict and no-profit duties, concluded that they existed because of the danger of the fiduciary being swayed by personal interest rather than duty and thus prejudicing those whom they were bound to protect.[97] In other words, the strict duties operate to insulate the fiduciary from distracting influences and ensure that the fiduciary resists the temptation to serve themself rather than the principal.[98]

(v) Deterrence

Another justification for the strict interpretation of fiduciary duties is deterrence of other fiduciaries, to ensure that they comply with the highest standards of behaviour. This is sometimes described as *'pour encourager les autres'*.[99]

(vi) Proper performance of non-fiduciary duties

According to Conaglen, fiduciary relationships are recognized and fiduciary duties are imposed to encourage the fiduciary to maintain high standards of behaviour, and so to increase the chance that their non-fiduciary duties will be properly performed.[100] The duties are interpreted strictly therefore to ensure that the chances of breaching a non-fiduciary

---

[93] [1896] AC 44, 50.   [94] *Murad v Al-Saraj* [2005] EWCA Civ 959, [2005] WTLR 1573, [82] (Arden LJ).

[95] Weinrib, 'The fiduciary obligation' (1975) 24 UTLJ 1, 9; Langbein (see n. 77), p. 657; Samet, 'Guarding the fiduciary's conscience: a justification of a stringent profit-stripping rule' (2008) 28 OJLS 763.

[96] [1896] AC 44, 50.

[97] Ibid., 51. See also *Murad v Al-Saraj* [2005] EWCA Civ 959, [2005] WTLR 1573, [74] (Arden LJ).

[98] Worthington (see n. 5), p. 506. See also Flannigan, 'The adulteration of fiduciary doctrine in corporate law' (2006) 122 LQR 449.

[99] *Murad v Al-Saraj* [2005] EWCA Civ 959, [2005] WTLR 1573, [74] (Arden LJ).

[100] Conaglen (see n. 5), p. 453.

duty, such as not acting in the principal's best interests or failing to comply with the reasonable standard of skill and care, are reduced by ensuring that the fiduciary avoids situations in which the breach of such a duty is more likely to occur. Conaglen considers that fiduciary law is consequently subsidiary, since it seeks to enhance the performance of non-fiduciary duties, and that it exists to remove or neutralize incentives that might tempt the fiduciary not to perform properly their non-fiduciary duties.[101]

(vii) Summary

Whilst some of these reasons are unconvincing, particularly those focusing on morality and evidential difficulties, the others are not necessarily incompatible with each other and in fact they are linked by a common thread. This is that the fiduciary duties are prophylactic, which means that they exist to prevent a particular state of affairs from occurring. That state of affairs is that the fiduciary acts in such a way as to be disloyal to the principal and Equity seeks to prevent such disloyalty by imposing the most severe duty of loyalty.[102] Whether this is analysed in terms of nullifying temptation, controlling discretion, deterring particular conduct, or ensuring the proper performance of non-fiduciary duties, the concern throughout is the prevention of disloyalty. All of these reasons provide sound justifications for the strictness of the fiduciary duties, although Conaglen's has the distinct advantage of identifying specifically what the fiduciary duties are seeking to prevent, namely breach of a fiduciary's other duties.

The prophylactic function of fiduciary duties has been summarized well by Samet:[103] 'the remedy [for breach of fiduciary duty] is not meant as an incentive to sincere and honest action in conditions of conflict of interest. Rather, it is a warning against getting involved in such situations in the first place.' This is the real reason why fiduciary duties are interpreted so strictly. Equity is not concerned with maintaining high standards of behaviour in carrying out work for or on behalf of the principal; that is what the non-fiduciary duties are for. Equity is concerned to ensure that the fiduciary does not place themself in a position in which they might be tempted to be disloyal. Where the fiduciary does place themself in such a position of personal interest, either because the fiduciary's personal interest conflicts with their duty to the principal or because the fiduciary has the opportunity to make a profit, there will be an automatic breach of fiduciary duty regardless of the reasons why the fiduciary placed themself in that position. The fiduciary duties are therefore simply imposed to ensure that the fiduciary remains personally disinterested throughout the time during which they are working for the principal.

Although reasons can therefore be identified for the strict interpretation of the fiduciary duties, there is one practical objection to those that have been suggested, an objection that is rarely canvassed in the cases or the literature. If these rules do have a prophylactic function, they exist to prevent the fiduciary from acting in particular ways. But the rules can be successful only if the fiduciary is actually aware of them and their potential ambit. Now, it is certainly fair to assume that professional fiduciaries are aware of the fiduciary duties, or at least should be aware of the duties, but is it really appropriate to assume that all fiduciaries have such knowledge of fiduciary law? Will the non-professional trustee or the inexperienced agent be aware of the strict standards required by fiduciary law? If they are not, the prophylactic aim must fail. It does not follow from this that the strict

---

[101] Conaglen (see n. 5), p. 469.
[102] Jones, 'Unjust enrichment and the fiduciary's duty of loyalty' (1968) 84 LQR 472, 474.
[103] See n. 95, p. 768.

standards required by fiduciary law should be rejected, since perhaps all that we can expect is an aspiration to the highest standards of behaviour; but it is important to be aware that the aims of fiduciary law may not always be fulfilled and that, where the fiduciary was unaware of the standards required, there might be a case to be made for those standards to be modified.

15.4.2 SHOULD THE HIGH STANDARDS BE LOWERED?

It follows that it is important to consider whether the very strict standards of conduct expected by fiduciary law can be defended. Conaglen and others justify the strictness to ensure that the fiduciary remains loyal to the principal without the distractions of preferring personal interest over the interests of the principal. But the very strict approach of Equity means that a fiduciary can be liable for breach of fiduciary duty even though there was no danger of the fiduciary breaching a non-fiduciary duty and even though the fiduciary's actions were beneficial to the principal. Consequently, Langbein[104] has argued that the strict prohibition of conflicts between personal interest and duty should be relaxed where the fiduciary has acted in the best interests of the principal. He considers that the strict rule imposes too high a cost, because it prohibits transactions that are beneficial to the principal, and that the imposition of a strict rule is unfair to honest fiduciaries.

As we will see, the strict interpretation of fiduciary duties might, in some cases,[105] be considered to produce unjust results where the acts of the fiduciary have actually benefited the principal, but the fiduciary is still held liable for breach of fiduciary duty. But the criticism of commentators such as Langbein ignores one vital feature of the law of fiduciary duties, which is that these duties are not absolute. The fiduciary is not prevented from entering into a transaction that conflicts with their duty to the principal or from profiting from their position as fiduciary, as long as the fiduciary has obtained prior authorization for their actions. The fiduciary can immunize themself against liability for breach of fiduciary duty either by ensuring that authorization for the conduct is provided for in the trust instrument or equivalent document, or by seeking the fully informed consent of the principal in advance of taking the action, or even by seeking the approval of the court. If such authorization, consent or approval is not forthcoming, the fiduciary should not take the action.

Whether the ability to obtain such consent or approval in advance of taking an action that would otherwise involve a breach of fiduciary duty is sufficient to mitigate against the otherwise strict interpretation of the fiduciary duties can be assessed only after the operation of those duties, and after the key cases that have interpreted and applied them, have been carefully considered.

15.5 NO-CONFLICT RULE

15.5.1 THE ESSENCE OF THE RULE

The essence of the no-conflict rule was recognized by Lord Cranworth in *Aberdeen Railway Company v Blaikie Bros*:[106]

---

[104] 'Questioning the trust law duty of loyalty: sole interest or best interest?' (2005) 114 Yale LJ 929.
[105] Notably *Boardman v Phipps* [1967] 2 AC 46. See Section 15.6.7.(iii), p. 444.
[106] (1854) 1 Macq 461, 471.

it is a rule of universal application, which no one having [fiduciary] duties to discharge, shall be allowed to enter into engagements in which he has, or can have, a personal interest conflicting, or which may possibly conflict, with the interests of those whom he is bound to protect.

This no-conflict rule has two distinct applications, as follows:

(1) Where a fiduciary finds themself in a position in which the fiduciary's personal interest does conflict with their duty to the principal, or may conflict in a real and sensible manner,[107] the fiduciary must prefer the duty to the principal to their personal interest,[108] save where the principal has given their free and fully informed consent to enable the fiduciary to prefer their own interest.

(2) Fiduciaries should avoid placing themselves in a position in which their duty to one principal conflicts with their duty to another principal, save where both principals have given their fully informed consent to such a conflict.[109] A fiduciary will breach this duty even if they have no personal interest in the transaction.

In both cases, the relevant duty that is owed to the principal is the fiduciary's non-fiduciary duty, such as the duty to act in the principal's best interests and in good faith.[110] So, for example, a fiduciary is prohibited from competing with the principal's business, for then the personal interests of the fiduciary will or might conflict with the interests of the principal that the fiduciary is bound to protect.[111] In both cases, the fiduciary is not permitted to adduce evidence to show that there was no actual conflict either of personal interest and duty or duty and duty; liability is founded on the existence of potential, rather than actual, conflict.

15.5.2 COMPANIES ACT 2006

As we have seen,[112] the fiduciary duties of directors are now provided for by the Companies Act 2006. This statute makes provision for the no-conflict rule, which embodies the essential features of that rule as it has been developed in Equity, but the terms of the statutory rule are defined more expansively and with particular provision for the corporate context.

Section 175 of that Act states that a director is subject to a duty to avoid a situation in which they have, or could have, a direct or indirect interest that conflicts, or may conflict, with the interests of the company,[113] other than an interest that arises in relation to a transaction or arrangement with the company.[114] The duty to avoid a conflict of interest is not infringed either if the situation cannot reasonably be regarded as likely to give rise to a conflict of interest,[115] or if the matter has been authorized by the directors.[116] Section 175 applies both to situations in which the director's own interest conflicts with their duty to the company and those in which the director's duty to the company conflicts with a duty they owe to another principal, such as where they are a director of another competing company.[117]

---

[107] *Boardman v Phipps* [1967] 2 AC 46, 124 (Lord Upjohn).
[108] *Swain v The Law Society* [1982] 1 WLR 17, 36 (Oliver LJ).
[109] *Clark Boyce v Mouat* [1994] 1 AC 428, 435.   [110] Conaglen (see n. 5), p. 462.
[111] *Re Thomson* [1930] 1 Ch 203.   [112] See Section 15.3.7, p. 428.
[113] Companies Act 2006, s. 175(1).
[114] Ibid., s. 175(3). This is covered by s. 177, considered in the next paragraph.
[115] Which is different from the equitable no-conflict rule.
[116] Companies Act 2006, s. 175(4).   [117] Ibid., s. 175(7).

If the director is directly or indirectly interested in a proposed transaction or arrangement with the company, they must disclose the nature and extent of that interest to the other directors of the company[118] before the company enters into the transaction or arrangement.[119] But this applies only where the director is aware, or ought reasonably to have been aware, of the interest or the transaction or arrangement.[120] The director need not disclose the interest if it cannot reasonably be regarded as likely to give rise to a conflict of interest or if the directors are already aware of the interest.[121]

15.5.3 DEALING RULES

During the administration of a trust, a trustee might wish to purchase either the trust property itself or a beneficiary's interest under the trust. Equity has developed two rules to resolve the particular conflict that may arise between the duty of the trustee to the beneficiaries and their personal interest in such circumstances, known as the self-dealing and the fair-dealing rules. Although the rules have been developed in the context of trusts, they are of general application to all fiduciary relationships because they are founded on the basic fiduciary duty to avoid a conflict between personal interest and duty.

Both the self-dealing and the fair-dealing rules were recognized by Megarry V-C in *Tito v Waddell (No 2)*[122] as two distinct, but allied, rules. The better view, however, is that both rules are applications of the no-conflict rule and that they operate in the same way, with liability turning on whether or not the beneficiary has given their fully informed consent to the transaction.[123]

(i) Self-dealing rule

The self-dealing rule provides that a fiduciary is barred from dealing on behalf of themself and the principal in the same transaction.[124] So, for example, a trustee cannot sell trust property to themself;[125] neither can the trustee sell their own property to the trust.[126] Breach of this rule renders the transaction voidable, so that the principal can seek rescission of it without needing to prove that the transaction is unfair.[127] Once the transaction has been rescinded, the fiduciary is liable to account to the principal for any profits that were made from the transaction. Rescission will not be possible if any of the usual bars apply, such as affirmation of the transaction by the principal.[128] The self-dealing rule can be excluded by the relevant instrument that governs the fiduciary relationship.[129]

The reason why self-dealing transactions are voidable is that where, for example, a trustee is seeking to buy property from the trust, there is a real danger of conflict between the trustee's personal interest in getting the cheapest price and their duty to the beneficiaries to obtain the highest price for the property. This risk exists regardless of the fairness of the transaction. The principal can consequently decide to set the transaction aside if they consider that they do not want the property to be sold to the fiduciary, but otherwise the transaction will be effective.

---

[118] Ibid., s. 177(1).   [119] Ibid., s. 177(4).   [120] Ibid., s. 177(5).

[121] Ibid., s. 177(6).   [122] [1977] Ch 106, 241.

[123] Conaglen, 'A re-appraisal of the fiduciary self-dealing and fair-dealing rules' (2006) 64 CLJ 366, 395.

[124] *Tito v Waddell (No 2)* [1977] Ch 106, 241 (Megarry V-C).

[125] *Ex p Lacey* (1802) 6 Ves 625, 626 (Lord Eldon LC); *ex p James* (1803) 8 Ves 337, 345 (Lord Eldon LC).

[126] *Armstrong v Jackson* [1917] 2 KB 822, 824 (McCardie J).

[127] *Tito v Waddell (No 2)* [1977] Ch 106, 241 (Megarry V-C).   [128] See Section 21.6.4, p. 646.

[129] *Sargeant v National Westminster Bank plc* (1990) 61 P & CR 518.

The transaction will not, however, be voidable where the fiduciary has obtained the consent of the court or the fully informed consent of the principal to the transaction.[130] The fairness of the transaction may then be relevant when assessing whether the consent was indeed fully informed. Since the principal will not have been a party to the transaction, clear evidence of consent to the transaction will need to be adduced before the court will be able to conclude that the principal had indeed consented to the transaction.

The operation of the self-dealing rule is illustrated by *Wright v Morgan*,[131] in which a testator had left land on trust for sale and provided that it should be offered to one of his sons, who was also a trustee, at a price to be fixed by valuers. If this son had purchased the land, this would not have involved a breach of the self-dealing rule, even though he was also a trustee, because the option to purchase was specifically provided for by the will. The son instead assigned his right of purchase to his brother, who later became a trustee, but who was not authorized to purchase the land by the terms of the will. The brother purchased the land at a price set by valuers, but it was held that this transaction could be set aside because the self-dealing rule had been infringed, even though the transaction had been fair.

This decision can be compared with *Holder v Holder*.[132] In that case the defendant was one of the testator's sons, who was tenant of one of the testator's farms and who was responsible for farming the remainder of the testator's land. On the testator's death, the defendant was appointed one of three executors and started to administer the estate. The testator had left his estate to be divided equally between his widow and children. The defendant sought to renounce his executorship and then purchased the farms at an auction for a fair price. The court needed to determine whether the sale could be set aside for breaching the self-dealing rule. The defendant had conceded at trial that his renunciation of his executorship was ineffective because he had already started to administer the estate. Consequently, he continued to be a fiduciary. But it was held that he had not breached the self-dealing rule by purchasing the farms. A number of reasons were given for this conclusion, including that he had not assumed any of the duties of executor; that he had acquired no special knowledge relating to the transaction whilst he had been acting as executor; and that he had never made any secret of the fact that he intended to purchase the farms.

This is a difficult decision to justify because it appears to undermine the strict interpretation of fiduciary duties. The defendant was a fiduciary as an executor and he had purchased property from the estate that he was administering, in what appeared to be a clear breach of the self-dealing rule. The result would have been easier to justify had he successfully renounced his executorship, for then he would cease to have been a fiduciary and would no longer have been bound by the self-dealing rule. The case may simply have involved a benevolent interpretation of the rule because of the concession that he had failed to renounce his executorship, a concession that was probably made incorrectly, and because the policy behind the self-dealing rule appeared not to be engaged, since the beneficiaries had not looked to the defendant to protect their interests and there were two other executors who could sell the property to the defendant, so that he did not need to be considered both the purchaser and the vendor of the farms. The result has subsequently been defended on the ground that the defendant had never acted as an executor in such a way as to amount to an acceptance of a duty to act in the interests of the beneficiaries.[133] But this still does not explain why the strict fiduciary duty was qualified at all on the facts of this case.

---

[130] *Ex p James* (1803) 8 Ves 337, 353 (Lord Eldon LC).   [131] [1926] AC 788.
[132] [1968] Ch 353.   [133] *Re Thompson's Settlement* [1986] Ch 99, 116 (Vinelott J).

There is an alternative explanation of the result in *Holder v Holder*, which is that the beneficiary who sought to have the transaction set aside had previously affirmed the transaction with full knowledge of the facts. Such affirmation bars rescission so that the transaction could not then be set aside. But, potentially, the most significant part of the decision was the recognition by Danckwerts LJ[134] that the court has a discretion to sanction a transaction even though it was made in breach of the self-dealing rule. This discretion has been recognized subsequently,[135] and if it is recognized generally, it has the potential to undermine the strict application of fiduciary duties generally and the self-dealing rule particularly.

The application of the self-dealing rule is not confined to the sale of property to the fiduciary. It was applied, for example, to set aside the assignment of leases in *Re Thompson's Settlement*,[136] in which land was held on trust for the settlor's grandchildren. The land had been leased to companies the directors of which included the trustees. Some of these leases were assigned to another company, of which one of the trustees was a managing director, and in which he and his family held a majority of the shares. The remaining leases were assigned to a partnership that had been formed by another trustee. It was held that the assignment of the leases was voidable by virtue of the self-dealing rule, because all of the trustees needed to agree to the assignment, and some of them were the assignees and so personally interested in the transaction. In *Kane v Radley-Kane*,[137] the self-dealing rule was applied to a sole personal representative who had taken shares in a private company from the testator's estate to satisfy a legacy due to her, but without the consent of the other beneficiaries. It was held that the transaction involving the appropriation of the shares could be set aside by the beneficiaries since it had infringed the self-dealing rule, primarily because it was difficult to value the shares, so it was unclear whether the personal representative had received more value from the estate than was actually due to her.

(ii) Fair-dealing rule

The fair-dealing rule provides that, where a fiduciary personally transacts with the principal, the transaction is voidable save where the fiduciary can show that they took no advantage of their fiduciary position, that they made full disclosure to the principal, and that the transaction was fair and honest.[138] So, for example, if a trustee purchases a beneficiary's interest in the trust property, the transaction can be set aside by the beneficiary unless the trustee can establish the fairness of the transaction.[139] Although a purchase from the beneficiary can be valid, therefore, it remains a hazardous transaction because the negotiations and the final agreement must be completely above board and reasonable, with no hint of fraud, concealment, or advantage of the principal taken by the fiduciary.[140] If the fair-dealing rule is breached, any transaction into which the fiduciary has entered is liable to be rescinded on the application of the principal and the fiduciary is liable to account for any profits that they made from the transaction. Rescission will be barred if any of the usual bars apply, such as affirmation[141] or lapse of time before the principal seeks rescission.

The fair-dealing rule clearly forms part of the no-conflict duty because the fiduciary will be tempted by their personal interest to obtain the cheapest price when dealing with the

---

[134] *Holder v Holder* [1968] Ch 353, 398.
[135] See also *Hillsdown Holdings plc v Pensions Ombudsman* [1997] 1 All ER 862, 895 (Knox J).
[136] [1986] Ch 99.   [137] [1999] Ch 274.
[138] *Tito v Waddell (No 2)* [1977] Ch 106, 241 (Megarry V-C).
[139] See *Thomson v Eatswood* (1877) 2 App Cas 215, 236 (Lord Cairns LC).
[140] See *Coles v Trecothick* (1804) 9 Ves 234, 247 (Lord Eldon LC).
[141] *Re Cape Breton Co Ltd* (1889) 29 Ch D 795.

principal in circumstances under which the fiduciary should be loyal to the principal and ensure that the best price is obtained. If the principal has given fully informed consent to the transaction, it will be valid, and the fact that the price for the purchase of the property is a good one from the principal's perspective will suggest that the consent was indeed fully informed.

The fair-dealing rule appears not to be applied as stringently as the self-dealing rule because the fiduciary is given the option of establishing the fairness of the transaction and showing that they had not taken advantage of the principal. The more flexible nature of the fair-dealing rule might be considered to be justified by the fact that there are genuinely two parties to the transaction, the fiduciary and the principal, whereas the self-dealing rule involves the fiduciary dealing with themself. But, even as regards the operation of the fair-dealing rule, the fiduciary will typically be in a superior bargaining position, so that they could take advantage of the principal. It is for this reason that Conaglen[142] has argued that the fair-dealing rule should be considered to involve the application of the no-conflict duty in the same way as the self-dealing rule. Whilst the cases do emphasize that the transaction cannot be rescinded where it can be considered to be fair, Conaglen argues that 'fairness' here does not relate to the substantive fairness of the transaction, but is simply an evidential factor that assists the court in determining whether the fiduciary did indeed give their fully informed consent to the transaction: if the transaction can be considered to be fair, it is legitimate to infer that the principal's consent was fully informed. If, however, there has not been full and frank disclosure, and the price was not a fair price, this will suggest that the principal's consent to the transaction was not fully informed, both because the principal was not aware of all of the relevant facts and because they are unlikely to have validly consented where the price was excessive. This is an appealing analysis because it removes the apparently artificial distinction between the self-dealing and fair-dealing rules turning on the fairness of the transaction. In both cases, breach of the rule will render the transaction voidable, but rescission will be defeated if the principal has given their fully informed consent to the transaction.

(iii) Acting for more than one principal

A fiduciary may also be liable for breaching the no-conflict duty even though there is no conflict between their personal interest and duty, but instead, where the fiduciary acts for more than one principal, there is a conflict between their duty owed to both principals.[143] A fiduciary is not prevented from acting for more than one principal, and professional fiduciaries such as solicitors and agents will often do so. Where, however, the interests of the two principals come into conflict, any transaction entered into by the fiduciary on behalf of one or both of the principals will be voidable and the fiduciary will be liable to account for any profit made or compensate for any loss suffered from the transaction.

This conflict of duties constitutes a breach of fiduciary duty because the fiduciary is not able to provide undivided loyalty to each one. So, for example, where the fiduciary negotiates a purchase of property between two principals, the fiduciary's duties to each will be conflicted. The purchaser will expect the fiduciary to negotiate the cheapest price and the vendor will expect the highest price to be obtained. Similarly, if the fiduciary obtains confidential information from one principal, Alan, which would be beneficial for the other

---

[142] See n. 123, p. 368.
[143] *Clarke Boyce v Mouat* [1994] 1 AC 428; *Marks and Spencer plc v Freshfields Bruckhaus Deringer (a firm)* [2004] EWHC 1337 (Ch), [2004] 1 WLR 2331. Conaglen considers this to be a fiduciary principle that is distinct from where there is a conflict between personal interest and duty, but which has the same prophylactic objectives: 'Fiduciary regulation of conflicts between duties' (2009) 125 LQR 111, 119.

principal, Brenda, to receive, the fiduciary's duty to each principal will conflict. Alan will expect the information to be kept confidential and Brenda will expect it to be disclosed. In such a situation it is no defence to the fiduciary that their duties to each principal conflict, since failure to disclose the information will breach the duty owed to Brenda and disclosing it will breach the duty owed to Alan.[144] It is the fact that the fiduciary has got themself into a position in which the duties owed to different principals inevitably conflict that constitutes the breach of fiduciary duty. As Lord Walker recognized,[145] 'the fact that he has chosen to put himself in an impossible position does not exonerate him from liability'.

That failing to disclose confidential information about one principal to another does constitute breach of the no-conflict rule is illustrated by *Hilton v Barker Booth and Eastwood (a firm)*.[146] In that case, Bromage had persuaded Hilton, a builder, to buy a property, develop it, and then sell it back to Bromage. Bromage paid a deposit in respect of the sale of the property, but failed to complete the sale, and Hilton then rescinded the transaction. Both parties had been represented by the same firm of solicitors. Hilton sued the firm for breach of fiduciary duty, on the ground that it had not informed him that, as the solicitors of the firm were aware, Bromage had been made bankrupt and been convicted for fraud, and that the firm had paid the deposit to make Bromage appear creditworthy. The firm was held liable for breach of contract, but it was acknowledged that it could also have been held liable for breach of fiduciary duty in failing to make full disclosure of the circumstances of the transaction to Hilton, even though such a disclosure might have breached the fiduciary duty it owed to Bromage because it would have meant that the development of the property would not have taken place, which would not have been in Bromage's best interests.

In addition to liability for breach of fiduciary duty where there is a potential or actual conflict between inconsistent duties owed to principals, in *Bristol and West Building Society v Mothew*[147] Millett LJ recognized that a fiduciary will be liable for breach of duty where their obligations to one principal are influenced by their relationship with another principal. This is a distinct and unusual type of fiduciary duty since the fiduciary will only be liable if they intentionally preferred one principal over another. The nature and function of this distinct duty has been identified by Conaglen.[148] It will be relevant where there is no actual or potential conflict of duty and duty, such as where each principal is aware that the fiduciary is acting for another, but where the fiduciary intentionally abuses the relationship by breaching a non-fiduciary duty owed to one principal in order to prefer the interests of the other. So, for example, if the fiduciary consciously fails to disclose relevant information to one fiduciary in breach of duty in order to favour the other principal, the fiduciary will be liable for breach of fiduciary duty.

Where the fiduciary does act for two principals so that there is a conflict of duties owed to each one, the fiduciary will not be liable for breach of fiduciary duty in two circumstances.

Fully informed consent

Where both principals have given their fully informed consent to the fiduciary acting for the other principal, the fiduciary cannot be liable where the interests of the two principals conflict.[149] This consent may be express or may be implied where the principal was aware

---

[144] *Moody v Cox and Hatt* [1917] 2 Ch 71.

[145] *Hilton v Barker, Booth and Eastwood* [2005] UKHL 8, [2005] 1 WLR 567, [44].

[146] Ibid.   [147] [1998] Ch 1, 19.   [148] See n. 143, p. 134.

[149] *Clark Boyce v Mouat* [1994] 1 AC 428. Cf. Conaglen, who argues that fully informed consent will negate liability only where there is a potential conflict of duties and not where there is an actual conflict of duties, nor where the fiduciary has consciously preferred the interests of one principal over another: 'Remedial ramifications of conflicts between a fiduciary's duties' (2010) 126 LQR 72.

that the fiduciary was acting for another principal. So, for example, where the fiduciary is a solicitor who was acting for both the mortgagor and the mortgagee, and both of the clients knew that the solicitor was acting for the other party, there will be no breach of the no-conflict rule.[150] But the principal's consent to the conflict of duty will be valid only where that consent can be considered to be fully informed. So, for example, in *Hilton v Barker Booth and Eastwood (a firm)*,[151] Hilton's consent to the firm of solicitors acting for Bromage could not have been fully informed because of the firm's failure to make full disclosure about Bromage's creditworthiness and background.

Contractual term

Liability for a conflict of duties owed to different principals can also be avoided by a term in the contract of appointment that allows the fiduciary to act for other principals. Such a term may be express or might be implied to reflect the objectively determined intention of the parties. So, for example, in *Kelly v Cooper*,[152] a term was implied in a contract with an estate agent to allow for the agent to act for more than one competing principal, since it was expected that estate agents would act for other clients and that the interests of different clients might conflict. The effect of implying such a term was that the fiduciary was not required to disclose information obtained from one client to all other clients. But a contractual term allowing conflict of duties will not be allowed where it does not reflect the expectations of the parties. Consequently, a term was not implied into the contract of retainer in *Hilton v Barker Booth and Eastwood (a firm)*[153] to permit the firm of solicitors to keep information about Bromage confidential.

15.6 NO-PROFIT RULE

15.6.1 THE ESSENCE OF THE NO-PROFIT RULE

The no-profit rule prohibits fiduciaries from obtaining a benefit by virtue of their position as fiduciary either for themselves or for a third party, save where the principal has given their fully informed consent to the fiduciary obtaining the profit following full and frank disclosure by the fiduciary,[154] or the profit is otherwise authorized, for example by the trust instrument.[155] So, for example, the fiduciary is prohibited from making a profit by using an opportunity or knowledge that they obtained by virtue of their position as a fiduciary. It is no defence that the fiduciary would still have made the profit even if they had acted properly,[156] nor that the fiduciary had acted honestly and in the principal's best interests, nor that the principal actually benefited, nor that the principal could not have obtained the benefit for themselves. The rationale behind this strict interpretation of the no-profit rule is that the fiduciary is precluded from using their position to advantage anybody's interests other than those of the principal, this being a vital component of the fundamental obligation of loyalty.

It does not follow that the fiduciary is prevented from obtaining any benefit at all whilst they acted as a fiduciary.[157] Many fiduciaries are professionals who are legitimately paid for

---

[150] *Bristol and West Building Society v Mothew* [1998] Ch 1, 19 (Millett LJ).
[151] [2005] UKHL 8, [2005] 1 WLR 567.   [152] [1993] AC 205.   [153] [2005] UKHL 8, [2005] 1 WLR 567.
[154] *Gwembe Valley Development Co Ltd v Koshy (No 3)* [2003] EWCA Civ 6048, [2004] 1 BCLC 131.
[155] *Ultraframe (UK) Ltd v Fielding* [2005] EWHC 1638 (Ch), [1318] (Lewison J).
[156] *Murad v Al-Saraj* [2005] EWCA Civ 959, [2005] WTLR 1573.
[157] Harpum, 'Fiduciary obligations and fiduciary powers: where are we going?', in *Privacy and Loyalty*, ed. Birks (Oxford: Clarendon Press, 1997), p. 154.

their work, including professional trustees.[158] The real concern is to ensure that the fiduciary does not make an unauthorized or secret profit from their position.[159] Consequently, where the principal gives their fully informed consent to the fiduciary obtaining the profit, there is no breach of the fiduciary's duty. Further, if the benefit is not obtained by reason of the fiduciary position, the fiduciary will not be liable to account for it.[160]

15.6.2 THE RELATIONSHIP WITH THE NO-CONFLICT RULE

In *Bray v Ford*,[161] Lord Herschell recognized both the no-conflict and the no-profit rule, but considered that the latter might simply be an application of the former, since, whenever the fiduciary makes a profit in breach of their fiduciary duty, this will inevitably involve a contravention of the no-conflict principle, because the personal interest of the fiduciary to obtain the maximum profit conflicts with their duty of loyalty to the principal. It would follow that the no-profit rule is simply a component of the wider no-conflict rule with no independent application.[162] It is certainly the case that the temptation of obtaining a profit from a fiduciary position could lead inexorably to a conflict between personal interest and duty to the principal, for the fiduciary will be tempted to act in their own best interests rather than those of the principal. Consequently, in the typical scenario of breach of fiduciary duty, both rules will have been breached. But it is still preferable to consider the rules as being distinct.[163] This is because they have different requirements and, consequently, there will be circumstances under which one rule operates and not the other. Certainly, the no-conflict rule can be contravened without the fiduciary making an unauthorized profit, such as where a director personally pursues a public call for a tender, knowing that their company is pursuing the same tender. The director's personal interest will conflict with their duty to the company, since the director will be competing with the company to make the best offer. But, if the director successfully obtains the tender for themself, the director will not have breached the no-profit rule because they did not obtain the profit as a result of their fiduciary position, since the offer was a public offer available to all and not to the fiduciary because of their fiduciary position.[164] The director would, however, have breached this rule had they known that the offer that they were making was less than that of the company, because the opportunity to make a lower offer would have been influenced by the information that they had obtained as a director. Another situation in which the no-conflict rule can be breached without infringing the no-profit rule is where the fiduciary starts up a business in competition with that of the principal.[165] The fiduciary will be liable to disgorge any profit made because of the conflict of personal interest and duty to the fiduciary even though this profit did not arise from the exploitation of the fiduciary's position as a fiduciary.

Where the fiduciary is alleged to have made a profit in breach of fiduciary duty, it should not be necessary to establish that this also involved a conflict of interest.[166] The fact that the fiduciary made an unauthorized profit should be sufficient to impose liability. So, for example, if a director has made a personal profit from a contract that they were able to obtain by virtue of their position as director, they will have profited from the fiduciary

---

[158] On remuneration of trustees generally, see Section 12.7.3, p. 357.   [159] Millett (see n. 25), p. 216.

[160] *Howard v Commissioner of Taxation* [2014] HCA 21, [37] (French CJ and Keane J).

[161] [1896] AC 44, 51.   [162] *Boardman v Phipps* [1967] 2 AC 46, 123 (Lord Upjohn).

[163] *Ultraframe (UK) Ltd v Fielding* [2005] EWHC 1638 (Ch), [1305] (Lewison J).

[164] Koh, 'Once a director, always a fiduciary?' (2003) 62 CLJ 403, 406.   [165] Simpson (see n. 91), p. 82.

[166] See Smith, 'Fiduciary relationships: ensuring the loyal exercise of judgement on behalf of another' (2014) 130 LQR 608, 626.

position, but the director will not have breached the no-conflict rule if the company had no interest in pursuing that contract.

It follows that, whilst in most cases a breach of fiduciary duty will inevitably involve a breach of the no-conflict and the no-profit rules, this will not always be the case, so the rules need to be analysed separately. Identifying the separate application of each rule is also useful when determining the appropriate remedy that should be awarded, since breach of the no-profit rule will engage a liability for the defendant to disgorge the profit to the principal,[167] whereas the remedy for breach of the no-conflict rule that does not involve the fiduciary obtaining a profit will be compensatory.

15.6.3 THE CORE CASE OF PROFITING

The leading case to recognize and apply the no-profit principle is *Keech v Sandford*,[168] which concerned a lease of the profits of Romford market in Essex. The lessee had devised his estate, including the lease, to a trustee to be held on trust for an infant. Before the lease was due to expire, the trustee applied to the lessor for its renewal for the benefit of the infant. The lessor refused because, being a lease of profits only, the remedy for recovery of rent could be enforced only under the covenant to pay, but this would not have bound the infant. The lessor was, however, willing to renew the lease for the trustee personally. The trustee took the renewed lease of the profits obtained from the market and the infant then sought the lease to be assigned to him. He succeeded in getting the lease assigned and also recovered the profits obtained by the trustee before the lease was assigned. Although the case is poorly reported, it is clear that the trustee's liability was founded on his breach of fiduciary duty since he obtained the opportunity to profit from the renewal of the lease in his capacity as trustee. King LC recognized that he should have let the lease expire rather than obtain it himself. The strictness of the fiduciary duty was recognized in the dictum that 'the trustee is the only person of all mankind who might not have the lease'.[169]

The rule in *Keech v Sandford* as regards renewal of leases has been applied to fiduciaries other than trustees. So, for example, it has been recognized that a partner who obtains a renewal of a lease of the partnership premises in his own name holds the lease on constructive trust for the partnership.[170] In *Chan v Zacharia*,[171] Deane J recognized that, where the lease is renewed for the benefit of a trustee, there is an irrebuttable presumption that the lease was obtained from the trustee's position of advantage, so that it is held on trust for the beneficiary. Where, however, the lease has been obtained by a partner, the presumption of exploitation of fiduciary position is rebuttable, so it will be presumed that the lease is held for the benefit of the partnership, save where the fiduciary can rebut this presumption.[172] This recognition of the variable duties of fiduciaries depending on the nature of the fiduciary relationship is difficult to justify, and may have derived from the view that a partner was not in a fiduciary relationship with the other partners.[173]

Even where the trustee has renewed the lease for themselves, this will not constitute a breach of fiduciary duty if the no-profit rule has been excluded, such as where a will states that the trustee can retain the renewed lease for themselves.[174]

---

[167] See Section 18.5, p. 525.
[168] (1726) Sel Cas 61. See Hicks, 'The remedial principle of *Keech v Sandford* reconsidered' (2010) 69 CLJ 287; Getzler, 'Rumford market and the genesis of fiduciary obligations', in *Mapping the Law*, ed. Burrows and Lord Rodger (Oxford: Oxford University Press, 2006), ch. 31.   [169] (1726) Sel Cas 61, 62.
[170] *Re Biss* [1903] 2 Ch 40.   [171] (1983) 53 ALR 417, 435 (High Court of Australia).
[172] As recognized in *Re Biss* [1903] 2 Ch 40.
[173] Cretney, 'The rationale of *Keech v Sandford*' (1969) 33 Conv 161, 176.
[174] *Re Knowles' Will Trusts* [1948] 1 All ER 866, 871 (Cohen LJ).

The principle in *Keech v Sandford* has been extended to cover all kinds of benefit obtained by a fiduciary as a result of being a fiduciary.[175] So, for example, if a fiduciary holds a leasehold interest for the principal and then acquires the freehold reversion in a personal capacity, the fiduciary must hold the reversion for the principal.[176] Also, if a trustee receives a payment in consideration of their retiring and appointing the payer as a new trustee, the former trustee will be liable to account for the payment.[177]

15.6.4 USE OF THE PRINCIPAL'S PROPERTY

The fiduciary will also be liable for breach of fiduciary duty where they save money by using the principal's property without permission to do so. For example, in *Brown v IRC*,[178] the defendant solicitor received clients' money, which he deposited in a bank account. The defendant then used the interest from this account for his own purposes. This constituted a breach of the no-profit rule because the defendant had used income that belonged to the clients for himself and without the authority of the clients. This was a clear breach of the no-profit principle. Although information is sometimes characterized as property that can be misappropriated,[179] the better view is that information lacks the key hallmarks of property and so it cannot be misappropriated,[180] so the fiduciary will consequently not be liable to account for profit obtained from the exploitation of such information.

15.6.5 INDIRECT PROFIT

The no-profit rule can be breached where the profit obtained by the fiduciary arises indirectly from their fiduciary position. So, for example, in *Re Macadam*,[181] trustees appointed themselves as directors of a company in which the trust owned shares. It was held that they were accountable to the trust for the payments that they had received as directors, because, as trustees, it was their duty to give the estate the benefit of their unfettered advice in choosing people to act as directors of the company and, as potential recipients of the remuneration of directors, it was in their interest to choose themselves for the job. They were liable to account for their remuneration even though the profit did not come directly from the trust and was earned for their work as directors, because they had acquired their position as directors by virtue of their position as trustees, since the company's articles of association expressly gave the power of appointing directors to the trustees, although it did not authorize the trustees to appoint themselves. Where, however, the trustees are legitimately appointed as directors of the company, they can keep any remuneration that they are paid as directors. Their appointment as directors will be legitimate where it is authorized by the trust settlement,[182] or where the trustees were appointed as directors independently of the votes from the trust's shares,[183] or the directors had already been appointed before becoming trustees.[184]

---

[175] *Re Edwards' Will Trusts* [1982] Ch 30, 41 (Buckley LJ).
[176] *Thompson's Trustee in Bankruptcy v Heaton* [1974] 1 WLR 605; *Popat v Schonchhatra* [1997] 1 WLR 1367, 1375 (Nourse LJ).
[177] *Sugden v Crossland* (1856) 3 Sm & G 192.   [178] [1965] AC 244.
[179] *Quarter Master UK Ltd v Pyke* [2005] 1 BCLC 245, [71] (Paul Morgan QC).
[180] *Boardman v Phipps* [1967] 2 AC 45.   [181] [1946] Ch 73. See also *Re Francis* (1905) 74 LJ Ch 198.
[182] *Re Keeler's Settlement Trusts* [1981] Ch 156.   [183] *Re Gee* [1948] Ch 284.
[184] *Re Orwell's Will Trusts* [1982] 1 WLR 1337. See also *Re Lewis* (1910) 103 LT 495.

15.6.6 STATUTORY DUTIES

(i) Directors of companies

In the same way that the no-conflict rule now applies to directors under the Companies Act 2006, provision is made in that statute for the operation of the no-profit rule. Although the Companies Act 2006 uses the language of a 'duty to avoid conflicts of interest', the language of 'not making a profit' is not used. But it is clear that the essence of the no-profit rule is covered by the Act. Two provisions are particularly significant:

(1)   The no-conflict rule is defined to include the exploitation of property,[185] regardless of whether the company could take advantage of that property.[186] Consequently, the director is under a duty to avoid a situation in which they have an interest in the exploitation of property that conflicts with the interests of the company. Such exploitation of property is legitimate, however, where the transaction has been authorized by the directors.[187] A director is under a duty not to exploit property even though they have ceased to be a director if they became aware of the possibility of exploiting the property whilst they were a director.[188]

(2)   A director is prohibited from accepting a benefit from a third party where the benefit is conferred either by reason of their being a director, or by doing or not doing anything as a director,[189] but only where the acceptance of the benefit is reasonably likely to give rise to a conflict of interest. A director who ceases to be a director is still prohibited from accepting a benefit from a third party where it is conferred by virtue of acts or omissions before they ceased to be a director.[190]

(ii) Partners

Section 30 of the Partnerships Act 1890 states that, if a partner carries on business of the same nature as the partnership and competes with it without the consent of the partner, the partners must account to the firm for all profits made.

15.6.7 EXPLOITATION OF OPPORTUNITIES

One of the most significant aspects of the no-profit rule is that the fiduciary must not exploit an opportunity to make a profit where the opportunity came to the defendant in their capacity as a fiduciary.[191] The fiduciary will be liable to disgorge to the principal any profits obtained by such a breach of duty, regardless of the fact that the defendant acted reasonably and in good faith, and even though the principal would not have been able to exploit the opportunity themself.[192]

(i) Nature of opportunity

The prohibition on the exploitation of an opportunity by a fiduciary can be traced back to the rule in *Keech v Sandford*,[193] in which the trustee had the opportunity to acquire the renewed lease for himself by virtue of his position as trustee. This case might, however, be better analysed as a case in which the trustee appropriated trust property because the practice at the time was that the opportunity to renew a tenancy was effectively recognized

---

[185] This also extends to the exploitation of information or opportunity. See Section 15.6.7.(i), p. 442.
[186] Companies Act 2006, s. 175(2).   [187] Ibid., s. 175(4).   [188] Ibid., s. 170(2).
[189] Ibid., s. 176(1).   [190] Ibid., s. 170(2).   [191] *Regal (Hastings) Ltd v Gulliver* [1967] 2 AC 134n.
[192] *Keech v Sandford* (1726) Sel Cas 61; *Regal (Hastings) Ltd v Gulliver* [1967] 2 AC 134n; *Boardman v Phipps* [1967] 2 AC 46.   [193] (1726) Sel Cas 61. See Section 15.6.3, p. 440.

as a legal right, so that the trustee had acquired a trust asset by seizing for his own benefit an opportunity that was effectively owned by the trust.[194] Similarly, in *Cook v Deeks*,[195] it was held that directors could not use their majority shareholding to divest the company of its beneficial interest in the future profits to be made on a contract originally negotiated for the company but which had been diverted to their private business, since this would involve the misappropriation of a corporate asset.

But there are many other cases in which the fiduciary has been held liable for exploiting an opportunity where the principal had no legal right to the opportunity, but only an interest in exploiting it. It has been suggested that, where the fiduciary has exploited such an opportunity in which the principal was interested, but had no legal right, known as a 'maturing business opportunity', the fiduciary's exploitation of the opportunity is like the appropriation of property from the claimant.[196] It is, however, doubtful whether such an opportunity should be characterized as proprietary, since it lacks many of the characteristics of property. Further, liability for a fiduciary exploiting an opportunity can arise even if the principal was not actively pursuing it.[197] This has been criticized as expanding the ambit of fiduciary law too widely, and it has been argued that an opportunity for these purposes should be defined as a business opportunity in which the principal already has an interest, or in the fruition of which the principal has a real and almost certain expectancy.[198] This does not, however, reflect the state of the law.

Where the fiduciary is a director, the law on exploiting opportunities is to be found in the Companies Act 2006. Section 175(2) prohibits the exploitation of information or an opportunity, even if the company could not have taken advantage of the information or opportunity. A person who has ceased to be a director will still be subject to this duty if they became aware of the information or opportunity whilst they were a director.[199] A director will not be liable for breaching this duty if the exploitation cannot reasonably be regarded as likely to give rise to a conflict of interest, or if the matter has been authorized by the directors.[200] This statutory duty broadly reflects the application of the no-profit rule in Equity.

(ii) Opportunity arising by virtue of fiduciary position

A fiduciary will be liable for exploiting an opportunity only where the opportunity was available by virtue of the fiduciary's position, such as where the fiduciary discovers the opportunity whilst acting as a fiduciary or exploits the opportunity for themself whilst negotiating with a third party on behalf of the principal. So, for example, in *Williams v Barton*,[201] the defendant was one of two trustees of a will who was employed as a clerk by a firm of stockbrokers on the terms that his salary would consist of half the commission earned by his firm on any business he introduced. He persuaded his co-trustee to employ him to value the testator's securities. It was held that he had breached his fiduciary duty and was liable to account to the trust for the commission that he had received. This was because he was subject to a duty to give unfettered advice in choosing stockbrokers, but, since he received commission for any business that he introduced, it was in his own interest to choose that firm to act for the estate. Consequently, the remuneration that he received for this introduction would not have been obtained but for his position as a trustee. This can be contrasted with *Re Dover Coalfield Extension Ltd*,[202] in which the defendant was a director

---

[194] *Sinclair Investments (UK) Ltd v Versailles Trade Finance Ltd* [2011] EWCA Civ 347, [2012] Ch 453, [58] (Lord Neuberger MR). See Hicks (n. 168).   [195] [1916] 1 AC 554.
[196] *CMS Dolphin Ltd v Simonet* [2001] 2 BCLC 704, [96] (Lawrence Collins J).
[197] See e.g. *Boardman v Phipps* [1967] 2 AC 46, discussed in Section 15.6.7.(iii), p. 444.
[198] Koh (see n. 164), p. 443.   [199] Companies Act 2006, s. 170(2).   [200] Ibid., s. 175(4).
[201] [1927] 2 Ch 9.   [202] [1908] 1 Ch 65, 70 (Cozens-Hardy MR).

who subsequently became a trustee. Since the opportunity of becoming a director did not arise from his being a trustee, he was not liable to account to the trust for his remuneration.

Liability for exploitation of an opportunity has also been imposed where the fiduciary discovered the opportunity in a different capacity. For example, in *Bhullar v Bhullar*,[203] a director of a company was held liable to the company for the profits that he obtained from the acquisition of a property that was located next to that of the company, even though the director discovered the property as a passer-by rather than as director. The director's liability was founded on his failure to inform the company of the opportunity and his subsequent exploitation of it. The liability is, however, better justified as involving breach of the no-conflict principle on the ground that, since the property was physically proximate to that of the company, it would have been in the company's best interests to purchase the property. Since the director was interested in purchasing the property for himself, it followed that his own interest conflicted with that of the company, so that there was a breach of fiduciary duty at the point at which he discovered the opportunity, whether or not he had profited from purchasing the property. If the case is analysed in this way, it follows that the crucial feature of the no-profit rule remains valid, namely that the opportunity that was exploited was available to the fiduciary only by virtue of their fiduciary position.

(iii) Liability is strict

That the fiduciary is strictly liable for exploiting an opportunity that they obtained because they were a fiduciary, and even though they acted reasonably and in good faith, is illustrated by the important decision of the House of Lords in *Boardman v Phipps*.[204] In that case 27 per cent of the shares in a company were held on trust for the testator's widow and his children. There were three trustees: the widow, a daughter of the testator, and an accountant. The claimant was one of the testator's sons. The defendants were another son, Tom, who was a beneficiary of the trust, and Boardman, the solicitor to the trust. The defendants had become dissatisfied with the way in which the company's business was being conducted. They attended the annual general meeting of the company with a view to getting Tom appointed as a director to represent the interests of the trust on the board of directors, but this was not successful. They then decided to buy the remainder of the company's shares in their own names, having obtained the approval of two of the trustees, who confirmed that the trust was not in a position to acquire the shares. The widow was senile and in failing health, and so was not consulted. Meanwhile, Boardman, acting on behalf of the trustees, tried to make the company more profitable and, in doing so, obtained more information about the company and the value of its shares. Boardman wrote to the testator's four children, as beneficiaries of the trust, asking for their approval to his taking a personal interest in the negotiations. He assumed that he had obtained this approval. The defendants eventually bought the rest of the company's shares and reorganized the business. They turned the business around to the financial benefit of themselves and the trust, which continued to have a significant shareholding in the company. The claimant then called on the defendants to account for the profits that they had made from the transaction. The House of Lords held, by a majority of three to two, that both defendants had breached their fiduciary duty to the trust since they had made a personal profit by virtue of their position as fiduciaries and were liable to account to the trust for the profit. But, since the solicitor had acted in good faith throughout, he was awarded a liberal allowance for his work.[205]

---

[203] [2003] EWCA Civ 424, [2003] 2 BCLC 241.
[204] [1967] 2 AC 46.   [205] See Section 18.5.3.(ii), p. 530.

Whilst the result of the case could not have been clearer, analysis of the reasoning of the judges is difficult, because each judge gave a judgment with a variety of different reasons being suggested for their conclusions. The approach of the different judges can be summarized as follows:

(1) Lords Hodson and Guest considered that the defendants had misappropriated confidential information from the trust, this information suggesting that purchasing shares in the company would be a good investment. The judges considered that such information could be characterized as property, so that the defendants had clearly profited from their fiduciary position by taking trust property and were liable to account for the fruits of that property.

(2) Lord Cohen concluded that confidential information lacked the hallmarks of property,[206] but considered that the defendants were liable for breach of fiduciary duty, because there was a conflict of interest and duty to the trust, although it is difficult to see what that conflict was when the trust was not able to purchase any more shares in the company.

(3) Lords Hodson and Guest also justified the defendants' liability on the ground that the opportunity to make the profit from the purchase of the shares in the company was available to the defendants because of the information that they had obtained whilst acting as fiduciaries.

(4) The minority, Viscount Dilhorne and Lord Upjohn, dissented, on the ground that there was no sensible possible conflict of interest and duty on the facts, and the defendants' actions had enhanced the value of the trust property.

Although the majority suggested a number of different reasons why the defendants should be held liable, the *ratio* of the case can be identified as being that the personal interests of the defendants conflicted with their duty to the trust and that they had profited from their position as fiduciaries by exploiting information that they had obtained whilst acting as fiduciaries.

Boardman v Phipps illustrates the strictness of the no-profit rule. In assessing whether the decision can be defended, a number of points need to be emphasized.

Fiduciary relationship

Whilst one defendant was a solicitor to the trust and so clearly owed fiduciary duties as a result, the other was a beneficiary and so does not appear to have owed fiduciary duties to the trust. But the beneficiary was considered to have been an agent for the trust and so owed fiduciary duties as a result, even though he had not been formally appointed to act as the trust's agent, and so was described as self-appointed.[207] The nature of this fiduciary relationship is preferably identified as not falling within one of the recognized categories of fiduciary relationship, but was a de facto relationship that arose from the beneficiary voluntarily undertaking to act for the trust,[208] or, preferably, that he was an intermeddler in the trust[209] and had assumed the authority of an agent, which he did not actually possess, so that he was an agent *de son tort*.[210]

Breach of duty

The breach of fiduciary duty related to the opportunity to purchase the shares in the company that the fiduciaries were able to exploit because they had obtained information

---

[206] This was also the view of Lord Upjohn, dissenting: [1967] 2 AC 46, 128.

[207] *Boardman v Phipps* [1964] 1 WLR 993, 1007 (Wilberforce J).   [208] Edelman (see n. 24), p. 311.

[209] *Boardman v Phipps* [1965] Ch 992, 1018 (Lord Denning). See Bryan, '*Boardman v Phipps*', in *Landmark Cases in Equity*, ed. Mitchell and Mitchell (Oxford: Hart, 2012), p. 581.

[210] For the doctrine of trustee *de son tort*, see Section 12.3.9, p. 345.

relating to the company in their capacity as fiduciaries. Although some of the judges had assumed that the breach of duty involved misappropriating trust property, namely the information that was considered to belong to the trust, the relevance of the information was not that it was property, but that it enabled the fiduciaries to exploit the opportunity of purchasing shares.[211] It was significant that the company was a private company, so that there was no public market for the shares, and consequently the information that the defendants obtained and the ability to purchase shares in the company came to them in a fiduciary capacity.

Informed consent

A fiduciary will not be liable for infringing the no-profit rule by exploiting an opportunity where the exploitation had the principal's fully informed consent. But whose consent would be relevant in *Boardman v Phipps*? Was it the consent of the trustees? Lord Cohen did suggest that the fiduciaries' only defence could have been that they purchased the shares with the knowledge and assent of the trustees.[212] It appears that two of the trustees had consented to the fiduciaries purchasing the shares, but the third, the testator's widow, was senile and unable to give her consent. In fact, she had died before the shares were purchased. It seems that the reason why informed consent did not negate liability was that the consent of the beneficiaries that was also obtained could not be considered to be fully informed—this consent being relevant because it was actually recognized that the fiduciary duty was owed to the beneficiaries and not to the trustees.[213]

In the light of these three key factors, the result in *Boardman v Phipps*, although strict, might be considered to be defensible, because the defendants were clearly fiduciaries, who had profited from the exploitation of an opportunity that they obtained as fiduciaries and when they would have been able to avoid liability had they obtained the fully informed consent of the beneficiaries. The strictness of the result in *Boardman v Phipps* was further mitigated by the fact that the solicitor was awarded an equitable allowance to reflect the value of his services in managing the company to make it profitable.[214]

But, despite this, the result in *Boardman v Phipps* has been criticized as producing an unjust result,[215] because there was nothing wrong with what the defendants had done. There was nothing to suggest that they had abused their relationship of trust and confidence. They had acted honestly and reasonably, but were still liable to account to the trust for the profit that they had obtained, and even though the trust had not been in a position to buy more shares, because this was not authorized by the investment clause in the will and there was no trust money available to buy shares, so there was no possibility of the fiduciaries competing with the trust.[216]

A similarly strict approach to the no-profit rule had been recognized by the House of Lords in an earlier case, *Regal (Hastings) Ltd v Gulliver*.[217] In that case, R Ltd had set up a subsidiary, A Ltd, to acquire the leases of two cinemas. The owner of the cinemas was willing to lease them to the company only if the share capital of A Ltd was fully subscribed. It was agreed that, since R Ltd could only afford to subscribe for 2,000 of A Ltd's 5,000 shares,

---

[211] Whether information could be properly characterized as property might also have been relevant to the determination of the appropriate remedy for breach of fiduciary duty. See Section 15.7.3, p. 451.

[212] [1967] 2 AC 46, 117. See also *Crown Dilmun v Sutton* [2004] EWHC 52, [2004] 1 BCLC 468, [202] (Peter Smith J).   [213] *Boardman v Phipps* [1967] 2 AC 46, 104 (Lord Cohen).

[214] See Section 18.5.3.(ii), p. 530.   [215] Jones (see n. 102); Langbein (see n. 104).

[216] This was not considered to negate liability in *Crown Dilmun v Sutton* [2004] EWHC 52, [2004] 1 BCLC 468.

[217] [1967] 2 AC 134n. See Nolan, '*Regal (Hastings) v Gulliver*', in *Landmark Cases in Equity*, ed. Mitchell and Mitchell (Oxford: Hart, 2012), p. 499.

the directors of R Ltd would subscribe for the remaining shares. The business of R Ltd was subsequently transferred to new controllers and the directors made a profit because of their holding in A Ltd. The new controllers of R Ltd procured the company to sue the ex-directors for their profit, who were held liable to account because they had acquired the shares only by reason of the fact that they were directors of the company and in the course of execution of that office.[218] It was accepted that they would not have been liable had they obtained shareholder approval for their subscription for the shares, either beforehand or afterwards.[219]

This was another case in which the fiduciaries were liable to account to the principal for their profit even though they had acted in good faith and for the benefit of the principal. The directors of R Ltd had enabled the company to obtain the leases that it would not have been able to do had the shares in A Ltd not been fully subscribed. The directors of R Ltd had taken the risk of the transaction failing, but it was the new controllers of R Ltd who obtained the benefits. So, again, the result would appear to be unjust. But the decision that R Ltd could not afford to subscribe for all of the shares was made by the directors who profited from the decision, so this was a situation in which a reasonable person who examined the circumstances might consider that there was a real sensible possibility of conflict between personal interest and duty.[220]

Whether *Boardman v Phipps* and *Regal v Gulliver* are considered to be unjust decisions requires careful analysis of the nature and function of fiduciary duties.[221] The strict application of the no-profit rule in these cases has subsequently been followed by the Court of Appeal.[222] This strict application of the rule can be justified for two reasons:[223] first, in the interests of efficiency, because the principal may not be able to monitor easily the fiduciary's actions on a daily basis; and, secondly, to provide an incentive to all fiduciaries to resist the temptation to conduct themselves improperly. Alternatively, where there is no hint of fraud in the conduct of the defendant, it might be considered to be more just to commend the defendant for what they had done rather than to hold them accountable to the claimant. This was the view of the minority in *Boardman v Phipps*.

(iv) Resignation followed by exploitation of the opportunity

Whether a fiduciary who resigns and then exploits an opportunity will have breached their fiduciary duty will turn on careful consideration of the facts. The courts adopt a pragmatic and flexible approach to liability in such circumstances that is based on common sense and the merits of the case.[224] At one extreme is a fiduciary who resigns for legitimate reasons, for example because of dissatisfaction with the principal, and subsequently obtains the opportunity to compete with the principal, which they exploit.[225] There will be

---

[218] [1967] 2 AC 134n, 145 (Lord Russell).

[219] Ibid., 150 (Lord Russell). It is now clear that approval from the board of directors is sufficient (Companies Act 2006, s. 175(5)), but all of the directors in *Regal (Hastings)* were interested in the opportunity and so they could not have passed a board resolution to reject the opportunity on behalf of the company, leaving them free to take the opportunity personally. Authorization by the shareholders was the only way in which their liability for breach of fiduciary duty could have been avoided.

[220] *Boardman v Phipps* [1967] 2 AC 46, 124 (Lord Upjohn).   [221] See Section 15.4, p. 428.

[222] *Murad v Al-Saraj* [2005] EWCA Civ 959, [2005] WTLR 1573. But Jonathan Parker and Arden LJJ did contemplate relaxation of the strict rule on a later occasion. See further Section 15.6.7.(v), p. 448.

[223] *Murad v Al-Saraj* [2005] EWCA Civ 959, [2005] WTLR 1573, [74] (Arden LJ).

[224] *Foster Bryant Surveying Ltd v Bryant* [2007] EWCA Civ 200, [2007] 2 BCLC 239.

[225] *Island Export Finance Ltd v Umunna* [1986] BCLC 460; *Ultraframe (UK) Ltd v Fielding* [2005] EWHC 1638 (Ch).

no breach of fiduciary duty in such circumstances, because there is no evidence of any disloyalty. Similarly, where the fiduciary relationship has broken down, but the fiduciary has not resigned, they will be able to exploit any opportunity and engage in competing business because they are no longer in a fiduciary relationship.[226] At the other extreme are cases in which the fiduciary has planned their resignation in order to exploit a business opportunity.[227] This will constitute a breach of fiduciary duty. This is illustrated by *Industrial Development Consultants Ltd v Cooley*,[228] in which the defendant was a director of the claimant company. The defendant sought to interest a gas board in a development project with the company. The gas board was not interested because it had a policy of not employing development companies. But it offered the contract to the defendant because of his experience in the gas industry. The defendant accepted the offer and resigned from his company by falsely representing that he was ill. He was held liable to account to the company for the profits that he had made from the contract. It was held to be irrelevant that the information about the contract with the gas board and the opportunity to enter into it came to him in a private capacity, and not as a director of the company. It was also irrelevant that the decision whether or not to contract with the company lay with the gas board and not the defendant. The key justification for imposing liability was that this was the type of opportunity that the company relied on the defendant to obtain and he had not acted in good faith by resigning with a false reason in order to obtain the opportunity for himself.

(v) A more flexible approach

In *Murad v Al-Saraj*,[229] the defendant was held liable for breach of the no-profit rule when he had profited from participation in a joint venture by failing to disclose that his contribution to the purchase of a hotel was made by offsetting unenforceable obligations that were owed to him by the vendor, including commission for his introduction of the claimants to the vendor. Arden LJ acknowledged[230] that the application of the no-profit rule was strict, so that the defendant was liable for breach of fiduciary duty even though, if he had made full disclosure of the nature of his financial contribution, the claimants would still have proceeded with the joint venture, although they would have demanded a greater share of the profit.[231] She considered that the time may have come:

> when the court should revisit the operation of the inflexible rule of equity in harsh circumstances, as where the trustee has acted in perfect good faith and without any deception or concealment, and in the belief that he was acting in the best interests of the beneficiary.[232]

She did not consider that this was such a case, because the fiduciary had made fraudulent misrepresentations to the claimants and so should be liable to disgorge all of the profits that he had obtained from the joint venture.

But the flexibility sought by Arden LJ already applies to breach of fiduciary duty: any fiduciary is able to profit from their position as a fiduciary if they obtain the fully informed consent of the principal before doing so.[233] Such consent will be considered to be

---

[226] *In Plus Group Ltd v Pyke* [2002] EWCA Civ 370, [2002] 2 BCLC 201.   [227] Ibid., [71] (Brooke LJ).
[228] [1972] 1 WLR 443. See also *CMS Dolphin Ltd v Simonet* [2001] 2 BCLC 704.
[229] [2005] EWCA Civ 959, [2005] WTLR 1573. See further Section 18.5.2, p. 527.
[230] [2005] EWCA Civ 959, [2005] WTLR 1573, at [82]. See also Jonathan Parker LJ, [121], and Clarke LJ, [158].
[231] The role of causation for breach of fiduciary duty is considered in Section 18.5.2, p. 526.
[232] [2005] EWCA Civ 959, [2005] WTLR 1573, [82].
[233] *Ultraframe (UK) Ltd v Fielding* [2005] EWHC 1638 (Ch), [1318] (Lewison J). See Conaglen, 'The extent of fiduciary accounting and the importance of authorisation mechanisms' (2011) 70 CLJ 548.

fully informed only where the fiduciary has made full and frank disclosure of all relevant matters.[234] Where this has occurred and the principal has then declined the possibility of exploiting the opportunity, there is no reason why the fiduciary should be prevented from retaining the profit that they make from the exploitation of the opportunity. It follows that the restrictions imposed on fiduciaries by virtue of the no-profit rule, and the no-conflict rule as well,[235] can be mitigated if the fiduciary obtains prior authorization for what they wish to do. This is consistent with the fundamental obligation of loyalty, since a loyal fiduciary will reveal their intentions about the exploitation of opportunities to the principal.

In the light of this, it might be concluded that the strictness of the no-profit rule is legitimate and defensible. But what the fiduciary is required to do in order to obtain the principal's consent might be reformed in certain ways. For example, the rule on whose consent should be obtained could be clarified. This has already occurred for directors, since the Companies Act 2006[236] now makes clear that the relevant authorization can be obtained from the board of directors rather than the shareholders in general meeting.[237] Similarly, in the trust context, clarification could usefully be provided as to whether it is appropriate to obtain the consent from the trustees or the beneficiaries. Further, if the fiduciary has not obtained the prior authorization of the principal, it might be legitimate to recognize a defence for the fiduciary if they were able to prove that, had there been full and frank disclosure before the opportunity was exploited, the principal would have authorized the fiduciary to proceed with the transaction.[238]

This more flexible approach to the imposition of liability for breach of fiduciary duty has been recognized by the Supreme Court of Canada in *Peso-Silver Mines Ltd v Cropper*,[239] in which it held that an account of profits would not be awarded where the fiduciary had exploited an opportunity after it had been declined by the principal. A flexible approach to liability was also recognized by the Privy Council in *Queensland Mines Ltd v Hudson*,[240] in which the claimant company had been interested in developing a mining operation and the defendant managing director successfully obtained the licences to enable it to do so. The company had been unable to proceed with the transaction because of financial difficulties. The defendant resigned as managing director and, with the knowledge of the board of directors, developed the mines himself. The Privy Council held that he was not liable to account for the profits that he had made because the company had rejected the opportunity and the defendant had acted with the full knowledge of the board of directors, so they should be considered to have given a fully informed consent to the activities. If this approach were adopted in England, it would mean that the defendant would not be liable for breach of fiduciary duty even though they had not formally obtained the fully informed consent of the principal, as long as it could be established that the principal would have consented to the fiduciary's exploitation of the opportunity had the principal sought that consent.

But the recognition of such a defence to liability for breach of the no-profit rule where the fiduciary had failed to obtain the prior authorization of the principal might be considered to undermine unacceptably the strict expectations of absolute loyalty from the fiduciary. That is certainly the present approach adopted by Equity in England and this will continue until the matter is considered by the Supreme Court.

---

[234] *Murad v Al-Saraj* [2005] EWCA Civ 959, [2005] WTLR 1573, [71] (Arden LJ).
[235] As recognized in *Bray v Ford* [1896] AC 44, 51 (Lord Herschell).   [236] s. 175(5).
[237] As had been suggested in *Regal (Hastings) Ltd v Gulliver* [1967] 2 AC 134n.
[238] *Murad v Al-Saraj* [2005] EWCA Civ 959, [2005] WTLR 1573, [82] (Arden LJ).
[239] [1966] SCR 673.   [240] [1978] 52 ALJR 379.

15.6.8 RECEIPT OF BRIBES AND SECRET COMMISSIONS

A fiduciary receiving a bribe to induce them to act against the interests of the principal is one of the clearest cases in which the fiduciary should be considered to have broken their fiduciary duty, by contravening both the no-conflict and the no-profit principles. Liability for breach of fiduciary duty in such cases is justified simply on the ground that fiduciaries should be deterred from accepting bribes, and so being influenced to act against the best interests of the principal. One of the best ways of deterring such conduct is by depriving the defendant of the bribe that they received.[241] This is illustrated by *Reading v Attorney-General*,[242] in which the defendant was a sergeant in the British Army serving in Egypt. He was bribed to sit on lorries whilst wearing military uniform, so that alcohol could be illegally transported without being stopped by the police. The defendant was convicted of a crime. Most of the bribes that he had received were seized by the Crown and he sought to recover them. His action failed because he had been acting in breach of his fiduciary duty and so he would have been liable to account for the bribes to the Crown had it not already received the money.

This liability has been extended to include the receipt of a secret commission by a fiduciary. In *Daryadan Holdings Ltd v Solland International Ltd*,[243] the defendant agent received a secret commission of 10 per cent of the contract price in return for him exerting his influence to obtain contracts between a third party and his principal. This secret commission was held to be an unauthorized profit that could be recovered by the principal. It was considered to be irrelevant whether the agent had solicited the secret commission or had been offered it by the third party.[244] In such a case, the fiduciary and briber may alternatively be liable for the torts of deceit and conspiracy to injure by unlawful means, for which compensatory damages may be available,[245] but the principal must elect between the remedies of account of profits for breach of fiduciary duty and compensatory damages for tort.[246]

Where a principal is induced to enter into a contract with a third party as a result of the fiduciary being bribed by the third party, the contract is voidable,[247] there being an irrebuttable presumption that the agent was influenced by the bribe.[248]

15.7 CONSEQUENCES OF BREACH OF FIDUCIARY DUTY

Where a fiduciary has breached their fiduciary duty, there are a number of possible consequences. Some are self-help remedies, such as sacking the fiduciary, although this will only prevent harm from occurring in the future and will not resolve the harm that has already occurred. It may also be possible to seek an injunction to restrain future behaviour,[249] but again this will not remedy existing harms.

---

[241] Receipt of a bribe is also likely to constitute a crime under the Bribery Act 2010.

[242] [1951] AC 507. See also *Attorney-General v Goddard* (1929) 98 LJKB 743; *Petrotrade Inc v Smith* [2000] 1 Lloyd's Rep 486.   [243] [2004] EWHC 622 (Ch), [2005] Ch 119.

[244] Ibid., [60] (Lawrence Collins J).

[245] Ibid., [54] (Lawrence Collins J). The briber may also be liable for dishonestly assisting a breach of fiduciary duty. See Section 20.3.2, p. 613.

[246] *Mahesan s/o Thambiah v Malaysia Officers' Co-operative Housing Society Ltd* [1979] AC 374, 383.

[247] *Logicrose Ltd v Southend United Football Club Ltd* [1988] 1 WLR 1256.

[248] *Hovenden and Sons v Millhof* (1900) 83 LT 41, 43.

[249] *Marks and Spencer plc v Freshfields Bruckhaus Deringer (a firm)* [2004] EWHC 1337 (Ch), [2004] 1 WLR 2331, [26] (Lawrence Collins J).

15.7.1 RESCISSION

Where a transaction has been entered into as a result of a breach of either the no-conflict or the no-profit rule, it will be voidable so that the principal can seek its rescission if the transaction is made with the fiduciary, but not if it is made with an innocent third party.[250] Rescission will be barred, however, if it is not possible to return the parties to their original position, if property has been transferred under the transaction to a bona fide purchaser for value, if the principal has affirmed the transaction, or if too much time has elapsed before the principal has sought to rescind it. Where the fiduciary breaches the conflict of duty and duty rules by acting for more than one principal, it is possible for a transaction entered into as a result to be rescinded, although this may be available only if the principal with whom the transaction was made was aware of the inconsistent duties.[251]

15.7.2 PERSONAL LIABILITY

Where the fiduciary has profited from the breach of fiduciary duty, they will be liable to disgorge the profit to the principal.[252] Where the fiduciary has been remunerated for work done in breach of fiduciary duty those payments can be forfeited to the principal.[253] Where the principal has suffered loss as a result of the breach of fiduciary duty, they may seek equitable compensation from the fiduciary.[254] These are alternative remedies and the principal will need to choose between them to avoid double recovery.

15.7.3 PROPRIETARY CLAIM

Where the fiduciary has profited from the breach of fiduciary duty it has been a matter of some controversy as to whether these profits should be held on constructive trust for the principal. The recognition of profit being held on trust for the principal is particularly significant where the fiduciary has become insolvent, for then the principal will be competing against the fiduciary's other creditors to obtain payment. But, if the fiduciary's profit is held on constructive trust for the principal, they will gain priority over the fiduciary's general creditors. The recognition that the profit is held on constructive trust will also be significant where the value of the profit has increased, such as where it has been invested and the value of the investment has increased; the principal will obtain the benefit of the increase in value. Further, the principal can assert proprietary rights against innocent third parties who have received the profits or their traceable substitute. These advantages will be available to the principal because the recognition of the constructive trust means that the principal has an equitable proprietary interest in the profit to enable them to bring a proprietary claim.[255]

It is consequently vital to determine when profit obtained from a breach of fiduciary duty will be held on constructive trust for the principal. Where the fiduciary has misappropriated an asset from the principal, it has long been recognized that the asset will be

---

[250] *Chancery Client Partners Ltd v MRC 957 Ltd* [2016] EWHC 2142 (Ch).

[251] *Transvaal Land Co v New Belgium (Transvaal) Land and Development Co* [1914] 2 Ch 488; Conaglen (see n. 149), p. 74.

[252] *Nocton v Lord Ashburton* [1914] AC 932, 956–7 (Viscount Haldane VC); *Murad v Al-Saraj* [2005] EWCA Civ 959, [2005] WTLR 1573, [56] (Arden LJ). See Section 18.5, p. 525.

[253] See *Hosking v Marathon Asset Management LLP* [2016] EWHC 2418 (Ch), [2017] Ch 157.

[254] *Bristol and West Building Society v Mothew* [1998] Ch 1, 19; *Swindle v Harrison* [1997] 4 All ER 705. See Section 18.4, p. 524.   [255] See Chapter 19 of this volume for discussion of these claims.

held on trust for the principal.[256] This includes where the fiduciary has obtained a bribe or a secret commission and it can be shown that this was derived from money paid by the principal to the fiduciary.[257] The recognition of a constructive trust in such circumstances is defensible because the profits made by the defendant can be considered to represent the fruits of the claimant's property. Consequently, it is entirely appropriate that the claimant should have an equitable proprietary interest in those profits. In addition, it is justifiable that the fiduciary should hold property on constructive trust where the consequence of the breach of duty is that the fiduciary obtains property which the principal would have obtained had the defendant not breached their duty. Goode has described the property which the defendant obtains in such circumstances as a 'deemed agency gain',[258] which should be held on constructive trust for the principal simply because the demands of the fiduciary relationship are such that it should be assumed that the defendant obtained the property for their principal rather than for themself. This is illustrated by *Cook v Deeks*[259] where the directors of the claimant company were negotiating a contract with a third party on behalf of the company. Rather than signing the contract on behalf of the company some of the directors signed it on behalf of themselves. It was held that the directors were liable for a breach of fiduciary duty and held the profits they had made on constructive trust for the company. This can be justified because, had the defendants not breached their duty, the company would have obtained the contract, so the defendants' gain could be presumed to have been made on behalf of the company.[260]

The most controversial issue arises where the fiduciary has obtained a benefit from a third party rather than depriving the claimant of property or the opportunity to make a profit. This has proved to be particularly controversial where the fiduciary has received a bribe or a secret commission from a third party. In such circumstances the profit cannot be considered to have derived from the principal. Consequently, the orthodox view was that only the personal remedy of an account of profits was available, and not a proprietary constructive trust. The leading case was *Lister and Co v Stubbs*,[261] in which the defendant was employed by the claimant company to purchase supplies for it. He bought goods from another company, having received secret commissions of over £5,000 to induce him to place orders with that company. The defendant invested this money in land. It was held that the bribes did not belong to the claimant, for otherwise the claimant would have priority over the defendant's unsecured creditors if the defendant were to become insolvent, and, if the bribes were invested in property that increased in value, the claimant would get the benefit of that increase. Neither of these conclusions was considered to be appropriate. The relationship between the parties was consequently not one of trustee and beneficiary, but was simply one of debtor and creditor.

In *Attorney-General for Hong Kong v Reid*,[262] however, the Privy Council recognized that a defendant fiduciary who had received a bribe held that bribe on constructive trust

---

[256] See *Primlake Ltd v Matthews Associates* [2006] EWHC 1227 (Ch), [2007] 1 BCLC 666, [334] (Lawrence Collins J); *Keown v Nahoor* [2015] EWHC 3418 (Ch) at [41] (D Halpern QC).

[257] *Daraydan Holdings Ltd v Solland International Ltd* [2004] EWHC 622 (Ch), [2005] Ch 119.

[258] 'Property and unjust enrichment', in *Essays on the Law of Restitution*, ed. Burrows (Oxford: Clarendon Press, 1991), p. 230.

[259] [1916] 1 AC 554. See Section 15.6.7.(i), p. 442. See also *Keech v Sandford* (1726) Sel Cas t King 61. See Section 15.6.3, p. 440.

[260] In *CMS Dolphin Ltd v Simonet* [2001] 2 BCLC 704, [96], Lawrence Collins J characterized the exploitation of a maturing business opportunity as appropriation of property belonging to the principal with the result that the defendant fiduciary would hold the profits of the exploitation on constructive trust for the principal. It is unprincipled, however, to treat a maturing business opportunity as the principal's property.

[261] (1890) 45 Ch D 1. See also *Metropolitan Bank v Heiron* (1880) LR 5 Ex D 319.   [262] [1994] 1 AC 324.

for the principal. The defendant fiduciary in this case held a number of public offices in Hong Kong, including that of Director of Public Prosecutions. He had accepted bribes to induce him to frustrate the prosecution of some criminals. He purchased land with this money and the claimant argued that the land was held on constructive trust for it. The Privy Council agreed and specifically rejected *Lister and Co v Stubbs* for the following reason. Where a defendant receives a bribe in breach of fiduciary duty it is clear that the defendant is liable to account to the principal for the value of the bribe immediately it is received, simply because it is the receipt of the bribe which constitutes the breach of duty. There is consequently a personal liability to account to the principal. But, by virtue of the equitable maxim that Equity treats as done what ought to be done,[263] Equity presumes that the fiduciary has accounted for the value of the bribe when it is received. It follows, therefore, that Equity considers the principal to have an equitable proprietary interest in the bribe immediately it is received, with the result that the defendant holds the bribe on constructive trust for the principal.

The Privy Council in *Reid* considered that it was appropriate to recognize that the principal had an equitable proprietary interest in the bribe as a matter of policy, even though this would mean that the unsecured creditors of the fiduciary would be deprived of their right to share in the money if the fiduciary were to become insolvent, because it was considered that the unsecured creditors could not be in a better position than their debtor. Also, it would not be appropriate for the fiduciary to retain any increase in the value of the bribe because of the principle that wrongdoers should not profit from their wrong. So, on the facts of *Reid*, although it was clear that the defendant was liable to account for the value of the bribe received, it was also inappropriate for him to retain the increase in the value of the land.

Reid was, however, a decision of the Privy Council which conflicted with earlier decisions of the House of Lords[264] and the Court of Appeal.[265] Despite this, *Reid* was followed in some cases[266] and can be considered to be consistent with earlier decisions, notably *Boardman v Phipps*,[267] where the shares which were purchased in breach of fiduciary duty were held on constructive trust even though there had been no interference with the claimant's property rights. The decision in *Reid* was, however, rejected by the Court of Appeal in *Sinclair Investments (UK) Ltd v Versailles Trade Finance Ltd*.[268] In that case the claimant had advanced money to a company to be used to purchase goods. The money was used fraudulently for other purposes. The defendant had sold shares in the company that he already owned for a profit. These shares had not been acquired with money in which the claimant had a proprietary interest, but the profit that he had obtained on their sale was attributable to his dishonest conduct in creating the appearance of trading which had not taken place, which had inflated the apparent turnover and profits of the company, so increasing its market value. It was held that the defendant had breached his fiduciary duty but he was only personally liable to account for the profits, which were not held on constructive trust for the claimant.

Although the profit in this case was not a bribe or a secret commission, the Court of Appeal considered that it should be analysed in the same way, because the profit made by the director was an unauthorized secret profit that had resulted from his breach of

---

[263] See Section 2.6, p. 32. [264] *Tyrrell v Bank of London* (1862) 10 HL Cas 26.
[265] Including *Metropolitan Bank v Heiron* (1880) 5 Ex D 319 and *Lister and Co v Stubbs* (1890) LR 45 Ch D 1.
[266] *Ocular Sciences Ltd v Aspect Vision Care Ltd* [1997] RPC 289, 412–13 (Laddie J); *Fyffes Group Ltd v Templeman* [2002] 2 Lloyd's Rep 643; *Daraydan Holdings Ltd v Solland International Ltd* [2004] EWHC 622 (Ch), [2005] Ch 119.
[267] [1967] 2 AC 46. See Section 15.6.7.(iii), p. 444. [268] [2011] EWCA Civ 347, [2012] 1 AC 776.

fiduciary duty.[269] The Court of Appeal held that the fact that a breach of fiduciary duty enabled the defendant to make a profit was not sufficient to give the claimant a proprietary interest in that profit. The rationale behind the recognition of the constructive trust in *Reid* was rejected as a matter of authority, as a matter of principle, and as a matter of policy. The key principle was that profits should only be held on constructive trust where they derived directly or indirectly from the principal's property or from the exploitation of an opportunity which had been available to the principal,[270] since the defendant will then have profited from interference with the principal's property rights, although this is difficult to justify where the defendant has only exploited an opportunity which should have been procured for the principal. The key policy was that the claims of the unsecured creditors of the fiduciary should not be defeated by recognizing that the fiduciary's property was held on constructive trust for the principal.

The decision of the Court of Appeal in *Sinclair Investments* was, however, overruled by the Supreme Court in *FHR European Ventures LLP v Cedar Capital Partners LLC*.[271] It was held that, wherever a fiduciary is liable to account for profits made as a result of a breach of fiduciary duty, those profits will be held on constructive trust for the principal, even though they did not derive from interference with the principal's property or from the exploitation of an opportunity which should have been exploited for the principal. Consequently, wherever a fiduciary receives a bribe or secret commission in breach of fiduciary duty, that bribe or secret commission will be held on constructive trust. The decision in *Lister v Stubbs* was also overruled. The constructive trust recognized by the Supreme Court is an institutional constructive trust[272] and is justified because the fiduciary is treated as though they had acquired the bribe or secret commission on behalf of the principal,[273] who therefore has an equitable proprietary interest in it. This assumption that the bribe has been acquired for the principal has been defended by virtue of the need to ensure fiduciary fidelity.[274]

In *FHR* the claimants had purchased the share capital of a company which owned the lease of the Monte Carlo Grand Hotel. Cedar Capital Partners LLC acted as the claimants' agent in negotiating the purchase of the shares and, as agent, owed fiduciary duties to the claimants. The defendant had earlier entered into an agreement with the vendor of the hotel by virtue of which the vendor would pay it €10 million following conclusion of the sale of the shares, but had failed to disclose this to the claimants in breach of fiduciary duty. It was held that the agent held the secret commission on constructive trust for the claimants.

The decision of the Supreme Court in *FHR* does at least resolve a long-standing controversy as to the role of the constructive trust where the fiduciary has profited from breach of their fiduciary duty. The Supreme Court cut through authorities to the contrary and rejected the principles and policies identified by the Court of Appeal in *Sinclair*.[275] The real difficulty with *FHR* relates to the Supreme Court's emphasis that the constructive trust was

---

[269] The decision was applied to a case involving bribes and secret commissions in *Cadogan Petroleum plc v Tolley* [2011] EWHC 2286 (Ch), [2015] WTLR 1505.

[270] *Sinclair Investments (UK) Ltd v Versailles Trade Finance Ltd* [2011] EWCA Civ 347, [2012] 1 AC 776, [88] (Lord Neuberger MR).

[271] [2014] UKSC 45, [2015] AC 250.   [272] See Section 9.2.1, p. 255.

[273] [2014] UKSC 45, [2015] AC 250, [7] (Lord Neuberger).

[274] Millett, 'Bribes and secret commissions again' (2012) 71 CLJ 583. See also Smith, 'Constructive trusts and the no-profit rule' (2013) 72 CLJ 260.

[275] The judgment of that court being delivered by Lord Neuberger MR, who, as President of the Supreme Court, delivered the unanimous judgment in the Supreme Court in *FHR*. See Gummow, 'Bribes and constructive trusts' (2015) 131 LQR 21.

institutional, arising by operation of law, rather than remedial,[276] which enables the operation of the trust to be modified through the exercise of judicial discretion.[277] Whether an institutional constructive trust is appropriate in this context depends on whether the three proprietary advantages of the trust[278] can necessarily be justified where the fiduciary has profited from breach of duty. If any of these advantages cannot be justified it would be appropriate to modify the institutional constructive trust through the operation of judicial discretion, such that not all the proprietary benefits are available.

First, where the defendant has profited from the investment of the profit made in breach of fiduciary duty, they should not benefit from this indirect profit, so that the institutional constructive trust should not be modified to exclude such profits, because of the strict nature of fiduciary duties. So, for example, it was not appropriate for the defendant in *Attorney-General for Hong Kong v Reid* to have benefited from the investment of the bribes in land.

The second advantage of the constructive trust is that the principal has priority over the fiduciary's unsecured creditors if the fiduciary has become insolvent. Lord Millett[279] has argued that such an advantage is justifiable, because the fiduciary's creditors claim through the fiduciary and should have no claim to property to which they are not entitled. But, even though the approach of the English courts in recognizing an institutional constructive trust appears to militate against flexibility in the operation of the constructive trust, in a very significant dictum in *FHR*[280] the Supreme Court recognized that concern about the position of unsecured creditors of the defendant fiduciary has considerable force in some contexts, although it has limited force in the context of bribes and secret commissions. The court did not elaborate beyond this and it is unclear why the position of unsecured creditors might matter more in some contexts, although it is unclear which, and why not where the profit took the form of bribes or secret commissions. But, acknowledging that the position of the unsecured creditors of the fiduciary might need to be considered in some cases is highly significant. It might suggest a willingness of the English court to recognize the constructive trust in principle, but then its effect might be modified to ensure that, whilst the fiduciary does not benefit from the profit, the relative positions of the principal and unsecured creditors are treated equally. Usually,[281] where the fiduciary has received a bribe or a secret commission, this should be held on constructive trust for the principal, but this should be modified to ensure that the principal's claim to the profits ranks equally with that of the fiduciary's unsecured creditors.

The third advantage of the institutional constructive trust is that the principal is able to assert a proprietary restitutionary claim against a third-party recipient of the property which was held on trust.[282] This result is much more difficult to justify where the third-party recipient is innocent of any wrongdoing,[283] for why should the claim of the principal, to profits which have not been taken from the principal, prevail over that of an innocent volunteer? In such circumstances it would be appropriate to modify the

---

[276] The Supreme Court specifically rejected the recognition of the remedial constructive trust. See further Section 9.4, p. 275.

[277] As is the case in Australia: *Grimaldi v Chameleon Mining NZ (No 2)* [2012] FCAFC 6, [569]–[584] (Finn J). See Ho, 'Bribes and the constructive trust as a chameleon' (2012) 128 LQR 486.

[278] See Section 15.7.3, p. 451.   [279] Millett (see n. 274).

[280] *FHR European Ventures LLP v Cedar Capital Partners LLC* [2014] UKSC 45, [2015] AC 250, [43].

[281] Where the secret commission has been obtained from the principal, holding it on constructive trust corrects the injustice of the fiduciary having gained from the principal and there is no reason to modify the trust. See Chapter 15.7.3, p. 452.   [282] See Chapter 19.1.3.(iii), p. 539.

[283] Where the third-party recipient has provided value and has acted in good faith the principal's proprietary claim will be defeated. See Section 19.5.1, p. 584.

institutional constructive trust so that the principal and third-party volunteer share the property equally. Where, however, the third party's receipt can be considered to be unconscionable, because the third party knew or suspected that the fiduciary had obtained the profit in breach of fiduciary duty, it is appropriate to enable the principal to assert their equitable proprietary rights against the third party, whose conscience has been tainted. So, for example, in *Attorney-General for Hong Kong v Reid*, assets were transferred to the fiduciary's wife and his solicitor who appear to have been aware that they had been purchased with bribe money. In such circumstances it is appropriate that the proprietary claim of the principal should prevail over such recipients whose consciences have been tainted by their knowledge of the breach of fiduciary duty. But, as English law stands, the principal has a proprietary claim against the third-party recipient who has received and retained the property or its substitute which was held on constructive trust, regardless of the recipient's ignorance of the breach of fiduciary duty. This is an unfortunate consequence of the recognition of the institutional constructive trust, which could be avoided if there was greater willingness to modify the proprietary impact of such a trust.

PART VII

VARIATION OF TRUSTS

16

THE VARIATION OF TRUSTS

16.1 GENERAL CONSIDERATIONS

A trustee must administer the trust in accordance with its terms, otherwise the trustee will commit a breach of trust. Sometimes, however, the observance of the terms of the trust is harmful to the beneficiaries, especially because circumstances affecting the beneficiaries may have changed. In particular, the structure of the trust may have adverse tax consequences for the beneficiaries. The question then arises as to whether it is ever possible to vary the terms of the trust.

16.1.1 TERMINATION OF THE TRUST

One extreme mechanism for varying a trust is by termination. Where the beneficiaries are of full age, under no disability, and absolutely entitled, then, if they all agree, they can terminate the trust[1] and either distribute the assets amongst themselves or resettle the property on different trusts. This will have the practical effect of varying the original trust, although that trust will have been destroyed and replaced by a new one. But this solution will not be available where there are beneficiaries who are minors, or who are not yet born, or who are not ascertained.

16.1.2 INHERENT JURISDICTION OF THE COURT

The court has an inherent jurisdiction to authorize trustees to do certain administrative acts that are beyond their powers, with the consequence of varying the trust temporarily and ad hoc, even though not all of the beneficiaries can consent to it because of incapacity or because they are not yet born. The exercise of this jurisdiction is exceptional, must clearly be for the benefit of all of the beneficiaries, and is confined to cases of emergency, such as the need to postpone the sale of property for a reasonable time, and not simply because the action would be advantageous to the beneficiaries.[2] But the court does not otherwise have an inherent jurisdiction to modify or vary trusts, save in exceptional circumstances under which a genuine dispute about the trust has arisen, such as where the court sanctions a genuine compromise of disputed rights on behalf of child and unborn beneficiaries.[3]

---

[1] Under the rule in *Saunders v Vautier* (1841) 4 Beav 115. See Section 11.4.1, p. 334.
[2] *Re New* [1901] 2 Ch 534; *Re Tollemache* [1903] 1 Ch 955.   [3] *Chapman v Chapman* [1954] AC 429.

16.1.3 EXPRESS POWERS OF VARIATION

The trust instrument may give the trustees the power to amend the trust.[4]

16.1.4 STATUTORY POWERS

There are certain statutory provisions that give the courts the power to vary the trust.

16.2 STATUTORY PROVISIONS TO VARY TRUSTS

16.2.1 POWERS TO DEAL WITH TRUST PROPERTY

Where the court considers that a particular transaction is expedient in the management or administration of trust property, but the trust instrument or the law does not give the trustee the power to undertake that transaction, the court can confer the power on the trustee where it is considered to be expedient to do so.[5] This power can be conferred generally or for a specific transaction, and on the application of a trustee or a person beneficially entitled under the trust. This provision can be used, for example, to give the trustees the power to sell, lease, or purchase trust property or to expand the powers of investment,[6] although this is less significant following the expansion of investment powers by the Trustee Act 2000,[7] but will remain useful where the statutory powers of investment have been restricted by the trust deed. The court can impose terms and conditions for the exercise of the power, which it can vary or rescind at any time.

This statutory provision only concerns the conferral of powers relating to trust property and cannot be used to alter any of the beneficial interests under the trust. The conferral of such administrative powers on the trustees could also be undertaken under the Variation of Trusts Act 1958,[8] but section 57 has certain advantages, including that it is not necessary to obtain the consent of all adult beneficiaries for the variation to take effect.

16.2.2 VARIATION OF TRUSTS ACT 1958

The Variation of Trusts Act 1958 gives the court the power to approve by order any arrangement that revokes or varies a trust or enlarges the powers of the trustees to manage or administer the trust property.[9] This Act covers some of the ground provided for by section 57 of the Trustee Act 1925,[10] but is wider, because it also enables beneficial interests to be varied. The function of the Act is to enable the court to approve the relevant arrangement on behalf of particular categories of person who are not in a position to consent to the variation. The court can approve the arrangement regardless of who proposes it and regardless of whether any other person who is beneficially entitled to the property is capable of assenting to the variation. But, generally, the court can approve the arrangement only if it is for the benefit of the person or people on whose behalf the court gives its approval.

---

[4] See e.g. *Society of Lloyd's v Robinson* [1999] 1 WLR 756.   [5] Trustee Act 1925, s. 57(1).

[6] *Mason v Farbrother* [1983] 2 All ER 1078; *Anker-Petersen v Anker-Petersen* (1998) 12 TLI 166. See Section 13.4.5, p. 390.   [7] See Section 13.4.2, p. 381.

[8] See Section 16.2.2, p. 460.

[9] Variation of Trusts Act 1958, s. 1(1). It has also been applied to trusts arising on the death of a testator: *Re Bernstein* [2008] EWHC 3454 (Ch), [2010] WTLR 559.

[10] And has been used to vary investment powers: *British Museum (Trustees) v Attorney-General* [1984] 1 All ER 337. See Section 13.4.5, p. 390.

(i) Function of the Variation of Trusts Act 1958

As we have seen, where the beneficiaries of the trust are adults, of full capacity, and fully entitled to the trust property, they may unanimously agree to terminate the trust and to resettle the trust property under the rule in *Saunders v Vautier*.[11] But this termination and resettlement will be available only where all of the beneficiaries consent. If any of the beneficiaries are incapable of consenting because, for example, they are infants or even not yet born, the rule in *Saunders v Vautier* will not apply. This is why the Variation of Trusts Act 1958 was needed: the function of that Act is simply to give the court the power to consent to the variation of the trust on behalf of those beneficiaries who are incapable of consenting.[12] In other words, it is a statutory extension of the consent principle embodied in the rule in *Saunders v Vautier*. When the court approves the variation on behalf of these beneficiaries, the approval binds the beneficiaries.[13] It does not, however, bind the adult beneficiaries who are capable of consenting and who must consent in their own right for the variation to be effective.

In the same way as settlors or testators cannot exclude the operation of the rule in *Saunders v Vautier*, so too they cannot exclude the application of the Variation of Trusts Act 1958.[14]

(ii) Variation and resettlement

The 1958 Act refers only to approval by the court of any arrangement that varies or revokes a trust or enlarges the administrative powers of the trustees, and no reference is made to a power to authorize the revocation and then resettlement of the trust. So it would appear that, if beneficiaries were to want to revoke and resettle the trust, they could not do so under the statute,[15] and the mechanism would be through the exercise of the rule in *Saunders v Vautier*, which consequently would not be applicable if any of the beneficiaries were to lack capacity or were unascertained. The Act has, however, been interpreted as extending to authorization of an arrangement that revokes an existing trust and establishing a new trust, but only where the new trust can be regarded in substance as similar to the old trust, so that, although the mechanism adopted is revocation and resettlement, this is in effect a variation under which the new trust is recognizable as the old trust.[16] Whether the new trust is recognizably similar to the old trust simply depends on whether the 'substratum' of the original trust can be identified in the new trust. This appears to be a very easy test to satisfy. So, for example, in *Re Ball's Settlement Trusts*,[17] the substratum of the original trusts was considered to continue in the new trusts since both the old and the new trusts involved funds being held for the settlor's two sons and their families, even though the variation was substantial since the settlor's life interest vanished, as did powers of appointment and many administrative powers. The key principle recognized by Megarry J was:

> If an arrangement changes the whole substratum of the trust, then it may well be that it cannot be regarded merely as varying that trust. But if an arrangement, while leaving the substratum, effectuates the purpose of the original trust by other means, it may still be possible to regard that arrangement as merely varying the original trusts, even though the means employed are wholly different and even though the form is completely changed.[18]

---

[11] See Section 11.4.1, p. 334.   [12] *Goulding v James* [1997] 2 All ER 239, 247 (Mummery LJ).
[13] *Inland Revenue Commissioners v Holmden* [1968] AC 685, 701 (Lord Reid).
[14] *Goulding v James* [1997] 2 All ER 239, 251 (Mummery LJ).
[15] See *Re Towler's Settlement Trust* [1964] Ch 158, 162 (Wilberforce J); *Allen v Distillers Co (Biochemical) Ltd* [1974] QB 384.   [16] *Re Holt's Settlement* [1969] 1 Ch 100.
[17] [1968] 1 WLR 899.   [18] Ibid., at 905.

This wide construction of the 1958 Act is consistent with the court's general attitude to the legislation, namely that the jurisdiction is beneficial and the court is only providing consent on behalf of those who cannot give it, so that there is no harm in adopting a wide interpretation of the legislation.

(iii) People on whose behalf approval may be given

At the heart of the 1958 Act is the need to identify the categories of person who are unable to consent to the variation of trust and on whose behalf the court is able to consent. Four such categories are identified:[19]

(1) anybody who has a direct or indirect interest under the trust, whether vested or contingent, but who is incapable of consenting to the arrangements because of infancy or incapacity,[20] including mental incapacity;[21]

(2) any person unborn;[22]

(3) any person in respect of a discretionary interest under protective trusts,[23] where the interest of the principal beneficiary has not failed or determined;[24] and

(4) anybody who may become directly or indirectly entitled to an interest under the trust in the future, either on a specified date or on the occurrence of a specified event.[25] Such a person may be of any specified description or a member of a specified class, but must not be a person who would meet that description or be a member of such a class if the future date or event had happened at the date on which the application for approval of the variation had been made to the court. The requirement that a person 'may' become entitled to an interest has been restrictively interpreted as excluding a person who is already entitled to an interest under a trust, albeit that this is a contingent and remote interest.[26] It follows that the provision applies only where the person has only a hope of an interest, such as being a next of kin of the beneficiary entitled to the income or a possible spouse.

Although the provision relating to this last category is rather complicated, the essence of it is that the court has jurisdiction to give consent for the variation on behalf of a person who cannot consent to a variation because they belong to a class that is ascertainable at a future date,[27] but not a person who could be ascertained if the relevant date or event had occurred by the time at which the application for variation had been made. Essentially, therefore, the provision enables the court to approve arrangements on behalf of people who could not consent because their identity is not yet ascertained.[28] The provision aims to draw a distinction between a person who is nowhere in sight, such as a future spouse, and someone whose identity could easily coincide with people at hand, such as a next of kin.[29] The court can approve the variation on behalf of the former, but not the latter.

The application of this last provision is illustrated by *Re Suffert's Settlement*,[30] in which the beneficiary sought a variation of a trust so that the bulk of the fund was transferred to her. She had a life interest in the fund, and, if she were to die without leaving any children, the fund would be held on trust for her statutory next of kin. When the application

---

[19] Variation of Trusts Act 1958, s. 1(1).   [20] Ibid., s. 1(1)(a).   [21] *Re CL* [1969] 1 Ch 587.
[22] Variation of Trusts Act 1958, s. 1(1)(c).
[23] Under the Trustee Act 1925, s. 33. See Section 3.6.2.(viii), p. 56.
[24] Variation of Trusts Act 1958, s. 1(1)(d).   [25] Ibid., s. 1(1)(b).
[26] *Knocker v Youle* [1986] 1 WLR 934. Criticized by Riddall, 'Does it or doesn't it? Contingent interests and the Variation of Trusts Act 1958' [1987] Conv 144.
[27] Watkin, 'Shifting interests overseas' (1976) 40 Conv 295.
[28] Harris, 'Ten years of variation of trusts' (1969) 33 Conv 113, 116.   [29] Ibid.
[30] [1961] Ch 1. See also *Knocker v Youle* [1986] 1 WLR 934.

for approval of the variation was made, she was unmarried and her nearest relatives were three adult cousins. It was held that the court could approve the variation on behalf of any unborn children of the beneficiary,[31] but not on behalf of the cousins. This was because the cousins' prospective interest under the trust was conditional on the occurrence of a particular event, namely the beneficiary's death. If it was assumed that she had died by the time the application for approval of the variation was made, the cousins would be members of the specified class. Consequently, the cousins needed to decide for themselves whether or not to agree to the variation; the court could not agree to the variation on their behalf. This can be compared with *Re Moncrieff's Settlement Trusts*,[32] in which the trust fund was held for the settlor for life, with remainder to such person as was appointed by the settlor and, in default of appointment, for her statutory next of kin. The settlor sought a variation of the trust. She had an adopted son at the time of the application. It was held that the court did not have jurisdiction to consent on his behalf, since he would be entitled to the fund if he survived the settlor and so would be entitled to the fund at the date of the application if his adopted mother had died. But the court did have jurisdiction to consent to the variation on behalf of the settlor's other next of kin, since they would be entitled to the fund only if two contingencies were satisfied, namely that the adopted son had died before the settlor and the settlor had also died. The essence of the difference between the approach adopted in *Re Suffert* and *Re Moncrieff* is that, in the latter case, the entitlement of the other next of kin to the fund depended on a double contingency test, whereas the entitlement of the cousins in *Re Suffert* and the adopted son in *Re Moncrieff* turned on a single contingency that is deemed to have been satisfied at the time of the application.[33] The effect of this is that, for example, the court will have jurisdiction to approve a variation on behalf of a widow of a beneficiary other than the present wife of the beneficiary, since any other person who would satisfy the condition of being a widow will need both to have married the beneficiary and to have survived the beneficiary.

The court cannot, however, give consent on behalf of somebody simply because they are untraceable or because it is difficult to obtain their consent, because, for example, they live abroad.[34]

(iv) Principles applicable to the exercise of the court's discretion

The court has a discretion to approve the variation of the trust if 'it thinks fit'.[35] In exercising this discretion where the court is approving the variation on behalf of a person who lacks capacity, who is unborn, or who is not yet ascertained, the court can approve the variation only if it is for the benefit of that person. If, however, the person on whose behalf the approval is given is a person who would be entitled under a protective trust if it had failed or determined, the court can approve the variation without it being a requirement that it is for the benefit of that person.

It follows that it is usually necessary to consider what is meant by 'benefit' for the purposes of approving a variation of the trust. Various principles can be identified to assist with this and the more general question of whether the court should think fit to approve the variation.

Tax-saving

The court will be willing to approve the variation of a trust even though its sole objective is to make a significant saving of tax, and this pecuniary advantage may outweigh any

---

[31] By virtue of the Variation of Trusts Act 1958, s. 1(1)(c).   [32] [1962] 1 WLR 1344.
[33] See Harris (see n. 28), p. 116.   [34] See *Knocker v Youle* [1986] 1 WLR 934.
[35] Variation of Trusts Act 1958, s. 1(1).

disadvantage, such as the children obtaining a benefit of substantial sums of money at an early age.[36]

Risk-taking

In determining whether the variation is likely to benefit the people who are unable to consent themselves, the court should be willing to take the same risk as an adult would take in approving the scheme.[37] Consequently, the scheme should be approved if it is highly likely to benefit the relevant people, even though there might be a small chance that the scheme might prove to be prejudicial.

Non-pecuniary benefit

Although the benefit to the person on whose behalf approval is given will usually be financial, and often through the saving of a tax liability, the courts are willing to consider non-financial benefits as well, such as moral and social benefits arising from the variation.[38] There have even been cases in which the variation was to the clear financial detriment of the beneficiary, but it was still approved because the beneficiary would have consented to the variation if they have had the capacity to do so. So, for example, in *Re CL*,[39] the court approved a variation whereby the beneficiary gave up her life interest to her adopted daughters in circumstances under which the beneficiary lacked the mental capacity to consent to the transaction, but it was considered that she would have done so had she not been incapacitated.

The significance of such non-pecuniary considerations was emphasized in *Re Weston's Settlements*,[40] which concerned an application to vary two settlements that the settlor had made in favour of his two sons. The settlor and the sons had moved to Jersey, and the settlor applied to the court to approve an arrangement under the 1958 Act to insert a power for the trustees to discharge the property from the trusts of the English settlements and to subject it to identical trusts of a Jersey settlement. The purpose behind seeking the variation was to avoid capital gains tax and to save estate duty, so that there would be considerable tax advantages from approving the variation and so an obvious financial benefit to the sons. Lord Denning MR recognized, however, that, in exercising its discretion, the function of the court was to protect those who could not protect themselves and to determine what was truly for their benefit. Whilst he acknowledged that the court could approve a variation of a trust that was motivated by tax avoidance, since this was usually the principal object of a scheme of variation, he held that the court should not only consider financial benefits to those on whose behalf approval was sought, but also the educational and social benefit arising from the variation. He considered that it was not for the benefit of the children to be uprooted from England and transported to another country simply to avoid tax, and so the court refused to approve the variation. It was acknowledged that it would have been different had the family permanently emigrated to a country and then sought a variation of the trust to enable its transportation to that country.[41] But, in *Re Weston's Settlement*, the family had only lived in Jersey for three months before the application for approval of the variation was made to the court. The detriment to the children outweighed the benefit and so the scheme was not approved.

---

[36] *Re Bernstein* [2008] EWHC 3454 (Ch), [2010] WTLR 559. See Evans, 'Variation classification' [2011] Conv 151.   [37] *Re Holt's Settlement* [1969] 1 Ch 100.
[38] Ibid., at 121 (Megarry J). See also the meaning of benefit for the purposes of the exercise of the power of advancement: Section 14.5.3, p. 416.   [39] [1969] 1 Ch 587.
[40] [1969] 1 Ch 223.   [41] See e.g. *Re Windeatt's Will Trusts* [1969] 1 WLR 692.

Family harmony

Another type of non-pecuniary benefit that might arise from the variation of trust is that the variation would contribute to family harmony. For example, in *Re Remnant's Settlement Trust*,[42] a trust fund was subject to forfeiture in respect of any one of the children of two sisters who practised Roman Catholicism or who was married to a Roman Catholic, with the forfeited portion accruing in favour of the other beneficiaries. One sister and her children were Protestants, and the other sister and her children were Roman Catholics. The sisters made an application to the court to approve an arrangement that deleted the forfeiture provision. This was approved, even though it was not for the financial benefit of the children of the Protestant sister, who would have benefited from the forfeiture of the interests of the other sister and her children. But the variation was approved because the forfeiture provisions represented a source of possible family dissension and so, taking a broad view of benefit, the deletion of the forfeiture provision was considered to be for the benefit of all of the children, born and unborn. The prevention of conflict and dissension within the family is, however, only one factor to be taken into account when considering whether or not to approve a scheme of variation and the scheme might not be approved even though it would remove a source of conflict.[43]

Observing the settlor's or testator's intention

A key factor in determining whether the variation should be approved concerns whether it is relevant to take into account the intention of the settlor or testator when establishing the trust. This was a key issue in *Goulding v James*.[44] The testatrix in that case had created a trust under her will in which her daughter had a life interest and her grandson would take absolutely on attaining the age of 40. The reason why the testatrix structured the trust in this way was that she did not want her daughter to have access to the capital of the fund, since she did not trust her daughter's husband, and she considered her grandson to be a 'free spirit' and likely to waste the money whilst he was young. The daughter and grandson sought to vary the trust, so that each had 45 per cent of the residuary estate, with the remaining 10 per cent held on trusts of a grandchildren's trust fund to benefit the unborn great-grandchildren of the testatrix. The court was required to approve the scheme of variation only on behalf of the unborn great-grandchildren and, since the scheme was considered to benefit them, the variation was approved. Mummery LJ emphasized that the purpose of the 1958 Act was to enable the court to supply consent to a variation of a trust for people who were incapable of consenting and the court was not standing in for the settlor or testatrix in varying the trust. Consequently, the fact that the variation was contrary to the clear wishes of the testatrix did not mean that the court could not approve the variation. The daughter and grandson were of full age and capacity, and so they were entitled to do what they wanted with their beneficial interests; the court was concerned only to protect the interests of the testatrix's unborn great-grandchildren, who would benefit from the proposed variation.

But Mummery LJ did suggest that, in determining whether the scheme should be approved, the court should have regard to the scheme as a whole and should not approve it simply because the scheme would benefit those who were unable to consent to it. In particular, the court could have regard to the intentions of the settlor or testator in determining whether the trust should be varied.[45] But it is unclear why this should be the case,[46] especially because the function of the court is to protect those who cannot protect

---

[42] [1970] Ch 560.   [43] *Re Tinker's Settlement* [1960] 1 WLR 1011.   [44] [1997] 2 All ER 239.
[45] Ibid., 251 (Mummery LJ).   [46] See ibid., 252 (Sir Ralph Gibson).

themselves.[47] If the court is approving the variation on behalf of unborn children, why should it be relevant that a consequence of the variation is to undermine the clearly expressed intention of the settlor or testator, save perhaps where this will result in such family conflict as not to be in the best interests of the children, born or unborn?

It is, indeed, sometimes the case that the courts have explicitly considered the settlor's or testator's intention in determining whether or not to approve a scheme of variation, most notably in *Re Steed's Will Trusts*.[48] In that case, a farm was held on a protective trust[49] for the testator's housekeeper for her life. The testator had expressed a wish that the housekeeper would have the use and enjoyment of the capital value during her life, and that, if the property were sold, the capital value should be applied for her benefit. The trustees wished to sell the farm, and the housekeeper sought to restrain the sale and brought a summons under the 1958 Act asking the court to approve an arrangement under which the trustees would hold the farm on trust for her absolutely rather than on a protective trust. The court refused to approve the variation, particularly because it would undermine the testator's intentions, since he had wanted the housekeeper to be provided for throughout her life and ensure that she would not be tempted to part with the money in favour of her brother, about whom the testator felt apprehension. But this was a very different case from *Goulding v James* for two reasons. First, the court was being asked to approve the scheme of variation on behalf of those who would benefit if the protective trust were to fail or to determine, and the approval of the variation in such circumstances need not be for the benefit of the people on whose behalf consent was sought.[50] So the absence of benefit to such people did not prevent the variation being approved and other factors could be taken into account, such as the testator's intention. Secondly, the testator's intention was vital, since he had intended to create a protective trust to protect the life tenant from improvident dealing, especially through exploitation by her brother, and the proposed variation would have undermined this objective completely.

Fraud on the power

The court will not approve a variation of trust where there is fraud on the power, namely where the variation is sought either for an ulterior purpose, notably to enable a life tenant to obtain as much as possible from the variation,[51] or where the variation constitutes a dishonest, inequitable, or otherwise improper act on the part of one or more of the beneficiaries.[52]

Summary

When the court is exercising its discretion to decide whether or not to approve the variation of trust, it is clear from the statute that there is a general discretion to decide whether or not it is appropriate to approve the variation and, for three groups of beneficiary, the variation must be for the benefit of those beneficiaries who are incapable of consenting. Even if the variation is for the benefit of those beneficiaries, it does not follow that the court will approve the scheme of variation.[53] It has been recognized that, because the court will approve the variation only if it thinks it fit, it is appropriate to consider the arrangement as a whole to determine whether it is in its nature fair and proper.[54] This involves 'a

---

[47] *Re Weston's Settlements* [1969] 1 Ch 223, 245 (Lord Denning MR).   [48] [1960] Ch 407.
[49] See Section 3.6.2.(viii), p. 56.   [50] See Section 16.2.2.(iv), p. 463.
[51] *Re Brook's Settlement Trust* [1968] 1 WLR 1661.
[52] *Goulding v James* [1997] 2 All ER 239, 252 (Sir Ralph Gibson).   [53] Ibid., 249 (Mummery LJ).
[54] *Re Remnant's Settlement Trusts* [1970] Ch 560, 565 (Pennycuick J).

practical and business-like consideration of the arrangement, including the total amounts of the advantages which the various parties obtain, and their bargaining strength'.[55]

Since, however, it is clear that the court is consenting only on behalf of those beneficiaries who are incapable of consenting to the variation, it is difficult to see why considerations other than the benefit to those beneficiaries should be relevant, save where there is evidence that those seeking the variation are wishing to perpetrate a fraud on the power, since the court should not associate itself with such unconscionable conduct. If the beneficiaries were capable of consenting to the variation, their only concern would be the benefit arising to them from the variation, whether it be pecuniary or non-pecuniary. Similarly, at least as a general rule, this should be the prime consideration for the court when determining whether the variation should be approved.[56]

(v) Effect of court approval

Since the function of the court's approval of the scheme of variation is merely to provide consent on behalf of those who cannot consent themselves, it follows that the approval of the scheme by the court does not make it effective automatically. Rather, the scheme becomes effective through the agreement of all of the beneficiaries.[57]

This is significant where a consequence of the scheme is to dispose of a beneficial interest in property, since such a disposition requires signed writing.[58] Such writing can be provided by those adult beneficiaries who consent to the scheme of variation. But is it required if the consent is approved by the court? It was held in *Re Holt's Settlement*[59] that, by conferring an express power on the court to do something by order, Parliament, in the 1958 Act, had provided by necessary implication an exception from the need for writing to dispose of an equitable interest. Bearing in mind that the court does not amend or vary the trusts of the original settlement, this occurring instead by the consent of the beneficiaries, the conclusion in *Re Holt's Settlement* is difficult to defend as a matter of principle, although it accords with practice. An alternative route to effect a disposition of the equitable interest without signed writing is where an agreement to vary the trust is specifically enforceable, for then a constructive trust arises as soon as the agreement is made, which will effect the disposition of the equitable interest without the need for writing.[60]

---

[55] *Re Van Gruisen's Will Trusts* [1964] 1 WLR 449, 450 (Ungoed-Thomas J).

[56] Cf. Luxton, 'Variation of trusts: settlors' intentions and the consent principle in *Saunders v Vautier*' (1997) 60 MLR 719, 722.

[57] *Goulding v James* [1997] 2 All ER 239, 239, 247 (Mummery LJ). See also *Inland Revenue Commissioners v Holmden* [1968] AC 685, 701 (Lord Wilberforce).

[58] Law of Property Act 1925, s. 53(1)(c). See Section 11.3, p. 324. [59] [1969] 1 Ch 100.

[60] Law of Property Act 1925, s. 53(2). See Section 11.3.6, p. 331.

PART VIII

BREACH OF TRUST AND FIDUCIARY DUTY

17

LIABILITY FOR BREACH OF TRUST AND FIDUCIARY DUTY

17.1 GENERAL CONSIDERATIONS

In the law of contract, where a contract has been validly made and one party to it does not do what they promised to do, the other party can sue for the wrong of breach of contract and obtain a remedy, usually compensatory damages, but sometimes an order that the promise be specifically performed.[1] In the law of tort, where a defendant breaches a duty, such as the duty of care, in circumstances that can be characterized as involving the commission of a wrong, a remedy will be available to the victim of the wrong, which again will usually be damages to compensate for loss suffered as a result of the wrong. This part of the book is concerned with liability for wrongdoing in Equity, specifically the wrongs[2] of breach of trust and breach of fiduciary duty. Although these 'wrongs' have sometimes been described as forming part of the law of tort, it is preferable to regard them as distinct, since, as will be seen, they have a number of peculiar characteristics. As with the law of contract and the law of tort, however, the breach of a duty owed in Equity will result in the award of a remedy, which is usually monetary.

To understand the nature of liability for breach of trust and breach of fiduciary duty, there is a useful formula that needs to be followed:

(1) Does the defendant owe an equitable duty to the claimant?

(2) Has that duty been breached?

(3) Has the breach infringed any rights of the claimant?

(4) Are there any defences to defeat the claim or to reduce the extent of liability?

(5) If the defendant is liable, what remedies might be available to vindicate the claimant's rights?

---

[1] This remedy of specific performance is a creation of Equity. See Section 21.4, p. 634.

[2] See *Target Holdings Ltd v Redferns* [1996] AC 421, 432 (Lord Browne-Wilkinson).

If these five questions are considered logically and carefully, the complex body of law that is examined in this part will be much easier to understand. The identification of a duty owed in Equity and whether that duty has been breached were considered in Chapters 13, 14, and 15. The determination of the appropriate remedy will be considered in Chapters 18 and 19. This chapter is concerned with the identification of liability, namely whether any rights have been infringed and whether the defendant can rely on any defences to the claim.

17.2 NATURE OF LIABILITY

The first two questions relating to liability in Equity concern the identification of a duty owed to the claimant and consideration of whether that duty has been breached. Once this has been established, it can be concluded that the claimant has a primary right that has been infringed and which should be vindicated by the award of a remedy. The right to a remedy is described as being a secondary right, since it will arise only once infringement of a primary right has been established.[3]

Whether the defendant owes a duty to the claimant in Equity will depend on whether they are a trustee or a fiduciary. Although a trustee will owe fiduciary duties, the category of fiduciaries is much wider,[4] and includes directors, agents, and solicitors. Whether the defendant is a trustee or a fiduciary, the nature of the duties that they owe and whether any of those duties have been breached was examined in Part VI. For present purposes, however, it is worth emphasizing that, although we readily talk about 'breach of trust' and 'breach of fiduciary duty', these are concepts that have never been formally defined.[5]

17.2.1 BREACH OF FIDUCIARY DUTY

Fiduciaries, including trustees, owe two distinct types of duty: fiduciary and non-fiduciary.[6] A breach of fiduciary duty involves a breach of those negative duties that arise from the fundamental obligation of loyalty to the principal, namely the no-conflict and the no-profit rules.[7] But fiduciaries may breach other non-fiduciary duties, triggering liability for breach of contract, or for the commission of a tort, or for unjust enrichment. We are not concerned with breach of these non-fiduciary duties here, since the normal rules of contract, tort, and unjust enrichment will apply regardless of the fact that the defendant also happens to be a fiduciary. So, for example, although a solicitor is in a fiduciary relationship with their client, the duty of the solicitor to that client will be primarily contractual and any breach of duty is likely to trigger a claim for breach of contract rather than for breach of fiduciary duty.[8]

17.2.2 BREACH OF TRUST

A trustee who breaches the no-conflict or the no-profit rule will have breached their fiduciary duty. But trustees will also be subject to non-fiduciary duties that arise in Equity and are peculiar to them as trustees. These duties relate to the administration of the trust[9]

---

[3] See further Section 18.1.2, p. 500.   [4] See Section 15.2, p. 420.

[5] *Tito v Wadell (No 2)* [1977] Ch 106, 247 (Megarry V-C).

[6] *Henderson v Merrett Syndicates Ltd* [1995] 2 AC 145, 205 (Lord Browne-Wilkinson); *Bristol and West Building Society v Mothew* [1998] Ch 1, 18 (Millett LJ).   [7] See Section 15.1.2, p. 418.

[8] *Hilton v Barker Booth and Eastwood (a firm)* [2005] UKHL 8, [2005] 1 WLR 567, 575 (Lord Walker).

[9] See Chapter 13 of this volume.

and the exercise of powers of appointment.[10] Breaches of these duties constitute breach of trust. It follows that a breach of trust can be defined as 'the violation of any duty which the trustee owes as trustee to the beneficiaries'.[11] This definition can encompass breach of fiduciary duty committed by a trustee, although, for convenience, it is preferable to distinguish between breaches of fiduciary duties imposed by virtue of being a fiduciary and breaches of trust duties arising from being a trustee.

A breach of trust may take many different forms,[12] but can be divided into two distinct categories.

(i) Unauthorized action

Trustees will be liable for breach of trust where they do what they should not do, so that their actions could be described as *ultra vires*.[13] Liability for this type of breach of trust is strict and includes misapplication of the trust property, making an unauthorized investment, or acting where there is a conflict between their personal interest and duty to the beneficiaries.

(ii) Inadequate action

Alternatively, trustees will be liable for acting badly, or failing to act, when, if the act were done properly, it would be an authorized action and so could be characterized as *intra vires*. Liability for this type of breach of trust requires proof of fault in the form of negligence. So, for example, a trustee with a power of investment will be liable for breach of trust if they mismanage the trust investments by unreasonably investing in authorized investments, but with a low yield, or by failing to invest at all.

Without the commission of some breach of duty owed in Equity to the claimant, there will be no equitable liability. Consequently, just because the trust or the principal suffers a loss, it does not follow automatically that there will be liability; the loss must arise from an equitable breach of duty. But, just because the defendant has breached a trust or acted in breach of a fiduciary duty, it does not follow that the defendant is automatically liable to the claimant. There may be a variety of reasons why such a defendant is not liable, including that the defendant did not cause a loss to the claimant or did not profit from the breach, or the defendant's liability might be excluded or limited for some reason. Although questions of causation and remoteness of loss or gain raise questions of liability, they are inextricably linked to the measure of that liability as regards the determination of the remedy which will be available, and so they will be considered in Chapters 18 and 19. Consequently, the key issue for this chapter concerns the exclusion and limitation of liability.

17.3 EXCLUSION AND LIMITATION OF LIABILITY

A variety of doctrines have been recognized by the courts to exclude or limit liability for breach of trust or breach of fiduciary duty. These doctrines are relevant only once the claimant has established that the defendant is liable for breach of trust or breach of fiduciary duty; in other words, that an equitable cause of action has been established. The burden then shifts to the defendant to show that one of these doctrines applies.

---

[10] See Chapter 14 of this volume.   [11] *Tito v Wadell (No 2)* [1977] Ch 106, 247 (Megarry V-C).

[12] *Armitage v Nurse* [1998] Ch 241, 251 (Millett LJ).

[13] Birks and Pretto, 'Preface', in *Breach of Trust*, ed. Birks and Pretto (Oxford: Hart, 2002), p. ix.

17.3.1 EXEMPTION CLAUSES

The liability of trustees for breach of trust might be excluded or limited by a clause in the trust instrument. These clauses are called exemption or exoneration clauses,[14] but they may take a variety of forms. For example, they may purport to exclude any liability for breach of trust or they may purport to modify the duties owed by trustees so that liability for breach of trust does not arise.[15] The same issues of policy arise for both types of clause, namely whether it is appropriate to enable the trustee's liability to be excluded or modified in any way to the prejudice of the beneficiaries or objects.

The validity of clauses excluding a trustee's personal liability for breach of non-fiduciary duties has been recognized by the courts.[16] The efficacy of such clauses in excluding liability for breach of the statutory duty of care has been recognized by the Trustee Act 2000.[17] The most significant issues relating to these clauses concerns the extent to which they can exclude or qualify liability for a trustee's breach of fiduciary duties and whether they can exclude liability for breach of trust regardless of the nature of the breach, particularly whether the trustee's fault in committing the breach is relevant.

As regards fiduciaries who are not trustees, the general rule in the law of contract on the exclusion of liability applies, so generally the liability of fiduciaries for breach of duty can be excluded.[18] But, as with trustees specifically, the issue concerns whether there are some core duties of fiduciaries that are so fundamental to the fiduciary relationship that it would not be appropriate to exclude liability for breach of them.[19] Although the key cases relate to the exclusion of liability for breach of trust by trustees, the principles identified in these cases are of general application to all fiduciaries.

(i) Ambit of exemption clauses

The extent to which exemption clauses can exclude liability for breach of trust was considered in *Armitage v Nurse*.[20] In that case, the claimant beneficiary sued her trustees for breach of trust following a variation of the trust, on the ground that the trustees had failed to protect her interests adequately when the trust was varied. A clause in the trust instrument stated that no trustee should be liable for any loss suffered by the trust fund save where the loss was caused by the trustee's 'own actual fraud'. The key questions for the court concerned the interpretation of this clause and the determination of its validity.

First, the court interpreted the clause to mean that the trustees would not be liable for any loss that they had caused to the trust property save where they had acted fraudulently, which was equated with them acting dishonestly. A trustee would be considered to have acted dishonestly if they intended to pursue a course of action either knowing that it was

---

[14] See generally Penner, 'Exemptions', in *Breach of Trust*, ed. Birks and Pretto (Oxford: Hart, 2002), p. 241.

[15] See e.g. *Citibank NA v MBIA Assurance SA* [2007] EWCA Civ 11, [2007] 1 All ER (Comm) 475.

[16] *Hayim v Citibank* [1987] AC 730 (PC).

[17] Sch. 1, para. 7. Specific statutory rules apply to exemption clauses in pension trusts (Pensions Act 1995, ss. 33 and 34(6): no exclusion of liability for investment functions), unit trusts (Financial Services and Markets Act 2000, s. 253: exemption for negligence is not permitted), and debenture trusts (Companies Act 2006, s. 750: exemption for negligence is not permitted).

[18] Except where the contract is with a consumer and the clause is considered to be unfair: Consumer Rights Act 2015, s. 62. See Section 17.3.1.(ii), p. 479.

[19] See Edelman, 'Four fiduciary puzzles', in *Exploring Private Law*, ed. Bant and Harding (Cambridge: Cambridge University Press, 2010), p. 305, who recognizes that those fiduciary duties that are imposed by law cannot be excluded.

[20] [1998] Ch 241. Lord Clarke in *Spread Trustee Co Ltd v Hutcheson* [2011] UKPC 13, [2012] 2 AC 194, [52], considered that *Armitage v Nurse* correctly states English law.

contrary to the best interests of the beneficiaries or being recklessly indifferent to those interests, regardless of whether the trustee intended to benefit personally from the conduct. This definition of dishonesty is a subjective one, since it is dependent on either the defendant's knowledge of the effects of their conduct, or recklessness, in the sense of a conscious awareness of the risk of detriment being suffered by the beneficiaries.[21] The court specifically recognized that dishonesty did not encompass constructive fraud or negligence. A trustee would have acted negligently where the reasonable person would have realized that the conduct was not in the best interests of the beneficiaries even though the defendant had not realized this. The court also concluded that a trustee would not be described as acting dishonestly if they had deliberately breached the trust, but in the honest belief that this was in the best interests of the beneficiaries: such a trustee would have been acting in good faith. So, for example, if the trust specifically excludes the power to invest in land, but the trustee considers that investment in land would give the best return for the trust and uses trust money to buy land, this would be a deliberate breach of trust, but it would not be dishonest. It follows that whether a trustee has acted fraudulently or dishonestly will turn on whether or not the trustee is purporting to act in the best interests of the beneficiaries, or is purporting to act selfishly or for the benefit of a third party.

Having construed the exemption clause in this way, the Court of Appeal needed to consider whether it was effective to exclude liability for all losses save for those that arose from dishonest conduct. In other words, would the clause exclude liability for negligence, even for gross negligence, involving conduct that fell below, or far below, the standard of a reasonable trustee? The court concluded that the clause would be effective to exclude such liability. This was because, as Millett LJ recognized, trustees owe an irreducible core of obligations to the beneficiaries that are fundamental to the concept of the trust and which are enforceable by the beneficiaries. Liability for breach of these fundamental duties cannot be excluded. The question then is which duties can be considered to be fundamental. Millett LJ concluded that the duties of skill and care, prudence, and diligence are not fundamental duties, because they involve negligence and not fraud, and so liability for them can be excluded. Fundamental duties include the duty to perform the trust honestly and in good faith for the benefit of the beneficiaries.[22] Breach of these duties equates to acting fraudulently and dishonestly, and so such liability cannot be excluded, because a trustee who acts in such a way strikes at the very core of the trust obligation.

On the facts of *Armitage v Nurse*, it was held that, since the pleadings had not alleged fraud or dishonesty but only negligence, the exemption clause was effective to exclude the trustees' liability for breach of trust. The claimant was given permission to amend her pleadings, although Millett LJ did suggest that, because one of the trustees was a professional, an allegation of fraud was implausible in the absence of some financial or other incentive to act selfishly.

The decision in *Armitage v Nurse* is of profound significance both as regards the law on exemption clauses and because it tells us a great deal about the essential nature of the trust and the duties of trustees. Although the case appears to adopt a single test of duties that form the irreducible core of trust obligations, there are, in fact, two distinct tests: one concerns the nature of the duty breached and whether it is fundamental or not; the other concerns the circumstances in which the duty was breached, having regard to the defendant's fault, if any. These tests overlap, but they can have a distinct operation such that liability for breach of a non-fundamental duty might not be excluded because of the defendant's fault in breaching the duty.

---

[21] Cf. the definition of dishonesty for purposes of the action for dishonest assistance. See Section 20.3.2.(iii), p. 621.   [22] [1998] Ch 241, 253.

The nature of fundamental duties

A key consequence of the decision in *Armitage v Nurse* is that it is vital to determine which duties of trustees are fundamental, since liability for such duties can never be excluded. So, for example, Millett LJ recognized that it is not possible to exclude liability for breach of the fiduciary fair-dealing principle,[23] where the trustee transacts with the beneficiary.[24] The same should be true of the self-dealing rule,[25] the no-conflict principle generally,[26] and the no-profit principle generally:[27] all of these duties should be considered to be fundamental because, being fiduciary duties, they are founded on the need to act in the best interests of the beneficiaries and not disloyally.[28] Nevertheless, it has been recognized that it is possible to avoid liability in respect of some of these fiduciary duties. In *Barnsley v Noble*[29] it was held that a clause which exonerated the trustee from liability for breach of the self-dealing rule, where the trustee had transacted in a personal capacity with the trust, was effective to exclude the trustee's liability for any loss caused to the trust by breach of fiduciary duty. It appears that the court was especially influenced by the fact that the focus of the clause was on loss caused. Presumably the clause would not have been effective to exclude liability if the trustee had made a profit from the breach of fiduciary duty. Further, the court was influenced by the fact that the breach of duty was not wilful in that the defendant had not deliberately or consciously acted in a way which he knew to be wrong. This indicates a blurring of the distinction between the nature of the breach and the fault relating to a particular breach of duty. More significantly, it suggests that fiduciary duties are not necessarily considered now to be so vital to the trustee–beneficiary relationship that it is possible to exclude liability for their breach. This is unfortunate and inconsistent with the strict interpretation of these duties.

But fundamental duties are not limited to fiduciary duties. Fox has identified the irreducible core of trust obligations as being that the trustee is barred from exploiting the beneficial incidents of their legal ownership of trust property for their own benefit.[30] It follows that the core duties of trustees that cannot be derogated from should include the duty to inform beneficiaries of their status as such and the duty to distribute assets to beneficiaries.

The determination of whether a breach of trust does involve a breach of a fundamental duty has proved particularly controversial in the context of commercial trusts. This is especially well illustrated by *Citibank NA v MBIA Assurance SA*,[31] in which the trust deed stated that a guarantor had the right to instruct the trustees as to the exercise of their discretion and that the trustees would not be liable for breach of trust if they followed these instructions. The Court of Appeal held that this clause effectively excluded liability for breach of trust. But, surely, the obligation of a trustee to exercise their discretion for the benefit of the beneficiaries and not for the benefit of a third party is a fundamental duty?[32] Arden LJ[33] concluded that, despite the guarantor's right to instruct the trustees, they were still subject to a duty of good faith and continued to have a real discretion to be exercised

---

[23] See Section 15.5.3.(ii), p. 435.   [24] [1998] Ch 241, 253.   [25] See Section 15.5.3.(i), p. 433.
[26] See Section 15.5, p. 431.   [27] See Section 15.6, p. 438.
[28] See also *Spread Trustee Co Ltd v Hutcheson* [2011] UKPC 13, [2012] 2 AC 194, [61] (Lord Clarke).
[29] [2016] EWCA Civ 799, [2017] Ch 191.
[30] 'The irreducible core for a valid trust' (2011) 17 T&T 16, 19.
[31] [2007] EWCA Civ 11, [2007] 1 All ER (Comm) 475.
[32] See Trukhantov, 'The irreducible core of trust obligations' (2007) 123 LQR 342.
[33] [2007] EWCA Civ 11, [2007] 1 All ER (Comm) 475, [82].

so that they retained sufficient independence. But this is difficult to square with the facts. The surrender of the trustee's discretion in a case such as *Citibank v MBIA Assurance* is inconsistent with the fundamental obligations of a trustee and liability for doing so should not have been validly excluded.

Fault in breaching the duty

A key determinant of whether liability can be excluded relates to the defendant's fault in breaching the duty. If the trustee has acted merely negligently, their liability can be excluded, even if the negligence is gross, whereas if they have acted fraudulently or dishonestly or in bad faith, their liability cannot be excluded.

In *Armitage v Nurse*, fraud was considered to mean dishonesty. Millett LJ defined it as:[34]

> an intention on the part of the trustee to pursue a particular course of action, either knowing that it is contrary to the interests of the beneficiaries or being recklessly indifferent whether it is contrary to their interests or not.

This creates a subjective test of fault with reference to the trustee's intention, knowledge, and recklessness, which means suspicion of adverse consequences arising from the trustee's actions.[35] It follows that if the trustee knew, or suspected, that the breach of trust would, or might, have a detrimental effect on the beneficiaries, the liability for breach could not be excluded. This requires an awareness of wrongdoing on the part of the trustee.[36] This is because a trustee who acts fraudulently or dishonestly is acting contrary to the essence of the core trust obligation, which requires the trustee to act honestly in the best interests of the beneficiaries. If, however, a trustee did believe that they were acting in the best interests of the beneficiaries, they would not have acted dishonestly, even if the conduct had adverse consequences for the beneficiaries.

In other fields of Equity, however, an objective test of dishonesty has been adopted, notably for the action of assisting a breach of trust or fiduciary duty.[37] According to this test, the dishonesty of the defendant's conduct is assessed objectively, by considering whether the reasonable person would consider the defendant's conduct to be dishonest, albeit in the light of the facts known by the defendant. This objective test of dishonesty has sometimes been applied even when determining whether liability for breach of trust can be excluded. In *Walker v Stones*,[38] the trustees of a discretionary trust were the partners in a firm of solicitors. The trust instrument included a clause that exempted trustees from all liability other than for 'wilful fraud or dishonesty'. The beneficiaries alleged that the trustees had acted in breach of trust by benefiting people who were not objects of the trust. The Court of Appeal accepted that a trustee-solicitor could have acted dishonestly even if they thought that they were acting in the best interests of the beneficiaries, if this belief was considered to be so unreasonable that no reasonable trustee acting in that profession could have held it. This stricter objective test of dishonesty was justified because of the higher standards expected of trustees who are solicitors.[39]

---

[34] [1998] Ch 241, 251.

[35] See *Barnes v Tomlinson* [2006] EWHC 3115 (Ch), [2007] WTLR 377. That recklessness means a conscious awareness of the risk was confirmed by the Privy Council in *Spread Trustee Co Ltd v Hutcheson* [2011] UKPC 13, [2012] 2 AC 194, [60] (Lord Clarke).

[36] *Barnsley v Noble* [2016] EWCA Civ 799, [2017] Ch 191, [54] (Sir Terence Etherton C).

[37] See *Royal Brunei Airlines Sdn Bhd v Tan* [1995] 2 AC 378, discussed in Section 20.3.2.(iii), p. 615.

[38] [2001] QB 902.

[39] See also *Barnes v Tomlinson* [2006] EWHC 3115 (Ch), [79] (Kitchin J); *Fattal v Walbrook Trustees (Jersey) Ltd* [2010] EWHC 2767 (Ch), [81] (Lewison J).

It follows that whether dishonesty is interpreted subjectively, as in *Armitage v Nurse*, or objectively, as in *Walker v Stones*, will depend on the circumstances of the trustee, with higher standards of conduct expected of professional trustees, such as solicitor-trustees.

(ii) The legitimacy of exemption clauses

Despite the focus in *Armitage v Nurse* on the irreducible core of the trust obligation, such that liability for obligations at the core cannot be excluded, either because of the nature of the duty breached or the way in which it was breached, the legitimacy of excluding the liability of trustees even for gross negligence needs to be considered carefully. The effect of *Armitage v Nurse* is that, if a trustee fails to comply with the standard of skill and care reasonably to be expected of a trustee and this causes loss to the trust, an exemption clause will be effective to exclude the trustee's liability, so that they will not be personally liable for the loss and the beneficiaries will not be compensated for any loss suffered as a result of the breach of trust. This may be acceptable where the trustee is an amateur, but is it defensible where the trustee is a professional and so is paid for their services as a trustee? The Privy Council has even contemplated that liability for ordinary negligence should not be excluded because it is an essential obligation of the trustee not to act negligently,[40] although it was accepted in that case that the state of the law was such that liability for negligence could be excluded and it would be for Parliament to change the law.

A number of arguments can be identified relating to whether or not the law should be changed to prevent the exclusion of liability for negligently breaching a trust.

Supervisory jurisdiction of Equity

An argument in favour of maintaining the status quo is that, if the settlor has decided that the trustee should have the benefit of the exemption clause, Equity should not interfere with the settlor's freedom to contract with the trustee as they wish. Before the trust is made, the beneficiaries have no rights. Any rights that they acquire are created by the trust instrument, and if the settlor wishes to circumscribe these rights by excluding the trustee's liability, it should be open to the settlor to do so. But the problem with this argument is that it undermines the fundamental purpose of Equity to protect beneficiaries. Equity has a general supervisory jurisdiction to protect their interests and it is not obvious why this can be excluded so easily by the inclusion of an exemption clause.

Personal rights do not bind third parties

The previous argument assumes that the law of trusts is essentially only a matter of the law of obligations, with rights and duties being created by the trust instrument as between trustee and beneficiaries so that it is acceptable for that instrument to exclude the trustee's liability to the beneficiaries. But, as we have previously seen,[41] the trust is much more than a collection of personal rights and obligations; the trust depends on there being property. The relevance of this to the validity of exemption clauses has been recognized by Penner:[42]

> from the proprietary perspective, the trustee is not like a 'contracting party', but is rather the *grantee* of a property which is burdened in a particular way, and so the incidents of the property he is granted must be incidents which can run with the property, and personal rights like the benefit of an exclusion clause cannot.

---

[40] *Spread Trustee Co Ltd v Hutcheson* [2011] UKPC 13, [2012] 2 AC 194, [62] (Lord Clarke).
[41] See Section 3.3.3, p. 42.   [42] See n. 14, p. 263.

The significance of this argument is that the trustee should only be able to rely on rights arising from the trust instrument as against the beneficiaries if the right is a proprietary right. Since the benefit of an exemption clause is a personal right, it should not bind a third party such as the beneficiary.

Professional trustees

Even if the validity of exemption clauses in trust instruments could be justified as a matter of principle, as a matter of policy is it really appropriate that professional trustees should be able to rely on such clauses to excuse their liability for negligence? Professionals would not normally be able to exclude liability for ordinary professional negligence by unreasonable clauses under the Unfair Contract Terms Act 1977, so why should they be able to do so in the trust context? It might be argued that these clauses are needed to encourage people to become trustees. This may well be true of amateurs, but it is common for professionals to protect themselves by insurance, so it is unclear why they need the additional protection of exemption clauses, which have the effect of the beneficiaries bearing losses arising from the breach of trust. The advantage of encouraging trustees to take out indemnity insurance is that the beneficiaries can still obtain a remedy where there has been a breach of trust. A disadvantage is that the cost of the insurance would be borne by the trust, which might be considered to be an unreasonable expense for the trust to bear, so that it is actually cheaper to allow clauses to exempt liability rather than to pay for indemnity insurance.[43]

That professional trustees should not be able to rely on exemption clauses in the same way as other trustees has been recognized by the courts, but essentially by ensuring that these clauses are interpreted restrictively rather than being rejected out of hand. So, for example in *Bogg v Raper*,[44] the Court of Appeal recognized that a solicitor trustee, who had included an exemption clause in a testamentary trust, could rely on it, but only if he had drawn the testator's attention to the clause and explained its effect. Similarly, in *Wight v Olswang*,[45] the Court of Appeal held that a clause that exempted solicitor trustees of liability had to be interpreted restrictively. Consequently, when one clause exempted them from all liability and another exempted only the liability of unpaid trustees, it was held that the latter prevailed.

Unfair Contract Terms Act 1977

The validity of exclusion clauses in contracts are covered by the Unfair Contract Terms Act 1977 (UCTA)[46] which invalidates exemption clauses that exclude liability for loss or damage arising from negligence,[47] or for certain breaches of contract[48] if the exclusion of liability is unreasonable. It has, however, been held that the Act does not apply to exemption clauses in trust deeds,[49] although the Act will be relevant to the exclusion of liability of other fiduciaries for breach of fiduciary duty if the clause exists in a contract between the principal and fiduciary if the clause is included in a parties' written standard terms of business.[50]

---

[43] *Spread Trustee Co Ltd v Hutcheson* [2011] UKPC 13, [2012] 2 AC 194, [74] (Lord Clarke).

[44] [1998] EWCA Civ 661, [1998] 1 ITELR 267, [53] (Millett LJ).   [45] [1999] EWCA Civ 1309.

[46] The fairness of exclusion clauses in consumer contracts is governed by the Consumer Rights Act 2015, which turns on whether the clause is unfair within section 62 of that Act, by virtue of a significant imbalance in the parties' rights and obligations under the contract to the detriment of the consumer, and having regard to the subject matter of the contract, all the circumstances which existed when the term was agreed and to other terms and contracts.   [47] Unfair Contract Terms Act 1977, s. 2(2).

[48] Ibid., s. 3.   [49] *Baker v JE Clark and Co* [2006] EWCA Civ 464.

[50] Unfair Contract Terms Act 1977, s. 3(1).

In principle, the inapplicability of UCTA to exemption clauses in trust deeds must be right, because the application of exemption clauses to a breach of trust does not operate in a contractual context. The typical context in which UCTA is significant involves a simple bilateral contractual relationship between the parties. It is for this reason that UCTA might be relevant to claims between a principal and a fiduciary, since this is typically a relationship that is founded on the contract containing the clause. But the trust context typically involves three parties, as illustrated in Figure 17.1: settlor, trustee, and beneficiary.

Settlor -------------------- Trustee ---------------------- Beneficiary

Figure 17.1 The typical context of a trust

In this context, the exemption clause will be contained in the trust instrument created by the settlor and trustee. But that instrument will not create any rights and obligations as between the settlor and trustee once the trust has been constituted, and, being typically a voluntary arrangement, even this relationship will not be founded on contract.[51] Rather, the trustee owes duties to the beneficiaries. This arises outside of the contract in Equity and so UCTA is of no relevance.

But should UCTA be extended to cover exemption clauses in trust documents? One argument in favour of such an expansion is that the statutory scheme, in so far as it applies to loss and damage arising from tort and liability for breach of contract, does not invalidate all exemption clauses, but only those that are considered to be unreasonable according to the statute.[52] Surely unreasonable exemption clauses in trust instruments should be similarly invalid. The case for invalidity of such clauses might even be considered to be stronger because the beneficiary will typically not have been involved in the negotiation of the clause, but the clause will have a direct effect on the trustee's liability to the beneficiaries.

(iii) Conclusions

It follows that it is difficult to find a convincing justification for exemption clauses being effective to exclude liability for many breaches of trust. Either they should be ineffective to exclude liability for negligence for all trustees or, if not, they should be ineffective for professional trustees. Alternatively, the application of UCTA should be extended so that exemption clauses can be invalidated if they are considered to be unreasonable. It is clear that reform of the law is required.

In *Armitage v Nurse*,[53] Millett LJ suggested that it was too late to conclude that the exclusion of a trustee's liability for negligence was contrary to public policy. Although he contemplated that it might be possible to draw a distinction between ordinary and gross negligence such that it would not be possible to exclude liability for the latter,[54] he concluded that such a distinction would be surprising, since even gross negligence is not the same as bad faith or fraud, whereas the distinction between negligence and gross negligence is simply a matter of degree.[55] In the Guernsey case of *Carlyle Capital Corporation*

---

[51] *Re Butlin's Settlement Trust* [1976] Ch 251, 260 (Brightman J).   [52] Sch. 2.

[53] [1998] Ch 241, 254.

[54] It appears that liability for gross negligence cannot be excluded in Scotland, as recognized by the Privy Council in *Spread Trustee Co Ltd v Hutcheson* [2011] UKPC 13, [2012] 2 AC 194.

[55] The distinction between mere negligence and gross negligence is, however, significant in the criminal law, especially in determining whether the crime of manslaughter by gross negligence has been committed: *Simester and Sullivan's Criminal Law: Theory and Doctrine*, 6th edn, ed. Simester et al. (Oxford: Hart, 2016), p. 416. It is also significant in other contexts. For example, a gratuitous bailee is only liable for gross negligence: *Spread Trustee Co Ltd v Hutcheson* [2011] UKPC 13, [2012] 2 AC 194, [50] (Lord Clarke).

Ltd v Conway[56] Lt Bailiff Marshall described gross negligence as 'jaw-dropping negligence'. Nevertheless, the Law Commission did, at one stage, consider that a distinction could legitimately be drawn between ordinary and gross negligence,[57] and Jersey in 1984 recognized that liability for fraud, wilful misconduct, and gross negligence could not be excluded,[58] as did Guernsey in 1990.[59]

The Law Commission[60] eventually concluded that statutory reform of the law relating to trustee exemption clauses was not required, it being sufficient that there was a rule of practice that could be enforced in accordance with the code of conduct of professional bodies, so that any paid trustee who might rely on a clause exempting liability for negligence should take reasonable steps to ensure that the settlor was aware of the meaning and effect of the clause before the trust was created. As a result, the Society of Trust and Estate Practitioners, for example, issued a Practice Rule that its members should disclose clauses exempting trustees and executors from liability.[61]

17.3.2 EXCUSABLE BREACHES OF TRUST

Where no exemption clause has been included in a trust deed, a trustee's liability for breach of trust may still be excused by statute.[62] Section 61 of the Trustee Act 1925[63] gives a judge a discretion to relieve a trustee[64] wholly or partly from personal liability for breach of trust where the trustee 'acted honestly and reasonably, and ought fairly to be excused for the breach of trust and for omitting to obtain the directions of the court'. This has been described as creating a 'dubious prerogative of mercy',[65] but this focus on mercy was rejected by Briggs LJ in *Santander UL plc v RA Legal Solicitors*,[66] who said:

> the requirement to balance fairness to the trustee with a proper appreciation of the consequences of the exercise of the discretion for the beneficiaries means this old-fashioned description of the nature of the section 61 jurisdiction should be abandoned. In this context mercy lies not in the free gift of the court. It comes at a price.

That price is that the beneficiaries may be denied a remedy, although the section only excuses the liability of the particular trustee; other trustees and third parties may still be liable to the beneficiaries. A further difficulty with this jurisdiction is that it remains unclear when the judicial discretion might be exercised. The courts are reluctant to identify any principles[67] to assist in the exercise of the discretion other than by reference to vague notions of fairness. But the jurisdiction to relieve the trustee of liability is defensible as a way of tempering the trustee's strict liability.[68]

---

[56] Unreported 38/2017.   [57] *Trustee Exemption Clauses*, CP No. 171 (London: HMSO, 2003).

[58] Trusts (Jersey) Law 1984, Art. 26(9), as amended by Trusts (Amendment) (Jersey) Law 1989, Art. 8.

[59] See now Trusts (Guernsey) Law 2007, s. 39(7)(a).

[60] *Trustee Exemption Clauses*, Law Com No. 301 (London: HMSO, 2006).

[61] *Trustee Exemption Clauses: STEP Practice Rule* (2009).

[62] See generally Lowry and Edmunds, 'Relieving the trustee-solicitor: a modern perspective on section 61 of the Trustee Act 1925?' (2017) 133 LQR 223; Haley, 'Section 61 of the Trustee Act 1925: a judicious breach of trust?' (2017) 76 CLJ 537..

[63] A similar power is given to the Charity Commission to relieve a charity trustee or trustee of a charity of liability for breach of trust or duty: Charities Act 2011, s. 199.

[64] The provision applies to all trustees, whether lay or professional: *Santander UL plc v RA Legal Solicitors* [2014] EWCA Civ 183, [2014] WTLR 813, [19] (Briggs LJ). But the type of trustee will be relevant to the exercise of the judge's discretion as to whether liability should be excused. See Section 17.3.2.(i), p. 482.

[65] Maugham, 'Excusable breaches of trust' (1898) 14 LQR 159.

[66] [2014] EWCA Civ 183, [2014] WTLR 813, [34].   [67] *Re Turner* [1897] 1 Ch 536.

[68] *Santander UL plc v RA Legal Solicitors* [2014] EWCA Civ 183, [2014] WTLR 813, [19] (Briggs LJ).

(i) Exercise of the discretion

It is clear from the statute that there are three tests that need to be satisfied before a judge can relieve the trustee of liability: namely that the trustee acted honestly; that they acted reasonably; and that it would be fair to relieve them of liability. The burden of proving that these three components are established is placed on the trustee.[69] The section is potentially applicable in respect of any breach of trust,[70] including where the trustee makes an unauthorized investment or distributes assets to the wrong objects. The section applies only once a breach of trust has been established, for only then will there be liability to be relieved. The effect of the provision is that the court determines that, although a trustee has committed a breach of trust, the circumstances of the breach are such that they should be excused wholly or partially from liability.[71]

Honesty

It is unclear whether a subjective or objective test of honesty should be adopted,[72] but, for consistency with the law on exemption clauses, the appropriate test should depend on whether or not the trustee is a professional, with an objective standard of honesty applied to professionals and a subjective standard for other trustees. This will be most significant where the trustee believes that they were acting in the best interests of the beneficiaries. If the trustee is a professional and no reasonable professional trustee would have held that belief, the trustee should be considered to be dishonest. If the trustee is a non-professional, their belief that they were benefiting the beneficiaries would mean that the trustee was acting honestly, even if this belief was unreasonable, although the trustee's conduct must still be reasonable to satisfy the statutory requirements of section 61.

Reasonableness

Morritt C recognized in *Nationwide Building Society v Davisons*[73] that the relevant 'standard is that of reasonableness not perfection'. Even if the trustee has acted unreasonably, this will not prevent section 61 from applying if the unreasonable conduct cannot be considered to have caused loss to the trust, such as where the unreasonable conduct occurred after the loss had been incurred,[74] although this will require careful consideration of the facts.[75] The introduction of a test of causation to determine whether it is reasonable to relieve the trustee of liability has been criticized by Lowry and Edmunds[76] for a number of reasons, including that it is not justified by the legislative language and causation of loss does not assist in determining reasonableness of conduct, although they acknowledge that it may be relevant when the judge is evaluating whether it is fair to excuse the breach of trust.

Where, however, a trustee falls below the expected standard of prudence, and this can be considered to have materially increased the risk of loss being suffered by the trust,[77] they will generally not be relieved of liability. But sometimes even a trustee who falls below such standards might be relieved of liability. In *Re Smith*,[78] the trustee was a widow who

---

[69] Ibid.   [70] *Re Stuart* [1897] 2 Ch 583.

[71] Maitland, *Equity: A Course of Lectures*, 2nd edn, ed. Brunyate (Cambridge: Cambridge University Press, 1936), p. 99.   [72] See Section 17.3.1.(i), p. 475.

[73] [2012] EWCA Civ 1626, [2013] WTLR 393, [48]. See also *Santander UL plc v RA Legal Solicitors* [2014] EWCA Civ 183, [2014] WTLR 813, [32] (Briggs LJ).

[74] *Ikbal v Sterling Law* [2013] EWHC 3291 (Ch); *Santander UL plc v RA Legal Solicitors* [2014] EWCA Civ 183, [2014] WTLR 813, [28] (Briggs LJ).   [75] Ibid., [29] (Briggs LJ).

[76] (2017) 133 LQR 223, 227.

[77] *Santander UL plc v RA Legal Solicitors* [2014] EWCA Civ 183, [2014] WTLR 813, [111] (Etherton C).

[78] (1902) 86 LT 401. See also *Nationwide Building Society v Davisons* [2012] EWCA Civ 1626.

lived in the country and employed a firm of solicitors to act as her agents. The firm's clerk fraudulently obtained the trustee's signature on certain cheques and induced her to initial alterations to the cheques. He then absconded with the money. The trustee was held to have breached the trust, but her liability was excused because she had acted honestly and reasonably, even though she had not taken all of the precautions against fraud that a reasonable trustee would have taken. *Re Smith* is probably explicable because of the peculiar position of the trustee, who was not a professional trustee and who had committed what might be considered to be a morally innocent breach of trust. Consequently, if a professional trustee acts negligently, they should not be considered to have acted reasonably and so their liability will not be excused.

An example of a case in which the court refused to relieve the defendant's liability on the grounds of unreasonable conduct is *Re Turner*,[79] in which the trustees had breached the trust by unauthorized lending of trust money on a mortgage. One of the trustees was a linen draper, who had relied for advice as to the legitimacy of the transaction from another of the trustees, who was a solicitor. Despite this reliance, the linen draper trustee was not excused because he had not acted with the care that he would have taken had the money been his own. It was considered that the trustee had acted honestly, but not reasonably.[80]

Where a trustee is doubtful as to whether their decision might involve a breach of trust, they should obtain legal advice. If the trustee relies on such advice and still commits a breach of trust, it is likely that the court will relieve them of liability under section 61 because they will have acted reasonably.

Fairness

In *Perrins v Bellamy*,[81] it was acknowledged that there may be some cases in which the trustee had acted reasonably, but it still would not be fair to excuse them from liability. In most cases, however, where the trustees are considered to have acted reasonably, their liability will be relieved because it is fair to do so.

The statutory power to relieve trustees is particularly significant as regards breaches of trust committed by amateur trustees. So, for example, in *Re Evans (deceased)*,[82] the deceased's daughter administered his estate. She assumed that her brother was dead and administered the estate accordingly. He reappeared four years later. She was found liable for breach of trust,[83] but was granted partial relief because she had acted on legal advice and her actions were considered to be reasonable in the light of that advice.

Higher standards are expected from professional trustees than amateurs,[84] but it will sometimes be appropriate to relieve even professionals of liability.[85] This is illustrated by *Re Pauling's Settlement Trusts*,[86] in which a power of advancement had been exercised improperly by the trustee, which was a bank. The breach of trust arose from the bank being improperly advised by its solicitors. It was held that more is expected from professional

---

[79] [1897] 1 Ch 536. See also *Lloyds TSB Bank plc v Markandan and Uddin* [2012] EWCA Civ 65, [2012] 2 All ER 884: payment of money by a firm of solicitors in breach of trust to fraudsters without making appropriate checks was held to be honest but unreasonable; *Santander UL plc v RA Legal Solicitors* [2014] EWCA Civ 183, [2014] WTLR 813.

[80] The solicitor trustee was, in fact, liable to indemnify the linen draper trustee. See Section 17.4.2.(ii), p. 496.

[81] [1898] 2 Ch 521, which concerned Judicial Trustees Act 1896, s. 3, the predecessor of s. 61.

[82] [1999] 2 All ER 777. See Section 14.3.2.(iv), p. 410.

[83] Since the administration of an estate is a trust: Judicial Trustees Act 1896, s. 1(2).

[84] *Re Rosenthal* [1972] 1 WLR 1273; *Bartlett v Barclays Bank Trust Co Ltd* [1980] Ch 515.

[85] *National Trustees Company of Australasia Ltd v General Finance Company of Australia Ltd* [1905] AC 373, 381.   [86] [1964] Ch 303.

trustees than amateurs and, without more, it would not be possible to relieve professional trustees of liability, even though they had acted honestly and reasonably. But the court did relieve the bank of liability because an additional factor was identified that made it fair to excuse it from liability, namely that the beneficiaries had consented in writing to the exercise of the power. Other factors which may be relevant to the question of fairness might include whether the beneficiaries were insured against loss.[87]

(ii) Assessment of section 61

Soon after the statutory power to relieve trustees of liability was first enacted at the end of the nineteenth century, there were a spate of cases that concerned its application and interpretation. But, since then, the power has rarely been used.[88] A number of reasons can be identified for this,[89] including the much greater use of professional trustees, indemnity insurance against liability, and exemption clauses.

Where section 61 applies, it will primarily be used where the trustee has innocently breached their trust, such as conduct following an innocent misconstruction of the trust instrument. Liability for breach of fiduciary duty by a trustee might also be relieved by the exercise of the court's statutory discretion,[90] although it will be difficult to show that it is fair to relieve the trustee of such liability,[91] especially because of the prophylactic policy of ensuring that trustees avoid a situation in which their personal interest and duty conflict, or in which they profit from their fiduciary position.[92]

Ultimately, it must not be forgotten that we expect the highest standards of conduct from trustees and it will not be appropriate to relieve trustees of their liability too readily, since it will undermine what we expect from them.

17.3.3 LIMITATION

In the same way that claims founded on tort, breach of contract, or unjust enrichment must be brought within certain time limits, so too claims for breach of trust or fiduciary duty are subject to limitation periods. There are two reasons why claims generally need to be subject to a limitation period:

(1) the longer the time between the cause of action accruing and the claim being pursued, the more likely it is that the evidence will become stale and unreliable; and

(2) otherwise, there will be uncertainty on the part of defendants as to whether or not a claim might be pursued against them, which can cause hardship.[93]

These concerns might not always be as significant in the context of trusts and equitable claims, and so such claims are not necessarily always subject to a defined limitation period.

Limitation periods in Equity can take two forms: first, there are specific statutory limitation periods that apply to certain types of equitable claim; and secondly, there is a residual equitable doctrine, known as laches, which gives the court discretion to bar an equitable claim if it is brought too long after the events that gave rise to the claim.

---

[87] *Santander UL plc v RA Legal Solicitors* [2014] EWCA Civ 183, [2014] WTLR 813, [33] (Briggs LJ).

[88] Although there have been a number of recent cases involving firms of solicitors seeking relief from liability for breach of trust.

[89] Lowry and Edmunds, 'Excuses', in *Breach of Trust*, ed. Birks and Pretto (Oxford: Hart, 2002), p. 280.

[90] Ibid., p. 293.   [91] Sheridan, 'Excusable breaches of trust' (1955) 19 Conv 420, 434.

[92] See Chapter 15 of this volume.   [93] *Re Richardson* [1920] 1 Ch 423, 440 (Warrington LJ).

(i) Statutory limitation periods

General limitation period

The Limitation Act 1980 makes specific provision for time limits for claims founded on tort[94] and contract.[95] In both cases, the limitation period is six years from the date on which the cause of action accrued. The usual limitation period for claims brought by a beneficiary, or by a trustee on behalf of a beneficiary,[96] to recover trust property or for any breach of trust is similarly six years from when the cause of action accrued.[97] For the purposes of the Limitation Act 1980, 'trustee' extends to implied and constructive trustees, and also to personal representatives.[98]

It has been held that the provision does not apply to an action brought by the Attorney-General to enforce a charitable trust, since there are no beneficiaries and the Attorney-General sues on behalf of the public at large, who cannot be considered to be beneficiaries because they do not have a right to property either present or future.[99] It follows that there is no statutory limitation period for such claims, but the doctrine of laches could still be applicable.[100]

Qualifications to the general limitation periods

This general limitation period is subject to certain qualifications.

Future interests

Where a beneficiary is entitled to a future interest, the cause of action will not accrue until that interest has fallen into possession.[101] This is because it would not be fair to require a beneficiary with a future interest to commence proceedings to protect an interest that they might never enjoy.[102] It follows that, once the interest becomes a present interest, the beneficiary will have six years to bring the claim for breach of trust and this may be a long time after the original breach. So, if the trustee breached the trust in 1966 and the claimant has an interest that comes into possession only on the death of his father, who died in 2015, the claimant will have to bring the claim by 2021. Such a claim might, however, become barred by virtue of the doctrine of laches.[103] The object of a discretionary trust does not have an interest in possession for these purposes.[104]

Fraudulent breach of trust

The usual six-year limitation period does not apply to claims brought by a beneficiary under a trust in respect of any fraud or fraudulent breach of trust to which the trustee was party.[105] Fraud is to be interpreted in the same way as it is in the context of exemption clauses, and so it encompasses dishonesty interpreted subjectively[106] and, presumably, objectively where the trustee is a professional,[107] and will not be established simply by showing that the breach of trust was deliberate.[108] Liability for non-fraudulent breach of trust, such as breach of the duty of care, will be subject to the usual six-year limitation period.[109]

---

[94] Limitation Act 1980, s. 2.   [95] Ibid., s. 5.

[96] *Cattley v Pollard* [2006] EWHC 3130 (Ch), [2007] Ch 353, 377 (Richard Sheldon QC).

[97] Limitation Act 1980, s. 21(3).   [98] Ibid., s. 38(1). See Trustee Act 1925, s. 68(17).

[99] *Attorney-General v Cocke* [1988] Ch 414.   [100] See Section 17.3.3.(ii), p. 489.

[101] Limitation Act 1980, s. 21(3).   [102] *Armitage v Nurse* [1998] Ch 241, 261 (Millett LJ).

[103] See Section 17.3.3.(ii), p. 489.   [104] *Armitage v Nurse* [1998] Ch 241, 261 (Millett LJ).

[105] Limitation Act 1980, s. 21(1)(a).   [106] See Section 17.3.1.(i), p. 477.

[107] See ibid.   [108] *Armitage v Nurse* [1998] Ch 241, 260 (Millett LJ).

[109] Limitation Act 1980, s. 21(3).

Claims relating to trust property

No time limit is prescribed by the statute for claims to recover trust property or the proceeds of such property that is in the possession of a trustee, or property that has been previously received by the trustee and has been converted to their own use.[110] A trustee will be considered to have received trust property where it has been transferred to a company which was directly or indirectly controlled by the trustee,[111] for otherwise the removal of a limitation period for claims relating to trust property could be easily avoided by the transfer of the property to a company. In *Burnden Holdings (UK) Ltd v Fielding*[112] David Richard LJ indicated that a claim for equitable compensation fell within the provision, so that no time limit was prescribed, whereas a claim for account of profits did not. The former remedy would be relevant to a claim involving trust property where such property had been received by the defendant who had then sold it and converted the proceeds to their own use; the beneficiaries could seek equitable compensation for the value of the property. But the beneficiaries could alternatively seek an account of profits, which would be preferable where the value of the property had increased between receipt and sale. This is still a claim relating to trust property which had subsequently been converted to the use of the trustee and there is no reason why the fact that the beneficiary is seeking a gain-based remedy of an account of profits should not fall within the provision, if a claim seeking equitable compensation falls within the provision.

Specific provision is made for the case in which a trustee is also a beneficiary and receives an excessive distribution of trust property.[113] Any claim against such a beneficiary to recover trust property or the proceeds of such property that is brought after the normal six-year limitation period has passed is limited to the amount exceeding the beneficiary's proper share, but only if the beneficiary acted honestly and reasonably in making the distribution.

Personal estates

Claims relating to the personal estate of a deceased person or any share or interest in such an estate, whether arising under a will or on an intestacy, are subject to a twelve-year limitation period starting from the date on which the right to receive the share or interest accrued.[114]

Action of account

The time limit for an action of account is the same as that for the claim, which is the basis of the duty to account.[115] So, for example, where the liability of an agent to account is contractual, the contractual limitation period applies.[116] Where the liability to account is not referable to a contract, the court will determine the limitation period by analogy with the statute[117] and will apply a six-year limitation period.[118] Where the liability to account arises from a trust, such as where an agent holds property as trustee, no statutory limitation period will apply.

---

[110] Ibid., s. 21(1)(b).
[111] *Burnden Holdings (UK) Ltd v Fielding* [2016] EWCA Civ 557, [2017] 1 WLR 39.   [112] Ibid., [38].
[113] Limitation At 1980, s. 21(2).   [114] Ibid., s. 22(a).   [115] Ibid., s. 23.
[116] *Paragon Finance v D B Thakerar and Co* [1999] 1 All ER 400, 415 (Millett LJ).
[117] The power to do so being preserved by the Limitation Act 1980, s. 36.
[118] *Tito v Waddell (No 2)* [1977] Ch 106, 251 (Megarry V-C).

Equitable relief

The general statutory limitation period is inapplicable to claims for equitable relief, including, but not confined to, specific performance and injunctions, except to the extent that such a limitation period can be applied by the court by analogy with the limitation periods that applied under any statute before 1940.[119] This means that if, before 1940, a claim for specific performance of a contract was subject to a statutory limitation period, that limitation period will apply today.

Ambit of the statutory provisions

The ambit of the statutory provisions on limitation periods has proved to be particularly controversial as regards claims involving constructive trusts and breach of fiduciary duty.

Constructive trust

Where a defendant holds property on constructive trust, this will be treated like an express trust, so that any claim to recover the property will not be time-barred,[120] neither will any claim involving fraudulent breach of that trust.[121] It then becomes important to determine when property is held on constructive trust. This was considered in *Paragon Finance v D B Thakerar and Co.*[122] Millett LJ recognized two uses of the language of 'constructive trust'. First, where the defendant had not been expressly appointed as a trustee, but had assumed the duties of one, the defendant would be a real trustee, albeit under a constructive trust, and would be treated just like an express trustee, so a claim for a fraudulent breach of such a trust or for the recovery of property held on such a trust would not be time-barred. This includes a person who interferes with a trust as trustee *de son tort*[123] or a fiduciary who misappropriates the property of the principal.[124] The second use of constructive trust is where the defendant is personally liable for being implicated in fraud, such as where they had unconscionably received property in breach of trust or fiduciary duty.[125] In such circumstances, the defendant is liable to account as though they were a constructive trustee. But this is simply a formula for equitable relief and there is no trust.[126] Consequently, the exclusion of the general statutory limitation period where the claim involves a fraudulent breach of trust will not apply. The liability of the unconscionable recipient is simply a personal liability to account such that they do not hold any property on trust.[127] Consequently, the normal six-year limitation period applies in respect of such claims.[128] Similarly, where the claim involves liability for dishonestly assisting a breach of trust,[129] the usual six-year limitation period is applicable.[130] Even though the assistant will have acted dishonestly, which might constitute fraudulent conduct, they are not a trustee and they are only subject

---

[119] When the Limitation Act 1939 came into force.

[120] By virtue of the Limitation Act 1980, s. 21(1)(b). See *James v Williams* [2000] Ch 1. This also applies to resulting trusts: *The High Commissioner for Pakistan in the United Kingdom v Prince Mukkuram Jah* [2016] EWHC 1465 (Ch), [2016] WTLR 1763, [125] (Henderson J).

[121] Limitation Act 1980, s. 21(1)(a). See Section 17.3.3.(i), p. 485.   [122] [1999] 1 ALL ER 400.

[123] See Section 12.3.9, p. 345.

[124] As recognized by Jonathan Parker J in *BCCI (overseas) v Jan* (unreported), 11 November 1999; *James v Williams* [2000] Ch 1.   [125] See Section 20.2.3.(i), p. 596.

[126] See Section 9.2.4, p. 257.

[127] *Soar v Ashwell* [1893] 2 QB 390, 393 (Lord Esher MR). See also *Peconic Industrial Development Ltd v Lau Kwok Fai* [2009] HKCFA 17, [23] (Lord Hoffmann NPJ).

[128] *Williams v Central Bank of Nigeria* [2014] UKSC 10, [2014] 1 AC 1189.

[129] See Section 20.3.2, p. 613, for discussion of the action for dishonest assistance.

[130] *Williams v Central Bank of Nigeria* [2014] UKSC 10, [2014] 1 AC 1189. See Hare, 'Trust law's limitations' [2014] RLR 110; Lee, 'Constructing and limiting liability in Equity' (2015) 131 LQR 39.

to a personal liability to the claimant, so cannot be characterized as a fraudulent trustee to disapply the limitation period.

Breach of fiduciary duty

Where the defendant is liable for breach of fiduciary duty, the appropriate limitation period depends on the nature of the claim.

(1) If the fiduciary holds property as a trustee, the limitation periods relating to trustees will apply in the normal way, regardless of whether they are an express or constructive trustee. So, for example, a fiduciary who takes the principal's property for themselves will hold that property on constructive trust for the principal,[131] so that any claim to recover that property or the proceeds of that property will not be subject to a statutory limitation period.[132]

(2) The liability of the fiduciary may relate to breach of a non-fiduciary duty[133] that constitutes a distinct cause of action, such as breach of contract or tort, and so the limitation period relating to that cause of action will apply.

(3) If the fiduciary is liable for deliberate and dishonest breach of fiduciary duty, this is a true breach of fiduciary duty, since this is a breach of the fundamental obligation of loyalty, but the six-year statutory limitation period will apply by analogy to the limitation period that applies to Common Law claims for deceit.[134]

(4) Similarly, where the relief sought is equitable compensation for a fiduciary's failure to act in the best interests of the principal, it has been held that the six-year statutory limitation period that applies to tort claims will apply by analogy.[135] In fact, breach of the duty to act in the principal's best interests is preferably treated as a non-fiduciary duty,[136] so that the contractual or tortious limitation periods should apply automatically rather than by analogy.

(5) We are left with the core liability for breach of fiduciary duty relating to innocent infringement of the no-conflict and no-profit rules where no property is held on trust for the principal.[137] It seems that no statutory limitation period applies to such claims, either directly or by analogy,[138] since breach of these duties has no equivalent at Common Law, but the doctrine of laches will be applicable.[139]

Extension or postponement of the statutory limitation periods

The statutory limitation periods may be extended or postponed in certain circumstances.

Extension

Where a right of action accrues to a person who is under a disability, their claim is subject to a six-year limitation period that does not begin to run until the person ceases to be

---

[131] See Section 15.7.3, p. 451.

[132] *JJ Harrison (Properties) Ltd v Harrison* [2001] EWCA Civ 1467, [2002] 1 BCLC 162, [39] (Chadwick LJ).

[133] See Section 15.3.2, p. 424.

[134] *Coulthard v Disco Mix Club Ltd* [2000] 1 WLR 707, 730 (Jules Sher QC). See also *Metropolitan Bank v Heiron* (1880) 5 Ex D 319.

[135] *Cia de Seguros Imperio v Health (REBX) Ltd* [2001] 1 WLR 112. See also *Paragon Finance v D B Thakerar and Co* [1999] 1 All ER 400, 416 (Millett LJ). [136] See Section 15.3.3, p. 424.

[137] See Chapter 15 of this volume.

[138] *Tito v Waddell (No 2)* [1977] Ch 106, 249 (Megarry V-C); *Attorney-General v Cocke* [1988] Ch 414, 421 (Harman J).

[139] See Section 17.3.3.(ii), p. 489.

under a disability or has died, even if the limitation period that would otherwise apply under the Limitation Act 1980 has expired.[140]

Where a right of action has accrued to recover a debt, or another type of liquidated pecuniary claim, or a claim to all or part of the estate of a deceased person and the person who is liable or accountable acknowledges the claim or makes a payment in respect of it, the right is deemed not to have accrued until the date of the acknowledgment or payment. It has been held that a claim for equitable compensation that related to a breach of fiduciary duty on the part of a solicitor, who facilitated the unauthorized transfer of money from a company, was not a liquidated pecuniary claim since the amount of compensation needed to be assessed.[141] It was recognized, however, that a classic breach of trust case involving the misappropriation of trust property could be characterized as a liquidated pecuniary claim.

Postponement

The statutory limitation period will be postponed in three situations:[142]

(1) where the action is based on the defendant's fraud;[143]

(2) where the defendant has deliberately concealed[144] from the claimant any fact relevant to the right of action; and

(3) where the action is for relief from the consequences of mistake.

In each case, the limitation period does not start until the claimant has discovered the fraud, concealment, or mistake as appropriate, or could, with reasonable diligence, have discovered it. This postponement of the limitation period does not apply to any claim to recover property or the value of property, or to enforce a charge against property or to set aside a transaction affecting property where the property was bought by a bona fide purchaser.[145] In determining what amounts to 'reasonable diligence' to make the relevant discovery, the court should have regard to what a person would have done if they had carried on a business of the relevant kind with adequate, but not unlimited, staff and resources, and motivated with a reasonable, but not excessive, sense of urgency.[146]

(ii) Laches

The equitable jurisdiction to refuse relief on the ground of laches is implicitly preserved by section 36(2) of the Limitation Act 1980.[147] Laches is a judge-made doctrine that defeats any claim in Equity where there has been an unreasonable delay before the claim is commenced,[148] and includes claims for breach of trust or breach of fiduciary duty. Laches can apply only where there is no statutory limitation period available in respect of the claim.[149] The doctrine will, however, be available where the Limitation Act states that there is no prescribed period of limitation under the Act, such as where the trustee is sued for a fraudulent breach of trust or where the claimant seeks to recover trust property.[150]

---

[140] Limitation Act 1980, s. 28(1).   [141] *Barnett v Creggy* [2016] EWCA Civ 1004, [2017] Ch 273.

[142] Limitation Act 1980, s. 32(1).   [143] *Eddis v Chichester Constable* [1969] 2 Ch 345.

[144] *Bartlett v Barclays Bank Trust Co Ltd* [1980] Ch 515, 537 (Brightman J).

[145] Limitation Act 1980, s. 32(3)(a).

[146] *Paragon Finance v D B Thakerar & Co* [1999] 1 All ER 400, 418 (Millett LJ).

[147] *Re Loftus (deceased)* [2006] EWCA Civ 1124, [2007] 1 WLR 591, [33] (Chadwick LJ).

[148] See generally Watt, 'Laches, estoppel and election', in *Breach of Trust*, ed. Birks and Pretto (Oxford: Hart, 2002), p. 353.   [149] *Re Loftus (deceased)* [2006] EWCA Civ 1124, [2007] 1 WLR 591, [37] (Chadwick LJ).

[150] Ibid., [41] (Chadwick LJ).

The rationale behind the doctrine of laches is that a court of Equity will not assist a claimant who has failed to exercise reasonable diligence in commencing proceedings.[151] The key test is whether the lapse of time in commencing proceedings is such that it would be unconscionable for the claimant to assert their beneficial right.[152] It was recognized in *Cattley v Pollard*[153] that establishing such unconscionability depends on all of the circumstances of the case, but usually requires some unconscionable conduct on the part of the claimant.

The application of these principles is illustrated by *Nelson v Rye*.[154] Although that decision was subsequently overruled,[155] this was on a different point,[156] and the analysis of laches was not criticized. The claimant in that case was a musician, who claimed that his manager had breached the fiduciary duty that he owed in receiving money on behalf of the claimant but not accounting to the claimant for it. Four factors were considered to be particularly significant when determining whether the claim would be barred by laches, namely the period of delay, the extent to which the defendant's position had been prejudiced by the delay, the extent to which that prejudice was caused by the claimant's actions, and the claimant's knowledge that delay would cause prejudice to the defendant. It was noted that the mere fact of delay in commencing proceedings will rarely suffice to establish laches. The court should examine all of the circumstances and consider whether the balance of justice or injustice is in favour of granting or denying the relevant remedy. The defence succeeded on the facts because the claimant had wilfully refused to involve himself in his own financial affairs, the defendant had destroyed most of the relevant paperwork, and because the oral evidence was unreliable, so that the delay had caused prejudice to the defendant.

(iii) Law reform

The law of limitation has been criticized for being outdated, uncertain, and unfair as regards its application to equitable claims and remedies.[157] The Law Commission reviewed the law of limitation in 2001 and recommended statutory reform, but there is still no sign of any legislation.[158] The essence of the Law Commission's recommendations was that there should be a primary limitation period that would run from the date of the claimant's actual or constructive knowledge of the facts giving rise to the claim, rather than from the date on which the cause of action accrued. This primary limitation period would be three years, but would be subject to an absolute maximum of ten years. Such a reform would specifically apply to claims for breach of trust. This would have the distinct advantage of assimilating the approaches at Common Law and Equity, and would ensure that the law on limitation would be covered in one statutory code, albeit that the doctrine of laches would continue to operate separately.

17.3.4 ACQUIESCENCE

The equitable jurisdiction to refuse relief on the ground of acquiescence is preserved by section 36(2) of the Limitation Act 1980. Acquiescence will be relevant where the claimant,

---

[151] *Erlanger v New Sombrero Phosphate Co* (1878) 3 App Cas 1218, 1279 (Lord Blackburn).

[152] *Re Loftus (deceased)* [2006] EWCA Civ 1124, [2007] 1 WLR 591, [42] (Chadwick LJ). See also *Lindsay Petroleum Co v Hurd* (1874) LR 5 PC 221, 240 (Sir Barnes Peacock).

[153] [2006] EWHC 3130 (Ch), [2007] Ch 353, [1514] (Richard Sheldon QC).

[154] [1996] 1 WLR 1378, 1392 (Laddie J).

[155] By *Paragon Finance v D B Thakerar & Co* [1999] 1 All ER 400.

[156] Namely that the claim was time-barred by statute since it related to breach of a contractual liability to account rather than breach of trust.

[157] See e.g. *Cia de Seguros Imperio v Heath (REBX) Ltd* [2001] 1 WLR 112, 124 (Sir Christopher Staughton LJ).

[158] *Limitation of Actions*, Law Com No. 270 (London: HMSO, 2001).

knowing of their rights, has stood by and allowed them to be interfered with by the defendant; in such a case, the claim in Equity for breach of trust or fiduciary duty may be barred completely.[159] Such acquiescence is passive and can be contrasted with the separate defence of consent where the claimant has actively concurred in the breach.[160] The rationale behind the doctrine of acquiescence is that, where the claimant stands by knowing that the defendant is about to infringe the claimant's rights, the claimant's consent to the defendant's acts can reasonably be inferred, so that the claimant cannot then complain of the defendant's actions.[161] Acquiescence is therefore a form of estoppel by conduct.[162] It will arise only where the claimant knows, or ought to know, of their rights against the defendant.[163]

The doctrine of acquiescence is closely related to laches, but is distinct. It does not depend on there being a delay in commencing proceedings, although evidence of delay may well indicate the claimant has acquiesced in the defendant's infringement of the claimant's rights.

The application of the doctrine of acquiescence is illustrated by *Allcard v Skinner*,[164] in which the claimant nun was unduly influenced by her mother superior to transfer her property to their convent. Although she had a claim in principle to recover this property on the ground of undue influence, this was barred because she had not taken steps to seek recovery until over five years after her rights had been explained to her by her brother, who was a barrister. This can be contrasted with *Re Pauling's Settlement*,[165] in which it was held that the beneficiaries could not be considered to have acquiesced in a breach of trust because they were only informed of their rights relating to a breach of trust much later, even though one of the claimants was a barrister, albeit not in Chancery chambers.

In *Holder v Holder*,[166] although it was held that the defendant executor was not liable for breach of trust in purchasing property from the deceased's estate,[167] the court considered what would have happened had such liability been established. Both the claimant and the defendant had thought that the defendant had renounced his executorship, but this had been unsuccessful. The defendant argued that the claimant had acquiesced in any breach of trust because he had failed to rescind the transaction, but the claimant argued that, since he was unaware that the defendant continued to be acting as a fiduciary, he was unaware of the breach of fiduciary duty and his right to rescind the purchase transaction. It was held that there was no absolute rule that ignorance of a legal right meant that the claimant could not have acquiesced and that all of the circumstances of the case should be considered to determine whether it was just that the claimant should be considered to have acquiesced.[168] On the assumed facts, it was recognized that the doctrine of acquiescence would have applied because, with full knowledge of the facts, the claimant had affirmed the sale, he had accepted part of the purchase price, and he had caused the defendant to incur liabilities that he could not recover, so it would not have been possible to return the parties to their original positions.

17.3.5 CONSENT

Where a beneficiary has consented to a breach of trust or fiduciary duty, they will be barred from suing the defendant.[169] Consent differs from acquiescence because it requires

---

[159] *De Bussche v Alt* (1878) 8 Ch D 286, 314 (Thesiger LJ).   [160] See Section 17.3.5, p. 491.
[161] *De Bussche v Alt* (1878) 8 Ch D 286, 314 (Thesiger LJ).   [162] Ibid.
[163] *Re Pauling's Settlement* [1964] Ch 303, 353 (Upjohn LJ).   [164] (1887) 36 Ch D 145.
[165] [1964] Ch 303.   [166] [1968] Ch 353.   [167] See Section 15.5.3.(i), p. 434.
[168] *Holder v Holder* [1968] Ch 353, 394 (Harman LJ).
[169] Payne, 'Consent', in *Breach of Trust*, ed. Birks and Pretto (Oxford: Hart, 2002), p. 300.

a positive act of affirmation.[170] The reason why the claimant's consent can bar a claim for equitable relief was recognized by Lord Eldon,[171] namely that the claimant who consents to acts that involve a breach of trust is considered to join with the trustees and cannot then complain of the breach.

Consent will bar only the claim of each claimant who consents and will not affect the rights of other claimants who did not consent to the defendant's actions. The consenting party must be of full age and sound mind; their consent must be freely given and must not be induced by duress or undue influence. The consent must also be fully informed, which means that the claimant must know of all of the key facts concerning what the trustee has done or plans to do and also the surrounding circumstances, but it is not necessary to show that the claimant knew that they were concurring in a breach of trust, as long as the claimant understood with what they were concurring.[172] The claimant need not have benefited from the breach for their consent to bar the claim for relief.[173]

The court has a discretion to determine whether it is fair and equitable in all of the circumstances for the claimant's consent to bar the claim.[174] How the court exercises its discretion is particularly well illustrated by *Re Pauling's Settlement Trust*,[175] which concerned a marriage settlement containing a power for the trustee, a bank, to advance property to the children of the marriage.[176] The power was exercised on a number of occasions, but the children subsequently claimed that it had been exercised improperly. On the assumption that there had been a breach of trust, the trustees pleaded that the beneficiaries had concurred in the exercise of the power in writing. It was accepted that, in some cases, this consent was ineffective, since it was uninformed and 'blindly given'. But, to the extent that the consent was effective, the bank was not liable. The consent given by each beneficiary was considered separately to determine whether or not it was uninformed. For example, one son, who was a student at university, was acquainted with his rights and was able to take care of himself. He had been advised about some of the trustees' transactions, so he knew the nature of the power that the trustees were exercising and was considered to have consented to their actions. The other son was older, but suffered from schizophrenia. He had studied at university and taught in a school. He had not been seen by any representative of the trustee, which was unaware of his mental health, but it was still held that he too had given valid consent to the actions of the trustees.

Consent may be given in a variety of circumstances. For, example, in *Evans v Benyon*,[177] the claimant actively encouraged the trustee to make a distribution from a trust fund. He subsequently discovered that he was a beneficiary under the trust and the distribution had been in breach of trust. It was held that his encouragement of the distribution barred his claim for equitable relief, even though he was not aware that he had an interest in the trust. Consent to the trustees' conduct may also operate through an express or implied agreement with the trustee that the claimant will not sue for breach of trust or fiduciary duty. Alternatively, the claimant will be estopped from reneging on a representation not to sue if the defendant has detrimentally relied on the representation. Consent may be given after the breach of trust to release the trustee from liability, but this will be effective only if consideration has been provided for the release[178] or if the defendant has detrimentally relied on the representation not to sue.

---

[170] *Re Pauling's Settlement Trusts* [1964] Ch 303.   [171] *Walker v Symonds* (1818) 3 Swans 1, 64.
[172] *Re Pauling's Settlement Trusts* [1962] 1 WLR 86, 108 (Wilberforce J).   [173] Ibid.
[174] Ibid.   [175] [1964] Ch 303.
[176] See Section 14.5, p. 414, for analysis of the power of advancement.   [177] (1887) 37 Ch D 329.
[178] *Stackhouse v Barnston* (1805) 10 Ves 453, 466 (Sir William Grant MR); *De Bussche v Alt* (1878) 8 Ch 286, 314 (Thesiger LJ).

Where the defendant has breached a fiduciary duty, they will not be liable if the principal has given their fully informed consent to the fiduciary's actions, such as where the fiduciary acts for two principals with potentially conflicting interests.[179]

The principal may consent to the defendant's breach of the no-conflict or no-profit rules after the breach of fiduciary duty has occurred, but only if the defendant had made full and frank disclosure of the breach.[180]

17.3.6 IMPOUNDING A BENEFICIARY'S INTEREST

The consequence of a beneficiary consenting to a breach of trust is not necessarily limited to the claim for equitable relief being barred; the beneficiary may also lose their beneficial interest. By virtue of section 62 of the Trustee Act 1925, where a trustee who breaches a trust at the instigation or request or with the written consent of a beneficiary, the court has a discretion to impound all or part of the beneficiary's interest in the trust estate in order to indemnify the trustee or any person claiming through the trustee. The effect of this provision is not to exclude the trustee's liability for breach, but to indemnify the trustee so that, in fact, they need not bear the expense of any liability. This has been justified on the basis that the trustee has a better right to the money than the beneficiary who instigated the breach.[181]

Where the beneficiary's interest is impounded, the effect is that compensation for the breach of trust will be provided out of the beneficiary's share of the trust fund rather than be paid by the trustee, but only up to the value of the beneficiary's interest. The beneficiary is not required to indemnify the trustee otherwise from their own assets.[182] The right to apply to the court for a beneficiary's interest to be impounded is available to a former trustee who had committed a breach of trust.[183]

The statutory discretion to impound the beneficiary's interest will be exercised only where it is just to impound the interest. This will only occur where the beneficiary actively encouraged the action or omission that constituted the breach of trust, knowing of the circumstances that would amount to the breach, although it is not necessary to show that the beneficiary was actually aware that the defendant had breached the trust as a matter of law.[184]

The operation of the discretion to impound the beneficiary's interest is illustrated by *Re Somerset*,[185] in which the trustees lent an excessive amount of money on a mortgage at the written request of the tenant for life. The security for the mortgage was inadequate and the life tenant sued the trustees for breach of trust. It was held that the life tenant's interest would not be impounded to meet the claim. This was because, although having approved the secured loan, the life tenant had not intended to be a party to the breach of trust and had left it to the trustees to determine whether the security was sufficient for the amount lent. In other words, she had consented to an authorized loan, but not to it exceeding the authorized limit, since this had been determined by the trustees themselves, and it was legitimate for the beneficiary to assume that the trustees would carry out her request in accordance with the terms of the trust. It would have been different had the beneficiary requested the trustees to make an investment that was unauthorized, even if she was unaware or had forgotten that the instrument was not authorized by the trust instrument.

---

[179] *Bristol and West Building Society v Mothew* [1998] Ch 1, 19 (Millett LJ). See Section 15.5.3.(iii), p. 436.
[180] *Gray v New Augarita Porcupine Mines Ltd* [1952] 3 DLR 1.
[181] *Re Pauling's Settlement Trust (No 2)* [1963] Ch 576, 584 (Wilberforce J).
[182] See further Section 17.4.2.(ii), p. 496.
[183] *Re Pauling's Settlement Trust (No 2)* [1963] Ch 576, 584 (Wilberforce J).
[184] *Re Somerset* [1894] 1 Ch 231. [185] Ibid.

There is a distinct, but related, rule where a trustee is also beneficially entitled to trust property and misappropriates part of the trust property. In such circumstances, the trustee is to be taken to have acted properly and already to have received their share of the trust property as beneficiary, so that the trustee, or anybody claiming through the trustee, is not entitled to receive any more property when the trust assets are distributed.[186]

17.4 LIABILITY BETWEEN TRUSTEES

17.4.1 PERSONAL LIABILITY

The liability of trustees to compensate the trust for loss suffered arising from a breach of trust is personal and not vicarious. Consequently, a trustee is not liable for the acts of their co-trustees. So if Ann, a trustee, commits a breach of trust, Brian, another trustee, will not be liable for it as well, unless he was independently liable in his own right. This will be the case where, for example, Brian let Ann do all of the work without participating in the decision-making process. This will be a breach of trust on Brian's part, since trustees are required to act jointly when making decisions.[187]

17.4.2 JOINT AND SEVERAL LIABILITY

Even though the liability of trustees is personal, it is also described as being 'joint and several'. What this means is that, where Ann and Brian are both responsible for the breach of trust, the claimant can choose to sue both Ann and Brian together (jointly) or to sue either Ann or Brian (severally). If only one of them is sued, that person will be liable to pay all of the compensation for the loss suffered as the result of the breach of trust.[188] A key factor in deciding whether to sue Ann or Brian separately or both jointly will be the perceived ability of Ann and Brian to meet the liability.

   Where Ann and Brian are both responsible for the breach of trust, but the claimant sues Ann only and obtains full compensation from her, she will wish to ensure that some or all of that liability is borne by Brian. There are two mechanisms for ensuring this distribution of liability: contribution and indemnity.

(i) Contribution

Where a trustee is liable for a breach of trust, it is possible for that trustee to apply to the court to require other trustees who were liable for the same breach to make a contribution towards the remedy. The power to order contribution between trustees was developed by the Equity courts, whereby the liability for breach of trust discharged by one trustee could be shared equally between all trustees, even if one trustee were more to blame than another.[189] Today, a statutory contribution regime operates under the Civil Liability (Contribution) Act 1978, which excludes the contribution regime developed at common law.[190] Where the Act applies, the court is given a discretion to award such contribution as is considered to be 'just and equitable',[191] so the distribution of liability is not necessarily equal between the parties.

---

[186] *Re Dacre* [1916] 1 Ch 344.   [187] *Bahin v Hughes* (1886) 31 Ch D 390.
[188] *Fletcher v Green* (1863) 33 Beav 426, 430 (Sir John Romilly MR).
[189] *Chillingworth v Chambers* [1896] 1 Ch 685.   [190] Civil Liability (Contribution) Act 1978, s. 7(3).
[191] Ibid., s. 2(1).

The Act will apply where two conditions are satisfied.

(1) *Damage suffered* According to section 1(1) of the 1978 Act, a person may recover contribution if they are liable for 'any damage suffered by another'. A person suffers damage for the purposes of this Act if they are entitled to recover compensation for that damage, whatever the legal basis of liability.[192] Consequently, damage for these purposes will include loss arising from breach of trust (which is specifically identified[193]) or breach of fiduciary duty.[194] Even though 'damage' is usually equated with compensation for loss suffered, it has been interpreted to include gains made by a defendant at the claimant's expense.[195]

(2) *Liability for the same damage* The person from whom contribution is sought must be liable for the same damage as the person who is seeking contribution.[196] Two defendants will be liable for the same damage even though one of them has caused loss to the claimant and the other has made a gain.[197]

It is likely that both of these conditions will be readily satisfied in the context of a breach of trust. So, for example, if Ann decides to make an unauthorized investment whilst Brian consciously stands by, they will both have breached their duty of care and so will be liable for breach of trust. If the beneficiary obtains compensation from Brian, he can then seek contribution from Ann. The trust will have suffered damage as a result of the breach of duty, and both Brian and Ann will be liable for the same damage, since the same loss will have resulted from their individual breaches. It is then necessary to assess the level of contribution that Ann should make to Brian. This is such an amount as the court considers to be just and equitable, having regard to the extent of Ann's responsibility for the damage.[198] The court has the power to exempt a party from making contribution or requiring a party to bear the full liability, by means of what is called an indemnity.[199] Since Ann was more responsible for the unauthorized investment than Brian, it is likely that Ann will be required to make more than a 50 per cent contribution to Brian.

The relevance of the Act to claims involving breach of trust is not confined to claims for contribution between trustees. One party may be liable for breach of trust and might seek a contribution from another party who is not a trustee, but is liable in tort or for breach of contract or in unjust enrichment; or a party who is liable in tort or for breach of contract or in unjust enrichment may seek contribution from a party who is liable for breach of trust. This is illustrated by *Friends' Provident Life Office v Hillier Parker May and Rowden*,[200] in which C had paid money to A by mistake as a result of B's negligence. B was sued by C for the tort of negligence and breach of contract, and was held liable. B then sought contribution from A, who held the money paid by C's mistake on constructive trust for C.[201] B argued that A had breached this trust by dissipating the money that had been

---

[192] Ibid., s. 6(1).   [193] Ibid.

[194] As well as for other equitable wrongs. See the action for unconscionable receipt, discussed in Section 20.2.3.(i), p. 596, and the action for dishonest assistance, discussed in Section 20.3.2, p. 613.

[195] *Friends' Provident Life Office v Hillier Parker May & Rowden* [1997] QB 85; *Niru Battery Manufacturing Co v Milestone Trading Ltd (No 2)* [2004] EWCA Civ 487, [2004] 2 All ER (Comm) 289; *City Index Ltd v Gawler* [2007] EWCA Civ 1382, [2008] Ch 313.   [196] Civil Liability (Contribution) Act 1978, s. 1(1).

[197] *Friends' Provident Life Office v Hillier Parker May & Rowden* [1997] QB 85; *City Index Ltd v Gawler* [2007] EWCA Civ 1382, [2008] Ch 313.

[198] Civil Liability (Contribution) Act 1978, s. 2(1). The amount awarded will be subject to a prior agreement as to the upper limit available: ibid., s. 2(3).   [199] Ibid., s. 2(2).

[200] [1997] QB 85.

[201] See Section 9.3, pp. 258 and 263, for analysis of the circumstances in which money paid by mistake will be held on constructive trust.

paid by mistake. The key issue for the Court of Appeal was whether A's liability for breach of trust could be considered to involve the 'same damage' as for C's liability in tort and for breach of contract. On the face of it, the damage was not the same, because B's liability was to compensate C for loss suffered, whereas A's liability was to give back the gain that it had made. Despite this, Auld LJ held that, regardless of whether the form of remedy was compensatory damages or disgorgement of a gain, both B and A were liable to C for the loss that it had suffered as a result of C's paying money by mistake to A, since B's liability in negligence and breach of contract contributed to the payment to A. So B and A were both liable for the same damage suffered by C, and so A was, in principle, liable to make a contribution to B for the liability that B had discharged.

(ii) Indemnity

Although the Civil Liability (Contribution) Act 1978 excludes the courts' inherent equitable jurisdiction to order a contribution between trustees, it does not exclude the right of one trustee who has borne a liability to the trust to obtain a full indemnity from another trustee.[202] One trustee will be required to indemnify another where the former bears the full liability for the breach of trust. The recognition of such full liability, however, is confined to three exceptional circumstances.

Benefit of breach

Where two trustees have breached the trust, but one of them obtained the benefit of the breach of trust, that trustee will be liable to indemnify the other.[203]

Sole responsibility of one trustee

If the relationship between the trustees is such that one of them can be considered to be solely responsible for the breach of trust, that trustee will be liable to indemnify the other. This is most likely to happen where one of the trustees is also a solicitor and the other trustee relies on the solicitor for guidance as to whether or not a particular course of action involves a breach of trust. If this guidance turns out to be incorrect, the solicitor trustee will be required to indemnify the other trustee, at least where the solicitor can be considered to have had such an influence on the other that that trustee was not able to exercise an independent judgement.[204] This is illustrated by *Re Partington*,[205] in which the two trustees of a fund were the testator's widow and a solicitor. The solicitor undertook the administration of the trust by himself. He made an unauthorized investment in breach of trust. It was held that the widow was entitled to a full indemnity from the solicitor in respect of her own liability, because he had not provided full information as to the nature of the investments and had acted negligently in his duty as a solicitor. The fact that the solicitor bore the full liability in this case is perfectly acceptable, since the widow's reliance on the solicitor's skill and experience was reasonable, and high standards of skill and care are expected from solicitors.

But an indemnity will not be awarded against trustee solicitors where they did not have a controlling influence over the other trustees. So, for example, in *Head v Gould*,[206] although the defendant was appointed as a trustee because he was a solicitor and he managed the trust's legal business, and was considered to be responsible for the breach of trust, the co-trustee, who was seeking the indemnity, was also found to be an active participant in the breach of trust, and his participation was not considered to be due to the advice

---

[202] Civil Liability (Contribution) Act 1978, s. 7(3).
[203] *Bahin v Hughes* (1886) 31 Ch D 390, 396 (Cotton LJ).   [204] Ibid.   [205] (1887) 57 LT 654.
[206] [1898] 2 Ch 250.

and control of the solicitor trustee. Since the solicitor trustee did not have any controlling influence over the other, an indemnity was not awarded.

Trustee also a beneficiary

Where one trustee is also a beneficiary of the trust, an indemnity may be awarded against that trustee if they benefited from the breach of trust. So, in *Chillingworth v Chambers*,[207] the claimant and defendant were co-trustees. The claimant was married to one of the beneficiaries and, on her death, he became a beneficiary of the trust. The trustees made unauthorized investments and the loss suffered by the trust was made good from the claimant's beneficial interest. The claimant unsuccessfully sought a contribution from the defendant. In rejecting this claim, it was recognized that a trustee who is also a beneficiary and who has benefited from the breach of trust should indemnify the co-trustee to the extent of their interest in the trust fund and not only to the extent of the benefit received. So, for example, where Ann is trustee and a beneficiary who is entitled to receive £3,000 from the trust, if there is a breach of trust causing loss to the trust of £5,000, which has been reimbursed by another trustee, Brian, he can seek an indemnity from Ann up to the value of Ann's interest as a beneficiary. Since this indemnity is limited by the value of the trustee-beneficiary's interest, Brian might be only partially indemnified.

17.5 LIABILITY OF TRUSTEES TO CREDITORS

Where a trustee is liable to a third-party creditor, either for breach of contract entered into on behalf of the trust or for tort arising from the operation of the trust, the trustee will be personally liable to the third-party creditor. So, for example, in *Perring v Draper*,[208] the trustees were personally liable for £96,000 rent arrears on the termination of a lease that was vested in them as trustees. Where the trustee is personally liable to a third-party creditor, they are entitled to be indemnified from the trust fund.[209] But the trust fund may not be sufficient to do this and it is also not possible to indemnify the trustee where the liability was not properly incurred, whether because of lack of capacity, lack of authorization, or breach of trust.[210]

If the trustee cannot be indemnified from the trust fund, as will be the case where they had committed a breach of trust, and the trustee does not have sufficient funds to discharge their own liability, the creditor cannot instead seek payment to discharge the liability from the trust assets.[211] This is because a trust is not a legal entity in its own right and so cannot be regarded as a principal, with the trustee acting as its agent.[212] The creditor may, however, be subrogated[213] to the trustee's right to an indemnity from the trust fund, but only to the extent that the trustee could have made a claim against the fund because the liability was properly incurred; so, if the trustee has committed a breach of trust, it follows that the creditor has no remedy.[214] This might be considered to be fair, because, if the creditor had entered into a contract with the trustee who was not acting in his capacity as trustee, such as where the trustee had contracted to buy a car from the creditor for his own

---

[207] [1896] 1 Ch 685.   [208] [1997] EGCS 109.

[209] Trustee Act 2000, s. 31(1), provides for a trustee to be reimbursed expenses from the trust fund, but only where the expense was properly incurred. See further Section 12.7.1.(i), p. 354.

[210] *Turner v Hancock* (1882) 20 Ch D 303, 305 (Sir George Jessel MR). See Trust Law Committee, *Rights of Creditors against Trustees and Trust Funds* (London: HMSO, 1999), pp. 3–5.

[211] *Perring v Draper* [1997] EGCS 109.   [212] Trust Law Committee (see n. 210), p. 2.

[213] For subrogation generally, see Section 19.4.3, p. 578.   [214] *Re Johnson* (1880) 15 Ch D 548.

personal use, the creditor would take the risk of insolvency in the normal way. Further, the rule protects the beneficiaries from some of the consequences of a breach of trust, since the trust fund cannot be used to compensate the third-party creditor. The rule is also consistent with the fundamental principle that the trust property is not regarded as belonging to the trustee absolutely, so that they cannot use it to defray all liabilities.

But the rule does still seem unfair: the trustee will have been acting for the benefit of the beneficiaries and, as between the beneficiaries and the creditor, is it really appropriate that the creditor bears the risk of the trustee's insolvency? It is for this reason that the Trust Law Committee recommended statutory reform of the law in this area,[215] so that, where the entry into the contract is in breach of the trustee's equitable duties, the creditor should still have a right of indemnity out of the trust fund, save where the trustee had acted dishonestly.

At one stage, the Law Commission indicated an intention to review the law on the rights of contractual creditors against trustees and trust funds, but only when current law reform projects were completed.[216] In 2011, however, the Law Commission announced that, following discussion with the Government, the project was not considered to be a sufficient priority to make the implementation of any recommendation a realistic proposal. Consequently, the liability of trustees to creditors no longer forms part of the Law Commission's law reform agenda and so the only chance of reform now is through the courts.

In the meantime, it remains possible for trustees to take out indemnity insurance to cover their liability for breach of trust, either to the beneficiaries or third parties, and it is possible for insurance premiums to be paid from the trust fund. Specific provision is made for such insurance cover being obtained by charity trustees. They can purchase insurance to indemnify themselves against any personal liability in respect of breach of trust or duty in their capacity as trustees, but only if they consider that the purchase of such insurance is in the best interests of the charity.[217] But the trustees cannot be insured against a liability incurred to the charity arising out of conduct that the trustees knew was not in the charity's best interests or did not care whether it was in the charity's best interests.

17.6 LIABILITY FOR BREACH OF TRUST BEFORE APPOINTMENT

A trustee will not be liable for breach of trust where the breach occurred before the trustee was appointed.[218] On appointment, if a trustee discovers that a breach of trust has occurred, they should commence proceedings against the former trustee; if the new trustee fails to do so, they may be liable for this breach of trust in their own right.

17.7 LIABILITY FOR BREACH OF TRUST AFTER RETIREMENT

A trustee remains liable for breaches of trust committed whilst they were a trustee even though they had retired from the trust. But a trustee will not be liable for breaches of trust that have occurred after the trustee retired, except if the trustee retired in order to facilitate a breach of trust[219] or if the trustee in retiring parts with the trust property without due regard to it, so that loss is suffered in the transfer of the property to the new trustees.[220]

---

[215] See n. 210.   [216] *Annual Report 2007/08*, Law Com No. 310 (London: HMSO, 2008).
[217] Charities Act 2011, s. 189.   [218] *Re Strahan* (1856) 8 De GM & G 291.
[219] *Head v Gould* [1898] 2 Ch 250, 272 (Kekewich J).   [220] Ibid., 269 (Kekewich J).

18

PERSONAL LIABILITY FOR BREACH OF TRUST AND FIDUCIARY DUTY

18.1 FUNDAMENTAL PRINCIPLES

18.1.1 PERSONAL AND PROPRIETARY REMEDIES

Where a trustee or a fiduciary has breached their duty causing a loss or making a gain, the beneficiary of the trust or the principal to whom the fiduciary duty is owed will usually seek a remedy. The nature of the remedy sought will depend on the consequences of the breach. The remedy may be proprietary, in the sense that the claimant might seek to recover property from the defendant or to obtain a security interest in the defendant's property. These remedies are considered in the next chapter. Where the defendant no longer has property belonging to the claimant or where the breach did not involve the defendant receiving any property, the remedy sought will be personal, in the sense that the claimant seeks to obtain a money remedy from the defendant representing the value of the claim.

There are certain key advantages and disadvantages in claiming personal or proprietary remedies. The key advantages of proprietary remedies are that the claimant will have priority over other creditors of the defendant, which will be significant where the defendant is insolvent. So, for example, if the defendant has taken money from the trust fund that they have credited to their bank account, but they subsequently become insolvent, the claimant will be able to claim the money by virtue of their title to it and will rank above all other creditors who have claims against the defendant. Another advantage of proprietary remedies where the claimant seeks to recover particular property retained by the defendant is that the claimant will gain the benefit of any increase in the value of that property. Of course, if the property has fallen in value, the claimant will bear the loss, which would make a personal remedy more attractive. Where, however, the defendant is not insolvent or facing insolvency, and where the property retained by the defendant has neither increased nor fallen in value, there may be little to choose between proprietary and personal remedies. A final advantage of proprietary remedies is that they can be obtained from a third-party recipient of the property even if they were unaware that the claimant had any proprietary rights to the property, save if the third party had also provided some value for the property.[1]

Where a trustee has misappropriated trust property and used it to acquire other property, the beneficiaries can elect whether to seek a personal remedy to recover the value of the property which has been misappropriated or, instead, adopt the substitute property as part of the trust fund.[2] The beneficiaries will, of course, prefer to recover the substitute property if its value is greater than the value of the property which was misappropriated.

This chapter will examine the personal remedies that may be available where the defendant has breached the trust or breached fiduciary duties.

18.1.2 PRIMARY AND SECONDARY DUTIES

Liability for breach of trust and breach of fiduciary duty might be considered to operate in a similar way to liability for breach of contract at Common Law. A contracting party has a primary duty to perform those obligations that arise under both the contract and the general law, and, if they fail to do so in breach of the contract, a secondary duty will arise whereby the party in breach must compensate the claimant for any loss suffered as a result of that breach,[3] or sometimes give up any gain made.[4] Similarly, a breach of trust or fiduciary duty can be analysed as a breach of the primary duty to comply with the standards that the law of trusts and fiduciary obligations expects the trustee or the fiduciary to meet, breach of which will result in a secondary duty to compensate the claimant for the loss suffered or to give up any gain made as a result of the breach.

Certainly, by analysing with reference to primary and secondary duties of the defendant and concomitant rights of the claimant, liability for breach of contract, breach of trust, and breach of fiduciary duty have a great deal in common. But there are some significant differences between them.

(i) Enforcement of primary duties

Primary duties are much more likely to be enforced in Equity than at Common Law. So, where a contract is breached, it is only exceptionally that the defendant will actually be required to perform their primary contractual duty by means of the equitable remedy of specific performance.[5] This remedy will be available, for example, where the contract relates to the sale of unique property, such as land, and even then, only where damages are an inadequate remedy. There is one contractual obligation that is enforceable directly at Common Law and that is where the defendant owes money to the claimant under the contract, for then the claimant will have a readily enforceable primary right to the money. This right can be enforced by an action in debt, which is effectively a Common Law action for specific performance of the promise to pay.[6]

Where, however, a trustee or fiduciary breaches or threatens to breach one of their primary duties, Equity will generally be willing to compel performance of the duty specifically even if monetary remedies would be an adequate substitute. The key duty of a trustee

---

[1] See Chapter 19 of this volume.

[2] *Tang Ying Loi v Tang Ying Yip* [2017] HKCFA 3, [2017] 2 HKC 502, [23] (Lord Millett). See Ho and Lee, 'The beneficiaries' right to elect remedies for misapplied funds' (2017) 133 LQR 565.

[3] *Photo Production Ltd v Securicor Transport Ltd* [1980] AC 827.

[4] *Attorney-General v Blake* [2001] 1 AC 268.   [5] See Section 21.4, p. 634.

[6] Smith, 'The measurement of compensation claims against trustees and fiduciaries', in *Exploring Private Law*, ed. Bant and Harding (Cambridge: Cambridge University Press, 2010), p. 371.

is to administer the trust in accordance with the trust instrument and the general law.[7] The courts will ensure that the trustee administers the trust properly by enforcing their duties, such as by compelling distribution of trust property to the beneficiaries,[8] preventing trustees from distributing trust property improperly,[9] or requiring the sale of unauthorized investments and reinvestment in authorized ones.

The courts have three methods for securing the enforcement of these duties: namely by directing that a particular duty be performed; by granting an injunction to stop the defendant from acting in a particular way; or by declaring that the trustees should act or not act in a particular way. A declaration might appear to be a rather weak response when the court has the option to direct performance, but a declaration may be appropriate where the court has clarified the law and expects the trustees to act accordingly. So, in *Cowan v Scargill*,[10] the court clarified the law about the considerations that trustees can take into account when objecting to the trusts' investment policy. As a result, half of the trustees were declared to be in breach of trust if they refused to concur with the other trustees, it being assumed that, since the law had been clarified, the trustees would comply with their primary duties to the trust.[11] Failure to do so would have resulted in secondary liability for any loss suffered by the trust as a result and, presumably, replacement by somebody else as trustee.

The different reactions to enforcing primary duties at Common Law and in Equity are significant. Equity's willingness to enforce primary duties is presumably a consequence of the general policy of expecting the highest standards of behaviour from trustees and fiduciaries in the fulfilment of their obligations, so that the courts are willing to make them perform their obligations for the benefit of the beneficiaries and the principal.

(ii) Taking of an account

Where a trustee or fiduciary has breached their duty, they will be liable for this breach and the beneficiary or the principal will have a secondary right to obtain a pecuniary remedy. As with breach of contract, breach of trust or breach of fiduciary duty is a wrong that constitutes a cause of action for which a variety of remedies are available. But, whereas for breach of contract the principal remedy is damages to compensate for loss by putting the claimant in the position in which they would have been had there not been a breach of contract, where a breach of trust has occurred, Equity's principal[12] mechanism for providing relief is the taking of an account, which in form is not even a remedy, but simply involves an assessment by the court of the state of the trust fund. Once the account has been taken, however, monetary relief may follow if the account reveals that a loss has been suffered by the trust or the defendant has made a gain. An account will also be available where a fiduciary who is not a trustee is responsible for managing the principal's property as a steward of it, such as where a fiduciary holds property as an executor or receiver; such a fiduciary will be accountable for the property. But not all fiduciaries are responsible for property and so, for convenience, references to account in this chapter will focus on trustees rather than fiduciaries.[13]

---

[7] *Target Holdings Ltd v Redferns* [1996] 1 AC 421, 434 (Lord Browne-Wilkinson); *AIB Group (UK) plc v Redler and Co* [2014] UKSC 58, [2015] AC 1503, [51] (Lord Toulson).

[8] *Re Locker's Settlement Trust* [1977] 1 WLR 1323.   [9] *Fox v Fox* (1870) LR 11 Eq 142.

[10] [1985] Ch 270. See Section 13.4.3.(ii), p. 385.   [11] [1985] Ch 270, 296 (Megarry V-C).

[12] Although, following the decision of the Supreme Court in *AIB Group (UK) plc v Redler and Co* [2014] UKSC 58, [2015] AC 1503, it is now a less significant remedy with growing emphasis on the remedy of equitable compensation. See also *Main v Giambrone and Law (a firm)* [2017] EWCA Civ 1193. See Section 18.2.3, p. 519.   [13] Liability of fiduciaries is considered in more detail in Section 18.4, p. 523.

The language of 'taking an account' is confusing. In fact, the account originated at Common Law as a remedy to recover money, originally from bailiffs of manors who were required to account for the money that they had collected on behalf of their landlords.[14] Eventually, this remedy was transformed into an action for the enforcement of a debt, and then for money had and received. A bill of account in Equity developed from this Common Law remedy and became especially significant because the administrative officers in Chancery had an auditing machinery[15] that made them particularly well suited to the taking of an account. The taking of an account remains a vital mechanism in Equity to ensure that trustees comply with their obligations to administer the trust properly, but the Common Law origins of the account and the fact that it operated as a remedy are highly relevant to the proper analysis of the account today.

To understand how the order to take an account actually operates, it is necessary to look behind the mechanics of the account to see that, whilst it actually involves the enforcement of a trustee's primary duty to account for their management of the trust, its effect may be to require trustees to compensate for loss arising from a breach of trust or to give up a gain. All express trustees are under a primary duty to account for their administration of the trust fund. This means that they are liable to account for all receipts, investments, and distributions, so that the court can identify the contents and value of the trust fund. When the account is taken, it might become apparent that there is a deficiency in the fund, either because of the actions or inactions of the trustees, and so the trustees will be personally liable to restore to the fund the value of the amount that is deficient. This is the reason why the taking of an account provides the mechanism for beneficiaries to obtain a remedy for a breach of trust. If, for example, a trustee has given a trust asset away to a third party without authority to do so, this will constitute a breach of trust. The beneficiaries may then apply to the court for an order that an account be taken. In taking the account, it will become apparent that the trust asset is missing as the result of an unauthorized transaction and without corresponding value being transferred to the trust fund. The trustee will be liable to make up the shortfall from their own resources by paying the amount that is missing into the trust fund.[16] Consequently, the account provides the mechanism for enforcing the trustee's secondary duty to compensate the trust fund for loss suffered as a result of the breach of trust, even though this operates in form as enforcing the primary duty of a trustee to account for the administration of the trust.[17] In form, it is comparable to an order for specific performance, to enforce the trustee's duty to account for the administration of the fund[18] and has been described as providing 'the pecuniary equivalent of performance of the trust'.[19] An analogy can also be drawn with the Common Law action of debt, since the account is similarly a claim to require payment of a liquidated sum that is due to the claimant.[20] But, where the money due represents the value of what the trust has lost as a result of a breach of trust, the order of an account undoubtedly has remedial implications.

The fact that this secondary duty to remedy a breach of trust is hidden behind the account has proved to be particularly confusing for judges and commentators. It is certainly

---

[14] Stoljar, 'The transformations of account' (1964) 80 LQR 203.   [15] Ibid., p. 220.

[16] The details of taking an account in such circumstances are considered in more detail in Section 18.2.1, p. 510.

[17] For the view that the account involves only enforcement of a primary duty, see Birks, 'Equity in the modern law: an exercise in taxonomy' (1996) 26 Univ WALR 1, 43; Lord Millett, 'Proprietary restitution', in *Equity in Commercial Law*, ed. Degeling and Edelman (Sydney: Law Book Co., 2005), p. 310.

[18] Elliott, 'Remoteness criteria in Equity' (2002) 65 MLR 588, 590.

[19] *AIB Group (UK) plc v Redler and Co* [2014] UKSC 58, [2015] AC 1503, [93] (Lord Reed).

[20] See ibid., [61] (Lord Toulson).

true that beneficiaries do not need to plead a breach of trust in order to obtain an account, and, in fact, the trustee is not even treated as a wrongdoer, since the account is taken on the assumption that the trustee acted properly throughout. But it does not follow that the breach of trust is irrelevant: the fact of the breach of trust will often provide the motivation for the beneficiaries to seek an account and explains why there is a shortfall that the trustee is liable to make up. The breach of trust essentially triggers a secondary personal duty to remedy the wrong, albeit hidden behind the beneficiaries' primary right to ensure that the trustee is accountable for the administration of the trust. The secondary duty to remedy the wrong is much more obvious where there has been a breach of fiduciary duty, where there is typically no liability to account for the administration of a particular fund, so the fiduciary in breach is obviously subject to a secondary remedial duty to the principal.[21]

18.1.3 WHO CAN SUE FOR BREACH?

Where a fiduciary has breached their fiduciary duty, the principal to whom the fiduciary duties were owed will sue and will benefit from the remedy that is awarded.

Where a trustee has breached the trust, the claimants will normally be the beneficiaries, no matter how remote their interest. So, for example, a beneficiary with a life interest or with an interest in remainder will have standing to sue for breach. But other trustees who are not responsible for the breach of trust will also have standing to sue on behalf of the trust. Where a trustee has breached a charitable trust, the Charity Commission or the Attorney-General will have standing to sue.[22] Where a trustee has breached a valid non-charitable purpose trust, the person who is entitled to the residue of the trust assets will be entitled to sue.[23] The settlor will not be able to sue for breach of trust, since the trustee's obligations are owed to the beneficiaries.

Where a beneficiary does sue for breach of trust, it does not follow that they will directly benefit from any remedy awarded. This is because, in many cases, an account will be taken and the trustee in breach will be liable to pay into the trust fund the identified shortfall. Where, however, the trust has come to an end, the trustee will be liable to pay the shortfall to the beneficiaries directly.[24]

18.1.4 FUNCTION OF REMEDIES AVAILABLE

There are a variety of personal remedies available for breach of trust and fiduciary duty, but each remedy potentially falls into one of six categories, depending on the function of that remedy: to compensate for loss suffered; to give back a gain made from the claimant; to give up a gain made from a third party; to unwind a transaction; to punish; or some other, less definite, function.[25]

(i) Compensation of loss

Although, by tradition, Equity does not use the language of damages,[26] that term being used to describe the Common Law pecuniary remedy to compensate for loss suffered as

---

[21] See Section 18.4, p. 523.   [22] See further Section 6.1.4, p. 148.

[23] *Re Astor's Settlement Trusts* [1952] Ch 534.

[24] *Target Holdings Ltd v Redferns* [1996] AC 421, 435 (Lord Browne-Wilkinson); *AIB Group (UK) plc v Redler and Co* [2014] UKSC 58, [2015] AC 1503, [99] (Lord Reed).

[25] See Chambers, 'Liability', in *Breach of Trust*, ed. Birks and Pretto (Oxford: Hart, 2002), p. 2; Edelman and Elliott, 'Money remedies against trustees' (2004) 18 TLI 116.

[26] *Ex p Adamson* (1878) 8 Ch D 807, 819 (James LJ). But the language of 'damages' was not unknown in Equity: see McDermott, *Equitable Damages* (London: Butterworths, 1994), ch. 1.

the result of breach of a contract or commission of a tort, Equity does award pecuniary remedies that operate to compensate the claimant for loss suffered as a result of a breach of trust or breach of fiduciary duty. This loss may arise, for example, from the unauthorized disposition of a trust asset or by a failure to manage the trust properly. The burden of proving the loss suffered is placed on the claimant.[27]

Where the cause of action is breach of trust, the mechanism for obtaining compensation will typically be the common account,[28] whereas, where the claim relates to a breach of fiduciary duty, the mechanism for obtaining compensation will usually be equitable compensation.[29] In each case, the effect of the remedy is just like the award of damages for breach of contract or tort, namely to put the claimant in the position in which they would have been had there been no breach.[30] Where the defendant has committed a breach of trust, the true function of the equitable compensatory remedy is 'to provide the pecuniary equivalent of performance of the trust'.[31]

It must be shown that the breach of trust or breach of fiduciary duty has caused a loss to the claimant[32] and the principles underlying causation at Common Law are accepted as applying in Equity, which adopts a common-sense approach to causation.[33] The relevant test is that of 'but for' causation, whereby it must be shown that, but for the breach, the loss would not have been suffered.[34] So, for example, the acts of a third party will not break the chain of causation if the loss suffered by the trust can still be considered to flow directly from the breach of trust,[35] such as where the trustee's neglect enabled a third party to default on payments which were due to the trust.[36] The acts of a third party may, however, break the chain of causation, where, for example, the third party's conduct contributed to the loss and was unrelated to the defendant's breach of fiduciary duty,[37] for then it cannot be established that but for the breach of duty the loss would not have occurred.

There are, however, some significant differences between the Common Law and equitable approaches to compensation:

(1) A key difference relates to remoteness of loss. In Equity, it usually does not have to be shown that the loss was foreseeable,[38] so the defendant will be liable to compensate for loss arising directly or indirectly as a result of the breach even if it was unforeseeable at the time of the breach.

---

[27] *Nestle v National Westminster Bank plc* [1993] 1 WLR 1260, 1269 (Dillon LJ).

[28] See Section 18.1.2.(ii), p. 501.   [29] See Section 18.4, p. 523.

[30] *Livingstone v Rawyards Coal Company* (1880) 5 App Cas 25, 39 (Lord Blackburn); *Nocton v Lord Ashburton* [1914] AC 932, 952 and 958 (Viscount Haldane LC); *Bartlett v Barclays Bank Trust Co Ltd (Nos 1 and 2)* [1980] 1 Ch 515, 535 (Brightman J); *AIB Group (UK) plc v Redler and Co* [2014] UKSC 58, [2015] AC 1503, [134] (Lord Reed).

[31] Ibid., [93] (Lord Reed).

[32] *Target Holdings Ltd v Redferns* [1996] AC 421, 437 (Lord Browne-Wilkinson); *AIB Group (UK) plc v Redler and Co* [2014] UKSC 58, [2015] AC 1503, [135] (Lord Reed).

[33] See *Canson Enterprises Ltd v Boughton and Co* (1991) 85 DLR (4th) 129, 163 (McLachlin J); affirmed by Lord Browne-Wilkinson in *Target Holdings Ltd v Redferns* [1996] AC 421, 438.

[34] *Re Miller's Deed Trusts* (1978) 75 LSG 454; *Nestle v National Westminster Bank plc* [1993] 1 WLR 1260, 1276 (Staughton LJ); *Swindle v Harrison* [1997] 4 All ER 705, 714 (Evans LJ). But note the different test that applies to claims to recover gains from the defendant: Section 18.5.2, p. 526.

[35] *AIB Group (UK) plc v Redler and Co* [2014] UKSC 58, [2015] AC 1503, [88] (Lord Reed).

[36] *Caffrey v Darby* (1801) 6 Ves 488.

[37] See *Canson Enterprises Ltd v Boughton and Co* (1991) 85 DLR (4th) 129.

[38] See ibid., 129, 160 (McLachlin J); affirmed by Lord Browne-Wilkinson in *Target Holdings Ltd v Redferns* [1996] AC 421, 438; *AIB Group (UK) plc v Redler and Co* [2014] UKSC 58, [2015] AC 1503, [135] (Lord Reed). But see Section 18.3.2, p. 522.

(2) In Equity, the loss is assessed at the date of trial,[39] with the benefit of hindsight, whereas for Common Law remedies, the loss is typically assessed at the time of the breach. This calculation of the loss at the date of the judgment in Equity is an inevitable result of taking an account. If, in taking the account, a deficiency is identified, the trustee will be liable to restore value to the fund that will be assessed at the time of the account, even though the deficiency may have occurred after the breach that triggered the account to be taken in the first place. This is different from the Common Law, under which changes in the amount of the loss that occur after the breach are usually not taken into account.[40] The significance of this difference is illustrated by the Australian decision of *Re Dawson (deceased)*,[41] in which the trustee was liable to repay the value of trust money that had been misapplied. The problem was that the rate of exchange had altered between the date of breach and the date of the judgment. It was held that the higher rate of exchange operating at the time of the judgment should apply, since this was the value of the deficiency in the trust fund at that time. As McLachlin J said in the Supreme Court of Canada in *Canson Enterprises Ltd v Boughton and Co*,[42] the loss 'should be assessed at the time of trial using the full benefit of hindsight' to ensure that the value of the trust fund is fully restored. The same approach to assessment of the loss at the time of judgment applies when awarding compensation for breach of fiduciary duty,[43] and should also apply when determining whether the defendant obtained any profit as a result of the breach of trust or fiduciary duty.[44]

(3) In Equity, there is generally no duty imposed on the claimant to mitigate their loss arising from a breach of trust or fiduciary duty.[45] This is a function of the obligations owed by the trustee or fiduciary to look after the interests of the beneficiary or the principal, so that the trustee or fiduciary will be responsible for causing the loss and cannot pass any blame to the claimant for not mitigating it. There may, however, be situations in which the claimant's failure to mitigate the loss is so unreasonable that it can no longer be concluded that the loss suffered was actually caused by the breach of duty.[46] So, for example, if the claimant is aware that the defendant trustee had invested trust property improperly, but the claimant decides not to request the sale of the investments, preferring to wait and see if they become profitable, and thinking that, if they are not, the trustee will bear the risk of loss, it might well be appropriate to regard the claimant's failure to intervene as breaking the chain of causation.[47] In *Magnus v Queensland National Bank*,[48] however, it was held that a trustee bank was liable where it had paid money to the wrong person, even though the beneficiaries were aware of this and had not taken steps to recover it from the recipient. This failure to intervene did not break the chain of causation.

Where there has been a breach of trust or fiduciary duty, it does not follow that there is an automatic right to compensation, since no loss may have been suffered as a result of the breach. Where, for example, there has been a judicious breach of trust that benefits the

---

[39] *Target Holdings Ltd v Redferns* [1996] AC 421, 437 (Lord Browne-Wilkinson); *AIB Group (UK) plc v Redler and Co* [2014] UKSC 58, [2015] AC 1503, [135] (Lord Reed).

[40] But sometimes they will be: see e.g. *Smith New Court Securities Ltd v Scrimgeour Vickers (Asset Management) Ltd* [1997] 1 AC 254 in respect of the tort of deceit.

[41] [1966] 2 NSWLR 211.   [42] (1991) 85 DLR (4th) 129, 162.

[43] *Swindle v Harrison* [1997] 4 All ER 705, 714 (Evans LJ).   [44] But see Section 18.5.3, p. 530.

[45] *Canson Enterprises Ltd v Boughton and Co* (1991) 85 DLR (4th) 129, 162 (McLachlin J).

[46] Ibid.; *AIB Group (UK) plc v Redler and Co* [2014] UKSC 58, [2015] AC 1503, [135] (Lord Reed). Smith (see n. 6), p. 368, suggests that this link to causation of the loss by the claimant is all that mitigation means.

[47] The claim for breach might be defeated in such circumstances by the bar of acquiescence. See Section 17.3.4, p. 490.   [48] (1888) 37 Ch D 466.

beneficiaries, there is no right to compensation, because no loss will have been suffered.[49] All that the beneficiary can insist on is that the consequences of the breach should be reversed. So, for example, if a trustee invests trust property in unauthorized investments that are profitable, the beneficiary could legitimately insist on the sale of the investments and the proceeds being invested instead in authorized investments—although this would be an odd thing to do where the unauthorized investments are profitable.

(ii) Restitution of gain

Another function of remedies for breach of trust or breach of fiduciary duties is to restore to the claimant the value of a gain made by the defendant as a result of the breach. This function is appropriately described as 'restitution' of the gain made since it is a mechanism to require the defendant to give back, or restore, the value of something that had been obtained from the claimant. It involves the award of remedies that focus on the gain made by the defendant rather than the loss suffered by the claimant.

The language of 'restitution' is, however, sometimes used in a different sense in Equity—a sense that is liable to confuse. Where, for example, a trustee has taken value from the trust fund and transferred this to a third party, as where value from the fund is used to buy unauthorized investments, the trustee is sometimes described as being liable to restore the fund to the position in which it was before the breach occurred—in other words, to make restitution to the fund.[50] But in this scenario 'restitution' is not being used in its technical sense to describe a gain-based remedy, since the trustee will not have personally gained from the unauthorized investment. Rather, a remedy will be awarded to compensate the trust for the loss suffered, albeit by restoring value to the fund.[51] The significance of the distinction is that, in one context, the remedy operates to deprive the defendant of a gain made and, in the other, to restore the value of the loss suffered by the claimant. Restitution is properly confined to only having a gain-based function and not having a compensatory function.

The typical scenario in which a restitutionary remedy, properly so-called, might be awarded is where a trustee has taken money from the trust fund for their own purposes. If the money has been invested, and the trustee still has the investment, the beneficiaries may pursue a proprietary claim.[52] If, however, the value has been dissipated, the trustee will be liable to restore the value of this property to the trust. The remedy that will be awarded to effect this restitution is that of account of profits,[53] whereby an account will be taken of the profit received by the trustee by misappropriating the trust property, which will then be restored to the trust.

It is important to make two significant observations about this restitutionary remedy. First, in many cases in which a trustee has taken value from the trust, it will not matter whether the remedy that is awarded has a compensatory or a restitutionary function, since the loss suffered by the trust will correspond precisely with the gain made by the defendant. So, where a trustee misappropriates £1,000 from the trust that they then spend on food and drink, the trust will have lost £1,000 and the defendant will have gained £1,000. If the defendant is required to pay £1,000 to the trust, this will both compensate the trust and deprive the defendant of the gain. But there will be some scenarios in which it matters whether the remedy is restitutionary or compensatory. In principle, this would arise where the value of the enrichment to the defendant is greater than the loss suffered by the

---

[49] *Target Holdings Ltd v Redferns* [1996] AC 421, 433 (Lord Browne-Wilkinson).

[50] Ibid., 434 (Lord Browne-Wilkinson); *AIB Group (UK) plc v Redler and Co* [2014] UKSC 58, [2015] AC 1503, [65] (Lord Toulson).   [51] See further Section 18.2.1, p. 510.

[52] See Chapter 19 of this volume.   [53] See Section 18.5, p. 525.

claimant. But, in the context of breaches of trust or fiduciary duty, the enrichment will typically be money, which means that the defendant's gain will correspond with the claimant's loss. Nevertheless, the measure of the remedy will still matter where, for example, the trust excludes liability to compensate for loss suffered, but does not exclude liability for gain made.

A second key observation is that the restitutionary remedies that are considered in this chapter are triggered by the commission of a breach of trust or breach of fiduciary duty; these are the underlying causes of action. Restitutionary remedies are also available where the defendant is liable for unjust enrichment. Unjust enrichment involves distinct type of cause of action, which will be established where the defendant has been enriched at the expense of the claimant, in circumstances falling within one of the recognized grounds of restitution, such as mistake.[54] Liability for unjust enrichment is distinct from that of breach of trust or breach of fiduciary duty, because it does not depend on the commission of a wrong. So, for example, if trust money is paid to a trustee by mistake, they will be liable to make restitution of the value of the money to the trust fund by virtue of their unjust enrichment. Although this is a potentially significant claim against trustees or fiduciaries, it is not relevant to the discussion in this chapter, since the underlying cause of action considered here is that founded on the commission of the wrong of breach of trust or fiduciary duty. Similarly, trustees or fiduciaries could be liable for breach of contract or a tort, but this liability does not depend on establishing a breach of trust or fiduciary duty.

(iii) Disgorgement of gain

Whereas the restitutionary measure focuses on the defendant giving *back* a gain made as a result of a breach of trust or fiduciary duty, a disgorgement remedy focuses on the defendant giving *up* a gain made as a result of the breach. The significance of this distinction is that disgorgement gains are obtained from a third party and do not involve a transfer being made from the claimant. The disgorgement measure has proved to be particularly significant in the law of trusts and fiduciaries, since there are numerous examples of trustees and fiduciaries profiting from breach of their duty by obtaining a benefit from a third party. In such cases it is irrelevant that the claimant has not suffered any loss as a result of the breach, or that any loss suffered is less than the gain made by the defendant. The focus of this measure is simply on the defendant's gain. So, for example, if the defendant fiduciary receives a bribe from a third party that induces them to act against the best interests of their principal, they will be liable to account for the value of that bribe even though the principal suffered no or little loss as a result.[55]

The mechanism for requiring the defendant to disgorge any profit made from a third party is the account of profits, which may also have a restitutionary function where the defendant's gain involved taking something from the claimant. In fact, it seems that for breaches of trust and fiduciary duty nothing turns on whether the account of profits involves restitution or disgorgement. In either case the focus is on the value of the defendant's gain and the remedy is awarded to ensure that a wrongdoer in Equity does not profit from the commission of their wrong,[56] regardless of whether the profit derives from the claimant or a third party. In either case the profit may be held on constructive trust for the beneficiary or the principal, such that the claimant would then have a proprietary claim to that gain.[57] There may be circumstances, however, where the personal remedy of

---

[54] *Banque Financière de la Cité v Parc (Battersea) Ltd* [1999] 1 AC 221, 227 (Lord Steyn). See further Section 8.5.1, p. 249.   [55] See Section 15.6.8, p. 450.

[56] *Attorney-General v Guardian Newspapers (No 2)* [1990] 1 AC 109, 286.

[57] *FHR European Ventures LLP v Cedar Capital Partners LLC* [2014] UKSC 45, [2015] AC 250.

an account of profits is more attractive, such as where the profits held on trust have been invested in property which has fallen in value.

(iv) Unwinding transactions

Another function of remedies following breach of fiduciary duty in particular is to unwind a transaction that was entered into in breach of duty. So, where a fiduciary enters into a contract with a third party on behalf of the principal in circumstances under which the fiduciary is to profit from the transaction, but this is not disclosed to the principal, the principal will wish the transaction to be set aside through rescission of the contract. Rescission operates to unwind the contract and to restore the parties to their original position. But, in doing so, rescission may have a variety of consequences. Apart from sometimes enabling the claimant to bring a proprietary claim to recover property transferred pursuant to the transaction,[58] rescission will also terminate any future obligations under the contract. But rescission may also have a pecuniary consequence. Where, for example, the property has been transferred pursuant to a voidable transaction, but that property cannot be returned to the claimant, the courts are willing to order the defendant to repay the value of the property to the claimant. For example, in *Mahoney v Purnell*,[59] a transaction involving the sale of shares by a father-in-law to his son-in-law was liable to be set aside by reason of presumed undue influence, but it was not possible to restore the parties to their original position because the company in which the shares had been sold had subsequently been wound up. It was held that, although recovery of the shares was no longer possible, the court had a power to award the claimant 'equitable compensation', which was assessed as the difference between the value of the shares sold by the claimant to the defendant and the purchase price that he had received. This had the effect of restoring the parties to their original position in so far as money was able to do this.

(v) Penal

In private law, where the defendant has committed a wrong, remedies can sometimes be awarded to punish the defendant. Such a remedy, which is often called 'exemplary damages' or 'punitive damages', is assessed neither by reference to the claimant's loss nor the defendant's gain, but involves the award of a sum that seeks to deter the wrongdoer from breaching their duty. Such remedies are exceptionally awarded where the defendant commits certain torts,[60] but not where the defendant has breached a contract.[61] There is no reason in principle why punishment should not motivate the award of remedies in Equity for breach of trust or fiduciary duty, and indeed, they are available in Canada[62] and New Zealand,[63] and the award of punitive damages for equitable wrongdoing has been recommended by the English Law Commission where the defendant has deliberately and outrageously disregarded the claimant's rights.[64] Punitive damages are not, however, presently available in England for equitable wrongdoing. Indeed, in *Vyse v Foster*,[65] James LJ said:

> This Court [of Equity] is not a Court of penal jurisdiction. It compels restitution of property unconscientiously withheld; it gives full compensation for any loss or damage through failure of some equitable duty; but it has no power of punishing anyone.

---

[58] See Section 9.3.2, p. 262.   [59] [1996] 3 All ER 61.

[60] See *Kuddus v Chief Constable of Leicestershire Constabulary* [2001] UKHL 29, [2002] 2 AC 122.

[61] *Addis v Gramohpone Co Ltd* [1909] AC 488.   [62] *Huff v Price* (1990) 76 DLR (4th) 138.

[63] *Aqualculture Corporation v New Zealand Green Mussels Ltd* [1990] 3 NZLR 299.

[64] *Aggravated, Exemplary and Restitutionary Damages*, Law Com No. 247 (London: HMSO, 1997), paras. 5.54–5.56.   [65] (1872) 8 Ch App 309, 333.

Most recently, the award of a penal remedy in Equity was specifically considered by the New South Wales Court of Appeal in *Harris v Digital Pulse Pty Ltd*,[66] in respect of breaches of fiduciary or other equitable duties, and was rejected by a majority of the judges, at least where the breach of fiduciary duty arose from a contractual relationship, since exemplary damages are not available for breach of contract. Mason P dissented, on the basis that the more appropriate analogy was with tort, under which exemplary damages are sometimes available, and he considered that a penal award for equitable wrongdoing was principled and compelling because of the need to deter such breaches. He would have been willing to make a penal award where the breach of duty was deliberate or was motivated by greed.

The arguments for and against the award of exemplary damages for equitable wrongdoing are finely balanced. One important argument in favour of making a penal award is founded on the fusion of Common Law and Equity.[67] Since such a remedy is available at Common Law for certain torts, such as the tort of deceit, it should also be awarded in Equity where, for example, a fiduciary has acted dishonestly.[68] This argument was rejected by the majority in *Harris v Digital Pulse*, since equitable wrongdoing and torts are distinct. The fusion argument could anyway be used against the recognition of exemplary damages, since they are not available for breach of contract, and breaches of trust and fiduciary duty are not that far removed from breach of contract, at least where the equitable obligation is voluntarily assumed rather than imposed by law. Another key argument in favour of awarding exemplary damages for equitable wrongdoing concerns the use of this award to deter equitable wrongdoing where the award of gain-based remedies cannot do so.[69]

But the key argument against the recognition of penal awards in Equity, which has proved influential for breach of contract as well, is that such awards are inherently uncertain, and the growing significance of Equity in the commercial world demands the identification of clear outcomes with reference to identified principles. Consequently, equitable remedies are not, and should not be, motivated by any desire to punish trustees or fiduciaries for breach of duty. It is sufficient that they compensate for loss suffered or give up gains made.[70]

It does not follow, however, that there will never be any penal consequences following a breach of trust or fiduciary duty, for this may involve the commission of a crime. So, for example, a trustee who misappropriates trust property could be guilty of theft[71] and a fiduciary who abuses their position may be guilty of fraud.[72]

(vi) Non-pecuniary remedies

It should not be forgotten that there are other non-pecuniary remedies available in Equity, following a breach of trust in particular, in addition to the proprietary remedies that are considered in Chapter 19. These non-pecuniary remedies have different functions from those considered so far. For example, the court may order that trustees are replaced following a breach of trust, to ensure that the trust is properly performed.[73] Alternatively, the court might appoint receivers or administrators to manage the trust property.

---

[66] (2003) 56 NSWLR 298. [67] See Section 1.6, p. 19.

[68] See Burrows, 'Remedial coherence and punitive damages in equity', in *Equity in Commercial Law*, ed. Degeling and Edelman (Sydney: Lawbook Co., 2005), p. 381.

[69] Duggan, 'Exemplary damages in Equity: a law and economics perspective' (2006) 26 OJLS 303, 322.

[70] See Hayton, 'Unique rules for the unique institution, the trust', in *Equity in Commercial Law*, ed. Degeling and Edelman (Sydney: Law Book Co., 2005), p. 301.

[71] Theft Act 1968, s. 1. See *R v Clowes (No 2)* [1994] 2 All ER 316. [72] Fraud Act 2006, s. 4.

[73] See Section 12.6.4, p. 353.

18.2 RECONSTITUTION OF THE TRUST FUND

Where a defendant trustee has misapplied assets from the trust fund, there is an immediate obligation on the trustee to remedy the breach. The beneficiaries will have two types of remedy available to them. One is a proprietary remedy to require the trustee to return the asset to the fund.[74] If, however, the asset or a substitute for it cannot be identified, the beneficiaries will seek a personal remedy to require the trustee to compensate the trust for the loss suffered as a result of the misappropriation.[75] The function of this remedy is preferably characterized as requiring the trustee to reconstitute the trust by returning the value of the asset that was misappropriated to the fund.[76]

18.2.1 FALSIFICATION OF THE ACCOUNT

The mechanism by which the trust fund is reconstituted is the common account, specifically by falsification of the account.[77] The language of falsification might appear artificial, but it explains perfectly the method by which the account is taken. Where there has been a breach of trust involving misapplication of trust assets, the beneficiary will typically apply to the court for an account to be taken. When the account is taken, if the trustee cannot give a satisfactory explanation as to what has happened to the assets for which they were responsible, the court will disallow the transaction that occurred in breach of trust from the account; this is the falsification. The effect of this will be that the trustee will be treated as having funded the transaction from their own assets. A consequence of the falsification is that value which once formed part of the trust fund, but which was taken by the trustee in breach of trust, will be deemed not to form part of the trust fund any more, and the trustee will be required either to restore the original asset or, if that is not possible, personally to reimburse the trust fund for the value missing.[78] The operation of falsification of the account was elegantly summarized by Lord Millett in *Libertarian Investments Ltd v Hall*:[79]

> If the account disclosed an unauthorised disbursement the [claimant] may falsify it, that is to say ask for the disbursement to be disallowed. This will produce a deficit which the defendant must make good, either *in specie* or in money.

Although the court has a discretion whether to order that an account should be taken, usually the discretion will be exercised in favour of it being done.[80]

The operation of falsification of the account as a remedy is illustrated by the following example. Alice is a trustee who made an unauthorized investment of £1,000 from the trust in shares that fell in value, so that they are now worth £750. The beneficiaries, Brian and Clare, will seek to falsify the account by asking the court to disallow the purchase of the

---

[74] *Nocton v Lord Ashburton* [1914] AC 932, 952, 958 (Viscount Haldane LC). See further Section 19.1.4.(i), p. 539.

[75] *Caffrey v Darby* (1801) 6 Ves 488; *Clough v Bond* (1838) 3 My & Cr 490. A restitutionary remedy of account of profits may be sought instead where the trustee has received the misappropriated asset, but, since the defendant's gain will typically correspond with the claimant's loss, there will usually be nothing to choose between these two remedies. See Section 18.1.4.(ii), p. 506.

[76] *Target Holdings Ltd v Redferns* [1996] AC 421, 434 (Lord Browne-Wilkinson). Edelman and Elliott (see n. 25), describe this as 'substitutive compensation'. See *AIB Group (UK) plc v Redler and Co* [2014] UKSC 58, [2015] AC 1503, [53] (Lord Toulson).

[77] See *AIB Group (UK) plc v Redler and Co* [2014] UKSC 58, [2015] AC 1503, [53] (Lord Toulson).

[78] Ibid., [90] (Lord Reed). See also *Williams v Central Bank of Nigeria* [2014] UKSC 10, [2014] 1 AC 1189, [13] (Lord Sumption).   [79] [2014] 1 HKC 368, [168].

[80] *Henchley v Thompson* [2017] EWHC 225 (Ch), [25] (Chief Master Marsh).

shares. The effect of this disallowance is that Alice will be treated as having purchased the shares from her own money. The shares will therefore be treated as belonging to Alice. But, once the account has been falsified, it will appear that £1,000 is missing from the trust fund, so Alice will be obliged to transfer £1,000 of her own money to reconstitute the fund and so restore it to its original position.

Typically, the beneficiaries will wish to falsify the account only where the investment has fallen in value. Where the investment has increased in value, they are much more likely to want to keep it and will authorize the transaction retrospectively by accepting the investment; they are not obliged to falsify the account. Where an unauthorized investment is adopted by the beneficiaries, the effect is that its purchase will be treated as having been authorized, so that it forms part of the trust fund. If such retrospective authorization were not allowed, it would follow that a trustee would be able to take money from the trust fund, make an unauthorized investment, and have the account falsified, so that the investment would be treated as belonging to the trustee, and would only have an obligation to repay the amount taken from the trust fund, pocketing the profit arising from the increase in value. Where, however, the investment has fallen in value, the beneficiaries will want the trustee to keep it and have the amount invested returned to the trust fund. That is what falsification of the account enables them to do.

The function of the account that is taken following a breach of trust which involved the misappropriation of assets is simply to return the trust to its original position—in other words, to reconstitute the trust. This is in effect, but not form, a compensatory remedy, since the effect of taking the account is that a loss is identified and the trustee will be obliged to compensate the fund for that loss.[81] The loss will obviously be a 'but for' cause of the breach of trust, since the relevant loss is the value taken from the trust; if the value had not been taken from the trust fund, it is clear that the trust would not have suffered the loss. The pecuniary award will be assessed at the date of judgment.[82] Liability will not be limited by the loss being too remote and unforeseeable, since the defendant is simply liable to reconstitute the fund. That is the relevant loss and it can never be too remote. Liability will not be limited by the obligation to mitigate loss, since the claimant is not responsible for the loss continuing. This is just the same for the Common Law action of debt: if the defendant owes money to the claimant under a contract, the defendant will be liable to pay that sum without the claimant having to prove loss, and remoteness and mitigation of loss are irrelevant.[83]

The significance of falsification of the account is illustrated by analysing two particular situations in which it will be of relevance in compensating the trust for breach, both of which involve breach of the trustee's custodial stewardship duty to preserve the trust assets.

(i) Purchase of unauthorized investments

In *Knott v Cottee*,[84] the testator left his estate to be held on trust and to be invested in British securities, but the executor invested the trust fund in foreign securities, which were sold at a loss. Had the securities been retained until the time of the trial, they could have been sold without loss. It was held that the purchase of the securities had been in breach of trust and the executor was to be treated as having made the purchase out of his own money, since the beneficiaries did not wish to recognize the investment. But, when the executor sold the securities, even though they were to be treated as belonging to him,

---

[81] See the decision of the High Court of Australia in *Youyang Pty Ltd v Minter Ellison Morris Fletcher* (2003) 196 ALR 482, [69].   [82] *Re Bell's Indenture* [1980] 1 WLR 1217, 1233 (Vinelott J).
[83] *Jervis v Harris* [1996] Ch 195, 202–3 (Millett LJ).   [84] (1852) 16 Beav 77.

the proceeds of sale were considered to have been refunded by the executor to the testator's estate. When the account was taken, it was appropriate to give credit for this amount, so that the executor was liable to pay to the trust only the difference between the amount taken from the trust originally to pay for the foreign securities and the proceeds of sale, in other words to compensate the trust for the loss arising from the sale of the securities. The fact that the securities could eventually have been sold without loss was irrelevant.

If the beneficiaries are of full capacity and all consent, they may adopt the unauthorized investment. If, at that point, the value of the investment is less than the purchase price, the trustee will be liable to compensate the trust for the difference.[85]

(ii) Improper sale of authorized investments

In *Re Massingberd's Settlement*,[86] the trustees sold an authorized trust investment and used the proceeds of sale to purchase mortgages, which were not authorized by the trust deed. It was held that the trust fund should be restored to the position in which it would have been had the authorized investments not been sold in the first place, so the loss arising from the sale of the authorized investment was assessed at the date of the judgment.

18.2.2 CAUSATION OF LOSS

One of the most controversial issues relating to the reconstitution of the trust concerns the identification of an appropriate test of causation: to what extent must the loss suffered by the trust be causatively linked to the breach of trust? It would be nonsense to assert that a trustee who has breached a trust is liable for every loss suffered by the trust, even if that loss is unrelated to the breach. So, for example, if a trustee makes an unauthorized investment of shares in company A and the trust suffers a loss from the fall in value of shares that it owns in company B, this loss is totally unrelated to the breach, and so the trustee should not be liable to compensate the trust for this loss. Consequently, causation of loss arising from the breach of trust must be established. The appropriate test to adopt is one of 'but for' causation, in the sense that it must be shown that, but for the breach, the loss would not have been suffered.

Applying the principles of causation where the account is falsified should be straightforward. If, for example, the trustee has misapplied trust funds, either by misappropriating them for themself or investing them in unauthorized investments, the trustee will have breached their custodial duty and must reconstitute the trust in full. The loss suffered by the trust is the value of the fund which has been misapplied. This loss was clearly caused by the breach of trust, since, but for the breach, the fund would not have been misapplied. It follows that this is the loss which should be remedied by reference to 'the objective value of the property lost, determined at the date when the account is taken and with the benefit of hindsight'.[87] The court is only concerned with the net value of the lost asset, so would need to offset any benefits which had already been returned to the trust fund. This analysis of falsification of the account, as incorporating the 'but for' test of causation, depends on careful analysis of the relevant breach and of the loss which arises from that breach. Where the trust fund has been misapplied the relevant breach is of the trustee's custodial duty which leads directly to the loss of the trust property, rather than a breach involving infidelity or failure to exercise reasonable standards of skill and care.[88] Focusing on the

---

[85] *Re Lake* [1903] 1 KB 439.   [86] (1890) 63 LT 296.

[87] *Libertarian Investments Ltd v Hall* [2014] 1 HKC 368, [168] (Millett NPJ); *Agricultural Land Management Ltd v Jackson (No 2)* [2014] WASC 102.

[88] See *Bank of New Zealand v New Zealand Guardian Trust Co Ltd* [1999] 1 NZLR 664, [687] (Tipping J).

relevant duty as being the custodial duty means that the relevant loss is the loss of the property itself, which typically will obviously have been caused by the breach of trust. This is illustrated by *Main v Giambrone and Law*,[89] where a firm of solicitors had paid deposits, which it held on trust for the purchasers of properties, to the vendors of the properties before valid guarantees had been obtained from the vendors. It was held that these payments had been made in breach of the firm's custodial duty to keep the money safe until valid guarantees had been made. This was a 'but for' cause of the loss of the money, so the firm was liable to compensate the claimants for this loss, which was assessed as the full value of the deposits which had been paid.

This orthodox analysis of the relevant loss and operation of the principles of causation where the relevant breach involves misapplication of the trust funds is not, however, reflected in two leading cases on the award of compensatory remedies for breach of trust, both of which require fundamental reconsideration of the nature of the loss and the operation of the test of causation where the beneficiaries seek to reconstitute the trust fund.

The first of these cases is *Target Holdings Ltd v Redferns*.[90] In that case Crowngate Developments Ltd (C Ltd) had entered into a contract to buy a property for £775,000. The claimant finance company, Target Holdings Ltd, received a loan application form from C Ltd, which stated that the property was valued at £2 million. The claimant agreed to lend C Ltd over £1.5 million in return for a mortgage on the property. This was all part of a fraudulent mortgage scheme to obtain twice the true value of the property that was the security for the loan. Redferns, the defendant firm of solicitors that was acting for both C Ltd and the claimant, received the loan money and held it on bare trust for the claimant, with implied authority to release the money to C Ltd only once the property had been conveyed to it and the charges had been executed. In breach of trust, the defendant released the money to a third party on 27 June, before the confirming documents were received and without the claimant's authority. These documents were eventually executed on 5 July and the money eventually received by C Ltd. The property was subsequently sold for £500,000. Clearly, this was a bad bargain for the claimant, which had a security on a property worth only one-third of the money lent. The claimant sued the defendant for breach of trust in releasing the money before the documents had been received. If, as may have been the case, the defendant firm of solicitors was implicated in the fraud, it could have been liable for the tort of deceit, for which compensatory damages are available for all losses arising from the fraud no matter how remote, since the defendant fraudster is prevented from arguing that the claimant would have acted in the same way had there been no fraud; this would have meant that the loss arising from the inadequate value of the property as security for the loan would have been recoverable.[91] But the claim was grounded instead on breach of trust, for which liability is strict, so avoiding the need to prove fraud.

The defendant denied liability on the ground that the claimant had suffered no loss as a result of the breach, because the loss arising from the inadequate security was not caused by the breach of trust; the claimant would have obtained the same valid security and suffered the same loss had the money been released after the documents had been executed. The Court of Appeal[92] held that, immediately the money had been transferred in breach of trust, the claimant had a right to have the trust fund reconstituted, even though the claimant had received the security that it was intending to obtain and regardless of the fact that

---

[89] [2017] EWCA Civ 1193.   [90] [1996] AC 421.

[91] *Smith New Court Securities Ltd v Scrimgeour Vickers (Asset Management) Ltd* [1997] AC 254. Such damages could not have been recovered had the defendant been merely negligent: *Banque Bruxelles Lambert SA v Eagle Star Insurance Co Ltd* [1997] AC 191. See further *Swindle v Harrison* [1997] 4 All ER 705, discussed in Section 18.4, p. 524.   [92] [1994] 1 WLR 1089.

the security was worth much less than anticipated, since Common Law principles of causation did not apply to a claim for breach of trust. This result does appear to be consistent with the theory underlying the falsification of the account.[93] The relevant breach of trust was the premature transfer of the loan money. Since this was an unauthorized transaction, it could be falsified and disregarded, meaning that the trust had suffered a loss of £1.5 million and the defendant trustee was liable to reconstitute the trust by that amount, with the claimant giving credit for the £500,000 that it had obtained as a result of selling the property. According to this analysis, causation need not be specifically considered, since it is implicit in the falsification of the account. Once the payment of £1.5 million was disregarded, the trust had suffered a loss of that amount minus the amount received from the sale; this was the loss which would not have been caused but for the breach.

When the case went on appeal to the House of Lords, the decision of the Court of Appeal was reversed on the ground that the claimant had obtained a valid security for the sum advanced, which it would still have obtained had there not been a breach of trust. Consequently, it appeared that the breach had not caused any loss to be suffered by the trust. The loss that it suffered was considered to have arisen from the inadequate security, which was not attributable to the breach.

Although it appears that this case decides that the claim for compensation failed because the loss suffered was not caused by the breach of trust, the decision is more limited than that and the analysis of the court is more complicated.

Crucial to our understanding of this decision is the distinction drawn by Lord Browne-Wilkinson between two different contexts in which express trusts might operate.

(i) Traditional trusts

Where, for example, Ann holds property on trust for Brian for life with remainder for Clare, this is considered to be a traditional trust. If Ann misapplies the trust fund and the trust continues, there is an obligation on her to put the trust fund back into its original position for the benefit of both beneficiaries, so that their equitable interests are satisfied when they fall into possession. Where, however, the trust has come to an end, such as where Brian has died and Clare has become absolutely entitled to the fund, Lord Browne-Wilkinson concluded that it would not be necessary to reconstitute the trust, because there would no longer be any trust to be reconstituted. Instead, Ann should pay compensation for the breach of trust to Clare directly, assessed by reference to what the value of the trust fund would have been but for the breach of trust.[94] The conclusion that Ann would be liable to reconstitute the trust only where it is subsisting is consistent with the decision of the Court of Appeal and the theoretical nature of the falsification of the account. Causation of loss here is obvious because the loss is the value of the property misapplied. But the trust in *Target Holdings* was not a traditional trust.

(ii) Bare commercial trusts

The other type of trust identified by Lord Browne-Wilkinson is a bare trust arising in a commercial context, which is what the trust was in *Target Holdings* itself. The money that had been paid to the defendant solicitors was to be held on bare trust for the claimant until the documentation was received. Lord Browne-Wilkinson considered it to be crucial that

---

[93] See Millett, 'Equity's place in the law of commerce' (1998) 114 LQR 214, 226. It is a result that was supported by the High Court of Australia in *Youyang Pty Ltd v Minter Ellison Morris Fletcher* (2003) 196 ALR 482.

[94] *Target Holdings Ltd v Redferns* [1996] AC 421, 435 (Lord Browne-Wilkinson). See *Bartlett v Barclays Bank Trust Co Ltd (Nos 1 and 2)* [1980] Ch 515.

this trust arose from a commercial transaction, so that the principles of Equity that have been developed in the context of traditional trusts were not applicable.

The significance of the distinction between traditional and commercial trusts was that, with the latter, until the underlying commercial transaction has been completed, the trustee could be required to restore the money that had been wrongly paid away. Once the underlying transaction had been completed, however, there was no obligation to reconstitute the trust fund,[95] but the trustee might still be liable to compensate the beneficiary directly for any loss suffered as a result of the breach. On the facts of *Target Holdings*, the commercial transaction had been completed, since the documentation for the loan was subsequently received, so that the bare trust was terminated and could not be reconstituted.

Once reconstitution of the trust has been ruled out, because the trust or the underlying transaction have been terminated, it is then necessary to determine whether the beneficiary has suffered any loss as a result of the breach of the trust.[96] In *Target Holdings*, that loss could not relate to the property being an inadequate security for the loan, because that was a loss that was not caused by the breach: the claimant would still have suffered that loss had the trust not been breached. Matters would be different, however, if it could be shown that, had the transfer of the money not occurred before the conveyance of the property was completed, the claimant would not have gone through with the transaction, for then the loss to the claimant arising from the much-reduced value of the property would not have been suffered but for the breach, because the claimant would not have lent the money.[97] The House of Lords considered that this was a matter that should be considered with reference to the evidence at the trial of the issue, this hearing simply being an appeal on a preliminary issue. So causation of a loss did remain a live issue on the facts. But the identification of the relevant loss is essential. It was not considered to be the loss arising from the premature payment of the loan, which is what the Court of Appeal had decided and which is consistent with the orthodox analysis of falsification of the account, but the loss from having an inadequate security on the property.

The significance of the distinction between traditional and commercial trusts is not as marked as may first be thought. This is because, in both cases, if the trust continues at the time of judgment, the trustee will be liable to reconstitute it. Further, in both cases, if the trust no longer continues, there is nothing to reconstitute, but the trustee may still be liable to compensate the beneficiary for any loss suffered as a result of the breach of trust. The only practical significance of the distinction between the two types of trust is that a bare commercial trust is more likely to be terminated, since the underlying commercial transaction on which the trust is founded is more likely to be completed. This is what happened in *Target Holdings*.

The distinction drawn by Lord Browne-Wilkinson between traditional and commercial trusts is artificial and, on closer inspection, is not significant. The crucial distinction does not relate to the context in which the trust arises, but only to whether the trust continues to subsist when the judgment is delivered: where the trust continues to subsist, whether it be a traditional or a bare commercial trust, the trustee will be liable to compensate the trust for the value transferred in breach of trust. This is the loss that was caused by the breach of the custodial duty. Where, however, the trust has come to an end, the trust cannot be reconstituted by compensating the trust fund. Instead, there will be a liability owed

---

[95] Cf. the approach in Australia: *Youyang Pty Ltd v Minter Ellison Morris Fletcher* (2003) 196 ALR 482, [49].

[96] *Swindle v Harrison* [1997] 4 All ER 705, 717 (Evans LJ).

[97] As occurred in *Alliance & Leicester Building Society v Edgestop Ltd* (unreported), 18 January 1991, in which, on similar facts to *Target Holdings*, it was found that, had the claimant known the true facts, it would not have lent the money.

to the beneficiary, but the relevant loss is no longer the amount which had been taken from the trust fund, but is the loss that would not have been suffered by the beneficiary but for the breach of trust, and the breach of trust appears not to be the breach of the custodial duty, which would trigger falsification of the account, but instead of the duty to act with reasonable skill and care, which triggers the remedy of compensation by reparation. But, if this different approach to the identification of the loss applies to commercial trusts, it should also apply to traditional trusts. If the vital distinguishing feature is that the trust has terminated, either because the beneficiary is absolutely entitled or the underlying transaction is completed, there will be no obligation to reconstitute since there is no fund to be reconstituted. But, in either case, the trustee is liable to the former beneficiary. The only real difference, which is a function of the different factual context, is that, where the trust is a traditional family trust, the claimant will be the beneficiary, who is absolutely entitled to the trust fund, whereas in the context of a commercial bare trust, as in *Target Holdings*, the claimant will be the former beneficiary, who is no longer entitled to the trust fund because the underlying transaction is complete. Beyond this, there is no need to distinguish between the different contexts in which the trusts arise.

It is, however, possible to justify the denial of the remedy in *Target Holdings* by focusing on the nature of the breach of trust. That breach involved the unauthorized payment of money from the trust fund. That payment became authorized, however, once the relevant documentation was received on 5 July. At that point, the trust terminated as the result of the payment becoming authorized and so there was no basis for compensating the beneficiary for the value of the money lent, because there was no continuing unauthorized act,[98] and no longer a breach of trust, although the beneficiary could still seek compensation for other losses that were caused by the earlier breach of trust. Such subsequent authorization resulting in the termination of the trust is much more likely to arise in respect of a commercial bare trust. Where, however, a transfer of money occurs in breach of a traditional family trust, that will be a continuing unauthorized transaction even after the trust is terminated, so the claimant beneficiary should be able to recover the value of the money transferred, unless the claimant had subsequently adopted the transaction. This focus on the subsequent authorization preserves the legitimacy of the distinction between traditional and commercial trusts (but largely as a matter of factual context rather than law), and means that the result of *Target Holdings* can be defended on policy grounds: in the commercial context, where the trustee transfers money in breach of trust in respect of a transaction that is subsequently authorized, it is not appropriate that the defendant trustee should bear the risk of events changing, so that there is a liability to restore the value of what has been transferred to the claimant. This allocation of risk is more defensible where the trust is a traditional one that arises in the family context.

It would follow from this argument that if in *Target Holdings* the trust had subsisted the defendant would have been liable to reconstitute the trust by paying £1.5 million, even though the breach of trust was technical and would not have occurred had the defendant simply waited a short time to receive the relevant documents before releasing the money. As a matter of policy this might be considered to be absurd. Similarly, on this view, the trustee would be liable to reconstitute the trust if the money paid in breach of trust were paid as the result of an innocent mistake, for example through a computer error. Who should bear the risk of that type of loss: the beneficiary or the trustee? The better view is

---

[98] As recognized by Lord Millett (see n. 17), p. 311. See also Millett (see n. 93), p. 226 and *Libertarian Investments Ltd v Hall* [2013] HKCFA 93, [2014] 1 HKC 368. The analysis of Lord Millett was approved by the High Court of Australia in *Youyang Pty Ltd v Minter Ellison Morris Fletcher* (2003) 196 ALR 482. See Elliott and Edelman, '*Target Holdings* considered in Australia' (2003) 119 LQR 545.

that it should be the trustee. Where a trustee has paid money by mistake, they should be strictly liable to compensate the trust for the loss, subject to a defence founded on section 61 of the Trustee Act 1925.[99] If the trustee is personally liable to reconstitute the trust in such circumstances, they would still be able to bring a claim against the recipient in unjust enrichment. This is because the effect of falsifying the account will be that the money transferred is deemed to belong to the trustee, so that the payee becomes unjustly enriched at the expense of the trustee rather than the trust, and it is the trustee who was mistaken in making the payment. More generally, to exclude liability on the basis of the triviality of the breach would undermine the basic premise of liability for breach of trust that the liability is strict.[100] Further, it is a fundamental principle that the trustee remains accountable to the trust regardless of the nature of the breach; the beneficiaries have a primary right to ensure that the trust fund is maintained.

It follows that, although the result in *Target Holdings* can be defended by focusing on the subsequent termination of the trust rendering the dissipation an authorized one, the reasoning of Lord Browne-Wilkinson in rejecting the orthodox analysis of the remedy of falsification of the account should itself be rejected as unprincipled. Nevertheless, Lord Browne-Wilkinson's reasoning was subsequently approved and applied by the Supreme Court in *AIB Group (UK) plc v Redler and Co.*[101] It follows that the orthodox analysis of the remedy of falsification of the account, by virtue of which unauthorized dissipation of trust assets involves a loss identified with reference to the value of the assets which have been dissipated, is no longer applicable, at least in respect of a commercial bare trust. The decision in *Redler* is, in fact, even more significant, because, unlike *Target Holdings*, the dissipation of the trust fund could not be considered to have been rendered authorized subsequently.

In *Redler* a married couple had applied for a loan of £3.3 million from the claimant bank. The loan was to be secured by a first legal charge over their home, which was worth £4.25 million. The home was already subject to a first legal charge in favour of Barclays Bank, which was secured on two accounts amounting to £1.5 million in total. The claimant bank had agreed to make the loan on condition that the secured loan in favour of Barclays was first redeemed. The defendant firm of solicitors acted for both the claimant bank and the borrowers. The claimant bank forwarded the loan to the defendant, which was held on trust for the claimant until completion. Barclays forwarded information to the defendant about the value of its loan, but this related to only one of the accounts. The defendant paid this amount to Barclays from the loan received from the claimant, assuming that this would discharge the Barclays loan completely, and the balance was paid to the borrowers. Since the loan was not fully discharged, Barclays was still owed £309,000 which was secured by a charge on the property which had priority over the claimant's charge. The borrowers defaulted and the property was sold for £1.2 million. The claimant recovered over £800,000 and sought to recover the outstanding amount of the loan from the defendant, amounting to £2.5 million, on the ground of breach of trust and fiduciary duty.[102] The defendant contended that it was only liable to pay what the claimant had lost by the defendant failing to do what it should have done, which was to have paid Barclays

---

[99] See Section 17.3.2, p. 481.

[100] In *Collins v Brebner* [2000] Lloyd's Rep PN 587, it was recognized that the decision in *Target Holdings* applies to all breaches of trust, regardless of whether the breach was fraudulent, negligent, or innocent.

[101] [2014] UKSC 58, [2015] AC 1503. See Turner, 'The new fundamental norm of recovery for losses to express trusts' (2015) 74 CLJ 188; Davies, 'Remedies for breach of trust' (2015) 78 MLR 681.

[102] The claimant also sued for breach of contract and negligence, liability for which was admitted by the defendant.

the full amount of its debt so as to redeem Barclays's charge on the property, amounting to £275,000.

Although the defendant had acted in good faith, it was accepted that it had acted in breach of trust by failing to comply with its instructions to discharge the full liability of Barclays before paying anything to the borrowers. Consequently, the breach of trust involved an unauthorized dissipation of the trust fund. Whilst Lord Reed considered that the unauthorized dissipation related only to that amount which was paid to the borrowers rather than to Barclays, the decision of the Court of the Appeal that the entire £3.3 million had been misapplied was not challenged.[103] It was still necessary for the Supreme Court to identify the loss which arose from this breach of trust. If the trust was to be reconstituted using the traditional accounting mechanism, then, since the breach involved paying money to the borrowers before discharging the money owed to Barclays, the defendant would be required to restore the whole £3.3 million, minus what the claimant had already received from the sale of the property. This was not the remedy which was awarded by the Supreme Court, because this was not considered to be the relevant loss which was caused by the breach of trust. The actual loss was instead identified as being that the claimant enjoyed less security for its loan than if there had not been a breach of trust. Consequently, the defendant was liable to compensate the claimant for what it had failed to do, namely to pay Barclays the additional amount of £275,000.

In reaching this decision the Supreme Court affirmed the reasoning of Lord Browne-Wilkinson in *Target Holdings*. Whilst the facts of *Redler* bore some similarity with those in *Target Holdings*, particularly that the relevant trust was a commercial bare trust, in *Redler* the underlying commercial transaction had never been completed because the shortfall of the money needed to discharge the Barclays loan had never been paid, so consequently the trust had not been terminated. This was, however, not considered to be a relevant distinction. What mattered was that the trust was a commercial bare trust, and this alone was considered to be sufficient to justify the court in characterizing the relevant breach as being a breach of the trustee's duty to exhibit reasonable skill and care, such that the loss was not the unauthorized disposition from the trust fund but rather the loss arising from the failure to comply with the trustee's instructions, namely the amount by which the value of the claimant's security was less than it should have been, which equated with the amount of the overpayment to the borrowers and the underpayment to Barclays. The award of such a remedy would put the beneficiary in the same position it would have been in had there not been a breach of trust,[104] and so equates the function of the compensatory remedy for breach of trust with that available for breach of contract and tort.[105]

Lord Toulson considered that the claimant's loss arising from the sale of the house at a significantly reduced amount was not a loss which was caused by the breach of trust, because it was a loss which would have been suffered even had the defendant done what it was instructed to do.[106] But this is not necessarily true and depends very much on the identification of the relevant breach and the relevant loss. If the breach was considered to be the unauthorized disposition of the money to the borrowers, then this was the loss which was caused by the breach of trust. But the Supreme Court considered that the commercial nature of the trust meant that it should focus on a different breach of trust and consequently a different characterization of the loss. It was recognized, however, that as regards a so-called traditional trust, where property is held on trust for potential beneficiaries over a lengthy period, the function of the remedy for breach of trust involving

[103] [2014] UKSC 58, [2015] AC 1503, [140] (Lord Reed).
[104] [2014] UKSC 58, [2015] AC 1503, [64] (Lord Toulson).
[105] Ibid., [71] (Lord Toulson), [136] (Lord Reed).   [106] Ibid., [62].

unauthorized disposition of trust assets is either to restore the assets to the trust or their monetary value to the trust, since[107] for such a trust the real loss to the trust is the loss of the trust asset. Lord Toulson unconvincingly sought to distinguish between traditional and commercial trusts on the basis that the former involves a transfer of property by way of gift whereas the latter arises out of a contract.[108] Whilst the reason for the transfer of property may well be different as between traditional and commercial trusts, this does not explain why the remedy awarded should be different. The implication of the decision, however, is that traditional trusts are typically longer lasting, so it is appropriate to treat the relevant loss as the loss of the asset which has been dissipated, whereas commercial bare trusts tend to be created for a particular defined purpose and, once that purpose has been fulfilled, the relevant loss should be that which would not have been suffered but for the breach of trust,[109] the relevant breach relating to the standard of skill and care rather than the custodial duty. The problem with this justification for the distinction, however, is that the trust in *AIB v Redler*, whilst being a commercial bare trust, had not been terminated because the underlying purpose had not been completely fulfilled.[110]

18.2.3 SUMMARY OF PRINCIPLES

Whilst the decisions of the House of Lords in *Target Holdings* and the Supreme Court in *AIB v Redler* can be criticized as unprincipled, they are authoritative and indicate that the law relating to the award of personal remedies for breach of trust has entered a new era. At the heart of this new law is the need to consider the context in which the trust was created. In a significant dictum in *AIB v Redler* Lord Reed said:[111]

> commercial trusts, usually arising out of contractual relationships rather than the transfer of property by way of gift, differ in a number of respects from the more traditional trust. That is not to say that there is a categorical distinction between trusts in commercial and non-commercial relationships, or to assert that there are trusts to which the fundamental principles of equity do not apply. It is, on the other hand, to recognise that the duties and liabilities of trustees may depend, in some respects, upon the terms of the trust in question and the relationship between the relevant parties
>
> In particular . . . where a trust is part of the machinery for the performance of a contract, that fact will be relevant in considering what loss has been suffered by reason of a breach of the trust.

The context in which the trust was created is clearly significant and, despite what Lord Reed said, whether or not that context is commercial will be especially important. Consequently, the following principles appear to reflect the state of the law:

(1) Where the trust is 'traditional', in that it does not arise in a commercial context and is intended to last for a significant period of time, if the trustee has made an unauthorized disposition of trust property, the relevant breach of trust should be considered to be breach of the custodial duty, with the relevant loss caused by the breach being the loss of the asset which has been dissipated. The relevant accounting mechanism will be to falsify the account. This could have the following implications:

(a) to require the trustee to reconstitute the trust by restoring the asset itself if they still have it;

---

[107] Ibid., [67] (Lord Toulson).   [108] Ibid., [70].   [109] Ibid.

[110] Although Lord Toulson, ibid. [74], assumed that the transaction was completed when the money was paid to the borrowers.   [111] Ibid., [102].

(b) to require the trustee to reconstitute the trust by restoring the value of the asset to the trust if the trust has not been terminated; or

(c) to require the trustee to transfer the value of the asset to the beneficiaries if the trust has been terminated.

(2) Where the trust is a bare trust which is part of the mechanism for the performance of a contract, and so will typically arise in a commercial context, if the trustee has made an unauthorized disposition of trust property then identifying whether a loss was a 'but for' cause of the breach of trust will depend on the nature of the underlying breach of duty.

(3) Where the breach was of an active duty to do something, such as in *Target*, where the breach was the defendant's failure to take active steps to secure a charge, or in *AIB*, where the relevant breach was the failure to remove prior charges before releasing the money which was held on trust, the relevant breach should be characterized as breach of the duty of reasonable skill and care, with the relevant loss being that which would not have been suffered but for the breach of trust.[112]

(4) Where, however, the breach can be characterized as breach of the custodial duty not to release money until the occurrence of a particular event, the trustee will be required to reconstitute the trust as though the trust was a 'traditional' trust. This distinction between breach of active and custodial duties was recognized by the Court of Appeal in *Main v Giambrone and Law*,[113] where a firm of solicitors had paid deposits in breach of its custodial duty to retain the money until valid guarantees were made. Since the firm was not responsible for obtaining the guarantees it was held that the firm had not breached any active duty, but only its custodial duty. *Target* and *AIB* were specifically distinguished because the relevant breaches in those cases was of a duty to take active steps to secure a result before money was released. Since the defendant in *Main v Giambrone and Law* had breached a custodial and not an active duty, the remedy which was awarded, albeit described as 'equitable compensation', involved paying the value of the deposits to the claimants because, but for the breach of trust, those deposits would not have been transferred since valid guarantees had not been obtained.

18.3   REPARATION OF THE TRUST FUND

18.3.1   GENERAL PRINCIPLES

Reconstitution of the trust will be relevant where the trust suffers loss from value being transferred out of the trust fund. A trust may suffer loss in another way, namely where a trustee fails to increase the value of the fund by missing an investment opportunity that would otherwise have been available to the trust, involving breach of the trustee's stewardship duty. So, for example, if a trustee negligently fails to invest trust money in shares so that the trust does not benefit from a subsequent increase in the share value, the trust will have suffered the difference between what it would have cost to purchase the shares and their later value. In this context of an omission to use the trust fund, the

---

[112] Whilst the Supreme Court in *AIB v Redler* [2014] UKSC 58, [2015] AC 1503 characterized this as equitable compensation, it could more accurately be characterized as surcharging the account. See further Section 18.3.1, p. 521.   [113] [2017] EWCA Civ 1193. See Section 18.2.2, p. 513.

remedy of reconstitution is not available, because there is nothing to put back into the fund since nothing has actually been taken out of it. Rather, a remedy is required to compensate the trust fund for the lost opportunity to profit. This can be described as a remedy of reparation of the fund.[114] Technically, again, Equity uses the account taken on the basis of wilful default to effect this compensation, but this time by surcharging the account.[115]

The essential feature of a surcharge of the account is that the trust account is altered so that it includes the profit that the beneficiaries can prove would have been made had the fund been invested properly and not in breach of trust;[116] this additional profit is added, or surcharged, to the account. This additional amount will not be reflected by the actual value of the fund and so the trustee will be personally liable to make up this discrepancy.

Where the account is surcharged, the consequence will be that the trust will be repaired by being placed into the position in which it would have been had there not been a breach of trust. Consequently, it is necessary to show that the loss suffered by the trust would not have been suffered but for the trustee's omission, so causation of loss must be established. So, for example, where the trustee has failed to invest trust assets in authorized investments, the remedy that should be awarded for breach of trust will be what the trust has lost by not obtaining those investments—in other words, the amount by which the investments that the trustee should have purchased have increased in value. This is illustrated by *Fry v Fry*,[117] in which a testator had provided in his will that the Langford Inn should be sold as soon as convenient after his death for the most money that could reasonably be obtained. The trustees advertised the property for sale for £1,000 and refused an offer for £900. Subsequently, the opening of a railway made the property more difficult to sell and, twenty years after the testator's death, it remained unsold. It was held that the trustees were liable for their negligence in not selling the property and were liable to compensate the trust for the difference in the amount that might eventually be received for the property and the offer of £900 that had been rejected.

The loss suffered by the trust as a result of the trustee's failure to administer the trust properly will be assessed at the time of the trial and not at the time of breach,[118] so there is more likely to be concrete evidence as to what profit could have been made. The loss will be measured only with reference to the value of a specific investment if the trustees were required to make that investment;[119] otherwise the loss will be calculated with reference to the most likely investments that a prudent trustee would have made in the circumstances.[120]

Crucially, however, the loss must arise from a breach of duty. Where a trustee retains an authorized security, they will not be liable for a loss suffered by the trust as a result of the fall in value of the security, provided that the trustee acted honestly and prudently in the belief that the retention of the security was in the best interests of the beneficiaries.[121]

[114] See Edelman and Elliott (see n. 25), p. 120; *AIB Group (UK) plc v Redler and Co* [2014] UKSC 58, [2015] AC 1503, [54] (Lord Toulson).

[115] *AIB Group (UK) plc v Redler and Co* [2014] UKSC 58, [2015] AC 1503, [91] (Lord Reed).

[116] By reason of failing to comply with the standard of the reasonable trustee. See Section 13.2.2, p. 376.

[117] (1859) 27 Beav 144.

[118] *Target Holdings Ltd v Redferns* [1996] AC 421, 437 (Lord Browne-Wilkinson).

[119] *Shepherd v Mouls* (1845) 4 Hare 500.

[120] See *Nestle v National Westminster Bank Plc* [1993] 1 WLR 1260, 1283 (Leggatt LJ).

[121] *Re Chapman* [1896] 2 Ch 763.

18.3.2 CAUSATION AND REMOTENESS

It is necessary to prove that, but for the breach of trust, the loss would not have been suffered. Although it has sometimes been asserted that it is not necessary to consider whether the loss was too remote, this has been challenged,[122] primarily on the ground that many of the cases that have asserted that remoteness is not relevant in Equity[123] involved breach of trust relating to misapplication of trust funds, requiring reconstitution of the trust, rather than negligent administration of the trust, requiring reparation. In *Bristol and West Building Society v Mothew*,[124] Millett LJ, albeit in the context of breach of fiduciary duty, recognized that Common Law rules of remoteness, causation, and the measure of damages should apply when assessing liability for breach of the equitable duty of skill and care. The same should apply where the claim relates to compensation for loss arising from a negligent failure to invest. Some limitation on the loss for which compensation is recoverable needs to be identified, and reasonable foreseeability of loss is a workable and acceptable test to do this.[125]

18.3.3 PROFIT MADE AND LOSS SUFFERED

Where the trustee has invested trust money in one transaction that has made a profit, but has negligently failed to dispose of trust assets, so suffering a loss, it is not possible to set the gain against the loss, because the profitable action and the negligent omission are distinct. This is illustrated by *Dimes v Scott*,[126] in which a testator had left his estate on trust for his widow for life and, on her death, on trust for the claimant. The estate included a mortgage that the will required the trustees to convert into money within a reasonable time following the testator's death. In breach of trust, the trustees retained the mortgage and paid the income from it to the widow. The mortgage was eventually discharged and the proceeds were reinvested by the trustees in securities, the price of which was lower than at the time after the testator's death, so the trustees were able to purchase more of them. It was recognized that the trustees had breached the trust by failing to redeem the mortgage following the testator's death, but they could not set off against that liability the value of the extra securities that they had been able to obtain as a result of the delay in redeeming the mortgage. This was described as an 'accidental advantage' from which the trustees could not benefit.

Where, however, a gain is made and a loss suffered in the course of the same transaction, the gain can be set off against the loss. So, in *Fletcher v Green*,[127] trustees made a secured loan to a firm of which one of the trustees was a partner. The security was sold at a loss, and the proceeds were paid into court and invested in shares that increased in value. It was held that this gain could be set off against the loss suffered from the sale of the security, presumably because this all formed part of the same transaction.

It may be difficult to identify whether the gain and the loss arose from a single or from distinct transactions, as is especially well illustrated by *Bartlett v Barclays Bank Trust Co Ltd (Nos 1 and 2)*.[128] In that case the trustee was a bank that had failed to oversee the actions of a company in which the trust held a majority of the shares. The directors of that company invested in two building developments, one of which was profitable and one of

---

[122] Elliott (see n. 18), p. 590.

[123] Including *Re Dawson (deceased)* [1966] 2 NSWLR 211; *Target Holdings Ltd v Redferns* [1996] AC 421; *Collins v Brebner* [2000] Lloyd's Rep PN 587.

[124] [1998] Ch 1, 16–18. See further Section 18.4, p. 523. See also *Bank of New Zealand v New Zealand Guardian Trust Co Ltd* [1999] 1 NZLR 213, (Fisher J); affirmed [1999] 1 NZLR 664 (CA).

[125] See Millett (see n. 93), p. 226.   [126] (1828) 4 Russ 195.   [127] (1864) 33 Beav 426.

[128] [1980] Ch 515. See further Section 13.4.4, p. 389.

which caused a huge loss to the company. Brightman J allowed the gain to be set off against the loss. This would seem to be difficult to justify on the ground that there was a single transaction, since the two building developments were distinct. Since, however, the breach of trust concerned a failure to supervise speculative property development, this could be collapsed into a single and continuing breach.

The general rule that gain cannot be set off against loss may be justified for two distinct reasons. One is that the trustee should not be allowed to benefit from the good luck that a gain might counteract a loss suffered, since this would undermine the principle that we expect the highest standards from trustees for the benefit of the beneficiaries, and the possibility of a future gain might encourage trustees to speculate in risky investments. Secondly, and more convincingly, it is all a matter of causation. Where the gain and the loss arise from the same transaction, they can be considered to be causally connected to a single breach, and so it is appropriate to set off the gain against the loss. But, where the loss and gain arise from two distinct decisions made by the trustee, they cannot be considered to be causally connected to the same breach of trust.

18.4 EQUITABLE COMPENSATION

In *Canson Enterprises Ltd v Boughton and Co*,[129] McLachlin J, sitting in the Supreme Court of Canada, said that 'compensation is an equitable monetary remedy which is available when the equitable remedies of restitution and account are not appropriate'. This was approved by Lord Browne-Wilkinson in *Target Holdings v Redferns*.[130] It has already been seen that the taking of an account, whilst involving the assertion of primary rights of the beneficiaries against the trustees to administer the trust properly, may have the effect of compensating the trust for loss suffered.[131] But there will be circumstances under which loss will have been caused by the commission of an equitable wrong, but it is not possible to take an account. This is most likely to be the case where loss has been caused to the claimant as a result of a fiduciary's breach of duty and where the fiduciary is not a steward of any property. Also, an account will not be available where it is no longer practical or helpful to pay money into the trust, typically because the trust has come to an end. In such cases, an equitable remedy can still be awarded, known as 'equitable compensation', to compensate the claimant for the loss suffered.[132] Although the name of the mechanism to compensate for loss suffered may be different, the principles that underpin account and equitable compensation are similar. A loss will need to be identified; it will need to have been caused by the breach;[133] and a pecuniary remedy will be paid to the beneficiary or the principal to place them in the position in which they would have been had the breach not occurred.

In considering liability for breach of duty by fiduciaries, a fundamental distinction needs to be drawn between non-fiduciary and fiduciary duties to take care.[134] The non-fiduciary duty to take reasonable care is similar to liability for negligence at Common Law

---

[129] (1991) 85 DLR (4th) 129, 163.   [130] [1996] 1 AC 421, 438.   [131] See Section 18.1.2.(ii), p. 502.

[132] *Cavendish Bentick v Fenn* (1887) 12 App Cas 652; *Nocton v Lord Ashburton* [1914] AC 932, 946; *Swindle v Harrison* [1997] 4 All ER 705; *JJ Harrison (Properties) Ltd v Harrison* [2001] 1 BCLC 158. See Conaglen, 'Equitable compensation for breach of fiduciary duty rules' (2003) 119 LQR 246.

[133] *Swindle v Harrison* [1997] 4 All ER 705.

[134] As recognized by Ipp J in *Permanent Building Society v Wheeler* (1994) 14 ACSR 109, 157–8. See also *Henderson v Merrett Syndicates Ltd* [1995] 2 AC 145, 205 (Lord Browne-Wilkinson); *Bristol and West Building Society v Mothew* [1998] Ch 1, 16–18 (Millett LJ); *Galambos v Perez* 2009 SCC 48, [2009] 3 SCR 247, [37] (Cromwell J) (not all duties owed by a lawyer to their clients are fiduciary duties).

and should be subject to the same tests of causation, mitigation, contributory negligence, and remoteness. So, for example, the defendant will be liable to compensate only for loss that was reasonably foreseeable.[135]

Where the fiduciary breaches a fiduciary duty and the principal seeks equitable compensation, the test of causation that is adopted is the usual 'but for' test.[136] So, for example, in *Swindle v Harrison*,[137] it was recognized that it had to be proved that the loss suffered by the claimant would not have occurred but for the defendant's failure to disclose a material fact in breach of fiduciary duty. In that case, the principal mortgaged her house to buy a restaurant. When another loan fell through, she sought a bridging loan. Her firm of solicitors provided this loan and took a mortgage over the restaurant, but her solicitor did not inform her that the firm would profit from the loan transaction. The restaurant failed and the principal lost her house. She sought equitable compensation on the grounds that, had the solicitor not breached his fiduciary duty, she would not have bought the restaurant and would not have lost her home. The claim failed because the breach had not caused her to lose her home; she would still have accepted the loan and completed the purchase even if full disclosure had been made.[138]

The test of remoteness that is adopted for breach of a fiduciary duty may depend on the nature of the breach. It has been recognized that, if the breach can be regarded 'as the equivalent of fraud', the defendant fiduciary will be liable to compensate the claimant for consequential loss, even if it was unforeseeable.[139] This is identical to the Common Law rule that liability for deceit[140] or for one of the intentional torts[141] is not limited by the foreseeability of the loss suffered. What might be meant by 'fraud' for these purposes is unclear, but it presumably equates with dishonesty or intentional breach of duty,[142] so that, where the fiduciary has acted dishonestly in breaching their fiduciary duty, they will be liable for all losses resulting from the breach even if they are unforeseeable.[143] Presumably, dishonesty is interpreted usually in an objective sense since fiduciaries tend to be professionals, so the fiduciary will have acted dishonestly even if they thought they were acting in the principal's best interests, if this belief was so unreasonable that no reasonable person acting in the fiduciary's profession could have held it.[144]

It also appears that the fiduciary who breaches their fiduciary duty intentionally cannot rely on the claimant's contributory negligence to reduce liability[145] and, because of the protective function of fiduciary law, the better view is that contributory negligence should never be relevant to any claim for breach of fiduciary duty.[146]

---

[135]   *Bristol and West Building Society v Mothew* [1998] Ch 1, 16–18 (Millett LJ). See Elliott (see n. 18).

[136]   *Swindle v Harrison* [1997] 4 All ER 705, 714 (Evans LJ).

[137]   Ibid. Compare *Brickenden v London Loan and Savings Co* (1934) 3 DLR 465, 469 (Lord Thankerton) (PC), which appears to recognize that causation of loss can be assumed. The actual meaning of Lord Thankerton's dictum is unclear and, being a Privy Council decision from Canada that is inconsistent with the clear decision of the Court of Appeal in *Swindle v Harrison*, it is best disregarded. See Conaglen, 'Remedial ramifications of conflicts between a fiduciary's duties' (2010) 126 LQR 72, 82–5.

[138]   This can be contrasted with the test of causation, which is adopted where the defendant has profited from the breach of fiduciary duty. See Section 18.5.2, p. 526.

[139]   *Swindle v Harrison* [1997] 4 All ER 705, 717 (Evans LJ).

[140]   *Smith New Court Securities Ltd v Scrimgeour Vickers (Asset Management) Ltd* [1997] 1 AC 254.

[141]   *Quinn v Leatham* [1901] AC 495, 537.

[142]   See *Nationwide Building Society v Balmor Radmore* [1999] Lloyd's Rep PN 241, 278 (Blackburne J).

[143]   Vos, 'Linking chains of causation: an examination of new approaches to causation in equity and the common law' (2001) 60 CLJ 337, 345.

[144]   By analogy with the test of dishonesty for professionals relating to the efficacy of exemption causes: *Walker v Stones* [2001] QB 902. See Section 17.3.1.(i), p. 477.

[145]   *Nationwide Building Society v Balmor Radmore* [1999] Lloyd's Rep PN 241, 278 (Blackburne J).

[146]   Conaglen (see n. 132), p. 96.

18.5 ACCOUNT OF PROFITS

18.5.1 GENERAL FEATURES

The remedies that have been considered so far have all been compensatory in function. But, where the defendant has profited from a breach of trust or breach of fiduciary duty and that profit exceeds any loss suffered by the claimant, the remedy of account of profits will be awarded as a mechanism to transfer the profit to the claimant.[147] Crucially, this remedy applies equally to breaches of trust and of fiduciary duty.

An account of profits is a mechanism to require an account to be taken in order to determine the profits made by the defendant from the breach, after deducting any expenses incurred. The defendant will be required to pay the net profit made to the claimant. The timing of the assessment of the gain is crucial. In *Nant-y-Glo and Blaina Ironworks Co v Grave*,[148] it was recognized that the defendant company director would be liable to account for the highest value of the shares improperly obtained within the period from the date of the breach to the date of the judgment. In that case, the defendant was liable to account for the shares at the value of £80 per share, even though each share had subsequently fallen to £1 each. This seems an especially harsh decision. The remedy of an account of profits seeks to prevent the defendant from profiting from the wrong. To the extent that the value of any benefit has fallen by the time of judgment, the defendant's profit will have reduced as well. Consequently, the better view is that the profit should be determined at the time of the judgment. This is consistent with those common accounts which operate as a mechanism to compensate the trust for loss suffered.[149]

The remedy of an account of profits can involve either literal restitution, where the defendant's profit was obtained from the claimant and is restored to the claimant,[150] or disgorgement, where the profit was made from a third party without causing any loss to the claimant.[151] Where the profit was made by taking something from the claimant, the account of profits requires the defendant to give the gain *back*; where it was made from a third party, the account of profits requires the defendant to give the benefit *up* to the claimant. In *Murad v Al-Saraj*,[152] a case involving breach of fiduciary duty, Arden LJ described the remedy as a 'procedure to ensure the restitution of profits which ought to have been made for the beneficiary'. On the other hand, Jonathan Parker LJ, in the same case,[153] described the remedy as being neither restitutionary nor compensatory, but designed to strip the fiduciary of profits. But a remedy that is focused on the stripping of the defendant's profits is properly analysed simply as being a gain-based remedy, albeit a remedy that may sometimes operate to disgorge profit rather than being literally restitutionary. The remedy is clearly gain-based rather than compensatory, because it does not depend on whether the claimant suffered loss from the breach,[154] or whether they could have made the profit.[155] Despite this, the Supreme Court has described the remedy as constituting

---

[147] *Vyse v Foster* (1872) 8 Ch App 309, 329 (James LJ).

[148] (1878) 12 Ch D 738.   [149] See Section 18.1.4.(i), p. 505.

[150] See Section 18.1.4.(ii), p. 506.   [151] See Section 18.1.4.(iii), p. 507.

[152] [2005] EWCA Civ 959, [2005] WTLR 1573, [85].

[153] Ibid., at [108].

[154] *Murad v Al-Saraj* [2005] EWCA Civ 959, [2005] WTLR 1573, [58] (Arden LJ). See also *Warman International Ltd v Dwyer* (1995) 182 CLR 541, 557.

[155] *Murad v Al-Saraj* [2005] EWCA Civ 959, [2005] WTLR 1573, [59] (Arden LJ). See also *Regal (Hastings) Ltd v Gulliver* [1967] 2 AC 46, 144 (Lord Russell of Killowen).

'equitable compensation'.[156] But compensation focuses on remedying the claimant's loss, whereas account of profits focuses on the defendant's gain, so using the language of compensation to describe account of profits can only cause categorical confusion.

18.5.2 CAUSATION AND REMOTENESS

Where the defendant has breached the trust or breached their fiduciary duty, it is necessary to ascertain what profits derive from the wrong by considering whether the profits fall within the scope of the fiduciary's duty of loyalty to the principal.[157] This is determined by identifying a reasonable connection between the breach and the profits obtained.[158] If the profit is not obtained by use or by reason of the fiduciary position, the fiduciary will not be liable to account for it.[159] Where the profit was obtained through the use of the fiduciary position it is still appropriate to deduct expenses incurred by the defendant in making the profit, as well as a sum to represent reasonable overheads.[160] The burden is placed on the defendant to show that a particular profit did not derive from the breach of duty.[161] If the defendant is unable to distinguish the profits made from the breach with the profits made legitimately from other sources, they will be liable to disgorge all of the profits, since it will be presumed that they all derive from the breach.[162] This is consistent with the equitable principle that everything is presumed against a fiduciary in breach.[163] This is justified because the special position of the fiduciary means that the breach of fiduciary duty is not the fact that the fiduciary had made a profit, but that the fiduciary seeks to keep this profit for themself.[164]

The usual 'but for' test of causation, which applies where the claimant seeks compensation for loss arising from breach of trust or fiduciary duty,[165] will be interpreted more flexibly when assessing the profits that the defendant obtained from committing a breach of trust or fiduciary duty. This was recognized in the important, but difficult, decision of the Court of Appeal in *Murad v Al-Saraj*,[166] in which it was held that the Court was not concerned with what would have happened but for the breach, but only with whether the fiduciary had profited following the breach. Consequently, a defendant fiduciary will be liable to account to the claimant for profits made from the breach of fiduciary duty even if the profit would have been made had the defendant not committed the wrong. The justifications for this relaxed approach to causation were that, first, for policy reasons, the courts refuse to speculate about what would have happened had the breach of duty not occurred,[167] and,

---

[156] *FHR European Ventures Ltd v Cedar Capital Partners LLC* [2014] UKSC 45, [2015] AC 250, [6] (Lord Neuberger).

[157] *Novoship (UK) Ltd v Mikhaylyuk* [2014] EWCA Civ 908, [2015] QB 499, [96] (Longmore LJ).

[158] *CMS Dolphin Ltd v Simonet* [2001] 2 BCLC 704, [97] (Lawrence Collins J). See also *Swain v The Law Society* [1982] 1 WLR 17.

[159] *Howard v Commissioner of Taxation* [2014] HCA 21, [37] (French CJ and Keane J), [62] (Hayne and Crennan J).

[160] *CMS Dolphin Ltd v Simonet* [2001] 2 BCLC 704, [97] (Lawrence Collins J); *Murad v Al-Saraj* [2005] EWCA Civ 959, [2005] WTLR 1573, [107] (Jonathan Parker LJ).

[161] *Murad v Al-Saraj* [2005] EWCA Civ 959, [2005] WTLR 1573, [77] (Arden LJ).

[162] Ibid., [77] (Arden LJ).

[163] *Warman International Ltd v Dwyer* (1995) 182 CLR 544. This presumption is also significant in the law of tracing: see Section 19.3.3.(iii), p. 562.

[164] Cf. where a non-fiduciary is liable as an accessory for assisting a breach of trust, where the liability to account for profits is dependent on the profits being caused by the assistance. See Section 20.3.3, p. 622.

[165] See Section 18.1.4.(i), p. 503.   [166] [2005] EWCA Civ 959, [2005] WTLR 1573.

[167] Ibid., [76] (Arden LJ). See also *Ex parte James* (1803) 8 Ves 337, 345 (Lord Eldon); *Gwembe Valley Development Co Ltd v Koshy* [2003] EWCA Civ 1048, [2004] BCLC 131, [145] (Mummery LJ).

secondly, there is a need to deter defendants from the temptation of abusing a relationship of trust and confidence.[168]

In *Murad v Al-Saraj*,[169] a majority of the Court of Appeal recognized that the fiduciary, who had failed to disclose a material fact to his principals in breach of fiduciary duty, was liable to account for the whole profit he had made as a result of the principals entering into a joint venture with him, even though some profit might still have been made had the fiduciary made the relevant disclosure. It was recognized that the fiduciary was not liable to account only for those profits which had arisen from a different transaction. The claimants and the defendant had entered into a joint venture to buy a hotel. The defendant fraudulently told the claimants that the purchase price was £4.1 million, when it was actually £3.6 million, and that he would contribute £500,000 in cash. This contribution actually took the form, in part, of a secret commission, which he received for introducing the claimants to the vendor, and a set-off of certain non-enforceable obligations. The trial judge found that, had the actual purchase price and the set-off been disclosed, the claimants would still have agreed to the joint venture, but with a higher profit share for themselves. The majority held that this was irrelevant and the defendant was liable to disgorge all of the profits, both income and capital, which he had made from the joint venture following the sale of the hotel, even though some profit would have been made had the defendant not breached his fiduciary duty.[170] Arden LJ cited the decision of the House of Lords in *Regal (Hastings) Ltd v Gulliver*[171] as authority for this proposition, although it is difficult to see how that case is of any relevance to the determination of the causation issue, other than to affirm that the profits must have been made 'by reason and in course of the fiduciary relationship'.[172] Other cases were cited by Jonathan Parker LJ,[173] but they simply affirmed that the fiduciary should not profit from the breach and that loss suffered by the principal need not be established when gain-based remedies are assessed; they do not engage with the question of how to determine what profit does derive from the breach. The majority appears to have assumed that, since 'but for' causation is relevant to establishing loss for the purposes of equitable compensation,[174] and because loss is not relevant to the account of profits, it must follow that 'but for' causation is not relevant either.[175] But this conclusion does not follow. Nevertheless, the conclusion is consistent with the earlier decision of the Court of Appeal in *United Pan-Europe Communications NV v Deutsche Bank AG*,[176] in which Morritt LJ[177] said: 'I see no justification for any further requirement that the profit shall have been obtained by the fiduciary "by virtue of his position". Such a condition suggests an element of causation which neither principle not the authorities require.' But this is clearly inconsistent with the decision of the House of Lords in *Regal v Gulliver*, in which

---

[168] [2005] EWCA Civ 959, [2005] WTLR 1573, [107] (Jonathan Parker LJ). See also *Bray v Ford* [1896] AC 44, 51 (Lord Herschell); *Consul Development Pty Ltd v DPC Estates Pty Ltd* (1975) 132 CLR 373, 397 (Gibbs J). See also Etherton, 'The legitimacy of proprietary relief' (2014) 2 Birkbeck LR 59, 74.

[169] [2005] EWCA Civ 959, [2005] WTLR 1573. See also *United Pan-Europe Communications NV v Deutsche Bank AG* [2002] 2 BCLC 461, [47] (Morritt LJ); *Gwembe Valley Development Co Ltd v Koshy (No 3)* [2003] EWCA Civ 1048, [2004] 1 BCLC 131; *Novoship (UK) Ltd v Mikhaylyuk* [2014] EWCA Civ 908, [2015] QB 499.

[170] [2005] EWCA Civ 959, [2005] WTLR 1573, [62] (Arden LJ).

[171] [1967] 2 AC 134n, particularly the dictum of Lord Russell of Killowen at 144–5. See Section 15.6.7.(iii), p. 446.

[172] [1967] 2 AC 134n, 143. See also ibid., 153; *Swain v The Law Society* [1982] 1 WLR 17, 36 (Fox LJ); *Warman International Ltd v Dwyer* (1995) 182 CLR 544, 559; *Attorney-General v Blake* [2001] 1 AC 268, 280 (Lord Nicholls).   [173] See e.g. *Parker v McKenna* (1874) LR 10 Ch App 96, 118.

[174] See Section 18.1.4.(i), p. 504.

[175] See also Conaglen, 'Strict fiduciary loyalty and account of profits' (2006) 65 CLJ 278.

[176] [2000] 2 BCLC 461.   [177] Ibid., [47].

this 'further requirement' of the profit arising in the course of the fiduciary relationship was recognized.[178] To confuse matters further, this requirement was even recognized by Jonathan Parker LJ in *Murad v Al-Saraj*[179] itself.

Clarke LJ in *Murad* dissented from the majority's approach on the basis that the question of whether the defendant would have made the profit even had there not been a breach of fiduciary duty was relevant to the extent of the account of profits, although he accepted that it was not relevant to whether there was any liability to account at all.[180] Clarke LJ preferred to treat the assessment of the profits as being dependent on what was an equitable result. But that way confusion and uncertainty lies.

The decision of the majority in *Murad v Al-Saraj* does create some significant difficulties when determining the extent of an account of profits. In assessing the validity of the approach adopted in that case, it is useful to return to first principles. It is clear that the remedy of an account of profits is the usual remedy where a defendant has breached their fiduciary duty. The alternative remedy is that of equitable compensation. To assess that remedy, it is necessary to show that, but for the commission of the wrong, the claimant would not have suffered loss. To obtain an account of profits, however, it is not necessary to show that the claimant had suffered any loss. But it is also clear that the fiduciary who has breached their duty need not account for all profits made from whatever source;[181] some link to the breach of duty must be established. It would be absurd to say, for example, that a defendant who has breached their fiduciary duty and who, at about the same time, won a large sum in a lottery would have to account for that lottery win. Some causative link needs to be shown between the breach and the profit.

So, if causation is relevant and, as the Court of Appeal in *Murad v Al-Saraj* recognized, the profit must arise 'within the scope and ambit of the relevant fiduciary duty',[182] what profit in that case did derive from the breach of fiduciary duty? Surely, if the defendant would have made a profit anyway had there not been a breach of fiduciary duty, the only profit that was caused by the breach must be the difference between the profit that was made and what would otherwise have been made? Now, it is true that Equity has been reluctant to speculate about what might have happened had there not been a breach of duty,[183] but in *Murad v Al-Saraj* the trial judge had been able to conclude that the claimants would have been willing to enter into a joint venture, albeit on different terms, had there been no breach of fiduciary duty. It is this fact that makes it difficult to conclude that the 'but for' test of causation was satisfied on the facts, save as regards the portion of the profit that the defendant would not have made had he made full disclosure of his financial arrangements, since the trial judge had recognized that the claimants would then have negotiated an arrangement under which they would have obtained more profit from the joint venture. It was this profit that the defendant obtained as a result of his breach of fiduciary duty. Further, the question of what might have happened but for the breach has to be considered for the assessment of equitable compensation,[184] and this was considered to be a live issue in *Target Holdings v Redferns*,[185] so there is no technical reason why Equity

---

[178] As it was in *Warman International Ltd v Dwyer* (1995) 182 CLR 544, 559.

[179] [2005] EWCA Civ 959, [2005] WTLR 1573, [116] (Jonathan Parker LJ).

[180] Ibid., at [141].   [181] [2005] EWCA Civ 959, [2005] WTLR 1573, [62] (Arden LJ).

[182] Ibid., [116] (Jonathan Parker LJ).

[183] See *Brickenden v London Loan and Savings Co* [1934] 3 DLR 465, 469 (Lord Thankerton) (Privy Council); *Gray v New Augarita Porcupine Mines Ltd* [1952] 3 DLR 1, 15 (Privy Council).

[184] *Murad v Al-Saraj* [2005] EWCA Civ 959, [110] (Jonathan Parker LJ). See *Bristol and West Building Society v Mothew* [1998] Ch 1, 17 (Millett LJ); *Target Holdings Ltd v Redferns* [1996] 1 AC 421, 436 (Lord Browne-Wilkinson).

[185] [1996] 1 AC 421, 436 (Lord Browne-Wilkinson). See Section 18.2.2.(ii), p. 515.

cannot speculate about this when ordering an account of profits.[186] Consequently, there is no justification for the rejection of the 'but for' test of causation when accounting for profits following a breach of fiduciary duty. It should be necessary to prove that, but for the breach,[187] the profit would not have been made. This does not involve the watering down of the policy of deterring breaches of fiduciary duty. It is simply a matter of ensuring that the profit that must be disgorged derives from the breach of duty.

It is not, however, necessary to prove that the profits obtained by the defendant arose directly from the commission of the wrong; the defendant will also be liable to account for profits indirectly obtained. Consequently, account of profits is not limited by a principle of remoteness. So, for example, in *Gwembe Valley Development Co Ltd v Koshy (No 3)*,[188] the defendant fiduciary was held liable to account for all of the profits that he had made from unauthorized loan transactions. The account included those profits that derived directly from the commission of the wrong, in the form of payments made to him, but also indirect benefits arising from the increase in the value of his shareholding in a company that had been purchased from the profits. It follows, for example, that, if a fiduciary has received a bribe, they should be liable to account for the value of the bribe and any income obtained from its investment.[189] This rejection of the Common Law rules on remoteness is justified by the policy to deter breaches of trust and fiduciary duty by ensuring that the defendant is deprived of all benefits that derive from the commission of the wrong. It was recognized by the Court of Appeal in *Sinclair Investments (UK) Ltd v Versailles Trade Finance Ltd*[190] that the effect of the defendant being required to account for profits indirectly obtained from the commission of the wrong meant that, if the defendant had received a bribe in breach of fiduciary duty and had invested the bribe in land which had increased in value, the defendant would be liable to account to the principal for the value of that land.[191]

This analysis of the cases concerning the award of an account of profits, and the policies underpinning the award of such a remedy, indicates that there is no justification for watering down the usual test of 'but for' causation, since it is vital to show that there is a causative link between the breach of duty and the profit made, for otherwise it is not possible to determine the profits for which the defendant should be accountable. As the High Court of Australia emphasized in *Warman International Ltd v Dwyer*:[192] 'In determining the proper basis for an account of profits, it is of first importance in this, as in other cases, to ascertain precisely what it was that was acquired in consequence of the fiduciary's breach of duty.' Despite this, the policy of deterring breaches of trust and fiduciary duty has resulted in English law recognizing that a fiduciary will be liable to account for any gain made no matter how remote it is from the commission of the breach, as long as there were some kind of causal connection between the breach and the gain, no matter how tenuous. Consequently, liability to account will not be limited to that gain which was a reasonably foreseeable consequence of the breach. So, if a fiduciary obtains a profit in breach of duty and uses it to buy lottery tickets, which they would not otherwise have bought and one of which wins the jackpot, they will be liable to account for the winnings. A causative link to the purchase of the lottery ticket can be established since, but for the profit, the ticket would not have been purchased and so the jackpot would not have been

---

[186] The High Court of Australia was willing to engage in such speculation for the purposes of taking an account in *Warman International Ltd v Dwyer* (1995) 182 CLR 544, 565–6.

[187] The language of 'but for' causation was used by Clarke LJ in his dissenting judgment in *Murad v Al-Saraj* [2005] EWCA Civ 959, [2005] WTLR 1573, [160].   [188] [2003] EWCA Civ 1048, [2004] 1 BCLC 131.

[189] *Murad v Al-Saraj* [2005] EWCA Civ 959, [2005] WTLR 1573, [85] (Arden LJ).

[190] [2001] EWCA Civ 347, [2012] 1 AC 776.

[191] Ibid., [90] (Lord Neuberger MR). Today all the profit, whether obtained directly or indirectly, could be held on constructive trust. See Section 15.7.3, p. 454.   [192] (1995) 182 CLR 544, [40].

won. The fact that the chances of winning the lottery are very small should be irrelevant. The fiduciary should not be allowed to profit from their breach of fiduciary duty and the jackpot win was a relevant gain that they should be required to disgorge.

18.5.3 LIMITING THE ACCOUNT

A problem with ordering an account of profits to be taken is that requiring the defendant to give up all profits made might unfairly benefit the claimant,[193] especially where all of the profit made cannot be attributed to the commission of the wrong. This might be resolved by simple application of the 'but for' test of causation, but two particular mechanisms have been identified that can assist in the assessment of the profits for which the defendant should account to the claimant. These are simply particular methods of showing that the profit made was not causatively linked to the breach of duty.

(i) Limiting the period for which the account must be taken

Where the nature of the wrong is such that the defendant earns a profit over a period of time, and is still earning the profit at the time of the trial, a difficult question arises as to whether the defendant should be required to account both for all of the profits that have already been made and also those that may be made in the future. This was a matter that was examined in *Warman International Ltd v Dwyer*,[194] in which the High Court of Australia recognized that, where it is equitable to do so, the defendant may be required to account only for the profits generated over a specified period of time. This was the type of account that was ordered in *Warman International Ltd v Dwyer* itself. The defendant in that case was an employee who had breached his fiduciary duty by taking a business opportunity for himself. It was held that the defendant was required to account only for those profits that he would not have acquired but for the breach of fiduciary duty,[195] which were found to be two years' profits made from the exploitation of the business opportunity.

(ii) The equitable allowance

Alternatively, the defendant may be awarded an equitable allowance in respect of those profits that were earned by virtue of the defendant's own efforts and this sum will be deducted from the amount for which the defendant has to account to the claimant.[196] The assessment of the allowance is not necessarily limited to the value of the fiduciary's work, but can also include part of the profit made from the venture if it is considered to be just to award this.[197] The award of the allowance is not automatic and will be awarded only where it is equitable to do so. The decision to award the allowance, and the amount awarded, depends on the operation of judicial discretion, which will be influenced by a variety of factors, including the good faith of the defendant.[198] So where there is an abuse of the fiduciary relationship by the fiduciary, the allowance might be reduced[199] or not awarded at all.

---

[193] See *Fyffes Group Ltd v Templeman* [2000] 2 Lloyd's Rep 643, 672 (Toulson J).

[194] (1995) 182 CLR 544. See also *Murad v Al-Saraj* [2005] EWCA Civ 959, [2005] WTLR 1573, [115] (Jonathan Parker LJ).

[195] The High Court also suggested that the profits might be split between the claimant and the defendant, but that this would normally be appropriate only where there was an antecedent profit-sharing arrangement.

[196] See *Re Jarvis (deceased)* [1958] 1 WLR 815; *Boardman v Phipps* [1967] 2 AC 46; *Warman International Ltd v Dwyer* (1995) 182 CLR 544, [33].

[197] *O'Sullivan and Management Agency and Music Ltd* [1985] QB 428, 468 (Fox LJ).

[198] *Boardman v Phipps* [1967] 2 AC 46; *Guinness v Saunders* [1990] 2 AC 663; *Warman International Ltd v Dwyer* (1995) 182 CLR 544.

[199] *O'Sullivan and Management Agency and Music Ltd* [1985] QB 428, 468 (Fox LJ); *Nottingham University v Fishel* [2000] IRLR 471, 485 (Elias J).

Although the award of the equitable allowance to a fiduciary who has breached their fiduciary duty was recognized by the House of Lords in *Boardman v Phipps*,[200] a subsequent decision of the same court, *Guinness plc v Saunders*,[201] casts doubt on the legitimacy of the award of an allowance to the fiduciary in such circumstances. In *Guinness plc v Saunders*, £5.2 million had been paid to a director of Guinness for the advice and services that he had given in respect of the takeover of another company by Guinness. It was accepted that this money had been received by the director in breach of his fiduciary duty and consequently he was liable to repay it to Guinness. But the director argued that he was entitled to an equitable allowance for the services that he had supplied to the company. The House of Lords rejected this claim on two grounds:

(1) Equity had no power to grant an allowance to a director who had breached their fiduciary duty if the company's articles made no provision for such a payment.[202] The reason for this is that the court is reluctant to interfere with the affairs of the company, and so the decision to award an allowance should be a matter for the company and not for the court.

(2) Because of the fundamental principle that trustees are not entitled to be remunerated for their services except where such remuneration is provided for in the trust deed, it was considered to follow that a fiduciary should not be awarded an equitable allowance save in the most exceptional circumstances under which the award of the allowance would not encourage the fiduciary to put themselves in a position in which their personal interest conflicted with the duty that was owed to the principal.[203] Since the nature of the director's breach of duty was to place him in a position in which his personal interest conflicted with his duty to the company, it followed that the equitable allowance was denied to him.

But neither of these reasons is convincing. First, why should the allowance be unavailable where the fiduciary is a director? If the defendant has incurred expense and provided services, particularly where the expense and services have benefited the claimant company, why should this not be taken into account when determining the extent of the defendant's liability to the claimant? Secondly, the award of the equitable allowance should not be considered to be encouraging the fiduciary to place themselves in a position in which personal interest and duty to the principal conflict. This is because the equitable allowance should not enable the fiduciary to profit from their breach of duty; rather it should simply ensure that the fiduciary is remunerated for expense incurred and services provided. There can surely be no objection to a fiduciary being remunerated, since this would not encourage the fiduciary to breach their fiduciary duty. It has, in fact, been recognized that there is nothing wrong with the court granting an allowance to remunerate a fiduciary for services provided to the principal.[204] The real objection arises where the fiduciary is allowed to profit from the breach of duty.[205] Despite this, *Guinness v Saunders* was followed in *Re Quarter Master UK Ltd v Pyke*,[206] in which an equitable allowance was not awarded to two directors who had exploited a business opportunity for themselves, on the ground that directors should not profit from their breach of fiduciary duty and that the directors concerned had not demonstrated special skills or taken unusual risks.

---

[200] [1967] 2 AC 46. See Section 15.6.7.(iii), p. 444.
[201] [1990] 2 AC 663.   [202] Ibid., 692 (Lord Templeman).   [203] Ibid., 701 (Lord Goff).
[204] *Dale v IRC* [1954] AC 11, 27 (Lord Normand). See Harpum, 'Fiduciary obligations and fiduciary powers: where are we going?', in *Privacy and Loyalty*, ed. Birks (Oxford: Clarendon Press, 1997), p. 159. See Section 12.7, p. 354, for analysis of when trustees can be remunerated.
[205] But note *O'Sullivan v Management Agency and Music Ltd* [1985] QB 428, in which the Court of Appeal contemplated that the allowance might include a profit element.   [206] [2005] 1 BCLC 245.

The major difficulty with the award of an equitable allowance arises from the uncertainty as to the reason for awarding the allowance. In fact, two justifications can be identified.[207]

Unjust enrichment

It might be possible to conclude that the award of an equitable allowance constitutes a mechanism to ensure that the claimant is not unjustly enriched at the fiduciary's expense. This unjust enrichment would otherwise arise because, if the effect of the defendant's work is that the claimant obtains a benefit, the claimant will have been enriched at the defendant's expense, with the ground of restitution being total failure of basis, in that the defendant would have expected to be remunerated for their services by retaining the profit, but they would receive nothing if they were liable to disgorge all of the profit to the claimant. Although this unjust enrichment explanation of the equitable allowance can be used to justify why the allowance was awarded in certain cases in which the principal was benefited by what the fiduciary had done,[208] this explanation has never been recognized by the courts and, crucially, the nature of the allowance that is awarded does not appear to be assessed by reference to the value of the benefit obtained by the principal. Rather, the allowance seeks only to remunerate the fiduciary for their work and skill.[209] Also this explanation of the equitable allowance would be inapplicable in any case in which the principal had not obtained a benefit from the fiduciary simply because the principal would not have been enriched at the fiduciary's expense.

Causation

The alternative, and preferable, explanation of the equitable allowance is that, where the defendant has made a profit as a result of the exercise of their time and skill, it is not possible to say that all of the defendant's profits derived from the commission of the wrong. Since the defendant should be required to disgorge only those profits that did arise from the wrongdoing, it follows that the equitable allowance seeks to apportion profits so that the claimant recovers only those profits that derive from the breach of trust or fiduciary duty, and the defendant is allowed to retain those profits that can be considered to derive from their work and skill. It will, of course, be very difficult to apportion the profits exactly, but at least the existence of the allowance gives the court the opportunity to determine in general terms how much of the profits derived from the defendant's contribution. This explanation of the award of the allowance was expressly recognized by the High Court of Australia in *Warman International Ltd v Dwyer*, which noted that the allowance was available:[210]

> when it appears that a significant proportion of an increase in profits has been generated by the skill, efforts, property and resources of the fiduciary, the capital which he has introduced and the risks he has taken, so long as they are not risks to which the principal's property has been exposed. Then it may be said that the relevant proportion of the increased

---

[207] See Harding, 'Justifying fiduciary allowances', in *The Goals of Private Law*, ed. Robertson and Wu (Oxford: Oxford University Press, 2009), ch. 14, who prefers to justify the allowance on the basis of desert in that the fiduciary's deserving conduct outweighs the application of policies of deterrence to the fiduciary, which is at least consistent with the award being assessed liberally.

[208] Most notably *Boardman v Phipps* [1967] 2 AC 46. But, if the equitable allowance does seek to ensure that the claimant is not unjustly enriched, it should also have been awarded in *Guinness plc v Saunders* [1990] 2 AC 663, in which the company had also been benefited by the defendant's services.

[209] See *Boardman v Phipps* [1967] 2 AC 46, 102 (Lord Cohen) and 112 (Lord Hodson).

[210] (1995) 128 ALR 201, 212.

profits is not the product or consequence of the plaintiff's property but the product of the fiduciary's skill, efforts, property and resources.

If the equitable allowance seeks to apportion the profits between those profits that derive from the breach and those deriving from the defendant's personal contribution, it should have followed that the director in *Guinness plc v Saunders* was awarded an allowance, because he had provided valuable services for the remuneration that he had received. But the denial of the allowance in that case might be justified on another ground, although it was a ground that was not specifically recognized by the court. Although the House of Lords assumed throughout that the director had been acting in good faith, there was clearly a suspicion of bad faith, since criminal charges had been brought as a result of the acquisition of the company by Guinness and an application had been made to extradite the director to the United States. If the House of Lords had been satisfied on the balance of probabilities that the director had been acting in bad faith, it would have been appropriate, in the exercise of the equitable jurisdiction, to decline to award an equitable allowance.

18.6 INTEREST

In addition to being liable to compensate the claimant for breach of trust or fiduciary duty, or liable to give up gains made as a result of the breach, the defendant trustee or fiduciary will be liable to pay interest on any amount due.[211]

18.6.1 FUNCTION OF INTEREST

In *Attorney-General v Alford*,[212] Lord Cranworth recognized that there were three circumstances under which the payment of interest might be relevant:

(1) Where the trustee received a payment of interest. This will be relevant where the trustee or fiduciary is liable to account for profits arising from breach of duty. Such a defendant will also be liable to account for any interest payments received from a third party. Here, the function of the interest award is to ensure that the defendant disgorges all profits arising from the wrongdoing.

(2) Where it is fairly to be presumed that the trustee did receive interest such that they are estopped from saying that they did not receive it. Here, the defendant is presumed to have made a profit from the wrong and will be liable to give up that amount of interest that they could have earned from having the money that they owed to the claimant.

(3) Where the trustee ought to have received interest. This will be relevant where, for example, a trustee has failed to invest trust property and so failed to obtain interest on the investment. The liability of the trustee to compensate the trust for the loss suffered will include an amount to compensate for the loss of interest that the trust did not obtain from the investment.

Where the breach of trust or fiduciary duty has caused a loss without any gain being made by the defendant, the claimant will seek only compensatory interest, to compensate the claimant for the loss that they failed to make. But, where the breach has caused a loss and resulted in a gain to the defendant, the claimant has a choice to claim either compensatory or disgorgement interest, with the latter reflecting the actual or presumed interest gained

---

[211] See generally Elliott, 'Rethinking interest on withheld and misapplied trust money' [2001] Conv 313.
[212] (1855) 4 De GM & G 843, 851.

by the defendant, and the claimant will exercise this choice depending on whether the loss or the gain is greater. An order for the payment of interest cannot be awarded to punish the defendant.[213] This is consistent with the rejection of penal awards for breach of trust or fiduciary duty.[214]

This approach to assessment of interest following breach of trust or fiduciary duty is reflected in the cases, notably *Wallersteiner v Moir (No 2)*.[215] In that case the defendant was a director of a company who breached his fiduciary duty by using company funds for his own purposes. He was liable to repay the amount taken and also to pay interest, which was assessed with reference to what the money was worth to him. Since he could have borrowed an equivalent amount of money at commercial rates of interest, this was considered to be the value of the benefit to him. Where, however, the breach of duty involves causing a loss to the claimant, the function of interest will similarly be to compensate the claimant for the loss suffered. So, in *Bartlett v Barclays Bank Trust Co Ltd (No 2)*,[216] Brightman LJ recognized that the function of the award of interest where a trustee failed to pay money to the trust was to compensate the beneficiaries for what they should have received. This was to be assessed with reference to the rate of interest paid on the courts' short-term investment account.

18.6.2 MEASURE OF INTEREST

English law recognizes two measures of interest. The first is simple interest, which is calculated by reference to the sum owed by the defendant to the claimant. Judges have a discretion to award simple interest by virtue of section 35A of the Senior Courts Act 1981. The other measure is compound interest, which is calculated with reference both to the sum owed by the defendant and also the interest that has already been incurred. Consequently, awarding compound interest is likely to give the claimant more money. Traditionally, there was only an equitable jurisdiction to award compound interest.[217] Consequently, it was necessary to establish a breach of trust or fiduciary duty, or the commission of some other equitable wrong, before compound interest was awarded. This proved to be a significant reason why claimants might wish to identify claims based on equitable wrongdoing rather than at Common Law.[218] In *Sempra Metals v IRC*[219] the House of Lords recognized that compound interest is now generally available regardless of whether the claim is equitable or one brought at Common Law, such as claims for breach of contract or unjust enrichment.

The award of compound interest for equitable wrongdoing can be justified by the general principle that wrongdoers should not profit from their wrongs and so the award of compound interest is consistent with the policy behind the award of the disgorgement measure of remedies. Where a trustee or a fiduciary is liable to the trust or the principal, a debt arises immediately the liability is incurred at the time of breach. At that point, the defendant should pay the money due to the claimant, even though assessment of any loss is not calculated until the date of judgment. The failure to discharge the liability immediately it is incurred means that the defendant will have profited from the use of this money,

---

[213] *Burdick v Garrick* (1870) LR 5 Ch App 233, 241 (Lord Hatherley LC). See Chambers (see n. 25), p. 36.

[214] See Section 18.1.4.(v), p. 508.

[215] [1975] QB 373.   [216] [1980] Ch 515.

[217] *Wallersteiner v Moir (No 2)* [1975] QB 373, 397 (Buckley LJ); *President of India v La Pintada Compania Navigacion SA* [1985] AC 104, 115 (Lord Brandon of Oakbrook).

[218] See e.g. *Westdeutsche Landesbank Girozentrale v Islington LBC* [1996] AC 669.

[219] [2007] UKHL 34, [2008] 1 AC 561. See Ridge, 'Pre-judgment compound interest' (2010) 126 LQR 279.

since the defendant does not need to borrow an equivalent amount of money from a bank. Consequently, the value of this benefit should be assessed as what the defendant has saved by not having to pay for this amount of money. Usually, interest that is paid to a bank will be assessed as compound interest, so this is what the defendant will have saved and this should be assessed at the commercial rate of interest, save if the claimant could have borrowed the money at a cheaper rate of interest.[220]

18.7 ELECTION BETWEEN INCONSISTENT REMEDIES

Both compensatory and gain-based remedies may be available in respect of the same breach of trust or breach of fiduciary duty. But, where these remedies are inconsistent,[221] the claimant will need to elect between them, usually before judgment is entered against the defendant, unless the claimant is not able to make an informed choice until later.[222] Once the election has been made, the claimant cannot then claim the other remedy. Although the cases use the language of remedies being inconsistent, in reality the real concern is to ensure that the claimant does not accumulate remedies excessively.[223]

The question whether loss-based and gain-based remedies are inconsistent can be difficult to determine, as illustrated by the decision of the Privy Council in *Personal Representatives of Tang Man Sit v Capacious Investments Ltd*.[224] In that case, a landowner had agreed to assign some houses to the claimant, but no deed of assignment was executed. The landowner let the houses without the claimant's agreement. The landowner died and the claimant sued his executors for breach of trust by virtue of the fact that the effect of the agreement to assign the houses was that the landowner held them on trust for the claimant. The trial judge had ordered the defendants to account for any profits made from the landowner letting the houses after the agreement was made, and to compensate the claimant for the loss arising from the lost rental on the houses and their loss of value. The Privy Council held that the remedies of account of profits and equitable compensation for loss of use of the properties were inconsistent. This was because the account of profits represented the money that the landowner had received from the use of the properties in breach of trust, whereas equitable compensation represented the financial return that the claimant would have received for the same period had it been able to use the properties. The wrong that enabled the defendant to gain the profit also caused the loss to the claimant.

It does not follow from the decision in *Tang Man Sit*, however, that compensatory and gain-based remedies are always inconsistent,[225] although great care must be taken to ensure that the two remedies are compatible. For example, in *Tang Man Sit* itself, if

---

[220] See *Benedetti v Sawiris* [2013] UKSC 50, [2014] AC 938; *Littlewoods Retail Ltd v HMRC (No 2)* [2015] EWCA Civ 515, [2016] Ch 373.

[221] *Tang Man Sit v Capacious Investments Ltd* [1996] AC 514, 521 (PC).

[222] *Island Records Ltd v Tring International plc* [1996] 1 WLR 1256, 1258. See also *Warman International Ltd v Dwyer* (1995) 182 CLR 544, 570.

[223] See Watterson, 'Alternative and cumulative remedies: what is the difference?' (2003) 11 RLR 7, who concludes that there should be no need for election between remedies, it being sufficient that the claimant is prohibited from accumulating remedies that exceed the minimum necessary to realize the aim of each remedy. See also Watterson, 'An account of profits or damages? The history of orthodoxy' (2004) 24 OJLS 471.

[224] [1996] AC 514.

[225] That an account of profits and equitable compensation are not necessarily inconsistent was accepted by the Privy Council: [1996] AC 514, 522.

the claimant had elected to take the profits, it is clear that it could not also have claimed compensation for the income that it had lost from being unable to lease the properties, since the defendant's profits arose from the same event that caused the claimant's loss, namely that the defendant, rather than the claimant, had leased the properties. But there would have been nothing to stop the claimant from claiming, in addition to an account of profits, compensation in respect of the capital loss to the properties arising from the breach of trust, namely that the tenancies had resulted in wear and tear to the properties, and that the value of the properties had decreased by reason of their being leased. In such circumstances, the remedies could be considered to be cumulative. In *Maheson s/o Thambiah v Malaysia Government Officers' Co-operative Housing Society Ltd*,[226] however, the defendant, in return for a bribe, had caused the claimant to buy land at an overvalue. The claimant sued the defendant both for the amount of the bribe and for damages for fraud for the loss caused by the purchase. It was held by the Privy Council that the two remedies were inconsistent, because, if the claimant were to recover the value of the bribe, this would reduce its loss in buying the land at an overvalue. Consequently, the claimant had to elect between the two remedies.

---

[226] [1979] AC 374. See also *Petrotrade Inc v Smith* [2000] 1 Lloyd's Rep 486; *Fyffes Group Ltd v Templeman* [2000] 2 Lloyd's Rep 643.

19

PROPRIETARY CLAIMS AND REMEDIES

19.1 FUNDAMENTAL PRINCIPLES

Where a trustee or fiduciary has breached a duty, they may, as we have seen in the last chapter, be personally liable to the beneficiaries or the principal either for the gain that he they have made or the loss that they have caused. Alternatively, if the breach of duty has involved the transfer of property to themselves, the trustee or fiduciary will be liable to restore that property to the trust or to the principal. But what is the basis of this liability? Alternatively, the trustee or fiduciary may have transferred that property to a third party in breach of duty, in return for which the trustee or fiduciary may have received substitute property. Can the beneficiaries or principal claim that substitute property, and, if they can, what is the basis for making such a claim? Or perhaps the trustee or fiduciary gave the property to a third party in breach of duty and that third party has retained the property, or has sold it and now retains the substitute property. Is the third party liable to give the original property or the substitute property to the beneficiaries or principal? These are the key questions that will be considered in this chapter.

19.1.1 PROPRIETARY CLAIMS AND REMEDIES

A crucial distinction needs to be drawn between proprietary claims and proprietary remedies, a distinction that has been judicially recognized.[1] A proprietary claim requires the claimant to show that the defendant has received an asset in which the claimant has a proprietary interest. Once the claimant has been able to establish the receipt of an asset in which they have such an interest, the emphasis then shifts to identify the appropriate remedy that should be awarded to enforce that right.

Where, for example, a trustee has misappropriated trust property in breach of trust, the beneficiary may bring a claim in respect of the property taken by the trustee. Such claims will be founded on the beneficiary's equitable right to the property and so are properly characterized as proprietary claims. But, although the claim is founded on the beneficiary's proprietary rights, the remedy that is awarded is not necessarily a proprietary one.[2]

---

[1] *Trustee of the Property of FC Jones and Sons (a firm) v Jones* [1997] Ch 159, 168 (Millett LJ).
[2] See *Boscawen v Bajwa* [1996] 1 WLR 328, 334 (Millett LJ).

There are two different types of remedy that are available in respect of equitable proprietary claims:

(1) One is a proprietary remedy that enables the claimant to assert rights against particular property that remains in the defendant's possession. This property may be the original property in which the claimant had property rights or property that has been substituted for the original property.

(2) The other is a personal remedy for the value of the property that has been received by the defendant, but has not been retained, so that the defendant no longer has any property against which the claimant can assert any property rights. This can still be characterized as a proprietary *claim*, because it depends on the defendant having received property in which the claimant had property rights, but the *remedy* sought will be personal, since the defendant no longer has the property, so the claimant can recover only the value of the property received by the defendant.

In both situations, however, it is necessary for the claimant to establish that the defendant had received property in which the claimant has an equitable proprietary interest. This will be examined in this chapter, as will the proprietary remedies that are available. Proprietary claims in which the claimant seeks a personal remedy will be examined in Chapter 20.[3]

19.1.2 THE NATURE OF PROPRIETARY REMEDIES

A proprietary remedy enables the claimant to assert rights against property that is in the defendant's possession.[4] There are two distinct categories of proprietary remedy:

(1) where the claimant is able to recover property that is in the defendant's possession in which the claimant has a property right, or an appropriate share of the value of that property; and

(2) where the claimant is able to recover only the value of the property that is in the defendant's possession, but the claimant has a security interest in the property in which the claimant has a property right.

19.1.3 THE ADVANTAGES OF PROPRIETARY REMEDIES

Proprietary remedies have three significant advantages over personal remedies.

(i) Priority over other creditors

Where the defendant has become insolvent, a personal remedy may be worthless, since such a remedy only creates a debt owed by the defendant to the claimant. Until this debt has been discharged, the claimant is merely a creditor of the defendant, without any security interest in the defendant's property. Consequently, the claimant's claim for payment will rank equally with other claims of the defendant's general creditors as regards the distribution of the defendant's assets. If the defendant has sufficient assets to pay off all of the creditors, this will not be a hardship. But, if the defendant has insufficient assets, the claimant may not receive the full amount that is due and may not receive anything at all. This is because, when assets are distributed upon the debtor's insolvency, they are distributed according to a list of priorities. Unsecured creditors will not receive anything

---

[3] See e.g. the action for unconscionable receipt of trust property, discussed in Section 20.2.3.(i), p. 596.

[4] The law relating to these remedies is examined in more detail in Section 19.4, p. 574.

until the claims of creditors with proprietary rights and the claims of preferential creditors have been satisfied, and the expenses of the insolvency proceedings paid. Consequently, if the claimant can show that they have an equitable proprietary or security interest in some of the assets in the defendant's possession, the claimant will rank above the general unsecured creditors in the distribution of those assets and the claim is more likely to be satisfied.[5] This will be an advantage regardless of whether the defendant is a trustee, a fiduciary,[6] or a third party.

(ii) Increase in value

Another advantage of some proprietary remedies arises where the property that has been received by the defendant has increased in value. In such circumstances, the claimant would clearly prefer to assert their rights against the property itself and so gain the benefit of the increased value. This advantage will arise only where the claimant can assert an equitable right in the asset rather than a security interest, since the latter interest secures only the value of the property assessed at the time of receipt and not any subsequent increase in the value of that property. Where the claimant can assert an equitable property interest in the asset that is in the defendant's possession, this will be disadvantageous if that property has fallen in value. In such circumstances, the claimant will elect to have a security interest in respect of a claim to the value of the property assessed at the time of receipt.

(iii) Claims against third parties

A further advantage of remedies involving the assertion of proprietary rights rather than a security interest is that they are available where the property in which the claimant has a proprietary interest has been received by a third party, without needing to prove that the third-party recipient was aware or should have been aware of the claimant's proprietary right. In other words, the award of proprietary remedies does not depend on the proof of fault.[7] This can be compared with the award of personal remedies for proprietary claims where typically fault must be proved before the remedy can be awarded.[8]

19.1.4 THE NATURE OF LIABILITY

One of the most controversial issues relating to proprietary claims and remedies concerns the legal basis for making such claims. This is a topic about which a great deal has been written, but it is possible to identify some clear principles to assist with the analysis of the law.

(i) Claims relating to the original property

Where the claimant has an equitable interest in property, such as the beneficial interest in property held on trust, and the defendant receives and retains the property that has been transferred in breach of trust, the claim of the beneficiaries to recover that property is founded on their continuing rights in that property.[9] So, for example, if Alan, a trustee, misappropriates £1,000 of shares from the trust, which he gives to his wife, Brenda, the beneficiaries will be able to rely on their equitable property rights to the shares and recover them from Brenda. Of course, they would alternatively have a claim against Alan for

---

[5] The extent of the priority that the claimant will gain over other creditors will depend upon the type of proprietary remedy that is awarded. See Section 19.4, p. 574.

[6] See *Re Hallett's Estate* (1880) 13 Ch D 696, concerning an insolvent solicitor.

[7] See Section 9.4, p. 278, for criticism of this advantage.

[8] See Section 20.2.3.(i), p. 600.

[9] See especially Birks, *Unjust Enrichment*, 2nd edn (Oxford: Oxford University Press, 2005), ch. 8.

breach of trust, but he may be insolvent or may have disappeared, so that the claim against Brenda will be significant. Also, if the shares have increased in value, the beneficiaries will wish to recover the shares from her and so get the benefit of the increased value.

The beneficiaries' claim to recover the original property that has been misappropriated from the trust will be founded on their continuing property rights in the shares. Since the transfer from the trust was in breach of trust, it was unauthorized and so no overreaching of the trust property will have taken place.[10] The beneficiaries continued to have equitable rights in the shares throughout and they will be able to rely on those rights to recover the shares. This can usefully be described as a claim to vindicate their equitable property rights arising within the law of equitable property.

(ii) Claims to substitute property

Much more difficult to explain is the situation in which the recipient of the property in which the claimant has an equitable property interest disposes of it and obtains substitute property in exchange, or the situation in which the original property is mixed with other property, such as where the claimant's money is mixed with the defendant's money so that the claimant's money is no longer identifiable. If the original property has been dissipated, the claimant will wish to claim the substitute property. For example, if Alan misappropriates £1,000 from the trust and gives it to Brenda, who then uses the money to buy shares, can the beneficiaries bring a proprietary claim in respect of the shares?[11]

This is a completely different scenario from the previous one, since in that case the claimant was simply continuing to assert the right that he or she had retained in respect of the original property. Where that property has been substituted for another piece of property, how can the claimant assert a right in respect of that new property? Although it is clear that the claimant can bring a claim in respect of the substitute property,[12] two different models for analysing this have been suggested.

Unjust enrichment

It has been suggested by a number of commentators[13] that the claimant can assert a right in respect of the substitute property by reference to the unjust enrichment principle. To establish that the defendant has been unjustly enriched, the claimant needs to show that the defendant has received an enrichment, at the expense of the claimant, within one of the recognized circumstances of injustice, known as grounds of restitution, and that none of the defences to such a claim apply.[14] In the simple case in which a trustee misappropriates trust property and gives it to a third party, who then exchanges it for substitute property, the beneficiaries will be able to assert an equitable right in this new property, according to this unjust enrichment theory, if the third party can be considered to have been unjustly enriched at the expense of the beneficiaries. It will be possible to show that the third party has been enriched because the substitute property will be valuable. If it can be shown that the value from the trust has been used to obtain the substitute property, it will be possible to establish that the third party has been enriched at the expense of the beneficiaries. As regards the identification of a ground of restitution, the beneficiaries will typically be

---

[10] See Section 3.5.4, p. 46.

[11] The beneficiaries will often not be able to claim the money paid to the vendor of the shares because he or she will typically have the defence of being a bona fide purchaser for value. See Section 19.5.1, p. 584.

[12] See Section 19.3.3, p. 559.

[13] Notably Birks, 'Property, unjust enrichment and tracing' [2001] CLP 231; and Burrows, 'Proprietary restitution: unmasking unjust enrichment' (2001) 117 LQR 412.

[14] *Banque Financière de la Cité v Parc (Battersea) Ltd* [1999] 1 AC 221, 227 (Lord Steyn).

unaware that the trustee has misappropriated property from the trust. It has been suggested that the ground of restitution might be ignorance of the misappropriation of the property,[15] or absence of authority or consent.[16] Assuming that the defendant had not changed his or her position as a result of receiving the substitute property,[17] the defendant would have been unjustly enriched at the expense of the beneficiaries and consequently an equitable right to the substitute property would be recognized.

The chief proponent of this unjust enrichment analysis of property claims to substitute property was Birks. Crucial to his argument was the proposition that rights to property can be generated only by events.[18] The event might be consensual, such as property rights arising from the express trust; or a result of wrongdoing, such as the constructive trust arising from breach of fiduciary duty;[19] or from unjust enrichment.[20] Where an innocent party has in their possession substitute property that represents the property misappropriated from the trust, it is not possible for the beneficiaries to assert rights to this new property by reference to a consensual transaction or to wrongdoing, but, according to Birks, it is possible to do so by reference to unjust enrichment.

This unjust enrichment analysis of claims to recover substitute property is fundamentally flawed in that it is not supported by authority, is unprincipled, is artificial, and has specifically been rejected by the House of Lords and the Supreme Court.[21] The proponents of the unjust enrichment theory of proprietary claims to substitute property have, at various times, identified a number of cases that they consider to be consistent with this approach, but there is no case that explicitly recognizes that rights to property can arise from the defendant's unjust enrichment. Birks[22] considered that *Foskett v McKeown*[23] was such a case, even though the majority judgments clearly contradict this, and that there are other cases that are consistent with this approach, including *Sinclair v Brougham*,[24] but this has been overruled,[25] and *Chase Manhattan Bank v Israel-British Bank*,[26] but this has been reinterpreted by the House of Lords.[27] Further, neither of these cases explicitly recognizes that property rights can derive from unjust enrichment. The Supreme Court in *Bank of Cyprus UK Ltd v Menelaou*[28] recognized that a claim to recover property in which the claimant had a proprietary interest, whether original or substitute property, was a claim to vindicate property rights rather than to reverse the defendant's unjust enrichment. It was, however, recognized that the proprietary remedy of subrogation,[29] which gives the claimant a security interest, did respond to the defendant's unjust enrichment,[30] although no explanation was given for this distinction.

If the unjust enrichment principle is to be used to enable claims to recover substitute property, the elements of that principle would need to be established in the usual way. The key difficulty concerns the identification of a recognized ground of restitution, especially

---

[15] Burrows, *The Law of Restitution*, 3rd edn (Oxford: Oxford University Press, 2011), ch. 16.

[16] Birks (see n. 13), p. 246. See also *Goff and Jones: The Law of Unjust Enrichment*, 9th edn, ed. Mitchell, Mitchell, and Watterson (London Sweet and Maxwell, 2016), ch. 8.

[17] See Section 19.5.2, p. 585, for analysis of the defence of change of position.

[18] Birks (see n. 13), p. 239.   [19] See Section 9.3.7, p. 273.

[20] Birks also recognized the category of miscellaneous events that might generate property rights, such as rights arising from prescription.

[21] *Foskett v McKeown* [2001] AC 102; *Bank of Cyprus UK Ltd v Menelaou* [2015] UKSC 66, [2016] AC 176, [37] (Lord Clarke) and [98] (Lord Neuberger).

[22] Birks (see n. 9), pp. 34–6.   [23] [2001] AC 102. See Section 19.1.6.(vi), p. 546.

[24] [1914] AC 398.   [25] *Westdeutsche Landesbank Girozentrale v Islington LBC* [1996] AC 669.

[26] [1981] Ch 105. See Section 9.3.1, p. 258.

[27] *Westdeutsche Landesbank Girozentrale v Islington LBC* [1996] AC 669. See Section 9.3.1, p. 258.

[28] [2015] UKSC 66, [2016] AC 176.   [29] See Section 19.4.3, p. 578.

[30] See also *Lowick Rose LLP v Swynson Ltd* [2017] UKSC 32, [2017] 2 WLR 1161.

where the claimant is unaware of the misappropriation of the property. The suggested grounds of ignorance or absence of authority or consent have not been recognized by the courts.[31] This absence of recognition of grounds of restitution relevant to proprietary claims is not surprising, because it is not necessary to rely on the unjust enrichment principle at all.[32] Rather, there is a different explanation as to how a claimant can successfully make a claim to substitute property. This is the vindication of property rights theory, the essence of which was recognized by the House of Lords in *Foskett v McKeown*,[33] which specifically rejected the unjust enrichment theory.

Vindication of property rights

According to the vindication of property rights theory, whether the claimant is able to assert rights in substitute property that is in the defendant's possession is a matter for the law of property and does not require the claim to be fitted artificially within the law of unjust enrichment.[34] As long as the claimant can show that he or she has an interest in property that had been taken from the claimant or transferred by the claimant, and the claimant continues to have that interest either in the original property or other property that can be shown to have been substituted for the original property, the claimant will be able to vindicate his or her property rights in respect of the property that is in the defendant's possession. It will be seen from this description of vindication of property rights that this theory operates both as regards claims to the original property and to substitute property. How the claimant proves that the property in the possession of the defendant is property in which the claimant has a proprietary interest depends on the application of the following and tracing rules, which will be examined later in this chapter.[35] But, crucially, once the claimant has shown that the defendant has property in which the claimant had a proprietary interest at the time of receipt, nothing else needs to be proved to establish the claimant's cause of action. If the defendant has the claimant's property, he or she should return it, or its value, to the claimant. So, for example, if the trustee, Alan, misappropriates money from the trust and gives it to his daughter, Carol, who uses the money to buy shares, the beneficiaries will be able to claim those shares by relying on their equitable proprietary rights to the money, because that money has been used to buy the shares. The original property rights can now be asserted against the substitute property simply because that property represents the original property and the rights to the original property are transmitted to the substitute property. There is no need to resort to the language of unjust enrichment to establish such a claim. No new right to property is created; an existing right to property continues to subsist.

Assessment of the principles

Despite the clear recognition of the vindication of property rights principle in *Foskett v McKeown*, some commentators have rejected this analysis of how claims to substitute property can be made, most notably Birks.[36] He argued that the vindication of property rights is not an event and so cannot explain how rights to new property can be created.[37] Clearly, vindication of property rights is not an event; rather it is a principle that is not

---

[31] See *Handayo v Tjong Very Sumito* [2013] SGA 44, [111] (Rajah JA) (Singapore High Court).

[32] *Foskett v McKeown* [2001] 1 AC 102, 127 (Lord Millett).

[33] Ibid. The language of vindicating property rights does have some judicial support: *Tinsley v Milligan* [1994] 1 AC 340, 368 (Lord Lowry); *Foskett v McKeown* [2001] 1 AC 102, 129 (Lord Millett).

[34] *Foskett v McKeown* [2001] 1 AC 102, 109 (Lord Browne-Wilkinson), 115 (Lord Hoffmann), 118 (Lord Hope), and 129 (Lord Millett); *Bank of Cyprus UK Ltd v Menelaou* [2015] UKSC 66, [2015] AC 176, [37] (Lord Clarke). See Grantham and Rickett, 'Tracing and property rights: the categorical truth' (2000) 63 MLR 905.

[35] See Section 19.3, p. 551.   [36] See n. 9, p. 35. See also Birks (see n. 13), p. 239.

[37] Birks (see n. 9), p. 35. See also Burrows (see n. 15), p. 186.

framed in those terms. But the principle could be rebranded into an event if it were necessary to do so. For example, the event could be that the defendant has interfered with the claimant's property rights in some way.[38] So analysing the claim with reference to 'events' does not get us any further in assessing which principle is the most appropriate.

At the heart of the debate about the legitimacy of the vindication of property rights principle is a basic question: how can a claimant bring a proprietary claim against substitute property when the claimant has never previously had a right in that property? Is it sufficient to conclude that the right to the original property is transferred to the substitute property simply because that property represents the original property by virtue of the principles of property law, as the House of Lords concluded in *Foskett v McKeown*,[39] or must the unjust enrichment principle be used? As we will see,[40] the principles of property law provide a satisfactory explanation of how property rights can be identified in substitute property without resorting to the law of unjust enrichment.

But there is another question that needs to be considered first: does it matter whether the unjust enrichment principle or the vindication of property rights principle is used to explain how claims can be asserted against substitute property? In practice, the method of analysis is usually irrelevant because the same result will be achieved. But there may be substantive consequences depending on the analysis adopted, especially as regards the application of the defence of change of position, which would be relevant only if the unjust enrichment analysis were adopted.[41] Further, what needs to be proven to establish the claim may vary depending on the analysis adopted, especially for unjust enrichment when seeking to identify the appropriate ground of restitution. Finally, it is important, when analysing the law, to have a clear and defensible mode of analysis and explanation. Clear thinking results in better understanding of the law. Consequently, although it will really matter only rarely, a choice does need to be made as regards the identification of the proper theory to explain how proprietary claims can be asserted against substitute property.

The vindication of property rights principle is consistent with the leading decision of the House of Lords and now the Supreme Court. It represents the state of English law and rightly so. It is logical and consistent with fundamental principles of Equity as to the nature of equitable rights in property.[42]

19.1.5 THE RELEVANCE OF DISCRETION

One of the other fundamental issues concerning equitable proprietary claims relates to the extent to which the recognition and vindication of property rights should be influenced by judicial discretion. This is an issue that was considered in Chapter 9 of this volume as regards the recognition of the remedial constructive trust in English law.[43] But this is also a significant issue when assessing how the courts should vindicate property rights. Should the courts apply the rules strictly or should they retain a discretion to determine whether—and, if so, how—the vindication of property rights is just and fair? If they should retain such a discretion, should it be grounded on principle or depend on the exercise of arbitrary choice?[44] A discretionary approach grounded on fairness and justice has been

---

[38] See Grantham and Rickett, 'Trust money as an unjust enrichment: a misconception' [1998] LMCLQ 514, 519.

[39] [2001] 1 AC 102.   [40] See Section 19.3, p. 551.   [41] See Section 19.5.2, p. 585.

[42] See Section 19.3.1.(ii), p. 554.   [43] See Section 9.4, p. 278.   [44] See Section 2.2, p. 24.

advocated by a number of commentators,[45] but it was rejected by a majority of the House of Lords in *Foskett v McKeown*,[46] most notably by Lord Millett, who said:[47]

> Property rights are determined by fixed rules and settled principles. They are not discretionary. They do not depend upon ideas of what is 'fair, just and reasonable'. Such concepts, which in reality mass decisions of legal policy, have no place in the law of property.

Lord Browne-Wilkinson also recognized that proprietary claims do not depend on any discretion vested in the court—such cases involve 'hard-nosed property rights'[48]—but he did accept that a proprietary interest might not be recognized if such recognition would be 'unfair'.[49] This notion of fairness is sometimes encountered in the context of the tracing rules,[50] but it contradicts the fundamental principle that the recognition of proprietary rights is rule-based and principled. It would be better to rationalize the decision not to recognize a proprietary interest by reference to principled defences rather than to rely on the uncertainty of concepts such as fairness and equity.[51] This is an area in which certainty is paramount for a number of reasons, particularly because a consequence of recognizing proprietary rights may be that the claimant gains priority over the defendant's unsecured creditors if the defendant becomes insolvent, so the award of such a remedy will be to the prejudice of these other creditors. Therefore, the court must always be vigilant against affording the claimant excessive protection at the expense of the defendant's other creditors. This has been recognized in a number of cases. For example, in *Re Stapylton Fletcher Ltd*,[52] Judge Paul Baker QC said that '[t]he court must be very cautious in devising . . . interests and remedies which erode the statutory scheme for distribution on insolvency. It cannot do so because of some perceived injustice arising as a consequence only of the insolvency.'[53]

Ultimately, the court must strive to balance the interests of two innocent parties, namely the claimant and the defendant's creditors, by reference to clear rules and principles rather than through the exercise of arbitrary choice depending on the facts in particular cases. In striving to balance these interests, one of the most important considerations relates to whether or not the claimant can be considered to have taken the risk of the defendant's insolvency:[54] if the claimant did take the risk, or can be deemed to have taken it, there is no reason why the claimant's proprietary claim should be preferred to the claims of the defendant's other creditors, and so the claimant should rank equally with those creditors.[55] This is most likely to be the case where the claimant transferred property to the defendant and had the opportunity to negotiate for a security, but failed to do so. In such a case it would not be appropriate for a proprietary claim to succeed. Where, however, the claimant was unaware that property had been taken from them, such as where a trustee has misappropriated trust property, it is perfectly acceptable that the proprietary claims of the

---

[45] Burrows (see n. 13), pp. 423–8; Rotherham, 'Tracing misconceptions in *Foskett v McKeown*' (2003) 11 RLR 57.   [46] [2001] 1 AC 102.

[47] Ibid., at 127. Compare Lord Hope (ibid., 120), who, dissenting, said that since there was no principle or authority to assist with the division of the property, in that case it should be divided in such proportions as were equitable, having regard to the equities affecting each party.

[48] Ibid., 109. Described by Master Clark in *FHR European Ventures LLP v Mankarious* [2016] EWHC 359 (Ch), [47], as 'fixed rules and settled principles of property law'.

[49] [2001] 1 AC 102.   [50] *Re Diplock's Estate* [1948] Ch 465, 548. See Section 19.3.3.(iv), p. 570.

[51] See Section 19.5, p. 583.   [52] [1994] 1 WLR 1181, 1203.

[53] See also *Re Polly Peck International plc (No 2)* [1998] 3 All ER 892, 827 (Mummery LJ).

[54] Burrows (see n. 13), pp. 423–8.

[55] This may be the case, for example, where the claimant entered into a transaction with the defendant that was void *ab initio*. See Lord Goff in *Westdeutsche Landesbank Girozentrale v Islington LBC* [1996] AC 669, 684.

beneficiaries of the trust should be preferred over those of the defendant's other creditors, since the claimant had not been given the opportunity to seek any security. Equally, if the claimant made arrangements to obtain a security, but this was invalid for some reason, the claimant should be afforded a degree of proprietary protection to fulfil their legitimate expectations that any claim against the defendant would be secured.[56] As we will see, these principles are reflected in the law relating to the identification of proprietary rights and the determination of appropriate remedies.

19.1.6 A FRAMEWORK FOR THE ANALYSIS OF PROPRIETARY CLAIMS

The law relating to equitable proprietary claims is complicated. This is partly because of the use of confusing terminology, but also because of confusion amongst the judiciary over the years as to what needs to be proved and why. The details of the law will be examined in the rest of this chapter, but to understand what is going on it is useful to have a clear framework for analysing any proprietary claim. The preferable structure for analysing such claims is as follows.

(i) The proprietary base

The claimant first needs to show that they have an equitable interest in particular property. This is known as the 'proprietary base' on which the claim is founded.[57] So, for example, in the simple case involving a breach of a fixed trust in which the trustee has misappropriated trust property, the beneficiaries will be able to show that they have a proprietary interest in the property that is held on trust.

(ii) Following and tracing

The claimant then needs to show that the property which was received by the defendant is property in which the claimant has an equitable interest. There are two ways of establishing this, depending on whether the claim relates to the original property or to substitute property. If it is a claim to the original property, the claimant needs to follow the property into the possession of the defendant.[58] If the claim relates to substitute property, the claimant needs to trace the value of the property from the original property in which the claimant had an equitable proprietary interest into the substitute property that was received by the defendant. So, for example, if the trustee has misappropriated shares from the trust that were sold and the proceeds of sale were used to buy a car that the trustee gave to the defendant, the beneficiaries will need to trace the value from the shares into the car that is in the possession of the defendant, and will then be able to assert their equitable rights against the car. The purpose of tracing is to identify what asset has been acquired with the value that was inherent in another asset. Sometimes tracing has been regarded as a remedy in its own right,[59] but that is patently incorrect. As Lord Steyn has recognized, tracing is 'a process of identifying assets: it belongs to the law of evidence. It tells us nothing about legal or equitable rights to the assets traced.'[60]

---

[56] See Section 19.4.3.(ii), p. 581.

[57] *Smalley v Bracken Partners* [2003] EWCA Civ 1875, [2004] WTLR 599; *Bainbridge v Bainbridge* [2016] EWHC 898 (Ch), [2016] WTLR 943, [32] (Master Matthews).

[58] See further Section 19.3.1.(i), p. 551.   [59] See *Sinclair v Brougham* [1914] AC 398.

[60] *Foskett v McKeown* [2001] 1 AC 102, 113; see also 109 (Lord Browne-Wilkinson), and 128 and 139 (Lord Millett).

(iii) Claiming

Once the defendant has been able to show that the defendant has received property in which the claimant has an equitable proprietary interest, the claimant will then be able to make a claim in respect of that property. Claiming is distinct from tracing.[61] Claiming involves the claimant's assertion of rights in the original asset or its traceable product.[62] The nature of the claim will be determined by whether the defendant has retained property in which the claimant has an interest or whether the defendant has dissipated the property and no longer has any property that represents the claimant's value. In the latter situation, the claimant will be able to bring only a personal claim to vindicate their property rights.[63] Where the proprietary claims relates to substitute property, the claimant will only be able to maintain the same claim to the substitute property as they could have made to the original property. So, for example, if the claimant only had a security interest in the original property, they will not be able to claim more than a security interest in the substitute property.

(iv) Identification of the remedy

Assuming that the claimant has been able to establish that the defendant received and retained property in which the claimant has an equitable proprietary interest, the claimant will seek a proprietary remedy to vindicate that right. The nature of the remedy will depend on the circumstances of the case, but may involve recovering the property from the defendant or obtaining a security interest in the property. Sometimes, the appropriate remedy will be a matter for the claimant to choose,[64] but this will depend on both remedies being available to the claimant as a matter of law.

(v) Defences

The liability of the defendant may be subject to a defence, which might negate the defendant's liability completely, if, for example, the defendant has purchased the property in good faith,[65] or the defence may restrict the liability, if, for example, the defendant changed their position in reliance on the receipt of the property.[66]

(vi) A model case

The application of this framework for analysing equitable proprietary claims is particularly well illustrated by the leading case of *Foskett v McKeown*.[67] In that case, a group of investors wished to invest in property on the Algarve in Portugal to develop as a golf course. A sum of £2.6 million was deposited by the investors and was settled on trust for them until the land was purchased; this was called the development trust. A few years earlier, one of the trustees had set up a life insurance policy on his life. The terms of the policy were such that, if he died, the sum of £1 million would be paid to him. He settled the policy on trust for his three children. He was required to pay an annual insurance premium of £10,220. On the receipt of a premium, units would be allocated which the insurers would cancel to

---

[61] *Boscawen v Bajwa* [1996] 1 WLR 328, 335 (Millett LJ). See also Birks, 'On taking seriously the difference between tracing and claiming' (1997) 11 TLI 2. Confusingly, in *Foskett v McKeown* despite earlier recognizing the distinction between tracing and claiming, Lord Millett considered the question of claiming under the heading of 'The tracing rules': [2001] 1 AC 102, 129–33.

[62] This could incorporate the identification of the proprietary base, but for ease of exposition it is useful to identify that as a separate and initial question, especially because the determination of whether the proprietary base is legal or equitable determines the tracing rules that apply, and so is necessarily a prior question.

[63] See Chapter 20 of this volume.   [64] *Foskett v McKeown* [2001] 1 AC 102, 130 (Lord Millett).

[65] See Section 19.5.1, p. 584.   [66] See Section 19.5.2, p. 585.   [67] [2001] AC 102.

meet the cost of life cover for the next year. If the premiums were to cease to be paid, the units would continue to be cancelled until there were no units left. Once there were no units left, the policy would lapse.

The trustee paid the first three premiums from his own money. He then stole £10,220 from the development trust to pay for the fourth premium and did the same the following year. He then committed suicide. The fact that he died at his own hand did not invalidate the policy. It followed that his children were eligible to receive a lump sum payment of £1 million from the insurance company.

The beneficiaries of the development trust discovered that the trustee had misappropriated £20,440 from the trust fund and brought a proprietary claim for restitution. There were four possible solutions to this dispute:

(1) As the beneficiaries argued, since their money had been used to pay two of the five premiums that had contributed to the payment of £1 million, it followed that they should have two-fifths of that sum, amounting to £400,000.

(2) The children should be required only to repay the £20,440 that had been stolen from the trust fund. This was argued by the children and was the solution adopted by the Court of Appeal.[68]

(3) The beneficiaries should recover nothing. This argument, which was also made by the children, was dependent on the peculiar nature of the insurance policy. The premiums that were paid were not automatically used to maintain the insurance policy, but were used to purchase units. The first three premiums had purchased sufficient units to mean that, even if the fourth and the fifth premiums had not been paid, the insurance policy would not have lapsed and the £1 million would still have been paid. Consequently, it was argued that the beneficiaries' money had not contributed to the receipt of the £1 million in any way.

(4) There was a fourth solution that was not argued in the case, namely that, because the fourth and the fifth premium had been stolen from the trust, which was a criminal offence, it followed that the £1 million was the proceeds of crime. English law has long recognized that recipients of the proceeds of crime should be required to give up those proceeds to the victim[69] and cannot be seen to benefit from them. Consequently, even though the children were innocent of the crime themselves, they could not be seen to benefit from their father's crime in any way and so the beneficiaries should recover the whole of the £1 million.

The House of Lords, by a bare majority, adopted the first solution, so that the beneficiaries recovered £400,000. In reaching this decision, it is possible to identify a number of distinct stages in the analysis of the majority:

(1) The beneficiaries had an equitable proprietary base. This was easily established because the trustee held the money that the investors had deposited on an express trust, so they clearly had an equitable proprietary interest in the money that had been misappropriated from the trust fund.[70]

(2) It was not possible to follow the money that was misappropriated into the £1 million death benefit. This was because the money that had been stolen had inevitably become mixed with other money, so that it had lost its identity. Consequently, it was necessary to trace the value of this money into substitute property, namely the death benefit. The process of tracing in this case was complex and controversial,[71] but the majority accepted that

---

[68] [1998] Ch 265.   [69] Or be confiscated by the State: see the Proceeds of Crime Act 2002.
[70] [2001] 1 AC 102, 126 (Lord Millett).   [71] See Section 19.3.1.(ii), p. 552.

it was possible to trace the trust funds into the premiums that were paid to the insurance company, then into the life insurance policy, and then into the death benefit.

(3) Having traced into the death benefit, and because the trustees of the insurance policy retained the £1 million death benefit, it was possible for the beneficiaries of the development trust to assert a proprietary claim against that money.

(4) The choice of remedy in this case was controversial,[72] but the majority held that the most appropriate way of vindicating the beneficiaries' equitable proprietary rights was by recognizing that the beneficiaries had a share of the death benefit in proportion to their contribution to the payment of the premiums, namely £400,000.

(5) The House of Lords also considered whether the children had any defences to the proprietary claims and concluded that they did not, primarily because they were volunteers who had received a gift.

The correctness of the decision will be considered subsequently, but what is important for now is to understand this logical approach that needs to be adopted when analysing proprietary claims.

(vii) Summary

The essence of equitable claims relating to property transferred in breach of trust was succinctly summarized by Briggs LJ in *Clegg v The Estate and Personal Representatives of Pache (deceased)*:[73]

> Where a trustee pays trust property in breach of trust to a person who is in fact a stranger to the trust (rather than a beneficiary) and who receives it as a pure volunteer, then the recipient is bound by the beneficiaries' interest in the property paid, so that the beneficiary may make a proprietary claim for its return, or a tracing claim for its proceeds, or a claim into a fund within which the recipient has mixed the property with his or her own property.

19.2 THE PROPRIETARY BASE

The first step in the analysis of a proprietary claim is to determine whether the claimant has a proprietary base, meaning an interest in identifiable property. Since we are concerned with equitable proprietary claims, the property interest must be an equitable one. This proprietary base will be established either by showing that a new proprietary interest has been created or that an existing proprietary interest has been retained by the claimant despite the transfer of property.

19.2.1 CREATION OF EQUITABLE PROPERTY INTERESTS

We have previously seen that equitable proprietary interests can be created by express intention in the form of an express trust,[74] or by presumed or imputed intention in the form of the resulting trust,[75] or can be imposed by operation of law in the form of the constructive trust.[76] In all of these cases, usually legal title[77] to the property will vest in the trustee and the beneficiaries of the trust will have an equitable interest in the property.

---

[72] See further Section 19.4.1.(ii), p. 575.   [73] [2017] EWCA Civ 256, [87].
[74] See Section 4.2, p. 72.   [75] See Chapter 8 of this volume.   [76] See Chapter 9 of this volume.
[77] Although a trustee could hold an equitable interest on sub-trust for the beneficiary.

It has also been recognized that a principal who has transferred property to a fiduciary will be able to bring an equitable proprietary claim against the fiduciary or a third party where that property has been misappropriated.[78] So, for example, in *Re Hallett's Estate*, a client of a solicitor transferred bonds to the solicitor for safe-keeping, who then sold the bonds and deposited the purchase money in his personal bank account; it was held that the client had a proprietary claim in Equity to the proceeds of sale.[79] The same will be true if the fiduciary is an agent or a bailee who is looking after the claimant's property and then misappropriates it. But it is not straightforward to identify an equitable proprietary base in such a case, because the defendant fiduciary will not have legal title to the property, which will remain with the principal, so it would appear that the fiduciary could not be considered to hold the property on trust for the principal. Indeed, this was specifically recognized in *Re Hallett's Estate*. So how can the principal establish an equitable proprietary base in order to bring a proprietary claim? Despite what was said in *Re Hallett's Estate*, this can be established only through the mechanism of a trust. Where the fiduciary has mixed the property, or the proceeds of the property, with his or her own property, the equitable proprietary base will be easily established. This is because, when the property is mixed, it loses its identity at Law,[80] so the legal title to the mixture will vest in the fiduciary. Since the fiduciary will have acted in breach of duty in mixing the principal's property, it is appropriate to conclude that the fiduciary holds that part of the mixture consisting of the principal's property on constructive trust for the principal.[81]

But if the principal's property has been retained by the fiduciary, or has been sold and the proceeds retained by the fiduciary without mixing them, how can the principal establish an equitable proprietary base, since it would appear that the principal will have retained the legal title to the property? This could be very significant if the fiduciary has become insolvent and the principal is trying to gain priority over the fiduciary's general creditors by means of a claim in Equity rather than one at Common Law. The preferable explanation of how the principal can establish an equitable proprietary base despite retaining legal title to the property is that, since the fiduciary has a possessory right to the property that is good against the world except for the principal, it is this right that can be held on trust for the principal[82] and this will then establish the equitable proprietary base. That a trustee can hold possessory rights on trust for the beneficiary is controversial and there is no authority explicitly in support of it. A further difficulty with this analysis is that the principal would then have both legal title to the property and an equitable right to the possession of the property, so that he or she would be allowed to elect to pursue the equitable rather than the legal right. But, at the very least, this possessory rights analysis does provide a mechanism for explaining how a principal can assert equitable proprietary rights to property that is in the defendant's possession even though the principal owns the property at Law. It also explains how the victim of theft can bring an equitable proprietary claim in respect of property that has been stolen against the person who is in possession of that property, even though the victim of the theft has retained legal title to the property.[83]

---

[78] *Re Hallett's Estate* (1880) 13 Ch D 696, 709 (Sir George Jessel MR).

[79] Ibid.   [80] See further Section 19.3.2.(iii), p. 557.   [81] See Section 9.3.7, p. 273.

[82] Tarrant, 'Property rights to stolen money' (2005) 32 UWALR 234, 245; Tarrant, 'Thieves as trustees: in defence of the theft principle' (2009) 3 J Eq 170, 172.

[83] See further Section 9.3.1.(i), p. 261. This has been recognized in Australia by the High Court in *Black v F S Freedman and Co* (1910) 12 CLR 105. See also *Westdeutsche Landesbank Girozentrale v Islington LBC* [1996] AC 669, 000 (Lord Browne-Wilkinson). For criticisms, see Barkehall Thomas, 'Thieves as trustees: the enduring legacy of *Black v S Freedman and Co*' (2009) 3 J Eq 52. See generally Chambers, 'Trust and theft', in *Exploring Private Law*, ed. Bant and Harding (Cambridge: Cambridge University Press, 2010), ch. 10, who adopts an unjust enrichment analysis of the proprietary right that arises in such cases.

But it does not follow that every fiduciary who has received property on behalf of the principal will necessarily hold that property on trust for the principal. It has been recognized that the mere existence of a fiduciary relationship is not sufficient in its own right to enable the claimant to assert a proprietary claim. As Millett LJ recognized in *Paragon Finance plc v DB Thakerar & Co*,[84] the question is not simply whether, for example, an agent is a fiduciary, because all agents owe fiduciary duties, but whether the agent owed fiduciary duties in respect of the property that they received so that they were trustee of it. This trust may be express or implied from an 'unexpressed but presumable intention of the parties, having regard to all the circumstances of the case'.[85] Such an intention will be implied, for example, where the fiduciary is entrusted with money to buy specific property so that the money and any property purchased with it will be held on trust for the principal.[86] The key indicator of whether a trust of the property can be identified is where the principal intended the fiduciary to keep the property that they had received separate from their own assets so that it cannot be used for the fiduciary's own purposes.[87] So, in *Lyell v Kennedy*,[88] rent was collected by the defendant as agent for the claimant and was paid into a separate bank account; it was held on trust for the claimant. This can be contrasted with *The West of England and South Wales District Bank, ex parte Dale*,[89] where a bank collected money as agent for the claimant. The money was not paid into a separate bank account and it was held that this had not been held on trust for the principal.

In all of these cases, if it can be shown that the claimant has an equitable proprietary interest in property, even though the claimant has retained legal title to the property and has only an equitable interest in the defendant's possessory title, the claimant will have been able to establish a proprietary base to bring an equitable proprietary claim.

19.2.2 RETENTION OF EQUITABLE PROPERTY INTEREST

Where the claimant has an existing equitable interest in property that is mixed with other property or is transferred to a third party, it is necessary to show that the claimant has retained that equitable interest in the original or substitute property. Normally, the interest will be retained, even if the property is transferred to a third party who is unaware of that interest.[90] So, for example, in *Foskett v McKeown*,[91] the claimants were able to establish that they had retained an equitable proprietary interest in money that was stolen by the trustee. Also, in *Re Diplock*,[92] the executors of the deceased's estate mistakenly paid part of the money from the estate to third parties. The deceased's next of kin, who should have received the property, were able to bring a proprietary claim to recover it on behalf of the estate, since they had retained an equitable proprietary interest in the property, despite the executors' mistaken transfer.

The claimant will not, however, retain an equitable property interest in certain circumstances. For example, if the property in which the claimant has an interest is dissipated without being substituted for any other property, the equitable interest will be extinguished. So, for example, if a trustee misappropriated £1,000 from the trust fund and

---

[84] [1999] 1 All ER 400.

[85] *Harris v Truman* (1881) 7 QBD 340, 356 (Manisty J).

[86] *Middleton v Pollock* (1876) 4 Ch D 49; *Harris v Truman* (1881) 7 QBD 340, approved by the Court of Appeal: (1882) 9 QBD 264; *Hancock v Smith* (1889) 41 Ch D 456, 461 (Lord Halsbury LC).

[87] So, for example, money paid into a client account by a solicitor will be held on trust for the client: *Plunkett v Barclays Bank Ltd* [1936] 2 KB 107, 117 (du Parcq LJ).   [88] (1889) 14 App Cas 437.

[89] (1879) 11 Ch D 722.   [90] *Re Diplock's Estate* [1948] Ch 465.

[91] [2001] 1 AC 102. See Section 19.1.6.(vi), p. 546.

[92] [1948] Ch 465. See also *Nelson v Larholt* [1948] 1 KB 339.

gave it to his son, who spent it on a holiday, there is no longer any property that represents the property in which the claimant has an interest and consequently that interest will be extinguished.[93] The interest will also be extinguished by overreaching where the property is received by a good-faith purchaser for value.[94]

19.3 FOLLOWING AND TRACING

Once an equitable proprietary interest has been identified, the claimant will then need to show that this interest can be identified in the property that has been received by the defendant. To do this, the claimant will need to rely on the following and tracing rules.

19.3.1 THE FUNCTION OF FOLLOWING AND TRACING

(i) The essence of following

The essence of following is that the claimant is able to show that the property in which they have has a proprietary interest has been received by the defendant.[95] If the identity of the claimant's property has been lost or the property has been destroyed, they will no longer be able to follow it. Where the claimant's property is transferred directly to the defendant, there is no difficulty in following the property. Where, however, the property is received indirectly by the defendant, the question of following may be more difficult to establish on the facts.

(ii) The essence of tracing

Where the original property cannot be followed (because, for example, it has been dissipated or has lost its identity in a mixture), it is necessary for the claimant to show that the value of the property in which they originally had a proprietary interest can be identified in substitute property that has been received by the defendant.[96] Whether the claimant can establish this depends on the application of the tracing rules,[97] which are evidential rules and presumptions that enable the claimant to prove that value in the original property is represented in the substitute property. The essence of tracing was identified by Lord Millett in *Foskett v McKeown*:[98]

> Tracing is thus neither a claim nor a remedy. It is merely the process by which the claimant demonstrates what has happened to his property, identifies its proceeds and the persons who have handled or received them, and justifies his claim that the proceeds can be regarded as representing his property. Tracing is also distinct from claiming. It identifies the traceable proceeds of the claimant's property. It enables the claimant to substitute the traceable proceeds for the original asset as the subject matter of his claim. But it does not affect or establish his claim.

More pithily, in *Shalson v Russo*,[99] Rimer J described tracing as 'the process by which a claimant seeks to show that an interest he had in an asset has become represented by an interest in a different asset'. McFarlane and Stevens describe tracing as enabling the claimant

---

[93] See further Section 19.5.2, p. 585.   [94] See Section 19.5.1, p. 584.

[95] *Foskett v McKeown* [2001] 1 AC 102, 127 (Lord Millett). See Smith, *The Law of Tracing* (Oxford: Clarendon Press, 1997), p. 4.   [96] *Foskett v McKeown* [2001] 1 AC 102, 128 (Lord Millett).

[97] See Section 19.3.2, p. 556 and Section 19.3.3, p. 559.

[98] [2001] 1 AC 102, 127.   [99] [2003] EWHC 1637 (Ch), [2005] Ch 281, [102].

'to identify a particular right as the product of another right',[100] where the right refers to a right against property.

In some cases it may be relatively easy for the claimant to show that value in one asset is now represented in another asset, such as where shares have been misappropriated from a trust and are sold for cash, and the cash is then used to buy a car. In such a case, value is cleanly transferred from one asset to another via the cash. But there will be other cases that are factually much more complicated, such as where many different amounts including the claimant's money are credited to a bank account, and many different amounts are paid from this bank account. In this situation, it will not be obvious whether the value of the claimant's money that has been credited to the account remains in the account, so rules are needed to break this 'evidential impasse'.[101]

The operation of the tracing rules is illustrated particularly well by the facts of *Foskett v McKeown*.[102] The beneficiaries of the development trust needed to show that part of the fund which was held on trust for them could be traced into the death benefit paid following the suicide of the trustee. The first part of the tracing exercise was straightforward, since it could be shown that the claimants' money had been used to pay two premiums. The difficulty in the case concerned tracing from the premiums into the payment of the death benefit, via the insurance policy, which turned on the appropriate analysis of the function of the premiums in the light of the unusual nature of the insurance policy. This was a unit-linked life policy under which the premiums were used to pay for the cost of life cover through the allocation of units that were exhausted over time. Each premium bought a number of units and each unit kept the policy going for a bit longer. The policy would lapse only once all of the units had been used up. Paying a premium was rather like topping up a parking meter: each time a payment is made, the car can be parked for an additional period of time. Since the first three premiums, which were paid from the trustee's own money, had purchased a substantial number of units, it followed that even if the fourth and fifth premiums had not been paid, the policy would not have lapsed at the time of the trustee's death, because the units purchased from the first three premiums were still operating. So what was the effect of the fourth and fifth premiums?

For Lord Steyn, who dissented,[103] the fact that the policy would not have lapsed had the fourth and fifth premiums not been paid meant that there was no link between the payment of those premiums and the receipt of the death benefit, so tracing was not possible. This involved a simple causative approach to the tracing exercise: the fourth and fifth premiums had not contributed to the death benefit being paid.

The majority adopted a different approach to the tracing exercise. Although the majority acknowledged that, in the events that happened, the premiums paid from the trust fund were not required to prevent the insurance policy from lapsing, they also recognized that this need not have been the case.[104] If, for example, the trustee had lived longer, the premiums would have contributed to the maintenance of the policy. Consequently, Lord Browne-Wilkinson recognized that:[105]

> the beneficial ownership of the policy, and therefore the policy moneys, cannot depend on how events turn out. The rights of the parties in the policy, one way or another, were fixed when the relevant premiums were paid when the future was unknown.

It followed that it was possible to trace the two premiums into the insurance policy, which was property in its own right because it consisted of a bundle of rights to which the policy

---

[100] 'The nature of equitable property' (2010) 4 J Eq 1, 20.   [101] Birks (see n. 61), p. 4.
[102] [2001] 1 AC 102. See Section 19.1.6.(vi), p. 546.   [103] [2001] 1 AC 102, 113.
[104] Ibid., 111 (Lord Browne-Wilkinson) and 138 (Lord Millett).   [105] Ibid., 111.

holder was entitled in return for payment of the premiums, and from the policy to the death benefit, which represented the traceable proceeds of the policy and indirectly of the premiums.

In reaching the conclusion that it was possible to trace into the death benefit, the majority identified two fundamental principles of tracing.

Attribution rather than causation

If the tracing rules were to depend on establishing a causal link between the receipt of the original asset and obtaining a substitute asset, in the sense that but for the receipt of the original asset the substitute would not have been obtained, tracing into the death benefit could not have been possible in *Foskett v McKeown* because the fourth and fifth premiums did not cause the death benefit to be obtained. But, since the majority recognized that tracing was possible on the facts, it follows that tracing cannot depend on identifying a causal link between the original and substitute asset. Rather, tracing can be established by attribution.[106] In *Foskett v McKeown*, it was sufficient that the death benefit could be attributed to the fourth and fifth premiums, and this could be shown because the death benefit was to be paid, according to the terms of the insurance policy, in consideration for all of the premiums paid, which therefore included the fourth and fifth premiums.[107] This shift away from causation to attribution is important to our understanding of tracing, especially when it is coupled with a second key conclusion about the nature of tracing.

Tracing value rather than identifying property

All of the judges in *Foskett v McKeown* recognized that tracing was not concerned with the identification of chains of property, but instead focused on the identification of value within property. It is this value that is the essence of the claimant's proprietary right and it is this value that is traced. This was expressly recognized by Lord Millett:[108]

> We speak of tracing one asset into another, but this too is inaccurate. The original asset still exists in the hands of the new owner, or it may have become untraceable. The claimant claims the new asset because it was acquired in whole or in part with the original asset. What he traces, therefore, is not the physical asset itself but the value inherent in it.

The recognition of these two principles in *Foskett v McKeown* means that the operation of the tracing rules should be easier. Tracing does not depend on causation in any meaningful sense. Rather, we are concerned only with logical progression: with the identification of value in various locations without regard to the effect of that value on particular property, in that it need not be shown that the property was acquired because of that value. In *Foskett v McKeown*, the claimants' value could be traced from the trust fund, through bank accounts, into two premiums, then into the policy itself, and finally into the proceeds of that policy. In a telling phrase, Lord Millett talked of establishing 'transactional links';[109] this is now the essential feature of tracing.

Although the decision of the majority in *Foskett v McKeown* is very significant to the modern understanding of the function of the law of tracing, the conclusion that it was possible to trace into the death benefit was dubious for two reasons. First, the assertion that the court is not concerned with how events turned out, but rather with proprietary rights at the time at which the premiums were paid, is inconsistent with the key conclusion that tracing is simply

---

[106] [2001] 1 AC 102, 137 (Lord Millett). Cf. Lord Hope who, dissenting, expressly stated that the death benefit was not attributable to the payment of the premiums: ibid., 122.

[107] Ibid., 116 (Lord Hoffmann), 119 (Lord Hope), and 133 (Lord Millett).

[108] Ibid., 128.   [109] Ibid.

a matter of evidence. Consequently, surely the court should have regard to all of the evidence, and so, if the premiums paid from the trust fund might have contributed to the payment of the death benefit, but did not actually do so, this should have defeated the tracing exercise. Secondly, even though the majority relied on the fact that the terms of the insurance policy stated that the £1 million was paid in consideration of all of the premiums, it is not clear why this contractual term was sufficient to influence proprietary rights to the money. In particular, the fourth and fifth premiums were used to buy units that formed part of a mixed fund of units, since the first three premiums had also purchased units that had not all been used up. Until the trustee's suicide, these units were gradually used to prevent the policy from lapsing. But which units would have been used first? The logical answer is that the first in time would have been used first, which would mean that the units attributable to the fourth and fifth premiums remained outstanding and this conclusion could not be changed by the inclusion of a contractual term that the premiums were paid in consideration of all premiums, unless that term stated explicitly that the most recently paid premiums were to be treated as used first. It follows that, for both of these reasons, the preferable view is that it should have been possible to trace the trust funds into the fourth and fifth premiums and into the purchase of units, but it should not have been possible to trace into the payment following the trustee's death.

Intention of the parties

In a significant article, Cutts[110] has identified another feature of tracing, which was not recognized in *Foskett v McKeown*, but which has proved to be significant in subsequent cases, namely that the content of a transaction cannot be determined without reference to the intentions of the parties, deduced from the agreement between them as a whole. Whilst Cutts prefers to focus on intention rather than transfer of value through a transaction as a means to establish tracing, the two concepts are not incompatible. Rather, there will be occasions where the intention of the parties will be important to determine whether value can be traced through multiple transactions, so that if the steps are intended to operate together to achieve a particular result, the intermediate steps can be ignored. This has, for example, been recognized as significant where the defendant has incurred a liability in purchasing property and then intends to use value from the claimant to discharge that liability; it is then possible to trace value into the previously acquired property because of the defendant's intent.[111] The focus on intention will also enable value to be traced through complex banking transactions involving multiple accounts, clearing and credit, despite the precise order of events.[112] As Cutts recognizes:[113]

> . . . in order to establish a transactional link in any case involving a bank payment, the claimant must show that the parties involved in the transaction intended to, and did in fact, bring about a debit to the account held by or for the claimant, and that into which the claimant seeks to trace. The precise mechanisms by which inter-bank payment instructions are executed by the participating banks have no bearing on the execution of this process.

(iii) Tracing into substitute assets

A matter of particular controversy as regards the application of the tracing rules concerns how a right in one piece of property can be asserted against a substitute asset. In particular,

---

[110] 'Tracing, value and transactions' (2016) 79 MLR 381.

[111] Section 19.3.3.(iv) ('Backward tracing'), p. 567.

[112] As recognized in *Relfo Ltd v Varsani* [2014] EWCA Civ 360, [2015] 1 BCLC 14. Section 19.3.3.(iv), p. 568.

[113] (2016) 79 MLR 381, 401.

does this right in the substitute property arise automatically or as a result of the exercise of a power by the claimant? The law on this point is confused. There is authority that suggests that the claimant obtains an immediate interest in the substitute asset,[114] and Lord Millett in *Foskett v McKeown* adopted such an approach.[115] Alternatively, there is authority that suggests that the claimant only has a power to crystallize his or her proprietary interest in the substitute asset.[116] *Foskett v McKeown* itself provides some support for this power analysis. Lord Millett did recognize that the claimant has a power,[117] but this relates to the choice to pursue a claim either against the original asset or its substitute, as long as both can still be identified. The preferable view is that, once the original asset cannot be identified, the equitable interest relating to that asset is extinguished and is automatically replaced by a proprietary interest in the substitute. Where, however, the original asset and the substitute can both be identified, the claimant can elect either to claim the original asset or its substitute.[118] If the claimant chooses to claim the substitute, this will extinguish the proprietary interest in the original asset and transfer it to the substitute, unless that substitute has been obtained by a bona fide purchaser for value.[119]

The significance of this election analysis is illustrated by the following example. The trustee, Alan, misappropriated £1,000 of shares from the trust and gave the shares to his wife, Belinda, who sold them to Clare. Belinda then used the proceeds of sale to buy a car from David. If Clare was aware that the shares had been given to Belinda in breach of trust, she cannot be a bona fide purchaser for value, but, if David was unaware of the breach of trust, he will be a bona fide purchaser for value. Consequently, the beneficiaries will not be able to pursue a proprietary claim against David, because he will have received the proceeds of sale of the shares free of the beneficiaries' equitable interest.[120] But the beneficiaries will potentially be able to trace the value of the shares from the trust fund into the car that is in Belinda's possession or to follow the shares into the possession of Clare. If the beneficiaries decide to pursue a claim against the car, perhaps because the value of the shares has fallen substantially, they will elect to assert their proprietary rights against the car rather than the shares. As a result of that election, Clare will take the shares free of the equitable proprietary interest.

This election analysis has a number of advantages. In particular, it explains why the claimant cannot bring proprietary claims against both the original property and the substituted property. By assuming that the claimant has a power to shift the proprietary interest from the original property to its substitute and that this can occur only once the power of election has been exercised, it follows that the claimant is able to bring only one proprietary claim at a time. But this election analysis does cause problems of its own.[121] For example, if the effect of this analysis is that the claimant has no interest in the substitute until the power of election has been exercised, it should follow that, if the defendant who is in possession of the substitute becomes insolvent before the claimant has made the election, the claimant's right to the substitute ought to be extinguished.[122]

---

[114] *Cave v Cave* (1880) 15 Ch D 639 (Fry J). See also *Re Diplock's Estate* [1948] Ch 465; Smith (see n. 95), pp. 356–61.

[115] [2001] 1 AC 102, 134.

[116] See *Lipkin Gorman v Karpnale Ltd* [1991] 2 AC 548, 573 (Lord Goff) as regards tracing at Common Law.

[117] [2001] 1 AC 102, 127.   [118] See *Boscawen v Bajwa* [1996] 1 WLR 328, 342 (Millett LJ).

[119] See Section 19.5.1, p. 584.   [120] Ibid.

[121] See Khurshid and Matthews, 'Tracing confusion' (1979) 95 LQR 78; and Andrews and Beatson, 'Common law tracing: springboard or swan-song?' (1997) 113 LQR 21, 24.

[122] Grantham, 'Doctrinal bases for the recognition of proprietary rights' (1996) 16 OJLS 561, 570.

(iv) Distinguishing between tracing at Common Law and in Equity

The tracing rules are complex essentially because of the fundamental differences between tracing at Common Law and in Equity.[123] Tracing at Law is relevant where the claimant has a legal proprietary base; the equitable tracing rules apply where a claim is founded on an equitable proprietary base. Separate tracing rules developed depending on whether the claim relates to legal or equitable property rights, because the Common Law courts would not recognize equitable rights and the Court of Chancery was not bound to apply the Common Law tracing rules.[124] Consequently, that court 'developed its own more sophisticated rules of identification and recognised a wider range of proprietary interests which the plaintiff could claim in a substituted asset'.[125] In fact, this is historically inaccurate, and there is no evidence of distinct tracing rules at Common Law and in Equity until the twentieth century.[126]

The essential difference between tracing at Law and in Equity is that the legal tracing rules treat property as a physical asset, whereas the equitable rules are more sophisticated and treat property as metaphysical,[127] in that Equity can see beyond the physical asset, and can identify the value inherent in it and the rights that relate to it. In *FHR European Ventures LLP v Cedar Capital Partners LLC*[128] the Supreme Court asserted that Common Law tracing is possible without a proprietary interest. No authority was provided for this *obiter dictum*, which is inconsistent with fundamental principles underpinning the law of tracing.

As will be seen,[129] this distinction between tracing at Common Law and in Equity is indefensible. It is another example of the historical divisions of the past being perpetuated without reason.[130] Although some commentators[131] and judges[132] have argued that there is no longer any distinction between tracing at Law and in Equity, it is not yet possible to reach such a conclusion, because the distinction has been clearly recognized in a number of authorities.[133] In *Foskett v McKeown*, some of the judges called for the unification of the tracing rules at Common Law and in Equity,[134] but this was *obiter* since the basic requirements for tracing in Equity were clearly established in that case. Despite the fusion of the administration of Common Law and Equity by the Judicature Act 1873, the distinction between tracing at Law and in Equity remains.[135]

19.3.2 TRACING AT COMMON LAW

Although we are concerned in this chapter with equitable proprietary claims for which the equitable tracing rules apply, to understand the nature and significance of those rules better, it is important to be aware of the Common Law tracing rules. Those rules apply where the claimant's proprietary base is a legal, rather than an equitable, proprietary right.

---

[123] *Re Diplock's Estate* [1948] Ch 465, 518–21.   [124] Ibid.   [125] Ibid.

[126] The wrong turning appears to have been made by Viscount Haldane in *Sinclair v Brougham* [1914] AC 348, 419–21. See Virgo, '*Re Hallett's Estate*', in *Landmark Cases in Equity*, ed. Mitchell and Mitchell (Oxford: Hart, 2012), p. 357.

[127] *Re Diplock's Estate* [1948] Ch 465, 520.   [128] [2014] UKSC 45, [2015] AC 250, [44].

[129] See Section 19.3.4, p. 572.   [130] See further Section 1.6, p. 19.

[131] See especially Smith (see n. 95), p. 5, and Khurshid and Matthews (see n. 121).

[132] *Bristol and West Building Society v Mothew* [1996] 4 All ER 698, 716 (Millett LJ).

[133] *Agip (Africa) Ltd v Jackson* [1990] Ch 265, 286 (Millett J), [1991] Ch 547, 566 (Fox LJ); *El Ajou v Dollar Land Holdings plc* [1993] 3 All ER 717, 733 (Millett J); *Boscawen v Bajwa* [1996] 1 WLR 328; *Shalson v Russo* [2005] Ch 281, 314 (Rimer J).

[134] [2001] 1 AC 102, 113 (Lord Steyn) and 128–9 (Lord Millett). Lord Browne-Wilkinson expressly did not consider this: ibid., 109.

[135] As recognized in *Shalson v Russo* [2003] EWHC 1637 (Ch), [2005] Ch 281, 314 (Rimer J).

(i) Tracing into pure substitutes and products

The Common Law tracing rules are logical, but restrictive. The fundamental principle underlying these rules is that the claimant will be able to identify the value of his or her property in the substitute for that property,[136] as long as the substitute has not become mixed with other property so that it loses its identity.[137]

(ii) Tracing into profits

In *Trustee of the Property of FC Jones v Jones*,[138] the Court of Appeal held that the claimant can also trace at Law into the profits that were made from the use of their property. In that case the partners in a firm of potato growers committed an act of bankruptcy. One of the partners drew cheques for £11,700 from a partnership bank account and paid them to his wife, who in turn paid the cheques into her account with a firm of commodity brokers. This money was applied on the potato futures market, and the wife made a large profit and deposited £50,760 into a deposit account at her bank. This money was never mixed with her own money. The trustee in bankruptcy of the partnership claimed this whole amount. The trustee was legally entitled to the money in the partnership bank account from the date of the bankruptcy, but the key question was whether he could trace at Law into the profits that had been credited to the wife's bank account.[139] It was held that he could, because there was a chain of straight substitutions from the money in the partnership account to the chose in action representing the funds deposited at the wife's bank account. It did not matter that the original money paid from the partnership bank account had nearly quintrupled in value; the trustee in bankruptcy was entitled to claim this profit simply because it derived from the original money without being mixed with any other money of the wife.

(iii) Tracing into mixed products

The major limitation on tracing at Common Law is that it is not possible to trace into a mixed product,[140] save where it is possible to separate the components of the product. There are two reasons why tracing into a mixed fund at Common Law is not possible: first, because of the inadequacies of legal proprietary remedies, especially that it is not possible to create a security interest over a mixed fund at Law by means of charging the fund for the amount due;[141] and, secondly, because the Common Law adopts a rigidly logical approach to tracing. Where there has been an irretrievable mixing, it is simply not possible to say in what property the claimant has a proprietary interest. Consequently, where such mixing has occurred, the claimant's legal title to the property will be extinguished.

The key implication of this restriction on tracing at Common Law arises where the claimant's money becomes mixed with other money that has been credited to the defendant's

---

[136] *Banque Belge pour l'Etranger v Hambrouck* [1921] 1 KB 321; *Lipkin Gorman v Karpnale Ltd* [1991] 2 AC 548.

[137] *Trustee of the Property of FC Jones v Jones* [1997] Ch 159, 169 (Millett LJ).   [138] [1997] Ch 159.

[139] An equitable proprietary claim could not be established because statute had passed the entire interest in the partnership money to the trustee in bankruptcy, so it could not have been held on trust by the wife.

[140] *Taylor v Plumer* (1815) 3 M & S 562; *Banque Belge pour l'Etranger v Hambrouck* [1921] 1 KB 321; *Agip (Africa) Ltd v Jackson* [1991] Ch 547; *El Ajou v Dollar Land Holdings* [1993] 3 All ER 717; *Bank of America v Arnell* [1999] Lloyd's Rep Bank 399. Smith, 'Tracing in *Taylor v Plumer*: Equity in the Court of King's Bench' [1995] LMCLQ 240 has argued that *Taylor v Plumer* actually turned on the application of equitable tracing rules. See also Khurshid and Matthews (see n. 121), p. 81. This was recognized by Millett LJ in *Trustee of the Property of FC Jones v Jones* [1997] Ch 159, 169, but he still affirmed the rule that tracing at Law is barred if the property has been mixed with other property.

[141] *Agip (Africa) Ltd v Jackson* [1991] Ch. 547, 563 (Fox LJ).

bank account, so that it is not possible to say which value belongs to the claimant and which to the defendant. It has sometimes been suggested that the effect of the restriction on Common Law tracing into mixed products is that, if the claimant's money is paid into a bank account, tracing will automatically fail. But that is not the case. The Common Law is willing to trace into and through a bank account, even though the property in which the claimant has a proprietary interest has changed its identity from a sum of money to a debt owed by the bank to the account holder. But, since this debt represents completely the sum of money that originally existed, assuming that no other money had been credited to this account either before or after the claimant's money had been credited to it, the debt can simply be regarded as the substitute for the claimant's money. A good example of tracing in such circumstances is *Banque Belge pour L'Etranger v Hambrouck*,[142] in which the first defendant forged a number of cheques, so that £6,000 was debited from the account of his employer at the claimant bank and this sum was then credited to his own bank account. The first defendant then drew sums from this account, which he paid to his mistress; she then paid these sums into her own bank account. The claimant bank sought to recover this money from the mistress. At the time of the bank's action, the mistress's account was credited with the sum of £315. The Court of Appeal held that the claimant was able to trace into this credit because only the proceeds of the fraud had been paid into the account of the first defendant and his mistress, so that there had not been any mixing of money. It did not matter that the tracing process did not relate to sums of money throughout, since credits had been substituted for actual money at various stages, because the credits simply represented the money and neither the credits nor the money were ever mixed with any other money or credits that did not derive from the fraud.

Modern banking practice is such that it is increasingly difficult to trace into and through a bank account. This is especially because of electronic transfers, which mean that the claimant is unable to show that the money received by the defendant necessarily represents the claimant's money. This limitation on the efficacy of tracing at Law was recognized in *Trustee of the Property of FC Jones v Jones*,[143] in which Millett LJ affirmed that it was not possible to trace through inter-bank clearing and that tracing at Law would be defeated where value is passed by an electronic funds transfer. The practical significance of this is illustrated by *Agip (Africa) Ltd v Jackson*,[144] in which the claimant bank had been defrauded of substantial sums of money by its chief accountant. The case focused on a payment to a company that had a bank account in London. Before the payment was made, the company had nothing credited to this account. Once the payment had been made, the balance was transferred to the defendant firm of accountants, and then to another company, and finally overseas to the fraudsters. The claimant sought to recover the value of the money received by the defendant. It succeeded in Equity,[145] but failed at Law because of mixing, since there had been a telegraphic transfer of the money between accounts, so nothing passed except for a stream of electrons.

The inability of the Common Law to trace through a mixed fund explains why tracing in Equity has proved so much more significant in practice, since Equity will trace through mixed funds. But, for the equitable tracing rules to be engaged, the claimant must first establish an equitable proprietary base; it is not yet possible to rely on the equitable tracing rules where the claimant has only a legal proprietary base. There are some signs, however, of greater flexibility being introduced into the Common Law tracing rules, albeit in jurisdictions other than England. For example, in *BMP Global Distribution Inc v Bank of Nova Scotia*,[146] the Supreme Court of Canada recognized that

---

[142] [1921] 1 KB 321.   [143] [1997] Ch 159, 168.
[144] [1990] Ch 265, affirmed by the Court of Appeal: [1991] Ch 547.
[145] For the personal claim in equity, see Section 20.2.3.(i), p. 596.   [146] [2009] SCC 15.

it is possible to trace at Law into a mixed bank account if it is possible to identify the funds.[147] This cannot yet be regarded as representing English law, but it does provide further evidence for the gradual breakdown of the long-standing distinction between the tracing rules at Law and in Equity.

19.3.3 TRACING IN EQUITY

The main advantage of tracing in Equity is that it will not be defeated by the irretrievable mixing of property.[148] This difference in approach between Law and Equity has been expressed in terms that the Common Law views property as physical assets, whereas Equity is able to view property metaphysically.[149] Consequently, where money in which the claimant has a proprietary interest is mixed in a bag with the defendant's money so that it is not possible to say which coins or notes belong to which party, tracing at Law will fail because the Common Law cannot identify the actual coins or notes in which the claimant has a proprietary interest. But Equity is able to assume that the claimant's property continues to exist in the mixture, albeit that it is not possible to say which coins or notes belong to which party. The reason Equity can do this is because, when the claimant has traced an equitable proprietary interest into a mixed fund, an equitable charge will be placed on the whole fund as security for the claim.[150] Consequently, Equity does not specifically regard any particular part of the fund as belonging to the claimant, but is prepared to assume that the claimant has an equitable interest in the mixture by means of a charge on the fund for the value of the claimant's contribution to the fund.

Since Equity is prepared to trace into and through a mixed fund, complex rules have been developed to determine how such tracing can occur. This will be examined after a further distinction between tracing at Law and Equity has been considered, namely that, to trace in Equity, it is first necessary to identify a fiduciary relationship.

(i) The fiduciary requirement

The orthodox requirement for tracing in Equity is that it is necessary to show that the property in which the claimant had an equitable proprietary interest passed to the defendant through the hands of a fiduciary in breach of duty.[151] In other words, there must have been an unauthorized disposition of property.[152] It is not, however, necessary to show that the defendant owed fiduciary duties to the claimant, since it suffices that the fiduciary through whose hands the property passed was an intermediary between the claimant

---

[147] This was considered to be consistent with *Banque Belge pour l' Étranger v Hambrouck* [1921] 1 KB 321; and *Agip (Africa) Ltd v Jackson* [1992] 4 All ER 451, although the latter case was specifically concerned with tracing in Equity.

[148] *Re Hallett's Estate* (1880) 13 Ch D 696; *Sinclair v Brougham* [1914] AC 398; *Agip (Africa) Ltd v Jackson* [1991] Ch 417.

[149] *Re Diplock* [1948] Ch 465, 520.

[150] *Re Hallett's Estate* (1880) 13 Ch D 696, 708–10 (Jessel MR); *Sinclair v Brougham* [1914] AC 398, 420–2 (Viscount Haldane LC), 441–2 (Lord Parker of Waddington), and 459–60 (Lord Sumner); *El Ajou v Dollar Land Holding* [1993] 3 All ER 717, 735–6 (Millett J).

[151] *Re Hallett's Estate* (1880) 13 Ch D 696, 710 (Jessel MR); *Re Diplock's Estate* [1948] Ch 465; *Agip (Africa) Ltd v Jackson* [1991] Ch 547, 566 (Fox LJ); *El Ajou v Dollar Land Holdings plc* [1993] 3 All ER 717, 733 (Millett J); *Boscawen v Bajwa* [1996] 1 WLR 328, 335 (Millett LJ); *Bank of America v Arnell* [1999] Lloyd's Rep Bank 399. *Re Diplock's Estate* was specifically affirmed by Lord Browne-Wilkinson in *Westdeutsche Landesbank Girozentrale v Islington LBC* [1996] AC 669, 714.

[152] *Space Investments Ltd v Canadian Imperial Bank of Commerce Trust Co (Bahamas) Ltd* [1986] 1 WLR 1072. If the disposition is authorized, the claimant's proprietary interest will be overreached, so that the claimant no longer has an equitable proprietary interest in the asset. See Section 3.5.4.(i), p. 47.

and the defendant.[153] This is illustrated by *Re Diplock*,[154] in which the executors of Caleb Diplock's will distributed £203,000 amongst 139 different charities. The validity of the will was successfully challenged by the next of kin,[155] who then sought to recover the money that had been paid to the charities. It was held that their equitable proprietary claim succeeded,[156] even though their money had been mixed in some cases with money already held by the charities in bank accounts. It did not matter that there was no fiduciary relationship between the next of kin and the charities, because it was sufficient that there was a prior fiduciary relationship between the next of kin and the executors, who had transferred the estate in breach of fiduciary duty.

Although the condition for tracing in Equity—namely, that the property has passed through the prism of a fiduciary relationship—has been recognized in many cases, it is controversial.[157] The requirement has been expressly rejected in New Zealand.[158] In *Agip (Africa) Ltd v Jackson*,[159] Millett J affirmed that, in England, a fiduciary relationship is required to permit the assistance of Equity to be invoked, but he accepted that this requirement has been widely condemned[160] and depended on authority rather than principle. He recognized that it was not necessary to show that the fund had been the subject of fiduciary obligations before it got into the wrong hands; it was sufficient that the transfer to the defendant had created the fiduciary relationship. This is significant to our understanding of what the fiduciary relationship is being required to do. This can also be identified from *Re Diplock* itself, in which the actual requirement for tracing in Equity was that there was 'a fiduciary or quasi-fiduciary relationship or of a continuing right of property recognised in Equity'.[161] We have already seen that, where the claimant has a relationship with the defendant that can be characterized as fiduciary, the claimant may be able to establish an equitable proprietary interest where the defendant has misappropriated property in breach of fiduciary duty.[162] The key requirement for tracing in Equity today should consequently be that the claimant has a 'right of property recognised in Equity', which is either a continuing right or one that is created as a result of a breach of a fiduciary or some other duty.[163] Rather than focusing on a fiduciary relationship, the only condition for the equitable tracing rules to apply should be that the claimant can establish an equitable proprietary base.[164] In fact, this approach was implicitly recognized in *Campden Hill Ltd v Chakrani*,[165] in which Hart J held that the fiduciary relationship can be established from the 'division of the legal and beneficial ownership' of the property,[166] and in *Re Diplock* itself, the court recognized that:[167]

---

[153] *Re Diplock's Estate* [1948] Ch 465. See also *Boscawen v Bajwa* [1996] 1 WLR 328.

[154] [1948] Ch 465.

[155] *Chichester Diocesan Fund and Board of Finance Inc v Simpson* [1944] AC 341. See Section 6.4.1, p. 175.

[156] For the personal claim, see Section 20.2.3.(ii), p. 607.

[157] For criticism of the requirement as being founded on a misreading of earlier authorities see Televantos, 'Losing the fiduciary requirement for equitable tracing claims' (2017) 133 LQR 492.

[158] *Elders Pastoral Ltd v Bank of New Zealand* [1989] 2 NZLR 180.   [159] [1990] Ch 265, 290.

[160] Including by himself: 'Tracing the proceeds of fraud' (1991) 107 LQR 71.

[161] [1948] Ch 465, 520.   [162] See Section 19.2.1, p. 541.

[163] See Oakley, 'The prerequisites of an equitable tracing claim' (1975) 28 CLP 64; Pearce, 'A tracing paper' [1976] Conv 277, 288.

[164] See *Westdeutsche Landesbank Girozentrale v Islington LBC* [1994] 1 WLR 938, 947 (Dillon LJ) and 953 (Leggatt LJ). Although this decision was overruled by the House of Lords, nothing was said about this point. See also Grantham (n. 122), p. 65, and Smith (see n. 95), pp. 123–30.

[165] [2005] EWHC 911 (Ch).

[166] Ibid., [74]. See also *El Ajou v Dollar Land Holdings* [1993] BCLC 735, 753, in which Millett J recognized the necessary equitable proprietary interest following rescission of a transaction for fraud, so that the property that had been transferred was held on resulting trust for the claimant. See Section 8.5.2, p. 253.

[167] [1948] Ch 465, 530.

equity may operate on the conscience not merely of those who acquire a legal title in breach of some trust, express or constructive, or of some other fiduciary obligation, but of volunteers provided that as a result of what has gone before some equitable proprietary interest has been created and attaches to the property in the hands of the volunteer.

This was actually highly significant on the facts of *Re Diplock* itself, because the next of kin, being the potential beneficiaries under a will, had no initial equitable interest in the undistributed property.[168] The only way in which such an equitable proprietary interest could be created was by treating the executors as owing a fiduciary duty to the next of kin that they breached by mistakenly transferring the estate to the charities. As a result of this breach of fiduciary duty, the charities should be treated as holding the money on constructive trust for the next of kin, because the property should have been transferred to them. The Court of Appeal in *Re Diplock's Estate* did not consider this aspect of the decision, but the creation of an equitable proprietary interest was clearly essential before the next of kin could trace in Equity and then bring an equitable proprietary claim.

(ii) Unmixed funds

It is clearly possible to trace value at Equity into an unmixed fund. So, for example, if a trustee misappropriates trust property, such as shares, which he or she sells and the proceeds of sale are credited to a bank account that has no other money credited to it, the beneficiary will be able to trace into that bank account. Similarly, if a trustee wrongly uses trust money to pay the whole purchase price in respect of a particular asset, the beneficiary can trace into that asset.[169]

(iii) Mixed funds

A mixed fund will arise where money in which the claimant has an equitable proprietary interest has become mixed with somebody else's money. This mixing may be a physical mixing, such as where £100 of the claimant's money is put into a bag that already contains £100 of the defendant's money. Alternatively, this may be a notional mixing, such as where the claimant's money is credited to the defendant's bank account that already has money credited to it. Equity allows tracing into and through a mixed fund, as was recognized by Millett J in *El Ajou v Dollar Land Holding*:[170]

> The victims of a fraud can follow[171] their money in equity through a bank account where it has been mixed with other moneys because equity treats the money in such accounts as charged with the repayment of their money. If the money in the account subject to the charge is afterwards paid out of the account and into a number of different accounts, the victims can claim a similar charge of each of the recipient accounts. They are not bound to choose between them . . . Equity's power to charge a mixed fund with the repayment of trust moneys . . . enables the claimant to follow the money not because it is theirs, but because it is derived from a fund which is treated as if it were subject to a charge in their favour.

Complex rules have developed to balance the interests of the different contributors to the mixed fund. Different rules and presumptions exist depending on whether the claimant's money has been mixed with that of a fiduciary or of an innocent third party.

---

[168] *Commissioner of Stamp Duties (Qld) v Livingston* [1965] AC 694. See Section 3.7.7, p. 64.
[169] *Re Hallett's Estate* (1880) 13 Ch D 696, 709 (Jessel MR).
[170] [1993] BCLC 735, 753.
[171] Despite using the language of following, Millett J is actually referring to tracing.

Mixing with the fiduciary's money

Where the fiduciary has wrongly mixed the claimant's money with the fiduciary's own money, either physically or notionally, the onus is on the fiduciary to distinguish the separate assets; to the extent that they are is unable to do so, they will belong to the claimant.[172] This is because, where a fiduciary wrongly mixes their own money with that of the claimant, the fiduciary has created an evidential difficulty as to what has happened to the claimant's money. In such a case, the evidential difficulty will be resolved against the interests of the fiduciary, save where the fiduciary can show otherwise on the balance of probabilities.[173] Whether the fiduciary is able to show this will turn on the facts. An example of a case in which it was held that the trustee had not used the trust fund to purchase an asset was *Re Tilley's Will Trust*,[174] in which the trustee had mixed trust funds with her own funds in her bank account and then bought some properties for development. It was held that these properties were not purchased with the trust money that had been credited to her bank account, but from the use of overdraft facilities that were available to her.

A consequence of the general principle relating to the fiduciary's creation of an evidential difficulty by mixing property is that the claimant is able to rely on one of two alternative presumptions to assist with the tracing exercise. The claimant can rely on whichever presumption is most favourable to him or her.

Fiduciary spent own money first

The first presumption is that the fiduciary spent their own money first, so the claimant will be able to trace into the sum remaining in the fund.[175] The significance of this presumption is illustrated by *Re Hallett's Estate*,[176] in which Hallett, a solicitor, had settled money on trust for himself, his wife, and his children. The trustees of the settlement transferred some of the trust property to Hallett to invest. He did so, but then sold the investments and paid the proceeds to his personal bank account. He had also been given some bonds by a client to look after. He sold those bonds and the proceeds of sale were also credited to his bank account. He made various payments from and into this account. He died insolvent, and the trustees of the settlement and the client brought proprietary claims to the money that was still credited to his bank account. At the date of his death, there were sufficient funds credited to that account to meet the claims of both the trustees and the client, but the crucial question for the Court of Appeal was whether they could both recover in priority to Hallett's general creditors. This turned on whether the payments that had been made from the account were made with Hallett's money or that of the claimants. It was held that Hallett, who was in a fiduciary relationship with both the trustees and the client, should be presumed to have drawn his own money out of the account first, so that the money that remained credited to the account could be distributed between the trustees and the client.

Fiduciary spent the claimant's money first

The alternative presumption is that the fiduciary spent the claimant's money first. The claimant will want to rely on this presumption where the fiduciary has used money from the mixed fund to purchase an asset and dissipated the remaining amount of the fund; the claimant can trace into the purchased asset by presuming that the fiduciary intended to

---

[172] *Lupton v White* (1805) 15 Ves Jun 432; *Re Tilley's Will Trust* [1967] 1 Ch 1179, 1183 (Ungoed-Thomas J).
[173] *Sinclair Investments (UK) Ltd v Versailles Trade Finance Ltd* [2011] EWCA Civ 347, [2012] 1 AC 776, [100] (Lord Neuberger MR).
[174] [1967] 1 Ch 1179.   [175] *Re Hallett's Estate* (1880) 13 Ch D 696.   [176] Ibid.

purchase that asset using the claimant's money rather than his or her own money.[177] The operation of this presumption is illustrated by *Re Oatway*,[178] in which the facts were the opposite of those in *Re Hallett's Estate*. The trustee in *Re Oatway* had paid trust money into his bank account that was already credited with his own money. The trustee then withdrew money from the account and used this to buy shares. The remaining money credited to the bank account was then dissipated. It was held that the beneficiary could trace into the shares, even though, when they were purchased, the balance to the credit of the bank account exceeded the value of the shares, so that there would still have been some money credited to the account that could meet the claimant's claim, before that amount was then dissipated. But the trustee was not entitled to withdraw anything from the bank account until the trust money had been restored to the trust. All of the money credited to the bank account was subject to a charge in favour of the trust, so that any asset purchased with value from the trust was also subject to a charge.

The implication of these dual presumptions is that the tracing rules can be manipulated to ensure that the interests of the beneficiaries are protected whenever possible. The result is inconsistent with one of the principles recognized in *Foskett v McKeown*, namely that proprietary rights should be vested at once and should not depend on subsequent events.[179] But, in *Re Oatway*, whether the claimant could trace into the money that was still credited to the account after the shares were purchased or into the shares themselves depended on events after the share purchase, namely the dissipation of the money credited to the bank account. The approach in *Re Oatway* is more consistent with the essentially evidential function of the tracing rules and the principle in *Foskett v McKeown* to the contrary should be rejected.

Mixing with the money of an innocent third party

General rule

Where the mixed fund consists of money in which the claimant has an equitable interest and also money from an innocent third party, such as the beneficiary of another trust fund, the general rule is that the money in the mixed fund will be assumed to belong equally to both parties.[180]

If the third party has mixed the claimant's money with their own, the third party is sometimes called an 'innocent volunteer', meaning someone who had not given consideration for the claimant's property and who had no reason to suspect that somebody else had a proprietary interest in the money. If the third party did know, or had reason to suspect, that somebody else had a proprietary interest in the property, they will be treated as a wrongdoer[181] and the tracing rules relating to mixing by fiduciaries will apply.

The essential features of the tracing rules relating to an innocent volunteer were identified by the Court of Appeal in *Re Diplock*, as follows:[182]

> In the case, however, of a volunteer who takes without notice ... if there is no question of mixing, he holds the money on behalf of the true owner whose equitable right to the money still persists as against him. On the other hand, if the volunteer mixes the money with money of his own, or receives it mixed from the fiduciary ... he must admit the claim of the true owner, but is not precluded from setting up his own claim in respect of the

---

[177] *Re Oatway* [1903] 2 Ch 356; *Re Tilley's Will Trusts* [1967] Ch 1179.
[178] [1903] 2 Ch 356.   [179] See Section 19.3.1.(ii), p. 552.
[180] *Sinclair v Brougham* [1914] AC 398; *Re Diplock's Estate* [1948] 1 Ch 465, 524.
[181] *Boscawen v Bajwa* [1996] 1 WLR 328, 337 (Millett LJ).   [182] [1948] Ch 465, 539.

moneys of his own which have been contributed to the mixed fund. The result is that they share *pari passu*.

Pari passu simply means that the claimant and the innocent volunteer share the fund in proportion to their contribution to it.[183] So, for example, if the fund consists of £1,000, with £250 derived from the claimant and £750 from the innocent volunteer, they will share the fund, and any increase or decrease in the value of that fund, in the proportion of one to three.[184]

The innocent volunteer may not have mixed the fund, but might receive the fund already mixed. For example, if Ann is a trustee of two trust funds, Trust A and Trust B, and misappropriates £250 from Trust A and £750 from Trust B, and gives the mixed fund to her daughter, then as between the beneficiaries of the two trusts 'there is no basis upon which any of the claims can be subordinated to any of the others',[185] so again the beneficiaries will share the fund in the proportion of one to three.

The rule in *Clayton's case*

An exception to this general rule that the claimant and third party rank equally in their claim to the fund arises where the mixing takes place in a current bank account, but not a deposit account, so that the rule in *Clayton's case*[186] applies, namely that the money that was first paid into the bank account is deemed to be the money that was first paid out of it. So, for example, if a trustee misappropriates £1,000 from trust fund B and deposits this in his current bank account, which is already credited with £1,000 that has been misappropriated from trust fund A, but no other money is credited to the account, and the trustee then withdraws and dissipates £750, it will be presumed that it was the money from trust fund A that was taken because this was the money that was credited to the bank account first. So the beneficiaries of trust fund A will suffer the loss.

The reason why the rule applies only to current accounts and not deposit accounts is that current accounts are active, so that there may be a large number of transactions involving the account every day, which makes it more difficult to establish whose money has been withdrawn from the account.

But the rule in *Clayton's case* is only a presumption and it will not operate if it can be rebutted, for example by proving that the defendant intended to withdraw the claimant's money from the bank account. The rule will not be applicable where the mixed fund is made up of contributions from the claimant and the fiduciary, simply because a different presumption operates in respect of such a mixed fund, namely the presumption that works best in favour of the claimant and against the fiduciary.[187] So the rule is applicable only where the mixed fund consists of contributions from different trusts or contributions from trust funds and innocent volunteers that have been wrongfully mixed.[188]

The rule in *Clayton's case* will also be inapplicable if it impracticable or unjust to rely on it,[189] or if another approach is more consistent with the intentions of the contributors to

---

[183] *Sinclair v Brougham* [1914] AC 398, 442 (Lord Parker).

[184] Hodgkinson, 'Tracing and mixed funds' [1983] Conv 135, who also suggests that the innocent volunteer should be awarded an allowance for effort where he or she has enhanced the value of the mixed fund.

[185] *Foskett v McKeown* [2001] 1 AC 102, 132 (Lord Millett).

[186] (1817) 1 Mer 572.

[187] *Re Hallett's Estate* (1880) 13 Ch D 696; *Re Oatway* [1903] 2 Ch 356. See Section 19.3.3.(iii), p. 562.

[188] *Barlow Clowes International Ltd v Vaughan* [1992] 4 All ER 22. See *Pennell v Deffell* (1853) 4 De GM & G 372.

[189] *Commerzbank AG v IMB Morgan plc* [2004] EWHC 2771 (Ch); *Charity Commission for England and Wales v Framjee* [2014] EWHC 2507 (Ch), [2015] 1 WLR 16.

the fund.[190] So, for example, in *Barlow Clowes International Ltd v Vaughan*,[191] the rule was not applied because the large number of proprietary claims made the operation of the rule impracticable. A rateable basis of distribution of assets amongst the claimants was adopted instead, so that withdrawals were apportioned according to the amount that had been contributed to the fund. In fact, the 'rule' in *Clayton's case* is increasingly being treated as an exception to a rule that the money should be distributed rateably between the innocent volunteers who contributed to the mixed fund.[192] In *Russell-Cooke Trust Co v Prentis*,[193] it was recognized that *Clayton's case* could be displaced very easily by reference to counter-intentions of the parties, the justice of the case, or where it could be seen that payments credited to a bank account had not led to payments out chronologically.

The rule is consequently very weak. It is fictional and has been described as apportioning 'a common misfortune through a test which has no relation whatever to the justice of the case'.[194] It can produce unjust results where, for example, a relatively small number of claimants become entitled to the bulk of the available assets because value misappropriated from them was credited to the bank account more recently. An alternative to the rule is the 'rolling charge', which is adopted in North America, whereby each debit to the account containing the mixed fund is attributable to all of the claimants pro rata, so that losses fall on all creditors proportionate to the value they have contributed to the fund.[195] But this has been rejected as too complicated and expensive, at least in a case in which there are a lot of claimants.[196] Where money is credited to a *deposit* account, losses following dissipation of money are borne proportionately in relation to the value of the contributions from the innocent volunteers. There is no reason of principle or logic why the same should not now apply to money deposited in current accounts. *Clayton's case* itself actually concerned the order of appropriation of payments from an account and was not about tracing, so that there is no reason to apply it in respect of proprietary claims. As McConville has convincingly argued,[197] the rule provided a mode of accounting as between a creditor, such as a trustee, and his or her debtor, such as a banker, and is immaterial to the assessment of who is entitled to the value credited to a bank account. Consequently the rule in *Clayton's case* should now be rejected,[198] and, where the mixed fund is not sufficient to meet the claims of all claimants, the losses should be attributed to all of them in proportion to their contribution.

Third-party and fiduciary contributions

Where the mixed fund comprises, for example, value that is derived from the defaulting fiduciary and two innocent claimants, the claimants will be treated as one party and the value contributed by the fiduciary will be treated according to the usual presumptions relating to fiduciaries to determine whether the fiduciary is deemed to have withdrawn their own money first. So, if money was withdrawn and was dissipated, this is deemed to have been the fiduciary's money, but, if the money was withdrawn and used to buy an

---

[190] *The National Crime Agency v Robb* [2014] EWHC 4384 (Ch), [2015] Ch 520, [64] (Etherton C).

[191] [1992] 4 All ER 22.

[192] *Russell-Cooke Trust Co v Prentis* [2002] EWHC 2227 (Ch), [2003] 2 All ER 478, [55] (Lindsay J); *Commerzbank AG v IMB Morgan plc* [2004] EWHC 2771 (Ch), [50] (Lawrence Collins J).

[193] [2002] EWHC 2227 (Ch), [2003] 2 All ER 478.

[194] *Re Walter J Schmidt & Co* 298 F 314, 316 (1923) (Judge Learned Hand).

[195] See *Charity Commission for England and Wales v Framjee* [2014] EWHC 2507 (Ch), [2015] 1 WLR 16, [48] (Henderson J).

[196] *Barlow Clowes International Ltd v Vaughan* [1992] 4 All ER 22, 28 (Dillon LJ).

[197] 'Tracing and the rule in *Clayton's Case*' (1963) 79 LQR 388, 407–8.

[198] As has occurred in New Zealand: *Re Registered Securities Ltd* [1991] 1 NZLR 545.

asset, this is deemed to have been the money of the two innocent parties. If the fiduciary is presumed to have dissipated their own money first, then any remaining value credited to the bank account will be apportioned between the claimants in proportion to their contribution to the mixed fund. Alternatively, if an asset has been purchased from the mixed fund and this is presumed to have been purchased with the claimants' contributions, they will have an interest in the asset that is proportionate to their contributions.[199] Consequently, any increase or decrease in the value of the asset will be borne rateably between them.

(iv) Restrictions on equitable tracing

Equitable tracing enables the claimant to trace value into a specific asset or fund only where it is possible to say that some or all of the value of the asset or fund represents the value of the property in which the claimant originally had an equitable interest. Consequently, equitable tracing will fail or will be restricted in the following circumstances.

Dissipation of the asset or fund

Where the asset in which the claimant has an equitable interest has been destroyed, or where the fund has been dissipated and no specific asset can be identified that derives from it, tracing will fail. So, for example, where the defendant buys wine with trust money and then drinks it, there is nothing into which the value can be traced.[200] Similarly, where the claimant's money is used to discharge a debt, such as where it is paid into an overdrawn bank account, there will usually[201] be no asset that can be considered to represent the claimant's property and so tracing will be defeated.[202] As the Privy Council has recognized, if a property interest has 'ceased to exist, it cannot metamorphose into a later property interest'.[203] Consequently, it is generally[204] not possible to trace *through* an overdrawn account. But it does not follow that it is not possible to trace *into* an overdrawn account to the discharged debt, since, exceptionally, a proprietary remedy involving the revival of the debt might be available.[205]

Lowest intermediate balance

If the claimant's money is mixed with other money, for example in a bank account, and subsequently the balance of that account is reduced to less than the amount of the claimant's money that had been deposited, the amount that the claimant can recover is necessarily limited to the maximum amount that can be regarded as representing their

---

[199] *Re Diplock's Estate* [1948] Ch 465, 539; *Lord Provost of Edinburgh v The Lord Advocate* (1879) 4 App Cas 823 (HL Sc).

[200] *Re Diplock's Estate* [1948] Ch 465, 521.

[201] If the overdraft was incurred in order to purchase an asset it might be possible to trace into that asset by virtue of the doctrine of 'backward tracing'. See further Section 19.3.3.(iv), p. 567.

[202] *Re Diplock's Estate* [1948] Ch 465, 521; *James Roscoe (Bolton) Ltd v Winder* [1915] 1 Ch 62; *Re Goldcorp Exchange Ltd* [1995] 1 AC 74; *Bishopsgate Investment Management Ltd v Homan* [1995] Ch 211; *Shalson v Russo* [2005] EWHC 1637 (Ch), [2005] Ch 281, [140] (Rimer J); *Serious Fraud Office v Lexi Holdings plc* [2009] EWCA Crim 1443, [2009] QB 376, [50] (Keene J); *Re BA Peters Ltd* [2008] EWCA Civ 1604, [2010] 1 BCLC 142, [15] (Lord Neuberger).

[203] *The Federal Republic of Brazil v Durant International Corporation* [2015] UKPC 35, [2016] AC 297, [17].

[204] This did, however, occur in *Shalson v Russo* [2003] EWHC 1637 (Ch), [2005] Ch 285, where the overdraft was incurred in order to purchase an asset; it was possible to trace into that asset. See also *The Federal Republic of Brazil v Durant International Corporation* [2015] UKPC 35, [2016] AC 297, [40]. See further Section 19.3.3.(iv), p. 569.

[205] See the remedy of subrogation, discussed in Section 19.4.3, p. 578.

money.[206] So, for example, if the defendant trustee paid £1,000 of the trust money into his own bank account, which already had £1,000 credited to it, and the defendant then dissipated £1,500, the maximum value that the claimant can claim is £500. This is because the first £1,000 that was spent is deemed to have been the defendant's money, because of the presumptions relating to fiduciaries.[207] But, since another £500 was spent, this must have been the claimant's money which has been dissipated, leaving only £500 left to satisfy the claimant's claim. The lowest intermediate balance rule will apply even if the defendant trustee has subsequently paid in their own money to the fund so as to restore the original balance. This is because the trustee could not be considered to intend to clothe their own money with a trust in favour of the claimant. It would be different, however, if the subsequent repayment was made to a separate trust bank account from which the trust funds had originally been taken, for then the payments could be considered to be a substitute for the trust money because there would then be a sufficient intention for the new money to be held on the old trust.[208]

The practical significance of the lowest intermediate balance rule is illustrated by *James Roscoe (Bolton) Ltd v Winder*,[209] in which over £455 of trust money was paid into a bank account by a trustee. The balance of that account then fell to £25, but, at the date of the trustee's death, it had increased to £358. It was held that the account could be charged only to £25 for the benefit of the trust, since this was the lowest intermediate balance in the account after the trust money had been paid in. What had clearly happened was that the trust money must have been spent except to the extent of £25. It was considered whether the amount that had subsequently been credited to the account could be regarded as being impressed with the trust. This was rejected because there was insufficient evidence that the trustee intended the subsequent payments to be subject to the trust. This aspect of the decision is difficult to defend and appears to be inconsistent with the general presumptions of intent relating to fiduciaries, as recognized in *Re Hallett's Estate*[210] in particular: the Court of Appeal accepted in that case that, where a trustee has acted, they should be regarded as acting in the best interests of the trust. It is for this reason that, when money is dissipated from a mixed fund, this is presumed to be the trustee's money. So, surely, this presumption should work in the same way when money is subsequently credited to a denuded bank account: the trustee should be presumed to be returning trust money to the account?

Backward tracing

The orthodox view of the law of equitable tracing has been that a claimant is not able to trace into property that was already in the defendant's possession before the claimant's money was received, because, in such circumstances, the defendant's property cannot be regarded as representing the claimant's money, even if the claimant's money was used to pay for the property by discharging a debt that had been incurred in respect of it.[211] In

---

[206] *James Roscoe (Bolton) Ltd v Winder* [1915] 1 Ch 62; *Re Goldcorp Exchange Ltd* [1995] 1 AC 74; *Bishopsgate Investment Management Ltd v Homan* [1995] Ch 211; *Campden Hill Ltd v Chakrani* [2005] EWHC 911 (Ch); *The Federal Republic of Brazil v Durant International Corporation* [2015] UKPC 35, [2016] AC 297, [41].

[207] See Section 19.3.3.(iii), p. 562.

[208] *James Roscoe (Bolton) Ltd v Winder* [1915] 1 Ch 62, 69 (Sargant J). See also *Re Diplock's Estate* [1948] Ch 465, 552 (unmixing of money by placing it in a separate bank account).

[209] [1915] 1 Ch 62.

[210] (1880) 13 Ch D 496.

[211] *Bishopsgate Investment Management Ltd v Homan* [1995] Ch 211, 221 (Leggatt LJ). See also *Re Tilley's Will Trust* [1967] 1 Ch 1179, in which the trust fund was used to reduce an overdraft that had been incurred to purchase properties and it was not contemplated that the claimant could trace into those properties.

other words, so-called 'backward tracing' is not available as part of the tracing exercise. So, for example, if the defendant purchases a car and incurs a debt to the vendor, the money that has been received from the claimant might be used by the defendant to discharge this debt. Although the claimant's money can be traced into the hands of the vendor of the car, to whom the debt was owed, it will usually not be possible to bring a proprietary claim against the vendor because they are likely to have a defence of being a good-faith purchaser.[212] But it is also not possible to trace into the defendant's car because the defendant had already acquired it, even though the claimant's money has actually been used to pay for it. It follows that tracing appears to be concerned only with forward-looking exchanges of value and cannot be considered to have any retrospective operation. This rejection of backward tracing has been defended by Conaglen[213] as being consistent with precedent, and with the principles and policies that underlie the law of tracing.

Nevertheless, in *Foskett v McKeown*[214] in the Court of Appeal, Sir Richard Scott V-C tentatively recognized the principle of backward tracing, although he declined to decide the point. He said that '[t]he availability of equitable remedies ought . . . to depend upon the substance of the transaction in question and not upon the strict order in which associated events happen'. Hobhouse LJ[215] and Morritt LJ[216] explicitly rejected the proposition that tracing could be used to identify value in a previously acquired asset.

Although the House of Lords in *Foskett v McKeown*[217] did not expressly consider the backward tracing principle, the approach adopted by the majority as regards equitable tracing is certainly consistent with it: if tracing is not concerned with causation as such, in the sense that but for the receipt of the claimant's property the substitute asset would not have been obtained, but is concerned with attribution of value, it is surely possible to attribute value from the original asset to the substitute asset if the claimant's money has been used to discharge a debt incurred in respect of the substitute asset. Consequently, the backward tracing principle should be recognized in English law.[218] If backward tracing were recognized, it would enable the claimant to trace into a previously acquired asset, both where the defendant used the claimant's money to discharge a debt that the defendant had incurred by borrowing money to acquire the asset, and where the claimant's money is paid into an overdrawn bank account where the overdraft resulted from the defendant purchasing the asset. This has been advocated by Smith on the ground that a payment that discharges a debt is 'just delayed payment, and the traceable proceeds are whatever was acquired in the past when the debt was incurred'.[219] In *Relfo Ltd v Varsani*,[220] Arden LJ recognized that, in order to trace money into substitute property, it is not necessary that the payments should occur in any particular order. So, for example, where a third party pays money to the defendant in the expectation that the third party would be reimbursed from money transferred from the trust of which the claimant is a beneficiary, the claimant could trace the value of their money to the defendant. This is a potentially significant expansion of the tracing rules, which does not limit tracing to direct substitutional transfers. Whilst not expressly recognizing backward tracing, Arden LJ's dictum is certainly consistent with its recognition.

---

[212] See Section 19.5.1, p. 584.

[213] 'Difficulties with tracing backwards' (2011) 127 LQR 432.

[214] [1998] Ch 265, 283–4. See also *Bishopsgate Investment Management Ltd v Homan* [1995] Ch 211, 217 (Dillon LJ); *Boscawen v Bajwa* [1996] 1 WLR 328, 341 (Millett LJ); *Jyske Bank (Gibraltar) Ltd v Spjeldnaes* (unreported) 23 July 1997; *Shalson v Russo* [2003] EWHC 1637 (Ch), [2005] Ch 285, [141] (Rimer J).

[215] [1998] Ch 265, 289.   [216] Ibid., at 296.   [217] [2001] 1 AC 102.

[218] See *Shalson v Russo* [2003] EWHC 1637 (Ch), [2005] Ch 285, [142] (Rimer J).

[219] 'Tracing into the payment of a debt' (1995) 54 CLJ 290, 292.

[220] [2014] EWCA Civ 360, [2015] 1 BCLC 14, [63].

There is, in fact, a decision of the Court of Appeal that is consistent with the recognition of backward tracing. In *Re Diplock's Estate*,[221] some of the money that should have been paid to the testator's next of kin by the executors had been paid by mistake to the Heritage Craft Schools, which had used the money to discharge a debt that had been incurred to enable it to improve a building. It was held that, even though the money had actually been used to discharge the debt, it had effectively been used to pay for the improvements and so it was possible to trace the value of the money into the improvements. This is consistent with the courts examining the substance of the transaction rather than being confined to a consideration of events in the exact order in which they occurred. But the proprietary claim did not succeed in that case, apparently because it was not considered to be just to allow such a claim where the recipient charity had innocently used the money to improve its own property.[222]

More recently, in *Shalson v Russo*,[223] it was recognized that the claimant could, in principle, trace through the payment of an overdraft debt into a yacht for which the defendant had partially paid through the overdraft borrowing, although it was necessary for the claimant to show that the overdraft could not have been paid off without the misappropriated money.

Backward tracing has now been explicitly recognized, albeit in a decision of the Privy Council, but it is likely to be followed by English courts.[224] In *The Federal Republic of Brazil v Durant International Corporation*,[225] the claimant had sued the defendant company for bribes which were held on constructive trust. The bribe money had been received by the controller of the company and paid into a bank account in New York, from which payments were made to the defendant's bank account in Jersey. The difficulty in this case was that it appeared that some of the bribe money which was paid into the New York bank account was credited to that account after money had been transferred to the Jersey account. Consequently, it was necessary for the Privy Council to consider whether it was possible to trace into the defendant's bank account even if it had been credited before the New York bank account had been debited. It was acknowledged that this was typical of modern banking practice. When a cheque is paid into a bank account, what actually happens is that the customer's bank will present the cheque to the bank on which the cheque is drawn and, assuming that the person who wrote the cheque, known as the 'drawer', has money credited to their bank account, their bank will credit the customer's bank with the amount of the cheque and will debit the drawer's bank account. But the reality of the banking system is such that the customer's bank may already have credited his bank account in anticipation of the cheque being cleared but before the drawer's bank account is debited.[226] If the cheque relates to money which has been dissipated from a trust fund, the fact that the customer's account is credited before the drawer's account is debited should not defeat the tracing exercise. The recognition of backward tracing would prevent such an artificial conclusion from being reached.

The Privy Council in *The Federal Republic of Brazil* did recognize backward tracing, but not without limits. The Privy Council did not wish to go so far as to recognize that it is possible to trace into whatever asset was acquired in return for the debt which was discharged with money in which the claimant had a proprietary interest. This was because the Privy Council

---

[221] [1948] Ch 465, 548–9.   [222] See further Section 19.3.3.(iv), p. 570.

[223] [2003] EWHC 1637 (Ch), [2005] Ch 285, 328.

[224] Since there is no conflicting English authority from a superior court: see *Wilers v Joyce* [2016] UKSC 44; [2016] 3 WLR 534, [16] (Lord Neuberger).

[225] [2015] UKPC 35, [2016] AC 297.   [226] Ibid., [27].

did not wish to expand equitable proprietary remedies in ways which may have adverse effects on innocent parties,[227] such as the unsecured creditors of the defendant. But the Privy Council did recognize that backward tracing would be possible where there was 'a close causal and transactional link between the incurring of a debt and the use of trust funds to discharge it'.[228] The focus should be on the substance of the transaction and not on the strict order in which associated events occur. This is consistent with the approach advocated by Arden LJ in *Relfo Ltd v Varsani*.[229] It follows that the principle of backward tracing was reognized such that it is possible to trace the value of an asset the proceeds of which are credited to an overdrawn account, but only where there is a connection between the depletion of the trust fund and the acquisition of the asset which is the subject of the proprietary claim. The Privy Council specifically recognized that this involves the attribution of value from the trust to the asset which the claimant claims. On the facts of the case it was possible to establish the necessary connection between the payment of the bribes from the New York account and the credit to the Jersey account, regardless of the precise order in which the debit and the credit occurred.

Although this was a decision of the Privy Council on appeal from the Court of Appeal of Jersey, it should be followed in English law. In addition, although the case concerned credits and debits between bank accounts, it will be of wider significance as regards proprietary claims involving previously purchased assets, but only where it can be shown that the purchase of the asset and the discharge of a consequent liability using value derived from the claimant is sufficiently coordinated. It is unclear when such coordination will be established. For example, where money has been borrowed from a third party to enable the defendant to purchase property from the vendor,[230] if the claimant's money is used to discharge this debt, it might be considered to be too great a jump to trace into the asset that the defendant purchased, because the contract of purchase and the contract of loan are distinct transactions. The key question of policy then is whether it should make any difference whether the money was borrowed from a third party or the vendor, which will turn on how wide is the notion of 'the same transaction'. Since it is clear that the Privy Council's recognition of backward tracing was, in part at least, motivated by concerns about fraud and money laundering, such that the 'court should not allow a camouflage of interconnected transactions to obscure its vision of their true overall purpose and effect',[231] a key factor to identifying a connected transaction will be whether the defendant took out any loan with a view to it being discharged with money taken from the claimant.

Although the decision in *The Federal Republic of Brazil* raises more questions than are answered, it clearly recognizes the doctrine of backward tracing. But the Privy Council also affirmed the continued existence of the lowest intermediate balance rule.[232] That rule is premised on the principle that, if it can be shown that the claimant's property interest has been dissipated, it cannot metamorphose into a later property interest. But backward tracing is different because, even though the asset in which the claimant has a proprietary interest has been dissipated through the discharge of a debt, it can be substituted for some other asset which the defendant already has.

Inequitable to trace

In *Re Diplock's Estate*,[233] the Court of Appeal recognized that tracing would be defeated where it would be inequitable to allow the claimant to trace into property held by the defendant. This will occur, for example, where an innocent volunteer has used the money

---

[227] Ibid., [33].   [228] Ibid., [34].   [229] [2014] EWCA Civ 360, [2015] 1 BCLC 14, [63].
[230] As in *Boscawen v Bajwa* [1996] 1 WLR 328.
[231] *The Federal Republic of Brazil v Durant International Corporation* [2015] UKPC 35, [2016] AC 297, [41].
[232] Ibid., [17]. See Chapter 19.3.3.(iv), p. 566.   [233] [1948] Ch 465, 546.

received to improve or alter their land.[234] In *Re Diplock's Estate*, one of the charities that received a mistaken payment was Guy's Hospital, which spent £14,000 on reconstructing two children's wards. It was held that it was not equitable to enable the next of kin to trace into this property. A number of reasons were identified as to why tracing should be barred in such a case, including that the value of the property might not have increased by the improvement; it might be difficult to determine whether a charge should attach to the whole property or just the part improved; and, most significantly, it may simply be unfair to expect an innocent volunteer to sell the property to discharge the liability. Similarly, where one of the charities had used the money paid by mistake to discharge a secured bank loan, it was held to be inequitable to compel the hospital to sell the land to satisfy the proprietary claim.[235]

This apparent bar to tracing should be rejected, or at least analysed more subtly. The better view is that this 'bar' does not defeat tracing. So, for example, the claimant should be able to trace into the defendant's improved property. Rather, the 'bar' operates at the subsequent claiming stage, when determining whether the claimant can assert a right against the traceable asset. Further, rather than being simply a matter of judicial discretion as to whether it is fair that a remedy should be awarded, the bar is better analysed as being a defence to the claim, specifically in the form of the defence of change of position,[236] although this raises a further issue as to whether it is appropriate for a proprietary claim to be defeated by the defendant's innocent change of position.[237]

(v) A move to a more pragmatic approach?

Despite the orthodox approach of equitable tracing, which requires clear representation of the value of the claimant's proprietary right in the asset or fund that is in the defendant's possession or under his or her control, dicta in some cases suggest that it is possible to trace into the defendant's general assets even though no specific asset can be identified as representing the claimant's right.[238] This has been described as the 'swollen assets' theory, since the defendant's assets will have been swollen by the receipt of value to which the claimant had a proprietary right. Tracing into the defendant's general assets can be justified on the basis that, if the defendant has dissipated those assets in which the claimant had a proprietary interest, then, because the defendant could have dissipated other assets that they owned, it is right that the claimant should be able to make a claim against those other assets.[239] But such a flexible approach to tracing is not consistent with the orthodox tracing rules, which require value to be identified in particular assets, and the 'swollen assets' theory has been confined to the specific situation in which an insolvent bank trustee wrongly deposits trust money with itself in a mixed fund and uses this money in its general business.[240] In such circumstances, a charge can be granted over the mixed fund. Recognizing this exception involving an insolvent bank trustee can be justified by reference to general principles underpinning equitable tracing.[241] If a bank is a trustee and trust money has been deposited with it, the bank will be required to keep that money in a

---

[234] Ibid., 548.   [235] Ibid., 550.

[236] See Section 19.5.2, p. 585. See *Boscawen v Bajwa* [1996] 1 WLR 328, 340 (Millett LJ).

[237] See Section 19.5.2, p. 587.

[238] See in particular *Space Investments Ltd v Canadian Imperial Bank of Commerce Trust Co (Bahamas) Ltd* [1986] 1 WLR 1072, 1074 (Lord Templeman).

[239] Ibid. For a defence of this theory, see Evans, 'Rethinking tracing and the law of restitution' (1999) 115 LQR 469.

[240] *Re Goldcorp Exchange Ltd* [1995] 1 AC 74, 105 (Lord Mustill); *Bishopsgate Investment Management Ltd v Homan* [1995] Ch 211, 218 (Dillon LJ).

[241] See Gullefer, 'Recovery of misappropriated assets: orthodoxy re-established?' [1995] LMCLQ 446, 447.

separate bank account. If the bank wrongly uses that money in its general banking business, it can be assumed that the trust money forms part of a mixed fund with all money
deposited with the bank. The beneficiaries will be able to trace into this fund, as long as the
value of that fund does not fall below the value of the claimant's contribution to it.

The courts have been right to reject the general incorporation of the swollen assets theory
into the tracing rules, since such a theory confuses the fundamental distinction between
proprietary claims in which the claimant seeks a personal remedy and those claims in which
he they seek a proprietary remedy: where the claimant seeks a personal remedy, it is sufficient for them to establish that the defendant received property in which the claimant had
a proprietary interest; it is irrelevant that this property was dissipated subsequently. Where,
however, the claimant seeks a proprietary remedy, they must establish that the defendant
has particular assets that can be considered to represent the claimant's property.[242] It is only
where particular assets can be identified that represent the claimant's original property that
it is appropriate that the claimant should gain priority over the defendant's general creditors.

Nevertheless, recent cases do suggest a trend towards the development of a more pragmatic approach to the equitable tracing rules. For example, where the claimant's money
is paid into different bank accounts, the courts have been prepared to place an equitable
charge on each account, even though the claimant was unable to identify which sums had
been credited to which accounts.[243] In *Shalson v Russo*,[244] however, the claimant's money
was deposited into the defendant's overdrawn bank account and tracing was defeated,
even though the defendant had other accounts in credit at other financial institutions.
Rimer J refused to treat all of the bank accounts as forming a single fund because it was
possible to show that the claimant's money had been deposited in the bank account that
was overdrawn. Other examples of a greater willingness to use tracing rules pragmatically
include focusing on the substance of transactions, rather than the precise order of payments,[245] and the emphasis on attribution rather than causation in *Foskett v McKeown*.[246]

19.3.4 THE FUTURE OF THE TRACING RULES

Although the orthodox approach to the law of tracing treats the tracing rules at Law and
Equity as distinct,[247] there have been calls for the assimilation of these rules.[248] Some commentators have asserted that the rules have always been assimilated[249] and there is some
indication from the case law that this view is shared by some members of the judiciary.[250]
Although the rules have not yet been formally assimilated, the artificial distinction between the rules at Common Law and Equity should be rejected. A unified approach to
tracing is required that incorporates the acceptable features of both regimes.[251] As Lord
Millett emphasized in *Foskett v McKeown*:[252]

---

[242] *Re Diplock's Estate* [1948] Ch 465, 521.   [243] *El Ajou v Dollar Land Holdings plc* [1993] 3 All ER 717.

[244] [2003] EWHC 1637 (Ch), [2005] Ch 281, [140] (Rimer J).

[245] See Section 19.3.3.(iv), p. 568.   [246] [2001] 1 AC 102.

[247] Confirmed by Rimer J in *Shalson v Russo* [2003] EWHC 1637 (Ch), [2005] Ch 281, [104].

[248] See Babafemi, 'Tracing assets: a case for the fusion of common law and Equity in English law' (1971)
34 MLR 12; Goode, 'The right to trace and its impact in commercial transactions' (1976) 92 LQR 360, 396;
Andrews and Beatson (see n. 121), p. 26; Birks (see n. 61).

[249] Smith (see n. 95), p. 5; Birks (see n. 61), p. 3; Birks, 'The necessity of a unitary law of tracing', in *Making
Commercial Law: Essays in Honour of Roy Goode*, ed. Cranston (Oxford: Oxford University Press, 1997), p. 239.

[250] See especially *Foskett v McKeown* [2001] 1 AC 102, 113 (Lord Steyn) and 129 (Lord Millett), both *obiter
dicta*. See also *Chief Constable of Kent v V* [1983] 1 QB 34, 41 (Lord Denning MR).

[251] See *Nelson v Larholt* [1948] 1 KB 339, 342–3 (Denning J); *Bristol and West Building Society v Mothew*
[1998] Ch 1, 23 (Millett LJ).

[252] [2001] 1 AC 102, 129.

Given its nature, there is nothing inherently legal or equitable about the tracing exercise. There is thus no sense in maintaining different rules of tracing at law and in equity. One set of tracing rules is enough . . . There is certainly no logical justification for allowing any distinction between them to produce capricious results in cases of mixed substitutions by insisting on the existence of a fiduciary relationship as a precondition for applying equity's tracing rules. The existence of such a relationship may be relevant to the nature of the claim which the plaintiff can maintain, whether personal or proprietary, but that is a different matter.

If the rules were assimilated, it would follow that, regardless of whether the proprietary base is legal or equitable, the claimant would be able to trace through a mixed fund without needing to establish a fiduciary relationship to do so. But such assimilation of the rules would not remove the distinction between proprietary claims at Common Law and in Equity. It would still be highly relevant that a claim was founded on a legal or an equitable proprietary base, since this would affect the nature of the claim and the nature of the remedy that would be available.[253] Assimilation of the tracing rules would not result in the assimilation of the rules on claiming or remedies.[254] For example, imagine a case in which a thief steals your money and deposits it in their bank account, which is already credited with other money. You will have retained legal title to the money. If the tracing rules were not changed, the mixing in the bank account would defeat the claim at Law, since legal title to the mixture would have passed to the thief. If tracing into a mixture were possible at Law, you would still retain legal title to the money in the mixture and would be able to bring a proprietary claim at Law. But the Common Law remedies to vindicate property rights are essentially limited to personal remedies,[255] so you would be able to recover only the value of the money paid plus profits obtained from the investment of that money,[256] but, being a personal remedy, if the defendant were to become insolvent, you would not have priority over any of the other creditors of the defendant.[257] This example shows that, even if the tracing rules were assimilated, in many cases this would be not be of any advantage to the claimant, who would prefer to obtain a proprietary remedy in Equity. There are two possible solutions to this problem. One is to recognize that the claimant who has retained legal title to property can elect to bring an equitable proprietary claim on the basis that the defendant who is in possession of the property holds the possessory title on trust for the claimant.[258] This is artificial,[259] but does at least give the claimant the option of obtaining more advantageous equitable remedies. The alternative solution is to assimilate the remedies that are available to vindicate property rights, so at the very least it would be possible to charge the defendant's property even though the claim were founded on a legal proprietary right, and maybe even to allow the claimant to recover stolen property or substitute property. This would be a radical reform that goes far beyond the relatively straightforward assimilation of the tracing rules. The assimilation of the claiming rules and the range of available remedies would drastically reduce the need to establish an equitable proprietary base outside of the express trust. But, without such assimilation of claiming, remedies, or even tracing, the equitable rules on proprietary claims remain incredibly important in the commercial world, as recognized by Briggs J in rejecting the view that these rules are old-fashioned, unduly restrictive, and 'inappropriate for the protection of investors in the modern world'.[260]

---

[253] See Section 19.4, p. 574.
[254] See Maudsley, 'Proprietary remedies for the recovery of money' (1959) 75 LQR 234.
[255] See Section 19.4, p. 574.   [256] *Trustee of the Property of FC Jones v Jones* [1997] Ch 159.
[257] Barkehall Thomas (see n. 83), p. 70.
[258] Tarrant (2005) (see n. 82), p. 245; Tarrant (2009) (see n. 82), p. 172.
[259] See Section 19.2.1, p. 549.
[260] *Re Lehman Brothers International (Europe) Ltd* [2009] EWHC 3228 (Ch), [2010] 2 BCLC 301, [198].

19.4 PROPRIETARY REMEDIES

Where the claimant has a legal proprietary base and has been able to trace at Common Law into property held by the defendant, as a general rule the claimant is able only to claim the value of the property received by the defendant rather than to recover the property itself.[261] This is the key reason why equitable property claims are preferable to Common Law claims, particularly where the property has increased in value or the defendant is insolvent. There are, however, two situations in which the Common Law does recognize proprietary remedies: first, where the claimant seeks to recover land, by the action of ejectment and, secondly, where the court orders the delivery of goods to the claimant where the defendant has committed a property tort, such as conversion.[262] But this latter remedy is available only where compensatory damages are inadequate and it lies in the discretion of the court.

Equity has developed much more extensive proprietary remedies that are available where the claimant has an equitable proprietary base and is able to trace into property received by the defendant by virtue of the equitable tracing rules. The award of these remedies is a matter of right rather than judicial discretion.[263]

19.4.1 CONSTRUCTIVE TRUST

The court may recognize that the defendant holds the property in his or her possession on trust for the claimant. Where the defendant is an express trustee, the substitute property will be held on the same trust.[264] But where the defendant is a third-party recipient of the trust property or substitute property, this property will be held on constructive trust,[265] since it arises by operation of law, even though the original equitable proprietary interest arose under an express trust,[266] because the recipient of the property will not be subject to the same duties as the express trustee. The effect of recognizing that property is held on constructive trust may be that the defendant becomes liable to transfer all, or a proportion, of the property to the claimant.

(i) Transfer of property

Where the claimant can show that he or she has an equitable proprietary interest in property that is in the possession of the defendant, the court may declare that the property is held on constructive trust for the claimant and it will order the defendant to transfer this property to the claimant.[267]

(ii) Proportionate share

A constructive trust may also be imposed where the claimant is considered to have an equitable proprietary interest in a proportionate share of the property that is in the defendant's possession. This remedy will be more attractive to the claimant than an equitable charge[268] where the property has increased in value.

---

[261] *Trustee of the Property of FC Jones v Jones* [1997] Ch 159.

[262] Torts (Interference with Goods Act) 1977, s. 3.

[263] *Foskett v McKeown* [2001] 1 AC 102, 109 (Lord Browne-Wilkinson).

[264] As in *Foskett v McKeown* itself.   [265] See Section 9.2.3, p. 256.

[266] But see, to the contrary, Lord Millett, 'Proprietary restitution', in *Equity in Commercial Law*, ed. Degeling and Edelman (Sydney: Law Book Co., 2005), pp. 315–16. See also *Foskett v McKeown* [2001] 1 AC 102, 108 (Lord Browne-Wilkinson).

[267] *Boscawen v Bajwa* [1996] 1 WLR 328, 334 (Millett LJ).   [268] See Section 19.4.2, p. 577.

When determining whether the claimant is able to claim a proportionate share of a mixture, it has been necessary to distinguish between those cases in which the defendant is a fiduciary and those where he or she is an innocent volunteer.

Fiduciary

In *Re Hallett's Estate*,[269] Jessel MR recognized that the claimant has a choice between asserting equitable title to property in the defendant's possession and obtaining a charge where the substitute property has been acquired solely with trust money. He went on to deny that the claimant could elect between these remedies where trust money had become mixed with that of the fiduciary. In such a situation, the claimant was confined to obtaining a charge to recover the value of the trust property that had been misappropriated. No convincing reason was given for this distinction, which was *obiter* because the claimant in that case sought only a charge. The distinction between the remedies for clean and mixed substitutions is particularly difficult to defend, because it means that, where a trustee has misappropriated trust funds and mixed them with their own, the trustee will be able to retain any increase in the value of the fund as long as the amount misappropriated is returned to the trust, and so they would be able to profit from the misappropriation.

The distinction between clean and mixed substitutions was ignored in some cases,[270] and was finally rejected by the House of Lords in *Foskett v McKeown*[271] specifically on the ground that a trustee should not be allowed to profit from the trust. Consequently, where a trustee wrongly uses trust money to provide part of the cost of acquiring an asset, the balance coming from the trustee's own money, the beneficiary can elect between claiming a proportionate share of the asset and enforcing a charge against the asset to secure their personal claim. This election is available regardless of whether the trustee mixed the trust money with their own and then paid for the asset from the mixture, or part-paid for the asset from their own funds and made a separate payment from the trust fund. The beneficiary will prefer to claim a proportionate share where the value of the asset has increased, so that the claimant will gain a proportionate share of the increased value. So, for example, if the asset were purchased for £1,000, and the trust fund contributed £750 and the trustee £250, the beneficiary would be able to claim three-quarters of the value of the asset. If the asset had increased in value to £2,000, the beneficiary would be able to claim a share worth £1,500. The claimant would be able to compel the trustee to sell the asset and transfer that amount to the claimant. It has been argued that the trustee who has misappropriated trust property should not be allowed to benefit at all from the increase in value of the property that has been purchased.[272] This does not reflect the law and it would be a harsh decision to deprive the trustee of all profit from the purchase, especially where the purchase has been beneficial to the claimant, who shares in the increase in value in proportion to their own contribution to the purchase price.

This remedy of a proportionate share was awarded in *Foskett v McKeown*.[273] Since the claimants were able to trace two of the five premiums into the death benefit, it was held by a majority that they were entitled to receive two-fifths of the death benefit. Whether it was appropriate to award the claimants such a remedy is a matter of some controversy. What is the just result in a case such as this, in which both claimants and defendants were innocent of any wrongdoing? The judges themselves expressed divergent views as to where the

---

[269] (1880) 13 Ch D 696, 709.

[270] Notably *Re Tilley's Will Trusts* [1967] Ch 1179, 1185–9 (Ungoed-Thomas J). See also the decision of the High Court of Australia in *Scott v Scott* (1963) 109 CLR 649.

[271] [2001] 1 AC 102, 131 (Lord Millett).   [272] Hodgkinson (see n. 184).

[273] [2001] 1 AC 102. See Section 19.1.6(vi), p. 546.

justice of the case lay on the facts.[274] It is certainly fair that the claimants should recover the amount that had been misappropriated from the trust and which was used to pay two of the premiums.[275] But should they get more than this? The claimants had been the victims of a criminal misappropriation of trust property, which had been used to make an involuntary contribution to the insurance policy. The children had made no such contribution and it was their father who committed the crime.[276] But should the sins of the father be visited upon the children? Is it of any use even to consider such matters? Lord Hope[277] was willing to consider the terms of the insurance policy, the conduct of the parties, and the consequences to them of allowing and rejecting the claim, in order to determine whether it was fair, just, and reasonable for the claimants to be awarded a proportionate interest in the proceeds of the insurance policy. But how are such factors to be weighed against each other? If such an approach had been adopted by all of the judges in the case, it is not clear what the decision would have been. The introduction of a vague discretion that is not 'directed by principled analysis of the facts' is unworkable[278] and involves the exercise of an arbitrary choice; it is no way in which to determine how property rights should be recognized and vindicated.

The awarding of a proportionate share in *Foskett v McKeown* has been criticized, by Berg especially,[279] not because the remedy was excessive, but because it did not go far enough. He considers that the claimants should have received the whole of the death benefit, by virtue of the policy that there should not be any incentive for trustees wrongfully to mix trust funds with their own. So, a trustee, or anybody who claims through a trustee such as the children in that case, should be required to disgorge the whole of the benefit that they had wrongfully obtained. But this argument fails to distinguish between claims grounded on the commission of the wrong of a breach of trust, in which disgorgement of all profits is the norm subject to the award of equitable allowances,[280] and claims grounded on the vindication of property rights, in which the law is essentially concerned only with identifying value in property and other policies have no part to play. Hard-nosed property rights do not always work solely for the benefit of the claimant.

Innocent volunteer

Where the claimant's money has been mixed with that of an innocent volunteer and the mixed fund has been used to purchase an asset, the claimant and the innocent volunteer will both have equitable interests in the asset in proportion to the value of their contribution.[281] In such circumstances, the claims of both parties are equal, so it is not appropriate for one to have priority over the other. The recognition that the parties share the asset proportionately means that any increase in the value of the property will be shared between them. Where the asset has fallen in value, this loss will be shared equally between the contributors in proportion to their contribution and the claimant will not be able to elect for a charge instead.[282]

---

[274] Cf. [2001] 1 AC 102, 115 (Lord Steyn) with [1998] Ch 265, 303 (Morritt LJ) and [2001] 1 AC 102, 140 (Lord Millett).

[275] [2001] 1 AC 102, 119 (Lord Hope).   [276] Ibid., 112 (Lord Steyn).   [277] Ibid., 120.

[278] See Sir Robert Walker, 'Tracing after *Foskett v McKeown*' (2000) 8 RLR 573, 575. See also [2001] 1 AC 102, 115 (Lord Steyn).

[279] 'Permitting a trustee to retain a profit' (2001) 117 LQR 366.

[280] See Section 18.5.3.(ii), p. 530.

[281] *Edinburgh Corporation v Lord Advocate* (1879) 4 App Cas 823, 841 (Lord Hatherley). See also *Re Hallett's Estate* (1879) 13 Ch D 606.

[282] *Re Diplock's Estate* [1948] Ch 465, 532; *Foskett v McKeown* [2001] 1 AC 102, 109 (Lord Browne-Wilkinson) and 132 (Lord Millett).

Fiduciary and innocent volunteer

Where a trustee, for example, has misappropriated trust money from two trusts, mixed this with the trustee's own money, and then used the mixture to purchase an asset, then, following the decision of the House of Lords in *Foskett v McKeown*, all of the contributors will share the property in proportion to their own respective contributions.

(iii) Remedial constructive trust

If the remedial constructive trust[283] were ever recognized in English law, it would mean that the courts would be given a discretion to determine what form the proprietary remedy should take. For example, the proprietary consequences of recognizing the constructive trust might be mitigated, so that the claimant would not be given priority over any of the other creditors of the defendant. Although the remedial constructive trust was rejected by the Supreme Court in *FHR European Ventures LLP v Cedar Capital Partners LLC*,[284] it was acknowledged that there may be circumstances where the rigidity of the constructive trust might be modified, particularly to ensure that the claimant did not gain priority over the defendant's unsecured creditors, although no indication was given as to when this might occur.[285]

19.4.2 EQUITABLE CHARGE OR LIEN

An alternative remedy to the recovery of particular property or the award of a proportionate share is to impose a charge, sometimes known as a lien, on the property to secure repayment of the amount that the defendant owes to the claimant. This enables the claimant to recover the value received and retained by the defendant plus interest but does not enable the claimant to recover any more; but the claimant does have a security interest that gives them priority over the defendant's other creditors should the defendant become insolvent.

Where the claimant's money has been used to acquire property, it is appropriate for the claimant to be able to recover that property where the claimant contributed all of the value to its acquisition, or to have a proportionate share in it where the claimant contributed some of the value. As has already been seen, even in cases involving acquisition of property, the claimant may elect to have a charge over the property.[286] Where, however, the claimant's contribution has been used only to improve or maintain property that is already in the defendant's possession rather than to acquire it, it will not be appropriate for the claimant to acquire a beneficial interest in the property so that they can benefit from any increase in its value. Consequently, where the value contributed by the claimant is used to improve or maintain the property, the court will treat the property as charged with a sum that represents the value of the claimant's contribution.[287] This applies whether the defendant is a fiduciary or an innocent volunteer, although, in the latter case, the charge will be imposed only where it would not be unfair to the defendant to do so,[288] which is why no charge was awarded on the improved building of the Heritage Craft School in *Re Diplock's Estate*.[289]

---

[283] See Section 9.4, p. 275.   [284] [2014] UKSC 45, [2015] AC 250, [43].

[285] See Section 9.4, p. 277, where a principled basis for modifying the constructive trust was identified.

[286] See Section 19.4.1.(ii), p. 575.   [287] *Boscawen v Bajwa* [1996] 1 WLR 328, 335 (Millett LJ).

[288] *Re Diplock's Estate* [1948] Ch 465, 547; *Foskett v McKeown* [2001] 1 AC 102, 109 (Lord Browne-Wilkinson).

[289] See Section 19.3.3.(iv), p. 570.

The function of the equitable charge as a remedy to vindicate property rights was considered in *Foskett v McKeown*. The key issue in that case was whether the appropriate remedy should be a charge over the proceeds of the policy to enable the claimants to recover the money that had been misappropriated, or whether they were entitled to a proportion of the proceeds calculated by reference to the amount of their money that was used to pay the premiums. The Court of Appeal[290] had concluded that a charge was the appropriate remedy, by analogy with cases in which trust money has been used to improve or maintain an asset. This is consistent with the nature of the life insurance policy in that case, since the death benefit would have been due even if the fourth and fifth premiums had not been paid; those premiums therefore did not contribute to the acquisition of the death benefit, but maintained the policy, so that additional units were purchased that would be available in future years. The majority in the House of Lords preferred the analogy with a trustee who has mixed trust money with their own money in a bank account, which has then been used to obtain another asset.[291] In such cases, awarding a proportionate share remedy is appropriate, and so that remedy was awarded in this case. This is consistent with the attribution approach to tracing, since the death benefit was analysed as being attributable in part to the fourth and fifth premiums that had therefore contributed to the death benefit being obtained.[292]

19.4.3 SUBROGATION

(i) The function of subrogation

Subrogation is a remedy that is designed to ensure 'a transfer of rights from one person to another . . . by operation of law'.[293] Essentially, the function of the remedy is to enable the claimant to rely on the rights of a third party against a defendant.[294] This is often described as the claimant being allowed to 'stand in the shoes' of the third party. The typical case in which subrogation will be an appropriate remedy in the context of an equitable proprietary claim is where the claimant's money is used by the defendant to discharge a debt that the defendant owed to a secured creditor. In such circumstances, the claimant can be subrogated to the secured creditor's charge and gain the benefit of that security as against other creditors of the borrower. In effect, the benefit of the charge is treated as though it had been assigned to the claimant,[295] so that they will obtain the benefit of that charge, but will obtain no other rights relating to the property.

The rationale for awarding the remedy of subrogation has proved to be controversial. In *Bank of Cyprus UK Ltd v Menelaou*[296] the Supreme Court specifically recognized that subrogation operated to reverse the defendant's unjust enrichment. It follows that it will be necessary to establish that the defendant was enriched at the expense of the claimant and

---

[290] [1998] Ch 265.

[291] [2001] 1 AC 102, 110 (Lord Browne-Wilkinson) and 115 (Lord Hoffmann). Lord Steyn did not consider this to be a useful analogy: ibid., at 114.

[292] See Section 19.3.1.(ii), p. 553.

[293] *Orakpo v Manson Investments Ltd* [1978] AC 95, 104 (Lord Diplock); *Re TH Knitwear (Wholesale) Ltd* [1988] Ch 275, 284 (Slade LJ).

[294] For detailed analysis, see Mitchell and Watterson, *Subrogation: Law and Practice* (Oxford: Oxford University Press, 2007).

[295] *Banque Financière de la Cité v Parc (Battersea) Ltd* [1999] 1 AC 221, 236 (Lord Hoffmann). See also *Boscawen v Bajwa* [1996] 1 WLR 328, 333 (Millett LJ).

[296] [2015] UKSC 66, [2016] AC 176. See also *Lowick Rose LLP v Swynson Ltd* [2017] UKSC 32, [2017] 2 WLR 1161. For criticism of *Menelaou* see Buckingham and Chambers, 'Subrogation, the straightjacket of unjust enrichment and legal taxonomy' [2016] Conv 219.

that a ground of restitution can be identified, which might be difficult to establish. In that case unjust enrichment was easier to establish, since the Bank which sought the remedy had mistakenly released charges on one property which enabled funds to become available so that the defendant's parents could purchase another property, which they gave to the defendant. The defendant was considered to have been enriched at the expense of the Bank, with the ground of restitution probably being that the Bank had mistakenly believed that it had a charge on the defendant's property when the charge was actually void. As a consequence the Bank was subrogated to the vendor's unpaid lien against the defendant, so that the Bank had a security interest in the defendant's property.[297]

In *Lowick Rose LLP v Swynson Ltd*[298] Lord Sumption warned against trying to fit subrogation into 'any broader category of unjust enrichment' and characterized it as *sui generis*. He identified various differences between unjust enrichment generally and unjust enrichment triggering subrogation, including that subrogation is not a restitutionary remedy as such, since it does not restore the parties to their pre-transfer position, but enforces a defeated expectation that the claimant would have security. In fact, and consistently with the approach to equitable proprietary claims which is adopted in this chapter, the preferable view is that subrogation is a remedy to vindicate the claimant's equitable property rights; such an approach has been endorsed by the High Court of Australia.[299] Consequently, the normal conditions for proprietary claims need to be established, namely that the claimant has an equitable proprietary interest that can be traced into property received by the defendant. It will then be appropriate to consider how best the claimant's property rights can be vindicated. The proprietary remedy of subrogation does, however, work differently from the other proprietary remedies that have been considered so far. Those remedies assume that the defendant has retained property in which the claimant has an equitable proprietary interest. The typical scenario in which subrogation will be relevant is where the claimant's value has been used to discharge a debt. As we have already seen,[300] the discharge of a debt will often defeat the tracing exercise.[301] But it is still possible to trace into the discharged debt, and then, if the conditions for awarding subrogation are satisfied, the proprietary right that has been destroyed through the discharge of the debt can be resurrected by allowing the claimant to stand in the shoes of another creditor of the defendant and obtain the benefit of any security that that creditor had against the defendant. In other words, subrogation provides a mechanism with which to obtain a charge over the defendant's property in circumstances under which the claimant has not been able to trace into property that remains in the defendant's possession, and so the claimant will gain priority over the defendant's general creditors if the defendant is insolvent. It is the defendant's insolvency that is the typical reason why the claimant seeks to be subrogated to the security of a third party against the defendant.

The reason why subrogation has been analysed as a remedy to reverse the defendant's unjust enrichment derives from the decision of the House of Lords in *Banque Financière de*

---

[297] Subsequently the court ordered the sale of the property so that the proceeds of sale could be used to discharge the defendant's liability: *Menelaou v Bank of Cyprus UK Ltd* [2016] EWHC 2656 (Ch).

[298] [2017] UKSC 32, [2017] 2 WLR 1161, [29].

[299] *Bofinger v Kingsway Group Ltd* [2009] HCA 44. See also the judgments of Lord Carnwath and Lord Neuberger in *Bank of Cyprus UK Ltd v Menelaou* [2015] UKSC 66, [2016] AC 176, with the former considering that subrogation could only be justified as a proprietary remedy to vindicate property rights and the latter, whilst acknowledging the legitimacy of subrogation being awarded to reverse the defendant's unjust enrichment, preferring the vindication of property rights analysis.

[300] See Section 19.3.3.(iv), p. 566.

[301] Save where the doctrine of backwards tracing applies, so that the claimant will be able to trace into the previously acquired asset in respect of which the debt was incurred. See Section 19.3.3.(iv), p. 567.

la Cité v Parc (Battersea) Ltd.[302] But the facts of that case were highly unusual and actually the remedy itself was personal rather than proprietary, since the claimant only obtained priority over the defendant and not as regards any of the other creditors of the debtor company.[303] Usually, however, subrogation will operate as a proprietary remedy since the claimant will obtain the benefit of the third party's security completely. Consequently, to the extent that the third party had priority over other creditors of the defendant, the claimant will gain equal priority. Indeed, in *Cheltenham and Gloucester plc v Appleyard*,[304] Neuberger J considered that the classic form of the subrogation remedy is proprietary, in that it enables a lender who expects to obtain a security to claim subrogation to another security and that the reference to *Banque Financière* is unlikely to be of assistance in a conventional case.

(ii) The principles underlying the remedy of subrogation

(1) The remedy of subrogation arises by operation of law and does not depend on the parties' intention that the remedy should be available.[305]

(2) The claimant may still get the benefit of a creditor's security against the defendant by means of the subrogation remedy even though that security has been discharged.[306] This was recognized in *Boscawen v Bajwa* by Millett LJ,[307] who accepted that a discharged security can be resurrected. So, for example, if the claimant's money has been used by the defendant to discharge a secured debt owed by the defendant to a third party, it will be possible for the claimant to get the benefit of the security even though it has been discharged. This has been described as subrogation to extinguished rights.[308]

An aspect of the decision of the Court of Appeal in *Re Diplock's Estate*[309] appears, however, to suggest a contrary conclusion. The executors of the testator's estate had mistakenly paid some money to the Leaf Homeopathic Hospital, which it used to discharge a mortgage over the hospital's property. It was held that the claimants could not trace into the discharged debt and so be subrogated to the mortgage, because the mortgage had ceased to exist once the debt had been discharged. The denial of the remedy in this case could be justified on the basis that the hospital had innocently changed its position by using the money to discharge a liability.[310] But this explanation is dubious for two reasons. First, it has been recognized in the law of unjust enrichment that the defence of change of position is not available where the defendant has used money paid by mistake to discharge a debt, because the defendant will not have suffered any detriment in doing so since he or they are simply substituting one creditor, the claimant, for another.[311] Secondly, the defence

---

[302] [1999] 1 AC 221, 231 (Lord Hoffmann). This decision was affirmed by the Supreme Court in *Bank of Cyprus UK Ltd v Menelaou* [2015] UKSC 66, [2016] AC 176.

[303] *Banque Financière de la Cité v Parc (Battersea) Ltd* [1999] 1 AC 221, 228 (Lord Steyn) and 237 (Lord Clyde).

[304] [2004] EWCA Civ 291.

[305] *Banque Financière de la Cité v Parc (Battersea) Ltd* [1999] 1 AC 221, 231 (Lord Hoffmann).

[306] That the claimant can obtain the benefit of a creditor's *undischarged* security was recognized by the House of Lords in *Banque Financière de la Cité v Parc (Battersea) Ltd* [1999] 1 AC 221.

[307] [1996] 1 WLR 328, 341.

[308] *Syed Ibrhaim v Barclays Bank plc* [2011] EWHC 1897 (Ch), [2012] 1 BCLC 33, [7] (Vos J). This can be contrasted with subrogation to subsisting rights that can arises in the context of insurance, where the insurer is subrogated to the rights of the insured against a tortfeasor. Here, subrogation arises by operation of contract. See *Alliance Bank JSC v Aquanta Corp* [2011] EWHC 3281 (Comm), [22] (Burton J).

[309] [1948] 1 Ch 465, 549–50.

[310] *Boscawen v Bajwa* [1996] 1 WLR 328, 341 (Millett LJ). See Section 19.5.2, p. 586.

[311] *Scottish Equitable plc v Derby* [2001] 3 All ER 818.

of change of position is probably not available to proprietary claims in which the claimant seeks a proprietary remedy.[312] The result in *Re Diplock's Estate* is better explained as turning on a question of evidence rather than law, namely that it could not be shown that the claimant's money had been used to discharge the mortgage. If the money could not be traced into the mortgage, it would not be possible to be subrogated to the discharged security.[313]

(3) Where the claimant has intentionally lent money that has been used to discharge a secured debt, the claimant will be subrogated to the discharged security only if they had intended the loan to be secured, but for some reason the security was not valid.[314] The award of the subrogation remedy can be justified on the ground that it is unconscionable to frustrate the claimant's intention that they were to obtain the benefit of a security.

The application of this principle is illustrated by *Boscawen v Bajwa*,[315] in which the Abbey National lent money to the purchaser of a house, with the loan being secured by a legal charge. This money was paid to the purchaser's solicitors. In breach of trust, that firm of solicitors transferred the money to the vendor's solicitors before completion and the money was used to discharge the vendor's mortgage with the Halifax. The sale of the house fell through. The creditors of the vendor had obtained a charging order against the property that was sold, with the proceeds of sale paid into court. The creditors claimed the proceeds of sale, but the Abbey National claimed that it was entitled by subrogation to the security right of the Halifax, being the vendor's former mortgagee, and so it was entitled to a charge on the proceeds of sale that ranked above the vendor's creditors. The Court of Appeal found for the Abbey National for the following reasons. An equitable proprietary base could be identified because the money was held on trust by the purchaser's solicitors for the Abbey National. It could trace its money in Equity into the payment that was used to discharge the mortgage by the vendor, despite mixing with other money in the vendor's solicitor's client account including some of the vendor's money. Subrogation was awarded to enable the Abbey National to vindicate its property rights because it was held that the vendor's solicitor must have intended to keep the mortgage alive for the benefit of the Abbey National. The Court of Appeal emphasized that it focused on the vendor's solicitor's intention to keep the security alive rather than the intention of the Abbey National when lending the money in the first place, because the Abbey National's money had not been paid directly to discharge the vendor's mortgage, but had been transferred via the purchaser's and the vendor's solicitors. This seems unnecessarily complicated. The key question should simply have been what the Abbey National's intention was in paying the money in the first place, and, since it had clearly intended to obtain the benefit of a security, it followed that a subrogation remedy was entirely appropriate.

(4) Where the claimant has not intentionally lent money, but the money has been misappropriated and has been used to discharge a secured debt, subrogation may be available even though the claimant was ignorant of the transfer and could not have intended to obtain any security. In this situation, the remedy will be triggered because it would be unconscionable for the defendant to deny the claimant's proprietary interest.[316] In other words, the remedy may be available because of the defendant's conduct. So, for example, if the defendant trustee misappropriates trust money and uses this to discharge a mortgage,

---

[312] See Section 19.5.2, p. 586.   [313] See Smith (see n. 140), p. 295.

[314] *Banque Financière de la Cité v Parc (Battersea) Ltd* [1999] 1 AC 221. See also *Cheltenham and Gloucester plc v Appleyard* [2004] EWCA Civ 291, [40] (Neuberger LJ); *Butler v Rice* [1910] 2 Ch 277; *Ghana Commercial Bank v Chandiram* [1960] AC 732.

[315] [1996] 1 WLR 328.   [316] Ibid., 335.

the claimant beneficiaries can be subrogated to the mortgagee's security interest by virtue of the defendant's unconscionable conduct.

(5) The claimant cannot obtain subrogation to put them in a better position than that in which they would have been had they obtained all of the rights for which they had bargained.[317]

(6) It is possible to exclude the remedy of subrogation expressly by contract. Similarly, the contract between the claimant and the defendant may impliedly exclude the remedy of subrogation. This is illustrated by *Capital Finance Co Ltd v Stokes*,[318] in which the claimant and the defendant had agreed that the claimant should obtain a security by way of a legal charge. This charge was unenforceable because it had not been registered, but it was held that, because a legal charge was a better interest than an equitable charge, the agreement between the parties prevented the claimant from being subrogated to a third party's equitable charge against the defendant. In other words, the intention that the claimant should have the benefit of a legal charge prevented the claimant from being subrogated to a lesser equitable charge. It was further recognized in *Re Beppler & Jacobson Ltd*[319] that subrogation will not be available if there is a subsisting contract between the parties.

(7) It was recognized in *Anfield (UK) Ltd v Bank of Scotland plc*[320] that a lender of money could be subrogated to a charge that had been redeemed in circumstances under which the lender had intended the loan to be secured, but had negligently failed to register the charge. Where, however, the borrower of the money had acted to its detriment in the reasonable, but false, belief that the loan was unsecured, as a consequence of the lender's negligence, then subrogation might not be available. This was justified on the ground that the borrower's enrichment would not then be unjust and that the defendant had changed its position in reliance on the loan being unsecured, which is consistent with the unjust enrichment analysis of subrogation.

(8) Subrogation will only be available where the defendant can be considered to have been enriched as the result of a defective transaction, such as a mistake or if the claimant did not obtain from the transaction what they expected to obtain. It was for this reason that subrogation was not available in *Lowick Rose LLP v Swynson Ltd*.[321] In that case the claimant intentionally discharged a debt owed by one company to another company, which was controlled by the claimant, in order to reduce the latter company's tax liability. Since there was no defect in the transaction involving the discharge of the debt, the claimant could not be subrogated to the company's claim against a third-party firm of accountants in professional negligence relating to the loan being made, it having been argued that the accountants had been enriched by the discharge of the debt which had relieved them of a substantial liability in the negligence claim since it had removed the loss suffered by the company.

19.4.4 SUMMARY OF PROPRIETARY REMEDIES

As an illustration of how the different proprietary remedies may operate and which of these may be better for the claimant to pursue, consider the following hypothetical problem.

---

[317] *Cheltenham and Gloucester plc v Appleyard* [2004] EWCA Civ 291, [41] (Neuberger LJ); *Filby v Mortgage Express (No 2) Ltd* [2004] EWCA Civ 759, [63] (May LJ).

[318] [1969] 1 Ch 261. See also *Liberty Mutual Insurance Co (UK) Ltd v HSBC Bank plc* [2002] EWCA Civ 691.

[319] [2016] EWHC 20 (Ch).   [320] [2010] EWHC 2374 (Ch), [2011] 1 WLR 2414.

[321] [2017] UKSC 32, [2017] 2 WLR 1161.

Alan, a trustee, misappropriates £250,000 from the trust fund, which he uses to discharge a mortgage that he had taken out with the Friendly Bank on his house. He had purchased his house for £400,000 and had borrowed the full amount from the bank. He had made monthly payments of capital and interest to the bank amounting to £250,000, and used the trust fund to discharge the rest, so the total payment to the Bank had been £500,000. Alan has since become insolvent and the house has been sold for £1 million. What remedies are available to the beneficiaries of the trust?

In such a case, it is clear that the beneficiaries have an equitable proprietary base and it will be possible for them to trace into the discharged mortgage. The key question then concerns the identification of the appropriate proprietary remedy. There are a number of options that are potentially available:

(1) Since money has been misappropriated from the trust fund and was used to discharge the mortgage, the beneficiaries can be subrogated to the bank's security even though it has been discharged. This means that the beneficiaries will be able to claim £250,000 of the proceeds of sale of the house in priority to other unsecured creditors of Alan.

This is most likely to be the solution that will be adopted by the courts. But, in the light of recent developments, in the law of tracing in particular, another solution might be available.

(2) Since Alan purchased the house and incurred a debt in doing so, and since money from the trust fund was used to discharge this liability, if the doctrine of backward tracing applied then, because there was a sufficiently close causal and transactional link between the incurring of the debt and the use of trust fund to discharge it,[322] it might be possible to trace into the house and then into the proceeds of sale even though the debt had been incurred by borrowing money from a third party rather than the vendor. If backward tracing were possible in such circumstances, which might be established if Alan intended from the start to use money from the trust to discharge the mortgage, the question then would be whether it would be appropriate for the beneficiaries to obtain a charge over the proceeds of sale or to obtain a proportionate share of the proceeds. Awarding a charge would simply replicate the effect of awarding the remedy of subrogation because the beneficiaries would recover £250,000 in priority to Alan's unsecured creditors. Awarding a proportionate share of the proceeds would be preferable to the beneficiaries, since, having contributed 50 per cent of the money to discharge the mortgage, they would be entitled to 50 per cent of the proceeds of sale, amounting to £500,000. Whether they would be able to claim a proportionate share rather than a charge would turn on whether their contribution should be analysed as money that assisted in the acquisition of the property. That is the preferable way of analysing their contribution and so they would be entitled to a proportionate share of the proceeds of sale. This solution depends, however, on backward tracing being recognized in such a case.

19.5 DEFENCES

Once the claimant has traced value into the property in the defendant's possession and claimed a proprietary right, the only remaining question is whether the defendant has any defence to the proprietary claim. Two defences are potentially available.

[322] See Section 19.3.1.(ii), p. 553.

19.5.1 BONA FIDE PURCHASE FOR VALUE

Where the recipient of property in which the claimant has an equitable proprietary interest has paid value for that property and has acted in good faith, the claimant's equitable proprietary interest will be defeated. The defence of bona fide purchase for value is consequently a defence that defeats the proprietary claim absolutely, because it defeats the claimant's equitable proprietary right and makes good defects in the defendant's title to property.[323]

The defence is generally not available at Common Law to defeat legal interests in property, save where money has been received by a bona fide purchaser for value who gets good title to it.[324] The defence is, however, very significant as regards equitable proprietary claims, regardless of the nature of the property that has been received, where the recipient has acquired legal title to the property.[325] Where, however, the recipient has purchased an equitable proprietary interest for value, the defence will not be available, because of the rule that the first equitable interest in time takes priority.[326]

The defence will be available as long as some recipient of the property is a bona fide purchaser for value; this need not have been the defendant. So, for example, if Alan, a trustee, misappropriates £1,000 of shares from the trust fund and sells them to Belinda, who is unaware of the breach of trust, and she then gives the shares to her son, Carl, a proprietary claim for the shares brought by the beneficiaries against Carl will be defeated because Belinda was a bona fide purchaser for value. She received the shares unencumbered by the beneficiaries' equitable proprietary interest, and will have passed legal title to the shares to Carl similarly unencumbered by any equitable proprietary interest. This will be significant to the beneficiaries of the trust if Alan has become insolvent, since then they will have no remedy available to them.

There are two key conditions for the bona fide purchase for value defence to apply. First, the recipient of property must have provided some value for it. Value includes the giving of money or money's worth, including the discharge of a debt,[327] or marriage consideration.[328] It is not necessary for the courts to consider whether the value that was given for the property was adequate; it is sufficient that some value was given. This value requirement means that the defence cannot be relied on by the recipient of a gift, simply because such a recipient will not have provided any value for the transfer. The value may be provided before or after the property was transferred to the recipient, as long as, when the property was transferred or the value was provided, whichever was the later, the recipient was not fixed with notice of the claimant's proprietary interest.[329] The defendant cannot be considered to have provided value for the property if it was transferred pursuant to an illegal transaction.[330]

Secondly, the recipient must have acted in good faith. The recipient will not have acted in good faith if he or she had actual notice of the claimant's equitable proprietary right, in that the claimant appreciated that the proprietary right probably existed, or had

---

[323] See *Boscawen v Bajwa* [1996] 1 WLR 328, 334 (Millett LJ).
[324] *Miller v Race* (1758) 1 Burr 452, 457–8 (Lord Mansfield).
[325] *Cave v Cave* (1880) 15 Ch D 639.
[326] *Macmillan Inc v Bishopsgate Investment Trust plc* [1995] 1 WLR 978, 1000 (Millett J). But the defence will defeat an earlier mere equity, such as the equity to rescind. See generally O'Sullivan, 'The rule in *Phillips v Phillips*' (2002) 118 LQR 296.
[327] *Taylor v Blakelock* (1886) 32 Ch D 560.
[328] *Pullan v Koe* [1913] 1 Ch 9. See Section 5.3.3.(iii), p. 133.
[329] *Ratcliffe v Barnard* (1871) LR 6 Ch App 652.
[330] *Lipkin Gorman (a firm) v Karpnale Ltd* [1991] 2 AC 548.

constructive notice of it.[331] The defendant will have constructive notice of the claimant's equitable proprietary right if the defendant failed to make enquiries that would have been made by a reasonable person in the defendant's position.[332] There will be an obligation to make such inquiries if there is a serious possibility of a third party having a proprietary right or if the facts known to the defendant would give a reasonable person in the position of the defendant serious cause to question the propriety of the transaction involving the transfer of property.[333] If the transaction appears to be proper then there is no duty to inquire, but, if the circumstances of the transaction are indicative of some form of wrongdoing, an explanation must be sought[334] and failure to do so will mean that the defendant is imputed with notice of the proprietary right. The defendant will not be prevented from relying on the bona fide purchase defence simply because they had notice of a doubtful claim of the claimant to recover the property,[335] presumably because the reasonable person would not have sought an explanation of the transaction in such circumstances.

Notice will also be imputed to the defendant if their agent had actual or constructive notice of the defect in title, as long as the agent acquired notice in the course of the transaction that involved the transfer of property that the claimant wishes to recover.

The burden of proving the defence is borne by the defendant on the balance of probabilities.[336] An equitable proprietary interest will not be defeated if the property is reacquired from the bona fide purchaser by the trustee[337] or where the transaction involving the transfer to the bona fide purchaser is rescinded, because the transaction will be a nullity and will operate retrospectively, converting the recipient into a volunteer.[338]

19.5.2 CHANGE OF POSITION

In the law of unjust enrichment, the defence of change of position has been recognized. The effect of this defence is that, to the extent that the defendant has changed their position in reliance on the receipt of an enrichment, the defendant is not required to make restitution to the claimant.[339] The defence is available either where the defendant loses the enrichment received, because it was spent or stolen, or, retaining that enrichment and in reliance on its receipt, the defendant changes their position in some other way. In either case, the defence will succeed only if it is not inequitable to require the defendant to make restitution in full.[340] It will be inequitable when the defendant has changed their position in bad faith, knowing or suspecting that there is a liability to make restitution to the claimant, or the defendant is a wrongdoer. So, within the law of unjust enrichment, it

---

[331] *Barclays Bank v O'Brien* [1994] 1 AC 180, 195 (Lord Browne-Wilkinson); *Crédit Agricole Corporation and Investment Bank v Papadimitriou* [2015] UKPC 13, [2015] 1 WLR 4265. See Watts, 'Tests of knowledge in the receipt of misapplied funds' (2015) 131 LQR 511.

[332] *Crédit Agricole Corporation and Investment Bank v Papadimitriou* [2015] UKPC 13, [2015] 1 WLR 4265, [20] (Lord Clarke). See also *Sinclair Investments (UK) Ltd v Versailles Trade Finance Ltd* [2011] EWCA Civ 347, [2012] Ch 453, [109] (Lord Neuberger MR). This is the same test as that which is used to establish liability for unconscionable receipt: *Crédit Agricole Corporation and Investment Bank v Papadimitriou* [2015] UKPC 13, 1 WLR 4265, [33] (Lord Sumption).

[333] Ibid., [20] (Lord Clarke).   [334] Ibid., [33] (Lord Sumption).

[335] *Carl-Zeiss Stiftung v Herbert Smith (No 2)* [1969] 2 Ch 276.

[336] *Crédit Agricole Corporation and Investment Bank v Papadimitriou* [2015] UKPC 13, [2015] 1 WLR 4265, [21] (Lord Clarke).

[337] *Wilkes v Spooner* [1911] 2 KB 473.

[338] *Independent Trustee Service Ltd v GP Noble Trustees Ltd* [2012] EWCA Civ 196, [2013] Ch 91.

[339] *Lipkin Gorman (a firm) v Karpnale Ltd* [1991] 2 AC 546, 578 (Lord Goff).

[340] Ibid.

the claimant pays £1,000 to the defendant by mistake and the defendant, not realizing that the money was mistakenly paid, spends it on a holiday that she would not otherwise have taken, she will not be required to make restitution because she has changed her position in good faith by spending the money.

Is the defence available in respect of equitable proprietary claims? If the claimant is seeking to recover the original misappropriated property from the defendant, there is no reason to think that the defence of change of position will be available. So, if the defendant has received this property and, in reliance on the receipt, changes her position in some other way, such as by selling another asset and using the proceeds to go on holiday, since the defendant still has the property in which the claimant has an equitable proprietary interest, the defendant should be required to restore that property to the claimant.

But what of the case in which the claimant wishes to claim substitute property, such as where the claimant's property has become mixed with other property? It was seen at the start of this chapter[341] that some commentators have analysed claims to substitute property by reference to the law of unjust enrichment. It should follow logically, therefore, that the claim to substitute property should be defeated to the extent that the defendant has changed their position in good faith. It has previously been seen that some of the cases involving tracing or claiming in which the proprietary claim has failed have been analysed with reference to the defence of change of position. So, in *Re Diplock's Estate*,[342] where money was used by a charity to improve property, the proprietary claim failed because it was not considered to be equitable for the claimant to obtain a proprietary remedy over a mixed asset to which an innocent volunteer had also contributed. In *Boscawen v Bajwa*,[343] Millett LJ explained this result on the basis that the defendant charity had changed its position in good faith by spending the money.

In this chapter, however, the unjust enrichment analysis of claims to substitute property has been rejected and, consistent with the decision of the House of Lords in *Foskett v McKeown*,[344] the assertion of rights to substitute property has been justified by reference to the vindication of property rights theory. Is a consequence of this analysis that the defence of change of position cannot defeat the claimant's proprietary claim? In *Foskett v McKeown*, there is an ambiguous dictum of Lord Millett that the defence of bona fide purchase applied to claims to vindicate property rights, whereas the change of position defence applies to claims to unjust enrichment.[345] Since the House of Lords held that the case was concerned with vindication of property rights and not unjust enrichment, it might follow that the defence of change of position was not applicable. This is ambiguous, both because the issue was *obiter*, since there was no evidence that the children had changed their position, and because Lord Millett did not explicitly say that the change of position defence was unavailable to proprietary claims.[346] He did, however, subsequently expand on this extra-judicially[347] and confirmed that he did not consider that a claim for a proprietary remedy should be subject to the defence of change of position. This has been recognized in other decisions.[348]

---

[341] See Section 19.1.4.(ii), p. 540.   [342] [1948] Ch 465, 548.   [343] [1996] 1 WLR 328.

[344] [2001] 1 AC 102.   [345] Ibid., 129.

[346] In *Campden Hill Ltd v Chakrani* [2005] EWHC 911 (Ch), [84], Hart J left open the question whether the defence affects the right to trace in Equity.

[347] See n. 266, pp. 315 and 325.

[348] *Papamichael v National Westminster Bank* [2003] 1 Lloyd's Rep 341, 376 (Judge Chambers QC); *Armstrong DLW GmbH v Winnington Networks Ltd* [2012] EWHC 10 (Ch), [2013] Ch 156, [99]–[103] (Stephen Morris QC); *Test Claimants in the FII Group Litigation v HMRC* [2014] EWHC 4302 (Ch), [2015] STC 1471, [348] (Henderson J).

Whether this is correct needs to be considered both as a matter of principle and of policy. Where the claimant seeks to obtain a proprietary remedy to vindicate equitable proprietary rights, there are three different scenarios in which change of position might operate:

(1) Where the defendant has received property in which the claimant has an equitable proprietary interest and then dissipates that property without there being any traceable substitute, the claimant will not be awarded an equitable proprietary remedy. But this is not because of the application of the defence of change of position, but simply because the defendant no longer has any property in their possession against which the claimant's proprietary right can be vindicated.

(2) The defendant may have received money in which the claimant has an equitable proprietary interest and have deposited that money in his bank account. In reliance on the receipt of that money, the defendant may have sold some existing property in their possession, such as shares, and used the proceeds of sale to pay for a holiday. This is a scenario in which the defence of change of position could have a role to play, since the defendant has changed their position in reliance on the receipt of the money from the claimant. The defence would not, however, be available if the defendant had acted in bad faith or was a wrongdoer; so, if the defendant is a trustee who has misappropriated trust property in breach of trust, the defence should not be available. But what if the defendant is an innocent recipient of money that has been misappropriated from the trust by somebody else? Should the defence of change of position apply? It might be argued that it would not be fair for the claimant to recover the money credited to the defendant's bank account, since the defendant has suffered a detriment by selling the shares. If the defendant were also required to pay back to the claimant the money that had been credited to the bank account, the defendant would have suffered a net loss. But, against this, the claimant is able to show that the defendant has received and retained the value of the misappropriated money that is credited to the defendant's bank account. Should equitable property rights be defeated by the defendant's innocent change of position? This is a matter of policy, but the better view is that the claimant's property rights should prevail and the defendant should not be able to plead the change of position defence. If the defendant has property in which the claimant has an equitable proprietary interest, that property will be held on constructive trust for the claimant who should be able to demand the transfer of that property, or a proportionate share of it.

(3) There is a third scenario in which there might be scope for the defence of change of position to apply, namely where the claimant's value has been used to discharge a debt owed by the defendant and the claimant seeks to be subrogated to the creditor's discharged security right. This is different from the other two scenarios because, although the property in which the claimant had an equitable proprietary interest has been dissipated through the discharge of the debt, the claimant is seeking to have a proprietary right created through the resurrection of the discharged security. This is the scenario in which Millett LJ in *Boscawen v Bajwa*[349] recognized that the claimant should have a defence of change of position. Although this may be more defensible because the claimant is not seeking to vindicate an existing property right, the defence of change of position is not available in the law of unjust enrichment where the defendant has used money paid by mistake to discharge a liability,[350] since the defendant will not suffer any detriment if they are

---

[349] [1996] 1 WLR 328, 341 (Millett LJ).   [350] See Section 19.4.3.(ii), p. 580.

held liable to the claimant who paid the money by mistake, because the defendant will simply owe liability to a new creditor; the claimant will be substituted for the creditor whose liability the defendant discharged. The same would be true were the claimant to seek the remedy of subrogation. Where the claimant's money has been used to discharge a secured debt, the resurrection of that debt in the claimant's favour will not cause any hardship to the defendant, because a secured liability to the claimant will simply be substituted for the liability owed to the original creditor.

20

PERSONAL LIABILITY OF THIRD PARTIES

20.1 GENERAL CONSIDERATIONS

When a trustee has breached the trust or a fiduciary has breached their fiduciary duty, we saw in Chapter 18 that they may be personally liable to the beneficiaries or the principal, either to compensate for loss suffered or to give up any gain made. Where the breach involves the misappropriation of property, we saw in Chapter 19 that, if the trustee or fiduciary has the property or its traceable substitute, the claimant will have a proprietary claim, and, if the property or its substitute has been transferred to a third party, the claimant may have a proprietary claim against that party instead, even if that party was unaware of the claimant's proprietary right.[1] In this chapter, we are concerned with the personal liability of third parties, meaning parties other than the trustee or fiduciary, where there has been a breach of trust or breach of fiduciary duty.

This personal liability of third parties may take two forms:

(1) *Receipt-based liability* Where a third party has received property in which the claimant has an equitable proprietary interest, but the third party no longer has that property or its traceable substitute, the third party may be liable to the claimant for the value of the property received if it was transferred following a breach of trust or fiduciary duty. It is not necessary to show that the third party has retained the property or its substitute, and, if the claimant could establish this, they would be likely to seek a proprietary remedy. It follows that personal liability of the third party is relevant where the property has been received and then dissipated without obtaining an identifiable substitute.

(2) *Accessorial liability* Where the third party has encouraged or assisted breach of trust or fiduciary duty, they may be personally liable to the beneficiaries or principal for the loss arising from the breach or consequent gain made by the defendant from the encouragement or assistance. It is irrelevant for accessorial liability that the third party had not received any property that was transferred in breach of trust or fiduciary duty. This is because accessorial liability is founded on the commission of a wrong by virtue of the third party's association with the trustee's or fiduciary's breach of duty.[2]

---

[1] Save if the recipient is a bona fide purchaser for value. See Section 19.5.1, p. 584.
[2] *Twinsectra Ltd v Yardley* [2002] UKHL 12, [2002] 2 AC 164, [107] (Lord Millett).

A third party's liability for receipt of property or as an accessory is of practical signifi-cance, especially as regards commercial and corporate fraud. For example, directors of a company might misappropriate corporate funds for their own purposes in breach of fiduciary duty and transfer these funds to third parties, often with the aim that the money should eventually be received by the directors themselves. The directors may have become insolvent or disappeared, and so the company will wish to pursue claims either against the recipient of the money or the people who assisted the directors to breach their duty, such as solicitors, accountants, or financial advisers. Since this third-party liability may arise in the context of ordinary commercial transactions, it is very important that the nature of the liability is clear and predictable.[3] As we will see, the lack of clarity of the law is a major weakness of third-party personal liability.

The personal liability of third parties may also arise in the context of a straightforward breach of trust. The significance of receipt-based and accessorial liability in this context is illustrated by the following example.

Amy is a trustee, who misappropriated £50,000 from the trust fund. She gave £20,000 to her daughter, Belinda, who used the money to buy shares. She gave £20,000 to her son, Carl, who lost all of the money whilst gambling at a casino. Amy retained £10,000, which she spent on a holiday that was booked by her personal assistant, David. Amy has just been declared bankrupt. The beneficiaries of the trust seek your advice as to any claims that they might have.

In this problem, four claims can be identified:

(1) Amy will be liable for breach of trust and so will be liable to reconstitute the trust by repaying £50,000.[4] Amy is, however, bankrupt and so the beneficiaries will rank with her general creditors, since there is no property in Amy's possession into which the benefi-ciaries can trace the value of the trust property that was misappropriated.

(2) Belinda will hold the shares on constructive trust for the beneficiaries. This is be-cause they will be able to trace the money that was misappropriated from the trust into the shares that she had purchased. As we saw in the last chapter, Belinda will be liable to transfer the shares to the trust even if she was unaware that her mother had transferred the money to her in breach of trust. Since the shares were given to her, she cannot plead the defence that she was a bona fide purchaser for value.

(3) Carl may be personally liable to the beneficiaries by virtue of his receipt of trust property that has been transferred following a breach of trust. The beneficiaries will not be able to bring a proprietary claim against him, because he no longer has any property that represents the value of the trust property. If Carl is liable for his receipt of the trust property, he may be required to repay the value of the property that he received, namely £20,000 plus interest. The conditions for establishing receipt-based liability will be consid-ered later in this chapter.[5]

(4) Although David did not receive any trust property, he might be considered to have assisted Amy to breach the trust by booking her holiday, which was purchased with funds from the trust. If David is liable for assisting a breach of trust, he will be liable to com-pensate the trust for the loss that it had suffered arising from his assistance, which would amount to £10,000. The conditions for establishing accessorial liability will be considered later in this chapter.[6]

---

[3] *Abou-Rahmah v Abacha* [2006] EWCA Civ 1492, [2007] 1 All ER (Comm) 827, [64] (Arden LJ).
[4] See Section 18.2, p. 510.   [5] See Section 20.2.3.(i), p. 596.   [6] See Section 20.3.2, p. 613.

20.1.1 FAULT OR STRICT LIABILITY?

The most controversial question relating to third-party personal liability is whether the third party's liability should be strict or fault-based, and, if the latter, what degree of fault should be required to establish liability. Crucially, is liability to be assessed subjectively, with reference to the defendant's own thought process, or should it be assessed objectively, by reference to whether a reasonable person would have known or suspected that the third party was receiving property that had been obtained in breach of trust or fiduciary duty, or was assisting a breach of trust or breach of fiduciary duty?

In assessing the appropriate levels of fault, reference is sometimes made to the so-called *Baden* classification of fault.[7] Although this classification of fault has been subjected to much criticism from judges and commentators, it remains of some use if only as a way of identifying the type of fault requirements that might be applicable to determine third-party personal liability. Traditionally, equitable receipt-based and accessorial liability has required proof of knowledge, which is what the *Baden* classification refers to. In that case, five different types of knowledge were identified:

(1) actual knowledge

(2) wilfully shutting one's eyes to the obvious (sometimes known as 'wilful blindness' or 'Nelsonian blindness', since it involves the defendant turning a blind eye to the obvious)

(3) wilfully and recklessly failing to make such inquiries as an honest and reasonable person would have made

(4) knowledge of circumstances that would indicate the facts to an honest and reasonable person

(5) knowledge of circumstances that would put an honest and reasonable person on inquiry.

The last four categories enable the court to impute knowledge of facts to the defendant even though they lacked actual knowledge of them, so categories (2)–(5) can be described as 'constructive knowledge'.

Although the *Baden* classification has often been referred to in subsequent cases,[8] it must be treated with significant caution. First, the categories that were suggested in the *Baden* case were put to the judge by counsel for the claimant and the defendant on an agreed basis. Secondly, the classification refers only to knowledge as the relevant fault concept, but, as will be seen, other concepts of fault have been suggested and recognized by the courts in respect of receipt-based and accessorial liability,[9] notably unconscionability, dishonesty, and notice. Thirdly, the distinction between the categories of knowledge are difficult to draw in practice and so may be too refined.[10] Indeed, they have been described as differences of degree rather than kind.[11] At this stage their relevance is simply to identify a hierarchy of potential fault requirements ranging from what the defendant actually knew, at one end of the spectrum, to knowledge of circumstances that would have prompted a reasonable person to make further inquiries, which constitutes a form of negligence, at the other end.

---

[7] *Baden v Société Générale pour Favoriser le Développement du Commerce et de l'Industrie en France SA* [1993] 1 WLR 509, 575–6 (Peter Gibson J).

[8] It was expressly adopted by the High Court of Australia in *Farah Constructions Pty Ltd v Say-Dee Pty Ltd* [2007] HCA 22.

[9] In *Royal Brunei Airlines Sdn Bhd v Tan* [1995] 2 AC 378, 392, the Privy Council indicated that, for accessorial liability at least, the *Baden* classification is best forgotten.

[10] *Agip (Africa) Ltd v Jackson* [1990] Ch 265, 293 (Millett J).

[11] *Royal Brunei Airlines v Tan* [1995] 2 AC 378, 390.

20.1.2 NATURE OF THE REMEDY

Traditionally, where a third party is held personally liable in Equity for receiving property transferred in breach of trust or breach of fiduciary duty, or as an accessory to such a breach, the third party will be liable to account as if they were a constructive trustee.[12] Although the use of the language of account indicates that the liability is personal, the reference to constructive trusteeship is potentially misleading, since it might suggest that the third party holds property on constructive trust for the claimant. But, where the third party's liability is receipt-based, typically they will no longer have the property that had been transferred, and liability as an accessory does not depend on the third party having received any property. Consequently, use of the language of constructive trusteeship should be avoided because of its proprietary connotations[13] and because it is easy to jump to the conclusion that the third party should be treated like a trustee. Further, the third party does not assume the position of trustee as regards the beneficiaries.[14] The language of constructive trusteeship has been used simply as a 'formula for equitable relief',[15] but, today, Equity does not need to rely on the artifice of such a formula to impose liability and the third party should simply be described as being personally liable in Equity. This rejection of the relevance of constructive trusteeship is also of practical significance as regards limitation periods in particular, since the normal limitation period under the Limitation Act 1980 will apply because the third party is not a trustee who is liable for breach of trust.[16]

Where the liability is receipt-based, the recipient is simply liable to account for the value of the property that has been received.[17] Where the liability is accessorial the usual remedy will be for the accessory to compensate the claimant for the loss that has been caused by their assistance or encouragement.[18] Since the liability is personal, no property is held on trust and fiduciary duties are not imposed on the defendant.[19]

20.2 RECEIPT-BASED LIABILITY

20.2.1 GENERAL PRINCIPLES

It is a fundamental feature of receipt-based liability that the claimant is able to show that the third party has received property in which the claimant has a proprietary interest. Many of the requirements for this form of liability have already been considered in Chapter 19, including the following in particular:

(1) The claimant must show that they have a proprietary base, consisting of an interest in property recognized in Equity.[20]

---

[12] *Westdeutsche Landesbank Girozentrale v Islington London Borough Council* [1996] AC 669, 705 (Lord Browne-Wilkinson).

[13] *Paragon Finance plc v DB Thakerar & Co* [1999] 1 All ER 400, 408 (Millett LJ); *Dubai Aluminium Co Ltd v Salaam* [2003] 2 AC 366, 404 (Lord Millett); *Williams v Central Bank of Nigeria* [2014] UKSC 10, [2014] 1 AC 1189, [64] (Lord Neuberger).

[14] Although Mitchell and Watterson, 'Remedies for knowing receipt', in *Constructive and Resulting Trusts*, ed. Mitchell (Oxford: Hart, 2010), p. 129, do argue that recipient liability does resemble the liability of express trustees to account for the trust property.

[15] *Selangor United Rubber Estates Ltd v Cradock (No 3)* [1968] 1 WLR 1555, 1582 (Ungoed-Thomas J).

[16] *Williams v Central Bank of Nigeria* [2014] UKSC 10, [2014] 1 AC 1189. See Section 17.3.3.(i), p. 487.

[17] See Section 20.2.3.(i), p. 604.   [18] See Section 20.3.3, p. 621.

[19] *Dubai Aluminium Co Ltd v Salaam* [2002] UKHL 48, [2003] 2 AC 366, [141] (Lord Millett) concerning the liability of the dishonest assistant.   [20] See Section 19.2, p. 548.

(2) The claimant must show that they can follow the property in which they have a proprietary interest into the hands of the third party. Alternatively, if the claimant's original property has been substituted for other property by the trustee, fiduciary, or somebody else, the claimant must be able to trace their value into the substitute property that was received by the third party.

(3) Once the claimant can show that the third party has received property in which the claimant has a proprietary interest, the claimant can then seek to assert a personal claim to recover the value of the property that had been received, even though the third party has not retained that property or its substitute.

It was seen in Chapter 19 that, where the claimant seeks to found a claim in respect of substitute property received by the defendant, the nature of the claim is a matter of some controversy.[21] Although some commentators have argued that all such claims are founded on the reversal of the defendant's unjust enrichment, regardless of whether the claimant seeks proprietary or personal remedies, the preferable view is that these claims are founded on the vindication of the claimant's property rights, even where the defendant has dissipated the property so that the claimant can only bring a personal claim. The key difficulty of analysing these cases as being founded on unjust enrichment is that, where the claimant's property has been misappropriated by a trustee or fiduciary and then transferred to the third party, it is not possible to conclude that the third party has been enriched at the expense of the claimant; rather, they will have been enriched at the expense of the trustee or the fiduciary.[22] Further, there are difficulties in identifying a recognized ground of restitution to show that the third party's enrichment is unjust.

The practical significance of analysing these claims as founded on the vindication of property rights is that the claimant does not need to establish the elements of an unjust enrichment claim; it is enough that the claimant can trace value from the property in which they have a proprietary interest into the property that was received by the defendant. As will be seen, however, some of the leading cases on personal claims founded on receipt-based liability have analysed the nature of the liability with reference to unjust enrichment, despite the difficulties in establishing the component elements of such a claim.

These personal receipt-based claims can arise at Law or in Equity, depending on the nature of the claimant's proprietary right in the property received. Although this book is concerned with equitable claims, it is important to be aware of the nature and operation of similar claims at Law, both because the limitations of such claims explains why the equitable claims are so significant and because there might be important lessons for Equity to learn from the developments at Common Law.

20.2.2 COMMON LAW PERSONAL CLAIMS

Where the claimant can establish that they had a legal interest in the property that was received by the defendant, the claimant may be able to recover the value of the property received by the defendant. Two Common Law personal claims founded on the defendant's receipt of property have been recognized.

(i) Action for money had and received

Where the defendant has received property in which the claimant has retained a legal proprietary interest, the claimant can recover the value of the property received by means of

---

[21] See Section 19.1.4.(ii), p. 540.
[22] See Bryan, 'The liability of the recipient: restitution at common law or wrongdoing in Equity?', in *Equity in Commercial Law*, ed. Degeling and Edelman (Sydney: Law Book Co., 2005), p. 339.

a claim traditionally called the 'action for money had and received'. It is sufficient that the defendant received the property in which the claimant has a legal proprietary interest; it is not necessary to show that the defendant has retained this property or anything representing the property.[23] It is also not necessary to show that the defendant was at fault in any way in receiving the property.

The leading case that illustrates this type of claim is *Lipkin Gorman (a firm) v Karpnale Ltd*.[24] In that case over £320,000 had been stolen from the client account of the claimant firm of solicitors by one of its partners, who had gambled with the money at the defendant's casino. The House of Lords held that the defendant was liable to make restitution to the claimant by means of a personal action for money had and received. The nature of this claim has been a matter of particular controversy. The House of Lords recognized that it was founded on the reversal of the defendant's unjust enrichment, although the ground of restitution was not identified. Some commentators have suggested that the ground of restitution was that the claimant was ignorant that its money had been stolen.[25] An alternative view is that this claim was simply concerned with the vindication of the claimant's property rights in the money, those rights having been retained because the money had been stolen.[26] The latter is the preferable view and is supported by the recognition of the House of Lords in *Foskett v McKeown*[27] of the vindication of proprietary rights principle.[28]

This analysis of *Lipkin Gorman* as a case that involved a proprietary restitutionary claim rather than a claim founded on the reversal of unjust enrichment is consistent with the leading judgments in the case itself: none of the judges identified a ground of restitution on which the claim could be founded. Lord Goff specifically referred to the fact that the claimant had a subsisting interest in the money that had been stolen.[29] Consequently, *Lipkin Gorman* should be treated as a case in which the reason why the claim for money had and received succeeded was because the defendant had received money in which the claimant had a legal proprietary right, rather than that the defendant was unjustly enriched. But this explanation seems difficult to defend on the facts for two reasons. First, legal title to the money had passed to the solicitor, who had authority to draw money from the client account. Despite this, Lord Goff concluded that, since the bank owed the money to the firm, the firm owned a chose in action at Law that it could trace into the cash drawn from the bank account by the solicitor and into the money received by the club. But this is highly artificial, especially because the firm's legal title to the debt was presumably destroyed when the solicitor withdrew the money from the bank, as he had authority to do, so that the bank no longer owed the firm that sum of money. But, even if the firm's legal title to the debt could be traced into the money that had been withdrawn from the account, this money was mixed in a fund with money that was credited to the solicitor personally. As we have previously seen,[30] the orthodox analysis of claims to legal proprietary rights is that they will be defeated once the claimant's property has become mixed with other property. Bizarrely and incorrectly, counsel

---

[23] See *Agip (Africa) Ltd v Jackson* [1990] Ch 265, 285 (Millett J).   [24] [1991] 2 AC 548.

[25] Birks, 'The English recognition of unjust enrichment' [1991] LMCLQ 473 and McKendrick, 'Restitution, misdirected funds and change of position' (1992) 55 MLR 377. Criticized by Swadling, 'Ignorance and unjust enrichment: the problem of title' (2008) 28 OJLS 627.

[26] See Virgo, *The Principles of the Law of Restitution*, 3rd edn (Oxford: Oxford University Press, 2015), pp. 560–5.

[27] [2001] 1 AC 102.   [28] See further Section 19.1.4.(ii), p. 542.

[29] Citing *Clarke v Shee and Johnson* (1774) 1 Cowp 197, 200 (Lord Mansfield).

[30] See Section 19.3.2.(iii), p. 557.

for the defendant casino had conceded that it would be possible to trace into a mixed fund and so, once the firm's legal title to property had been identified, it was able to trace into the money received by the defendant.

Another explanation for the result in *Lipkin Gorman* has been suggested by Smith,[31] namely that, although the claimant was bringing a claim for money had and received at Common Law, this could have been founded on the claimant's equitable proprietary interest in money. Smith has identified a number of old cases[32] that recognized that money had and received is available as a remedy to vindicate equitable proprietary rights under a trust. This is not how the House of Lords decided *Lipkin Gorman*, since that decision was explicitly founded on a legal property right, but this does provide a useful way of justifying the result in the case. Lord Goff did acknowledge that, if legal title had vested in the solicitor, he would have held the money on trust for the firm.[33] As a thief and a solicitor, this would have been an institutional constructive trust triggered by the defendant's unconscionable retention of the money.[34] The firm would then have been able to trace in Equity through the mixed fund into the money received by the defendant. If this approach of recognizing a Common Law claim where there is an equitable proprietary right were to be developed, it would enable equitable proprietary rights to be vindicated by the award of personal remedies without the proof of fault. That is inconsistent with the general tenor of personal claims against third parties in Equity, in which fault is usually required,[35] and this might be a significant policy reason against allowing a Common Law claim to be used to vindicate an equitable proprietary right.

However it is analysed, *Lipkin Gorman* is a difficult case to explain and justify. But, in line with the approach adopted by the judges in the case, it should simply be treated as involving the vindication of Common Law property rights by means of a personal claim for money had and received, without the need to prove fault. The defendant will then be liable to pay to the claimant the value of the property that has been received, judged at the time of receipt, but subject to the application of the defence of change of position.[36]

(ii) Action for debt

It was recognized by the Court of Appeal in *Trustee of the Property of FC Jones and Sons (a firm) v Jones*[37] that, where the claimant could establish that the defendant had received property in which the claimant had a legal proprietary right, the claimant could bring an action for debt against the defendant and obtain an order for payment of the money. This is a personal claim, which has the same practical consequences as the action for money had and received, namely that the claimant is able to recover the value of the money that was received by the defendant. The advantage of bringing a claim in debt is that, if the defendant has invested the money received and obtained income from that investment, this income must also be paid to the claimant. This makes the action for debt look increasingly proprietary in its operation, save that, if the defendant becomes insolvent, the claimant will not have priority over any of the defendant's other creditors, but will rank as a general unsecured creditor.

---

[31] 'Simplifying claims to traceable proceeds' (2009) 125 LQR 338.
[32] Such as *Case v Roberts* (1817) Holt 500 and *Bartlett v Dimond* (1845) 14 M & W 49.
[33] [1991] 2 AC 548, 572. [34] See Section 9.3.1, p. 258. [35] See further Section 20.2.3.(i), p. 600.
[36] See Section 19.5.2, p. 586. [37] [1997] Ch 159.

20.2.3 EQUITABLE PERSONAL CLAIMS

(i) Action for unconscionable receipt

Although the main form of receipt-based liability in Equity has traditionally been called 'knowing receipt',[38] following recent developments in the law, it is now properly called 'unconscionable receipt'.

The equitable action for unconscionable receipt can be considered to be the equitable equivalent of the Common Law claim for money had and received. Both claims are dependent on proof that the defendant had received property in which the claimant had a proprietary interest: either a legal interest for the action for money had and received, or an equitable interest for the action for unconscionable receipt. A further similarity between the two claims is that they will both succeed as long as it can be shown that the defendant received the property without it being necessary to show that the defendant had retained this property. Further, the remedy that is awarded for both types of claim is a personal restitutionary remedy, since it is assessed by reference to the value of the property that the defendant received at the time of its receipt. Despite these similarities between the two claims, there is one fundamental difference between them: whereas liability in the action for money had and received is strict, liability for the action for unconscionable receipt depends on proof that the defendant was at fault in some way. The degree of fault that must be proved is a matter of particular controversy, especially as to whether it is to be assessed subjectively (with regard to the defendant's thought processes) or objectively (with regard to the standard of the reasonable person). But the reason why fault must be established is also a controversial matter that will require careful consideration.[39]

Liability for unconscionable receipt is sometimes described as secondary liability,[40] since it is assumed that the defendant's liability depends on there having been a breach of trust or fiduciary duty. This is not correct. Secondary liability requires proof that the accessory has caused, encouraged, or assisted the breach of trust or fiduciary duty. That does not need to be proved to establish liability for unconscionable receipt, especially because such liability arises after the relevant breach and sometimes after a number of transfers of property between different parties. Such a remote recipient cannot be considered to have caused, encouraged, or assisted the breach of trust or fiduciary duty.

The conditions of liability

In order to establish liability for unconscionable receipt, the following conditions need to be met.

Receipt of property

The defendant must have received property directly or indirectly[41] in which the beneficiary beneficiary or principal has an equitable proprietary interest.[42] This is established by applying the equitable following and tracing rules.[43] Where the property is registered land, an equitable proprietary interest will be avoided where the land has been transferred for valuable consideration,[44] so a claim for unconscionable receipt would not then be available.[45]

---

[38] This language is still used. See e.g. *Williams v Central Bank of Nigeria* [2014] UKSC 10, [2014] AC 1189, [35] (Lord Sumption).   [39] See Section 20.2.3.(iii), p. 600.

[40] *Novoship (UK) Ltd v Mikhaylyuk* [2014] EWCA Civ 908, [2015] QB 499, [68] (Longmore LJ).

[41] *Fistar v Riverwood Legion and Community Club Ltd* [2016] NWSCA 81, [63] (Leeming JA).

[42] *Arthur v Attorney General of the Turks and Caicos Islands* [2012] UKPC 30, [38] (Sir Terence Etherton). He left open, at [53], whether the receipt of an equitable interest suffices to establish a claim for unconscionable receipt.   [43] *Boscawen v Bajwa* [1996] 1 WLR 328, 334 (Millett LJ).

[44] Land Registration Act 2002, s. 29.

[45] See Conaglen and Goymour, 'Knowing receipt and registered land', in *Constructive and Resulting Trusts*, ed. Mitchell (Oxford: Hart, 2010), p. 181. A claim for dishonest assistance might still be available, however. See Section 20.3.2, p. 613.

Property includes chattels and money, but contractual rights arising under an executory contract do not count as property for the purposes of a claim in unconscionable receipt.[46] Although it has sometimes been suggested that the receipt of confidential information might be regarded as the receipt of property,[47] the better view is that information cannot be characterized as property for these purposes,[48] because it lacks the characteristics of property.

Whether the defendant has received property may sometimes raise difficult questions. So, for example, in *Trustor v AB Smallbone (No 2)*,[49] it was held that, where property has been received by a company, its receipt cannot be attributed to an individual who controls the company because of the fundamental doctrine that a company has a separate corporate personality from its directors and shareholders. But receipt by a company may be attributed to the controller of it where the recipient company was acting as agent for the controller or where the veil of incorporation can be pierced, such as where the company has been used as an artificial device to conceal the true facts. Where the veil cannot be pierced then, although receipt-based liability cannot be imposed on the controller, the company can be still liable for unconscionable receipt in its own right,[50] but it will be necessary to attribute the relevant fault to the company from the fault of the person who is the directing mind and will of the company.

Breach of trust or fiduciary duty

The transfer of property to the defendant must have arisen from a breach of trust[51] or fiduciary duty. Where property has been transferred in breach of trust, the claimant will have a prior equitable proprietary interest which can be vindicated. It has been recognized that the action is also available where property has been transferred in breach of fiduciary duty,[52] such as where directors transfer the company's property in breach of fiduciary duty. But, for such a claim to be treated as grounded on the vindication of property rights, it would be necessary to establish that the claimant had a proprietary interest in the property which was transferred in breach of fiduciary duty. Following the recognition by the Supreme Court that property received in breach of fiduciary duty by the fiduciary will be held on constructive trust for the principal,[53] it will be much easier to establish this equitable proprietary interest.

The nature of the breach of trust or fiduciary duty is irrelevant. In particular, it need not be a fraudulent breach.[54] We have seen that a breach of trust encompasses breach of administrative and dispositive duties and powers of trustees.[55] We have also seen that trustees may be subject to fiduciary duties, as are others who are in fiduciary relationships, but the notion of fiduciary duty has been interpreted restrictively to encompass acting where there is a conflict of interest and duty, and making an unauthorized profit.[56] But fiduciaries will be subject to other non-fiduciary duties, such as the duty of care, the duty to act in good faith, and the duty to act in the best interests of the principal. If a fiduciary transfers property to the defendant in breach of one of these

---

[46] *Criterion Properties Ltd v Stratford UK Properties Ltd* [2004] UKHL 28, [2004] 1 WLR 1846, [27] (Lord Scott).

[47] *Satnam Investments Ltd v Dunlop Heywood* [1999] 3 All ER 652.

[48] *Farah Constructions Pty Ltd v Say-Dee Pty Ltd* [2007] HCA 22, [118]–[119]. See also *OBG Ltd v Allan* [2007] UKHL 21, [2008] AC 1, [275] (Lord Walker). [49] [2001] 1 WLR 1177.

[50] *Ultraframe (UK) Ltd v Fielding* [2005] EWHC 1638, [2006] FSR 16, [1576] (Lewison J).

[51] *Novoship (UK) Ltd v Mikhaylyuk* [2014] EWCA Civ 908, [2015] QB 499, [89] (Longmore LJ).

[52] *Arthur v Attorney General of the Turks and Caicos Islands* [2012] UKPC 30, [31] (Sir Terence Etherton).

[53] *FHR European Ventures LLP v Cedar Capital Partners LLC* [2014] UKSC 45, [2015] AC 250. See Section 9.3.7, p. 274. [54] *Agip (Africa) Ltd v Jackson* [1990] Ch 265, 292 (Millett J).

[55] See Chapters 13 and 14 of this volume. [56] See Chapter 15 of this volume.

non-fiduciary duties, can the defendant be liable for unconscionable receipt? If the fiduciary was a trustee, there will have been a breach of trust, even though it is not strictly a breach of fiduciary duty, so the action for unconscionable receipt is potentially available. But, if the fiduciary is not a trustee, such as a director or a solicitor, and has transferred property to the defendant in breach of a non-fiduciary duty, such as failing to comply with the reasonable standard of skill and care, it is unclear whether this will be sufficient to establish a claim in unconscionable receipt; by analogy with liability for breach of trust, it might be.[57]

It appears that the receipt of property by the defendant must have been a direct consequence of the relevant breach of trust or fiduciary duty. This was recognized in *Brown v Bennett*,[58] in which receivers of a company that had gone into administrative receivership sold the business to the defendant. Some of the former shareholders and directors of the company, to whom the receivers had assigned their causes of action, sued the defendant for unconscionable receipt of the company's assets, knowing that the directors of the company had breached their fiduciary duty. It was held that the receipt of the company's assets was not a direct consequence of the breach of fiduciary duty, because the assets had been purchased from independent sellers, namely the receivers. The effect of this decision is that, if the receipt of property arises from a separate legitimate transaction, the defendant cannot be liable for the receipt, regardless of the state of their knowledge of the background to the transfer. This was illustrated by an example suggested by Morritt LJ in *Brown v Bennett*.[59] A mansion house was vested in trustees, who, in breach of trust, let it fall into disrepair over a number of years. The trustees were replaced and the new trustees decided to sell the property to a neighbour, who had seen the property fall into disrepair. The purchase of the property by the neighbour would not render them liable for unconscionable receipt, even though they were well aware of the old trustees' breaches of duty of care, because, assuming that the transaction was at a proper price, those breaches of duty had not caused the neighbour to acquire the land; this arose from a separate, valid transaction that consequently broke the chain of causation.

But this emphasis on the receipt being a direct result of the breach of duty appears inconsistent with the prime requirement of the claim, namely that it is enough that the value of the claimant's property can be traced to the defendant's receipt, even if the property has passed through various hands and has been substituted on the way. A better explanation for the result in *Brown v Bennett*, and for Morritt LJ's hypothetical example, is that the defendant was a bona fide purchaser for value, which will defeat the claimant's equitable proprietary interest, or, alternatively, that the vendors of the property were not acting in breach of trust in selling the property. This is a preferable way of denying liability than by reference to causation.

Beneficial receipt

The property must be received by the defendant for their own use and benefit,[60] rather than ministerially. This means that, if the property is received by the defendant merely as agent for another, the defendant cannot be liable for unconscionable receipt, unless the defendant subsequently misappropriates the property for their own use, since then the defendant will be benefiting from the property.

---

[57] Conaglen, 'The nature and function of fiduciary loyalty' (2005) 121 LQR 452, 479.

[58] [1999] 1 BCLC 649.   [59] Ibid., 655.

[60] *Agip (Africa) Ltd v Jackson* [1990] Ch 265, affirmed [1991] Ch 547 (CA); *Trustor AB v Smallbone (No 2)* [2001] 1 WLR 1177.

Where the defendant has received the property ministerially, they might still be liable for dishonest assistance.[61] Alternatively, if the defendant deals with trust money in breach of trust, they might become a trustee *de son tort* in their own right and so be liable for breach of trust as a trustee.[62] So, for example, in *Blyth v Fladgate*,[63] trust money had been invested in securities that were deposited with the solicitor's bankers. The sole trustee of the trust died and the proceeds of sale were paid to the credit of the solicitor's bank account. The proceeds of sale were then paid by the solicitors to a mortgagor, who executed a mortgage in favour of three people, who were subsequently appointed trustees. The loan of this money to the mortgagor was held to be an improper investment and in breach of trust. The solicitors were held liable as constructive trustees,[64] because they had money in their possession that they knew to be trust money and they had made an improper investment without instructions from any principal. Crucially, the solicitors were liable not because they had received trust property, but because they were treated as trustees. Their liability was strict.

Apart from this exceptional case in which a third party's receipt renders them a trustee, a third party who receives property, but not for their own use or benefit, cannot be liable for unconscionable receipt. This limitation on receipt-based claims can be of real practical significance. For example, where money is transferred to a bank in breach of trust, it cannot be liable for unconscionable receipt, even though the bank might know of the breach of trust, because it will not have received the money for itself, but ministerially for its customer. That, at least, is the orthodox view. An exception has been recognized where the money was paid into an overdrawn account, which has the effect of discharging a debt owed by the customer, so that then the bank will have received the money beneficially rather than ministerially.[65] But, surely, all money that is paid to a bank is received by it beneficially rather than ministerially, because the relationship between bank and customer is one of debtor and creditor, so the bank receives the money for itself and is liable only to pay to the customer the amount that has been received rather than the actual money that has been transferred?[66] In other words, payment to a bank simply creates a debt owed to the customer and the bank is free to do what it wants with the money that was transferred to it. In *Uzinterimpex JSC v Standard Bank plc*,[67] the Court of Appeal confirmed the general principle that receipt-based liability turns on the defendant receiving property for their own use and benefit, but Moore-Bick LJ did suggest *obiter* that, since a bank has the benefit of its customers' money until it is called upon to repay, it should follow that a bank could be liable for unconscionable receipt when money is credited to a customer's bank account. If correct, it follows that the ambit of liability for unconscionable receipt is potentially very significant, although it must not be forgotten that a bank could not be liable for receiving property transferred in breach of trust or fiduciary duty unless it is at fault as regards the receipt.[68]

---

[61] See Section 20.3.2, p. 613.   [62] See Section 12.3.9, p. 345.   [63] [1891] 1 Ch 337.

[64] Not having been expressly appointed, the trust arose by operation of law. But it was a real trust; they were not simply liable to account as though they were constructive trustees. See Section 12.3.9, p. 346, for the view that trustees *de son tort* are express trustees.

[65] *Agip (Africa) Ltd v Jackson* [1990] Ch 265, 292 (Millett J).

[66] Gleeson, 'The involuntary launderer: the banker's liability for deposits of the proceeds of crime', in *Laundering and Tracing*, ed. Birks (Oxford: Clarendon Press, 1995), pp. 126–7; Bryan, 'Recovering misdirected money from banks: ministerial receipt at Law and in Equity', in *Restitution and Banking Law*, ed. Rose (Oxford: Mansfield Press, 1998), p. 182.   [67] [2008] EWCA Civ 819, [2008] Lloyd's Rep. 456.

[68] But note the discussion of strict liability for receipt-based claims in Section 20.2.3.(iii), p. 608.

Fault

The defendant must have been at fault either at the time that they received the property in breach of trust or breach of fiduciary duty or, if the receipt was innocent, the defendant was at fault subsequently.

It has been a matter of controversy for some years as to what should be the appropriate level of fault for equitable receipt-based liability. Many cases have held that an objective test of fault applies, sometimes described as 'constructive knowledge', so that it is sufficient that the defendant had failed to make such inquiries as a reasonable person would have made as to whether property had been transferred in breach of trust or breach of fiduciary duty.[69] Other cases have held that constructive fault is not sufficient and that a subjective test applies, so it must be established that the defendant actually knew or suspected that the property had been received in breach of trust or breach of fiduciary duty.[70]

The applicable level of fault was considered by the Court of Appeal in *Bank of Credit and Commerce International (Overseas) Ltd v Akindele*,[71] in which it was held that the appropriate test is one of unconscionability as regards the retention of the benefit of the property received.[72] In *Akindele*, employees of a company breached their fiduciary duty by procuring the company to enter into an artificial investment agreement with the defendant, the effect of which was that the defendant invested US$10 million and subsequently received a payment of nearly US$17 million from the company. The claimants, who were the company's liquidators, sued the defendant for knowing receipt of the money on the ground that he had received the money knowing of the employees' breach of fiduciary duty. The Court of Appeal held that it was not necessary to show that the defendant had acted dishonestly to be liable for a receipt-based claim, because the receipt might be passive and dishonesty was considered only to relate to actions;[73] similarly, it was not necessary to establish that the defendant had knowingly participated in any fraud. Rather, the key test was whether the defendant's knowledge of the circumstances relating to the breach of trust or fiduciary duty made it unconscionable for them to retain the benefit of the property that had been received. This could be established if the defendant actually knew of the circumstances in which the money was transferred; constructive knowledge would not be sufficient. On the facts, there was insufficient evidence that the defendant knew enough to make retention of the value of the money received unconscionable. He was unaware of any facts that questioned the propriety of the loan transaction, despite the very high rate of interest (which he assumed was because he was considered to be a high-worth customer). Unconscionability could not be established from the defendant's suspicions about the general reputation of the company; any suspicion had to relate to

---

[69] See e.g. *Karak Rubber Co Ltd v Burden (No 2)* [1972] 1 WLR 602, 632 (Brightman J); *Belmont Finance Corp Ltd v Williams Furniture Ltd (No 2)* [1980] 1 All ER 393, 405 (Buckley LJ) and 412 (Goff LJ); *International Sales and Agencies Ltd v Marcus* [1982] 3 All ER 551; *Rolled Steel Products (Holdings) Ltd v British Steel Corp* [1986] Ch 246, 306 (Browne-Wilkinson LJ); *Agip (Africa) Ltd v Jackson* [1990] Ch 265, 291 (Millett J); *Houghton v Fayers* [2000] 1 BCLC 511, 516 (Nourse LJ). Similarly in New Zealand: *Westpac Banking Corpn v Savin* [1985] 2 NZLR 41; and Canada: *Citadel General Assurance Co v Lloyds Bank Canada* (1997) 152 DLR (4th) 411.

[70] *Re Montagu's Settlement Trust* [1987] Ch 264; *Eagle Trust plc v SBC Securities Ltd* [1993] 1 WLR 484, 503 (Vinelott J); *Cowan de Groot Property Ltd v Eagle Trust plc* [1992] 4 All ER 700; *Eagle Trust plc v SBC Securities Ltd (No. 2)* [1996] 1 BCLC 121; *Hillsdown Holdings plc v Pensions Ombudsman* [1997] 1 All ER 862; *Templeton Insurance Ltd v Brunswick* [2012] EWHC 1522 (Ch), [80] (HHJ Simon Barker QC); *Williams v Central Bank of Nigeria* [2014] UKSC 10, [2014] AC 1189, [31] (Lord Sumption). See Havelock, 'The transformation of knowing receipt' [2014] RLR 1.   [71] [2001] Ch 437.

[72] Ibid., 455 (Nourse LJ).

[73] Dishonesty is required to establish liability for assisting a breach of trust or breach of fiduciary duty. See Section 20.3.2(iii), p. 614.

the particular transaction. Consequently, he was not liable to account for the value of the profit that he had received.

Although the Court of Appeal gave no real guidance to the courts as to what constitutes 'unconscionable conduct' for these purposes, it is clear that a subjective test was contemplated.[74] Clearly, a defendant's receipt will be considered to be unconscionable if they knew of the breach of trust or fiduciary duty and, presumably, also if they turned a blind eye to the breach. It is not, however, clear whether the receipt of a defendant who was suspicious about the breach can be considered to have been unconscionable.

The House of Lords was presented with the opportunity to clarify the appropriate test of fault in *Criterion Properties plc v Stratford UK Properties LLC*.[75] This case concerned a 'poison pill' agreement, whereby the managing director and another director of Criterion signed an agreement, purportedly on behalf of Criterion, with the defendant Oaktree, which gave Oaktree the contractual right to be bought out of a partnership with Criterion on favourable terms if another party were to gain control of Criterion or if its chairman or managing director were to cease to be involved in the management of the company. The managing director of Criterion was dismissed and Oaktree sought to exercise its option to be bought out. Criterion sought to set the agreement aside on the ground that it was unauthorized. The Court of Appeal[76] held that, although the directors of Criterion might have lacked authority to make the agreement, whether Oaktree could enforce the agreement turned on whether it was unconscionable for Oaktree to hold Criterion to the agreement, a matter that needed to be considered at trial. A variety of factors and considerations were identified to determine such unconscionability, including the fault of both parties to the agreement; the defendant's knowledge of the circumstances constituting the breach of duty; whether the parties had obtained legal advice; and the actions and knowledge of the parties in the context of the commercial relationship as a whole. It appears from this that 'unconscionable' is given a subjective interpretation, but also that relative fault and factual context are significant.

The decision went on appeal to the House of Lords,[77] where the court was given the opportunity to clarify what 'unconscionability' means for these purposes. But the court concluded that the unconscionability test generally, and unconscionable receipt in particular, were not relevant to the case, since no property had been received by the defendant pursuant to the agreement. It was held that the only issue to resolve was whether there was a valid poison pill agreement, which turned on whether the directors of Criterion were authorized to sign the agreement on behalf of the company.[78] Since this matter had not yet been determined, it was directed to go to trial.

Crucially, the House of Lords rejected the approach adopted by the Court of Appeal in *BCCI v Akindele*,[79] which was also considered to have turned on the question of authority to enter into the loan agreement rather than unconscionability. As Lord Nicholls said:[80]

> If a company (A) enters into an agreement with B under which B acquires benefits from A, A's ability to recover these benefits from B depends essentially on whether the agreement is binding on A. If the directors of A were acting for an improper purpose when they entered into the agreement, A's ability to have the agreement set aside depends upon the

---

[74] Cf. Birks, 'Receipt', in *Breach of Trust*, ed. Birks and Pretto (Oxford: Hart, 2002), p. 227, who considered that unconscionability involved an unreasonable failure to appreciate the trust provenance of the property received, which would constitute an objective test.   [75] [2004] UKHL 28, [2004] 1 WLR 1846.
[76] [2002] EWCA Civ 1883, [2003] 1 WLR 2108.   [77] [2004] UKHL 28, [2004] 1 WLR 1846.
[78] Although it was acknowledged that the defendant's knowledge of the circumstances was relevant when considering whether there was apparent authority to sign: [2004] UKHL 28, [2004] 1 WLR 1846, [30] (Lord Scott).
[79] [2001] Ch 437.   [80] [2004] UKHL 28, [2004] 1 WLR 1846, [4].

application of familiar principles of agency and company law. If, applying these principles, the agreement is found to be valid and is therefore not set aside, questions of 'knowing receipt' by B do not arise. So far as B is concerned there can be no question of A's assets having been misapplied. B acquired the assets from A, the legal and beneficial owner of the assets, under a valid agreement made between him and A.

So the primary issue in cases such as *Criterion* and *Akindele* concerns the validity of the agreement, determined with reference to the principles of agency and corporate law. If the agreement is valid, any property acquired by B would have been acquired legitimately and there would not have been any misapplication of A's assets. It is only if the underlying agreement is invalid that the receipt-based claim could arise. We know from the decision of the Court of Appeal in *Criterion Properties* that the test of unconscionability remains relevant to the equitable receipt-based claim and nothing said in the decision of the House of Lords undermines that. In particular, the factors identified by the Court of Appeal remain relevant to determine what is meant by 'unconscionability' for these purposes, although the essence of unconscionability remains unclear.

In *Armstrong DLW Gmbh v Winnington Networks Ltd*[81] Stephen Morris QC held that unconscionability for the purposes of a claim in unconscionable receipt encompassed both subjective awareness by the defendant of possible impropriety and also where, on the facts actually known to the defendant, a reasonable person would have appreciated that the transfer was in breach of trust or would have made such inquiries or sought advice which would have revealed the probability of breach of trust. In *Arthur v Attorney-General of the Turks and Caicos Islands*[82] Sir Terence Etherton described knowing receipt as 'involving unconscionable conduct amounting to equitable fraud. It is a classic example of lack of *bona fides*'. But this confirms the ambiguity of unconscionability, since equitable fraud and absence of good faith can incorporate objective notions of fault.

In *Dubai Aluminium Co Ltd v Salaam*[83] Lord Millett had confirmed that the liability for the receipt claim is fault-based, but he concluded that it was founded on allegations of dishonesty and described it as involving dishonest receipt. It is unclear whether this was because of the way in which the case was argued or whether his analysis is of more general significance to our understanding of the fault requirement for this cause of action. More recently in *Williams v Central Bank of Nigeria*,[84] Lord Neuberger emphasized three times in the space of one paragraph that the liability of the recipient is founded on dishonesty. As will be seen later,[85] dishonesty, for the purposes of the action of dishonest assistance, is interpreted as involving conduct objectively assessed in the light of the defendant's own knowledge or suspicion of the facts.

Unconscionability has also proved significant in determining whether the defence of change of position to claims in unjust enrichment can be established.[86] That defence is not available if the defendant has acted in bad faith in changing their position, which has been equated with unconscionability. In that context unconscionability has been interpreted as including dishonesty, a failure to act in a commercially acceptable way,[87] and wilfully and

---

[81] [2012] EWHC 10 (Ch), [2013] Ch 156, [132].   [82] [2012] UKPC 30, [40].
[83] [2002] UKHL 48, [2003] 2 AC 366, 391.
[84] [2014] UKSC 10, [2014] 1 AC 1189, [64]. See also *Vestergaard Frandsen v Bestnet Europe Ltd* [2013] UKSC 31, [2013] 1 WLR 1556, at [42] (Lord Neuberger). Although in *Williams* Lord Sumption asserted that liability for knowing receipt does not require proof of dishonesty on anybody's part: [35].
[85] See Section 20.3.2.(iii), p. 620.   [86] See Section 19.5.2, p. 586.
[87] *Niru Battery Manufacturing Co v Milestone Trading Ltd* [2002] EWHC 1425 (Comm), [2002] 2 All ER (Comm) 705, 741. This was endorsed in the Court of Appeal: [2003] EWCA 1446 (Civ); *Abou-Rahmah v Abacha* [2006] EWCA Civ 1492, [2007] 1 All ER (Comm) 827.

recklessly failing to make such inquiries as an honest and reasonable person would make.[88] It does not, however, include negligence.[89] There is no reason to think that this is anything other than an objective assessment of the defendant's conduct, but in the light of the facts as the defendant knew or suspected them to be.[90] Presumably, these interpretations of unconscionability for the purposes of the defence of change of position will also apply to the action for unconscionable receipt. That unconscionability for the receipt-based claim and for change of position should be interpreted in the same way was recognized by the Court of Appeal in *Abou-Rahmah v Abacha*,[91] in which it was held that general suspicions on the part of the defendant about the nature of the trustee's or fiduciary's conduct is not sufficient to constitute unconscionability; the defendant must be suspicious about the particular transaction involving the transfer of property.[92]

This objective interpretation of unconscionability was recognized by the Privy Council in *Crédit Agricole Corporation and Investment Bank v Papadimitriou*,[93] where the Privy Council considered the definition of bad faith which would prevent the defendant from establishing the bona fide purchase defence.[94] It was recognized that a defendant will not have acted in good faith if they had actual notice of the claimant's equitable proprietary right or had constructive notice of it. The defendant will have constructive notice of the proprietary right if the facts known to the defendant would give a reasonable person in the position of the defendant serious cause to question the propriety of the transaction involving the transfer of property.[95] Lord Sumption specifically recognized that this is the same test as for unconscionable receipt.[96]

It is appropriate for the fault requirement for the action in unconscionable receipt to be interpreted objectively, since this is consistent with the equitable notions of conscience and unconscionability.[97] In a receipt-based claim the defendant's behaviour should be considered to be unconscionable when they should have made restitution of the value of the property received in the light of the facts involving breach of trust or fiduciary duty which the defendant knew or suspected. Since this is consistent with the interpretation of dishonesty for the assistance claim,[98] it might be preferable to name this the claim for dishonest receipt, but only if the interpretation of dishonesty is considered to be sufficiently robust to be interpreted objectively in the light of the defendant's own awareness of the facts. It might even be appropriate to revert to the original nomenclature of 'knowing receipt', although the danger of using the language of knowledge is that it has subjective connotations. The key feature of the interpretation of fault[99] for the receipt-based claim is that it should embody all aspects of the *Baden* test,[100] since, in the light of the defendant's knowledge (which should encompass belief and suspicion) the question is whether the defendant's behaviour in not making restitution to the claimant was appropriate, which will be assessed objectively with reference to what the reasonable person would have done.

---

[88] *Papamichael v National Westminster Bank* [2003] Lloyd's Rep. 341, 369 (Judge Chambers QC).

[89] *Maersk Air Ltd v Expeditors International (UK) Ltd* [2003] 1 Lloyd's Rep 491, 499.

[90] As was recognized in *Re Hampton Capital Ltd* [2015] EWHC 1905 (Ch), [2016] 1 BCLC 374, [67] (George Bompas QC).

[91] *Abou-Rahmah v Abacha* [2006] EWCA Civ 1492, [2007] 1 All ER (Comm) 827.

[92] Criticized by Lee, 'Changing position on change of position' [2007] RLR 135, 139.

[93] [2015] UKPC 13, [2015] 1 WLR 4265.   [94] See Section 19.5.1, p. 584.

[95] [2015] UKPC 13, [2015] 1 WLR 4265, [20] (Lord Clarke).   [96] Ibid., [33].

[97] See Section 2.3.3.(i), p. 30. Cf. Havelock (see n. 70), who argues that actual knowledge should be required to impose such personal liability because otherwise the defendant's conscience is not sufficiently affected; there is a danger of judicial discretion in imposing liability; and there is a need to protect the security of receipt and integrity of commercial transactions.   [98] See Section 20.3.2.(iii), p. 620.

[99] Whether liability should depend on fault at all is considered in Section 20.2.3.(iii), p. 608.

[100] See Section 20.1.1, p. 591.

The remedies for unconscionable receipt

Once these conditions for establishing liability have been satisfied, the defendant would have been held liable to the claimant as a constructive trustee.[101] This form of liability has now been convincingly rejected as fictional and unnecessary.[102] As Millett LJ said in *Paragon Finance plc v DB Thakerar and Co:*[103] 'the expressions "constructive trust" and "constructive trustee" are misleading for there is no trust and usually no possibility of a proprietary remedy; they are nothing more than a formula for equitable relief'. Where the defendant is held liable for unconscionable receipt, the remedy is a personal liability to account for the value of property received.[104] It is a gain-based, restitutionary remedy.[105] There is no obligation to transfer specific property to the claimant. Rather, the defendant is liable to account for the gain made and regardless of the amount of loss, if any, suffered by the claimant.[106] Although in *Arthur v Attorney General of the Turks and Caicos Islands*,[107] Sir Terence Etherton assumed that the liability to account as a constructive trustee meant that the recipient was subject to the same custodial duties as those voluntarily assumed by an express trustee, such that the recipient's core duty was to restore the misapplied trust property, this confuses proprietary and personal claims: the recipient is only liable to restore the value of the property received in a personal claim for unconscionable receipt.

In assessing this remedy, it is important to be clear as to the date on which the property should be valued: is it at the point of receipt by the defendant or at the time of judgment? This will be significant if the value of the property has fallen or increased after it was received. If the action for unconscionable receipt is considered to be the equitable counterpart of the Common Law action for money had and received,[108] the remedy should be assessed at the point of receipt. But the traditional description of the defendant's liability as being accountable as if they were a constructive trustee would suggest that the defendant recipient should be liable for all benefits received, so any increase in the value of the property should be taken into account[109] and the remedy should therefore be assessed at the time of judgment, which is consistent with the equitable practice relating to the taking of an account.[110] Indeed, in *Crown Dilmun v Sutton*,[111] Peter Smith J held that a defendant who had unconscionably received property in breach of fiduciary duty was liable to account for all of the profits that he had received or would subsequently make. The only restriction was that the account would have to be taken before the end of the six-year limitation period after the claimant first became aware of its claim.[112] Further, the judge recognized that, in taking the account, the defendant might be awarded a personal allowance

[101] See *Gwembe Valley Development Co Ltd v Koshy* [2003] EWCA Civ 1048, [2004] 1 BCLC 131, [88].

[102] *Paragon Finance plc v DB Thakerar and Co* [1999] 1 All ER 400, 408 (Millett LJ). See also *Williams v Central Bank of Nigeria* [2014] UKSC 10, [2014] AC 1189.

[103] *Paragon Finance plc v DB Thakerar and Co* [1999] 1 All ER 400; *Dubai Aluminium Co Ltd v Salaam* [2002] UKHL 48, [2003] 2 AC 366, 404 (Lord Millett).

[104] *Paragon Finance plc v DB Thakerar and Co* [1999] 1 All ER 400, 408 (Millett LJ); *Crown Dilmun v Sutton* [2004] EWHC 52, [2004] 1 BCLC 468, [204] (Peter Smith J).

[105] *Royal Brunei Airlines v Tan* [1995] 2 AC 378, 386; *Twinsectra v Yardley* [2002] UKHL 12, [2002] 2 AC 164, 194 (Lord Millett).

[106] *Akita Holdings Ltd v The Honourable Attorney General of the Turks and Caicos Islands* [2017] UKPC 7, [2017] AC 590.   [107] [2012] UKPC 30, [37]. Mitchell and Watterson (see n. 14).

[108] As advocated by Lord Nicholls of Birkenhead writing extra-judicially: 'Knowing receipt: the need for a new landmark', in *Restitution: Past, Present and Future*, ed. Cornish et al. (Oxford: Hart, 1998), p. 231.

[109] Mitchell and Watterson (see n. 14), p. 138.   [110] See Section 18.1.4.(i), p. 505.

[111] [2004] EWHC 52, [2004] 1 BCLC 468, [27]. See also *Ultraframe v Fielding* [2005] EWHC 1638, [2006] FSR 16, [1577] (Lewison J); *City Index Ltd v Gawler* [2007] EWCA Civ 1382, [2008] Ch 313, [64] (Arden LJ).

[112] [2004] EWHC 52, [2004] 1 BCLC 468, [30].

to reflect their own contribution to making the profit, although such an allowance might be denied by virtue of the defendant's conduct.[113] Since the defendant's receipt will already have been shown to have been unconscionable in order for the defendant to be held liable, this will probably prevent the defendant from obtaining the personal allowance.

Exceptionally, there may be circumstances under which the gain to the defendant is smaller than the value of the loss suffered by the claimant. In such a situation, the claimant can elect for the remedy of equitable compensation[114] rather than the value of the defendant's gain.[115]

Contribution

It was seen in Chapter 17 that, where two or more people are jointly liable in respect of the same damage and one party discharges the liability of them both, that party can seek a contribution from the other under the Civil Liability (Contribution) Act 1978, the extent of the contribution lying in the discretion of the court.[116] A contribution claim may be made where one party is liable for unconscionable receipt. In *City Index Ltd v Gawler*,[117] an employee of a company had stolen £9 million in breach of fiduciary duty. The money had been received by City Index, which knew of the breach of fiduciary duty, and was liable for unconscionable receipt of the money. This claim was settled for £5.5 million. City Index then sought contributions from some of the company's directors and its auditor, on the ground that they had negligently failed to detect the theft. A contribution claim could have succeeded only if City Index and the directors were liable for the same damage, which is defined by section 6(1) of the 1978 Act as a liability to pay compensation in respect of the damage. The liabilities did not appear to involve the same damage, since liability in the tort of negligence is loss-based, whereas that for unconscionable receipt is gain-based, being assessed by reference to the value of the property received. Nevertheless, the Court of Appeal held that the claims were deemed to involve the same damage, since even unconscionable receipt can be analysed as loss-based and compensatory.[118] This is because, the defendant having received property in which the claimant has a proprietary interest, the remedy of accounting for the value of the property received involves restoring value to the claimant, so essentially the claimant is compensated for the loss suffered from the misapplication of property.

From a purely doctrinal perspective, the analysis of the Court of Appeal is incorrect, since the remedy for unconscionable receipt cannot be equated with that for the tort of negligence; it is assessed with reference to the value of the property at the time of the receipt, which may be different to the loss suffered by the claimant at the time of transfer. This difference between the function of the remedies is even more marked if the defendant is liable to account for profits that they received subsequently from the use of the property. Nonetheless, the result of the decision can be defended on policy grounds, since it is only fair that one defendant, who has discharged their own liability as well as that of another defendant, should be able to obtain contribution from the other defendant where that liability relates to the same series of events. But such a liability to make contribution should operate only to the extent that the value of the claimant's loss corresponds to the value of the defendant's gain,[119] for only then can they be considered to be liable for the same damage.

---

[113] See Section 18.5.3.(ii), p. 530.   [114] See Section 18.4, p. 523.

[115] See *City Index Ltd v Gawler* [2007] EWCA Civ 1382, [2008] Ch 313, [64] (Arden LJ).

[116] See Section 17.4.2.(i), p. 494.   [117] [2007] EWCA Civ 1382, [2008] Ch 313.

[118] Consistent with *Friends' Provident Life Office v Hillier Parker May and Rowden* [1997] QB 85. Cf. *Royal Brompton Hospital NHS Trust v Hammond (No 3)* [2002] UKHL 14, [2002] 1 WLR 1397.

[119] Goymour, 'A contribution to knowing receipt liability? (*City Index v Gawler*)' [2008] RLR 113, 118.

The decision in *City Index* is also significant as regards the determination of the extent of the contribution. According to the 1978 Act, the court can order contribution as appears just and equitable, having regard to the extent of the parties' responsibility for the damage. The Court of Appeal held that, where the defendant has received property in breach of trust or fiduciary duty, then, to the extent that the defendant has retained the value of that benefit, they should not be able to obtain contribution from the other defendant. So, for example, consider a case in which Ann was jointly liable with Brian to Carol, with Ann being liable for unconscionably receiving £10,000, which was transferred in breach of trust, and Brian for the tort of negligence in not stopping this. Ann then discharged the joint liability by settling with Carol for £5,000. If Ann had retained £3,000 of the money that she received, she should only be able to seek a maximum contribution from Brian of £2,000. In exercising its discretion as to the award of contribution, the court should have regard to the circumstances in which the money was dissipated and the relative fault of the party. In this example, the fact that Ann had acted unconscionably, whereas Brian acted only negligently, might be a reason to reduce, or even eliminate, the contribution claim, although this will turn on careful assessment of the facts, and also whether unconscionability is interpreted subjectively or objectively. In *City Index* itself, the question of contribution between the parties as regards the value of the benefit lost by the defendant was left for decision at trial.

Defences

The claim for unconscionable receipt could potentially be defeated or qualified by two defences.

Bona fide purchase

If the defendant has received the property in good faith and for value, this will defeat the claimant's equitable proprietary interest, so that a key requirement for the claim could not be established. But the defence will not be available to a defendant who is sued for unconscionable receipt. This is because the claimant will already have had to prove that the defendant's receipt was unconscionable in order to establish the claim.[120] Proof of such fault will negate the defendant's good faith, so that the defendant will not be able to plead the defence successfully. If, however, the defendant had received the property from a third party who was a bona fide purchaser for value, the claimant's equitable proprietary interest will already have been defeated, so the defendant would not be liable for unconscionable receipt, even if the defendant was aware of the initial breach of trust or breach of fiduciary duty.

Change of position

It is unclear whether the defence of change of position is available to the defendant who is liable for unconscionable receipt. The defence is available where the claimant sues the defendant for money had and received where the defendant has received property in which the claimant has a legal proprietary interest.[121] Since the equitable action for unconscionable receipt appears to be the equitable equivalent of the Common Law action for money had and received,[122] it might be considered to follow that the defence of change of position

---

[120] In *Crédit Agricole Corporation and Investment Bank v Papadimitriou* [2015] UKPC 13, [2015] 1 WLR 4265, Lord Sumption, [33], recognized that bad faith for the purposes of the bona fide purchase defence is the same as that to establish unconscionability.

[121] *Lipkin Gorman (a firm) v Karpnale Ltd* [1991] 2 AC 548.   [122] See further Section 20.2.2.(i), p. 593.

should be available, so that the defendant would not be liable to account to the claimant for the value of the property they had received, to the extent that the defendant had changed their position in reliance on the receipt of the property.

In fact, even if the defence of change of position is available in principle, it will not be available on the facts. This is because the defence cannot be established if the defendant has acted in bad faith. As we have already seen, bad faith has been equated with unconscionability,[123] so that a defendant who is liable for unconscionable receipt will necessarily have been acting in bad faith and so change of position will not be available to them.

(ii) Administration of estates

The House of Lords in *Ministry of Health v Simpson*,[124] recognized an apparently limited personal claim in Equity, whereby beneficiaries of a testator's estate were able to recover money that had been paid to the defendants by the personal representatives who were administering the estate and who mistakenly believed that the money was properly paid to the defendants. This equitable action has two unusual features. First, unlike many equitable claims which depend on the defendant's conscience having been affected in some way before equitable liability is imposed, the defendant's liability is strict, so that no fault needs to be proved. Secondly, the beneficiaries are able to bring an action against the recipients of the estate only once they had exhausted their remedies against the personal representatives, which they would have done had the personal representatives been impecunious or had a defence, such as that under section 61 of the Trustee Act 1925.[125]

The proper analysis of this equitable action is a matter of some controversy. It might be analysed as a strict liability equitable proprietary claim, with the beneficiaries vindicating their equitable proprietary rights against the defendants who had received property from the estate by mistake. But this proprietary analysis will not work, since the beneficiaries of an unadministered estate have neither a legal nor an equitable interest in the estate until the personal representatives have discharged all of the deceased's debts.[126] Until this has occurred, the beneficiary has only an expectation of the property being distributed, which is characterized as a mere equity.[127] Consequently, the beneficiaries have no equitable property interest to vindicate. The preferable way of analysing the claim in *Ministry of Health v Simpson* is that the beneficiaries are bringing a claim on behalf of the estate rather than themselves to vindicate the distribution scheme of the administration of the estate.[128] The personal representatives are responsible for bringing the claim for recovery of property transferred by mistake. But, if they do not do so, the potential beneficiaries should sue the personal representatives to restore the value of the estate. If they are not able to do that successfully, Equity enables them to bring a claim against the defendant recipient of the property. If they are successful, the value of the property received is not paid to the beneficiaries, but is returned to the estate, which still needs to be administered. Throughout this process, the beneficiaries cannot benefit directly, since they have only an expectation that they will receive something in the administration of the estate. This expectation will be defeated if the third-party recipient of the property was a bona fide purchaser for value.[129]

---

[123] See Section 20.2.3.(i), p. 602.   [124] [1951] AC 251, on appeal from *Re Diplock's Estate* [1948] Ch 465.

[125] See Section 17.3.2, p. 481.

[126] *Commissioner of Stamp Duties (Queensland) v Livingston* [1965] AC 694; *Eastbourne Mutual Building Society v Hastings Corporation* [1965] 1 WLR 861. See Section 3.7.7, p. 65.

[127] See Smith, 'Unjust enrichment, property, and the structure of trusts' (2000) 116 LQR 412, 444.

[128] See Sheehan, 'Disentangling equitable personal liability for receipt and assistance' [2008] RLR 41, 61.

[129] See e.g. *Baker (GL) Ltd v Medway Building and Supplies Ltd* [1958] 1 WLR 1216, 1220 (Danckwerts J); *Re J Leslie Engineers Co Ltd* [1976] 1 WLR 292, 299 (Oliver J).

It follows that this strict liability personal claim arises in the very specific context of a defective transfer of property in the administration of an estate. The requirements for the claim are dependent on this particular context and this cannot be extrapolated to establish a general strict liability personal claim in Equity. Nevertheless, the strict liability claim has been recognized outside the administration of estates context. For example, in *GL Baker Ltd v Medway Building and Supplies Ltd*,[130] the principle was applied to enable a beneficiary to recover money mistakenly transferred by a trustee in the administration of an inter vivos trust. This may be treated as an aberration or perhaps as a logical extension of the principle recognized in *Ministry of Health v Simpson*, under which the beneficiary has a right to sue the third-party recipient in Equity, where the right to sue is derived from the trustee and the beneficiary cannot benefit personally from this claim. If the claim were successful, the recipient would be liable to repay the money to the trust fund rather than to the beneficiary directly.

(iii) The future of personal receipt-based claims in Equity

The action of unconscionable receipt has proved to be controversial, both as regards the conditions of liability, but also, and more significantly, as regards the rationale of liability. The key concern is that liability involves both wrongdoing, because of the need to establish that the defendant was at fault in some way, and vindication of proprietary rights, which depends on the defendant having received property in which the claimant had an equitable proprietary interest. The need to establish fault has been criticized, most notably by Lord Nicholls of Birkenhead, writing extra-judicially.[131] According to Lord Nicholls, it would be more appropriate to distinguish between two distinct forms of liability.[132] The first would be grounded on the commission of a wrong, for which fault would be required in the form of dishonesty, in the objective sense that the defendant's conduct would be characterized by a reasonable person as dishonest, and for which the defence of change of position would not be available because a dishonest defendant would inevitably have acted in bad faith. The second would be receipt-based and would be founded on the vindication of equitable property rights; it would be the exact counterpart of the Common Law action for money had and received. Where the defendant had received, but no longer retains, property in which the claimant had an equitable proprietary right, the fact that the defendant has interfered with the claimant's equitable proprietary rights means that it is appropriate that the defendant's liability should be strict, subject to the defences of change of position and bona fide purchase.

But, as a matter of policy and principle, should Equity develop such a strict liability personal claim where the defendant has received property in which the claimant had an equitable interest and which would be the mirror-image of the Common Law claim? The imposition of strict liability could be justified both at Law and in Equity because, where a defendant has received property in which the claimant has a proprietary interest, the strength of that proprietary interest requires the defendant to make restitution of its value regardless of the defendant's fault and even though the defendant has not retained the property. The *quid pro quo* for recognizing a strict liability claim should be that the defendant is able to rely on the defence of change of position. This is what happened in *Lipkin*

---

[130]   [1958] 1 WLR 1216.

[131]   Lord Nicholls (see n. 108), p. 231. See also Lord Millett, 'Proprietary restitution', in *Equity in Commercial Law*, ed. Degeling and Edelman (Sydney: Law Book Co., 2005), pp. 311–12; Lord Walker, 'Dishonesty and unconscionable conduct in commercial life: some reflections on accessory liability and knowing receipt' (2005) 27 Sydney LR 187.   [132]   See also Birks (see n. 74), p. 224.

Gorman (a firm) v Karpnale Ltd[133] at Common Law and, by virtue of the need for consistency, the same could follow in Equity.

But, is it appropriate to require Equity to develop a new cause of action simply to reflect what occurs at Law? Smith[134] has argued that this is not appropriate, because equitable proprietary rights are not protected in the same way as legal ones. For example, most legal proprietary rights are not defeated by the bona fide purchase defence and beneficiaries with equitable proprietary rights do not have direct claims in the torts of conversion[135] or negligence.[136] Legal and equitable proprietary rights are different, and cannot be assimilated. Gardner[137] has defended the need to establish fault before personal liability is imposed in Equity on third-party recipients on the ground that receipt-based liability derives from the failure to preserve trust property and, for such liability to arise, the recipient must have been aware of the need to preserve the property, hence the need to prove unconscionability.

The distinct approach to personal liability in Equity can also be justified for policy reasons. It is simply not appropriate for third-party recipients of property in which the claimant has an equitable proprietary interest to be held strictly liable for the value of the property received, because equitable interests tend to be hidden. It is only where the third-party recipient knew, or suspected, that there might be such interests in the property received that it is appropriate to hold the third party personally liable.[138] If such strict liability were recognized in Equity, it would place unacceptable burdens on third-party recipients, such as banks, which have no reason to suspect that the claimant might have a proprietary interest in the property received. Whilst it is true that the imposition of such strict liability would require there to be generous defences of bona fide purchase for value and change of position to protect defendants, this would still place an onerous burden on an innocent recipient to establish the defences.[139]

In Australia, the recognition of a strict liability receipt-based claim has been rejected as a 'grave error', primarily on the ground that it is unjust to impose such liability on the defendant who has no idea that they had received property in breach of trust or fiduciary duty.[140] As the law stands in England, the strict liability receipt-based claim is not recognized in Equity,[141] although certain senior members of the judiciary have contemplated the introduction of such a claim. For example, in *Dubai Aluminium Co Ltd v Salaam*,[142] Lord Millett supported the recognition of an equitable strict liability claim. He described the action

---

[133] [1991] 2 AC 548.

[134] See n. 127. See also Barkehall Thomas, '"Goodbye" knowing receipt; "Hello" unconscientious receipt' (2001) 21 OJLS 239.

[135] *MCC Proceeds Inc v Lehman Brothers International (Europe) Ltd* [1998] 4 All ER 675. See Section 3.5.5.(i), p. 48.

[136] *Leigh and Sillivan Ltd v Aliakmon Shipping Co Ltd* [1986] AC 785, 812 (Lord Brandon). See Section 3.5.5.(i), p. 48.

[137] 'Moment of trust for knowing receipt?' (2009) 125 LQR 20, 23. See also Jaffey, 'The nature of knowing receipt' (2001) 14 TLI 151.

[138] Sheehan (see n. 128); Low, 'Recipient liability in Equity: resisting the siren's lure' [2008] RLR 96.

[139] Dietrich and Ridge, 'Receipt of what? Questions concerning third-party recipient liability in Equity an unjust enrichment' (2007) 31 MULR 47.

[140] *Farah Constructions Pty Ltd v Say-Dee Pty Ltd* [2007] HCA 292, [155]. See Hayton, 'Lessons from knowing receipt liability and unjust enrichment in Australia' (2007) 21 TLI 55.

[141] The introduction of such a claim was doubted in *Bank of Credit and Commerce International (Overseas) Ltd v Akindele* [2001] Ch 437.

[142] [2002] UKHL 48, [2003] 2 AC 366, 391. See also *Twinsectra v Yardley* [2002] UKHL 12, [2002] 2 AC 164, 194 (Lord Millett).

of unconscionable receipt as involving concurrent liability. One claim was fault-based and required proof of the defendant's unconscionable conduct. For this type of claim, the receipt of property is incidental; it is the defendant's fault that grounds liability. Here, the claim is founded on the defendant's wrongdoing. The other claim is receipt-based and does not require proof of fault. Here, the claim is founded on the vindication of proprietary rights. This is broadly consistent with the extra-judicial analysis of Lord Nicholls.[143]

Further, in a significant dictum in *Criterion Properties plc v Stratford UK Properties LLC*,[144] Lord Nicholls himself appeared to recognize a general strict liability claim in Equity founded on receipt-based liability. In considering the nature of the liability that would arise if an agreement, by virtue of which party B acquired benefits from party A, were set aside, he said:[145]

> If, however, the agreement is set aside, B will be accountable for any benefits he may have received from A under the agreement. A will have a proprietary claim, if B still has the assets. Additionally, and irrespective of whether B still has the assets in question, A will have a personal claim against B for unjust enrichment, subject always to a defence of change of position. B's personal accountability will not be dependent upon proof of fault or 'unconscionable' conduct on his part. B's accountability, in this regard, will be strict.

But this strict liability claim in unjust enrichment does not replace the claim in unconscionable receipt. Lord Nicholls was considering a simple case in which property is transferred by one party to another pursuant to a transaction that was void for want of authority. In such a case the claimant can recover the value of the property transferred to the defendant by virtue of the defendant's unjust enrichment. The value of the property will be the enrichment. This will have been obtained directly at the expense of the claimant and one of the recognized grounds of restitution can be established, namely that there has been a failure of basis for the transfer by virtue of the invalidity of the underlying transaction. In fact, a claim in unjust enrichment succeeded in this way in *Westdeutsche Landesbank Girozentrale v Islington LBC*,[146] as regards payments made to a bank under a contract that was void *ab initio*. There is nothing unusual about such a claim; but this is not the usual scenario of the claim in unconscionable receipt. That claim is relevant where property in which Ann has an equitable proprietary interest is misappropriated by Bill, a trustee, and it is then received by Clare and dissipated. Ann cannot sue Clare in unjust enrichment because Clare has been enriched at Bill's expense and not at the expense of Ann.[147] That is why Ann needs to rely on her equitable proprietary right to establish a claim against Clare and unjust enrichment cannot help. Lord Nicholls's dictum in *Criterion Properties* is concerned with a two-party situation, in which a claim in unjust enrichment is available. Unconscionable receipt is available in a three-party situation, involving typically the beneficiary, the trustee, and a third party, and the law of unjust enrichment is not engaged.

We are left with a scenario in which Equity continues to recognize a receipt-based personal claim that requires proof of fault,[148] regardless of the demands from senior members of the judiciary and many commentators that a strict liability claim should be recognized. The main reason for recognizing such a claim is because of the perceived need to assimilate the rules between what happens at Common Law and what happens in Equity. But

---

[143] Lord Nicholls (see n. 108), pp. 231–45.   [144] [2004] UKHL 28, [2004] 1 WLR 1846.
[145] Ibid., [4].   [146] [1996] AC 669.
[147] To establish unjust enrichment, the claimant must be enriched directly at the expense of the claimant: *Commissioners for Her Majesty's Revenue and Customs v The Investment Trust Companies* [2017] UKHL 29, [2017] 2 WLR 1200.
[148] This is defended by Salmons, 'Claims against third-party recipients of trust property' (2017) 76 CLJ 399.

the equitable rules and their context are different. Recognition of a strict liability claim in Equity can be criticized for policy reasons as well. Further, even if a strict liability claim were introduced in Equity, it would not change the law dramatically. Any strict liability claim would be subject to the defence of change of position. That defence will be defeated if the defendant has acted in bad faith and, as has already been seen,[149] cases on the defence of change of position have relied on the notion of unconscionability to determine whether or not the defendant can be considered to have acted in bad faith. It follows that, even if the receipt-based claim becomes one of strict liability, the question of unconscionability cannot be avoided. The only difference between a strict liability claim and a fault-based claim would turn on who bears the burden of proof. As the law stands, the claimant must prove that the defendant's receipt was unconscionable. If a strict liability claim were introduced, the burden would shift to the defendant to prove that their receipt and subsequent conduct was not unconscionable. Since it is difficult to justify shifting the burden of disproof on to the defendant, the preferable view is that a strict liability receipt-based claim should not be recognized in Equity.

20.3 ACCESSORIAL LIABILITY

20.3.1 THE NATURE OF ACCESSORIAL LIABILITY

Where a third party assists the trustee in committing a breach of trust, or a fiduciary in committing a breach of fiduciary duty, the third party may be personally liable to the beneficiary or the fiduciary's principal.[150] This has been described as an 'equitable tort',[151] and liability is certainly dependent on the third party being at fault and so a wrongdoer.

Liability for assisting a breach of trust or fiduciary duty has been justified by analogy with the tort of procuring a breach of contract.[152] That tort exists because a defendant who knowingly encourages a breach of contract is liable for interfering with the proper performance of the institution of the contract. The same is true of a defendant who interferes with a trust or fiduciary relationship. Liability is justified both because it ensures that the beneficiary or principal is recompensed for the loss that they had suffered if the trustee or fiduciary lacks the financial means to do so, and because it deters others from undermining the institution of the trust or the fiduciary relationship.

Although the question of the appropriate level of fault has been the most controversial aspect of this cause of action, more recently a new controversy has emerged, concerning the very nature of the liability for dishonest assistance. There are three possible models of liability.

(i) Civil secondary liability

Elliott and Mitchell[153] have suggested that equitable accessorial liability is a form of civil secondary liability,[154] in which the assistant is held jointly and severally liable along with the trustee or fiduciary whose breach of duty is assisted.[155] This is therefore a derivative

---

[149] See Section 20.2.3.(i), p. 602.   [150] See Davies, *Accessory Liability* (Oxford: Hart, 2015), ch. 4.

[151] *Abou-Rahmah v Abacha* [2006] EWCA Civ 1492, [2007] 1 All ER (Comm) 827, [2] (Rix LJ).

[152] See *Royal Brunei Airlines v Tan* [1995] 2 AC 378, 387; *Twinsectra v Yardley* [2002] UKHL 12, [2002] 2 AC 164, [127] (Lord Millett).   [153] 'Remedies for dishonest assistance' (2004) 67 MLR 16.

[154] Building on the work of Sales, 'The tort of conspiracy and civil secondary liability' (1990) 49 CLJ 491.

[155] Approved by Lewison J in *Ultraframe (UK) Ltd v Fielding* [2005] EWHC 1638 (Ch), [2006] FSR 16, [1600].

form of liability, which is equivalent to the doctrine of secondary liability in the criminal law where a criminal who encourages or assists a principal to commit a crime is guilty of that crime.[156] Consequently, the accessory is liable for the same wrong as the primary wrongdoer. Elliott and Mitchell use this analysis to explain why the accessory is traditionally treated as liable to account as a constructive trustee, because the accessory's personal liability may be enforced by claims of the same type as the personal claims that lie against an express trustee.[157] In other words, the accessory is treated as liable as if they were a trustee. It follows that the accessory may be liable to compensate the claimant for loss suffered from the breach of trust or fiduciary duty even if the defendant has not directly caused that loss by assisting the breach, since the accessory's liability derives from that of the primary wrongdoer rather than because the accessory caused that wrong to be committed.

But treating the accessory's liability as derived from that of the trustee or fiduciary does cause some theoretical and practical difficulties. For example, if the trustee can rely on an exclusion of liability clause, presumably this would negate the accessory's liability as well.[158] It would also logically follow that the accessory should be liable to pay the value of any profits made by the trustee or fiduciary as a result of the breach of duty, even if the accessory had not personally profited from the breach. This is difficult to defend.[159]

(ii) Primary liability

An alternative model of accessorial liability is that the accessory is liable because of a commission of a primary wrong,[160] namely the accessory's exploitation of the claimant's vulnerability.[161] In other words, there is something inherently wrong in assisting or encouraging another person to breach their duty. It follows that the accessory is liable in their own right, and the nature of that liability and the determination of appropriate remedies do not depend on the liability of the trustee or fiduciary, but turn instead on the loss caused by the accessory or the gain that they had made. But it would follow that the accessory could only be liable for the loss suffered or gain made as a result of their act of encouragement or assistance, which would restrict the ambit of accessorial liability, since it will often be difficult to establish such a causative link.[162] Also, this model of accessorial liability does not explain all of the elements of the existing law, especially that the liability of accessory and principal is joint and several,[163] and that the principal needs to have committed a breach of trust or fiduciary duty before the assister or encourager can be liable as an accessory. If there has been no breach of trust or fiduciary duty, there is nothing to which the accessory's liability can attach.

(iii) A mixed model

Neither the purely secondary nor primary liability model adequately explain the liability of the accessory in Equity. The reality is that the accessory's liability straddles primary and secondary liability.[164] This is what happens as regards accessorial liability in the criminal law, where the notion of derivative liability is not absolute. Whilst a principal offender

---

[156] As recognized by Lewison J, ibid., [1506].   [157] See n. 153, p. 22.

[158] See Ridge, 'Justifying the remedies for dishonest assistance' (2008) 124 LQR 445, 450.

[159] Elliott and Mitchell do not take their thesis this far: see n. 153, p. 42. See Section 20.3.3, p. 622.

[160] Ridge (see n. 158).

[161] Loughlin, 'Liability for assistance in breach of fiduciary duty' (1989) 9 OJLS 260.

[162] See further Section 20.3.3, p. 622.   [163] See further Section 20.3.3, p. 623.

[164] As was subsequently acknowledged by Mitchell and Watterson (see n. 14), p. 152. See also Campbell, 'The honest truth about dishonest assistance' [2015] Conv 159.

must have committed a crime, the accessory need not be convicted of the same offence, and there are even circumstances under which the accessory is convicted even though the principal has been acquitted because of a personal defence. For civil accessorial liability, although it must be established that the third party is a wrongdoer in their own right, hence the need to prove fault, the liability is still properly regarded as derivative, since it derives from the commission of an equitable wrong by the trustee or fiduciary. Without the commission of that wrong, there is nothing to which the third party can be an accessory. But the liability of the accessory need not correspond precisely with the liability of the trustee or fiduciary, in the same way as the punishment of an accessory in the criminal law need not be the same as the principal. So, where the trustee or fiduciary is exempt from liability by virtue of an exemption clause, there is no reason why that should exempt the accessory from liability as well. The trustee or fiduciary must have breached a duty for the exemption clause to bite, for otherwise there will be no liability to exempt. The exemption clause should be treated as operating to exempt an individual liability and not as negating the underlying breach of duty completely. So there will still have been a wrong to which the accessory's liability can attach. The same result should arise where the trustee is exempt from liability as a result of the exercise of statutory discretion.[165]

20.3.2 CONDITIONS FOR ESTABLISHING LIABILITY FOR DISHONEST ASSISTANCE

(i) Breach of trust or breach of fiduciary duty

A breach of trust or breach of fiduciary duty[166] needs to be established. Although it was once recognized that, at least as regards breach of trust, the trustee's breach must have been dishonest and fraudulent,[167] this requirement has since been rejected; it is sufficient that a breach of trust has occurred without needing to consider the nature of that breach.[168] The court is concerned with the state of mind of the third party and not that of the trustee or fiduciary. It follows that if, for example, a dishonest solicitor were to persuade an honest trustee to apply money in breach of trust, the solicitor could be held liable to compensate the beneficiaries for loss arising from the breach, even though the trustee honestly believed that they were acting properly. It is appropriate to hold the dishonest solicitor liable in such circumstances because they had caused the trust property to be misapplied.

Where the trustee or fiduciary has innocently breached their duty, they will still be personally liable to the beneficiaries or the principal, but there may be a number of reasons why the claimant might wish to sue the accessory instead. For example, the trustee or fiduciary may be insolvent, or may be able to rely on an exemption clause,[169] or might be relieved from liability.[170]

(ii) Inducing, encouraging, or assisting the breach

The third party can be liable as an accessory to the breach of trust or fiduciary duty by inducing, encouraging, or assisting the breach.[171] The third party will have procured the

---

[165] See Section 17.3.2, p. 481. Similarly, whereas the liability of the principal for a fraudulent breach of trust will not be time-barred, the liability of the dishonest assistant is subject to a six-year limitation period: *Williams v Central Bank of Nigeria* [2014] UKSC 10, [2014] 1 AC 1189. See Section 17.3.3.(i), p. 485.

[166] *Barlow Clowes International Ltd v Eurotrust International Ltd* [2005] UKPC 37, [2006] 1 WLR 1476, [28].

[167] *Barnes v Addy* (1874) 9 Ch App 244, 251 (Lord Selborne LC).

[168] *Royal Brunei Airlines Sdn Bhd v Tan* [1995] 2 AC 378.   [169] See Section 17.3.1, p. 474.

[170] See Section 17.3.2, p. 481.

[171] *Royal Brunei Airlines Sdn Bhd v Tan* [1995] 2 AC 378. See Davies (see n. 150), pp. 104–9.

breach where they caused the breach to occur, for example by instigating the breach by the trustee. The third party will have encouraged the breach where they suggested that the trustee should act in breach of duty. The third party will have assisted the breach where, for example, they prepared paperwork in order to transfer property in breach of trust. The assistance may take place at the time of the original breach of trust or fiduciary duty, but can extend to everyone who assists in the continuing diversion of property,[172] such as by helping to cover up the breach by laundering money that has been transferred in breach of trust or fiduciary duty.

Where the breach by the trustee or fiduciary was procured, it must be established that the accessory caused it. Where the accessory has encouraged or assisted the breach, it must be shown that the encouragement or assistance is connected to the breach of trust or fiduciary duty in some way, although it is not necessary to show that the assistance directly caused the loss to be suffered by the claimant.[173] So, for example, where a wife accompanied her husband in a car on money-laundering trips abroad, this was not sufficient assistance to make her an accessory, because merely accompanying her husband had not contributed to his breach of duty.[174] This emphasis on connection, rather than direct causative effect, is consistent with the approach to accessorial liability that is adopted in the criminal law.[175]

(iii) Fault

There have been various suggestions as to the type of fault that is required to found accessorial liability. It is clear that some fault is required, since it is an obligation-based, rather than a receipt-based, liability,[176] so that an innocent third party with no reason to suspect the breach of trust or fiduciary duty will not be liable. Where a defendant has received trust property, then, as we have already seen,[177] a case can be made for strict liability because of the need to protect property rights, even if that case is ultimately unconvincing. But, where the defendant has assisted a breach of trust or fiduciary duty, something else needs to be shown to establish liability. Further, if accessorial liability were strict, ordinary business would become impossible, because anybody who did anything that assisted a breach of trust or fiduciary duty could be potentially liable to the beneficiary or the principal, even if they had no reason to think that they were dealing with a trustee or fiduciary or were involved in a transaction that was inconsistent with the trust or the fiduciary relationship.

Some cases have recognized that the appropriate test of fault is constructive notice of the breach of trust,[178] whilst other decisions have held that want of probity[179] or dishonesty[180] is required. In *Williams v Central Bank of Nigeria*[181] Lord Sumption described this claim

---

[172] *Twinsectra Ltd v Yardley* [2002] UKHL 12, [2002] 2 AC 164, [107] (Lord Millett).

[173] *Brown v Bennett* [1999] 1 BCLC 649, 659 (Morritt LJ); *Grupo Torras SA v Al-Sabah (No 5)* [2001] Lloyd's Rep Bank 36, 61; *Casio Computer Ltd v Sayo* [2001] EWCA Civ 661, [15] (Tuckey LJ).

[174] *Brinks Ltd v Abu-Saleh* [1999] CLC 133.

[175] See *Simester and Sullivan's Criminal Law: Theory and Doctrine*, 6th edn, ed. Simester et al. (Oxford: Hart, 2016), p. 223.   [176] *Royal Brunei Airlines Sdn Bhd v Tan* [1995] 2 AC 378, 387.

[177] See Section 20.2.3.(iii), p. 608.

[178] *Selangor United Rubber Estates Ltd v Cradock (No 3)* [1968] 1 WLR 1555, 1590 (Ungoed-Thomas J); *Karak Rubber Co Ltd v Burden (No 2)* [1972] 1 WLR 602; *Baden v Société Générale pour Favoriser le Développement du Commerce et de l'Industrie en France SA* [1993] 1 WLR 509n.

[179] *Carl Zeiss Stiftung v Herbert Smith & Co (No 2)* [1969] 2 Ch 276; *Belmont Finance Corpn Ltd v Williams Furniture Ltd* [1979] Ch 250; *Lipkin Gorman v Karpnale Ltd* [1989] 1 WLR 1340; *Polly Peck International plc v Nadir (No 2)* [1992] 4 All ER 769; *Eagle Trust plc v SBC Securities Ltd* [1993] 1 WLR 263, 293 (Vinelott J).

[180] *Re Montagu's Settlement Trusts* [1987] Ch 264, 286 (Sir Robert Megarry V-C); *Agip Africa Ltd v Jackson* [1990] Ch 265, 293 (Millett J).

[181] [2014] UKSC 10, [2014] AC 1189, [35].

as 'knowing assistance'[182] and considered it to be based on fraud, but also added that the 'liability of a knowing assister has always depended on the unconscionability of *his* conduct'.[183] In the space of one paragraph the whole gamut of equitable fault is encompassed without any apparent awareness that these terms might bear different meanings. The requirement of dishonesty had previously been recognized by the House of Lords.[184] The meaning of 'dishonesty' for this claim has been considered in a number of key decisions.

Royal Brunei Airlines v Tan

In *Royal Brunei Airlines v Tan*,[185] the Privy Council recognized that the appropriate level of fault for accessorial liability was dishonesty and that the old language of 'knowing assistance' should be rejected. The Privy Council also considered that the five categories of knowledge, as recognized in *Baden*,[186] were 'best forgotten'.

In *Royal Brunei* the claimant airline appointed Borneo Leisure Travel as its travel agent to sell tickets. Borneo was expected to account to the claimant for the net proceeds of ticket sales and was made an express trustee of the proceeds. In breach of trust, Borneo failed to pay the proceeds into a separate bank account and used the proceeds in its general business. Borneo became insolvent and the claimant sought a remedy from the defendant, who was the principal shareholder and controlling director of Borneo, on the ground that the defendant had assisted Borneo to breach the trust. Lord Nicholls, delivering the advice of the Privy Council, held that the defendant was indeed liable as an accessory. The appropriate test of fault was considered to be dishonesty rather than simply knowledge of the breach of trust or fiduciary duty. This is a necessary, and also a sufficient, condition of accessorial liability; no other fault element needs to be proved. Dishonesty was equated with a want of probity and commercially unacceptable conduct. It involved the defendant 'simply not acting as an honest person would in the circumstances'. This is essentially an objective test, but it still requires conscious impropriety on the part of the defendant. In identifying such dishonesty, two questions need to be considered, as follows:

(1) What did the defendant know about the circumstances at the time relating to the proposed transaction and their participation in it?

(2) In the light of that knowledge, would the reasonable person have considered the defendant's condut to be dishonest? In assessing this, the court will have regard to personal attributes of the defendant, such as their experience and intelligence, and the reason why the defendant acted as they did. So, if the defendant is a professional, such as a solicitor, the objective standard of honesty will be higher.

The significance of this test of dishonesty is that the defendant is not the arbiter as to what is or is not dishonest. The defendant might consider their conduct to be honest, but, in the light of the defendant's knowledge of the circumstances, the reasonable person might disagree. On the facts of *Tan*, since the defendant had caused Borneo to apply the money in a way that he knew was not authorized, it followed that the defendant was considered to have acted dishonestly.

The Privy Council considered that, in many cases, it would be clear whether the defendant was dishonest. So for example, if the defendant had intentionally deceived someone, deliberately participated in a misapplication of trust property, or turned a blind eye to

---

[182] See also *Vestergaard Frandsen v Bestnet Europe Ltd* [2013] UKSC 31, [2013] 1 WLR 1556, [26] (Lord Neuberger). [183] [2014] UKSC 10, [2014] AC 1189, [35] (emphasis in original).
[184] *Twinsectra Ltd v Yardley* [2002] UKHL 12, [2002] 2 AC 164. [185] [1995] 2 AC 378.
[186] See Section 20.1.1, p. 591.

misconduct, this would be dishonest. There will, however, sometimes be some difficult borderline cases, such as that in which the defendant assists a trustee to enter into a transaction on behalf of the trust where there is a genuine doubt as to whether the trustee has the power to do so, such as to invest trust property in a particular way. In such cases, the facts will need to be considered carefully to determine whether the reasonable person would consider the conduct to be dishonest in the light of the defendant's knowledge and, where relevant, professional experience.

The Privy Council considered that negligence, in the sense of the defendant failing to exercise reasonable diligence, was not an appropriate test of fault for accessorial liability, because negligence required the defendant to owe a duty of care and there is no reason why the accessory should be considered to owe a duty of care to the beneficiaries, especially when many third parties, such as solicitors, agents, and financial advisers, will already owe a duty of reasonable skill and care to the trust. Even where the trustees are behaving dishonestly, it was not considered to be appropriate to require third parties to owe a duty of care to the beneficiaries to exercise reasonable diligence.

Twinsectra Ltd v Yardley

The definition of dishonesty for the purposes of accessorial liability was further considered by the House of Lords in *Twinsectra Ltd v Yardley*.[187] Yardley negotiated a £1 million loan from the claimant. The money was paid by the claimant to Sims, who had undertaken to the claimant that the money would be retained until it was used by Yardley to purchase property. Consequently, the money was held on trust.[188] In breach of trust, the money was paid by Sims to Yardley's solicitor, Leach, for the benefit of Yardley. Leach was aware of the undertaking that the money would be used only to acquire property, but he paid the money to Yardley without ensuring that it would be used only for that purpose. The claimant sued Leach for dishonestly assisting Sims's breach of trust. The trial judge found that Leach had shut his eyes to the details of the transaction, but he did believe that the money was available for him to transfer to Yardley at the latter's request, because he believed that, as a matter of law, the payment of the money was not subject to any undertaking. The key question for the House of Lords was whether this constituted dishonesty. Lord Hutton, for the majority, identified three different tests of dishonesty:

(1) purely subjective, under which the defendant can be considered to have acted dishonestly only if they considered the conduct to be dishonest by their own standards, even if this is contrary to the standard of reasonable and honest people (which test was rejected);

(2) purely objective, under which honesty is assessed with reference to the ordinary standards of reasonable and honest people, even if the defendant does not realize that such people would consider the conduct to be dishonest; and

(3) a hybrid test, under which the defendant's conduct is assessed with reference to the standard of reasonable and honest people, but the defendant can be regarded as dishonest only if they realized that the conduct would be considered to be dishonest by those standards, even if the defendant did not consider the conduct to be dishonest by their own standards.

This last is the test of dishonesty that was applied in the criminal law for purposes of the crimes of theft and fraud.[189] Lord Hutton considered that this test was that which was

---

[187] [2002] UKHL 12, [2002] 2 AC 164. See Section 8.4.2.(ii), p. 241.

[188] Either an express or a *Quistclose* trust. See Section 8.4.2.(ii), p. 241.

[189] See *Ghosh* [1982] QB 1053. Se now *Ivey v Genting Casinos (UK) Ltd* [2017] UKSC 67, [2017] 3 WLR 1212, Section 20.3.2.(iii), p. 620.

intended to be adopted by the Privy Council in *Tan*. This is essentially a subjective test of dishonesty, since the defendant can be considered to be dishonest only if they perceived that the reasonable person would consider the conduct to be dishonest.

Applying the hybrid test, the majority concluded that Leach had not acted dishonestly, because, although he was aware of Sims's undertaking about the use of the money, he honestly believed that, once he had received the money on behalf of Yardley, he received it unconditionally and so was entitled to use it as he wished. A solicitor who held such a view would not be considered to be dishonest.

That this hybrid test was the one that had been recognized in *Tan* is simply wrong, since the Privy Council in that case had specifically rejected the criminal test of dishonesty, which is the hybrid test. The Privy Council actually applied the objective test. It is true that reference was made to the defendant's knowledge of the circumstances of the transaction, but this was to enable the reasonable person to assess whether the defendant's conduct was dishonest in the light of the defendant's awareness of the circumstances. This was recognized by Lord Millett in *Twinsectra* in a dissenting judgment. He considered that the Privy Council in *Tan* had used dishonesty in a purely objective sense and not in the hybrid sense, with the focus being on dishonest conduct rather than a dishonest state of mind. That is why a different test of dishonesty has been used in the criminal law, where the focus is on the defendant's state of mind to establish criminal culpability. He analysed the approach of the Privy Council as involving:[190]

> an objective standard of dishonesty by which the defendant is expected to attain the standard which would be observed by an honest person placed in similar circumstances. Account must be taken of subjective considerations such as the defendant's experience and intelligence and his actual state of knowledge at the relevant time. But it is not necessary that he should actually have appreciated that he was acting dishonestly; it is sufficient that he was.

Lord Millett considered that Leach should be liable for dishonestly assisting a breach of trust, since he knew of Sims's undertaking to use the money borrowed from the claimant for specific purposes and he participated in the transfer of the money in a manner that he knew was unauthorized—conduct that Lord Millett considered that the man in the street would regard as culpable.

The different approaches of the majority and of Lord Millett as regards the determination of fault for accessorial liability have real practical significance: the majority, by focusing on an essentially subjective test of dishonesty, held that the defendant was not liable, whereas Lord Millett, by focusing on the third party's actual knowledge, but with regard to objective standards of honesty, considered the defendant should be liable. But, with the majority focusing on a hybrid test of dishonesty, there appeared to be a conflict with the decision of the Privy Council in *Tan*. In such circumstances, the usual rules of precedent would mean that the decision of the House of Lords prevailed. The next opportunity to consider the test of fault for accessorial liability was another decision of the Privy Council.

Barlow Clowes v Eurotrust International

In *Barlow Clowes International Ltd v Eurotrust International Ltd*,[191] the claimant company had been used to perpetrate a fraudulent offshore investment scheme. Clowes, the perpetrator of the scheme, was convicted of fraud. Some of the investors' money had been paid through bank accounts maintained by the defendant company, which was administered

---

[190] Ibid., [121].   [191] [2005] UKPC 37, [2006] 1 WLR 1476.

from the Isle of Man. The claimants alleged that the defendant company and its directors had dishonestly assisted Clowes to misappropriate the investors' money in breach of trust. The defendant company was held liable, but one of its directors, Henwood, had been held not liable on the ground that he had not acted dishonestly. The claimants appealed to the Privy Council as regards Henwood's liability, which consequently required the Board to consider the appropriate test of dishonesty.

Lord Hoffmann, delivering the advice of the Board, said that the test of dishonesty was the objective test as had been formulated in *Tan*. So the issue was whether the defendant's conduct could be considered to be contrary to the ordinary standards of honest behaviour.[192] He considered a dishonest state of mind to be a subjective mental state, but the standard by which the law determined this is an objective one. If the defendant's mental state would be characterized as dishonest by ordinary standards, then the fact that the defendant did not consider it to be dishonest was irrelevant. But it is still necessary to consider first what the defendant's mental state was, by reference either to what the defendant knew about the transaction in which they were assisting, or suspicion about the transaction combined with a conscious decision not to make inquiries about it that might result in knowledge of the transaction. Once this subjective mental state had been identified, the court should then focus on the objective standard of dishonesty.

In applying this test to Henwood, the trial judge had found that Henwood had strongly suspected that the money had been paid by members of the public who thought that they were investing in securities, whereas, as Henwood knew, the money was being transferred to Clowes for his personal use. Consequently, Henwood suspected that the money was either being transferred in breach of trust or in breach of fiduciary duty. It was not necessary to show that he knew that the money was held on trust; knowledge or suspicion of misappropriation was sufficient. Henwood had consciously decided not to make inquiries about the source of the money because he did not wish to discover the truth. This state of mind was considered to be dishonest by ordinary standards, and it was irrelevant that Henwood might have had different moral standards and saw nothing wrong in what he was doing, preferring to follow his clients' instructions at all costs because of an exaggerated notion of duty to them. This would not have been dishonest according to the hybrid test, except if Henwood were consciously aware that his standards of conduct were different from the normal standards of honesty, but it was dishonest according to the objective test of dishonesty.

This appears simply to be a useful restatement and application of what the Privy Council had previously said in *Tan*. But, to complicate matters, Lord Hoffmann said that this was consistent with both what Lord Hutton and he had said in *Twinsectra*. He acknowledged that there was an element of ambiguity in what Lord Hutton had said, but there had been no intention to adopt the hybrid test of dishonesty. Similarly, in *Twinsectra*, Lord Hoffmann himself had said[193] that a dishonest state of mind meant 'consciousness that one is transgressing ordinary standards of honest behaviour'. This was reinterpreted in *Barlow Clowes* as meaning 'consciousness of those elements of the transaction which make participation transgress ordinary standards of honest behaviour. It did not also require him to have thought about what those standards were.'[194] This is a radical reformulation of the definition of dishonesty to seek reconciliation of dicta in *Twinsectra* with those in *Tan*. This is not simply a matter of wordplay. The approach adopted by the majority in *Twinsectra* had resulted in a conclusion that the defendant was not dishonest. But, if the

---

[192] Ibid., [10].   [193] [2002] UKHL 12, [2002] 2 AC 164, [35].
[194] [2005] UKPC 37, [2006] 1 WLR 1476, [16] (Lord Hoffmann).

focus had been on the defendant's knowledge as assessed by the reasonable person rather than the defendant's perception of the standard of his conduct, he should have been held liable, because, as Lord Millett had observed in that case, he had been aware of the unauthorized nature of the payment of money even though he believed that he was not bound by the undertaking as a matter of law.

Abou-Rahmah v Abacha

Although the Privy Council in *Barlow Clowes* sought to reconcile *Tan* and *Twinsectra*, we are still left with a decision of the House of Lords in *Twinsectra* that appears to be inconsistent with *Tan*. At the very least, as Lord Hoffmann acknowledged in *Barlow Clowes*, some of the dicta in *Twinsectra* are ambiguous. But the decision of the Privy Council in *Barlow Clowes* could not be clearer as to what the proper interpretation of dishonesty should be. So, which test should prevail: the hybrid test, as appears to have been recognized by the House of Lords,[195] or the objective test clearly recognized by two decisions of the Privy Council? Although decisions of the House of Lords are binding on lower courts, with decisions of the Privy Council being of persuasive value only, in recent years there are a number of examples in which lower courts have followed decisions of the Privy Council where there is an inconsistency between its decision and that of the House of Lords. This is invariably where the decision of the Privy Council is more recent and involves many of the same judges who gave judgments in the House of Lords.[196]

In *Abou-Rahmah v Abacha*,[197] Arden LJ in the Court of Appeal was willing to apply the definition of dishonesty as recognized by the Privy Council. In *Abou-Rahmah* the claimants had been the victims of a fraud that involved two payments being made to the defendant bank that were then transferred to the fraudsters. The claimants sued the defendant for dishonestly assisting a breach of trust. The defendant had suspected that fraudsters might be using its banking facilities to assist corrupt politicians to launder money, but it had no suspicions that the two payments that had been credited to the account had been obtained by fraud.

Arden LJ recognized that *Barlow Clowes* had clarified that *Twinsectra* had not recognized a hybrid test of dishonesty, so that the defendant was not required to be conscious of their wrongdoing.[198] She acknowledged that, exceptionally, the High Court or Court of Appeal might follow a decision of the Privy Council rather than a decision of the House of Lords. *Abou-Rahmah* was such an exceptional case, because *Barlow Clowes* did not depart from *Twinsectra* but simply gave guidance as to its proper interpretation, the members of the Privy Council were all members of the House of Lords, and two members of the majority in *Twinsectra* were also in *Barlow Clowes*.[199] She also considered that, as a matter of policy, there was no reason, when considering civil liability, why the law should have regard to the

---

[195] And was followed by the Court of Appeal in *Bultitude v The Law Society* [2004] EWCA Civ 1853. See also *Ultraframe (UK) Ltd v Fielding* [2005] EWHC 1638 (Ch), [2006] FSR 16, [1481] (Lewison J).

[196] See especially the conflict in the criminal law as regards the interpretation of the old defence of provocation between a decision of the House of Lords (*R v Morgan (Smith)* [2001] 1 AC 146) and the Privy Council (*Attorney-General for Jersey v Holley* [2005] UKPC 23, [2005] 2 AC 580). The Court of Appeal subsequently followed the decision of the Privy Council: *James and Karimi* [2006] EWCA Crim 14, [2006] QB 588.

[197] [2006] EWCA Civ 1492, [2007] 1 All ER (Comm) 827.   [198] Ibid., [65].

[199] In *Sinclair Investments (UK) Ltd v Versailles Trade Finance Ltd* [2011] EWCA Civ 347, [2012] Ch 453 the Court of Appeal approved the approach adopted in *Abou-Rahmah* because it was a foregone conclusion that if the case had gone to the House of Lords, the decision of the Privy Council would have been followed: [74] (Neuberger LJ). See also *Starglade Properties Ltd v Nash* [2010] EWCA Civ 1314; *Fiona Trust & Holding Corp v Privalov* [2010] EWHC 3199 (Comm), [1437] (Andrew Smith J); *Vivendi SA v Richards* [2013] EWHC 3006 (Ch), [2013] BCC 771, [183] (Newey J).

defendant's views as to the morality of their actions. But, even applying the objective test of dishonesty, she did not consider that the defendant's general, rather than specific, suspicions about fraudulent activities were sufficient to render the defendant dishonest.

The other two judges agreed that the defendant was not dishonest, but they did not consider that it was necessary to consider the conflict between *Twinsectra* and *Barlow Clowes*, since the defendant's conduct was not even objectively dishonest, because the defendant was not suspicious about the legitimacy of the particular payments, although Pill LJ did acknowledge the value of *Barlow Clowes* in interpreting *Twinsectra*[200] and Rix LJ referred to dishonesty 'in the *Twinsectra* sense … as clarified in *Barlow Clowes*'.[201]

Summary of the law on dishonesty

So where does this leave the law on the definition of dishonesty for the purposes of establishing accessorial liability? As a matter of authority, the preferable view is that the objective test of dishonesty prevails. This was recognized in *Starglade Properties Ltd v Nash*,[202] a case in which the defendant was a director of a company who, knowing that the company was insolvent, paid other creditors in preference to the claimant with money that was held on trust by the company for the claimant. The defendant was sued for dishonestly assisting a breach of trust and the key question for the Court of Appeal was whether this conduct could be considered to be dishonest. Morritt LJ recognized that '[t]here is a single standard of honesty objectively determined by the court. That standard is applied to specific conduct of a specific individual possessing the knowledge and qualities he actually enjoyed'.[203] Although the defendant was not setting out to prefer some creditors over others, but simply to frustrate the claimant's claim by removing assets from his company, this was considered not to be conduct in accordance with ordinary standards of honest commercial behaviour and so was dishonest.

This objective test of dishonesty can also be justified for policy reasons. It is appropriate to require defendants to comply with objectively determined standards of honesty.[204] This objective test of dishonesty, which has regard to the defendant's knowledge of and suspicions about the facts, is consistent with the core meanings of conscience and unconscionability which underpin equitable liability.[205] A different test of dishonesty has been adopted in the criminal law, whereby the defendant is only dishonest if they realize that the reasonable person would consider their conduct to be dishonest, so the test is primarily subjective. This difference between criminal law and Equity can be justified, because the criminal law is concerned to ensure that the defendant is aware of their moral wrongdoing, since that establishes culpability and justifies punishment; the focus is on a dishonest state of mind. The civil law is not concerned with establishing culpability, since the aim is not to punish the defendant, but simply to compensate the claimant for loss suffered. Consequently, the focus is placed on the dishonesty of the defendant's conduct rather than their state of mind, and this can be determined objectively, albeit with regard to the defendant's knowledge and suspicions of the circumstances. This distinction between the criminal law and Equity has, however, been removed, with the criminal law now adopting the equitable objective test of dishonesty.[206]

---

[200] [2006] EWCA Civ 1492, [2007] 1 All ER (Comm) 827, [94].   [201] Ibid., [40].

[202] [2010] EWCA Civ 1314.   [203] Ibid., [26].

[204] Cf. Davies (see n. 150), p. 130, who argues that the appropriate test should be one of knowledge, with a defence of justification, because a lesser test would expand liability too far. But this ignores the significance of unconscionability underpinning the identification of fault in Equity. See Section 2.3.3, p. 29.

[205] See Section 2.3, p. 27.

[206] *Ivey v Genting Casinos (UK) Ltd* [2017] UKSC 67 [2017] 3 WLR 1212. See Virgo, 'Cheating and dishonesty' (2018) 17 CLJ 18.

It follows that, to establish dishonesty, it is necessary to have regard to two separate questions. First, the court must assess the defendant's knowledge or suspicion about the particular transaction or transactions that they are procuring, encouraging, or assisting. The defendant need not know that they are procuring, encouraging, or assisting a breach of trust or breach of fiduciary duty, but must be aware of the facts that would indicate this and be aware of the broad terms of the design with which they are involved.[207] So, for example, the defendant must know that they are assisting or encouraging somebody to do something that they are not entitled to do,[208] such as the transfer of money to somebody who is not entitled to receive it, or suspects this and fails to make appropriate inquiries.

Secondly, in the light of the defendant's knowledge or suspicion, and their experience and intelligence, and reasons for acting, the court needs to assess whether the defendant's conduct falls below ordinary standards of honesty. It is irrelevant that the defendant did not consider their own conduct to be dishonest.

This was usefully summarized by Lord Mance in *Central Bank of Ecuador v Conticorp SA*:[209]

> In short, a defendant must be conscious of those elements of the transaction which makes his participation transgress ordinary standards of honest behaviour, but there is no requirement that he should have thought about what those standards were.

20.3.3 REMEDIES FOR DISHONEST ASSISTANCE

Whereas liability for unconscionable receipt is generally restitutionary, assessed by reference to the value of the property received, liability for dishonest assistance is typically different because the defendant will usually not have received any property the value of which can be restored to the claimant. Rather the liability is generally compensatory,[210] although the claimant will be able to elect between equitable compensation and disgorgement where the defendant has profited from the assistance.[211] Where, however, the defendant has not profited from assisting the breach of duty, or where the claimant's loss exceeds any gain made, the claimant will elect for a compensatory remedy. The defendant will then be required to compensate the claimant for the loss that resulted from the breach of trust or breach of fiduciary duty that the defendant procured, encouraged, or assisted.[212] So, for example, in *Fyffes Group Ltd v Templeman*,[213] the defendant had bribed an employee of the claimant company to enter into a contract with the defendant on favourable terms for the defendant. It was held that the defendant was liable for dishonestly assisting the employee's breach of fiduciary duty. It was accepted that the claimant's loss was the difference between the terms as agreed and the terms that would have been agreed had the employee not been bribed.

The nature of this compensatory liability is significant, however. The accessory is regarded as jointly and severally liable with the trustee or fiduciary.[214] This means that the claimant can sue the accessory and recover all losses suffered as a result of the breach of

---

[207] *Barlow Clowes International Ltd v Eurotrust International Ltd* [2005] UKPC 37, [2006] 1 WLR 1476, [28].

[208] *Twinsectra v Yardley* [2002] UKHL 12, [2002] 2 AC 164, 171 (Lord Hoffmann); *Ultraframe (UK) Ltd v Fielding* [2005] EWHC 1638 (Ch), [2006] FSR 16, [1506] (Lewison J).

[209] [2015] UKPC 11, [2016] 1 BCLC 26, [9].

[210] *Twinsectra Ltd v Yardley* [2002] UKHL 12, [2002] 2 AC 164, [107] (Lord Millett).

[211] *Fyffes Group Ltd v Templeman* [2000] 2 Lloyd's Rep 643.

[212] *Grupo Torras SA v Al-Sabah (No 5)* [2001] Lloyd's Rep Bank 36; *Casio Computer Ltd v Sayo (No 3)* [2001] EWCA Civ 661.   [213] [2000] 2 Lloyd's Rep 643.

[214] *Cowper v Stoneham* (1898) 68 LT 18; *Ultraframe (UK) Ltd v Fielding* [2005] EWHC 1638 (Ch), [2006] FSR 16, [1600] (Lewison J).

trust or fiduciary duty. It is not necessary to show that this loss was caused by the accessory's assistance or encouragement. This is consistent with Elliott and Mitchell's thesis[215] that the liability of the dishonest assistant is derivative and duplicative of that of the trustee or fiduciary, so that the remedies available against the assistant should replicate those that are available against the trustee or fiduciary. Ridge,[216] who prefers to analyse accessorial liability as primary, rather than secondary, liability, justifies the joint and several liability of accessories to compensate the claimant on policy and pragmatic grounds, namely that, by virtue of the prophylactic characteristics of fiduciary law, it is sufficient for the claimant to show that loss has been caused by the breach of trust or fiduciary duty, even as regards a claim against the accessory, and this can be justified because the accessory can be liable only if they acted dishonestly. The accessory can then bring a claim for contribution against the trustee or fiduciary whose liability the accessory has discharged.

Elliott and Mitchell acknowledge that their civil secondary liability thesis should lead them to conclude that, if the trustee or fiduciary profited from their breach of fiduciary duty, the accessory should be liable to disgorge this profit to the claimant even though the accessory may not have derived any profit from the encouragement or assistance provided.[217] But they conclude that this is not justifiable and that the accessory should be liable to disgorge only the gains that they obtained as a result of encouraging or assisting the breach of trust or fiduciary duty.[218] This was recognized by Lewison J in *Ultraframe (UK) Ltd v Fielding*[219] on the basis that the liability of the accessory is personal and is not punitive.

In *Novoship (UK) Ltd v Mikhaylyuk*[220] the Court of Appeal recognized that it was possible to award the remedy of an account of profits where the defendant had profited from dishonestly assisting a breach of fiduciary duty.[221] This remedy was justified on the ground that the dishonest assister is liable to account as if he was a trustee, so is liable to account for any profits made as a result of the assistance. But the court also emphasized that the dishonest assister is not a fiduciary, and this had implications for the assessment of the remedy. In particular, unlike where a fiduciary is liable to account for all profits made which fall within the scope of the duty of loyalty,[222] the dishonest assister is only liable to account for those profits which were directly causally connected to the assistance. The appropriate test of causation is not that of simple 'but for' cause, but rather whether the assistance or encouragement was a real or effective cause of the profits. On the facts of the case, the defendant had assisted the fiduciary in breaching his fiduciary duty by negotiating shipping charters when he knew that the fiduciary had paid bribes. The assister had profited from these shipping charters but, since these profits had arisen from an unexpected change in the market, this was held to be insufficiently connected to the assistance to be caused by it. Further, the court held that, even where the profits were directly caused by the assistance, the award of an account of profits was not automatic, and the remedy would be withheld if it was considered to be disproportionate in the light of the form and extent of the wrongdoing.[223] These are two significant restrictions on the award of a gain-based remedy for dishonest assistance.

---

[215] See n. 153, pp. 18–20. See Section 20.3.1.(i), p. 612.   [216] See n. 158, p. 458.

[217] (2004) 67 MLR 16,40   [218] Ibid., 42.   [219] [2005] EWHC 1638 (Ch), [2006] FSR 16, [1600].

[220] [2014] EWCA Civ 908, [2015] QB 499. See Davies, 'Gain-based remedies for dishonest assistance' (2015) 131 LQR 173. See also *Fyffes Group Ltd v Templeman* [2000] 2 Lloyd's Rep 643.

[221] This is criticized by Devonshire, 'Account of profits for dishonest assistance' (2015) 74 CLJ 222, who wishes liability for dishonest assistance to be treated like a Common Law tort, so that disgorgement remedies are not available. But such remedies are available for some torts. Virgo (see n. 26), ch. 17.

[222] See *Murad v Al-Saraj* [2005] EWCA Civ 959, [2005] WTLR 1573. See Section 18.5.2, p. 527.

[223] *Novoship (UK) Ltd v Mikhaylyuk* [2014] EWCA Civ 908, [2015] Ch 499, [119] (Longmore LJ).

The law relating to the remedies available for accessorial liability is confusing and difficult. Whilst it appears that the accessory is jointly and severally liable with the principal as regards compensation for the claimant's loss, the accessory is solely liable as regards disgorgement of gains. This might be justified for policy and pragmatic reasons, but it is not doctrinally coherent. It was suggested above[224] that the strict derivative nature of civil secondary liability does not represent the law; neither does treating the accessory as personally liable in their own right. The preferable view is that the accessory's liability is a hybrid of the two. It is derivative, in that it depends on the trustee or fiduciary having committed a wrong, but, once this is established, the accessory is regarded as personally liable for their own wrongdoing. So, the accessory should be liable only to compensate the claimant for loss suffered as a result of the accessory's encouragement or assistance of the breach of trust or fiduciary duty, or liable to disgorge a gain arising from the encouragement or assistance; joint and several liability should be rejected. Liability for the tort of inducing a breach of contract, with which equitable accessorial liability is analogous,[225] does not involve joint and several liability,[226] and there is no reason why accessorial liability should be joint and several either. It is true that liability of the accessory has traditionally been described as a liability to account as if the accessory were a constructive trustee and the liability of trustees is joint and several,[227] but the accessory is not a constructive trustee since the liability is only personal. Consequently, the nature of accessorial liability cannot be deduced from the old formula used to describe the nature of liability, especially because such a formula has been rejected by the Supreme Court.[228]

But the rejection of joint and several liability for accessories will not result in significant differences in the operation of the law. Consider a simple case in which a trustee misappropriates trust money from a trust fund, being encouraged to do so by his wife. As long as that encouragement had an effect on her husband, she can be considered to have contributed to the misappropriation and she should be personally liable in her own right for the whole loss, assuming that she was dishonest. In other words, contribution to the loss will usually be readily established.

But there will be other circumstances under which such contribution cannot be established. Consider another case in which a trustee misappropriates £2,000 worth of shares from a trust, with the documentation for the transfer of half of the shares being completed by Albert and the documentation for the other half being completed by Brenda. Assuming that both Albert and Brenda acted dishonestly, they should be liable only for the loss caused in respect of the particular transaction that they facilitated and not for the total loss suffered by the trust.

By focusing on the accessory's personal liability, no artificial distinction is drawn between the award of compensatory and gain-based remedies. The result is logical and doctrinally coherent. Crucially, accessorial liability should not be considered to be joint and several.

20.3.4 CONTRIBUTION

Where a third party is liable for dishonest assistance, they, or another party who is vicariously liable for their wrong,[229] will be able to seek contribution from another party who is liable for the 'same damage' where the third party has discharged their joint liability.[230]

---

[224] See Section 20.3.1.(iii), p. 612.   [225] See *Royal Brunei Airlines v Tan* [1995] 2 AC 378, 386.
[226] *OBG v Allan* [2007] UKHL 21, [2008] 1 AC 1, [39] (Lord Hoffmann). See Carty, 'Joint tortfeasance and assistance liability' (1999) 19 LS 489, 506–7.   [227] See Section 17.4.2, p. 494.
[228] *Williams v Central Bank of Nigeria* [2014] UKSC 10, [2014] 1 AC 1189.
[229] *Dubai Aluminium Co Ltd v Salaam* [2002] UKHL 48, [2003] 2 AC 366.
[230] Under the Contribution Act 1978. See further Section 17.4.2.(i), p. 494.

20.3.5 VICARIOUS LIABILITY

Where a partner in a firm of solicitors is held liable for dishonestly assisting a breach of trust, the firm will be liable as well for loss caused to the claimant if the partner was acting in the ordinary course of the firm's business or with the authority of co-partners.[231] The significance of this liability was considered by the House of Lords in *Dubai Aluminium Co Ltd v Salaam*.[232] In that case, a solicitor had dishonestly assisted a fraudulent scheme by drafting various documents in furtherance of the fraud. It was held that the firm was vicariously liable to compensate the claimant even though the acts of the solicitor had not been authorized and had been done for a dishonest purpose, because the assistance to the fraudulent scheme provided by the solicitor was closely connected with the acts that he was authorized to do, namely to draft commercial agreements, and so fell within the description of being in the ordinary course of the firm's business.

This vicarious liability extends only to those cases in which the liability of the partner can be considered to be wrongful and which cause damage to the claimant, such as dishonest assistance, since it is fault-based liability.[233] Whether vicarious liability would extend to liability for unconscionable receipt depends on whether that conduct can be characterized as wrongful. Since fault must be proved, it follows that this should be characterized as a wrong, and so the partnership will be liable for a partner's unconscionable receipt. If, however, the receipt-based liability were to become strict,[234] it would no longer be fault-based and so the partnership would no longer be vicariously liable for a partner's receipt.

It has been recognized that a firm of solicitors will not be vicariously liable for a solicitor who has committed a wrong as an express trustee[235] or as a trustee *de son tort*, because it is not within the ordinary scope of a solicitor's practice to act as a trustee.[236]

---

[231] Partnership Act 1890, s. 10.

[232] [2002] UKHL 48, [2003] 2 AC 366. See also *Northampton Regional Livestock Centre Co Ltd v Cowling* [2015] EWCA Civ 651, [2016] 1 BCLC 431.

[233] [2002] UKHL 48, [2003] 2 AC 366, at [111] (Lord Millett).   [234] See Section 20.2.3.(iii), p. 608.

[235] *Walker v Stones* [2001] QB 902.

[236] *Dubai Aluminium Co Ltd v Salaam* [2002] UKHL 48, [2003] 2 AC 366, [143] (Lord Millett).

PART IX

EQUITABLE ORDERS

21

EQUITABLE ORDERS

Throughout this book a variety of equitable remedies have been examined. Although the focus has been on those remedies that relate to breach of trust, particularly remedies involving account,[1] other remedies have been considered, including proprietary estoppel[2] and remedies relating to proprietary claims, such as liens and subrogation.[3] But Equity has had other significant impacts on the remedial landscape of English law. This chapter will illustrate that remedial impact by considering other equitable remedies. For reasons of space, this cannot be comprehensive—both as regards the range of remedies that are identified[4] and also as regards the detailed analysis of each one. The focus will instead be on the essential nature and function of each remedy.

21.1 GENERAL PRINCIPLES

The equitable jurisdiction to make orders is influenced by a number of key principles:

(1) The equitable jurisdiction can be used to enforce and protect both legal and equitable rights, and is available both where there is an actual infringement of such a right and where there is a threatened infringement.

(2) Although the jurisdiction to grant equitable remedies is discretionary, the exercise of the jurisdiction is dependent on recognized principles. Nevertheless, the jurisdiction is flexible and can be adapted to deal with new situations,[5] which has proved to be especially significant with the growth of international commercial litigation.

(3) These remedies and orders are available only where compensatory damages are not an adequate remedy. This is because the equitable jurisdiction to do justice can be engaged only where there is an inadequacy in the remedies available at Common Law; Equity here is subordinate to the Common Law. Compensatory damages will be inadequate if no damages are available at Common Law for the infringement of the particular wrong; if the

---

[1] See Section 18.1.2.(ii), p. 501.   [2] See Section 10.4, p. 305.   [3] See Chapter 19 of this volume.
[4] Other examples of equitable relief and orders that will not be considered include the relief of penalties and relief against forfeiture. See generally *Snell's Equity*, 33rd edn, ed. McGhee (London: Sweet & Maxwell, 2014), ch. 13.
[5] *Co-operative Insurance Society v Argyll Stores (Holdings) Ltd* [1998] AC 1, 9 (Lord Hoffmann).

damages would be nominal or small; if the loss would be difficult to quantify; or if the damages would compensate only for past loss and not for loss that might arise in the future. Damages would also be an inadequate remedy if the defendant was unable to afford to pay them. The principle that damages must be inadequate before an equitable order will be granted was considered by the Court of Appeal in *AB v CD*.[6] In that case the claimant sought an interim injunction to require the defendant to honour an agreement between them. The agreement contained a clause which limited the damages which would be available for breach of contract to below what might have been available under the general law. It was held that, because of the agreed clause, damages would be an inadequate remedy for breach of contract and so the interim injunction was awarded. At first sight, this conclusion seems to be odd, since it appears to undermine the bargain agreed by the parties. But the court emphasized the importance of distinguishing between primary and secondary obligations. The agreed damages clause provided for damages as a secondary obligation following breach, whereas the interim injunction operated to enforce the primary obligation to perform the contract and sought to avoid the claimant needing to have recourse to the agreed damages clause. It followed that, if the agreed damages clause provided for less damages than would otherwise have been available for breach, damages could be considered to be an inadequate remedy for breach, enabling the injunction to be awarded.

(4) Breach of an equitable order constitutes the crime of contempt of court for which the punishment is imprisonment,[7] the imposition of a fine, or seizure of the defendant's assets. A third party who encourages or assists the commission of contempt of court may be criminally liable as an accessory.

(5) There are a variety of defences available to the defendant, including that the claimant did not come to Equity with clean hands,[8] laches,[9] estoppel, acquiescence, prejudice to any third-party interests, and hardship to the defendant. The usual six-year limitation period does not, however, apply where the claimant seeks equitable relief such as specific performance or an injunction.[10]

(6) Sometimes, rather than make the requested order, the court can instead order that damages should be paid to the claimant.[11]

21.2 INJUNCTIONS

The injunction remains one of the most significant creations of the equitable jurisdiction, which is wide-ranging in effect because it can prohibit the defendant from acting or make the defendant act in a particular way.[12] Today, the authority to grant injunctions is statutory,[13] whereby the court may grant an injunction where it appears to the court to be just[14] and convenient to do so—but the equitable origin of the order continues to explain some of its significant features. There are a number of different types of injunction that will be identified in this chapter to illustrate the scope and adaptability of Equity to respond to

---

[6] [2014] EWCA Civ 229, [2015] 1 WLR 771, relying on the earlier decision in *Bath and North East Somerset DC v Mowlem plc* [2014] EWCA Civ 115, [2015] 1 WLR 785.

[7] See *Shalson v Russo* [2003] EWHC 1637 (Ch), [2005] Ch 281 (imprisonment for two years for breaching an injunction).   [8] See Section 2.5, p. 31.

[9] See Section 17.3.3.(ii), p. 489.   [10] Limitation Act 1980, s. 36(1).

[11] See further Section 21.5, p. 636.   [12] See generally *Snell's Equity* (see n. 4), ch. 18.

[13] Senior Courts Act 1981, s. 37(1).

[14] *AB v CD* [2014] EWCA Civ 229, [2015] 1 WLR 771, [33] (Ryder LJ).

different circumstances. But it is first important to identify some general principles relating to all injunctions.

21.2.1 GENERAL PRINCIPLES

(1) The court will grant an injunction only to protect a person's legal or equitable rights, whether they are proprietary or personal.[15] So, for example, an injunction may be awarded to protect the claimant's right to the enjoyment of their property free from tortious interference by the defendant.

(2) An injunction will not be granted if the court considers that remedies available at Common Law are adequate.[16] It follows that, if the defendant did interfere with a right of the claimant and damages would adequately compensate the claimant for this wrong, an injunction will not be granted, unless it appears that the defendant would not be able to afford to pay damages if they were found liable.[17]

(3) There is no right to an injunction, since the decision to order one is a matter for the court in the exercise of its discretion, depending on the particular circumstances of the case.

(4) The court's jurisdiction to award an injunction will be barred in certain circumstances, such as where the party seeking the injunction has acquiesced in the defendant's infringement of the claimant's right,[18] or there has been an unreasonable delay before the injunction is sought,[19] or granting the injunction would cause hardship to the defendant,[20] or the claimant's misconduct means that they do not come to the court with clean hands.[21]

21.2.2 TYPES OF INJUNCTION

(i) Mandatory injunctions

A mandatory injunction is an order made at trial to require the defendant to act in a particular way. The equitable jurisdiction to grant such an injunction supplements the Common Law where the defendant's infringement of the claimant's rights is continuing.

In *Redland Bricks Ltd v Morris*[22] Lord Upjohn identified certain key principles relating to the exercise of the court's discretion to grant a mandatory injunction:

(1) The claimant must show a very strong probability on the facts that grave damage will accrue to them in the future if an injunction is not granted. The jurisdiction to grant such an injunction is to be exercised sparingly and with caution, but in the proper case without hesitation.

(2) The cost to the defendant to take action to avoid or reduce the risk[23] of future harm must be taken into account by the court when determining whether an injunction should be awarded. Where the defendant has acted unreasonably, the injunction might be awarded even though the expense to the defendant is out of all proportion to the advantage that accrues to the claimant. Where, however, the defendant has acted reasonably, the cost to the defendant of avoiding the harm must be taken into account.

---

[15] *North London Railway Co v Great Northern Railway Co* (1883) 11 QBD 30.
[16] See *AB and CD* [2014] EWCA Civ 229, [2015] 1 WLR 771. See Section 21.1, p. 628.
[17] *American Cyanamid Co v Ethicon Ltd* [1975] AC 396, 408 (Lord Diplock).
[18] *Shaw v Applegate* [1977] 1 WLR 970.   [19] *Shepherd Homes Ltd v Sandham* [1971] Ch 340.
[20] *Shell UK Ltd v Lostock Garage Ltd* [1976] 1 WLR 1187.   [21] Ibid., 1199 (Lord Denning MR).
[22] [1970] AC 652, 665–6.   [23] *Kennard v Cory Bros and Co Ltd* [1922] 1 Ch 265, 274 (Sargant J).

(3) If an injunction is to be granted, it is important that the defendant knows precisely what they are expected to do or to refrain from doing.

(ii) Negative injunctions

A negative injunction is granted to prevent the continuance or recurrence of a wrongful act. The decision to grant such an injunction is influenced by the same principles as apply to the order of a mandatory injunction, except that the court will be more willing to grant a negative injunction to stop the defendant from acting in a particular way, rather than to make the defendant act, since this is considered to involve less interference with the defendant's autonomy. Further, the question of the cost to the defendant in not acting in a particular way is not considered to be a relevant consideration.[24]

(iii) *Quia timet* injunctions

Quia timet (meaning 'because he fears') injunctions can be granted where interference with the claimant's rights is threatened or feared, but has not yet occurred. In such circumstances, the injunction may be granted even though the defendant is not yet liable to the claimant at Common Law, for example, because the claimant has suffered no harm but such harm is threatened. A *quia timet* injunction will be granted to prevent an apprehended legal wrong in two particular circumstances:[25]

(1) When the defendant is threatening and intending to act in such a way as to harm the claimant, the defendant may be ordered not to act in such a way.

(2) When the claimant has been fully compensated for loss or damage that has already occurred, but the earlier actions of the defendant might lead to future claims brought by the claimant, the defendant may be ordered to act in a particular way, by means of a mandatory injunction, to ensure that the loss or damage does not occur again.

(iv) Interim injunctions

The interim injunction is awarded before the trial at a preliminary hearing, usually to maintain the status quo to ensure that the defendant does not violate any of the claimant's legal rights until the court has determined whether the proposed action will indeed violate such rights. The task of the court in such cases is difficult because the existence of the right and its violation will be uncertain until final judgment.

The leading case on the award of interim injunctions is *American Cyanamid Co v Ethicon Ltd*,[26] in which Lord Diplock[27] recognized that the interim injunction is a temporary and discretionary remedy that is awarded to protect the claimant against injury arising from the violation of a right for which they could not be adequately compensated by damages if liability were established at trial. An interim injunction will be awarded only where there is a serious question to be tried, the claim is not considered to be frivolous or vexatious, and there is a real prospect of the claimant obtaining a permanent injunction at trial. When there is doubt as to whether damages would be an adequate remedy, the court should consider where the balance of convenience lies, with reference to a variety of factors depending on the particular facts of the case. Where these factors are evenly balanced, it is appropriate for the court to be prudent and to maintain the status quo by granting the injunction. When an interim injunction is granted, the claimant must give an undertaking to pay damages to the defendant for any loss sustained by reason of the injunction

---

[24] *Redland Bricks Ltd v Morris* [1970] AC 652, 666 (Lord Upjohn).
[25] Ibid., at 665 (Lord Upjohn).   [26] [1975] AC 396.   [27] Ibid., 405.

being granted, which would be relevant if, at trial, it were held that the defendant had not infringed any of the claimant's rights.

(v) Freezing orders

The creative function of Equity is particularly well illustrated by an important remedy developed in the 1970s to deal with the problem of a defendant who seeks to hide their assets or to take them out of the jurisdiction to prevent the claimant from enforcing a judgment for damages against them. To avoid this problem, the equitable jurisdiction was used to create a new form of prohibitory injunction, known then as a *Mareva* injunction (named after one[28] of the early cases that first recognized it, involving a ship of that name[29]) and now known as a freezing injunction or freezing order.[30] The jurisdiction to grant such an injunction is now recognized by statute.[31]

The freezing order is an injunction that can be used by judges to freeze some or all of the defendant's assets to prevent them from being removed from the jurisdiction or dissipated. For example, the injunction might mean that the defendant is unable to gain access to money that has been credited to their bank account. Such injunctions can be granted either before or after[32] judgment has been obtained. This is an injunction that has proved to be a significant feature of the English law of civil procedure. It was described by Lord Denning extra-judicially as 'the greatest piece of judicial law reform in my time'.[33]

The purpose of a freezing injunction is to restrain the defendant from dealing with their assets in such a way as to defeat, wholly or in part, a likely judgment against them, such as by hiding assets, transferring them abroad, or dissipating them. Crucially, the purpose is not to give the claimant any security for the claim against the defendant to rank above the defendant's other creditors if they become insolvent,[34] or a proprietary interest in the asset that is frozen.[35] Consequently, the injunction does not change the ownership of assets or create new rights in the defendant's assets; it only modifies the defendant's right to deal with the asset as they wish.[36] The freezing order can extend to assets which are held by a third party in respect of which the defendant retains the beneficial ownership or control.[37] It follows that assets which are held on trust for the defendant can be subject to a freezing order.[38] It is even possible to extend a freezing order to require the defendant to disclose any interest they have as an object under a discretionary trust, even though it is not possible to require trust assets under a discretionary trust to be the subject of a freezing order since the objects do not have a proprietary interest in the assets until the trustee's discretion has been exercised to make an appointment to the object.[39]

In *JSC BTA Bank v Ablyazov (No 10)*[40] Beatson LJ recognized three principles to guide the decision as to whether to grant a freezing order:

---

[28] The first case to recognize this injunction was *Nippon Yusen Kaisha v Karageogis* [1975] 1 WLR 1093.

[29] *Mareva Compania Naviera SA v International Bulkcarriers SA* [1975] 2 Lloyd's Rep 509.

[30] See generally Merrett, 'Worldwide freezing orders in Europe' [2008] LMCLQ 71; Hartley, 'Jurisdiction in conflict of laws: disclosure, third-party debts and freezing orders' (2010) 126 LQR 194.

[31] The Senior Courts Act 1981, s. 37(3). See also the Civil Procedure Rules 1998, r. 25.1(f).

[32] *Babanaft International Co SA v Bassatne* [1990] Ch 13.

[33] *The Due Process of Law* (London: Butterworths, 1980), p. 134.

[34] *Camdex International Ltd v Bank of Zambia (No 2)* [1997] 1 WLR 632, 638 (Aldous LJ).

[35] *Gangway Ltd v Caledonian Park Investments (Jersey) Ltd* [2001] 2 Lloyd's Rep 715, [14] (Colman J).

[36] *Customs and Excise Commissioners v Barclays Bank plc* [2006] UKHL 28, [2007] 1 AC 181, [10] (Lord Bingham).

[37] *JSC BTA Bank v Solodchenko* [2010] EWCA Civ 1436, [2011] 1 WLR 888, [31] (Patten LJ).

[38] *JSC Mezhdunarodniy Promyshlenniy Bank v Pugachev* [2015] EWCA Civ 139, [2016] 1 WLR 160, [14] (Lewison LJ).

[39] Ibid., [15].　　[40] [2013] EWCA Civ 928, [2014] 1 WLR 1414.

(1) The enforcement principle: the function of the freezing order is to stop the defendant from dissipating assets which could be the subject of a claim to enforce a judgment if the claimant won the case.

(2) The flexibility principle: the equitable jurisdiction should be flexible and adaptable to enable the courts to respond to defendants who seek new ways to thwart the enforcement of the orders.

(3) The strict interpretation principle: since breach of a freezing order has penal consequences, the order should be clear, unequivocal, and strictly construed.

The court has jurisdiction to grant a freezing injunction whether or not the party who is restrained from removing their assets is domiciled, resident, or present within the jurisdiction.[41] It has been recognized that freezing injunctions can be granted to restrain the dissipation of assets abroad, to require the defendant to disclose the location of its assets abroad,[42] and even to order transfer of assets from one jurisdiction to another in aid of a freezing order.[43] But a freezing injunction will have an extra-territorial effect only if there is a sufficient connection with England, either because the English court has jurisdiction over the defendant, or there are assets located in England. A freezing injunction with extra-territorial effect has been called a 'worldwide freezing order', but, if a defendant breaches such an injunction by dissipating assets in another country in contravention of the terms of the injunction, this will only constitute contempt of court in England and it will be enforceable only if the defendant is present in England or has assets in England. If the defendant is located abroad and has no assets within the jurisdiction, the injunction is effectively unenforceable.

A freezing injunction can be granted only if the claimant has satisfied the usual requirements for the award of an interim injunction as recognized in *American Cyanamid Co v Ethicon Ltd*[44]—namely, that there is a serious issue to be tried and the balance of convenience favours the grant of the injunction. The claimant must also have issued, or must undertake to issue, proceedings against the defendant.[45] Factors that are relevant to the decision to grant a freezing injunction include[46] that the claimant must have some grounds for believing that the defendant has assets in the jurisdiction, such as a bank account, and must have grounds for believing that there is a risk of the assets being removed or destroyed. The claimant must give an undertaking in damages in case they fail in their claim or the order of the injunction is subsequently considered to have been unjustified.[47]

A matter of particular practical significance relates to the effect of freezing injunctions on third parties. This was considered by the House of Lords in *Customs and Excise Commissioners v Barclays Bank plc*,[48] in which a bank had been informed of the award of a freezing injunction over a customer's bank account, but failed to prevent payment out of the account. The claimant sued the bank for negligence, but it was held that no duty of care was owed. It was, however, acknowledged that a third party, such as a bank, which knows of the order would be held in contempt of court if it were to assist intentionally in or permit a breach of the order; carelessly allowing the order to be breached will not amount to contempt.

---

[41] See *Dadourian Group International Inc v Simms* [2006] EWCA Civ 399, [2006] 1 WLR 2499.
[42] *Derby and Co Ltd v Weldon* [1990] Ch 48.
[43] *Derby and Co Ltd v Weldon (No 6)* [1990] 1 WLR 1139.
[44] [1975] AC 396. See Section 21.2.2.(iv), p. 630.
[45] *Fourie v Le Roux* [2007] UKHL 1, [2007] 1 WLR 320.
[46] *Third Chandris Shipping Corp v Unimarine SA* [1979] QB 645.
[47] See *Energy Venture Partners Ltd v Malebu Oil and Gas Ltd* [2014] EWCA Civ 1295, [2015] 1 WLR 2309.
[48] [2006] UKHL 28, [2007] 1 AC 181. See Gee, 'The remedies carried by a freezing injunction' (2006) 122 LQR 535.

21.3 SEARCH ORDERS

Another significant application of the equitable jurisdiction to supplement domestic and international litigation is the search order, formerly known as the *Anton Piller* order after one of the first cases[49] to recognize the jurisdiction to grant an order to permit the claimant to search premises and to seize property so as to assist the claimant in establishing a claim against the defendant. That case illustrates the potential significance of this exercise of the equitable jurisdiction. In *Anton Pillar KG v Manufacturing Process Ltd*[50] the claimant claimed that the defendant had given confidential information to manufacturers that was damaging to the claimant's business. The Court of Appeal granted the claimant an order giving it permission to enter the defendant's premises to remove documents. Lord Denning considered that these orders were exceptional, and that they only authorized entry and inspection with the permission of the defendant, albeit that the effect of the order was that the defendant was ordered to permit entry when it was essential in the interests of justice, for example to avoid the destruction of evidence or the removal of evidence out of the jurisdiction. If the defendant were not to give permission to allow entry, they would be guilty of contempt of court.

Three conditions need to be satisfied before a search order will be granted:

(1) The claimant has to establish an extremely strong prima facie case that the defendant is liable.

(2) The potential or actual damage arising from the search order not being granted has to be very serious for the applicant.

(3) There has to be clear evidence that the defendant had incriminating documents or assets in their possession and that there was a real possibility that such material might be destroyed. Consequently, the essential rationale of the search order is to preserve evidence for use at a later trial.

The jurisdiction to make such an order to preserve evidence or property has now been recognized by statute.[51] This enables the court to order that a person is permitted to enter premises and, for example, to search for items described in the order and to take copies of them. The defendant has been allowed to claim the privilege against self-incrimination[52] as a legitimate reason for refusing to comply with a search order.[53] Although this privilege is no longer available in the context of intellectual property disputes,[54] it may still be pleaded in respect of other disputes in which the execution of the search order may assist with a criminal prosecution. In *C plc v P*,[55] however, it was held that the privilege did not extend to documents or things that have 'an existence independent of the will' of the person who sought to plead it. It followed in that case that the privilege was not available to a defendant who had been required, pursuant to a search order, to hand over to an independent expert a computer, on the hard drive of which were found indecent images of children.

If a search order is granted and it is subsequently discovered that the claimant did not make full and frank disclosure to the court, the claimant will be liable to compensate the

---

[49] The very first reported case to make such an order was *EMI Ltd v Pandit* [1975] 1 WLR 302 (Templeman J).

[50] [1976] Ch 55.

[51] Civil Procedure Act 1997, s. 7. Supplemented by the Civil Procedure Rules, r. 25.1(i). The execution of a search order does not violate Art. 8 of the European Convention on Human Rights: *Columbia Picture Industries Inc v Robinson* [1987] Ch 38.   [52] Civil Evidence Act 1968, s. 14.

[53] *Rank Film Distributors Ltd v Video Information Centre* [1982] AC 380.

[54] Senior Courts Act 1981, s. 72.   [55] [2007] EWCA Civ 493, [2008] Ch 1.

defendant for the subsequent loss of any business arising from the claimant seizing items
that were not relevant to its claim.[56]

21.4 SPECIFIC PERFORMANCE

Another equitable remedy that is of great practical significance is specific performance,[57]
which requires a party to perform a particular positive obligation, usually arising from a
contract.

The operation of this remedy is particularly well illustrated by the decision of the House
of Lords in *Co-operative Insurance Society v Argyll Stores (Holdings) Ltd*.[58] In this case the
claimant had leased a unit in a shopping centre to the defendant, who had covenanted to
keep the premises open for retail trade during usual business hours. The defendant subsequently announced that it planned to close the shop and the claimant sought specific
performance of the covenant. It was held that the defendant would not be required to
continue with the business, but was required to compensate the claimant for the loss suffered from the breach of covenant. Lord Hoffmann recognized that specific performance
was an exceptional remedy that was available to do justice where Common Law remedies
were inadequate. It followed that, where the defendant threatened to breach their contract,
the usual remedy would be for the defendant to compensate the claimant for any loss that
would be suffered rather than the defendant being required to perform their contractual
obligation.

Even where damages for breach of contract are available, they might still be considered
to be an inadequate remedy, because, for example, the loss arising from the breach of contract might be difficult to quantify or because the claimant bargained for unique property,
such as land[59] or unusual chattels,[60] which cannot be readily acquired on the open market,
so that receipt of a pecuniary award would not adequately compensate the claimant for not
obtaining the property. This was recognized by the House of Lords in *Beswick v Beswick*,[61]
in which it was held that, were a defendant to be bound by contract to pay a regular annuity to the claimant and the defendant had failed to do so, the claimant would be able to
sue the defendant for breach of contract at Common Law. But the claimant would only be
able to bring a claim for each payment when that payment had not been made. In other
words, the claimant could bring a claim only following each breach of the promise to make
a payment and it would not be possible to obtain damages in respect of a future breach of
contract. This is a significant limitation of the Common Law, but Equity can come to the
claimant's assistance by specifically enforcing the contract now and for the future, and so
avoid the trouble and expense of a multiplicity of actions.

Even where damages are considered to be an inadequate remedy, the court will not
necessarily order specific performance of the defendant's obligations. This remains a discretionary remedy that is not ordered as a matter of course, but with reference to careful
consideration of the facts. In *Co-operative Insurance Society v Argyll Stores (Holdings) Ltd*[62]
the following factors were identified as being relevant to determine whether the defendant
should have been compelled to carry on with its business, on the assumption that damages
for breach of contract would not have been an adequate remedy:

---

[56] *Columbia Picture Industries Inc v Robinson* [1987] Ch 38.

[57] Jones and Goodhart, *Specific Performance*, 2nd edn (London: Butterworths, 1996); *Snell's Equity* (see
n. 4), ch. 17.

[58] [1998] AC 1.   [59] *Sudbrook Trading Estate Ltd v Eggleton* [1983] 1 AC 444, 478.

[60] *Falcke v Gray* (1859) 4 Dr 651.   [61] [1968] AC 58.   [62] [1998] AC 1.

(1) The court will not order a defendant to carry on a business where the order would require constant supervision by the court in the form of rulings on applications by the parties as to whether the order had been breached. For similar reasons, the courts will not specifically enforce an employment contract.[63] But it would be different if, rather than the defendant being required to carry on a business, they were simply required to achieve a particular result that could be adjudicated by the court once the work had been completed. Consequently, the court would be willing to order specific performance of a building contract,[64] since compliance with such an order could be determined once the work has been completed.

(2) The court's only weapon for breach of an order for specific performance is punishment for contempt of court, but this is a powerful weapon which might be considered to be heavy-handed. Where the threat of punishment influences the defendant to carry on with performance of their contractual obligation, even though it might not have been in their economic interests to do so, this would be a reason why specific performance should not be awarded.

(3) The order for specific performance is less likely to be made where its enforcement would be expensive, with the possibility of repeated applications over time rather than a once-and-for-all inquiry as to damages. Similarly, if the terms of the order could not be precisely drawn, the possibility of wasteful litigation relating to compliance with the order would be increased, such that the order would be less likely to be made.

(4) The court should also consider whether the loss suffered by the defendant in carrying out the order would be far greater than the loss that would be suffered by the claimant if the contract were breached. If the claimant were able to secure more than the performance that was due to them under the contract, ordering specific performance would be considered to be unjust.

Further, the court will not grant an order of specific performance in favour of a volunteer who has not provided consideration. So, for example, a party to a deed of covenant will not be able to obtain an order of specific performance to enforce the covenant,[65] except where the party fell within the marriage consideration, since they are no longer a volunteer in Equity.[66] A third party to a contract may be able to enforce rights under that contract even though they have not provided consideration, by virtue of the Contracts (Rights of Third Parties) Act 1999. Section 1(5) of that Act states that such a third party will have any remedy that would have been available had they been party to the contract 'and the rules relating to . . . specific performance and other relief shall apply accordingly'. But, since the existing rule relating to specific performance is that this relief is not available in favour of a volunteer, there is no reason to conclude that this rule has been changed by the 1999 Act.[67] Specific performance will, however, be available even though a volunteer will benefit from the performance of the contractual obligation.[68]

In determining whether to exercise its discretion, there are certain factors that may cause the court to refuse to order specific performance of an obligation. These factors include the poor conduct of the party seeking specific performance, so that a claimant who is not ready and willing to perform their own contractual obligations will not be able to

---

[63] Trade Union and Labour Relations (Consolidation) Act 1992, s. 236.

[64] *Wolverhampton Corporation v Emmons* [1901] 1 KB 515.

[65] *Cannon v Hartley* [1949] Ch 213. See Section 5.3.3.(iii), p. 135.   [66] See Section 5.3.3.(iii), p. 133.

[67] Cf. Andrews, 'Strangers to justice no longer: the reversal of the privity rule under the Contracts (Rights of Third Parties) Act 1999' (2001) 60 CLJ 353, who argues to the contrary. See Section 5.3.3.(iii), p. 133.

[68] *Beswick v Beswick* [1968] AC 58.

obtain an order for specific performance[69]—such a claimant does not have clean hands;[70] similarly if the claimant delays unreasonably in seeking the order;[71] or if the grant of specific performance would cause unnecessary hardship to either party, or to a third party.[72]

21.5 DAMAGES IN LIEU OF EQUITABLE ORDERS

By section 50 of the Senior Courts Act 1981, where the court has jurisdiction to grant an injunction or specific performance, it may award damages in addition to, or in substitution for, the equitable order. This provision replaced section 2 of the Chancery Amendment Act 1858, which was known as Lord Cairns' Act. The object of that Act was to ensure that a claimant who did not obtain equitable relief in the form of an injunction or specific performance was not left to a remedy at Common Law that would require the claimant to be sent back to the Common Law courts. But the statute also enabled the Chancery court to award damages in cases in which the Common Law courts could not do so, and so it was not necessary to establish that the claimant would have had a claim for damages at Common Law. So, for example, damages under the Act could be awarded once and for all for future harm that was only threatened, where an injunction had not been granted to prevent such harm,[73] whereas damages at Common Law could be awarded only for past harm. The jurisdiction under the Act applies regardless of whether the underlying cause of action is breach of contract or tort, but the statutory jurisdiction will apply only if the court had the jurisdiction to grant an injunction or specific performance. Consequently, the claimant must establish that they are prima facie entitled to an equitable order, by showing that they have a right with which the defendant has already interfered and that interference is continuing, or that the defendant has threatened to interfere with the right, and also that the claim is not defeated by any equitable defence such as laches or acquiescence.[74]

The court has a discretion to withhold equitable relief and to order damages instead. The Supreme Court in *Coventry v Lawrence*[75] emphasized that the exercise of this discretion is essentially fact-sensitive and must not be fettered by the mechanical application of rules. It was, however, recognized that four factors identified by A. L. Smith LJ in *Shelfer v City of London Electric Lighting Co*[76] remain significant. Those factors are: the injury to the claimant's right is small; the injury can be valued in money; the injury can be adequately compensated by a small money payment; and it would be oppressive to the defendant to grant an equitable order. Lord Neuberger[77] accepted that, if these four factors were established, normally an injunction would be refused and damages would be awarded in lieu. But, if any of the factors were not established, it did not follow that an injunction would necessarily be awarded. Lord Neuberger also considered that other factors were relevant, particularly the public interest, which meant that it was relevant to consider the effect of granting an injunction on the defendant's business and their employees. It was also relevant to consider the effect of not granting an injunction on third parties, such as the claimant's neighbours. *Coventry v Lawrence* concerned a claim

---

[69] *Cornish v Brook Green Laundry* [1959] 1 KB 394.   [70] See Section 2.5, p. 31.
[71] *MEPC Ltd v Christian-Edwards* [1981] AC 205.   [72] *Patel v Ali* [1984] Ch 283.
[73] *Leeds Industrial Co-operative Society Ltd v Slack* [1924] AC 851, in which damages were awarded under the Act in lieu of granting a *quia timet* injunction. See Section 21.2.2.(iii), p. 630.
[74] See Section 21.1, p. 628.   [75] [2014] UKSC 13, [2014] AC 822.
[76] *Shelfer v City of London Electric Lighting Co* [1895] 1 Ch 287, 322–3 (A. L. Smith LJ).
[77] [2014] UKSC 13, [2014] AC 822, [123].

relating to the tort of nuisance, arising from noise caused by stock-car racing, which operated with planning permission, in close proximity to the claimant's property. The tort was established and the Supreme Court recognized that, in such circumstances, an injunction should be granted and the defendant bore the burden of establishing why it should not be granted.[78]

The function of the statutory jurisdiction is essentially to make a financial award in substitution for an injunction or specific performance, with the claimant being compensated for the defendant's commission of wrongdoing in the future. But, once damages have been awarded in lieu of an equitable order being made, the claimant will be estopped from seeking damages for the defendant's future commission of that particular wrong. It follows that the consequence of the exercise of the statutory jurisdiction is that the defendant is free to continue to infringe the claimant's right, whether it be by the continued breach of a promise under a contract or a continued tortious interference with the claimant's property right, but that this infringement can no longer be considered to be wrongful because the defendant has effectively purchased the right to infringe the claimant's right in the future, albeit that this is a purchase of a right that is sanctioned by the court and can arise only once the court has decided not to grant the equitable order of an injunction or specific performance.

The application of this provision is illustrated by *Jaggard v Sawyer*,[79] in which the defendant had built a house in a private cul-de-sac, the access to which involved the breach of a covenant made with the nine other residents in the cul-de-sac. The claimant, one of the residents, sought an injunction to restrain the defendant's continuing breach of the covenant and the commission of the tort of trespass. The award of an injunction was refused on the ground that it would have been oppressive to the defendant because its effect on the defendant would have been out of proportion to the loss suffered by the claimant. Damages were awarded in lieu of the injunction, which were assessed as one-ninth of what the defendant might reasonably have been required to pay the residents for release of the covenant.[80]

In assessing the appropriate measure of damages, it appears that a distinction should be drawn between a case in which the infringement of the claimant's right is finished and cases in which the infringement, or potential infringement, continues. In the former case, the damages will be assessed, as at Common Law, with reference to the loss actually suffered by the claimant. So, in *Johnson v Agnew*,[81] the vendor of land obtained a decree of specific performance to compel the purchaser to complete the transaction. The purchaser failed to do so and the vendor's mortgagee then sold the land. Consequently, the vendor applied to have the decree set aside and for damages to be awarded in lieu of the order. Damages were awarded in the exercise of the statutory jurisdiction by reference to the value of the land at the time when specific performance became impossible. This was because the breach was not a continuing breach of contract, so that the assessment of the remedy at Common Law and under the statute would be the same. Where, however, the infringement of the right is continuing, as in *Jaggard v Sawyer*, the damages are assessed with reference to the future loss and can be determined by reference to the claimant's lost opportunity to negotiate with the defendant, which requires the court to identify a hypothetical bargain between the parties relating to how much the claimant would have

---

[78] Lord Sumption, ibid. [161], thought that damages should be the general remedy and an injunction to restrain nuisance should only be awarded exceptionally.   [79] [1995] 1 WLR 269.

[80] A measure of damages that had been adopted in *Wrotham Park Estate Co Ltd v Parkside Homes Ltd* [1974] 1 WLR 798.   [81] [1980] AC 367.

demanded from the defendant to release the right.[82] Although the justification for this measure of damages is that it is necessarily different from the Common Law measure because the Common Law cannot compensate for future losses,[83] in fact the lost opportunity to bargain can be regarded as a past loss, and so this measure has been used at Common Law as well to compensate for loss arising from a breach of contract even where the claimant could not have sought an injunction or specific performance.[84] This is, consequently, another scenario in which there has been fusion of Common Law and Equity, this time as regards the method of assessing damages.[85]

21.6 RESCISSION

21.6.1 THE NATURE OF RESCISSION

Rescission is a remedy that enables a transaction, typically a voidable contract, to be treated as though it had never come into existence.[86] A contract will be voidable where there was a flaw in its making that impaired the consent of one of the parties to it, such as where they were induced to enter into it as a result of a misrepresentation or undue influence. Such a contract remains valid until it is rescinded. Once a contract is rescinded, it is nullified and everything that has been done under it is liable to be undone, so that the parties are restored to their original pre-contractual position; there is a giving and a taking back on both sides.[87]

Although the remedy of rescission is usually relevant to set aside a contract, it is also relevant to setting aside other transactions, including wills,[88] deeds of gift, and other voluntary settlements, such as a disposition to trusts.[89] Rescission is not necessary to enable the recovery of gifts where there is no deed, since there is no transaction that needs to be set aside.

The essence of the remedy of rescission was usefully summarized by Master Matthews in *Bainbridge v Bainbridge*[90] as being an

> equitable remedy available in appropriate circumstances to undo (or set aside) otherwise consensual transactions between two or more parties where there is a factor or element vitiating consent.

21.6.2 RESCISSION AT COMMON LAW AND IN EQUITY[91]

The nature of the remedy of rescission depends on whether rescission occurs at Common Law or in Equity.[92] Whether rescission is effected at Common Law or in Equity will depend on the type of vitiating factor that is engaged. The Common Law recognizes far fewer

---

[82] In *Coventry v Lawrence* [2014] UKSC 13, [2014] AC 822, some Justices contemplated that damages in lieu of an injunction to restrain a nuisance might be assessed with reference to the defendant's gain from committing the tort.   [83] *Jaggard v Sawyer* [1995] 1 WLR 269, 291 (Millett LJ).

[84] *Frischmann Engineering Ltd v Bow Valley Iran Ltd* [2009] UKPC 45, [2011] 1 WLR 2370, [49] (Lord Walker). See also *Vercoe v Rutland Fund Management Ltd* [2010] EWHC 424 (Ch), [292] (Sales J); *Force India Formula One Team Ltd v 1 Malaysia Racing Team Sdn Bhd* [2012] EWHC 616 (Ch), [384] (Arnold J).

[85] See Section 1.6.2, p. 20.   [86] *Johnson v Agnew* [1980] AC 367, 393 (Lord Wilberforce).

[87] *Shalson v Russo* [2003] EWHC 1637 (Ch), [2005] Ch 281, [122] (Rimer J).

[88] *Re Edwards (deceased)* [2007] EWHC 1119 (Ch).

[89] *Pitt v Holt* [2013] UKSC 26, [2013] 2 AC 108. See Section 9.3.3, p. 264.

[90] [2016] EWHC 898 (Ch), [2].

[91] See generally McBride, 'Rescission' in *Commercial Remedies: Resolving Controversies* (ed. Virgo and Worthington), (CUP, 2017), ch. 7.

[92] O'Sullivan, 'Rescission as a self-help remedy: a critical analysis' (2000) 59 CLJ 509.

vitiating factors than Equity, but all the factors that are recognized at Common Law are also recognized in Equity by virtue of Equity's concurrent jurisdiction, so that the party who wishes a contract to be rescinded may have a choice as to whether to seek rescission at Common Law or in Equity. Depending on the facts of the case, there may be certain advantages in seeking rescission at Common Law or in Equity, although usually equitable rescission will be preferable, because of the more extensive vitiating factors that are recognized, the less restrictive approach to the bars on rescission,[93] and the remedial consequences which are more likely to be beneficial to the party who seeks rescission.[94]

(i) Rescission at Common Law

Rescission at Common Law will be available only where a contract has been made as a result of a fraudulent misrepresentation; the non-disclosure of a material fact for certain types of contract; duress; or where a contracting party's consent to enter into a contract has been impaired by incapacity. Rescission at Common Law is a self-help remedy that takes effect by the act of the party seeking rescission,[95] which is usually effected by communication to the other party to the contract and without requiring a court order.[96]

(ii) Rescission in Equity

In Equity, rescission is a form of equitable relief that is determined and effected by the court.[97] The judges have a discretion both as to whether to order rescission and, if so, as to the nature and extent of that relief, which might be subject to conditions.[98] The discretion is exercised with reference to recognized principles, so it is still correct to describe the claimant as having a right to rescission if an equitable vitiating factor is identified and none of the bars to rescission apply.[99] When making an application to the court, the claimant can either expressly ask for the court to rescind the contract or this may be implicit, for example in an application to commence proceeding to recover property from the defendant.[100]

Where the contract is rescinded in Equity by the court, a condition will be imposed to ensure that the parties are restored to their original positions.[101] Before the contract is rescinded by the court, the claimant will have only an equity to rescind if one of the equitable vitiating factors applies. This gives the claimant an entitlement to apply to the court for an order to rescind the contract.[102]

In addition to Equity's concurrent jurisdiction to rescind by virtue of the grounds recognized at Common Law, there is an exclusive equitable jurisdiction of rescission in Equity where a contract has been induced by non-fraudulent misrepresentation, or undue influence, or where the defendant has procured the contract in breach of fiduciary duty, or where the contract can be considered to be an unconscionable bargain.[103]

---

[93] See Section 21.6.4, p. 646.   [94] See Section 21.6.5, p. 650.

[95] *Halpern v Halpern (No 2)* [2006] EWHC 1728 (Comm), [2007] QB 88, [26] (Nigel Teare QC).

[96] *Brotherton v Aseguradora Cobeguros (No 2)* [2003] EWCA Civ 705, [2003] 3 All ER (Comm) 298, [27] (Mance LJ) and [45] (Buxton LJ).

[97] *Erlanger v New Sombrero Phosphate Co* (1878) 3 App Cas 1218, 1278 (Lord Blackburn); *Spence v Crawford* [1939] 3 All ER 271, 288 (Lord Wright).

[98] *Hurstanger Ltd v Wilson* [2007] EWCA Civ 299, [2007] 4 All ER 1118, [48] (Tuckey LJ).

[99] *Lagunas Nitrate Co v Lagunas Syndicate* [1899] 2 Ch 392, 457 (Rigby LJ); *Spence v Crawford* [1939] 3 All ER 271, 281 (Lord Thankerton).

[100] *Shalson v Russo* [2003] EWHC 1637 (Ch), [2005] Ch 281, [120] (Rimer J).

[101] See further Section 21.6.4.(i), p. 646.

[102] *Phillips v Phillips* (1861) 4 De GF & J 208, 218 (Lord Westbury); *Goldsworthy v Bricknell* [1987] Ch 378, 409 (Nourse LJ).   [103] See further Section 21.6.3, p. 640.

(iii) Fusion

Although the distinction between the process of rescission at Common Law and in Equity has long been recognized,[104] the continued legitimacy of this distinction has been challenged on the ground that there is no reason why different grounds for rescission should be recognized at Common Law and in Equity,[105] and there is no reason why the process of rescission should be different at Common Law and in Equity, with a preference being expressed that the self-help approach of the Common Law should prevail.[106]

In fact, the Judicature Act 1873 might have been applied to ensure that the equitable rules of rescission prevailed over those of the Common Law, so that all rescission would be effected by order of the court. This is because that Act provided that, where there is a conflict or variance between the rules of Equity and the Common Law with reference to the same matter, the rules of Equity will prevail.[107] This might be interpreted to mean that, where there is a concurrent jurisdiction to rescind in Equity and the Common Law, the equitable rules should apply to the extent that they conflict. This interpretation of the legislation was acknowledged by Carnwath LJ in *Halpern v Halpern (No 2)*,[108] in which, in a case concerning rescission of a contract for duress, it was recognized that rescission for duress at Common Law should be subject to the more flexible, equitable interpretation of the bar that rescission will be denied if the claimant cannot restore the defendant to their pre-contractual position, so that rescission would not be barred if the claimant could only restore the defendant substantially to their pre-contractual position.[109]

It has been argued, however, that the distinction between rescission at Common Law and in Equity has survived the Judicature Act because the difference between the two jurisdictions is not a consequence of differences in the application of particular rules, but is simply a consequence of the different mechanisms employed by the Common Law and Equity to effect rescission, so that there is no reason for the equitable rules of rescission to prevail over those of the Common Law.[110] The more restrictive approach to rescission at Common Law has been defended as proportionate and justified,[111] because such self-help rescission is appropriate where the defendant's conduct is fraudulent or the commercial context calls for a clear mechanism for rescission without the need for a court order. Nevertheless, the limitations of rescission at Common Law are difficult to defend, especially when compared with the more flexible equitable jurisdiction. Consequently, the equitable jurisdiction should be preferred, so that all rescission should be effected by means of a judicial order to which terms can be attached if necessary, rather than be treated simply as a self-help remedy.[112]

21.6.3 THE GROUNDS OF RESCISSION

Various grounds of rescission are recognized in Equity, by virtue of which the claimant's consent to enter into a transaction can be considered to have been impaired by virtue of some defect operating at the time the contract was made.

---

[104] *Erlanger v The New Sombrero Phosphate Co* (1878) 3 App Cas 1218, 1278 (Lord Blackburn); *Spence v Crawford* [1939] 3 All ER 271, 290 (Lord Wright); *O'Sullivan v Management Agency and Music Ltd* [1985] QB 428, 457 (Dunn LJ).

[105] See *Halpern v Halpern (No 2)* [2008] QB 88, [70] (Carnwath LJ). See further Section 1.6.2, p. 21.

[106] See e.g. Burrows, *The Law of Restitution*, 3rd edn (Oxford: Oxford University Press, 2011), p. 15.

[107] Judicature Act 1873, s. 25(11). See now Senior Courts Act 1981, s. 49.

[108] [2007] EWCA Civ 291, [2008] QB 88, [70].   [109] See further Section 21.6.4.(i), p. 646.

[110] O'Sullivan, Elliott, and Zakrzewski, *The Law of Rescission*, 2nd edn (Oxford: Oxford University Press, 2014), 10.13.   [111] Ibid., 10.22.

[112] This was assumed by Dyson LJ in *Islington LBC v UKCAC* [2006] EWCA Civ 340, [2006] 1 WLR 1303, [26]. See also O'Sullivan, Elliott, and Zakrzewski (n. 110), 11.57.

(i) Misrepresentation

A contract that was induced[113] by misrepresentation as to an existing fact[114] or as to the law[115] is voidable in Equity, regardless of whether the misrepresentation was fraudulent,[116] negligent, or innocent.[117] Where the representee enters into a contract with the defendant as the result of a misrepresentation made by a third party, that contract can be rescinded if the representee can establish that the defendant had actual or constructive notice of the misrepresentation.[118] So, for example, where a wife has been induced to agree to the matrimonial home being used as security for a loan made by a bank to her husband as a result of a misrepresentation made by the husband to the wife, the security transaction with the bank can be rescinded if it can be considered to have constructive notice of the misrepresentation, because the transaction is not, on its face, to the wife's advantage and there was a substantial risk that the husband had made a misrepresentation to induce the wife to enter into the transaction.[119] Where, however, the bank can show that it had taken reasonable steps to ensure that the wife had not been induced to act by a misrepresentation, the contract cannot be rescinded, such as where the bank receives confirmation from a solicitor that the wife received independent legal advice before she entered into the transaction.[120]

(ii) Mistake

Where a contract has been made as a result of a common mistake shared by the parties, the effect of which is that the non-existence of a state of affairs that was assumed to exist renders the performance of the contract impossible, the contract will be void at Common Law,[121] so there will be no role for rescission. Where one party has made a unilateral mistake as to the identity of the other party to the contract or the subject matter of the contract,[122] that contract will also be void;[123] and similarly where the mistake related to the terms of the contract, but only then if the other party knew of the mistake.[124]

For many years, there was an equitable jurisdiction to rescind a contract for a common mistake that was characterized as fundamental.[125] But this equitable jurisdiction was rejected by the Court of Appeal in *Great Peace Shipping Ltd v Tsavliris Salvage (International) Ltd*.[126] Certain cases decided before *Great Peace* had recognized an equitable jurisdiction to rescind a contract for a unilateral mistake where the other party had engaged in sharp practice or unconscionable conduct.[127] The existence of this jurisdiction to rescind for

---

[113] *Zurich Insurance Co plc v Hayward* [2016] UKSC 48, [2017] AC 142.

[114] *Spence v Crawford* [1939] 3 All ER 271.

[115] *Brennan v Bolt Burdon* [2004] EWCA Civ 1017, [2005] QB 303, 317 (Bodey J).

[116] *Derry v Peek* (1889) 14 App Cas 337, 374 (Lord Herschell). In *The National Crime Agency v Robb* [2014] EWHC 3484 (Ch), [2015] Ch 520, [5] Etherton C held that a transaction is voidable for fraud even though the transaction was initially legitimate and the fraud arose subsequently.

[117] *Redgrave v Hurd* (1881) 20 Ch D 1.   [118] *Barclays Bank plc v O'Brien* [1994] 1 AC 180.

[119] *Royal Bank of Scotland v Etridge (No 2)* [2001] UKHL 44, [2002] AC 773.   [120] Ibid.

[121] *Great Peace Shipping Ltd v Tsavliris Salvage (International) Ltd* [2002] EWCA Civ 1407, [2003] QB 679.

[122] *Raffles v Wichelhaus* (1864) 2 H & C 906.

[123] *Shogun Finance Ltd v Hudson* [2003] UKHL 62, [2004] 1 AC 919.

[124] *Hartog v Colin and Shields* [1939] 3 All ER 566.

[125] *Solle v Butcher* [1950] 1 KB 671; *Grist v Bailey* [1967] Ch 532.

[126] [2002] EWCA Civ 1407, [2003] QB 679.

[127] *OT Africa Ltd v Vickers plc* [1996] 1 Lloyd's Rep 700, 704 (Mance J); *Huyton v Dipasa* [2003] 2 Lloyd's Rep 780, 838 (Andrew Smith J). See also *Thames Trains Ltd v Adams* [2006] EWHC 3291, [56] (Nelson J), which was decided after *Great Peace*.

unilateral mistake in Equity was, however, rejected[128] and, following the decision in *Great Peace*, the preferable view is that there is no jurisdiction in Equity to rescind a contract for any mistake, whether common or unilateral,[129] although it remains possible to rescind a contract in Equity where a party's mistake was induced by a misrepresentation.[130] That a common fundamental mistake renders the contract void rather than voidable was criticized by the Court of Appeal in *Great Peace Shipping Ltd v Tsavliris Salvage Ltd*,[131] in which it was recognized that an equitable jurisdiction to grant rescission on terms for such a mistake would be preferable because it gives greater flexibility as to the appropriate result. It was considered, however, that it was a matter for Parliament rather than the courts to introduce such a flexible regime, by analogy with the Law Reform (Frustrated Contracts) Act 1943.

There continues to be an equitable jurisdiction to set aside deeds of gift and voluntary dispositions to trusts that have been made by mistake.[132] This jurisdiction is available only where the mistake was sufficiently serious and was of such gravity as to make it unjust for the donee to retain the property transferred.

(iii) Undue pressure

A contract is voidable at Common Law for duress when one party has exerted unlawful pressure to induce a contract to be made. In Equity, the doctrine of undue pressure is recognized where the defendant has threatened to do something lawful, but their conduct can be characterized as unconscionable, typically because of inequality between the parties so that the defendant can be considered to have taken unfair advantage of the claimant.[133] The lawful threat may be a threat to invoke the criminal process if a contract is not made, in circumstances under which the person who might be prosecuted has actually committed a crime,[134] or a threat to commence civil proceedings,[135] or to publish information.[136]

(iv) Undue influence

When the claimant can be considered to have entered into a contract with the defendant as the result of undue influence, the contract is voidable in Equity. The essential feature of undue influence is that the relationship between the defendant and the claimant is one of ascendancy and dependency,[137] and the defendant either abuses that relationship or is presumed to have abused it to induce the claimant to enter into a contract with them.

Undue influence will be established where the relationship between the claimant and the defendant was such that the claimant trusted and had confidence in the defendant,[138] the defendant exercised influence over the claimant, the exercise can be characterized as undue,[139] such as by tricking the claimant to enter into a contract, and the undue influence caused the claimant to enter into the contract.

---

[128] *Riverlate Properties Ltd v Paul* [1975] Ch 133, 144 (Russell LJ).

[129] *Statoil ASA v Louis Dreyfus Energy Services LP, The Harriette N* [2008] EWHC 2257 (Comm).

[130] See Section 21.6.3.(i), p. 641.   [131] [2002] EWCA Civ 1407, [2003] AC 679, [161].

[132] *Pitt v Holt* [2013] UKSC 26, [2013] 2 AC 108. See Section 9.3.3, p. 264.

[133] *Lloyd's Bank v Bundy* [1975] QB 326, 338–9 (Lord Denning MR).

[134] *Williams v Bayley* (1866) LR 1 HL 200.   [135] *Unwin v Leaper* (1840) 1 Man & G 747.

[136] *Norreys v Zeffert* [1939] 2 All ER 187.

[137] *Royal Bank of Scotland plc v Etridge (No 2)* [2001] UKHL 44, [2002] 2 AC 773, 795 (Lord Nicholls).

[138] *Morley v Laughnan* [1893] 1 Ch 736.

[139] *Dunbar Bank plc v Nadeem* [1998] 3 All ER 876, 883 (Millett LJ).

Where it is not possible for the claimant to establish that they were unduly influenced to enter into the contract, it may be possible to presume undue influence if two conditions are satisfied.[140] First, the relationship between the parties must be one of influence. Certain relationships are always treated as relationships of influence without the claimant needing to prove that they placed particular trust and confidence in the defendant, such as the relationship of solicitor and client.[141] Other relationships can be treated as relationships of influence on the facts by the claimant showing that they placed such a degree of trust and confidence in the defendant that they were under the defendant's influence, so that the defendant could take advantage of the claimant, such as the relationship between husband and wife[142] and between a junior employee and their employer's agent.[143] Secondly, the nature of the transaction must be such that it cannot reasonably be explained by the relationship of the parties.[144] It is this second condition that triggers the presumption that the influence which was presumed to have been exerted was undue,[145] because, for example, the terms of the transaction make it disadvantageous to the claimant, such as a sale at an undervalue[146] or a liability as surety beyond the means of the claimant.[147] Once the presumption of undue influence has been triggered, the burden shifts to the defendant to rebut it, by showing that the claimant entered into the contract voluntarily and was not induced to do so by the defendant's influence.[148] This might be established by showing that the claimant entered into the contract having obtained independent, relevant, and competent advice from a qualified person who was independent of any influence from the defendant,[149] and who advised that the claimant should enter into the contract, having explained the nature and effect of the transaction to them.[150]

Where the claimant has entered into a contract with the defendant as the result of undue influence exerted by a third party, as a general rule the contract cannot be rescinded, save in two circumstances:[151] first, where the defendant can be considered to have acted as agent for the third party; secondly, where the defendant had actual or constructive notice of the undue influence.[152] A defendant will have constructive notice if, having regard to the relationship between the parties, the transaction could not be explained by the ordinary motives of the parties. The defendant would then be put on inquiry about the possibility of undue influence.[153] If the defendant is put on inquiry, they will avoid being fixed with constructive notice of the undue influence only if the defendant had taken reasonable steps to ensure that the claimant was not affected by undue influence at the time the contract was signed. These reasonable steps would typically involve the defendant arranging a private meeting to ensure that the claimant was properly advised about the nature and effect of the transaction in the absence of the third party.[154]

---

[140] *Royal Bank of Scotland plc v Etridge (No 2)* [2001] UKHL 44, [2002] 2 AC 773, 796, (Lord Nicholls of Birkenhead).   [141] *Wright v Carter* [1903] 1 Ch 27.

[142] *Barclays Bank plc v O'Brien* [1994] 1 AC 180, 190 (Lord Browne-Wilkinson).

[143] *Crédit Lyonnais Bank Nederland NV v Burch* [1997] 1 All ER 144.

[144] *Royal Bank of Scotland plc v Etridge (No 2)* [2001] UKHL 44, [2002] 2 AC 773, 796 (Lord Nicholls).

[145] *BCCI v Aboody* [1990] 1 QB 923, 957 (Slade LJ).   [146] *Leeder v Stevens* [2005] EWCA Civ 50.

[147] *Crédit Lyonnais Bank Nederland NV v Burch* [1997] 1 All ER 144.

[148] *Allcard v Skinner* (1887) 36 Ch D 145, 171 (Cotton LJ).

[149] *Inche Noriah v Shaik Allie Bin Omar* [1929] AC 127, 135 (Lord Hailsham LC).

[150] *Niersmans v Pesticcio* [2004] EWCA Civ 372, [23] (Mummery LJ).

[151] *Royal Bank of Scotland plc v Etridge (No 2)* [2001] UKHL 44, [2002] 2 AC 773 [144] (Lord Scott). See also where the contract was induced by a third party's misrepresentation. See Section 21.6.3.(i), p. 641.

[152] *Barclays Bank plc v O'Brien* [1994] 1 AC 180.

[153] *Chater v Mortgage Agency Services Number Two Ltd* [2003] EWCA Civ 490, [67] (Scott Baker LJ).

[154] *Royal Bank of Scotland plc v Etridge (No 2)* [2001] UKHL 44, [2002] 2 AC 773.

(v) Unconscionable conduct

Contracts can be rescinded in Equity where the claimant's consent to enter into the contract can be considered to have been procured by unconscionable conduct,[155] or what is sometimes described as constructive or equitable fraud.[156] Unlike the ground of undue influence, a contract can be rescinded for unconscionable conduct without needing to identify an existing relationship of influence or dependency between the parties. Unconscionable conduct will be established where the defendant has unconscientiously exploited their superior bargaining position to the detriment of the claimant who is in a much weaker position.[157]

The defendant will be considered to have unconscionably exploited the claimant if the following conditions are satisfied:

(1) The claimant suffered from a special disability or disadvantage that placed them in a disadvantageous position as against the defendant, so that there was a reasonable degree of inequality between the parties.[158] This includes: contracts made with somebody who is poor and ignorant,[159] although this is now interpreted as meaning a member of a lower income group and somebody who is less highly educated;[160] contracts made with expectant heirs who expect to receive an inheritance in the future, and who are particularly vulnerable to exploitation by virtue of inexperience and immaturity;[161] and contracts made with people suffering from infirmity of body or mind, or some other disadvantage, which has been held to encompass a claimant who was illiterate and had a poor command of English.[162] Exceptionally, a gross inequality of bargaining power between the parties may also constitute a special disadvantage.[163] Such inequality may even arise in a purely commercial context.[164]

(2) The defendant acted unconscionably[165] in exploiting the claimant's disadvantage in a morally culpable manner, having regard to the defendant's knowledge of that disadvantage. This is a requirement of procedural unconscionability. But simple exploitation of the inequality of bargaining power between the parties is not sufficient.[166] The defendant needs to have acted in a morally reprehensible manner,[167] either because they actually knew of the claimant's special disability or disadvantage, or should have known this since the defendant was aware of particular facts that would have put the reasonable person on notice that the claimant had a special disability or disadvantage.[168] In *Hart v O'Connor*[169] the Privy Council recognized that a transaction for the sale of land could not be set aside, even though the vendor was suffering from senile dementia, because the purchaser was unaware of her condition and there was nothing to put him on notice of it, since it appeared that the vendor was acting in accordance with the most full and careful

---

[155] *Hart v O'Connor* [1985] AC 1000; *Crédit Lyonnais Bank Nederland NV v Burch* [1997] 1 All ER 144, 151 (Nourse LJ).　　　　　　　　　[156] *Earl of Chesterfield v Janssen* (1751) 2 Ves Sen 125, 157 (Lord Hardwicke).

[157] *Lloyd's Bank Ltd v Bundy* [1975] QB 326, 337 (Lord Denning MR).

[158] *Cresswell v Potter* [1978] 1 WLR 255n.

[159] *Fry v Lane* (1888) 40 Ch D 312. See also *Evans v Llewllin* (1787) 1 Cox 333.

[160] *Cresswell v Potter* [1978] 1 WLR 255n; *Portman Building Society v Dusangh* [2000] EWCA Civ 142, [2000] 2 All ER (Comm) 221.　　　　　　　　　[161] *Earl of Aylesford v Morris* (1873) LR 8 Ch App 484.

[162] *Singla v Bashir* [2002] EWHC 883, [7] (Park J).

[163] *Backhouse v Backhouse* [1978] 1 WLR 243 (divorcing couple).

[164] *Multiservice Bookbinding Ltd v Marden* [1979] Ch 84, 110 (Browne-Wilkinson J).

[165] *Alec Lobb (Garages) Ltd v Total Oil Great Britain Ltd* [1985] 1 WLR 173, 182 (Dillon LJ).

[166] *National Westminster Bank plc v Morgan* [1985] AC 686, 708 (Lord Scarman).

[167] *Yorkshire Bank plc v Tinsley* [2004] EWCA Civ 816, [2004] 1 WLR 2380.

[168] *Owen and Gutch v Homan* (1853) 4 HLC 997, 1035 (Lord Cranworth LC).　　　　[169] [1985] AC 1000.

legal advice. The potential for abuse as regards contracts with the poor and ignorant and with expectant heirs might be so great that unconscionability on the part of the defendant may even be presumed, at least where the transaction is oppressive, such as a sale at a significant undervalue.[170]

(3) The contract must have been overreaching and oppressive, rather than simply harsh or improvident.[171] This means that the conscience of the court must be shocked, for example because a contract of sale was at a substantial undervalue. This requirement focuses on the substantive unconscionability of the transaction.

The contract will not be voidable where the defendant can establish that it was fair, just, and reasonable.[172] The defendant will be able to establish this by showing, for example, that the claimant had obtained independent legal advice, since this places the parties on equal terms.[173] But obtaining such advice will be relevant only if its effect really is to place the parties on equal terms. So, for example, in *Boustany v Piggott*,[174] a renegotiated lease was set aside by reason of the defendant's unconscionable conduct, even though the disadvantages of the transaction had been forcibly pointed out to the claimant by a barrister, because the defendant was present and was taking advantage of the claimant whilst the advice was taken.

Where the claimant is induced to enter into a transaction with the defendant as a result of the unconscionable conduct of a third party, and the defendant's own conduct cannot be characterized as unconscionable, the defendant will be able to enforce the transaction unless they had notice, whether actual or constructive, of the claimant's equity to set the transaction aside.[175] So, for example, if an employer induces an employee to provide security for the employer's debts in favour of a bank and this can be characterized as unconscionable by virtue of the employer's conduct, the bank will still be able to enforce the security unless it has notice of the employer's impropriety.[176]

(vi) Breach of fiduciary duty

Any contract made in breach of fiduciary duty is liable to be rescinded in Equity.[177] So, for example, where a fiduciary breaches the self-dealing rule by dealing on behalf of themself and the principal in the same transaction,[178] that transaction is voidable,[179] so that the principal can rescind it without needing to prove that the transaction was unfair,[180] except where the fiduciary has obtained the consent of the court or the fully informed consent of the principal to the transaction.[181] Similarly, where the fair-dealing rule is breached, where the fiduciary contracts with the principal in their own right, the contract will be voidable,[182] except where the fiduciary can show that they took no advantage of the fiduciary

---

[170] *Fry v Lane* (1888) 40 Ch D 312, 321 (Kay J); *Alec Lobb (Garages) Ltd v Total Oil Great Britain Ltd* [1985] 1 WLR 173, 182 (Dillon LJ).

[171] *Portman Building Society v Dusangh* [2000] EWCA Civ 142, [2000] 2 All ER (Comm) 221.

[172] *Earl of Aylesford v Morris* (1873) LR 8 Ch App 484, 491 (Lord Selborne LC).

[173] *Fry v Lane* (1888) 40 Ch D 312.   [174] (1993) 69 P & CR 298.

[175] See *Yorkshire Bank plc v Tinsley* [2004] EWCA Civ 816, [2004] 1 WLR 2380.

[176] See *Crédit Lyonnais Nederland NV v Burch* [1997] 1 All ER 144, 153 (Millett LJ).

[177] See Section 15.7.1, p. 451.

[178] *Tito v Waddell (No 2)* [1977] Ch 106, 241 (Sir Robert Megarry V-C). See Section 15.5.3.(i), p. 433.

[179] *Holder v Holder* [1968] 1 Ch 353, 398.

[180] *Tito v Waddell (No 2)* [1977] Ch 106, 241 (Sir Robert Megarry V-C).

[181] *Ex p James* (1803) 8 Ves 337, 353 (Lord Eldon LC); *Tito v Waddell (No 2)* [1977] 1 Ch 106, 225 (Megarry V-C).

[182] *Re Cape Breton Co* (1885) 29 Ch D 795, 803 (Cotton LJ); *Burland v Earle* [1902] AC 83, 99 (Lord Davey). See Section 15.5.3.(ii), p. 435.

position, that the transaction was fair,[183] and that there had been full disclosure of every-thing that was or might be material to the principal's decision to enter into the transaction.[184] Where a principal is induced to enter into a contract with a third party as a result of the fiduciary being bribed by the third party, the contract may be voidable in Equity by virtue of breach of the no-conflict rule,[185] there being an irrebuttable presumption that the agent was influenced by the bribe.[186] The contract will be voidable, however, only if the third party knew[187] that the principal was deprived of the fiduciary's disinterested advice;[188] that the principal neither knew nor consented to the payment to the fiduciary;[189] and that the bribe was paid or mentioned before the contract was made.[190]

21.6.4 THE BARS TO RESCISSION

Various bars to rescission have been recognized that generally apply regardless of the ground for rescission and regardless of whether rescission occurs at Common Law or in Equity, although the bars are interpreted more restrictively in Equity than at Common Law. In addition, where rescission is sought in Equity, the court has a discretion as to whether the remedy will be awarded and that discretion will not be exercised if the consequences of rescission are considered to be unfair and disproportionate[191] or if the party seeking rescission does not come to the court 'with clean hands'.[192]

(i) Complete restoration not possible

Rescission will be barred if it would not be possible to restore the defendant to the position in which they were before the contract was made.[193] This is also called the bar of *restitutio in integrum* being impossible. The justification for this bar is both to ensure that the claimant is not unjustly enriched at the expense of the defendant,[194] which would occur if the claimant were able to recover benefits from the defendant, but were not required to restore benefits to the defendant, and also to protect the defendant from being in a worse position following the rescission of the contract than they occupied before the contract was made. In Equity, the bar can be justified by reference to the maxim that 'Those who seek Equity must do Equity'.[195]

Although this bar is often described as requiring both parties to be restored to their pre-contractual position,[196] the doctrine operates as a bar to rescission only when the

---

[183] *Moody v Cox and Hatt* [1917] 2 Ch 71; *Tito v Waddell (No 2)* [1977] Ch 106, 241 (Megarry V-C).

[184] *Demerara Bauxite Co Ltd v Hubbard* [1923] AC 673.

[185] *Logicrose Ltd v Southend United Football Club* [1988] 1 WLR 1256, 1260 (Millett J).

[186] *Hovenden and Sons v Millhof* (1900) 83 LT 41, 43 (Romer LJ).

[187] This includes wilful blindness: *Logicrose Ltd v Southend United Football Club* [1988] 1 WLR 1256, 1261 (Millett J).   [188] Ibid.

[189] *Ross River Ltd v Cambridge City Football Club Ltd* [2007] EWHC 2115 (Ch), [2008] 1 All ER 1004, [203] (Briggs J).   [190] Ibid., at [228] (Briggs J).

[191] *Hurstanger Ltd v Wilson* [2007] EWCA Civ 299, [2007] 1 WLR 2351.

[192] *Royal Bank of Scotland Plc v Highland Financial Partners LP* [2013] EWCA Civ 328, at [158] (Aikens LJ). See *UBS AG (London Branch) v Kommunale Wasserwerke Leipzig GmbH* [2014] EWHC 3615 (Comm), at [703] (Males J).

[193] *Clarke v Dickson* (1858) El Bl & El 148; *Spence v Crawford* [1939] 3 All ER 271, 288–9 (Lord Wright); *Smith New Court Securities Ltd v Scrimgeour Vickers (Asset Management) Ltd* [1994] 1 WLR 1271, 1280 (Nourse LJ); *Halpern v Halpern (Nos 1 and 2)* [2007] EWCA Civ 291, [2008] QB 195.

[194] *Spence v Crawford* [1939] 3 All ER 271, 288–9 (Lord Wright).

[195] *O'Sullivan v Management Agency and Music Ltd* [1985] 1 QB 428, 458 (Dunn LJ). See further Section 2.4, p. 30.

[196] See e.g. *Erlanger v The New Sombrero Phosphate Co* (1878) 3 App Cas 1218, 1278 (Lord Blackburn).

defendant cannot be restored to their original position.[197] The fact that a claimant cannot be restored to their pre-contractual position precisely will not bar rescission,[198] presumably because the claimant has elected to rescind the contract and takes the risk of not being restored. If the defendant can be restored to their original position but the claimant is unwilling to do so, rescission will be barred.[199]

At Common Law this bar is interpreted very strictly, so that if the defendant cannot be restored precisely to the position in which they were before entering into the contract, rescission will be barred.[200] So, for example, if the claimant has consumed or disposed of property that was received from the defendant under a voidable contract, the claimant will be barred from rescinding the contract because the property cannot be restored, such as where documents have been received under the contract that are then destroyed.[201] The reason why the requirement to make *restitutio in integrum* is interpreted so strictly at Common Law is that the Common Law lacks the adjudicative machinery to make financial adjustments on rescission, so that it is unable to value benefits received.[202] But this strict interpretation is also a function of the nature of rescission at Common Law, which occurs automatically once the claimant has given notice of their intention to rescind without judicial intervention, so that there is no scope for the operation of judicial discretion to authorize substantial restoration of the defendant to their pre-contractual position.

The bar of complete restoration not being possible is interpreted more flexibly in Equity, both because Equity has the adjudicative mechanism with which to make financial adjustments and because these adjustments can be effected through the exercise of judicial discretion. It is sufficient that the defendant can be restored substantially to their pre-contractual position, by reference to a more flexible criterion of 'practical justice'.[203] It follows that the bar of *restitutio in integrum* being impossible is of much more limited significance in Equity. Equity effects this substantial restoration by directing accounts and making allowances.[204]

It is possible for the court to value the benefit that has been received by the claimant and to ensure that the defendant is restored to their original position financially, if not precisely. So, rescission will still be possible in Equity where the defendant had transferred property to the claimant who had disposed of or destroyed it,[205] or where services had been provided by the defendant to the claimant,[206] because the claimant will be required to pay to the defendant the reasonable value of the property or service, as assessed at the time the order for rescission is made. So, for example, in *Erlanger v New Sombrero Phosphate Co*[207] the claimant sought to rescind a contract for the purchase of a phosphate mine on the ground of non-disclosure of a material fact by the defendant. Since the mine had been worked by the claimant, it was held that the contract could be rescinded only if the claimant returned the mine to the defendant and accounted for the profits made from working it. Lord Blackburn recognized that a court of Equity would grant relief 'whenever, by the

---

[197] *Spence v Crawford* [1939] 3 All ER 271, 289 (Lord Wright).

[198] Ibid., 279 (Lord Thankerton); *Halpern v Halpern* [2007] EWCA Civ 291, [2008] QB 195, [75] (Carnwath LJ).

[199] *Gamatronic (UK) Ltd v Hamilton* [2016] EWHC 2225 (QB), [224] (Akhlaq Choudhury QC).

[200] *Erlanger v The New Sombrero Phosphate Co* (1878) 3 App Cas 1218, 1278 (Lord Blackburn).

[201] See *Halpern v Halpern (Nos 1 and 2)* [2007] EWCA Civ 291, [2008] QB 195.

[202] *Erlanger v The New Sombrero Phosphate Co* (1878) 3 App Cas 1218, 1278 (Lord Blackburn); cf. *Smith New Court Securities Ltd v Scrimgeour Vickers (Asset Management) Ltd* [1997] AC 254, 262 (Lord Browne-Wilkinson); and *Halpern v Halpern (Nos 1 and 2)* [2007] EWCA Civ 291, [2008] QB 195, [74] (Carnwath LJ).

[203] *Erlanger v New Sombrero Phosphate Co* (1878) 3 App Cas 1218, 1278 (Lord Blackburn).

[204] *Cheese v Thomas* [1994] 1 WLR 129, 136 (Sir Donald Nicholls V-C).

[205] *Erlanger v New Sombrero Phosphate Co* (1878) 3 App Cas 1218, 1278 (Lord Blackburn).

[206] *O'Sullivan v Management Agency and Music Ltd* [1985] 1 QB 428.   [207] (1878) 3 App Cas 1218.

use of its powers, it can do what is practically just, though it cannot restore the parties precisely to the state they were in before the contract'.[208] In the exercise of this power, the court will also be prepared to grant the defendant an allowance in respect of the deterioration in value of any property that is returned to them, to compensate the defendant for any loss suffered,[209] or to compensate the defendant for incurring a liability to a third party,[210] in each case to ensure that the defendant is restored to their pre-contractual position. In *Salt v Stratstone Specialist Ltd*[211] it was recognized that a contract for the purchase of a car could be rescinded for misrepresentation that the car was new, even though title to the car had been registered with the claimant, because the *restitutio in integrum* bar was concerned with changes in the car as a physical entity, rather than its legal condition. Further, the fact that the car had depreciated in value or the claimant had intermittently used it did not bar rescission, but could be reflected in a compensatory award for the other party if practical justice required this.[212]

Rescission will, however, be barred in Equity if it is not possible to restore the defendant to their pre-contractual position because it is not possible to value the property or the service that had been transferred with any degree of accuracy, or because the property that had been transferred to the claimant had changed in its nature so that it is no longer identifiable in any reasonable sense.[213] So, for example, in *Thomas Witter Ltd v TBP Industries Ltd*[214] rescission was barred as being impractical where a company had been sold to the claimant, but the nature of the business changed from being the operator of licensed premises to a property holding company and there had been numerous changes of staff.

(ii) Affirmation

The right to rescission will be waived if the person entitled to rescind elects to waive the right and affirms the contract. A contract will have been affirmed only if the claimant knew of the circumstances that enabled them to rescind the transaction and knew of the legal right to rescind,[215] or deliberately decided not to investigate these rights.[216] The claimant must have unequivocally manifested an intention to affirm the contract[217] once they were free from the effects of the vitiating factor that gave rise to the right to rescind in the first place. The bar of affirmation applies regardless of the effect of the affirmation on the defendant, who is not required to prove any detrimental reliance on the act of affirmation or even awareness that it had occurred, since affirmation depends on an objective manifestation of a choice to affirm by the party who has a right to rescind.[218]

(iii) Lapse of time

The claimant may be barred from rescinding a contract if a substantial period of time has elapsed before they sought to rescind it.[219] What constitutes a substantial period of time is a question of fact that depends on the particular circumstances of the case. The time

---

[208] Ibid., 1278.

[209] *Erlanger v New Sombrero Phosphate Co* (1878) 3 App Cas 1218, 1278 (Lord Blackburn); *Lagunas Nitrate Co v Lagunas Syndicate* [1899] 2 Ch 392, 457 (Rigby LJ).

[210] *Spence v Crawford* [1939] 3 All ER 271, 283 (Lord Thankerton).

[211] [2015] EWCA Civ .745, [2015] 2 CLC 269.   [212] Ibid., [24] (Longmore LJ).

[213] *Spence v Crawford* [1939] 3 All ER 271, 279 (Lord Thankerton).

[214] [1996] 2 All ER 573, 587 (Jacob J).   [215] *Evans v Bartlam* [1937] AC 473, 479 (Lord Atkin).

[216] *Allcard v Skinner* (1887) 36 Ch D 145, 188 (Lindley LJ) and 192 (Bowen LJ).

[217] *Clough v London and North Western Rly Co* (1871) LR 7 Exch 26, 34 (Mellor J); *Abram Steamship Co Ltd v Westville Shipping Co Ltd* [1923] AC 773, 789 (Lord Atkinson).

[218] *ICCI Ltd v The Royal Hotel Ltd* [1998] Lloyd's Rep IR 151, 163 (Mance J).

[219] *Leaf v International Galleries* [1950] 2 KB 86.

should begin to run only once the claimant was aware of the material facts that trigger the ground of rescission[220] and where the claimant is free from the effects of any pressure or exploitation.[221] This bar is recognized because it is unreasonable and unjust for the claimant to seek to rescind a contract after a substantial period of time has passed, since delay enables the claimant to speculate whether it is beneficial for them to rescind the contract.[222]

(iv) Third-party rights

Rescission is also traditionally barred where the effect of rescission of the contract made by the claimant and the defendant would be to harm the rights of third parties.[223] In particular, the right of rescission will be barred if a third party subsequently acquires a legal[224] interest in property that was transferred to the defendant under a voidable contract, where the third party acquired the property for value and without notice of the defect that provides the reason for the claimant wishing to rescind it.

The existence of the third-party rights bar is difficult to defend. Whilst it is clear that, if a third party has acquired proprietary rights in good faith and for value, the claimant should not be able to bring a claim against the third party to recover the property,[225] it does not necessarily follow that the acquisition of third-party proprietary rights should prevent the claimant from rescinding the contract with the defendant[226] and so protect the defendant. Although an effect of rescission is traditionally to revest title in property to the claimant, it would not be appropriate for rescission to have this effect where a third party has acquired rights in the property transferred for value; the security of the third party's receipt is then paramount. But there is no reason why this should bar rescission completely, since rescission has other consequences, such as to avoid future contractual obligations and to enable the claimant to recover the value of the property transferred to the defendant, but this can still occur and the third party's proprietary right can be left unaffected.[227]

(v) Damages in lieu of rescission

Whilst the bars that have been considered so far are of general application regardless of the ground for rescission, there is one specific bar that is potentially applicable only where a contract has been induced by non-fraudulent misrepresentation. In such circumstances, section 2(2) of the Misrepresentation Act 1967 provides that the court has a discretion to declare that the contract subsists and to award damages in lieu of rescission. This discretionary bar to rescission can apply only where rescission would otherwise be available and where the court considers it equitable to award damages instead of rescinding the contract.

The court has jurisdiction only to award damages in lieu of rescission where the contract has been induced by a non-fraudulent misrepresentation[228] and the claimant must still be entitled to rescind the contract, so the jurisdiction to award damages will not be available

---

[220] At least where the ground of rescission involves fraud: *Redgrave v Hurd* (1881) 20 Ch D 1, 13 (Sir George Jessel MR). In *Leaf v International Galleries* [1950] 2 KB 86 the claim for rescission on the ground of innocent misrepresentation was barred after five years, even though the claimant had not been aware that a misrepresentation had been made for most of that time. It is difficult to characterize the delay in such circumstances as unreasonable.   [221] *Allcard v Skinner* (1887) 36 Ch D 145, 192 (Bowen LJ).

[222] *Erlanger v The New Sombrero Phosphate Co* (1878) 3 App Cas 1218, 1279 (Lord Blackburn).

[223] *Tennent v The City of Glasgow Bank and Liquidators* (1879) 4 App Cas 615, 621 (Earl Cairns LC).

[224] *Phillips v Brooks Ltd* [1919] 2 KB 243.   [225] See Section 19.5.1, p. 584.

[226] Nahan, 'Rescission: a case for rejecting the classical model?' (1997) 27 Univ WALR 66, 74.

[227] Häcker, 'Rescission and third party rights' [2006] RLR 21, 36.

[228] *Government of Zanzibar v British Aerospace (Lancaster House) Ltd* [2000] 1 WLR 2333, 2342 (Judge Raymond Jack QC).

if rescission is barred.[229] Section 2(2) of the Misrepresentation Act 1967 identifies certain factors that should be considered by the court when determining whether it is equitable to award damages instead of rescission—namely, the nature of the misrepresentation, the loss to the representee if the contract were not rescinded, and the loss to the representor that would arise from rescission. The court may declare the contract to be subsisting even though the claimant has suffered no relevant loss, so that no damages will be awarded in lieu of rescission.[230]

21.6.5 THE CONSEQUENCES OF RESCISSION

(i) Termination of the transaction

The most significant consequence of the transaction being rescinded is that it is treated as void *ab initio*, meaning that the transaction is treated as though it had never taken place. It follows that all future obligations arising under a contract which has been rescinded should be treated as terminated, and any liabilities which had already accrued but not yet performed would no longer be enforceable. Consequently, if the transaction triggered a tax liability but the transaction is subsequently rescinded, the liability to pay tax is discharged as well.[231] Although these are fundamental consequences of the contract being treated as never having been made, the implications of this are sometimes ignored. For example, in *Hardy v Griffiths*[232] it was held that rescission of a contract for the sale of land did not vitiate the purchaser's liability to pay a deposit, because the vendor's right to receive the deposit had already accrued before rescission. The only possible justification for this conclusion is that the contract had not actually been rescinded but had been discharged for breach, the effect of which being that obligations which had accrued before breach would continue to subsist.

Where a transaction is rescinded, the orthodox approach is that it can be set aside only in its entirety and not partially so that some of it remains effective,[233] even if the claimant would have entered into the contract, albeit on different terms, had there not been an operating vitiating factor. For example, in *TSB Bank plc v Camfield*[234] a mortgage was set aside completely as a result of a husband's misrepresentation to his wife and was not treated as valid to the extent of the liability that the wife had intended to accept. Although this reflects the orthodox position as regards rescission of a contract, more recent cases have shown a willingness to rescind a non-contractual voluntary transaction in part only. For example, it has been recognized that it is possible to rescind a self-contained and severable part of a voluntary transaction, such as a disposition to a trust made by a deed which is voidable for mistake.[235] This has been justified on the unconvincing ground that in such a transaction there is no need to restore both parties to their pre-transaction position, since, being a voluntary disposition, only the recipient will have received a benefit. Further, in *Bainbridge v Bainbridge*[236] it was recognized that, where various properties had been

---

[229] *William Sindall plc v Cambridgeshire County Council* [1994] 1 WLR 1016, 1044 (Evans LJ); *Salt v Stratstone Specialist Ltd* [2015] EWCA Civ 745, [2015] 2 CLC 269, [17] (Longmore LJ).

[230] *Huyton SA v Distribuidora Internacional de Productos Agricolas SA de CV* [2003] 2 Lloyd's Rep 780, 846.

[231] *AC v DC* [2012] EWHC 2032, [2013] WTLR 745.   [232] [2014] EWHC 3947 (Ch), [2015] Ch 417.

[233] *TSB Bank plc v Camfield* [1995] 1 WLR 430, 436 (Nourse LJ); *Kennedy v Kennedy* [2014] EWHC 4129 (Ch), [2015] WTLR 837, [46] (Etherton C).

[234] [1995] 1 WLR 430. In Australia, partial rescission is accepted: *Vadasz v Pioneer Concrete (SA) Pty Ltd* (1995) 184 CLR 102.

[235] *Kennedy v Kennedy* [2014] EWHC 4129 (Ch), [2015] WTLR 837, [46] (Etherton C).

[236] [2016] EWHC 898 (Ch), [2016] WTLR 943.

voluntarily transferred to the defendant to be held on trust, it was possible to rescind the disposition for mistake in respect of one property only, since that disposition was severable from the others. It appears that the reason why a contract can only be rescinded entirely and not in part is because the courts should not seek to impose a different contract to the one which the parties had made, whereas this objection does not apply to rescission of a non-contractual voluntary transaction.[237] But, even though a contract cannot be rescinded partially for fear of imposing a different contract on the parties, it is possible instead to rescind a contract on terms in Equity. This is different because it involves the contract being rescinded completely, but the court imposing terms as a condition of this rescission being ordered. Such terms may include that a new, fairer contract replaces the original one,[238] or that losses arising from the contract are allocated between the parties.[239] The recognition of this equitable jurisdiction more generally to enable rescission on terms would mean that, for example, if the claimant entered into a transaction as a result of misrepresentation, thinking that they had entered into a surety transaction for £5,000, but in fact the transaction was for £50,000, the original surety transaction should be rescinded, but terms could be imposed that a £5,000 surety transaction should be substituted, since this is the amount that the claimant actually consented to guarantee. The effect of this would actually be to rescind the contract partially, and thus impose a different contract on the parties, although the mechanism adopted would be complete rescission of the contract and then judicial construction of a new contract. Such flexibility of rescission would be consistent with the rationale of rescission in Equity, which is to seek practical justice,[240] and so rescission on terms that might effect partial rescission should be recognized in Equity.

It is not possible to rescind a contract made as a result of breach of fiduciary duty where the other party to the contract did not participate in the conduct which constitutes the vitiating factor. So, for example, if Adam enters into a contract with Brenda as a result of a fraudulent misrepresentation made by Clive, the contract cannot be rescinded.[241] Adam will instead have a claim in deceit against Clive. Similarly, if Clive is Adam's agent and negotiates a contract with Brenda following receipt of a bribe from David, who has no connection with Brenda, the contract cannot be rescinded, and Adam will be confined to a claim for breach of fiduciary duty against Clive.[242]

(ii) Restitution to prevent unjust enrichment

It is a fundamental consequence of rescission that the parties are restored to their pre-contractual position. It follows that the defendant must make restitution to the claimant of any benefits that they had received pursuant to the transaction, and the claimant will be required to make counter-restitution to the defendant of the value of any benefit that the claimant has received.[243] The relevant benefit might be money,[244] goods,[245] or services.[246]

---

[237] *Kennedy v Kennedy* [2014] EWHC 4129 (Ch), [2015] WTLR 837, [46] (Etherton C).

[238] In some of the cases on rescission in Equity for mistake, the claimant was permitted to rescind the transaction, but only on condition that a new contract was made: *Solle v Butcher* [1950] 1 KB 671 and *Grist v Bailey* [1967] Ch 532. Today, rescission in Equity would not be allowed for mistake in such cases: *Great Peace Shipping Ltd v Tsavliris Salvage (International) Ltd* [2002] EWCA Civ 1407, [2003] QB 679. See Section 21.6.3.(ii), p. 641.   [239] *Cheese v Thomas* [1994] 1 WLR 129.

[240] *Erlanger v The New Sombrero Phosphate Co* (1878) 3 App Cas 1218, 1278 (Lord Blackburn).

[241] *Pulsford v Richards* (1857) 17 Beav 87.

[242] *Chancery Client Partners Ltd v MRC 957 Ltd* [2016] EWHC 2142 (Ch).

[243] *Clough v London and North Western Railway Co* (1871) LR 7 Ex 26, 37 (Mellor J).

[244] *Erlanger v New Sombrero Phosphate Co* (1878) 3 App Cas 1218.

[245] *Mahoney v Purnell* [1996] 3 All ER 61.

[246] *O'Sullivan v Management Agency and Music Ltd* [1985] AC 686.

Since rescission in Equity occurs by order of the court, restitution and counter-restitution of the value of benefits transferred will be required as a condition of the contract being rescinded, so a separate claim in unjust enrichment will not need to be pursued. But the requirement to make restitution and counter-restitution can still be analysed in terms of the need to prevent one party being unjustly enriched at the expense of the other.

(iii) Vindication of proprietary rights

Where one party has transferred an asset to the other party pursuant to a contract that is voidable, legal title to the asset will still be transferred to the other party.[247] Where a contract is rescinded in Equity, the court will recognize that the party who sought rescission has an equitable proprietary interest in the property that was transferred to the defendant, who will consequently hold this property on trust for the rescinding party.[248] This trust is preferably characterized as a constructive trust.[249] Since rescission in Equity takes effect only on the order of the court, it follows that the claimant has no equitable proprietary interest in the asset until the court order is made, which will then have the effect of vesting equitable title in the claimant, who can then recover the property.[250] Before the court order is made, the claimant has only a mere equity to rescind the contract, which creates an entitlement to the equitable relief that is conferred by the order of the court.[251] It has, however, been recognized that, where the contract was induced by fraud, the claimant will obtain an equitable proprietary interest in the property transferred from the time at which they make the election to rescind.[252] Where the claimant has paid money to the defendant having been fraudulently induced by the defendant to enter into a contract to do so, following the election to rescind the contract, the claimant will have an immediate proprietary claim to the money.[253]

The equity to rescind that enables the claimant to recover property on rescission is preferably treated as an inchoate proprietary right.[254] The equity to rescind can be enforced against any party who receives the property from the defendant, other than a bona fide purchaser for value; it is a right that can be left in a will and passes on death; it can be traced through substitute property.[255] Once rescission is barred so that the contract can no longer be set aside, the equity to rescind will be defeated and the claimant will not be able to assert a proprietary claim to recover property.[256]

(iv) Indemnity

A further consequence of rescission of the contract in Equity is that both parties to the contract acquire a right to be indemnified for any detriment or disadvantage that they suffered under the contract, but only where they were required to suffer the detriment or

---

[247] *Load v Green* (1846) 15 M & W 216, 221 (Parke B).

[248] *Lonrho plc v Fayed (No 2)* [1992] 1 WLR 1, 11–12 (Millett J); *El Ajou v Dollar Land Holdings plc* [1993] 3 All ER 717, 734 (Millett J); *Bristol and West Building Society v Mothew* [1998] Ch 1, 22–3 (Millett LJ); *Shalson v Russo* [2003] EWHC 1637 (Ch), [2005] Ch 281, 316, [122] (Rimer J); *Bainbridge v Bainbridge* [2016] EWHC 898 (Ch), [2016] WTLR 943, [32] (Master Matthews).

[249] *The National Crime Agency v Robb* [2014] EWHC 4384 (Ch), [2015] Ch 520 [49] (Etherton C). See Section 9.3.2, p. 263.   [250] *Bristol and West Building Society v Mothew* [1998] 1 Ch 1, 23 (Millett LJ).

[251] *Phillips v Phillips* (1861) 4 De GF & J 208, 218 (Lord Westbury).

[252] *Shalson v Russo* [2003] EWHC 1637 (Ch), [2005] Ch 281, 316, [122] (Rimer J).

[253] *El Ajou v Dollar Land Holdings plc* [1993] 3 All ER 717, 735 (Millett J); *Bank Tejarat v Hong Kong and Shanghai Bank* [1995] 1 Lloyd's Rep 239, 248 (Tuckey J); *Shalson v Russo* [2003] EWHC 1637 (Ch), [2005].

[254] O'Sullivan, Elliott, and Zakrzewski (see n. 110), 16.40.

[255] *Bainbridge v Bainbridge* [2016] EWHC 898 (Ch), [2016] WTLR 943.

[256] *Lonrho plc v Fayed (No 2)* [1992] 1 WLR 1, 12 (Millett J).

disadvantage by the contract. For example, if either party incurred a necessary expense in performing the contract, or conferred a benefit on another or incurred a liability to another under the contract, that party can be indemnified by the other for the value of the benefit or the liability incurred.[257]

(v) Compensation

Where one party has suffered loss in carrying out the contract, then, as a function of the need to restore the parties substantially to their pre-contractual position, the other party will be required to compensate for this loss. So, for example, the claimant can recover compensation for improvements or repairs to property purchased under the contract.[258] Where the claimant is required by the contract to make such repairs or improvements, they will be able to seek an indemnity for the cost of the work; compensation for loss will be available where the claimant was not contractually obliged to do the work.

(vi) Apportionment of loss

Although, normally, a consequence of rescission is to require one party to make restitution of gains to the other, there will sometimes be circumstances under which the contract has resulted in a loss and the court may seek to allocate the loss between the parties. This is illustrated by *Cheese v Thomas*,[259] in which a contract for the joint purchase of a house was rescinded for undue influence. Both the claimant and the defendant had contributed to the purchase of the property, which had fallen in value. Rather than setting aside the transaction in its entirety and requiring the defendant to make restitution of the claimant's contribution, the court imposed a condition on rescission—namely, that the loss should be apportioned between the parties in proportion to their contribution to the purchase price. This was justified because the parties were considered to have entered into a joint venture so that they should be treated as equal participants and so share the loss between them, although this joint-venture analysis is difficult to defend because the defendant's presumed undue influence meant that the parties should have been treated as unequal participants.

(vii) Concurrent claims

A claimant who seeks rescission may also have a concurrent claim in Equity for wrongdoing, typically for breach of fiduciary duty for which a pecuniary award may be made to compensate the claimant for loss suffered as a result of the breach of duty, such as consequential financial loss.[260] If rescission is barred, the claimant could simply seek equitable compensation for the wrong.[261]

Where a fiduciary has entered into a contract on behalf of the principal in breach of fiduciary duty and obtains a profit as a result, if the contract is rescinded, the fiduciary will also be liable to account for the profits made in breach of fiduciary duty. Where, however, the contract cannot be rescinded because one of the bars to rescission applies, it has been recognized that the fiduciary cannot be liable to account for profits made from breach of fiduciary duty, at least where the fiduciary sold property to the principal that they had

---

[257] *Whittington v Seale-Hayne* (1900) 82 LT 49, 51 (Farwell LJ).

[258] *Ex p Bennett* (1805) 10 Ves 381, 400 (Lord Eldon LC); *Lagunas Nitrate Co v Lagunas Syndicate* [1899] 2 Ch 293, 456 (Rigby LJ). [259] [1994] 1 WLR 129.

[260] *Nocton v Lord Ashburton* [1914] AC 932; *Mahoney v Purnell* [1996] 3 All ER 61; *Swindle v Harrison* [1997] 4 All ER 705, 718 (Evans LJ), 726 (Hobhouse LJ), and 733 (Mummery LJ); *Bristol and West Building Society v Mothew* [1998] Ch 1, 17 (Millett LJ). See Section 18.4, p. 523.

[261] *JJ Harrison (Properties) Ltd v Harrison* [2001] 1 BCLC 158.

obtained before they were in a fiduciary relationship with the principal and the breach of duty involved the failure to disclose that interest to the principal.[262] But this is unjustifiable. The claim for rescission and the claim for profits made in breach of fiduciary duty should be regarded as distinct claims, and the fact that rescission is barred should not bar a claim for an account of profits.[263] There are situations, however, in which it has been recognized that a principal who has entered into a contract with a fiduciary involving breach of the fiduciary's duty can seek disgorgement from the fiduciary regardless of whether the contract has been rescinded, such as where the fiduciary sells an asset to the principal that was the principal's property;[264] where the breach of fiduciary duty was dishonest;[265] or where the impossibility of rescission was due to the acts of the fiduciary.[266]

21.7 RECTIFICATION

21.7.1 THE ESSENCE OF RECTIFICATION

Rectification is an equitable remedy that enables a written document to be amended by order of the court when one or both of the parties has been mistaken about the terms of the document. Usually, the document will be a contract, but it may be a will or a deed of settlement.

Rectification is a drastic equitable remedy because it enables the court to rewrite a written document. Although, being an equitable remedy, it is discretionary, the equitable jurisdiction is founded on clear principles.[267] The remedy is justified by the principle that Equity looks to the substance rather than the form of the transaction.[268] The Common Law looks only to the form of the document, without regard to the parties' prior intentions before the document was drafted.[269] Equity can, however, have regard to prior intentions,[270] as reflected for example in antecedent negotiations.[271]

Being an equitable remedy, rectification is subject to the usual defences, such as delay or acquiescence,[272] or where a bona fide purchaser for value has acquired an interest as a result of the transaction.[273]

21.7.2 RECTIFICATION OF WILLS AND SETTLEMENTS

Where a will fails to carry out the testator's intentions as the result of a clerical error or a failure on the part of the drafter of the will to understand the testator's instructions, the court may order that the will should be rectified so that it accords with the testator's

---

[262] *Re Cape Breton Co* (1885) 29 Ch D 795; *Burland v Earle* [1902] AC 83, 99 (Lord Davey); *Jacobus Marler Estates Ltd v Marler* (1916) 114 LT 640n.

[263] See *Re Cape Breton Co* (1885) 29 Ch D 795, 808–9 (Bowen LJ, dissenting).

[264] Ibid., 811 (Fry LJ); *Gluckstein v Barnes* [1900] AC 240; *Jacobus Marler Estates Ltd v Marler* (1916) 114 LT 640n.

[265] *Gwembe Valley Development Co v Koshy* [2003] EWCA Civ 1478, [2004] 1 BCLC 131, 177 (Mummery LJ).

[266] *Re Cape Breton Co* (1885) 29 Ch D 795, 811 (Fry LJ).

[267] *Daventry District Council v Daventry and District Housing Ltd* [2011] EWCA Civ 1153, [2012] 1 WLR 1333, [194] (Lord Neuberger MR).

[268] See Section 2.11, p. 35.   [269] *BCCI v Ali* [2001] UKHL 8, [2002] 1 AC 251.

[270] The test is whether the document accords with intent rather than motive: *Kennedy v Kennedy* [2014] EWHC 4129 (Ch), [2015] WTLR 837, [43] (Etherton C).

[271] *Daventry District Council v Daventry and District Housing Ltd* [2011] EWCA Civ 1153, [2012] 1 WLR 1333, [198] (Lord Neuberger MR).

[272] *Beale v Kyte* [1907] 1 Ch 564.   [273] *Smith v Jones* [1954] 1 WLR 1089.

intentions.[274] The exercise of this power is illustrated by *Marley v Rawlings*,[275] where the claimant's parents had drafted mirror wills by virtue of which each had left their entire estate to the other and, in the event that the other died first, the whole estate was to be left to the claimant. By mistake the parents had signed each other's wills, which were consequently invalid. The Supreme Court rectified the wills so that the text of the will signed by the mother was transposed into the will signed by the father. It follows that rectification may cure formality defects in wills. Similarly, the parties can seek rectification of a deed of settlement so that it accords with the intentions of the settlor,[276] or a deed of appointment executed by trustees.[277] Even though there is a statutory jurisdiction for the rectification of wills in certain defined circumstances, Hodge has argued that the courts should recognize that they have an inherent power to rectify a will which is wider than the power conferred by the legislature.[278]

21.7.3 RECTIFICATION OF CONTRACTS

Before the remedy of rectification is considered, it is important first to determine whether any mistake in the drafting of the contract can be resolved through interpretation of what the words used objectively mean.[279] But the doctrine of contractual interpretation should not be strained at the expense of the remedy of rectification.[280] If the words used in the contract have a clear meaning objectively, but those words do not reflect the intention of one or both of the parties, there is scope for the remedy of rectification to alter the words used in the contract.

In most cases rectification will simply ensure that contractual documentation reflects the intentions of the parties. But there will be some cases where rectification may have other consequences, such as extinguishing rights which would otherwise be enjoyed by the defendant according to the face of the contract or enabling the claimant to recover property which had been transferred to the defendant. This is illustrated by *Day v Day*,[281] where a written conveyance was rectified as a consequence of there being a mistake relating to its legal effect. Property had been settled on trust. The settlor had intended the property to be used simply as security to enable the defendant to raise funds, whereas the effect of the settlement was to give the defendant a beneficial interest in the property. The effect of rectification was to enable the settlor's estate to recover the property which had been mistakenly transferred to the defendant.

In assessing the operation of this equitable remedy to rectify contracts, it is important to draw a fundamental distinction between those cases in which the mistake about the terms of the written contract are shared by all of the parties to the contract, so-called common mistake, and those in which the mistake is made by only one of the parties, so-called unilateral mistake.

---

[274] Administration of Justice Act 1982, s. 20(1). See *Re Segelman* [1996] Ch 171; *Giles v The Royal National Institute for the Blind* [2014] EWHC 1373 (Ch). The Law Commission having reviewed the law in this area has concluded that statutory reform is not warranted: *Making a Will* (Law Com CP No. 231, 2017), p. 184.

[275] [2014] UKSC 2, [2015] AC 129. See Goodwin and Granger, 'Where there's a will there's a way: *Marley v Rawlings*' (2015) 78 MLR 140.

[276] *Re Butlin's Settlement* [1976] Ch 251; *RBC Trustees v Stubbs* [2017] EWHC 180 (Ch).

[277] *Price v Williams-Wynn* [2006] WTLR 1633; *Prowting 1968 Trustee Ltd v Amos-Yeo* [2015] EWHC 2480, [2015] BTC 33.   [278] 'The correction of mirror wills: interpretation versus rectification' [2017] Conv 45.

[279] See *Chartbrook v Persimmon Homes Ltd* [2009] UKHL 38, [2009] 1 AC 1101.

[280] Buxton, 'Construction and rectification after *Chartbrook*' (2010) 69 CLJ 253, 262. See also Davies, 'Rectification versus interpretation: the nature and scope of the equitable jurisdiction' (2016) 72 CLJ 62.

[281] [2013] EWCA Civ 280, [2014] Ch 114.

(i) Common mistake

Where there has been a mistake in recording the agreed terms of the contract so that the written document does not accord with the intention of the parties, the equitable remedy of rectification can be used to alter the document so that it does accord with the parties' agreement. Rectification for common mistake does not depend on proof of any culpability, whereas that is crucial for unilateral mistake.[282]

The common mistake of the parties must relate to the terms of the document that purports to record a previous transaction rather than a mistake relating to the transaction itself. This previous transaction may be either a prior concluded agreement or a continuing common intention in respect of a particular matter in the document. It was recognized by Lord Hoffmann in *Chartbrook v Persimmon Homes Ltd*[283] that, when determining whether there was a continuing common intention, an objective test should be adopted, so that the court is concerned with what a reasonable person would have understood the parties to have agreed, rather than what the particular parties in question subjectively believed the consensus to have been.[284] Although this dictum of Lord Hoffmann was *obiter*, it was delivered after full argument, was approved by the other members of the court, and set out established principles rather than seeking to change them. It has subsequently been recognized by the Court of Appeal as representing the law and as being defensible as a matter of policy.[285]

The key requirements for identifying a common intention have been summarized by Etherton LJ[286] as follows:

(1) The parties had a common continuing intention, whether or not amounting to an agreement, in respect of a particular matter in the instrument to be rectified.

(2) This common intention must have existed at the time of execution of the instrument which is sought to be rectified.

(3) The common continuing intention is to be established by reference to what an objective observer aware of all the relevant facts known to both parties[287] would have thought the intentions of the parties to be.

(4) By mistake the instrument did not reflect the common intention.

Convincing proof is required that the document does not represent the common intention of the parties.[288]

This recognition that the common continuing intention is to be determined objectively rather than subjectively means that it is possible to identify a common mistake shared by both parties, even if one party was not subjectively mistaken. That this is the effect of recognizing the objective test is illustrated by *Daventry District Council v Daventry and District Housing Ltd*.[289] The parties in that case had been negotiating who should take responsibility for making up the deficit in a pension fund. During their negotiations, the parties reached an agreement in principle that Daventry and District Housing Ltd (DDH)

---

[282] *Daventry District Council v Daventry and District Housing Ltd* [2011] EWCA Civ 1153, [2012] 1 WLR 1333, [91] (Etherton LJ). See further Section 21.7.3.(ii), p. 657.

[283] [2009] UKHL 38, [2009] 1 AC 1101, [60].

[284] This is criticized by Davies (n. 280) 74, who argues that the equitable jurisdiction of rectification should only be engaged if both parties' consciences had been affected, requiring a subjective test to be adopted.

[285] *Daventry District Council v Daventry and District Housing Ltd* [2011] EWCA Civ 1153, [2012] 1 WLR 1333, [89] (Etherton LJ).

[286] Ibid., [80].   [287] Ibid., [197] (Lord Neuberger MR).

[288] *Crane v Hegeman-Harris Co* [1939] 1 All ER 662, 664 (Simonds J); *Joscelyne v Nissen* [1970] 2 QB 86.

[289] [2011] EWCA Civ 1153, [2012] 1 WLR 1333.

would make up the deficit. The board of DDH did not consider that it was responsible for the deficit. When a draft contract was drawn up, a term was included that Daventry District Council (DDC) would be responsible for the deficit. The chief negotiator for DDC misunderstood the meaning of this clause and did not consider that DDC would be liable for the deficit. The final contract contained this clause and, when DDC discovered that it was liable for the deficit, it sought rectification of the contract on the ground that the written document did not reflect the continuing common intention of the parties. A majority of the Court of Appeal accepted that the parties had objectively made a mistake that the final contract accorded with their prior agreement in principle that DDH would be responsible for the deficit and that this objective common belief continued until the document was executed, so that the contract could be rectified. Etherton LJ dissented on the facts on the ground that the objective common intention of the parties had not continued until the final document was signed, since DDH had objectively changed its mind about who would be responsible for the deficit when the clause allocating responsibility for the deficit to DDC was inserted into the contract.[290]

The effect of the decision in *Daventry* is that a contract was rectified on the ground of common mistake even though the final contract reflected the actual belief of DDH, which consequently was not mistaken. This unacceptably confuses the clear distinction between common and unilateral mistakes,[291] a distinction that is of significance because a contract can be rectified for a unilateral mistake only where the defendant has acted unconscionably in some way and this could not be established on the facts of the case. The real difficulty for rectification for common mistake arises from the objective test being used to identify a continuing common intention. This difficulty was identified by Toulson LJ[292] by reference to the following example:

A and B reach what they consider to be an agreement in principle, but A believes that this agreement means x and B believes that it means y. They then enter into a written contract that they both believe gives effect to their agreement in principle. If the agreement in principle is objectively construed as meaning x, but the written contract is objectively construed as meaning y, a common mistake can be identified even though the written contract accords with the subjective intention of B.

This problem can be avoided by adopting a subjective approach to the identification of a common mistake. This would reflect the different approaches to construction adopted at Common Law and in Equity. At Common Law, an objective approach is adopted for the interpretation of contracts. This should logically leave no room for the adoption of an objective test for the identification of a common continuing intention in Equity. Rather, a subjective test should be adopted in Equity. It follows that, if the contract as drafted reflects the subjective intentions of one of the parties to the contract, the doctrine of common mistake is not engaged and the contract should not be rectified for that reason. Instead, the focus should shift to the doctrine of rectification for unilateral mistake.

(ii) Unilateral mistake

Where one party to a contract mistakenly believes that the contract contains a term that is not included in the written contract, that contract may be rectified to accord with

---

[290] Ibid., [110].   [291] Ibid., [114] (Etherton LJ).   [292] Ibid., [176]–[177].

the party's belief even though that mistaken belief was not shared by the other party. Rectification for unilateral mistake is much more controversial than rectification for a common mistake, because the effect of rectification for unilateral mistake is to impose on the defendant a contract that they did not make and did not intend to make.[293] It is for that reason that rectification for unilateral mistake will be awarded only where the other party has acted unconscionably in some way.

To establish a unilateral mistake, the following requirements need to be satisfied:[294]

(1) Party A must have erroneously believed that the document contained a particular term or provision or believed that it did not contain a term or provision that it did contain.

(2) Party B was aware of the omission or inclusion of the term and was aware of A's mistake. It is sufficient that B knows, is wilfully blind, or suspects that A was mistaken.[295]

(3) B omitted to draw the mistake to the notice of A.

(4) This was calculated to benefit B.

If these conditions are satisfied, it would then be inequitable or unconscionable to allow B to resist rectification. Since, however, rectification is a discretionary remedy, the claimant's own carelessness, for example, may result in refusal of the remedy.[296]

The key justification for allowing rectification for unilateral mistake is that the defendant has acted unconscionably in allowing the claimant to enter into the contract despite the defendant's conscious awareness that the claimant was or might be mistaken as to the terms of the agreement—what Etherton LJ has described as dishonest conduct on the part of the defendant.[297] It has been suggested that it should be sufficient to trigger rectification for unilateral mistake if the defendant ought to have been aware of the claimant's mistake.[298] Such a purely objective conception of fault is, however, inconsistent with the proper interpretation of unconscionability,[299] which refers to an assessment of the defendant's conduct, albeit in light of the facts as the defendant knew, believed, or suspected them to be. This is an objective test, but one which is assessed with regard to the defendant's awareness of the facts. It is this notion of unconscionability, or dishonesty, which was recognized by Etherton LJ and which is consistent with the notion of unconscionability which, as we have seen throughout this book, is at the heart of the equitable jurisdiction.

---

[293] *Rowallan Group Ltd v Edgehill Portfolio No 1 Ltd* [2007] EWHC 32 (Ch), [14] (Lightman J).

[294] *Thomas Bates and Son Ltd v Windham's (Lingerie) Ltd* [1981] 1 WLR 505, 515–16 (Buckley LJ); *George Wimpey UK Ltd v VI Construction Ltd* [2005] EWCA Civ 7, [38] (Peter Gibson LJ).

[295] *Commission for the New Towns v Cooper (Great Britain) Ltd* [1995] Ch 259.

[296] *Agip SpA v Navigazione Alta Italia SpA* [1984] 1 Lloyd's Rep 353.

[297] *Daventry District Council v Daventry and District Housing Ltd* [2011] EWCA Civ 1153, [2012] 1 WLR 1333, [96].

[298] Ibid., [184] (Toulson LJ) and [226] (Lord Neuberger MR). See also McLauchlan, 'The "drastic" remedy of rectification for unilateral mistake' (2008) 124 LQR 608; Burrows, 'Construction and rectification', in *Contract Terms*, ed. Burrows and Peel (Oxford: Oxford University Press, 2007), ch. 5.

[299] See further Section 2.3.3.(i), p. 29.

GLOSSARY

APPOINTMENT The distribution of trust property to beneficiaries of the trust

BARE TRUST A trust to hold property for the benefit of one person who is of full age

BENEFICIAL INTEREST The right to enjoy the benefits of property, such as the right to receive the income from property

BENEFICIARY A person who is entitled to the benefit of property

BONA VACANTIA Ownerless property, which can be claimed by the Crown

CAPITAL The assets that form the trust fund

CHARGE A security interest in property

CODICIL A formal supplement or annex to a will

CONDITION PRECEDENT A requirement that must be satisfied before an interest in property can be vested

CONDITION SUBSEQUENT A requirement that, once satisfied, will deprive a person of his or her interest in property

CONSIDERATION The promise or provision of value in return for a promise. But see marriage consideration

CONTINGENT INTEREST An interest in property that will arise only after a condition has been satisfied

DONATIO MORTIS CAUSA A gift made in prospect of the donor's death

EQUITABLE INTEREST A right in property recognized by Equity

FIDUCIARY RELATIONSHIP A relationship of trust and confidence such as that between trustee and beneficiary or agent and principal

INCOME The value earned on the capital trust assets

INTER VIVOS TRUST A trust declared by a settlor whilst he or she is alive

INTEREST IN POSSESSION A beneficiary who has an immediate entitlement to the income of the trust property

INTEREST IN SUCCESSION A situation in which beneficiaries have different interests over time

JOINT TENANTS Co-owners of property who are treated together as the single owner; on the death of one joint tenant, their interest passes to the others. Cf. tenants in common

LEGATEE A beneficiary under a will

LIEN A security interest in property

LIFE TENANT The person who has an entitlement to the income or capital during his or her lifetime

MARRIAGE CONSIDERATION The husband, wife, and children of the marriage

PERSONALTY Personal property, such as chattels and shares

REALTY Land

REMAINDER INTEREST An interest in property that is disposed of by the creator of a trust, but the enjoyment of which is postponed

RESIDUARY ESTATE That part of a deceased person's estate that is left after their debts have been paid and legacies fulfilled

REVERSIONARY INTEREST Part of an interest in property that is not disposed of, such as when a trust of a life interest is declared with the property to revert to the creator of the trust on the death of the life tenant

SETTLEMENT The transfer of property, but sometimes used as shorthand for a trust

SETTLOR A person who creates a trust that takes effect whilst they are alive

TENANTS IN COMMON Co-owners of property who have distinct, but undivided, shares in one asset, the size of which is not affected by the death of one of the tenants in common. Cf. joint tenants

TESTATOR A person who makes a will

VESTED IN INTEREST A right to the future enjoyment of property

VESTED IN POSSESSION A right to the present enjoyment of property

VESTED INTEREST An interest in property that does not depend on a prior condition being fulfilled, such as attaining a specified age or the exercise of a trustee's discretion

VOLUNTEER A person who has not provided consideration, such as a recipient of a gift

BIBLIOGRAPHY

ALLAN, 'Once a fraud, forever a fraud: the time-honoured doctrine of parol agreement trusts' (2014) 34 LS 419

ANDREWS, 'Strangers to justice no longer: the reversal of the privity rule under the Contracts (Rights of Third Parties) Act 1999' (2001) 60 CLJ 353

ANDREWS and BEATSON, 'Common law tracing: springboard or swan-song?' (1997) 113 LQR 21

ASHBURNER's *Principles of Equity*, 2nd edn, ed. BROWNE (London: Butterworth and Co., 1933)

BABAFEMI, 'Tracing assets: a case for the fusion of common law and Equity in English law' (1971) 34 MLR 12

BAILEY, 'Equitable interests: position of beneficiaries under will or intestacy—whether administration complete: tracing' (1965) 23 CLJ 44

BAKER, *Introduction to Legal History*, 4th edn (Oxford: Oxford University Press, 2002)

BARKEHALL THOMAS, ' "Goodbye" knowing receipt; "Hello" unconscientious receipt' (2001) 21 OJLS 239

BARKEHALL THOMAS, 'Thieves as trustees: the enduring legacy of *Black v S Freedman and Co*' (2009) 3 Journal of Equity 52

BARLOW, 'The appointment of trustees: a disappointing decision' [2003] Conv 15

BARTLETT and STEBBING, 'Trust powers: a reappraisal' [1984] Conv 227

BARTON, 'Trusts and covenants' (1975) 91 LQR 236

BATTERSBY, 'Some thoughts on the Statute of Frauds in relation to trusts' (1975) 7 Ottawa LR 483

BATTERSBY, 'Formalities for the disposition of equitable interests under a trust' [1979] Conv 17

BAUGHEN, 'Performing animals and the dissolution of unincorporated associations: the "contract-holding theory" vindicated' [2010] Conv 216

BERG, 'Permitting a trustee to retain a profit' (2001) 117 LQR 366

BIRKS, 'The remedies for abuse of confidential information' [1990] LMCLQ 460

BIRKS, 'The English recognition of unjust enrichment' [1991] LMCLQ 473

BIRKS, 'Equity in the modern law: an exercise in taxonomy' (1996) 26 Univ WALR 1

BIRKS, 'Trusts raised to reverse unjust enrichment: the *Westdeutsche* case' [1996] 4 RLR 3

BIRKS, 'The necessity of a unitary law of tracing', in *Making Commercial Law: Essays in Honour of Roy Goode*, ed. CRANSTON (Oxford: Oxford University Press, 1997), p. 239

BIRKS, 'On taking seriously the difference between tracing and claiming' (1997) 11 TLI 2

BIRKS, 'Property and unjust enrichment: categorical truths' [1997] NZ Law Rev 623

BIRKS, 'Property, Unjust enrichment and tracing' (2001) 54 CLP 231

BIRKS, 'Receipt', in *Breach of Trust*, ed. BIRKS and PRETTO (Oxford: Hart, 2002), p. 227

BIRKS, 'Retrieving tied money', in *The Quistclose Trust*, ed. SWADLING (Oxford: Hart, 2004), p. 126

BIRKS, *Unjust Enrichment*, 2nd edn (Oxford: Oxford University Press, 2005)

BIRKS and PRETTO, 'Preface', in *Breach of Trust*, ed. BIRKS and PRETTO (Oxford: Hart, 2002)

BRIGGS, '*Akers v Samba*: Equity's darling reigns supreme' (Chancery Bar Association Annual Lecture, 5 April 2017)

BROOK, 'King v Dubrey: a donatio mortis causa too far?' [2014] Conv 525

BROWN, 'What are we to do with testamentary trusts of imperfect obligation?' [2007] Conv 148

BRYAN, 'Recovering misdirected money from banks: ministerial receipt at Law and in Equity', in Restitution and Banking Law, ed. ROSE (Oxford: Mansfield Press, 1998), ch. 10

BRYAN, 'The liability of the recipient: restitution at common law or wrongdoing in Equity?', in Equity in Commercial Law, ed. DEGELING and EDELMAN (Sydney: Law Book Co., 2005), p. 339

BRYAN, 'Boardman v Phipps', in Landmark Cases in Equity, ed. MITCHELL and MITCHELL (Oxford: Hart, 2012), p. 581

BUCKINGHAM and CHAMBERS, 'Subrogation, the straitjacket of unjust enrichment and legal taxonomy' [2016] Conv 219

BURROWS, 'Proprietary restitution: unmasking unjust enrichment' (2001) 117 LQR 412

BURROWS, 'We do this at Common Law but that in Equity' (2002) 22 OJLS 1

BURROWS, 'Remedial coherence and punitive damages in equity', in Equity in Commercial Law, ed. DEGELING and EDELMAN (Sydney: Law Book Co., 2005), p. 381

BURROWS, 'Construction and rectification', in Contract Terms, ed. BURROWS and PEEL (Oxford: Oxford University Press, 2007), ch. 5

BURROWS, The Law of Restitution, 3rd edn (Oxford: Oxford University Press, 2011)

BUXTON, '"Construction" and rectification after Chartbrook' (2010) 69 CLJ 253

CAMPBELL, 'The honest truth about dishonest assistance' [2015] Conv 159

CARTY, 'Joint tortfeasance and assistance liability' (1999) 19 LS 489

CHAFEE, 'Coming into Equity with clean hands' (1949) 47 Mich L Rev 877 and 1065

CHAMBERS, Resulting Trusts (Oxford: Clarendon Press, 1997)

CHAMBERS, 'Liability', in Breach of Trust, ed. BIRKS and PRETTO (Oxford: Hart, 2002), p. 2

CHAMBERS, 'Resulting trusts', in Mapping the Law, ed. BURROWS and LORD RODGER (Oxford: Oxford University Press, 2006), ch. 13

CHAMBERS, 'Is there a presumption of resulting trust?', in Constructive and Resulting Trusts, ed. MITCHELL (Oxford: Hart, 2010), ch. 9

CHAMBERS, 'Trust and theft', in Exploring Private Law, ed. BANT and HARDING (Cambridge: Cambridge University Press, 2010), ch. 10

CHARITY COMMISSION, Students' Unions: A Guide, OG48.C3 (2001)

CHARITY COMMISSION, Charities and Public Benefit (January 2008)

CHARITY COMMISSION, Speaking Out: Guidance on Campaigning and Political Activities by Charities, CC9 (2008)

CHARITY COMMISSION, Charities and Investment Matters: A Guide for Trustees, CC14 (2011)

CHARITY COMMISSION, Trustee Expenses and Payments, CC11 (2011)

CHARITY COMMISSION, Guidance on Charitable Purposes (2013)

CHARITY COMMISSION, Public Benefit: the Public Benefit Requirement (2013)

CHARITY COMMISSION, Campaigning and Political Issues Arising in the Run-Up to the 2017 General Election (2017)

CLOHERTY and FOX, 'Proving a trust of a shared home' (2007) 66 CLJ 517

CONAGLEN, 'Equitable compensation for breach of fiduciary duty rules' (2003) 119 LQR 246

CONAGLEN, 'The nature and function of fiduciary loyalty' (2005) 121 LQR 452

CONAGLEN, 'A re-appraisal of the fiduciary self-dealing and fair-dealing rules' (2006) 64 CLJ 366

CONAGLEN, 'Strict fiduciary loyalty and account of profits' (2006) 65 CLJ 278

CONAGLEN, 'Sham trusts' (2008) 67 CLJ 176

CONAGLEN, 'Fiduciary regulation of conflicts between duties' (2009) 125 LQR 111

CONAGLEN, *Fiduciary Loyalty: Protecting the Due Performance of Non-Fiduciary Duties* (Oxford: Hart, 2010)

CONAGLEN, 'Remedial ramifications of conflicts between a fiduciary's duties' (2010) 126 LQR 72

CONAGLEN, 'Difficulties with tracing backwards' (2011) 127 LQR 432

CONAGLEN, 'The extent of fiduciary accounting and the importance of authorisation mechanisms' (2011) 70 CLJ 548

CONAGLEN, 'Fiduciary duties and voluntary undertakings' (2013) 7 Journal of Equity 105

CONAGLEN and GOYMOUR, 'Knowing receipt and registered land', in *Constructive and Resulting Trusts*, ed. MITCHELL (Oxford: Hart, 2010), p. 181

CRETNEY, 'The rationale of *Keech v Sandford*' (1969) 33 Conv 161

CRITCHLEY, 'Instruments of fraud, testamentary dispositions and the doctrine of secret trusts' (1999) 115 LQR 631

CROSS, 'Some recent developments in the law of charity' (1956) 72 LQR 187

CUMBER, '*Donatio mortis causa*: a doctrine on its deathbed?' [2016] Conv 56

CUTTS, 'Tracing, value and transactions' (2016) 79 MLR 381

DAVIES, *Accessory Liability* (Oxford: Hart, 2015)

DAVIES, 'Gain-based remedies for dishonest assistance' (2015) 131 LQR 173

DAVIES, 'Remedies for breach of trust' (2015) 78 MLR 681

DAVIES, 'Rectification versus interpretation: the nature and scope of the equitable jurisdiction' (2016) 72 CLJ 62

DAVIES and VIRGO, 'Relieving trustees' mistakes' [2013] RLR 73

DAWSON, 'The rule against inalienability: a rule without a purpose' (2006) 26 LS 414

DENNING, 'The need for a new Equity' (1952) 5 CLP 8

DENNING, *The Due Process of Law* (London: Butterworths, 1980)

DEVONSHIRE, 'Account of profits for dishonest assistance' (2015) 74 CLJ 222

DIETRICH and RIDGE, 'Receipt of what? Questions concerning third-party recipient liability in Equity an unjust enrichment' (2007) 31 MULR 47

DIXON, 'The never-ending story: co-ownership after *Stack v Dowden*' [2007] Conv 456

DIXON, 'Confining and defining proprietary estoppels: the role of unconscionability' (2010) 30 LS 408

DOGGETT, 'Explaining *Re Rose*: the search goes on?' (2003) 62 CLJ 263

DOUGLAS and MCFARLANE, 'Sham Trusts', *Modern Studies in Property Law*, Vol. 9 (eds. CONWAY and HICKEY) (2017, Hart Publishing), ch. 13

DOWLING, 'Can roses survive on registered land?' (1999) 50 NILQ 90

DUGGAN, 'Is Equity efficient?' (1997) 113 LQR 601, 624

DUGGAN, 'Exemplary damages in Equity: a law and economics perspective' (2006) 26 OJLS 303

DUGGAN, 'Contracts, fiduciaries and the primacy of the deal', in *Exploring Private Law*, ed. BANT and HARDING (Cambridge: Cambridge University Press, 2010), ch. 12

DUNN, 'As "cold as charity"? Property, Equity and the charitable trust' (2000) 20 LS 222

EASTERBROOK and FISCHEL, 'Contract and fiduciary duty' (1993) 36 J L & Econ 425

EDELMAN, 'Four fiduciary puzzles', in *Exploring Private Law*, ed. BANT and HARDING (Cambridge: Cambridge University Press, 2010), p. 305

EDELMAN, 'When do fiduciary duties arise?' (2010) 126 LQR 302

EDELMAN, 'Two fundamental questions for the law of trusts' (2013) 129 LQR 66

EDELMAN and ELLIOTT, 'Money remedies against trustees' (2004) 18 TLI 116

EDGE and LOUGHREY, 'Religious charities and the juridification of the Charity Commission' (2001) 21 LS 36

ELLIOTT, D., 'The power of trustees to enforce covenants in favour of volunteers' (1960) 76 LQR 100

ELLIOTT, S., 'Rethinking interest on withheld and misapplied trust money' [2001] Conv 313

ELLIOTT, S., 'Remoteness criteria in Equity' (2002) 65 MLR 588

ELLIOTT and EDELMAN, '*Target Holdings* considered in Australia' (2003) 119 LQR 545

ELLIOTT and MITCHELL, 'Remedies for dishonest assistance' (2004) 67 MLR 16

EMERY, 'The most hallowed principle: certainty of beneficiaries of trusts and powers of appointment' (1982) 98 LQR 551

ETHERTON, 'Constructive trusts: a new model for Equity and unjust enrichment' (2008) 67 CLJ 265

ETHERTON, 'Constructive trusts and proprietary estoppel: the search for clarity and principle' [2009] Conv 104

ETHERTON, 'The role of equity in mistaken transactions' (2013) 27 TLI 159

ETHERTON, 'The legitimacy of proprietary relief' (2014) 2 Birkbeck LR 59

EVANS, 'Rethinking tracing and the law of restitution' (1999) 115 LQR 469

EVANS, 'Variation classification' [2011] Conv 151

EVERSHED, 'Reflections on the fusion of Law and Equity after seventy-five years' (1954) 70 LQR 326

FELTHAM, 'Intention to create a trust of a promise to settle property' (1982) 98 LQR 17

FELTHAM, 'Informal trusts and third parties' [1987] Conv 246

FINN, *Fiduciary Obligations* (Sydney: Law Book Co., 1977)

FINN, 'Fiduciary law and the modern commercial world', in *Commercial Aspects of Trusts and Fiduciary Obligations*, ed.

McKENDRICK (Oxford: Clarendon Press, 1992), p. 9

FINN, 'Unconscionable conduct' (1994) 8 JCL 37

FLANNIGAN, 'The adulteration of fiduciary doctrine in corporate law' (2006) 122 LQR 449

FLANNIGAN, 'The [fiduciary] duty of fidelity' (2008) 124 LQR 274

FLANNIGAN, 'A revised Canadian test for fact-based fiduciary accountability' (2011) 127 LQR 505

FORD, 'Trustee investment and modern portfolio theory' (1996) 10 TLI 102

FOX, 'Overreaching', in *Breach of Trust*, ed. BIRKS and PRETTO (Oxford: Hart, 2002), ch. 4

FOX, *Property Rights in Money* (Oxford: Oxford University Press, 2008)

FOX, 'Discretion and moral hazard in pension trusts' (2010) 69 CLJ 240

FOX, 'The irreducible core for a valid trust' (2011) 17 T&T 16

FULLER, 'Consideration and form' (1941) 41 Columbia L Rev 799

FUNG, 'The scope of the rule in *Shephard v Cartwright*' (2006) 122 LQR 651

GARDNER, J., 'Ashworth on principles', in *Principles and Values in Criminal Law and Criminal Justice: Essays in Honour of Andrew Ashworth*, ed. ZEDNER and ROBERTS (Oxford, Oxford University Press, 2012), p. 9

GARDNER, S., 'Fiduciary powers in Toytown' (1991) 107 LQR 214

GARDNER, S., 'Rethinking family property' (1993) 109 LQR 263

GARDNER, S., 'The remedial discretion in proprietary estoppel' (1999) 115 LQR 438

GARDNER, S., 'Quantum in *Gissing v Gissing* constructive trusts' (2004) 120 LQR 541

GARDNER, S., 'The remedial discretion in proprietary estoppel: again' (2006) 112 LQR 492

GARDNER, S., 'Family property today' (2008) 124 LQR 422

GARDNER, S., 'Moment of trust for knowing receipt?' (2009) 125 LQR 20

GARDNER, S., 'Problems in family property' (2013) 72 CLJ 301

GARTON, 'National Anti-Vivisection Society v Inland Revenue Commissioners', in Landmark Cases in Equity, ed. MITCHELL and MITCHELL (Oxford: Hart, 2012), p. 555

GEE, 'The remedies carried by a freezing injunction' (2006) 122 LQR 535

GEORGE and SLOAN, 'Presuming too little about resulting and constructive trusts?' [2017] Conv 303

GETZLER, 'Duty of care', in Breach of Trust, ed. BIRKS and PRETTO (Oxford: Hart, 2002), ch. 2

GETZLER, 'Rumford market and the genesis of fiduciary obligations', in Mapping the Law, ed. BURROWS and LORD RODGER (Oxford: Oxford University Press, 2006), ch. 31

GLEESON, 'The involuntary launderer: the banker's liability for deposits of the proceeds of crime', in Laundering and Tracing, ed. BIRKS (Oxford: Clarendon Press, 1995), ch. 5

GLISTER, 'The nature of Quistclose trusts: classification and reconciliation' (2004) 63 CLJ 632

GLISTER, 'The presumption of advancement', in Constructive and Resulting Trusts, ed. MITCHELL (Oxford: Hart, 2010), ch. 10

GLISTER, 'Disclaimer and secret trusts' [2014] Conv 11

GLOVER, 'The identification of fiduciaries', in Privacy and Loyalty, ed. BIRKS (Oxford: Clarendon Press, 1997), ch. 10

GLOVER and TODD, 'The myth of common intention' (1996) 16 LS 325

GODDARD, 'Equity, volunteers and ducks' [1988] Conv 19

GOFF and JONES, The Law of Unjust Enrichment, 9th edn, ed. MITCHELL, MITCHELL and WATTERSON (London: Sweet and Maxwell, 2016)

GOODE, 'The right to trace and its impact in commercial transactions' (1976) 92 LQR 360

GOODE, 'Property and unjust enrichment', in Essays on the Law of Restitution, ed. BURROWS (Oxford: Clarendon Press, 1991), p. 230

GOODE, 'Are intangible assets fungible?' [2003] LMCLQ 379

GOODWIN and GRANGER, 'Where there's a will there's a way: Marley v Rawlings' (2015) 78 MLR 140

GORDON, 'Delegation of will-making powers' (1953) 69 LQR 334

GOYMOUR, 'A contribution to knowing receipt liability? (City Index v Gawler)' [2008] RLR 113

GRANTHAM, 'Doctrinal bases for the recognition of proprietary rights' (1996) 16 OJLS 561

GRANTHAM and RICKETT, 'Trust money as an unjust enrichment: a misconception' [1998] LMCLQ 514

GRANTHAM and RICKETT, 'Tracing and property rights: the categorical truth' (2000) 63 MLR 905

GRAVELLS, 'Charitable trusts and ancillary purposes' [1978] Conv 92

GRAY, 'Property in thin air' (1991) 50 CLJ 252

GRBICH, 'Baden: awakening the conceptually moribund trust' (1974) 37 MLR 643

GROWER, 'Explaining the 'Pallant v Morgan equity' [2016] Conv 434

GULLEFER, 'Recovery of misappropriated assets; orthodoxy re-established?' [1995] LMCLQ 446

GUMMOW, 'Bribes and constructive trusts' (2015) 131 LQR 21

HÄCKER, 'Rescission and third party rights' [2006] RLR 21

HÄCKER, 'Proprietary restitution after impaired consent transfers: a generalized power model' (2009) 68 CLJ 324

HARDCASTLE, 'Administrative unworkability: a reassessment of an abiding problem' [1990] Conv 24

HARDING, 'Two fiduciary fallacies' (2007) 2 Journal of Equity 1

HARDING, 'Trusts for religious purposes and the question of public benefit' (2008) 71 MLR 159

HARDING, 'Justifying fiduciary allowances', in *The Goals of Private Law*, ed. ROBERTSON and WU (Oxford: Oxford University Press, 2009), ch. 14

HARDING, 'Equity and the rule of law' (2016) 132 LQR 278

HARE, 'Trust law's limitations' [2014] RLR 110

HARPUM, 'Administrative unworkability and purpose trusts' (1986) 45 CLJ 391

HARPUM, 'Overreaching, trustees' powers and the reform of the 1925 legislation' (1990) 49 CLJ 277

HARPUM, 'Fiduciary obligations and fiduciary powers: where are we going?', in *Privacy and Loyalty*, ed. BIRKS (Oxford: Clarendon Press, 1997), p. 154

HARRIS, 'Ten years of variation of trusts' (1969) 33 Conv 113

HARRIS, 'Trust, power and duty' (1971) 87 LQR 31

HART, H. L. A., 'Discretion' (2013) 127 Harvard Law Review 652

HART, W. G., 'What is a trust?' (1899) 15 LQR 294

HARTLEY, 'Jurisdiction in conflict of laws: disclosure, third-party debts and freezing orders' (2010) 126 LQR 194

HAVELOCK, 'The evolution of equitable conscience' (2014) 8 Journal of Equity 128

HAVELOCK, 'The transformation of knowing receipt' [2014] RLR 1

HAVELOCK, 'Conscience and unconscionability in modern equity' (2015) 9 Journal of Equity 1

HAYTON, '*Dingle v Turner*' [1972] Conv 209

HAYTON, '*Ottaway v Norman*' [1972] Conv 129

HAYTON, 'Uncertainty of subject-matter of trusts' (1994) 110 LQR 335

HAYTON, 'The irreducible core content of trusteeship', in *Trends in Contemporary Trust Law*, ed. OAKLEY (Oxford: Clarendon Press, 1996), ch. 3

HAYTON, 'Developing the obligation characteristic of the trust' (2001) 117 LQR 96

HAYTON, 'Pension trusts and traditional trusts: drastically different species of trusts' [2005] Conv 229

HAYTON, 'Unique rules for the unique institution, the trust', in *Equity in Commercial Law*, ed. DEGELING and EDELMAN (Sydney: Law Book Co., 2005), p. 301

HAYTON, 'Lessons from knowing receipt liability and unjust enrichment in Australia' (2007) 21 TLI 55

HAYTON, 'The development of Equity and the "good person" philosophy in Common Law systems' [2012] Conv 263

HICKS, 'The remedial principle of *Keech v Sandford* reconsidered' (2010) 69 CLJ 287

HO, 'Trustees' duties to provide information', in *Exploring Private Law*, ed. BANT and HARDING (Cambridge: Cambridge University Press, 2010), ch. 15

HO, 'Bribes and the constructive trust as a chameleon' (2012) 128 LQR 486

HO and LEE, 'A director's duty to confess: a matter of good faith?' (2007) 66 CLJ 348

HO and LEE, 'The beneficiaries' right to elect remedies for misapplied funds' (2017) 133 LQR 565

HO and SMART, 'Re-interpreting the *Quistclose* trust: a critique of Chambers' analysis' (2001) 21 OJLS 267

HODGE, 'Secret trusts: the fraud theory revisited' [1980] Conv 341

HODGE, D., 'The correction of mirror wills: interpretation versus rectification' [2017] Conv 45

HODGKINSON, 'Tracing and mixed funds' [1983] Conv 135

HOLDSWORTH, 'Secret trusts' (1937) 53 LQR 501

HOPKINS, J., 'Certain uncertainties of trusts and powers' (1971) 29 CLJ 68

HOPKINS, N., 'The Trusts of Land and Appointment of Trustees Act 1996' [1996] Conv 411

HOPKINS, N., 'The *Pallant v Morgan* equity' [2002] Conv 35

HOPKINS, N., 'Conscience, discretion and the creation of property rights' (2006) 26 LS 475

HUDSON, J., 'A Normative approach to the *Quistclose* trust' (2017) 80 MLR 775

HUDSON, S., and Sloan, 'Testamentary freedom: mutual wills might let you down', in *Modern Studies in Property Law*, Vol. 8 (ed. BARR) (Oxford: Hart, 2015), p. 157

HUGHES, 'The right of a trustee to a personal indemnity from beneficiaries' (1990) 64 ALJ 567

IBBETSON, 'The *Earl of Oxford's Case*', in *Landmark Cases in Equity*, ed. MITCHELL (Oxford: Hart, 2012), ch. 1

IWOBI, '"Out with the old, in with the new": religion, charitable status and the Charities Act 2006' (2009) 29 LS 619

JACONELLI, 'Decision-taking by private and charitable trustees' [1991] Conv 30

JACONELLI, 'Problems in the rule in *Strong v Bird*' [2006] Conv 432

JAFFEY, 'The nature of knowing receipt' (2001) 14 TLI 151

JAFFEY, 'Explaining the trust' (2015) 131 LQR 377

JONES, 'Unjust enrichment and the fiduciary's duty of loyalty' (1968) 84 LQR 472

JONES and GOODHART, *Specific Performance*, 2nd edn (London: Butterworths, 1996)

KEPPEL-PALMER, 'Discretion no more?' (1996) 146 NLJ 1779

KHURSHID and MATTHEWS, 'Tracing confusion' (1979) 95 LQR 78

KINCAID, 'Secret and semi-secret trusts: justifying distinctions between the two' [1995] Conv 366

KINCAID, 'The tangled web: the relationship between a secret trust and the will' [2000] Conv 420

KITTO, 'Foreword', in *Equity: Doctrine and Remedies*, ed. MEAGHER, GUMMOW, and LEHANE (London: Butterworths, 1975)

KLINCK, 'The unexamined "conscience" of contemporary Canadian Equity' (2001) 46 McGill LJ 571

KLUCK, *Conscience, Equity and the Court of Chancery in Early Modern England* (Farnham: Ashgate, 2010)

KODILINYE, 'A fresh look at the rule in *Strong v Bird*' [1982] Conv 14

KOH, 'Once a director, always a fiduciary?' (2003) 62 CLJ 403

LANGBEIN, 'The contractarian basis of the law of trusts' (1995) 105 Yale LJ 625

LANGBEIN, 'The secret life of the trust: the trust as an instrument of commerce' (1997) 107 Yale LJ 165

LANGBEIN, 'Questioning the trust law duty of loyalty: sole interest or best interest?' (2005) 114 Yale LJ 929

LAW COMMISSION, *Aggravated, Exemplary and Restitutionary Damages*, Law Com No. 247 (London: HMSO, 1997)

LAW COMMISSION, *Trustees' Powers and Duties*, Law Com No. 260 (London: HMSO, 1999)

LAW COMMISSION, *Cohabitation: The Financial Consequences of Relationship Breakdown*, Law Com No. 307 (London: HMSO, 2007)

LAW COMMISSION, *Annual Report 2007/08*, Law Com No. 310 (London: HMSO, 2008)

LAW COMMISSION, *Capital and Income in Trusts: Classification and Apportionment*, Law Com No. 315 (London: HMSO, 2009)

LAW COMMISSION, *The Illegality Defence*, Law Com No. 320 (London: HMSO, 2010)

LEE, J., 'Changing position on change of position' [2007] RLR 135

LEE, J., 'Constructing and limiting liability in Equity' (2015) 131 LQR 39

LEE, R., 'In search of the nature and function of fiduciary loyalty: some observations on Conaglen's analysis' (2007) 27 OJLS 327

LEE, R., '*Stack v Dowden*: a sequel' (2008) 124 LQR 209

LEGAIR, 'Modern portfolio theory: a primer' (2000) 14 TLI 75

Liew, 'Reanalysing institutional and remedial constructive trusts' (2016) 74 CLJ 528

Liew. 'The ambit of the mutal wills doctrine' (2016) 132 LQR 664

Loughlin, 'Liability for assistance in breach of fiduciary duty' (1989) 9 OJLS 260

Low, 'Recipient liability in Equity: resisting the siren's lure' [2008] RLR 96

Lowrie and Todd, 'Re Rose revisited' (1998) 57 CLJ 46

Lowry and Edmunds, 'Excuses', in Breach of Trust, ed. Birks and Pretto (Oxford: Hart, 2002), p. 280

Luxton, 'Cy-près and the ghost of things that might have been' [1983] Conv 107

Luxton, 'Variation of trusts: settlors' intentions and the consent principle in Saunders v Vautier' (1997) 60 MLR 719

Luxton and Evans, 'Cogent and cohesive? Two recent Charity Commission decisions on the advancement of religion' [2011] Conv 144

McBride, 'On the classification of trusts', in Restitution and Equity, Volume 1: Resulting Trusts and Equitable Compensation, ed. Birks and Rose (Oxford: Mansfield Press, 2000), p. 24

McBride, 'Rescission' in Commercial Remedies: Resolving Controversies (ed. Virgo and Worthington), (Cambridge: Cambridge University Press, 2017), ch. 7

McConvill and Bagaric, 'The yoking of unconscionability and unjust enrichment in Australia' (2002) 7 Deakin LR 225

McConville, 'Tracing and the rule in Clayton's Case' (1963) 79 LQR 388

McDermott, Equitable Damages (London: Butterworths, 1994), ch. 1

McFarlane, 'Constructive trusts arising on a receipt of property sub conditione' (2004) 120 LQR 667

McFarlane, 'Proprietary estoppel and failed contractual negotiations' [2005] Conv 501

McFarlane, The Structure of Property Law (Oxford: Hart, 2008)

McFarlane, The Law of Proprietary Estoppel (Oxford: Oxford University Press, 2013)

McFarlane and Robertson, 'The death of proprietary estoppel' [2008] LMCLQ 449

McFarlane and Robertson, 'Apocalypse averted: proprietary estoppel in the House of Lords' (2009) 125 LQR 535

McFarlane and Sales, 'Promises, detriment, and liability: lessons from proprietary estoppel' (2015) 131 LQR 610

McFarlane and Stevens, 'The nature of equitable property' (2010) 4 Journal of Equity 1

McInnes, 'Cohabitation, trusts and unjust enrichment in the Supreme Court of Canada' (2011) 127 LQR 339

McKay, 'Re Baden and the third class of uncertainty' [1974] Conv 269

McKay, 'Share transfers and the complete and perfect rule' (1976) 40 Conv 139

McKendrick, 'Restitution, misdirected funds and change of position' (1992) 55 MLR 377

McLauchlan, 'The "drastic" remedy of rectification for unilateral mistake' (2008) 124 LQR 608

McNair, 'Equity and conscience' [2007] OJLS 659

Maitland, Equity: A Course of Lectures, 2nd edn, ed. Brunyate (Cambridge: Cambridge University Press, 1936)

Man Yip, 'The Pallant v Morgan equity reconsidered' (2013) 33 LS 549

Marshall, 'The failure of the Astor trust' (1953) 6 CLP 151

Martin, 'The construction of charitable gifts' (1974) 38 Conv (NS) 187

Martin, 'Fusion, fallacy and confusion; a comparative study' [1994] Conv 13

Mason, 'Themes and prospects', in Essays in Equity, ed. Finn (Sydney: Law Book Co., 1985), p. 246

Mason, 'The place of Equity and equitable remedies in the contemporary common law world' (1994) 110 LQR 238

MATTHEWS, 'The true basis of the half-secret trust?' [1979] Conv 360

MATTHEWS, 'A problem in the construction of gifts to unincorporated associations' [1995] Conv 302

MATTHEWS, 'The new trust: obligations without rights?', in *Trends in Contemporary Trust Law*, ed. OAKLEY (Oxford: Clarendon Press, 1996), p. 3

MATTHEWS, 'The comparative importance of the rule in *Saunders v Vautier*' (2006) 122 LQR 266

MAUDSLEY, 'Proprietary remedies for the recovery of money' (1959) 75 LQR 234

MAUGHAM, 'Excusable breaches of trust' (1898) 14 LQR 159

MAURICE, 'The office of custodian trustee' (1960) 24 Conv 196

MEAGHER and LEHANE, 'Trusts of voluntary covenants' (1976) 92 LQR 427

MEAGHER, GUMMOW, and LEHANE, *Equity: Doctrines and Remedies,* 5th edn, ed. HEYDON, LEEMING, and TURNER (London: Butterworths, 2014)

MEE, '"Automatic" resulting trusts: retention, restitution or reposing trust?', in *Constructive and Resulting Trusts*, ed. MITCHELL (Oxford: Hart, 2010), ch. 7

MEE, 'Resulting trusts and voluntary conveyances of land' (2012) Conv 307

MEE, 'Proprietary estoppel and inheritance: enough is enough?' [2013] Conv 280

MEE, 'Presumed resulting trusts, intention and declaration' (2014) 73 CLJ 86

MEE, 'The past, present, and future of resulting trusts' (2017) CLP 1

MERRETT, 'Worldwide freezing orders in Europe' [2008] LMCLQ 71

MIDWINTER, 'Subrogation finds some "well-settled principles"' [2003] LMCLQ 6

MILLETT, 'The *Quistclose* trust: who can enforce it?' (1985) 101 LQR 269

MILLETT, 'Tracing the proceeds of fraud' (1991) 107 LQR 71

MILLETT, 'Equity: the road ahead' (1995) 9 TLI 35

MILLETT, 'Equity's place in the law of commerce' (1998) 114 LQR 214

MILLETT, 'Restitution and constructive trusts' (1998) 114 LQR 399

MILLETT, 'Pension schemes and the law of trusts; the tail wagging the dog?' (2000) 14 TLI 66

MILLETT, 'Foreword', in *The Quistclose Trust*, ed. SWADLING (Oxford: Hart, 2004)

MILLETT, 'Proprietary restitution', in *Equity in Commercial Law*, ed. DEGELING and EDELMAN (Sydney: Law Book Co., 2005), p. 309

MILLETT, '*Quistclose* trusts: *Twinsectra v Yardley* explained' (2011) 1 T&T 7

MILLETT, 'Bribes and secret commissions again' (2012) 71 CLJ 583

MILNER, 'Pension trust: a new trust forum' [1997] Conv 89

MILSOM, *Historical Foundations of the Common Law*, 2nd edn (London: Butterworths, 1981)

MITCHELL and WATTERSON, *Subrogation: Law and Practice* (Oxford: Oxford University Press, 2007)

MITCHELL and WATTERSON, 'Remedies for knowing receipt', in *Constructive and Resulting Trusts*, ed. MITCHELL (Oxford: Hart, 2010), p. 129

MOFFAT, 'Pension funds: a fragmentation of trust law?' (1993) 56 MLR 471

MOFFAT, *Trusts Law*, 6th edn, ed. GARTON (Cambridge: Cambridge University Press, 2015)

MORE, *Utopia* (1516) Book 1, 45

MORRIS and LEACH, *Rule against Perpetuities*, 2nd edn (London: Stevens, 1962)

NAHAN, 'Rescission: A case for rejecting the classical model?' (1997) 27 Univ WALR 66

NEUBERGER, 'The stuffing of Minerva's owl? Taxonomy and taxidermy in Equity' (2009) 68 CLJ 537

NEUBERGER, 'The remedial constructive trust: fact or fiction', delivered in August 2014 to the Banking Services and Finance Law Association Conference, New Zealand

NICHOLLS, 'Trustees and their broader community: where duty, morality and ethics converge' (1995) 9 TLI 71

NICHOLLS, 'Knowing receipt: the need for a new landmark', in *Restitution: Past, Present and Future*, ed. CORNISH et al. (Oxford: Hart, 1998), p. 231

NOBLES, 'Charities and ethical investment' [1992] Conv 115

NOBLES, 'Pensions Act 1995' (1996) 59 MLR 241

NOLAN, '*Vandervell v IRC*: a case of overreaching' (2002) 61 CLJ 169

NOLAN, 'Property in a fund' (2004) 120 LQR 108

NOLAN, 'Equitable property' (2006) 122 LQR 232

NOLAN, 'Understanding the limits of equitable property' (2006) 1 Journal of Equity 18

NOLAN, 'Controlling fiduciary power' (2009) 68 CLJ 293

NOLAN, '*Regal (Hastings) v Gulliver*', in *Landmark Cases in Equity*, ed. MITCHELL and MITCHELL (Oxford: Hart, 2012), p. 499

NOLAN and CLOHERTY, 'The rule in *Pitt v Holt*?' (2011) 127 LQR 499

NOLAN and CONAGLEN, 'Good faith: what does it mean for fiduciaries and what does it tell us about them?', in *Exploring Private Law*, ed. BANT and HARDING (Cambridge: Cambridge University Press, 2010), ch. 14

OAKLEY, 'The prerequisites of an equitable tracing claim' (1975) 28 CLP 64

OAKLEY, *Constructive Trusts*, 3rd edn (London: Sweet and Maxwell, 1996)

O'DELL, 'The resulting trust', in *Structure and Justification in Private Law*, ed. RICKETT and GRANTHAM (Oxford: Hart, 2008), ch. 19

O'SULLIVAN, D., 'The rule in *Phillips v Phillips*' (2002) 118 LQR 296

O'SULLIVAN, D., ELLIOTT, and ZAKRZEWSKI, *The Law of Rescission*, 2nd edn (Oxford: Oxford University Press, 2014)

O'SULLIVAN, J., 'Rescission as a self-help remedy: a critical analysis' (2000) 59 CLJ 509

PARKINSON, 'Reconceptualising the express trust' (2002) 61 CLJ 657

PAWLOWSKI, 'Imputing a common intention in single ownership cases' (2015) 29 TLI 3

PAWLOWSKI and BROWN, 'Constituting a secret trust by estoppel' [2004] Conv 388

PAWLOWSKI and SUMMERS, 'Private purpose trusts: a reform proposal' [2007] Conv 440

PAYNE, '*Quistclose* and resulting trusts', in *Restitution and Equity*, Volume 1: *Resulting Trusts and Equitable Compensation*, ed. BIRKS and ROSE (Oxford: Mansfield Press, 2000), ch. 5

PAYNE, 'Consent', in *Breach of Trust*, ed. BIRKS and PRETTO (Oxford: Hart, 2002), p. 300

PEARCE, 'A tracing paper' [1976] Conv 277

PENNER, 'Exemptions', in *Breach of Trust*, ed. BIRKS and PRETTO (Oxford: Hart, 2002), p. 241

PENNER, 'Resulting trusts and unjust enrichment: three controversies', in *Constructive and Resulting Trusts*, ed. MITCHELL (Oxford: Hart, 2010), p. 240

PERRINS, 'Can you keep half a secret?' (1972) 88 LQR 225

PETTIT, 'He who comes to Equity must come with clean hands' [1990] Conv 416

PISKA, 'Distinctions without a difference? Explaining *Stack v Dowden*' [2008] Conv 451

POLLOCK (ed.), *Table Talk of John Selden* (London: Selden Society, 1927)

Report of the Radcliffe Commission, Cmd 9474 (London: HMSO, 1955)

RICKETT, 'The constitution of trusts: contracts to create trusts' [1979] CLP 1

RICKETT, 'Two propositions in the constitution of trusts' [1981] CLP 189

RICKETT, 'Different views on the scope of the *Quistclose* analysis: English and Antipodean insights' (1991) 107 LQR 608

RICKETT, 'Thoughts on secret trusts from New Zealand' [1996] Conv 302

RICKETT, 'Completely constituting an *inter vivos* trust: property rules?' [2001] Conv 515

RICKETT and GRANTHAM, 'Resulting trusts: a rather limited doctrine', in *Restitution and Equity*, Volume 1: *Resulting Trusts and Equitable Compensation*, ed. BIRKS and ROSE (Oxford: Mansfield Press, 2000), p. 59

RICKETT and GRANTHAM, 'Resulting trusts: the true nature of the failing trust cases' (2000) 116 LQR 15

RIDDALL, 'Does it or doesn't it? Contingent interests and the Variation of Trusts Act 1958' [1987] Conv 144

RIDGE, 'Justifying the remedies for dishonest assistance' (2008) 124 LQR 445

RIDGE, 'Pre-judgment compound interest' (2010) 126 LQR 279

ROSSITER and STONE, 'The Chancellor's new shoe' (1988) 11 UNSWLJ 11

ROTHERHAM, 'Tracing misconceptions in *Foskett v McKeown*' (2003) 11 RLR 57

ST GERMAN'S *Doctor and Student* (1523, 1531)

SALES, 'The tort of conspiracy and civil secondary liability' (1990) 49 CLJ 491

SALMONS, 'Claims against third party recipients of trust property' (2017) 76 CLJ 399

SAMET, 'Guarding the fiduciary's conscience: a justification of a stringent profit-stripping rule' (2008) 28 OJLS 763

SAMET, '*Locus poenitentiae*: repentance, withdrawal and luck', in *Constructive and Resulting Trusts*, ed. MITCHELL (Oxford: Hart, 2010), ch. 12

SAMET, 'Proprietary estoppel and responsibility for omissions' (2015) 78 MLR 85

SAMUELS, 'The duty of trustees to obtain the best price' [1975] Conv 177

SANTOW, 'Charity in its political voice: a tinkling cymbol or a sounding brass?' [1999] CLP 255

SCOTT, 'The nature of the rights of the *cestuis que* trust' (1917) 17 Columbia L Rev 269

SELDEN, *Table Talk of John Selden* (London: Selden Society, 1927)

SHEEHAN, 'Disentangling equitable personal liability for receipt and assistance' [2008] RLR 41

SHEPHERD, 'Towards a unified concept of fiduciary relationships' (1981) 97 LQR 51

SHERIDAN, 'English and Irish secret trusts' (1951) 67 LQR 314

SHERIDAN, 'Excusable breaches of trust' (1955) 19 Conv 420

SHERIDAN, 'Protective trusts' (1957) 21 Conv 110

SHERIDAN, *Simester and Sullivan's Criminal Law: Theory and Doctrine*, 5th edn, ed. SIMESTER et al. (Oxford: Hart, 2013)

SIMPSON, 'On the nature of resulting trusts: the *Vandervell* legislation revisited', in *Restitution and Equity*, Volume 1: *Resulting Trusts and Equitable Compensation*, ed. BIRKS and ROSE (Oxford: Mansfield Press, 2000), ch. 1

SIMPSON, 'Conflicts', in *Breach of Trust*, ed. BIRKS and PRETTO (Oxford: Hart, 2002), p. 77

SLOAN, 'Keeping up with the *Jones* case: establishing constructive trusts in the sole legal owner scenarios' (2015) 35 LS 226

SMART, 'Holding property for non-charitable purposes: mandates, conditions and estoppels' [1987] Conv 415

SMITH, 'Tracing in *Taylor v Plumer*: Equity in the Court of King's Bench' [1995] LMCLQ 240

SMITH, 'Tracing into the payment of a debt' (1995) 54 CLJ 290,

SMITH, 'Constructive fiduciaries', in *Privacy and Loyalty*, ed. BIRKS (Oxford: Clarendon Press, 1997), ch. 9

SMITH, *The Law of Tracing* (Oxford: Clarendon Press, 1997)

SMITH, 'Unjust enrichment, property, and the structure of trusts' (2000) 116 LQR 412

SMITH, 'Trust and patrimony' (2008) 38 Revue générale de droit 379

SMITH, 'Simplifying claims to traceable proceeds' (2009) 125 LQR 338

SMITH, 'The measurement of compensation claims against trustees and fiduciaries', in *Exploring Private Law*, ed. BANT
and HARDING (Cambridge: Cambridge
University Press, 2010), p. 371

SMITH, 'Constructive trusts and the no-profit
rule' (2013) 72 CLJ 260

SMITH, 'Fiduciary relationships: ensuring the
loyal exercise of judgement on behalf of
another' (2014) 130 LQR 608

Snell's Equity, 33rd edn, ed. McGHEE
(London: Sweet and Maxwell, 2014)

STEP, *Trustee Exemption Clauses: STEP
Practice Rule* (2009)

STEVENS and FELDMAN, 'Broadcasting advertisements by bodies with political objects,
judicial review, and the influence of charities law' [1997] PL 615

STOLJAR, 'The transformations of account'
(1964) 80 LQR 203

SWADLING, 'A new role for resulting trusts?'
(1996) 16 LS 110

SWADLING, 'A hard look at *Hodgson
v Marks*', in *Restitution and Equity*,
Volume 1: *Resulting Trusts and Equitable
Compensation*, ed. BIRKS and ROSE
(London: Mansfield Press, 2000), p. 74

SWADLING, 'Orthodoxy', in *The Quistclose
Trust: Critical Essays*, ed. SWADLING
(Oxford: Hart, 2004), p. 19

SWADLING, 'Explaining resulting trusts'
(2008) 124 LQR 72

SWADLING, 'Ignorance and unjust enrichment: the problem of title' (2008) 28 OJLS
627

SWADLING, 'The nature of the trust in
Rochefoucauld v Boustead', in *Resulting
and Constructive Trusts*, ed. MITCHELL
(Oxford: Hart, 2010), ch. 3

SWADLING, 'The fiction of the constructive
trust' (2011) 64 CLP 1

SWADLING (ed.), *The Quistclose Trust: Critical
Essays* (Oxford: Hart, 2004)

SYNGE, *The 'New' Public Benefit Requirement:
Making Sense of Charity Law?* (Oxford,
Hart, 2015)

SYNGE, 'Charitable status: not a negligible
matter' (2016) 132 LQR 303

TARRANT, 'Property rights to stolen money'
(2005) 32 UWALR 234, 245

TARRANT, 'Thieves as trustees: in defence
of the theft principle' (2009) 3 Journal of
Equity 170

TELEVANTOS, 'Losing the fiduciary requirement for equitable tracing claims' (2017)
133 LQR 492

TETTENBORN, 'Resulting trusts and insolvency', in *Restitution and Insolvency*, ed. ROSE
(London: Mansfield Press, 2000), p. 167

THAM, 'Exploding the myth that bare sub-
trustees "drop out"' (2017) TLI 76

THOMAS, 'Conditions in favour of third parties' (1952) 11 CLJ 240

THOMPSON [1996] Conv 366

THORNLEY, 'Trusts of personalty: dispositions
of interests—formality' (1960) 20 CLJ 31

THORNTON, 'Ethical investments: a case of
disjointed thinking' (2008) 67 CLJ 396

TRUKHANTOV, 'The irreducible core of trust
obligations' (2007) 123 LQR 342

TRUST LAW COMMITTEE, *Rights of Creditors
against Trustees and Trust Funds* (London:
HMSO, 1999)

TURNER, 'The High Court of Australia on
contracts to assign equitable rights' [2006]
Conv 390

TURNER, 'Charitable trusts with political
objects' [2011] CLJ 504

TURNER, 'Understanding the constructive
trust between vendor and purchaser'
(2012) 128 LQR 582

TURNER, 'The new fundamental norm of
recovery for losses to express trusts' (2015)
74 CLJ 188

VINELOTT, 'Equity and its relevance to
superannuation schemes today' (1992) 62
TLI 119

VIRGO, 'Restitution through the looking glass:
restitution within Equity and Equity within
restitution', in *Rationalizing Property,
Equity and Trusts: Essays in Honour of*

Edward Burn, ed. GETZLER (Oxford: Oxford University Press, 2003), p. 106

VIRGO, '*Re Hallett's Estate*', in *Landmark Cases in Equity*, ed. MITCHELL and MITCHELL (Oxford: Hart, 2012), p. 357

VIRGO, *The Principles of the Law of Restitution*, 3rd edn (Oxford: Oxford University Press, 2015)

VIRGO, 'The genetically modified constructive trust' (2016) 2(2) Canadian Journal of Comparative and Contemporary Law 579

Vos, 'Linking chains of causation: an examination of new approaches to causation in equity and the common law' (2001) 60 CLJ 337

WAGGONER, 'US perpetual trusts' (2011) 127 LQR 423

WALKER, 'Tracing after *Foskett v McKeown*' (2000) 8 RLR 573

WALKER, 'Dishonesty and unconscionable conduct in commercial life: some reflections on accessory liability and knowing receipt' (2005) 27 Sydney LR 187

WALTON, '*McGovern v Attorney-General*: constraints on judicial assessment of charitable benefit' [2014] Conv 317

WARBURTON, 'The holding of property by unincorporated associations' [1985] Conv 318

WATERS, 'The nature of the trust beneficiary's interest' (1967) 45 Canadian Bar Review 219

WATERS, 'The protector: new wine in old bottles', in *Trends in Contemporary Trust Law*, ed. OAKLEY (Oxford: Clarendon Press, 1996), ch. 4

WATKIN, 'Shifting interests overseas' (1976) Conv 295

WATKIN, 'Charity: the purport of "purpose"' [1978] Conv 277

WATKIN, 'Cloaking a contravention' [1981] Conv 335

WATT, 'Laches, estoppel and election', in *Breach of Trust*, ed. BIRKS and PRETTO (Oxford: Hart, 2002), p. 353

WATT, *Equity Stirring* (Oxford: Hart, 2009)

WATTERSON, 'Alternative and cumulative remedies: what is the difference?' [2003] 11 RLR 7

WATTERSON, 'An account of profits or damages? The history of orthodoxy' (2004) 24 OJLS 471

WATTS, 'Tests of knowledge in the receipt of misapplied funds' (2015) 131 LQR 511

WATTS, 'The insolvency of agents' (2017) 133 LQR 11

WEINRIB, 'The fiduciary obligation' (1975) 24 UTLJ 1

WILDE, 'Secret and semi-secret trusts: justifying distinctions between the two' [1995] Conv 366

WORTHINGTON, 'Proprietary restitution: void, voidable and uncompleted contracts' (1995) 9 TLI 113

WORTHINGTON, 'Fiduciaries: when is self-denial obligatory?' (1999) 58 CLJ 500

WORTHINGTON, *Equity*, 2nd edn (Oxford: Oxford University Press, 2006)

YIP, 'The commercial context in trust law' [2016] Conv 347

YOUDAN, 'Formalities for trusts of land, and the doctrine in *Rochefoucauld v Bousted*' (1984) 43 CLJ 306, 314

INDEX